The Routledge Handbook of Deviant Behavior

The Routledge Handbook of Deviant Behavior presents a comprehensive, integrative, and accessible overview of the contemporary body of knowledge in the field of social deviance in the 21st century.

This book addresses the full range of scholarly concerns within this area—including theoretical, methodological, and substantive issues—in over 70 original chapters, written by an international mix of recognized scholars. Each of these essays not only provides insight into the historical and sociological evolution of the topic addressed, but highlights associated notable thinkers, research findings, and key published works for further reference. As a whole, this *Handbook* undertakes an in-depth evaluation of the contemporary state of knowledge within the area of social deviance, and beyond this considers future directions and concerns that will engage scholars in the decades ahead.

The inclusion of comparative and cross-cultural examples and discussions, relevant case studies and other pedagogical features makes this book an invaluable learning tool for undergraduate and postgraduate students in such disciplines as criminology, mental health studies, criminal theory, and contemporary sociology.

Clifton D. Bryant was Professor Emeritus of Sociology at Virginia Tech, US. He was the editor-in-chief of the *Encyclopedia of Criminology and Deviant Behavior* (Routledge, 2001), editor of the *Handbook of Death & Dying* (Sage, 2003), co-editor of *21st Century Sociology: A Reference Handbook* (Sage, 2007), and co-editor of the *Encyclopedia of Death and the Human Experience* (Sage, 2009). Other publications include *Deviant Behavior: Readings in the Sociology of Norm Violations* (Hemisphere Publishing Corporation, 1990), *Sexual Deviancy and Social Proscription: The Social Context of Carnal Behavior* (Human Sciences Press, 1982), and *Khaki-Collar Crime: Deviant Behaviour in the Military Context* (The Free Press, 1979). He was also the founding editor of the journal *Deviant Behavior*.

The Routledge Handbook of Deviant Behavior

Edited by Clifton D. Bryant

LONDON AND NEW YORK

Published 2011
by Routledge
2 Park Square, Milton Park, Abingdon, Oxon, OX14 4RN

Simultaneously published in the USA and Canada
by Routledge
711 Third Avenue, New York, NY 10017

Routledge is an imprint of the Taylor & Francis Group, an informa business

British Library Cataloguing in Publication Data
A catalogue record for this book is available from the British Library

Library of Congress Cataloging in Publication Data
Routledge handbook of deviant behavior / edited by Clifton D. Bryant.
p. cm.
1. Deviant behavior. 2. Deviant behavior—Handbooks, manuals, etc.
I. Bryant, Clifton D., 1932–2010 II. Title: Handbook of deviant behavior.
HM811.R68 2010
302.5′42—dc22
2010010082

ISBN: 978–0–415–48274–5 (hbk)
ISBN: 978–0–203–88054–8 (ebk)

Typeset in Baskerville
by Keystroke, Station Road, Codsall, Wolverhampton

Printed and bound in Great Britain by
CPI Antony Rowe, Chippenham, Wiltshire

This volume is affectionately dedicated to Patty Bryant, my partner of 53 years

Contents

Contents

Contents

Illustrations

Figures

Tables

Contributors

Jeff Ackerman is an Assistant Professor of Sociology at Texas A&M University. He received his Ph.D. in the Crime, Law, and Justice Program in the Department of Sociology at Penn State University. His research interests include intimate partner violence, female crime, and juvenile delinquency.

Robert Agnew is Professor of Sociology at Emory University. His research focuses on the causes of crime and delinquency, particularly general strain theory. His books include *Pressured into Crime: An Overview of General Strain Theory* (Oxford University Press, 2006) and *Why Do Criminals Offend? A General Theory of Crime and Delinquency* (Oxford University Press, 2005).

Ronald L. Akers is a Professor of Criminology and Sociology at the University of Florida. He has published widely on many topics in the field, but is best known for his development and testing of social learning and social structure–social learning as a general theory of crime and deviant behavior.

David Allen is a Professor of Sociology at the University of New Orleans, where he has taught for forty years. For about half of that time, including the present, he has been Chair of the Department of Sociology. He has occasionally written on the subjects of classical social theory, violence, drugs, and alcohol. His Ph.D. is from Vanderbilt University.

Stephen J. Bahr is Professor of Sociology at Brigham Young University. He received his Ph.D. from Washington State University and previously taught at the University of Texas at Austin. Recent publications have focused on prisoner reentry, desistance from crime, and adolescent drinking and drug use.

Carol A. Bailey is an Associate Professor of Sociology at Virginia Tech. She specializes in qualitative methodology and conducts evaluation research, primarily on programs that serve youth with severe mental health problems. Her most recent book is the second edition of *A Guide to Field Research* (Pine Forge/Sage).

Richard A. Ball is a Professor of Administration of Justice at Penn State-Fayette. He received his Ph.D. from Ohio State University. His recent publications include articles and book chapters on white-collar crime, and the fifth edition of his co-authored *Criminological Theory*, published in 2011.

Nachman Ben-Yehuda received his Ph.D. in Sociology from the University of Chicago and is a Professor of Sociology at the Hebrew University, Jerusalem. He has been a visiting scholar in US, Canadian, and British universities. His recent publications include *Moral Panics* (with Erich Goode, Wiley-Blackwell, 2009) and *Theocratic Democracy* (Oxford University Press, forthcoming).

Joel Best is Professor of Sociology and Criminal Justice at the University of Delaware. His books include: *Organizing Deviance* (with David F. Luckenbill, 2nd edn 1994), *Controlling Vice* (1998), *Random Violence* (1999), *Damned Lies and Statistics* (2001), *Deviance: Career of a Concept* (2004), and *Social Problems* (2008).

Kathleen A. Bogle is an Assistant Professor of Sociology and Criminal Justice at La Salle University in Philadelphia. She received her doctoral degree in Sociology from the University of Delaware. Her book, *Hooking up: Sex, Dating, and Relationships on Campus*, was published by New York University Press in 2008.

Stacey J. Bosick is an Assistant Professor of Sociology at the University of Colorado Denver with a secondary appointment to the School of Public Affairs. She received her Ph.D. from Harvard University. Her recent work focuses on crime and inequality from a life-course perspective.

Joseph Boyle is an Associate Professor of Sociology and Criminal Justice as well as Chair of the Department of Anthropology and Sociology at Brookdale Community College in Lincroft, New Jersey. He received his Ph.D. from Virginia Tech University. His career has also included teaching at Texas State University and Rowan University.

Mindy S. Bradley-Engen is an Associate Professor of Sociology and Criminal Justice at the University of Arkansas. She received her Ph.D. in Sociology from Pennsylvania State University. She has published in numerous outlets, and is the author of *Naked Lives: Inside the Worlds of Exotic Dance* (SUNY Press).

Timothy Brezina is Associate Professor of Criminal Justice at Georgia State University. His research and teaching interests include criminological theory and youth violence. Currently, he is pursuing innovative multi-methods research in these areas, combining quantitative and qualitative data. Recent publications appear in the journals *Criminology* and *Justice Quarterly*.

Gregory C. Brown is Assistant Professor of Criminal Justice at California State University, Fullerton. He received his MA in Sociology from University of California, Santa Cruz and his Ph.D. in Social Ecology from University of California, Irvine. His research interests include corrections, gangs, and white-collar and corporate crime, and his publications cover such topics as identity theft, correctional overcrowding, and internet gambling.

Clifton D. Bryant was Professor Emeritus in Sociology at Virginia Tech University. He was the founding editor of the journal *Deviant Behavior* and the editor of the four-volume *Encyclopedia of Criminology and Deviant Behavior* (Routledge, 2001). He was a president of the Southern Sociological Association, and in 2009 was inducted into the Role of Honor of that organization.

Patty M. Bryant served as assistant editor and later managing editor of the journal *Deviant Behavior*. She was managing editor of the *Encyclopedia of Criminology and Deviant Behavior* (Routledge 2001), managing editor of *The Handbook of Death and Dying* (Sage 2003), and managing editor of *21st Century Sociology: A Reference Handbook* (Sage 2007).

Michael Cherbonneau is a doctoral student in the Criminology Program at the University of Texas at Dallas. His primary research interest focuses on the situational and interactional influences on participation in street crime and violence. His current research concerns the decision-making strategies of currently active auto thieves. His work appears in the *British Journal of Criminology*, *Journal of Research in Crime and Delinquency*, and *Justice Quarterly*.

Addrain Conyers is a Criminal Justice Professor at the State University of New York, Brockport. He received his Ph.D. in Sociology from Southern Illinois University, Carbondale. He is a coauthor of the popular *Readings in Deviant Behavior* (Pearson).

Heith Copes is an Associate Professor in the Department of Justice Sciences at the University of Alabama at Birmingham. His primary research explores the criminal decision-making process. His recent publications appear in the *British Journal of Criminology*, *Justice Quarterly*, *Criminology and Public Policy*, and *Social Problems*.

Mary Dodge is an Associate Professor of Criminology at the University of Colorado, Denver. She received her Ph.D. in Criminology, Law and Society from the University of California, Irvine. Her research interests include white-collar crime, policing, and women and crime. Her most recent book, *Women and White-Collar Crime*, was published in 2009 by Prentice-Hall.

Keith F. Durkin is Professor and Chair of the Department of Psychology and Sociology at Ohio Northern University. His primary research interests are internet crime and deviance.

Stephen Farrall is Professor of Criminology at Sheffield University, UK. He is the author/co-author of *Rethinking What Works with Offenders* (Willan) and *Understanding Desistance from Crime* (Open University Press).

Charles E. Faupel was Professor of Sociology at Auburn University until his retirement in the summer of 2010. He received his Ph.D. from the University of Delaware in 1981 and taught at Auburn from 1983. He has published primarily in the areas of the sociology of drug use and the sociology of disasters and the environment.

Bonnie S. Fisher is a Professor in the School of Criminal Justice at the University of Cincinnati. She received her Ph.D. in Political Science from Northwestern University. Her recent publications include: *Unsafe in the Ivory Tower: The Sexual Victimization of College Women* (Sage) and *The Dark Side of the Ivory Tower: Campus Crime as a Social Problem* (Cambridge University Press).

Craig J. Forsyth is Professor and the Head of the Department of Criminal Justice and Professor of Sociology at the University of Louisiana at Lafayette. He received his Ph.D. from Louisiana State University in 1983. He is the author of over 170 journal articles, books, and book chapters. His principal research interests are in the areas of deviance and crime.

Gilbert Geis is Professor Emeritus, Department of Criminology, Law and Society, University of California, Irvine. He is a former President of the American Society of Criminology and a recipient of the society's Edwin Sutherland Award for research. His most recent book is *White Collar and Corporate Crime* (Prentice-Hall).

Professor Martin Gill is Director of Perpetuity Research and Consultancy International (PRCI), a spin-out company from the University of Leicester. He has published thirteen books and over a hundred journal and magazines articles, and is editor of the *Handbook of Security* (Palgrave) and co-editor of the *Security Journal*.

Barry Goetz is an Associate Professor of Sociology at Western Michigan University, where he also teaches in the Criminal Justice Studies Program. He received his Ph.D. from the University of California at Berkeley. He is currently working on a book that views community policing and crime prevention measures as aspects of the welfare state.

Erich Goode is Sociology Professor Emeritus at Stony Brook University. Goode is the author of ten books, including: *Moral Panics* (with Nachman Ben-Yehuda, Wiley-Blackwell, 2nd edn 2009) and *Deviant Behavior* (Pearson/Prentice-Hall, 9th edn 2011).

Angela R. Gover is an Associate Professor in the School of Public Affairs at the University of Colorado, Denver. She received her Ph.D. in Criminology and Criminal Justice at the University of Maryland. Her primary research interests include violence against women and children. Her recent work has appeared in *Violence and Victims, Journal of Interpersonal Violence*, and *Justice Quarterly*.

Ryken Grattet is a Professor of Sociology at the University of California, Davis. He is the author of *Making Hate a Crime: From Social Movement to Law Enforcement* (with Valerie Jenness, Russell Sage Foundation Press) and *Parole Violations and Revocations* (with Joan Petersilia and Jeff Lin, National Institute of Justice).

Dee Wood Harper is Professor of Sociology and Criminal Justice at Loyola University, New Orleans. He received his Ph.D. from Louisiana State University. He has published on a wide variety of sociological topics, including violent crime, most recently *Crime and Criminal Justice in Disaster* (2010).

James Hawdon is a Professor of Sociology at Virginia Tech. Previously, he was an Associate Professor at Clemson University. His recent publications include *Social Capital, Social Control and Crime* and *Drugs and Alcohol Consumption as a Function of Social Structure: A Cross-cultural Sociology*.

Keith Hayward is Professor of Criminology at the University of Kent, UK. His research interests include criminological theory, cultural criminology, popular culture, youth crime, social theory, and terrorism and fanaticism. He is the author, coauthor, editor, or co-editor of eight books, the most recent being *Framing Crime: Cultural Criminology and the Image* (Routledge).

Druann Maria Heckert received her BA from Frostburg State University, MA from the University of Delaware, and Ph.D. from the University of New Hampshire. She teaches at Fayetteville State University. Her publications have focused on topics including labeling theory and stigmatized appearance, positive deviance, and deviance theory.

Robert Heiner is Professor of Sociology at Plymouth State University. He is the author of *Social Problems: An Introduction to Critical Constructionism* (3rd edn, Oxford University Press, 2010) and the editor of *Deviance across Cultures* (Oxford University Press, 2008). He has also edited readers in social problems and in criminology.

Nancy A. Heitzeg, Ph.D., is a professor of Sociology and Critical Studies of Race/Ethnicity at St. Catherine University. She is the author of *Deviance: Rule-makers and Rule-breakers*, and has written and presented widely on the intersection of race, class, gender, and social control.

Ronald M. Holmes is a Professor Emeritus of Jusice Administration at the Universty of Louisville. He is the author of several books on violent crime, among them *Profiling Violent Crimes* (2009) and *Serial Murder* (2008) and over 50 articles in scholarly publications.

Stephen T. Holmes is an Associate Vice-President for Academic Initiatives at the University of Central Florida. He received his Ph.D. from the University of Cincinnati in Criminal Justice. During his career he has published more than ten books and scores of articles in academic outlets in the fields of violence, policing, drug testing, and probation and parole.

Jonathan Ilan is a Lecturer in Criminology at the University of Kent, UK. His research interests include ethnography; youth crime, justice and policing, urban sociology, and cultural criminology. As a DJ and music writer, he is also interested in exploring how urban and dance musics have been sites of autonomy, resistance, and control for several generations.

Valerie Jenness is a Professor in the Department of Criminology, Law and Society and the Department of Sociology and is Dean of the School of Social Ecology at the University of California, Irvine. As a sociologist and a criminologist, her empirical research has focused on prostitution, hate crime, and prison violence to explore the links between deviance and social control; the politics of crime control; social movements and social change; and corrections and public policy.

Wesley G. Jennings, Ph.D., is an Assistant Professor in the Department of Criminology at the University of South Florida. He received his doctorate degree in Criminology from the University of Florida in 2007. His major research interests include longitudinal data analysis, semi-parametric group-based modeling, sex offending, gender, and race/ethnicity.

Gary Jensen is a Professor of Sociology at Vanderbilt University. His research specialties include the sociology of deviance, criminology, and the sociology of religion. His most recent works are *The Path of the Devil* (2007), *Delinquency and Youth Crime* (2009), and articles dealing with American Wicca and various religious cosmologies.

Paul Jesilow is a Professor in Criminology, Law and Society at the University of California, Irvine. He has studied healthcare regulation for three decades and published in leading healthcare and criminology journals. His 1993 co-authored book *Prescription for Profit: How Doctors Defraud Medicaid* continues to be regularly cited.

Spyridon Kodellas is a Fulbright Scholar and Ph.D. candidate at the School of Criminal Justice, University of Cincinnati, OH. He holds a master's degree in Political Communication and New Technologies from the University of Athens, Greece. He does research in the areas of victimization, mass media and crime, and public attitudes toward crime and criminal justice.

Mark Konty received his Ph.D. from the University of Arizona in 2002. He is a public scholar conducting research and writing on social control from an interactionist perspective. His articles appear in the top criminology and sociology journals. He is currently the President-elect of the Mid-South Sociological Association.

Nancy Kutner, Professor of Rehabilitation Medicine and Sociology at Emory University, has NIH support for research on quality of life outcomes in chronic kidney disease. Publications include chapters in *21st Century Sociology: A Reference Handbook* (2006), *The Sociology of Health and Illness: Critical Perspectives* (2009), and the *International Encyclopedia of Rehabilitation* (2010).

Pat Lauderdale, Ph.D. (Stanford University), is Professor of Justice at Arizona State University and Director of their Ph.D. /J.D. Program. His recent publications include research on deviance, the world system, global indigenous struggles, and a new book on international terrorism coauthored with Annamarie Oliverio, titled *Terrorism: A New Testament* (Sage).

Bruce G. Link is a research scientist at New York State Psychiatric Institute, in addition to his responsibilities at the Mailman School. His interests are centered on topics in psychiatric and social epidemiology. He has written on the connection between socioeconomic status and health, homelessness, violence, stigma, and discrimination. Currently he is conducting research aimed at understanding health disparities by race/ethnicity and socioeconomic status, the consequences of social stigma for people with mental illnesses, and the connection between mental illnesses and violent behaviors. He is Director of the Psychiatric Epidemiology Training Program, Director of the Center for Violence Research and Prevention, and a Director of the Robert Wood Johnson Health and Society Scholars Program at Columbia University.

Donileen R. Loseke received her Ph.D. from the University of California, Santa Barbara, and currently is Professor of Sociology at the University of South Florida. Her books include *The Battered Woman and Shelters* and *Thinking about Social Problems*. Her current research explores identity in a globalized world.

David F. Luckenbill is Professor Emeritus of Sociology at Northern Illinois University. He received his Ph.D. in Sociology from the University of California at Santa Barbara in 1978. His primary research interest is the violation and protection of intellectual property.

Penelope A. McLorg has a Ph.D. in Anthropology and is Director of the Gerontology Program at Indiana University–Purdue University, Fort Wayne. She specializes in biological and sociocultural aspects of aging, particularly in health and aging. She has published on such topics as body composition, bone loss, and eating disorders.

Jody Miller is Professor of Criminal Justice at Rutgers University. She is author of *Getting Played: African American Girls, Urban Inequality, and Gendered Violence* (New York University Press, 2008) and *One of the Guys: Girls, Gangs, and Gender* (Oxford University Press, 2001), as well as numerous articles and chapters.

Kirk Miller is Department Chair and Associate Professor of Sociology at Northern Illinois University. His intellectual focus is broadly framed by questions of social control as process and outcome, with special attention to the criminal justice system as a focus for race, class, and gender inequalities. His current research is concerned with aspects of police decision-making, socio-historical and political forces affecting the police industry, intellectual property law and its violation, and gun culture.

John P. Minkes lectures in Criminology and Criminal Justice at Swansea University. His main research interests are corporate crime and the history of the criminal justice system. Recent publications include chapters on "Corporate Financial Crimes" and "Tax Evasion and Benefit Fraud" (with Leonard Minkes) in the *Handbook on Crime* (Willan, 2010).

Leonard Minkes is Emeritus Professor of Business Organisation, University of Birmingham, UK, and has had extensive academic experience in Britain and internationally. He has had international consulting experience in public and private sector organizations and has published widely on corporate management and strategy.

Robert G. Morris, Assistant Professor of Criminology at the University of Texas at Dallas, received a Ph.D. in Criminal Justice from Sam Houston State University in 2007. He has published numerous peer-reviewed articles on topics including fraud, computer hacking, digital piracy, identity theft, inmate behavior, and corrections policy.

Elizabeth Ehrhardt Mustaine is an Associate Professor of Sociology at the University of Central Florida. She received her Ph.D. from Ohio State University. During her career she has published numerous articles on routine activity theory, victimization risks, sexual offenders, and child abuse. Recently, she published the book *Hard Lives, Mean Streets: Violence in the Lives of Homeless Women* (Northeastern University Press).

Staci Newmahr is an ethnographer and Assistant Professor of Sociology at Buffalo State College. Her substantive areas of interest include gender, risk-taking, emotions, sexuality, deviance, and qualitative methodology. Her first book, *Playing on the Edge: Risk, Intimacy and Sadomasochism*, was published by Indiana University Press in 2011.

Stacey Nofziger is an Associate Professor of Sociology at the University of Akron. She received her Ph.D. in Sociology from the University of Arizona in 1999. Her areas of research are examinations of self-control and lifestyle theories and intersections of violence and victimization.

C. Eddie Palmer is currently Professor of Sociology and Dean of the Graduate School at the University of Louisiana at Lafayette. Earlier, he taught at the University of Texas at El Paso and Texas Tech University. He received his Ph.D. from Virginia Polytechnic Institute and State University in 1975.

Denay Patterson received bachelor's degrees in Sociology and Psychology from Ohio Northern University in Ada. She is currently a graduate student in Sociology at Indiana University. Her research interests include gender roles, female sexuality, and bisexuality.

Lynn Pazzani, MA, is finishing her Ph.D. in Criminology, Law and Society at the University of California, Irvine. She is an experienced research methodologist and statistician and much of her work focuses on violence against women.

Jo C. Phelan is an Associate Professor of Sociomedical Sciences at Columbia University. Her research interests include social stigma, conceptions of mental illness, the impact of the "genetics revolution" on the stigma of mental illness, attitudes and beliefs relating to social inequality and its legitimation, and social inequalities in health and mortality.

David Polizzi is an Assistant Professor of Criminology and Criminal Justice at Indiana State University. He received his Ph.D. in Clinical Psychology from Duquesne University. He has taught a variety of courses in offender treatment, corrections, and ethics. He has recently co-edited *Transforming Corrections: Humanistic Approaches in Corrections and Offender Treatment* and *Surviving Your Clinical Placement*. He also edits the *Journal of Theoretical and Philosophical Criminology*.

Henry N. Pontell is Professor of Criminology, Law and Society and of Sociology at the University of California, Irvine. His work has covered a number of areas in criminology, criminal justice, and the sociology of law, including, most recently, white-collar and corporate crime, identity theft, and comparative criminology. He is a past Vice-President of the American Society of Criminology, and a past President of the Western Society of Criminology, and is a Fellow of both organizations.

John Pruit is a graduate student in the Department of Sociology at the University of Missouri-Columbia. He received his MA in Sociology from the University of Memphis. His interests include narrative ethnography, qualitative research methods, culture and identity, and deviance. He is currently researching internet peak oil blogs.

Ethel Quayle is from the University of Edinburgh and was formerly Director of COPINE at University College Cork, Ireland. She is a clinical psychologist and for the last twelve years has worked in the area of technology-mediated crime. She has authored three books in this area.

James F. Quinn is a criminologist who currently heads the Addictions Program at the University of North Texas. He received his Ph.D. in Sociology from Louisiana State University. The author of over thirty articles and four books, his main areas of expertise are motorcycle gangs, drugs and crime, and corrections.

Carol Rambo is Associate Professor of Sociology at the University of Memphis, TN, and editor of *Symbolic Interaction*. She has published in journals such as *Deviant Behavior, Mental Retardation, Qualitative Inquiry,* and the *Journal of Aging Studies*. Her research interests include the intersection of trauma, narrative, the economy, and the environment.

Stephen M. Rosoff was Professor of Sociology and director of the Criminology Program at the University of Houston-Clear Lake. He received his BA in Psychology from Harvard, and his MA and Ph.D. in Social Ecology from the University of California, Irvine. His published work spans numerous areas, including medical sociology, deviance and social control, law and psychology, and white-collar and corporate crime. He is the lead author of the classic text *Profit without Honor: White-Collar Crime and the Looting of America* (Prentice-Hall, 5th edn 2010).

Steven Stack is Professor of Psychiatry and Criminology at Wayne State University. He has authored 270 articles and chapters, mostly on the social risk and protective factors for suicide, which have received 2,700 citations. In 2004 he received the Louis Dublin Award for lifetime contributions from the American Association of Suicidology.

Robert A. Stebbins is Faculty Professor in the Department of Sociology, University of Calgary. He received his Ph.D. in Sociology from the University of Minnesota. He has taught at two other universities. His books include: *Leisure and Consumption* and *Personal Decisions in the Public Square: Beyond Problem Solving into a Positive Sociology*.

Diane E. Taub is Professor of Sociology at Indiana University–Purdue University, Fort Wayne. Her research primarily involves the sociology of deviance, with a focus on issues related to identity formation and the management of a deviant identity. Recent publications concern eating disorders and the lived experiences of women with physical disabilities.

Jimmy D. Taylor received his Ph.D. in Sociology from Ohio State University. He is currently Assistant Professor of Sociology and Criminology at Ohio University-Zanesville. He specializes in masculinity and stigma management. His publications include a book on American gun culture, and articles on stigma management and self-injury.

Steven J. Taylor, Ph.D., is Centennial Professor of Disability Studies at Syracuse University. He has published on disability policy, the sociology of disability, and qualitative research. His books include *Introduction to Qualitative Research Methods* and *Acts of Conscience: World War II, Mental Institutions, and Religious Objectors*.

Richard Tewksbury is Professor of Justice Administration at the University of Louisville. He holds a Ph.D. in Sociology from Ohio State University. He is former editor of both *Justice Quarterly* and the *American Journal of Criminal Justice*. He has published thirteen books and over two hundred articles and book chapters.

Marie Skubak Tillyer is an Assistant Professor in the Department of Criminal Justice at the University of Texas at San Antonio. She received her Ph.D. in Criminal Justice from the University of Cincinnati in 2008. Her research focuses on criminological theory, victimization, violence prevention, and environmental criminology.

Emilio C. Viano is a Professor at the American University and Washington College of Law, Washington, DC. He has earned a Ph.D. in Sociology at New York University, an LLB (Hons.), College of Law of England and Wales/Open University, and three LLM degrees. Most recently he was member of the Permanent Commission for the Revision of the UN Minimum Rules for the Treatment of Prisoners. His most recent publication is a legal review of NAFTA in the *Denning Law Journal*.

Patrick Walsh was an Assistant Professor of Criminal Justice at Loyola University, New Orleans. He received his Ph.D. from the University of Southern Mississippi. He specialized in security, drug markets and thought processes leading up to the commission of crime. Dr. Walsh died suddenly in February 2010 and is sadly missed by his students and colleagues.

Charles Walton is an Associate Professor of Sociology and Chair of Sociology and Criminology at Lynchburg College. He received his Ph.D. in Sociology from Virginia Tech. His specializations include the sociology of music and deviance.

Thomas S. Weinberg is Professor of Sociology at Buffalo State College. His research interests include theory building, the sociology of emotions, alcohol studies, deviance and sexuality. He teaches contemporary sociological theory, social psychology, group dynamics, deviant behavior, the sociology of sexual behavior, and the sociology of addiction.

Ronald Weitzer is a Professor of Sociology at George Washington University. His main areas of expertise are policing and the sex industry, and he recently published the second edition of his edited book, *Sex for Sale: Prostitution, Pornography, and the Sex Industry* (Routledge, 2010).

Rob White is Professor of Criminology in the School of Sociology and Social Work at the University of Tasmania, Australia. He has published extensively in the areas of youth studies and criminology. Recent books include *Crimes against Nature: Environmental Criminology and Ecological Justice* and *Global Environmental Harm: Criminological Perspectives*.

Diane Kholos Wysocki is a Professor of Sociology at the University of Nebraska at Kearney. She received her Ph.D. in Sociology from the University of California, Santa Barbara. During her career she has published a number of articles on sex and the internet.

Preface

The challenge of trying to compress a contemporary overview of the field of deviant behavior into one reference volume is formidable. The *Encyclopedia of Criminology and Deviant Behavior*, published by Brunner-Routledge in 2001, required four volumes and approximately 2,000 pages, in excess of 500 entries, and more than 500 authors and co-authors to present a truly comprehensive survey of the field of deviant behavior at the beginning of the 21st century. At the end of the decade, we sought to accomplish much the same, albeit in a much more concise fashion. Obviously a high degree of selectivity was used in choosing topics to cover, and in chapter authors as well. The *Handbook of Deviant Behavior* includes 71 chapter topics that we feel will adequately inform the reader in regard to the contemporary state of the sub-discipline. The chapter topics were carefully assembled. This process involved a review of the initial preliminary list of topics by a set of very accomplished outside reviewers, who provided very generous input and many suggestions.

After the outline and list of chapter topics were finalized, I then identified, recruited, and assembled a very distinguished and informed international group of scholars in the field of deviance to serve as members of an advisory board for the *Handbook* project, and they provided many suggestions regarding topics and possible authors.

After reviewing all of the ideas and suggestions from the advisory board editors, a final list of 71 chapter topics was compiled. These editors provided very helpful comments in regard to the selection of authors. Invitations were extended and, in time, all chapters were assigned.

The 71 chapter topics were arranged into 15 parts, each addressing a seminal area in deviant behavior. Part I, "Conceptualizing Deviance," examines the nature of deviance, including social control, the construction and deconstruction of deviance, positive deviance, social change and deviance, differentials in deviance, and moral panics.

Part II, "Research Methodology in Studying Deviance," looks at quantitative, qualitative, cross-cultural, and historical research techniques. All of these techniques are currently being employed in deviance research.

Part III, "Theories of Deviance," surveys the array of theoretical perspectives on deviant behavior that drive research on this topic. Eleven chapters on theories of deviance make this part quite comprehensive.

Part IV, "Becoming Deviant as a Process," explores the dynamics of entering deviance, the social impact of stigma and the resultant deviant identity, and how the deviant career proceeds.

Part V, "Deviant Lifestyles and Subcultures," explores both generic and particularistic perspectives on deviant lifestyles and deviant subcultures. The generic chapters explore the concepts of deviant lifestyle and subculture. The particularistic chapters describe the transgender lifestyle and the Hassidim subculture in Israel.

Not all deviance elicits consensus in its condemnation. There are many forms of deviance where there is disputatious public debate concerning whether or not a particular mode of behavior should be labeled as "deviant." Part VI, "Contentious Deviance," explores four varieties of disputed deviance: homosexuality, premarital adolescent sexual activity, vegetarianism, and cybersex.

Part VII, "Self-destructive Behavior as Deviance," examines the phenomenon of self-directed deviance. In this type of deviance, the individual deliberately inflicts harm on himself or herself. This self-directed deviance is illustrated by chapters that address alcohol abuse, drug use, eating disorders, self-mutilization, and suicide.

Part VIII, "Deviance in Social Institutions," explains that deviant behavior does not take place within a social vacuum, but rather occurs within a social context. Some forms of deviance are relatively unique to particular contexts. Examples might be specific forms of deviance that take place within the context of social institutions. In addition to the traditional core institutions—family, education, religion, the polity, and the economy and work—there are the additional social institutions: the military, medicine, and sports and recreation. All harbor specific types of crime and deviance. The nature of the normative system of each social institution and the opportunity structure attendant to particular social institutions would seem to engender unique configurations of deviance and crime. This part offers chapters that examine deviance constituent to the family, the polity, occupations and organizations, sports and leisure, and medicine.

Part IX, "Sexual Deviance," reviews several sexual normative systems and the social contexts in which they operate. The violation of sexual norms can range from very serious sexual crimes to relatively innocuous sexual miscreance, and chapters in this section address topics such as female prostitution, sex tourism, pedophilia, and stripping and erotic dancing, among others. These chapters afford a broad perspective on sexual deviance.

Some forms of crime are as "durable" as granite, and have occurred for thousands of years in many, if not most, societies. But many varieties of crime and deviance are the offspring of recent social and technological change and are, accordingly, quite new and unique to the times. Part X, "Crimes of the Times," features configurations of crime that are both relatively new and reflect contemporary times and the social/technological milieu. Some of the topics in this part address such timely subjects as cyber crime, identity theft, ecological crimes, intellectual property crime, and terrorism, to mention some.

Part XI, "Crime: Traditional Non-violent Modes," addresses some of the more common and conventional varieties, such as burglary, motor vehicle theft, and fraud and embezzlement. Crimes of this variety are hoary with age, but still ubiquitous in occurrence in many societies.

Violent crimes date back thousands of years, but are still quite prevalent, albeit, sometimes, with modern embellishment. The chapters in Part XII, "Crime: Traditional Violent Modes," focus on several such varieties of criminal violent crime, such as homicide (of different varieties), rape, and armed robbery.

Deviance does not always refer to some physical violation of a given norm. Instead, the deviant stigma may derive from someone simply looking different or physically functioning in a disparate fashion, or whose mental abilities depart from the social norm to a notable degree. Physical appearance, or intellectual or cognitive deficiencies, may result in being labeled "deviant," with the attendant stigma that accompanies labeling. The chapters in Part XIII, "Handicap, Disability, and Impairment as Deviance," analyze four configurations of physical and mental deviance and stigma. These include deviant physical appearance, deviant physical functioning, mental retardation and intellectual disabilities, and mental illness and psychiatric disorders.

Part XIV, "Exiting Deviance," addresses the process of becoming "undeviant." Exiting deviance may often result from volitional motivation. Just as deviants are more likely to be "made" than "born," so, too, may they often be "unmade," rather than die a deviant. Much deviance is ephemeral in nature and the culprit may often thereafter turn away from such miscreant deeds and subsequently live a life of more or less social conformity. Exiting deviance may also occur because of structural factors. There are also social mechanisms that facilitate exiting deviance. The chapters in this part examine two main modes for exiting deviance, coerced and imposed exits from deviance, and cessation and desistance from deviance.

Some of the "New Horizons in Deviance," explored in Part XV, may simply involve the "discovery" of overlooked or previously unrecognized configurations of deviance; but in other instances, social or technological change may produce new and unique forms of deviant behavior. Both modes of "new" deviance will provide vast new opportunities for scholars in the field.

The development of the *Handbook of Deviant Behavior* has been, in every way, a collective enterprise. A great many individuals have been involved and have made signal contributions to the effort. These contributors need to be acknowledged and the individuals thanked. Gerhard Boomgaarden, senior publisher at Routledge, originally conceptualized the notion of a reference handbook on deviant behavior and I am most grateful to him for having entrusted the stewardship for operationalizing his concept. Hopefully the final product meets his original expectations.

Miranda Thirkettle, assistant to Mr. Boomgaarden, provided invaluable services in the initial organization stages of the project, serving as liaison with the editorial group at Routledge, providing advice regarding start-up protocols, and assisting in the paperwork of early development tasks.

Ms. Thirkettle was succeeded by Jennifer Dodd, who also was of great help in dealing with administrative concerns, getting information passed on to the proper persons at Routledge and advising on manuscript development matters. I am most grateful to Jennifer for her tolerance in accommodating my poorly organized and often convoluted workflow.

I am extremely grateful to the group of advisory editors for their tireless work in providing me with their reactions to the *Handbook* outline and list of topics, and their advice and suggestions on changes, deletions, additions, and new ways of framing chapter topics. I am also very appreciative for their many splendid suggestions for possible contributing authors. Their very knowledgeable advice on this matter made it possible to invite a group of extraordinarily well-qualified scholars to develop the topics. I think that the reader will find the chapters to be of uniformly high quality, interesting, informative, insightful and meticulously well documented. The contributors were a pleasure to work with—completing their chapters promptly and developing manuscripts that were extremely well crafted and sophisticated, and very professional in responding to suggestions for minor changes.

Heidi Browne, the assistant editor, has been indispensable from the very first days of the project. Her contributions were, indeed, quite broad in scope and included library research, computer research, compiling lists, sending e-mails, assisting with layouts and outlines, editing and proofreading, verifying references, generating bibliographies, and reviewing credentials, to mention but some. I am most grateful for her loyal efforts in this regard. At the very end of the project, while developing the editorial overview for one of the parts, I became quite ill, requiring hospitalization, surgery, and lengthy recuperation. Fortunately Heidi, my son, Clifton Bryant II, a commercial writer, and a colleague at another college, Charles Walton, came to my rescue and completed the commentary material. I offer them my profound thanks.

An enormous supply of thanks is due to my managing editor, Patty Bryant. She was involved in all of the activities listed above and many others in addition. She and I collaborated on every aspect of the *Handbook* project, from the initial compilation of a working outline and the framing of the reference work theme and orientation to the construction of this Preface. She has had to coordinate an enormous amount of e-mail correspondence, manuscript processing, editing and revisions, reference topic selection, and a host of other developmental tasks. She and I have been publishing books for more than 40 years and work as a very harmonious team. I owe her a trainload of love and gratitude for her enthusiastic and untiring efforts and contributions to our publishing enterprise.

Clifton D. Bryant
June 24, 2010

Clifton Dow Bryant

(1932–2010)

Dr. Clifton Dow Bryant, Professor Emeritus of Sociology at Virginia Tech University, was born December 25, 1932 and died September 13, 2010. A memorial service was held for Cliff in Blacksburg, Virginia, on September 16, 2010 and graveside services were held at Lakewood Memorial Park in Jackson, Mississippi, on September 18, 2010. Cliff is survived by his wife of 53 years, Patty Watts Bryant, four children, and five grandchildren.

Cliff had a long and productive career, taking degrees in Sociology from the University of Mississippi and Louisiana State University and studying Labor Economics at the University of North Carolina. He was a prolific writer and editor, having produced eleven books, numerous articles and book chapters, and scores of papers read at professional conferences. He served in several administrative and teaching posts, including being department chair at Millsaps College, Western Kentucky University, and Virginia Tech after an early teaching stint at the University of Georgia. He held research positions with the US Army, Mississippi State University, and Oak Ridge Associated Universities. He was also Visiting Professor at National Taiwan University and at Xavier University in Mindanao, Philippines, and participated in two Fulbright-Hays summer seminars, one in the People's Republic of China and one in Hungary.

Cliff had an outstanding service record, having served as president of the Southern Sociological Society (1978–79) and the Mid-South Sociological Association (1981–82). The SSS bestowed awards upon Cliff for his teaching and service, and in 2009 he received their Roll of Honor Award. The MSSA recognized Cliff for his distinguished career and also presented him their distinguished book award (in 2001 and again in 2004). Cliff organized sessions and presented papers at numerous professional meetings over the span of his fifty-year career as a sociologist. He also founded the journals *Sociological Symposium* and *Deviant Behavior* and served several other journals in advisory or editorial capacities. Cliff was also proud of another service record, his service as detachment commander in the Military Police Corps in the US Army (1953–55). In fact, Cliff is known for his work in the field of military sociology, writing cogently about "khaki-collar crime" and deviant behavior in the military.

Cliff was an award-winning teacher, known by his students as being insightful, inspiring, and creative. I am fortunate to have been one of Cliff's doctoral students who later became a colleague and friend. His graduate courses were challenging but delightful, entertaining, imaginative, and engaging. His enthusiasm for conceptualization and discovery of new connections in the social world was contagious. Cliff's lecture style was one filled with humorous anecdotes and skillful linguistic banter. In fact, Cliff will be remembered not only for his significant contributions made to the sociological literature but also for the slightly irreverent titles found on his papers and articles, titles which grab the attention of readers and entice them to come along on exploratory sociological journeys. Some of this irreverence stemmed from the part of Cliff's personality that reflected an enjoyment of exploration, travel, and discovering new and exciting things. Cliff and Patty were world travelers and Cliff would often come back from a trip with a new sociological toy that would find its way into print in some form or fashion. Cliff's participation in five African safaris, his collection of art and antiques from the places he visited, and his excitement for new discoveries indicate that he did not like things dull. This is summed up in an inscription Cliff placed in a book he gave to me some years back, to wit, "Living is what you do while you are waiting to die. Have as much fun as possible while you wait." Cliff liked real-life adventures as well as adventures of the mind. He also participated vicariously in the adventures of his students, with lively conversations with Cliff about what they had recently learned or experienced often prompting the students to develop theses, dissertations, papers, or articles on these topics.

Cliff was an organizer (with Patty's professional assistance) and collaborator. His forty-page curriculum vitae demonstrates just how much others owe to Cliff for providing them with research and publishing opportunities. The works of scores of authors have found expression in Cliff's edited books and anthologies over the years, with this volume the latest and last testament to Cliff's collaborative nature. The field of sociology and sociologists who benefited from Cliff's insights, generosity, and encouragement have lost a dear friend and an inspirational colleague. He will be missed greatly by family, friends, students, and others who interacted with him on a wide variety of sociological stages.

C. Eddie Palmer, Ph.D., CCS

Part I
Conceptualizing deviance

Overview

The notion of deviance is not a monolithic construct. Rather it is a far more nebulous concept with fuzzy borders and shifting parameters. Different individuals perceive and conceptualize deviance quite differently. The variations may be a matter of individual and idiosyncratic inclination, but the variations of perceptions and conceptualizations of deviance may also be a function of time, place, and circumstances. Perceptions and conceptualizations of deviance vary from culture to culture, from generation to generation (old or young), from sub-culture to sub-group, from social class to social class, from ethnic group to ethnic group, and from century to century and decade to decade, to list but some of the factors that may produce differential perceptions and conceptualizations of deviance. The confrontation of social norm and norm violator occurs as much in the eye and mind of the individual as in the actual context of behavior and interaction. It is the public or the onlooker, generically speaking, who, in effect, socially "processes" deviance. Social norms may be effected by various mechanisms and contrivances, but it is the populace, generally speaking, who will have to perceive and interpret the violation of such norms, and what response is appropriate, if in fact any is called for.

Deviance and social control

In the initial chapter in this book, Gary Jensen indicates that there are two basic and instrumental concepts in the study of deviant behavior. This sub-field of sociology dates back to the 1950s when sociologists first introduced the concept of deviance. Initially, the concept referred to objectification of some type of social norm, such as a law or some type of acceptable behavior in a given situation. But by the 1960s, the concept had become contentious, with many scholars asserting that labeling processes and stigmatization were the main elements of the concept rather than the simple violation of a norm. Using the "violation of a norm" perspective, the concept of deviance was intended to be non-judgmental. Further, because reactions and normative standards governing reaction were considered to be culturally and temporally relative, it was felt that the forms, degree, and nature of reactions could be established through empirical research.

Jensen points out that the concept of deviance did, however, become judgmental, especially as used by the general public. The misinterpretation or stigmatization is likely the reason that the use of the concept in major journals declined.

In the study of deviance, the subject matter includes behavior that violates legal norms, forms of conduct that are stigmatized by the members of society, and the condemnation and stigma applied to some because of their appearance or past behavior. There has not been complete agreement among scholars on the properties of deviance. The perspective that deviance is norm-violating behavior has been especially relevant in criminology, a major field of sociology. In this area, inappropriate behaviors that violate legal codes are defined as misdemeanors or felonies. Researchers here assume that "there are real, measurable, variations in conduct that violate such codes." There is less debate about the subject matter of criminological research than is the case of deviance research.

Some critics of the "actual behavior defined as deviance" have posited a "reactive" or "constructionist" perspective. Using this orientation, scholars may define deviance as "behavior that people so label," or "how people and conduct come to be defined or labeled in certain ways." Jensen indicates that the social constructionists take deviance as "subjectively problematic," rather than "objectively given." He cites one scholar as asserting that "reality depends on perspective and perspective is to a degree arbitrary." He also mentions another scholar who sums up the reactive constructionist perspective by defining deviance as "a property conferred upon these forms by audiences which directly or indirectly witness them."

Some deviance scholars have utilized another perspective in their research that focuses on a specific type of normative standard. Jensen recalls that for several decades, the traditional subject matter of both the sociology of deviance and criminology has been criticized for including social biases in the definition of the subject matter. He mentions that in the mid-1970s, two scholars proposed a "deviance as the violation of rights" perspective on the proper subject matter of criminology. Specifically, they proposed that "crime" should be defined by conduct and social arrangements that violate "the historically determined rights of individuals." This strategy would open up a variety of new research opportunities.

Jensen then moves on to examine several pending issues in social control. Some scholars proposed "theories of social control." One of these scholars defined social control as "reactions to deviance." Later, one of these same scholars observed, "the quantity of social control defines the rate of deviant behavior." It was concluded that "the study of social control included far more than the study of reaction to crime."

Jensen concludes his chapter with a discussion of an "integrated approach." He suggests that "there has been relatively little attention paid to the intersection of the study of social control with the study of deviance." This new research direction seems indicated.

Constructing deviance

In the second chapter, Joel Best walks the reader through the process of "constructing deviance." He initially points out that while some contend that deviance is an objective quality of behavior (i.e. certain behavior simply is deviant behavior), such is not the case. Most sociologists support the contention that deviance is very much a subjective, socially constructed category of behavior whose definition varies across time and space.

The concept of deviance being constructed is simply a subset of the notion of the social construction of all sorts of reality. Best notes that the construction of deviance depends on language to make the world meaningful, and as he phrases it, "language is inherently social;

all knowledge is shaped by the social arrangements within which it is produced." He indicates that in his chapter he seeks to identify and describe some of the processes by which deviance is created.

While there are some types of social behavior that have been considered to have been deviant at some place or time, Best reports that a number of other behaviors "may display wild variations in whether they are considered deviant and, if so, just why they are deviant."

The process of emerging deviant categories in a given society at a given moment in history has been analyzed from a number of theoretical perspectives. Best indicates that conflict theorists following a Marxist perspective have asserted that elites play a significant role in creating new categories of deviance. These theorists believe that social control is a mechanism for elites maintaining their position in, and control over, a society. Sociologists using the Durkheimian perspective contend that deviance is necessary for society because it "reinforces the social solidarity of its members." Punishing those who break the rules "affirms the importance of the social ties that bind society together."

Theorists of Weberian persuasion view "deviance and social control as products of cultural and structural changes that lead to status competition, shifts in authority structures, and the like." In the 20th century, some forms of deviance became "medicalized." Alcoholism, previously considered to be a moral or legal problem, instead became a "disease" to be medically treated. According to Best, by mid-century, alcoholism was most often medicalized as a manifestation of mental illness. He further indicated that, by century's end, there was a new emphasis on an individual's genetic make-up, and there was a search for genetic markers for alcoholism. Sometimes social movements or the media create new categories of deviance.

Once a new category of deviance has been constructed, the deviant label must be applied. Some deviant labels are never applied, and others may be applied selectively. Best observes that deviant categories are a "resource for social control agents." Social control agents evaluate the behavior of individuals and make decisions about which ones will qualify for the application of the deviant label.

Deviant labels are not always permanent. Over time, they will be altered, reconstructed, replaced with new constructions, or removed. Critics may argue that social control is inadequate and demand that social control agents be more active. On the other hand, critics may assert that social control is too harsh or excessive. Some may call for the decriminalization of certain deviant activities. According to Best, over time there are often shifts or changes "in what is considered deviant, why it is considered deviant, the circumstances under which it is considered deviant, what sort of deviance it is thought to be, and what is thought to be the best way to respond." Reconstruction of deviant categories, in some instances, may be in the form of vindication. Vindication occurs when a deviant category is abandoned, or when society redefines the behavior categorized as deviance as respectable or at least acceptable. Best concludes his chapter with a brief discussion of the importance of selectivity and observes that, "whatever is counted must first be defined, and understanding what is defined as deviant has proved to be a rich topic for scholars of deviance."

Tolerable, acceptable, and positive deviance

In his chapter, Robert Stebbins compares and analyses three encountered configurations of deviant behavior—*tolerable*, *acceptable*, and *positive* deviance. He addresses these topics as a nominal or separate scheme. They cannot be fitted into a continuum at this time.

He defines deviance as "behavior judged as violating one or more of the community's *moral norms*." Moral norms derive from the community's collective judgment regarding right or wrong behavior and activities in everyday life. Stebbins indicates that moral norms stand apart from other types of norms, such as folkways, customs, regulations, and ordinances.

Some deviant acts are tolerated. *Tolerance*, according to Stebbins, is "an attitude or orientation that individuals hold toward certain activities or thoughts of others that differ substantially from their own." It is a relatively passive reaction midway between scorn and embracement. Tolerated behavior is only mildly threatening. It is accorded legitimacy, although only grudgingly. Others have little interest in actually adopting or accepting tolerated behavior. With tolerable deviance, the welfare of the community is believed to be preserved.

Stebbins defines *intolerable deviance* as behavior "which greatly threatens the established order, causing the community to scorn it and therefore try to eliminate it." He observes that members of the community "know they ought to refrain from engaging in them [tolerable deviance activities], yet they find it difficult to escape their magnetic pull."

He articulates three varieties of tolerable deviance: criminal tolerable deviance; noncriminal tolerable deviance; and legitimate tolerable deviance. *Criminal tolerable deviance* is actually illegal, according to criminal law, but the community and law enforcement agencies view it as of minor importance. *Noncriminal tolerable deviance* lies outside the jurisdiction of the law, but it still violates community norms. An example would be adultery. *Legitimate tolerable deviance* is guaranteed by law. Everyone can legally engage in unconventional religious or political activities or beliefs about the supernatural that differ significantly from those of the majority in the community. *Intolerable deviance* is behavior in violation of criminal law and the violation of very serious noncriminal moral norms.

Stebbins reports that there are three broad reasons why people engage in tolerable deviance. They do so because it is interesting and pleasurable to do so as leisure. They do so because it is a livelihood or a serious amateur pursuit. Or they do so because it serves as a mode of adjustment—"a way of arriving at a behavioral balance between personal needs and goals, on the one hand, and the demands of other people and society, on the other."

Stebbins cites another scholar as having posited the notion of *acceptable deviance*. This form of deviance is defined as "behavior which deviates from the norm, such that it is not entirely predictable, yet which conforms enough to the norm to be acceptable as signifying membership." To illustrate this variety of deviance, one author provides observations on fashion and slang. This scholar observes that, "to be fashionable is to be acceptably deviant," and "going beyond acceptability to forms of dress regarded as serious observations" would constitute "outrageous" fashion. In regard to slang, there must be ways of introducing new slang words to the group. If members of the group refuse to incorporate the new term into their vocabulary, then it stands as an "outrageous" word in the existing lexicon and is therefore deviant and unacceptable. If some members of the group begin to use the new slang word, its outrageousness declines, and the new slang word gradually becomes conceptualized as "fashionableness."

Stebbins then devotes the remainder of his chapter to a detailed analysis of the contentious notion of "positive deviance." He concludes with the observation that "each perspective contributes to our understanding of how individuals differ along one or more important dimensions—tolerance, acceptability, excellence—from the large majority of people in their group or the larger local community."

The deconstruction of deviance

Mark Konty, in his chapter, critically examines the concepts of the construction of deviance and the deconstruction of deviance. Konty points out that the notion of the *construction of social reality* appeared in the 1960s and the concept of *deconstruction* was first used a bit later. Deconstruction initially focused on literary analysis, but later became a component of the "new" social theories, such as postmodernism. The author provides the simple definition of deconstruction as "the analytical process that examines the assumptions and experiences that shape meaning." He further adds that, "rather than taking these for granted, deconstruction identifies how assumptions and experiences result in shared cultural meaning." Deconstruction, in effect, explores the dynamics by which definitions of deviance came about. Often there are self-serving factors or considerations that influence the shaping of deviant definitions. Some might, for example, label women with active sex lives as "sluts," because this might benefit male interest, or such behavior simply fails to live up to the female ideal. Konty suggests that reality is not an objective fact that can be discovered through the use of empirical methods, but instead must be subjectively and uniquely experienced by particular individuals who have unique circumstances and experience. To explain deconstruction better, Konty provides the "history of sociology's interest in the topic."

He begins this history with a discussion of Durkheim's positing the existence of "social facts"—intangible dimensions of reality that exist outside the body, but are real. Examining the effects of something is one way of demonstrating it is "real." Durkheim went on to deconstruct crime, bifurcating it into "normal" crime and "pathological," depending on the effects it has on society. Normal crime results in social change and strengthens social solidarity. Pathological crime produces disorder and disintegration in society. Konty indicates that Durkheim's notions led later sociologists to search for other ways that crime can be deconstructed into good and bad.

Some functionalists did this in their research, but scholars of other theoretical persuasion took the lead in perusing the deconstructionist strategy. Labeling theorists asserted that the label of "deviant" derives not so much from the unconventional behavior itself, but rather it is the product of the response of the community to the behavior. Konty observes that, "deconstructing the labeling process soon revealed the role that power and status play in applying deviant labels."

Critical theorists followed by demonstrating that norms and social control maintain the status order for the benefit of the elite. In effect, as Konty phases it, "the law and criminal justice system are used to maintain the stratification system."

Feminist sociology insisted that men and women were treated differently in the criminal justice system and that this disparate treatment was a tool to maintain the male power and status system. Feminist researchers used deconstruction to reveal that patriarchal society acted to maintain male status and keep women in their inferior place in the status order by making them play the feminine role.

Konty then turns to discussion of deconstruction of the deconstruction. Here he seeks to deconstruct "the interests of those studying deviance." He asserts that researchers are attracted to the study of deviance because it is titillating, interesting to study, and articles and books about the subject are quite marketable. Some scholars, however, believe that studying the deviant is exploitative. As Konty phases it, "by studying and deconstructing deviance, the researcher reifies the very definition of deviance they claim to destroy . . . [and] instead is aiding and abetting the further exploitation of the powerless deviant."

The remaining part of the chapter is devoted to a discussion of what Konty labels "deconstruction by the damned." This refers to deviants themselves deconstructing their own "untoward behavior" in an attempt to explain their miscreance to their interaction partner or the general audience in terms that they will accept. He provides a description of two previously published conceptualizations of how this is accomplished. In one of these conceptualizations, termed "techniques of neutralization," the efforts preceded the deviant behavior and "had a causal effect by reducing informal control mechanisms." In the second such conceptualization, termed "accounts," the author asserted that individuals who commit deviant acts use one of two strategies to make their acts acceptable. In one strategy, the deviant offers an "excuse" that "admits the act was wrong, but claims that uncontrollable circumstances are responsible." In employing the second strategy, the deviant offers a "justification," where he or she "admits culpability for the act, but 'denies the pejorative' quality of the act."

Deconstruction has had its detractors over the years, but as Konty observes in concluding his chapter, the ideas in this process have "proven to be a powerful methodology for the sociology of deviance."

Social change and deviance

In his chapter, Nachman Ben-Yehuda explores the relationship between deviance and social change. He begins his narrative by reminding the reader that Durkheim, in his day, declared that "deviance is an inevitable aspect of all societies." Durkheim had also observed that "crime implies not only that the way remains open to necessary changes, but that in certain cases, it directly prepares these changes." Ben-Yehuda interprets Durkheim's writings to say that crime (and thus deviance) challenges the moral care of society and this invokes a punitive response, which, in turn, strengthens social cohesion and helps maintain societal boundaries. Ben-Yehuda argues that unconventional behavior results in "a sphere of ambiguity and uncertainty," but they are two different perspectives that can be taken on this state. One perspective is that the unconventional behavior can be viewed as deviant behavior that challenges the status quo, and this results in a punitive reaction that underscores "symbolic-moral boundaries" and helps maintain social solidarity and societal stability. On the other hand, the perspective can be taken that unconventional behavior can be seen as challenging the status quo "and introducing vital elements of changes into culture" that help create "different symbolic-moral universes and new social environments." Thus, deviance may help facilitate social change. These two perspectives may shift over time. For example, Nelson Mandela was once considered to be a terrorist, but years later was perceived as a heroic leader and occupied a position of "hegemonic power."

According to Ben-Yehuda, this shift in perspective can be vividly demonstrated by examining deviant textbooks over a period of several decades and noting what behaviors are considered to be deviant in different time periods. He notes a number of scholars have emphasized the linkage of deviance to change, and mentions that some have spoken of "creative deviance" and that deviance is "the only major source of creative adaptation of rules to new life situations." He also notes that various kinds of deviance have become socially acceptable through the process of "normalization." Some scholars have even posited the notion of "positive deviance."

He suggests that changes in the symbolic-moral universe involve changes in consciousness and social identities. Morality is a seminal concept in an examination of the deviance–social linkage. Ben-Yehuda observes that, "morality is a resource that is created and used by moral entrepreneurs, sometimes in moral panics and crusades, many times in competitive and antagonistic social and cultural landscapes." The creation of morality involves power in terms of who defines what is deviant, and who has the power to enforce the definition.

Ben-Yehuda suggests that there are three basic types of deviance in terms of where they come from: "the periphery and aimed at the center"; "the center and aimed at periphery"; and "either the center or the periphery and aimed at the same level (center to center, periphery to periphery)." He then notes that such types of deviance are always linked to "issues of political justice," "political trials," and "criminals as heroes and political criminals." Much of the remainder of the chapter is devoted to a discussion of these three topics.

Some deviance is motivated by strong feelings of injustice or political causes. The perpetrators often use "language of justice/injustice in justifying" such acts. Ben-Yehuda also points out that the processes of deviantization are used for political purposes, and asserts that trials of individuals who are accused of challenging the legitimacy of the regime or attempting to alter the existing distribution of power are political. Political trials produce political prisoners, which may lead to the politicization of prisons. As examples, he indicates that the trials of some historically significant individuals, such as Giordano Bruno and Galileo, were very political.

Deviants and criminals are treated as heroes—the Robin Hood syndrome. Politicians are criminals. Examples here might be Joseph Stalin, Adolf Hitler, Pol Pot, and Mao Zedong. Ben-Yehuda concludes his chapter with the observation that "The creation of rules and penal punishments implies that the lifestyle, values and morality of specific social groups gained ascendancy over those of other groups, many times at the other groups' expense."

Moral panic

In their chapter, Erich Goode and Nachman Ben-Yehuda examine in detail the curious phenomenon of *moral panic*—"an episode of exaggerated concern about a threatening condition which many members or sectors of a society blame on 'folk devils' or deviants." They indicate that the distinguishing characteristic of a moral panic is that the concern "is *substantially above and beyond what evidence suggests is the actual threat or danger of the condition* that generated the concern." The concept was first used in 1972, and Goode and Nachman assert it is one of the most influential concepts produced by sociologists.

They explain that a variety of "actors" are components in the concept. These actors include the public or society at large, the media and the internet, law enforcement (the police and the courts), politicians and legislators, and social movements or action groups. When a moral panic occurs, concern is expressed among one or more of the actors, or some combination of them. Goode and Ben-Yehuda report that "we observe a discrepancy between this concern and the imputed threat that the concern reflects."

They suggest that moral panics are episodes that contain five elements: *concern* about a threat; *hostility* toward a folk devil; a degree of *consensus* among the public; *disproportion* between the threat and the concern; and *volatility* in the concern. In regard to *concern*, they indicate that five relevant "actors" express their felt concern in overt actions. First, the *public* expresses indignation; second, because of the public concern, the *media* runs news stories stoking up the threat and concern; third, *politicians* make speeches about folk devils and propose legislation to criminalize the threatening behavior; fourth, *law enforcement* steps up legal control; and, fifth, *activists* form social movement organizations.

They suggest that in moral panics, society expresses an increased level of *hostility* toward the folk devil. The folk devil is designated as an enemy of decent, respectable society. Moral panic actors *stereotype* the folk devil in exaggerated, demeaning ways.

Concerning *disproportion*, Goode and Ben-Yehuda point out that "the lynchpin of the moral panics concept is disproportion—the disparity between concern and threat." Some critics of the concept argue that disproportion cannot be objectively determined. They assert that, for the most part in moral panics, disproportion can be calibrated and suggest several indicators. Among these indicators are *imaginary threats* that generate much concern and even fear, but prove to be entirely imaginary. There are also *exaggerated claims*. In some moral panics, the dimensions of the threats are obviously greatly exaggerated. In such cases, the authors contend that "the criterion of disproportion has been met." Another indicator they offer is *other harmful conditions*. In this connection, Goode and Ben-Yehuda point out that "some less harmful conditions, dangers, or threats attract vastly more concern, fear, anxiety, and attention than other, more harmful conditions do." Yet another indicator they offer is *other times, other places*. In a fashion similar to the previous indicator, the authors suggest that "often, when we compare one time or place with another, we find more concern when and where the objective threat is lower, and less concern when and where the objective threat is higher."

The fifth element of a moral panic is *volatility*. Moral panics, by their very nature, are volatile. They ignite quite suddenly and may subside equally suddenly. In regard to the actors in moral panics, the *media and the internet*, as opposed to the word-of-mouth of times past, are "the most effective generators and conveyors of moral panics in the history of humanity." Today's world is *multimediated* and this fact permits *competing* moral panics, and even the possibility that "a diversity of panics may break out among different audiences."

In the instance of another actor, the *public*, for a full-blown moral panic to be ignited, there must be some potential for a reaction from the public. The threat in a moral panic must resonate with at least some sectors of the audience. *Law enforcement* must display formal actions of social control that forcefully demonstrate that a moral panic is actually occurring. According to the authors, when a moral panic ignites, it must "generate appeals, campaigns, and finally, fully fledged social movement organizations or action groups which arise to cope with the newly existing threat."

Goode and Ben-Yehuda conclude their chapter with a detailed discussion of three theories of moral panics: *elite engineered* theory, *grass roots* theory, and *interest group* theory.

The differentials in deviance: race, class, gender, and age

Deviance does not occur uniformly across the population. There is variance based on a number of social and socioeconomic factors. In her chapter, Nancy A. Heitzeg explores the variances attendant to the factors of race, class, gender, and age. She indicates that these categories— "cornerstones of stratification," as she phrases it—"shape access to social opportunity, demarcate social inequality, inform identity, and provide common ground for social movements and resistance." These four social categories enjoy a degree of centrality in sociology, but the research literature on them has been quite varied. They have been examined as separate variables in some research, but other research has viewed them as intersecting variables. Heitzeg suggests that they can also be understood as "part of an interlocking system of oppression." She also observes that race, class, gender, and age are "stigmatized statuses that are targets for deviant labeling."

She indicates that these four categories have long been cited as variables that contribute to deviant behavior. One perspective of these variables viewed them as representing "structural conditions that impelled deviance," in effect, primary factors.

Research during much of the 20th century tended to focus on deviants who were identified as "poor, they were young 'delinquents,' they were racial/ethnic minorities, and they were often male." These deviants were engaged in activities such as drug addiction, alcoholism, street crime, and gang membership, and were mostly encountered in inner-city urban areas. Heitzeg reports that two early explanations of the role of race, class, gender, and age in deviant behavior were *cultural deviance* and *strain theory*. The cultural deviance thesis posited that "structural position and location produced subcultural interactions that give rise to deviant values." Strain theory held that class variables "lead to blocked opportunities in achieving the shared 'American Dream' which then fostered deviant alternatives for economic success." Poverty may contribute to economic crime such as armed robbery, theft, and burglary. On the other hand, "white-collar crime" or "crimes of the suite," requires positions of wealth, power, and prestige. Strain theory posits that "race and gender discrimination are negative strains that may pressure youth into delinquency." Such variables as youth, being poor, and being black may contribute to the development of an alternative set of norms and standards of respect, which may increase the likelihood of gang involvement and violence.

According to Heitzeg, the relationship between race, class, gender, and age and deviant behavior can be viewed through an alternate perspective. Rather than concern with differentials in deviant behavior, this alternate perspective focuses on differentials in social control. In effect, "race, class, gender, and age are stigmatized statuses that are subject to social control by those with the power to create and apply deviant labels." Stigmatized statuses are controlled relative to their social status. The informal stigmatized statuses of race, class, gender, and age are vulnerable to escalations in social control, and may be subject to differential treatment in the criminal justice system and media stereotyping and distortions. Heitzeg reveals that, "despite no real statistical differences in rates of offending, the poor, the under-educated, the young and people of color are over-represented in every phase of the criminal and juvenile justice system, from arrest to death row." Race, class, gender, and age are powerful indicators of stigma and subsequent social control. They also "shape access to both the power label and the powerlessness of being subjected to social control."

As to future research directions in this area, Heitzeg suggests the study of the interplay between "deviants" and social control, and an investigation into "how systemic racism, classism, sexism, and ageism may both create and encourage deviance, or indeed how these systems may represent a mega-level of deviance unto themselves."

1

Deviance and social control

Gary Jensen

The conception of deviance as behavior that violates normative standards governing accept-able and unacceptable conduct in a society was first used by sociologists in the 1950s and has persisted in that form for over fifty years (Best 2004). However, debates about features of that conception began in the 1960s with numerous scholars emphasizing labeling processes and stigmatization as the defining features of the concept rather than the behavioral violation of normative standards per se (Becker 1963; Goffman 1963). By the mid-1960s, some scholars began differentiating between deviant behavior and "social control," with the latter defined as "reactions to deviance" (Gibbs 1966; Cohen 1966). Although the differentiation between the concept of deviance as behavior and the concept of social control is quite widely accepted, the concept of social control itself is used in diverse ways in the sociological literature. The variable uses of that concept will be specified toward the end of this chapter.

When defined in terms of the violation of norms, the concept of deviance was intended to be a non-judgmental, neutral concept encompassing behavior and characteristics of people that are subject to condemnation or stigmatization within a social system. Because reactions and the normative standards governing reactions vary among societies, among groups within societies as well as over time, the exact subject matter encompassed by the concept is both culturally and temporally relative. The specific forms, the degree of condemnation, and the nature of reactions are meant to be established through empirical research.

Unfortunately, although the concept was chosen because it was not widely used in everyday life, the label "deviant" has become a judgmental term used by the general public. This evolution complicates use of the concept because categorizing behaviors as violating widely shared normative standards is not a judgment of those behaviors or the people engaged in them (e.g. homosexuality). Best (2004) notes that use of the concept has declined in major journals and concern that it is misinterpreted as a stigmatizing public label may be one of the sources of that decline.

The specific subject matter typically includes the study of behaviors that violate legal norms, such as crime and delinquency, and forms of conduct that are disapproved of or stigmatized by a sizeable proportion of members of a society, including suicide, mental illness, certain forms of alcohol and drug use, and some forms of sexuality. The concept was originally applied to viola-tions of shared norms defining disapproved *behavior*. However, because people can experience condemnation or stigma based on their past behavior and their appearance, contemporary use of the concept of deviance includes forms of expression, beliefs, and appearance and labels applied based on prior behavior or characteristics.

The choice of deviance as an objective concept intended to encompass a subject matter with shared properties has not been accompanied by complete agreement on those properties. Some social scientists highlight behavioral violations of norms in a community or society. Others highlight the way in which behaviors, people, and circumstances come to be designated as instances of some type of deviance. Yet others propose that the phenomena included should be violations of justice norms or normative standards defining rights.

Deviance as norm-violating behavior

Most textbook definitions of deviance emphasize behavior that violates definitions of appropriate conduct shared by the members of a social system (Akers 1985; Clinard and Meier 2004; Stark 2007). The normative definition requires that definitions must be shared to some degree and some scholars actually specify defining cutting points. For example, Charles Tittle (1995: 124) limits the normative version of the concept to instances where "the majority of a given group" regards a form of behavior as "unacceptable." Since norms (i.e. definitions of acceptable and unacceptable conduct) can vary over time, among societies, and among groups, the appropriate subject matter of the study of deviance is quite variable using this definition. Most scholars using the concept do not specify exact cutting points but, rather, treat the prevalence and severity of disapproval as variable properties of normative phenomena (see Gibbs 1981).

A major field in the sociology of deviance is criminology, which can be defined as the scientific study of crime, including the relevant forms of law-making, law-breaking, and reactions to law-breaking (Luckenbill, Cressey and Sutherland 1992). Definitions of inappropriate conduct that come to be embodied in legal codes as felonies and misdemeanors have been particularly central to the study of deviance, and scholars in this tradition assume that there are real, measurable variations in conduct that violate such codes. Thousands of research projects have focused on variations among people, social settings, and over time in activities subject to state intervention as criminal or delinquent offenses (Jensen and Rojek 2009). Because the relevant forms of conduct are defined by written codes, there is less debate about the subject matter encompassed by crime than is the case for the concept of deviance. Moreover, because legal codes and the normative definitions of conduct shared by people in a social system do not perfectly coincide, some forms of criminal or delinquent conduct may not be viewed as worthy of condemnation by the public, and some forms of conduct condemned by the public may not be illegal. Because laws and their enforcement change, the subject matter of criminology can change as well.

Deviance as a reactive construction

As one of the critics of the focus on forms of actual behavior defined as deviant by reference to potentially measurable and widely shared social norms, Kai Erikson (1962: 308) defined deviance as "a property *conferred upon* these forms by audiences which directly or indirectly witness them." This "reactive" or "constructionist" definition is reflected in other definitions, such as "conduct that is subject to social control" (Black 1976: 9) and "behavior that people so label" (Becker 1963: 9). From this perspective, the focus is not on what offenders are "doing" or have done but on how people and conduct come to be defined or labeled in certain ways.

A very simple definition of social constructionism in the study of deviance is expressed in Rubington and Weinberg's (2005: 1–2) statement that social constructionists take deviance as "subjectively problematic" as opposed to "objectively given." Goode (1994: 32–33) proposes that "to the constructionist, definitions have no absolute, objective validity" and that *"reality depends on perspective, and perspective is to a degree arbitrary."* The typical approach to delineating the features of the constructionist perspective is to contrast it with an opposing, "traditional," and "quantitative" alternative referred to under terms such as "absolutism," "realism," "naturalism," or "positivism." When taken to the extreme, the alleged positivist takes for granted that the problems or problem people studied are really "out there" and that people fall in such judgmental categories because they have violated widely accepted societal norms. Because these problems and problem people are real, positivists ask what other measurable characteristics of people or their social world determined that reality.

James Richardson, Joel Best and David Bromley (1991: 4) stress that the most basic questions asked by constructionists are: "Who is making claims? Why are they making them? What do they say? And, how do others respond?" The constructionist conception of deviance is particularly applicable to the study of situations where the actual conduct is: quite common; can be transformed into a serious problem through definitional activity and labeling; and where there are conflicting norms held by groups with differential ability to invoke some types of labeling process and/or where the deviance has an artificial, fabricated quality. Even for conduct where there is widely shared and strong consensus on the impropriety of the conduct (intentional killing), there are other beliefs, definitions, or norms defining "mitigating circumstances" (e.g. self-defense, in the line of duty, mental capacity, etc.) that affect the way in which the conduct and people involved are categorized.

Deviance as the violation of rights

The traditional subject matter of both the sociology of deviance and criminology has been criticized for several decades for incorporating societal biases in the definition of its subject matter. In his dramatic presentation on the "poverty" of the sociology of deviance in the 1970s, Alexander Liazos (1972) chided the field for focusing on "nuts, sluts and perverts" and ignoring forms of crime involving the powerful. In fact, some scholars view the sociology of deviance as so fundamentally biased that the field is either dying or dead (see Sumner 1994: vii). The criticism is similar to arguments by constructionists, but the resolution to the perceived problem takes the form of a new definition of deviance and/or crime—a definition that focuses on a specific type of normative standard.

In the mid-1970s, Herman and Julia Schwendinger (1975: 132) proposed a human rights conception of the appropriate subject matter for criminology. They proposed that "crime" should be defined as conduct and social arrangements that violate "the historically determined rights of individuals." Since rights are a specific type of normative standard (justice norms), the definition attempts to redefine the subject matter of the field rather than provide a requiem for its demise. The range of topics encompassed by a rights definition includes much of the subject matter that falls within the sociology of deviance and the wider sociological study of social problems.

One of the appealing features of this approach is that offenses that affect collectivities would be central to the field and forms of activity involving whole societies and powerful interests would be highlighted. In fact, to the degree that animals are defined as possessing rights, the subject matter could extend to animal rights. Moreover, topics involving "culture wars" (Hunter 1991) would be encompassed within the sociology of deviance as power struggles over "rights." For example, one side to the abortion controversy extends the right to life from the moment of conception, and some anti-abortionists would accord the right to life of the unborn priority over the life and health of the mother. In contrast, there is strong support for women's rights to make their own choices. Even Americans who disapprove of abortion are likely to accord primacy to the life and health of the mother. Pro-life advocates anchor their arguments in what they define as self-evident rights of the unborn, and pro-choice advocates anchor their arguments in what they define as self-evident rights of women to control matters involving their own lives and health.

Social control: pending issues

For most of the history of sociology there were no general theories specifically addressing and defining social control. However, between the mid-1970s and the present, two prominent theorists proposed "theories of social control"—Donald Black (1976, 1979, 1983, 1984, 1989) and Jack Gibbs (1981, 1989, 1994, 2008). In an early discussion of the subject matter of social control, Gibbs (1972: 4) defined it as the search for answers to the question: "What are the causes and consequences of variation in the character of reaction to deviance among social units over time?" This question highlighted what he later called the "prophylactic" conception of social control—i.e. that social control was defined as "reactions to deviance." Donald Black (1976: 9, 2) defines deviant behavior "as conduct that is subject to social control" and social control as "the normative aspect of social life, or the definition of deviant behavior and the response to it, such as prohibitions, accusations, punishment, and compensation." This distinguishes social control from deviance, but Black (1976: 9) also proposes that "The quantity of social control defines the rate of deviant behavior." These concepts need to be more clearly distinguished from one another. If they are distinct concepts, then deviant behavior needs to be clearly distinguished from social control. One cannot "define" the other.

Gibbs undertakes the task of differentiating between deviance and social control in subsequent works where he rejects the "prophylactic" conception of social control (1981). He ultimately rejects the prophylactic conception on the grounds that the concept includes more than "reactions to deviance" and that not all reactions to deviance are instances of social control. According to Gibbs, any attempt to get someone else to do something or refrain from doing something can be considered an attempt at "control," but social control has certain special qualities.

To qualify as "social" control, such attempts must involve three parties. Social control is an attempt by one or more individuals to manipulate the behavior of another individual or individuals by or through a third party (by means other than a chain of command or sequence of orders). Gibbs' "third party"can be an actual person or a reference to "society," "expecta- tions," or "norms." For example, if one party attempts to influence another by invoking reference to a third party assumed to have authority (such as "I'll tell Mom!"), it is a type of "referential" social control. If one party attempts to control another by punishing a third (e.g. general deterrence), it is a form of "vicarious" social control. Numerous categories and subcategories of social control are delineated by Gibbs, but the major point is that the third party distinguishes *social* control from mere external behavioral control, simple interpersonal responses, or issuing orders for someone to do something.

This definition clearly distinguishes social control from "prophylactic" conceptions of social control. A variety of phenomena typically thought of as types of social control are not clearly "reactions to deviance" (such as propaganda, advertising, education, strikes, protests, and governmental regulations). Moreover, deviant behavior, itself, can be a type of social control (in terms of Gibbs' final definition of it). If deviant behavior can be a form of social control and social control can involve more than reactions to deviance, then the two concepts cannot be equated; nor can one be subsumed by the other. Gibbs' elaboration has to be noted because it highlights the fact that the study of social control includes far more than the study of reactions to deviance. Further specification of the relation between the two concepts should take the study of social control and deviance in new directions.

An integrated approach

The fact that the public has come to view the concept of "deviance" and the label "deviant" as pejorative terms is a topic for sociological inquiry itself and should not be allowed to bring about the demise of the sociology of deviance (see Jensen 2007). Each of the conceptions highlights distinct issues and questions about "properties" of norm-violating behavior, appearance and expression, and variable reactions to people and characteristics that fit into those categories (Jensen 2000). Constructionists point to the types of group conflicts, negotiations, and decisions that are made in the process of designating episodes, events, behaviors, and people as instances of some type of deviance. They lead scholars to ask whether there is a behavioral basis for the events and people assigned to some "official" category of deviance. The reactive component of deviant phenomena can obey its own principles quite independent of the behavioral component (see Gibbs 1981).

A normative perspective directs inquiry toward a behavioral foundation. Actual conduct in violation of legal or social norms is one of the best predictors for designations of people as criminal by different audiences, and activities that violate widely shared norms and beliefs about rights have a long history of prohibition in legal codes. Self-evident human rights might provide a more universal standard for such decisions but that approach does not eliminate disagreement on the exact nature of those self-evident standards nor on the proper adjudication among conflicting standards when rights are in conflict.

For some types of phenomenon, the subject matter will overlap and there will be considerable agreement about their propriety as subject matter in the study of deviance. For example, forcible rape is strongly condemned, reacted to as a problem requiring a response, and it is certainly a violation of the rights of the victim. On the other hand, controversies about such issues as date rape, rape processing, and spousal rape involve conflict over specific definitions of what constitutes rape, conflicting conceptions of "real" victims, and conflicting definitions of rights.

When a "rights" approach to the conception of deviance is adopted, new issues have to be addressed. If animals have rights, then a growing range of research activities may become subject to social control. At present, some animals having "more rights" than others and mistreatment of certain categories of animal are subject to more sanctions by funding agencies than others. It is not clear at present whether research activities that harm animals are defined as worthy of condemnation by any sizeable segment of the public.

Additional questions about rights can be explored. Do plants have rights? Does the planet earth have rights? These questions may strike some people as silly or absurd, but new environmental movements are beginning to raise such issues. Again, one and the same phenomenon can begin to move from the edges of one category toward the center where different conceptions overlap. Different emphases stem from different conceptions of deviance and consideration of their overlap and independence raises questions which illuminate the complexities of the subject matter.

Finally, compared to the amount of debate about the subject matter of the study of deviance, relatively little attention has been paid to the intersection of the study of social control with the study of deviance. The overlap seems quite apparent when social control is defined as reactions to deviance, but less than obvious when the study of social control is approached as a field of its own, independent of deviance. There has yet to be a dialogue over the intersection of such concepts despite the fact that prominent theorists have quite distinct approaches to the relation between deviance and social control.

References

Akers, R. L. (1985). *Deviant Behavior: A Social Learning Approach*. Third Edition. Belmont, California: Wadsworth.

Becker, H. S. (1963*). Outsiders: Studies in the Sociology of Deviance*. New York: The Free Press.

Best, J. (2004). *Deviance: Career of a Concept*. Belmont, California: Wadsworth/Thomson Learning.

Black, D. (1976). *The Behavior of Law*. New York: Academic Press.

——. (1979). "Common Sense in the Sociology of Law." *American Sociological Review* 44: 18–27.

——. (1983). "Crime as Social Control." *American Sociological Review* 48: 34–45.

——. (1984). *Toward a General Theory of Social Control*. Volume 1: *Fundamentals*; Volume 2: *Selected Problems*. Orlando, Florida: Academic Press.

——. (1989). *Sociological Justice*. New York: Oxford University Press.

Clinard, M. B., and R. F. Meier (2004). *Sociology of Deviant Behavior*. Twelfth Edition. Belmont, California: Wadsworth.

Cohen, A. K. (1966). *Deviance and Control*. Englewood Cliffs, New Jersey: Prentice-Hall.

Erikson, K. T. (1962). "Notes on the Sociology of Deviance." *Social Problems* 9: 307–14.

Gibbs, J. (1966). "Conceptions of Deviant Behavior: The Old and the New." *Pacific Sociological Review* 9: 9–14.

——. 1972. *Social Control*. New York: Warner Modular Publications, Module 1.

——. (1981). *Norms, Deviance and Social Control*. New York: Elsevier.

——. (1989). *Control: Sociology's Central Notion*. Urbana: University of Illinois Press.

——. (1994). *A Theory about Control*. Boulder, Colorado: Westview Press.

——. (2008). *Colossal Control Failures*. Boulder, Colorado: Paradigm.

Goffman, E. (1963). *Stigma: Notes on the Management of Spoiled Identity*. Englewood Cliffs, New Jersey: Prentice-Hall.

Goode, E. (1994). *Deviant Behavior*. Englewood Cliffs, New Jersey: Prentice-Hall.

Hunter, J. D. (1991). *Culture Wars: The Struggle to Define America*. New York: Basic Books.

Jensen, G. F. (2000). "Deviance, Definition of." In Clifford Bryant (Editor), *Encyclopedia of Criminology and Deviant Behavior*. Volume 1: *Historical, Conceptual, and Theoretical Issues*. New York: Taylor and Francis.

——. (2007). "The Sociology of Deviance" In Clifton D. Bryant and Dennis L. Peck (Editors), *The Handbook of 21st Century Sociology*. Thousand Oaks, California: Sage.

—— and D. G. Rojek (2009). *Delinquency and Youth Crime*. Long Grove, Illinois: Waveland Press.

Liazos, A. (1972). "Nuts, Sluts, and Perverts: The Poverty of the Sociology of Deviance." *Social Problems* 20:103–20.

Luckenbill, D.F., D. R. Cressey, and E. H. Sutherland (1992). *Principles of Criminology*. Eleventh Edition. Dix Hills, New York: General Hall.

Richardson, J. T., J. Best, and D. G. Bromley (1991). *The Satanism Scare*. New York: Aldine De Gruyter.

Rubington, R. and M. Weinberg (Editors). (2005). *Deviance: The Interactionist Perspective*. Boston: Allyn & Bacon.

Schwendinger, H. and J. Schwendinger (1975). "Defenders of Order or Guardians of Human Rights?" In I. Taylor and J. Young (Editors), *Critical Criminology*. London: Routledge and Kegan Paul.

Stark, R. (2007). *Sociology*. Belmont, California: Wadsworth.

Sumner, C. (1994). *The Sociology of Deviance: An Obituary*. New York: Continuum.

Tittle, C. R. (1995). *Control Balance: Toward a General Theory of Deviance*. Boulder, Colorado: Westview Press.

2

Constructing deviance

Joel Best

In *Outsiders*, Howard S. Becker (1963, p. 9) declared: "The deviant is one to whom that label has successfully been applied; deviant behavior is behavior that people so label." Becker's analysis was pivotal, in that it directed sociologists' attention to the centrality of subjective, definitional processes for understanding deviance (Best 2004). Although sociologists sometimes pretend that deviance is an objective quality of behavior—that some acts simply *are* deviant—most acknowledge that definitions of deviance vary across time and space.

Analysts adopt a variety of verbs to characterize these definitional processes. They speak of becoming deviant, of creating, defining, making, framing, manufacturing, inventing, or discovering deviance. This chapter favors another term—constructing. Speaking of constructing deviance links the study of deviance to the larger literature on the social construction of all sorts of reality (Berger and Luckmann 1966; Holstein and Gubrium 2008). To say that something is socially constructed is to acknowledge that people depend upon language to make the world meaningful, and language is inherently social; all knowledge is shaped by the social arrangements within which it is produced. This is fundamental: any claim that some act or condition is deviant depends upon a set of shared, subjective understandings about the nature of the social order.

The general statement that deviance is socially constructed encompasses a variety of definitional processes. This chapter seeks to identify some of the more significant ways in which deviance is constructed. It begins by considering the creation of new forms of deviance, before considering how deviant categories can be changed or eliminated.

Creating deviance

All varieties of deviance have histories and geographies. Definitions of deviant categories shift over time, and they also vary from place to place. Even acts that seem to be universally deplored, such as murder, show such variation. Particular sorts of killing may be considered deviant at some time or place, but as legitimate or justified at others (Spierenburg 2008). And of course other offenses—the use of a particular drug, a specific sexual practice, and so on—may display wild variation in whether they are considered deviant and, if so, just why they are deviant.

Analysts who adopt a constructionist perspective tend to focus on the creation or emergence of deviance. Defining an act or condition that has been considered respectable as now deviant is a fairly dramatic event, and a substantial literature has emerged around understanding this process.

Creating deviant categories

Many of these analyses adopt a macrosociological framework; they look at how deviant categories emerge in particular societies and at given historical moments. This is a topic that attracts the interest of analysts rooted in very different theoretical perspectives.

Conflict theorists, working in the intellectual tradition of Marx, tend to see the hand of elites in creating new categories of deviance. Viewing social control as a means for maintaining elites' position in and control over a society, they interpret creating deviant categories (by, say, passing laws against new criminal offenses) as a mechanism for preserving the status quo. In particular, shifts in society's economic base can threaten the established order, leading elites to protect their interests by designating activities as deviant. Thus, Chambliss (1964) argues that English vagrancy laws evolved to reflect shifting elite interests, first insuring that landowners would have access to cheap labor when the collapse of feudalism and the Black Death coincided to cause a labor shortage, and, later, as commerce became a more important economic sector, serving to protect merchants from idle rogues who might prey upon shipments of goods. By designating poor vagrants as deviant, the law protected the interests of the rich.

If conflict theorists emphasize the role of elite interests in creating deviant categories, sociologists working in the Durkheimian tradition focus on deviance's role in affirming social values. From this perspective, deviance is necessary for society, because it reinforces the social solidarity of its members ("the respectable") by devising rules; punishing those who break those rules ("the deviants") affirms the importance of the social ties that bind society together. New rules—creating new categories of deviance—allow society to adapt to social changes that may have threatened social solidarity or blurred old boundaries between respectability and deviance. For example, Erikson (1966) describes how the New England Puritans, who understood everything in religious terms and found their small, vulnerable colony beset by a sense of isolation and the hardships of building a new world, constructed witchcraft and other heresies as threatening their community, and sought to drive these deviants out. By identifying threats to the spiritual order, they reaffirmed the bonds of faith that held them together.

Sociologists adopting a third, rather broader theoretical approach emphasize Weberian concerns. That is, they see deviance and social control as products of cultural and structural changes that lead to status competition, shifts in authority structures, and the like. Their arguments can take various forms. For example, Gusfield (1963) traces the history of disputes over alcohol: during most of the 19th century, those opposed to drink promoted Temperance campaigns designed to persuade drinkers to abstain; however, as that century came to a close, anti-alcohol crusaders shifted to calls for Prohibition—for making alcohol illegal. In Gusfield's view, this shift reflected a status competition within American society: opposition to drink was concentrated among small-town Protestants of English descent—people who saw their political dominance and once-considerable status being challenged by the wave of immigrants from Eastern and Southern Europe who were settling in large cities. These new immigrants came from different cultures and religions, and they often took drinking for granted; their growing prominence challenged the status dominance of the native-born. In this status conflict, alcohol became an important status symbol, and banning drink served to demonstrate that the old elite still had power.

The shift from Temperance to Prohibition illustrates a second important Weberian process: a transformation in the authority to define and control deviance. The Temperance campaign had been rooted in religious authority; it understood drinking to be a moral lapse, a sin. Religious leaders had considerable authority in pre-Civil War America, but their influence was in decline by the late 19th century. The rise of Prohibition reflected a growing emphasis on the role of legal authority; under Prohibition, drinking's morality was irrelevant—it was now criminal behavior. Of course, national Prohibition was quickly repealed, and as the 20th century progressed, drinking increasingly came to be understood in yet another way—as an illness. This reflected another shift in authority. The 20th century saw a marked increase in the prestige of medical professionals, and a medical vocabulary (e.g. "disease," "symptom," treatment," etc.) was used to reframe all sorts of deviance—including drinking—that had previously been understood as moral or legal problems (Conrad 2007). The process of medicalization has itself evolved: in the mid-20th century, deviance was most often medicalized by psychiatrists who argued that deviant behavior was a manifestation of mental illness; however, by century's end, there was a new emphasis on explaining deviance in terms of an individual's genetic make-up, and recent decades have witnessed repeated efforts to identify the genetic markers for alcoholism. Thus, the creation of alcoholism as a deviant category reveals broader shifts in the relative authority of religion, law, and medicine.

While most sociological attention has focused on how these institutions' elites compete for the authority to define and control deviance, definitional campaigns can be mounted from outside elite circles. Some social movements seek to define particular acts or conditions as deviant, or to argue that authorities should devote more attention to controlling forms of deviance. For instance, while drunk driving has long been a criminal offense, offenders were not always subject to harsh sanctions. However, the highly visible campaign by the social movement organization Mothers Against Drunk Driving (MAAD) pressured officials to define drunk driving as a serious crime, and to pass and enforce tougher laws. Such movements, often mobilizing people who have been victimized, display popular support for creating deviant categories (Reinarman 1988).

Similarly, the mass media sometimes mount their own campaigns for deviance creation. Criminologists have long understood that crime waves are best understood as waves in media coverage. Media—sometimes, but not always, prompted by activists or elites—can focus attention on some variety of troubling behavior, perhaps giving it a dramatic name (e.g. "road rage" or "identity theft"), and suggesting that it is an increasing menace that demands action. Such coverage can draw public attention to troubling conditions and prompt the creation of new deviant categories (Chermak 2002).

In sum, the creation of new categories of deviance has attracted the attention of scholars working within a range of theoretical traditions. Different schools tend to emphasize particular actors and motivations: for Marxists, economic and political elites manufacture deviant categories to protect their interests; for Durkheimians, deviant categories are expressions of shared values that reinforce social solidarity; while Weberians recognize the importance of an array of status and professional interests that operate within a context of social movements and media organizations. In each case, however, there is the recognition that deviant categories are social constructions, created by actors who identify what is problematic, and presume that social control offers a solution.

Applying deviant labels

After new deviant categories are in place—a law is on the books, a disease is granted official recognition, or whatever—work remains to be done. Some deviant categories are never applied. Many US states, for instance, have had laws prohibiting all sorts of common sexual behavior, yet those laws were virtually never enforced. In other cases, labels may be used fairly frequently, yet be applied to only a small proportion of those engaged in the deviant act. Contrast the many millions of times Americans smoke marijuana annually with the vastly smaller number of pot busts.

The application of available social control categories to specific instances of deviance also involves social construction; social control agents must construct—label— particular actors as deviant. Traditionally, studies of labeling deviance adopt a microsociological stance, examining how social control agents identify deviants, how deviants seek to avoid being labeled, and the social psychological consequences of having been labeled. There are countless case studies that examine labeling processes in particular settings: how police officers maintain order on skid row by choosing when to make arrests (Bittner 1967); how psychiatrists determine which patients can be involuntarily committed for observation (Scheff 1966); how prosecutors decide which sexual assault cases ought to be taken to court (Frohmann 1998); and so on. However, these same labeling practices also have macrosociological significance.

The creation of a deviant category creates a resource for social control agents, a new label that might be applied to some offenders. Just as the construction of deviant categories is an accomplishment, in that it creates a new label and thereby a new way of categorizing the world, so too is each individual application of that label a form of social construction, in which particular acts and people are designated—by social control agents, other deviants, ordinary folks, and even themselves—as offenders. In most cases, this work is done by social control agents, who evaluate the behavior of many individuals and identify some as warranting being labeled as deviants. This process should not be imagined to be some straightforward, mechanistic enforcement of rules; rather, particular decisions always occur within and are shaped by particular contexts. What exactly is the prospective deviant thought to have done? Who does this individual seem to be (e.g. gender, race, age, class, demeanor)? Are other people observing the interaction between this individual and the social control agent? What sorts of work pressures are affecting the social control agents (e.g. is the agency demanding that more cases of deviance be processed; how much discretion do individual agents have; is the agent's shift about to end)? There are all manner of considerations that can affect decisions whether to label a particular act, committed by a specific individual, as an instance of deviance. Deviance is not simply detected by social control agents; it must be actively constructed, so that this act—or this individual—is deemed deviant.

In sum, deviance must be created at both the macro and the micro levels. Acts and conditions need to be created as categories of deviance, through the construction of deviant categories. And, once those categories are available for the use of social control agents, they can be applied as labels to particular cases, so that individuals are constructed as deviants.

Altering deviance

The activities of social control agents often come under criticism. Critics adopt a range of positions. They may argue that social control is inadequate, insufficient to meet the need. Such critiques warn that social control is not doing enough to curb deviance, that agents need to be more active. Thus, warnings that crime is out of control may lead to calls for increasing the numbers of police, passing new laws that identify more crimes or specify tougher penalties, and so on. Alternatively, critics may warn that social control is excessive, too harsh. For instance, there are arguments that marijuana should be decriminalized, and treated more like alcohol as an acceptable—within limits—intoxicant; or that particular methods of execution are inhumane and ought to be replaced. A third form of critique views social control policy as not so much too lenient or too harsh, but as misguided. Calls to medicalize deviance, for instance, often insist that punitive approaches fail and cannot help but fall short, while treatment offers the only hope of success.

Any of these critiques has the potential to lead to new constructions—or reconstructions— of deviant categories. Most deviant categories have complex histories. Cultural and structural changes in the larger society often lead to shifts in what is considered deviant, why it is considered deviant, the circumstances under which it is considered deviant, what sort of deviance it is thought to be, and what is thought to be the best way to respond. The history of homosexuality illustrates this complexity: at various times and in various places, homosexual relations have been valorized, ignored, and denounced; homosexuality has been variously understood as a sin, a crime, a psychological disorder, a genetic predisposition, and so on; and homosexuals have been characterized as constituting everything from conspiracies to political minorities (Greenberg 1988). It is not that homosexuality was simply created, at some particular moment, as a deviant category. Rather, time and again, existing ideas about homosexuality have been denounced by all manner of critics, who have claimed various sorts of authority—ecclesiastical, moral, legal, medical, and scientific. Each set of critics has argued that currently dominant ideas about homosexuality are wrongheaded and require revision, so that homosexuality can be constructed in a new, superior fashion. It is important to understand that analogous cycles— critique leading to a new construction that in turn inspires a new critique—characterize the histories of most deviant categories.

Note, too, that these critics often direct their attention not just to the abstract deviant categories but also to the practical social control policies that label deviants. Critiques identify ways in which existing control agents need to alter their practices in dealing with deviants, or they may call for more sweeping changes—for the establishment of entirely new social control arrangements. For instance, the history of policing has been marked by continual calls for reform, with critics attacking all manner of police excesses and insufficiencies—including corruption, brutality, racial profiling, and other abuses of police powers—as well as failures to live up to others' expectations of police (Klockars 1985).

Reconstructions are often linked to cultural or structural changes in the larger society. Thus, the 20th century saw such fundamental transformations in medicine as: the effort to professionalize medical care by standardizing medical education, setting standards for hospitals, and so on; the development of new, more effective treatments (most especially the emergence of antibiotics); the spread of medical insurance; and the explosion in biological knowledge that followed the discovery of DNA (and the spread of medical applications of that knowledge) (Starr 1982). These changes served to raise the prestige of medicine, leading more people to defer to medical authority. For deviance, this had the consequence that more forms of deviance were medicalized, with medical professionals assuming much of the responsibility for social control. Not only were new categories of deviance created, but existing deviant categories were reconstructed as medical problems. This in turn meant that labeling—the application of deviant categories in particular cases—was more likely to involve social control agents adopting medical language to justify their actions.

Social control agents prefer to present their activities as correct, justified, to imply that their approach is not merely the best but really the only sensible reaction to deviance. Taking this sort of confident stance helps ward off criticism that social control is arbitrary or unfair. But, in fact, social control agents often find their activities—to say nothing of the rationales that justify those activities—under attack. There are constant calls—from deviants, activists, the general public, the mass media, politicians, and even from within the social control agencies themselves—to reorient or reconstruct deviant categories and the ways in which those categories are applied.

Vindicating deviance

One variety of reconstruction deserves special mention—vindication. This occurs when a deviant category is abandoned, when behavior that has been considered deviant is redefined as respectable, or at least acceptable (Best 1979). When a criminal statute is struck down, and formally illegal behavior is legalized or decriminalized, it is a form of vindication. When the members of the American Psychiatric Association voted to remove homosexuality from the APA's *Diagnostic and Statistical Manual* (the *DSM* is widely acknowledged to be the authoritative catalog of mental disorders), homosexuality went from being defined as a form of mental illness to be reconstructed as an alternative form of sexual behavior (Kirk and Kutchins 1992).

Explanations for vindication parallel those for the creation of deviant categories. Conflict theorists emphasize the role of shifting economic interests (e.g. the early 20th-century public relations campaigns by tobacco and alcohol producers to redefine women's smoking and drinking as glamorous and sophisticated, rather than immoral). Functionalists point to shifting moral consensus (e.g. public opinion polls revealing growing tolerance for homosexuality). Scholars working in the Weberian tradition describe shifting status interests and changes in the social control apparatus (e.g. vindication campaigns by gay-rights activists). Note, too, that vindication can be viewed from a micro—as well as a macro—perspective; redefinitions of formerly deviant behavior as respectable must be turned into practical activities by social control agents. That is, agents must change their routines, so that they now treat formerly deviant behavior as outside their purview. Vindication, while less studied by sociologists, is undoubtedly as complex and multifaceted as the creation of deviant categories.

Since the Second World War, there have been a number of campaigns—several successful— to vindicate various forms of deviant exchange (so-called victimless crimes). Abortion has been legalized, many US states have reformed their laws governing sexual behavior between consenting adults, restrictions against pornography have been reduced, and there are currently far more forms of legalized gambling than in the mid-20th century. On the other hand, campaigns to legalize, criminalize, or medicalize illicit drug use have been relatively unsuccessful. Moreover, all of these redefinitions remain fairly controversial: there is a visible anti-abortion movement; critics continue to speak out against sexual promiscuity, pornography, and gambling; and would-be reformers advocating legalized marijuana or assisted suicide find that they have active, vocal opposition (Dombrink and Hillyard 2007). Recalling the complicated histories of many deviant categories, in which reconstruction and redefinition are sometimes quite common, we should be careful about assuming that recent reforms will be permanent. In the long run, we know that change—not constancy—characterizes definitions of deviance.

The importance of subjectivity

However much analysts may prefer to assume that some act or condition *is* deviant, that it can be identified, counted, and the resulting numbers subjected to sophisticated statistical analyses, deviance is, as Becker noted, a product of subjective judgments. Deviant categories emerge, evolve, and fall out of favor, just as social control agents choose to apply or ignore particular deviant categories. Whatever is counted must first be defined, and understanding what is defined as deviant has proven to be a rich topic for scholars of deviance.

References

Becker, Howard S. 1963. *Outsiders*. New York: Free Press.

Berger, Peter L., and Thomas Luckmann. 1966. *The Social Construction of Reality*. New York: Doubleday.

Best, Joel. 1979. "Economic Interests and the Vindication of Deviance." *Sociological Quarterly* 20: 171–82.

———. 2004. *Deviance: Career of a Concept*. Belmont, CA: Wadsworth.

Bittner, Egon. 1967. "The Police on Skid Row." *American Sociological Review* 32: 699–715.

Chambliss, William J. 1964. "A Sociological Analysis of the Law of Vagrancy." *Social Problems* 12: 177–94.

Chermak, Steven M. 2002. *Searching for a Demon*. Boston, MA: Northeastern University Press.

Conrad, Peter. 2007. *The Medicalization of Society*. Baltimore, MD: Johns Hopkins University Press.

Dombrink, John, and Daniel Hillyard. 2007. *Sin No More*. New York: New York University Press.

Erikson, Kai T. 1966. *Wayward Puritans*. New York: Wiley.

Frohmann, Lisa. 1998. "Constituting Power in Sexual Assault Cases." *Social Problems* 45: 393–407.

Greenberg, David F. 1988. *The Construction of Homosexuality*. Chicago, IL: University of Chicago Press.

Gusfield, Joseph R. 1963. *Symbolic Crusade*. Urbana: University of Illinois Press.

Holstein, James A., and Jaber F. Gubrium (eds.). 2008. *Handbook of Constructionist Research*. New York: Guilford.

Kirk, Stuart A., and Herb Kutchins. 1992. *The Selling of DSM*. Hawthorne, NY: Aldine de Gruyter.

Klockars, Carl B. 1985. *The Idea of Police*. Beverly Hills, CA: Sage.

Reinarman, Craig. 1988. "The Social Construction of an Alcohol Problem." *Theory and Society* 17: 91–120.

Scheff, Thomas J. 1966. *Being Mentally Ill*. Chicago, IL: Aldine.

Spierenburg, Pieter. 2008. *A History of Murder*. Malden, MA: Polity.

Starr, Paul. 1982. *The Social Transformation of American Medicine*. New York: Basic Books.

3

Tolerable, acceptable, and positive deviance

Robert A. Stebbins

Tolerable, acceptable, and positive deviance have in common the fact that each explains how individuals differ along one or more important dimensions from the large majority of others in their group or the larger local community in which they live. From what is known at present about deviance viewed from these three perspectives, it is best to treat each as a nominal, or separate, scheme. Placing them on a continuum of some sort is not logically possible at this time, and may never be.

This chapter looks first at tolerable deviance, the approach most closely aligned with mainstream theory in deviance and criminology. Acceptable deviance, which resembles its tolerable cousin in certain ways, is covered next. With these two as background we are in a good position to examine positive deviance.

Tolerable deviance

This perspective dates to 1988 and the first edition of the author's book *Deviance: Tolerable Differences.* The present statement is drawn from the second edition (Stebbins 1996), however, where I define deviance as behavior judged as violating one or more of the community's *moral norms.* This judgment is collective, a result of many people having sufficient power or influence to make the judgment stick. Moral norms emerge from the community's definition of right and wrong behavior and activity in certain emotionally charged areas of everyday life. They serve as the broad directives by which community members implement their institutionalized solutions to problems significantly affecting their valued way of life. These norms indicate in a general way what the community expects of its members in particular areas of social life and what it considers rejections of those expectations. Moral norms stand apart from other kinds of expectations, such as ordinances, regulations, customs, and folkways.

Notwithstanding their moral overtones, some deviant acts are tolerated by most members of the community. *Tolerance* is an attitude or orientation that individuals hold toward certain activities or thoughts of others that differ substantially from their own (Stebbins 1996: 3). It is a relatively passive disposition, falling roughly midway between scorn, or disdain, toward an activity or thought pattern, on the one hand, and embracement or acceptance of it, on the other. Both scorn and embracement, in contrast to tolerance, are active approaches to the behavior in question. When something is tolerated it is accorded legitimacy, though perhaps grudgingly.

At the same time, because tolerated thought and behavior are nonetheless mildly threatening, people have little interest in actually adopting tolerated behaviors or thought patterns as their own, or even accepting them as alternatives they might conceivably adopt in the future.

The presence of tolerance in society gives *tolerable deviance* its special status. With such deviance, the welfare of the community is still believed to be preserved. But this outlook holds true only just so long as such behavior is enacted by only a small proportion of members in a way that is only mildly threatening to the community's majority. Tolerable deviance stands in contrast to *intolerable deviance*, which greatly threatens the established order, causing the community to scorn it and therefore to try to eliminate it. Hagan (1991: 11–12) developed three measures for empirically distinguishing mildly threatening tolerable deviance from the highly threatening intolerable variety. Intolerable deviance is likely to be accompanied by the following: considerable agreement about its wrongfulness; a harsh community reaction; and a judgment that it is especially harmful. With tolerable deviance there is a significantly lower level of agreement about its wrongfulness; a significantly more lenient community reaction; and a belief that only the deviant is harmed, and then not seriously.

Many people are ambivalent about one or more of the activities falling under the heading of tolerable deviance. They know they ought to refrain from engaging in them, yet they find it difficult to escape their magnetic pull. This is the type of deviance Becker (1963: 26) had in mind when he observed that "it is much more likely that most people experience deviant impulses frequently. At least in fantasy, people are much more deviant than they appear." Little wonder that tolerable deviance is the classificatory home of most forms of deviant leisure (see Chapter 41).

Types of tolerable and intolerable deviance

The relationship between tolerable and intolerable deviance is, however, more complicated than just described. Thus tolerable deviance may be classed as criminal, noncriminal, or legitimate. *Criminal tolerable deviance*, though actually illegal according to criminal law, is generally treated by police and wider community alike as having minor importance compared with mainstream intolerable deviance. That is, criminal tolerable deviance is seldom officially challenged. Several conditions explain this response. The laws in question may be vague, exemplified well by those pertaining to the production and sale of pornography. Or they may be difficult to enforce, as are those pertaining to group sex, cheating at gambling, and player violence in sport. And some laws have, at certain points in history, low enforcement priority—for instance, those controlling disorderliness, marijuana consumption, and recreational use of prescription drugs. In short, people who tolerate a form of deviance fail to see it as inherently evil.

Noncriminal tolerable deviance lies outside the jurisdiction of law. At present in many countries in the West no laws exist prohibiting adultery (when morals of minor children are not endangered) or striptease work (when done within legal limits of undress). Nudism practiced in private resorts is frequently not illegal, nor are heavy drinking and nonpublic drunkenness. Many political jurisdictions define as illegal only certain forms of gambling, while saying nothing about others.

Legitimate tolerable deviance is guaranteed by law. In most Westernized countries people may legally think as they wish, with some holding religious and political beliefs that diverge significantly from those of the majority in the community. They may also embrace beliefs about the supernatural, rejecting thereby scientific explanations of physical and psychological reality. Certain minor forms of mental disorder are also tolerable and within the law if, according to the general public, they amount to no more than "warped" sets of beliefs. Neuroses, as opposed to psychoses (which must be classified as intolerable deviance), include such reactions as phobias, neurotic anxiety, partial personality impairment, and obsessive-compulsive acts.

The relationship between tolerable and intolerable deviance is portrayed in Table 3.1.

Of course, much more of a case must be made for classifying a type of deviance as tolerable or intolerable than can be considered in this chapter. This is done, in part, in Stebbins (1996: chs. 3–10) and in Chapter 41 of this book. In the meantime, it should be understood that the types of tolerable and intolerable deviance in a community extant at a particular time in history reflect the current values of people collectively powerful enough to influence public opinion and shape legislative, enforcement, and judicial practice. In other words, their definition of threat is the one by which some forms of deviance are officially treated as intolerable, while other forms are unofficially treated as tolerable. Groups lacking such power may look askance on some of these generally tolerated forms of deviance, as do, for example, many smokers when reflecting on today's restrictive laws governing smoking in public places.

The foregoing three types of tolerable deviance constitute an incomplete list, because as the distribution of power changes, the list tends to change as well. Some forms of intolerable deviance may gradually become tolerable, as is presently evident to a greater or lesser degree for abortion, use of marijuana, and production and consumption of pornography. Meanwhile, tolerable forms may drift toward intolerability, which appears to be happening today for smoking and has already happened, in a way, for use of performance-enhancing drugs in sport.

By contrast, intolerable deviance is behavior in violation of powerful criminal and non-criminal moral norms. Its core forms are illegal—what Daniel Glaser (1974: 60) poetically labelled "crimes of predation." These acts include theft, rape, burglary, murder, forgery, and assault as well as swindling, embezzlement, and other types of fraud. Bribery fits in this category, too. Noncriminal forms of intolerable deviance are seen as bizarre mental aberrations or severe, destructive addictions; they include suicide, alcoholism, drug addiction, compulsive gambling, and severe mental disorder (e.g. psychosis). They violate the moral precept that people be in control of their thoughts, behavior, and emotions. Clearly, some forms of deviance are tolerated when carried out at a certain level, for example heavy drinking or habitual gambling, but become ever more scorned as they become addictive. Because intolerable deviance compared with the other types is covered elsewhere in this book and because space is limited, it will not be considered in this chapter.

Table 3.1 Tolerable and intolerable deviance

Threat scale	Norms	Criminal deviance	Noncriminal deviance	Legitimate deviance
Great	Mores	ID	ID	–
↓	Criminal laws	ID/TD	–	–
Mild	Other moral norms	–	TD	TD

Key: ID = Intolerable deviance
TD = Tolerable deviance
– = Logically impossible cross-classification

Source: Stebbins 1996: 5

Why engage in tolerable deviance?

The tolerable deviance perspective offers three broad reasons that help explain why people engage in such behavior. One, sometimes they turn to such deviance because it is interesting or pleasurable to do as *leisure*. Two, in general terms, people sometimes engage in tolerable deviance as a *livelihood* or an aid to a livelihood or as a serious amateur pursuit. Three, some tolerable deviance serves as a mode of *adjustment*, as a way of arriving at a behavioral balance between personal needs and goals, on the one hand, and the demands of other people and society, on the other. This is ordinarily a long-term process taking several years. While most, if not all, tolerable deviance can be seen as a form of adjustment, much of it can also be identified and justified as leisure or work or both. Still, a residual category of deviant adjustment exists for which, in our culture, there is no explicit term. Residual adjustments, known as "residual rule breaking" (Scheff 1984: 38), are sometimes lumped by professionals and the general public under the heading of mental illness or mental disorder.

While theories of crime and deviance abound, only the foregoing perspective bears directly on tolerable deviance. Certain other theories, though they never directly refer to such deviance, do nonetheless help explain indirectly its emergence, persistence, decline, and place in the larger society. These theories—they are anomie-strain, labeling, value-conflict, functionalism, and medicalization—cannot be adequately covered here, but interested readers will find detailed reviews of them elsewhere in this book.

Acceptable deviance

Lesley Harman (1985) pioneered the idea of *acceptable deviance*. Her goal was to shed additional light on the imprecise and complicated line separating conformity and deviation. She defined acceptable deviance as "behavior which deviates enough from the norm such that it is not entirely predictable, yet which conforms enough to the norm to be acceptable as signifying membership" (Harman 1985: 2). She observed that a liberal democratic ethic prevails in Western society, an ideology that asserts that individuals have the right and the freedom to express their unique identities. Increases in society's individuality and creativity are encouraged. Still the existence of society as a collection of rule-governed individuals interested in the common goal of social order requires members to share basic conceptions about what it is that makes them a group. These two demands of conformity and deviation are contradictory.

Harman points out that people ordinarily care to avoid being seen as "over-involved." That is, an acceptable member of society arrives at a negotiated accommodation between the extreme demands of conformity and deviance, with acceptable deviance being an apparent solution to this "paradox." Seen from another angle the individual, in being acceptably deviant, is engaging in "rule bending." "One may bend rules to the extent that the individual appears to have control over them, but not to the point that s/he poses a threat to the social order" (Harman 1985: 2–3). In this regard Harman extends Erving Goffman's ideas on involvements—main and side, dominant and subordinate—as well as his observations on rule distance. She says it is acceptable for an individual to bend the rules of social interaction (by engaging in subordinate involvements) as long as it is clear that he can account for the deviant action (by being prepared to engage in the dominant involvement when it arises), and as long as, once made, subordinate involvement does not become dominant. Actors must always demonstrate their commitment to the group, which frees them to express themselves through side and main involvements.

Harman illustrated her conceptualization of acceptable deviance with observations on fashion and slang. To be fashionable is to be acceptably deviant. Personal good taste keeps the fashionable individual safe, from going beyond acceptability to forms of dress regarded as serious aberrations. The latter is "outrageous" fashion.

As for slang, Harman says there must be ways to introduce new colloquialisms in the group. Yet, any member doing this undertakes a risky innovation, since other members may refuse the new term. If it lingers as an outrageous item in their lexicon, it is deviant and unacceptable. If a few members begin using the new word or phrase, its outrageousness declines, drifting toward fashionableness. If the trend continues, the new term becomes increasingly common in the group's vocabulary, its use becoming a mark of membership there.

Mutunda (2007) analyzed patterns of Nyanja slang among young adults in Lusaka, Nambia. Of the fifteen reasons for using slang identified in an earlier study, among them sheer high spirits and an exercise of wit or ingenuity, one stood out. It was "the desire to break away from the conventions of the past, or even of the present, and achieve originality, if only in a small way, by using a new, or if not a new, an unconventional word or expression." This reason, Mutunda observes, is especially relevant to youth slang, for it is acceptable deviance. Members of the group who use such terms display an appropriate sense of being fashionable. Being in fashion through introduction and use of new slang is also a mark of the user's distinctive identity.

So far the idea of acceptable deviance has failed to generate much research. The term is sporadically encountered in scholarly articles, but rarely as an explanatory concept as Mutunda used it.

Positive deviance

Discussion is limited here to the positive deviance/negative deviance debate, also starting in 1985, which has added theoretic color to the sociological study of deviance. Excluded for reasons of space is use of the positive perspective as a management and leadership tool in various organizations and its several applications in other areas of life.

Brad West (2003) has written a thoughtful article in which he summarizes the debate about the idea of positive deviance and weighs in with his own conclusions as a suggested resolution of differences. David Dodge (1985) ignited the controversy, in its contemporary version, in an article in which he examined the "over-negativized conceptualization of deviance." He urged specialists in deviance studies to recognize as positively deviant, "those persons and acts that are evaluated as superior because they surpass conventional expectations" (Dodge 1985: 18). Admired, honorable exceptions in, for example, sport, art, science, and politics, compared with what is usually achieved, should be studied. Such people are deviant, too, albeit positively. There has been, Dodge argued, too much concentration on the negative, condemnable kinds of deviance.

Erich Goode (1991) and Edward Sagarin (1985), among others, countered that the idea of positive deviance is oxymoronic, a contradiction in terms. Nothing may be gained by injecting such confusion into deviance theory, for the idea of deviance as the tails of a bell-curved distribution of behavior calculated along a common dimension has already been convincingly rejected (see Sagarin 1985). The two ends of the putative dimension are very different.

Dodge argued, however, that some people highly honored for their achievements are also negatively deviant, albeit, it should be added here, in circles outside those doing the honoring. An exceptionally able pickpocket might be highly regarded for his abilities among local thieves of the same bent, but scorned by police and victims alike. A charismatic leader of a deviant religious group or an outstanding poker player would have similarly contrasting images.

Of course it can be observed that negative deviance sometimes has positive consequences, as in a serial rapist or arsonist whose activities bring the local community together to try to end the scourge. Yet, we could hardly label as positive the precipitating deviant activities. The same holds for the deviant behavior of one era that forces social change leading to a positive understanding of it in a future era. Christ was deviant in his time, even if Christianity is now an honorable religion in many parts of the world.

Of course the public, or a sizeable part of it, may be ambivalent in their judgment of certain deviants. West (2003) cites a number of examples of such "antiheros," celebrated murderers, bank robbers, and the like who have attracted substantial crowds of nondeviant followers. These Jesse Jameses and Robin Hoods have acquired a mythical status and level of charisma with some segments of the population. Yet, this might be more accurately seen as a problem of interpretation: does the community believe these people are bad enough to be tagged as deviants and, as time goes by, does it continue to believe in its judgment? This is less about positiveness or negativeness per se than about the antecedent process of judging the individual and his questionable activities.

In his concluding remarks West sides substantially with the negative, or traditional, approach:

> The conceptualisation of positive deviance in this article argues against the original advocacy that it refer to "persons and acts that are evaluated as superior" due to a deviation of norms, in that "they surpass conventional expectations" (Dodge 1985: 18). The critics of the positive deviance concept are correct in their judgement that use of the term in this way is oxymoronic and would take the field in directions that are inconsistent with deviance.

Nevertheless, we should also be attending to the positive side of life, says West, even in its deviant forms. In this murky sphere of life, too, all is not negative.

On a broader plane, the emphasis on positive deviance must be seen in the light of a much larger concern in sociology, which I have identified as its penchant for "problem solving" (Stebbins 2009). This discipline has long been centered on the negative, on life's many problems, including deviant behavior. It is time now for a "positive sociology," which looks into how, why, and when people pursue those things in life that they desire, and the things they do to make their existence attractive and worth living. Positive sociology is the study of what people do to organize their lives such that those lives become, in combination, substantially rewarding, satisfying, and fulfilling, which sometimes takes the form of positive deviance. This is not to suggest that we abandon the study of negative deviance. Rather we should avoid trying to graft the study of positive deviance onto it, and consider the second as a separate, albeit sometimes related, avenue for developing a positive sociology. This new field has roots in the sociology of leisure, whose relationship to deviance is explored elsewhere in this book.

Conclusions

Tolerable and intolerable deviance are identifiable through violation of moral norms, a condition not shared by the other two perspectives. By contrast, in acceptable deviance, the norm in question is not violated at all, only stretched somewhat in its interpretation by the acceptably deviant person. Moreover, any norm (moral, non-moral) may be examined for acceptable deviance from it.

In positive deviance the norms by which judgments of deviance are made are not usually moral; they are not essentially about what is morally right and wrong in the community. Rather the norms in question, at bottom, establish levels of excellence, which, through positive deviance, a few notable people manage to meet exceptionally and hence admirably. Though, as just noted, such norms may be morally tinged, their essence lies in their capacity to guide and measure achievement, this achievement being honored by the majority of those concerned.

Each perspective contributes to our understanding of how individuals differ along one or more important dimensions—tolerance, acceptability, excellence—from the large majority of people in their group or the larger local community.

References

Becker, H. S. (1963) *Outsiders: Studies in the Sociology of Deviance*, New York: Free Press.

Dodge, D. L. (1985) "The over-negativized conceptualization of deviance: a programmatic exploration," *Deviant Behavior*, 6: 17–37.

Glaser, D. (1974) "The classification of offenses and offenders," in D. Glaser (ed.), *Handbook of Criminology*, Chicago, IL: Rand McNally.

Goode, E. (1991) "Positive deviance: a viable concept," *Deviant Behavior*, 12: 289–309.

Hagan, J. (1991) *The Disreputable Pleasures: Crime and Deviance in Canada* (3rd edn), Toronto, ON: McGraw-Hill Ryerson.

Harman, L. D. (1985) "Acceptable deviance as social control: the cases of fashion and slang," *Deviant Behavior*, 6: 1–15.

Mutunda, S. (2007) "Language behavior in Lusaka: the use of Nyanja slang," *International Journal of Language Society and Culture*, 21 (published online).

Sagarin, E. (1985) "Positive deviance: an oxymoron," *Deviant* Behavior, 6: 169–81.

Scheff, T. J. (1984) *Being Mentally Ill: A Sociological Theory* (2nd edn), New York: Aldine.

Stebbins, R. A. (1996) *Tolerable Differences: Living with Deviance* (2nd edn), Toronto, ON: McGraw-Hill Ryerson.

——(2009) *Personal Decisions in the Public Square: Beyond Problem Solving into a Positive Sociology*, New Brunswick, NJ: Transaction.

West, B. (2003) "Synergies in deviance: revisiting the positive deviance debate," *Electronic Journal of Sociology*, 7 (published online).

4

The deconstruction of deviance

Mark Konty

When social science offered the metaphor of the *construction* of social reality (Berger and Luckman 1966) the *deconstruction* of that reality soon followed. Jacques Derrida introduced the term in *Of Grammatology* (1967). While Derrida focused narrowly on literary text in his early work, the theory and method of deconstruction became an integral part of the "new" social theories: poststructuralism, postmodernism and various veins of critical theory (Agger 1991, Lyman 1997, Leledakis 2000).

One can become dizzy considering the voluminous debate over what Derrida or his intellectual predecessor Heidegger *really* meant with the concept of deconstruction. Moreover, its meaning appears to have broadened as it was applied to the various perspectives of the different social sciences and humanities. Perhaps the broadest view of deconstruction is the analytical process that examines the assumptions and experiences that shape meaning. Rather than taking these for granted, deconstruction identifies how assumptions and experiences result in shared cultural meaning.

As inexorably related social phenomena pregnant with assumptions, experience and shared cultural meaning, deviance and social control can be deconstructed. What then is meant by the "deconstruction of deviance"?

One way to think about deconstruction is to contrast it with the concept of construction. The social construction of deviance refers to the conditions, processes and effects of social interaction and cultural meanings that together invent and reify the designation of a behavior as *deviance* and the people we call *deviants* (see Chapter 2, this volume). Deviance is not a "thing" that is objectively real and tangible; rather it is created and recreated through human interaction. Deviants are not a "type" of person that can be diagnosed with a checklist of symptoms but simply any person to whom the deviant label has successfully been applied (Becker 1963).

In this sense the deconstruction of deviance calls attention to the conditions, processes and effects that construct deviance. The deconstruction of deviance would note, for example, that certain conditions like material deprivation more easily produce "moral panics," extreme reactions to a perceived threat when there is not an actual increase in the level of threat. Some social processes, socialization for example, more readily transmit definitions of deviance than the non-verbal impersonal processes that guide us through the subway. Some effects, child abuse for example, are more likely to produce a deviant label for the perpetrator than a fistfight between two barflies. The deconstruction of deviance, in this sense, literally takes the building materials of the social construction of deviance and examines each independently.

In the hands of critical theory deconstruction becomes a method for identifying where social inequalities are manifest and a theory for explaining how elites manage to maintain the false consciousness of the plebs. For the critical theorist, deconstruction is not simply an analytical tool but a weapon to fight oppression, a means to lift the blinders of false consciousness away and demonstrate how specific ontological assumptions are used to justify status inequality while people's experiences in that status order reify the existing system. In this view the deconstruction of deviance would not just examine the assumptions of femininity that produce the deviant "slut" label for women with active sex lives, but also how this assumption benefits male interests and can be applied to women for simply challenging the patriarchal hegemony. Many women, it turns out, are actually "falsely accused," guilty of nothing more than failing to live up to the feminine ideal (Tanenbaum 2000). The horrible period of lynching in the United States reveals not only how whites used terrorism to confine the black population to the bottom of the status hierarchy, but also how white male identity was constructed through its practice (Messerschmidt 1997)

All these variations on deconstructionism are true to Heidegger's and Derrida's argument to focus inquiry on subjective reality as experienced by individuals rather than the positivists' world of observation and objectivity. Reality is not something to be discovered by the careful use of the scientific method but rather something that is experienced uniquely by individuals living in particular settings, under particular assumptions and with particular experiences. Examining how these constituent parts construct meaning is the goal of deconstruction.

This chapter describes the deconstruction of deviance over the history of sociology's interest in the topic. It begins with the preconstructionist Durkheim parsing the "normal" and the "pathological," and the functionalist counterintuitive notion that deviance is good for society. Sociology then takes the allegorical critical turn where the method of deconstruction comes to the fore as a means of identifying the power and status relations in deviance. Deconstruction finally comes full circle as the study of deviance is declared dead, reports of which were greatly exaggerated. Stepping away from deconstruction as a research methodology, the chapter identifies the everyday use of deconstruction in social interaction.

The preconstructionists

Before there was a social construction of reality there were "social facts," an intangible nature to reality that exists outside the individual but is nevertheless as real as food and bullets. In *The Rules of the Sociological Method*, Emile Durkheim (1938) laid out a methodology for identifying aspects of society that are "real." Determining the effects of a "thing" is one way of telling if it is real or not. For example, he deconstructs "crime" into the "normal" and the "pathological," depending upon the effects it has on the society. Crime that delineates social boundaries, improves social solidarity and produces social change is "normal" and in this sense the fact of "normal crime" is real. Conversely, an amount of crime that produces disorder and disintegration is pathological, bad for the society, and just as real as normal crime. Crime, universally considered bad for a society, is deconstructed into crime that is good and crime that is bad. Durkheim takes apart the taken-for-granted assumption that crime is bad and launches several generations of sociologists in a search for other ways that crime can be deconstructed into the good and the bad.

The prototype of this search is Kingsley Davis' (1937) "The Sociology of Prostitution." Davis insists that the persistence of prostitution, condemned in the Bible and outlawed in

America, must have some benefit to a society. The act of sex is considered quite normal and encouraged in specific social relations. What separates the "crime" of prostitution from the "normal" act of marital coitus is simply a transactional nature, the exchange of money for sex. Davis also notes that society limits approved sex to marriage, but some men seek satisfaction outside marriage. This is a problem for marriage and the important family unit it buttresses as the man may form emotional attachments to other females. Prostitution, however, is simply a monetary rather than an emotional transaction and is thus free from this kind of complication. Prostitution provides access to sex without threatening a marriage, and is thus "good."

To be sure, the preconstructionists were not the intellectual source of Derrida's deconstruction. Nonetheless the functionalists took something with taken-for-granted meaning, and examined and challenged that meaning by identifying elements of the meaning in a way that actually opposed the taken-for-granted assumption that deviance is "bad." The preconstructionists, however, did not consider the role of power and status in producing the meanings they deconstructed; that turn was just down the road.

The critical turn (around)

The "critical turn" is a much used, abused, disabused, and misused phrase, often used to describe the time in American sociology when the dominant functionalist paradigm was challenged by a handful of scholars who insisted that not everyone shared the fruits of society's functions. The turn away from functionalist theory would eventually see functionalism relegated to sociology textbooks.

The sociology of deviance was one of the subject areas to turn the fastest and this was due in no small part to the use of deconstruction by sociologists studying deviance. The labeling perspective started the turn. Perhaps not intentionally, but it offered the first challenge to the notion that social control has only positive consequences. Later, social conflict theory and other critical perspectives would implicate the elite's control over the labeling process as a means to maintain the status order. The full deconstruction of power and social control turns functionalism back on itself and argues for the complete dismantling of existing power relations.

Labeling perspective

Someone steals a bicycle and is caught with the bike. The people in the community have a new label for that person: thief. With that new label comes new meaning about the person. The new meaning is not inert. It is not simply another label among labels. The "deviant" label imputes a negative character to the individual and begins a ceremony segregating the individual from the society in a "dramatization of evil" (Tannenbaum 1938). Lemert (1951) further deconstructs the deviant label and demonstrates that the relevant feature is not the act itself, but rather the response of the community. One can break rules many times without detection and escape the effects of labeling (primary deviance), but the real effects begin when the person is caught and labeled (secondary deviance). The negative reactions of others are part of the constructed meaning. The "normal" is now the "deviant." For even if one commits numerous foul and heinous acts, one is neither foul nor heinous until someone else detects and labels the act.

Managing these deviant labels is not easy. In *Stigma*, Erving Goffman (1963) describes the various strategies people use to avoid or attenuate the "stigma" associated with the deviant label. Again, the act itself may be irrelevant, as even the "falsely accused" must treat the label as real in its consequences. Howard Becker (1963), in the seminal *Outsiders*, adds to this the observation that the deviant label is more potent than all others as it becomes a "master status." He too

33

advances the proposition that the rule and the act are themselves irrelevant to the label; all that matters are the responses of others. Goffman and Becker both deconstruct the deviant label to find the source of its meaning and find that it is not the action and not the rule that make the deviant label, it is the negative responses of others that create the consequences for the "person so labeled."

Deconstructing the labeling process soon revealed the role that power and status play in applying deviant labels. William Chambliss' "The Saints and the Roughnecks" (1973b) illustrates how two groups of youth, one high status and one low status, both involved in criminal behavior, could face entirely different labels and entirely different outcomes. The Saints committed delinquent and frequently dangerous acts, yet, by virtue of their resources and high status, faced few sanctions, were considered the "good kids," and went on to successful, happy lives. The Roughnecks committed criminal but rarely dangerous acts, yet, by virtue of their meager resources and low status, were considered the "bad seeds," were constantly punished and for the most part lived miserable, short lives. Chambliss deconstructed the meaning of "deviant" in the town of "Hannibal" and explained how economic and status relations affect the constructed meaning of a youth as a Saint or a Roughneck.

Critical theories

Conflict criminology pushed the critical turn by identifying how the law and criminal justice system are used to maintain the stratification system. Criminal laws harshly punish small-time property criminals but slap white-collar criminals on the wrist. Justice can be purchased through a good lawyer and the scales of justice tip heavily toward those with more status and resources. Deviance scholars were already on this path of course, identifying the ways that norms and social control maintained the status order to the benefit of the elite. Thus we begin to see Derrida's concept and view social constructions like deviance as the result of unequal power relations.

Dozens of studies over the years described this process, but the work of Chambliss particularly stands out as deconstructing the law as a tool to serve elite interests (see, for example, Chambliss 1973a; Chambliss and Zatz 1993). Over two decades Chambliss deconstructed the legal process, property crimes, corruption and even mundane laws like vagrancy, finding in each case how the interests of the elite and their power to make law produced a "criminal" where before there was none. Elites use this same process to shield themselves from those same laws, redefining their own actions as part of a normally functioning society. Messerschmidt (1997) summed up Chambliss' and others' observations with a general theory that deconstructed deviance in terms of race, class and gender, demonstrating how the meanings and privileges associated with race, class and gender "structured" what gets defined and reacted to as deviant and who becomes deviant.

While the conflict theorists deconstructed deviance in terms of the economic status order, feminist sociology gave the discipline a harder turn, insisting that gender deviance was nothing more than a tool to maintain male power and status. Feminist criminologists pointed to the ways in which the criminal justice system treated men and women differently, enforcing laws, like prostitution, on women that were rarely enforced on men. In the field of deviance, feminist scholars enumerate the methods used by a patriarchal society to maintain male status. Numerous pejorative terms were applied to women who refused to act feminine, who wanted to rise in the labor or political hierarchy, play sports or simply wanted an erotic sex life. Sexually active women were not just devalued next to other women (the whore/Madonna dichotomy), but were stigmatized for the exact same behavior for which males were praised! Women athletes face the "lesbian stigma" and practice stigma avoidance (Blinde and Taub 2005). Feminist researchers deployed the method of deconstruction and laid bare the patriarchal underpinnings of a world that most took for granted as grounded in biological necessity.

The critical turn in social science, and deviance studies particularly, benefited from deconstructionism. It is not enough to say that deviance is socially constructed, unique to specific times and places, without explaining how it is that those constructions happen. The method of deconstruction exposed the role of power, interests, status and resources in both defining deviance and determining who would be defined as a deviant. Deviance and deviants are not natural a priori categories but arise out of human relations and more often than not out of unequal relations (Konty 2007).

Deconstruction of the deconstruction

Every deconstruction can be deconstructed.

(Agger 1991: 115)

The alternative rock band REM released an album in 1985 titled *Fables of the Reconstruction*. On the album cover the phrase "of the" is also written after the word "Reconstruction." So the title of the album actually reads: "Fables of the Reconstruction of the Fables of the Reconstruction of the Fables . . .," and so on. The implication is that the process is never-ending, much like the process of deconstruction. Once elites have been exposed by the deconstruction of deviance, what is left? Why, the deconstruction of the deconstruction of deviance, of course.

In an article that now finds its way into every deviance reader, Liazos (1972) critiques the study of deviance itself and rather than deconstructing the interests of those involved in the social control enterprise he deconstructs the interests of those studying deviance. "Nuts, sluts and perverts," it seems, are titillating. Students want to hear about them, faculty want to write about them, and publishers know they can sell articles and books about them. But titillation and marketing are fine and dandy until someone gets exploited, and Liazos argues that simply studying the deviant is exploitative. Here the deconstruction leads to an entirely new conclusion, that by studying and deconstructing deviance, the researcher reifies the very definitions of deviance they claim to destroy! The researcher may wax poetically about "elite deviance" and "power relations" but does nothing tangible to stop it. The researcher instead is aiding and abetting the further exploitation of the powerless deviant.

Summers (1994) goes still farther and claims that the deconstruction of deviance has "demolished the terrain"—there is nothing left to fight over but "empty trenches" and "unexploded mines." Deviance, it seems, has been deconstructed to death. Summers proposes that sociologists should move on to the more promising area of the social movements that create deviance and drive the resistance. Henderschott (2002) aims one parting blow at the dead horse. In her deconstructive analysis the power relation is political, the liberals are trying to silence the conservatives by deconstructing all the deviance conservatives hold dear (homosexuality, drug use), while failing to deconstruct deviance as defined by liberals (political correctness, sexual harassment). Deviance studies are a one-sided political struggle, defining deviance up (Krauthammer 1993) or down (Moynihan 1993) according to leftist political goals. Since leftist ideals reign supreme in the academy, the only deviance being deconstructed is deviance with which liberals disagree.

Erich Goode (2002) takes up the defense of the "empty castle," claiming that deviance is still a viable field with many students, publications and research projects. Joel Best (2004) finds this argument unconvincing, arguing, much as Liazos did, that just because scholars and students are still titillated by deviance, that does not mean that deviance studies are a robust field. These two protagonists and several other writers take up the discussion in a special issue of *Sociological Spectrum* (2006, vol. 26). The conclusion? According to Konty (2006), as long as there is a subject to be studied, a process to be explained, and perhaps most importantly a robust debate about the subject, the subject's death has been greatly exaggerated (see also Konty 2007). The deconstruction of the deconstruction of the deconstruction continues.

Deconstruction by the damned

As scholars, we often have the conceit that only we can do what we do. Perhaps this conceit is merited on occasion and on first blush it seems likely that most people could not care less about the deconstruction of deviance, much less employ it as a methodology in their daily lives. Or do they?

Scott and Lyman's (1968) notion of "accounts" proposed that people offer verbal statements to explain their "untoward behavior" to one another. Actors are not required to explain their "routine, common sense behavior," only that behavior which may cause problems for the interaction or the relationship. In other words, people are motivated to explain their deviant behavior in terms that their interaction partners or general audience will accept. The purpose is to convince the other that the untoward, or deviant, behavior is actually acceptable, given the circumstances described in the account.

Building on Sykes and Matza's (1957) "techniques of neutralization," Scott and Lyman argued that people pursue one of two strategies. The first is an "excuse" where the deviant admits the act was wrong but claims that uncontrollable circumstances are responsible. For example, "I am late because of traffic" is an excuse that recognizes the violation of a punctuality norm but claims the tardiness was unavoidable. The second type of account is a "justification," where the deviant admits culpability for the act, but "denies the pejorative" quality of the act. For example, "I was late because I had to take my kid to the doctor" is a justification that admits intention and accepts responsibility but claims that the punctuality norm is nullified by a more important norm to care for one's children. Like Sykes and Matza, Scott and Lyman offer several subtypes of excuses and justifications, thus revealing a breadth and depth to people's explanations for their deviance.

Unlike Sykes and Matza, who claimed their techniques of neutralization preceded the deviant act and had a causal effect by reducing informal control mechanisms, Scott and Lyman make no such causal claim. In fact, the actual cause of the act is irrelevant as the important element is the way in which the deviant act is explained to one's interaction partners. In essence, Scott and Lyman make the claim that people are lay deconstructionists, deconstructing their own deviance via language into two elements: the responsibility for the act and the wrongness of the act. In so doing they change the meaning of the act from an act of wrongdoing to one that is excused or justified. The need to deconstruct one's deviance even surfaces when attempting to explain a heinous event like rape, with almost no hope of winning approval by the other (Scully and Marolla 1984).

Coda

The deconstruction of deviance is as old as the subject of deviance. While some took up Derrida's challenge to use deconstruction as a tool to uncover power relations, functionalists and the early proponents of labeling theory had already discerned the utility of deconstructing deviance into constituent elements and thereby uncover features of deviance not readily seen. In everyday interaction, people generally intuit the utility of deconstructing deviance as they deconstruct their own deviance as a means of restoring social relationships. The metaphor of deconstruction at last measure invites a recursive process where the language of deconstruction is itself deconstructed and criticized. Still, there is no arguing with the utility of the concept. While Derrida's vision and purpose may have been limited to literary texts, his ideas proved to be a powerful methodology for the sociology of deviance.

References

Agger, B. (1991) "Critical theory, poststructuralism, and postmodernism: their sociological relevance," *Annual Review of Sociology*, 17: 105–31.

Becker, H. (1963) *Outsiders: Studies in the Sociology of Deviance*. New York: Free Press.

Berger, P. L. and T. Luckman (1966) *The Social Construction of Reality*. Garden City, NY: Anchor Books.

Best, J. (2004) *Deviance: Career of a Concept*. Belmont, CA: Wadsworth.

Blinde, E. M. and D. E. Taub (2005) "Women athletes as falsely accused deviants: managing the lesbian stigma," *Sociological Quarterly*, 33: 521–33.

Chambliss, W. (1973a) "Elites and the creation of criminal law," in W. Chambliss (Ed.) *Sociological Readings in the Conflict Perspective* (pp. 430–44). Reading, MA: Addison-Wesley.

—— (1973b) "The saints and the roughnecks," *Society*, 11: 24–31.

Chambliss, W. and M. Zatz (1993) *Making Law: The State, the Law, and Structural Contradictions*. Bloomington: Indiana University Press.

Davis, K. (1937) "The sociology of prostitution," *American Sociological Review*, 5: 744–55.

Derrida, J. (1967) *De La Grammatologie*. Paris: Les Éditions de Minuit.

Durkheim, E. (1938) *The Rules of the Sociological Method*. New York: Free Press.

Goffman, E. (1963) *Stigma: Notes on the Management of Spoiled Identity*. Englewood Cliffs, NJ: Prentice-Hall.

Goode, E. (2002) "Does the death of the sociology of deviance make sense?," *The American Sociologist*, 33: 107–18.

Henderschott, A. (2002) *The Politics of Deviance*. San Francisco: Encounter Books.

Konty, M. (2006) "Of deviance and deviants," *Sociological Spectrum*, 26: 621–31.

—— (2007) "When in doubt, tell the truth: pragmatism and the sociology of deviance," *Deviant Behavior*, 28: 153–70.

Krauthammer, C. (1993) "Defining deviancy up: the new assault on bourgeois life," *The New Republic*, 21: 20–25.

Leledakis, K. (2000) "Derrida, deconstruction and social theory," *European Journal of Social Theory*, 3: 175–93.

Lemert, E. (1951) *Social Pathology*. New York: McGraw-Hill.

Liazos, A. (1972) "The poverty of the sociology of deviance: nuts, sluts, and perverts," *Social Problems*, 20: 103–20.

Lyman, S. (1997) *Postmodernism and a Sociology of the Absurd and Other Essays on the "Nouvelle Vague" in American Social Science*. Fayetteville: University of Arkansas Press.

Messerschmidt, J. W. (1997) *Crime as Structured Action: Gender, Race, Class and Crime in the Making*. Thousand Oaks, CA: Sage.

Moynihan, P. (1993) "Defining deviancy down," *American Scholar*, 62: 17–31.

Scott, M. B. and S. Lyman (1968) "Accounts," *American Sociological Review*, 33: 46–62.

Scully, D. and J. Marolla (1984) "Convicted rapists' vocabulary of motive: excuses and justifications," *Social Problems*, 31: 530–44.

Summers, C. (1994) *The Sociology of Deviance: An Obituary*. Buckingham: Open University Press.

Sykes, G. M. and D. Matz (1957) "Techniques of neutralization: a theory of delinquency," *American Sociological Review*, 22: 664–70.

Tannenbaum, F. (1938) *Crime and Community*. Boston, MA: Ginn.

Tanenbaum, L. (2000) *Slut! Growing up Female with a Bad Reputation*. New York: HarperCollins.

5

Social change and deviance

Nachman Ben-Yehuda

I am that part of the power that eternally wants bad and eternally does only good.

(Goethe's Faust)

Many researchers portray "deviance" in negative terms. That is, deviance as a characteristic of behavior that elicits negative social reactions is typically stigmatized and tends to endow those who are assumed to present such behavior with a deviantized and stigmatized identity.

Can such behavior be involved in processes of social change? Theoretical and empirical evidence suggest that indeed it can, and does.

Enter Durkheim

Emile Durkheim set the parameters for this issue. He first set out to establish that deviance is an inevitable aspect of all societies: "Crime . . . is . . . an integral part of all healthy societies . . . Crime is . . . necessary; it is bound up with the fundamental conditions of all social life, and . . . is useful" (Durkheim 1938: 67, 70).

Next, Durkheim attempted to specify exactly why this is so. His answer consists of two interconnected foci. In *The Rules of Sociological Method* (1938: 65–73), he argues:

> Crime is normal because a society exempt from it is utterly impossible . . . Crime implies not only that the way remains open to necessary changes, but that in certain cases it directly prepares these changes. Where crime exists, collective sentiments are sufficiently flexible to take on a new form, and crime sometimes helps to determine the form they will take.

This formulation implies that crime is a necessary and vital part of social systems because it can create and sustain the flexibility necessary for the social system to adapt itself to varying conditions. Crime and deviance are thus viewed as a mechanism for social change. Durkheim offers as evidence the example of a renowned criminal, Socrates: "According to Athenian law Socrates was a criminal, and his condemnation was no more than just. However, his crime, namely the independence of his thought . . . served to prepare a new morality and faith" (Durkheim 1938: 73).

However, in *The Division of Labor in Society*, Durkheim (1933: 70–110) notes:

> The only common characteristic of all crimes is that they consist . . . in acts universally
> disapproved of by members of each society . . . An act is criminal when it offends strong
> and defined states of the collective conscience . . . Crime is everywhere essentially the same,
> since it everywhere calls forth the same effect . . . Its primary and principal function is to
> create respect for . . . beliefs, traditions, and collective practices . . . Crime damages . . .
> unanimity [and] since it is the common conscience which is attacked, it must be that which
> resists, and accordingly the resistance must be collective. [Punishment's] true function is to
> maintain social cohesion intact.

Even more specifically, Durkheim (1933:102) notes:

> Crime brings together upright consciences and concentrates them. We have only to notice
> what happens, particularly in a small town, when some moral scandal has just been com-
> mitted. They stop each other on the street, they visit each other, they seek to come together
> to talk of the event and wax indignant in common. From all the similar impressions which
> are exchanged, for all the temper that gets itself expressed, there emerges a unique temper—
> which is everybody's without being anybody's in particular. That is the public temper.

What Durkheim implies in these passages is that crime threatens the moral core of society.
Crime's main function is therefore to invoke punishment, which in turn facilitates cohesion and
maintains societal boundaries. That is, crime helps to maintain stability. The idea that deviance
helps to solidify symbolic-moral boundaries is echoed by quite a few sociologists.

The main lesson from Durkheim's work is clear: we need to view crime, deviance and
reactions to them as essential ingredients in central processes of social change and in its prevention: that is, in processes which maintain social stability.

Durkheim's formulations imply that the essence of deviance has something unstable, or
ambiguous, about it. Indeed, Downes and Rock (2007) emphasize that deviance eludes
definitions and that much of it has to do with the difficulties involved in predicting and controlling
the implications of moral rules. Taking all this into consideration, one can argue that some
behaviors may be regarded as unconventional. Reacting to these unconventional behaviors can
assume a few forms. One, ignore it. Two, define it in negative terms and attempt to initiate a
process that will deviantize and stigmatize that behavior. Three, define the behavior in question
as innovative, support it and help new conduct norms ascend.

In summary, then, unconventional behavior creates a sphere of ambiguity and uncertainty.
However, one can examine such behavior from two very different points of view. One, deviant
behavior as challenging the status quo, and eliciting a punitive response which tends to reaffirm
symbolic-moral boundaries and thus help maintain cultural stability (and ossification). Two, as
challenging the status quo and introducing vital elements of change into cultures, mutations, if
you like, which enable cultures to adapt to (and create) different symbolic-moral universes and
new social environments. In this evolutionary biological analogy Durkheim's view may be
interpreted to imply that unconventional behaviors have always been part of human cultures,
and will continue to be so. Some of these will help solidify cultures against the perpetrators while
others may become beacons for processes of social change. Indeed, Durkheim did not fail to
note that a culture without deviance is not possible.

To use a brief illustration, let me paraphrase Pat Lauderdale's (2003) observation that some
of those defined today as terrorists may become tomorrow's heroes. Nelson Mandela is but one

example from the recent past. The terms "terrorist" and "hero" themselves may be relativistic and thus Mandela was an heroic figure for nonwhites in South Africa when hegemonic whites defined him as a terrorist. Moreover, from being defined as a "terrorist" by hegemonic powers, Mandela occupied—years later—a position of hegemonic power himself. It is not too difficult to understand that this transformation could not have taken place without a major social, cultural and political change in South Africa. The personal price paid by Mandela in this process was extremely high. His best biological years were spent in prison.

The Nazi-controlled collaborative Vichy government, presented at the time as a new, positive and bold political order for France, had no difficulties to appoint a court-martial which in 1940 sentenced Charles de Gaulle (then in London) to a term in prison on charges of treason and in 1944 to replace this sentence with a death sentence. Once the Vichy regime was gone and its verdicts were annulled, different moral boundaries were drawn. Years later, the very same Charles de Gaulle became president of France.[1]

An added complication may be that what is regarded as deviance at one point in time and culture may not be regarded in this way in another time and culture, or vice versa. To illustrate this fact vividly one only needs to pick up Robert R. Bell's textbook on deviance (1971). Following an introductory conceptual part, the second part presents—in different chapters—various cases of deviance. Obviously, it should not be too difficult to view these chapters as presenting what the field of deviance views as deviance. Moreover, one can infer that the order of the presentation of the cases may have something to do with the importance of the topics. How, then, did Bell in 1971 present the empirical bread and butter of the field? The *first* empirical chapter which presents a case of deviance, twenty-four pages long, is devoted to and focused on—you better believe this—"premarital sex." The last three chapters in the book cover "militant women," "militant students" and "the Hippie movement." Furthermore, if one looks at the development of one of the long-lasting and established textbooks on deviant behavior, that of Erich Goode,[2] one can see that from its second edition[3] such cases of deviance as drug usage, homosexuality, violent behavior (including homicide and rape), property crimes and mental disorders, starred in it (as well as in another established textbook—that by Alex Thio[4]). However, in its fifth edition (1997), but much more forcefully in its sixth and seventh editions (2001 and 2005, respectively), a chapter on ideological, ethical and moral implications of studying deviance was added, and the sixth and seventh editions already had chapters on cognitive deviance (focusing on religious deviance, parapsychology, UFOlogy, urban legends—a category which, by the way, had appeared in Jack D. Douglas and Frances C. Waksler's textbook back in 1982) and physical aberrations, as a result of which, previous subjects were condensed and presented in a much more concise manner. The seventh edition even had a chapter on the "death" of the sociology of deviance. Moreover, such deviancies as shoplifting and massage parlors, which appeared quite saliently in the 1978 edition, disappeared completely in the 2005 edition.

Deviance and change

While many scholars accepted the idea that reactions to deviance enhance stability by reaffirming moral boundaries and the status quo, fewer pursued the idea that it produces change by challenging the status quo. For example, Douglas's (1977: 60) analysis suggests the term "creative deviance" and argues that "deviance is the mutation that is generally destructive of society, but it is also the only major source of creative adaptations of rules to new life situations." Thus, he suggests that entire cultures and societies can change through deviance. And, indeed, Dombrink and Hillyard (2007) point out that as moralities changed in the USA, gambling went through a process of normalization. They suggest that more normalization processes will probably occur with respect to abortion, gay rights, assisted suicide and stem-cell research. Legalizing the use of psychoactive substances may be on the horizon as well. Moreover, the relevant debate which developed in the literature (mostly in the journal *Deviant Behavior*) in the late 1980s and early 1990s about the possibility of the existence of "positive deviance" testifies to this. Viewing deviance within such central processes as change and stability inevitably requires that we examine deviance from a very different perspective.

Locus of change

Utilizing the rhetoric of "change" requires that we clarify what it means. Following Durkheim's lead, and his more general perspective, the term should mean—first and foremost—changes in the boundaries of the symbolic-moral universes of which cultures are structured and the relevant configurations of power. In micro terms, this means change(s) in consciousness, and consequently in social identities. This conceptualization necessarily directs us to examine the moral structure of cultures as well as diving into politics and deviance. On the micro level, this approach requires that we look into issues of identities and the factors that help structure these identities.

Although Durkheim's formulations are basic and important, our understanding of morality has developed much further.[5] The idea that societies are structured from different, many times competing, symbolic-moral universes takes us away from Durkheim's concept of coherency in societal moral systems, which are—supposedly—internalized in more or less uniform processes of socialization. Morality is a resource that is created and used by moral entrepreneurs, sometimes in moral panics and crusades, many times in competitive and antagonistic social and cultural landscapes. The different symbolic-moral universes that inhabit a society provide cognitive dwellers in them with motivational accounting systems with which they can explain and understand their past and justify future behaviors. These, in turn, form the basis for different cultural identities.

However, these symbolic-moral universes, in and by themselves, are not sufficient to understand deviance and social change—or its prevention. One important element that is missing is power: that is, politics.

Politics and deviance

Examining politics and deviance requires that we look at such issues as those involving power and morality. For example, who defines what as deviance? Who has the power to enforce such a definition? Two main possibilities exist here. The first includes all those types of deviance where the issues of power and morality are explicitly at the forefront as the challenge (and potential threat) to the status quo. The second includes deviancies where this challenge is implicit. Many deviant acts which are referred to as "political" are in the first category. Roebuck and Weeber (1978), for example, created three categories in this area: first, crimes against the state as assassinations, political bombing, bribery, tax and/or tax evasion, conscientious objection, and spying; second, crimes against society as false advertisements, medical fraud, environmental pollution, occupational hazards, and unsafe machines; third, crimes committed by the government as police corruption and/or violence, violation of human rights, genocide, and discrimination (see also Ross 2002).

On a more general level of abstraction, all these forms of crime and deviance can be classified into three basic types of deviance which come from: the periphery and aimed at the center; the center and aimed at the periphery; either the center or the periphery and aimed at the same level (center to center, periphery to periphery). These forms of deviance are always connected to issues of political justice, political trials, criminals as heroes and political criminals.

Political deviance versus political justice

Clearly, strong feelings of injustice could motivate people into actions aimed to rectify what they feel is unjust. Criteria for these feelings and actions are not, and cannot, be objective or absolute. Many deviant acts classified as "terror" may use the language of justice/injustice in justifying or condoning these acts. And, indeed, rhetorics capitalizing on "victim accounts (or narratives)" have become quite popular in justifying some nasty and problematic behaviors. Such behaviors may challenge (or threaten) the foundations of a social order. A closely related issue is that of using processes of deviantization (sometimes by the criminal justice system itself) for political purposes: for example, police involvement in riot control, capture and trials of terrorists, enforcement of immigration laws or treating political opponents as criminals.

Political trials

While the exact nature and characterization of political trials are not entirely clear, these trials involve those who are accused, directly and explicitly, in threatening and challenging the legitimacy of the regime: treason, sedition, mutiny, civil unrest. Political trials may produce political prisoners, which in turn may lead to another interesting process—politicization of prisons. Political deviance always entails some form of a conflict which is presented as one between two, or more, symbolic-moral universes: that of the challengers (real or imaginary) and that of those being challenged. Therefore, the history of political deviance is also, in an inverse fashion, the history of morality and the distribution of power.

However, in the popular and older professional literature, political deviance was usually taken to mean challenges against the power and legitimacy of the rulers, and not vice versa. In the culture where Socrates lived, his persecutors had more legitimized power, so that when the two symbolic-moral universes and opposing systems of vocabularies of motives collided, Socrates lost.

In today's liberal democratic societies, freedom of thought and speech are hailed as primary virtues. In other regimes, individuals who exercise freedom of thought, or challenge the "order," are liable to find themselves imprisoned or committed to an insane asylum. Science is no exception. Giordano Bruno died for challenging the Ptolemaic worldview and the morality which supported it; Galileo suffered because of this worldview, too. Freud's theory, which revolutionized psychology and psychiatry and enriched other disciplines, was originally criticized heavily on moral grounds. Likewise, the first innovators in radio astronomy, and some developers of a number of the most central concepts in astronomy (e.g. black holes, the Big Bang theory and background microwave radiation) were isolated and kept away from the main halls of science. It is not too difficult to find cases of innovations, some quite significant, in the sciences and the arts, that were reacted to as deviance, and the innovators treated as bona fide deviants— deviantized, ostracized, stigmatized and ridiculed. Discovery of the role of the bacteria *Helicobacter pylori* in the development of peptic ulcers is a good and recent illustration.

Apparently, the question of who interprets whose behavior, why, where and when is crucial. Pat Lauderdale's insightful observation (2003: 5) is very relevant here:

> Is, for example, the leader of loose-knit bands of hit-and-run killers of British soldiers a "homicidal maniac," a "crazed cult killer," or a "bandit"? Or is George Washington a revolutionary hero? Is Nat Turner, who executed Virginia slave owners and their families

in 1830, in the same category? Is the Jewish terrorist in Palestine in 1948 distinguishable from the Palestinian terrorist in Israel in 1978?

Criminals as heroes and political criminals

History teaches us that deviants and criminals have often been treated as heroes. The famous Robin Hood syndrome received a strong validation in Kooistra's (1989) work where he examined a large variety of such cases. However, the existence of this category also raises the reverse possibility—of politicians as criminals. Suffice it to point out that some of the vilest and most despicable mass murderers of the 20th century were politicians—for example, Adolf Hitler, Joseph Stalin, Mao Zedong and Pol Pot.

Power and morality in regular deviance

The second possibility, very different from the first, consists of regular forms of deviance which, prima facie, do not seem to present any explicit challenge to the status quo. Finding out the implicit power/morality challenge in these forms of behavior requires some "excavations of knowledge" (paraphrasing Foucault). Doing this may mean following different, yet comple-mentary, routes: for example, examining the ways in which criminal laws are created, passed and enforced. The very act of defining a particular behavioral pattern as deviant is inherently political—it uses power to impose the view of a specific symbolic-moral universe upon other universes. This process, referred to by Schur (1980) as "deviantization" and consisting of stigma contests, typically begins when some moral entrepreneurs get organized and try to change public attitudes and law. That is, cause change. Such a process may involve shaming (Braithwaite 1989), vilification, degradation ceremonies (Garfinkel 1950) and stigmatization (Goffman 1963). Clearly, since power and morality are the basis of deviantization processes, reversal of these processes can be achieved by using the same resources (e.g., see Ben-Yehuda 1990: 221–50). As Schur pointed out, a process of deviantization is a key element in the social stratification order because it intervenes in the process of resource allocation. Thus, actors in societal centers who negotiate power and morality, attempting to define particular patterns of behavior as deviant (or non-deviant) are necessarily engaged in constructing the boundaries of symbolic-moral universes and affecting processes of change or stability. These moral entrepreneurs seek constantly to manipulate political, as well as moral, symbols in order to mobilize support, generate power and control or influence public opinion.

Some interesting insights may be gained here by examining how specified behaviors once considered "deviant" or "criminal" become legitimized at other times and vice versa. There are some good examples for that.

Gusfield's (1963: 122–23) work on the Temperance Movement's anti-liquor struggle illustrates this:

> What prohibition symbolized was the superior power and prestige of the old middle class in American society. The threat of decline in that position had made explicit actions of government necessary to defend it. Legislation did this in two ways. It demonstrated the power of the old middle classes by showing that they could mobilize sufficient politi-cal strength to bring it about, and it gave dominance to the character and style of old middle-class life in contrast to that of the urban lower and middle classes. The power of the Protestant, rural, native American was greater than that of the Eastern upper classes, the Catholic and Jewish immigrants, and the urbanized middle class.

What Gusfield's work implies is that a contemporary "problem," perceived as excessive use of alcohol, was socially constructed. Furthermore, Zurcher *et al.* (1971) showed that in two anti-pornography campaigns, the moral crusaders emphasized a general lifestyle and sets of values instead of the specific steps they demanded in order to abolish pornography.

Parties to a potential moral–political conflict, and therefore to negotiations, are engaged in an effort to create or maintain a collective identity by defining the moral boundaries of the symbolic-moral universe of that collective. Hence, collective definitions of deviance always result in stigma contests and in deviantization processes. The creation of rules and penal punishments implies that the lifestyles, values and moralities of specific social groups gained ascendancy over those of other groups, many times at the other groups' expense (Gusfield 1963). Two illustrations will suffice.

First, until the first two decades of the 20th century, many psychoactive drugs were freely available in commercial and medical markets. Then, during these decades, a very effective campaign of various moral entrepreneurs made us all experience an interesting exercise in criminalization as slowly but surely most psychoactive substances were defined as dangerous and their use as criminal. Only toward the end of the century did some loud voices begin to be heard demanding a reevaluation of this criminalization and its results, suggesting that a "harm reduction" policy be introduced instead and that decriminalization, and even full legalization, be considered.

Second, rape, which for many decades was considered as a "sexual deviance," was reinterpreted as a crime which has sexual tones, but which is primarily a crime of violence reflecting an unequal distribution of power between the sexes.

Notes

1 For a short description, see Ben-Yehuda 2001: 157–58.
2 Now in its seventh edition, all by Prentice-Hall.
3 1984; the first (1978) edition was packaged in a symbolic interactionism perspective.
4 Published by Houghton Mifflin and later Harper and Row.
5 E.g., see Lowe 2006; Boltanski and Thévenot 2006.

References

Bell, Robert R. 1971. *Social Deviance: A Substantive Analysis*, Homewood, IL: The Dorsey Press.
Ben-Yehuda, Nachman. 1990. *The Politics and Morality of Deviance*, Albany: State University of New York Press.
——. 2001. *Betrayal and Treason*, Boulder, CO: Westview.
Boltanski, Luc and Laurent Thévenot. 2006. *On Justification: The Economies of Worth*, Princeton, NJ: Princeton University Press.
Braithwaite, John. 1989. *Crime, Shame, and Reintegration*, New York: Cambridge University Press.
Dombrink, John and Daniel Hillyard. 2007. *Sin No More: From Abortion to Stem Cells, Understanding Crime, Law, and Morality in America*, New York: New York University Press.
Douglas, J. 1977. "Shame and Deceit in Creative Deviance," in E. Sagarin (ed.), *Deviance and Social Change* (pp. 59–86), Beverly Hills, CA: Sage.
Douglas, Jack D. and Frances C. Waksler. 1982. *The Sociology of Deviance: An Introduction*, Boston, MA: Little, Brown and Company.
Downes, David and Paul Rock. 2007. *Understanding Deviance: A Guide to the Sociology of Crime and Rule Breaking*, 5th edn, Oxford: Oxford University Press.
Durkheim, E. 1933. *The Division of Labor in Society*, 1964 edn, New York: The Free Press.
——. 1938. *The Rules of Sociological Method*, New York: The Free Press.
Garfinkel, Harold. 1950. "Conditions of Successful Degradation Ceremonies," *American Journal of Sociology*, 61: 420–24.

Goffman, Erving. 1963. *Stigma*. Englewood Cliffs, NJ: Prentice-Hall.

Gusfield, J. R. 1963. *Symbolic Crusade: Status Politics and the American Temperance Movement*, Chicago: University of Illinois Press.

Lauderdale, Pat (ed.). 2003. *A Political Analysis of Deviance*, Toronto: de Sitter.

Lowe, Brian M. 2006. *Emerging Moral Vocabularies: The Creation and Establishment of New Forms of Moral and Ethical Meanings*, Oxford: Lexington.

Kooistra, Paul G. 1989. *Criminals as Heroes*, Bowling Green, OH: Bowling Green State University Popular Press.

Roebuck, J. and Weeber, S. C. 1978. *Political Crime in the United States*, New York: Praeger.

Ross, Jeffrey Ian. 2002. *Dynamics of Political Crime*, Thousand Oaks, CA: Sage.

Schur, E. M. 1980. *The Politics of Deviance*, Englewood Cliffs, NJ: Prentice-Hall.

Zurcher, Louis A. Jr., George R. Kirkpatrick, Robert G. Cushing and Charles K. Bowman. 1971. "The Anti-Pornography Campaign: A Symbolic Crusade," *Social Problems*, 19 (2): 217–38.

6

Moral panic

Erich Goode and Nachman Ben-Yehuda

A *moral panic* is an episode of exaggerated concern about a threatening, or supposedly threatening, condition which many members or sectors of a society blame on "folk devils," or deviants. What *defines* an episode of moral panic is that the concern the public, or sectors of the public, and the media express *is substantially above and beyond what evidence suggests is the actual threat or danger of the condition* that generated the concern.

Stanley Cohen used the term "moral panic" (coined a year earlier by Jock Young) in 1972, in a study of social reactions to "mods" and "rockers," two British youth groups. Roving crowds of rowdy rock-and-roller teens and young adults committed acts of vandalism, causing the police to make a hundred arrests. This episode shocked the country, representing the disintegration of the traditional British social order. While critics of the moral panics concept abound (e.g., Waddington, 1986; Cornwell and Linders, 2002; Waiton, 2008), in fact, measured by the volume of research, publications, and citations it has generated, it is one of the most influential concepts produced by a sociologist.

The moral panic is *conveyed* or *expressed* by the following "actors": the public or society at large; the media and the internet; politicians and legislators; law enforcement—the police and the courts; and social movements or action groups. In a given moral panic, concern is expressed among one or more of these social actors, or any combination of them; and for all of these actors, we observe a discrepancy between this concern and the imputed threat that that concern reflects.

In sum, the moral panic is a social episode that contains the following elements: substantial *concern* about a threat or putative threat; *hostility* toward a deviant or folk devil; a degree of *consensus* among the public, or sectors of the public, that the threat is real and caused by designated deviants; *disproportion* between the threat and the concern; and *volatility* in the concern—a substantial rise and fall in its intensity over time.

Concern

The concern that our five relevant actors or sectors of society feel is expressed in overt actions. First, the *public* expresses indignation, engages in informal "chatter" or talk about the issue, verbalizes its feelings in opinion polls, supports and votes for politicians who propose legislation to address the threat, reads or watches media accounts about the threat and the designated folk devils, and—very occasionally—vents outrage in the form of collective violence. Second, as cause and/or consequence of the public's concern, the *media* run news stories embodying, expressing, and stoking up the threat and the concern, and, in addition, the internet broadcasts and regenerates a "buzz." Third, *politicians* make speeches about folk devils and propose legislation to criminalize the presumably threatening behavior. Fourth, *law enforcement* steps up legal control by increasing the surveillance and arrest of suspects, and the courts increase the likelihood of convicting, imprisoning, and handing down stiffer sentences for the relevant illegal behavior. Fifth, *activists* form social movement organizations march, demonstrate, and hold rallies protesting the relevant threat and the actions of folk devils.

These actors usually justify the acts that express their concern within a rationalistic frame-work. Action should be taken, they believe, to ensure that the damage the threat causes be minimized. Actors argue that the immoral acts they try to prevent cause or represent objectively harmful conditions or more serious behavior. They explain their acts as reactions to a very real, concrete, and present threat; hence, the concern they express and act out should *not* be referred to or dismissed as mere "panic."

Hostility

In a moral panic, sectors of the society express an increased level of *hostility* toward the group or category said to engage in the behavior or cause the threatening condition in question. Folk devils are designated as the—or at least an—enemy of decent, respectable society. The deviant's behavior is seen as objectively harmful, threatening to the values, the core beliefs, the interests of the society. Moral panic actors tend to *stereotype* folk devils in exaggerated, demeaning ways (Cohen, 1972).

Consensus

To qualify as a moral panic, we must see a substantial and fairly widespread consensus: that is, a minimal level of agreement—either in the society as a whole or in certain social sectors of the society—that the threat exists, that it is serious, and that it is caused by specific members of a group and their harmful and deviant behavior. The proportion of the population that feels this way need not be universal or even make up a majority. Moral panics come in different sizes, with some gripping most members of society, and others more localized to one or more communities, social circles, groups, or categories. A large number of individuals might be panicking, but if they are scattered haphazardly throughout the society, *as a sociological phenomenon*, this is *not* a moral panic. However, if there is consensus that a threat exists and should be dealt with, and if this grips a large proportion of a particular group or residents of a certain community, this *is* a moral panic. Hence, by *consensus*, we mean that fairly widespread agreement exists among members of *identifiable social categories*—possibly, but not necessarily, society as a whole—that there is a problem or threat, and that something should be done to address it.

Disproportion

Sociologists who use the moral panic concept do not argue that certain actions that generate panics are harmless. The lynchpin of the moral panics concept is *disproportion*—the disparity between concern and threat. Some critics have argued that disproportion cannot be objectively determined, that it rests on a value judgment rather than scientific criteria (Cornwell and Linders, 2002). We agree that, for *some* issues, the relationship between concern and threat is difficult to measure; but in fact, for most, disproportion can be roughly calibrated. Here are several indicators of disproportion.

Imaginary threats

A few supposed threats that generate a great deal of concern, even fear and great anxiety, do not even exist; they are entirely imaginary. During the 1980s, many fundamentalist Christians believed that Satanists kidnapped and ritually murdered tens of thousands of children each year in the United States and the UK in loathsome, gruesome ceremonies that represented a mockery of Christian services. Careful examination of the claim has produced no evidence whatsoever to support it—no satanic rituals, satanic kidnappings, or murders of children by Satanists (de Young, 2004). During the European Renaissance (1400s–1600s), hundreds of thousands of people, mostly women, were put to death for practicing witchcraft—mainly, consorting with the devil. Clearly, no such action took place, and the concern and fear, as manifested by these executions, along with the mass panic that such accusations generated, were unwarranted and misplaced (Ben-Yehuda, 1985). Typically, when we find the conjunction of great concern with the complete absence of an actual threat, we know that a moral panic is taking place.

Exaggerated claims

If the evidence cited to *measure* the scope of the problem is grossly exaggerated, the criterion of disproportion has been met. Exaggeration of a claim may reside in number of victims, extent of harm to the victims, how widespread the harm is, and financial cost to the society. In 1982, an Israeli politician and several representatives of the police released figures to the media that half of all Israeli schoolchildren used hashish. This claim attracted a flurry of media and public attention, but careful, systematic studies indicated that the actual figure was just 3 to 5 percent (Ben-Yehuda, 1986)—so the exaggeration was in the order of ten times. Spokespersons have claimed that, yearly, 50,000 or more "slaves" are "pouring" into the United States. After spending millions of dollars to find these victims, law enforcement and the government were able to locate only three (Markon, 2007). Claims as discrepant as these suggest that we have a moral panic on our hands.

Other harmful conditions

Some less harmful conditions, dangers, or threats attract *vastly* more concern, fear, anxiety, and attention than do other, more harmful conditions. Why? Tobacco smoking, according to figures released periodically by the federal Centers for Disease Control, kills 440,000 people in the United States every year. In contrast, illicit drug abuse kills 20,000–30,000 people annually (Goode, 2008). Why has drug abuse stirred up intense and recurrent moral panics over the years (Goode and Ben-Yehuda, 2009), while cigarette smoking panics pale in comparison?

Likewise, beginning in the late 1980s, a huge volume of media attention focused on the spread of methamphetamine ("meth") abuse and the harm that the drug causes to users. The drug was supposedly "sweeping the country like wildfire." We are "awash" in meth—and the East Coast has been "invaded" by the drug. In 2004 and 2005, the *Oregonian* ran some 250 stories proclaiming that we are in the midst of a meth "epidemic." In August 2005, *Newsweek* proclaimed meth "America's most dangerous drug."

In truth, harmful as methamphetamine is, surveys indicate that its use remains below that of the country's most popular drugs, and hospital and coroners' reports indicate that, every year, cocaine, heroin, sedatives, antidepressants, and alcohol in combination with other drugs cause substantially more lethal and non-lethal overdoses—yet those drugs have attracted vastly less media hysteria than meth (Goode, 2008). Clearly, in recent years American society has experienced a meth panic, with the concern and fear expressed about the threat much greater than objective evidence suggests is warranted.

Other times, other places

Often, when we compare one time or place with another, we find more concern when and where the objective threat is lower, and less concern when and where the objective threat is higher. School shootings, a horrific phenomenon that has caused the deaths of hundreds of children in the Anglophone world provides an example here. Between the late 1990s and early 2000s, school shootings and killings attracted an immense volume of media attention at precisely the time when their incidence was actually *declining* (Cornell, 2006).

In March 2001, after an incident involving the deaths of two teenagers and the injury of thirteen others, CNN proclaimed an "epidemic" of school shooting. The headline of its story read: "The Incidents in Schools Rise Sharply." The *CBS Evening News* agreed, with its anchor saying: "School shootings in the country have become an epidemic." According to sociologist Joel Best (2002), during the late 1990s the number of stories about school deaths increased eight times; but between 1998 and 2001 the actual number of violent deaths in schools *dropped* from 35 to 15. Dewey Cornell (2006), a forensic psychologist, found that the number of juvenile arrests for murder declined from 3,284 in 1993 to 973 in 2002; the number of victims of school homicides dropped from 42 in 1993 to 8 in 2001, 2 in 2002 and 4 in 2003. For schoolchildren nationwide, schools are safer places to be than their own homes, and they are becoming increasingly safe. A small number of newsworthy, high-profile cases of violence do not represent the country as a whole; and school violence actually substantially *declined* between the 1990s and the 2000s. There is no "epidemic" of school violence. When the media used this exaggerated, overheated term, they not only expressed but contributed to a moral panic of school shootings.

Volatility

By their very nature, moral panics are *volatile*: they erupt fairly suddenly (although they may lie latent for long periods and reappear from time to time) and subside just as suddenly. Some moral panics become *routinized* or *institutionalized*: after the panic has run its course, the concern about the target behavior results in, or remains in place in the form of, social movement organizations, legislation, enforcement practices, and informal interpersonal norms or practices for punishing transgressors. Other moral panics vanish, almost without trace: the legal, cultural, moral, and social fabric of the society after the panic is essentially no different from the way it was before; no new social control mechanisms are instituted as a consequence of its eruption. But whether it has a long-term impact or not, the hostility generated during a moral panic tends to be fairly temporally limited. The fever pitch that characterizes the trajectory of a moral panic is not typically sustainable over a long stretch of time. In that respect, it is similar to the fad and the craze, and, hence, a form of collective behavior.

Actors in the moral panic

The media and the internet

Prior to the institutionalization of newspapers, radio, and television, moral panics developed by word of mouth, religious sermons, and religious and imperial decrees and proclamations. Thus, they disseminated more slowly than they do today. The media and the internet are the most effective generators and conveyors of moral panics in the history of humanity. Whenever the media and the internet address a story about wrongdoing with exaggerated attention, inventions, distortion, and stereotyping, we have a good idea that there's a moral panic erupting or in process. In the past generation or so, the sources and diversity of the media have proliferated and ramified to the point where we find competing claims about a supposed threat; indeed, *competing* moral panics. We live, in other words, in a *multimediated* world (McRobbie and Thornton, 1995). Not all media sources agree with one another, so a diversity of panics may break out among different audiences. This tendency has increased with the development of the internet, which combines instant and widespread communicability with little or no professional filter on verifiability. It is possible that competing definitions of threats and folk devils, plus the explosion of the internet, may increase the number of (albeit smaller) moral panics, not decrease them.

The public

For a classic, full-blown moral panic to erupt, there must be some potential on the part of the public, or sectors of the public, to react to an issue. The issue must have resonance with at least some sectors of the public. A media campaign cannot whip the public into a frenzy over an issue to which the public at large is initially indifferent. In September 1989, following a series of speeches by President Ronald Reagan pumping up several proposed drug bills, a *New York Times*/CBS poll revealed that nearly two-thirds (64%) of the American public thought that drug abuse was the number-one problem facing the country at that time. Given the other, objectively more serious problems the country faced, this was an unlikely assertion; hence, it represented an exaggeration of a less serious problem. On the other hand, word-of-mouth rumors, usually in the form of urban or contemporary legends, both convey and energize moral panics, but they often spread *without* being reported or valorized by the media. Hence, the public's concern is one dimension of the moral panic—sometimes independent from, yet often codependent with, the others, especially the media.

Law enforcement

In addition to the press and general public, the actions of formal social control demonstrate that a moral panic is taking place. During a moral panic, police officers make efforts to broaden the scope of legal surveillance and law enforcement, and often increase its intensity: that is, they arrest more often on less provocation. In addition, the courts step up social control when judges send persons convicted of a crime to jail or prison rather than probation or the suspension of a sentence. Today, we see such forces at work in both the United States and the United Kingdom in an increase in the deportation of illegal immigrants and stepped-up surveillance against the possibility of terrorism.

Politicians and legislators

In a moral panic, legislators escalate proposing and enacting legislation to curb a putative threat. In 1988, the Anti-Drug Law called for the death penalty for major drug traffickers as well as anyone causing someone's death during the course of committing a felony. Some panics, however, fail to ignite legislation: all the laws proposed against pornography in the late 1980s and early 1990s by anti-porn feminists failed to be sustained by executive or judicial review (Goode and Ben-Yehuda, 2009).

Action groups and social movements

At some point, moral panics generate appeals, campaigns, and, finally, fully fledged social movement organizations or action groups which arise to cope with the newly existing threat. Social movement activists are *moral entrepreneurs* who believe that existing remedies are insufficient, that "something must be done" to remedy the threat. The emergence of such social action groups in the heat of the moment is one sign that a moral panic is developing.

Three theories of moral panic

Why do moral panics occur? Why do the public, the media, law enforcement agencies, politicians, and action groups in a particular society at a particular time express intense concern over a condition, phenomenon, issue, behavior, or would-be threat that—as a sober assessment of the evidence would reveal—does not merit such concern? Scholars have proposed three main theories to explain the emergence of moral panic.

Of the many dimensions along which we might array theories of moral panic, the *grassroots* versus *elitism* dimension comes most readily to mind. Are *many* actors responsible for the creation and maintenance of the panic or just *a few*? Does the panic start from the bottom and progress up, or does it work from the top down? Or, to cite a third possibility, might a panic begin in the *middle* of society's status and power hierarchy rather than from the elite at the top or from the undifferentiated general grassroots public: from directors and administrators of middle-level organizations, agencies, associations, and interest groups?

The explanation that moral panics are caused at the top of the society by a small number of powerful actors, usually on behalf of their own, typically economic, interests, might be called the *elitist* or "elite engineered" theory. The explanation that moral panics arise out of the genuinely felt concerns of the public at large might be labeled the *grassroots* theory. And the explanation that moral panics emerge out of the efforts of representatives that advocate the ideology and interests of a specific, organized clientele—such as teachers, the Catholic Church, gun owners, physicians, labor unions, veterans, the media itself, and so on—might be called the *interest group* theory.

The classic orthodox Marxist approach is the *elitist* model. It argues that elites "orchestrate" moral panics so that they will gain some material or status or ideological advantage therefrom. According to this model, elites fabricate, orchestrate, or engineer a panic from a nonexistent or trivial threat—usually one about which they themselves feel little moral concern—in order to gain something of value or divert attention away from issues that, if addressed, would threaten their own interests. Advocates of this theory see the general public or grassroots as possessing relatively little independent agency; instead, they are manipulated from above. On their own, the public would not stampede into a scare; their participation in moral panics is a result of the machinations of the rich and the powerful (Hall *et al.*, 1978). In this model, big business interests control the actions of "the state," which is conceived of as a more or less homogeneous entity, acting in a more or less coordinated fashion.

In contrast, advocates of the *interest group* theory hold that occupants of the middle level of power in a society act independently of the elite either to express or to maximize their own political, material, ideological or professional advantage. Moreover, they argue that moral panics originate somewhere in society's middle strata: professional associations, religious groups, social movement organizations, educational institutions, labor organizations—middle-level associations, organizations, groups, and institutions of every description (Jenkins, 1992). The media may make up one of these interest groups: the concern that media figures seemingly express in a panic may not even be felt by owners, publishers, or journalists; their motives may simply be to stir up a story; moreover, their efforts do not always work. The interest group model sees society as neither controlled from the top nor as an open or grassroots democracy. Members of middle-level groups, organizations, and associations often initiate crusades, panics, and campaigns in the face of elite opposition *and* (sometimes) societal or grassroots indifference.

The *grassroots* model argues that moral panics are initiated from the bottom up and, concomitantly, that morality and ideology are dominant motives for activists and concerned citizens. To the grassroots theorist, moral panics are more or less spontaneous eruptions of fear and concern on the part of large numbers of people about a given threat or putative threat. This "large number" need not be a majority of the entire population. In fact, it could be a small minority yet still comprise substantial numbers (1 percent of the US population equates to three million people).

Often a particular issue will inflame members of particular *sectors* of society, such as evangelical Christians, conservatives, homosexuals, or feminists. The panic and exaggerated fear expressed in many legends, tales, and rumors exemplify a genuinely grassroots dynamic. Likewise, most conspiracy theories are populist in nature and express fears that begin in society's socioeconomic rank and file (Ramsay, 2006).

References

Ben-Yehuda, Nachman. 1985. *Deviance and Moral Boundaries*. Chicago, IL: University of Chicago Press.
——. 1986. "The Sociology of Moral Panics: Toward a New Synthesis." *Sociological Quarterly*, 27 (4): 496–513.
Best, Joel. 2002. "Monster Hype." *Education Next*, Summer: 51–55.
Cohen, Stanley. 1972. *Folk Devils and Moral Panics*. London: MacGibbon & Kee.
Cornell, Dewey G. 2006. *School Violence: Fears versus Facts*. Mahwah, NJ: Lawrence Erlbaum.
Cornwell, Benjamin and Annula Linders. 2002. "The Myth of 'Moral Panic': An Alternative Account of LSD Prohibition." *Deviant Behavior*, 23 (4): 307–30.
de Young, Mary. 2004. *The Day Care Ritual Abuse Moral Panic*. Jefferson, NC: McFarland.
Goode, Erich. 2008. *Drugs in American Society* (7th edn). New York: McGraw-Hill.
Goode, Erich and Nachman Ben-Yehuda. 2009. *Moral Panics: The Social Construction of Deviance* (2nd edn). Oxford: Wiley-Blackwell.
Hall, Stuart, Chas Critcher, Tony Jefferson, John Clarke, and Brian Roberts. 1978. *Policing the Crisis: Mugging, the State, and Law and Order*. London: Macmillan.
Jenkins, Philip. 1992. *Intimate Enemies: Moral Panics in Contemporary Britain*. New York: Aldine de Gruyter.
Markon, Jerry. 2007. "Human Trafficking Evokes Outrage, Little Evidence." *Washington Post*, September 23: A1 ff.
McRobbie, Angela and Sarah L. Thornton. 1995. "Rethinking 'Moral Panic' for Multi-Mediated Social Worlds." *British Journal of Sociology*, 46 (4): 559–74.
Ramsay, Robin. 2006. *Conspiracy Theories*. New York: Barnes & Noble.
Waddington, P. A. J. 1986. "Mugging as a Social Panic: A Question of Proportion." *British Journal of Sociology*, 37 (2): 245–59.
Waiton, Stuart. 2008. *The Politics of Antisocial Behaviour: Amoral Panics*. New York and London: Routledge.

7

Differentials in deviance

Race, class, gender, and age

Nancy A. Heitzeg

> The story of deviance and social control is a battle story . . . Deviants never exist except in relation to those who attempt to control them. Deviants exist in opposition to those whom they threaten and those who have enough power control against such threats.
>
> *(Pfohl 1994: 3)*

Social structure is central to the sociological endeavor; indeed, the analysis of structured inequality is the essence of the "sociological imagination" (Mills 1959). Race, class, gender and age—those cornerstones of stratification—shape access to social opportunity, demarcate social inequality, inform identity, and provide common ground for social movements and resistance. So too they shape our understanding of deviance. Race, class, gender, and age create the contours of that battle story of deviant response and societal reaction.

Despite their centrality to sociology, the treatment of these statuses in the literature on deviance has been varied, and occasionally confounding. Race, class, gender, and age have been at both the margins and the center of the sociology of deviance. At times, they have been the unspoken, unexamined subtext of analyses of particular deviant behaviors, lurking unnamed and unattended. Conversely, race, class, gender, and age have also been the central focus of scholarship on deviance, the very variables held as crucial to an understanding of both behaviors and labeling. Race, class, gender, and age have been addressed singularly as separate influences, with class and age the primary focal points. Still others have called for their examination as intersecting variables whose relationship to deviance must be understood as part of an interlocking system of oppression, an approach resulting in the most profound research. Finally, race, class, gender, and age are alternately seen as direct contributors to deviant behavior, as stigmatized statuses that are targets for deviant labeling, and as sources of power to exert that very same social control.

This latter point is perhaps the most fruitful framework for a discussion of the role of race, class, gender, and age in the deviance literature. The sociology of deviance has variously attempted to explain both the deviant and the ensuing societal reaction. In both the classic and contemporary literature, these variables have largely been examined through one lens or the other: that is, as either differential shapers of deviant behavior or as precursors to differential social control.

Race, class, gender, and age: differentials in deviant behavior

> When alienation becomes so entrenched, an oppositional culture can develop and flourish. This culture, especially among the young, can gain strength and legitimacy by opposing dominant society and its agents.
>
> *(Anderson 1999: 216)*

From the outset, race, class, gender, and age have been cited as variables that contribute to deviant behavior. The prevailing question of the field early on was: "*Why* are people deviant?" One set of answers involved a look at the structural conditions that impelled deviance: that is, a look at race, class, gender, and age as primary factors. The initial interpretation of the role of these variables was decidedly deterministic, and partly limited by a reliance on official statistics that over-represented the poor, the young, people of color, and men. This flaw was further compounded by an acceptance of official statistics on crime, arrest, and mental illness as comprehensive accounts that captured the universe of all deviants in their measures.

The "deviants" who were the subjects of study through much of the 20th century were poor, they were young "delinquents," they were racial/ethnic minorities, and they were often male. The deviance they were engaged in was street crime, mental illness, drug addiction, alcoholism, and gang membership. Discussion of female deviance was largely ignored or limited to issues of sexual activity or sexually stereotyped mental disorders and was later explained by the influence of either men or feminism. Of course, these "deviants" could largely be found in inner-city urban areas and so attributes of those areas and their inhabitants became the locus of explanations for deviance. The question "*Why* are people deviant?" became "*Why* are the poor, people of color, urban youth, and women deviant?"

Two early explanations emerged to explain the role of race, class, gender, and age in deviant behavior—cultural deviance and strain theories. Both held social class as a central variable in shaping either values or access to opportunities. According to cultural deviance, structural position and location produced subcultural interactions that gave rise to deviant values (Cohen 1955). Strain theory argued that these variables, particularly class, lead to blocked opportunities in achieving the shared "American Dream" which then fostered deviant alternatives for economic success (Cloward and Ohlin 1960). Later, a third approach, differential association, offered additional insight into *how* deviance was learned in interaction with others (Sutherland and Cressey 1960). These theories persist to date in less deterministic versions, and related research has offered insight into the complex relationships between these statuses and deviant behavior.

Race, class, gender, and age are statuses that do shape access to the opportunity structure, and may give rise to values that legitimate deviance. Certain types of deviant activity do require knowledge, skills, rationales, and avenues for engagement. Class continues to be the primary consideration, and to the extent that it interacts with race, gender, and age, these variables are often implied if not explicitly addressed. Until recently, the focus has been on poverty as a contributor to deviance, and, yes, some types of deviance are more available to the poor, often not by choice but by access to institutional means. Poverty may increase the inclination of people to commit economic crimes such as theft, burglary, armed robbery, and street-level drug dealing and prostitution (Merton 1997). Other deviance requires positions of wealth, power, and prestige, a point finally elucidated in the literature with the acknowledgment of "white-collar" crime and later "elite deviance" (Simon 2003; Sutherland 1983). The decision to dump toxic waste illegally, pollute, expose employees to hazardous work conditions, embezzle, engage in insider trading on Wall Street, or participate in elaborate cyber crimes necessarily is dependent on socio-economic status and occupational/organizational position. It is the middle class or the rich—in other words, mostly white, male, and middle-aged—who can commit these "crimes of the suite," often while rationalizing their activity with an array of techniques of neutralization (Simon 2003; Coleman 2002).

Age is also a variable that continues to be linked with deviant behavior in this literature. Scholars and the public remain fascinated with the propensity of youth to become deviants. A plethora of literature addresses informal, medical, and formal deviance: youth subcultures of style, teen suicide, youth crime and violence ranging from gangs to school shootings, teen drug use and sexual activity, and dire predictions of a generation of "super-predators" (Wilson 1995; Males 1996; Hancock 2001).

Recent work has a more complex accounting of race and gender differentials in deviant behavior. General strain theory argues that race and gender discriminations are negative strains that may pressure youth into delinquency. Initial studies verify this: discrimination gives rise to a sense of injustice, which in turn is positively correlated with delinquency (Agnew 2006; Eitle 2002; Moon *et al.* 2009) The most fruitful research clarifies how the intersection of race, class, gender, and age creates a complex impetus for deviance. Analysis of youth gangs, "cool pose," and "the code of street" reveals how these variables combine to produce subcultural norms and collective responses that encourage violence, teen pregnancies, stringent norms of respect, and a rejection of the mainstream values of work and conformity (Shihadeh 2003; Majors and Mancini-Billson 1992; Anderson 1999; Stewart and Simmons 2009). Being young, poor, and black in the context of institutionalized racism and isolated neighborhoods may contribute to the adoption of an alternative set of norms and standards for respect; this may, in turn, be correlated with involvement in gangs and/or violence.

The relationship between race, class, gender, age, and deviance is a complicated one. The best thinking on how these variables contribute to deviance now indicates that it is insufficient to choose one of these variables alone as the primary focal point; they are intertwined with both social structure and social identity. Further, race, class, gender, and age cannot be isolated from consideration of the role of systems of oppression in fueling alienation and deviant response. That is, the experience of racism or sexism or classism or ageism may contribute to the rejection of dominant societal norms and subsequently be correlated with deviant behavior.

Race, class, gender, and age: differentials in labeling and social control

> All domination is, in the last instance, maintained through social control strategies.
>
> *(Bonilla-Silva 2001: 25)*

An alternative tradition in the sociology of deviance focuses on the relationship between deviant labeling and race, class, gender, and age. The concern here is less with differentials in deviant behavior but rather with differentials in social control. This approach begins with the question "Who is labeled deviant and who has the power to create and apply the labels?" Race, class, gender, and age are key components of the answer; these statuses give rise to power or oppression and are central to labeling and social control. It is this theoretical tradition that provided the most insight into the role that race, class, gender, and age play in the definition and control of deviance.

This analysis has its roots in the early works of both Marx and Durkheim as well as the later perspectives of critical/conflict theory, labeling, and functional-labeling theory. The initial work relied heavily on the examination of social class/class interests in shaping the law and its enforcement against the poor and created the framework for further examination of inequality, power, and labeling (Black 1989; Quinney 1970; Lauderdale 2003), while Goffman's classic *Stigma: Notes on the Management of Spoiled Identity* (1963) expanded the discussion to race, and gender and age were included in analyses soon after. These foundational perspectives laid the groundwork for understanding race, class, gender, and age as stigmatized statuses that are subject to social control by those with the power to create and apply deviant labels.

To the extent that the privileged and empowered "norm" is white, male, financially well off, heterosexual, and adult, then systems of social control maintain their interests, while people of color, women, the poor, GLBT persons, and the young become "the Other," the "abnormal," the "deviant" (Goffman 1963; Bonilla-Silva 2001). These stigmatized "Others" have been subject to labeling and social control based on the intersection of race, class, gender, and age. And, while there are "deviants" of all classes, all races, all genders, and all ages, the ways they are controlled reflect their relative social status. A substantial literature on stigma and related stereotypes explores how these statuses alone or in combination give rise to informal, medical, and legal social control; the homeless, female athletes, AIDS patients, style subcultures, and the young, black male have all been examined through the lens of stigma (Gans 1995; Lynxweiler and Gay 2000; Perry 2001; Weitz 2009; Zellner 1995).

The informal stigmas of race, class, gender, and age often provide the foundation for escalations in social control. Much current literature focuses attention on the systems of social control and how they operate to create and enforce rules that direct attention to select "deviants" relative to race, class, gender, and age. Increasingly, media is cited as a force in shaping public perceptions of deviance. Corporate crime and governmental deviance are minimized, reframed or ignored, while "street crime" and various epidemics of deviance rule the airwaves. Media perpetuates stereotypes and fuels "moral panics" and the "culture of fear" (Frymer 2009; Glassner 1999; McCorkle and Miethe 1998)

Media stereotypes relative to race, class, gender, and age become precursors to social policies that escalate social control, leading to medicalization of the "redeemable" white middle and upper classes and criminalization for the poor and communities of color (Conrad and Schneider 1998; Heitzeg 2008). Media has furthered the medicalization of deviance: epidemics of disorders of infancy, childhood and adolescence, eating disorders, self-mutilations, addictions, depression, and suicide are a news cycle staple raising concerns especially for youthful and female deviance (Birkland and Lawrence 2009; Ferrell and Websdale 1999; Males 1996; Weitz 2009). Perhaps mostly significantly the media endlessly regale the public with stories of crime—drug epidemics, school-shooting sprees, gang proliferation, and exaggerated accounts of violent crime, most often with young men of color as the perpetrators. The research indicates that violent crime and youth crime are dramatically over-represented, crime coverage has increased in spite of falling crime rates, African Americans and Latinos are over-represented as offenders and under-represented as victims, and inter-racial crime, especially crimes involving white victims, is over-reported (Hancock 2001; Walker, Spohn, and Delone 2007).

A large body of work documents the relationship between race, class, gender, and age and formal social control by the juvenile and adult criminal justice systems. Topics of study include: racial profiling, increased police attention to youth gangs, the "war on drugs," the proliferation of zero-tolerance policies in schools and the shift toward punitive policies in juvenile justice, the school–prison pipeline, the rise of mass incarceration and the prison industrial complex, the death penalty, and the proliferation of "collateral consequences" for many felony convictions such as voter disenfranchisement, denial of federal welfare, medical, housing or educational benefits, accelerated time-lines for loss of parental rights, and exclusion from any number of employment opportunities (Brewer and Heitzeg 2008; Heitzeg 2008; Mauer and Chesney-Lind 2002; Brownfield, Sorenson, and Thompson 2001; Zatz and Krecker 2003). It is clear from the research that these variables are indeed better predictors of arrest, criminal processing, sentencing, incarceration, and execution than actual participation in criminal behavior may be.

Again, the best analyses examine the intersection of race, class, gender, and age and their relationship to social control. A brief glimpse into criminal justice statistics immediately reveals these intersections. Despite no real statistical differences in rates of offending, the poor, the under-educated, the young, and people of color are over-represented in every phase of the United States' criminal and juvenile justice systems, from arrest to death row. While 1 in 35 adults is under correctional supervision and 1 in every 100 adults is in prison, 1 in every 36 Latino adults, 1 in every 15 black men, 1 in every 100 black women, and 1 in 9 black men between the ages of 20 and 34 are incarcerated (PEW 2008). The number of women incarcerated has increased tenfold during the past two decades, and they are overwhelmingly women of color (BJS 2007). The race and class disparities are even greater for youth. Black youth are two times more likely than white youth to be arrested, to be referred to juvenile court, to be adjudicated as delinquent or referred to the adult justice system, and they are three times more likely than white youth to be sentenced to out-of-home residential placement. And while boys are five times as likely to be incarcerated as girls, girls are at increasing risk (Walker, Spohn and Delone 2007). Race, class, gender, and age collide and combine to create these extreme disparities of formal social control.

Race, class, gender, and age, then, are major factors in the social control of deviance. These variables and their intersection are powerful indicators of both stigma and subsequent social control. While race, class, gender, and age may play a role in creating opportunities for deviant behavior, their real significance is in shaping the differential direction of power and social control. The intersection of these statuses shapes access to both the power to label and the powerlessness of being subjected to social control.

Future directions

> The sociology of deviance must speak of oppression, conflict, persecution, and suffering. It must examine the conditions of inequality, powerlessness, institutional violence . . . which lie at the base of our society.
>
> *(Liazos 1972: 120)*

At various points in its history, the sociology of deviance has been called into question for failure to address the structural impact of race, class, gender, and age (Liazos 1972; Sumner 1994). Certainly the critics have been, at least partly, answered. Recent scholarship in the field has contributed to an understanding of how these positions in the social structure intersect to create both differential opportunities to engage in deviant behavior and differential chances for stigma, deviant labeling, and social control. The most compelling research examines race, class, gender, and age not in isolation, but in combination—illustrating how these statuses interact to create a complex process of deviance and social control.

Some of the early critiques remain unanswered. The sociology of deviance should further explore the interplay between "deviants" and social control, the deviance of elites and institutions, and the extent to which power/privilege shape the definition and control of deviance. The field could also more completely outline the interconnections between race, class, gender, and age as sources of identity and resistance, and subsequent societal efforts at escalating social control. Although current research is pointed toward this direction, the sociology of deviance has yet fully to interrogate how systemic racism, classism, sexism, and ageism may both create and encourage deviance, or indeed how these systems may represent a meta-level of deviance unto themselves.

The sociology of deviance may be informed here by the scholarship that examines the impact of racism and sexism on deviant behavior and by the literature that exposes the propensity of systems of social control to target deviants—not by behavior—but by race, class, gender, and age. Research in other areas of sociology—inequality, race/ethnicity, gender and social movements—may additionally augment this line of inquiry, as might critical legal studies, critical race and feminist theory, and interdisciplinary studies of race/ethnicity, women/gender, and youth. These fields have done much to uncover the social processes and consequences of "othering" and the roots of systems of inequality.

Yes, race, class, gender, and age are central to the sociological endeavor, and they must remain so to the sociology of deviance. Their intersection forms the "matrix of domination" that is at the very root of deviation, definition, and control (Andersen and Hill-Collins 2007). The most pressing questions of 21st-century research in the field may well center on the role of race, class, gender, and age in demarcating those battle lines of deviance and social control.

References

Agnew, R. (2006) *Pressured into Crime: An Overview of General Strain Theory*. Los Angeles, CA: Roxbury.

Anderson, E. (1999). *Code of the Street*. New York: W. W. Norton.

Andersen, M. and P. Hill Collins (eds.). (2007) *Race, Class, and Gender*. 6th edn. Belmont, CA: Wadsworth.

Birkland, T. A. and R. Lawrence. (2009) "Media Framing after Columbine." *American Behavioral Scientist* 52: 1405–1425.

Black, D. (1989) *Sociological Justice*. New York: Oxford University Press.

Bonilla-Silva, E. (2001) *White Supremacy and Racism in the Post-Civil Rights Era*. Boulder, CO: Lynne Rienner.

Brewer, R. M and N.A. Heitzeg. (2008) "The Racialization of Crime and Punishment: Criminal Justice, Color-Blind Racism and the Political Economy of the Prison Industrial Complex." *American Behavioral Scientist* 51: 625–643.

Brownfield, D., A. M. Sorenson and K. M. Thompson (2001). "Gang Membership, Race, and Social Class: A Test of the Group Hazard and Master Status Hypotheses." *Deviant Behavior* 22: 73—89.

Bureau of Justice Statistics (BJS). (2007) *Sourcebook of Criminal Justice Statistics*. Washington, DC: US Government Printing Office.

Cloward, R. A. and L. E. Ohlin. (1960) *Delinquency and Opportunity*. New York: Free Press.

Cohen, A. K. (1955) *Delinquent Boys*. Glencoe, IL: Free Press.

Coleman, J. W. (2002) *The Criminal Elite: Understanding White-Collar Crime*. New York: Macmillan.

Conrad, P. and J. W. Schneider. (1998) *Deviance and Medicalization: From Badness to Sickness*. Philadelphia, PA: Temple University Press.

Eitle, D. J. (2002) "Exploring a Source of Deviance-Producing Strain for Females: Perceived Discrimination and General Strain Theory." *Journal of Criminal Justice* 3: 429–42.

Ferrell, J. and N. Websdale (eds.). (1999) *Making Trouble: Cultural Constructions of Crime, Deviance, and Control*. New York: Aldine de Gruyte.

Frymer, B. (2009) "The Media Spectacle of Columbine: Alienated Youth as an Object of Fear." *American Behavioral Scientist* 52: 1387–1404.

Gans, H. (1995) The *War against the Poor: The Underclass and Antipoverty Policy*. New York: Basic Books.

Glassner, B. (1999) *The Culture of Fear: Why Americans Are Afraid of the Wrong Things*. New York: Basic Books.

Goffman, E. (1963) *Stigma: Notes on the Management of Spoiled Identity*. New York: Prentice-Hall.

Hancock, L. (2001) "Framing Children in the News: The Face and Color of Youth Crime in America." In Valerie Polakow (ed.), *The Public Assault on America's Children: Poverty, Violence and Juvenile Justice* (pp. 78–100). New York: Teacher's College, Columbia University.

Heitzeg, N. A. (2008) "Race, Class and Legal Risk in the United States: Youth of Color and Colluding Systems of Social Control." *Forum on Public Policy*, summer. Available at: www.forumonpublicpolicy.com/summer08papers/archivesummer08/heitzeg1.pdf.

Lauderdale, P. (2003) *A Political Analysis of Deviance: New Edition*. Willowdale: de Sitter.

Liazos, A. (1972) "The Poverty of the Sociology of Deviance: Nuts, Sluts, and Perverts." *Social Problems* 20: 103–20.

Lynxweiler, J. and D. Gay. (2000) "Moral Boundaries and Deviant Music: Public Attitudes toward Heavy Metal and Rap." *Deviant Behavior* 21 (1): 63–85.

Majors, R. and J. Mancini-Billson. (1992) *Cool Pose: The Dilemmas of Black Manhood in America*. New York: Touchstone.

Males, M. A. (1996) *Scapegoat Generation: The War on America's Adolescents*. Monroe, ME: Common Courage Press.

Mauer, M. and M. Chesney-Lind (eds.). (2002) *Invisible Punishment: The Collateral Consequences of Mass Imprisonment*. New York: The New Press.

McCorkle, R. C. and T. D. Miethe. (1998) "The Political and Organizational Response to Gangs: An Examination of a Moral Panic in Nevada." *Justice Quarterly* 15: 41–64.

Merton, R. (1997) "On the Evolving Synthesis of Differential Association and Anomie Theory: A Perspective from the Sociology of Science." *Criminology* 35: 517–25.

Mills, C. W. (1959) *The Sociological Imagination*. New York: Oxford University Press.

Moon, B. *et al.* (2009) "General Strain Theory, Key Strains, and Deviance." *Journal of Criminal Justice* 37: 98–106.

Perry, B. (2001) *In the Name of Hate: Understanding Hate Crime*. New York: Routledge.

PEW Center on the States. (2008) *One in 100: Behind Bars in America 2008*. Washington, DC: PEW.

Pfohl, S. (1994) *Images of Deviance and Social Control: A Sociological History*. 2nd edn. New York: McGraw-Hill.

Quinney, R. (1970) *The Social Reality of Crime*. Boston, MA: Little, Brown.

Sheldon, R. G., S. K. Tracy and W. B. Brown. (2001) *Youth Gangs in American Society*. Belmont, CA: Wadsworth.

Shihadeh, E. S. (2003) "Race, Class, and Crime: Reconsidering the Spatial Effects of Social Isolation on Rates of Urban Offending." *Deviant Behavior* 26: 5–27.

Simon, D. (2007) *Elite Deviance*. Upper Saddle River, NJ: Pearson.

Stewart, E. and R. Simmons. (2009) *The Code of the Street and African American Violence*. Washington, DC: National Institute of Justice.

Sumner, C. (1994) *The Sociology of Deviance: An Obituary*. New York: Continuum.

Sutherland, D. and R. Cressey. (1960) *Principles of Criminology*. Chicago, IL: Lippincott.

Sutherland, E. (1983) *White Collar Crime*. New Haven, CT: Yale University Press.

Walker, S., C. Spohn and M. DeLone. (2007) *The Color of Justice: Race, Ethnicity and Crime in America*. 4th edn. Belmont, CA: Wadsworth.

Weitz, R. (ed.). (2009) *The Politics of Women's Bodies: Sexuality, Appearance, and Behavior*. 2nd edn. New York: Oxford University Press.

Wilson, J. Q. (1995) *Crime*. San Francisco, CA: Institute for Contemporary Studies.

Zatz, M. and R. Krecker Jr. (2003) "Anti-Gang Initiatives as Racialized Policy." In Daniel Hawkins, Samuel Meyers and Randolph Stone (eds.), *Crime Social Control and Social Justice: The Delicate Balance*. Westport, CT: Greenwood.

Zellner, W. (1995) *Countercultures*. New York: St. Martin's Press.

Part II
Research methodology in studying deviance

Overview

Deviant behavior invites research and understanding. All human social behavior is subject to scientific inquiry and explanation, and numerous protocols, procedures, and strategies are available to the scholarly researcher for accomplishing this. Deviant behavior is, perhaps, the most compelling configuration of human social behavior, because the aberrant is always more interesting than the normal. Conducting research on deviance offers some unique problems and challenges, however, not the least of which is that deviant behavior is usually furtive, if not clandestine or secret. Deviants do not want intrusion. Outsiders are not welcome in deviant subcultures. Deviants tend to be non-communicative about their behavior. It is difficult to gain an entrée into deviant circles. All of these handicaps and others have to be overcome in order to conduct research.

Quantitative methodology

Jeff Ackerman, in his chapter, addresses the matter of the statistical analysis of research data—so-called "hard sociology," as it were. He defines quantitative methodology as "any of a variety of systematic processes that scholars use to detect, understand, and summarize patterns among phenomena measured in a numerical way." Some use the term "statistics" synony-mously with the phrase "quantitative." The two do overlap considerably, but "methods" most often refers to data-gathering techniques, while "statistics" and "statistical techniques" properly identify the ways in which researchers analyze, summarize, and present information about previously obtained data.

Ackerman notes that with the exception of Durkheim, almost all of the "pioneers" of sociology relied on qualitative methodology in their research. This continued through the time of the Chicago School, with their urban ethnographies. Later, when criminology emerged as a sub-discipline of sociology, some criminological researchers began using analytical induction methods.

Ackerman relates that some of Sutherland's data were increasingly of such a nature that they lent themselves to quantitative analysis. A number of mid-20th-century sociologists began to argue for the incorporation of quantitative methods. As Ackerman phrases it, "a growing unrest emerged among crime and deviance scholars of the mid-20th century that the field would benefit from increases in methodological rigor of the type that would permit a clearer understanding of the factors causally related to deviance." While the faculty of various schools such as the "second Chicago School," which emerged in the 1950s, "remained reliant primarily upon qualitative methods, they gradually introduced quantitative-probabilistic analyses to the discipline of sociology and subsequently to the study of deviant behavior."

Ackerman then turns to a lengthy and detailed exposition contrasting qualitative and quantitative methodology. He relates that qualitative methodology relies on observation or other forms of information-gathering that "produces little or no numerical measurement. Proponents of quantitative methodology assert that research employing this methodology is value-free."

Ackerman suggests that scholars who rely solely on a single methodology may tend to "write essays that are somewhat biased by the author's methodological preferences." In general, quantitative methodology tends to be probabilistic while qualitative methodology is more likely to be deterministic. Statistical models seek "to generalize a study's results to a larger population of interest, even when the scholar was able to include only a small fraction of the population in the study." Qualitative scholars, however, do not want to generalize the findings of their research beyond those in the observed cases. Qualitative methodology tends to be idiographic in orientation (providing a full explanation of the unique characteristics in all subjects). On the other hand, quantitative scholars tend to have a nomothetic orientation (here the intent is to "detect patterns across a larger group of individuals without specific intent to enumerate all factors influencing the outcome for particular individuals"). Qualitative scholars seek to produce "broad, overarching, and relatively complete descriptions or explanations of a particular phenomenon which emphasize a thorough evaluation and interpretation of limited observation." They do not intend to generalize beyond their observed cases. Quantitative scholars, on the other hand, "typically intend their work to focus on smaller aspects of a narrowly defined question, to rely upon a large number of observations, and to make inferences about conditions that exist beyond the group of cases examined." In short, quantitative methodology has the goal of providing knowledge of a limited position of a complex question while qualitative methodology "will likely provide a thorough description of most aspects of the sampled offenders' lives in a way that permits the qualitative sociologists to explain the many ways that each offender differs."

Ackerman concludes his chapter with a discussion of the tools of quantitative methodology. This discussion addresses a variety of research techniques, such as summary (descriptive) statistics, univariate statistics, central tendencies (mean, median, and mode), measures of dispersion, inferential statistics, calculating confidence intervals surrounding an estimate of how strongly one factor affects the magnitude of another, and prediction models, to mention but some.

Qualitative methodology

In his chapter, Richard Tewksbury reviews the usage of qualitative methodology in the study of deviant behavior. Tewksbury points out that qualitative methodology is particularly well suited for the study of deviance, inasmuch as scholars seek to "gain true understandings of the social aspects of how deviant acts occur and how the social responses to deviance are experienced within culturally situated contexts." Quantitative methodology, with its incidence rates, covariates or statistical relationships, simply cannot capture the depth of understanding desired by researchers. Qualitative methodology, relying on such techniques as interviews and observations, can more effectively "explore issues and their context, clarifying what, how, when, where and among whom behaviors and processes operate."

Tewksbury reports that qualitative methodology often produces taxonomies (or typologies), theoretical constructs and arguments, and explanations of cultural settings. Qualitative methodology relies on a variety of collection methods to generate data. These methods include interviews, observations and immersion, to mention but some. Tewksbury goes on to provide details about some of these methods.

Interviews are structured conversations with subjects for the purpose of obtaining information about their experiences and activities, and/or their views on social events and causes. Interview information can be a rich source of data but interviewers must establish a productive relationship with the subject, and keep the conversation on target.

Participant observation, as the name implies, refers to a researcher who actively engages in the "actual routines and behavioral sets" of the activity and people being studied. Participant observation, in effect, means "getting inside" of the phenomenon under investigation. Sometimes, the identity of the participant observed is known to all, but in other instances, only a few of those involved actually understand the purposes of the observer.

In some situations, the researcher may necessarily have to be a *covert participant observer*. Here the researcher will have to misrepresent himself or herself and their reason for being there. This method is sometimes labeled "disguised observation." Secrecy must be maintained and this raises ethical questions. In some cases, it might become very problematic if those being studied learn about the real reason why the covert observer is there.

Ethnography is another technique used by qualitative research. This technique generates a more complete picture of how a deviant social world is structured and how it operates. Ethnography is sometimes accomplished by having the researcher become totally "immersed" in the setting in order to provide an analytic description of the dynamics of the deviance occurring in the setting being studied.

A variation on this technique is *"edge ethnography."* This is essentially an ethnography of the subject of study "beyond the margins of society, often with some type or element of danger." With edge ethnography, the researcher may well actually have to engage in the deviance being studied, in order to do his or her research. Edge ethnography seeks "a depth and detailed understanding of groups, settings, and activities that are not necessarily available or accessible" to other types of researcher. In engaging in edge ethnography, the researcher may be exposed to physical, legal, and/or social danger.

According to Tewksbury, *extreme methods* are research techniques that call for "highly unusual or creative approaches" to gathering data on deviant behavior. This might involve innovative ways of getting access to subjects and settings and how data is collected in a very unusual fashion, for example. To study some types of deviance, it may be necessary to "go beyond simple immersion, and observation of those being studied." Tewksbury observes that extreme measures are "methodologies that push the limits of ethical interaction with those being studied."

Tewksbury stresses that, for a variety of reasons, qualitative research methods are especially useful for the study of deviance. Among these reasons is the fact that qualitative research collects data in a naturalistic setting and also collects information about the setting. This is important because some settings "often serve to encourage, facilitate or inhibit many forms of behavior," including deviant behavior. Qualitative data may be more likely than quantitative data to provide insights and understanding of "experiences, behaviors, and social responses to behaviors in context and from the perspective of those being studied." Another significant contribution of qualitative methodology is "the development of theoretical constructs and explanations for phenomena."

Qualitative methods for the study of deviance and deviants also have some limitations. These limitations include the fact that it may be very difficult, if not impossible, to access deviants and some forms of deviance. Most criminals and deviants would not likely agree to being interviewed, or to permit an observer to accompany them as they engage in illegal acts. Covert observation might be possible, but this may be very dangerous for the researcher.

Tewksbury concludes his chapter with a lengthy discussion of ethical challenges in qualitative deviance studies. In this connection, he observes that "There are some unique ethical concerns and considerations that are introduced by the use of qualitative methods, but these are not so great that they cannot be overcome."

Cross-cultural and historical methodology

Robert Heiner, in his chapter, explores research journeys in time and space. He begins by citing Durkheim as one of the sociological pioneers in the utilization of cross-cultural and historical research methodology, inasmuch as he employed both strategies in his classic research on suicide. He points out that researchers in almost all disciplines use comparative methodology in their research. Heiner also notes that cross-cultural and historical research are similar in that both use comparative techniques. As Heiner observes, "comparing different historical periods is essentially the same as comparing different cultures." The aim of comparative research is to obtain data that yield generalizations applicable to a wider range of social units than is the case with one-dimensional research. But, he cautions, there are two caveats relative to his discussion of deviance. First, while there is a large body of literature on cross-cultural and historical sociological research, there is relatively little literature on cross-cultural and historical methods that are distinctive to the sociology of deviance. His second caveat is that it is difficult (if not impossible) to obtain "reliable, comparable data from the past and from other cultures."

Heiner warns that data on deviance is often flawed because of various reasons, not the least of which is that offenders actively try to keep their deviance secret. He cites one researcher who sums up some of the problems inherent in comparative research and observes there are "cultural variations in the definition of crime, sentiments of severity, degree of reportability, probabilities of discovery, types of penalties, and the methods of collecting criminal statistics."

In regard to cross-cultural research, such studies are always burdened from the start by the fact that definitions and measurements are not consistent across cultures, and data come from a variety of official sources. Working from a consensus model, cross-cultural researchers often assert that, "there is near-universal condemnation, at least, for certain criminal offenses." Such offenses are labeled "moral minima"; an illustration would be homicide.

Heiner reports that conflict theorists take exception to the use of official data in cross-cultural research, and assert that official data are not so much a reflector of the incidence of criminal behavior as an indicator of the activities of the police, the courts, the prison, and the type of people who are being processed by the criminal justice system.

Historical research, according to Heiner, is similar to cross-cultural research inasmuch as it involves the examination of a different culture—the culture of the past. If data from a number of different time periods are used, the research is considered to be comparative. If a single time period is examined, the research is more properly labeled as a case study. Heiner suggests that historical research is often quite productive in providing revealing insights into the nature of social control. He then discusses several well-known historical studies of deviant behavior and offers some predictions regarding future directions in comparative research. In this regard,

Heiner suggests that there will be more research on deviance within the context of global-ization. Research in transnational crime will increase. The internet has opened up vast new opportunities for crime and deviance, which, in many instances, will know no national boundaries. Some crimes now fall within the jurisdiction of several countries. Among the effects of globalization has been the homogenization of culture, which, in turn, has expedited the proliferation of Western culture and values in many other cultures globally. This may well have "implications for the construction of deviant categories throughout the world." Heiner concludes his chapter with the observation that "popularly held beliefs about deviant behavior being inherently wrong, harmful, or offensive have been and will continue to be put to the test by cross-cultural and historical research."

8

Quantitative methodology

Jeff Ackerman

General introduction

Quantitative methodology (or quantitative research) is any of a variety of systematic processes that scholars use to detect, understand, and summarize patterns among phenomena measured in a numerical way (Babbie 2001; Neuman 2003). Quantitative methods are closely associated with the field of statistics and the two terms overlap considerably. Although scholars often use these expressions synonymously, when academics make distinctions between the terms, *methods* most often refers to data-gathering techniques, and *statistics* and *statistical techniques* most often refer to the ways researchers analyze, summarize, and present information about previously obtained data.

Often, the phrase *quantitative methods* is used as a universal phrase that subsumes the term *statistics*. For example, although university courses addressing statistical techniques may be labeled *quantitative methods*, it is less common to discuss data-gathering techniques in a university course called *statistics*.

Antecedents of quantitative methodology in crime and deviance scholarship

With the exception of a very few individuals such as Durkheim (e.g., 1938, 1951), sociology relied upon *qualitative* methodology until the mid-20th century. The early works of the Chicago School, for example, focused largely upon qualitative ethnographic work in urban sociology (e.g., Thomas and Znaniecki 1918; Wirth 1928). Crime and deviance research, another Chicago School sub-specialty, was similarly focused on qualitative scholarship, epitomized by classic ethnographies of deviant occupations such as *The Jack-Roller* (Shaw 1930), *The Hobo* (Anderson 1923), and *The Gang* (Thrasher 1927).

During this early period, when criminology developed as a sub-discipline of sociology, the technique of *analytic induction* emerged. A brief explanation of this technique provides background information illuminating the context in which quantitative methodology came to be used in deviance research and helps contrast the goals of quantitative and qualitative methods as used in this field.

Although scholars had relied upon the essence of analytic induction throughout earlier history, Znaniecki (1934) first described its principles in the sociological literature. According to

Znaniecki, the method's objective was to develop universal propositions that purported to explain human behavior. When a theorist discovered exceptions to preliminary propositions, the theorist was tasked with modifying the framework to conform to the newly revealed observations. After extensive revision, the end result was the development of a general framework presumed an exhaustive understanding of the particular phenomenon of interest. In other words, the goal of analytic induction, in Znaniecki's view, was a comprehensive explanation for all known cases of a particular phenomenon, such as deviant behavior.

Changes eventually occurred in the ways scholars viewed analytic induction techniques. Lindesmith (1947) and Cressey (1950, 1953) refined its principles while other authors repudiated Znaniecki's implication that theorists could develop comprehensive universal laws of human behavior (e.g., Robinson 1951). Although scholars of those times were refining their views about this and other qualitative methodologies, a belief emerged among several mid-20th-century deviance scholars that an alteration of existing methods was insufficient to advance the discipline adequately. What was needed, in their view, was the incorporation of quantitative techniques.

Sutherland's differential association theory—an example antecedent

As explained by Akers (1998), Edwin Sutherland (e.g., 1924, 1942), an early and influential criminologist who obtained his Ph.D. from the University of Chicago in 1913, relied upon analytic induction principles to express his theory of *differential association*. Sutherland was strongly influenced by Chicago School theorists Shaw and McKay (e.g., 1942), who argued against pathological and biological explanations of crime by attributing offending to the social contexts of individuals.

Starting in the 1920s, Sutherland gradually refined his theory, which purported to differentiate offenders from non-offenders by the quantity and quality of various pro- and anti-criminal *definitions* to which individuals are exposed. Although Sutherland modified his theory over several editions of his criminology text (Gaylord and Galliher 1988), most contemporary scholars suggest that he was unable fully to operationalize his concept of (pro-criminal) *definitions* in a way that permitted others to test specific hypotheses based upon his articulated framework (e.g., Matsueda 1988; Pfohl 1994). Although many scholars would strongly argue against dismissing Sutherland's differential association theory as excessively vague (e.g., Tittle, Burke, and Jackson 1986), and would also caution that Sutherland's critics often misinterpreted his writings (e.g., Cressey 1953), even supporters like Akers (1998) suggested that we can attribute the sparse detail in Sutherland's writings (and perhaps the writings of other early crime and deviance scholars as well) to the non-probabilistic nature of the analytic induction methods common to that era.

Because the conventions of Znaniecki's methods required theoretical modification when exceptions to an initial proposition were realized, the approach required proponents either to express generalized theoretical frameworks in an abstract, imprecise manner; or write in an extraordinarily detailed fashion whereby the scholar describes a comprehensive array of relationships and the conditions under which all associations are both observed and modified. Articulating a framework between these extremes would negate the usefulness of a general theory intended to provide full explanation of all aspects of deviance. Although contemporary examples exist within the quantitative literature of the successful application of an extraordinarily detailed theoretical framework (e.g., Kaplan 2009), the stringent requirements and lofty goals of the analytic induction methods of this early era likely hindered Sutherland and others from articulating precise operationalized definitions for their key constructs.

The advent of probabilistic models in the study of deviant behavior

While the degree to which Sutherland's classic theory is sufficiently precise is debatable, there is less doubt that a growing unrest emerged among crime and deviance scholars of the mid-20th century that the field would benefit from increases in methodological rigor of the type that would permit a clearer understanding of the factors causally related to deviance. Although speculative, a large portion of this dissatisfaction might be attributed to the sometimes nebulous theoretical statements produced by deviance scholars who adhered to Znaniecki's version of analytic induction. Subsequently, their dissatisfaction may have pushed later authors away from comprehensive, grand theorizing and toward more probabilistic and specific frameworks. In other words, it is likely that as the early sociologists gained greater awareness of the expansive array of factors associated with deviant behavior, they gradually focused upon more limited segments of these many factors and evaluated their findings in a more formalized way.

We can clearly observe the unrest among deviance scholars during the mid-20th century in the early volumes of the crime and deviance specialty journals, which were increasingly founded at that time. The inaugural issue of *Crime and Delinquency*, for example, featured an article strongly arguing for the expanded use of the scientific method in the discipline (Fischer 1955). Cohen (1951) also authored a pervasive critique of deviance research when he wrote that "we do not definitely link [research] to specific and clearly worded hypotheses capable of verification."

In this environment, a second Chicago School emerged during the 1950s (Fine 1995). While the second school's members remained reliant primarily upon qualitative methods, they gradually introduced quantitative-probabilistic analyses to the discipline of sociology and subsequently to the study of deviant behavior.

Contrasting qualitative and quantitative methodology

Social and behavioral scientists frequently contrast *quantitative and qualitative methodology* as a way to illustrate the fundamental elements of each. The latter includes a variety of techniques related most obviously by a reliance upon observation or upon other forms of information-gathering that produce little or no numerical measurement. Beyond this obvious difference, broad and oversimplified summaries of each method are sometimes contentious. This fact is soon realized when we consider that some scholars believe that both methods may accomplish identical or similar goals using alternative techniques, while others suggest that the two methods have inherently different objectives (Creswell 1994). Moreover, the differences discussed both herein and by others are generally suggested as universal ideals that may be overdrawn and contain many exceptions in practice.

We can see an illustration of the views suggestive of strong goal differences between the methods by noting that proponents of quantitative research claim their work is accomplished within a value-free framework (Babbie 2001), while qualitative work typically stresses the inability to be completely objective; the value-laden nature of inquiry; and the advantages of subjectivity (Denzin and Lincoln 2005).

Although some scholars suggest that the choice of quantitative versus qualitative approaches can be determined only after a proper articulation of goals for a given study (e.g., Tewksbury 2009), until recently, when mixed/combined methods have become more prevalent, most scholars in the social and behavioral sciences consistently relied upon one method over the other (Vogt 1998). This fact suggests that more traditional authors who rely solely upon a single methodology may write essays that are somewhat biased by the author's methodological preferences.

One of the less contentious contrasts between the two approaches is the reasonably consistent agreement that quantitative approaches, but generally not qualitative ones, specifically include probabilistic elements. Unlike approaches used by the sociologists of Sutherland's era, probabilistic (or stochastic) models assume that selected characteristics or circumstances of individuals increase or decrease the *probability* of deviance but do not necessitate it (Bailey 2007). In other words, probabilistic models acknowledge a degree of randomness and inaccuracy. Knowledge about a specific characteristic (a predictor or independent variable) helps forecast to some imperfect but useful way the magnitude (or presence) of another characteristic (an outcome or dependent variable), and the model should specifically acknowledge the degree to which forecasting error occurs.

A deterministic model is the opposite of a probabilistic one. A deterministic model assumes that no randomness or error exists after a scholar uses a set of antecedent characteristics or conditions intended to forecast the magnitude or presence of an interesting outcome. In other words, when a given set of factor(s) is present (or absent), a particular outcome (deviant behavior in this case) is felt to always occur.

Because Sutherland's theory both a) suggested that individuals choose a path of crime when the [weighted] balance of definitions for law-breaking to which the individual was exposed exceeds their law-abiding exposure, and b) rejected other theoretical perspectives proposing alternative factors in the production of deviant behavior, an argument can be made that Sutherland's theory was deterministic. Very clearly, however, proponents of Sutherland's work have revised his original propositions to include probabilistic language (e.g. Akers and Jennings 2009).

A second traditional but diminishing distinction between quantitative and qualitative methodologies is that statistical models aim to provide insight about individuals or conditions beyond the sample from which the researcher obtained the data used in model formulation. In other words, a quantitative model intends to generalize a study's results to a larger population of interest even when the scholar was able to include only a small fraction of the population in the study. In contrast, a majority of traditional qualitative scholars do not intend their findings to generalize beyond observed cases. A trend toward generalizing is emerging, however, among some qualitative methodologists and to an even greater extent among advocates of mixed methodology (e.g., Maruna 2001; Hagan, Hirshfeld, and Shedd 2002).

An alternative delineation between these methods emphasizes the idiographic approach that qualitative techniques sometimes contain versus the nomothetic approach used by quantitative studies. An ideographic approach documents distinctiveness among individuals by providing a full explanation for the uniqueness present in each. In contrast, nomothetic approaches intend to detect patterns across a larger group of individuals without specific intent to enumerate all factors influencing the outcome for particular individuals (Luthans and Davis 1982; Neuman 2003).

Most qualitative scholars state goals of broad, overarching, and relatively complete descriptions or explanations of a particular phenomenon, which emphasize a thorough evaluation and interpretation of limited observations. These scholars routinely call attention to the fact that they do not intend their studies to produce information generalizable beyond their observed cases. In contrast, quantitative methodologists typically intend their work to focus on smaller aspects of a narrowly defined question, to rely upon a large number of observations, and to make inferences about conditions that exist beyond the group of cases examined (Babbie 2001).

A qualitative methodologist studying a small group of offenders, for example, might describe a wide variety of factors intended as relatively inclusive of the comprehensive influences upon the group's deviant behavior. In contrast, a quantitative methodologist is likely to examine patterns in a much larger sample of offenders and emphasize the measurement of a few key factors hypothesized to distinguish between high-frequency offenders and those who offend on a limited basis.

Unlike quantitative research, qualitative methodologists seldom emphasize formalized methods for gauging the degree to which the researcher's conclusions are reproducible in a different offender group. The result of the qualitative study will likely provide a thorough description of most aspects of the sampled offenders' lives in a way that permits the qualitative methodologist to explain the many ways that each offender differs. That methodologist is likely to describe the reasons that one offender acted in a particular way and how those reasons diverged from those underlying the behavior of other offenders.

Unlike qualitative methods, uniqueness in one offender that is absent in others is treated as unexplained error or randomness by quantitative methods. These approaches typically emphasize a thorough examination of limited factors, a precise way to measure these factors, and some form of mathematical technique intended both to quantify the degree to which each factor affects the phenomena of interest and the degree of evidence supporting the study's results and conclusions.

The fact that quantitative methods are generally intended to provide knowledge about a limited portion of a complex question is often a source of misunderstanding about quantitative methodology. Those unfamiliar with quantitative techniques sometimes criticize quantitative studies for failing to consider all possible factors. In other words, some critics may not understand that a thorough examination of the effect of limited factors on a single outcome, rather than a full and complete explanation of an elaborate question, is the articulated goal of most quantitative work.

Absent claims that a model encompasses all factors producing deviance and is thus deterministic, the qualitative methodologist who intends no generalizability beyond his or her sample of observations can certainly produce a valid and meaningful product that adheres to the scholar's stated goals more directly than a scholar intending to develop a framework purportedly capable of perfect and comprehensive explanation. The exception, of course, is a deterministic model intended to be fully inclusive and generalizable to a larger population where the model, in reality, retains sufficient ambiguity to permit multiple interpretations or is formulated in a way that otherwise inhibits precise empirical testing in samples beyond the one used to construct the initial model.

In sum, quantitative methods gradually became widespread due to the belief among many scholars that very generalized and overarching theoretical frameworks of crime and deviance that evidenced a deterministic component were insufficient to advance the discipline. Quantitative methods are generally, but somewhat contentiously, described as probabilistic rather than deterministic, nomothetic rather than ideographic, intended to provide more detailed and formalized information about their applicability to cases beyond the sample, and concerned with providing a partial explanation for a particular phenomenon rather than a comprehensive and generalized account of all factors associated with deviant outcomes.

The tools of quantitative methodology

Among the least complex forms of quantitative methodology are summary (descriptive) statistics, which deal with a single variable or measurement (univariate) obtained for each member of a group or sample of cases. Many consider univariate statistics *descriptive* because they describe or summarize more extensive and more complex information.

The most common summary statistics are *central tendency* measures, such as the mean, median, and mode. The summary's objective is a synopsis of the group's basic features that researchers may use in place of presenting all available information for each group member. For example, rather than discussing the heights of all 100 individuals in an offender group, a quantitative methodologist might discuss the group's mean height (less precisely but frequently termed the *average*) as a single summary statistic. The benefits of doing so include the ability to present information in an understandable, useful, and parsimonious way, while the drawbacks include information loss. In this example, providing only the mean height of the group is easily understandable; however, the summary fails to provide detailed information about each of the 100 individual heights and the ways in which height differs across members.

Other common descriptive statistics intended to summarize information include measures of dispersion, such as the variance, standard deviation, and range. These statistics quantify the homogeneity of the group/sample in related, but alternative ways. In other words, measures of dispersion summarize the degree to which we might expect individual cases to deviate from each other or from the group's mean.

Although descriptive statistics clearly are the most basic type of quantitative methodology, they form the foundation of the more complex techniques of *inferential statistics*, which extend description by reaching conclusions beyond the immediate data alone (see, for example, Felson, Ackerman, and Yeon 2003). Included in this overarching methodological category are techniques intended to determine whether patterns exist between two or more measurements/variables. Also included are techniques to gauge the dependability of conclusions and whether data patterns observed in a sample of cases are *real* (statistically significant) and therefore expected to be consistently found in similar data sources. In other words, quantitative methods are intended to ascertain the probability that data patterns may be present due solely to coincidence (chance) and therefore how likely we are to observe similar patterns consistently elsewhere (e.g., in the population of cases from which the analyzed sample was drawn).

It is perhaps important to note that the use of statistical significance tests to determine whether observed data are consistent with existing theory is a traditional quantitative approach in the social sciences. More recently, however, several scholars have advocated that we downplay this traditional approach in favor of an emphasis on calculating confidence intervals surrounding an estimate of how strongly one factor affects the magnitude of another (see Ritchey 2000).

Regardless of whether used to test hypotheses or produce confidence intervals around predicted population parameters, inferential statistics are the type that contain the probabilistic aspect previously described as intending to forecast to some imperfect but useful way the magnitude (or presence) of another measurement or characteristic. In the majority of research questions, even prediction models containing a great amount of error can be extremely useful and informative. For example, years ago, innovative individuals discovered that the number of "10" cards remaining in a deck predicted a greater probability that a player would win a hand from a dealer in the casino game of blackjack. Although the number of "10" cards increased the player's probability of winning the hand from roughly 50 percent only to a maximum of around 55 percent, these individuals were able to win fortunes by increasing bet sizes when their chances of winning increased (Thorp 1962). Although the "10"-card proportion was far from a perfect predictor of winning, knowledge about the number of such cards proved extremely useful to the players. In a similar fashion, knowledge about how parental supervision and parental attachment affect juvenile delinquency may provide information useful to the reduction of juvenile offending even if that information is insufficient to eliminate offending completely or explain why all offending occurs.

In sum, in order to produce usable knowledge, inferential statistics (and quantitative methodology more generally) attempts to discover new knowledge by discovering patterns in numerically coded data; recognizing that the new knowledge is uncertain; and simultaneously determining the magnitude of uncertainty in the newly discovered knowledge (Rao 1999).

References

Akers, Ronald L. (1998) *Social Learning and Social Structure: A General Theory of Crime and Deviance.* Boston, MA: Northeastern University Press.

Akers, Ronald L. and W. G. Jennings. (2009) "Social Learning Theory." In *21st Century Criminology: A Reference Handbook*, edited by J. M. Miller. Thousand Oaks, CA: Sage.

Anderson, Nels. (1923) *The Hobo: The Sociology of the Homeless Man.* Chicago, IL: University of Chicago Press.

Babbie, Earl R. (2001) *The Practice of Social Research.* Belmont, CA: Wadsworth.

Bailey, Kenneth D. (2007) "Quantitative Methodology." In *21st Century Sociology*, edited by C. D. Bryant and D. L. Peck. Thousand Oaks, CA: Sage.

Cohen, Albert K. (1951) "Juvenile Delinquency and the Social Structure." Unpublished doctoral dissertation. Department of Social Relations, Harvard University, Boston, MA.

Cressey, Donald R. (1950) "The Criminal Violation of Financial Trust." *American Sociological Review* 15:738–743.

——. (1953) *Other People's Money: A Study in the Social Psychology of Embezzlement.* Montclair, NJ: Patterson Smith.

Creswell, John W. (1994) *Research Design: Qualitative and Quantitative Approaches.* London: Sage.

Denzin, Norman K. and Yvonna S. Lincoln. (2005) *Handbook of Qualitative Research.* Thousand Oaks, CA: Sage.

Durkheim, Emile. (1938) *Rules of Sociological Method.* Chicago, IL: University of Chicago Press.

——. (1951) *Suicide: A Study in Sociology.* Glencoe, IL: Free Press.

Felson, Richard B., Jeff Ackerman, and Seong-Jin Yeon. (2003) "The Infrequency of Family Violence." *Journal of Marriage and Family* 65:622–634.

Fine, Gary Alan. (1995) *A Second Chicago School? The Development of a Postwar American Sociology.* Chicago, IL: University of Chicago Press.

Fischer, Coverly. (1955) "Research and Evaluation: Applying the Scientific Method to Problems in Business and Social Work." *Crime and Delinquency* 1:41–50.

Gaylord, Mark S. and John F. Galliher. (1988) *The Criminology of Edwin Sutherland.* Piscataway, NJ: Transaction.

Hagan, John, Paul Hirshfeld, and Carla Shedd. (2002) "First and Last Words: Apprehending the Social and Legal Facts of an Urban High School Shooting." *Sociological Methods and Research* 31:218–254.

Kaplan, Howard B. (2009) "Self-Referent Processes and the Explanation of Deviant Behavior." In *Handbook on Crime and Deviance*, edited by M. D. Krohn, A. J. Lizotte, and G. P. Hall. New York: Springer.

Lindesmith, Alfred. (1947) *Opiate Addiction.* Bloomington, IN: Principia Press.

Luthans, Fred and Tim R. V. Davis. (1982) "An Idiographic Approach to Organizational Behavior Research: The Use of Single Case Experimental Designs and Direct Measures." *Academy of Management Review* 7:380–391.

Maruna, Shadd. (2001) *Making Good: How Ex-convicts Reform and Rebuild Their Lives.* Washington, DC: American Psychological Association.

Matsueda, Ross L. (1988) "The Current State of Differential Association Theory." *Crime and Delinquency* 34:277–306.

Neuman, William L. (2003) *Social Research Methods: Qualitative and Quantitative Approaches.* Boston, MA: Allyn and Bacon.

Pfohl, Stephen J. (1994) *Images of Deviance and Social Control: A Sociological History.* New York: McGraw-Hill.

Rao, C. Radhakrishna. (1999) *Statistics and Truth: Putting Chance to Work.* Singapore: World Scientific.

Ritchey, Ferris. (2000) *The Statistical Imagination: Elementary Statistics for the Social Sciences.* Boston, MA: McGraw-Hill.

Robinson, W. S. (1951) "The Logical Structure of Analytic Induction." *American Sociological Review* 16:812–818.

Shaw, Clifford R. (1930) *The Jack-Roller: A Delinquent Boy's Own Story.* Chicago, IL: University of Chicago Press.

Shaw, Clifford Robe, and Henry Donald McKay. (1942) *Juvenile Delinquency and Urban Areas: A Study of Rates of Delinquents in Relation to Differential Characteristics of Local Communities in American Cities*. Chicago, IL: University of Chicago Press.

Sutherland, Edwin H. (1924) *Criminology*. Philadelphia, PA: Lippincott.

——. (1942) "Development of the Theory." In *The Sutherland Papers*, edited by A. K. Cohen, A. Lindesmith, and K. F. Schuessler. Bloomington: Indiana University Press.

Tewksbury, Richard. (2009) "Qualitative versus Quantitative Methods: Understanding Why Qualitative Methods Are Superior for Criminology and Criminal Justice." *Journal of Theoretical and Philosophical Criminology* 1. Available at: jtpcrim.org/archives.htm.

Thomas, William I. and Florian Znaniecki. (1918) *The Polish Peasant in Europe and America*, vol. IV. Boston, MA: Gorham Press.

Thorp, Edward O. (1962) *Beat the Dealer: A Winning Strategy for 21*. New York: Random House.

Thrasher, Frederic. (1927) *The Gang: A Study of 1313 Gangs*. Chicago, IL: University of Chicago Press.

Tittle, Charles R., Mary Jean Burke, and Elton F. Jackson. (1986) "Modeling Sutherland's Theory of Differential Association: Toward an Empirical Clarification." *Social Forces* 65:405–432.

Vogt, Paul W. (1998) *Dictionary of Statistics & Methodology: A Nontechnical Guide for the Social Sciences*. Thousand Oaks, CA: Sage.

Wirth, Louis. (1928) *The Ghetto*. Chicago, IL: University of Chicago Press.

Znaniecki, Florian. (1934) *The Method of Sociology*. New York: Farrar and Rinehart.

9

Qualitative methodology

Richard Tewksbury

Studies of deviant behavior and deviant persons are one of the primary areas where qualitative methods are common and most productive. Systematic approaches to understanding behaviors that violate social norms and the persons who engage in such behaviors have long been the province of scientific efforts centered on understanding of experience, motivation, and experienced consequences. Efforts to yield knowledge about what it is like to be involved in socially unacceptable, stigmatized, and devalued forms of social activities commonly emphasize understanding such behaviors from the perspective of those engaged in such, and how the processes of such behaviors are structured and enacted. Understandings on such a level are much more thoroughly, effectively, and efficiently achieved through the use of qualitative research methods (see Tewksbury, 2009).

Qualitative research methods are those that highlight understandings of processes and experiences over understanding rates, covariates or statistical relationships. The most common data used in qualitative methods are interviews and observations.

The great value and contribution provided by all forms of qualitative methods are that they allow scholars to gain true understandings of the social aspects of how deviant acts occur and how the social responses to deviance are experienced within culturally situated contexts. The insights that qualitative methods provide typically yield a depth of understanding not possible through the use of quantitative, statistically based investigations. Qualitative methods are the social science methods that centralize complete understandings, and how people experience and operate within milieus that are dynamic, and social in their foundation and structure.

Qualitative research provides in-depth, detailed information which, while perhaps limited in generalizability, explores issues and their context, clarifying what, how, when, where, and by and among whom behaviors and processes operate. Additionally, when qualitative research is reported it describes in detail the actions, interactions, and ways that environments are involved in the structuring of behavior. This is especially valuable for studies of deviance, whether the goal is simply to understand how such behaviors exist or to develop and implement prevention, intervention or social control measures. As with any social science, qualitative deviance research seeks to identify and explain patterns and themes across people and their behaviors as well as if and how such patterns and themes vary across divergent social contexts. Similar to Weber's concept of *Verstehen*, qualitative researchers seek to provide a fully rounded, empathetic understanding of issues, concepts, processes, and experiences.

The results of qualitative research can be presented in several different ways, which are contingent on both the goals of a particular project and the forms of data that the research gathers (Richardson, 1990; Wolcott, 1990). Most often the products of qualitative research are delineations and explanations of taxonomies, explanations of cultural settings, and the development of theoretical constructs and arguments. Taxonomies, or typologies, are explications of types of a particular thing, person, event, etc. A taxonomy outlines a number of categories that reflect the variety of forms that a particular event, etc., may take, and ideally also explains the characteristics that define that particular variation. Explanations of settings and subcultures most often are presented in the form of ethnography. Such a document is an explanation of how a setting or group of people operates, focusing on what is actually done and the contextual details of the actions.

Approaches to data collection in qualitative deviance studies

Qualitative research in deviance relies on data that come from a range of collection methods. These include interviews with individuals, observations of people, places and actions/interactions, and immersion in settings so as to understand the what, how, when, and where of behaviors, structures, and actions/interactions. Each approach differs in the source(s) of and activities to collect information. What is common, however, is that all qualitative research centers on aggregating and analyzing specific instances of behavior and experiences.

Interviews are (typically) structured conversations that researchers have with individuals for purposes of learning about experiences, activities, and views on social events. Interview data are very rich in that not only does the researcher learn how the interviewee sees and knows something, but so too does the qualitative researcher get an explanation of that observation or knowledge. When doing interviews, researchers need to attend to cultural issues that may or may not influence their relationship with interviewees, manage their personal and professional persona, and work to keep the interview conversation focused on target. The quality of data that are gained via interviews (e.g. comprehensiveness, accuracy, depth, etc.) is largely contingent on the nature and quality of the relationship that is established between the interviewer and the interviewee. Hence, an ability to establish a good rapport with others quickly is a key skill for qualitative interview researchers. When conducting deviance studies, however, finding commonalities and experiences that can help establish a bond with those being studied can be a significant challenge.

Participant observation occurs when a researcher engages in activities with others who are being studied. The researcher participates, to some extent, in the actual routines and behavioral sets of individuals and groups, being present and observing actions "from the inside." Participant observer researchers engage in the activities of the group or setting being studied to varying degrees, and can adopt a number of roles in regard to their degree of participation and openness about their role. In some instances participant observer researchers are known to everyone in the study setting as a researcher; sometimes they are known to only a few others (typically those in gatekeeping roles); and sometimes their presence may be known but not fully understood by others who are present. Balancing active engagement in the setting with systematically observing and recording what transpires can be a major challenge for the participant observer, and it is often stress-inducing. In the study of deviance, engagement in the activities of the setting can be a psychological, emotional or legal challenge for scholars, and anticipating these barriers is an important pre-study task for researchers. Furthermore, participant observers need to be aware of how their presence in the setting may or may not influence the activities of others in that setting.

Covert participant observation involves a researcher engaging in the activities of others, but doing so without the others having knowledge of the fact that the researcher is there for purposes other than simply to be someone engaged in the behaviors in question. Sometimes referred to as "disguised observation," the goals of this approach are the same as in participant observation: exploration, description, and (with a few endeavors) evaluation. Covert participation most notably differs from participant observation in that those in the setting do not know of the researcher's "real" reason for being present, and the ways that the researcher gains access to the setting necessarily must be through the same channels as any real setting participant. This usually means that the researcher has to misrepresent his/her intentions and motivations, which can lead to questions about the ethics of the approach (however, see Miller, 1995). Once in the setting, the researcher also has the added responsibility of maintaining his/her role and not being discovered as a researcher. This means that note-taking, probing others for information and being at events, activities and in settings where regular participation would not otherwise be a problem can be difficult (if not impossible) to maintain.

Ethnography is the approach of qualitative research that seeks to provide a complete picture of the ways that a social world is structured, how it operates, how roles are established and fulfilled and how the participants in a world both experience that world and reciprocally influence and construct the setting. Ethnographic research is typically completed by the researcher immersing him/herself in the setting of study and seeking to provide an analytic description of the setting under study that allows readers not only to understand how the setting is structured and operates but why it is the way that it is.

Edge ethnography is an approach that builds on the basics of ethnographic methods but adds in the fact that the subject of study is on or beyond the margins of society, often with some element of danger—either to the researcher or inherent in the activities of those being studied— added to the context (Ferrell and Hamm, 1998). The goals of edge ethnography are basically to do ethnography, but to do so in ways and in regard to populations and behaviors that go beyond the limits of traditional social actions and thinking. Edge ethnography seeks to provide a depth and detailed understanding of groups, settings, and activities that are not necessarily available or accessible to either empirically based quantitative researchers or traditional qualitative researchers (including ethnographers). Hence, edge ethnography fits very well with the study of deviants and in deviant social settings. It emphasizes understanding deviant groups and settings through the process of risk taking and the researcher immersing him/herself in the culture or setting being studied. This is an approach to scholarship that is done on, in, and with populations and subcultures that are in some way physically, emotionally, psychologically or socially dangerous and in which those persons involved in the social world being studied are at risk of (usually official or legal) sanctioning for their behavior.

Because of the marginalized status of the typical foci of the edge ethnographer, and the necessity of gaining and demonstrating full immersion in the world(s) being studied by the edge ethnographer, there is a de facto need for scholars practicing this approach to engage in behavior that is physically, legally, socially or otherwise dangerous. In many respects, in order to engage in edge ethnography, the researcher him/herself must engage in deviance while doing his/her research. Hence, this approach to research considers that the researcher is working "on the edge."

Extreme methods are similar to those of edge ethnography, but include researcher activities and data-collection methods that go beyond simple immersion and observation of those being studied. The field of deviance is the primary area where extreme methods are utilized, because of the difficulties inherent in entering deviant settings and obtaining interviews and observation opportunities (Miller and Tewksbury, 2001). Extreme methods are unconventional approaches to at least one of three aspects of a research project: how a project is conceptualized; how researchers go about gaining access to subjects and settings; and how data are actually collected in a way that is outside the boundaries of traditional social science approaches. As explained by Miller and Tewksbury (2001, p. 1), "Extreme research methods are those that involved either highly unusual or creative approaches to finding answers to difficult-to-answer questions. Researchers using extreme methods are thus usually thought of as individuals (or teams) that go about their work in ways that many other researchers would see as dangerous, innovative, and sometimes unethical." Almost by necessity and definition, extreme methods are qualitative approaches. They involve researchers immersing themselves in settings and activities via creative approaches that prioritize large amounts and degrees of involvement with study subjects and their activities. In many instances, extreme methods can be thought of as ethnographic approaches that include dangers, non-traditional roles for researchers as setting participants, and/or methodologies that push the limits of ethical interactions with those being studied.

Why are qualitative methods especially useful for the study of deviance?

Qualitative research is most often collected in a naturalistic setting, and therefore brings with it the environment in which it is housed. This is important for the study of deviance as the settings in which people act and interact often serve to encourage, facilitate or inhibit many forms of behavior. As such, by definition (and necessity), qualitative research provides a more thorough understanding of how the collected data are impacted by, and reciprocally impact upon, their context than can quantitative research (Higgins, 2009; Tewksbury, 2009). This means that qualitative data allow, and actually facilitate, understandings of experiences, behaviors and social responses to behaviors in context and from the perspective of those being studied. The benefit for greater understandings of deviance and deviants, then, is that the knowledge that is created by qualitative research is contextualized and grounded in the specific settings in which deviant behavior occurs and deviant persons act. In this way it is possible to understand the variations in behavior more clearly and to see if and how behaviors can be expected to vary across specific types of setting.

Qualitative research methods are also especially well suited for the study of deviance because of the emphasis of such data on understanding experiences of social actors. While it is valuable to know how various forms of behavior are enacted, and when, where, and how they occur, it is also very valuable to understand how the people who do deviant behaviors think, feel, and reflect on their activities. It is only through talking with and observing people doing the behaviors we are interested in that it is possible to gain their own insights into their actions. Quantitative, statistical research projects cannot tell anything about what it is like to engage in deviant behavior, nor what one benefits emotionally, psychologically or socially from such activities. By talking with people and being present to see—and jointly experience—their engagement in deviance, it is fairly easy to understand the benefits people derive from their behaviors, as well as their motivations for such behaviors.

One of the most significant contributions that qualitative research makes to the study of deviance is the development of theoretical constructs and explanations for phenomena. To understand how qualitative research contributes to the development of theory, it is important to recognize that qualitative research relies on analytic descriptions for

> identification of recurrent patterns or themes and attempting to construct a cohesive representation of the data. These recurrent themes are then linked to concerns or issues in the . . . literature—theoretical, conceptual, or applied—as you develop interpretations of

what is happening in your setting (or interviews or documents or images) and what their words or images mean to the participants.

(Warren and Karner, 2005, p. 190)

As such, the analytic process in qualitative research is centered on researchers looking at their data, finding patterns and similarities across cases, times, and instances, and interpreting what these issues mean. This process of interpretation is the development and proposing of theory.

Qualitative research methods, then, have important advantages over quantitative methods in the knowledge that can be generated by research endeavors. This is not to say that the knowledge generated by quantitative methods is inferior or of less value, but rather that the complementary contributions of each general approach allow a greater, more comprehensive understanding of deviance.

Limitations on the use of qualitative methods to study deviance

There are several limitations to the use of qualitative methods for the study of deviance and deviants (Worrall, 2000). Perhaps the greatest drawback to using qualitative methods to study deviance is that some forms of deviant behavior and deviants may be extremely difficult, if not impossible, to access. It may not be possible to gain access to observational opportunities or secure interviews with individuals involved in illegal, highly stigmatized, and closed from public observation/access behaviors. In such instances it may be possible to conduct covert observations, although such approaches may be very dangerous for researchers. For instance, homicide offenders, criminal organizations, and individuals who are sexually interested in children or animals are not likely to agree to conduct an interview or allow a researcher to accompany them as they engage in their deviant behaviors. Although it may be possible to access such individuals once they are apprehended and processed by the criminal justice system, the data that would be accessible would be very different from what would be gained by studying them prior to their apprehension.

The difficulties in accessing certain populations also means that some research questions may not be amenable to qualitative study, either. And the questions that a researcher asks and seeks to find answers to must be questions that require qualitative data. This means understanding how common a particular form of deviant behavior is or what background characteristics are related to particular forms of deviance are not questions that are appropriate for qualitative methods. Finally, the use of qualitative methods is also not very good for the study of unplanned and unorganized forms of deviance. When a particular type of deviance is believed to be spontaneous or to occur only as a result of unanticipated opportunities (such as children shoplifting or violence among spectators at sporting events), while it may be possible to use qualitative methods to study the behavior and its participants, it is not an efficient approach. While a researcher could observe children and hope to be present if and when they shoplift, or attend sporting events in the hope of seeing violence break out, the investment of time and resources would be quite high and the opportunities for data collection quite low. As a result, such forms of deviance are not considered amenable to qualitative study.

Ethical challenges in qualitative deviance studies

Qualitative research in general, and especially qualitative research in deviance, carries with it several potentially significant ethical challenges in how research is conducted. Qualitative research generally brings with it concerns about informed consent and confidentiality of research subjects. Questions may arise regarding when individuals are observed in their natural environments: is the researcher required to inform people that they are being studied? Generally speaking, if the people and behaviors being observed are in a public place, or if the people are public officials functioning in their official capacities, then there is no need to secure informed consent to collect data about their activities. When studying deviant behavior, however, many times the activities being observed or about which an individual is interviewed are not performed in public settings. However, how can a researcher secure informed consent from someone who is likely not to want their behavior publicized? For many researchers, the answer is that research needs to be covert in nature, and the individual(s) being studied should not be informed of the research. Many researchers treat this as a balancing act, weighing the benefit of the knowledge gained against the privacy rights of the study subjects. For institutional review boards—official bodies that review proposed research to ensure that it is conducted ethically—this is usually an easy issue. The typical response here is that informed consent is necessary, as the rights of those being studied outweigh the rights of the researcher and the potential value of the knowledge that is to be gained. For qualitative deviance researchers, then, this may mean that some studies simply cannot be conducted, at least not in an ethical manner (see Bryant, 1999; Goode, 1999).

Ethics also encompass the need to ensure that the researcher, as well as the general public, is protected. Regarding protection of the researcher, for many deviance studies the researcher necessarily must immerse him/herself in situations that are physically dangerous, professionally dangerous, or even illegal. Ensuring that one's research does not bring physical harm to oneself can be a tricky situation to manage. Researchers are encouraged to establish safety plans for their own protection, and to limit their immersion and engagement in activities, settings, and groups where danger can be predicted. Professional dangers can come to the qualitative deviance researcher who immerses and studies stigmatized topics and populations. As many sex, drug culture, violence, and marginal political group researchers know, outsiders often perceive that mere interest and willingness to become involved in such topics indicates a "natural interest" in such behaviors. Stigmatization of researchers as deviants themselves can carry with it limitations on professional success, prestige, and future opportunities.

Qualitative deviance researchers also need to consider the ethical question of whether the people and behaviors they study pose undue risks of harm to people outside of the deviant settings where they work. What should a qualitative scholar do when observing criminal activity? What are the responsibilities of a researcher who learns in an interview of a study subject's plans to commit crimes or participate in activities that either directly or indirectly might harm others? These are ethical questions, as well as legal questions, that qualitative deviance researchers must prepare for and address as they enter the worlds of deviance and deviants.

Summary

Qualitative research methods in the study of deviance are those approaches such as interviews, participant observation, covert observation, ethnography, edge ethnography, and extreme methods which highlight the contextualized understandings of how people engage in deviant behavior, how they perceive and understand their activities, and how deviant behaviors are conducted and experienced. Qualitative methods are highly beneficial for understanding deviance and deviants from the perspective of the individuals being studied, and they offer a depth of insight and understanding that is not available with quantitative methods. Qualitative methods are not appropriate for answering all types of social science question, but when a researcher wants to understand the experience of deviants and the actual process and conduct of deviant behavior, they may be indispensable. Some unique ethical concerns and considerations are introduced by the use of qualitative methods, but these are not so great that they cannot be overcome. Despite some potential problems and unique challenges, qualitative methods are very valuable to the study of deviance.

References

Bryant, Clifton D. 1999. Gratuitous Sex in Field Research: "Carnal Lagniappe" or "Inappropriate Behavior"? *Deviant Behavior*, 20, 325–329.

Ferrell, Jeff and Mark Hamm. 1998. *Ethnography at the Edge: Crime, Deviance and Field Research*. Boston: Northeastern University Press.

Goode, Erich. 1999. Sex with Informants as Deviant Behavior: An Account and Commentary. *Deviant Behavior*, 20, 301–324.

Higgins, George E. 2009. Quantitative versus Qualitative Methods: Understanding Why Quantitative Methods are Predominant in Criminology and Criminal Justice. *Journal of Theoretical and Philosophical Criminology*, 1 (1). Available at: jtpcrim.org/archives.htm.

Miller, J. Mitchell. 1995. Covert Participant Observation: Reconsidering the Least Used Method. *Journal of Contemporary Criminal Justice*, 11 (2), 97–105.

Miller, J. Mitchell and Richard Tewksbury. 2001 *Extreme Methods: Innovative Approaches to Social Science Research*. Boston: Allyn and Bacon.

Richardson, Laurel. 1990. *Writing Strategies: Reaching Diverse Audiences*. Newbury Park: Sage.

Tewksbury, Richard. 2009. Qualitative versus Quantitative Methods: Understanding Why Qualitative Methods Are Superior for Criminology and Criminal Justice. *Journal of Theoretical and Philosophical Criminology*, 1, (1). Available at: jtpcrim.org/archives.htm.

Warren, Carol A. B. and Tracy X. Karner. 2005. *Discovering Qualitative Methods: Field Research, Interviews, and Analysis*. Los Angeles: Roxbury.

Wolcott, Harry F. 1990. *Writing up Qualitative Research*. Newbury Park: Sage.

Worrall, John L. 2000. In Defense of the "Quantoids": More on the Reasons for the Quantitative Emphasis in Criminal Justice Education and Research. *Journal of Criminal Justice Education*, 11, 353–360.

10

Cross-cultural and historical methodology

Robert Heiner

> Crime is present not only in the majority of societies of one particular species but in all societies of all types. There is no society that is not confronted with the problem of criminality. Its form changes; the acts thus characterized are not the same everywhere; but, everywhere and always, there have been men who have behaved in such a way as to draw upon themselves penal repression.
>
> *(Durkheim, 1938: 65)*

The above passage could well be the most definitive, most often reprinted, comparative statement in the sociology of deviance. Writing in his classic *The Rules of the Sociological Method* (originally published in 1895), Durkheim provides the basis for the functionalist approach to the understanding of deviance, arguing that since crime occurs in all societies and always has occurred in all societies, it should be regarded as a normal phenomenon and not as an indicator of social pathology. The basis of his assertion is both cross-cultural ("all societies") and historical ("always"). Interestingly, this statement is not based on systematically acquired empirical data, yet few have challenged its validity.

A couple of years after the publication of *The Rules of the Sociological Method*, Durkheim published *Suicide* (1897). This book, like so many of Durkheim's works, became a classic in sociology, serving as a model of data-driven comparative research. Using secondary data collected in many countries, Durkheim concludes that suicide rates are directly affected by the degree to which a society fosters the integration of its individual members. Namely, suicide rates are high in societies that do not effectively integrate individuals into group affiliations *and* in societies that are overly effective in integrating individuals into groups. In the former, individuals are isolated and lack social support. In the latter, individuals are over-committed to the group and may sacrifice themselves for the sake of the group (Durkheim, 1951).

The comparative method

A discussion of the comparative method begins with the recognition that virtually all scientific methods employ comparisons: the comparison of fossils formed in one geo-historical period to those formed in another; the comparison of different chemical combinations mixed in differing amounts; the comparison of the ability of a mouse who has received repeated rewards to go through a maze to the ability of one who has not been rewarded; and so on.

In the social sciences, the comparative method usually refers to the comparison of data pertaining to different cultures or to different historical periods. (Historical and cross-cultural research are similar in that comparing different historical periods is essentially the same as comparing different cultures, given that cultures change over time.) Comparative methods are useful, some would argue necessary, in testing the validity of a social theory or the limits of its application. More specifically, "The goal of comparative [research]," write Clinard and Abbott (1973: 2), "should be to develop concepts and generalizations at a level that distinguishes between universals applicable to all societies and unique characteristics representative of one or a small set of societies."

There are, however, two important caveats relevant to our discussion of deviance. First, while there is a great deal of literature on deviance in the past and in cultures around the world, and while there are volumes upon volumes written on sociological methods, a literature on cross-cultural and historical methods distinctive to the sociology of deviance is relatively spare. Second, one of the most often repeated caveats in the literature on both historical and cross-cultural methods in the social sciences concerns the difficulty (or impossibility) of obtaining reliable, comparable data from the past and from other cultures. Depending on how one looks at it, this latter caveat either applies especially to the study of deviance or it applies not at all—because the data on deviance have always been notoriously flawed in all cultures in all time periods, if only because those who engage in deviant behavior actively try to keep it secret.

Criminologists have long recognized that official crime statistics *within* a given country are problematic; *cross-cultural* comparisons of criminological data are even more problematic. Marvin Wolfgang (1967: 65) summed up the problems as involving "cultural variations in the definition of crime, sentiments of severity, degrees of reportability, probabilities of discovery, types of penalties, and the methods of collecting criminal statistics." When it comes to "deviance," a broader category which includes both criminal and non-criminal behaviors, cross-cultural comparisons become all the more problematic.

Just as researchers in the United States have tried to circumvent the pitfalls of official statistics by using self-report surveys, the same has been done in cross-cultural research. For example, Vazsonyi and his colleagues (2001) measured the "lifetime deviance" of several thousand adolescents in Hungary, the Netherlands, Switzerland, and the United States using the Normative Deviance Scale. The NDS was designed to measure deviant behaviors that are "independent of penal code and legal definitions" (p. 104) and includes behaviors related to vandalism, alcohol use, drug use, school misconduct, general deviance, theft, and assault. But, while measures included in the NDS are certainly better separated from legal definitions and the biases of social control agents than official statistics, they are still dependent on culturally specific norms and values. For example, several of the items included in the scale deal with drinking alcohol under the age of twenty-one. No matter what the drinking age is in the countries surveyed, such behavior is likely to be more deviant in one country than in another and perhaps not at all deviant in another.

Cross-cultural methods

It is perhaps more so with cross-cultural research than other methodologies that one can see how theory informs method as much as method informs theory. Quantitative cross-cultural studies almost always begin with the obligatory warning that one cannot assume that definitions and measurements are consistent across cultures and then they proceed to use and compare official data from a variety of societies. Most often, they work from a consensus model arguing that there is near-universal condemnation, at least, for certain criminal offenses. These offenses have been called "moral minima" (Scott and Zatz, 1981) and those working from the consensus model argue that while there may be some variation in how these offenses are defined and how the law is applied to such cases, there is not enough variation to invalidate the use of cross-cultural data. Homicide is often taken to be such an offense. In his book *Comparative Deviance: Perceptions and Law in Six Cultures* (1976), Graeme Newman, for example, found strong consensus (disapproval) among survey respondents in India, Indonesia, Iran, Italy, the United States, and Yugoslavia for the acts of robbery and the misappropriation of public funds. Disapproval rates were well above 90 percent in all of these countries. These offenses, then, might also be considered moral minima. Contrary, perhaps, to popular expectations, incest did not reach this threshold because in the New York sample "the proportion disapproving it was down to 75 percent" (Newman, 1976: 113). The exceptionality of New York leaves it an unexplained outlier or calls into question the survey results.

Conflict theorists often take strong exception to the use of official data in the conduct of cross-cultural research, arguing that one cannot assume a consensus with regard to deviance and crime—not even in one's own society, let alone in other societies. They hold that definitions of crime and the application of the law reflect elite interests and how power is distributed in a society. "[W]hen particular kinds of strife become issues of elite or general concern," write Gurr and his colleagues, "a typical response is the passage of laws that criminalize some of the behaviors in question" (Gurr *et al.*, 1977: 753). For example, while Newman (1976) identified near-universal disapproval of the misappropriation of funds in his survey research, since this could be seen as a political crime, it could be that his results may have depended on the timing of the survey and the shifting political winds in one or more countries. (After all, a significant drop in disapproval in only one country would negate the consensus.) That is, the mis-appropriation of public funds is likely to become the object of public scorn when one regime is losing its grip on power and another is angling to take its place. Thus, the supposed consensus regarding the act would be a temporal reflection of the struggle for power between two or more groups.

The consensus theorist believes that official statistics are generated by the deviant acts of individuals and, therefore, are reflective of the incidence of such behavior in a society; conflict theorists believe them to be a reflection of economic and political conflict in a society. When conflict theorists do use official data, they use them as indicators of the activities of the police, the courts and the prisons. For the conflict theorist, the data do not reflect the kinds of deviance that are being committed in a population; instead, they reflect the activities of social control agents and/or the types of people who are being processed by the criminal justice system. Seeing, for example, that more than half of the prisoners in the United States are racial and ethnic minorities (Bureau of Justice Statistics, 2003) and that immigrants make up more than half the prison population in the Netherlands (Heiner, 2005), the conflict theorist might conclude that the prisons are a tool of oppression in these two societies, while the consensus theorist might conclude that minorities commit most of the serious crime in these societies.

Discussions of consensus and conflict perspectives take place within the realm of sociology. Then, of course, there is the work of anthropologists who have contributed enormously to the body of literature on cross-cultural deviance. It is largely their work over the past century or more that has sparked the public imagination with the cultural variability of human behavior. The works of Ruth Benedict and Margaret Mead drew attention to the variability of sexual practices in different parts of the world and encouraged tolerance of practices considered deviant in our own culture. In 1951, *Patterns of Sexual Behavior*, a classic work by Clellan Ford and Frank

Beach (1972), catalogued the sexual practices of 190 preindustrial societies (plus those of the United States) using the Human Relations Area Files. Such works effectively challenge prevailing notions about supposed natural sexual behaviors and deviant sexual behaviors. Perceptions of the difference between "natural" and "deviant" behavior, accordingly, are almost always the product of culture. Ford and Beach (1972: 250) conclude,

> One essential way of looking at the evidence involves the achievement of a cross-cultural perspective. Only in this manner can the behavior of men and women in any given society be compared and contrasted with the peoples belonging to quite different societies. The results of our cross-cultural analysis emphasize the important fact that the members of no one society can safely be regarded as "representative" of the human race as a whole.

Historical methods

Historical research is quite similar to cross-cultural research in that it involves the examination of a culture different from the investigator's own—that is, the culture of the past. Historical research may or may not be comparative, depending on whether data are compared over a number of periods of time; if not, they are more appropriately considered case studies (Jones, 1985). Historical investigators often encounter similar problems to those of the cross-cultural researcher as regards the reliability and comparability of data.

Historical research in deviance often yields considerable insight into the nature of social control. One of the best-known examples of such research is Kai Erikson's *Wayward Puritans* (1966). Using mostly older published histories, journals, and documentary evidence, including court records, Erikson reconstructed patterns of social control among the Puritans of Massachusetts in the 17th century to develop his theory of the societal functions of deviance, a theory inspired by Durkheim's assertion some seventy years earlier that "crime is an integral part of all healthy societies" (*The Rules of the Sociological Method*, quoted by Erikson, 1966: 3). Accordingly, a healthy community is one that proudly identifies itself as a community that is morally distinct from other communities. Deviance enables the community to establish and publicize the moral boundaries that distinguish it from other communities. "[D]eviant persons," Ericson writes, "often supply an important service by patrolling the outer edges of group space and by providing a contrast which gives the rest of the community some sense of their own territorial identity" (p. 196).

Another fine example of historical research in social control is David Musto's *The American Disease: The Origins of Narcotic Control* (1987). Using an extensive array of historical documents, legislative records, court records, and the personal papers of people connected to various drug control efforts, Musto reveals a number of important insights into the evolution of drug control in American society. He deftly demonstrates a good deal of disingenuousness behind many historical efforts to control drug use, with those behind such efforts motivated less by concerns about public health or even public morality than by concerns about furthering more personal or political agendas. Most notably, a common thread behind most of the more significant drug control efforts has been racism and/or xenophobia. Musto (1987: 244) writes,

> The most passionate support for legal prohibition of narcotics has been associated with fear of a given drug's effect on a specific minority. Certain drugs were dreaded because they seemed to undermine essential social restrictions which kept these groups under control: cocaine was supposed to enable blacks to withstand bullets which would kill normal persons and to stimulate sexual assault. Fear that smoking opium facilitated sexual contact between

85

Chinese and white Americans was also a factor in its total prohibition. Chicanos in the Southwest were believed to be incited to violence by smoking marijuana. Heroin was linked in the 1920s with a turbulent age group: adolescents in reckless and promiscuous urban gangs. Alcohol was associated with immigrants crowding into large and corrupt cities. In each instance, use of a particular drug was attributed to an identifiable and threatening minority group.

As regards alcohol control and urban immigrants, Musto confirms the earlier historical analysis by Joseph Gusfield (1963); and analogous conclusions regarding the control of marijuana and Chicanos were derived in the historical work of Richard Bonnie and Charles Whitebread (1974). These and similar historical analyses of drug control reflect a conflict perspective and challenge the popularly held consensus view that certain drugs are illegal because they are inherently wrong or injurious to the user or society.

Those interested in the application of historical methods to the study of deviance might also be interested in a number of treatises on the history of modes of perceiving deviance—both inside and outside the ivory tower. Anne Hendershott's *The Politics of Deviance* (2002), for example, examines fluctuations in definitions of deviance and reactions to deviance since the 1960s, and the cultural and political forces that explain these fluctuations. In *Deviance: Career of a Concept* (2004), Joel Best traces the career of the study of deviance, beginning with the "predecessors" to the study of deviance proper (Durkheim and Merton), proceeding to a discussion of the powerful emphasis on labeling theory in the 1960s and early 1970s, and then to the vigorous attacks on labeling theory in subsequent years. Best also describes the convergence and conflict between the studies of deviance and of crime. Both Hendershott and Best contest the claim that the study of deviance is "dead." Best concludes that, though it is not dead, the field lacks agreement on definitions of deviance and domains of study and is, therefore, too fragmented and in need of revitalization. He writes (Best, 2004: 85),

> The initial focus on crime, mental illness, drug abuse, and sexual misbehavior was soon extended to include disabilities, obesity, nudism, cult membership, red hair and all manner of other phenomena that had relatively little in common with one another except, as the labeling theorists suggested, some degree of social disapproval . . . No wonder, then, that the field of deviance became fragmented.

Future directions in comparative research

Despite the sometimes fragmented research in the study of deviance, globalization perhaps offers the opportunity for the revitalization of the field that is called for by Best. These are interesting times for comparativists and it is likely that there will be more work emerging in cross-cultural research in the coming decades. Research in transnational crime is increasing and will certainly continue to do so. Globalization has made national borders less relevant and, for some crimes, it has become increasingly difficult to establish the country in which they originated (Beirne and Messerschmitt, 2006). The internet has provided pathways for a host of crimes and deviant indulgences that know no national boundaries, including money laundering, fraud, pornography, and sabotage. Crimes are frequently committed that fall within the jurisdictions of several countries. In the case of child pornography, for example, law enforcement authorities occasionally conduct coordinated international sting operations. Thorsten Sellin (1938) identified the problem of culture conflict which was especially relevant in the wake of massive immigration to the United States in the early twentieth century and has become relevant again with recent waves of immigration and the influx of refugees in countries throughout the world. And the drug trade, in particular, is notorious for its lack of respect for national boundaries. The market for illegal drugs in the United States, for example, has led to widespread violence in Mexico, some of which spills back into the United States.

Another effect of globalization has been the homogenization of cultures. Cultures are becoming less distinct. Smaller pre-industrial cultures are being assimilated or overrun by larger, more "modern" cultures in the latter's efforts to expropriate their land and natural resources. Another homogenizing influence has been the proliferation of Western culture and values largely through the media and the export of popular culture. These processes have implications for the construction of deviant categories throughout the world. For example, what Westerners would consider "lesbian" relations have been common, perhaps even normative, among women in Lesotho; but because no penis was involved, local women did not consider these relations "sexual" and, therefore, not as lesbian or deviant. Limakatso Kendall, however, reports the non-deviant status of this behavior is changing as the people of Lesotho become increasingly exposed to Western culture. "I believe that one pressure leading to the demise of batsoalle [the "special friends" relationship] is the increasing Westernization of Lesotho and the arrival, at least in the urban and semi-urban areas and the middle class, of the social construction of 'homophobia' with and without its name" (Kendall, 2008: 104). It is quite possible, even likely, that globalization is similarly affecting deviant categories in cultures throughout the world. The changes—in terms of the types of behavior considered deviant, the frequency of deviance, and the application of sanctions—could be profound and the subject is ripe for investigation by students of deviance.

Conclusions

Cross-cultural and historical research in deviance is fraught with methodological peril, but considerable knowledge and insight have been derived from these methods. Separately and together, cross-cultural and historical methods have added invaluable breadth to the body of knowledge on deviance. They allow us to understand and appreciate the diversity of human behavior as well as its cultural and historical relativity. They have provided us with tools for better understanding the human condition and allow us to challenge conventional wisdom. They both provide an invaluable aid in understanding the social forces that influence the construction of deviant categories. And popularly held beliefs about deviant behavior being inherently wrong, harmful or offensive have been and will continue to be put to the test by cross-cultural and historical research.

References

Beirne, Piers and James W. Messerschmitt, *Criminology* (4th edn). Los Angeles: Roxbury, 2006.

Best, Joel, *Deviance: Career of a Concept*. Belmont, CA: Wadsworth, 2004.

Bonnie, Richard J. and Charles H. Whitebread, *The Marihuana Conviction: A History of Marihuana Prohibition in the United States*. Charlottesville: University of Virginia Press, 1974.

Bureau of Justice Statistics, "Table 6.34: Prisoners in Federal State and Private Correction Facilities," in *Sourcebook of Criminal Justice Statistics*. Washington, DC: US Department of Justice, 2003. Available at: www.albany.edu/sourcebook/pdf/t634.pdf.

Clinard, Marshall B. and Daniel J. Abbott, *Crime in Developing Countries: A Comparative Perspective*. New York: John Wiley, 1973.

Durkheim, Emile, *The Rules of the Sociological Method*, translated by S. Soloway and J. H. Mueller, edited by G. Catlin. Chicago: University of Chicago Press, 1938 [originally published 1895].

Durkheim, Emile, *Suicide: A Study in Sociology*, translated by J. Spaulding and G. Simpson. New York: Free Press, 1951 [originally published 1897].

Erikson, Kai T., *Wayward Puritans: A Study in the Sociology of Deviance*. New York: John Wiley, 1966.

Ford, Clellan S. and Frank A. Beach, *Patterns of Sexual Behavior*. New York: Harper and Row, 1972 [originally published 1951].

Gurr, Ted Robert, Peter N. Graboski and Richard C. Hula, *The Politics of Crime and Conflict: A Comparative History of Four Cities*. Beverly Hills: Sage, 1977.

Gusfield, Joseph, *Symbolic Crusade: Status Politics and the American Temperance Movement*. Urbana: University of Illinois Press, 1963.

Heiner, Robert, "The Growth of Incarceration in the Netherlands," *Federal Sentencing Reporter*, vol. 17, no. 3, February 2005, pp. 227–230.

Hendershott, Anne, *The Politics of Deviance*. San Francisco: Encounter Books, 2002.

Jones, T. Anthony, "The Evolution of Crime in Pre-industrial Society," in *Comparative Social Research: Deviance*, R. F. Tomasson, ed. Greenwich, CT: JAI Press, 1985.

Kendall, K. Limokatso, "Women in Lesotho and the (Western) Construction of Homophobia," in *Deviance across Cultures*, R. Heiner, ed. New York: Oxford University Press, 2008.

Musto, David F., *The American Disease: Origins of Narcotic Control* (expanded edn). New York: Oxford University Press, 1987 [originally published 1973].

Newman, Graeme, *Comparative Deviance: Perception and Law in Six Cultures*. New York: Elsevier, 1976.

Scott, Carolyn and Marjorie S. Zatz, "Comparative Deviance and Criminology," *International Journal of Comparative Sociology*, vol. 12, nos. 3–4, 1981, pp. 237–256.

Sellin, Thorsten, *Culture Conflict and Crime*. Bulletin No. 41. New York: Social Science Research Council, 1938.

Vazsonyi, Alexander, Lloyd Pickering, Marianne Junger and Dick Hessing, "An Empirical Test of a General Theory of Crime: Comparative Study of Self-Control and the Prediction of Deviance," *Journal of Research in Crime and Delinquency*, vol. 38, no. 2, May 2001, pp. 91–131.

Wolfgang, Marvin E., "International Criminal Statistics: A Proposal," *Journal of Criminal Law, Criminology and Police Science*, vol. 58, no. 1, 1967, pp. 65–69.

Part III
Theories of deviance

Overview

Deviant behavior can be, and is, viewed from numerous perspectives. There have been equally numerous efforts to explain deviance. Over the last half century, many scholars in the field have advanced theories that they felt explained, or at least provided insights into, the dynamics of certain kinds of deviance. Some of these theories have tended to be relatively similar, while others have been quite disparate. Over the years, extensive research has been conducted to examine the validity and utility of these various theories, and there is a significant body of published research literature in support of them.

By and large, most of the theories that have been posited fit into one of several broad categories. Some of them can be classified as *structural*, which is to say that there are various aspects of society which, because of their very existence, put some individuals in a position where they may be motivated to commit deviant acts while attempting to conform to societal norms (or even to exist, in some extreme instances). An example here might be US society, whose norms strongly encourage members of society to be successful, but do not provide suitable opportunities for everyone to accomplish such a goal. Thus, a young, highly success-motivated person who is economically deprived might be driven to commit theft in order to pay for their college tuition. A number of structural theories are based on variations of this theme.

Other theories of deviant behavior might be more aptly classified as *processual*, because they tend to focus more on the dynamics of persons committing deviance. Here the emphasis is on the sequence of events that occurs and may propel an individual into deviance. An example of such a process might be that of a family moving into a new neighborhood where many of the teenagers are involved in recreational delinquency. If the new family has teenaged children, when they meet and begin to interact with the local youngsters, they may very likely acquire some of the values of the neighborhood teenagers and begin to participate with them in their delinquent behavior, and come to feel that it is normal behavior. They would effectively have "learned" to be deviant, and the deviance would be reinforced by peer pressure from the neighborhood children. A number of very sophisticated processual theories have proven to be useful to scholars of deviant behavior.

Throughout the history of the study of deviance there has also been persistent interest in biological and physiological motivation of such behavior, and various theories have been posited which fit into this category. This part of the *Handbook* includes eleven chapters that present and review a variety of such theories. The list of theories is very diverse and very comprehensive. The reader will therefore be well informed in regard to the range of contemporary theories of deviant behavior that are being used by researchers today.

Anomie-strain theory

In his chapter, Timothy Brezina outlines the historical antecedents of anomie-strain theories. He traces the development of anomie from its classical beginnings with Durkheim through the reformulations of Merton. The latter's classic strain theory is very much in evidence as contemporary criminologists continue to refine and extend this seminal theoretical perspective.

The anomie tradition in criminology can be traced back to the classical sociologist, Emile Durkheim, who assumed that humans were essentially insatiable and primal creatures, relentlessly pursuing pleasure and egoistic goals. Society's moral institutions placed limits on individuals, channeling their energies into collective activities that provided meaning and fulfillment. Without societal restraints, anomie, according to Durkheim, was the condition where "institutionalized norms lose their force and no longer guide behavior, individuals are freed to pursue egoistic goals, and rates of various deviant behaviors tend to increase."

Robert K. Merton reformulated anomie in "Social Structure and Anomie," one of the most influential offerings to the study of crime and deviance. His formulation of anomie maintained the notion of insatiable pursuit of desires but located it within culture and viewed it as a product of socialization. In this classic typology of strain, Merton proposed five types of adaptation that play roles in anomie and strain theories, ideal types of alternative modes of adjustment or adaptation by individuals within the culture-bearing society or groups: *conformity, innovation, ritualism, retreatism,* and *rebellion.* Key to understanding anomie and strain is that society, through approved cultural *goals*, encourages everyone to pursue these goals while at the same time preventing certain individuals or groups from acquiring the access to the opportunity structure that would allow the attaining of those goals (the *means*). The lack of high integration between the means and ends elements of the cultural pattern and the particular class structure combine to favor a heightened frequency of antisocial conduct in some groups.

There have been a number of revisions to Merton's classic strain theory; prominent among these revisions are the contributions of Albert Cohen and Cloward and Ohlin. These revisions attempted to make strain theory more applicable to juvenile delinquency. For Cohen, strain contributes to the formation of gangs, which then encourages delinquent adaptations. In Cloward and Ohlin's revision, strain provides the motivation for juvenile crime and deviance, but the illegitimate opportunity structure dictates which adaptations will come about.

Even though strain theory is a compelling theoretical perspective, it was sharply criticized in the 1970s. In an attempt to address these critiques, contemporary strain theorists have also reformulated and expanded on strain. Brezina provides descriptions of Agnew's general strain theory and Messner and Rosenfeld's institutional anomie theory. Throughout this section of the chapter, the author provides some examples of research into these expansions of strain theory, but he concludes that a complete assessment of anomie-strain theories is still in the offing. Nevertheless, Brezina also concludes that anomie-strain theories will continue to stimulate criminological research.

Social learning theory

In the chapter by Wesley G. Jennings and Ronald L. Akers, Jennings reviews Akers' social learning theory, outlining the specific elements comprising the theory, and reviews empirical studies and evidence that support the theory.

Sutherland's differential association theory forms the basis of Akers' work in this area. Sutherland posited that criminal behavior is learned through individual and group interaction, and as the individual develops an excess of favorable definitions of behaviors that are normally considered deviant, most often from others who have participated or are participating in these behaviors, he or she becomes more likely to engage in the behaviors.

Akers later built on Sutherland's work and looked at four core elements that he viewed as underlying social learning theory: *definitions, differential associations, differential reinforcement,* and *imitation*. He first looked at the wide continuum of perceptions that lead individuals to develop unfavorable or favorable "definitions" for various deviant behaviors or activities. Differential associations experienced by an individual with other individuals or groups who espouse pro-criminal attitudes increase the likelihood that the individual will engage in those types of activity. As the individual engages in these deviant behaviors or activities, differential reinforcements from peers and peer groups affect his or her attitudes, either rewarding or punishing the individual's involvement in "deviant" behavior. Differential association is reinforced by the general attraction of imitation, as the individual sees peers engage in, enjoy, and benefit from involvement in deviant activities or behaviors.

Jennings demonstrates that a large body of empirical evidence provides support for Akers' theories regarding these four core elements underlying social learning theory, then proceeds to outline Akers' expansion of his theory to include four macro-level factors: *differential social organization; differential location in the social structure; theoretically defined structural variables* (including a wide range of dysfunctional social and class issues); and *differential social location*. In addition to the four core elements discussed earlier, operating on an individual or peer-group level, these four macro-level variables complete the overarching social construct that supports and explains Akers' social learning theory.

Control and social disorganization theory

In his chapter, Robert Agnew indicates that control and social disorganization theories focus on the restraints that keep people from engaging in deviant behavior. What distinguishes these theories from each other is the unit of analysis: control theories focus on the individual level while social disorganization theories center on the macro-level of society (community level). Further, what distinguishes control and social disorganization theories from other theories of crime and deviance is that they focus on the factors that restrain people from engaging in deviance rather than strains, favorable definitions, and/or exposure to deviance.

Agnew briefly reviews the historical background of these theories, citing the contributions to social control theory of Reiss, Toby, Nye, Reckless, Matza, and Briar and Piliavin. These theorists identified the major types of social control while describing the role taken by social control in explaining crime and deviance. Agnew also highlights Hirschi's work in his classic *Causes of Delinquency*, which was based upon and extended the contributions of the early theorists. Research by Vold, Patterson *et al.*, Gottfredson, and others found that there was a relationship between social controls and crime and deviance. Agnew briefly discusses Gottfredson's and Hirschi's work on self-control and its influence as a factor in both the level of social control exerted on the individual and through the life-course. Research by Goode, Gottfredson, and Pratt and Cullen indicates that this is a strong relationship.

Agnew rounds out his historical review of these theories with Shaw and McKay's social disorganization theory. Communities with high rates of crime, poverty, and residential mobility are posited as disorganized, with residents unable to exert effective control over one another. While this theory enjoyed a good deal of popularity during the first half of the 20th century, it fell into disuse until Sampson and Groves, Kornhauser, Sampson and Wilson, and Bursik and Grasmick revived it in the 1990s. Social disorganization theory, with its emphasis on sources of disorganization, continues as a leading theory in contemporary studies of community differences in rates of crime and deviance.

Agnew follows the history of social control and disorganization with the central tenets of social control, self-control, and social disorganization theories. Included in this discussion are key studies that examine these theories. He concludes his chapter with a brief discussion of the large amount of empirical support for these theories but ultimately concludes that they do not support all the variation. Nevertheless, these theories do contribute a great deal and should be regarded as leading theories in the study of crime and deviance.

Labeling theory

Ryken Grattet provides an overview of the origins and current understanding of labeling theory, with a specific focus on labeling as it applies to crime and criminal deviance.

In a detailed review of the origins of the theory over the course of the 20th century, including increasingly detailed critiques and expansions of the theory beginning in the 1960s, labeling theory is shown to explain deviance "as a product of the social interaction between individuals and various types of audience, such as parents, peer groups, anonymous onlookers, and, perhaps most extensively, representatives of formal social control organizations."

Deviance is a label that is often applied disproportionately to different individuals or groups, and it has consequences for the individual's propensity to engage in deviant behavior, their treatment in the justice system, and their ability to reintegrate into society at some point in the future.

Grattet takes a detailed look at the consequences of labeling, beginning with a shift in focus from the perceived effects of labeling by official social control agents to labeling by parents and other significant personal players in the individual's life.

The specific effects of labeling within the context of mental illness are another specific area of study. Perceptions of a patient's dangerousness, or untreatability, can have particularly harmful effects for the individual being treated for mental illness related to deviant behavior.

Collateral consequences associated with labeling is another area of recent study, with an understanding of how labeling can result in structural social impediments for the individual, including interference with voting rights, employment, and housing opportunities. These and other collateral consequences of labeling can have specific harmful effects not just on the deviant individual but on their families, and can make desistance and any potential reintegration into society particularly difficult.

Grattet concludes with a look at the organizational context of social control decision-making, and how a "theory of office" involving probation officers and legal officials draws on labels, with officers vacillating between frameworks of legal/social control concerns and casework/counseling considerations. Within this context of social control decision-making, sentencing itself is heavily influenced by labeling.

While Grattet points out that labeling theory continues to be controversial, and subject to ongoing expansion and alteration, it has "become part of the orthodoxy of the sociological study of deviant behavior."

Phenomenological theory

In his chapter, David Polizzi looks past the causal determinants of criminal behavior to phenomenology, or the ways in which deviance and a deviant lifestyle are understood by the individuals engaged in this behavior. This type of study—of behavior such as gang involvement or drug use and addiction—focuses on subjective accounts of the individual's experiences, and their individual rituals of deviance and criminality. But further, the shared social world, and the specific social context surrounding the deviant individual, is also paramount.

A phenomenology of deviance must first examine phenomenology in general, looking at the ever-present question: does the perception of the world reflect a true representation of the world as it actually exists or is it simply an experience of the world from a unique perspective? The perception and explication of an individual's reality are always limited and unique.

Polizzi looks at the concept of intentionality, stating that individual perception of objects and events does not create these things, but it does create the point of reference, the "lived-meaning" that surrounds them. Intentionality extends to a shared context, a "they–self," whereby others help shape the unique experience of the individual.

The concept of "thrownness"—being thrown into social and human situations—explains how these shared experiences can affect individuals, but there are limitations. Situations such as racism, sexism, poverty, and so on may be beyond the control of the individual, but they nonetheless generate powerful and defining realities.

Polizzi uses gang experience to represent and demonstrate the tenets of phenomenology. Gangs usually form as reactions to perceived threats, and members develop and live with a radically different perception of their own "deviance" than that perceived by the larger community or agents of social control. As Polizzi states, "gang activity, like all types of deviant behavior, occurs in contested space, space that is defined by competing manifestations of the they–self, which attempt to impose or validate a specific meaning upon this encounter. What one manifestation of the they–self validates, the other denies."

This perception of deviance, Polizzi concludes, is not limited to one notion of defiance, self-protection, or criminality, but can be a complicated intertwining of all three. Individual perception, the "they–self," and the concept of "thrownness" all contribute to the individual phenomenology of the deviant experience. But while thrownness can often be seen as destiny, the possibility of individual action always remains.

For the social scientist, it is important always to attempt to understand deviance and criminality from a more holistic vantage point, as part of a complex system of perceptions and influences.

Conflict theory

Addrain Conyers explains that conflict can be seen as a more effective way than consensus to categorize society. Conflict theorists question the true intent of the creation of norms and laws, and suggest that dominant groups in a society maintain power through subjection of subordinate groups through these norms and laws.

Conflict theory's origins lie in Marxism, particularly in the exploitative culture of capitalism, which leads to class divisions, with a small elite and a larger, less powerful bourgeoisie. In opposition to this elite, the less powerful classes organize in opposition and fight their own exploitation, hence the conflict. Yet this same emergent class consciousness leads the working classes to begin to desire the dominant cultural norms.

Conyers reviews the development of the theory over the 20th century, looking at Dahrendorf (1958), who suggests that conflict plays a useful role in the development of society, fostering creativity and innovation in social structures. Bonger, writing in 1969, examines how class distinctions do not mean that only the lower classes engage in deviance and crime, but instead that different types of crime develop for different levels of society. Vold (1958) examines how common group interests lead to broad social conflict, and Quinney (1970) develops a much broader and more integrated theory of societal deviance and its causes.

The most recent thought on conflict theory includes the British left realist theory, promoting "realistic" policies to address issues of crime, and its impact on the working classes. Peacemaking criminology attempts to refocus the reaction to crime and deviance not on offenders but on the well-being of the individual in general, hopefully ameliorating broader conflict. Critical race theory focuses on race and how it relates to law and society. And causal explanation theory ties earlier study of the causes of crime and deviance with the broader social study of conflict theory.

Conyers concludes by noting that "as long as social stratification is in existence," conflict theory will always be a critical tool in examining the causes and consequences of societal patterns of crime and deviance.

Routine activities theory and rational choice theory

In her chapter, Marie Skubak Tillyer examines these complementary approaches to understanding the occurrence and distribution of deviance within populations.

Both approaches begin with a classical assumption that human beings are rational, and make decisions to participate in deviant or criminal behavior for "rational" reasons related to perceived consequences and rewards. While most criminological theories focus on distal causes of criminality, routine activities and rational choice "emphasize the importance of proximate environmental and situational factors and their influence on how opportunities for crime are created and perceived by offenders."

Routine activities theory looks first at all of the disparate elements that must come together to lead to deviant behavior. In addition to a motivated potential offender, there must be suitable targets and the absence of capable guardians. Target suitability itself is a function of four characteristics: value, visibility, access, and inertia against illegal treatment.

The notion of "capable guardians" is further explored as including *guardians*, who protect potential targets from victimization; *handlers*, who supervise potential offenders; and *managers*, who monitor and prevent crime at specific places. These guardians can range from family members to employees of stores or workplaces to members of the general public.

Routine activities theory, comprising as it does such a wide range of potential influences on the commission of crime, points to how changes in crime trends and patterns can be explained by changes in the supply of suitable targets, and how instances of repeat victimization can be studied and prevented.

While routine activities theory explains the elements necessary for a crime to occur and those actors which have the ability to prevent crime, rational choice theory explains the process by which offenders make decisions, looking at six core concepts. First and second, crime is seen as purposive and rational, with decisions made with direct considerations of consequence and reward. Third, criminal decision-making is crime-specific, with different types of criminality and deviance having their own unique qualities. Fourth, the decision to commit crime is actually made up of two decision points—an involvement decision and an event decision. Fifth, the involvement decision, which is shaped by prior learning and experiences, comprises three stages: initiation, continuance, and desistance. And sixth, criminal events unfold in a sequence of stages and decisions, heavily influenced by situational factors.

In conclusion, Tillyer emphasizes how routine activities theory and rational choice theory provide paths both to understand the general distribution of crime and deviance, and to employ strategies to prevent criminal activity.

Marxist and critical theory

Rob White states that Marxist criminology and critical criminology "deal with issues of inequality and power as core concerns," but with varying explanations, theoretical concerns, and analytical emphasis.

Marxist criminology is first concerned with class, looking at how "the concentration of disadvantage" in individuals and communities engaged in deviance provides the context for the types of criminality evidenced. This link between socioeconomic status and criminality is visible across jurisdictions, regions, and nationalities.

Specific areas of inquiry demonstrate how underclass criminality is characterized by a survival component driven by disconnection and marginalization, or by basic economic subsistence. Beyond individual needs, families and communities faced with shared deprivation and oppression are seen to organize into criminal groups and organizations. In comparison, privileged groups develop their own criminal instincts, resulting in so-called "white-collar" crime.

Marxist criminology recognizes the importance of institutionalized power (police, judiciary, prisons) in not only controlling behavior but setting the very parameters of what defines "deviance."

Unlike Marxist criminology, critical criminology looks at a broader set of specific social inequalities implicated in deviant behavior, including social constructions of class, gender and sexuality, ethnicity, political structures, age, and many others. There are two general trends in critical criminology theory: the structuralist approach, focusing on power structures; and the postmodern approach, looking at language and knowledge production itself as a critical component of the social construction of deviance. While postmodern theory shows how language itself can be used to define certain groups as deviant, theorists also point out the possibilities to turn the tables, and empower the disadvantaged and "deviant" to regain control over discourse involving their own subjugation.

Issues of oppression and injustice unify the various strands of Marxist and critical theory. As White concludes, "institutional reform is not seen as an end in itself, but as part of a more profound transition towards a more equal, fairer society."

Biological and biosocial theory

Richard A. Ball begins his chapter with a look at 19th-century and early 20th-century theories emphasizing purely biological roots of deviance, including phrenology, atavism, and "criminal diathesis," all pointing to the biological inferiority of deviant individuals. In the 20th century, we saw the expansion of these theories, leading to the development of organized eugenics, and mass genocide.

By the late 20th century, medical knowledge advanced beyond these simplistic theories, and we saw the discovery of true organic origins of deviant conditions such as drug and alcohol addition, eating disorders, and various types of mental illness. With the advent of medical technologies such as MRI and genetic mapping, we are now even closer to discovering causes and possibly treatments for specific deviant behaviors.

Biosocial theory now looks at genetics, evolutionary psychology, neuroscience, and other emergent fields as critical areas of the study of deviance. Genetics looks at the relationship between genotypes and phenotypes; epigenetics studies how environmental factors can alter gene function; while behavioral genetics combines evolution with behavioral studies. Molecular genetics continues to take these studies into new areas.

Evolutionary psychology looks at possible specific evolutionary and biological origins of a wide range of deviant behaviors, from adolescent angst and sensation-seeking to infidelity.

Neuroscience provides a third area of interest for studying causes of deviance, focusing on brain chemicals such as dopamine and serotonin, and their influence on the mind and body, as key to the understanding of deviant conditions.

While all of these areas of research are nascent, each provides potentially rich insight into the causes and potential cures of deviant behavior.

Feminist theory

Carol Bailey's chapter provides a comprehensive overview of feminist thought and research, comprising both a history of the development of feminist thought and a delineation of current areas of feminist research.

Bailey first asserts that feminist theory is founded on recognition that it is women's differences, rather than their sameness, that underlie this field of study. Issues of race, ethnicity, class, age, nationality, and disability are as important as gender in understanding the place of women in society.

Feminist theory has a long history of intersecting with other strands of sociological study, including Marxist theory, ethnic studies, and various types of psychological and political theory.

Liberal feminism, in the 1960s and 1970s, was one of the first major strands of feminist study, tied to the women's liberation movement and focused primarily on college-educated, white, heterosexual women. It pointed out some of the most basic inequalities facing women in society, education, and the workplace.

Radical feminists took the feminist critique further, introducing a notion of male patriarchy, a deliberate system of codified male control, maintained through institutional and cultural arrangements, and requiring radical solutions.

Marxist feminists provide a unique focus on feminist issues through an economic lens, seeing "women's work" as devalued and the role of women as child-bearer as a further impediment to their social and economic equivalency.

A more recent strand of feminist theory takes a multicultural approach, looking past the white, middle-class, Western critique of women's social standing and instead examining women's conditions across countries, continents, and cultures. Multicultural feminists look at the condition of women within the broader context of all problems facing people in the developing world. Issues of globalization, capitalism, patriarchy, and colonialism are identified as participating in the oppression of women.

Bailey also investigates "feminist criminology," looking at how some elements of crime and deviance are specifically related to issues of feminism. The broad category of female "sex work" is explored, with discussion of whether such work is truly deviant or deviant only in the context of female oppression. Another area of discussion is the global practice of female genital mutilation, which can be considered a legitimate religious practice or an agent of female subjugation. Finally, Bailey turns to the subject of eating disorders, uniquely associated with women, and looks at whether these disorders are caused by patriarchal, misogynistic standards of beauty or are related to broader issues of oppression, including sexism, racism, and homophobia.

Bailey concludes by asserting the enormous range of research in feminist theory, but the shared goal of working to end oppression and subordination.

Postmodern theory

Charles Walton's chapter explores the contemporary turn toward pluralistic theories of deviance, which are adept at dealing with the preponderance of media in our lives as well as the cultural contradictions that inform deviance today. Theorists such a Foucault, Pfohl, and Kellner offer a variety of postmodern interpretations of deviance.

One of the most distinctive aspects of postmodern theories of deviance has to do with the epistemological challenges to modernist theories of deviance that are posed by such perspectives. Contrary to modernist perspectives, postmodern theory claims no conduit to any objective truth regarding deviance, but rather offers a variety of partial explanations, partial truths, and partial depictions of the reality of deviance. Walton addresses the many criticisms that are often leveled at postmodern perspectives: that the postmodern turn is no more than a fad; and that the suspicion of positivism robs the attempt to explain phenomena of its scientific claim to knowledge. However, the fact of the matter is that postmodern theory offers the study of deviance a much-needed critical stance; moreover, such a perspective is adept at theorizing media, which so informs deviance, in a fashion that more staid perspectives lack.

Walton begins by offering some basic distinctions between modernism and postmodernism in general. For example, modernist theories have a tendency to overemphasize a singular normative order and to represent society as a totality, or a coherent whole. In contrast, postmodern theories are more heterogeneous, recognize the contemporary fragmentation of self and society, and, moreover, offer a conceptual framework to deal with cultural contradictions.

While adept at dealing with cultural contradictions that inform deviance (e.g. violence, sex, drugs) postmodern perspectives resist framing the world in terms of dichotomies. Walton illustrates such resistance in relating the *Time* magazine vignette that featured an interview with Stephen Pfohl, who was sought out as a "drug expert" for a story on the efficacy of the "War on Drugs." The *Time* reporter framed the drug problem as being solved either by stiffer penalties or more opportunity for treatment. When Pfohl began to reference the cultural contradictions regarding drug use in American society and sought to explain the socio-historical circumstances that gave rise to this very complex problem, the reporter still tried to force him into the dichotomy. None of what Pfohl offered in his analysis made its way into the article because it might not be so easy to digest for the reader in the waiting room.

Kellner's attempt to highlight the role of simulation in the media with respect to school shootings (e.g. the Virginia Tech Massacre) exemplifies one of the strengths of postmodern theory in understanding the spectacle of deviance that is offered up for consumption via television, film, and the internet. Media may play a critical role in reflecting as well as shaping deviance in the larger culture.

Walton also highlights Foucault's work regarding the so-called "disciplinary society" which details the relationship between power–knowledge and social regulation as yet another example of such critical perspectives on deviance. Those who fear what they deem an emerging technocracy are concerned about a society of individuals increasingly under surveillance and subject to social regulation via technological means.

Criticisms abound regarding postmodern theories, given the absence of so-called hypothesis testing associated with such discourse. Empirical evidence in the positivist sense is lacking in postmodern work. However, it is the cultural primacy of positivism in scientific discourse that postmodern perspectives challenge in the first place.

11

Anomie-strain theory

Timothy Brezina

The anomie tradition in criminology (also referred to as strain theory) can be traced to the early pioneering work of the French sociologist Emile Durkheim. Similar to Freud's notion of the "id," Durkheim assumed that individuals possessed a primal self that, in the absence of society, expressed itself through selfish wants and desires. Furthermore, Durkheim argued that the wants and desires of the primal self are more or less insatiable; in other words, the primal self is characterized by a relentless appetite "for more." In the context of modern society, this condition—when not adequately restrained—tends to express itself in an unquenchable thirst for pleasure or success, "overweening ambition," a "longing for infinity," and "perpetual dissatisfaction."

Given this view of human nature, Durkheim stressed the critical role played by society's moral institutions (such as family and religion) in placing limits on ambition, keeping egoistic or selfish desires "in check," and directing the energy of individuals into collective tasks and pursuits that provide meaning and fulfillment. In the absence of such restraint, society is at risk of degenerating into a state of *anomie*, in which the insatiable and potentially destructive desires of individuals are no longer regulated. In this condition, institutionalized norms lose their force and no longer guide behavior, individuals are freed to pursue egoistic goals, and rates of various deviant behaviors tend to increase, including crime and suicide.

In the 1930s, a young sociologist by the name of Robert K. Merton reformulated the anomie framework and applied it directly to deviant behavior in the United States. This seminal work, titled "Social Structure and Anomie" (Merton 1938), would become one of the most influential contributions to the study of crime and deviance, helping to shape all subsequent developments in the anomie-strain theory tradition.

Merton's reformulation retained the notion of insatiable desires, but instead of rooting such desires in human nature, they were now seen as products of culture and socialization. In particular, Merton observed that the cultural ethos known as the "American Dream" serves to promote the very type of overweening ambition and "longing for affinity" that Durkheim viewed as a threat to social order. Regardless of their current position in the stratification system, Americans are encouraged "never to stop trying," and to aspire to success, with an overwhelming emphasis on the accumulation of monetary wealth.

At the same time, Merton recognized that the opportunities required for monetary success are unevenly distributed in society, with large segments of society lacking prosocial means to achieve the ends they have been encouraged to pursue. Thus, for disadvantaged segments of the population, there exists a mismatch or *disjunction* between culturally prescribed success goals and the legitimate means available to achieve these goals. This disjunction between means and ends generates *strain* in the social structure and, especially among disadvantaged groups, contributes to a state of anomie. When large segments of the population have internalized a strong desire for material success, yet lack the legitimate means to attain this goal, the norms governing the legitimate ways to achieve success lose their relevance and force. When people no longer believe they can get ahead through "hard work" or "playing by the rules," their commitment to conformity weakens. This fact frees individuals to cheat, or to "innovate," by pursuing alternative and illegitimate avenues to success.

Merton recognized that innovation was not the only possible response to strain or anomie. Other adaptations to strain are possible, including *conformity* (in which individuals remain committed to legitimate means and goals, despite the odds), *ritualism* (in which individuals accept failure but remain committed to legitimate means, perhaps because they have simply become resigned to their fate), *retreatism* (in which individuals give up on society's prescribed goals *and* means, as exhibited by such escapist behaviors as alcoholism, drug abuse, and suicide), and *rebellion* (in which individuals or groups struggle to redefine the culturally approved goals and means). Nevertheless, while alternative adaptations are possible, strain is said to increase the rate of innovative behavior, including crime.

Thus, a defining feature of Merton's anomie-strain theory is that it locates the origins of deviant behavior in a contradictory configuration of cultural and structural arrangements. In fact, the theory was developed in reaction to biological and psychological theories that were popular at the time and located the roots of crime in individual pathology. Rejecting a pathological approach, Merton argued that crime more often represented "the normal reaction, by normal persons, to abnormal conditions" (Merton 1938: 672, note 2).

The alternative image of the offender suggested by strain theory, then, is that of a more or less rational, goal-seeking individual who has opted for non-conventional means to attain conventional goals. Offenders, therefore, are not distinct from conformists in terms of their biological or psychological makeup, or even in terms of the nature of their desires or goals. Indeed, a unique feature of Merton's anomie-strain theory is the implication that *both* conformist and deviant behaviors are motivated by a strong commitment to conventional success goals.

Contemporary research on drug dealers provides a useful illustration. This research indicates that successful participants in the illicit drug trade tend to share a number of traits in common. Not only do they share a particularly strong desire for monetary success but, in comparison to less successful dealers, individuals who reap high monetary returns from the illicit drug trade also tend to be relatively intelligent, willing to take risks, and willing to network with other dealers in order to secure advantages in the drug market (McCarthy and Hagan 2001). In short, the desires and traits exhibited by these dealers do not appear to differ substantially from the characteristics normally attributed to successful and legitimate business entrepreneurs. From a strain theory perspective, the key difference is that the former have rejected legitimate means of goal attainment in favor of illegitimate means.

Revised strain theories of crime and delinquency

Merton's strain theory was followed by a number of attempts to revise and expand the theory, and to make it more applicable to specific types of deviant group, especially juvenile gangs. In general agreement with Merton, Albert Cohen (1955) observed that much delinquency stems from the blockage of success goals experienced disproportionately by lower-class juveniles, especially in relation to the goal of middle-class status. Specifically, lower-class juveniles often arrive at school without the knowledge, values, and skills necessary to achieve success through legitimate means. As a result, they fall behind their middle-class peers and fail to meet the expectations of their middle-class teachers. In short, these juveniles are unable to live up to the middle-class "measuring rod." They are defined as problems by school officials and are effectively denied a legitimate pathway to middle-class status.

At the same time, however, Cohen observed that much juvenile delinquency is non-utilitarian in nature and is not specifically concerned with the goal of monetary success or conventional status. Vandalism, fights, and other "expressive" delinquencies can hardly be construed as innovative means to acquire middle-class status, for example. To explain such behavior, Cohen interpreted the delinquency of lower-class juveniles as an indirect response to strain. When strained juveniles come together, they cope with their collective frustration by setting up an alternative status system, which expresses hostility to the middle class and emphasizes goals they *can* achieve, such as toughness and fighting ability. Thus, according to Cohen's account, strain contributes to the formation of delinquent peer groups, which in turn encourage delinquent adaptations.

Cloward and Ohlin (1960) also explained the formation of juvenile gangs in terms of strain. Many lower-class juveniles desire monetary success but realize they will be unable to achieve this goal through legal channels. When these strained juveniles interact regularly and blame their goal blockage on the larger society, they may form gangs that facilitate and justify criminal activity. In contrast to Cohen, however, Cloward and Ohlin argue that delinquent gangs tend to specialize. Some gangs, for example, focus primarily on fighting, while others focus on theft or drug use. This specialization is believed to be a function, in part, of the "illegitimate opportunities" available to strained youth. In some communities, youth receive instruction and support from older individuals and are directed into theft and other money-oriented crimes. In other communities, strained youth receive little direction and may cope by forming gangs that are oriented toward violence. Thus, according to Cloward and Ohlin, strain provides the motivation for juvenile crime, but the illegitimate opportunity structure plays a crucial role in the type of delinquent adaptations that ultimately arise.

Recent developments in the anomie-strain theory tradition

The "classic" strain theories of Merton, Cohen, and Cloward and Ohlin were highly influential during much of the 20th century, but were sharply criticized during the 1970s. Prominent criminologists criticized classic strain theories for their failure to explain the delinquency of middle-class individuals, their failure to explain why only *some* strained individuals turn to crime or delinquency, and their neglect of goals other than monetary success or middle-class status. Classic strain theories were also seen as lacking in empirical support. If such theories were correct, one would expect to find high levels of crime and delinquency among "strained" individuals; namely, among individuals who experience a disjunction between their aspirations and expectations. Yet, contrary to expectations, researchers observed that the highest levels of offending were to be found among individuals who lack aspirations for conventional success (e.g., among individuals who do *not* aspire to a college education or high-status occupation).

To address these criticisms, contemporary theorists have reformulated and reinvigorated the anomie-strain framework. The most influential of these reformulations include Agnew's (1992) general strain theory and Messner and Rosenfeld's (2001) institutional-anomie theory.

Agnew's general strain theory

To address some of the criticisms associated with classic strain theories, Agnew broadened the conception of strain to include a wider array of potential stressors, including stressors that are not limited to lower-class individuals but can also be experienced by individuals from middle-class backgrounds. According to Agnew's general strain theory (GST), the goals and outcomes that are important to individuals are not limited to income or middle-class status. Additional goals and outcomes that are recognized by the theory, and appear to be especially important to young males, include respect and masculine status (e.g., the expectation that one be treated "like a man"), autonomy (e.g., the goal or desire to enjoy a certain amount of personal independence), and the desire for thrills or excitement. GST, then, recognizes that individuals pursue a variety of goals beyond economic success and it expands the notion of goal-blockage accordingly. In particular, GST defines goal-blockage more broadly to include *the failure to achieve positively valued goals* (Agnew 1992, 2006).

In addition, Agnew highlights two other categories of strain, including *the loss of positively valued stimuli* and *the presentation of noxious or negatively valued stimuli*. The loss of positively valued stimuli includes a potentially wide range of negative events or experiences, including the theft of valued property, the loss of a romantic relationship, or the withdrawal of parental love. The presentation of noxious stimuli also includes a wide range of negative experiences, such as harassment and bullying from peers, negative relations with parents and teachers, and criminal victimization (Agnew 1992, 2006).

According to GST, strain increases the likelihood that individuals will experience negative emotions. Anger is one possible response and is of special interest to general strain theorists. Anger occurs when strain is blamed on others and it is believed to be especially conducive to crime and delinquency. Among other things, anger reduces one's tolerance for injury or insult, lowers inhibitions, energizes the individual to action, and creates desires for retaliation and revenge.

Of course, many people experience strains and stressors of various types, yet most do not resort to crime. In fact, GST recognizes that strain does not *automatically* lead to crime or delinquency. Rather, the theory specifies a number of conditions that are said to make a criminal/delinquent response to strain more or less likely. These conditions involve the nature of the strain in question, the coping abilities and resources available to the strained individual, and the extent to which the strained individual is predisposed to crime. Individuals may instead cope in legal or conventional ways. According to GST, for example, a criminal or delinquent response to strain is most likely to occur when conventional coping strategies are unavailable, when they prove ineffective, or when the coping resources of the individual become taxed (as may occur when the individual is subjected to chronic or repeated strain).

Like other strain theories, GST interprets offending behavior as an adaptation to strain—one that may allow individuals to cope with strain in the short run. However, the theory does *not* contend that crime is an effective solution (Agnew 2006). Crime is only one possible response to strain and, in the long run, may prove to be maladaptive, especially if it leads to other problems for the individual. Moreover, the intent of GST is not to excuse or justify criminal behavior. As Agnew is careful to note, the main purpose of the theory is to identify the processes that foster criminal conduct in the hopes that such knowledge may lead to improved strategies for the prevention and control of crime. The major crime control strategies that follow from GST include efforts that are designed to reduce or alleviate the strains that are conducive to crime or delinquency, equip individuals with the tools and skills that will allow them to avoid such strains, and reduce the likelihood that individuals will cope with strain in a criminal or delinquent manner (Agnew 1995).

A number of studies have attempted to assess the validity of GST. Although a comprehensive test of GST has yet to be conducted, researchers have managed to assess some of the core propositions of the theory. While the results of these research efforts have not always been consistent (Agnew 2006), the findings appear to indicate that, overall, GST has some potential for explaining crime, delinquency, and drug use.

Messner and Rosenfeld's institutional anomie theory

Although Agnew (1999) contends that GST can be extended and applied to community-level crime rates, the primary focus of GST is on individual-level, social psychological processes. Messner and Rosenfeld's (2001) institutional anomie theory (IAT) concentrates on macro-level forces. In particular, IAT represents a contemporary elaboration and extension of Merton's earlier anomie-strain framework, with a special focus on the specific institutional arrangements that serve to magnify (or weaken) criminogenic aspects of the American Dream.

Like Merton, Messner and Rosenfeld highlight the criminogenic consequences of the American value system, with its exaggerated emphasis on achievement and competition. Although the American Dream fosters high levels of motivation and innovation, this cultural ethos defines success in excessively narrow and materialistic terms. Individual achievement and monetary success are glorified, while alternative measures of success (e.g., social or educational contributions to one's community) are implicitly devalued. In addition, the ethos of the American Dream tends to place greater emphasis on goal outcomes rather than the means used to attain success goals. In short, the American Dream generates strong pressures to succeed at any cost, and it does not discourage individuals from pursuing monetary success by the "technically most efficient means, that is, by any means necessary" (Messner and Rosenfeld 2001: 8).

According to Messner and Rosenfeld, at least two factors serve to magnify the criminogenic effects of the American Dream. The first factor involves the extent to which the economy dominates the institutional landscape. When, in a market society, "the pursuit of private gain becomes the organizing principle of all areas of social life" (Elliott Currie quoted in Messner and Rosenfeld 2001: 70), and when non-economic roles associated with family, school, and the larger community are consistently devalued, the norms surrounding prosocial means of goal attainment lose their perceived importance and become difficult to enforce. When, in turn, the normative order is weakened and individuals are not sufficiently restrained in terms of the means they select to pursue success, the result is a condition of anomie. At the individual level, this anomic condition is reflected in extreme competition, individualism, and an "anything goes" mentality (see also Konty 2005).

A second factor involves high levels of economic inequality. In light of extreme economic differences, the perceived consequences of winning or losing in the competitive struggle for society's rewards become all the more significant. Given extensive inequality, large segments of the population are positioned at the bottom rungs of the economic ladder and, by the standards of the American Dream, are relegated to the role of "failure." The desire to avoid this fate intensifies the pressure to succeed at any cost. As a result, normative means of goal attainment lose their restraining force and anomie prevails.

As IAT locates the major causes of crime in the dominant culture, the implications of the theory for crime control are fairly radical and go beyond traditional policy prescriptions. The crime control recommendations that follow from IAT involve nothing short of a cultural transformation, including alternative definitions of success and increased commitment to community, responsibility, and public altruism. Policies that strengthen non-economic institutions such as the family and school would facilitate this transformation, as these institutions help to restrain antisocial behavior (by enforcing norms that govern socially acceptable means of goal attainment). These institutions also provide a buffer against the corrosive forces of the market.

In an important test of IAT, Baumer and Gustafson (2007) examined the relationship between monetary success goals, commitment to legitimate means of goal attainment, and instrumental crime rates (robberies, burglaries, larcenies, and auto thefts) across 77 geographic units in the United States, including metropolitan areas and non-metropolitan counties. Several findings of the study are noteworthy. First, the authors observe significant variation in relevant value orientations across the communities they examined. For example, the percentage of survey respondents from each area who expressed a strong commitment to monetary success (agreeing that, "next to health, money is the most important thing") ranged from a low of 15 percent to a high of 49 percent. Likewise, the percentage of respondents from each area who expressed weak commitment to the legitimate means of pursuing monetary success (agreeing that "there are no right or wrong ways to make money, only hard and easy ways") ranged from 5 percent to 41 percent. These findings highlight the fact that, despite a shared American culture, individuals differ in the extent to which they internalize the values associated with the "dark side" of the American Dream. Moreover, these values appear to be exaggerated only in select communities.

Second, the authors observe a relationship between instrumental crime rates and commitment to monetary success, but only under certain conditions. As predicted by both classic and contemporary anomie-strain theories, strong commitment to monetary success is associated with relatively high crime rates only in those areas where commitment to legitimate means is weak. (In areas where people's commitment to legitimate means remains strong, the importance of monetary success has no bearing on the crime rate.) Furthermore, this particular value configuration tends to have the strongest impact on instrumental crime in those areas that suffer from extensive economic inequality and where many residents occupy positions of low economic standing.

Third, consistent with IAT, the authors find some evidence that non-economic institutions can lessen the pressures that contribute to instrumental crime. Specifically, they observe that values related to monetary success and legitimate means have no impact on the crime rate in those areas where family ties are strong and where the poor receive above-average levels of welfare assistance. According to the authors of the study, these results lend support to the policy recommendations that follow from IAT. In particular, policies that strengthen families and buffer people from the effects of poverty and unemployment "would contribute significantly to a comprehensive crime control policy" in the United States (Baumer and Gustafson 2007: 655).

Conclusion

Although additional research will be required before a complete assessment of anomie-strain theories can be made, the results of existing studies indicate that such theories have some potential to explain crime and deviance at both the micro- and macro-levels of analyses. Anomie-strain theories, then, may help to supplement the leading crime theories, including alternative theories that are rooted in the concepts of social learning or informal social control (Akers and Sellers 2008). Contemporary anomie-strain theories are intuitively compelling, have received considerable attention from criminologists, have helped to revitalize the anomie-strain theory tradition, and are certain to stimulate criminological research for years to come.

References

Agnew, Robert. 1992. "Foundation for a General Strain Theory of Crime and Delinquency." *Criminology* 30:47–87.

Agnew, Robert. 1995. "Controlling Delinquency: Recommendations from General Strain Theory." In H. Barlow (Ed.), *Crime and Public Policy* (pp. 43–70). Boulder, CO: Westview.

Agnew, Robert. 1999. "A General Strain Theory of Community Differences in Crime Rates." *Journal of Research in Crime and Delinquency* 36:123–155.

Agnew, Robert. 2006. *Pressured into Crime: An Overview of General Strain Theory.* Los Angeles, CA: Roxbury.

Agnew, Robert, Francis T. Cullen, Velmer S. Burton Jr., T. David Evans, and R. Gregory Dunaway. 1996. "A New Test of Classic Strain Theory." *Justice Quarterly* 13:681–704.

Akers, Ronald L. and Christine S. Sellers. 2008. *Criminological Theories.* 5th edition. New York: Oxford University Press.

Baumer, Eric P. and Regan Gustafson. 2007. "Social Organization and Instrumental Crime: Assessing the Empirical Validity of Classic and Contemporary Anomie Theories." *Criminology* 45:617–663.

Brezina, Timothy. 1996. "Adapting to Strain: An Examination of Delinquent Coping Responses." *Criminology* 34:39–60.

Cloward, Richard A. and Lloyd E. Ohlin. 1960. *Delinquency and Opportunity.* New York: Free Press.

Cohen, Albert. 1955. *Delinquent Boys.* New York: Free Press.

Durkheim, Emile. (1951 [1897]). *Suicide: A Study in Sociology.* Translated by J. A. Spaulding and G. Simpson. New York: Free Press.

Konty, Mark. 2005. "Microanomie: The Cognitive Foundations of the Relationship between Anomie and Deviance." *Criminology* 43:107–132.

McCarthy, Bill and John Hagan. 2001. "Capital, Competence, and Criminal Success." *Social Forces* 79:1035–1059.

Merton, Robert K. 1938. "Social Structure and Anomie." *American Sociological Review* 3:672–682.

Messner, Steven F. and Richard Rosenfeld. 2001. *Crime and the American Dream.* 3rd edition. Belmont, CA: Wadsworth.

12

Social learning theory

Wesley G. Jennings and Ronald L. Akers

Introduction

This chapter provides an overview of Akers' social learning theory as an explanation for crime and deviance. It begins with a discussion of the theoretical origins of social learning theory and provides an overview of the four core elements of the theory. The following section offers a brief review of the empirical research testing the applicability of social learning theory for explaining variation in crime and deviance. The recent macro-level theoretical extension of social learning theory (e.g., social structure and social learning theory) and relevant empirical tests are also briefly discussed. The chapter concludes by offering suggestions for future research investigating the utility of social learning theory as a general theory of crime and deviance.

Social learning theory: theoretical origins and framework

Burgess and Akers' (1966) differential association-reinforcement theory was first cast as a theoretical effort to mesh Sutherland's differential association theory with principles of behavioral psychology. Specifically, Sutherland's (1947: 6–7) differential association theory provided the following nine propositions:

1 Criminal behavior is learned.
2 Criminal behavior is learned in interaction with other persons in a process of communication.
3 The principal part of the learning of criminal behavior occurs within intimate personal groups.
4 When criminal behavior is learned, the learning includes (a) techniques of committing the crime, which are sometimes very complicated, sometimes very simple, and (b) the specific direction of motives, drives, rationalizations, and attitudes.
5 The specific direction of motives and drives is learned from definitions of the legal codes as favorable or unfavorable.
6 A person becomes delinquent because of an excess of definitions favorable to violation of law over definitions unfavorable to violation of the law.
7 Differential associations may vary in frequency, duration, priority, and intensity.
8 The process of learning criminal behavior by association with criminal and anti-criminal patterns involves all of the mechanisms that are involved in any other learning.

9 Although criminal behavior is an expression of general needs and values, it is not explained by those general needs and values, because non-criminal behavior is an expression of the same needs and values.

Most germane to Burgess and Akers' differential association-reinforcement theory is Sutherland's sixth principle, the "principle of differential association." For Sutherland, an individual learns two types of definition for a particular behavior—a favorable and an unfavorable definition. A favorable definition will increase the likelihood that an individual will choose to participate in a particular behavior, whereas an unfavorable definition will decrease an individual's likelihood for participating in a particular behavior. Furthermore, these contrasting definitions should be considered in terms of their frequency. For example, as applied to involvement in crime and deviance, the theoretical assumption is that when an individual learns favorable definitions toward violations of the law in "excess" of unfavorable definitions toward violations of the law, then the individual is more likely to choose to participate in the particular criminal or deviant act.

Considering this theoretical assumption, it is logical to expect (as well as having been empirically supported) that an individual will learn pro-criminal definitions (e.g., favorable definitions toward violations of the law) from individuals who are already participating or have participated in crime and deviance themselves. Similarly, it is reasonable to expect that unfavorable definitions toward violations of the law will be learned from law-abiding individuals (e.g., non-criminals or non-deviants). Having said this, it is not necessarily impossible for non-criminal/non-deviants to express pro-criminal (favorable) definitions, just as it is not improbable for a criminal/deviant to express anti-criminal (unfavorable) definitions for violations of the law. Nevertheless, it is more often the case that the pro-criminal definitions will be learned from the criminals/deviants and the conforming definitions will be learned from the non-criminals/non-deviants. In addition, Sutherland does not argue that merely associating with criminals/deviants or with non-criminals/non-deviants will result in participation or lack of participation in a particular behavior (e.g., the seventh principle). Rather, the nature, the characteristics, and the balance of the differential association all contribute to the individual's likelihood for engaging in the criminal/deviant act. Specifically, if an individual is exposed to favorable definitions for violations of the law first (priority), and these definitions increase in frequency and strength (intensity) and persist over time (duration), then the individual's likelihood for participating in criminal/deviant acts is amplified.

Drawing from Sutherland's differential association theory and the specific assumptions reviewed above, Burgess and Akers (1966: 132–145) presented the following modified serial list of the principles describing the process wherein the learning occurs:

1 Criminal behavior is learned according to the principles of operant conditioning (reformulation of Sutherland's first and eighth principles).
2 Criminal behavior is learned both in non-social situations that are reinforcing or discriminative and through that social interaction in which the behavior of other persons is reinforcing or discriminative for criminal behavior (reformulation of Sutherland's second principle).
3 The principal part of the learning of criminal behavior occurs in those groups which comprise the individual's major source of reinforcements (reformulation of Sutherland's third principle).
4 The learning of criminal behavior, including specific techniques, attitudes, and avoidance procedures, is a function of the effective and available reinforcers, and the existing reinforcement contingencies (reformulation of Sutherland's fourth principle).

5   The specific class of behaviors which are learned and their frequency of occurrence are functions of the reinforcers which are effective and available, and the rules or norms by which these reinforcers are applied (reformulation of Sutherland's fifth principle).
6   Criminal behavior is a function of norms which are discriminative for criminal behavior, the learning of which takes place when such behavior is more highly reinforced than non-criminal behavior (reformulation of Sutherland's sixth principle).
7   The strength of criminal behavior is a direct function of the amount, frequency, and probability of its reinforcement (reformulation of Sutherland's seventh principle).[1]

Thus, informed by these revised principles, Burgess and Akers made an effort to integrate these principles with the principles of differential reinforcement from behavioral psychology (e.g., operant conditioning). Their reformulated theoretical perspective, differential association-reinforcement theory, emphasizes the balance of rewards and punishments as they operate during social interaction. Yet, this process also accounts for the influence of non-social variables. Following some theoretical criticism, Akers later made refinements and theoretical modifications and specifications moving away from the original serial list of the seven revised principles and classic operant behaviorism in favor of focusing on four core elements (definitions, differential association, differential reinforcement, and imitation) and Bandura's (1979) social behaviorism (for review, see Akers and Sellers, 2009).

In light of these theoretical revisions and modifications, the essential underlying assumption of Akers' social learning theory remains intact. Specifically, the theory emphasizes "that the same learning process in a context of social structure, interaction, and situation produces both conforming and deviant behavior. The difference lies in the direction . . . [of] the balance of influences on behavior" (Akers, 1998: 50). It is in this regard that social learning theory can be considered a general theory of crime and deviance because its basic underlying assumption seeks to explain why individuals participate in criminal and deviant acts as well as explaining why they do not participate in criminal and deviant behaviors. The following statement best summarizes Akers' social learning theory as presented and understood in the literature:

> The probability that persons will engage in criminal and deviant behavior is increased and the probability of their conforming to the norm is decreased when they differentially associate with others who commit criminal behavior and espouse definitions favorable to it, are relatively more exposed in-person or symbolically to salient criminal/deviant models, define it as desirable or justified in a situation discriminative for the behavior, and have received in the past and anticipate in the current or future situation relatively greater reward than punishment for the behavior.
>
> *(Akers, 1998: 50)*

Social learning theory: four core elements

As mentioned previously, Akers' social learning theory comprises four core elements: definitions, differential association, differential reinforcement, and imitation. The definitions component of social learning theory focuses on the values, orientations, and attitudes toward criminal and/or deviant behavior. The range in these values, orientations, and attitudes shapes an individual's "definitions" toward certain behavior as being more right or wrong, good or bad, desirable or undesirable, justified or unjustified, appropriate or inappropriate, excusable or inexcusable. These definitions can be either general or specific. General definitions refer to an individual's conventional, moral, and religious beliefs that are held for a variety of behaviors in a number of situations. Comparatively, specific definitions refer more to a person's attitudes of permissiveness or proscription toward a specific behavior or a specific behavior in a specific situation. Although general and specific definitions are described as conceptually distinct, it is important to note that these definitions are often intertwined and overlap. Nevertheless, it is best to consider the definitions component of social learning theory along the following continua that reflects the balance of personal definitions favorable and unfavorable toward violations of law (Akers, 1998: 83):

> Definitions favorable to deviance include weakly held general beliefs and more strongly held deviant justifications and definitions of the situation; those unfavorable to deviance include more strongly held conventional beliefs and deviant definitions that are weakly subscribed to . . . Think of two parallel continua running in opposite directions:

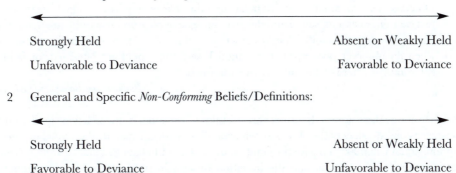

1   General and Specific *Conforming* Beliefs/Definitions:

Strongly Held   Absent or Weakly Held

Unfavorable to Deviance   Favorable to Deviance

2   General and Specific *Non-Conforming* Beliefs/Definitions:

Strongly Held   Absent or Weakly Held

Favorable to Deviance   Unfavorable to Deviance

The differential association component of social learning theory acknowledges and emphasizes the importance of the individuals/groups that an individual interacts with insofar as this interaction provides the social context wherein the social learning process operates. Although this component is often referenced in the literature as "delinquent peer association," social learning theory cannot and should not be merely reduced to a theory of "hanging out with the bad kids." More specifically, this element recognizes the effect that family members, intimate peer groups, and even secondary peer groups (including neighbors, churches, schoolteachers, law and authority figures) as well as "virtual groups," such as those established through the mass media, the internet, cell phones, and so on (see Warr, 2002), may have on an individual's participation or lack of participation in crime and deviance. Akers argues that the more an individual is differentially associated with individuals who are involved in criminal and deviant behavior and/or differentially associated with individuals who espouse pro-criminal attitudes toward criminal and deviant behavior, the higher is the likelihood for the individual to engage in the particular behavior that their "associates" are participating in or expressing pro-criminal definitions for. Akers also mentions the importance of the "modalities" of association (e.g., intensity, priority, frequency, and duration) as having an effect on the ratio of criminal to non-criminal associations.

The differential reinforcement component of social learning theory is similar to the mechanism of differential association whereby an imbalance of norms, values, and attitudes favorable toward violations of the law will increase an individual's likelihood for participating in a particular criminal or deviant act. Yet, this component emphasizes the effect that past, present, and future anticipated and/or experienced rewards and punishments have on whether an individual initiates their participation in a particular criminal or deviant act and whether or not the individual will continue their participation in the criminal or deviant act in the future. This differential reinforcement process operates in several ways: positive reinforcement (increase in status among a peer group as a result of participating in a particular criminal or deviant behavior), negative reinforcement (participation in a particular criminal or deviant behavior allows the individual to escape or avoid adverse stimuli or consequences), positive punishment (experiencing an unwanted punishment, such as making a decision to smoke marijuana and throwing up as a result), and negative punishment (the removal of something valuable to an individual, such as smoking marijuana and getting arrested for this behavior: that is, loss/removal of freedom).

The final component of Akers' social learning theory is imitation. This involves the observation of behavior modeled by others and the consequences of the behavior modeled by others. The latter is often referred to as vicarious reinforcement (see Bandura, 1979) and can best be explained as follows:

> Observers tend to imitate modeled behavior if they like or respect the model, see the model receive reinforcement, see the model give off signs of pleasure, or are in an environment where imitating the model's performance is reinforced . . . Inverse imitation is common when an observer does not like the model, sees the model get punished, or is in an environment where conformity is being punished.
>
> *(Baldwin and Baldwin, 1981: 187)*

Furthermore, Akers argues that the characteristics of the models, the behavior itself, and the observed consequences of the observed behavior all have an effect on the likelihood of whether an individual will make a decision to imitate the observed behavior. Finally, while the social learning process in general and the imitation process in particular occur throughout an individual's life-course, Akers suggests that the process of imitation is likely to have the strongest effect on an individual's decision to perform the particular act in the first place (e.g., the initial criminal or deviant act).

Empirical support for social learning theory

As research now spanning over five decades has tested the theoretical assumptions of social learning theory, there is certainly not enough space here to provide a detailed description of each and every empirical study. However, it is important to highlight the fact that empirical research by Akers and his associates, as well as work done by others, has generally found modest support for social learning theory as an explanation of crime and deviance. More specifically, Akers and his associates found that when full social learning models were tested incorporating all of the four core elements of the theory (e.g., definitions, differential association, differential reinforcement, and imitation), these theoretical constructs explained a number of behaviors, including minor deviance, substance use, delinquent behavior, and serious delinquent/criminal behavior. Furthermore, each of the core elements of social learning theory (for the most part) was able to explain the variation in behavior individually as well as collectively. These models consistently explained a rather large portion of the variance in the dependent variable(s), and the effects of the social learning variables were often stronger than the effects of other theoretical models (for a review of these studies, see Akers and Jennings, 2009).

Comparatively, Warr (2002: 40) provides the best statement for summarizing the large body of literature conducted by researchers testing social learning theory (in addition to the research performed by Akers and his associates) when he states:

No characteristic of individuals known to criminologists is a better predictor of criminal behavior than the number of delinquent friends an individual has. The strong correlation between delinquent behavior and delinquent friends has been documented in scores of studies from the 1950s up to the present day using alternative kinds of criminological data (self-reports, official records, perceptual data) on subjects and friends, alternative research designs, and data on a wide variety of criminal offenses. Few, if any, empirical regularities in criminology have been documented as often or over as long a period as the association between delinquency and delinquent friends.

Social structure and social learning

Acknowledging the long line of empirical research supporting the robust relationship between social learning variables and crime and deviance, Akers (1998) more recently extended his theory to include macro-level factors. Akers' social structure and social learning theory rests on the assumption that there are key social structural factors that have an indirect effect on an individual's behavior. The effect of these social structural variables is hypothesized as indirect because Akers argues that the influence of the macro-level variables operates through the four individual-level social learning variables (definitions, differential association, differential rein-forcement, and imitation), which all have a direct effect on crime and deviance. Akers (1998; see also Akers and Sellers, 2004: 91) identifies four specific domains wherein the social learning process takes place in his social structure and social learning model:

1 *Differential social organization* refers to the structural correlates of crime in the community or society that affect the rates of crime and delinquency, including age composition, population density, and other attributes that lean societies, communities, and other social systems "toward relatively high or relatively low crime rates" (Akers, 1998: 332).
2 *Differential location in the social structure* refers to sociodemographic characteristics of individuals and social groups that indicate their niches within the larger social structure. Class, gender, race, ethnicity, marital status, and age locate the positions and standing of persons and their roles, groups, or social categories in the overall social structure.
3 *Theoretically defined structural variables* refer to anomie, class oppression, social disorganization, group conflict, patriarchy, and other concepts that have been used in one or more theories to identify criminogenic conditions of societies, communities, or groups.
4 *Differential social location* refers to individuals' membership in and relationship to primary, secondary, and reference groups, such as the family, friendship/peer groups, leisure groups, colleagues, and work groups.

Empirical support for social structure and social learning theory

Given that Akers' theoretical extension of social learning theory with macro-level factors occurred only recently, there have been few explicit tests of the social structure and social learning theory model. For example, Bellair, Roscigno, and Velez (2003) tested a partial social structure and social learning model, and their results indicated that the professional sector effects (concentration of low-wage service employment) on adolescent violence was almost entirely mediated by the social learning process. Lee *et al.* (2004) performed one of the first complete tests of the social structure and social learning model, and their findings suggested that "variations in the behavioral and cognitive variables specified in the social learning process . . . substantially mediate most, if not virtually all, of the effects of gender, socio-economic status, age, family structure, and community size on these forms of adolescent deviance" (Lee *et al.*, 2004: 29).

Two more recent explicit tests of the social structure and social learning model demonstrated support for the macro-level extension of social learning theory for mediating the effects of some of the structural variables (Holland-Davis, 2006; Verrill, 2008). Nevertheless, both of these researchers suggested that social structure and social learning theory should be modified in order to take into account the moderated-mediation process regarding gender and/or directly express the direction of the moderation mediation.

Conclusion

This chapter set out to provide a description of Akers' social learning theory and its recent theoretical extension incorporating macro-level factors (social structure and social learning theory), and to highlight some of the research findings that have tested social learning theory and its macro-level extension. There can be little argument that social learning theory has come to be recognized as an important general theory of crime. Similarly, its recent theoretical extension to a cross-level integration of meso- and macro-level social structural variables provides a fresh and new area for empirical research. Unfortunately, having said this, researchers too often test only one or a few of the social learning variables at a time or try to compare the effects of one of the social learning variables against another. Future research should attempt to collect and analyze data with measures of all four core elements of social learning theory (definitions, differential association, differential reinforcement, and imitation), and recognize that it is not necessary (or appropriate) to compare and contrast the effects of one particular social learning variable in relation to another because they are all part of the same underlying learning process.

Finally, for every theory that claims to be a general theory of crime, it follows that the theory should be put to the test across a variety of samples, time periods, race/ethnic groups, cultural contexts, and so on. Therefore, future research testing either social learning theory or social structure and social learning theory should focus on taking it "global" in an effort to establish its generality as an explanation for crime and deviance.

Note

1   In their reformulation of the theory, Burgess and Akers (1966) chose to omit Sutherland's ninth principle.

References

Akers, R. L. (1998). *Social learning and social structure: A general theory of crime and deviance*. Boston, MA: Northeastern University Press.

Akers, R. L. and Jennings, W. G. (2009). "Social learning theory." In J. M. Miller (Ed.), *21st century criminology: A reference handbook*. Thousand Oaks, CA: Sage.

Akers, R. L. and Sellers, C. S. (2004). *Criminological theories: Introduction, evaluation, and application*. Fourth edition. Los Angeles, CA: Roxbury.

Akers, R.L. and Sellers, C. S. (2009). *Criminological theories: Introduction, evaluation, and application*. Fifth edition. New York: Oxford University Press.

Baldwin, J. D. and Baldwin, J. I. (1981). *Beyond sociobiology*. New York: Elsevier.

Bandura, A. (1979). *Social learning theory*. Englewood Cliffs, NJ: Prentice-Hall.

Bellair, P. E., Roscigno, V. J., and Velez, M. B. (2003). "Occupational structure, social learning, and adolescent violence." In R. L. Akers and G. F. Jensen (Eds.), *Advances in criminological theory*, Volume 11: *Social learning theory and the explanation of crime: A guide for the new century*. New Brunswick, NJ: Transaction.

Burgess, R. L. and Akers, R. L. (1966). "A differential association-reinforcement theory of criminal behavior." *Social Problems*, 14: 128–147.

Holland-Davis, L. (2006). "Putting behavior in context: A test of the social structure social learning model." Ph.D. dissertation. Gainesville: University of Florida.

Lee, G., Akers, R. L., and Borg, M. (2004). "Social learning and structural factors in adolescent substance use." *Western Criminology Review*, 5: 17–34.

Sutherland, E. H. (1947). *Principles of criminology*. Fourth edition. Philadelphia, PA: J. B. Lippincott.

Verrill, S. W. (2008). *Social structure, social learning, and criminal behavior: Cross-level moderator effects*. New York: LFB Scholarly.

Warr, M. (2002). *Companions in crime: The social aspects of criminal conduct*. Cambridge: Cambridge University Press.

13

Control and social disorganization theory

Robert Agnew

Control and social disorganization theories are distinguished by their focus on those factors that restrain people from engaging in deviance. Control theories examine those restraints operating at the individual level, while social disorganization theories examine those operating at the community level. Deviance is said to result from weak restraints or controls. When controls are weak, individuals are free to satisfy their needs and desires in the most expedient manner—which is often deviance. This argument stands in contrast to most other theories, which argue that deviance is positively motivated by such factors as strains or stresses, exposure to deviant models, and beliefs favorable to deviance.

This chapter begins with a brief history of control and social disorganization theories, followed by an overview of the central arguments and research on social control, self-control, and social disorganization theory.

Historic overview

Numerous scholars contributed to the development of social control theory, most notably Reiss (1951), Toby (1957), Nye (1958), Reckless (1961), Matza (1964), and Briar and Piliavin (1965). Social control refers to the controls stemming from the relations among people, as when parents sanction their children, or adults refrain from deviance for fear of jeopardizing their jobs. These scholars described the role of control in explaining deviance and identified the major types of social control. Hirschi (1969) drew on and extended their work in his classic book on *Causes of Delinquency*. This book presented a very popular typology of the major forms of social control, as well as data suggesting that these controls are strongly related to delinquency. Subsequent research has generally found a relationship between social controls and deviance (Agnew 2009a; Gottfredson 2006; Kubrin *et al.* 2009; Patterson *et al.* 1992; Vold *et al.* 2009). Also, the theory has been applied to new areas, such as the explanation of offending over the life course (Sampson and Laub 1993). As a consequence, social control theory is one of the leading theories of deviance.

In 1990, however, Gottfredson and Hirschi published *A General Theory of Crime*, which argued that variations in the level of *self*-control are the primary cause of deviance. "Self-control" refers to the ability of individuals to restrain themselves from acting on their immediate impulses and desires. This internal characteristic was said to originate during the early childhood years, being a function of the level of *social* control exercised by parents. In particular, children develop self-control if their parents closely monitor their behavior and consistently sanction them if they misbehave. Once self-control is formed in childhood, it is said to be relatively stable over the life course, and variations in social control are said to be unimportant in explaining deviance. Much data suggest that low self-control is an important cause of deviance, and it too is one of the leading theories of deviance (Goode 2008; Gottfredson 2006; Pratt and Cullen 2000).

Social disorganization theory was developed primarily by Shaw and McKay (1942) during the first half of the twentieth century. The theory explains why some urban areas have much higher rates of crime than others. High-crime areas are said to be disorganized, with residents failing to exercise effective social control over one another. Further, this disorganization is explained in terms of community characteristics, such as poverty and high rates of mobility. The theory remained popular for many years, but then fell into decline; partly because the research on deviance became increasingly individualistic in nature (see Sampson and Groves 1989). Social disorganization theory, however, experienced a revival in the 1990s, due in large part to the work of scholars such as Kornhauser (1978), Sampson and associates (Sampson and Groves 1989; Sampson and Raudenbush 1999; Sampson and Wilson 1995), and Bursik and Grasmick (1993). This new work better describes the nature of disorganized communities and the sources of this disorganization. As a consequence, social disorganization theory is now the leading theory of community differences in rates of crime and deviance.

Social control theory

Contemporary social control theories focus on three major types of control: direct control, stake in conformity, and beliefs regarding deviance. These types of control are mainly used to explain individual differences in deviance but, more recently, they have been used to explain patterns of deviance over the life course and group differences in deviance.

Direct control

Direct control is perhaps the most obvious form of social control. People refrain from deviance out of fear that they will be caught and sanctioned. Direct control may be informal or exercised by such individuals as family members, friends, teachers, and employers. Direct control may also be formal or exercised by representatives of the justice system, such as police and judges. Informal control is far more common and plays a much larger role in the control of deviance than formal control. This is because individuals such as family and friends are in much better positions to monitor individuals and sanction them if they misbehave. These sanctions may be as subtle as a disapproving look from a friend or as blatant as a husband severely beating his wife. Research suggests that direct control must have several elements if it is to be effective in controlling deviance (Agnew 2009a; Patterson *et al.* 1992).

First, the agents of control must clearly communicate rules that prohibit deviance and related behaviors, such as associating with criminals. Second, individuals must be monitored to make sure that they obey these rules. This monitoring may be direct, as when parent and teachers watch over the children in their care. It may also be indirect, as when parents ask their children about what they have done and periodically talk to their children's teachers and friends. Third, individuals must be consistently sanctioned for rule violations. These sanctions should be meaningful, but not excessive or abusive.

Such direct control can be quite effective in reducing deviance, regardless of whether it is exercised by parents, teachers, police, or others. Individuals, however, differ in the direct control to which they are subject. Most research has focused on the family, and studies suggest that parents may fail to exercise effective direct control for several reasons. They may lack the knowledge to be effective parents; they may have "difficult" children who exasperate them; they may be overwhelmed with such stressors as poverty and family violence; and they may have personality traits which undermine effective parenting, such as low self-control (Agnew 2009a; Colvin 2000; Patterson *et al.* 1992).

Stake in conformity

Some individuals are more responsive than others to direct control. One reason for this is that individuals differ in their stake in conformity or in what they have to lose if caught engaging in deviance. Some individuals have a high stake in conformity. This stake includes the individual's emotional bond to conventional others, such as parents, teachers, friends, and religious figures. Deviance may upset these others and jeopardize relations with them. This stake also includes the individual's achievements and possessions, including educational and occupational achievements, material possessions, and reputation. Further, it includes the individual's plans for the future, such as attending college or becoming a lawyer. These things may also be jeopardized by deviance. Deviance, in short, is more likely among those who have little to lose if caught.

Beliefs regarding deviance

Individuals often refrain from deviance even if there is little or no chance they will be caught and their stake in conformity jeopardized. A major reason for this is that they have been taught that deviance is wrong and they have internalized this belief. According to control theorists, however, some people are not properly socialized and are amoral, believing that deviance is neither wrong nor right. Control theorists disagree with subcultural deviance and social learning theorists, who argue that some people are taught to approve of, justify, or excuse deviance. Rather, these individuals are simply amoral in their orientation, or their beliefs condemning deviance are not strongly held.

The research on social control theory

Studies suggest that there is a strong association between the above types of social control and deviance (Agnew 2009a; Britt and Gottfredson 2003; Colvin 2000; Gottfredson 2006; Kubrin *et al.* 2009). Most of the research has involved surveys and has focused on the explanation of crime and delinquency. Such research routinely finds that crime is lower among individuals who report that their parents closely monitor them and consistently sanction their deviance, they love and respect their parents, they are doing well in school, they plan to obtain advanced education, they have good jobs, and they think that various types of delinquency are "very wrong." This cross-sectional research, however, does not demonstrate that low social control *causes* deviance. It is possible that deviance causes a reduction in social control. Delinquency, for example, may disrupt the juvenile's emotional bond to his/her parents. Longitudinal studies that take account of causal order find somewhat less support for social control theory, although social control variables do have a weak to moderate effect on subsequent deviance in such studies (see Kubrin *et al.* 2009).

Extensions of social control theory

Most of the theory and research on social control theory has focused on explaining individual differences in delinquency. Recent work, however, has used the theory to explain offending over the life course and group differences in delinquency. In their classic work on *Crime in the Making*, Sampson and Laub (1993) use control theory to explain why some offenders substantially reduce their crime when they move from adolescence to adulthood, while others continue to offend well into the adult years. They argue that the sources of social control change over the life course. Ties to family and school are most important during childhood, while ties to spouse and work are critical during adulthood. Those juvenile offenders who become involved in good marriages and form strong commitments to work are able to desist from crime, while those who fail to form such social bonds continue to offend. It is not entirely clear why some offenders are able to form strong bonds while others are not, although such factors as arrest and incarceration can make it more difficult to form such bonds.

Social control theory has also been used to explain such things as the large gender difference in offending. There is some evidence that females are less likely to offend than males partly because they are higher in social control. In particular, females are more closely supervised than males, more likely to be sanctioned for many deviant acts, more strongly bonded to school, and more likely to condemn deviance (Agnew 2009b). Given the support for and applicability of social control theory, it is not surprising that it has also been used to guide efforts to control and prevent crime (Agnew 2009a; Kennedy 1998; Patterson *et al.* 1992).

Self-control theory

Self-control theory does not deny the importance of social control. In fact, Gottfredson and Hirschi (1990) state that the social control exercised by family members during the early childhood years is largely responsible for the development of self-control. Self-control refers to the ability to exercise self-restraint when tempted to engage in deviance. Individuals develop self-control when their parents set clear rules for them, regularly monitor them, and consistently sanction them in a meaningful way for rule violations. Individuals who fail to develop self-control have several characteristics. They tend to act before thinking, prefer immediate over delayed rewards, like risky activities, have high activity levels, have trouble controlling their anger, and have little ambition or motivation. Self-control is typically measured in terms of such characteristics (Goode, 2008; Grasmick *et al.*, 1993; Kubrin *et al.*, 2009; Pratt and Cullen, 2000).

Gottfedson and Hirschi argue that one's level of self-control is relatively stable beyond childhood. Individuals who are relatively low in self-control as adolescents, then, will be relatively low as adults. Further, self-control is said to be the primary cause of deviance. Levels of *social* control and most other factors should have little effect on deviance once level of self-control is taken into account. Gottfredson and Hirschi (1990, 2006), however, do state that the opportunity to engage in deviance has an effect on deviance. Individuals low in self-control cannot engage in particular deviant acts unless they have the opportunity to do so. For example, they cannot engage in drug use unless they come into contact with individuals who possess drugs. Finally, self-control is said to explain most of the major facts about deviance, such as the greater involvement of males in most forms of deviance.

Much research suggests that level of self-control is one of the strongest correlates of crime and deviance (Agnew 2009a; Goode 2008; Gottfredson 2006; Pratt and Cullen 2000). At the same time, certain of the claims made by Gottfredson and Hirschi have been challenged. While level of self-control is influenced by social control in the family, it is also influenced by other factors, particularly such biological factors as genetic inheritance (Wright and Beaver 2005). While self-control is moderately stable over the life course, it is not as stable as Gottfredson and Hirschi suggest. Individuals relatively low in self-control at one point in time are not always low at another (Hay and Forrest 2006). This is because self-control is influenced by factors beyond childhood, such as the level of social control in adolescence and adulthood (Sampson and Laub 1993; Wright *et al.* 1999). While low self-control is a major cause of offending, other causes also affect offending—even after researchers take self-control into account (Pratt and Cullen 2000). And while self-control helps explain group differences in offending, such as gender differences, it does not fully account for such differences (Greenberg 2008). Nevertheless, low self-control clearly stands as a major cause of crime and deviance. And it too has inspired efforts to control and prevent crime (Agnew 2009a).

Social disorganization theory

Criminologists have long noted that some communities have much higher rates of crime than others. Social disorganization theory draws on social control theory to explain this fact. It is said that certain communities are disorganized, with the residents unable or unwilling to exercise social control over one another. These communities are low in direct control, with residents being less likely to monitor public spaces and sanction individuals for crime and deviance. Residents in these communities also have a lower stake in conformity. They are less likely to have close ties to their neighbors and community, to help one another secure good educations and jobs, and to support community organizations that assist residents. Further, residents are less likely to foster a community culture that condemns crime. Research suggests that such factors do help account for the higher rates of crime in some communities (Agnew 2009a; Kubrin *et al.* 2009; Sampson and Groves 1989; Vold *et al.* 2009). For example, recent research has found that crime rates are strongly related to the level of "collective efficacy" in a community—the extent to which community residents know and trust one another and report that their neighbors would intervene if they encountered various forms of deviance (Sampson 2006; Sampson and Raudenbush 1999).

Social disorganization theorists have also devoted much attention to those factors that contribute to low social control in a community. Such factors include high levels of economic deprivation, residential instability, and family disruption; as well as close proximity to other economically deprived and high-crime communities. Individuals in such communities often lack the ability to exercise effective social control; for example, they are single parents preoccupied with a range of financial and other problems. Also, the high rates of residential instability mean that residents are less likely to get to know their neighbors and develop strong ties to the community. Further, residents are less able to draw on the resources of surrounding communities, since these communities are also poor and plagued by crime.

It is important to note that race and ethnicity are *not* strongly related to community crime rates once such factors as economic deprivation are taken into account. At the same time, African Americans are more likely to live in the types of community with high crime rates: that is, very poor communities with high rates of mobility and family disruption. This is due to the effects of past and present discrimination. As a result of past housing discrimination, African Americans of all classes were more likely to live in the inner cities of metropolitan areas. As housing discrimination declined, working- and middle-class African Americans left the inner city, leaving the poor behind. Public housing projects were more likely to be placed in these poor, largely African-American communities. And the loss of well-paid blue-collar jobs in recent decades had a particularly severe effect on these same communities (see Sampson and Wilson 1995). So while race does not have a causal effect on urban crime rates, the history of discrimination in the US has created a situation where African Americans are disproportionately likely to suffer from such crime rates.

Summary

Control and social disorganization theories play a special role in the explanation of deviance, with both focusing on the restraints or controls which prevent deviance. Such theories have amassed a good amount of empirical support, and are able to account for a significant portion of the individual, group, and community variation deviance; as well as variations in the level of deviance over the life course. They do not fully explain such variations, however; other theories focusing on those factors that positively motivate deviance are also important. Nevertheless, control and disorganization theories are clearly among the leading theories of deviance.

References

Agnew, R. (2009) *Juvenile Delinquency: Causes and Control*. New York: Oxford University Press.

Agnew, R. (2009) "The contribution of "mainstream theories" to the explanation of female delinquency," in M. Zahn (ed.) *The Delinquent Girl*. Philadelphia, PA: Temple University Press.

Briar, S. and Piliavin, I. (1965) "Delinquency, situational inducements, and commitments to conformity." *Social Problems* 13:35–45.

Britt, C. L. and Gottfredson, M. R. (eds.) (2003) *Control Theories of Crime and Delinquency*. New Brunswick, NJ: Transaction.

Bursik, R. J., Jr. and Grasmick, H. G. (1993) *Neighborhoods and Crime*. New York: Lexington.

Colvin, M. (2000) *Crime & Coercion*. New York: St. Martin's Press.

Goode, E. (ed.) (2008) *Out of Control: Assessing the General Theory of Crime*. Stanford, CA: Stanford University Press.

Gottfredson, M. R. (2006) "The empirical status of control theory in criminology," in F. T. Cullen, J. P. Wright, and K. R. Blevins (eds.) *Taking Stock: The Status of Criminological Theory*. New Brunswick, NJ: Transaction.

Gottfredson, M. R. and Hirschi, T. (1990) *A General Theory of Crime*. Stanford, CA: Stanford University Press.

Gottfredson, M. R. and Hirschi, T. (2006) "Self-control and opportunity," in C. L. Britt and M. R. Gottfredson (eds.) *Control Theories of Crime and Delinquency*. New Brunswick, NJ: Transaction.

Grasmick, H. G., Tittle, C. R., Bursik, R. J., and Arneklev, B. J. (1993) "Testing the core empirical implications of Gottfredson and Hirschi's general theory of crime." *Journal of Research in Crime and Delinquency* 30:5–29.

Greenberg, D. F. (2008) "Age, sex, and racial distributions of crime," in E. Goode (ed.) *Out of Control: Assessing the General Theory of Crime*. Stanford, CA: Stanford University Press.

Hay, C. and Forrest, W. (2006) "The development of self-control: Examining self-control's stability thesis." *Criminology* 44:739–774.

Hirschi, T. (1969) *Causes of Delinquency*. Berkeley: University of California Press.

Kennedy, D. M. (1998) "Pulling levers: Getting deterrence right." *National Institute of Justice Journal* 236:2–8.

Kornhauser, R. R. (1978) *Social Sources of Delinquency*. Chicago, IL: University of Chicago Press.

Kubrin, C. E., Stuck, T. D., and Krohn, M. D. (2009) *Researching Theories of Crime and Deviance*. New York: Oxford University Press.

Matza, D. (1964) *Delinquency and Drift*. New York: Wiley.

Nye, I. F. (1958) *Family Relationships and Delinquent Behavior*. New York: Wiley.

Patterson, G. R., Reid, J. B., and Dishion, T. J. (1992) *Antisocial Boys*. Eugene, OR: Castalia.

Pratt, T. C. and Cullen, F. T. (2000) "The empirical status of Gottfredson and Hirschi's general theory of crime." *Criminology* 38:931–964.

Reckless, W. C. (1961) "A new theory of crime and delinquency." *Federal Probation* 25:42–46.

Reiss, A. J., Jr. (1951) "Delinquency as the failure of personal and social controls." *American Sociological Review* 16:196–207.

Sampson, Robert J. (2006) "Collective efficacy theory: Lessons learned and directions for further inquiry," in Francis T. Cullen, John Paul Wright, and Kristie R. Blevins (eds.) *Taking Stock: The Status of Criminological Theory*. New Brunswick, NJ: Transaction.

Sampson, R. J. and Groves, W. B. (1989) "Community structure and crime: Testing social-disorganization theory." *American Journal of Sociology* 94:774–802.

Sampson, R. J. and Laub, J. H. (1993) *Crime in the Making*. Cambridge, MA: Harvard University Press.

Sampson, R. J. and Raudenbush, S. W. (1999) "Systematic observation of public spaces: A new look at disorder in urban neighborhoods." *American Journal of Sociology* 105:603–651.

Sampson, R. J. and Wilson, W. J. (1995) "Toward a theory of race, crime, and urban inequality," in J. Hagan and R. Peterson (eds.) *Crime and Inequality*. Stanford, CA: Stanford University Press.

Shaw, Clifford R. and McKay, Henry D. (1942) *Juvenile Delinquency and Urban Areas*. Chicago, IL: University of Chicago Press.

Toby, J. (1957) "Social disorganization and stake in conformity: Complementary factors in the predatory behavior of hoodlums." *Journal of Criminal Law, Criminology, and Police Science* 48:17–19.

Vold, G. B., Bernard, T. J., and Snipes, J. B. (2009) *Theoretical Criminology*. New York: Oxford university Press.

Wright, B. R. E., Caspi, A., Moffitt, T. E., and Silva, P. A. (1999) "Low self control, social bonds, and crime: Social causation, social selection, or both?" *Criminology* 37:479–514.

Wright, J. P. and Beaver, K. M. (2005) "Do parents matter in creating self-control in their children?" *Criminology* 43:1169–1202.

14

Labeling theory

Ryken Grattet

Labeling theory views deviance as a product of the social interaction between individuals and various types of audience, such as parents, peer groups, anonymous onlookers, and, perhaps most extensively, representatives of formal social control organizations. Deviance is a designation—a label—that is attached to some individuals and not others. Individuals labeled deviant can experience a number of psychological and social consequences by being labeled, including the cultivation of deviant identity, increased likelihood of further involvement in deviant behavior, stigma, and blocked opportunities for social advancement. While labeling theory is a broad perspective on all sorts of deviance (e.g., mental illness, crime, welfare dependency) it emerged as a critique of mainstream approaches in criminology that focused on psychological, biological, and environmental causes of crime. The term "labeling theory" is frequently used interchangeably with the "interactionist" approach to deviance and "societal reaction theory".

Labeling theory was the subject of intense criticism during the late 1960s and 1970s (Gove 1970, 1980 [1975], Hagan 1973, Lemert 1981, Manning 1973, Tittle 1980 [1975]), as well as a spirited defense (Lemert 1981, Petrunik 1980, Schur 1969, Scheff 1974). Some have declared that labeling ideas have become "orthodoxy" (Plummer 2001), while others have declared it "dead" (see Paternoster and Iovanni 1989). The former seems more apt than the latter, as many of the core themes of labeling theory are manifest in recent work on deviance and social control decision-making, although seldom is the tradition explicitly invoked.

The origins and early foundations of the labeling perspective

The earliest roots of labeling theory lie in George Herbert Mead's 1918 essay on "The Psychology of Punitive Justice," which focused on the social significance of community and legal responses to criminals and other kinds of social enemies (Mead 1918, Schur 1969). Another foundational text is Frank Tannenbaum's (1938) *Crime and the Community*, which focused on the role of "tagging" young delinquents in the criminal justice system. According to Tannenbaum, the first imposition of a label—a "dramatization of evil"—sets in motion a psychological process by which the juvenile comes to self-identify as a "criminal." "The process of making the criminal, therefore, is a process of tagging, defining, identifying, segregating, describing, emphasizing, making conscious and self-conscious; it becomes a way of stimulating, suggesting, emphasizing, and evoking the very traits that are complained of". (Tannenbaum 1938: 19)

However, a fuller and more influential point of origin is Edwin Lemert's book *Social Pathology* (1951). *Social Pathology* put forward a broad analytical framework and programmatic statement on deviance and social control—although it is replete with examples as well—which Lemert envisioned as a counter to the biological, psychological, psychiatric, social disorganization, and other prevailing etiological approaches to social pathologies. Lemert later wrote that his aim in developing the societal reaction approach was "to show how deviance was shaped and stabilized by efforts to eliminate or ameliorate it" (1974: 458). Among the most enduring contributions was his delineation of "primary" and "secondary" deviation. Lemert regarded deviance as "polygenetic"; in other words, the "original causes and antecedents of deviant behaviors are many and diversified" (1951: 603) and, in doing so, he set aside, somewhat dismissively, the pursuit of further etiological analyses of deviant behavior. Instead, he argued that the sociologically significant aspect of deviant behavior lies not in understanding involvement in deviant activities, some portion of which never rises to the attention or concern of others, but in those circumstances where the reaction of others results in a reorganization of the self. The former was primary and the latter—the sociologically significant part—secondary deviation. *"When a person begins to employ his deviant behavior or a role based upon it as a means of defense, attack, or adjustment to the overt and problems created by the consequent societal reaction to him, his deviation is secondary"* (Lemert 1951: 640; original italics).

In the early 1960s, the perspective began to be elaborated. John Kitsuse (1962) published "Societal Reaction to Deviant Behavior: Problems of Theory and Method," which, among other things, directed attention to the operation of social control organizations.

> A sociological theory of deviance must focus specifically upon the interactions which not only define behaviors as deviant but also organize and activate the application of sanctions by individuals, groups, or agencies. For in modern society, the socially significant differentiation of deviants from the non-deviant population is increasingly contingent upon circumstances of situation, place, social and personal biography, and the bureaucratically organized activities of agencies of control.
>
> *(Kitsuse 1962: 256)*

Howard Becker followed with *Outsiders* in 1963, which put forward several important conceptual tools, such as the sequential model of deviance, moral entrepreneurs, and "secret deviance," as well as a definition of deviance—later made controversial by Gibbs (1966)—as *"not* a quality of the act the person commits, but rather a consequence of the application by others of rules and sanctions to the 'offender'" (Becker 1963: 9; emphasis in original). *Outsiders* also included an analysis of the role of "moral entrepreneurs" in the legal construction of deviant labels (see also Gusfield 1963). In doing so, Becker initiated another line of research that was less about the social interactions involved in labeling and more about the social and political origins of the labels themselves (Jenness 2004).

Becker amplified the attitude of earlier research that deviants were best studied naturalistically—"in their natural habitat" (1963: 170)—rather than through surveys or official records, as earlier social pathology research had tended to do. The naturalistic approach linked societal reaction proponents to the American interpretivist tradition in sociology, with roots in the Chicago School and its "West Coast" manifestation in the 1950s and 1960s (Lemert 1974). Interpretive studies of deviants and deviance proliferated for a time (Becker 1963, Goffman 1961, Lofland 1969, Matza 1969, Scheff 1966, Sykes and Matza 1957) and were a direct reaction to the prevailing scholarship and popular wisdom about crime and other kinds of deviance—that these subjects could be understood through an assessment of psychological precursors or as a result of structural conditions and where the central question was etiological: that is, what caused someone to be deviant? At least some of the labeling proponents trace their perspective back to symbolic interactionism (Schur 1969), which gained popularity in the 1950s and 1960s in response to the dominance of structural functionalism during the previous decades (Fine 1993, Pfohl 1994). Links to conflict perspectives on crime, law, and deviance are also apparent (Chambliss 1964, Lofland 1969, Gusfield 1963, Schur 1971).

For a short time, roughly from the late 1960s to the mid-1970s, the labeling perspective was a key battlefield upon which the ongoing debate between positivist and interpretivist wings of American sociology took place. During this period, articles informed by the perspective, as well as critical assessments of it, proliferated in mainstream sociological journals (Petrunik 1980, Paternoster and Iovanni 1989). These criticisms and the debates that followed them were frequently quite bitter in tone and, three decades later, it is clear that there were many instances when each side misconstrued, mischaracterized, or narrowly represented the other's point.

Criticisms emerged from both within and without the perspective. Critics argued many of the core concepts were poorly defined (Gibbs 1966, Gove 1970, Hagan 1973, Manning 1973); that it was not a theory because most or all of its central arguments did not lead to testable propositions about the causes of deviance (Akers 1968, Becker 1973, Bernstein, Kelly, and Doyle 1977, Bordua 1967, Gibbs 1966); that the perspective was freighted with political and moral overtones—that its proponents identified and sometimes championed the deviants and demonized the social control agents (Liazos 1972); that it often advocated a radical constructionism in which an individual's actual behavior was deemed irrelevant to the labeling process (Gove 1980 [1975]); and that it produced many facile analyses of deviants and the labeling process (Lemert 1981).[1]

Critics also focused on testing what they thought were two key empirical implications of the labeling perspective (Tittle 1975, 1980 [1975]). The first hypothesis is that social variables unrelated to the rule-breaking behavior, particularly such indicators of social disadvantage as race and class, are influential in the application of labels by sanctioning agents and organizations. The second hypothesis is that a consequence of labeling is further involvement in deviant behavior. Paternoster and Iovanni (1989) call the first hypothesis the "status characteristics" hypothesis and the second the "secondary deviation" hypothesis. According to Tittle (1980 [1975]: 259),

> Neither of the major propositions of labeling theory finds much support in the available data concerning crime. It does not appear that disadvantage has more influence on criminal labeling than actual rule-breaking, nor does it appear that labeling leads generally to crime or even that it increases the probability of rule-breaking more often than it decreases it.

However, Tittle's empirical critique of labeling theory has been rejected by subsequent writers (Paternoster and Iovanni 1989, Pfohl 1994, Triplett 1993), and research has continued to accumulate on both the status characteristics and secondary deviation hypotheses, as well as other aspects of the perspective.

Consequences of labeling

Paternoster and Iovanni (1989) offered a review and synthesis of labeling research since the 1970s. They argue that, despite the critical responses of the 1970s, most of the theoretical nuances of labeling arguments remain untested. They reformulate both the status characteristics and secondary deviation hypotheses, building in more contingency, such that how status characteristics affect labeling and how labeling affects subsequent involvement in deviance are dependent upon attributes of offenders, their offending backgrounds, as well as environmental and organizational conditions (see also Bernburg and Krohn 2003, Bernburg, Krohn, and Rivera 2006, Chiricos, Barrick, Bales, and Bontrager 2007, Sherman, Smith, Schmidt, and Rogan 1992). Paternoster and Iovanni conclude that the potential of labeling remains untapped as yet, arguing that "work conducted thus far says more about its critics than about labeling theory itself" (1989: 389).

In the last two decades, contributions and refinements to the perspective have continued. Ross Matsueda's (1992) study of delinquents shifted the focus from labeling by official social control agents and agencies to the informal social control involved in labeling by parents. He showed that "reflected appraisals"—appraisals by significant others regarding a juvenile's behavior—affects the juvenile's self-conception and, in turn, their involvement in delinquency. "Those who see themselves (from the standpoint of others) as persons who engage in delinquent behavior in certain situations are more likely to engage in delinquency" (Matsueda 1992: 1582).

Work on labeling in mental illness has also been a fertile area for refinements labeling theory, focusing mostly on elaborating Goffman's concept of stigma. Link and Phelan (2001: 363) note that "research since Goffman's seminal essay has been incredibly productive, leading to elaborations, conceptual refinements, and repeated demonstrations of the negative impact of stigma on the lives of the stigmatized." Link himself put forward a "modified labeling theory" of mental illness which moderates the older assumption that the actual behavior of the mental patient is irrelevant, or of little relevance, in the labeling process. In doing so, he and his colleagues sought a middle ground where behavior need not be seen as irrelevant to labeling and where the focus could shift to the kinds of intervening processes and factors—attributes of individuals, actions, or situations—that increase or decrease the effect of labeling. For example, in a 1989 paper, Link and his colleagues examined how the social control agent's perceptions of patient dangerousness and social distance make the labeling effect more pronounced (Link, Cullen, Struening, Shrout, and Dohrenwend 1989).

Other work focuses on the collateral consequences associated with labeling. This work suggests that labeling affects subsequent deviance not by a transformation of the deviant's identity but by the creation of structural impediments to successful reintegration into society (e.g., voting rights, occupational prohibitions, residential restrictions). Sampson and Laub (1997) focus on the structural impediments produced by labeling in their work on the life-course criminology. They contend that there is only "one theoretical perspective in criminology that is inherently developmental in nature—labeling theory" (Sampson and Laub 1997: 3). They put forward the notion of "cumulative disadvantage," which refers to the consequences of iterative involvement in criminal sanctioning over the life course.

Cumulative disadvantage is generated most explicitly by the negative structural consequences of criminal offending and official sanctions for life chances. The theory specifically suggests a "snowball" effect—that adolescent delinquency and its negative consequences (e.g., arrest, official labeling, incarceration) increasingly "mortgage" one's future, especially later life chances molded by school and employment (Sampson and Laub 1997: 15).

The structural consequences they refer to represent products of labeling that, in turn, make desistance more difficult. The obstacles faced by convicted felons in reintegrating is a central theme of recent research on parole and reentry (Petersilia 2003, Travis 2005). Uggen and Manza (2006) focus on the consequences of felon disenfranchisement for both the felons themselves and the larger polity. Western (2006) examines the effects of incarceration on work, marriage, and family outcomes—all potential turning points in the process of desistance and all of which are made more challenging by incarceration.

Pager's recent book *Marked* (2007), which makes no explicit links to the labeling tradition, examines the effect of a criminal record on employment outcomes. She uses the concept of a "negative credential" to describe these effects. "Negative credentials are those official markers that restrict access and opportunity rather than enabling them" (Pager 2007: 32). Pager finds that negative credentialing is particularly consequential for blacks—that black offenders have "two strikes" against them when it comes to securing a job by virtue of their race and their criminal histories. Her work is also useful for countering the simplistic treatments of the secondary deviation hypothesis—that labeling leads directly to further involvement in deviance. She details the way criminal labeling affects employment opportunities, which leads to greater likelihood of reinvolvement in crime (see also Uggen 2000). The lesson, which resonates with Link's focus on the contingency of labeling effects, is that labeling produces intervening processes that themselves may generate further involvement, or, in some cases, desistance. Thus, despite the declarations of its demise, a few studies in criminology continue to expand and deepen our understanding of the interactional dynamics and consequences of labeling.

Social control decision-making

In addition to work on the consequences of labeling, other work has continued on the causes of labeling. This work has moved beyond the status characteristics hypothesis (e.g., race, gender, disadvantage) to a wider focus on the organizational context of social control decision-making. Drass and Spencer (1987; see also Spencer 1983) found that probation officers' decision-making is rooted in a "theory of office," which is a kind of working ideology (or conceptual toolkit) officers use to deal with probationer deviance. In the case of probation officers, the theory of office vacillates between a legalistic/social control framework and a casework/counseling framework. Labeling decisions are contingent upon the ideological frameworks and circumstances of social control agents. Cavender and Knepper (1992: 398) found similar processes in their study of juvenile parole revocation decision-making: "We see a theory of office, its organizational context, and accompanying accounts as integrated features of the decision-making gestalt." From this work, it is clear that how social control agencies operate requires explication of both the cognitive frameworks social control decision-makers use and the organizational constraints they face.

Along these lines, another important development in research on social control decision-making comes from sentencing research. This work is most associated with Darrell Steffensmeier, Jeffrey Ulmer, and their colleagues (Kramer and Ulmer 2002, Steffensmeier, Ulmer, and Kramer 1998, Ulmer and Kramer 1996, Ulmer 1997, Ulmer and Bradley 2006) on the "focal concerns" of social control decision-makers, which contends that sanctioning decisions are made with respect to three general criteria: estimations of the blameworthiness of the deviant; assessments of the deviant's dangerousness and risk to participate in further deviant behavior; and bureaucratic constraints. For example, Ulmer and Bradley (2006: 658) found that differences in the "perceived group threats and in practical political constraints and incentives between court community contexts—are key reasons behind the patterns in jury trial penalties we have found among serious violent offenses." Also, confirming Emerson's (1983) emphasis on caseload management as a key factor in understanding social control decision-making, Ulmer and Bradley found some evidence that bureaucratic constraints stemming from caseload pressures impacted sanctions.

As such, research on social control decision-making has moved beyond assessing the impact of status characteristics on labeling to consider a broader array of organizational and ideological factors.

Conclusion

Although it is seldom referred to by name in much of the recent research, the labeling perspective is not dead. Perhaps the best indicator of its enduring impact is the degree to which its ideas have bled into adjacent areas. As discussed above, labeling ideas have begun to make inroads into life-course criminology, research on social control organizations (e.g., minority group threat), and research (not reviewed here) on the social construction of social problems and "criminalization" (see Jenness 2004). In this sense, Plummer (2001) is right: for better or worse, labeling has quietly become part of the orthodoxy of the sociological study of deviant behavior.

Note

1 These latter points, regarding radical constructionist, overly politicized, and facile analyses, mostly relate to the execution of research done under the banner of labeling theory, and thus do not represent inherent problems with perspective. For example, most analyses in the labeling perspective did not embrace radical constructionism, denying entirely the role of behavior and "objective" influences on the labeling process. Moreover, it is not essential to hold that the individuals labeled deviant are heroic figures and the social control agents evil-doers. And if overly simplistic analyses were a serious criticism then many other perspectives in sociology would be equally problematic.

References

Akers, Ronald L. 1968. "Problems in the Sociology of Deviance: Social Definitions and Behavior." *Social Forces* 46(4): 455–465.

Albonetti, Celesta. 1991. "An Integration of Theories to Explain Judicial Discretion." *Social Problems* 38: 247–266.

Becker, Howard S. 1963. *Outsiders*. Glencoe, IL: The Free Press.

——. 1973. "Labeling Theory Reconsidered." In Howard S. Becker, *Outsiders*, revised edition. New York: The Free Press.

Bernburg, Jon Gunnar, and Marvin D. Krohn. 2003. "Labeling, Life Chances and Adult Crime: The Direct and Indirect Effects of Official Intervention in Adolescence on Crime in Early Adulthood." *Criminology* 41: 1287–1318.

Bernburg, Jon Gunnar, Marvin D. Krohn, and Craig J. Rivera. 2006. "Official Labeling, Criminal Embeddedness, and Subsequent Delinquency: A Longitudinal Test of Labeling Theory." *Journal of Research in Crime and Delinquency* 43: 67–88.

Bernstein, Ilene Nagel, William R. Kelly, and Patricia A. Doyle. 1977. "Societal Reaction to Deviants: The Case of Criminal Defendants." *American Sociological Review* 42(5): 743–755.

Bordua, David. 1967. "Recent Trends: Deviant Behavior and Social Control." *Annals of the American Academy of Political and Social Science* 369: 149–163.

Cavender, Gray and Paul Knepper. 1992. "Strange Interlude: An Analysis of Juvenile Parole Revocation Decision Making." *Social Problems* 39(4): 387–399.

Chambliss, William. J. 1964. "A Sociological Analysis of the Law of Vagrancy." *Social Problems* 12: 67–77.

Chiricos, Ted, Kellie Barrick, William Bales, and Stephanie Bontrager. 2007. "The Labeling of Convicted Felons and Its Consequences for Recidivism." *Criminology* 45(2): 547–581.

Drass, Kriss A., and J. William Spencer. 1987. "Accounting for Pre-Sentencing Recommendations: Typologies and Probation Officers' Theory of Office." *Social Problems* 34(3): 277–293.

Emerson, Robert. 1983. "Holistic Effects in Social Control Decision-Making." *Law and Society Review* 17(3): 425–455.

Fine, Gary Alan. 1993. "The Sad Demise, Mysterious Disappearance, and Glorious Triumph of Symbolic Interactionism." *Annual Review of Sociology* 19: 61–87.

Gibbs, Jack P. 1966. "Conceptions of Deviant Behavior: The Old and the New." *Pacific Sociological Review* 9: 9–19.

Goffman, Erving. 1961. *Asylums*. New York: Doubleday Anchor.

Gove, Walter R. 1970. "Societal Reaction as an Explanation of Mental Illness: An Evaluation." *American Sociological Review* 35(5): 873–884.

—— (ed.). 1980 [1975]. *The Labelling of Deviance: Evaluating a Perspective*. New York: Halsted.

Gusfield, Joseph. 1963. *Symbolic Crusade*. Urbana: University of Illinois Press.

Hagan, John L. 1973. "Conceptual Deficiencies of an Interactionist Perspective in 'Deviance.'" *Criminology* 11: 383–404.

Jenness, Valerie. 2004. "Explaining Criminalization: From Demography and Status Politics to Globalization and Modernization." *Annual Review of Sociology* 30: 141–171.

Kitsuse, John I. 1962. "Societal Reaction to Deviant Behavior: Problems of Theory and Method." *Social Problems* 9(3): 247–256.

Kramer, John H., and Jeffery T. Ulmer. 2002. "Downward Departures for Serious Violent Offenders: Local Court 'Corrections' to Pennsylvania's Sentencing Guidelines." *Criminology* 40: 601–636.

Lemert, Edwin M. 1951. *Social Pathology: A Systematic Approach to the Theory of Sociopathic Behavior*. New York: McGraw-Hill.

——. 1974. "Beyond Mead: The Societal Reaction to Deviance." *Social Problems* 21 (4): 457–468.

——. 1981. "Issues in the Study of Deviance." *Sociological Quarterly* 22 (2): 285–305.

Liazos, Alexander. 1972. "The Poverty of the Sociology of Deviance: Nuts, Sluts, and Perverts." *Social Problems* 20: 103–120.

Link, Bruce, Francis T. Cullen, Elmer Struening, Patrick E. Shrout, and Bruce Dohrenwend. 1989. "A Modified Labeling Theory Approach to Mental Disorders: An Empirical Assessment." *American Sociological Review* 54: 400–423.

Link, Bruce G., and Jo C. Phelan. 2001. "Conceptualizing Stigma." *Annual Review of Sociology* 27: 363–385.

Lofland, John. 1969. *Deviance and Identity*. Englewood Cliffs, NJ: Prentice-Hall.

Manning, Peter K. 1973. "Review of *Images of Deviance* by Stanley Cohen, *Social Deviance* by Daniel Glaser, *Human Deviance, Social Problems, and Social Control* by Edwin Lemert, *Becoming Deviant* by David Matza, *Labeling Deviant Behavior* by Edwin M. Schur." *Contemporary Sociology* 2 (2): 123–128.

Matsueda, Ross L. 1992. "Reflected Appraisals, Parental Labeling and Delinquency: Specifying a Symbolic Interactionist Theory." *American Journal of Sociology* 97: 1577–1611.

Matza, David. 1969. *Becoming Deviant*. Englewood Cliffs, NJ: Prentice-Hall.

Mead, Georg Herbert. 1918. "The Psychology of Punitive Justice." *American Journal of Sociology* 23 (5): 577–602.

Pager, Devah. 2007. *Marked: Race, Crime, and Finding Work in the Era of Mass Incarceration*. Chicago, IL: University of Chicago Press.

Paternoster, Raymond, and Leeann Iovanni. 1989. "The Labeling Perspective and Delinquency: An Elaboration of the Theory and an Assessment of the Evidence." *Justice Quarterly* 6 (3): 359–394.

Petersilia, Joan. 2003. *When Prisoners Come Home: Parole and Prisoner Reentry*. New York: Oxford University Press.

Petrunik, Michael. 1980. "The Rise and Fall of 'Labelling Theory': The Construction and Destruction of a Sociological Strawman." *Canadian Journal of Sociology / Cahiers canadiens de sociologie* 5 (3): 213–233.

Pfohl, Stephen J. 1994. *Images of Deviance and Social Control: A Sociological History*. New York: McGraw-Hill.

Plummer, Kenneth. 2001. "Labeling Theory." In Clifton Bryant (ed.) *Encyclopedia of Criminology and Deviant Behavior*, Volume 1. New York: Routledge.

Sampson, Robert J. and John Laub. 1997. "A Life-Course Theory of Cumulative Disadvantage and the Stability of Delinquency." In Terry Thornberry (ed.) *Developmental Theories of Crime and Delinquency*. New Brunswick, NJ: Transaction.

Scheff, Thomas J. 1966. *Being Mentally Ill*. Chicago, IL: Aldine.

——. 1974. "The Labelling Theory of Mental Illness." *American Sociological Review* 39 (3): 444–452.

Schur, Edwin M. 1969. "Reactions to Deviance: A Critical Assessment." *American Journal of Sociology* 75 (3): 309–322.

——. 1971. *Labeling Deviant Behavior*. New York: Harper and Row.

Sherman, Lawrence W., Douglas A. Smith, Janell D. Schmidt, and Dennis P. Rogan. 1992. "Crime, Punishment and Stake in Conformity: Legal and Informal Control of Domestic Violence." *American Sociological Review* 57: 680–690.

Spencer, Jack W. 1983. "Accounts, Attitudes, and Solutions: Probation Officer–Defendant Negotiations of Subjective Orientations." *Social Problems* 30 (5): 570–581.

Steffensmeier, Darrell. 1980. "Assessing the Impact of the Women's Movement on Sex-Based Differences in the Handling of Adult Criminal Defendants." *Crime & Delinquency* 26: 344–357.

Steffensmeier, Darrell, Jeffery T. Ulmer, and John Kramer. 1998. "The Interaction of Race, Gender, and Age in Criminal Sentencing: The Punishment Cost of Being Young, Black, and Male." *Criminology* 36: 763–798.

Sykes, Gresham, and Matza, David. 1957. "Techniques of Neutralization: A Theory of Delinquency." *American Sociological Review* 22 (2): 664–670.

Tannenbaum, Frank. 1938. *Crime and the Community*. New York: Columbia University Press.

Tittle, Charles. R. 1975. "Deterrents or Labeling?" *Social Forces* 53 (3): 399–410.

——. 1980 [1975]. "The Labelling Perspective: An Overview." In Walter Gove (ed.) *The Labelling of Deviance: Evaluating a Perspective*. New York: John Wiley and Sons.

Travis, Jeremy. 2005. *But They All Come Back: Facing the Challenges of Prisoner Reentry*. Washington, DC: Urban Institute.

Triplett, Ruth. 1993. "The Conflict Perspective, Symbolic Interactionism, and the Status Characteristics Hypothesis." *Justice Quarterly* 10 (4): 541–558.

Uggen, Christopher. 2000. "Work as a Turning Point in the Life Course of Criminals: A Duration Model of Age, Employment, and Recidivism." *American Sociological Review* 67: 529–546.

Uggen, Christopher, and Jeff Manza. 2006. *Locked out: Felon Disenfranchisement and American Democracy*. New York: Oxford University Press.

Ulmer, Jeffery T. 1997. *Social Worlds of Sentencing: Court Communities under Sentencing Guidelines*. Albany: State University of New York Press.

Ulmer, Jeffrey T., and Mindy S. Bradley. 2006. "Variation in Trial Penalties among Serious Violent Offenses." *Criminology* 44 (3): 631–670.

Ulmer, Jeffery T., and John Kramer. 1996. "Court Communities under Sentencing Guidelines: Dilemmas of Formal Rationality and Sentencing Disparity." *Criminology* 3: 306–332.

Western, Bruce. 2006. *Punishment and Inequality in America*. New York: Russell Sage Foundation Press.

15

Phenomenological theory

David Polizzi

Introduction

The study of crime has traditionally focused on the relationship between criminal behavior and its causal determinants. Whether situated within the individual or identified as the artifact of pre-existing social structures, criminal behavior or deviance has been understood and explained as the result of an underlying set of individual or social deficits (Arrigo, Milovanovic, 2009). However, such a formulation of deviance seems to ignore perhaps the most important aspect of this type of behavior: that is, the way in which this experience is understood and made meaningful by those involved in a deviant lifestyle (Katz, 1988). Such a focus demands that we turn away from causal explanations of criminal behavior and begin to explore the subjective contours of such experiences, which seem to defy or go beyond objectified or generalizable conclusions related to the meaning and nature of the criminal act. Phenomenology provides an appropriate theoretical frame of reference by which to explore these concerns.

It is important to keep in mind that this chapter will not be proposing a theory of deviance but, rather, a phenomenology of deviance. Such a distinction is an important one and needs to be explored further. A phenomenology of deviance is focused on the subjective experience of the deviant act that may or may not be viewed as deviant or problematic by the individual. The experience of gang involvement or the experience of drug use or addiction takes on a much different hue when viewed from a phenomenological frame of reference. Within this context, causal explanations are replaced by subjective accounts of the event, which in turn provide this experience its unique lived-meaning from the perspective of the individual. For example, the fact of gang membership does not explain or describe the way in which each respective member comes to understand their participation in the gang lifestyle. The fact of illegal drug use tells us very little about the individualized ritual of addiction, which each addict undergoes in pursuit of their drug of choice.

The phenomenology of deviance, then, attempts to study the experience of the criminal act from the perspective of the individual. Individual experience, rather than being a collection of objective facts, is a collection of lived-meanings that emerge from one's involvement with a specific shared social world (Giorgi, 2009). The attempt to understand the various nuances of the gang experience is fundamentally predicated upon and limited by the specific perspective each individual brings to that project. What this implies is that individual experience is always perspectival and always influenced by a specific social context, which in turn evokes a variety of social meanings consistent with the lived-reality of that context. However, before we go any further, a brief exploration of the theoretical assumptions of phenomenology is in order.

Toward a phenomenology of deviance: a brief theoretical overview

Taken in its strictest sense, the term "phenomenology," whose origin dates back to the mid-18th century, is concerned with the way the world is perceived (Spinelli, 2005). However, in order to understand this reality better, a distinction must be made between the world as perceived and the world as it actually is. To be able to clarify this distinction, a question needs to be asked: does the perception of the world reflect a true representation of the world as it actually exists or is it simply an experience of the world from a unique perspective? (Hart, 2007). Edmund Husserl, the founder of phenomenology, made this question a central focus of his philosophy (Cerbone, 2006; Giorgi, 2009; Hart, 2007; Marion, 1998 [1989]; Spinelli, 2005).

Most fundamental to the project of Husserl's transcendental phenomenology is the way in which the world appears to a perceiving consciousness, a process which provides both structure and meaning to the perceptual field (Cerbone, 2006; Gurwitsch, 1964; Polizzi and Arrigo, 2009). Because consciousness is always a consciousness of something for Husserl, little emphasis is given to the study of the objective reality of the world as a separate philosophical category (Edie, 1987; Kohak, 1978; Marion, 1998 [1989]). However, this does not imply that the existence of the world is somehow contingent upon a perceiving consciousness; only that the experience of the world always emerges from a specific perspective that is always limited in its ability to capture the reality of the world in a complete or total way (Marion, 2008 [2005]). The same would be true concerning the perception of a specific experience, situation or event.

Take, for example, the experience of illegal drug use. Though the phenomenology of this experience may share a variety of characteristics that are more or less specific to this phenomenon, its actual lived-meaning will likely be perceived differently depending upon the unique perspective of the individual. The meaning of illegal drug use is obviously perceived much differently when taken from the perspective of a law enforcement officer than it is from the perspective of someone who is seeking to buy or sell the substance (Polizzi, 2007). The fact of the illegality of such behavior reflects only one perspectival concern that may not even be perceived as important or significant when contextualized from the perspective of the active drug user. The experiential variability of these lived-meanings is explained by Husserl through his concept of intentionality (Giorgi, 2009; Hart, 2007; Sokolowski, 2000).

Intentionality is concerned with the way in which consciousness directs or intends conscious awareness toward a specific target of perception from a specific point of view (Caputo, 2007; Cerbone, 2006; Gurwitsch, 1964; Husserl, 1982; Natanson, 1973; Sokolowski, 2000). It is through this intentional engagement with the world that the world appears and becomes meaningful to human consciousness. However, it is important to reiterate that individual perception does not create those "objects" which appear to consciousness and does not create the world, only the point of reference from which the object becomes accessible and meaningful to the perceiving subject (Edie, 1987; Natanson, 1973). Perhaps stated more simply, there is always more to the object than meets the eye. Much like the above example of illegal drug use, the meaning of individual experience always remains contingent to that experience and, given this limitation, can never exhaust the possibility of its meaning.

However, individual perception is never without its context, a context which is also shared by others. Included within this intentional relationship with a world is the relationship with other people and the way in which their influence also helps to provide meaning to the world as perceived experience. However, such a formulation departs from the transcendental phenomenology of Edmund Husserl, away from the specific focus upon consciousness and perception, and toward what has been labeled phenomenology's existential turn, initiated by the work of Martin Heidegger (Spinelli, 2005).

Heidegger (1962 [1927]), in his classic text *Being and Time*, redirects the project of phenomenology toward a reexamination of the meaning of being (Sheehan, 2007). Being-in-the-world—or Dasein—describes for Heidegger the basic ontological character of human existence. Heidegger uses this term to designate the uniqueness of human being, through its ability both to consider and illuminate the possibilities and limits of existence (Cohn, 2002; Letteri, 2009; Spinelli, 2005). For Heidegger, "Dasein's relation to the world is not to be thought of as the formal relations between one thing (Dasein) and another (that with which Dasein concerns itself)" (Macann, 1993: 72). Rather, for Heidegger, the world is the fundamental characteristic of Dasein itself (Sheehan, 2007). Stated more simply, human being is not possible in the absence of a world. As such, being-in-the-world always finds itself situated within a variety of social contexts that are not of its own exclusive making or control. The possibilities for the meaning of human experience become predicated upon the realities of one's social existence, which may hinder or evoke being-in-the-world's unique potentiality. Though being-in-the-world may pursue a specific set of projects or experiences, these actions are never isolated and must always take into account the social reality or context from which they emerge. Heidegger has defined the social character of being-in-the-world with his term "publicness."

For Heidegger, publicness describes the ontological social character of human existence. It is that which structures our social relatedness and gives shared meaning to our everyday experience (Heidegger, 1962 [1927]; Zimmerman, 1981). Heidegger has defined this possibility as the "they–self." It is the they–self which defines the meaning of the world and removes that burden from us. Heidegger (1962 [1927]: 165), in his discussion of the "they," states,

> Thus the "they" maintains itself factically in the averageness of that which belongs to it, of that which it regards as valid, and that which it does not, and of that to which it grants success and to that which it denies. In this averageness with which it prescribes what can and cannot be ventured, it keeps watch over everything exceptional that thrusts itself to the fore.

From this perspective, social reality can never be understood as a construct solely derived by an individual subject; rather, it becomes that possibility for human experience which is brought forth through being-in-the-world's intervolvement with the they–self. Being-in-the-world always finds itself thrown into social situations or contexts that attempt to define the possibilities for human experience. Heidegger's concept of "thrownness" recognizes the powerful influence that culture and history impose relative to the way in which human being is defined and lived. The possibilities open to being-in-the-world are recognized or denied based on the quality and openness of this thrown reality.

Thrownness, then, implies the specific contextualized ground for human existence that is both open to possibility and yet limited by preexisting cultural and social meanings concerning the limits of human expression and potential (Cerbone, 2006; May, 1986). "As such, my existence is always *situated* in a structure, or set of thrown conditions, whose presence I neither chose nor can truly control" (Spinelli, 2005: 113; emphasis in original). What remains for human existence is the way in which these structures are made meaningful and actually lived. For example, the individual who finds him- or herself situated within the social context of racism, sexism, poverty, and so on may have little control over the overwhelming realities these types of meaning-generating processes impose upon human experience. However, the way in which these processes become defined and made meaningful for existence remains up to individual choice. An example of this can be witnessed in the gang lifestyle.

The phenomenology of the gang experience and its relationship to a theory of deviance

As has been suggested above, it would be theoretically inappropriate, if not incorrect, to attempt to offer a phenomenological formulation concerning the theory of deviant behavior. Such an approach would, by necessity, need to establish a certain set of factors or variables that would identify this construct, while at the same time rejecting or ignoring those aspects of this experience that are not reflected within the specific set of legalistic assumptions this definition would evoke. A phenomenology of deviance is most concerned with the experience and meaning that this type of behavior has for the individual, prior to its construction as deviant or criminal, or in spite of the presence of these socially contextualized meanings. However, it is also important to note that such a formulation does not preclude the inclusion of more legalistic constructions, which must also be recognized as part of this phenomenon; only that its meaning cannot be limited to them.

An example of this process can be witnessed in the phenomenology of the gang lifestyle. Though it is certainly true that a variety of gang behaviors or activities can be identified as being deviant or criminal, it is equally true that such formulations provide very little insight into the actual meaning this experience has for gang members. Take, for example, the now infamous Central American gang Mara Salvatrucha (or MS-13).

The roots of MS-13 can be found in the ruinous civil conflict that ravaged El Salvador for a good portion of the 1970s through the early 1990s; a conflict which was fueled and funded by the competing ideological interests of the Cold War (Dunn, 2007; Kovacic, 2007–2008). As a result, many individuals uprooted their families and settled in the Los Angeles area in an attempt to flee the violence in their own country (Kovacic, 2007–2008; Reisman, 2006). However, many of these same individuals were forced to live in poverty-ridden sections of East LA that were already home to a variety of local gangs who saw this influx of immigrants as an intrusion into their territory (Logan, 2009). These Salvadorian refugees become the targets of gang-related urban violence and banded together in an attempt to protect one another from these violent assaults, and MS-13 was born (Kovacic, 2007–2008).

When explored from the perspective of phenomenology, the creation and perpetuation of gang identity and gang violence emerge from the thrownness experienced by Salvadorian refugees who needed to respond to the reality of their new social context. Here, we witness the way in which thrownness and choice come together to construct the meaning of a specific set social experiences. Rather than continue to be victimized by local gangs, these individuals decided to join together and fight back. It is also important to note that many of these same individuals either fought with leftist guerrilla forces in El Salvador's bloody civil war or experienced first hand the tragic effects of that conflict and were intimately familiar with the realities and use of violence (Dunn, 2007; Kovacic, 2007–2008).

Gang organization and the use of violence to respond to this perceived threat became the way in which this new social context is constructed and lived. However, this response to the new reality of life in America, though deviant when viewed from outside this social frame of reference, is not experienced as such by those directly involved in this activity. Even as the function and identity of MS-13 turned away from concerns related to self-protection and toward those of criminal predation and violence, such formulations must be seen as only one perspective on this phenomenon that cannot capture the totality of its lived-meaning. Gang membership, then, not only comes to represent a specific response to the thrownness of these individuals but comes to represent a very different relationship to the "they."

What we witness within this description of the phenomenology of deviance—or, better stated, the phenomenology of the gang experience—is the way in which these behaviors and activities are made meaningful. However, this meaning-generating process and the specific choices which emerge from it, are directly related to a specific manifestation of the they–self that, in turn, identifies those behaviors granted validity and those that are not. Gang activity, like all types of "deviant behavior," occurs in contested space, space that is defined by competing manifestations of the they–self, which attempt to impose or validate a specific meaning upon this encounter. What one manifestation of the they–self validates, the other denies (Polizzi, 2003, 2010, 2011).

Within this context, the defining of certain behaviors as deviant, as invalid, emerge as such, relative to their relationship to the law and the way in which this manifestation of the they–self invalidates or labels these encounters as criminal. The same gang activity or behavior takes on a very different meaning when constructed from the context of the they represented in gang identity. Now, violence becomes validated as an expression of gang and ethnic loyalty, as an expression of the member's individual courage and fidelity to the they–self, represented by MS-13. Though the possibility for choice always remains, being-in-the-world as gang member or as member of MS-13 will always find itself situated within the overlap of these two competing meaning-generating processes which demand a certain degree of compliance and fidelity.

The possibilities or potential for human experience or being-in-the-world become drastically limited when constructed within the rigid confines of gang membership or criminal deviance. Though gang membership may be seen as a legitimate response to the realities of one's thrown-ness, it offers little beyond the trappings of one's immediate existence. Compliance with the law, with the they–self of the legal social order, may prevent regular confrontations with the criminal justice system, but it offers little else relative to the transformation of those conditions that help to legitimate gang involvement as the only seemingly "rational" response one has to the realities imposed upon lived-experience.

The experience of deviance, when seen within this context, does not emerge as an act of defiance, self-defense or criminal wrongdoing; rather, it becomes a complicated intertwining of all three. Because individual choice or expression remains inseparably linked to a complex layering of different and sometimes competing manifestations of the they–self, it is often very difficult to determine where the contours of one experience ends and the other begins. However, it is through this choosing that being-in-the-world proclaims a specific fidelity to the they–self and, by implication, a specific meaning for existence. Though it would be theoretically accurate to maintain that thrownness is destiny, that thrownness is the ontological reality of human existence or being-in-the-world, human possibility still remains, regardless how faintly.

Some concluding remarks

Deviant behavior or the phenomenology of deviance evokes a specific set of lived-meanings that collide at the place of the criminal act. Gang behavior or activity can be seen as that gesture which evokes the attention of a variety of manifestations of the they–self, each of which attempts to inscribe a specific meaning on this set of experiences (Polizzi, 2003, 2010, 2011). Though it is certainly true that most of this gang-related activity falls under the auspices of illegal behavior, this definition alone does not exhaust the totality of possible meanings for these experiences (Agnew, 2006; Polizzi, 2010). Any analysis of the meaning of deviant behavior most also include the way in which this behavior is defined by the perpetrator of these acts. Such a theoretical position should not be read as an apologetic stance toward this behavior, only that, if we are truly to understand this phenomenon in the complexity of its lived-meaning, we must attempt to understand it not solely from the perspective of its illegality but from a more holistic vantage point so as to include those more subtle and nuanced meanings that often defy easy generalization.

References

Agnew, R. (2006). Storylines as a neglected cause of crime. *Journal of Research in Crime and Delinquency*, 43: 119–147. doi: 10.1177/00224278052800052.

Arrigo, B. A., Milovanovic, D. (2009). *Revolution in penology: Rethinking the society of captives*. Lanham, MD: Rowman & Littlefield.

Caputo, J. D. (2007). The hyperbolization of phenomenology: Two possibilities for religion in recent continental philosophy. In K. Hart (Ed.), *Counter-experiences: Reading Jean-Luc Marion* (pp. 67–93). Notre Dame, IN: University of Notre Dame Press.

Cerbone, D. R. (2006). *Understanding phenomenology*. Chesham: Acumen.

Cohn, H. W. (2002). *Heidegger and the roots of existential therapy*. London and New York: Continuum.

Dunn, W. (2007). *The gangs of Los Angeles*. New York: iUniverse.

Edie, J. (1987). *Edmund Husserl's phenomenology: A critical critique*. Bloomington: Indiana University Press.

Giorgi, A. (2009) *The descriptive phenomenological method in psychology: A modified Husserlian approach*. Pittsburgh, PA: Duquesne University Press.

Gurwitsch, A. (1964). *The field of consciousness*. Pittsburgh, PA: Duquesne University Press.

Hart, K. (2007). Introduction. In K. Hart (Ed.), *Counter-Experiences: Reading Jean-Luc Marion* (pp. 1–54). Notre Dame, IN: Notre Dame University Press.

Heidegger, M. (1962 [1927]). *Being and Time*. Translated by J. Macquarie and E. Robinson. New York: Harper & Row.

Husserl, E. (1982). *Ideas pertaining to a pure phenomenology and to a phenomenological philosophy: First book*. Translated by F. Kersten. Dordrecht: Kluwer.

Katz, J. (1988). *Seductions of crime*. New York: Basic Books.

Kohak, E. (1978). *Idea & experience: Edmund Husserl's project phenomenology in Ideas I*. Chicago, IL: University of Chicago Press.

Kovacic, K. (2007–2008). Creating a monster: MS-13 and how United States immigration policy produced "the world's most dangerous gang." *Gonzaga Journal of International Law*, 11 (1). Available at www.gonzagajil.org/content/view/183/26/.

Letteri, M. (2009). *Heidegger and the question of psychology: Zolikon and beyond*. Amsterdam and New York: Rodopi.

Logan, S. (2009). *This is for the Mara Salvatrucha: Inside the MS-13, America's most violent gang*. New York: Hyperion.

Macann, C. (1993). *Four phenomenological philosophers: Husserl, Heidegger, Sartre, Merleau-Ponty*. London: Routledge.

Marion, J. L. (1998 [1989]). *Reduction and givenness: Investigations of Husserl, Heidegger and phenomenology*. Translated by Thomas A. Carlson. Evanston, IL: Northwestern University Press.

—— (2008 [2005]). *The visible and the revealed*. Translated by Christina M. Gschwandtner *et al*. New York: Fordham University Press.

May, R. (1986). *The discovery of being: Writings in existential psychology*. New York: W.W. Norton.

Natanson, M. (1973). *Edmund Husserl: Philosopher of infinite tasks*. Evanston, IL: Northwestern University Press.

Polizzi, D. (2003). *The experience of antiblack racism: A phenomenological-hermeneutic of the Autobiography of Malcolm X*. Available from UMI Dissertation Services (UMI NO. 3069293).

Polizzi, D. (2007). The social construction of race and crime: The image of the black offender. *International Journal of Restorative Justice*, 3 (1): 6–20.

Polizzi, D. (2010). Agnew's General Strain Theory reconsidered: A phenomenological perspective. *International Journal of Offender Therapy and Comparative Criminology*, published online, August 31, 2010, doi: 10.1177/0306624X10380846.

Polizzi, D. (2011). Heidegger, restorative justice and desistance: A phenomenological perspective. In R. Lippens and J. Hardie-Bick (Eds.) *Crime, Governance and Existential Predicaments*. Basingstoke, UK: Palgrave Macmillan Ltd. In Press.

Polizzi, D., Arrigo, B. A. (2009). Phenomenology, postmodernism and philosophical criminology: A conversational critique. *Journal of Theoretical and Philosophical Criminology*, 1 (2): 113–145.

Reisman, L. (2006). Breaking the vicious cycle: Responding to Central American youth gang violence. *SAIS Review*, 26 (2): 147–152.

Sheehan, T. (2007). Dasein. In H. Dreyfus and M. Wrathall (Eds.), *A companion to Heidegger* (pp. 193–213). Oxford: Blackwell.

Sokolowski, R. (2000). *Introduction to phenomenology*. Cambridge: Cambridge University Press.

Spinelli, E. (2005). *The interpreted world: An introduction to phenomenological psychology*. 2nd edition. London/ Thousand Oaks, CA: Sage.

Zimmerman, M. (1981). *The eclipse of the self*. Athens, OH: Ohio University Press.

16

Conflict theory

Addrain Conyers

Conflict theory is a general concept used to categorize a set of social structural theories with a common perspective: society is better categorized by conflict than consensus (Williams and McShane 2010). In reference to crime and deviance, this perspective challenges the source of lawmaking. The dominant group holds power in defining laws, norms, and values; consequently, the subordinate group will be viewed as deviant if they do not meet or pursue the dominant norms of society. The dominant group's goal is to maintain power at the cost of oppressing subordinate groups (Chambliss and Seidman 1971; Quinney 1970; Turk 1969); therefore, conflict theorists actually question the true intent and purpose of the laws and norms created (Turner 2003). This perspective is in opposition to consensus theories of crime and deviance which assume there is an objective social agreement on what constitutes deviance and law violation (Chamlin 2009). It has been argued that conflict is even at the foundation of consensus (Rawls 2003). Unlike other perspectives, conflict theorists do not focus their attention on the actual deviant behavior, but rather on the norms and values which define deviance. This chapter is designed to give a general overview of the perspective and a current review of the existing literature.

Heritage

Conflict theory is traced back to the work of Marx and Engels (1992 [1848]) (Savur 1975). The Marxist perspective does not focus on deviant behavior itself, but on the exploitative culture of capitalism. According to Marx, two social classes exist in a capitalist society, the bourgeoisie and the proletarians. Capitalism leads to this division and creates a small amount in power and many in subordination. The bourgeoisie are the ruling class. The proletarians are a class of laborers who are exploited by the bourgeoisie. Despite having less power, the proletarians are many in number. They become class conscious and aware of their social status. They mass together and fight against the exploitation of the powerful, hence the conflict. Capitalism is viewed as the cause of the conflict because of the economic and social disparity it creates.

Class consciousness is constant in a stratified society. This class consciousness not only causes conflict but leads to the proletarians desiring to be a part of the dominant group. The strength of the dominant exists not only in their economic power but in their ability to have the working class believe and desire the dominant cultural norms. Marx and Engels did not speak on crime or deviance specifically, but their work guided future theorists to explore the high correlation between conflict and crime. Weber acknowledged there are other strands of power which can cause conflict besides economic class; however, many of the early conflict theorists assessed crime and deviance from the Marxist perspective and focused more on class struggle and how the law is an instrument of power for the dominant group (Platt 1974; Spitzer 1975; Michalowski and Bohlander 1976; Quinney 1977; Bohm 1982; Reiman 2003).

Simmel

Georg Simmel (1950) is another German philosopher who is given credit for being one of the founders of the conflict perspective. Simmel viewed conflict as a normal part of social life (Turner 1978; Spykman 1964). Overall, he argued that conflict serves a function in society. Spykman (1964: 113) quotes Simmel: "Struggles and conflicts have a positive sociological significance in contrast with dissolutions and repudiations of socialization, which are both negative." Turner (1975) notes the major contrast between Marx's and Simmel's perspectives on conflict: Marx focused on the causes and Simmel focused on the consequences.

Dahrendorf

Like Simmel, Ralf Dahrendorf (1958: 126) viewed conflict as a normal process in society: "Not the presence but absence of conflict is surprising and abnormal, and we have good reason to be suspicious if we find a society or social organization that displays no evidence of conflict." He argued that a conflict model should be adopted to explain social problems, swaying away from the structural-functionalist approach that dominated that era. Even in an unrealistic utopian society, he argues the social system can produce a deviant. Dahrendorf also argues that conflict plays a useful function in the development of society. He states "that all that is creativity, innovation, and development in the life of the individual, his group, and his society is due, to no small extent, to the operation of conflict between group and group . . . This fundamental fact alone seems to me to justify the value judgment that conflict is essentially 'good' and 'desirable'" (Dahrendorf 1959: 208).

Bonger

Willem Bonger, in *Criminality and Economic Conditions* (1969), discusses how the economic conditions of capitalism will lead to an increase in crime rates. Capitalism will divide society into segments, and will consequently lead to egoism. This type of egoism brings about a criminal mind. An individual's position and skills will determine the type of crime he/she will commit. This is important because it introduces the idea that the upper class, as well as the lower class, is susceptible to this egoistic state of mind which can lead to economic crimes. Bonger (1969: 90) states:

> A man who knows how to make counterfeit bank-notes will commit this crime, whenever he wishes for any reason to enrich himself in a dishonest fashion, but he will become neither an incendiary nor a procurer. A former prostitute, on the contrary, will not think of making bank-notes, but will become a procuress. The kind of economic crime committed by the person who has a mind to commit such a crime depends principally upon chance (occupation, etc.).

Bonger clearly acknowledges that everyone in a capitalist society is liable to commit economic crimes due to their egoism. What differs is the type of crime they will commit because of their status and class.

Vold

George Vold's (1958) conflict theory, also known as group conflict theory, changes the focus from capitalism and value conflict to conflict based on group interests. Different groups come into conflict when there are opposing viewpoints, more specifically competition "in the same general field of interaction." If the groups do not have to interact, conflict will not occur. Groups are formed based on similarities and common goals between individuals. These individuals identify with one another and come together for the greater good of their group. Vold argues that the conflict between opposing groups helps solidify the loyalty of group members and develops their *group-mindedness* attitudes. "The individual is most loyal to the group for which he has had to fight the hardest and to which he had to give the greatest measure of self for the common end of group achievement" (Vold and Bernard 1986: 272). Groups can be segmented on a number of common traits such as race, gender, class, age, and religion. When the group is relatively subordinate, such as youth gangs, it is known as a *minority power group*. Vold's conflict theory is distinctive because of the focus on group interest, rather than capitalism.

Quinney

Richard Quinney (1970) is best known for his integrated social reality of crime theory. His focus on capitalism and power as the cause of crime grounds his theory in the conflict perspective; however, different aspects of the theory clearly integrate social constructionism, labeling, and differential association. His theory is best summarized in his six propositions (Quinney 1970: 15–23):

- Proposition 1 (Definition of Crime): Crime is a definition of human conduct that is created by authorized agents in a politically organized society.
- Proposition 2 (Formulation of Criminal Definition): Criminal definitions describe behaviors that conflict with the interests of the segments of society that have the power to shape public policy.
- Proposition 3 (Application of Criminal Definitions): Criminal definitions are applied by the segments of society that have the power to shape the enforcement and administration of criminal law.
- Proposition 4 (Development of Behavior in Relation to Criminal Definitions): Behavior patterns are structured in segmentally organized society in relation to criminal definitions, and within this context persons engage in actions that have relative probabilities of being defined as criminal.
- Proposition 5 (Construction of Criminal Conceptions): Conceptions of crime are constructed and diffused in the segments of society by various means of communication.
- Proposition 6 (The Social Reality of Crime): The social reality of crime is constructed by the formulation and application of criminal definitions, the developments of behavior patterns related to criminal definitions, and the construction of criminal conceptions.

Throughout the six propositions Quinney's reference to power and conflict is evident, but he also incorporates concepts of earlier established sociological and criminological theories. His first proposition focuses on the definition of crime as created by those in power. The manner in which one defines and constructs their reality is based on their personal background and experiences (Berger and Luckman 1966). In reference to the definition of crime, it is based on the formulation of those in power. His second and third propositions focus on the division of groups and specifically how the segment in power will have the leverage to enforce their definitions. This is related to Vold, Bernard, and Snipes' (1998) view on group conflict and how those in power will be able to control and dominate the law. The second proposition is also grounded in the labeling perspective due to the focus on moral entrepreneurs (Becker 1963). Quinney's fourth proposition references Sutherland's (1947) *differential association* theory as criminal behavior is learned based on one's surrounding norms. Quinney (1970: 20) states: "Therefore all persons—whether they create criminal definitions or are the objects of criminal definitions—act according to normative systems learned in relative social and cultural settings." The fifth proposition also has roots in social construction and the labeling perspective due to the constructed conceptions being "diffused" throughout society. The diffusion refers to the media's ability to spread the constructed definitions of crime in a manner which disguises its dominant origins. His last proposition summarizes the focus of his theory: crime is socially constructed based on criminal definitions of the powerful.

Other major contributors

There were many other chief proponents who contributed to the foundation of this perspective in contemporary criminological research. Chambliss (1969) and Chambliss and Seidman (1971) focused on lawmaking and how it favors the dominant group. The oppressive laws criminalize the behavior and values of the lower class. Chambliss and Seidman's (1971) theory is summarized in five propositions which emphasize how every stage of the criminal justice system benefits the powerful at the cost of oppressing the powerless.

Blalock (1957, 1967) is known for his power threat theory, which views race and ethnicity as the key variables in explaining oppressive norms and laws (Corzine, Creech, and Corzine 1983). Blalock (1967) argues that the population increase in racial minorities would threaten whites. Consequently, whites will request authorities to provide more crime control.

Turk (1966, 1969) focused on the authority–subject relationship in reference to law and society. In his *Criminality and the Legal Order* (1969), greatly influenced by Dahrendoff and Simmel, he focused on the criminalization process. This process acknowledges the role of authority in the criminalization process. Subjects who conflict with the norms and demands of authority are more likely to be labeled criminal; therefore, authority plays a bigger role in criminalizing behavior compared to subjects committing the behavior. Overall, the conflict perspective has many different perspectives which all view crime and deviance as a consequence of conflict.

Contemporary trends

Current literature in the conflict perspective has different focal points which complement and supplement the traditional views. The intent is to advance the perspective as society evolves. Contemporary conflict theorists also focus on other forms of stratification outside of economic class (e.g., race, gender, and sexuality). This research critically assesses every aspect of society from family relations to the criminal justice system (Messerschmidt 1986, 1993; Rudy 2001; Sharp 2006; Walker, Spohn, and DeLone 2007; Franklin and Fearn 2008; Holmes, Smith, Freng, and Munoz 2008).

Left realist

Left realists emerged in the 1980s in Great Britain. Their main objective was to produce "real" policies to address the issue of crime. In essence, crime is a social problem which needs to be realistically addressed. Young (1992: 26) argues that "criminology should be faithful to the nature of crime." Realists confront previous strands of conflict theory which focused on the definition of laws and norms:

> It is unrealistic to suggest that the problem of crime like mugging is merely the problem of mis-categorization and concomitant moral panics. If we choose to embrace this liberal position, we leave the political arena open to conservative campaigns for law and order . . . the reality of crime in the streets can be the reality of human suffering and personal disaster.
>
> *(Young 1976: 89)*

Left realists focus their concerns on the impact of crime on the working class (Young 1986). The working class is viewed as the victim because they are the most vulnerable and constantly in position to be violated. Young (1992) argues there are four variables that should be used to explain crime: a victim, an offender, the public, and social control. The social relationships between these four variables can explain crime rates. In other strands of conflict theory the deviant is viewed as a victim, but in left realism the "real" victim is the vulnerable working-class citizen. Left realist ideology has its beginnings in Europe and has influenced North America's view of conflict and crime (Platt 1985).

Peacemaking criminology

Quinney has traveled from his Marxist roots to a different position (Anderson 2002). Although still best known for his *Social Reality of Crime*, he has now joined other theorists in a more recent movement known as "peacemaking criminology" (Pepinsky 1988, 1999; Quinney 1988; Pepinsky and Quinney 1991; Quinney and Wilderman 1991). The focus veers from traditional conflict theories by focusing on positive interaction which can reduce conflict, and consequently reduce crime (Pepinsky 1999). Peacemaking encourages self-reflection of the individual to see how one can positively contribute to a peaceful community (Pepinsky and Quinney 1991). The government should be more concerned with the well-being of others, and not cause division by focusing on offenders. This division feeds the existing conflict. The justice system can promote positive interaction and community cohesiveness through changing the police, court, and correctional philosophies. For example, if the police were to focus more on community policing rather than watchmen style it could promote positive interaction in the community. Overall, the peacemaking approach is designed to ameliorate conflict.

Race

Current research has challenged the limitations of traditional conflict theory's focus on class (Hawkins 1987; Mitchell and Sidanius 1995; Hagan, Shedd, and Payne 2005; Buckler and Unnever 2008). Demographics change and consequently the system of stratification changes. Hagan *et al.* (2005) developed a comparative conflict theory. This theory is based on the notion of perceived injustices from racial minority groups. These perceptions have been shown to be a cause of criminal behavior (Sherman 1993). The theory is based on six hypotheses, with Buckler and Unnever (2008: 276) noting that three of these are key: "(1) there should be a racial and ethnic divide in perceptions of injustice, (2) Hispanics should perceive greater injustices than Whites but less injustice than African Americans, and (3) Hispanics should perceive more injustice than African Americans after having a negative run-in with the police." This theory encompasses two new trends in conflict theory. First, it acknowledges the role of race in conflict. Second, it provides a causal explanation of crime by arguing that the perceived injustice will lead to more conflict between minorities and the criminal justice system.

Critical race theory (CRT) focuses specifically on race and how it relates to law and society. It challenges the experience of white European Americans as the normative standard. This is critical because it challenges America's legal, social, and cultural texts' oppressive and subordinating features (Crenshaw 1995: xiv). CRT identifies the values and norms that have been disguised and subordinated in the law, and acknowledges that racism is a normal daily fact of life in society (Russell 1998). It is an intellectual movement that challenges the dominant norms as they relate specifically to race, so it is not limited to class and economics.

Causal explanation

The causal relationship between economic conditions and crime has been well documented in criminological theories (e.g., social disorganization and strain theories). These criminological theories do not provide an explanation for one's economic status. Through the conflict perspective, theorists have attempted to explain crime rates based on economic conditions. In essence, the cause of the economic deprivation can explain the type of deviant behavior and crime which may occur (Lilly, Cullen, and Ball 1995; Pratt and Lowenkamp 2002). Pratt and Lowenkamp (2002) researched how resource deprivations have a stronger effect on instrumental homicides compared to expressive homicides. Case (2008) discusses how economic conditions for minority ex-offenders can lead to a higher rate of recidivism. Having an ex-offender status and being non-white (i.e., subordinate) presents greater issues of securing employment compared to white ex-offenders (Western 2002). Case (2008) argues that the difference between black and white recidivism rates are more structural than cultural. The oppressive system cripples blacks more economically and can lead them back to crime for survival. Explaining the causes of crime and deviance provides an additional tool for conflict theorists in addressing social problems.

Discussion

The conflict perspective is not limited to crime and law, but can also be applied to societal norms. For example, beauty norms (i.e., hair, complexion, and figure) in America are commonly associated with the physical characteristics of Euro-Americans, the dominant group in the country. Any deviation from the norms can result in a spoiled identity based solely on physical characteristics. Conflict theorists, like labeling theorists, are not necessarily concerned with the cause of the behavior, but who defines it. The focus, commonly, is on the oppressive system. This oppressive system can vary based on the demographics of a population (e.g., race, class, gender, and religion) and which group possesses the power. Despite many theorists' attention to the dominant group's use of power, many have also directed their attention to conflict between groups of comparable power (Simmel 1950; Vold 1958; Dahrendorf 1958, 1959). It is also important to note that the conflict perspective has led to the creation of a conflict resolution theory (Hansen 2008).

The conflict perspective provides an overview and framework of what causes conflict and can help practitioners regulate conflict between opposing parties. It will always serve a purpose in addressing crime and deviance as long as social stratification is in existence. As society evolves, the dynamics of the stratification may change, but this perspective will always be relevant in explaining the consequences of the conflict.

References

Anderson, K. B. (2002) "Richard Quinney's journey: The Marxist dimension," *Crime delinquency*, 48:232–241.

Becker, H. S. (1963) *Outsiders: studies in the sociology of deviance*, New York: The Free Press.

Berger, P. L. and Luckman, T. (1966) *The social construction of reality: A treatise in the sociology of knowledge*, New York: Anchor Books.

Blalock, H. M., Jr. (1957) "Per cent non-white and discrimination in the South," *American Sociological Review*, 22:677–682.

—— (1967) *Toward a theory of minority-group relations*, New York: John Wiley.

Bohm, R. M. (1982) "Radical criminology: An explication," *Criminology*, 19:565–589.

Bonger, W. (1969) *Criminality and economic conditions*, Bloomington: Indiana University Press.

Buckler, K. and Unnever, J. D. (2008) "Racial and ethnic perceptions of injustice: Testing the core hypotheses of comparative conflict theory," *Journal of criminal justice*, 36:270–278.

Case, P. F. (2008) "The relationship of race and criminal behavior: Challenging cultural explanations for a structural problem," *Critical sociology*, 34:213–238.

Chambliss, W. J. (1969) *Crime and the legal process*, New York: McGraw-Hill.

Chambliss, W. J. and Seidman, R. T. (1971) *Law, order, and power*, Reading, MA: Addison-Wesley.

Chamlin, M. B. (2009) "Threat to whom? Conflict, consensus, and social control," *Deviant behavior*, 30:539–559.

Corzine, J., Creech J., and Corzine, L. (1983) "Black concentration and lynchings in the South: Testing Blalock's power-threat hypothesis," *Social forces*, 61:774–796.

Crenshaw, K. (1995) *Critical race theory: The key writings that formed the movement*, New York: The New Press.

Dahrendorf, R. (1958) "Out of utopia: Toward a reorientation of sociological analysis," *American journal of sociology*, 64:115–127.

—— (1959) *Class and class conflict in industrial society*, Stanford, CA: Stanford University Press.

Franklin, C. A. and Fearn, N. E. (2008) "Gender, race, and formal court decision-making outcomes: Chivalry/paternalism, conflict theory or gender conflict?," *Journal of criminal justice*, 36:279–290.

Hagan, J., Shedd, C., and Payne, M. R. (2005) "Race, ethnicity, and youth perceptions of injustice," *American sociological review*, 70:381–407.

Hansen, T. (2008) "Critical conflict resolution theory and practice," *Conflict resolution quarterly*, 25:403–427.

Hawkins, D. (1987) "Beyond anomalies: Rethinking the conflict perspective on race and criminal punishment," *Social forces*, 65:719–745.

Holmes, M. D., Smith, B. W., Freng, A. B., and Munoz, E. A. (2008) "Minority threat, crime control, and police resource allocation in the southwestern United States," *Crime and delinquency*, 54:128–152.

Lilly, J. R., Cullen, F. T., and Ball, R. A. (1995) *Criminological theory: Context and consequences*, 2nd edn, Thousand Oaks, CA: Sage.

Marx, K. and Engels, F. (1992 [1848]) *Communist manifesto*, New York: Bantam.

Messerschmidt, J. (1986) *Capitalism, patriarchy and crime: Toward a socialist feminist criminology*, Totowa, NJ: Rowman and Littlefield.

—— (1993) *Masculinities and crime: Critique and reconceptualization of theory*, Lanham, MD: Rowman and Littlefield.

Michalowski, R. J. and Bohlander, E. W. (1976) "Repression and criminal justice in capitalist America," *Sociological inquiry*, 46:95–106.

Mitchell, M. and Sidanius, J. (1995) "Social hierarchy and the death penalty: A social dominance perspective," *Political psychology*, 16:591–619.

Pepinsky, H. E. (1988) "Violence as unresponsiveness: Toward a mew conception of crime," *Justice quarterly*, 5:539–563.

—— (1999) "Peacemaking primer," in B. A. Arrigo (ed.), *Social justice: Criminal justice*, Belmont, CA: Wadsworth.

Pepinsky, H. and Quinney, R. (eds.) (1991) *Criminology as peacemaking*, Bloomington: Indiana University Press.

Platt, T. (1974) "Prospect for a radical criminology in the United States," *Crime and social justice*, 1:2–10.

—— (1985) "Criminology in the 1980s: Progressive alternative to law and order," *Crime and social justice*, 21:191–199.

Pratt, T. C. and Lowenkamp, C. T. (2002) "Conflict theory, economic conditions, and homicide," *Homicide studies*, 6:61–83.

Quinney, R. (1970) *The social reality of crime*, Boston, MA: Little, Brown.

—— (1977) *Class, state and crime: On the theory and practice of criminal justice*, New York: McKay.

—— (1988) "Crime, suffering, service: Toward a criminology of peacemaking," *Quest*, 1:66–75.

Quinney, R. and Wilderman, J. (1991) *The problem of crime: A peace and social justice perspective*, 3rd edn, Mountain View, CA: Mayfield.

Rawls, A. (2003) "Conflict as a foundation for consensus: Contradictions of industrial capitalism in book III of Durkheim's *Division of Labor*," *Critical Sociology*, 29:295–335.

Reiman, J. (2003) *The rich get richer and the poor get prison: Ideology, class, and criminal justice*, 7th edn, New York: Pearson, Allyn and Bacon.

Rudy, K. (2001) "Radical feminism, lesbian separatism, and queer theory," *Feminist studies*, 27:191–222.

Russell, K. K. (1998) *The color of crime: Racial hoaxes, white fear, black protectionism, police harassment and other macro aggressions*, New York: New York University Press.

Savur, M. (1975) "Sociology of conflict theory," *Social scientist*, 3:29–42.

Sharp, E. (2006) "Policing urban America: A new look at the politics of agency size," *Social science quarterly*, 87:291–307.

Sherman, L. (1993) "Defiance, deterrence, and irrelevance: A theory of the criminal sanction," *Journal of research in crime and delinquency*, 30:445–473.

Simmel, G. (1950) *The sociology of Georg Simmel*, New York: The Free Press.

Spitzer, S. (1975) "Towards a Marxian theory of deviance," *Social problems*, 22:638–651.

Spykman, N. J. (1964) *The social theory of Georg Simmel*, New York: Russell & Russell.

Sutherland, E. H. (1947) *Principles of criminology*, 3rd edn, Philadelphia, PA: Lippincott.

Turk, A. T. (1966) "Conflict and criminality," *American sociological review*, 31:338–352.

—— (1969) *Criminality and the legal order*, Chicago, IL: Rand McNally.

Turner, J. H. (1975) "Marx and Simmel revisited: Reassessing the foundations of conflict theory," *Social forces*, 53:618–627.

—— (1978) *The structure of sociological theory*, Homewood, IL: Dorsey.

—— (2003) *The structure of sociological theory*, 7th edn, Belmont, CA: Wadsworth.

Vold, George B. (1958) *Theoretical criminology*, New York: Oxford University Press.

Vold, G. B. and Bernard, T. J. (1986) *Theoretical criminology*, 3rd edn, New York: Oxford University Press.

Vold, G. B., Bernard, T. J., and Snipes, J. (1998) *Theoretical Criminology*, 4th edn, New York: Oxford University Press.

Walker, S., Spohn, C., and DeLone, M. (2007) *The color of justice: Race, ethnicity and crime in America*, 4th edn, Stamford, CT: Wadsworth.

Western, B. (2002) "The impact of incarceration on wage mobility and inequality," *American sociological review*, 67:526–546.

Williams, F. P., III, and McShane, M. D. (2010) *Criminological theory*, 5th edn, Upper Saddle River, NJ: Pearson Education.

Young, J. (1976) "Working class criminology," in I. Taylor, P. Walton, and J. Young (eds.), *Critical criminology*, London: Croom Helm.

—— (1986) "The failure of criminology: The need for radical realism," in J. Young and R. Matthews (eds.), *Confronting crime*, London: Sage.

—— (1992) "Ten points of realism," in J. Young and R. Matthews (eds.), *Rethinking criminology: The realist debate*, London: Sage.

17

Routine activities theory and rational choice theory

Marie Skubak Tillyer

Routine activities theory and rational choice theory are complementary explanations for the occurrence and distribution of crime and deviance. Routine activities theory describes the necessary elements of crime and those who have the potential to prevent it, while rational choice theory articulates the process by which offenders make decisions. Unlike many other explanations for crime and deviance, routine activities theory and rational choice theory emphasize the importance of immediate situational and environmental factors in explaining the distribution of crime and deviance across time and space. These two perspectives, which share similar theoretical roots and assumptions, have inspired substantial empirical exploration by criminologists. Further, the prevention implications offered by these perspectives add to their considerable influence.

Common theoretical roots and assumptions

With common theoretical roots in "classical" criminology, routine activities theory and rational choice theory share many similar assumptions, making the two approaches complementary rather than competing explanations. The basic premise of classical theory is that humans are naturally self-serving, rational beings who pursue their own interests, attempting to maximize their pleasure and minimize their pain. Therefore, classical criminologists argued that consequences for crime must be sufficiently swift, certain, and severe to ensure that the resulting "pain" following crime outweighs the anticipated "pleasure" to ensure that individuals do not choose to commit crime as they pursue their own self-interests.

Consistent with classical criminology, routine activities theory and rational choice theory are grounded in the assumption that humans are rational beings who make decisions based on their calculation of costs and benefits. Therefore, both point to offenders' perceptions of criminal opportunity as key to understanding the distribution of crime and deviant behavior. Unlike most criminological theories, which focus on distal causes of criminality, routine activities and rational choice emphasize the importance of proximate environmental and situational factors and their influence on how opportunities for crime are created and perceived by offenders.

Routine activities theory

Unlike many criminological theories, which seek to understand the motivation behind deviant behavior, routine activities theory explains the elements that must come together for such behavior to occur. First introduced by Cohen and Felson in 1979, routine activities is distinct from many other criminological theories in that it suggests that the motivated offender is but one element necessary for the occurrence of crime. According to Cohen and Felson (1979), structural routine activity patterns influence crime rates by affecting the convergence in time and space of three minimal elements of crime events: motivated offenders, suitable targets, and the absence of capable guardians. Influenced by human ecological theories, routine activities theory suggests that the ordinary activities of people structure the patterns for criminal opportunity, and thus the patterns of crime across time and space.

According to Cohen and Felson (1979), target suitability is a function of four characteristics: value, visibility, access, and inertia against illegal treatment. In other words, people and things that have perceived value, are visible by and accessible to offenders, and are of the size and weight that make victimization possible are more likely to be perceived as suitable targets. Clarke (1999) extended this conceptualization of suitable targets to include *hot products*, or those items that are repeatedly targeted for theft. According to Clarke, relatively few products make up a large proportion of all items targeted for theft and these products share six key attributes which increase their target suitability. Crime is concentrated on products that are concealable, removable, available, valuable, enjoyable, and disposable—*CRAVED* (Clarke 1999).

The concept of guardianship has also been expanded by criminologists to explicate the role these actors play in the prevention of crime. Guardians, now collectively referred to as *controllers*, have been further divided based on whom or what they supervise—targets, offenders, or places. *Guardians* are those who protect potential targets from victimization, *handlers* are those who supervise potential offenders (Felson 1986), and *managers* monitor and prevent crime at specific places (Eck 1994). According to Felson (1995), controllers' tendency to intervene and discourage crime varies with their degree of responsibility. Felson describes responsibility as an ordinal variable with four categories: personal, such as owners, families, and friends; assigned, such as employees with specific assignments; diffuse, such as employees with more general assignments; and general, such as strangers or the general public. Those most closely associated with potential targets, offenders, and places of crime are more likely to intervene successfully and prevent the occurrence of crime (Felson 1995).

Interestingly, routine activities theory suggests that crime and deviance can increase and decrease without any change in the supply of motivated offenders. Because the theory points to a range of factors which must intersect in time and space to produce criminal opportunities, changes in crime trends and patterns can be explained by changes in the supply of suitable targets, the supply or ability of controllers to prevent crime, or changes in routine activities which affect the likelihood of convergence in time and space of the necessary elements of crime. Consistent with this rationale, prevention implications derived from routine activities generally focus on altering opportunities for crime rather than directly addressing offender motivation. Eck (2001) has argued that specific types of crime and disorder problems can be linked to elements from routine activities theory. Problems of repeat victimization, repeat places of crime (i.e., hotspots), and repeat offending can be interpreted as functions of the routine activities of potential victims, places, and/or offenders, as well as the absence of potential guardians, managers, and handlers. For example, a repeat victimization problem can be attributed to the routine activities and target attractiveness of the victim, as well as the absence or ineffectiveness of guardians. This conceptualization of crime problems can be used to understand the factors which facilitate crime, as well as the controller who is most likely to be effective in addressing the problem.

Routine activities theory has influenced a broad range of research activity aimed at understanding crime patterns. Cohen and Felson (1979) initially introduced the theory to explain changes in national-level crime trends. They argued that the increase in urban violent crime rates in the 1960s was a function of changes in the structure of routine activities which increased the convergence in time and space of motivated offenders and suitable targets in the absence of capable guardians. Specifically, target suitability rose as sales of small, durable goods increased. In addition, guardianship decreased with dispersion of activities away from households. Not only did these non-household activities leave suitable targets at home unguarded, but they exposed individuals as targets to potentially motivated offenders. Cohen and Felson (1979) tested their hypotheses by calculating a household activity ratio which represented the proportion of households in the United States likely to be left unattended during the day. Controlling for changes in demographics and unemployment, they found a statistically significant relationship between their household activity ratio and rates of forcible rape, aggravated assault, robbery, burglary, and homicide from 1947 and 1974. Based on these findings, Cohen and Felson concluded that routine activities may be the source of criminal opportunities, thus accounting for the distribution of crime.

Since then, routine activities theory has been used in numerous ways, including to examine the non-random distribution of crime across space using cross-sectional data (e.g., Messner and Blau 1987; Sherman, Gartin and Buerger 1989). For example, Messner and Blau (1987) found that aggregate levels of television viewing—an activity that takes place inside the home and provides guardianship for household goods as well as residents—maintained a significant negative relationship with rates of rape, robbery, aggravated assault, burglary, larceny, and auto theft. Conversely, the supply of sports and entertainment establishments—an indicator of activities which take place outside of the home and leave household goods unguarded and residents exposed to potentially motivated offenders—was significantly and positively associated with murder, rape, robbery, aggravated assault, burglary, and larceny.

Researchers have also used measures of routine activities in victimization surveys to understand patterns of victimization (e.g., Cohen, Kluegel and Land 1981; Miethe, Stafford and Long 1987; Fisher et al. 1998). For example, Cohen, Kluegel and Land (1981) found that indicators of routine activities, such as household composition, labor force status, and neighborhood characteristics, are significantly related to predatory victimization, mediating the relationship between victimization and income, race, and age. Fisher et al. (1998), in a study of college students, found that measures of routine activities, including proximity to crime, target attractiveness, exposure, and lack of guardianship, significantly increased the risk of property victimization. Further, violent victimization risk was significantly increased by such routine activities as partying on campus at night and using recreational drugs.

Routine activities theory has also been used to explain variation in offending (Osgood et al. 1996; Osgood and Anderson 2004). For example, Osgood et al. (1996) argued that unstructured socializing with peers in the absence of authority figures presents opportunities for deviant behavior. Not only is deviance easier and more rewarding when with peers, but the absence of authority reduces the likelihood of social control. Further, the unstructured nature of these activities provides the time available for the deviance. Osgood et al. found support for their hypothesis that these routine activities are associated with deviance, including criminal behavior, heavy alcohol use, drug use, and dangerous driving behavior.

In addition to being used to explain the non-random distribution of crime and deviance across places, victims, and offenders, routine activities theory has been used to explain many forms of crime and deviance. Examples include property crime (e.g., Mustaine and Tewksbury 1998), violence (e.g., Kennedy and Forde 1990; Sampson 1987), sexual assault (e.g., Schwartz *et al.* 2001), and stalking (e.g., Fisher, Cullen and Turner 2002; Mustaine and Tewksbury 1999).

Rational choice theory

While routine activities theory explains the elements necessary for a crime to occur and those actors which have the ability to prevent crime, rational choice theory explains the process by which offenders make decisions. Clarke and Cornish (1985), drawing from a multidisciplinary literature on rationality, put forth a rational choice theory which moves beyond the strict classical school of rationality to acknowledge the "bounded" or "limited" nature of offender rationality. Their rational choice perspective is built around six core concepts (Cornish and Clarke 2008). First, criminal behavior is purposive. That is, individuals have needs and desires, as well as beliefs about how these can be fulfilled; these beliefs inform our actions as we try to achieve specific goals. Therefore, human actions, including deviant behavior and crime, tend to be instrumental and intended to benefit the offender in some way.

Second, criminal behavior is rational (Cornish and Clarke 2008). Consistent with the purposive nature of criminal behavior, the concept of rationality suggests that individuals attempt to select the best available means to achieve their goals. Yet rational choice theory moves beyond the strict classical assumptions to acknowledge the "bounded" or "limited" nature of offender rationality. Offenders often operate with limited information in high-stress situations. Further, decision-making may be further influenced by individual skills, experiences, knowledge, and so on.

Third, criminal decision-making is crime-specific. Cornish and Clarke (2008) assert that each crime has its own specific motives, purposes, and payoffs for the offender; in turn, the factors influencing offender decision-making vary by offense. This does not mean that offenders necessarily restrict their offending to a specific crime type; rather, to understand why a particular crime occurred, one must examine the benefits this particular crime offers to the offender.

Fourth, the decision to commit crime is actually made up of two decision points—an involvement decision and an event decision (Clarke and Cornish 1985). The involvement decision reflects the individual's willingness to do crime, while the event decision reflects the choice of particular criminal acts.

Fifth, the involvement decision, which is shaped by prior learning and experiences, comprises three stages: initiation, continuance, and desistance. During initiation, offenders become aware of their "readiness" to commit a crime (Clarke and Cornish 1985). This readiness goes beyond simply being receptive to the possibility of crime. Rather, offenders weigh potential options for meeting their needs and conclude that they are ready to commit this type of crime under certain circumstances. During the continuance stage, the offender's involvement decision continues to be shaped by experiences, with positive reinforcement during criminal events increasing the frequency of offending until it reaches an optimum level. In addition, personal circumstances may change to support continued involvement in crime. For example, Clarke and Cornish (1985) cite increased professionalism in offending, changes in lifestyle, and changes in network of associates as personal circumstances that can shift to confirm the offender's willingness to be involved in crime. During the desistance stage, offenders may revisit the involvement decision and choose to stop offending after reevaluating their alternatives to crime. The decision to desist may follow an aversive experience during a crime, changes in personal circumstances, or changes in the neighborhood that alter the offender's perceptions of criminal opportunity. The decision to desist does not necessarily mean offenders will never commit crime again; they may displace to another form of crime or stop offending only temporarily.

Sixth, criminal events unfold in a sequence of stages and decisions (Cornish and Clarke 2008). The event decision, or the decision to commit a particular crime, is highly influenced by situational factors. The offender's perceptions of criminal opportunity influence the selection of targets. Clarke and Cornish's (1985) rational choice model acknowledges that situations are not perceived the same by all. The offender's prior experiences and information-processing abilities influence criminal decision-making. Further, sometimes the information used to assess the risks and rewards of crime is inaccurate. Decision-making can also be influenced by situational changes, drugs, and alcohol. In other words, although the decision-making process is guided by rational principles, rationality is bounded or limited due to a number of factors.

Clarke and Cornish's (1985) rational choice models of involvement and event decisions reflect a "modified classicism." In other words, they share the assumption of the classical school that individuals make choices in pursuit of their interests, yet the choices available to individuals, as well as their ability to assess them accurately, may be limited.

Clarke (1980) has also argued that conceptualizing crime as the result of immediate choices made by offenders offers promising prevention possibilities. Situational crime prevention has evolved into the set of techniques that aims to alter offender decision-making by addressing the perceived opportunity for crime by systematically manipulating or managing the immediate environment (Clarke 1983). Recent extensions of situational crime prevention recognize that environments and situations create not only opportunities for crime but at times provide the motivation (Wortley 2001; Cornish and Clarke 2003). Wortley (2001) suggests that the motivation to commit a particular offense may be situationally dependent, arguing that situations precipitate criminal responses in at least four ways: present cues that prompt the criminal behavior; exert social pressure to offend; permit behavior by weakening moral prohibitions; and produce emotional arousal that provokes a criminal response. Therefore, Cornish and Clarke (2003) suggest situational crime prevention techniques should focus on effectively altering opportunity structures and/or motivations of a particular crime by: increasing the efforts; increasing the risks; reducing the rewards; reducing provocations; and removing excuses.

Rational choice theory has been broadly applied by researchers to study a wide range of crime and deviant behavior. Examples include suicide (Clarke and Mayhew 1988), terrorism (Dugan, LaFree and Piquero 2005), traffic law violations (Corbett and Simon 1992), shoplifting (Weaver and Carroll 1985), corporate crime (Piquero, Exum and Simpson 2005; Stretesky 2006), assault (Carmichael and Piquero 2004; Exum 2002), and drunk driving (Grasmick, Bursik and Arneklev 1993).

Conclusion

Routine activities theory and rational choice theory have been used to understand the distribution of many forms of crime and deviance. Because of their similar theoretical roots, these two perspectives can be viewed as complementary approaches to understanding crime and deviance in that they emphasize the importance of immediate situational and environmental factors in shaping offender decision-making. Each of these perspectives has been influential in the explanation as well as prevention of crime and deviant behavior.

References

Carmichael, S. and Piquero, A. R. (2004) "Sanctions, perceived anger, and criminal offending," *Journal of Quantitative Criminology*, 20: 371–93.

Clarke, R. V. (1980) "'Situational' crime prevention: Theory and practice," *British Journal of Criminology*, 20: 136–47.

Clarke, R. V. (1983) "Situational crime prevention: Its theoretical basis and practical scope," in M. Tonry and N. Morris (eds) *Crime and Justice: An Annual Review of Research*, Vol. 4, Chicago, IL: University of Chicago Press.

Clarke, R. V. (1999) "Hot products: Understanding, anticipating and reducing demand for stolen goods," Paper 112, edited by B. Webb. London: Home Office, Research Development and Statistics Directorate.

Clarke, R. V. and Cornish, D. B. (1985) "Modeling offenders' decisions: A framework for research and policy," in M. Tonry and N. Morris (eds) *Crime and Justice: A Review of Research*, Vol. 6, Chicago, IL: University of Chicago Press.

Clarke, R. V. and Mayhew, P. (1988) "The British gas suicide story and its criminological implications," in M. Tonry and N. Morris (eds) *Crime and Justice: A Review of Research*, Vol. 10, Chicago, IL: University of Chicago Press.

Cohen, L. E. and Felson, M. (1979) "Social change and crime rate trends: A routine activities approach," *American Sociological Review*, 44: 88–100.

Cohen, L. E., Kluegel, J. R., and Land, K. C. (1981) "Social inequality and predatory criminal victimization: An exposition and test of a formal theory," *American Sociological Review*, 46: 505–24.

Corbett, C. and Simon, F. (1992) "Decisions to break or adhere to the rules of the road, viewed from the rational choice perspective," *British Journal of Criminology*, 32: 537–49.

Cornish, D. B. and Clarke, R. V. (2003) "Opportunities, precipitators and criminal decisions: A reply to Wortley's critique of situation crime prevention," in M. J. Smith and D. B. Cornish (eds) *Theory for Practice in Situational Crime Prevention*, Monsey, NY: Criminal Justice Press.

Cornish, D. B. and Clarke, R. V. (2008) "The rational choice perspective," in R. Wortley and L. Mazerolle (eds) *Environmental Criminology and Crime Analysis*, Cullompton: Willan.

Dugan, L., LaFree, G., and Piquero, A. R. (2005) "Testing a rational choice model of airline hijackings," *Criminology*, 43: 1031–65.

Eck, J. E. (1994) "Drug markets and drug places: A case-control study of the spatial structure of illicit drug dealing," unpublished doctoral dissertation, University of Maryland.

Eck, J. E. (2001) "Policing and crime event concentration," in R. Meier, L. Kennedy and V. Sacco (eds) *The Process and Structure of Crime: Criminal Events and Crime Analysis, Theoretical Advances in Criminology*, New Brunswick, NJ: Transaction.

Exum, M. L. (2002) "The application of robustness of the rational choice perspective in the study of intoxicated and angry intentions to aggress," *Criminology*, 40: 933–66.

Felson, M. (1986) "Routine activities, social controls, rational decisions, and criminal outcomes," in D. Cornish and R. V. Clarke (eds) *The Reasoning Criminal*, New York: Springer-Verlag.

Felson, M. (1995) "Those who discourage crime," in J. E. Eck and D. Weisburd (eds) *Crime and Place*, Monsey, NY: Criminal Justice Press.

Fisher, B. S., Cullen, F. T., and Turner, M. G. (2002) "Being pursued: A national-level study of stalking among college women," *Criminology and Public Policy*, 1: 257–308.

Fisher, B. S., Sloan, J. J., Cullen, F. T., and Lu, C. (1998) "Crime in the ivory tower: The level and sources of student victimization," *Criminology*, 36: 671–710.

Grasmick, H. G., Bursik, R. J., and Arneklev, B. J. (1993) "Reduction in drunk driving as a response to increased threats of shame, embarrassment, and legal sanctions," *Criminology*, 31: 41–67.

Kennedy, L. W. and Forde D. R. (1990) "Routine activities and crime: An analysis of victimization in Canada," *Criminology*, 28: 137–52.

Messner, S. F. and Blau, J. R. (1987) "Routine leisure activities and rates of crime: A macro-level analysis," *Social Forces*, 65: 1035–52.

Miethe, T. D., Stafford, M. C., and Long, J. S. (1987) "Social differentiation in criminal victimization: A test of routine activities/lifestyle theories," *American Sociological Review*, 52: 184–94.

Mustaine, E. E. and Tewksbury, R. (1998) "Predicting risks of larceny theft victimization: A routine activity analysis using refined lifestyle measures," *Criminology*, 36: 829–58.

Mustaine, E. E. and Tewksbury, R. (1999) "A routine activity theory explanation for women's stalking victimizations," *Violence Against Women*, 5: 43–62.

Osgood, D. W. and Anderson, A. L. (2004) "Unstructured socializing and rates of delinquency," *Criminology*, 42: 519–49.

Osgood, D. W., Wilson, J. K., O'Malley, P. M., Bachman, J. G., and Johnston, L. D. (1996) "Routine activities and individual deviant behavior," *American Sociological Review*, 61: 635–55.

Piquero, N. L., Exum, M. L., and Simpson, S. S. (2005) "Integrating the desire-for-control and rational choice in a corporate crime context," *Justice Quarterly*, 22: 252–80.

Sampson, R. J. (1987) "Personal violence by stranger: An extension and test of the opportunity model," *Journal of Criminal Law and Criminology*, 78: 327–56.

Schwartz, M. D., DeKeseredy, W. S., Tait, D., and Alvi, S. (2001) "Male peer support and a feminist routine activities theory: Understanding sexual assault on the college campus," *Justice Quarterly*, 18: 623–49.

Sherman, L. W., Gartin, P. R., and Buerger, M. E. (1989) "Hot spots of predatory crime: Routine activities and the criminology of place," *Criminology*, 27: 27–55.

Stretesky, P. B. (2006) "Corporate self-policing and the environment," *Criminology*, 44: 671–708.

Weaver, R. and Carroll, J. (1985) "Crime perceptions in a natural setting by expert and novice shoplifters," *Social Psychology Quarterly*, 48: 349–59.

Wortley, R. (2001) "A classification of techniques for controlling situational precipitators of crime," *Security Journal*, 14: 63–82.

18

Marxist and critical theory

Rob White

Introduction

Social inequality fundamentally determines who does what when it comes to deviancy and crime, and who ends where when it comes to social reactions to deviancy and crime. The defining feature of Marxist criminology and critical criminology is that they deal with issues of inequality and power as core concerns. However, in doing so, they vary somewhat in the explanations put forward, in the use of particular theoretical concepts, and in analytical emphasis.

Marxism and class analysis

Class and criminality

The concentration of disadvantage in particular individuals and in particular communities is at the root of most street crime. That is, it is the structurally unequal and socially disadvantaged position of people that provides the context for certain types of criminality and the commission of certain types of crime. To put it differently, typical patterns of crime are linked with specific classes and particular motivational factors. Certain behaviours emerge out of very specific class circumstances and are subject to particular limits and pressures associated with class location (see White and van der Velden, 1995; Reiman, 1998; White, 2008). Class situation is thus a prime influence in type of criminality. There is, indeed, a strong link between the socio-economic status of individuals (and communities) and the incidence of criminal offending. For example, offenders who are deepest within the criminal justice system, especially in prisons, disproportionately come from disadvantaged situations and backgrounds featuring low socio-economic status and highly volatile family relationships.

This is a cross-national and cross-jurisdictional phenomenon, as evidenced in a wide variety of reports, research studies, and discussion papers dealing with socio-economic status and offending patterns (see, for example, Michalowski and Carlson, 1999; Papps and Winkelmann, 2000; Kitchen, 2006; Fougere, Kramarz and Pouget, 2006). While the specific conditions and influences that mark the relationship between socio-economic hardship and crime vary (depending upon such factors as local neighbourhood social cohesion, state interventions to address mass unemployment, and the nature of law enforcement), overall there is a strong positive correlation. This holds for cross-country comparisons as well as nation-specific analysis (Fajnzylber, Lederman and Loayza, 2002).

Where there is persistent and intergenerational disadvantage, this sometimes manifests in the form of criminal families. Indeed, a network of professional offenders and lifestyle offending are characteristic features of an underclass (White, 2008). In essence, deprived individuals, families, and communities will organise their own means and forms of subsistence and enjoyment. They will especially do so under circumstances in which they are excluded from desirable areas in which to live and separated from opportunities to find paid work. Moreover, even if work is there to be had, illegality may be far more rewarding, secure, and satisfying as a source of income than the insecurities and exploitations of precarious employment in the formal sectors of the economy.

In the case of working-class and underclass criminality, the generating force for much of this crime is subsistence or to supplement one's income relative to subsistence levels. With regard to underclass criminality specifically, crime has more of a survival component and plays a greater part in basic economic subsistence. The extreme marginalisation and disconnection experienced by members of the underclass translates into a greater dependency upon alternative survival measures – and this often means a greater chance that this will include serious crime linked to a criminal career and the criminal economy. Working-class economic crime is more supplementary in character, and includes such things as stealing from job sites, avoiding tax through payment by cash-in-hand, and low-level social security fraud.

In general, there are major differences in the motivations behind working-class criminality (for example, theft of money for purposes of immediate consumption) and capitalist criminality (for example, theft of money linked to start-up capital for investment). Moreover, the alienations experienced by members of the working class resurface in antisocial behaviour and crimes of violence that often reflect the economic and social tensions associated with class situation.

A key characteristic of Marxist conceptions of crime and criminality is the focus on how institutionalised power is organised and exercised in society (see White and Haines, 2008). The general tendency of state institutions (such as the police, the judiciary, prisons, and community programmes) is to concentrate on specific kinds of behaviour (usually associated with working-class crime) as being "deviant" and "harmful." Other kinds of destructive or exploitative behaviour (usually associated with crimes of the powerful) are deemed to be less worthy of state intervention.

Historical development

Early Marxist writings on crime in the first few decades of the twentieth century discussed the ways in which crime is an outcome of the precipitating economic and social conditions of capitalism. Bonger (1916; see also Taylor *et al.*, 1973), for example, argued that criminal thought is generated by the conditions of want and misery foisted upon sections of the working class, and is also the result of the greed that underpins the capitalist competitive process. However, generally speaking, these writings went against the mainstream of criminology of the time. It was not until the 1970s that Marxist criminology was incorporated into the field as a significant and popular perspective in its own right.

During the 1960s and 1970s, criminologists such as Quinney and Chambliss directly challenged the prevailing approaches in criminology. It was argued that where there are class divisions in a society, one will find different capacities to determine the content of the laws of that society. The powerful ruling class will thus be able to shape the criminalisation process in such a way as to protect its own collective interests, which reflect the interconnection between this class and a particular state form (see Chambliss, 1975; Chambliss and Mankoff, 1976; Quinney, 1970, 1974).

In developing a new typology of crime, one that dealt with both crimes of the powerful and crimes of the less powerful, Quinney (1977) argued that analysis of the relationship between class, state and crime is essential. It was proposed that, on the one hand, there are *crimes of domination*. These are crimes committed by the capitalist class, the state, and the agents of the capitalist class and the state. They include crimes of control (such as police brutality, violation of civil liberties), crimes of government (such as warfare, political assassination) and crimes of economic domination (such as pollution, price-fixing). On the other hand, there are *crimes of accommodation and resistance*, which are associated with the working class. These include predatory crimes (such as burglary, robbery), personal crimes (such as murder, assault, rape), and crimes of resistance (such as workplace sabotage, protests).

Criminality, according to Marxists, is intimately tied to class position, and the logic of a system that is geared towards capital accumulation rather than the meeting of social need (see Greenberg, 1993). An important concept is that of *surplus population*, in that much of the existing forms of criminalisation and public concern with street crime are seen to be targeted at those layers or sections of the population that are surplus to the labour market and the requirements of capitalism generally (Spitzer, 1975). A broad political economic analysis of capitalism is needed in order to set the scene for research and writing on more specific aspects of class conflict and class processes relating to crime, such as youth subcultures (see Hall and Jefferson, 1976).

The ongoing contribution of a Marxist framework to understanding contemporary developments in society, and criminal justice specifically, has long been highlighted in the work and writings of Jeffrey Reiman (1998). Reiman first published *The Rich Get Richer and the Poor Get Prison* in 1979. As the title suggests, this book is an analysis of the economic biases, ideological processes, and social inequalities associated with the criminal justice system. In later editions, the book includes an appendix that provides a detailed outline of the Marxist critique of criminal justice. Marxism as an analytical framework may have declined in popularity among academic intellectuals, but Reiman (1999) argues that the issues with which it is concerned have not lost any of their potency or relevance.

The Marxist criminological approach highlights the inequalities of a class society (for example, wealth versus poverty, business profits versus low wages), and the impact these have on the criminalisation process. The powerful are seen as designing the laws in their own collective interest, while having greater capacity to defend themselves individually if they do break and bend existing rules and regulations. The less powerful in society are seen as propelled to commit crime through economic need and social alienation. They are also the main targets of law enforcement and wider criminal-justice agencies, something reflected in statistics that show an overrepresentation of the unemployed and poor in prisons, police lock-ups and criminal courts.

Critical criminology and social inequality

Social inequality and the question of power

The location of different categories and groups of people in the social structure has major implications for their well-being, social opportunities, and life prospects. Such social differentiation is institutionally and ideologically legitimated, and contested, across a range of social domains. These include, for example (White and Perrone, 2010):

- *inequalities associated with class relations and economic processes*, e.g., disparities in income and wealth; labour market opportunities and unemployment; poverty and homelessness;

- *inequalities associated with gender relations and social constructions of sexuality*, e.g., differential treatment of women and men in paid work settings, in education and the public sphere; negative social sanctions against gays and lesbians; domestic violence and different roles in domestic labour;
- *inequalities associated with ethnic and cultural relations and racist ideologies and practices*, e.g., differential access to economic, social and political resources and decision-making depending upon ethnic and cultural background; persistent denial of human rights;
- *inequalities associated with community relations and state political structures*, e.g., difficulties in access to decision-making at local, state, and federal government levels; different access to the provision and delivery of important services (such as childcare, education, sport, and recreation) according to factors such as geography and disability;
- *inequalities associated with age*, e.g., disparities in access to economic, social and political resources, and decision-making due to arbitrary and inconsistent legal rules and administrative procedures (in areas such as welfare provision, voting rights, and wages and employment conditions).

These inequalities cross over and intersect in many different ways. Likewise, there are many different types of social exclusion and social marginalisation. While there are various intersections between inequalities relating to class, gender, ethnicity, race, and age, it is nevertheless important to bear in mind the specific nature of each as well. For instance, class inequality can be explained in terms of exploitation and the appropriation of surplus in any society (e.g., concentrations of private property in a capitalist society); while colonialism provides the best description of inequalities pertaining to indigenous peoples (e.g., physical and cultural dispossession).

Critical criminology represents a further development of the broad radical strands within criminology. In particular, it builds upon the basic concepts and strategic concerns of the Marxist and feminist perspectives. For example, there is a consensus among critical criminologists that the present operation of the criminal justice system is unfair, biased, and operates in ways that advantage certain groups or classes above others.

The focal point of critique within this perspective is how power is mobilised within the broad sphere of criminal justice. There are two general trends in the critical criminological literature (White and Haines, 2008). The "structuralist" approach tends to focus on power as something that is ingrained in social structures, and that manifests itself in the form of the action of institutions and the activities of sectional interest groups (see Scraton and Chadwick, 1991). The "postmodern" approach, on the other hand, sees power in terms of language, and the ways in which knowledge production shapes human experience while simultaneously engendering conflict over meaning (see Arrigo and Bernard, 1997; Lea, 1998; Henry and Milovanovic, 1994). What unifies the different approaches within the critical criminology perspective is a deep concern with issues of oppression and injustice. These are seen to stem from structural inequalities in resource allocation and decision-making power.

Historical development

In the late 1980s and early 1990s, critical criminologists still thought it was essential to examine the structural relations of power in society, and to view crime in the context of the social relations, state institutions, and political economy of advanced capitalism (Scraton and Chadwick, 1991). However, earlier narrow versions of Marxism were criticised insofar as issues such as racism, sexism, and heterosexism were by and large ignored or insufficiently explained.

The acknowledgement of differences (in terms of specific needs, experiences, and histories) and recognition of commonalities (in relation to marginalisation and criminalisation processes) were translated into a concern with all forms of oppression within the critical criminology framework. Issues of class, gender, and ethnicity were seen to be interrelated, and to reflect the general institutional processes of capitalism.

The conceptual legacy of Marxism was to establish a firm interest in examining questions relating to the nature and exercise of class power and state power. In a similar vein, and reinforced by feminist studies informed by postmodernist theories on the cultural and psychological basis of oppression, research was directed at the role of ideology in shaping lived experience. Racism, sexism and individualism are all bound up with certain ways in which the world is described and categorised – the definition of who is "dangerous" or who is a "victim," and who is not, for example. How and why this occurs were made problematic.

Foucault's approach to the history of discipline and punishment, for example, focused on the micro-processes of authority and the exercise of power (Foucault, 1977). In doing so, he highlighted the role of professionals in imposing control over their subjects (such as prisoners). He also described the mechanism by which social domination is achieved. This includes the development of special languages or discourses (such as "delinquents"), which establish the boundaries between the "normal" and the "deviant." The prison regime, prison language, and prison architecture shape and constrain the inmate in ways that profoundly affect how they speak, move, interact, feel, and think – in short, the essence of their social being. Converted into social outcasts through a continuous cycle of segregation, supervision, and labelling, offenders are thereby rendered both politically and socially harmless. They become the scapegoats for society's crime problem, thus diverting public attention away from crimes perpetrated by the powerful.

Much of this type of critical criminological research, scholarship, and commentary has been informed by a concern to publicise existing injustices, and potential abuses, of criminal justice institutions (Schissel and Brooks, 2002; Carrington and Hogg, 2002; Anthony and Cunneen, 2008). For example, the victimisation, and empowerment of such groups as indigenous people, immigrant communities, refugees, gay men and lesbians, and working-class young people have been the subject of probing analysis and insightful discussion (see Taylor, 1999; Lynch and Michalowski, 2006). The discussions of specific groups (such as indigenous people and female prisoners) and particular institutions (especially special police tactical response units and private prisons) are usually framed within a general perspective that views the state and powerful social interests (especially the corporate sector) as hegemonic forces that reproduce social inequalities.

Other writers point to the way postmodernism or social constructivist approaches can empower those with little voice (Einstadter and Henry, 1995). In this view, reality is always constituted and reconstituted through language, and according to very specific discourses. Many critical criminologists are concerned to give a voice to those views that are currently underplayed or ignored by those who have power: for example, the views of indigenous people, women, and lesbians and gay men. Meaning is present in everything we do, but it is the task of postmodernism to unpack the complex nature of everyday "realities," and the discourses of these realities, including those realities concerned with crime and criminality.

In addition to the focus on the powerless, critical criminology has been concerned with the harm directly perpetrated by those in positions of power. Studies of white-collar crime and corporate crime (crime specifically resulting from the actions of organisations) have pointed to the enormity of harm perpetrated by the powerful. A consistent focus of this research has been to label such acts criminal, and to call for their inclusion as quintessentially criminal acts to be dealt with accordingly (see, for examples, Shover and Wright, 2001; Friedrichs, 1996; Pearce and Tombs, 1998). This has also involved rethinking the nature of harm, for example viewing violations of human rights as significant acts of harm (Schwendinger and Schwendinger, 1975) that can also be applied to an analysis of state crime (Green and Ward, 2004).

Conclusion

What unifies the many different approaches within the Marxist tradition and within critical criminology is a deep concern with issues of oppression and injustice. These issues are seen to stem from structural inequalities in resource allocation and decision-making power (Young, 1999, 2007).

Accordingly, institutional reform is not seen as an end in itself, but as part of a more profound transition towards a more equal, fairer society. To take a specific example, a call for the abolition of prisons (or at least a radical reduction in the prison population) may reflect the position that those who end up in prison are the most vulnerable sections of the population (in terms of income, employment, and educational background) and hence are unfairly criminalised and further penalised for their predicament. But to abolish prisons is not enough. Until the conditions that give rise to the creation of "surplus populations" and ethnically and racially based social divisions are confronted, piecemeal institutional reform will not be sufficient to forestall suffering and pain in the future.

References

Anthony, T. and Cunneen, C. (eds) (2008). *The Critical Criminology Companion*. Sydney: Federation Press.

Arrigo, B. and Bernard, T. (1997). "Postmodern Criminology in Relation to Radical and Conflict Criminology," *Critical Criminology*, 8(2): 39–60.

Bonger, W. (1916). *Criminality and Economic Conditions*. Boston, MA: Little, Brown and Company.

Carrington, K. and Hogg, R. (eds) (2002). *Critical Criminology: Issues, Debates, Challenges*. Devon: Willan.

Chambliss, W. (1975). "The Political Economy of Crime: A Comparative Study of Nigeria and USA," in I. Taylor, P. Walton, and J. Young (eds), *Critical Criminology*. London: Routledge & Kegan Paul.

Chambliss, W. and Mankoff, M. (1976). *Whose Law What Order? A Conflict Approach to Criminology*. Toronto: John Wiley & Sons.

Einstadter, W. and Henry, S. (1995). *Criminological Theory: An Analysis of Its Underlying Assumptions*. New York: Harcourt Brace.

Fajnzylber, P., Lederman, D., and Loayza, N. (2002). "Inequality and Violent Crime," *Journal of Law and Economics*, 45(1): 1–40.

Foucault, M. (1977). *Discipline and Punish: The Birth of the Prison*. London: Penguin.

Fougere, D., Kramarz, F., and Pouget, J. (2006). *Youth Unemployment and Crime in France*. Paris: Centre for Research in Economics and Statistics.

Friedrichs, D. (1996). *Trusted Criminals: White Collar Crime in Contemporary Society*. Belmont, CA: Wadsworth.

Green, P. and Ward, T. (2004). *State Crime: Governments, Violence and Corruption*. London: Pluto.

Greenberg, D. (ed.) (1993). *Crime and Capitalism: Readings in Marxist Criminology*. Philadelphia, PA: Temple University Press.

Hall, S. and Jefferson, T. (eds) (1976). *Resistance through Rituals: Youth Subcultures in Post-war Britain*. London: Hutchinson.

Henry, S. and Milovanovic, D. (1994). "The Constitution of Constitutive Criminology: A Postmodern Approach to Criminological Theory," in D. Nelken (ed.), *The Futures of Criminology*. London: Sage.

Kitchen, P. (2006). *Exploring the Link between Crime and Socio-economic Status in Ottawa and Saskatoon: A Small-Area Geographical Analysis*. Report prepared for the Department of Justice Canada. Ottawa: Department of Justice.

Lea, J. (1998). "Criminology and Postmodernity," in P. Walton and J. Young (eds), *The New Criminology Revisited*. London: Macmillan.

Lynch, M. and Michalowski, R. (2006). *Primer in Radical Criminology: Critical Perspectives on Crime, Power and Identity*. New York: Criminal Justice Press.

Michalowski, R. and Carlson, S. (1999). "Unemployment, Imprisonment, and Social Structures of Accumulation: Historical Contingency in the Rusche-Kirchheimer Hypothesis," *Criminology*, 37(2): 217–249.

Papps, K. and Winkelmann, R. (2000). "Unemployment and Crime: New Evidence for an Old Question," *New Zealand Economic Papers*, 34(1): 53–72.

Pearce, F. and Tombs, S. (1998). *Toxic Capitalism: Corporate Crime and the Chemical Industry*. Aldershot: Dartmouth.

Quinney, R. (1970). *The Social Reality of Crime*. Boston, MA: Little, Brown and Company.

Quinney, R. (ed.) (1974). *Crime and Justice in America: A Critical Understanding*. Boston, MA: Little, Brown and Company.

Quinney, R. (1977). *Class, State and Crime: On the Theory and Practice of Criminal Justice*. New York: David McKay.

Reiman, J. (1998). *The Rich Get Richer and the Poor Get Prison*. Boston, MA: Allyn & Bacon.

Reiman, J. (1999). "The Rich (Still) Get Richer: Understanding Ideology, Outrage and Economic Bias," *Critical Criminologist*, 9 (2): 1, 4–5.

Schissel, B. and Brooks, C. (eds) (2002). *Marginality and Condemnation: An Introduction to Critical Criminology*. Halifax, NS: Fernwood.

Schwendinger, H. and Schwendinger, J. (1975). "Defenders of Order or Guardians of Human Rights," in I. Taylor, P. Walton, and J. Young (eds), *Critical Criminology*. London: Routledge & Kegan Paul.

Scraton, P. and Chadwick, K. (1991). "The Theoretical and Political Priorities of Critical Criminology," in K. Stenson and D. Cowell (eds), *The Politics of Crime Control*. London: Sage.

Shover, N. and Wright, J. (2001). *Crimes of Privilege: Readings in White-Collar Crime*. New York: Oxford University Press.

Spitzer, S. (1975). "Toward a Marxian Theory of Deviance," *Social Problems*, 22: 638–651.

Taylor, I. (1999). *Crime in Context: A Critical Criminology of Market Societies*. Cambridge: Polity Press.

Taylor, I., Walton, P., and Young, J. (1973). *The New Criminology*. London: Routledge & Kegan Paul.

White, R. (2008). "Class Analysis and the Crime Problem," in T. Anthony and C. Cunneen (eds), *The Critical Criminology Companion*. Sydney: Federation Press.

White, R. and Haines, F. (2008). *Crime and Criminology*. Melbourne: Oxford University Press.

White, R. and Perrone, S. (2010). *Crime, Criminality and Criminal Justice*. Melbourne: Oxford University Press.

White, R. and van der Velden, J. (1995). "Class and Criminality," *Social Justice*, 22(1): 51–74.

Young, J. (1999). *The Exclusive Society*. London: Sage.

Young, J. (2007) *The Vertigo of Late Modernity*. London: Sage.

19

Biological and biosocial theory

Richard A. Ball

Biological and biosocial theories of deviance have a long and checkered history. Nineteenth-century and early 20th-century theories emphasized the purely biological roots of deviance, with phrenology, for example, positing a connection between head shape, personality, and behavior. Body type theories traced different forms of deviance to variations in body type, variously defined. Under the influence of Darwin, the Italian physician Cesare Lombroso (1876) gained fame with his thesis that deviance was a consequence of atavism and that the criminal was in effect an evolutionary "throwback" who should have been born among prehistoric people, whom he mistakenly believed to have been more violent and less altruistic than contemporary Europeans. Refuting Lombroso's notion of atavism, Charles Goring (1913) found evidence which he took to mean that criminals were typified by a "criminal diathesis," a combination of biological features which rendered them biologically inferior, and this sort of theory was embraced by the anthropologist Ernest Hooton (1939).

By the mid-twentieth century, William Sheldon (1949) was arguing for his own brand of body type theory which asserted that deviance was associated with the muscular mesomorph rather than the slender ectomorph or more rotund endomorph. Such theories lacked significant research support, but they were used to support political ideologies extolling those of higher socioeconomic status as biologically superior beings and political practices such as eugenics, entailing horrifying efforts to "weed out" the inferior types through techniques ranging from forced sterilization to euthanasia, an approach which, among other things, resulted in the death of hundreds of thousands of homosexuals, gypsies, Slavs, people with disabilities, and others labeled "inferior," along with more than six million Jews in the Holocaust. As a consequence, such approaches became stigmatized as "unscientific," "racist," and worse.

Recent developments

By the late 20th century, however, fairly sophisticated biological research had been discovering what seemed to be organic predispositions to such problems as alcoholism and other forms of drug abuse. Specific genes have been linked to such forms of "deviance" as depression, anorexia, bulimia, attention deficit hyperactivity disorder (ADHD), and various forms of conduct disorder (CD). Types of schizophrenia have been tied to deficiencies in enzymes helpful in dealing with environmental stress. The more these things were studied, however, the clearer it became that the old argument of "nature versus nurture" had to be overcome by an interactive approach which would try to untangle the contributions of each to a dialectical or synergistic phenomenon, leading to the emphasis upon *biosocial* theorizing rather than *biological* theorizing. Partly because of disputes about the meaning of the term "deviance," most of these theories seek to explain what they term "antisocial behavior," by which they mean behavior defined as such by authorities empowered to define them.

The resurgence of biological and biosocial theories of deviance owes a lot to new research methods (Lilly *et al.* 2007). Thus, for example, computerized tomography (CT), magnetic resonance imaging (MRI), positron emission tomography (PET), and the mapping of the human genome through the Human Genome Project (HGP) have opened a plethora of research possibilities. The first two approaches provide pictures of such biological organs as the brain, while the third can measure such dynamics as metabolic activity occurring in various locations.

Recent research using these tools has shown what appear to be temporal lobe abnormalities in both sex offenders and violent criminals. Various forms of antisocial behavior have been traced to low self-control, and brain research has disclosed associated dysfunctions of the frontal and prefrontal cortex where the so-called "executive functions" of the brain are centered.

Biosocial theory follows several approaches, including genetics, evolutionary psychology, and neuroscience (Walsh and Beaver 2009). The first of these concentrates upon inherited genes and their possible connection to various forms of deviance. Here it is important to make a distinction between *genetic* and *biological* factors. Upon conception, the zygote represents a combination of *genetic* contributions from each parent. These represent predispositions. All sorts of *biological* factors, however, may alter these predispositions in the womb and beyond. The genital features by which we identify gender, for example, may tell us that the newborn baby is a male, but the neurological components develop last, and if the fetus has been exposed to drastically different conditions during the last months of pregnancy, the structure of the brain may not "match" the genital features, leading to one reason for some people feeling that they are women born in the bodies of men or vice versa and eventually undergoing medical transgender procedures to "correct" the problem.

Biosocial theorists do not suggest that this is the only explanation for such phenomena as homosexuality and transsexuality, but they are investigating a variety of environmental factors, and for biological theorists the womb is defined as an environment. Neither biological nor biosocial theorists any longer argue that genes code for particular behaviors. There is no anticipated one-to-one relationship. No one expects to find a particular gene for anger or a specific gene for armed robbery. Certain tendencies such as impulsivity, however, may be related to certain combinations of genetic predispositions, depending upon how the environment has encouraged or discouraged the genetic tendencies.

The genetic approach

The genetic approach can be subdivided into behavior genetics, molecular genetics, and epigenetics (Walsh and Beaver 2009.) All of them try to elucidate relationships between *genotypes* (genetic endowments) and *phenotypes* (observable traits and behaviors). The first tries to tease out the relative contributions of heredity and environment to various traits and behaviors, including deviance, and many studies of such attributes as IQ have been done along these lines. The second is focused upon analysis of the molecular structure of substances such as deoxyribonucleic acid (DNA) and has found, for example, particular genes associated with aggression. The newest of these fields, epigenetics, focuses upon the relatively new discovery that environmental factors tend to alter gene functioning without changing the DNA structure at all, a discovery which may lead to some reconsideration of limited aspects of the long-rejected Lamarkian hypothesis suggesting the inheritance of acquired characteristics.

Behavior genetics began with the observation that behaviors defined as "deviant" are more common among males than among females in virtually all societies, and biosocial theory suggests that this may be traced in part to the fact that during hundreds of millennia of evolution the more aggressive men were more successful in passing on their genes, thus leading to a tendency toward greater aggressiveness in males. Males not only engage in more deviant activities but exhibit less self-control and much more aggressiveness in such behavior. Girls show fear much earlier than boys and are more fearful as adults, even when research controls for socialization effects. In most societies, behaviors defined as "deviance" are also more likely to appear among adolescents than among either very young children or adults. For more than a century, the notion of this developmental period as one of *Sturm und Drang*, of "raging hormones" and impulsivity, was generally accepted. In the mid-20th century, however, writers such as Margaret Mead (1928) and others gained considerable popularity by insisting that their data showed adolescence to be a fairly tranquil period in most preliterate societies. This interpretation remained influential for several decades, until some of this work was discredited, juvenile delinquency soared, and biological and biosocial investigations began to reveal some of the mechanisms behind the unsettling behavior of adolescents.

As had long been argued, the influx of testosterone during adolescence seems to be a significant part of the equation, with MRI studies showing juveniles, for example, to have more dominant nucleus accumbens activity compared to activity in the prefrontal cortex (PFC) relative to younger children and adults. The nucleus accumbens is associated with the push toward immediate gratification, while the prefrontal cortex tends to operate as an impulse inhibitor, and the biological shift in adolescence appears to be triggered in part by testosterone. Neither biological nor biosocial theory argues that such factors as testosterone produce "deviance" directly, only that they are associated with brain structures and functions which are linked to impulse control, the lack of which is sometimes tied to behaviors defined as deviant (Booth and Osgood 1993). Recent research has emphasized, however, that in primates testosterone seems to be more associated with dominance behaviors than aggressiveness toward others. Thus, testosterone is also linked to behaviors defined as socially desirable, including sports and business success.

Molecular genetics studies the structure and function of genes at the molecular level of the cell and how they are transferred from one generation to another. Its best-known work involves the recent progress in DNA research, including the HGP, which successfully sequenced all human DNA (Lilly *et al.* 2007). Nearly 1,200 diseases, including cystic fibrosis, sickle-cell anemia and Huntington's disease, are caused by a single gene (Beaver 2009). When it comes to traits or behavior defined as deviant, however, few expect the discovery of any OGOD (one gene–one disorder) relationship. Part of this is because genes are defined biologically while "disorders" are defined socially and psychologically, and most biosocial researchers expect complex traits such as self-control or complex behaviors such as aggression to be associated with combinations of genes in a so-called polygenic effect. Searching for such effects, molecular genetics often focuses upon either neurological or biochemical factors.

Biological and biosocial theories are directing considerable attention toward such biochemical factors as sex hormones and neurotransmitters. Thus, the effects of sex hormones such as testosterone have been studied for more than a century with increasing precision. The so-called hypoarousal of the autonomic nervous system (ANS) has been connected to low levels of the neurotransmitter dopamine, and low glucose metabolism in the orbitofrontal lobes has been tied to neuronal deficits associated with both conduct disorder (CD) and antisocial personality disorder (ASPD). Along with dopamine, the neurotransmitters serotonin and norepinephrine continue to receive the most research attention.

Recent biological and biosocial research has reinforced and extended earlier findings on the relationship between ADHD, CD and various genetic factors, including some associated with predispositions at the level of molecular biology. Robinson (2009) has recently reviewed some of this research. Thus, for example, the low levels of prefrontal cortical functioning linked to such behavioral disorders has been connected to a variant of the COMT gene (Thapar *et al.* 2005), while a variant of the 5HTT serotonin transporter gene has been tied to substance abuse, school problems and aggression in adolescents (Gerra *et al.* 2005) and extreme forms of violence in adult males (Liao *et al.* 2004), and a variant of the DRD4 dopamine regulating gene has been shown to be associated with diminished executive functioning of the brain and tied in turn to poor planning and ADHD (Robinson 2009).

The relationship between genes and deviance is also complicated by the recent development of a new field called epigenetics, which has changed many traditional ideas in biology. While such areas as molecular genetics study what some have compared to the "hardware" of genetics, epigenetics refers to little-understood processes by which "software" is developed to regulate the "expression" of the genes, "turning them on," "turning them off," modulating them, and otherwise affecting their functioning. Genes contain information for structuring and functioning of the organism, but they need more particular instructions themselves, which are found in an array of chemical "switches" called the epigenome. It is widely recognized, for example, that what a pregnant woman eats will affect the fetus, not by altering its basic genetics, which are passed on by a combination of the DNA of male and female, but by altering the expression of these inherited predispositions through an "imprinting" process. Less widely known is the fact that the mother's diet may affect her grandchildren and great-grandchildren because some epigenetic effects seem to last through several generations, a discovery which has revived interest in the discredited Lamarkian hypothesis suggesting the possible inheritance of characteristics acquired by parents which were never part of the original gene pool (Bird 2007).

Even less widely known is the research showing that factors such as poverty, parenting, and environmental toxins also have a significant epigenetic effect, actually altering the "expression" or "behavior" of the inherited genes and changing the structure of the brain and other neurological components of the body. Thus, for example, research has shown that child abuse may lower the expression of glucocorticoid receptors, which affects the instructions provided in the DNA inherited from the parents and alters the hypothalamic-pituitary-adrenal (HPA) function, a brain activity associated with antisocial behavior. The genetic inheritance is not altered, but the epigenetic effect of the abuse seems to alter its expression by shifting the "imprinting" on the epigenome. It is possible that antisocial behavior is "passed down" several generations not by genetics but by a cycle of abuse which is imprinting the epigenome of each successive generation. Environmental toxins may have similar effects. If this proves to be the case, it suggests that efforts to eliminate the environmental forces altering the epigenomes in ways associated with antisocial behavior represent a much better preventive strategy than such policies as eugenics that aim to sterilize "deviants" and prevent the reproduction entirely.

Evolutionary psychology

In addition to the general area of genetics as divided roughly into behavior genetics, molecular genetics, and epigenetics, the second general area of biological and biosocial investigation of deviance is evolutionary psychology. It begins with the assumption that we are products of successful natural selection over millions of years of evolution and attempts to connect variations in antisocial behavior between, for example, males and females, emphasizing such characteristics as tendencies toward high-risk behavior (which are presumably associated with evolutionary success among males) and higher levels of fear (which are presumably associated with evolutionary success among females). Evolutionary psychology also stresses that many of the impulsive activities associated with adolescence, such as sensation-seeking experimentation and competitiveness, were probably once highly adaptive as means of increasing the reproductive success of certain adolescents, who then passed on their genes to later generations, contributing to behavior not regarded as deviant in less regimented societies. Trying to explain why it should be that the flood of testosterone seems to trigger antisocial behavior in adolescents, Ellis (2003) has developed an "evolutionary neuroandrogenic theory" which argues that testosterone lowers neurological sensitivity to environmental stimuli, which may have once been an evolutionary advantage to adolescents but which is also tied to problems with emotional control and can result in activities defined as deviant.

Other examples of evolutionary psychology include cheater theory, r/K theory, alternative adaptation theory, conditional adaptation theory, and evolutionary expropriative theory (Lilly et al. 2007). The first argues that while most males have evolved reproduction strategies along the lines of "dads," who fulfill female desires for a mate willing to support offspring, the opposite "cads," who are inclined to deviance, are the product of the evolution of a reproductive modality focused upon use of force and deception to impregnate females. The second suggests that some males follow a "K" reproductive strategy aimed at slower reproduction and special care for each offspring, while the more antisocial types represent an "r" reproductive strategy aimed at producing a large number of offspring with minimum energy devoted to caring for each one. Alternative adaptation theory argues that people inclined to antisocial behavior have inherited a predominance of mating rather than parenting urges, while conditional adaptation theory assumes that the inherited potential for antisocial behavior may be equally distributed but that much antisocial behavior is part of an evolutionary adaptive strategy for success in unstable or hostile environments, such as the large cities of today.

Interesting as they are, evolutionary theories are very hard to prove or disprove (Rowe 2002). Even if we could prove that the various differences cited above were inherited, how could we establish that they were a consequence of evolutionary adaptation, especially when almost opposite tendencies are so explained? Evolutionary theories sometimes seem more directed toward the "why" rather than the "how," and the latter is generally considered the hallmark of scientific theories.

Many studies have found large heritability coefficients (ranging from .20 to .82) for various traits associated with behaviors defined as deviant, such as fearlessness, aggressiveness, sensation seeking, impulsivity, and low IQ (Walsh and Beaver, 2009). Of course, the relationship between the genetic heritability and such personality traits is not as great as that between the genetic endowment and actual behavior, because the environment may function to inhibit behaviors congenial to certain personalities.

The neuroscience approach

Although these research approaches clearly overlap, a third major area of investigation for biological and biosocial approaches to deviance is centered in neuroscience. Psychopathy, for example, is associated with low levels of fear and anxiety, and research has shown that one of the important factors underlying this lack of fear seems to be an imbalance between the behavioral activation system (BAS) and the behavioral inhibition system (BIS), and a low arousal level for the ANS. While the BAS is very sensitive to the neurotransmitter dopamine, which facilitates goal-direct behavior, the BAS is sensitive to serotonin, which helps to manage risk. Psychopaths tend to be more determined to achieve their goals and less able to manage the risks involved. They tend to persist in trying to get what they want even when punished for behaviors for which they were previously rewarded. Biological and biosocial research has suggested that such characteristics may be associated with a dysfunctional amygdala, a key component of the neurology of the brain's limbic system. Psychopaths appear to be characterized by low startle potentials, which are associated with limited capacity for empathy.

Alcoholism and other forms of drug addiction have long been a major target for biological and biosocial investigation. Researchers claim to have established the neural circuits associated with these problems, with the principal one being the mesolimbic reward system of the brain. This is the neural network providing the positive reinforcement for eating, drinking, and other survival behaviors. Research here has been precise enough to identify the particular brain receptors involved. Such research is aimed at development of particular treatment modalities, such as those which attempt to "train" the identified brain components of executive function, production of what are called "antagonists" to bind to the identified receptor sites and block the effects of a drug, or creation of "agonists" which bind to other receptor sites and stimulate them into activity considered more desirable.

The biological and biosocial approaches to deviance bear the stigma associated with their employment in prevention efforts, especially those centering on eugenics, policies aimed at fostering the breeding of people with characteristics theoretically related to low levels of deviance and preventing the breeding of people with characteristics linked to high levels of deviance, through interventions such as sterilization. Recent research and policy development, however, have stressed that a deviance prevention approach based on biosocial models has applicability at multiple levels. Thus, Robinson (2009) has pointed to work indicating that it may soon be possible to alter genetic makeup and/or replace particular genes so as to reduce the likelihood of antisocial behavior. Of course, it has been pointed out that from the perspective of cost–benefit analysis, it makes more sense to intervene at the environmental level in terms of those features identified as "triggers" for the expression of genetic predispositions, especially because many people are exposed to such conditions simultaneously. In the event that behaviors defined as sufficiently deviant to call forth a public response cannot be prevented in either manner, the third level of biosocial intervention involves the medicalization of deviant behavior, meaning the treatment of such behavior with a variety of drugs to regulate neurotransmitters, enzymes, and hormones.

References

Beaver, K. (2009) "Molecular genetics and crime," in A. Walsh and K. Beaver (eds.) *Biosocial Criminology: New Directions in Theory and Research*, New York: Routledge, pp. 50–72.

Bird, A. (2007) "Perceptions of epigenetics," *Nature*, 447: 396–398.

Booth, A. and Osgood, D. (1993) "The influence of testosterone on deviance in adulthood: assessing and explaining the relationship," *Criminology*, 31: 93–118.

Ellis, L. (2003) "Genes, crime, and the evolutionary neuroandrogenic theory," in A. Walsh and L. Ellis (eds.) *Biosocial Criminology: Challenging Environmentalism's Supremacy*, Hauppauge, NY: Nova Science, pp. 13–34.

Gerra, G., Garofano, L., Castaldini, L., Rovetto, F., Zamovic, A., and Moi, G. (2005) "Serotonin transporter promoter polymorphism genotype is associated with temperament, personality traits and illegal drug use among adolescents," *Journal of Neural Transmission*, 112: 1435–1463.

Goring, C. (1913) *The English Convict: A Statistical Study*, London: Her Majesty's Stationery Office.

Hooton, E. A. (1939) *Crime and the Man*, Cambridge, MA: Harvard University Press.

Liao, D., Hong, C., Shih, H., and Tsai, S. (2004) "Possible association between serotonin transporter promoter region polymorphism and extremely violent crime in Chinese males," *Neuropsychobiology*, 50: 284–287.

Lilly, J., Cullen, F., and Ball, R. (2007) *Criminological Theory: Context and Consequences*, 4th edn, Thousand Oaks, CA: Sage.

Lombroso, C. (1876) *On Criminal Man*, Milan: Hoepli.

Mead, M. (1928) *Growing up in Samoa: A Psychological Study of Primitive Youth for Western Civilization*, Oxford: Morrow.

Robinson, M. (2009) "No longer taboo: crime prevention implications of biosocial criminology," in A. Walsh and K.M. Beaver (eds.) *Biosocial Criminology: New Directions in Theory and Research*, New York: Routledge, pp. 243–263.

Rowe, D. (2002) *Biology and Crime*, Los Angeles, CA: Roxbury.

Sheldon, W. H. (1949) *Varieties of Delinquent Youth*, New York: Harpers.

Thapar, A., Langley, K., Fowler, T., Rice, F., Turic, D., and Whittinger, N. (2005) "Catechol O- methyltransferase gene variant and birth weight predict early-onset antisocial behavior in children with attention deficit/hyperactivity disorder," *Archives of General Psychiatry*, 62: 1275–1278.

Walsh, A. and Beaver, K. (2009) "Introduction to biosocial criminology," in A. Walsh and K. M. Beaver (eds.) *Biosocial Criminology: New Directions in Theory and Research*, New York: Routledge, pp. 7–28.

20

Feminist theory

Carol A. Bailey

Feminist theory is a loosely codified, interdisciplinary, and intellectually vibrant body of theory that has women as a central feature of the theorizing. Feminist theorists examine the complex ways that the social world is gendered, affected by cultural, structural, and historical contexts (Miller, 2003). Within the last two decades, the recognition of women's differences, rather than implicit assumptions of sameness, has led feminists to extend their focus on women to include the complex intersections of gender with other structural locations and identities, such as race, ethnicity, class, sexualities, age, nationality, and disabilities (Davis, 2008; Wendell, 1997). The emphasis on an intersectional framework is one of the many reasons that feminist theory continues to make significant contributions to broad academic audiences (Davis, 2008). However, feminist theory is not just an academic pursuit as it is also developed and practiced by non-academics. Feminist theory often provides, but is not limited to, explanations of inequality that have implications for social transformation, with feminism being the corresponding social and political movement to end oppression. Feminist methodologies have contributed to new ways of conducting research, and feminist pedagogy has helped reform educational practices.

This broad and oversimplified summary is no doubt contentious because of the large array of feminist theories that are sometimes in sharp contrast with each other. The differences among feminists have resulted in a long list of adjectival feminist theories, such as liberal, Marxist, socialist, radical, Latin American/Hispanic, Asian American, Native American, black, lesbian, cultural, eco-, multiracial, multicultural, French, critical race, post-, youth, locational (DeKoven, 2001), global, "third world," transnational, psychoanalytic, postcolonial, care-focused, indigenous, postmodern, African, aboriginal, fashion (Genz, 2006), and standpoint. Some of these have multiple sub-types. For example, there are libertarian and cultural perspectives within the radical feminist camp (Tong, 2009).

In discussions of feminist theories, a common convention is to organize them into three waves. Of late, the popular wave metaphor has been criticized as yet another example of excluding some women and prioritizing others. For example, claiming that the suffragettes were the first wave of feminists ignores actions by women of color that occurred long before the fight to obtain the right to vote for white women (Potter, 2006). The time period specified for the second wave does not recognize women between the 1920s and 1960s who fought against male domination, often outside mainstream politics, particularly women of color and working-class women (Cott,

1987; Genz, 2006; Potter, 2006). Given these and other critiques, the organization of theories by waves is not used here.

The following, extremely simplified, summaries of some of the major strands of feminist theory mask the incredibly complex and rigorous arguments and diversity within and across feminist traditions; references to key scholars are largely omitted. What is included is intended as a barebones introduction to feminist discourse. The number of variants worthy of inclusion is large, but only those feminist theories that have been used extensively in the study of deviant behavior are included here. The brief overviews are followed by illustrations of how some feminist theories have specifically been applied in the study of deviant behavior.

Liberal feminism gained attention in the 1960s and 1970s as an outgrowth of the women's liberation movement and primarily focused on white, middle-class, heterosexual, educated women. Based on the premise of a distinction between sex, a biological characteristic, and gender, a social construction, liberal feminists contend that gender role socialization is at the root of gender inequality. They posit that the more restrictive gender roles for women unfairly resulted in men having greater power, status, and opportunities. Concomitantly, women and things traditionally associated with women are devalued (Lorber, 2005). A goal of liberal feminists is to eliminate gender inequality by engaging in activities that promote equal opportunities and calling upon legal solutions when needed. A key issue that has divided feminists within the liberal tradition is whether they view men and women as the same or different and what should follow therefrom. The concepts of difference and sameness also permeate other feminist theories; however, issues of difference or sameness *among women* take the forefront in some other articulations of feminist theory.

Radical feminists have a considerably less benign view than liberal feminists of the sources of gender inequality. The former begin with the assertion that patriarchy, a system of male dominance, is a deliberate system of injustice that is codified and maintained through institutional and cultural arrangements and social interactions. The pervasiveness of patriarchy, historically and cross-culturally, suggests that only a radical transformation of the social order will result in women's freedom. Similar to liberal feminists, radical feminists were criticized for assuming universality of women's experiences, in this case by ignoring the fact that male power and privilege do not affect all women in the same ways (Tong, 2009).

Marxist feminists critique liberal and radical feminists for ignoring capitalism as a system of inequality. From a Marxist feminist perspective, the owners of the means of production, who are predominately men, hold power over others who are exploited for their labor. For example, women's labor is devalued in the market place and the home, where women are expected to support a capitalistic system through their reproductive and other forms of free labor. Further, the interests of powerful men are maintained and reflected in other domains—education, law, religion, medicine, and so on. To eliminate gender inequality, Marxist feminists assert that women should join men of the same class to fight against oppression (Reed, 1970)

Socialist feminists claim that Marxist and radical feminists are reductionist in attempting to explain gender inequality by either patriarchy *or* capitalism. In speaking to the relationships between patriarchy and capitalism, Hartman (2003: 206, 207) writes, "the accumulation of capital both accommodates itself to patriarchal social structure and helps to perpetuate it . . . sexist ideology has assumed a peculiarly capitalist form in the present, illustrating one way that patriarchal relationships tend to bolster capitalism." For socialist feminists, it is this partnership that explains why males dominate in both the workplace and the home.

Arguably, the first move toward an intersectional approach to the study of inequality began with a series of theories variously named black feminism, womanism, women of color feminism, and multiracial feminism. Black feminists critique liberal feminists, in particular, for their concentration on the concerns of white women and the exclusion of women of color from their analysis. From black and multiracial feminist perspectives, race should hold the central position in feminist theorizing because it is race that intersects with class, sexuality, age, and other structural locations to construct gender (Baca Zinn and Thornton Dill, 1996: 324). The intersections are dynamic, socially constructed, cross-cutting, and multiplicative systems of power relationships that operate at both the micro-structural and macro-structural levels (Baca Zinn and Thornton Dill, 1996; Burgess-Proctor, 2006). This "matrix of domination" places people in locations in relationship to power such that, depending upon the circumstances, one can be the oppressor, the oppressed, or both (Collins, 2000).

Multicultural feminists argue that "first world" women who claim to "speak for all women" or "give voice to other women" are demeaning, exclusionary, and elitist because they are unaware of, fail to acknowledge, or ignore the huge differences among women within and across the same nation-state or geographical area (Tong, 2009). Thus, they do not serve the cause of women who do not share similar characteristics. Multicultural feminists claim that examining women's conditions within a worldwide context illuminates even greater variation and complexity of injustices against women served by the hands of men (Tong, 2009).

Global, postcolonial, and transnational feminists examine the complex ways that "first world/developed/Northern/Western nations" exploit "third world/developing/Southern/Eastern nations." Of particular interest is how the processes of globalization, capitalism, patriarchy, and colonialism oppress some women, privilege others, and link women in differential ways within and across local and global contexts (Bunch, 1993; Dhruvarajan and Vickers, 2002; Mohanty, 2003; Tong, 2009).

Postmodern theories are yet another set of theories that are loosely related. Postmodern theories break from the trajectory of previous feminist theories by rejecting the notion of universal, stable, and binary classifications, such as man/woman, body/mind, and sex/gender. Particularly relevant for the study of deviance, they suggest that intersexuality, transsexuality, sexual indeterminacy, transgendered, and queer are examples of the multiplicity of sexes and genders (Braidott, 2001; Hird, 2000). Thus, for postmodernists, gender is not a stable category but a language with a system of meanings and symbols (Burgess-Proctor, 2006; Hird, 2000; Wilchins, 2004).

Yet another conceptualization of gender is that it is situated action or situated accomplishment that reflects and helps reproduce social structures of inequality. It is not just an individual characteristic. People "do gender"; they "perform gender" (Miller, 2002; West and Fenstermaker, 1995).

All of the theories reviewed thus far, and others, have been utilized in the study of deviance. A common assertion by feminist researchers who study deviance is that what is defined as normal and deviant is affected by gender and the intersection of other social locations and structures which then result in differential risks of being labeled deviant and engaging in deviant behavior (Burgess-Proctor, 2006). Feminists' interest in criminology has resulted in the well-developed area of feminist criminology (Burgess-Proctor, 2006; Chesney-Lind, 2006). A major accomplishment in the early days of feminist criminology resulted from liberal feminists' effective efforts to have crimes against women, such as intimate partner violence and sexual assault, treated as crimes worthy of systematic analysis when they heretofore had received scant attention (Burgess-Proctor, 2006; Chesney-Lind, 2006). As an example of the range of substantive interests of feminists in criminology, global feminists argue that increases in the imprisonment of women throughout the world are related to globalization, the war on drugs, and the prison-building industry (Reynolds, 2008), and Meyer and Post (2006) use a feminist ecological model to study fear of crime among older women.

Issues related to women's bodies are perennial concerns of feminists, and thus will be the focus of the remainder of this review. A central debate among feminists who study the body is whether women are active agents, victims of patriarchal structures, such as misogynistic standards of beauty, medicalization of women's bodies, and compulsive heterosexuality, or engaging in acts of resistance. Examples of substantive interests of feminists include foot binding, suttee, clitoridectomy, witch burning, "sex work," trafficking in women, eating disorders, self-mutilation, surrogate motherhood, cosmetic surgery, and genital surgery (Tong, 2009).

"Sex work" has garnered considerable attention by liberal, Marxist, radical, black, global, postmodern, and other feminists. The disagreements among the theoretical perspectives are so volatile that they have been referred to as the "feminist sex wars" (Wahab, 2003). As an example of how feminist interpretations can be polar opposites, even radical feminists have major disagreements among themselves about pornography. Radical cultural feminists insist that pornography is degrading to women and reifies men's views of women as second-class citizens, thus justifying rape, sexual harassment, and other forms of violence often portrayed in pornography (MacKinnon, 1982; Tong, 2009). In contrast, radical libertarian feminists contend that pornography should be used for women's pleasure, to explore their sexuality, and to free them from sexual inhibitions (Tong, 2009). When radical cultural feminists got anti-pornography laws passed in two major cities, liberal feminists organized to have the laws repealed (Tong, 2009).

Feminist views on prostitution show even more divergence. Radical cultural feminists passionately assert that prostitution is degrading, an example of women's sexual and economic subordination (Scoular, 2004), physically and emotionally violent, "the absolute embodiment of patriarchal privilege" (Kesler, 2002: 219), and harmful to prostitutes and all women. Radical libertarian feminists assert that women should be free to express their sexuality in any way they want, including "sex work." An alternative view is that women are entrepreneurs and sex is the commodity they sell (Jolin, 1994). Marxist and socialist feminists counter that women sell their bodies because, under a capitalist system, poor and unemployed women have few available routes to earn money; thus the "choice" made for economic survival is tantamount to coercion (Scoular, 2004; Tong, 2009). In contrast, some global feminists assert that other feminists need to include an analysis of migrant "sex workers" who are engaging in a form of resistance as they voluntarily escape the patriarchal forms of marriage and family by earning their own money (Scoular, 2004). Postmodern feminists enter the fray by challenging the view that sex for money has any inherent meaning (Scoular, 2004). Some prostitutes who are self-identified feminists report that they do not see themselves as victims of male domination but rather victims of a system that criminalizes their work (Scoular, 2004; Wahab, 2003). Critical race legal feminists examine the ways in which the laws regarding "sex work" are not gender neutral (Jolin, 1994).

Another area addressed by feminists is female genital "cosmetic" surgery. Some feminists assert that the practice is violent and harmful, but sold to women under the guise that their bodies are inadequate and require a medicalized solution. Thus, women are the hapless victims of a misogynistic and capitalist system that profits from the mutilation of their bodies. A contrasting feminists' view is that women are active agents in making the decision to have the surgery, although they make the decision within a limited context (Tiefer, 2008). From this perspective, women should have a right to decide what is done to them, and they should be supported for finding a mechanism that improves their lives, self-esteem, and self-identity (Tiefer, 2008).

Another topic that has engendered bitter disagreements is female circumcision, clitoridectomy, or female genital mutilation; the different terminology immediately identifies the divergent views. "Western" feminists who passionately speak out against the practice are charged with imposing their values on "non-Western" women, and, as such, they become part of the colonial discourse. Some "third world" feminists support the practice. Others suggest that critics should be more willing to engage in a more nuanced and fuller discussion rather than demonize the practice (Mohanty, 2003; Njambi, 2004). Part of the response to these criticisms is that women should not be subjected to violence, regardless of the culture; thus, cultural relativity is not an acceptable reason not to speak out against violence against women (Nussbaum, 1999). Also, these feminists remind others that they are acting in solidarity with women who oppose the practice within their own culture. Another perspective is that the discussions should include questioning the nature/cultural dualism and colonial notions of sexuality, body, and culture, and consider the body not as distinct from culture but a place of enculturation (Njambi, 2004).

Another area addressed by feminist theorists is eating disorders. Among the first to conduct research on eating disorders, liberal feminists focused primarily on white, young, and educated women and found that eating disorders developed in response to patriarchal, heterosexual, and misogynistic standards of beauty that were often unattainable (Hesse-Biber *et al.*, 2006). More recent work by multiracial feminists has pointed out that ignoring or viewing race as a protective factor has led to the under-diagnosis of black women. Rather than responding to standards of beauty, eating disorders among women of color may be a way to cope with sexism, racism, and homophobia (Hesse-Biber *et al.*, 2006; Thompson, 1994). Katzman and Lee (1997) suggest that defining anorexia as a body image disorder ignores food refusal in a transcultural context as a possible response to generational disparity, disconnection, transition, and oppression. Because of the awareness of the differences among women, such practices as multicultural feminist informed therapy have been developed for the treatment of Asian American women with eating disorders (Cummins and Lehman, 2007).

Scholars in feminist disability studies suggest that feminist theorists should take into account the ways that gender intersects with disabilities, along with race, age, sexualities, and other systems of repression (Garland-Thomson, 2002; Hall, 2002). Compulsory ablebodiness should be added to mutually reinforcing systems of patriarchy, race and class privilege, and compulsory heterosexuality that lead to women's oppression (Hall, 2002). Further, multicultural feminists assert that an analysis of gender and disabilities should include how bodily differences are interpreted in different cultures (Garland-Thomson, 2002; Jung, 2002). Jung (2002) submits that feminist analysis should not only focus on fixing problems related to disabilities, although action is important, but should include an analysis of the negative effects of a normalizing society.

As the above illustrates, feminist theory is a diverse body of theories that vary by level of analysis, substantive problem, disciplinary origins, major concepts, perspectives on the sources of inequality, social and political agendas for eradicating inequality, and the identities and structures that are included at the center of the theorizing. What almost all feminists share is a desire to end oppression and subordination.

References

Baca Zinn, M. and Thornton Dill, B. (1996) "Theorizing differences from multiracial feminism," *Feminist Studies*, 22: 321–331.

Braidott, R. (2001) "Becoming-woman: Rethinking the positivity of difference," in E. Bronfen and M. Kavka (eds.) *Feminist Consequences: Theory for the New Century* (pp. 353–380), New York: Columbia University Press.

Bunch, C. (1993) "Prospects for global feminism," in A. Jaggar and P. Rothenberg (eds.) *Feminist Frameworks* (3rd edn) (pp. 249-252), New York: McGraw-Hill.

Burgess-Proctor, A. (2006) "Intersections of race, class, gender, and crime," *Feminist Criminology*, 1: 27–47.

Chesney-Lind, M. (2006) "Patriarchy, crime, and justice: Feminist criminology in an era of backlash," *Feminist Criminology*, 1: 6–26.

Collins, P. H. (2000) *Black Feminist Thought: Knowledge, Consciousness, and the Politics of Empowerment* (2nd edn), New York: Routledge.

Cott, N. F. (1987) *The Grounding of Modern Feminism*, New Haven, CT: Yale University Press.

Cummins, L. and Lehman, J. (2007) "Eating disorders and body image concerns in Asian American women: Assessment and treatment from a multicultural and feminist perspective," *Eating Disorders*, 15: 217–230.

Davis, K. (2008) "Intersectionality as buzzword: A sociology of science perspective on what makes a feminist theory successful," *Feminist Theory*, 9: 67–85.

DeKoven, M. (2001) *Feminist Locations: Global and Local, Theory and Practice*, New Brunswick, NJ: Rutgers University Press.

Dhruvarajan, V. and Vickers, J. (2002) *Gender, Race, and Nation: Global Perspective*, Toronto: University of Toronto Press.

Garland-Thomson, R. (2002) "Integrating disability, transforming feminist theory," *NWSA Journal*, 14: 1–32.

Genz, S. (2006) "Third way/ve: The politics of postfeminism," *Feminist Theory*, 7: 333–353.

Hall, K. (2002) "Feminism, disability, and embodiment," *NWSA Journal*, 14: vii–xiii.

Hartman, H. (2003) "The unhappy marriage of Marxism and feminism: Towards a more progressive union," in C. McCann and S.-K. Kim (eds.) *Feminist Theory Reader: Local and Global Perspectives* (pp. 206–221), New York: Routledge.

Hesse-Biber, S., Leavy, P., Quinn, C., and Zoino, J. (2006) "The mass marketing of disordered eating and eating disorders: The social psychology of women, thinness and culture!," *Women's Studies International Forum*, 29: 208–224.

Hird, M. (2000) "Gender's nature: Intersexuality, transsexualism and the 'sex'/'gender' binary," *Feminist Theory*, 1: 347–354.

Jolin, A. (1994) "On the backs of working prostitutes: Feminist theory and prostitution policy," *Crime & Delinquency*, 40: 69–83.

Jung, K. (2002) "Chronic illness and educational equity: The politics of visibility," *NWSA Journal*, 14: 178–200.

Katzman, M. and Lee, S. (1997) "Beyond body image: The interpretation of feminist and transcultural theories in the understanding of self-starvation," *International Journal of Eating Disorders*, 1: 385–394.

Kesler, K. (2002) "Is a feminist stance in support of prostitution possible? An exploration of current trends," *Sexualities*, 5: 219–235.

Lorber, J. (2005) *Gender Inequality: Feminist Theories and Politic* (3rd edn), Los Angeles, CA: Roxbury.

MacKinnon, C. (1982) "Feminism, Marxism, method and the state: An agenda for theory," *Signs: Journal of Women in Culture and Society*, 7: 515–544.

Meyer, E. and Post, L. (2006) "Alone at night: A feminist ecological model of community violence," *Feminist Criminology*, 1: 207–227.

Miller, J. (2002) "The strengths and limits of 'doing gender' for understanding street crime," *Theoretical Criminology*, 6: 433–460.

—— (2003) "Gender, crime, and (in)justice: Introduction to the special issue," *Journal of Contemporary Ethnography*, 32: 3–8.

Mohanty, C. (2003) *Feminism without Borders: Decolonizing Theory, Practicing Solidarity*, Durham, NC: Duke University Press.

Njambi, W. (2004) "Dualism and female bodies in representation of African female circumcision: A feminist critique," *Feminist Theory*, 5: 281–303.

Nussbaum, M. (1999) *Sex and Social Justice*, New York: Oxford University Press.

Potter, H. (2006) "An argument for black feminist criminology: Understanding AA women's experiences with intimate partner abuse using an integrated approach," *Feminist Criminology*, 1: 106–124.

Reed, E. (1970) "Women: Caste, class, or oppressed sex?," *International Socialist Review*, 31: 15–41.

Reynolds, M. (2008) "The war on drugs, prison building, and globalization: Catalysts for the global incarceration of women," *NWSA Journal*, 20: 72–95.

Scoular, J. (2004) "The 'subject' of prostitution: Interpreting the discursive, symbolic material positions of sex/work in feminist theory," *Feminists Theory*, 5: 343–355.

Thompson, B. (1994) *A Hunger So Wide and So Deep: A Multiracial View of Women's Eating Problems*, Minneapolis: University of Minnesota Press.

Tiefer, L. (2008) "Female genital cosmetic surgery: Freakish or inevitable? Analysis from medical marketing, bioethics, and feminist theory," *Feminism & Psychology*, 18: 466–479.

Tong, R. (2009) *Feminist Thought: A More Comprehensive Introduction*, Boulder, CO: Westview Press.

Wahab, S. (2003) "Creating knowledge collaboratively with female sex workers: Insights from a qualitative, feminist, and participatory study," *Qualitative Inquiry*, 9: 635–642.

Wendell, S. (1997) "Toward a feminist theory of disability," in Lennard Davis (ed.) *Disability Studies Reader* (pp. 260–278), New York: Routledge.

West, C. and Fenstermaker, S. (1995) "Doing difference," *Gender & Society*, 9: 8–37.

Wilchins, R. (2004) *Queer Theory, Gender Theory: An Instant Primer*, Los Angeles, CA: Alyson Books.

21

Postmodern theory

Charles Walton

The emergence of postmodern theory has signified a challenge to the traditional sociological discourse regarding deviance. One of the most distinctive aspects of the relatively new theoretical turn toward postmodernism is the fact that there are important epistemological differences relative to most modern theories of deviance. For example, postmodern theory promises only a partial explanation, to uncover partial truths, to reveal a partial reality. Postmodern theory, unlike its modern counterpart, does not pretend to explain deviance in its totality, and so it is less ambitious in its reach.

Postmodern theory has, on occasion, been dismissed by critics as being trendy or evidence of the latest theoretical fad:

> While some sociological theorists, and many sociologists, still consider postmodern social theory to be a fad, and it continues to look to some [but not this author] more like a carnival (Norris, 1990) than a serious scholarly endeavor, the simple fact is that sociological theorists can no longer view postmodernism as little more than an interesting side- (if not freak-) show. A good deal of the most interesting and important contemporary social theory swirls in and around the postmodern scene.
>
> *(Ritzer 1997:1)*

The intent here is to offer an account of how postmodern theory has been used and may be used in the future to account for and analyze deviance in a nuanced fashion.

Some basic distinctions between the attributes of modernism and those of postmodernism may clarify the varied conceptualizations of self and society regarding the respective types of theory. Modernist theories tend to hold a view that society represents a coherent entity, that it is a totality of sorts, informed by a singular normative order. Postmodern theories, though not homogeneous, tend to suggest a fragmentation of society and self, characterized by pluralism and cultural contradictions. Modernist theories tend to valorize rationality and linear thinking. By contrast, postmodern theories tend to highlight the irrationality of rationality, hypertext thinking, and may well elevate the absurd and ironic to cultural primacy. Science is not so privileged in postmodern accounts—rather it offers us simply "another way of knowing." Lastly, modernists tend to believe in absolutes—Art, with a capital "A," Beauty with a capital "B," Truth with a capital "T"—that is, there are definitive ideas as to what is art and what is not art, what is beauty and what is not beauty, what is truth and what is not truth. Duchamp's found objects are elevated to the status of art. Dichotomous thinking is deconstructed and truth is, at best, partial.

Postmodern theory is most often considered a critical perspective. Pfohl (1994:404) attempts to capture the umbrella of critical perspectives by highlighting both theoretical and practical concerns germane to postmodern approaches to deviance:

> Theoretically, critical perspectives attempt to make sense of the relationship between human struggles for power in history and the ritual construction, deconstruction, and reconstruction of normative social boundaries. Practically, people who engage in critical theorizing ally themselves with people who are committed to the uprooting of hierarchical social forms and the realization of social justice. This combination of theoretical and practical concerns leads critical theorists to examine the material and symbolic relationships between power, social control, and actions which resist control.

Moreover, critical theories call into question the dominant perspectives that serve to colonize deviance theory and reify deviance in some essentialist fashion acting as a force of knowledge-based social control. Such theories serve the interest of power as tools in the maintenance of the cultural hegemony.

Postmodern theories of deviance represent a compilation of multifarious perspectives to include Marxist, feminist, multicultural, anarchist, societal reactionist, deconstructionist, situationist, nihilist, semiotic, and radical standpoints. Like most of contemporary theory, the emphasis in postmodern theory is on a synthesis, recombining elements of various perspectives in the hopes of finding a suitable frame given distinct social circumstances that change from scene to scene. Such free appropriation and synthesis is misunderstood when confronted by the positivist gaze. Criticisms of postmodern theory, like those exemplified in *The Poverty of Postmodernism* (O'Neill 1995), hold the theory to be trendy and illogical, the textbook example of navel gazing. O'Neill (1995:16, 191) laments the "insanity of postmodernism," suggesting it offers only "a great black sky of nonsense." More substantive criticisms charge that the decentered nature of postmodern theories fosters a lack of clarity with regard to concepts and assumptions; it is, in fact, this very notion of ordered, linear thought that results in the standardized knowledge construction that postmodern theories rail against. Given that positivism has cultural primacy and is privileged in science, coupled with the fact that positivist perspectives see themselves as value neutral, one can easily venture to comprehend the dominant ideological resistance to such emerging perspectives.

> The supposed "facts" of positivist research, like pornographic images of women's bodies, are objectified but not objective. To be truly objective, positivism would have to forsake its desires to blast free of human–animal interdependence and to recognize the socially situated character of all claims to knowledge.
>
> *(Pfohl 1994:471)*

Cultural contradictions, deconstruction, and deviance

Contradictions have a long history as a theoretical concept of import in sociology. They are a prominent theoretical feature in the workings of Marx's theory. Bell's *The Cultural Contradictions of Capitalism* (1976) rethinks the concept in light of Weber's work regarding the Protestant ethic. The rampant rise of technology in the service of the industrial revolution, followed by a resultant post-industrial information society, fueled by what Virillio (1991) refers to as "dromology," makes the potential for fragmentation and contradiction manifold.

Weinstein and Weinstein (1993) argue that Simmel may have been one of the first classical sociologists to anticipate the postmodern condition with his theory regarding what he called the "tragedy of culture." The tragedy of culture is the result of the exponential growth of what is termed the "objective culture," the whole of cultural products produced throughout time, juxtaposed with the relatively constant "individual culture," which is the individual's ability to produce and interpret the objective culture. The tragedy of culture ensues and grows more grave with each generation. Such a theory could serve as an alternative means in sense-making of some postmodern maladies (e.g. ADHD, CFS, eating disorders, OCD, and so on). These so-called diseases exemplify the medicalization of deviance in most cases, and ultimately may be socially constructed as well as having some organic component. The argument here is that individuals in the postmodern era are overwhelmed by stimuli in the increasingly simulated world of media, popular culture, and advertising. In the case of ADHD, for example, the incredible rises in rates of diagnosis of the disorder raise the question as to whether people's bodies, physiologically, have changed all that much over time to explain why there is no evidence of the disease prior to 1980? Or, rather, has the culture changed? The ascension of television and the internet in the 20th century are cultural changes that have had irrevocable consequences for how leisure and work have been refashioned. Individuals are socialized relative to the new rapid-fire media and the old pastime of "storytelling" is regarded as somewhat anachronistic. Or still another possibility is that the new diagnostic language of the 1980s ushered in these patients by the thousands.

In any event, one can easily observe that the volume of images, soundbites, and texts has increased at such a rate that the potential for contradictory representations regarding so-called core values is more salient.

> In an arena of intense competition with 24/7 cable TV networks, talk radio, Internet sites, and blogs, and ever proliferating new media like Facebook, Myspace, and YouTube, competition is ever more intense leading the media to go to sensationalistic tabloidized stories which they construct in the forms of media spectacle that attempt to attract maximum audiences for as much time as possible.
>
> *(Kellner 2008:29)*

The sense of fragmentation that permeates postmodern life is buoyed by such cultural contradictions as those that inform violence in our society. On the one hand, we abhor violence, loathe its finality and injustice; it is, as Marx argued, the power of last resort. Yet we are transfixed by violence, and prone to consume the spectacle of someone else's demise. The level of hyperreal violence represented through a variety of media attests to the cultural primacy of violence in contemporary society, whether it be military violence, gang violence, domestic violence, or the spectacular violence of the unhinged spree killer. It is the *hyperreal* simulation of violence without *real* consequences that is problematic as the subjective attempts to reconcile these disparate values. Especially, given that violence is the "trump card on both sides in the battle of deviance and social control" (Pfohl 1994:409).

The term "deconstruction" is a method endorsed by French literary theorist Jacques Derrida, understood as a means to tease out the contradictions of any text. Murderers for whom we should have contempt are made over as reality television stars, given their fifteen minutes of fame, in the Warhol vernacular. Deviance is informed by a plethora of cultural contradictions, from those related to violence, to sex, to substance abuse, and power. "Thus in doing deconstruction, Derrida often focuses on the small, tell-tale moments in the text. The goal is to locate the key moment, the key contradiction" (Ritzer 1997:121).

The vignette that Pfohl (1994) offers in *Images of Deviance and Social Control* exemplifies just such a testimony of the media's role in facilitating such contradictions, relative to deviance. Pfohl explains that he once received a phone call from a *Time* magazine reporter hunting for an "expert" to quote for a story on the socially constructed "War on Drugs." America was besieged by a *nouveau* crack epidemic. The 1970s saw the expansion of freebasing in the community of drug users whose drug of choice was cocaine. Comedian Richard Pryor infamously set himself on fire during one such episode. By the mid-1980s a less volatile version of smokable cocaine was in fashion, referred to as "crack." The War on Drugs was a federal government campaign, initiated by the Nixon administration but most salient in the Reagan administration, aimed at curbing recreational drug use of all sorts. Pfohl was chosen as an "expert" because of his published work in the area of deviant behavior. He was perplexed from the start, given that the reporter had already framed the problem in a dichotomy: that is, he wanted to know whether Pfohl thought the correct response to such rampant drug use was "stricter punishments" or "more treatment." Pfohl explains his consternation at the frame offered by the journalist:

> I tried to offer the journalist an alternative perspective. I suggested that an exclusive focus on either punishment or rehabilitation ignores the more complex and contradictory context of contemporary drug use. I was speaking about the mass marketing of both legal and illegal drugs as a solution to the widespread experience of powerlessness, social alienation, and personal anxiety.
>
> *(Pfohl 1994:401)*

The reporter was not impressed with Pfohl's nuanced response and was looking for something that was easily digestible for the mass market audience his magazine targeted. The historical and structural conditions that Pfohl suggested were important in more fully conceptualizing the so-called drug problem fell on deaf ears, even after Pfohl pointed to the alleged CIA involvement in the drug trafficking amid the backdrop of the Iran Contra Affair (Scott and Marshall 1991). The deviance theorist recommended several articles and books the reporter might reference, and in the end none of what Pfohl said in the forty-five-minute interview made it into the magazine.

The simulation of deviance

The accelerated cultural primacy of the electronic media has wrought consequences for our understanding of representations of deviance in the postmodern era. Representations of deviance become more important in a culture wherein the secondary agents of socialization, particularly media and the culture industry, are ascendant, given the perpetually fracturing postmodern family's declining role in primary socialization (e.g. the rise of divorce rates in the last half century, childcare increasingly farmed out to other institutions). The sheer volume of time that contemporary individuals spend consuming some form of electronic visual media, whether through television or the internet, is an invitation to sociologists to think critically about the social construction of such content. Surette (1998) found that from the 1960s through the 1990s television programming devoted toward crime and justice accounted for approximately a quarter of all prime-time broadcasts. Since then there has emerged a new hybrid news–entertainment genre of television which is dominated by shows in the style of *Nancy Grace* which fetishize crime and deviance, especially if it involves death. True-crime news documentaries featured on major networks like *Dateline* (NBC) or *48 Hours Mystery* (CBS) usually offer some hyperreal narrative involving an innocent person's tragic death and the sensational investigations that follow. Ordinary death is rarely represented currently in the culture; it is virtually invisible as the simulations of extraordinary death become the norm.

Writers like Townsend (1998) have argued that the end of the 20th century was characterized by a "radical change" in which culture depicting natural death gave way to increasingly hyperreal depictions of cinematic death and violence. Coverage of such high-profile spree killers as Virginia Tech Massacre perpetrator Seung-Hui Cho and Fort Hood Army psychiatrist Nadil Hasan, and such serial killers as the DC snipers, John Allen Muhammad and Lee Boyd Malvo, serves to elevate individuals who are thought to be the worst society has to offer into media anti-celebrities starring in something just shy of their own mini-series. The media is oddly positioned as both the engine of spectacle in flashing these haunting images across the screen as well as owing some responsibility with respect to sense-making in this arena and, if at all possible, assisting with the investigation. "On the one hand, the media are accused of spreading glamorous images of crime, which can lead to copycat behavior; but on the other hand, the media are expected to aid in reducing crime, assisting in manhunts, and bolstering the criminal justice system" (Alexander and Thompson 2008:356–7).

The aforementioned Cho, who killed thirty-two people and himself on April 16, 2007, on the campus of Virginia Tech, presents an interesting case relative to the mixing of reality and the fiction of media. Cho, a disturbed, otherwise non-descript twenty-three-year-old Korean-American English major, not only knew he would kill several of his fellow students and faculty that day. He knew he would create a media spectacle that few would rival. "A multimedia package that Cho mailed to NBC News on April 16, apparently after the first murder in the dorm, and widely shown on April 18, revealed that Cho indeed was planning a media spectacle in the tradition of the Columbine shooters whom he celebrated as 'martyrs'" (Kellner 2008: 38–9). Cho had assembled a veritable press kit that contained video clips, photos with captions, and a lengthy document to attest to his extreme alienation. The killer had created his own ready-made simulation which was immediately media accessible.

Several aspects of Cho's partial account of the prelude to the Virginia Tech Massacre are compelling. The fact that he had celebrated Harris and Klebold, the Columbine killers, even calling them "martyrs," as if they had died for the cause of some misfit religion, is interesting in that his only knowledge of those ill-fated youth came from the media spectacle, the characters that were borne out of the Columbine High School surveillance video replayed without end. Media also played a distinct role in the construction of Cho, as evidenced in one of the photographs he included in the multimedia package.

> One of the photos in which Cho posed with a hammer in his hand reprises the Korean "Asian Extreme" film *Oldboy*, which itself is a revenge fantasy in which a young Korean inexplicably imprisoned in a room goes on a rampage of revenge against one of his captors. Another pose shows Cho pointing a gun at his own head, another iconic image of *Oldboy*, which in turn is quoting Robert de Niro's famous scene in *Taxi Driver*, in which he follows a slaughter of perceived villains with a suicidal blowing of his head apart, just as Cho did.
>
> *(Kellner 2008:39)*

The shy introvert with an odd speech pattern struggled throughout life to assimilate socially, not part of his Korean parents' cultural pluralism and yet not part of his largely white American middle-class fellow students' socially compulsory conformity. His violent fantasies, though fragmented and full of hyperbole, would find "voice" in the centrifuge of media spectacle whirling around, spilling little distortions of the truth here and there for the consumers of this tragedy to piece together, as if some order could be made of this chaos and mayhem.

Power-knowledge and social regulation

Postmodern theories tend to recognize the salience of emotion as well as the physicality of bodies in deviance and crime. Foucault, perhaps more than anyone, has fashioned a theory that highlights the manner in which the social regulation of people's bodies and emotions has been transformed throughout history. "Each major historical epoch, he argued, is distinguished by a predominant form of regulation or control" (Alexander and Thompson 2008:358). For example, in *Discipline and Punish* (1977), Foucault offers the reader a history of torture and execution, beginning with traditional feudal society, through the "total institutions" that are the subject of Goffman's *Asylums* (1961), and eventually to an account of the scientific discourses that are employed to discipline the mind and body of the prisoner.

In *The Condition of Postmodernity* (1990), Harvey interprets Foucault's conceptualization of the relationship between knowledge and power in the social regulation of deviance as embodied in a loosely wound, yet pervasive, web of societies under surveillance.

> Close scrutiny of the micro-politics of power relations in different localities, contexts, and social situations leads him to conclude that there is a intimate relation between the systems of knowledge ("discourses") which codify techniques and practices for the exercise of social control and domination within particular localized contexts. The prison, the asylum, the hospital, the university, the school, the psychiatrist's office, are all examples of sites where a dispersed and piecemeal organization of power is built up independently of any systematic strategy of class domination.
>
> *(Harvey 1990:45)*

The disciplinary society that emerges from Foucault's work serves to regulate the individual at every turn, even as individuals imagine themselves to be free and able to choose their own destinies.

> By way of summary we can say that disciplines involve a series of procedures for distributing individuals, fixing them in space, classifying them, extracting from them maximum time and energy, training their bodies, coding their continuous behavior, maintaining them in perfect visibility, surrounding them with mechanisms of observation, registering and recording them, and constituting in them a body of knowledge that is accumulated and centralized.
>
> *(Ritzer 1997:58)*

Ultimately Foucault is conflicted about the prospects of the disciplinary society. He sees its advantages in the administration of large factories and the military, but worries about the ways in which the disciplinary society permeates the private lives of individuals, tracking them, and scanning them, even as they are unaware.

At the root of the disciplinary society is the full threat of violence. May's *Power and Innocence* (1972) is interesting in this vein as the author considers how the resistance that blocked power may create, might play in the ritual structure of social interaction. "Violence is thus a power-play, a final and dramatic gesture through which we assert control over a world which appears to escape our grasp" (Pfohl 1994:407). Pfohl (1994), in his reading of May (1972), is suggesting that violence is *always* the trump card, no matter if you are in the establishment or part of the resistance.

Summary

Postmodern theories of deviance are interdisciplinary and nearly impossible to herd as far as representing a coherent group. Perhaps it is not in the interest of postmodernism to have its theoretical definition so neatly arranged. All the variety of such theories has not been expressed here. As mentioned earlier, postmodern theories are adept at the synthesis of any number of perspectives and do not privilege one particular ontology above another. Nevertheless, postmodern theories of deviance do appear critical of the formulaic bias of positivist theories of deviance. One of the main sources of critique would be something on the order of a suspicion of any such study or perspective as being capable of offering an authentic understanding of the phenomenon in question. Moreover, postmodern thinkers are likely to suspect that positivist-type work that is done in the area of criminology and deviance is likely to objectify the subjects and serve the interests of law and normative order.

Postmodern theories of deviance are more likely to embrace perspectives that lend themselves to cultural studies and an appreciation for the role that media plays in constructing deviance. Postmodern theories seem adept at dealing with cultural contradictions, simulation and the problem of representation, and the ways in which technology has informed our understanding of deviance. Some have raised questions as to the utility of such theories with respect to hypothesis testing even as postmodernism resists the invitation. However, postmodern theories do not claim to be the "final answer," as do most competing paradigms. Ironically, in that sense, perhaps postmodern theory is the most realistic.

References

Alexander, J. and Thompson, K. (2008) *A Contemporary Introduction to Sociology: Culture and Society in Transition*. Boulder, CO: Paradigm.

Bell, D. (1976) *The Cultural Contradictions of Capitalism*. New York: Basic Books.

Foucault, M. (1977) *Discipline and Punish: The Birth of the Prison*. New York: Pantheon.

Goffman, E. (1961) *Asylums: Essays on the Social Situation of Mental Patients and Other Inmates*. Garden City, NY: Anchor.

Harvey, D. (1990) *The Condition of Postmodernity*. Cambridge, MA: Blackwell.

Kellner, D. (2008) "Media spectacle and the massacre at Virginia Tech," in B. Agger and T. Luke (eds.) *There is a Gunman on Campus: Tragedy and Terror at Virginia Tech* (pp.29–54). Lanham, MD: Rowman & Littlefield.

May, R. (1972) *Power and Innocence: A Search for the Source of Violence*. New York: Norton.

Norris, C. (1990) *What's Wrong with Postmodernism?* Baltimore, MA: Johns Hopkins University Press.

O'Neill, J. (1995) *The Poverty of Postmodernism*. London: Routledge.

Pfohl, S. (1994) *Images of Deviance and Social Control*. New York: McGraw-Hill.

Ritzer, G. (1997) *Postmodern Social Theory*. New York: McGraw-Hill.

Scott, P. and Marshall, J. (1991) *Cocaine Politics: Drugs, Armies, and the CIA in Central America*. Berkeley: University of California Press.

Surette, R. (1998) *Media, Crime, and Criminal Justice: Images and Realities*. Belmont, CA: Wadsworth.

Townsend, C. (1998) *Vile Bodies: Photography and the Crisis of Looking*. New York: Prestel .

Virillio, P. (1991) *Lost Dimension*. New York: Semiotext(e).

Weinstein, D. and Weinstein, M. (1993) *Postmodern(ized) Simmel*. London: Routledge.

Part IV

Becoming deviant as a process

Overview

Some individuals may be born deviant by virtue of being physiologically different in the sense of having some deformity, disfiguring characteristic, unusual appearance, or mental deficiency or dysfunction. Behavior may sometimes be a function of constitutional or physiological predisposition. In most instances, deviance is likely ascribed or learned. Individuals may learn deviant behavior in a very direct fashion, such as by instruction. They may also learn it in an indirect fashion by example, or observation, or from information they receive. People may also acquire their deviant tendencies in a more generalized manner from the mass media or through experiential inference.

Individuals may learn about the existence of a particular form of deviance that has some attraction for them. Then, they subsequently learn the techniques of the deviant activities. At some point, they may encounter an opportunity structure that will facilitate this type of deviance, and then take advantage of it. While some persons "discover" deviance by themselves, or with minimal direct or indirect suggestions from others, many are more closely instructed or guided into deviant activities—mentored, as it were. Paths to deviance are both numerous and diverse.

This part includes three chapters that each examines a particular path. Stacey Nofziger addresses one path to deviance that puts heavy emphasis on the onset of deviance during childhood, lack of self-control, and parenting protocols. Mindy Bradley-Engen looks at another path that is a function of acquiring a stigmatized identity that evolves into a deviant identity, and the subsequent deviant behavior that attends the identity. Charles Faupel employs the concept of career to explore deviant behavior over the life course.

Entering deviance

In her chapter, Stacey Nofziger asserts that early involvement in deviant behavior is a key predictor of adult deviance. On the basis of the existing body of knowledge regarding the process of becoming deviant, she indicates that there are two "empirical realities" that provide insight into this process. It appears that the earlier an individual first becomes involved in deviant behavior, the more likely it is that that person will later engage in "long-term patterns of criminal and deviant activities." She also reports that the research literature further suggests that "the family plays a vital role" in the process of becoming deviant.

She does concede that there are other events, circumstances, and changes that occur during the life course of an individual that may lead to increased deviance or, conversely, may motivate "exit or desistance" from such behavior. For Nofziger, the age of onset of deviant behaviors is one of the key factors that increase the likelihood of the individual engaging in "serious and chronic antisocial behaviors" in later stages of life. This factor is also related to the problem of more serious offending, a greater variety of offending behaviors, and engaging in deviance over a longer period of time. Nofziger also suggests that, based on the research literature, parenting and self-control are also powerful factors in predicting deviance and criminal activity in adulthood.

Research has demonstrated that self-control is a strong indicator of deviant and criminal behavior. Nofziger reports that this has been defined as "the extent to which individuals are likely to give in to temptations of the moment." Self-control is therefore considered to be crucial in preventing entrance into deviance. It develops early in life and remains relatively stable through the life course. It is very much related to effective parenting. Parents are role models and should provide warmth, affection, clear rules and restrictions, and discipline, and demonstrate strong self-control themselves. Deviant parents often produce deviant children since parents who have poor self-control cannot properly teach their children self-control. The relationship between parenting, socialization of children in a fashion that promotes self-control, and the children's later involvement in deviance and crime is forcefully demonstrated by research.

Stigma and the deviant identity

In her chapter, Mindy Bradley-Engen addresses the concept of *identity* and the process of *stigmatization.* She describes identity as the "way people think about and describe themselves." Identity also includes the image by which others recognize someone. Bradley-Engen defines *stigma* as having a characteristic (or characteristics) or attribute, behavioral or physical, that makes one "different" from others, but in a "less desirable way." Because of something unique, in an unfavorable or disvalued fashion, the individual is stigmatized. As a result, their identity is "tainted" and, thus, socially degraded, and, accordingly, deemed a deviant identity.

Bradley-Engen, citing the literature, reports that there are two levels of stigma. One of these levels is that of the *discredited.* This label refers to an individual whose stigma is known or apparent. This fact impacts on the stigmatized individual and those with whom he or she interacts. Because the stigma is apparent, the quality of the relationship and the interaction between the stigmatized individual and others is degraded and strained. The second level of stigma is that of the *discreditable.* In this instance, the individual's disvalued uniqueness or stigma is not apparent but concealed. Discreditable individuals attempt to maintain the concealed stigma through impression management and information control. By doing so, they can control the reaction of others by manipulation of what they disclose. Should the stigma be revealed, others will react to the stigmatized individual in a negative or unfavorable fashion, socially discrediting them, "spoiling their normal identity," and labeling them as deviant. This may result in rejection and social exclusion.

Bradley-Engen suggests that the individual who is labeled deviant may then internalize their label and it will become incorporated into their sense of self. Others will continue to label and socially reject them. Bradley-Engen indicates that inasmuch as they no longer "belong" to previous social groups, they may seek out, or be sought out by, other deviants like themselves. She goes on to say that because of their deviant identity, they will likely think of themselves in this way and transition from primary deviance to secondary deviance. This deviant identity will likely impact their behavior in the future.

Deviants may try to negotiate their label and stigma within the context of their ongoing relationships and interactions with others, through a variety of stigma management techniques. These might include avoiding interaction with others (*disassociation*); disguising or hiding the stigma (*passing*); acknowledging the stigma but seeking to minimize its influence on interaction with others (*covering*); using proactive mechanisms such as levity or sarcasm to manage tension with others (*coping*); or working with others, such as family and friends, to manage impressions jointly (*teamwork*).

Some individuals try to avoid or diminish their deviant labels, while others may turn to *tertiary deviance*, which involves *role embracement*. Here the deviant identifies with their deviance and works with stigmatized others to combat their mutual deviant label through advocacy and social protests to change the public image and alter social views on their form of deviance. Deviants may experience *charismatic destigmatization* which involves "individual purification," "individual transcendence," and "collective aristocratization" (advocacy to destigmatize their category of deviance).

Bradley-Engen concludes her chapter with a brief overview of a number of research studies that address deviant identities and stigma management.

The deviant career

In his chapter, Charles Faupel uses the concept of "career" to explore criminal and deviant activities over the life course. He points out that "career" has been a neglected concept prior to the time that it was introduced to sociology through the research and writing of Everett C. Hughes and Oswald Hall, who used it to great advantage in their research on work and occupation in the 1940s. Faupel indicates that it was "pivotal" in their research in explaining the lifestyles of workers. It came to be used in the deviant behavior research and writings of Goffman and Becker and later became a very utilitarian concept in the works of many researchers in the field.

Previously, it was felt by many scholars that criminal activities could be characterized as "pathological." "Career" came to be a far more productive concept when doing research on deviant behavior. Faupel reports that researchers identified three "essential qualities common to all careers": careers are temporal and single actions do not constitute a career; a career is a series of related activities that serves as a reference point around which individuals organize their lives; and a career entails a subjective experience and identity, derived from the meanings attached to these activities. He suggests that careers can be bifurcated into two categories, which he labels *deviant* and *respectable*. He further posits that the concept of "careers" can also be bifurcated into two categories on another dimension, resulting in the categories of *occupational* and *non-occupational*. This double categorization results in a matrix paradigm of "careers."

Faupel indicates that some researchers have pointed out that there are significant points of divergence between deviant and respectable careers. One of these is the fact that deviant careers operate under "the threat of legal sanctions" and, therefore, "deviant careerists must carry out their activities in secret." Another divergence is the fact that "deviant careers are not normally pursued within the context of a highly structured environment." Accordingly, such careers are not as predictable as respectable careers, which do occur "within the context of a highly structured environment."

On the other dimension, occupational careers are associated with activities by which one earns a living. The non-occupational career may involve avocational, civic, religious, or patriotic activities.

There is a temporal quality to both deviant and respectable careers. They both proceed over time and involve phases or stages. Some of these stages are *career choice and entry*, *career mobility*, and *exiting the career*, among others. As Faupel concludes, "*career* captures most faithfully the way in which deviant actors understand their own activities and lives."

22

Entering deviance

Stacey Nofziger

Introduction

The question of how individuals become deviant has been the focus of many criminological theories and empirical studies. Theories may focus on either the socially constructed nature of deviance or the processes involved in the entrance into deviance. Some perspectives argue that once started on a deviant path, the individual will be persistent in their criminal and deviant behaviors. Others argue this is a more fluid relationship, which accounts for transitions in and out of deviance throughout the life course. Regardless of the specific processes and mechanisms that are hypothesized to predict deviance, two empirical realities are acknowledged as central in the understanding of deviant behavior. First, the earlier one begins engaging in deviant behaviors, the more likely one is to have relatively stable, long-term patterns of criminal and deviant activity. Second, the family plays a vital role in becoming deviant.

This chapter examines the importance of early onset and stability of deviant behavior and focuses on experiences within the family that affect early childhood entrance into deviance.

Onset and stability of deviance

The majority of research on crime and deviance has focused on the reasons why individuals engage in antisocial behaviors. Nearly every theory proposes different explanations, ranging from larger structural and cultural causes to individual differences and various social processes. While there is continued debate about the mechanisms and processes involved, most theories attempt to explain the initial cause or entrance into deviant behaviors. In contrast, some recent theory has focused more on processes that influence not only the entrance of individuals into deviance but their persistence and exit or desistance from these behaviors. For example, life-course theories argue that different trajectories of behavior are interwoven and influenced by specific, relatively abrupt or gradual, transitions that lead to increased deviance or a movement away from deviance (Sampson and Laub 1993, 1997; Thornberry 1997; Elder 1985, 1994; Laub and Sampson 2003). These perspectives emphasize changes that occur during the life course of the individual that influence their deviant career (Inciardi 1975; Luckenbill and Best 1981). While these new perspectives expand our understanding of changes in deviant behavior and bring attention to a relatively neglected area of study, they also still acknowledge the importance of the first step of entering deviance.

One important issue related to entrance is the age at which individuals begin such behaviors. The assumption is that an earlier age of onset will increase the likelihood that individuals engage in serious and chronic antisocial behaviors. Research on whether the age of onset matters typically compares those who have their first incident of either official or self-reported deviance in childhood or young adolescence to those who do not begin such behaviors until they are older. For example, a review of research found that those who began criminal acts in childhood "continued committing crime at a higher rate all through adolescence and early adulthood" compared to those who started at later points in life (Loeber 1982: 1438). In general, those who enter deviance during childhood are more likely to engage in antisocial behaviors at later stages in life (Farrington 1992; Hirschi and Gottfredson 1995). In addition to simply increasing the likelihood of later offending, studies find that younger onset is associated with more serious offending, a greater variety of offending behaviors, higher frequency of offending, and engaging in deviance over a longer period of time (Loeber 1982; Blumstein *et al.* 1986; Tolan 1987; Farrington and Hawkins 1991; Tolan and Thomas 1995). The implication of these studies is that understanding, and potentially correcting, the processes that lead to entrance into deviance at young ages will have a substantial impact on long-term behavior.

The age of entrance into deviance is vital to understand due to the high level of stability in deviant behavior. The concept of stability has been defined in a number of ways, and many of these interpretations are dependent on whether the focus is on "within" or "between" individual stability. For within individual stability, the essential argument is that individuals involved in deviant behaviors early in life are likely to be engaged in similar behaviors later in life. For example, most studies of adults who are defined as criminal find that these individuals participated in deviant behaviors as juveniles and that involvement in such behavior early in life predicts later antisocial behaviors (Olweus 1979; Loeber 1982; Moffitt 1993; Laub and Sampson 2003). While studies find that juveniles who are deviant as children do not always persist in deviance as adults (Gove 1985; Sampson and Laub 1997; Laub and Sampson 2003), the dominant trend in research supports within-person stability in that "the antisocial child tends to become the antisocial teenager and the antisocial adult" (Farrington 1992: 258).

In addition to stability *within* individuals, there is a great deal of relative stability in deviant behavior *between* individuals. This form of stability focuses on how much "people differ in the likelihood that they will commit crimes" (Gottfredson and Hirschi 1990: 108). While the absolute levels, or the manifestations, of deviance may shift, the relative involvement between individuals remains consistent over time. In other words, individuals who are highly deviant as children will be more deviant as adults compared to individuals who were less deviant as children. For example, in a review of longitudinal studies, Olweus (1979: 870) found that individual differences in aggression emerge very early, as young as three years old, and are maintained to a "considerable degree" through adolescence and adulthood. Thus, differences in relative levels of participation in deviant behaviors emerge early and persist over time (Robbins 1966; Loeber 1982; Farrington 1992; Sampson and Laub 1993). These findings again point to the importance of understanding early entrance into deviance as it may be possible to differentiate between individuals who are at high and low risk for chronic deviance early in life.

One important example of these stability findings is provided by Sampson and Laub through their work with the data originally collected by Sheldon and Eleanor Glueck. In *Unraveling Juvenile Delinquency* (1950), the Gluecks compared 500 boys who had been officially classified as delinquent by the State of Massachusetts with 500 "non-delinquent" comparable boys. This control group may have engaged in various forms of deviant behavior, but they were not involved in "official, or serious, persistent delinquency" (Sampson and Laub 1993: 26) according to police records or key reporters, such as their parents or teachers. While these data do not represent a random sample of the population, and are limited in important ways (such as not including females in the sample), the richness of these data, and the fact that subsequent follow-up studies have followed these individuals through youth, adolescence, young adulthood, middle age, and the beginnings of old age, makes these some of the most useful data for understanding patterns of stability in deviant behavior.

While Laub and Sampson emphasized the need to examine social bonds and experiences through the life course that can change participation in deviance, they found substantial stability. Boys who were identified as deviant children were much more heavily involved in crime, as well as other deviant and analogous behaviors, throughout their lives (Sampson and Laub 1997; Laub and Sampson 2003). Therefore, they concluded that there was a great deal of consistency in behaviors from childhood through adulthood. Such findings suggest that "individual traits and childhood experiences" (Laub and Sampson 2003: 6) are both important in understanding deviant behaviors.

Findings regarding age of onset and stability in deviance indicate that a useful focus of research would be to identify a characteristic or trait that develops in childhood and maintains a relatively stable influence on behavior over time. In *Becoming Deviant*, Matza (1969) argued that individuals develop an affinity, or predisposition, toward crime. He argued that people "develop predispositions to certain phenomena, say delinquency, as a result of their *circumstances*" (Matza 1969: 90–91). One circumstance that may produce an affinity toward deviance is the type or quality of childrearing practices. Specifically, the lack of self-control, which results from circumstances that produce inadequate parenting, can be regarded as a specific form of affinity toward deviance. The remainder of this chapter examines the role of the parents in developing self-control in children.

Parenting and self-control

Research on self-control has firmly established that this trait predicts a wide range of deviant and analogous behaviors (see Pratt and Cullen 2000 and Gottfredson 2008 for reviews). Defined as the extent to which individuals are likely to give in to temptations of the moment (Gottfredson and Hirschi 1990: 87), self-control has been found to develop early in life and to remain fairly stable across time (Arneklev, Cochran, and Gainey 1998; Tuner and Piquero 2002; Hay and Forest 2006; Beaver and Wright 2007). In addition, self-control has been used to predict behaviors in childhood and adolescence as well as adulthood, in general and criminal samples, across different racial groups and for both sexes (Pratt and Cullen 2000). Due to the consistency in these findings about the importance of self-control, it is argued that it is crucial to develop this characteristic in order to prevent entrance into deviance.

The processes necessary to develop self-control are said to be best carried out in early childhood and within the home. However, this is not always successful. The assumption in most research is that the home is a place of safety and security and parents engage in socialization processes that encourage law-abiding, non-deviant activities in children. Parents are presumed to serve the role of providing "conventional, anti-criminal definitions, conforming role models, and the reinforcement of conformity" (Akers and Jensen 2008: 50). Unfortunately, that is not always the case. Parents who are themselves engaged in a variety of deviant behaviors often produce high levels of deviance in their children (West and Farrington 1977; Loeber and Stouthamer-Loeber 1986; Farrington 1992). For example, Glueck and Glueck (1950; 1962) and Sampson and Laub (1993) found that delinquent boys were more likely to have parents who had problems with criminal behavior and alcoholism than their non-delinquent counterparts.

Parents do not need to have criminal records or to be involved in serious forms of deviance to increase their children's entrance to deviance. Simple tolerance for deviant behavior is adequate. In a meta-analysis on the ways that families are important in the prediction of juvenile delinquency (Loeber and Stouthamer-Loeber 1986), it was found that both parental criminality and lenient attitudes toward deviance increased deviance in children. In fact, nearly every study (eight out of nine) that included a measure of parents' tolerance for deviance found this led to increased deviance in children. These findings indicate that deviant parents increase the likelihood that children enter into deviant activities. What is needed is to understand the mechanisms that link parental and child deviance. One argument is that deviant parents do not engage in behaviors that will produce adequate self-control in their children.

Gottfredson and Hirschi (1990: 101) proposed that self-control develops when parents monitor the child, recognize when deviance occurs, and correct these behaviors. Parents who fail in these steps increase the risk that their children will enter into deviant behavior. An underlying necessary condition for these behaviors is that the parents are invested in their children as evidenced through feelings of concern and affection (Gottfredson and Hirschi 1990: 98). The importance of both affection and various parenting styles and processes are well established in existing research. Studies of different forms of parenting find that "authoritative" parents, who provide warmth and affection as well as clear rules and restrictions, are most likely to develop children who follow the rules of society and are non-deviant (Baumrind 1978; 1991). In addition, poor supervision and erratic or harsh discipline are consistently found to differentiate between deviant and non-deviant juveniles (Glueck and Glueck 1962; Loeber and Stouthamer-Loeber 1986; Gibbs, Giever and Martin 1998; Unnever, Cullen and Pratt 2003; Akers and Jensen 2008). The need for affection is also clear. Poor relationships between parents and children lead to problems with hostility on the part of children (Glueck and Glueck 1962: 128), and generally increase antisocial behaviors in juveniles (Loeber and Stouthamer-Loeber 1986).

While there is a great deal of work that establishes the importance of parenting practices, most of these studies were conducted prior to the development of self-control theory and thus do not specifically test whether these practices influence the self-control of the child. However, there is a growing body of literature that specifically examines the three parenting practices advocated by the theory that tests whether these steps are associated with self-control in children. A recent review by Cullen *et al.* (2008) examines thirteen different studies conducted since 1994 that test specific pieces of the necessary steps for developing self-control. Of these studies, the majority focus on the role of supervision and various forms of punishment (Cullen *et al.* 2008: 70–71). Across all these studies, higher self-control was related to adequate and consistent supervision or monitoring, as well as various measures of parenting which included appropriate discipline, parental warmth and affection for children. One thing that may result in poor parenting performance is whether the parents are deviant, and thus low in self-control, themselves.

Many studies find that adults who are deviant engage in practices that do not fulfill the requirements of developing their children's self-control. For example, parents who have a history of criminal involvement use punishment inconsistently, and when they do discipline their children, their methods rely on actions that are "easy, short-term, and insensitive—that is, yelling and screaming, slapping and hitting" (Gottfredson and Hirschi 1990: 101). Further, deviant parents do not perceive their child's activities to be problematic or simply ignore acts of deviance (Patterson and Dishion 1985; Laub and Sampson 1988). Therefore, parents who are deviant themselves are more likely to engage in practices that will lead to the development of low self-control in their children and thus to an early entrance into deviance.

Deviant parents may not adequately instill self-control in their children because of their own poorly developed self-control. Characteristics of low self-control include impulsivity, having a short temper, and being self-centered (Gottfredson and Hirschi 1990: 90). Since successful parenting requires a great deal of effort, time, patience, and self-sacrifice, adults with poor self-control are unlikely to engage in parenting practices that are adequate to teach their children self-control and thus prevent them from entering into deviance. In fact, Gottfredson and Hirschi (1990: 100) argue that the self-control of the parent will be the primary predictor in the self-control of their children. Parental self-control is expected to affect whether they engage in the types of parenting that will produce self-control in their children. In spite of this growing attention to building an understanding of how parenting leads to self-control, most studies do not directly measure the self-control of the parent. One recent exception (Nofziger 2008) found that mothers with low self-control were more likely to engage in such parenting practices as ignoring the child when they misbehave (thus, not acknowledging or correcting such behavior) and failing to monitor certain activities. These parenting practices ultimately led to lower self-control, and subsequent deviant behavior, in their children.

The large, and continually growing, body of literature on self-control theory supports the importance of the relationship between parenting processes, the development of self-control, and ultimately deviant behavior. While there are many other factors that may influence individual entrance into deviance, this research clearly establishes the importance of these family processes. Thus, entrance into deviance cannot be fully understood without a consideration of the role of parenting and self-control.

Conclusion

The step of entering deviance is arguably the most important process to understand due to the findings that, once started on a deviant path, there is a great deal of stability in such behavior. Therefore, preventing entrance is the key to avoiding a lifetime of antisocial behaviors. This chapter argues that the processes related to the family, and in particular parental practices that produce self-control in children, are vital in producing or preventing deviance. Specifically, parents who have poor self-control and are themselves deviant inadequately socialize their children. They fail to form close attachments with their children, provide inadequate supervision, discipline inconsistently or inappropriately, and ultimately fail to instill adequate self-control in their children.

Of course, such "family factors never operate in a vacuum but take place against a backdrop of other influence such as those exercised by children's peers, their school, and society in general" (Loeber and Stouthamer-Loeber 1986: 128). Therefore, while the processes involved in the family are important to consider, it must be remembered that entering into deviance is a highly complex process with multiple causes. While early processes may be those that have the longest and therefore most important impact, it is conceivable that later developing realities may also influence other pathways into deviance.

References

Akers, R. L. and Jensen, G. F. (2008) "The empirical status of social learning theory of crime and deviance: The past, present, and future," pp. 37–76 in F. T. Cullen, J. P. Wright, and K. R. Blevins, (eds), *Taking Stock, The Status of Criminological Theory: Advances in Criminological Theory*, Volume 15, New Brunswick, NJ: Transaction.

Arneklev, B. J., Cochran, J. K., and Gainey, R. R. (1998) "Testing Gottfredson and Hirschi's 'low self-control' stability hypothesis: An exploratory study," *American Journal of Criminal Justice*, 23: 107–127.

Baumrind, D. (1978) "Parental disciplinary patterns and social competence in children," *Youth and Society*, 9: 239–276.

—— (1991) "The influence of parenting style on adolescent competence and substance use," *Journal of Early Adolescence,* 11: 56–95.

Beaver, K. M. and Wright, J. P. (2007) "The stability of low self-control from kindergarten through first grade," *Journal of Crime and Justice,* 30: 63–86.

Blumstein, A., Cohen, J., Roth, J. A., and Visher, C. A. (eds) (1986) *Criminal Careers and Career Criminals,* Washington, DC: National Academy Press.

Cullen, F. T., Unnever, J. D., Wright, J. P., and Beaver, K. M. (2008) "Parenting and self-control," pp. 61–74 in E. Goode (ed.) *Out of Control: Assessing the General Theory of Crime,* Stanford, CA: Stanford University Press.

Elder, G. H., Jr. (1985) "Perspectives on the life-course," pp. 23–49 in G. H. Elder, Jr. (ed.) *Life-Course Dynamics,* Ithaca, NY: Cornell University Press.

—— (1994) "Time, human agency, and social change: Perspectives on the life course," *Social Psychology Quarterly,* 57: 4–15.

Farrington, D. P. (1992) "Explaining the beginning, progress and ending of antisocial behavior from birth to adulthood," in J. McCord (ed.) *Facts, Frameworks and Forecasts: Advances in Criminological Theory,* Volume 3, New Brunswick, NJ: Transaction.

Farrington, D. P. and Hawkins, J. D. (1991) "Predicting participation, early onset, and later persistence in officially recorded offending," *Criminal Behavior and Mental Health,* 1: 1–33.

Gibbs, J. J., Giever, D., and Martin, J. S. (1998) "Parental management and self-control: An empirical test of Gottfredson and Hirschi's general theory," *Journal of Research in Crime and Delinquency,* 35: 40–70.

Glueck, S. and Glueck, E. (1950) *Unraveling Juvenile Delinquency,* New York: The Commonwealth Fund.

—— (1962) *Family Environment and Delinquency,* Boston, MA: Houghton Mifflin.

Gottfredson, M. R. (2008) "The empirical status of control theory in criminology," pp. 77–100 in F. T. Cullen, J.P. Wright, and K. R. Blevins (eds) *Taking Stock: The Status of Criminological Theory, Advances in Criminological Theory,* Volume 15, New Brunswick, NJ: Transaction.

Gottfredson, M. R. and Hirschi, T. (1990) *A General Theory of Crime,* Stanford, CA: Stanford University Press.

Gove, W. R. (1985) "The effect of age and gender on deviant behavior: A biopsychosocial perspective," pp. 115–144 in A. S. Rossi (ed.) *Gender and the Life Course,* New York: Aldine.

Hay, C. and Forest, W. (2006) "The development of self-control: Examining self-control theory's stability thesis," *Criminology,* 44: 739–774.

Hirschi, T. and Gottfredson, M. R. (1995) "Control theory and the life course perspective," *Studies on Crime and Crime Prevention,* 4: 131–142.

Inciardi, J. A. (1975) *Careers in Crime,* Chicago, IL: Rand McNally.

Laub, J. H. and Sampson, R. J. (1988) "Unraveling families and delinquency: A reanalysis of the Gluecks' data," *Criminology,* 26: 355–380.

—— (2003) *Shared Beginnings, Divergent Lives: Delinquent Boys to Age 70,* Cambridge, MA: Harvard University Press.

Loeber, R. (1982) "The stability of antisocial and delinquent child behavior: A review," *Child Development,* 53: 1431–1446.

Loeber, R. and Stouthamer-Loeber, M. (1986) "Family factors as correlates and predictors of juvenile conduct problems and delinquency," pp. 29–149 in M. Tonry and N. Morris (eds) *Crime and Justice,* Volume 7, Chicago, IL: University of Chicago Press.

Luckenbill, D. F. and Best, J. (1981) "Careers in deviance and respectability: The analogy's limitations," *Social Problems,* 29: 197–206.

Matza, D. (1969) *Becoming Deviant,* Englewood Cliffs, NJ: Prentice-Hall

Moffitt, T. E. (1993) "Adolescent-limited and life-course persistent antisocial behavior: A developmental taxonomy," *Psychological Review,* 100: 674–910.

Nofziger, S. (2008) "The 'cause' of low self-control: The influence of maternal self-control," *Journal of Research in Crime and Delinquency,* 45: 191–224.

Olweus, D. (1979) "Stability of aggressive reaction patterns in males: A review," *Psychological Bulletin,* 86: 852–875.

Patterson, G. R. and Dishion, T. J. (1985) "Contributions of families and peers to delinquency," *Criminology,* 23: 63–79.

Pratt, T. and Cullen, F. T. (2000) "The empirical status of Gottfredon and Hirschi's general theory of crime: A meta-analysis," *Criminology,* 38: 931–964.

Robbins, L. (1966) *Deviant Children Grown up,* Baltimore, MD: Williams and Wilkins.

Sampson, R. J. and Laub, J. H. (1993) *Crime in the Making*, Cambridge, MA: Harvard University Press.

—— (1997) "A life-course theory of cumulative disadvantage and stability of delinquency," pp. 133–161 in T. P. Thornberry (ed.) *Developmental Theories of Crime and Delinquency: Advances in Criminological Theory*, New Brunswick, NJ: Transaction.

Thornberry, T. P. (1997) "Introduction: Some advantages of developmental and life-course perspectives for the study of crime and delinquency," pp. 1–10 in T. P. Thornberry (ed.) *Developmental Theories of Crime and Delinquency: Advances in Criminological Theory*, New Brunswick, NJ: Transaction.

Tolan, P. H. (1987) "Implications of age of onset for delinquency risk," *Journal of Abnormal Child Psychology*, 17: 47–65.

Tolan, P. H. and Thomas, P. (1995) "The implications of age of onset for delinquency risk II: Longitudinal data," *Journal of Abnormal Child Psychology*, 23: 157–181.

Tuner, M. G. and Piquero, A. R. (2002) "The stability of self-control," *Journal of Criminal Justice*, 30: 457–471.

Unnever, J. D., Cullen, F. T. and Pratt, T. C. (2003) "Parental management, ADHD, and delinquent involvement: Reassessing Gottfredson and Hirschi's general theory," *Justice Quarterly*, 20: 471–500.

West, D. J. and Farrington, D. P. (1977) *The Delinquent Way of Life*, London: Heinemann.

23

Stigma and the deviant identity

Mindy S. Bradley-Engen

In sociology, the term *identity* is generally defined as the way people think about and describe themselves as belonging to particular groups. *Stigma* refers to the process through which one's possession of a particular attribute makes one different from others in a less desirable way. A stigmatized individual is one who has been reduced from a "whole and usual person to a tainted, discounted one" in the minds of others (Goffman, 1963: 3). Thus, the concept of a "deviant identity" refers to one's perception and interpretation of self as atypical or acting beyond the boundaries of normative behavior. A person with a deviant identity is one who has been stigmatized by others, and incorporated that stigma into his/her sense of self. S/he comes to see himself/herself as an "outsider" (Becker, 1963), someone who does not fit in or engages in behavior deemed inappropriate by conventional social norms.

Explaining stigma

Research on stigma and the deviant identity has explored the processes through which people acquire deviant identities, the management of stigma and consequences of having a deviant identity, and the various ways in which people remove or exit the stigma of the deviant label. The study of stigma is perhaps most associated with the work of Erving Goffman, a renowned sociologist and one of the first scholars to explore stigma as a social phenomenon. Goffman describes stigma as a "language of relationships." He characterizes it as a process involving unique disjuncture between the *virtual social identity* (the presumed behavioral demands and imputed character society deems normative) and the *actual social identity* (the actual character and attributes an individual does in fact possess).

In his analysis, Goffman (1963) identifies two levels of stigma—the *discredited* and the *discreditable*. These types of stigma present individuals with fundamentally different concerns. For the *discredited*, the stigma has been revealed. It is known, and thus affects both their behavior as well as the behaviors of those around them. Since their stigma is assumedly identified, discredited persons confront problems connected with managing the social tension that stigma creates during interactions with others. In contrast, when people's negative attributes are not immediately evident, they are *discreditable*. Their stigma may be successfully concealed or revealed. Discreditable persons focus on managing information or concealment so that others do not become aware of their stigma. The disclosure of stigma may take place either intentionally by them or through unintended means beyond their control. For these people, efforts focus primarily on impression management or information control, as those with the "undesired differentness" try to control the reactions of others by manipulating what they reveal about themselves.

The formation of a deviant identity

The literature on deviant identity formation generally conceptualizes it as a process that focuses on the interplay between self-perception and the perceptions of others. The initial impetus is the discovery of the behavior by others and public identification of the individuals. In the well-known work *Outsiders: Studies in the Sociology of Deviance* (1963), Becker outlines the multi-stage progression of deviant identity development. Once their deviance becomes publicly known, negative social reaction ensues. Others begin to think of them differently, reconsidering their assessment of them, and perhaps even scrutinizing the deviants' past behavior. This process of "retrospective reinterpretation" involves reevaluating what heretofore may have been considered unremarkable behavior in light of this new information (Kitsuse, 1962).

As others begin to think of and respond to their behavior, either formally (such as processing them through the justice system) or informally (such as shunning and social exclusion), individuals develop tarnished reputations and subsequent "spoiled identities" (Goffman, 1963). Socially discrediting them, the reactions of others spoil their previously held normal identity. Through these formal and informal social control mechanisms, individuals become labeled as deviant. They are publicly shunned and socially rejected. They are often excluded from clubs, friendships, professional associations, job opportunities, and other conventional social groups. Ostracized from these social groups, they may consequently develop associations with others who are also engaged in the same or similar non-normative activities. That is, finding that they no longer "belong" to their previous groups, these individuals may seek out or be sought out by other outsiders, like themselves.

Those who have been labeled deviant may find that others no longer want to associate with them or indicate that feelings toward them have changed. Cast out by conventional others, with new associations with deviant others, they begin to change the way they think about themselves and integrate this deviant label into their role performance. That is, as a result of continued stigmatization, these outcast individuals internalize their deviant label. Having internalized the deviant label, the deviant status becomes incorporated into their sense of self. The extent and significance of the deviant identity label are typically more profound when people go through official labeling processes (such as through the criminal justice system) than when they are informally labeled. Nevertheless, similar to Merton's (1968) concept of a "self-fulfilling prophecy," once they think of themselves in this light, their newly acquired deviant identity is likely to impact their future behavior.

These stages outlined above parallel Lemert's (1967) processual explanation of deviant labeling as a transition from *primary deviance* to *secondary deviance*. Often people commit deviant acts, but these activities go unrecognized. As a result, they do not receive a deviant label; they do not form a deviant identity nor perform a deviant role. Similarly, Becker (1963) suggests that, should the behavior go undetected, these "secret deviants" may avoid public scrutiny and internalization of the deviant label. Consequently, they are unlikely to consider themselves as outside the norm and develop a deviant identity.

However, should these acts become known, the processes of exclusion and labeling commence. Others begin to view and treat them as deviant. While they may resist, they continually confront stigmatization in their interactions with others; despite their efforts, the deviant label is pressed upon them. As a result, they may ultimately begin to see themselves in this way as well. As individuals move from primary to secondary deviance, they reluctantly come to accept their deviant status, and allow this identity to impact future social interactions and behavior.

Managing the deviant label

How do people negotiate the deviant label and stigma in their everyday interactions? Goffman specifies a number of stigma management techniques. First, they may avoid interactions altogether. By "disassociating" themselves or "retreating backstage," they steer clear of social contact, both positive and negative, in order to avoid the reactions of others. *Passing* is the act of hiding or disguising the stigma. Goffman (1963) suggests that visibility is a critical determinant of successful "passing." For individuals to "pass," they must make their stigma undetectable so that it is known only to themselves and to other similarly situated individuals.

Alternatively, they may cover or normalize their stigma. When *covering*, individuals acknowledge the stigma, yet seek to minimize its influence in interaction. That is, they do not deny the stigma, yet attempt to minimize the prominence of their spoiled identity. By making the stigma less obtrusive, individuals seek to minimize the social tension associated with the stigma and engage in more normative social interactions (Anderson, Snow, and Cress, 1994).

They may also engage in *coping*, using proactive mechanisms, such as levity, sarcasm, or avoidance in order to manage tension in interactions. Those who are associated with the discreditable may also be instrumental in the management of his/her stigma. That is, the potentially stigmatized individual's friends and family may take part in *teamwork* both to prevent leakage of discrediting information and to manage impressions jointly.

Destigmatization and exiting the deviant identity

How do people free themselves of deviant labels and escape stigmatization? Those who possesses a stigma and have been discredited may find shedding the deviant label particularly challenging. Much of the early research on the destigmatization focused on the reformation of the individual (including treatment or self-help/habilitation), or on the improvement of social attitudes toward the individual's stigma characteristics, such as through social movements or increased public acceptance (for some excellent examples, see Lofland, 1969; Trice and Roman, 1972).

Whereas most people attempt to avoid or diminish their deviant label, others engage in what Kituse (1980) refers to as *tertiary deviance*. In contrast to primary deviants (who engage in deviance denial/resistance) and secondary deviants (who engage in deviance acceptance), tertiary deviants engage in role embracement. They may denounce the negative assessment of their stigma as socially constructed, not intrinsic to their behavior. In this way, they may argue that their stigma is positive, in that it distinguishes them in an affirmative or superior way from "normal." In addition, they may identify with their deviance and work collectively with stigmatized others to combat the deviant label that is applied to them. They may engage in various forms of advocacy and social protest to change social views regarding their deviance.

Relatedly, Warren (1980), drawing on the work of Katz (1975), discusses the role of the *charismatic deviant*. Whereas normals are those who meet expectations, and deviants are those who do not, charismatics are defined as those who surpass the normative. In this way, the charismatic is a role that allows for both destigmatization and representation of the "deviant collectivity to the general public" (Warren, 1980: 59). Warren proposes a systematic theory of destigmatization, specifying three modes of charismatic destigmatization:

1   individual purification (the cleansing of the old moral self and substitution of a new one, such as through newfound devotion to religion or cessation and denouncement of drug or alcohol use);

2   individual transcendence (the expression of an alternative better self through superior performances or "overcoming adversity"); and

3   collective aristocratization (the advocacy and projection of a collective image by the members of the deviant group in order to destigmatize the category and redefine themselves as supranormal or better than normals).

Studies on deviant identity and stigma management

Much of the research in this area draws on the conceptualizations defined above to explain stigma management, identity formation, and deviant label resistance among various stigmatized groups. In his writing, Goffman drew on autobiographies and case studies from individuals with various forms of stigma, including individuals with physical deformities, those with physical or developmental handicaps, the mentally ill, those with addictions, convicted criminals, prostitutes, and racial/ethnic minority statuses. Contemporary applications of theories and concepts related to stigma and deviant identity management include a wide array of social phenomena. For example, recent work by Rodner (2005) explored strategies among drug *users* to resist stigma and reject the deviant drug *abuser* identity. Meanwhile, Adler and Adler (2005) discussed self-perceptions and understanding of behavior among people who intentionally self-injure. Other work examined homosexual stigma and self-perceptions among men who have sex with other men ("on the down low"), yet self-identify as heterosexual (Boykin, 2005). Additionally, in their work on adolescents, Kaplan and Lin (2005) examined the role of social bonding in moderating the relationship between deviant identity and subsequent later deviant behavior.

Indeed, the literature on stigma and the deviant identity covers a wide range of stigmatized groups. A number of studies have explored resistance strategies and pro-deviant social movements, including such groups as "pro-anorexics" (Fox, Ward, and O'Rourke, 2005), and members of the "fat acceptance" movement (Kirkland, 2008). Theories on stigma management, deviant identity formation, and label resistance are continually being applied to and/or tested with previously underexplored and/or newly recognized phenomena, including people with HIV (Sandstrom, 1990; Siegel, Lune, and Meyer, 1998), overweight people (Degher and Hughes, 1991), epileptics (Schneider and Conrad, 1981), childless couples (Park, 2002), and cross-dressers (Ekins, 1997).

Most scholars view the labeling of deviance in relativist terms, understanding that whether a behavior or individual is labeled as deviant, and subsequently becomes the focus of stigmatization, depends upon social reaction to the behavior, the relative power of the individual and any victim or object of the activity, and the consequences of the behavior. Symbolic interactionists explore the dualism of identity, and demonstrate how identity can both influence and be influenced by social reality at large. The definition of a behavior or characteristic as deviant (and thus a source of deviant identity) is not static. The ever-changing dynamics of politics, economies, religion, education, and family mean that some previously stigmatized behaviors may eventually be considered normative, while entirely new activities and social groups become the subject of stigmatization and deviant labeling.

References

Adler, P. A. and Adler, P. (2005). "Self-injurers as loners: The social organization of solitary deviance." *Deviant Behavior*, 26: 345–378.

Anderson, L., Snow, D., and Cress, D. (1994). "Negotiating the public realm: Stigma management and collective action among the homeless." In S. Cahill and L. Lofland (eds.) *The community of "the streets."* Greenwich, CT: JAI Press.

Becker, H. S. (1963). *Outsiders: Studies in the sociology of deviance*. New York: Free Press.

Boykin, K. (2005). *Beyond the down low: Sex, lies, and denial in Black America*. New York: Dafina Books.

Degher, D. and Hughes, G. (1991). "The identity change process: A field study of obesity." *Deviant Behavior*, 12(4): 385–401.

Ekins, R. (1997). *Male femaling: A grounded theory approach to cross-dressing and sex-changing*. New York: Routledge.

Erikson, K. T. (1966). *Wayward Puritans*. New York: Wiley.

Fox, N., Ward, K., and O'Rourke, A. (2005). "Pro-anorexia, weight-loss drugs, and the internet: An 'anti-recovery' explanatory model of anorexia." *Sociology of Health and Illness*, 27: 944–971.

Goffman, E. (1963). *Stigma: Notes on the concept of spoiled identity*. Englewood Cliffs, NJ: Prentice-Hall.

Kaplan, H. B. and Lin, C. (2005). "Deviant identity, negative self-feelings, and decreases in deviant behavior: The moderating influence of conventional social bonding." *Psychology, Crime, and Law*, 11: 289–303.

Katz, J. (1975). "Essences as moral identities: Verifiability and responsibility in imputation of deviance and charisma." *American Journal of Sociology*, 80: 1369–1389.

Kirkland, A. (2008). "Think of the hippopotamus: Rights consciousness in the fat acceptance movement." *Law and Society Review*, 42: 397–431.

Kitsuse, J. (1962). "Societal reactions to deviant behavior: Problems of theory and method." *Social Problems*, 9: 247–256.

Kitsuse, J. (1980). "Coming out all over: Deviants and the politics of social problems." *Social Problems*, 28: 1–13.

Lemert, E. (1951). *Social pathology*. New York: McGraw-Hill.

Lemert, E. (1967). *Human deviance, social problems, and social control*. New York: Prentice-Hall.

Lofland, J. (1969). *Deviance and identity*. Englewood Cliffs, NJ: Prentice-Hall.

Merton, R. K. (1968). *Social theory and social structure*. New York: Free Press.

Park, K. (2002). "Stigma management among the voluntary childless." *Sociological Perspectives*, 45: 21–45.

Rodner, S. (2005). "I am not a drug abuser, I am a drug user: A discourse analysis of 44 drug users' construction of identity." *Addiction Research and Theory*, 13: 333–346.

Sandstrom, M. (1990). "Confronting deadly disease: The drama of identity construction among gay men with AIDS." *Journal of Contemporary Ethnography*, 19: 271–294.

Schneider, J. W. and Conrad, P. (1981). "Medical and sociological typologies: The case of epilepsy." *Social Science and Medicine*, 15: 212–219.

Siegel, K., Lune, H., and Meyer, I. (1998). "Stigma management among gay/bisexual men with HIV/AIDS." *Qualitative Sociology*, 21: 3–24.

Trice, H. M. and Roman, P. M. (1972). "Delabeling, relabeling, and Alcoholics Anonymous." In F. Scarpitti and P. Y. MacFarlane (eds.) *Deviance: Action, reaction, interaction*. Reading, MA: Addision-Wesley.

Warren, C. A. (1980). "Destigmatization of identity: From deviant to charismatic." *Qualitative Sociology*, 3: 59–72.

24

The deviant career

Charles Faupel

The concept of *career* is, in my view, the most effective vocabulary authentically to interpret the experiences of those who engage in many, if not most, forms of deviant behavior. This is a departure from much research on deviance, particularly early research which interpreted such behaviors through a framework of social pathology. This essay will begin with a brief history of *career*: its early use, sociological definition, and its eventual application to deviant behavior. Following that discussion, I will examine how deviant careers fit within a broader typology of careers. Finally, I will examine the temporal character of deviant careers as analogous to conventional careers, such as those of lawyers, doctors and other professionals.

Sociology discovers career

Derived from the French *carriere*, meaning road or race course, the term *career* was first employed in 1534 to refer to "a running course." While our current use of the concept to capture the course of one's working life is etymologically related, this application did not make its way into our vocabulary until the first decade of the nineteenth century. The term was introduced to sociology with the writings of Everett C. Hughes and Oswald Hall, who were studying work and occupations at the University of Chicago in the 1940s (see, especially, Hall, 1948; and Hughes, 1958). With their pioneering work, the concept became pivotal in explaining the occupational lifestyles of workers. Hughes would later write another book in 1961 entitled *Boys in White: Student Culture in Medical School* with the young, aspiring sociologist Howard Becker (along with Blanche Geer and Anselm Strauss). As Becker was also writing on the sociology of deviance at this time, his participation in this project resulted in an application of career to deviant and non-occupational lifestyles as well.

The idea of a *deviant career* was first introduced into the literature with Goffman's (1959, 1961) works on the moral careers of mental patients, and later extended by Becker (1963) to deviant careers generally. Subsequent to these early works, career has been used as an interpretive framework to study numerous forms of deviance, including prostitution and other forms of sexual deviance (Best, 1982; Weinberg, 1966); fencing (Klockars, 1974); professional crime (Inciardi, 1975; Letkeman, 1973); skid row alcoholism (Wiseman, 1970); gambling (Hayano, 1982; Lesieur, 1977); narcotics addiction (Coombs, 1981; Faupel, 1991; Rubington, 1967); and even illness (Pavalko, 2004).

A starting point for a broad sociological understanding of career is a definition by Van Maanen (1977: 1), who defines it as "a series of separate but related experiences and adventures through which a person passes during a lifetime." As Van Maanen understands it, these experiences are encountered by all manner of individuals, including prostitutes, doctors, factory workers, housewives and criminals. His definition includes lines of activity not customarily considered to be careers. Housewives, for example, care for their families, cook meals and get kids off to school, but we do not readily see these activities as comprising a "career." Similarly, criminals engage in activity that, even in the professional literature, is characterized as "pathological," but is not usually regarded as part of a career, and certainly is not viewed through the same lens as the career activities of a lawyer or a doctor. Nevertheless, these otherwise disparate lines of activity do share important features in common, and in understanding the commonality of these lifestyles we are able to understand them more appreciatively. Hughes (1958: 48) understood this when he wrote:

> we need to rid ourselves of any concepts which keep us from seeing that the essential problems of men at work are the same whether they do their work in some famous laboratory or in the messiest vat room of a pickle factory. Until we can find a point of view and concepts which will enable us to make comparisons between the junk peddler and the professor without intent to debunk the one and patronize the other, we cannot do our best work in this field.

Van Maanen distinguishes three essential qualities common to all careers. First, careers are *temporal*; a single action does not constitute a career. A career consists of a series of activities carried out over time in a given status or series of statuses. Second, this sequence of related activities serves as a significant reference point around which an individual organizes his or her life. Hence, attending church on Sunday mornings, reciting prayers before turning in for the night, and other religious or spiritual activities that represent a "time out" from normal routines do not constitute a career. By contrast, the individual who has abandoned or curtailed the other activities in her life and who has embarked on a pursuit of God through a regular regimen of prayer, study of scripture, involvement with others in daily spiritual fellowship, and other activities related to the quest for God is indeed involved in a spiritual *career*. This constellation of activities now makes up a coherent framework from which she organizes her life. Finally, a career entails a subjective experience and identity deriving from meanings attached to these activities. Based on these considerations, I suggest the following sociological definition of career: *a career is a series of meaningfully related statuses, roles, and activities around which an individual organizes some aspect of his or her life.*

A typology of careers

While the adoption of career as a common conceptual framework to describe the activities of prostitutes, shoplifters, homemakers, and spiritual visionaries, along with doctors, lawyers, and other occupational specialists, has been extremely valuable in providing a more realistic paradigm for understanding deviant behavior, it is also important to recognize that these patterns of activities do not look exactly alike. While careers can vary in any number of ways, two broad dimensions are discussed in the literature on careers that capture most of these differences. The first is a normative dimension, distinguishing between *deviant* and *respectable* careers. The second dimension distinguishes between *occupational* and *non-occupational* careers.

Deviant versus respectable careers

Since Goffman (1959) and later Becker (1963) extended the application of career to deviant conduct, subsequent research has revealed numerous qualities of deviant biographies that make them analogous to conventional careers. As discussed below, this literature reveals how deviant careers are initiated, how they are terminated, and all of the movements between, commonly referred to as "career mobility." These studies also highlight the norms and ethics that guide the conduct of prostitutes, drug users, and other criminals, in much the same way that doctors and lawyers are strongly guided by a professional code of ethics.

It has also been recognized, however, that there are important points of divergence between deviant and respectable careers. These differences have been most clearly addressed, perhaps, by Luckenbill and Best (1981). The feature of deviant careers that most sets them apart from their respectable counterparts is the threat of legal sanctions. Because of this, deviant careerists often carry out their activities in secret. Punitive sanctions, moreover, introduce a potential cost of being publicly shamed, and possibly even arrested and incarcerated, which is not shared by individuals pursuing respectable careers. A second distinguishing feature is that deviant careers are not normally pursued within the context of a highly structured environment.[1] Because of these divergent environments, the sequence of statuses and roles characterizing the deviant career is less predictable than for most respectable careers, particularly those in highly structured organizations. The deviant career does not, for example, normally begin with any formal educational training; nor are there formal rites of passage such as official promotions or scheduled salary increases. Hence, the pattern of progression through the deviant career is not nearly as clear as that for most respectable careers.

Occupational versus non-occupational careers

Occupational careers are organized around those statuses and roles associated with the activities in which one engages for the purpose of making a living. Much of the work on careers at least implicitly equates career with occupations. It is, however, possible to understand careers apart from occupations:

> Careers in our society are thought of very much in terms of jobs . . . But the career is by no means exhausted in a series of business and professional achievements . . . A woman may have a career in holding together a family or in raising it to a new position. Some people of quite modest occupational achievements have careers in patriotic, religious, and civic organizations . . . It is possible to have a career in an avocation as well as in a vocation.
>
> *(Hughes, 1958: 64)*

Most sociologists of deviance who employ the concept understand career to include a much broader array of activities than merely those associated with occupational or income-producing work.

The typology presented in Figure 24.1 illustrates the polytypic nature of careers. It should be pointed out that the normative and occupational dimensions are represented here as continua; any given career is *more or less* deviant and *more or less* occupational in nature. Moreover, some careers may contain features of more than one of these types. Nevertheless, this typology does sensitize us to the multidimensional nature of career, and provides a useful framework for locating deviant careers within the broad spectrum of activities that are properly understood as careers.

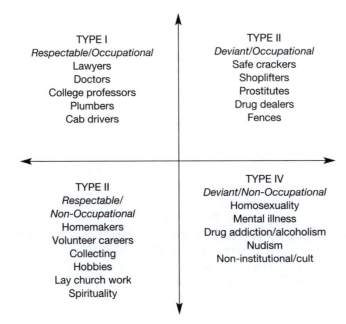

Figure 24.1 Types of career

Deviance as career

The career typology presented in Figure 24.1 distinguishes deviant from non-deviant career tracks, with deviant activities comprising Type III and Type IV careers. Figure 24.1 further distinguishes between *occupational* and *non-occupational* careers in deviance. Many forms of deviance involve making a living, just like individuals in respectable occupational careers. Deviant careerists do indeed understand their behaviors as making a living. Pagie, a dealer-addict in my research on heroin-using careers, explained, "It was business to me then. My addiction was business. What I had to sell was business. I was very businesslike in manner too. Because it wasn't a game I was playing" (Faupel, 1991: 29). Figure 24.1 also identifies many deviant activities which are not occupational in nature. Nudists, alcoholics and cult participants are not, in these capacities, engaged in patterned activities that are organized in pursuit of compensation.

In reality, many deviant careers incorporate both Type III (occupational) and Type IV (non-occupational) types of behaviors. In some cases, for example, homosexuals become involved in prostitution, thereby embarking on a career that has both occupational and non-occupational attributes. Drug-using careers almost always entail both occupational and non-occupational features as most regular users of expensive drugs such as heroin and cocaine not only pursue the consumer activities of purchasing, preparing, and ingesting their drug of choice but are involved in income-generating criminal activities that support this expensive consumer lifestyle.

Finally, I must point out that involvement in deviant careers does not preclude involvement in respectable careers. Indeed, respectable career activities may well contribute to deviant careers, and vice versa. Members of religious cults, for example, may carry on very conventional strategies for fundraising, including selling donuts at a WalMart store next to a Girl Scout table selling cookies. More importantly, these deviant careerists live multifaceted lives that may entail patterned activities that would be regarded as respectable careers as well. It is not uncommon for drug addicts, for example, to be working in very respectable occupations, and to be very involved in community affairs. Sudhir Venkatish (2008) highlights the extensive level of community involvement of J.T., a gang leader and drug dealer in Chicago's renowned Robert Taylor housing project. J.T. took great pride in the good that he was doing in his community. His career as a community activist was an important part of his self-identity.

The temporal nature of deviant careers: entry, mobility, and retirement

There is a temporal quality to deviant careers which closely resembles conventional careers. They unfold over time, which means that they pass through stages or phases, each of which poses certain obstacles and opportunities that, in turn, further define the direction of a given career. Research on occupational careers has identified various phases that can also be recognized in deviant careers.

Career choice and entry

The early period that marks the beginning of a career has been variously labeled, but it generally consists of the related processes of career choice and career entry. Stereotypically, this is a very rational, carefully planned process in occupational careers, though sociologists recognize that even with professional careers, the process may be quite situational and unplanned in character. Rather than a carefully planned process, individuals pursuing professional and other respectable occupational careers often wake up to find themselves in their careers after stumbling upon a major in college almost serendipitously. Perhaps quite by accident, after several "dead-end" attempts at choosing a major, a future young lawyer took a course in criminology or political science that piqued her interest. This positive experience led to further courses, meaningful relationships with professors, internships, declaring a major, and eventually entering law school on her way toward a career as a lawyer.

Deviant careers, I contend, are similarly initiated. Almost without exception, research on drug use reports that beginning users are first *turned on* to a drug by close friends and acquaintances who are themselves just experimenting with the drug. My research on heroin addicts (Faupel, 1991) revealed that while the circumstances of initial use were varied, this initiation was quite unintentional. Frequently, the setting is a party or similar social occasion at which the drug is being shared. Moreover, experimental users often try using several drugs before settling on a primary drug of choice. Similarly, individuals pursuing criminal careers will often experiment with several types of crime before settling into their *main hustle*, which is their primary means of criminal support. Indeed, this street parlance conveys a sense of career specialization, similar to respectable careers, though also recognizes that there are other fallback criminal skills if it is impossible to carry out one's main, or primary, hustle.

Career mobility

Somewhere between entering and exiting a career are encountered the opportunities, obstacles, decisions, and activities that comprise the span of one's career. This period we often term *career mobility*. Typically, the literature on conventional occupational careers depicts career mobility in terms of a rather predictable upward progression of statuses culminating at some "peak" in one's career at some point prior to "retirement." This is an idealized version of occupational careers, of course, and the fact is that many such careers are not so predictable and are, as Wilensky (1961) has characterized them, "disorderly" in nature. My research (Faupel, 2000) has revealed this disorderly quality of careers in the music industry. Deviant careers much more closely approximate Wilensky's *disorderly career* than the stereotyped predictable career depicted in the literature on conventional occupations. These careers are by nature composed of multiple career shifts and temporary exiting and reentering. Lesieur (1977), for example, finds that compulsive gamblers experience repeated cycles of abstinence and relapse in their careers. Similarly, Irwin (1970) found that risk of arrest frequently forces habitual property offenders to engage temporarily in some other type of work. Failing to do so before getting caught often results in arrest and confinement, which serve to interrupt one's career substantially. Drug-using careers also manifest a disorderly quality. Rosenbaum (1981: 50–51) has described the career of the female addict as "chaotic":

> The activities that are part of the addict's life make establishing a structured routine nearly impossible. With the first event of the day—waking up sick—chaos begins. A woman who is desperate does not have the patience to think out her moves, to execute an ordered plan; therefore, her hustling patterns are both sporadic and chaotic. She may prostitute one day, boost the next, forge after that—each without much plan or attention to detail.

Because of the disorderly nature of deviant careers, the casual observer fails to see anything resembling a career in routine deviant activities. This is because the mental lens that we have from which to understand careers is that of an orderly, upward progression of statuses within an organizational framework. The deviant career, however, is not normally played out within an organizational context, and there is certainly no orderly upward progression here. There is, nevertheless, movement through a series of statuses that provide a context for meaning to these activities and serve to provide an identity for the actor.

Exiting the career

Conventional occupational careerists eventually "retire," which is regarded as an earned right, the logical culmination of many years of work. This experience of a recognized retirement, of course, presupposes an orderly career. Here again, deviant careers much more resemble *disorderly* careers, characterized by frequent disruptions and forced changes such that even the word "retirement" seems totally inappropriate for the exiting process. Irwin (1970), for example, found that the return to a non-criminal lifestyle was a very uneasy transition for the felon. Similarly, heroin-using criminals do not usually maintain the same main hustle, but pursue a series of criminal enterprises throughout their careers. Many hold legitimate jobs and perhaps moonlight at night and on the weekends while at the same time carrying out their criminal hustles (Faupel, 1991). As they get older, when the stressful lifestyle of criminal hustling begins to take its toll, their "retirement" consists of gradually becoming more involved in legitimate money-making activities instead. Similarly, exiting non-occupational drug *consumption* careers is usually disorderly in nature. In some cases, addicts are said to "mature out" (Winick, 1962) of the lifestyle associated with their addiction, almost suggesting an informal rite of passage analogous to the retirement experience of respectable-occupational careerists. Waldorf (1983) suggests, however, that "retiring" addicts more typically become alcoholics or join the ranks of those imputed to be mentally ill. Still others become involved in social or religious causes.

Clearly, deviant careers end at some point in time. The exit is not likely to be recognized through formal ceremonies or acknowledgment of a lifetime of service. On the contrary, these careers may end somewhere in prison; or in a treatment program after an overdose; or very quietly, following a decision to get out of "the life."

Conclusion

I have attempted to interpret the activities of those engaged in deviant lifestyles through the conceptual framework of "career." Deviant careers are, in some ways, unique, to be sure. They are "deviant," after all, and often illegal. This imposes certain conditions, including the fact that these careers are not typically carried out in formal organizational contexts, and that they are not orderly and predictable, as are many conventional careers. Nevertheless, deviant actors are involved in patterned activities around which they organize their lives and their identities. If the task of the social scientist is to describe and interpret social reality accurately, I contend that the most accurate rendition is that which faithfully represents the perspective of the social actor him- or herself. *Career* captures most faithfully the way in which deviant actors understand their own activities and lives.

Note

1 Many respectable careers are pursued in less structured environments as well. My research (Faupel, 2000) revealed that careers in country music are extremely unstructured and opportunistic, and as early as 1937 Hughes recognized less structured respectable careers. On the other hand, Inciardi (1975) and Letkeman (1973) both suggest a relatively highly structured context for some criminal careers, analogous to careers in highly structured organizations.

References

Best, Joel. 1982. "Careers in Brothel Prostitution." *Journal of Interdisciplinary History* 12, 4 (Spring), pp. 597–619.

Becker, Howard S. 1963. *Outsiders: Studies in the Sociology of Deviance*. Glencoe, IL: Free Press.

Becker, Howard S., Blanche Geer, Everett C. Hughes, Anselm L. Strauss. 1961. *Boys in White: Student Culture in Medical School*. Chicago, IL: University of Chicago Press.

Coombs, Robert H. 1981. "Drug Abuse as Career." *Journal of Drug Issues* 11 (Fall), pp. 369–387.

Faupel, Charles E. 1991. *Shooting Dope: Career Patterns of Hard-Core Heroin Users*. Gainesville: University of Florida Press.

Faupel, Charles, with Ray Wix and Carolyn Wix. 2000. "Careers in Country Music." In Charles K. Wolfe and James E. Adenson (eds.), *Country Music 2000 Annual* (pp. 30–45). Lexington: University Press of Kentucky.

Goffman, Erving. 1959. "The Moral Career of the Mental Patient." *Psychiatry* 22, pp. 123–142

——. 1961. *Asylums*. Garden City, NY: Doubleday.

Hall, Oswald. 1948. "The Stages of a Medical Career." *American Journal of Sociology* 53, 5 (March), pp. 327–336.

Hayano, David M. 1982. *Poker Faces: The Life and Work of Professional Card Players*. Berkeley: University of California Press.

Hughes, Everett C. 1958. *Men and Their Work*. Glencoe, IL: Free Press.

Inciardi, James A. 1975. *Careers in Crime*. Chicago, IL: Rand McNally.

Irwin, John. 1970. *The Felon*. Englewood Cliffs, NJ: Prentice-Hall.

Klockars, Carl B. 1974. *The Professional Fence*. New York: Free Press.

Lesieur, Henry R. 1977. *The Chase*. Garden City, NY: Anchor Books.

Letkeman, Peter. 1973. *Crime as Work*. Englewood Cliffs, NJ: Prentice-Hall.

Luckenbill, David F. and Joel Best. 1981. "Careers in Deviance and Respectability: The Analogy's Limitations." *Social Problems* 29, 2 (December), pp. 197–206.

Pavalko, Eliza K. (2004) "The Illness Career: Intersecting Dynamics of Individual Health and Health Institutions." Paper presented at the annual meeting of the American Sociological Association, San Francisco, CA, August.

Rosenbaum, Marsha. 1981. *Women on Heroin*. New Brunswick, NJ: Rutgers University Press.

Rubington, Earl. 1967. "Drug Addiction as a Deviant Career." *International Journal of the Addictions* 2, 1 (Spring), pp. 3–20.

Van Maanen, John. 1977. *Organizational Careers: Some New Perspectives*. New York: John Wiley & Sons.

Venkatish, Sudhir. 2008. *Gang Leader for a Day: A Rogue Sociologist Takes to the Streets*. New York: Penguin Press.

Waldorf, Dan. 1983. "Natural Recovery from Opiate Addiction: Some Social-Psychological Processes of Untreated Recovery." *Journal of Drug Issues* 13, 2 (Spring), pp. 237–280.

Weinberg, Martin S. 1966. "Becoming a Nudist." *Psychiatry: Journal for the Study of Interpersonal Processes* 29, 1 (February), pp. 15–25.

Wilensky, Harold L. 1961. "Orderly Careers and Social Participation: The Impact of Work History on Social Integration in the Middle Class." *American Sociological Review* 26, pp. 521–539.

Winick, Charles. 1962. "Maturing out of Narcotic Addiction." *Bulletin on Narcotics* 14 (January–March), pp. 1–7.

Wiseman, Jacqueline P. 1970. *Stations of the Lost: The Treatment of Skid Row Alcoholics*. Englewood Cliffs, NJ: Prentice-Hall.

Part V

Deviant lifestyles and subcultures

Overview

To some degree, every individual and every family have something of an individualized and unique lifestyle, but only within the relatively narrow prescriptive template imposed by the culture of a society. Lifestyle involves many constituent elements. These elements may vary somewhat within the cultural template, but the template limits the variability of lifestyle parameters. There are normative lifestyles just as norms shape our social behavior. Extreme variations of lifestyle are considered deviant, but as with other social norms, some adopt lifestyles that cannot be accommodated within the cultural template. Deviant lifestyles may differ from conventional lifestyles only along one or two dimensions.

Culture is not a monolithic concept but instead, in large societies, there may be many smaller subcultures that are components of the larger and more generic panoply of culture. Subcultures may develop around certain groupings of persons based on religion, ethnic group, occupation, avocation, age category, or social class, to mention but some. Subcultures possess their own unique value systems and normative structures. They socialize and inculcate these values and norms in their members. Some subcultures have deviant value systems and norms, and the members are so socialized.

The deviant lifestyle

In the first chapter in this part, Craig Forsyth and Clifton Bryant posit a new conceptualization of the notion of deviant lifestyle. Traditionally, in public use, the concept of "lifestyle" has been used in a very broad fashion to refer to economic levels of lifestyle, such as "an affluent lifestyle," a "modest lifestyle," or a "poverty-stricken lifestyle." Alternatively, the word "lifestyle" has sometimes been used publicly to convey levels of health, such as a "wholesome lifestyle" or a "healthy lifestyle." The sociological use of the concept has generally not expanded its descriptive utility other than to use it to convey an example of day-to-day activities and patterns of behavior in a generic location, such as "an urban lifestyle" or "a suburban lifestyle." Sociologists also use the label "deviant lifestyle" to describe the characteristic behavior of members of a deviant subculture, such as "a homosexual lifestyle" or "a criminal lifestyle. Forsyth and Bryant have a far more elaborate, multidimensional, nuanced notion of lifestyle.

They propose that "consistent patterns of everyday behavior, or "routines," are the "building blocks" of lifestyles. These routines are essentially protocols that program our lives. Routines are templates that provide the scripts for what an individual eats, what they wear, their degree of cleanliness, their manner of speaking, and their choice of words. Other examples of scripted behavior that are constituent to routines include how an individual entertains and/or amuses himself or herself, how he or she elects to relate to a supreme being, how he or she obtains sexual gratification, and how he or she makes a living. Forsyth and Bryant point out that this is not an exhaustive list of routines.

The routines of some individuals may be conventional and the routines of others may be deviant. One individual may pursue a mixture of routines—some conventional and some deviant. Deviant routines or deviant elements of routines are sometimes relatively subtle.

To illustrate better their notion of deviant lifestyle, the authors offer an illustration of a two-dimensional conceptual paradigm. This paradigm articulates the eight routines to lifestyle on the horizontal dimension. It also articulates five patterns of frequency on the vertical dimension. The resulting matrix therefore contains forty cells. Forsyth and Bryant devote most of the chapter to filling in the cells with examples of particular routines at varying levels of frequency. All examples are described and discussed. They conclude with the observation that "Many deviant behaviors are merely exaggerated versions of familiar components or ordinary behaviors."

Transgender lives and lifestyles

In their chapter, Valerie Jenness and Gilbert Geis begin by indicating that the concept of *transgender* is not widely or well understood by the public, and is nebulous in meaning, inasmuch as it is difficult to define because it encompasses so many different kinds of non-normative gender variations and characteristics. Some of the variations include: male-to-female transsexual (and individuals at various stages of transition); female-to-male transsexuals (and individuals at various stages of transition); male cross-dressers; and bigendered; to name but a few. They relate that "Transgender is an umbrella term that captures a range of identities, orientations, and behaviors."

Recently, when Chastity Sun Bono, the daughter of entertainers Sonny and Cher, born in 1969, announced that she was undergoing female-to-male gender transition, it made national news and vividly acquainted the public with the phenomenon of gender change. As Jenness and Geis write, "It has elevated 'transgender' to the evening news."

Jenness and Geis report that demography research on transgender is limited, but a recent survey of 3,474 transgender respondents revealed that 90% were US citizens, 90% were white or European American, 76% indicated that their gender assignment at birth was male, 47% were 32 or younger, 40% reported that they express themselves as female, 26% express themselves as male, and 25% express themselves as transgender.

Because the traditional cultural belief systems have included only two genders, this has tended to make transgender life "invisible." "Gender dysphoria" is a condition recognized by the American Psychiatric Association's *Diagnostic and Statistical Manual of Mental Disorders*, making it clinically "abnormal." Inasmuch as culture dictates a binary division of gender, transgendered individuals are identified as deviant and their non-normative lifestyle is viewed as deviance. Being "different" defines the concept of "abnormal," and transgendered individuals have the "stigma of difference." This shapes the lives of such people and creates challenges that are "inextricably linked to being transgender." Many challenges arise from the need to conform to an array of cultural gender expectations.

At this point, Jenness and Geis proceed to a very detailed examination of the etiology and process of the female-to-male transgender shift with special emphasis on some of the challenges and adversities inherent in the process.

They then look at the problem of civil rights for transgender individuals. A transgender movement in the late 20th century was mounted "on the heels of well-institutionalized feminist and gay and lesbian movements." The transgender movement has experienced significant success. Jenness and Geis point out that more than "sixty colleges and universities," and "more than two hundred employers, including some Fortune 500 companies," now "include gender identity in their non-discrimination policies." In 2004, a federal court of appeal ruled that transgender individuals who experience workplace discrimination "are protected by Title VII of the Federal Civil Rights Act of 1964." Jenness and Geis conclude that "the line between deviance and normalcy has been considerably blurred."

Deviant subcultures

In the third chapter in Part V, Keith Hayward and Jonathan Ilan provide a very detailed and quite comprehensive overview of the development and research use of the concept of *deviant subculture*. They define deviant subculture as "a subgroup whose distinctive shared attitudes and cultural practices are considered sufficiently illicit or subversive to pose a threat—whether perceived or real—to the prevailing values of the mainstream population." They suggest that it first appeared in the mid-20th century, when researchers began to employ anthropological perspectives on culture as strategies in the study of crime and deviance.

Hayward and Ilan assert that the genesis of the use of deviant subculture as a conceptual research tool came with the various ethnographic studies of deviance and delinquency conducted by the scholars of the Chicago School of Sociology. They point to Albert Cohen's (1955) study of a Chicago street gang as having established the "theoretical base" for all deviant behavior research that followed. Subsequent research by other scholars looking at street gangs noted that they were products of lower-class culture, which had focal concerns that "encouraged deviance as opposed to conformity." These lower-class focal concerns were the foundation for the cultural outlook and values of street gang members. The focal concerns included, *trouble, toughness, smartness, excitement, fate,* and *autonomy*. The focus of research on deviant subcultures used the same template to examine other deviant subcultures beyond street gangs. Some examples included studies of the world of the jazz musician, life in the closed community of the mental hospital, and the ethnography of pool hustlers.

In the 1970s, some very notable research on deviant subcultures was conducted by scholars at the University of Birmingham's Centre for Contemporary Cultural Studies (CCCS). The focus of the studies continued the examination of "socio-cultural" relations within lower-/working-class neighborhoods, but broadened to include the backdrop of the leisure and consumer society and the cultural themes of consumerism, self-expression, and "rabid individualism."

Hayward and Ilan note that subcultural analysis is still flourishing within the venue of "cultural criminology." The dynamics and symbols of deviant subcultures, and the larger cultural background of modernity, have become significant research concerns. The interplay between the media, notions of deviance, and deviant subcultures has also started to interest researchers.

Hayward and Ilan review and analyze shifts in thinking about changing social, philosophical, and political postures concerning the definition and meaning of deviance, and they point out that deviance and deviant subculture as concepts have become quite nebulous. As they phrase it: "Stated bluntly, in the absence of an identifiable moral consensus, there is now no clear benchmark against which to define the deviant."

They end with the conclusion that the notion of deviant subculture has been an important and influential concept that has provided a very productive intellectual legacy. It helped shape such new perspectives as "cultural criminology, which provide crucial alternatives to the administrative and control-centered approaches to understanding criminality that otherwise prevail."

Theocrats versus democrats: unconventionality and deviance in a *Kulturkampf*

In his chapter, Nachman Ben-Yehuda provides a case study of subcultural deviance or a deviant subculture. In this instance, the case study is a national case study of the nation of Israel and events transpiring there, particularly the conflict between democrats and theocrats.

Ben-Yehuda relates that the state of Israel was established in 1948 as a "Jewish democracy." This morally based political characterization of the country was problematic from the beginning. The term "democracy" connotes equality, options, and freedom to make informed choices. On the other hand, as Ben-Yehuda phases it, "one of the very central cultural 'building blocks' of Judaism is the Torah-based religion, which—by definition—is non-democratic." This political and identity conundrum may lead some readers to consider the label "Jewish democracy" to be an oxymoron. The social tensions inherent in this name raise numerous philosophical, political, moral, and identity questions.

Ben-Yehuda points out that there are serious religious ideology divisions in Israeli society and that these differences effectively divide the population into five categories: orthodox, ultra-orthodox (*Haredim*), conservative, reform, and secular. These various religious persuasions are also expressed in the different political parties. The population can generically be bifurcated between religious theocrats and secular democrats. Tensions and cultural conflicts are constituent to this division, resulting in what Ben-Yehuda terms a *Kulturkampf*, especially between the *Haredim* and seculars.

Ben-Yehuda describes characteristics of the *Haredim* as "a deep faith in the Almighty," "keeping religious dictates in the most pious way," "intensive community life within defined geographical enclaves," "distinctive clothing," "strong emphasis on family life," "a neo-traditionalist lifestyle," and a "deep commitment to study Jewish scriptures, mostly the Talmud," among others. The *Haredim* have a lifestyle and ideology that are quite "different" from those of most Israelis and are considered deviant by many who follow a mainstream lifestyle. Some *Haredim* engage in deviant behavior.

To explore *Haredim* patterns of deviant behavior, Ben-Yehuda examined reports of *Haredim* violence in secular, religious, and *Haredim* newspapers for a period of fifty years. Based on an analysis of the newspaper reports, he concludes that "the *Haredim* contribute very little to the overall crime picture in Israel." Their deviant patterns tended to be "public-order, politically and ideologically oriented violence," physical and verbal, directed against reform, conservative, and secular Jews. At the most basic level, the *Haredim* attempt to "enforce Halakhic rules about what they consider the appropriate lifestyle upon others." Beyond this, they want to move Israel toward a theocracy. The *Haredim* consider their violent actions as justified on moral and religious grounds, and the non-*Haredim* consider such behavior as deviant, if not criminal.

Ben-Yehuda devotes the remainder of his chapter to an interpretation of this cultural clash, and relates it to larger global events and trends.

Deviant lifestyles

25

The deviant lifestyle

Craig J. Forsyth and Clifton D. Bryant

Everyday life can be conceptualized as a behavioral cafeteria—everyone can pick and choose according to their whims, inclinations, and idiosyncratic persuasions. The resulting smorgasbord of behavioral lifestyle is the equivalent of the assortment of food on the cafeteria tray. Within the boundaries of biological imperative, cultural imprint, and societal dictates, the elements of our everyday activities are largely a matter of volitional choice.

The building blocks of lifestyles are routines or consistent patterns of everyday behavior. In time, these routines become veritable protocols that program our lives. Examples of lifestyle routines might include what an individual eats (diet), the type of clothing that an individual wears (apparel or dress), the degree of cleanliness (hygiene), and the manner of speaking and the choice of words (verbal behavior). Other illustrations of routines are how an individual entertains and/or amuses himself or herself (recreational behavior or avocation), how an individual elects to relate to a supreme being (religious behavior), the manner in which an individual obtains sexual gratification (sexual behavior), and the way in which he or she makes a living (occupational behavior). This enumeration of routines is far from exhaustive and there are many other routines that are components of lifestyle.

A deviant lifestyle is a more or less unconventional way of life or style of living that reflects the markedly different attitudes and values of a person or group. Such lifestyles can be voluntary or involuntary; full-time or part-time; hidden or manifest. Indeed, many individuals who may pursue some deviant routines alongside other, more conventional routines may succeed in keeping their deviant routines completely obscured from public awareness, and effectively pursue them in a clandestine fashion.

Non-normative activities imbedded within routines do not have to be flamboyant or criminal to qualify as deviant. Deviant routines or deviant elements of routines are often relatively subtle. Defective verbal behavior as innocuous as stuttering could be sufficiently stigmatizing, and perceived as deviant enough, to degrade an individual's identity, possibly weaken the individual's legitimacy, and handicap social interaction with others. Crumbling crackers in one's soup during a meal in certain public places (such as country-club dining room or at a dinner party) might garner such a label as "boor" and the stigmatization that would result from the label.

The complexity of lifestyles can be better visualized with a two-dimensional conceptual paradigm. This paradigm is depicted in Table 25.1. The horizontal dimension articulates the eight routines constituent to lifestyles, mentioned above. The behaviors that are components of

Table 25.1 Conceptual paradigm of deviant lifestyle

Frequency of occurance	Dietary behavior	Dressing behavior (Apparel)	Hygienic behavior	Verbal behavior	Recreational behavior	Religious behavior	Sexual behavior	Occupational behavior
COMPULSIVE	Anorexia nervosa; Bulima nervosa	Habitually wearing a particular item of old clothing because it is "lucky" or because of other superstition	Compulsive hand-washing	Tourette's syndrome (uncontrolled verbal outbursts and other odd noises)	Compulsive gambling; Kleptomania	Nodding by Orthodox Jews and Muslims; Shouting "Amen" and "Hallelujah" by fundamentalist Protestants	Sexual addiction (nympho-mania and satyriasis)	"Workaholism"; Japanese "salaryman"
ONGOING	Vegetarianism; Improper table manners; Unacceptable eating behavior	Transvestitism	Bikers; Street people; Hippies; Hobos	Habitual swearing (cursing); Profanity		Cult membership; Practicing Wicca; Satanic worship	Sexual promiscuity	Prostitution; Massage parlor masseuse; Stripping; Professional criminal (burglar)
INTERMITTENT	Fasting; Dirt eating; Chalk eating	Occasional cross-dressing		Glossolalia (speaking in tongues)	Cock-fighting; Dog-fighting	Snake handling during religious services	"Swingers"; Voyeurism; Visiting prostitutes	Sexual harassment; Embezzlement

EPISODIC	Eating bizarre food (i.e. dog or monkey meat) in another culture.	Dressing like animals ("furries")	Not bathing for several days while camping	Libel; Slander; Verbal abuse; Use of profanity when angry; Sedition	Vandalizing property; "Binge drinking" at a frat party; Girls exposing their breasts at Mardi Gras; "Joy-riding"; Shoplifting for thrills	"Backsliding"	Adulterous affairs; Exhibitionism; "One-night stands"	Violent behavior at work; Sexual behavior in the office
ENFORCED	Unusual food taboos because of cultural, religious, allergenic or other health concerns	Convict uniform or straitjacket for inmates	Limited showers for inmates	Speech codes; Vows of silence (Trappist monks)		Forcibly converting Aborigines to Christianity; "Rice Bowl" Christians	"Sex slaves"; Vows of celibacy (monks and priests) and chastity (nuns)	Employees coerced into doing shoddy work or committing deviant or illegal acts ("cooking the books")

routines do not take place uniformly, but rather occur with different patterns of frequency. The vertical dimension of the paradigm includes five patterns of frequency. The resulting matrix therefore contains forty cells. All cells provide examples of deviant elements of particular routines at varying frequencies of occurrence.

Dietary behavior

Eating is a biological imperative, but it takes place within a cultural context that universally prescribes what, when, why, and how certain foods should be eaten. These normative dictates are known as foodways (Boyle and Bryant 2001: 415; McIntosh 1995). These foodways circumscribe dietary behavior in a given society.

Compulsive deviant dietary behavior

Some deviant dietary habits are compulsive. These include bulimia nervosa, anorexia nervosa, and binge eating. All three are classified as eating disorders (Bailey 2001), and can also be labeled pathological and a form of deviant behavior.

Dietary deviance on an ongoing basis

Some dietary deviance may occur on an ongoing basis. An example here might be the practice of vegetarianism. Since the Greek era, vegetarianism has been viewed as a deviant foodway. Pythagoreans considered the abstinence from meat to be "subversive" (Spencer 1995). Later, in the Christian period, because various religious orders practiced vegetarianism, some Christian writers accused vegetarians of being religious heretics. Vegetarianism continues to be thought of by some as a deviant foodway and those who practice it as "odd" and or stigmatized (Boyle and Bryant 2001).

Dietary deviance on an intermittent basis

Dietary deviance may not be routine or continual but rather may occur at intervals or sporadically. Some eating disorders may be considered compulsive, but the bizarre practice of eating dirt (specially certain fine clay soils), known as geophagia, occurs on a somewhat more irregular basis. Forsyth and Benoit (1989: 61–62) report that dirt eating is common in many societies, including some rural parts of the United States. It is a stigmatized activity in the US, which has caused many of those who engage in the practice to attempt to hide the fact.

Dietary deviance on an episodic basis

On some occasions, individuals may travel to a foreign country that has (by US standards) alien foodways, especially in regard to the type of food that is considered edible and appropriate (or even a delicacy). To be a good guest ("when in Rome, do as the Romans do"), an individual may be obliged to eat unusual, if not bizarre, food that is considered normal in the country being visited, but might be considered taboo, and therefore deviant, in the West.

Enforced deviant dietary behavior

In some instances, deviant dietary behavior is not volitional but enforced. In US society, some individuals observe some very unusual food taboos because of compelling cultural, religious, allergenic, or other health concerns.

Apparel (dress) behavior

Individuals usually wear clothes and other accessories for useful reasons: hats to diminish the effects of the sun; heavy coats and ear muffs to stay warm; boots to keep feet dry. Repeatedly wearing your "lucky socks" (or other garments), men wearing women's clothes, and dressing like an animal would appear to be rather irrational, but these acts do have a purpose, albeit while reflecting varying degrees of deviance.

Compulsive deviant dress behavior

Some individuals are compulsive in choosing what to wear. Articles of clothing or accessories can be seen to have powers to alter outcomes. Sports fans and athletes alike are often superstitious. Some basketball players have lucky socks that they wear over or under their official uniforms. Football players have lucky undershirts. Baseball players wear jewelry around their necks. Sports fans are no less compulsive in their apparel. Such dress has produced satisfactory outcomes in the past so the athlete or sport fan feels they must wear the same accessories to avoid the pangs of defeat.

Dress deviance on an ongoing basis

Transvestitism is the wearing of clothes of the opposite sex. The transvestite is a person who feels compelled to dress in the clothes of the opposite sex, or to cross-dress. This is usually seen as a sexual deviation that is used for sexual arousal and attainment of orgasm. The transvestite is content with his cross-dressing; and he is basically content with his morphological sex. The transvestite is also comfortable with his role as a male. The transvestite is not necessarily homosexual; indeed, most male transvestites are straight. Transvestites are often confused with transsexuals. Transvestitism can be a stage toward transsexualism, and until 1953 the two terms were used interchangeably. There are also female transvestites and transsexuals (Fournet, Forsyth and Schranm 1988).

Dress deviance on an intermittent basis

The occasional cross-dresser fits into this intermittent category. The most conspicuous display of occasional cross-dressing occurs at the New Orleans Mardi Gras or other such celebrations. The dressing in this case is compartmentalized into very concentrated periods of time. This frequency of cross-dressing does not intrude into the individual's lifestyle.

Dress deviance on an episodic basis

Furries are people who enjoy dressing like animals. They are apart from other groups, who see their wearing of animal costumes as a route to socializing with others who share common interests, such as anthropomorphic art and costumes. Indeed, the furries see their costumes (fursuits) as part of a lifestyle. A furry is a person with an important emotional/spiritual connection with an animal or animals, be they real, fictional or symbolic. They see themselves as something other than human and desire to become more like the furry species with which they identify. Indeed, a small percentage of furries do not consider themselves to be human at all. Another small subgroup within the furry fandom attaches a sexuality to their activity, dressing like an animal while having sex.

Enforced deviant dress behavior

The uniform that a convict is forced to wear reflects his or her social status. Even within the institution there are different statuses, usually reflecting the degree of freedom the prisoner is allowed. Certain uniforms are restricted to places within the prison. For example, a trusty will have a different uniform from others. The wearing of the prison uniform, like the criminal conviction, confers an immediate deviant status. Stripes or an orange jump suit denotes a deviant identity.

Hygienic behavior

Proper hygiene represents conformity. We receive messages from our parents, schools, and the media about the benefits of good hygiene. Obviously not everyone adopts these rules; some become compulsive in their cleanliness to an extent that labels their behavior deviant. Others, either forced or voluntarily, have adopted different modes of hygienic behavior, or a lack of hygiene, either of which would be viewed as deviant. Cultures differ in their degree of hygiene— for example, whether one needs to bathe every day.

Compulsive deviant hygienic behavior

Compulsive hand-washing reflects a recurrent obsession with cleanliness. The hand-washing has become severe enough to be time-consuming. The need to wash one's hands becomes distressful to the individual and is generally seen as unreasonable by those around them. The person may feel they have been contaminated by touching objects or people. Generally, compulsive deviant hygienic behaviors are not related to any real-life problems but are fictions.

Hygienic deviance on an ongoing basis

Bikers, street people, hippies, and hobos do not practice good hygiene on an ongoing basis. For some, the necessary amenities are not available; but for others, it is a lifestyle choice. Their lack of good hygiene sets them apart from others as they are seen as dirty, smelly, or diseased. Their lives have no requirements (work) that dictate good hygiene. For bikers, the "dirty status," whether real or fictional, is part of the mystique which intimidates and keeps people away from them, partly through fear.

Hygienic deviance on an intermittent basis

Many men and couples change their identities each weekend. They change from suits and/or work clothes to biker costumes and hit the open road on their motorcycles. They do not bathe; they uncover their tattoos; and they stay away from Starbucks and other middle-class affectations. In effect, they become weekend deviants (Quinn and Forsyth 2009).

Hygienic deviance on an episodic basis

Not bathing for several days while on a hunting or camping trip represents an episode of deviant behavior. Even if amenities (showers, shaving) are available, they are not used because the rules of hygiene have changed for the duration of the trip. "Real men" hunt, use profanity, tell dirty jokes and "war stories," and stay dirty and stink.

Enforced deviant hygienic behavior

Showers are "rationed" for prison inmates, who are routinely denied them as punishment. Those on death row or in solitary confinement are denied showers/shaving for longer periods. The fact that the denial of hygiene represents a punishment is indicative of the positive mode of good hygienic behavior.

Verbal behavior

The way in which people speak, what they have to say, and the manner in which they say it are all indicators of social status, and subject to normative dictate and social assessment. Verbal behavior may enhance (or degrade) an individual's social status, reveal or announce their persona, strengthen or weaken their social skills, and augment their argumentative strategies.

Compulsive verbal deviance behavior

Some "defective" speech is compulsive in nature. Certain neurological afflictions produce defective and stigmatizing verbal behavior. One of the most vivid and compelling examples of defective speech is that caused by Tourette's syndrome. Individuals so afflicted display a variety of symptoms, including complex muscle tics, uncontrolled verbal outbursts that may include obscenities (words related to feces, copralalia, are common), grunting, snorting, barking like a dog, and/or involuntary bouts of cursing (Beers 2003: 400). The individual who has Tourette's is very ineffective in communicating, is socially handicapped, and is often subject to ridicule and derisive, sometimes abusive, reactions. Being stigmatized and marginalized is not uncommon.

Verbal deviance on an ongoing basis

Lack of education and effort may result in deficient language skills (poor grammar, poor spelling, poor pronunciation, and limited vocabulary), and individuals with such deficiencies will have their social skills severely handicapped. Inadequate verbal abilities are stigmatized and considered deviant, especially by those who are noticeably articulate and able to converse in a grammatically correct fashion.

The most extreme case of deficient language skills is the individual who is totally illiterate. Such a person is very much a deviant because he or she cannot function adequately in wider society.

Some persons may have adequate verbal abilities but engage in inappropriate verbal behavior, such as an individual who habitually engages in profanity ("cursing" or "swearing"). Such verbal behavior is offensive, a violation of the social norms of proper manners, gentility, civility, and decency.

Verbal deviance on an intermittent basis

Deviant verbal behavior does not necessarily have to be offensive on a habitual basis. Sometimes, individuals who observe the requirements of "polite" and non-derisive speech may occasionally "lapse" into inappropriate verbal behavior. Even entertainers, politicians, and other celebrities often "forget" the rules of polite speech and occasionally "slip" and use profanity, the "N" word, or some other racial or ethnic epithet. Lapsing into "non-politically correct" speech is not uncommon. Apologies are usually extended.

Verbal behavior does not necessarily have to be offensive to be deviant. It merely has to be sufficiently different or unusual from, or alien to, conventional verbal behavior. A colorful illustration of this is glossolalia (speaking in tongues). Glossolalia is a fabricated, non-meaningful, non-interpretive babble or language uttered by members of some fundamentalist Christian denominations (derisively called "Holy Rollers" by some skeptics) (Goodman 1971). Such persons speak it during highly emotional religious services. For the faithful believers, speaking in tongues is believed to be divinely inspired and a highly personalized communication with the divinity. Non-believers tend to ridicule the practice because they see it as nonsensical babble uttered by less educated lower-class persons.

Deviant verbal behavior on an episodic basis

Some verbal deviancy occurs only on an irregular basis. An individual who is not normally inclined to use profanity might well do so if he or she hits their thumb while hammering a nail. Similarly, an individual who loses his or her temper in the middle of an argument might suddenly and inadvertently lapse into a cursing mode of communication.

Enforced deviant verbal behavior

Sometimes modes of verbal communication are enforced or imposed. Some institutions, such as schools, may have "speech codes." To violate the rules of the speech code is to invite sanctions.

In Marine boot training, the recruits are instructed that when they speak to a drill instructor or any other superior, the first and last word uttered must be "Sir." Failure to do so results in punishment. Just as there are speech codes, there are also "silence codes." Trappist monks, for example, take vows of absolute silence.

Recreational behavior

For many individuals, some of their recreational activity is deviant. Mainstream theories about deviance have given scant attention to the role of pleasure or fun as possible motivational underpinnings for certain forms of deviance (Reimer 1981). Many individuals seem to be motivated by the excitement, challenge, and relief from boredom that deviant activities offer.

Compulsive deviant recreational behavior

Gambling is to bet on an uncertain outcome. Compulsive gambling is to be preoccupied with gambling. The compulsive gambler wishes to relive past gambling experiences, plans the next gambling experience, and thinks of ways to get money to gamble. They seek and are aroused by the action of gambling.

Kleptomania is the recurrent failure to resist impulses to steal items. These items may not be for personal use and/or monetary gain. Like the compulsive gambler when placing a bet, the kleptomaniac gets pleasure and gratification when committing a theft. They usually work alone and do little planning.

Recreational deviance on an ongoing basis

Nude sunbathing is a form of recreational deviance for all participants: the sunbathers themselves and the voyeurs who watch. Voyeurism poses a dilemma for the nude beach naturalists, and voyeurs have become the plague of the nude scene. The abstract vision of the beach does not see it as in any way a sex trip, but the casual vision of life in general certainly does not exclude or downgrade sex (Douglas, Rasmussen and Flanagan 1977).

Suspension involves the hanging of an individual from hooks that have been inserted through either the skin or existing body piercings. For the most part, it is a social activity that occurs in front of a group. Usually it is done as a "performance," in which case the group can be sizeable (Forsyth and Simpson 2008).

Recreational deviance on an intermittent basis

Cock-fighting dates back to antiquity, and it has enjoyed widespread popularity in many parts of the world. Throughout its history, though, it has also had its critics and detractors. In the US for most of the 20th century it has been labeled deviant, and in some instances has been designated a crime. It involves attaching steel spurs to the legs of two roosters, placing them in a small pit, and letting them fight to the death. The fights provide the basis for gambling on the outcome (Bryant 1991; Forsyth 1996; Worden and Darden 1992). The spectators are often portrayed as sinister, brutish, and criminally inclined.

Dog-fighting results in a great deal of stigma on the participants (Evans and Forsyth 1998), and the activity has never had general support. There is a supporting subculture, but it is very small and the activity occurs at times and places unknown to all but a small group. Indeed, the time and location of an upcoming dog-fight are generally not announced until the last minute. Dog-fighting is considered to be an even more heinous form of deviance than cock-fighting, and may result in arrest on a felony charge, conviction, and a prison sentence.

Recreational deviance on an episodic basis

"Bead whores" are women who expose their breasts at the New Orleans Mardi Gras in exchange for beads thrown by float riders. They play to several groups of voyeurs. The ostensible "audience" are the individuals on the parade floats, who notice the girls in the crowd exposing their breasts and throw the beads as a kind of "reward." Also in the crowds are many males who like to stare at the women. The attentions of some are welcomed while those of others are not, but many of the women say they enjoy being watched (Forsyth 1992).

Enforced deviant recreational behavior

Many drinking groups enforce drinking behavior. The non-drinker is excluded from the group, or is constantly asked, "Why aren't you drinking?" or "Do you want a drink?" The fact that one is forced to carry a drink in one's hand (and presumably drink it) in order to be accepted as part of the group indicates enforcement.

Religious behavior

Religion plays a seminal role in the lives and lifestyles of many people. Muslims must face Mecca, kneel, touch their heads to the ground, and pray five times a day. Orthodox Jews, and many reform Jews, must plan their dietary habits carefully, eating only kosher food and avoiding pork. Members of some religious denominations do not imbibe alcoholic beverages; members of others refuse blood transfusions; and members of yet others do not seek medical care when ill. Some religious groups eschew smoking, gambling, and even dancing.

Compulsive deviant religious behavior

Once indoctrinated into a religious faith or denomination, many individuals develop certain seemingly spontaneous or compulsive religious habits. Orthodox Jewish men stand in front of the "Wailing Wall" in Jerusalem nodding their heads up and down for a period of time. This nodding is also frequently observed in Orthodox Jewish men reading the Torah. Such behavior is not dictated by the Jewish faith, but the habit is acquired from others who share the Judaic culture and becomes reflexive and habitual. The nodding also seemingly aids concentration and reflection.

Deviant religious behavior on an ongoing basis

Religions and religious denominations differ greatly in belief, doctrine, and practices. Certainly, American culture accommodates religious diversity, and, accordingly, there is an extraordinarily broad range of religions and religious denominations represented in US society.

Some religious practices, however, are less accommodated and may unsuccessfully test public tolerance and be labeled and stigmatized as deviant, while their practitioners are derisively termed "crackpots," if not "sinful" or "sinister." An example of such a stigmatized religious practice might be membership of a cult such as Hare Krishna.

Other stigmatized religious behavior is practicing Wicca, a kind of benign witchcraft that members claim is simply worship of nature (Lamond 2004). Satanic worship is perceived as more sinister and more deviant than Wicca.

Deviant religious behavior on an intermittent basis

All religions and religious denominations have their own unique, idiosyncratic beliefs and practices, but some are bizarre by any set of standards. In some fundamentalist Protestant churches (often of localized affiliation) the members of the congregation handle snakes (mostly rattlesnakes) during services on an irregular basis. Having handled the snakes, they pass them on, often throwing them, to other members of the congregation. By the end of the service, a majority of the congregation will probably have had some physical contact with the snakes. This behavior occurs primarily in rural parts of Appalachia.

Deviant religious behavior on an episodic basis

No matter how devout a religious person tries to be—whether they are Christian, Jew, Muslim, or Buddhist—there are occasions, even if episodic, when an individual may "cross the line" and engage in behavior that is considered deviant within the context of that religion's normative structure. Members of all religious denominations may sometimes err.

Baptists have a label for such behavior: "backsliding." An example might be a devout Christian who embraces the Baptist doctrine, faithfully follows the teachings of the Church, and fulfills all the religious behavioral requirements, but then engages in some sinful act.

Enforced deviant religious behavior

Belief in a particular religious doctrine and participation in the practices of that faith are not always volitional. In some instances, they are enforced. Historically, under Shariah law, the punishment for abandoning the Islamic religion and converting to another has been death. Toward the goal of keeping their population Islamic, most Islamic countries still do not allow Christian missionaries into their territory.

All forms of religious coercion are forms of domination and, therefore, deviance. Much religious behavior is dramaturgical and designed to curry favor or elicit social or personal gain, and is thus insincere and deviant. Finally, forced religious conversions tend to marginalize the convert, thereby stigmatizing him or her, labeling them deviant.

Sexual behavior

Humans obviously are biologically motivated to engage in sexual relations. While fundamental human sex drives undeniably exist, it is also clear that this sexual behavior takes many diverse forms. Norms vary widely regarding sexual attractiveness, the availability of sexual partners, the acceptance of non-procreative sexual practices, and a wide range of other normative sexual proscriptive and prescriptive behaviors. Standards of sexual behavior change rapidly in any given society

Compulsive deviant sexual behavior

Sexual addiction is a compulsive deviant sexual behavior. Nymphomania and satyriasis are two examples. Nymphomania is excessive sexual desire in, and behavior of, a female. Satyriasis is the male version of the same level of sexual desire. In both instances, the level of sexual desire and frequency of sexual interaction far exceed that of "normal" sexual motivation and activity.

Sexual deviance on an ongoing basis

Sexual promiscuity is a label given to the behavior of males or females who have sex with greater frequency and with more sexual partners than the norm (although the label is rarely applied to heterosexual males). Since the norm is rather elastic, the label is indicative of era, geography, and culture. Promiscuity is generally seen as having casual sexual relations frequently with many different partners.

Sexual deviance on an intermittent basis

Swinging is the phenomenon of mate swapping. Seen as an alternative to monogamous marriage, there was a flurry of attention from researchers and the popular press to swinging during the 1960s and 1970s. However, it never reached the levels of the attention given to it.

Voyeurism is watching persons who are undressing, naked, or in the act of sexual intercourse. Vicarious sexual gratification as a symbolic replacement for physical sexual fulfillment represents a socially acceptable substitute (Bryant 1977).

Sexual deviance on an episodic basis

The one-night stand is an example of an episode of sexual deviance. Many "groupies" engage in one-night stands. "Groupie" is a term usually used to refer to young women who follow rock groups on tour, but the groupie subculture also surrounds professional athletics, with each sport having specific names for these women. Baseball players refer to the women as "Annies," hockey players call them "puck bunnies," and rodeo cowboys term them "buckle bunnies" (Gauthier and Forsyth 2000).

Enforced deviant sexual behavior

In many countries the debts of the family are paid off with the forced labor of the children. Sexual slavery is an extension of this forced labor. The erotic tour industry supports this in an indirect way (Evans, Forsyth and Wooddell 2000). The whore houses of the ports of the Panama Canal, for example, are full of women brought in from Central and South America who live, eat, and work in these establishments.

Occupational behavior

For many, work is the master routine in their lifestyle. It provides sustenance, social identity, challenge, companionship, and security, among other consequences. Work as social activity is a pervasive phenomenon and a significant portion of our life and group existence is labeled as such. As one author (Edholm 1967: 16) phrased it, "work really includes all, or nearly all, human activity." Work impacts on our lives and our lifestyles. In most instances, it is conventional, normative, and functional, but it can also be unconventional, deviant, and dysfunctional.

Compulsive deviant occupational behavior

For most individuals, work can be and is a "good thing," but, for some, it can be "too much of a good thing." Many people enjoy their work, some are "wedded to their work," others take on too much work, and some are addicted to their work to the point of being chronically and voluntarily overworked. Individuals with this affliction are often derisively labeled "workaholics."

Deviant occupational behavior on an ongoing basis

There are many occupations that are deviant (and, in some instances, criminal) on an ongoing basis: "sex workers," such as prostitutes, massage parlor masseuses (Bryant and Palmer 1973), strippers and other erotic dancers (Deshotels and Forsyth 2006, 2008; Forsyth and Deshotels 1997), and pornographic movie actors and actresses. Other deviant occupations are pool and shuffleboard hustlers (Gillespie 1974), professional gamblers, some carnival workers (Bryant 1972), and pornographic authors. There are also "career" illegal vocational pursuits, such as moonshiners, burglars, pickpockets, and narcotic distributors, among others.

Deviant occupational behavior on an intermittent basis

Deviant occupational behavior also occurs in most work systems on a sporadic or intermittent basis. Police officers, when investigating a burglary, might go into the unoccupied store and, while there, help themselves to small items, such as cigarettes and candy bars. Some might even "shop" for more expensive items, such as steaks or hams (Stoddard 1968: 231–232). Some law enforcement officers, from time to time, may accept bribes of money or sexual services, or steal narcotics from evidence rooms.

Deviant occupational behavior on an episodic basis

The workplace is a fertile context for flirtation, romance, and/or erotic behavior. Work frequently throws together persons of the opposite sex. A male worker, for example, may have one or more females as subordinates, peers, or even superiors. Some mixed-sex dyadic arrangements are quite institutionalized. Examples here might include the male executive and his female secretary, the male physician and his female nurse, and the male artist and his female model. Additionally, many occupational practitioners interact (perhaps intimately) with a clientele of the opposite sex in the course of their work. It should not be surprising that romances and affectionate affairs, including sexual activities, sometimes occur in spite of workplace rules or professional ethics to the contrary.

The workplace—office, store, factory, classroom, and so on—is also sometimes the focus of violence. The nature of this violence may range from a simple altercation between two employees on the workplace premises to mass murder by a disgruntled or alienated employee, student, or customer (Knefel and Bryant 2004).

Enforced deviant occupational behavior

There are instances when workers or employees may be encouraged, instructed, ordered, or coerced to break the formal norms by superiors from within the formal work structure or the informal work group, or agents of authority from without the work structure. In effect, workers may be pressured to commit deviance.

Sometimes factory workers may be encouraged, if not ordered, by supervisors to use forbidden procedures or tools as shortcut techniques to meet quotas or schedules, or to conceal mistakes or shoddy workmanship (Bensman and Gerver 1963).

Discussion

Compulsive behaviors are for the most part not under the individual's control. Some are forms of mental disorder. Others are more or less deviant identities or behaviors which are the consequence of choice within the confines of cultural and structural experiences. The degree one curses, or not, depends on others in the cultural environment also using profanity. Many deviant behaviors are merely exaggerated versions of familiar components of ordinary behaviors (Sagarin 1975). The borderline between normal and deviant is sometimes blurred.

References

Bailey, C. L. (2001) "Eating disorders," pp. 326–330 in Clifton D. Bryant (ed.) *Encyclopedia of Criminology and Deviant Behavior*, Vol. IV. Philadelphia, PA: Brunner-Routledge.

Beers, M. H. (2003) *The Merk Manual of Medical Information*. New York: Pocket Books.

Bensman, J. and I. Gerver (1963) "Crime and punishment in the factory: The functions of deviancy in maintaining the social system," *American Sociological Review* 28 (4) (August): 588–598.

Boyle, J. E. and C. D. Bryant (2001) "Vegetarianism as deviance," pp. 415–416 in Clifton D. Bryant (ed.) *Encyclopedia of Criminology and Deviant Behavior*, Vol. I. Philadelphia, PA: Brunner-Routledge.

Bryant, Clifton D. (1972) "Sawdust in their shoes: The carnival as a neglected complex organization and work culture," pp. 180–203 in C. D. Bryant (ed.) *The Social Dimensions of Work*. Englewood Cliffs, NJ: Prentice-Hall.

—— (1977) *Sexual Deviancy in Social Context*. New York: New Viewpoints.

—— (1991) "Deviant leisure and clandestine lifestyle: Cockfighting as a socially disvalued sport," *Work Leisure and Recreation* 33 (2) (Summer): 117–121.

Bryant, C. D. and C. D. Palmer (1973) "Massage parlors, sexual service, and 'hand whores': Some sociological observations," *Journal of Sex Research* 2 (3) (August): 227–241.

Deshotels, Tina and Craig J. Forsyth (2006) "Strategic flirting and the emotional tab of exotic dancing," *Deviant Behavior* 27 (2): 223–241.

—— (2008) "Sex rules: The edicts of income in exotic dancing," *Deviant Behavior* 29 (5): 484–500.

Douglas, Jack D., Paul K. Rasmussen, and Carol A. Flanagan (1977) *The Nude Beach*. Beverly Hills, CA: Sage.

Edholm, O. G. (1967) *The Biology of Work*. New York: McGraw Hill.

Evans, Rhonda D. and Craig J. Forsyth (1998) "The social milieu of dogmen and dogfights," *Deviant Behavior* 19 (1): 51–71.

Evans, Rhonda D., Craig J. Forsyth and George Wooddell (2000) "Macro and micro view of erotic tourism," *Deviant Behavior* 21 (6): 537–550.

Forsyth, Craig J. (1992) "Parade strippers: A note on being naked in public," *Deviant Behavior* 13 (4): 391–403.

—— (1996) "A pecking disorder: Cockfighting in Louisiana," *International Review of Modern Sociology* 26 (1): 15–25.

Forsyth, C. J. and G. M. Benoit (1989) "Rare, ole, dirty snacks: Some research notes on dirt eating," *Deviant Behavior* 10 (1): 6–68.

Forsyth, Craig J. and Tina H. Deshotels (1997) "The occupational milieu of the nude dancer," *Deviant Behavior* 18 (2): 125–142.

Forsyth, Craig J. and Jessica Simpson (2008) "Everything changes once you hang: Flesh hook suspension," *Deviant Behavior* 29 (4): 367–387.

Fournet, Lee, Craig J. Forsyth, and Catherine Schranm (1988) "The process of deviance designation: The case of the homosexual transvestite," *Free Inquiry in Creative Sociology* 16 (November): 177–182.

Gauthier, DeAnn K., and Craig J. Forsyth (2000) "Buckle bunnies: Groupies of the rodeo circuit," *Deviant Behavior* 21 (4): 349–365.

Gillespie, Charles (1974) "The open road for boys: Meet Glen Young, master shuffleboard hustler," pp. 278-285 in Clifton D. Bryant (ed.) *Deviant Behavior: Occupational and Organizational Bases*. Chicago, IL: Rand McNally College Publishing.

Goodman, F. D. (1971) *Speaking in Tongues: A Cross-Cultural Study of Glossolalia*. Chicago, IL: Chicago University Press.

Knefel, A. M. C. and C. D. Bryant (2004) "Workplace as combat zone: Reconceptualizing occupational and organizational violence," *Deviant Behavior* 25 (6): 579–601.

Kurotani, S. (2009) "Karoshi," pp. 625–626 in C. D. Bryant and D. L. Peck (eds.) *Encyclopedia of Death and the Human Experience*. Thousand Oaks, CA: Sage.

Lamond, Frederic (2004) *Fifty Years of Wicca*. Sutton Mallet: Green Magic.

McIntosh, E. N. (1995) *American Food Habits in Historical Perspective*. Westport, CT: Praeger.

Quinn, James F. and Craig J. Forsyth (2009) "Leathers and Rolexes: The symbolism and values of the motorcycle club," *Deviant Behavior* 30 (3): 235–265.

Reimer, J. W. (1981) "Deviance as fun," *Adolescence* 61: 39–43.

Sagarin, Edward (1975) *Deviants and Deviance*. New York: Praeger.

Spencer, C. (1995) *The Heretics: A History of Vegetarianism*. Hanover, NH: University Press of New England.

Stoddard, Ellwyn (1968) "The informal 'code' of police deviancy: A group approach to 'blue-coat' crime," pp. 218–238 in Clifton D. Bryant (ed.) *Deviant Behavior: Occupational and Organizational Bases*. Chicago, IL: Rand McNally College Publishing.

Worden, Steve and Donna Darden (1992) "Knives and gaffs: Definitions in the deviant world of cockfighting," *Deviant Behavior* 3 (3): 271–289.

26

Transgender lives and lifestyles

Valerie Jenness and Gil Geis

In 2007, *Newsweek*, the sixteenth most circulated magazine in the US (tellingly, right behind *Sports Illustrated* and right before *Playboy*), introduced transgender America to the public when it ran a cover story on "The Mystery of Gender: Aside from the Obvious, What Makes Us Male or Female? The New Visibility of Transgender America is Shedding Light on the Ancient Riddle of Identity" (Rosenberg, 2007). This article did not offer a definitive definition of what it means to be transgender, nor did it provide a social-science-informed portrayal of transgender lives and lifestyles. This is not particularly surprising because experts, activists, researchers, and members of transgender communities do not agree on what it means to be transgender and there is only a nascent body of literature on transgender lives.

Two years after the *Newsweek* article appeared, in 2009, Chaz Bono (born Chastity Sun Bono on March 4, 1969), the celebrity offspring of legendary entertainers and popular culture icons Sonny and Cher, made national headlines when his publicist announced that he was undergoing female-to-male gender transition. As Bono's publicist said in a press release:

> Yes, it's true—Chaz, after many years of consideration, has made the courageous decision to honor his true identity. He is proud of his decision and grateful for the support and respect that has already been shown by his loved ones. It is Chaz's hope that his choice to transition will open the hearts and minds of the public regarding this issue, just as his "coming out" did nearly 20 years ago.[1]

The reference to "coming out" is explained in *Family Outing*, in which Bono (1998) wrote:

> As a child, I always felt there was something different about me. I'd look at other girls my age and feel perplexed by their obvious interest in the latest fashion, which boy in class was the cutest, and who looked the most like cover girl Christie Brinkley. When I was 13, I finally found a name for exactly how I was different. I realized I was gay.

Bono's life story is increasingly a central piece of the iconography of transgender America and it has elevated "transgender" to the evening news.

Transgender as an umbrella term: capturing variation

Although there is a growing academic literature on transgender people and their lives, there is not a concomitant consensus on how best to define transgender. In one of the most recent books on the topic, *Transgender Voices: Beyond Women and Men*, Girshick (2008: 13) ultimately concedes: "Writing this book, I was immediately constrained by the limitations of the English language, which does not capture the wide diversity of sex and gender characteristics of the people I interviewed." Participants in Girshick's study identified themselves as: male-to-female and female-to-male transsexuals (not necessarily living as such full time, and individuals at various stages of transition); male cross-dressers; female (including transsexuals and non-transsexuals); male (including transsexuals and non-transsexuals); transgender (along with other identities); butch (including labels of butch lesbian, stone butch, dyke, soft butch, and masculine woman); intersex; genderqueer; transgender; femme; woman-born transsexual; androgyne male; femme androgyne; ungendered; bigendered; transman; gender variant; transmale performing butch; trans; femme dyke or transdyke; tranny fag; tranny; or trans. Clearly, transgender is a term that is used to refer to a plethora of non-normative gender identities and sexual orientations as well as non-normative gender presentations and lifestyles.

Transgender is a term that captures a range of identities, orientations, and behaviors. At one end of a range of definitions, it is used as an umbrella term to refer to gender variant individuals. Gender variance refers to individuals whose gender expression and behavior do not match the expectations associated with a binary understanding of sex/gender (i.e., that there are males and there are females, but nothing else). This understanding includes all non-normative sexual and gender identities and lifestyles. At the other end, transgender is used as a proxy for transsexuals or transvestites. This offers a narrower sense of the term. Either broadly or narrowly construed, transgender references a population with a unique social location in a culture that values a dichotomous sex/gender system with mutually exclusive components (i.e., male and female) (Girshick 2008; Stryker 2008).

The demography of transgender America

Social science has only recently begun to produce a systematic demographic profile of transgender people and communities. For example, in a book that is slated to be published soon, *Understanding Transgender Lives*, Brett Genny Beemyn and Sue Rankin present empirical data from a survey of 3,474 transgender respondents in the US. The majority (76%) reported that their assigned gender at birth was male and 23% reported their assigned gender at birth as female. Also, 38% of the respondents described their gender identity as female, 35% as transgender, and less than 20% as male. Among the respondents who identified as transgender, the most common descriptions were "male-to-female," "crossdresser," "female-to-male," "genderqueer," and "transvestite." In terms of gender expression, 40% reported that they express themselves as female, 26% express themselves as male, and 25% express themselves as transgender. Nine percent selected "other," and most often expressed as "ambiguous," "androgynous," "bigender," "both female and male," "butch," "crossdresser," "fluid," "genderqueer," and "varies." Their sexual orientation is equally variable as almost a third of respondents (32%) reported that their sexual orientation is bisexual; 30% identified as heterosexual; and 16% identified as "other," which included but was not limited to "a mix of asexual, gay, and heterosexual," "ambivalent," "attracted to genderqueer people," "autobisexual," "bisexual when dressed in female clothes otherwise heterosexual," "pansexual," "queer," and "transgender lesbian"; 12% identified as lesbian; 4% identified as gay; and 5% identified as asexual. There was a wide range in age for the respondents (18 and under: 10%; 19–22: 17% ; 23–32: 20%; 33–42: 27%; 43–52: 21%; 53

and over: 5%). Eleven percent reported having a physical attribute that substantially affects a major life activity, and 22% reported having a cognitive or emotional attribute that substantially affects a major life activity. The majority of the respondents (90%) were US citizens, while 8% identified as non-permanent residents. Finally, the majority of respondents indicated that they were white or European American (90%), while the remainder of the sample chose a racial identity that was other than white (African/African American/black: 2%; American Indian: 4%; Alaskan Native: less than 1%; Asian/Asian American: 2%; Latino(a) or Hispanic/Chicano(a): 3%; Middle Eastern: less than 1%; Pacific Islander: less than 1%; Hawaiian Native: less than 1%). (Participants could choose more than one racial-ethnic identity, meaning the percentages total more than 100.) In short, transgender people are, demographically speaking, as diverse as the country. What they share is their relationship to a sex/gender system that privileges heterosexuality, a dichotomous gender order, and an alignment between the two.

The invisible and visible lives of transgender people

The institutionalized cultural belief that the sex/gender system includes two, and only two, sexes serves to render transgender lives and lifestyles invisible, both historically and in the 21st century. Although clinicians have long taken an interest in "gender dysphoria" as a condition recognized by the American Psychiatric Association's *Diagnostic and Statistical Manual of Mental Disorders*, the public in general and social scientists in particular have been slow to take a sustained interest in the daily lives of transgender people. As Namaste (2000: 1) explains in *Invisible Lives: The Erasure of Transsexual and Transgendered People*: "To date, very few of the monographs, articles, and books written about us deal with the nitty-gritty realities of our lives, our bodies, and our experience of the everyday world." She goes on to explain:

> Our lives and bodies are constituted in the mundane and uneventful; going to a pawn shop; finding a doctor; bad clients; electrolysis; looking for a job, losing a lover; perfecting the art of binding breasts; trying to get a date; fixing junk; watching films featuring psychotic transsexual characters; learning how to inject hormones; recovering from surgery; electrolysis; Norvir, Crixivan, and Interferon; overdoses; visiting the hospital; trying to find a surgeon willing to perform sex reassignment surgery on a seropositive transsexual; attending funerals; and changing legal documents.
>
> *(Namatse 2000: 1–2)*

To the degree that transgender lives are increasingly rendered visible in the modern age—in both the popular press and scholarly publications—two things are clear. First, a diverse population comprises the transgender community, including Stu Rasmussen, the mayor of a small town in rural Oregon, and hundreds of prisoners in California (Sexton, Jenness, and Sumner 2010). Second, diversity aside, their lives are commonly marked as non-normative from the point of view of a heterosexist culture and a culture wedded to a gender binary. This marking serves to identify them as "deviant" and makes their lifestyles easily categorized as "deviance," in large part because of the stigma—in the classic Goffmanian sense (Goffman 1963)—that accompanies their social location and daily lives. To quote Girschick (2008: 155), "the experience of being different very much defines the notion of 'abnormal.'" This is the stigma of difference (see also Minow 1990).

The stigma of difference that accompanies being transgender shapes the contours of daily life for transgender people in a plethora of ways. For example, it creates challenges as they navigate what Hines (2007: 74) calls "gender performance and hierarchies of authenticity" and what Snow and Anderson (1987) call "identity work": coming out to family, friends, and coworkers; (pre- and post-) identities—both legally and socially—that are not in alignment with institutional structures and social expectations; and what Girshick (2008: ch. 5) calls "gender policing" in the public sphere. Gender policing relates to the subtle but nonetheless powerful enforcement of taken-for-granted social expectations related to clothing, demeanor, and temperament; the use of sex-segregated bathrooms; the rules associated with medical gate-keeping; the routine use of gender pronouns; and, in the most severe forms, bullying, hostility, and hate crimes related to homophobia.

Seen in this way, the lives of transgender people are distinct from the lives of their non-transgender counterparts. Their social location requires that they cope with an array of challenges inextricably linked to being transgender. To understand features of transgender lives and lifestyles, it is useful to take an extended example, the case of female-to-male transgender people, as illustrative.

Female-to-male: an illustration

No reliable numbers exist that tally the extent of the transgender shift from female to male, labeled FTM, transman, or transguy, but there is no question that it takes place considerably less often than male-to-female gender reconfigurations. The striking discrepancy in the number of FTMs to MTFs raises questions about whether transgendering is or is not a response to genetic imperatives.

Nonetheless, for most biological females who alter their presentation of self, the switch is declared to be genetically dictated. They will recite how as youngsters they were tomboys and how they persistently felt more comfortable acting in what are regarded as masculine ways. Sarah Morgan and Patricia E. Stevens, who carried out in-depth interviews with four FTMs, found that each of them emphasized they self-identified as boys at a very early age and were characterized by a mind–body dissonance. Often they resented and resisted wearing dresses. One of the respondents, for instance, told the researchers: "I was just like all the other little boys. We didn't take our clothes off, so we couldn't tell there was any difference between what we looked like (Morgan and Stevens 2008: 588).

The theory of "penis envy" among females (Sandler, Person, and Fonagy 1991) has long been heavily criticized by feminists, but it can nonetheless be noted that half of the FTMs interviewed by Morgan and Stevens (2008) called specific attention to their dismay when they viewed the penis of a male infant joining the family and asked their mothers why they did not have such equipment. A common response was that of a transgender man interviewed by David Schleifer. He said that he always felt that "there was something missing down there." To try to rectify that absence, he said: "I would always roll up a sheet or bunch my pajamas or make a little dick out of Kleenex and put it in my pants" (Schleifer 2006: 64). Johnny Giovani Righini writes that when in sixth grade he filled a ziplock bag with water and placed it in the front of his panties. "This is the first time I can truly remember feeling power," he said (Righini 2004: 77). The FTMs also reported feeling particular unease in early adolescence when bodily changes—menstruation and developing breasts—pushed them toward an unwanted female identification.

There are inherent difficulties with the FTM transformation. The competitive element of male behavior and their generally taller build places some transgender females at a disadvantage. Women posing as men can urinate only by sitting on the toilet if they are likely to be visible to others to whom they wish to validate the gender role they have assumed. The American military once sought to develop a device that would allow female soldiers to urinate while standing to make them less vulnerable targets and more rapid eliminators (Dickerson 2000), but its utility was ultimately deemed minimal.

In terms of sexual intercourse, some FTMs form homosexual attachments to males. In Schleifer's (2006) study of five gay FTMs, two had once lived as lesbians, but found themselves erotically attached to men after they themselves took on a male identity. The remaining three gay FTMs had been attracted to men as women and remained so after their gender orientation change. Chivers and Bailey (2000) compared homosexual and non-homosexual FTMs and found that homosexual FTMs manifested greater childhood nonconformity, were more sexually assertive, had more sexual partners, were more intent on undergoing phalloplasty, and were more interested than the non-homosexuals in sexual stimuli. They emphasize that FTMs can by no means be regarded as a homogeneous grouping.

FTM situations may involve complexities in heterosexual intercourse. For the FTM, oral sex can help to overcome the absence of a penis, and the use of a dildo can simulate a penis. Sexual arrangements depend on a mutuality that can be more difficult to negotiate than a "regular" heterosexual relationship. The self-image of another of Morgan and Stevens' (2008: 591–592) interviewees is informative:

> I consider myself heterosexual . . . and I like females. Some people might consider me lesbian or gay, but in the relationships I've had, I've had only two in my life, they were both women, they both were interested in me because of my male attributes. They weren't interested in being with females.

The fact that this FTM, who fits in the 39–45-year age group, had only two relationships with women would indicate, if characteristic of others as well, that such relationships might be difficult to obtain and sustain.

The FTM transformation is likely to involve hormone treatment to enhance masculine characteristics. This typically includes bi-monthly injections of testosterone that stop menstruation, lead to a deeper voice, and produce an increased growth of facial and bodily hair. Surgical procedures may involve bilateral mastectomies ("top surgery"), treatments to enlarge the clitoris, and less frequently phalloplasty (the attachment of a penis, often called "bottom surgery"). (For an excellent description of the medical options for FTMs, see Green 2004: 102–119.) In a mail survey of 150 persons who had undergone phalloplasty, Hage and his colleagues (1993) found that all but one desired to be able to void in a standing position. Ninety-six percent said they desired a scrotum and 86 percent wanted penile rigidity.

A medical team suggests that women who transition to men "are at increased risk for having polycystic ovarian syndrome, contracting HIV, experiencing violence, and committing suicide" (Dutton, Koenig, and Fenie 2008: 331). However, they grant that these conclusions are based on limited evidence and write that they ought to be regarded at best as tentative. The Dutton team seems on more solid ground when it points out that women who transition to men are reluctant to take their problems to doctors because of shyness about the discrepancy between their self-image and their physiological makeup.

There are a number of personal accounts by those who have gone through female-to-male transformations, but perhaps the most comprehensive and well-known study of the subject was by sociologist Holly Devor in the book *FTM* (1997). Devor, who at the time was a lesbian, later, at the age of fifty, made the transition that she had written about, becoming Aaron Devor. He is presently dean of graduate studies at the University of Victoria in British Columbia, Canada. In 46 interviews with self-defined FTMs, Devor focused on how they go about redefining their lives as much as possible in order to be credible and to appear and function as though they originated as males. She emphasized that her results came from a non-clinical sample, and thereby hopefully avoided responses that were tailored to seek approval and treatment from social work and medical professionals.

Devor's respondents ranged in age from 22 to 53, with a mean of 37. Six had not yet taken steps to transition, a stage that she defined as taking place with the beginning of hormone therapy. A plurality of her subjects had been sexually attracted to women prior to their transition. Their recollections echo those of one of their number:

> I remember the first girl I had a crush on. It was in nursery school and her name was Betsy Ann. I can remember playing with the boys and they were talking about who they really liked. I said that I really liked her and they just jumped all over me, ooh! They said, "well you can't like another girl, you're a girl."
>
> *(Devor 1993: 308)*

Subsequently, the pattern of gendered sexual attractions shifted, most notably away from straight men and bisexuality. Some avoided sex, Devor comments, because they were "trapped in a conundrum. They would not have sexual relations until they were complete. Medical technology cannot yet make them that way" (Devor 1993: 309). For many FTMs, routine acceptance as a male is a paramount goal that often can involve nerve-racking setbacks. It may sometimes be achieved only by jettisoning previous relationships when the person was recognized as female-bodied. Those FTMs who merge into the general population usually do not become involved in social science portraits of the transgender community, which perhaps skews published results (Cromwell 1999).

The rights revolution

Falling on the heels of well-institutionalized feminist and gay and lesbian movements, a transgender movement emerged in the latter part of the 20th century to ensure transgender rights have a home in larger discussions about legal and social equality. As Currah, Juang, and Mintor (2006: xiii) explain in their book, simply and tellingly titled *Transgender Rights*:

> In the past thirty years, the transgender movement in the United States has gained surprising visibility and strength. In the legislative arena, transgender advocates have successfully fought for inclusion in non-discrimination and hate crime laws in several states and dozens of municipalities. More than two hundred employers, including some Fortune 500 companies, and more than sixty colleges and universities now include gender identity in their non-discrimination policies. In 2004, overturning decades of prior case law, a federal court of appeals ruled for the first time that transgender people who are discriminated against in the workplace are protected under Title VII of the Federal Civil Rights Act of 1964.

In large part, these significant changes parallel the fact that during the latter part of the 20th century almost every major lesbian, gay, and bisexual national organization changed its mission statement to include transgender people. In this way, to be transgender has been normalized even as it remains a visible instance of "deviance" (as delineated above). As a result, the line between deviance and normalcy has been considerably blurred.

Note

1   Cited at: http://www.people.com/people/article/0,,20284698,00.html, last visited December 13, 2009.

References

Bono, Chaz [as Chastity] (1998). *Family Outing: A Guide to the Coming-Out Process for Gays, Lesbians & Their Families*. Boston, MA: Little, Brown.

Chivers, Meredith and Michael J. Bailey (2000). Sexual orientation of female-to-male transsexuals: A comparison of homosexual and nonhomosexual types. *Archives of Sexual Behavior*, 29:259–278.

Cromwell, Jason (1999). *Transmen and FTMs: Identities, Bodies, Genders and Sexualities*. Urbana: University of Illinois Press.

Currah, Paisley, Richard M. Juang, and Shanon Price Mintor (eds.) (2006). *Transgender Rights*. Minneapolis: University of Minnesota Press.

Devor, Holly (1993). Sexual orientation identities, attractions, and practices of female-to-male transsexuals. *Journal of Sex Research*, 30:303–318.

Devor, Holly (1997). *FTM: Female-to-Male Transsexuals in Society*. Bloomington: Indiana University Press.

Dickerson, Debra (2000). *An American Story*. New York: Pantheon.

Dutton, Lauren, Karel Koenig, and Kristopher Fennie (2008). Gynecological care of female-to-male transgender men. *Journal of Midwifery and Women's Health*, 53:331–337.

Girschick, Lori (2008). *Transgender Voices: Beyond Women and Men*. Hanover, NH: University Press of New England.

Goffman, Erving (1963). *Stigma: Notes on the Management of a Spoiled Identity*. Englewood Cliffs, NJ: Prentice-Hall.

Green, Jamieson (2004). *Becoming a Visible Man*. Nashville, TN: Vanderbilt University Press.

Hage, J. Joris, C. A. Bout, Joannes J. A. M. Bloem, and Jos A. Megens (1993). Phalloplasty on male-to-female transsexuals: What do our patients want? *Annals of Plastic Surgery*, 30:323–326.

Hines, Sally (2007). *Transforming Gender: Gender Practices of Identity, Intimacy, and Care*. Bristol: The Policy Press.

Minow, Martha (1990). *Making all the Difference: Inclusion, Exclusion, and American Law*. Ithaca, NY: Cornell University Press.

Morgan, Sarah W. and Patricia E. Stevens (2008). Transgender identity development as represented by a group of female-to-male adults. *Issues in Mental Health Nursing*, 29:583–599.

Namaste, Viviane (2000). *Invisible Lives: The Erasure of Transsexual and Transgendered People*. Chicago, IL: University of Chicago Press.

Righini, Johnny Giovani (2004). Male-to-male. In Monty Diamond (ed.), *From the Insider Out: Radical Gender Transformation, FTM and Beyond* (pp. 76–79). San Francisco, CA: Manic D Press.

Rosenberg, Debra. (2007). Rethinking gender. *Newsweek*, May 21.

Sandler, Joseph, Ethel Spector Person, and Peter Fonagy (eds.) (1991). *Freud's "On Narcissism"—An Introduction*. New Haven, CT: Yale University Press.

Schleifer, David (2006). Make me feel mighty real: Gay female-to-male transgenders negotiating sex, gender, and sexology. *Sexualities*, 9:57–75.

Sexton, Lori, Valerie Jenness, and Jennifer Macy Sumner (2010). Where the margins meet: A demographic assessment of transgender inmates in men's prisons." *Justice Quarterly*, 27:835–860.

Shapiro, Eve (2004). "Trans"cending barriers: Transgender organizing on the internet. *Journal of Gay and Lesbian Social Services*, 16:165–179.

Snow, David and Leon Anderson (1987). Identity work among the homeless: The verbal construction and avowal of personal identities. *American Journal of Sociology*, 19:1336–1371.

Stryker, Susan (2008). *Transgender History*. Berkeley, CA: Seal Press.

Deviant subcultures

27

Deviant subcultures

Keith Hayward and Jonathan Ilan

Introduction: the origins of deviant subcultures

The term 'deviant subculture' dates back to the mid-20th century when sociology of deviance scholars began applying anthropological notions of culture to the study of crime. Put simply, if 'subculture' is a term used to describe a subsection of a wider population (whether distinct or hidden) whose cultural norms and values differentiate that subgroup from the larger culture to which it belongs, then a *deviant* subculture (as the name clearly implies) is a subgroup whose distinctive shared attitudes and cultural practices are considered sufficiently illicit or subversive to pose a threat – whether perceived or real – to the prevailing values of the mainstream population.

As one might presume, there can be no understanding of the criminological concept of the deviant subculture without some understanding of the term 'deviance'. As a social science designation, the term emerged in the United States during the Great Depression of the 1930s (Sumner 1994). Roosevelt was rolling out an expanded welfare state, and the concept of deviance quickly found favour with the new battalions of social policy-makers seeking to categorize deleterious social behaviours such as drug taking, homosexuality, intellectual radicalism and various forms of mental "illness". In terms of our story, though, one deviation stood out above all others – *delinquency*. The concept of delinquency, of course, already had a long-established history dating back to the early 19th century (May 1973). It had been a major cause for concern among Victorian social reformers such as Henry Mayhew and Charles Booth in England, while in the United States it was likewise a source of much agitation for everyone from Jane Addams to W.E.B. DuBois. However, it was scholars from the Chicago School of Sociology in the early decades of the 20th century who did most to develop delinquency in terms of theoretical and empirical inquiry; and it is here, in the pioneering studies of the Chicagoans, that one finds the roots of the deviant subculture. Virtually all the key figures of the Chicago School studied youthful delinquents in one form or another, from Thrasher's work on street gangs to Shaw and McKay's famous concentric-circle map of juvenile delinquency court statistics. It was this rich history of Chicagoan delinquency studies that inspired the first key figure to develop the notion of deviant subcultures.

Albert Cohen and the delinquent subculture

Albert Cohen's (1955) research on the culture of the American street gang arguably set out the theoretical base for all subsequent analyses of (at least youthful) deviant subcultures. During his time at Indiana University, Cohen was greatly influenced by former Chicago School titans Edwin Sutherland and Alfred Lindesmith. In particular, he was schooled in the Chicago traditions of 'differential association' and 'cultural transmission', especially in their application to youthful delinquency. His Ph.D. thesis, entitled 'Juvenile Delinquency and the Social Structure', was an attempt to develop 'a general theory of subcultures' applied to the specific problem of delinquency. This research eventually became *Delinquent Boys: The Culture of the Gang*, his 1955 classic which reinvented Chicago School thinking to produce a theory of both the cultural origins and transmission of delinquent values. *Delinquent Boys* is far-reaching in its scope – at various points touching on such diverse topics as masculinity, Malinowskian anthropology, social movements research, and social and individual psychology. However, its significance for criminology stems from Cohen's constructs of *social frustration* and *reaction formation*. Cohen's observations of gangs led him to proffer that, in contrast to the utilitarian, means–ends model of delinquency proposed by Robert Merton, most delinquency in fact was 'non-utilitarian, malicious and negativistic'. According to Cohen, lower-class delinquent subcultures are products of so-called *social frustration/humiliation*, as certain young boys quickly recognize that they will never measure up to the exacting middle-class standards imposed on them in school and elsewhere in society. These boys gather together to create deviant subcultures characterized by working-class membership, group allegiances, aggressive masculinity, and a lust for transgressive hedonism (see Matza and Sykes, 1961). While these groups develop their own nuanced, stylistic codes and norms, their delinquency in fact stems from the same source – *a reaction formation* whereby middle-class values are rejected/inverted and subcultural status is attained through this process of cultural rebellion.

    Delinquent Boys was hugely influential and triggered a mass of subsequent studies of delinquent subcultures. Much of this research was problematic, often dramatically overemphasizing the negativistic or destructive aspects of subcultural deviance while ignoring certain positive aspects, such as friendship, attachment and plain old fun. However, while not perfect, Cohen's observations in *Delinquent Boys* firmly established the value of studying collective subcultural behaviour and its role in generating and fostering deviant behaviour.

Youth deviance and the subculture of the gang

In the wake of Cohen's study, subcultural theories of deviance emerged as the predominant mode of analysis within the burgeoning sociology of deviance. In particular, attention was trained on how distinct and oppositional norms tended to coalesce within discrete communities of interest and/or identity. Undoubtedly the most influential of these studies was Walter Miller's (1958) work on lower-class urban gang delinquency. Miller contested Cohen's argument that deviant subcultures emerged as a negativistic reaction to the expectations of dominant middle-class culture. Rather, for the anthropologically trained Miller, deviant subcultures such as the 'delinquent street gang' were products of a distinct *lower-class culture* whose 'focal concerns' encouraged deviance as opposed to conformity. Miller's observations about how gangs functioned in disadvantaged communities prompted him to categorize a number of key *focal concerns* that underpinned the cultural outlook of the gang members he studied. These included:

- *Trouble*: a commitment to law-violating behaviour or being noticed as a problem to others;

- *Toughness*: an admiration for physical prowess, bravery and masculinity;
- *Smartness*: agile wit and canniness, as opposed to academic achievement;
- *Excitement*: thrilling sensations often generated by illicit acts;
- *Fate*: rationalizing the consequences of low social status or particular occurrences by reference to 'luck'; and
- *Autonomy*: a resentment of external controls and interference.

While Miller's terminology may now seem somewhat anachronistic and conservative, the emphasis he attached to the lived experience of poverty and social exclusion continues to be prescient. His analysis endows his subjects with a greater sense of independent agency: they are not merely railing against the strictures of elite norms, but are actively interpreting their world and positively enacting their particular culturally informed values.

Miller's approach marked a key moment in the interpretation of deviant subcultures, especially when read in conjunction with Richard Cloward and Lloyd Ohlin's 1960 work *Delinquency and Opportunity*. Put simply, if Miller claimed that delinquent gang subcultures were products of particular socializing and acculturating effects within disadvantaged communities, then Cloward and Ohlin went one step further and attempted to explain how these effects vary across different disadvantaged communities. Their starting position was that Mertonian strain theory was only 'half right'. While Robert Merton had correctly identified the pressures on lower-class youth to commit delinquency, he had not accounted for the variable range of deviant subcultures that existed in these areas – or why youths chose one particular subculture over another. Put another way, just as the legitimate economy provides a host of contingent paths to success and achievement for entrepreneurs, the *illegitimate means* to achieve subcultural delinquency are also highly differentiated. For example, acquisitive *criminal subcultures* require a certain stability, trust and solidarity within the surrounding community. Where these conditions exist, markets for illicit goods can be sustained and theft becomes economically viable; established criminal figures tend to be more involved and visible, thus capable of providing local youth with 'role models' and or 'apprenticeships'. Where there are no senior players to emulate accessible routes to illicit entrepreneurialism, Cloward and Ohlin concluded that young people are drawn towards *conflict subcultures*. Between conflict groups, violence can create meaning and solidify collective identity for those excluded from both legitimate and illegitimate paths to status and financial gain. Finally, they identified the *retreatist subculture* as the refuge for those whose surroundings and/or circumstances deny them even the opportunity to form conflict gangs. The retreatists were described as seeking an alternative reality to that around them through immersing themselves in cultures of intoxication.

Not only did Cloward and Ohlin's focus on micro-community cultures provide important texture to both strain and subcultural theories, in terms of our specific concern – the deviant subculture – their work was important in that it focused attention on the interface between youth crime and the wider cultures and practices of adults. In doing so, it expanded the scope of sociologists and criminologists to study a wider array of adult deviant subcultures right across the social structure; a legacy that found expression in some of the most celebrated works in criminology, including the likes of Howard Becker's (1963) study of jazz musicians, Erving Goffman's (1961) account of life in the closed community of the mental hospital, and Ned Polsky's (1967) ethnography of poolroom hustlers.

That said, the close association of deviant subcultures with the lifestyles and practices of young people would endure. Indeed, as the 1960s gave way to the 1970s, subcultural research into young people's deviance would enter arguably its most productive and creative phase.

The Birmingham School and beyond: subcultural style and social structure

During the 1970s, the most notable research on deviant subcultures was produced in Britain at the Centre for Contemporary Cultural Studies (CCCS), University of Birmingham. Most notably, *Resistance through Rituals* (Hall and Jefferson, 1976), an edited collection of the centre's output, became a canonical work, illustrating and analysing the social world of Britain's colourful post-war subcultures. While the focus of the Birmingham School continued to be trained on the socio-cultural relations within lower-/working-class neighbourhoods, this time it was augmented by an abiding concern with the expanding so-called 'leisure society', with its attendant traits of consumerism and self-expression. Suddenly the deviant subculture was of interest to sociologists as much for its stylistic nuance and media exposure as it was for its putative criminality. For example, much attention was afforded working-class 'skinheads', a British youth subculture that caricatured working-class style in order magically to preserve a sense of community solidarity that was seen to be fast diminishing as a consequence of rapid deindustrialization and the influx of immigrant populations. Similarly, the 'mod' subculture was much observed for the way its protagonists playfully obscured the humdrum routines of workaday life via a combination of fashion styles that embraced tasteful displays of affluent consumerism and extended bouts of hedonistic partying fuelled by soul music and amphetamines.

Importantly, the CCCS's perspective on subculture did much to expand debates beyond straightforward questions of deviance. By fusing Marxist analysis with Gramscian theory, the centre posited the deviant subculture as a strategy for working-class youth to respond to, play with, and resist their place in the lower echelons of the social structure. Subcultural style, then, was vitally important for the Birmingham School – but only to the extent that it allowed one to 'read' and interpret ideology and thus understand how the vectors of political power coursed through society.

This approach was never more in evidence than in *Subculture: The Meaning of Style*, Dick Hebdige's benchmark study of 1970s youth culture. Here, *style* was used symbolically to resist the dictates of mainstream normativity through infusing quotidian choices and behaviours with subversive meaning. Hebdige acknowledged, however, that these transformative processes were ultimately tamed by the market, as subversive subcultural style was quickly packaged up and resold to mainstream youthful customers.

This concern with the way deviant subcultures could be subject to appropriation and commodification by wider social forces such as the market and the media was further explored by Stan Cohen (1972). Introducing his now-ubiquitous concept of *moral panic*, Cohen showed how the deviant subculture could be constructed as a *folk devil* – a readily identifiable enemy around which fear and symbolic crusade could coagulate. While the now-infamous clashes between 'mods' and 'rockers' were actually relatively minor in nature, the press reaction to these skirmishes was anything but. The idea that marauding deviant subcultures were apparently running amok and disrupting the genteel idyll of the British seaside resort crystallized public fear about the nature and future of society. Cohen showed how vested *moral entrepreneurs*, functioning at various levels of the state and civil society, utilized this combination of sensational press coverage and public anxiety to advance a more punitive crime agenda.

Later work by Stuart Hall showed that it was not just overt, highly stylized deviant subcultures that could be the subject of intense criminalization. In *Policing the Crisis* (1978), Hall and his co-authors demonstrated how the problem of 'mugging' was constructed by a cosy interplay of media reportage and so-called expert opinion that surfaced in response to a small spike in rates of street robbery. Through the propagation of a media stereotype that cast the 'mugger' as young, black, working class and male, the state essentially manufactured a phantasmal deviant subculture. Inevitably, the public's fear of crime intensified. The state responded to this public concern by implementing police practices that disproportionately targeted black teenagers. Thus, the state reaffirmed its 'legitimacy' by restoring public confidence in the police's ability to maintain law and order.

The work of the Birmingham School and the mass of subcultural studies that appeared in its wake served to highlight the contested cultural context that defines the complex interrelationships between subcultures and the law. However, while the dynamic tension between youth subcultures and aggressive legal regulation is well established, public anxieties about youthful subcultures show no sign of abating. Be they politicians attempting to curry favour with the 'moral majority' or sensationalist newspaper editors seeking to boost circulation, moral entrepreneurs are as keen today as they ever were to depict deviant subcultures as the very embodiment of social decay.

Stuart Hall and the Birmingham School's insights into the representation and politicization of deviant subcultures would be given a further twist by the next generation of American gang researchers. During the 1980s and 1990s, criminologists once again returned to the subject of entrenched urban violence. However, rather than drawing on the rich body of research outlined above, much of this work adopted a more moralizing tone, seeking to identify aetiological links between rising rates of violent crime and the growth of an urban 'underclass' supposedly characterized by broken homes, drug markets and welfare dependency. Worse still, on occasion, certain researchers even went as far as to explain cultures of poverty and high crime via a thinly veiled return to discredited forms of constitutional positivism.

It was in a bid to respond to this controversial body of work that a small but influential group of urban ethnographers began to revisit and reinvigorate the subcultural tradition. Drawing on the 'appreciative' approach of the Chicago School, these scholars entered into the economic hinterlands of the late modern city to investigate and give voice to a disparate array of deviant street (sub)cultures too often subsumed by the totalizing gaze of the 'new right'. For example, Phillipe Bourgois (1995) illustrated how socially marginalized Latino males used the drug market to carve out a sense of 'respect' and dignity denied them by the crumbling landscape of the post-industrial urban economy. Likewise, Elijah Anderson (1999) illustrated the complex ballet within certain disadvantaged communities between *decent* families (who share goals, aspirations and behavioural norms with mainstream society) and those individuals and groups embedded in the competitive, violent *code of the street*. The legacy of Cohen and Miller is clear in such studies – only this time these analyses are updated and enhanced by being set against the backdrop of a hyper-mediated consumer society and a world of rabid individualism.

Cultural criminology, post subcultures and 'neo-tribes'

In recent years subcultural analysis has continued to flourish, especially within the field of 'cultural criminology' – a theoretical, methodological and interventionist approach to the study of crime and deviance that places criminality and its control in the context of culture. Alongside its abiding interest in, *inter alia*, the labelling perspective, theories of power and desire, phenomenology and postmodern social theory, cultural criminologists also prioritize the study of subcultures – whether via deep or 'liquid' ethnography or media analysis. Striving for a deeper and more critical understanding of crime and criminal justice, cultural criminologists focus not just on the way criminal subcultures recruit and retain members through secretive shared experiences and symbolic styles but on the policing of subcultures and the way surveillance and control agents 'read' subcultural displays for indications of conflict or danger.

Cultural criminologists use a series of theoretical models to explore the dynamic between crime and criminal justice further – in particular the way this dynamic manifests itself within subcultural practice. For example, the concept of 'edgework' (Lyng, 1990) has been used to understand such practices as illegal car racing, street fighting and graffiti writing. Likewise, Jack Katz's (1988) work on 'the seductions of crime' is utilized to explain the existential attractions of certain forms of subcultural deviance, such as gang membership. These approaches are then fused with a wider focus on the contemporary economic and cultural dynamics associated with late modernity (see Ferrell et al., 2008: ch 3).

Echoing the likes of Anderson and Bourgois, cultural criminologists further elucidate subcultural deviance by situating it in a world transitioning from an *inclusive society* (characterized by the social stability, cultural homogeneity and high modernity of the post-war period up to the 1960s) to a late modern *exclusive society* (characterized by hyper-pluralism, casino capitalism and the unravelling of consensual politics and the traditional ties of community, family and stable employment).

Finally, augmenting the Birmingham School's approach, cultural criminology's theory of *media loops and spirals* argues that we have gone well beyond simple questions of how accurately the media reports crime or whether media images cause copycat crimes. Rather, our world today is so saturated with media images and technology that any distinction between an event and its mediated image is replaced by a shifting interplay of the real and the virtual, the factual and the fictional (Ferrell et al., 2008: ch 5). Such a situation has major implications for subcultural theory. For example, not only are subcultural symbols and styles reappropriated by the media, but crime itself has been seized upon, packaged and marketed to young people as a romantic, exciting and cool cultural symbol.

It is in this cultural context that subcultural transgression becomes a desirable consumer choice (Hayward, 2004: 166–173). Consider how graffiti and rap music – once considered subcultural manifestations of America's urban decay – are now readily restyled and redeployed to sell late modernity's hot new commodities, from game consoles to branded fast food. Thus, in late modernity it becomes even more difficult to view subcultures as necessarily deviant when there is such considerable interplay with mainstream social forces.

Such difficulties in deploying deviant subculture as an analytical tool have been compounded by movements within academic discourse which problematize both constituent elements of the term. First, as is eloquently captured by Colin Sumner (1994), the notion of deviance has been stripped of much of its utility. It had been used in an overly politicized manner: falsely imbued with connotations of nascent social rebellion while failing to account adequately for the experiences of women and immigrant groups. Ultimately the growth of liberal pluralism also made it difficult to consider political radicals, homosexuals and those suffering from mental illness within the same analytical category as street criminals and sex offenders. Furthermore, a lens had been cast upwards to the sanctioned 'deviance' of the elite political and industrial classes: rampant corruption, savage war-mongering and environmental plunder. Stated bluntly, in the absence of an identifiable moral consensus, there is now no clear benchmark against which to define the deviant.

Second, subcultures lost categorical cohesion as late modernity unfolded (see Muggleton and Weinzierl, 2004). In contrast to the rather monolithic, class-based subcultures described by the CCCS, the wider democratization of consumption, prevalence of hyper-communicativity and globalized plurality of today's world is said to have produced communities of identity and interest in a manifestly different manner (see, e.g., Snyder, 2009 on how certain deviant subcultural practices now segue into so-called 'subcultural careers'). Thus, the French sociologist Michel Maffesoli (1996) has argued for an understanding of *neo-tribes*: loose alliances of consumers who draw upon a range of stylistic sources to construct temporary and ever-shifting self and group identities. Offending street groups, however, remain a prime social concern and focus of criminological interest, regardless of whether it remains appropriate to describe them as 'deviant subcultures'. The notion of the deviant subculture thus remains an important stream of thought in terms of both its intellectual legacy and its influence on such contemporary discourses as cultural criminology which provide crucial alternatives to the administrative and control-centred approaches to understanding criminality that otherwise prevail.

References

Anderson, E. (1999) *Code of the Street: Decency, Violence and the Moral Life of the Inner City*, New York: Norton & Co.

Becker, H. (1963) *Outsiders*. New York: Free Press.

Bourgois, P, (1995) *In Search of Respect*, Cambridge: Cambridge University Press.

Cloward, R. and Ohlin, L. (1960) *Delinquency and Opportunity: A Theory of Delinquent Gangs*, London: Routledge.

Cohen, A, (1955) *Delinquent Boys: The Culture of the Gang*, New York: The Free Press.

Cohen, S. (1972) *Folk Devils and Moral Panic*, London: MacGibbon and Kee.

Ferrell, J., Hayward, K. and Young, J. (2008) *Cultural Criminology: An Invitation*, London: Sage.

Goffman, E. (1961) *Asylums*. New York: Doubleday.

Hall, S. and Jefferson, T. (eds) (1976) *Resistance through Rituals: Youth Subcultures in Post-war Britain*, London: Hutchinson.

Hall, S., Critcher C., Jefferson, T., Clarke, J. and Robert, B. (1978) *Policing the Crisis: Mugging, the State and Law and Order*, London: Palgrave Macmillan.

Hayward, K. (2004) *City Limits: Crime, Consumer Culture and the Urban Experience*, London: GlassHouse.

Hebdige, D. (1979) *Subculture: The Meaning of Style*, London: Routledge.

Katz, J. (1988) *Seductions of Crime*, New York: Basic Books.

Lyng, S. (1990) 'Edgework: a social psychological analysis of voluntary risk-taking', *American Journal of Sociology* 95: 876–921.

Maffesoli, M. (1996) *The Time of the Tribes: The Decline of Individualism in Mass Society*, London: Sage.

Matza, D. and Sykes, G. (1961) 'Juvenile delinquency and subterranean values', *American Sociological Review* 26: 712–719.

May, M. (1973) 'Innocence and experience: the evolution of the concept of juvenile delinquency in the mid-nineteenth century', *Victorian Studies* 17: 7–29.

Miller, W. (1958) 'Lower class culture as a generating milieu of gang delinquency', *Journal of Social Issues* 14(3): 5–19.

Muggleton, D. and Weinzierl, R. (2004) *The Post-Subcultures Reader*, Oxford: Berg.

Polsky, N. (1967) *Hustlers, Beats and Others*. New York: Anchor.

Snyder, G. (2009) *Graffiti Lives: Beyond the Tag in New York's Urban Underground*, New York: New York University Press.

Sumner, C. (1994) *The Sociology of Deviance: An Obituary*, Buckingham: Open University Press.

28

Theocrats versus democrats*

Unconventionality and deviance in a *Kulturkampf*

Nachman Ben-Yehuda

Context and background

Issues of religious deviance and violence have climbed to the top of our early 21st-century agenda.[1] This chapter examines how forms of deviance and unconventional behavior can be understood as part of a *Kulturkampf* that takes place between democrats and theocrats. While this chapter is based on a study in one country, the global implications and meanings are explored and discussed.

The state of Israel was established in 1948 as a "Jewish democracy." The problem created by this morally based political characterization has accompanied the state from its very first day. On the one hand, "democracy" denotes a political structure associated with equality, options, freedom to make informed choices among competing alternatives, and increasingly with universalistic human rights. On the other hand, one of the very central cultural "building blocks" of Judaism is the Torah-based religion, which—by definition—is non-democratic. Some interesting and often implicit dimensions of tension thus characterize the idea of a "Jewish democracy." For example, what about non-Jews living in Israel? What is the basis for the (cultural) definition of a Jew?

By not separating state from religion, and declaring itself a "Jewish democracy," an inherent and essential structural and conceptual tension was introduced into the political nature and fabric of the state.[2] This tension has focused on the moral boundaries of the nation, but has also radiated into a number of other areas.[3] Indeed, this tension gave rise to a number of documents,[4] and the issue of whether a Jewish state can or should be democratic or theocratic has been long debated and often obfuscated. This problematic characteristic of Israel has even propelled some researchers to refer to that state as an "ethnic democracy."[5]

Cases of pure democracies and pure theocracies are rare (if there are any). The degree to which a country presents more characteristics, or practices, of a theocracy or a democracy is an open question. One can certainly find countries that practice a separation of state from religion, and yet such countries may be rife with strong religious elements that exert powerful national influences despite, or perhaps because of, the separation. The tension inherent in a "Jewish democracy" has also created some difficult and painful dilemmas relating to answering a question of primary importance for identity.

The question "Who is a Jew?" has generated public, bitter, at times violent, political and moral debates.[6] It is the answer—yet to be found—to this question that will create the moral boundaries of the symbolic-moral universe within which the Jewish and non-Jewish citizens of Israel must live. Pending this answer, the boundaries are not clear, allowing for political flexibility and attempts to bend and stretch them by various groups within Israeli society.

These boundaries are not only a matter for legal and political debate, but go right to the heart of the personal and national identity of Israeli citizens and their daily lives. For individual Jewish citizens, this issue boils down to such simple, yet crucially important, questions as: "What kind of a Jew am I? What is the meaning of this definition in terms of values, daily appearance and conduct?" Thus, this issue involves not only national questions but personal questions whose answers give citizens a sense of belonging to (or separation from) a collective and of a shared culture.[7] Resolving this identity issue not only paints the symbolic-moral boundaries of the state and its individual members, but structures inner and distinguishing moral fibers.

Forms of Judaism

Judaism can be expressed in a number of ways, with five major interpretations easily discernible. Each of these interpretations constitutes an ideological-moral core toward which thousands of Jews flock and maintain different cultural and social systems. Each provides a symbolic-moral universe with distinct boundaries. Sometimes, these universes are also expressed in political parties.[8] The five main divisions are: the orthodox; ultra-orthodox (*Haredim*); conservative; reform; and secular. Some ultra-orthodox Jewish groups present traits that resemble sects which fill the ranks of the "new religions." However, the stigma often associated with sects is something these groups were able to avoid very successfully. These different forms of religious groups are not homogeneous. There are further sub-divisions and rivalries within each of them, and the variance within these groups can be substantial. For example, seculars can range from those whose lifestyle is secular (probably the majority in Israel) and a much smaller minority that has developed secular consciousness and practices.[9] The ultra-orthodox are divided among different (and competing) fractions and factions, for example various Hassiduyot (small or large groups of Hassidim weaving social, moral and political networks around one rabbi or admor). These groups are also divided along the line of how tolerant they are in accepting Israel as a Jewish state (or a state of the Jews). Some accept this happily (e.g., the Lubavitchers), others uncomfortably, and still others are overtly anti-Zionist and anti-Israeli (e.g., the Satmars, Neturey Karta).

Most orthodox Jews in Israel are not *Haredim*, and are known collectively, especially by the non-orthodox, simply as *Dati* (religious). They, too, are not a homogeneous group, yet all observe the rules of Shabbat and kashrut, although they differ in attire and lifestyle from each other.

The main general division between Jews in the country is probably between "secular" and "religious." Like so many other concepts in social sciences, reaching an accurate definition of these terms is all but impossible. To illustrate: does secularism mean atheism? Certainly not. Many secular people believe in some form of transcendence. Equally, does "religious" denote an automatic belief in the Almighty and rejection of such modern institutions as higher education? Certainly not. However, when it comes to more specific issues like resurrection, the messiah, belief in life after death, and trust in magical practices, differences between the two categories may become more pronounced,[10] so there is not a complete blurring of the boundaries between them. Overall, there are significant differences on such technical issues as food they are willing to eat and the clothes they are willing to wear (kosher versus non-kosher), as well as education, politics and ideology.

The Israeli *Kulturkampf*

A central expression of the structural tension in Israel is the cultural conflict between religious theocrats and secular democrats, mostly between *Haredim* and seculars. *Haredim* comprise between 7 and 12 percent of the Jewish population in Israel. They can be subdivided into numerous—and sometimes competing—sub-groups, but some of their more general characteristics[11] are a deep faith in the Almighty, keeping religious dictates in the most pious way, specific and recognizable clothing, intensive community life within defined geographical enclaves, anti-Zionism (in most, if not all), deep commitment to study the Jewish scriptures, mostly the Talmud, a very strong emphasis on family life, and a neo-traditionalist lifestyle.

Haredi activists tend to clash with secular activists on a variety of topics and issues—symbolic and physical—all focused on the type of country each side wants to have. This cultural conflict has accompanied the state of Israel since the day of its birth, and even before.[12]

Focusing on the *Kulturkampf*

Niklas Luhmann's (1995, 1996) system theory asserts that the essence of social systems is that they are systems of communication. These systems of communication define the boundaries between social systems and give individual residents of these systems a sense of identity, belonging and purpose. It is through these systems of mass-media communications that modern-day complex cultures create the symbolic reality within which their members live and function. The contents of these systems of communication are very important and one is invited to enter here the constructionist theory by assuming that symbolic-moral universes are the unique entities that fill up Luhmannian social systems. Documenting the communications/media used in the different symbolic-moral universes provides us with an excellent opportunity to understand how these systems define their boundaries in communication terms.

Consequently, examining the nature and contents of communications in any one particular culture, centering on specific issues, can give us interesting clues and insights into that culture.

One arena where the Israeli *Kulturkampf* is played out and empowered is the media. Secular and religious media tend to clash, sometimes very harshly, over a series of issues. Following Luhmann's formulation, secular, religious, and *Haredi* newspapers were examined for a period of 50 years—1948–1998. Between two and four independent teams surveyed each year, day by day, documenting all cases of reported deviance by *Haredim* in the various newspapers. Once this database had been compiled, the different acts and affairs were placed into categories. This yielded some interesting results.

Main results

When annual data about *Haredi* deviance and unconventionality—as based on media reports—are compared with annual reports of the Israeli police, it is evident that the *Haredim* are very far from manufacturing any significant quantity of deviance. Clearly, they contribute very little to the overall crime picture in Israel. However, if we examine the media-based data, a few conclusions emerge. First, *Haredi* press rarely reports on deviance and unconventionality among *Haredim*. Thus, most reports are based on the secular press. This is consistent with *Haredi* press policy of "the right of the people not to know," which aims to shield *Haredi* readers from exposure to information about such issues as rape, robbery, suicide, prostitution, and so on. Second, *Haredi* deviance and unconventionality show a persistent upward trajectory between 1948 and 1998. However, this trajectory is not consistent and is characterized by ups and downs. Third, a close examination of the data reveals that the most salient, consistent, and repeated infraction reported in the press centers on violence—accounting for at least 63 percent of the cases. *Haredi* violence, both verbal and non-verbal, is expressed forcefully in a number of areas: against those perceived as violating the Shabbat and religious holidays; attitudes toward the dead; violent expressions against pathologists and archaeologists; violence against non-*Haredi* Jews (especially reform and conservative, but seculars did not escape this violence, either); objections to church music; and so on. Intra-*Haredi* violence is also salient (although probably under-reported). *Haredim* have also expressed violence against Zionism, and have subverted and shown disrespect toward the state of Israel (for example, by not recognizing the state, mocking its symbols, actively ignoring its holidays, and so on). The term used here—"violence"—refers to physical violence, such verbal violence as threats and curses, and the accompanying behavior that often goes hand in hand with physical violence.

Thus, clearly, the most salient category of *Haredi* nonconformity and deviance is violence. This is somewhat consistent with Bromley and Melton's (2002) work on violence among cults. Their main conclusion is that, while instances of violence are infrequent within cults and cults rarely resort to violence, any such violence attracts much political, media, and social attention.

It is important to remember that, while violence is the number-one deviant behavior recorded for the *Haredim*, there are examples of the "usual criminological suspects" as well—sex offenses, smuggling, drug use, cheating, tax fraud, stealing, wife beatings, juvenile delinquency, rape, arson, suicide, and so on.

Interpretation

Viewing the saliency and content of public-order, politically, and ideologically oriented violence practiced by *Haredi* activists, it is not too difficult to interpret these findings by pointing out that they indicate *Haredi* attempts to enforce *Halakhic* rules about what they consider the appropriate lifestyle upon others. Most *Haredi* violence recorded in the media—verbal and nonverbal—is organized and planned. It represents *Haredim's* attempts to direct themselves and Israel towards a theocracy. This violence aims to alter Israel's symbolic-moral boundaries and signify their own boundaries to the *Haredim*. Media constructions make it clear that while *Haredim* view this behavior as justified deviance, non-*Haredim* view it negatively, as unjustified, worthy and deserving of punishment. *Haredim* tend to frame and rationalize this behavior in accounts that imply a "no-choice" struggle to preserve Judaism and a Jewish way of life in a Jewish state. It needs to be added that most *Haredim* seem to treat the state in a pragmatic way—that is, they try to live with and exploit it, while theologically stating that this is not the state the Almighty wanted.

Haredi theocratic challenges to the authority, legitimacy, and morality of the state of Israel encompass a number of areas. The demographic minority status of the *Haredim* (and wider orthodoxy) and its potential low impact are counterbalanced by a number of factors that challenge the fragile and tense coexistence of religion and democracy in Israel, such as the reliance of Israeli governments on coalitions, the presence of theocratic parliamentarians, separate educational systems for the religious theocrats, and the willingness of theocratic activists to use violence and direct action to achieve their goals.

Israeli religious theocrats and secular democrats differ in almost all aspects of life—they live separately and read different cultural texts which they study in different educational systems. Members of these cultures tend to dress differently, eat different foods, have different architecture and media, use different verbal expressions (sometimes they even use different languages—Hebrew and Yiddish), have different dating practices and marriage patterns, different perceptions of gender, and so on.

Haredi religious theocratic challenges are counteracted by political pressures and by parties who carry strong anti-clerical banners. Two public devices used in these negotiations are the "status quo" and "public arena." They create enough cultural ambiguity that gives rise to never-ending debates about the nature of moral boundaries. They also serve as an effective focus on which waves of meaning can clash and create areas where cultural interaction, innovations and coexistence can (and do) occur.

The main thrust of this cultural conflict is between theocrats and democrats, between the secular and the religious. A major ingredient in cultural conflicts is morality or moral authority, and the competing definitions of symbolic-moral boundaries (Hunter 1991). Following criticisms of Hunter's work,[13] Kidd (2006) suggested a reconceptualization of cultural conflicts in terms of social policies. Aware of the problems involved in defining cultural conflicts and wars, Kidd (2006: 5) proposes that "a cultural war is a media-grabbing multi-vocal conflict within and across institutions that has consequences for the kinds of demands that institutions make on public policy." Steven Dubin's work on cultural wars in Africa prompted him to characterize such wars as "the impassioned clashes of opinion between groups within the same society, polarized over so-called hot button issues falling broadly within the realms of race and ethnicity; the body, sexuality and sexual orientation; identity politics; religion; and patriotism and national identity."[14] The methodological and substantial focus on the media in this chapter is coherent with Kidd's and Dubin's approaches.

So far, the cultural war in Israel has been expressed in a number of areas and issues, many in the symbolic realm, but also in practical matters. Might the Israeli *Kulturkampf* erupt to a full-scale civil war? While caution dictates being careful making such a claim, Jewish violence in the past[15] and the study reported here suggest that a strong, real, and threatening potential for a civil war between democrats and theocrats does exist. Whether this potential will materialize is a different question. One process that charges this cultural war with extra tension is that the different factions tend to align along different nationalistic lines, which bear directly on the Israeli–Palestinian conflict. Religious theocrats tend to present extreme nationalistic positions while seculars tend to be more differentiated, and many are skewed to the center and the left. This means that the Israeli–Palestinian conflict is reinterpreted with religious narratives from the Israeli Jewish side (and, with the ascent of the Islamic fundamentalist Hamas in the Palestinian Authority, there too). These developments add warning signs along the way to a potential civil war. Obviously, such a war can be avoided if politicians on all sides have the wisdom to negotiate and navigate the daily life away from it.

Globally speaking, one almost has no choice but to rethink Huntington's (1996) provocative work in more finely tuned terms, such as those of global confrontations between religious fundamentalist theocrats and secular democrats.[16] Moreover, these confrontations may take place within gray and unstable political structures.[17] The variance within countries facing such conflicts is impressive, the simple one of which is between those that practice a separation of state from religion and those that do not.[18] Many democracies have become open arenas for theocrats and democrats to develop cultural struggles and mechanisms that enable the different parties to live together. Viewed in this way, the conflict is not between East and West, North and South, Islam and Judeo-Christianity, but between two diametrically opposed ways of thinking, systems of morality, and ways of life. It stands to reason, for example, that secular democratic Muslims have more in common with Jewish or Christian secular democrats than with fundamentalist Muslims. Likewise, Jewish fundamentalists may find an easier common ground with fundamentalist Christians than they would with secular Jews. The global perspective focuses on how these different worldviews can negotiate among themselves, manage their conflicts and—if necessary—live together. One needs to add that this conflict may overlap other conflicts, such as political (e.g., right–left in the Israeli cases), economic (e.g., class), or symbolic (e.g., gender). Structurally speaking, it is along the rifts of this global conflict and the different *Kulturkampfs* that we find clusters of unconventional and deviant behavior.

Notes

*This chapter is based on my book *Theocratic Democracy* (New York: Oxford University Press, 2010).

1 E.g., see Eller 2006: 176–204 and McClymond and Freedman 2008.
2 For more on this tension within the context of citizenship and law, see Soffer and Korenstein 1998.
3 Including civil rights—see Shetreet 1999.
4 E.g., see Ravitsky 1997, 1998, 2005.
5 E.g., Smooha 1990. A more general statement on the relevant majority–minority relations is Hasson's 2007 work.
6 E.g., Sela 2001.
7 Zisser and Cohen 1999.
8 E.g., Shas, Yahadut HaTorah, Mafdal, or Shinui in Israel.
9 E.g., see http://www.tkasim.org.il.
10 See, for example, Shachar's survey-based views in *Ha'aretz*, June 1, 2006, p. 7.
11 Based on Levi 1988; Samet 1979; Shilhav and Friedman 1985; Anaki 1999.
12 E.g., see Rosenthal 1954.
13 E.g., by DiMaggio *et al.* 1996; Evans *et al.* 1995; Evans 2002.
14 Columbia University, personal communication.
15 E.g., see Ben-Yehuda 1993, 2000; Sprinzak 1999; Peri 2000.
16 The chronic tension between Islamists and seculars in Turkey provides another focused illustration.
17 For a fascinating analysis of the religious crisis in Europe concerning Islam, Christianity, and secularism, see Jenkins 2007.
18 For more on the history and contemporary meaning of this separation, see Lilla's 2007 fascinating work.

References

Anaki, Ofer. 1999. *Who and Who in the Religious World*, Tel Aviv: Or-Am (Hebrew).
Ben-Yehuda, Nachman. 1993. *Political Assassinations by Jews: A Rhetorical Device for Justice*, Albany: State University of New York Press.
——. 2000. "One More Political Murder by Jews," pp. 63–95 in Yoram Peri (ed.) *The Assassination of Yitzhak Rabin*, Stanford, CA: Stanford University Press.
Bromley, David and Gordon J. Melton (eds.). 2002. *Cults, Religion, and Violence*, Cambridge and New York: Cambridge University Press.
DiMaggio, Paul, John H. Evans, and Bethany Bryson. 1996. "Have Americans' Social Attitudes Become More Polarized?," *American Journal of Sociology*, 102: 690–755.
Eller, David J. 2006. *Violence and Culture: A Cross-Cultural and Interdisciplinary Approach*, Belmont, CA: Thomson Wadsworth.
Evans, David T., Francis T. Cullen, R. Gregory Dunaway, and Velmer S. Burton, Jr. 1995. "Religion and Crime Reexamined: The Impact of Religion, Secular Controls, and Social Ecology on Adult Criminality," *Criminology*, 33(2): 195–224.
Evans, John H. 2002. *Have American Attitudes Become More Polarized? An Update*, Princeton University Center for Arts and Cultural Policy Studies Working Paper 24 [quoted in Kidd 2006].
Hasson, Shlomo. 2007. *Between Nationalism and Democracy: Scenarios on Majority and Minority Relations in Israel*, Jerusalem: Floersheimer Institute for Policy Studies (Hebrew).
Hunter, James Davison. 1991. *Culture Wars: The Struggle to Define America*, New York: Basic Books.
Huntington, S. P. 1996. *The Clash of Civilizations and the Remaking of World Order*, New York: Simon and Schuster.
Jenkins, Philip. 2007. *God's Continent. Christianity, Islam and Europe's Religious Crisis*, New York: Oxford University Press.
Kidd, Dustin. 2006. "Rethinking the Culture Wars Concept," *Culture* [newsletter of the Sociology of Culture Section of the American Sociological Association], 20(2): 1, 4–6.

Levi, Amnon. 1988. *The Haredim*, Jerusalem: Keter (Hebrew).

Lilla, Mark. 2007. *The Stillborn God: Religion, Politics and the Modern West*, New York: Knopf.

Luhmann, Niklas. 1995. *Social Systems*, Stanford, CA: Stanford University Press.

——. 1996. *The Reality of the Mass Media*. Stanford, CA: Stanford University Press.

McClymond, Michael J. and David N. Freedman. 2008. "Religious Traditions, Violence and Nonviolence," pp. 1860–1869 in Lester Kurtz (ed.) *Encyclopedia of Violence, Peace, & Conflict*, San Diego, CA: Academic Press, Elsevier.

Peri, Yoram (ed.). 2000. *The Assassination of Yitzhak Rabin*, Stanford, CA: Stanford University Press.

Ravitsky, Aviezer. 1997. "Religious and Seculars in Israel: A Post-Zionist Cultural War?," *Alpaim*, 14: 80–96 (Hebrew).

——. 1998. *Religion and State in Jewish Philosophy: Models of Unity, Division, Collision and Subordination*, Jerusalem: Israel Democracy Institute (Hebrew).

—— (ed.) 2005. *Religion and State in Twentieth-Century Jewish Thought*, Jerusalem: Israel Democracy Institute (Hebrew).

Rosenthal, Celia Stopnicka. 1954. "Deviation and Social Change in the Jewish Community of a Small Polish Town," *American Journal of Sociology*, 60(2): 177–181.

Samet, Moshe. 1979. *Religion and State in Israel*, Jerusalem: Eliezer Kaplan School of Economics and Social Sciences, The Hebrew University (Hebrew).

Sela, Michal. 2001. *Between Declaration and Reality: State and Religion in Israel*, Jerusalem: Center for Jewish Pluralism (Hebrew).

Shetreet, Shimon. 1999. *Between Three Branches of Government: The Balance of Rights in Matters of Religion in Israel*, Jerusalem: Floersheimer Institute for Policy Studies (Hebrew).

Shilhav, Yoseph and Menachem Friedman. 1985. *Growth and Segregation: The Ultra Orthodox Community of Jerusalem*, Jerusalem: Jerusalem Institute for the Study of Israel (Hebrew).

Smooha, Sammy. 1990. "Minority Status in an Ethnic Democracy: The Status of the Arab Minority in Israel," *Ethnic and Racial Studies*, 13(3): 389–412.

Soffer, Oren and Aliza Korenstein. 1998. *Ethnocentricity, Citizenship, and the Rule of Law in Israel*, report submitted to the Friedrich Ebert Foundation, Tel Aviv: Israeli Institute for Economic and Social Research (Hebrew).

Sprinzak, Ehud. 1999. *Brother against Brother: Violence and Extremism in Israeli Politics from Altalena to the Rabin Assassination*, New York: The Free Press.

Zisser, Baruch and Asher Cohen. 1999. "From an Arranged Democracy to a Democracy under a Crisis: The Struggle for Collective Identity in Israel," *Politika*, 3: 9–30 (Hebrew).

Part VI
Contentious deviance

Overview

Deviance is not an absolute concept; rather, it is very much a relative concept. Its conceptualization is relative to time, place, context, and circumstances, among other considerations. Because it is viewed differently by different people, in different times, in different places, in different contexts, in different circumstances, and from different points of view, there is seldom consensus in regard to what, or who, is deviant, and to what degree a particular type of behavior is considered deviance, as well as the extent to which it poses a problem for or harm to society.

Deviance is viewed differently by various segments of society and the resulting viewpoints are often strongly felt. Many may be quite vocal and even militant in the strength of their conviction in regard to different kinds of deviance. In effect, some varieties of deviance may be very contentious, with some viewing the deviant behavior as of no social consequence and even denying that the behavior in question qualifies for the label, while others take an opposing judgmental posture and argue that the behavior in question is quite serious, possibly pathological, if not degenerate, and poses a serious threat to the public and the social fabric.

This part addresses four such modes of contentious deviance: homosexuality, premarital adolescent sexual activity, vegetarianism and fruitarianism, and cybersex/computer sex addiction/cyberpornography. There has long been disputatious debate regarding the appropriateness of the label "deviance" and the possible social harm of the first three behavioral modes. The fourth, "cybersex/computer sex addiction/cyberpornography," is a relatively new phenomenon. Proponents and opponents of each are just beginning to become vociferous in their debate on these very controversial issues. The four chapters in this part examine and analyze each of these four contentious configurations of deviance.

Homosexuality

Of all the variations of sexual expression socially labeled "deviant," perhaps none has traditionally tended to elicit more controversy than homosexuality. The roots of homophobia are imbedded in Judeo-Christian ideology. The historical Judeo-Christian posture toward homosexual activity was, in large measure, one of uncompromising condemnation. Sodomy or homosexual intercourse was considered to be the "*vicium contra naturam*" or vice against nature. Homosexuality was categorized as a form of religious deviance. Historically, it has also been viewed as cultural deviance.

The condemnation of homosexuality has not been historically consistent, however. Rather, over the centuries, negative views concerning it have waxed and waned. Over the last 50 years or so of the 20th century, there was increasing toleration of homosexuality to the point of it being normalized, and accepted as such by many. Today, in the US and most other Western cultures, homosexuality is legal and tolerated (if not accepted) as simply an alternative sexual persuasion and a variation of normal sexual gratification modes.

Staci Newmahr, in her chapter, points out that the inclusion of a chapter on homosexuality in a handbook of deviant behavior is contentious in itself, and that labeling this behavior deviant is stigmatizing and often politically and ideologically troubling. One of the contentious aspects of homosexuality is the fact that there is little agreement regarding its definition. Over the centuries, the explanation of homosexuality has ranged from the "demonic perspective," to "spiritual or paranormal [deviance] . . . intertwined with evil," "to a medical problem rather than a moral problem." Later attempts at defining it have ranged from "something social in origin," to a "social role," to a "social identity."

Newmahr provides a historical account of the metamorphosis of homosexuality from sin and pathology to normal variation from the traditional "ideal of heterosexuality." In her richly detailed chronicle of the history of homosexuality, she includes a discussion on the emergence of "gay identity," the "gay rights movement," the attendant conservative backlash, the counter-attack from the "religious right," and the evolution of legal rights and legal protection of gays. She concludes with the observation that debates on homosexuality "have exploded into nearly all aspects of social life," which suggests that "an increasing number of people want to have these conversations. They remain, however, challenging—and often contentious—conversations."

Premarital adolescent sexual activity

Traditionally, in the US, sexual activity among adolescents was theoretically taboo or deviant. Females were theoretically supposed to abstain from sexual intercourse before marriage and go to their wedding bed as a virgin. *Very* theoretically, males were supposed to do the same, although the norm was not remotely as rigid. Similar restrictions are still in place today in many parts of the world (such as in Islamic cultures).

The fear of pregnancy, venereal disease, getting a "bad reputation," and concern that losing their virginity would make them less marriageable to an upwardly mobile man tended to discourage adolescent girls from engaging in premarital sexual intercourse. Instead, many girls engaged in alternative forms of sexual gratification with the boys they dated in an attempt to maintain their "technical virginity."

Kathleen Bogle, in her chapter, examines changes in sexual interaction between young men and women prior to marriage. She reports that the median age for women and men to marry is at an all-time high at 26 for women and 28 for men, but most young people have been sexually active since adolescence.

She found that in terms of adolescent sexual activity outside of marriage, the technical norms of sexual behavior have changed. During the first half of the 20th century, unmarried adolescents engaged in "kissing, necking, and petting; however, oral sex and sexual intercourse were considered to be off-limits." In the latter half of the 20th century, oral sex and sexual intercourse have been parts of the adolescent sexual repertoire. Such a change can be traced to a number of factors, including the women's rights movement and "the pill." Since the risks of unwanted pregnancy were minimized, sexual intercourse could be engaged in for pleasure rather than just procreation.

Bogle reveals that a new sexual arrangement has emerged—"hooking up." This consists of meeting someone of the opposite sex, perhaps even a stranger, and engaging in a physical encounter with no romantic involvement. Hooking up can involve anything from kissing to full sexual intercourse. Such behavior is especially popular among college-age people. Hooking-up partners see the encounter as simply enjoyable behavior; no romantic involvement is expected, and may not even be wanted.

Bogle relates that sex education has had some impact on adolescent sexual behavior. The official goal was to teach young people to use birth-control measures to reduce unwanted pregnancy, and to use condoms as protection against sexually transmitted diseases. Such programs have been very controversial. Some objected to the lack of effort to prevent adolescent sexual intercourse. Some religious groups and particularly the "religious right" have insisted on an abstinence-only curriculum, which opposing groups claim is much less effective in reducing high-risk adolescent sexual behavior. Thus, even the context of sex education programs has become highly contentious.

Vegetarianism and fruitarianism as deviance

There are norms that govern almost every aspect of our lives, including dietary behavior. These normative dictates are known as *foodways*. Foodways address dietary concerns such as specifying what is considered to be edible, what can and should be eaten, in what quantity, how it should be prepared, the context within which it can be consumed, the appropriate time in which certain foods can be eaten and in what sequence, the combination in which foods should be eaten, how food is to be eaten, and the appropriate behavior involved in eating, among many culturally mandated concerns. Violation of any of these foodways constitutes dietary deviance.

Many individuals may commit dietary deviance from time to time, but some do so on an ongoing basis. An example here might be the practice of vegetarianism. In most societies, meat in some form or another (including seafood) plays a cultural role in the diet of the members of society. This is the case today and has been the case throughout most of history.

Since the Greek era, vegetarianism has been viewed as a deviant foodway. Pythagoreans considered abstinence from meat to be "subversive." Later, in the Christian period, because various religious orders practiced vegetarianism, some writers accused vegetarians of being heretics. Although in the Western world in recent times the supremacy of meat in a diet has declined, vegetarianism continues to be viewed by many as a deviant foodway. Those who practice it are often seen as "odd" and are stigmatized.

Joe Boyle points out that in the US, since colonial times, meat has been the center of the human diet, starting with wild game, then pork (because of the pig's ability to live in a woodland environment without much care), and later beef (after the West was settled, cattle were raised on huge ranches, and railroads were built to transport the animals to Eastern towns and cities for consumption).

Against this historical backdrop, those who eschew meat and restrict their diet to vegetables, fruits, nuts, and grain clearly are outside the mainstream, marginalized, and stigmatized. Boyle indicates that not all "vegetarians" follow the same diet, but rather there are degrees of vegetarianism resulting in eight types of eating pattern that still fit the label of vegetarian. He relates that vegetarianism might be classified as "positive deviance" because it promotes a healthy lifestyle. Some vegetarians are motivated to eat vegetables, fruits, and grains not only for health reasons but because of compassion for the animals that are slaughtered for the production of food.

Like all deviants, vegetarians feel the need to explain and justify their behavior when they are questioned about their motivation. Toward this end, deviants develop vocabularies of motive known as "accounts" which will legitimate their behavior. Boyle has identified ten vegetarian accounts which they use to justify their variation from the traditional meat-centered diet and provides a detailed analysis of each. He concludes that, over time, vegetarianism has "transformed itself from a most serious heretical offense . . . into a foodway that is accepted in its more common form, but still occupies a very deviant status at the strictest levels." Some vegetarian groups now use the phrase "plant-based diet" as a means of deflecting the negative connotations of the "vegetarian" label.

Cybersex, computer sex addiction, and cyberpornography

Cybersex

In her chapter, Diane Kholos Wysocki acquaints the reader with the intricacies of relatively new and contentious forms of sexual deviance made possible by the computer. The computer was not invented with any erotic purposes in mind. Once in use in connection with the internet, however, many users quickly discovered (likely in a serendipitous fashion) that the computer had numerous salacious latent functions. In fact, the computer offered almost unlimited vistas of carnal opportunity, ranging from the retrieval of online pornography to locating and connecting with other individuals who shared similar interests. Users also quickly grasped the concept of virtual sex. Cybersex was the result. Wysocki defines cybersex as "a range of sexual activities that takes place on the internet and typically begins when two or more people engage in conversations about their sexual fantasies." The computer is the ideal venue for sharing sexual fantasies with others. She also informs us that 60 percent of all visits to the internet involve sexual purposes.

The computer offers anonymity. One can safely interact with another individual without fear of having one's identity known. Anonymity also has the advantage of being "liberated" to say anything or do anything. To share one's perverse fantasies with someone known has the risk of shocking or disgusting that individual to the point that they withdraw from all interaction or contact with the person describing their erotic fantasy. With a stranger, if they are offended by the fantasy, the sender can simply move on to the next person with the click of a mouse.

Cybersex is contentious because it involves behavior that many would find offensive, if not repulsive. Wysocki reports that the spouses of individuals who participate in cybersex may even view this activity as infidelity and betrayal.

Computer sex addiction

Computer sex, like anything pleasurable, often becomes addictive. Wysocki suggests that what begins as a simple entertaining activity may take over the individual's life until they become powerless to control the practice. As they devote ever more time and energy to this activity, they neglect their face-to-face relationships and those relationships may fail as a result. Cybersex is as addictive as narcotics or alcohol abuse and could result in loss of job, breakdown of marriage, or worse. Wysocki also discloses that cybersex addicts "use [computer] sex as a way to cope, handle boredom anxiety and other powerful feelings." Cybersex may also make the addict feel important, powerful, or wanted. Breaking the addiction may require a professional therapist and long-term counseling.

Cyberpornography

Wysocki asserts that pornography dates back to pornographic images in cave paintings in prehistoric times. Cyberpornography, however, is a relatively new venue for erotic pictures that provide salacious entertainment and vicarious sexual gratification for viewers. She asserts that, among its other functions, cyberpornography provides inspiration and instruction for new sexual ideas to try out on the viewer's sexual partner.

Cyberpornography has many advantages over traditional forms of visual porn. Wysocki points out that it is inexpensive, easy to use, readily available, almost limitless, and easy to access anonymously.

Viewing cyberpornogaphy is not without legal risks, however. As Wysocki indicates, it is sometimes difficult to determine the age of the person in the pictures. If they are underage, then the viewer is involved with child pornography, which is a serious felony that could incur a long prison term if detected by the authorities.

29

Homosexuality

Staci Newmahr

The inclusion of "homosexuality" in a handbook of "deviant behavior" is itself contentious, on multiple levels. At the most basic, the consideration of homosexuality as a *behavior* is problematic. In addition, the term "deviant" is stigmatic, and is often politically and ideologically troubling.

The disagreement over whether homosexuality is deviant underscores the more fundamental dissentions within the literature—and, increasingly, in mainstream conversations—regarding sexuality and deviance. The question of whether homosexuality constitutes deviance cannot be settled without knowing what we mean when we say "homosexuality." Further, the issue of what deviance is, and is not, is far from settled. The changes in these terms throughout history intersect in interesting ways. What emerges from this is a complex portrayal of Western sexuality, social control and dissonance over the last hundred years.

Although same-sex sexual activities between adults have been recorded since at least the fifth century BCE, the word "homosexuality" did not enter mainstream vernacular until Krafft-Ebing's *Psychopathia Sexualis* in 1886. Before this, deviance—and, within it, same-sex sexual behavior and attraction—was understood broadly in accordance with what has been called the "demonic perspective" (Pfohl 1985); the deviation from social expectations was understood in spiritual or paranormal terms, and intertwined with evil. In the early medical literature, homosexuality was framed as a medical problem rather than a moral problem, as same-sex sexual contact had previously been understood. This shift "from badness to sickness" (Conrad and Schneider 1980) absolved "the homosexual" of responsibility for his "condition," attributing it to physiological misfortune.

Though this shift to a medical perspective marked a change, the study of deviance continued its focus on attempting to discover the source of deviance within individuals who committed deviant acts. Because social conformity was the default expectation, "deviants" were assumed to have particular characteristics in common that would render them likely to engage in deviant activities. The study of deviance was most concerned with discovering and understanding these characteristics.

Deviance and homosexuality: early thinking

Throughout the early part of the 20th century, homosexuality was a source of repulsion and a cause for pity in the popular imagination, and most certainly a kind of deviance in scholarly literature. By the 1930s, it had become a source of fear, paving the way for policy decisions against it. The longstanding public and political aversion to gays in the military was formalized in 1943, and during the late 1940s suspicion of homosexuality was the grounds for the denial of 1,700 federal job applications, the discharge of 4,380 people from the military, and the firing of 420 government employees (Adam 1987). In 1953, President Eisenhower signed an executive order mandating the dismissal of federal employees found to be guilty of "sexual perversion."

In the meantime, sexologist Alfred Kinsey was studying sexual behavior among Americans. The first of his two book-length reports was published in 1948. The findings were highly controversial and ultimately influential. Kinsey argued that sexuality was not static, that it changed over time, and that it existed along a continuum between heterosexuality and homosexuality, rather than as a mutually exclusive binary model (Kinsey 1948). The fluidity that Kinsey found in human sexuality laid the groundwork for later social constructionist work on sexuality, blurring the dichotomous distinction between heterosexual and homosexual as fixed categories.

As the seeds of what later became known as the "sexual revolution" were being planted, the study of deviance was undergoing conceptually similar changes. Having been traditionally understood as something a deviant did—that is, actions chosen by actors in whom the propensity to deviate from cultural norms resided—deviance began to shift from the actor to the social world. In 1963, Erving Goffman and Howard Becker each produced a major work that reframed deviance as something social in origin. Becker's *Outsiders* reached an academic audience more prepared to think of deviance as residing in the dominant values of society rather than in the body of the individual deviant. Becker (1963: 9; emphasis in original) argued that "*social groups create deviance by making the rules whose infractions constitute deviance* . . . deviance is *not* a quality of the act the person commits, but rather a consequence of the application by others of rules and sanctions to an 'offender.'" In this context, Becker articulated the still-useful idea of "becoming" deviant, focusing on the ways in which an actor learns to engage in behaviors and adopt an identity that we *regard* as deviant.

The moral condemnation that once accompanied the study of deviance, and the term itself, thus began to erode. The "deviant" ceased to be a kind of person and became instead a person who learned to engage in deviant things through, by, and because of social factors. Increasingly, deviance scholars engaged in this conceptual shift; but in regard to homosexuality, many did not shift quite so easily.

Within this changing intellectual climate, the notion of "role theory" emerged. The concept of "roles" focused necessarily on the social world rather than the body of the individual, further de-naturalizing perspectives on deviance. The application of this to homosexuality, however, was resisted from multiple directions. In a 1968 essay, Mary McIntosh called for precisely this shift in the context of homosexuality, arguing against viewing it as a condition and instead framing it as a social role. However, despite the prevalence of role theory within the sociology of deviance a decade later, scholars continued to reject this formulation for homosexuality (Whitam 1981).

The attempted shift from the "nature" of "the homosexual" to the homosexual role in academic literature did little to assuage mainstream concerns about homosexuality. In the midst of the broader sexual revolution and the civil rights movement, gays and lesbians became more visible, more organized, and less willing to feign heterosexuality. In 1969, during what would otherwise have been a fairly routine raid of a gay bar by New York City police, the patrons at the Stonewall Inn refused to cooperate. The resistance at Stonewall led to riots that lasted for three days, and it is widely recognized as a pivotal moment in the gay rights movement.

The emergence of gay identity

Post-Stonewall, a gay and lesbian "community" began to crystallize, in a more visible way than previously. In the aftermath of the early civil rights movement, which had achieved success in a cultural context in which race was a relevant, biologically based distinction, the gay rights movement adhered to essentialist notions of sexual difference between homosexuals and heterosexuals. The work of scholars such as Kinsey and McIntosh were claimed for their pro-gay undertones, but not for their challenges to the category of homosexuality.

Throughout the 1970s, amid a new sexual empowerment of women, demand for equal rights for and by African Americans and a literature on deviance that quite radically shifted to look at the rule-makers rather than the rule-breakers, "homosexuality" began to change again. In 1973, after heavy social pressure from increasingly influential gay and lesbian activist groups, the American Psychological Association removed homosexuality as a diagnostic category.

The term itself began to crumble, as lesbians sought to distinguish themselves from homosexual men, who, in turn, increasingly turned to the word "gay" as an identity label. While male homosexuality had been cast as (misdirected) hypersexuality, female homosexuality began to be conflated with feminism; lesbianism became not a medical condition, nor a deviant role, but a feminist political choice.

By this time, the "gay rights" movement was well under way and faced increasingly vocal and visible resistance. Anita Bryant, a devoutly Christian pop singer and advertisement celebrity, spearheaded a powerful and highly public battle against gay rights. In response to a Florida ordinance that prohibited discrimination against gays and lesbians, Bryant formed "Save Our Children, Inc." Over the next two years, she and her coalition (assisted by Jerry Falwell) battled the quickly organizing gay community for the rights of public schools to fire openly gay employees, and of real estate agencies to refuse to sell houses to gays and lesbians. Based on the premise that homosexuals were "trying to recruit our children into homosexuality," Save Our Children crusaded throughout multiple states.

Sociological and social-psychological literature shifted from the homosexual role to the less politically problematic issue of identity (Weinberg 1978; Troiden 1979). This thinking followed Becker in the exploration of "becoming," and McIntosh in the emphasis on social worlds, by emphasizing the process of coming to terms with one's homosexuality. However, it sometimes held the potential to solidify an essentialist perspective on sexuality, in which people "are" gay and form a gay identity alongside or through a coming-out process.

By the early 1980s, the anti-gay movement was energized by Bryant's success, but the gay rights movement had countered her progress, having caused so much negative publicity that Bryant's career suffered. Bolstered by this momentum and growing community identity, the battleground shifted to gays and lesbians in the military. In 1981, the Department of Defense issued an update to the military's policy regarding homosexuality, declaring that the presence of homosexuals in the military "seriously impairs the accomplishment of the military mission . . . adversely affects the ability of the armed forces to maintain discipline, good order, and morale; to foster mutual trust and confidence among service members . . . and to prevent breaches of security" (Department of Defense Directive 1332.14).

Not an official change in policy, the directive served to clarify the US government's position that homosexuals are not appropriate for military service. Increasingly, gays and lesbians began to take legal action for being dismissed for their sexual orientation. Despite occasional legal victories and the reinstatement of individual gay men and lesbians into their military commands, this effort spanned over a decade before resulting in any change to the policy.

Six months later, in June 1981, the American public learned of a tragic and deadly disease that was suddenly being detected in epidemic numbers. Initially identified overwhelmingly in gay men, the HIV virus was known as GRID, or Gay Related Immune Disorder, for a short time. As health officials scrambled to understand the sudden epidemic, the gay community mobilized to acquire and share information and resources. The backlash against the gay community, and homosexual behavior more specifically, gained ground and vitality. Throughout the 1980s, this conservative backlash against the visibility of the gay community drew strength from the widespread fear of AIDS, and permeated various aspects of public life.

In the wake of the AIDS crisis, Christian evangelicals also mobilized to respond. Reverend Jerry Falwell announced that AIDS was "the wrath of God upon homosexuals," and Charles Stanley, then-president of the American Southern Baptist Convention, concurred: "AIDS is God indicating his displeasure toward a sinful lifestyle" (Ross 1988, cited in Murphy 1988: 155).

Verbal violence escalated to physical violence against the gay community, particularly against gay men. Incidents of "gay-bashing" were reported on television news and in newspapers; arguably for the first time, gay men were being portrayed in mass media as sympathetic victims of what would soon be considered "hate crimes." In 1982, Harvey Fierstein's play *Torch Song Trilogy* opened on Broadway. The story of a gay man's life in the 1960s and 1970s, it moved audiences with its depiction of the gay-bashing death of the lead character's partner. Hate-crime discourse as it related to gays and lesbians gained ground throughout the decade, but did not become a particularly salient mainstream issue until later.

Impacts of postmodern thought

By 1990, the climate had changed significantly regarding gays and lesbians. In academia, the tide was turning toward postmodern and poststructuralist thought that challenged the ideas of absolute "truths," in the first place, and underlying socio-linguistic structure as sites of truth, in the second. The destabilizing threads in early work by Kinsey, McIntosh and Becker had been continued in Michel Foucault's three-volume *History of Sexuality*. Foucault's work succeeded in facilitating a wider-ranging paradigm shift from sexuality as a set of behaviors to a discursive, conceptual and analytical category.

Poststructuralism called for the destabilization of categories, including both homosexuality and deviance. Queer theory developed the assault on not only the heterosexual/homosexual binary, but the gender binary, as well as its own identity in the scholarly literature (see Seidman 1991, 1994; Halberstam 1998; Butler 1990, 1993; Sedgwick 1991; Lovaas, Elia and Yep 2007). With sexuality itself repositioned in academic thought as a discursive tool for social control, "homosexuality" made little sense. The inclusive terms LGBT and LGBTQ—for lesbian, gay, bisexual, trans, queer—replaced the "gay and lesbian" designation of the 1980s.

The study of deviance did not fare so well in this intellectual climate. Deviance itself became a category to destabilize; the very concept of deviance was rooted in the notion of a social order from which to deviate. Deviance scholars debated its relevance as a concept as well as a discipline (Sumner 1994; Miller, Wright and Dannels 2001; Goode 2002, 2004). In regard to homosexuality specifically, the study of deviance suffered from a lack of direction, for "whereas gay identity politics aims to change the status of homosexuality from a deviant identity to a normal identity, queer politics struggle against normalizing any identity" (Seidman 2002: 9). In the context of gay identity politics, the study of deviance was embroiled in debates over whether homosexuality ought to be considered deviant. In the context of queer politics, however, the concept of homosexuality is as problematic as that of deviance.

The year 1992 saw the removal of homosexuality as a disease from the International Classification of Diseases. Several well-known and popular celebrities "came out" publicly, including k.d. lang in 1992, Melissa Etheridge in 1993, and Ellen De Generes in 1997. The issue of gays in the military, still unsettled, occupied center stage again during Bill Clinton's presidency. (For a thorough historical exploration of this issue, see Shilts 1993, Knapp 2008 and Sinclair 2009.) The administration, which had initially sought to end the ban, ultimately did not do so, instead enforcing a code of silence around the issue. The "Don't Ask, Don't Tell" policy sought to reduce sexuality-based dismissals by encouraging lesbians and gay men to keep their sexuality a secret while prohibiting military officials from asking for information regarding sexual orientation. The new policy stated that the propensity or intention to engage in homosexual acts "would create an unacceptable risk to the high standards of morale, good order and discipline, and unit cohesion that are the essence of military capability" (US Code 654, 1993).

The gay and lesbian communities were torn about whether the new policy constituted progress, but the backlash against the Clinton administration from vocal objectors was well publicized. In 1995, gay elected officials traveled to the White House for a meeting. When they arrived, guards donned latex gloves, "for protection," it was reportedly said. Partially in response to pressure from the increasingly powerful gay and lesbian activist groups, Clinton created the first White House liaison to gay and lesbian communities in 1995.

In 1998, twenty-one-year-old Matthew Shepard was brutally murdered by two young men who reportedly told him that they were gay and wanted to discuss the state of the community. Instead, they tied him to a fence and beat him to death. Shepard's death came to symbolize the violent potential of homophobia, the fight for gay rights and for the special treatment of hate crimes. The murder was highly publicized, and many Americans were taken aback by protesters at Shepard's funeral carrying billboards reading, "Matt Shepard Rots in Hell" and "God Hates Fags."

In part, the sympathies of the public were also related to the transgender movement. The shift to LGBTQ language reflected an increasing visibility of transgendered and transsexual people and activists. This visibility served also to neutralize some of the concern with homosexuality; suddenly, there were signs of a "queerer" movement—one that threatened not only the heterosexual/homosexual binary, but the gender binary on which it is based. The 1999 film *Boys Don't Cry*, released soon after Shepard's murder, dramatized the life of Brandon Teena, an FTM (female-to-male) transgendered adolescent who was beaten, raped and killed by his friends when they discovered his transgendered status. The film received critical acclaim and a Best Actress Oscar for Hillary Swank, who played Teena.

Amid this increasing public awareness of, and perhaps sensitivity to, transgender issues, the term "queer" has become all-inclusive, replacing LGBT in some circles. The proliferation of "queer" in academia has led to a re-stigmatization of the term "homosexuality," with the latter now generally taken as an indicator of less queer-friendly spaces than the former.

Conclusion

Perhaps no recent story captures this battleground better than the debates over same-sex marriage. In particular, the saga over California's Proposition 8 illustrates not only the degree of controversy surrounding homosexuality but the acceptable interpretations and parameters of homosexuality. In May 2008, the California Supreme Court decided that the longstanding prohibition of same-sex marriage was a violation of state constitutional rights. However, the November ballot included the opportunity for Californians to overturn the decision. Proposition 8 read that "Only marriage between a man and a woman is valid and recognized in California." The November 2008 vote on Proposition 8 was preceded by a good deal of controversy and political activism. The proposition was passed, overturning the May decision, and therefore continuing the prohibition of same-sex marriage in California.

In contemporary sexuality theory, it is not entirely clear what "homosexuality" is: whether it is best understood as an identity, a label, an analytical category or a behavior. It is no longer clear to everyone what we are talking about when we say "homosexuality." Therefore, it is not clear what precisely is objectionable, to whom and for what reasons.

What homosexuality is, or is not, and what deviance is, or is not, appear to have little impact on the sensibilities of most Americans, many of whom continue to believe in the significance of both "homosexuality" and "deviance" as categories of social organization. Heterosexual couples remain by far the norm on television, in mainstream film and in advertisements. Adolescents and young adults in the first decade of the new millennium casually deployed the phrase "That's so gay" to refer to anything substandard. Reformist groups, such as Exodus International, practice "reparative" or "conversion" therapy, harkening back to a medical model and using such language as "healing" homosexuality (Fetner 2005; Erzin 2006); states seek to overturn equal marriage amendments. In 2008, a fifteen-year-old openly gay boy named Lawrence King was shot to death by a classmate. At the time of writing, the Westboro Baptist Church's website, "www.godhatesfags.com," was quoting Leviticus in its masthead: "therefore I abhorred them," and was maintaining an up-to-the-minute "picket schedule" of sites at which WBC members carry signs that read: "Aids Cures Fags" and "Fags Are Nature Freaks."

Although homosexuality is no longer generally understood as an illness, nor a role, nor a behavior, nor an identity, it is still understood by many people as something different than— and most certainly less than—an ideal of heterosexuality. Despite indicators that this is changing, including such television shows as *Will and Grace* (1998), *Queer as Folk* (2000), *Queer Eye for the Straight Guy* (2003), and *The L Word* (2004), and public opinion polls (Hicks and Lee 2006; Massey 2009), the homosexual/heterosexual binary appears to be alive and well.

Irrespective of whether homosexuality is relevant as an analytical category, many people view deviation from the cultural norm of heterosexual dyadic partnerships as deeply problematic. This clash manifests itself in debates over marriage rights, in battles over HIV funding, political elections, questions of censorship in the media and religious and spiritual guidance. The fact that these debates have exploded into nearly all aspects of social life suggests that an increasing number of people want to have these conversations. They remain, however, challenging—and often contentious—conversations.

References

Adam, B. (1987) *The Rise of a Gay and Lesbian Movement*. New York: Twayne.

Becker, H. (1963) *Outsiders: Studies in the Sociology of Deviance*. New York: The Free Press.

Butler, J. (1990) *Gender Trouble: Feminism and the Subversion of Identity*. New York: Routledge.

—— (1993) *Bodies That Matter: On the Discursive Limits of "Sex."* New York: Routledge.

Conrad, P. and Schneider, J. (1980) *Deviance and Medicalization: From Badness to Sickness*. St. Louis, MO: C. V. Mosby.

Erzin, T. (2006) *Straight to Jesus: Sexual and Christian Conversions in the Ex-Gay Movement*. Berkeley: University of California Press.

Fetner, T. (2005) "The Christian Antigay/Pro-Family Movement's 'Truth in Love' Ad Campaign." *Journal of Homosexuality*, 50: 71–95.

Foucault, M. (1978) *The History of Sexuality*, Vol. I: *An Introduction*, translated by Robert Hurley. New York: Pantheon.

—— (1985) *The History of Sexuality*, Vol. II: *The Use of Pleasure*, translated by Robert Hurley. New York: Pantheon.

—— (1986) *The History of Sexuality*, Vol. III: *The Care of the Self*, translated by Robert Hurley. New York: Pantheon.

Goffman, E. (1963) *Stigma: Notes on the Management of Spoiled Identity*. Englewood Cliffs, NJ: Prentice-Hall

Goode, E. (2002) "Does the Death of the Sociology of Deviance Claim Make Sense?" *American Sociologist*, 33(3): 107–118.

—— (2004) "Is the Sociology of Deviance Still Relevant?" *American Sociologist*, 35(4): 46–57.

Halberstam, J. (1998) *Female Masculinity*. Durham, NC: Duke University Press.

Hicks, G. R. and Lee, T. (2006) "Pubic Attitudes toward Gays and Lesbians: Trends and Predictors." *Journal of Homosexuality*, 51(2): 57–77.

Kinsey, A. C. *et al.* (1948) *Sexual Behavior in the Human Male*. Philadelphia, PA: W. B. Saunders.

Knapp, D. E. (2008) "Ready or Not? Homosexuality, Unit Cohesion, and Military Readiness." *Employee Responsibilities and Rights Journal*, 20: 227–247.

Krafft-Ebbing, R. (1965 [1886]) *Psychopathia Sexualis*, edited by F. S. Klaf. London: Staples Press.

Lovaas, K. E., Elia, J. P. and Yep, G. A. (2007) "Surveying the Contested Terrain of LGBT Studies and Queer Theory." *Journal of Homosexuality*, 52: 1–18.

Massey, S. G. (2009) "Polymorphous Prejudice: Liberating the Measurement of Heterosexuals' Attitudes toward Lesbians and Gay Men." *Journal of Homosexuality*, 56: 147–172.

McIntosh, M. (1968) "The Homosexual Role." *Social Problems*, 16: 182–192.

Miller, J. M., Wright, R. A. and Dannels, D. (2001) "Is Deviance 'Dead'? The Decline of a Sociological Research Specialization." *American Sociologist*, 32 (3): 43–59.

Murphy, T. F. (1988) "Is AIDS a Just Punishment?" *Journal of Medical Ethics*, 14: 154–160.

Pfohl, S. (1985) *Images of Deviance and Social Control: A Sociological History*. New York: McGraw-Hill.

Ross, J. W. (1988) "Ethics and the Language of AIDS." In C. Pierce and D. Van DeVeer (eds.) *AIDS, Ethics and Public Policy*. Belmont, CA: Wadsworth.

Sedgwick, E. K. (1991) *Epistemology of the Closet*. Berkeley: University of California Press.

Seidman, S. (1991) "The End of Postmodern Theory: The Postmodern Hope." *Sociological Theory*, 9: 131–146.

—— (1994) "Queer-Ing Sociology, Sociologizing Queer Theory: An Introduction." *Sociological Theory*, 12: 166–177.

—— (2002) *Beyond the Closet: The Transformation of Gay and Lesbian Life*. New York: Routledge.

Shilts, R. (1993) *Conduct Unbecoming: Lesbians and Gays in the US Military: Vietnam to the Persian Gulf*. New York: St. Martin's Press.

Sinclair, G. D. (2009) "Homosexuality and the Military: A Review of the Literature." *Journal of Homosexuality*, 56: 701–718.

Sumner, C. (1994) *The Sociology of Deviance: An Obituary*. New York: Continuum.

Troiden, R. (1979) "Becoming Homosexual: A Model of Gay Identity Acquisition." *Psychiatry*, 42: 362–373.

US Code 654 (1993) Pub. L. 103-160 571, 107 Stat. 1547. Washington, DC: Government Printing Office.

Weinberg, T. (1978) "On 'Doing' and 'Being' Gay: Sexual Behavior and Homosexual Male Self-Identity." *Journal of Homosexuality*, 4: 143–156.

Whitam, F. (1981) "A Reply to Goode on 'The Homosexual Role.'" *Journal of Sex Research*, 17: 66–72.

30

Premarital adolescent sexual activity

Kathleen Bogle

Premarital adolescent sexual activity refers to sexual interaction between young men and women prior to marriage. Currently, the median age at first marriage is at an all-time high of approximately 26 for women and 28 for men.[1] Although young people are delaying marriage, they are often sexually active from adolescence (the average age of first intercourse is approximately 17).[2] Adolescent sexual interaction, like that of adults, can encompass a range of behavior, including kissing, fondling, oral sex, intercourse (vaginal penetration) and, less often, anal sex.

The prevalence rates for various types of sexual behavior among adolescents is tracked via a variety of nationally representative surveys, including the Youth Risk Behavior Surveillance Survey (YRBSS), which is administered by the Centers for Disease Control every two years (beginning in 1991). The most recent data, gathered in 2007 on high-school-age students in ninth through twelfth grade, indicates that rates of teenagers experiencing sexual intercourse has dropped in recent years (47.8% in 2007 compared to 54.1% in 1991).[3] Department of Health and Human Services data from 2002 support a downward trend concerning adolescent sex, finding that 30% of 15–17-year-old girls (down from 38% in 1995) and 31% of 15–17-year-old boys (down from 43% in 1995) had experienced sexual intercourse. Additionally, this study found that 13% of girls and 15% of boys had intercourse prior to age 15 (down from about 20% in 1995).[4]

The data on adolescent intercourse stand in contrast to the media-hyped image of teens spiraling out of control and sexualized images of youth in America. However, adult concern over the sexual behavior of youth stems not only from intercourse but from other sexual activities that have traditionally been seen as "high risk" or "deviant." According to the 2002 National Survey of Family Growth, 55% of males and 54% of females aged 15–19 had engaged in oral sex with someone of the opposite sex and 11% of males and females aged 15–19 had engaged in anal sex with someone of the opposite sex (Mosher *et al.* 2005).

In addition to researchers examining the correlations between gender and sexual behavior, they gather information on social class and race. Adolescents from poor families tend to have sex earlier than their counterparts from middle- or high-income families (Meier 2007). Likewise, African-American adolescents are more likely to have intercourse at younger ages than those of Hispanic or White backgrounds. For example, data from the 2007 YRBSS show the disparate breakdown by race of high school students reporting having had intercourse: Blacks 66.5%, Hispanics 52%, and Whites 43.7%. Blacks and Hispanics also are more likely to have had sex prior to age 13 (Blacks: 16.3%; Hispanics: 8.2%; Whites: 4.4%) and to have had four or more partners than their White counterparts (Blacks: 27.6%; Hispanics: 17.3%; Whites: 11.5%). Although minority students are more likely to have sex, have it younger, and have it with more partners, White students engage in some risky behaviors more than minorities. For instance, they are more likely to report that they drank alcohol or used drugs prior to their last intercourse (24.8%), compared to 21.4% of Hispanic students and 16.4% of Black students.[5]

Mark Regnerus, author of *Forbidden Fruit: Sex and Religion in the Lives of American Teenagers* (2007), has attempted to make sense of the survey data on teens in his sociological analysis of adolescent sexual behavior. He argues that a new middle-class morality of "everything but intercourse" is guiding the sex lives of many contemporary adolescents. However, teens are not abstaining from intercourse in order to maintain their "technical virginity," as some have claimed; rather, some teens favor sexual practices other than intercourse because they are trying to avoid risks, such as pregnancy and sexually transmitted diseases (Regnerus 2007). Teens' fear of the risks associated with intercourse does not always affect behavior, however. According to the 2007 YRBSS, among high schools students who were sexually active, approximately 45% of girls and 32% of boys indicated that they did not use a condom during their last intercourse.[6]

Adolescent sexuality and social problems

Many scholars chart changes in both attitudes and behavior related to adolescent sexuality in order to explore the connection between sexual behavior and an array of social problems, such as teen pregnancy and the spread of sexually transmitted diseases. Regarding teen pregnancy, although the rate of teen childbearing has fallen sharply since the 1950s, according to the Centers for Disease Control, in 2002 12% of all pregnancies, which equates to 757,000, occurred among adolescents aged 15–19 (Ventura *et al.* 2006). It is not only adults who have concerns about the timing of teen pregnancy. Only 12% of mothers who give birth prior to age 18 (in the five years preceding the survey) said they believed their pregnancy occurred at "the right time" (Abma *et al.* 2004).

The concern over teen pregnancy stems from concern about how it connects to other social problems, such as poverty and crime. In Edin and Kefalas's (2007) groundbreaking study on inner-city, unwed pregnancy, they found girls from poor families are more likely to get pregnant and most will not be in a romantic relationship with the father of their baby by the time the child turns one year old. Children born in these circumstances often grow up without their biological father in the home and are more likely to suffer a variety of negative outcomes, including lower achievement in school and involvement with drugs and crime.

Although some believe lack of access to or education about birth control is to blame for teen pregnancy, Edin and Kefalas found that was not the real problem. Rather, poor teen girls revere motherhood as a productive, high-status role that will keep them out of trouble and give them a purpose in life. Although the girls interviewed were not necessarily trying to get pregnant, they were not doing anything to prevent it either. These girls were aware that an "unplanned" pregnancy could be a consequence of their actions, yet some hoped that having a child would help them transition to becoming an adult and escape their own, often difficult, childhood. However, these young women learned that their dreams of having a stable family life were far from the reality of raising a child as a poor, single parent.

Although boys and girls are both engaging in unprotected sex, which in some cases leads to unplanned pregnancies, scholars have found that their motivations for doing so vary greatly by gender. In Anderson's (1999) classic study on urban poverty in Philadelphia, he found that while young girls dreamed of settling down and "playing house" with their sexual partners, young men often viewed sex as a conquest that helped boost their status in the eyes of their same-sex peers. For example, Anderson found that some young men callously referred to getting a girl pregnant and leaving her and the unborn child as a "hit and run."[7] Such terminology underscores why many adults are concerned about the choices adolescents make in the realm of sex and mating.

Another area of concern pertaining to adolescents and sex relates to sexually transmitted diseases. The Centers for Disease Control estimate that approximately 19 million new sexually transmitted infections occur each year, with almost half among people aged 15–24 (Weinstock *et al.* 2004). In 2006, an estimated 5,259 young people aged 13–24 in the 33 states reporting to the CDC were diagnosed with HIV/AIDS, representing about 14% of the persons diagnosed that year.[8] Teens with multiple sexual partners are more at risk of contracting a sexually transmitted infection. Since minority youth are more likely to have had four or more partners, they are more likely to contract a sexually transmitted infection. Data indicates that Black youth are at particularly high risk of getting a sexually transmitted infection or disease. For example, according to CDC data, 70% of those aged 13–19 who were diagnosed with HIV/AIDS in 2006 were Black, compared to 14% Hispanic and 14% White.[9]

Context for premarital adolescent sex

With the average age of first marriage in the middle to late twenties, most adolescents experience sexual activity outside the context of marriage. For most of the first half of the 20th century, the primary context for early sexual experiences was dating (Bailey 1988). The sexual norms for the dating era included kissing, necking, and petting; however, oral sex and sexual intercourse were considered off-limits. Despite these standards, Alfred Kinsey's mid-20th-century reports on male and female sexual behavior shocked Americans by suggesting that many were not abstaining from intercourse. Although Kinsey's study was not representative, he found that over half of women lost their virginity prior to marriage (Kinsey *et al.* 1953).

The decades that followed brought about the most significant changes in attitudes and behavior for premarital sex, particularly for women. Some of these changes were brought about by women's rights activists in the 1960s and 1970s demanding equality with men in all areas of life, including sex. In this era, the increasing availability of birth control, including "the pill," made it possible for sexual intercourse to occur without a significant risk of pregnancy. This technological advance fueled the change, which was already under way, that sexual intercourse could be for pleasure, not just procreation (D'Emilio and Freedman 1988). Attitudes toward premarital sex changed as a result of this sexual revolution. Youth cultures in particular began to reject premarital chastity as an ideal. At this time, it increasingly became socially acceptable for men and women to have sexual intercourse outside of the context of marriage (Rubin 1990).

One study of sex and relationships on college campuses (Bogle 2008) found that these changes ushered in a new context for early sexual experience, called "hooking up," which has largely replaced traditional dating as the means to begin a sexual or romantic relationship. In the first national study on hooking up among college women, Glenn and Marquardt (2001: 4) define a hook-up as: "when a girl and a guy get together for a physical encounter and don't necessarily expect anything further." Hooking up can mean anything from kissing to sexual intercourse (or anything generally seen as falling between these two extremes) between partners who are strangers, brief acquaintances or friends (Bogle 2008; Glenn and Marquardt 2001).

Both quantitative and qualitative data suggest that hooking up is common among college-age populations. For example, in their representative study of a large college in the northeastern US, Paul *et al.* (2000) found that 78% of students had engaged in a hook-up encounter. Although most of the data on hooking up thus far have focused on college populations, researchers have found that hooking up does not begin in college. In fact, college students report that they are familiar with both the term and the practice from their high school years (Bogle 2008).

Hooking up differs from traditional dating in many ways. Two key differences are the sexual norms and the timing of certain types of sexual activity. In the dating era, sexual intercourse prior to marriage was seen as taboo. However, dating partners would typically become more sexually intimate as the relationship grew in closeness or intensity. Unlike the dating era, the norms guiding the development of sexual intimacy among hook-up partners are less clear. With hooking up, the degree of sexual intimacy varies dramatically and is not as clearly tied to relationship development or emotional closeness (Bogle 2007, 2008). For example, some college students will be *more* sexually intimate with a hook-up partner if they believe that an ongoing romantic relationship with that person is unlikely (Bogle 2008).

Thus, sexual intercourse for young singles is not only possible but can happen between hook-up partners or, in other words, outside the context of an exclusive, committed relationship. Drawing on data from the National Longitudinal Study of Adolescent Health, Manning *et al.* (2005) found that 60% of sexually active teens have had sex in both romantic and non-romantic contexts. This distinction is important because, in spite of more relaxed rules pertaining to premarital sex over the last several decades, the context for sexual intercourse did not change from "marriage only" to "anything goes," as is often assumed. Most Americans still approve of premarital sex only in the confines of a committed relationship between consenting adults (Widner *et al.* 1998). As a result, the phenomenon of hooking up and the idea that many adolescents are not only having sex but having sex outside the milieu of a committed, romantic relationship has set off a firestorm of media attention (e.g. Stepp 2007; Denizet-Lewis 2004) and has led to a sustained public debate over how adolescent sex should be controlled.

Controlling adolescent sexual behavior

Although the statistical data do not support the idea that adolescent sexual behavior is "out of control," some are concerned that approximately half of adolescents are sexually active; many adolescent sexual encounters, if they include intercourse or not, occur outside the context of a committed relationship; and engaging in sexual behavior puts teens at risk of unplanned pregnancies and sexually transmitted diseases. Given societal concern about teen sexuality, there is much debate over how to control adolescent sex.

Historically, religious leaders played a major role in encouraging premarital chastity. However, recent data suggest that there is a complex relationship between religious influence and adolescents' sexual attitudes and behavior. For example, Regnerus (2007) found that many teens belonging to evangelical Christian denominations take "abstinence pledges" where they promise not to have sex until after marriage. While most of these youth break their pledge, they do tend to have their first sexual experience later than those who do not take the pledge, which many adolescent health experts view as positive. Regnerus also found that evangelical youth were just as likely to be sexually active as other young men and women; however, they were more likely to feel guilty about it. This underscores one of Regnerus's major findings: that is, religion often affects sexual *attitudes* more than sexual *behavior*. Despite the dwindling influence of religion on contemporary adolescent sexual behavior, Regnerus found that religiosity (i.e., level of devotion to one's religious beliefs) mattered more than belonging to any particular denomination.

In addition to the influence of religion, schools try to exert influence over adolescent sexuality, particularly through sex education. When sex education is offered prior to sexual onset, it has been found to affect adolescent sexual behavior with regard to delaying first intercourse and using contraception at first intercourse (Mueller *et al.* 2008). Regardless of the effectiveness of sex education programming, the content of sex education programs has led to heated debate throughout society for decades (Irvine 2004). In *Talk about Sex: The Battles over Sex Education in the United States*, Irvine argues that although most Americans claim to favor comprehensive sex education in public schools, only 10% of school districts offer a comprehensive program. Instead, the conservative Christian movement, often referred to as the "religious right," has waged (and largely won) the battle to limit sex education to an abstinence-only curriculum. The problem with the abstinence-only approach is that it has been found to be less effective in reducing high-risk adolescent sexual behavior than a more comprehensive approach (Kirby 2008).

Given the ineffectiveness of organized religion's attempts to promote abstinence among adolescents and the lack of comprehensive sex education in most schools, adolescent health advocates call upon parents to play an active role in educating their children about sex. Fortunately, recent research indicates that parental influence does matter. Longmore *et al.* (2009) found that parental caring and parents' preferences that their child should postpone sex were both significant predictors in delaying teen initiation to sexual activity.

Notes

1   US Bureau of the Census 2008.
2   Data from National Center for Health Statistics, US Department of Health and Human Services.
3   Centers for Disease Control 2007.
4   Reported in Parker-Pope 2009.
5   Centers for Disease Control 2007.
6   Centers for Disease Control 2007.
7   "Hit" is a slang term for sexual intercourse.
8   Centers for Disease Control 2006a.
9   Centers for Disease Control 2006b.

References

Abma, J.C., Martinez, G.M., Mosher, W.D., and Dawson, B.S. (2004) *Teenagers in the United States: Sexual Activity, Contraceptive Use, and Childbearing, 2002*. Hyattsville, MD: National Center for Health Statistics.

Anderson, E. (1999) *Code of the Street: Decency, Violence, and the Moral Life of the Inner City*. New York: W.W. Norton & Company.

Bailey, B.L. (1988) *From Front Porch to Back Seat: Courtship in Twentieth-Century America*. Baltimore, MD: Johns Hopkins University Press.

Bogle, K.A. (2007) "The Shift from Dating to Hooking up in College: What Scholars Have Missed." *Sociology Compass* 1 (2): 775–788.

Bogle, K.A. (2008) *Hooking up: Sex, Dating, and Relationships on Campus*. New York: New York University Press.

Centers for Disease Control (2006a) "HIV/AIDS Surveillance Report, 2006." Atlanta, GA: US Department of Health and Human Services, Centers for Disease Control and Prevention.

Centers for Disease Control (2006b) "HIV Related Risk Behaviors among African American Youth." Atlanta, GA: US Department of Health and Human Services, Centers for Disease Control and Prevention

Centers for Disease Control (2007) "Youth Risk Behavior Surveillance—United States." Atlanta, GA: US Department of Health and Human Services, Centers for Disease Control and Prevention.

D'Emilio, J. and Freedman, E.B. (1988) *Intimate Matters: A History of Sexuality in America*. New York: Harper & Row.

Denizet-Lewis, B. (2004) "Friends with Benefits and the Benefits of the Local Mall." *New York Times Magazine*, May 30.

Edin, K. and Kefalas, M. (2007) *Promises I Can Keep: Why Poor Women Put Motherhood before Marriage*. Berkeley: University of California Press.

Glenn, N. and Marquardt, E. (2001) *Hooking up, Hanging out and Hoping for Mr. Right: College Women on Dating and Mating Today*. Institute for American Values report for the Independent Women's Forum.

Irvine, J. (2004) *Talk about Sex: The Battles over Sex Education in the United States*. Berkeley: University of California Press.

Kinsey, A.C., Wardell, B.P., Clyde E.M., and Gebhard, P. (1953) *Sexual Behavior in the Human Female*. Philadelphia, PA: W.B. Saunders.

Kirby, D. (2008) "The Impact of Abstinence and Comprehensive Sex and STD/HIV Education Programs on Adolescent Sexual Behavior." *Sexuality Research and Social Policy* 5: 18–27.

Lambert, T.A., Kahn, A.S., and Apple, K.J. (2003) "Pluralistic Ignorance and Hooking up." *Journal of Sex Research* 40: 129–133.

Longmore, M.A., Eng, A.L., Giordano, P.C., and Manning, W.D. (2009) "Parenting and Adolescents' Sexual Initiation." *Journal of Marriage and Family* 71: 969–982.

Manning, W.D., Longmore, M.A., and Giordano, P.C. (2005) "Adolescents' Involvement in Non-romantic Sexual Activity." *Social Science Research* 34: 384–407.

Meier, A.M. (2007) "Adolescent First Sex and Subsequent Mental Health." *American Journal of Sociology* 112: 1811–1847.

Mosher, W., Chandra, A., and Jones, J. (2005) "Sexual Behavior and Selected Health Measures: Men and Women 15–44 Years of Age, United States, 2002." *Advance Data from Vital and Health Statistics* 362: 21–26.

Mueller, T.E., Gavin, L.E., and Kulkarni, A. (2008) "The Association between Sex Education and Youth's Engagement in Sexual Intercourse, Age at First Intercourse, and Birth Control Use at First Sex." *Journal of Adolescent Health* 42: 89–96.

Parker-Pope, T. (2009) "The Myth of Rampant Teenage Promiscuity." *New York Times Magazine*, January 26.

Paul, E.L. and Hayes, K.A. (2002) "The Casualties of Casual Sex: A Qualitative Exploration of the Phenomenology of College Students' Hookups." *Journal of Social and Personal Relationships* 19: 639–661.

Paul, E.L., McManus, B., and Hayes, A. (2000) "Hookups: Characteristics and Correlates of College Students' Spontaneous and Anonymous Sexual Experiences." *Journal of Sex Research* 37: 76–88.

Regnerus, M.D. (2007) *Forbidden Fruit: Sex and Religion in the Lives of American Teenagers*. New York: Oxford University Press.

Rubin, L. (1990) *Erotic Wars: What Happened to the Sexual Revolution?* New York: Farrar, Straus & Giroux.

Stepp, L.S. (2007) *Unhooked: How Young Women Pursue Sex, Delay Love and Lose at Both*. Riverhead Books.

US Bureau of the Census (2008) *Estimated Median Age at First Marriage by Sex, 1890 to the Present*. Washington, DC: US Bureau of the Census.

Ventura, S.J., Abma, J.C., Mosher, W.D., and Henshaw, S.K. (2006) *Recent Trends in Teenage Pregnancy in the United States, 1990–2002*. Hyattsville, MD: National Center for Health Statistics.

Weinstock, H., Berman, S., Cates, W. (2004) "Sexually Transmitted Diseases among American Youth: Incidence and Prevalence Estimates, 2000." *Perspectives on Sexual and Reproductive Health* 36: 6–10.

Widner, E.D., Treas, J., and Newcomb, R. (1998) "Attitudes toward Nonmarital Sex in 24 Countries." *Journal of Sex Research* 35: 349–358.

31

Vegetarianism and fruitarianism as deviance

Joe Boyle

With a vegetarian option in nearly every restaurant in North America, it is arguable whether vegetarianism can even be considered deviant. Many people who are not familiar with vegetarianism see a difficult, yet conscientious, dietary preference. However, people who choose to be vegetarian usually view it as a lifestyle that includes much reasoning (Maurer 2002). The contention that vegetarianism is deviant rests in the potential extreme forms of vegetarianism as well as the ideology behind the movement. Historically, vegetarianism rejects the dominant cultural prescription for food production and consumption in Western industrialized nations. These foundations of meat eating in the West can be directly traced back to the Bible and the first chapter of the book of Genesis (Stuart 2006). The early Church stood by the doctrine concerning man's dominion over animals, and human beings were insulting God by not eating what He provided for them (Spencer 1995).

In early North American history, meat as the center of the human diet can be seen in the agricultural practices of the American Indians. Wild game was second only to maize in importance to the Native Americans of the eastern and coastal areas (Drache 1996). The arrival of the European settlers did nothing to quell the taste for meat. Colonial Americans ate primarily pork because of the pig's ability to live in a woodland environment without much care (Ross 1980). Cattle held its place in colonial life by producing dairy products, and the well-to-do ate beef as an occasional treat (McIntosh 1995). The ordinary citizen ate salted pork, fish, and various kinds of bread. The change to beef began with the expansion of the American West. Rifkin (1992) noted that the railroad system and the technological advances that came with it forged the groundwork for beef to dominate well into the latter half of the 20th century. The core eating pattern developed to include meat regularly at both lunch and dinner in American households (Levenstein 1988).

The beginning of the 21st century has seen the continuation of the "core" eating pattern as well as the entrenchment of the fast-food industry. The latter accounts for nearly 50% of all the money spent on meals away from home (Harper 2007). Since the hamburger was introduced in 1904 at the World's Fair in St. Louis, it has become the trademark of modern American life (Rifkin 1992). Willard (1997) points out that even though Americans are slowly moving away from red meat, the practice of meat eating in general has not declined. It has only shifted from red meat to more poultry products. The influence of the American lifestyle has driven the world's consumption of meat to an all-time high.

Types and numbers of vegetarians

Essentially, vegetarians construct diets that avoid certain kinds of food. The limitations vegetarians place on themselves can be classified by seven categories of food: red meat, poultry, seafood, eggs, dairy products, root and leaf vegetables, and fruits/nuts/ grains. The only food grouping that is eaten by all types of vegetarian is the last: fruits/nuts/grains. Avoidance of one or several of the other six categories creates the eight types of eating pattern that can be considered "vegetarian" (Meister 1997).

First, the semi-vegetarian eats seafood and poultry but rejects red meats, such as beef and pork. The pollo-vegetarian and pesco-vegetarian reject red meat but consume poultry and seafood, respectively. The classic, and most common, lacto-ovo-vegetarian eats eggs and dairy products but abstains from all forms of meat. Then there are two subgroups of this category: the lacto-vegetarian, who eats dairy but excludes eggs; and the ovo-vegetarian, who excludes dairy but eats eggs. Finally, the last two types of vegetarian do not consume any product derived from animals, even excluding the use of animal products as clothing or other household items. One of these two types, the vegan, will eat root and leaf vegetables. However, the strictest form of vegetarian, the fruitarian, abstains from all but one of the seven categories of food—the fruit of plants. This means they can eat fruit vegetables, such as peppers and cucumbers, as well as nuts and some grains. The aim is to avoid injury to either animals or plants (Meister 1997). Moreover, the fruit is preferably consumed in a raw, uncooked state (Carrington 2005).

Recently, a new form of vegetarianism that is closer to veganism but retains aspects of the fruitarian diet has become popular. Raw food diets center on food that is preferably grown organically and is eaten in its uncooked form. However, there is a split within the raw food movement between simply raw diets and living food diets. Both of these forms of vegetarianism require the participant to avoid heating the food above 110 °F (39 °C). The living food diet differs from the simply raw diet in that the only raw fruit and vegetables consumed are in the closest possible state to the time the foods were harvested in order to provide the highest possible nutritional value (Russo 2008).

The total number of vegetarians is difficult to calculate due to the varied categories of the vegetarians themselves. Maurer (2002) estimates the number of North American vegetarians at just 1% of the population, while others suggest it could be as high as 7%, if one includes semi-vegetarians (Meister 1997; Deitz et al. 1995). Vegetarianism in the United Kingdom produces similar percentages. The oldest current vegetarian group, the Vegetarian Society of Great Britain, reports that the percentage of complete vegetarians is as low as 1% in Scotland. However, it also claims that the number of residents with a partly or semi-vegetarian diet in the United Kingdom is 7% (www.vegsoc.org/info/statorg.html). So there seems to be a consistency among the North American and UK populations regarding the percentage of the population who claim to be vegetarian. The stricter forms of vegetarianism that eliminate meat consumption float in the 1% to 5% range. Expanding the definition to include semi-vegetarians increases the range to about 7%.

Vegetarianism as positive deviance

Sociologists have questioned whether vegetarianism will always be considered "marginal" and/or "deviant" (McIntosh 1996; Maurer 1997; Hamilton 2000). Voluntary vegetarianism is said to have begun approximately at the point in history, around 500 BCE, when Buddha in India and Pythagoras in Greece were expounding the virtue of life and the rejection of meat. However, Pythagoras is considered the father of Western vegetarianism due to the nature of the ideals that have passed down in Western philosophy (Gregerson 1994). Abstinence from meat was considered subversive in the Greek city-states (Spencer 1995). And the existence of vegetarian sects during the time of early Christianity brought about accusations that those practicing this type of foodway were religious heretics. Being vegetarian was not the only reason that practicing sects were ostracized. The ideology behind the sects usually refuted the dominant church leaders of the time. Vegetarian sects went against the Church by allowing women to be treated as equals, opening their doors to homosexuals, and denouncing the accumulation of wealth. Later, meat consumption and the owning of livestock showed that the proprietor had wealth, power, and status in the community. In this context, vegetarianism was seen as a threat to the fundamental philosophies of Western, capitalistic, and democratic societies such as the United States and those in Western Europe (Spencer 1995).

Any deviant act that is believed to contribute to the moral, economic, or intellectual growth of a society can be classified as positive deviance. Vegetarians usually do not engage in active social protest, but they do have organized structures for disseminating information and perpetuating the criticism of meat eating in the West (Maurer 2002). Vegetarian organizations walk the line between subversive social critics and beneficial educators for a healthy lifestyle. For the most part, they espouse a positive message regarding social justice and healthy living. The study of positive deviance attempts to tie together both the future social benefits of the marginalized movement with the negative reactions of the current social context.

Vegetarianism could be viewed as "superior" behavior that is nonetheless rejected, meaning it meets Heckert's (1998) criterion for positive deviance. Many people see it as a difficult and even noble attempt at personal and/or societal benefit, so it could be classified under supra-conformity in her typology. Vegetarianism represents the ideal, whether it is the drive for ideal health, an ideal society, or the ideal treatment of animals. It even has the potential to become overly ideological and incredibly strict in its variations. For example, vegans and fruitarians are extreme forms of vegetarianism that require supra-conforming behavior in order to reach that goal. Overall, vegetarianism has historically been a violation of major foodways in Western civilization. Today, it has succeeded in moving away from the heretical offenses of Old World Europe to a marginal behavior that is seen as having positive value for those who practice it. However, those who practice vegetarianism must negotiate their decision to participate in behavior outside the norm in similar ways to any other person who engages in deviant behavior.

Vegetarian vocabularies of motive

An eating pattern alone is not the barometer of whether someone has become vegetarian. Vegetarians must justify or rationalize their behavior to others when they are questioned. The ideology behind the decision may be radical, which results in a very strict form of vegetarianism, such as veganism. Or an individual might choose to abstain from certain types of meat simply because they are worried about their health.

Vegetarians, like other deviants, will find a way of validating themselves and selling the behavior to others. The most accepted application of the vocabulary of motive is the conceptualization of accounts outlined by Marvin Scott and Stanford Lyman (1968). The necessity of legitimacy in the life of the vegetarian forces them to offer accounts for their deviance. Scott and Lyman (1968: 46) note that every person engages in some form of deviance at some time, and individuals need verbal mechanisms to bridge "the gap between action and expectation" and to foster a positive self-image. Arguably the most comprehensive organization of accounts and accounting techniques was Nichols' (1990) expansion of the work of Scott and

Lyman that adds two other forms of remedial account: admissions and denials. Vegetarians use remedial accounts when consistently defending their identity after conversion. This is the defining feature of a deviant who is in the final stage of signification (Matza 1969). The person practicing vegetarianism then becomes a vegetarian.

Initially, vegetarians, as well as other deviants who are early in their careers, are still learning the how and the why of the vegetarian way. Developing vegetarians usually offer just a simple monothematic account to alleviate the conflict that arises between their actions and societal expectations (Boyle 2007). This monothematic account serves as a "starting point." The initial vegetarian accounts can be classified within the framework of the accounting typology developed by Nichols (1990). However, Nichols overlooked an important account from his "admissions" category: the notion of deviance avowal. This concept was introduced by Ralph Turner in 1972 and described a coping or stigma management technique in which deviants attempt to portray their marginal behavior in a positive light. Adler and Adler (1997) note that deviance avowal is a way of managing contentious behavior in that the deviant person understands both the deviant lifestyle and the "normal" viewpoint.

In any form of deviance, certain accounts will be more prevalent within certain subcultures. Vegetarians are no different. There are essentially ten major accounts given by vegetarians to minimize stigma attached to their behavior. The first category, admissions, allows the person to admit the wrongfulness of the act while simultaneously accepting responsibility for the behavior. Of that first category, only the generally overlooked admission—deviance avowal— is slightly relevant to vegetarianism. Deviance avowal necessitates the ability of vegetarians to acknowledge the marginalized dietary habit openly and present themselves as positively as possible. Vegetarians will minimize the impact of their behavior within social interaction, especially during eating activities. Many vegetarians attempt to "get by" with eating what is readily available.

The second category of accounts—excuses—are defined by Nichols (1990) as behaviors that admit the wrongfulness or deviant nature of the act but deny personal responsibility for the act in question. Excuses are made up of four distinct accounts, of which two are relevant to vegetarians. (Vegetarians do not employ appeal to accidents or appeal to defeasibility because becoming vegetarian is a lifestyle choice, not a result of a hazard or a mental lapse.) The first of these, an appeal to biological drives, can be defined as the belief that the body and/or biological factors can determine human behavior (Scott and Lyman 1968). Here, the belief is that the body can influence certain social choices. Many vegetarians claim that they do not like the taste of meat or that they cannot handle the aesthetic qualities of meat, such as the touch, smell, or even the sight of raw meat. Twigg (1979) argues that the aesthetic properties of meat that vegetarians find repulsive are based on the association of meat with death. The other excuse used by vegetarians is scapegoating. This denies the responsibility of the questioned behavior by alleging that the deviance is in response to another's behavior. Vegetarians scapegoat by placing responsibility with other people who are in their lives at the time of conversion. Parents are common scapegoats for vegetarians.

The third major category of remedial accounts—justification—denies the wrongfulness of the behavior, but the person accepts responsibility for the deviance (Nichols 1990). Justification is the primary type of remedial account used by vegetarians, especially denial of injury. This can be described as an account that presents the deviance as acceptable because no person or thing was injured. This parallels the classic vegetarian argument for social justice (Beardsworth and Keil 1997). Rejecting meat for this reason rejects the current dominant social structure in Western societies. Vegetarianism is a form of protest that stands up against the exploitation of people under a capitalistic and patriarchal system.

The argument for animal rights essentially can be classified as another justification, known as an appeal to higher loyalties. This admits responsibility for the action because it was done out of allegiance to another group (Scott and Lyman 1968), with the other group in this instance being the animal kingdom. Beardsworth and Keil (1997) note that this argument is based on the concept of "speciesism," originally popularized by the philosopher Peter Singer (1976). For those adopting this position, it is a moral imperative to reduce the suffering of animals.

The next justification for vegetarianism is self-fulfillment. This resides in the belief that the deviant behavior helps the individual become a better person. When a vegetarian claims better health as a reason for their vegetarianism, he or she is essentially arguing for self-fulfillment. This health position states that eating meat is essentially opening the person up to the ill effects of meat consumption (Beardsworth and Keil 1997).

The way in which Western societies produce food and use the environment can also be classified as a justification. More specifically, this remedial account falls into the type known as condemnation of the condemners. As Scott and Lyman (1968) state, when a deviant uses this accounting mechanism, he or she is volleying back the negative connotation of the behavior by stating that others commit much worse acts. The mass production of beef, veal, pork, and poultry and the unpleasant realization of the subsequent environmental degradation can cause many people to adopt the vegetarian lifestyle.

The final justification vegetarians employ is the sad tale. This presents the person as a victim of certain circumstances, but the deviance has now "saved" them from that dismal situation (Scott and Lyman 1968). This is very similar to the health argument, but in this case the vegetarian says that the vegetarian lifestyle saved them from continuing down the path of sickness and disease.

The final category in Nichols' typology is denial. This involves the deviant's rejection of both the wrongfulness of the act and their responsibility for it. The two types of denial are passing and deviance disavowal. Passing can be described as the deviant's unwillingness to tell anyone about the stigma in question (Goffman 1963). Vegetarianism is a type of deviance that lends itself to passing quite nicely, as the only time vegetarianism really must be acknowledged is during the course of a meal.

Fred Davis (1961: 120) defined deviance disavowal as "the refusal of those who are viewed as deviant to concur with the verdict." The purpose of the disavowal is for the deviant to normalize him- or herself in relation to others (Adler and Adler 1997). Vegetarians attempt to disavow their deviance by trying to show "normals" that they can participate in ordinary eating activities. The development of meat analogs has helped them to do this. (A meat analog is a food designed to replace meat in a traditional meal, but it is made primarily out of vegetables and grain. The most recognizable example is the "veggie burger.") Meat analogs allow a vegetarian to acknowledge the difficulties of being deviant but simultaneously participate in "regular" eating.

In conclusion, Western vegetarianism has transformed itself from a most serious, heretical offense that often resulted in a death by stoning (Stuart 2006; Spencer 1995) into a foodway that is accepted in its more common forms but still carries very deviant status at the strictest levels. Even though vegetarianism has become more accepted, the stigma has remained as vegetarian groups prefer to promote a "plant-based diet" as a way to deflect the negative connotation of "vegetarian" (Maurer 2002). The sometimes radical ideology behind the movement has fed into the contentious nature of the debate. As a result, vegetarianism may always be considered a deviant and marginalized lifestyle choice in modern Western culture.

References

Adler, Patricia A. and Peter Adler. (1997). *Constructions of Deviance*, 2nd edn. Belmont, CA: Wadsworth.

Beardsworth, Alan and Teresa Keil. (1997). *Sociology on the Menu: An Invitation to the Study of Food and Society*. London: Routledge.

Boyle, Joseph. (2007). Becoming vegetarian: An analysis of the vegetarian career using an integrated model of deviance. Unpublished doctoral dissertation. Virginia Polytechnic Institute and State University.

Carrington, Hereward. (2005). *The Fruitarian Diet*. New York: Kessinger.

Davis, Fred. (1961). Deviance disavowal: The management of strained interaction by the visually handicapped. *Social Problems*, 9: 120–132.

Deitz, Thomas, Ann Stirling Frisch, Linda Kalof, Paul C. Stern, and Gregory A. Guagnano. (1995). Values and vegetarianism: An exploratory analysis. *Rural Sociology*, 60: 533–542.

Drache, Hiram M. (1996). *History of US Agriculture and Its Relevance to Today*. Danville, IL: Interstate.

Goffman, Erving. (1963). *Stigma*. Englewood Cliffs, NJ: Prentice-Hall.

Gregerson, Jon. (1994). *Vegetarianism: A History*. Fremont, CA: Jain.

Hamilton, Malcolm. (2000). Eating ethically: "Spiritual" and "quasi-religious" aspects of vegetarianism. *Journal of Contemporary Religion*, 15: 65–88.

Harper, Charles. (2007). *Food, Society, and Environment*, 2nd edn. London: Trafford.

Heckert, D.M. (1998). Positive deviance: A classificatory model. *Free Inquiry in Creative Sociology*, 26: 23–30.

Hughes, J.D. (1980). The environmental ethics of the Pythagoreans. *Environmental Ethics*, 2: 401–412.

Levenstein, H.A. (1988). *Revolution at the Table*. New York: Oxford University Press.

Matza, D. (1969). *Becoming Deviant*. Englewood Cliffs, NJ: Prentice-Hall.

Maurer, Donna. (1997). The vegetarian movement: Ideology and strategy in a collective identity movement. Unpublished doctoral dissertation. Southern Illinois University-Carbondale.

Maurer, Donna. (2002). *Vegetarianism: Movement or Moment?* Philadelphia, PA: Temple University Press.

McIntosh, Elaine N. (1995). *American Food Habits in Historical Perspective*. Westport, CT: Praeger.

McIntosh, Wm. Alex. (1996). *Sociologies of Food and Nutrition*. New York: Plenum Press.

Meister, Kathleen. (1997). *Vegetarianism*. New York: American Council on Science and Health.

Nichols, Lawrence. (1990). Reconceptualizing social accounts: An agenda for theory building and empirical research. *Current Perspectives in Social Theory*, 10: 113–144.

Rifkin, Jeremy. (1992). *Beyond Beef*. New York: Plume.

Ross, E.B. (1980). Patterns of diet and forces of production: An economic and ecological history of the ascending nature of beef in the US diet. In E.B. Ross (ed.) *Beyond Myths of Culture*. New York: Academic Press.

Russo, Ruthann. (2008). *The Raw Food Diet Myth*. Bethlehem, PA: DJ Iber.

Scott, Marvin B. and Stanford Lyman. (1968). Accounts. *American Sociological Review*, 33: 46–62.

Singer, Peter. (1976). *Animal Liberation*. New York: Avon Books.

Spencer, Colin. (1995). *The Heretic's Feast: A History of Vegetarianism*. Hanover, NH: University Press of New England.

Stuart, Tristram. (2006). *The Bloodless Revolution*. New York: W.W. Norton.

Sykes, Gresham and David Matza. (1957). Techniques of neutralization: A theory of delinquency. *American Sociological Review*, 22: 664–670.

Turner, Ralph H. (1972). Deviance avowal as neutralization of commitment. *Social Problems*, 19: 308–324.

Twigg, J. (1979). Food for thought: Purity and vegetarianism. *Religion*, 9: 13–35.

Willard, Barbara Ellen. (1997). What's for dinner? Articulating and antagonizing the American foodway. Unpublished doctoral dissertation. University of Iowa.

32

Cybersex, computer sex addiction, and cyberpornography

Diane Kholos Wysocki

Introduction

Individuals are not born with an innate ability to be sexual. They might know how to have intercourse, which they learn from friends, media, and sometimes their parents, if they are lucky. However, people typically don't know how to give and receive sexual pleasure. Pleasure is taught and learned in various ways. One is that an individual is lucky enough to have a partner who is open to all kinds of sexual pleasure and who is willing to partake in those activities. However, this isn't always the case. Instead, people learn very early on what is considered "normal" sexual behavior versus "abnormal" or deviant sexual behavior. Many learn that masturbation is bad and that touching oneself can cause damage. Some religions teach that oral sex is deviant and sex is only for procreation. It is no wonder that the two main reasons why people divorce are money and sex. This is because what an individual likes when they are young might change over time. And such a change is more likely because of the internet, which enables individuals to learn about types of sexual behavior they might not have imagined before.

Cybersexualities

Cybersex is a range of sexual activities that takes place on the internet and typically begins when two or more people engage in conversations about their sexual fantasies (Whitty and Carr, 2006). Sexual activities happen over the internet for a number of reasons. First, research has found that at least one person has access to the internet in 71% of households (US Census Bureau, 2007). If the internet is not in the household, then it only takes a trip to the library, coffee shop, or internet café to hook up. It should be no surprise that computers, email, and various chat-rooms provide outlets for people interested in fulfilling their sexual fantasies. Furthermore, more than 60% of all visits to the internet involve sexual purposes (Schneider and Weiss, 2001) .

Meeting another person online for sexual purposes is much easier than meeting someone face-to-face and trying to decide if that person has the same sexual interests (Wysocki, 1998). For instance, if two people meet in a chat-room dedicated to sadomasochism, they already know that they share an interest in the same kind of sexual activity and so are able to divulge their fantasies early in the "relationship" (Wysocki and Thalken, 2007) . If they like one another, they can then act out their sexual fantasy online, often with the addition of a video camera and microphone so they can see and hear what the other person is doing (Levine, 1998). Most often the act of having "sex" online involves masturbation and it usually ends in an orgasm (Ross, *et al.*, 2004). All this happens without bodies ever even touching each other.

Another reason why cybersex occurs is because it allows individuals to be much more liberated than they might otherwise be (Screenseductress, 2005). Telling one's partner that one wants something outside the typical sexual repertoire might involve some risk to the relationship which is not worth the reward. A face-to-face partner might think the desired sexual act is abnormal, if not perverted, and would consider it deviant. The risk is much lower online, where it is easy to find someone with similar sexual interests. And if two individuals do not connect, with the click of the mouse they can move on to the next person.

Many studies have found that people have very satisfying sexual experiences on the internet (Ben-Ze'ev, 2004; Bright, 1992; Schneider and Weiss, 2001; Wysocki, 1998). Sometimes, cybersex also leads to meeting the person face-to-face to have an offline sexual experience (Ross *et al.*, 2004; Whitty, 2003; Wysocki, 1998).

A study of 1,026 Latino men who stated they had sex with other men found that cybersex gave them a feeling of anonymity—they could be anyone they wanted to be online and cybersex kept them free from HIV transmission (Ross *et al.*, 2004). The men also stated that cybersex allowed them to be more truthful about what turned them on; it was easier and less hassle than meeting someone in real life; and they were able to meet men who were more attractive than those they would meet in bars. Other research studies echo this, revealing that the looks of the person, and other qualities, do not matter as much as they would in face-to-face relationships (Wysocki, 1998)

Is cybersex considered cheating on a real-life partner? That depends on who you ask (Whitty, 2005). Oftentimes the partner of the person who is online for sexual reasons does not know the activity is taking place. It is something that is hidden and done behind closed doors, at work, or after the partner has gone to bed (Wysocki, 1998). In a recent study of 1,100 women who responded to a survey about their online sexual behavior, the younger women were about 1.5 times more likely than the older women to find sexual pleasure in viewing explicit websites. However, they were also more anxious about being caught and tried to erase their cyber-trails (Wysocki and Childers, forthcoming).

In another study, Kitzinger and Powell (1995) explored men's and women's understandings of internet infidelity. The 234 participants each wrote a story to a cue relating to internet infidelity. Although not all participants saw this as a real act of betrayal, the majority saw cybersex not only as real infidelity but as just as damaging to a relationship as a traditional offline affair. The most important finding in this study was that emotional infidelity was given as much attention as sexual infidelity. Moreover, Monica Whitty (2003) surveyed 1,117 respondents about their attitudes toward both online and offline infidelity and found that cybersex was considered *more* of an act of betrayal among her respondents.

While it is impossible to tell how many people are using the internet for cybersex, we know that it is the number-one reason why individuals go online. They use cybersex as a way to learn about other types of sexual behavior, for masturbation, and to meet people with similar ideas. The notion that it is deviant behavior is really in the eye of the beholder. It is easy to say that it is deviant, but who gets to decide what is deviant and what is not?

Computer sex addiction

Addiction is common in society. One definition of addiction is the condition of being habitually or compulsively occupied with or involved in something. We are used to hearing about people who are addicted to alcohol, drugs, shopping, and food, and addiction to cybersex is now becoming more common, too. It is also increasingly cited as a reason for divorce.

Addiction to cybersex is similar to more traditional addictions. What begins as a simple activity may soon take over the individual's life as they become powerless to control their behavior (Alcoholics Anonymous, 2002b). Sex addicts use sex as a way to cope, handle boredom, and reduce anxiety. They also use it as a means to feel important, wanted or powerful (Schneider and Weiss, 2001). As the addict becomes more involved in their sexual activities, they spend ever more time away from their face-to-face relationships, which typically causes those relationships to fail (Alcoholics Anonymous, 2002a; Schneider and Weiss, 2001; Sexaholics Anonymous, 2001). Levine (1998), whose book tells people how to participate in cybersex, warns that many of those involved in online sex are already addicted. However, she does not explain in her "how-to" book how to avoid becoming addicted yourself.

Sex Rehab with Dr. Drew (VHR, 2009) is a reality TV show in which celebrities seek guidance from Dr. Drew, a medical doctor who specializes in addictions. The celebrity talks about how their sex addiction is ruining their life and Dr. Drew works on helping them begin the long path toward recovery. What is interesting about this series is that it brings sexual addiction to the forefront and puts a face to this addiction. Many of those who participate in the show are hooked on cybersex and cyberporn. They expend considerable time and money fueling their addictions, which leads to many problems in their face-to-face lives. The celebrities often talk about sexual abuse in their past or other traumatic events that led them to sex addiction and sometimes other addictions, too (Morahan-Martin, 2005; Young, 2004, 2008).

As with other addictions, it is difficult to keep sexual activity on the internet to a minimum. Once a person starts and it becomes good, they lose sleep, do not pay their bills, and lose the emotional exclusivity they once had with their face-to-face partner (Ben-Ze'ev, 2004). This is when the behavior goes over the edge and becomes an addiction, which causes changes in the face-to-face life of the individual involved.

As we have seen, what starts as a simple curiosity with sex on the internet can turn into a full-blown addiction. This addiction, which is similar to other addictions, has the power to change the addicted person's life in many negative ways. Once they become all-consumed with internet sex, they tend to take less care with their day-to-day life, which ultimately suffers and could end up in divorce, loss of a job, or worse.

Cyberpornography

Pornography is defined as sexually explicit pictures, writing, or other material whose primary purpose is to cause sexual arousal. It is nothing new, dating all the way back to cave paintings (Stephenson, 2003), and has featured in the work of many well-known authors and artists (although sometimes such artistic endeavors are termed erotica, rather than pornography). Print and film pornography has been mass produced for decades, but the advent of the internet has caused it to be more widespread than ever. In this medium, it is known as cyberpornography.

Cyberporn is relatively inexpensive and easy to access anonymously, and it is now so ubiquitous that it has become impossible to estimate how much of it is on the internet (Berne, 2007; Elmer-Dewitt, 1995). A comprehensive research project in the mid-1990s found that men were more interested in pornography than women (Michael *et al.*, 1994). However, times have changed, and women are now looking at more pornography than ever before (personal communications with friends and students, 2009). Cyberporn not only gives both men and women sexual ideas to use with their partner but aids individuals in fantasizing while masturbating (Screenseductress, 2005).

While viewing a computer image of adults having sex poses little legal risk, being unable to determine the age of a younger couple involved in erotic behavior on the screen might prove to be legally problematic. For example, a friend's fourteen-year-old daughter took a picture of her face and breasts and sent the picture to one person at her junior high school. That person forwarded it to someone else, who sent it on to others. Before the girl in the picture was even aware it was happening, her image had been widely circulated to students in both the junior high and the high school of her small town (personal communication, 2009). The girl was suspended from school, but the first eighteen-year-old to forward her picture could well have been arrested and prosecuted in a federal court. The girl also had no rights to her own picture. Once she hit send, anyone could use it, see it, and display it.

While pornography itself is controversial because some see it as deviant behavior, this is another case when deviance is essentially in the eye of the beholder. Some researchers believe that pornography is based on the idea of morality or sexual innocence (Dworkin, 1991; McKinnon, 1996). McKinnon (1996) believes that any type of pornography both subordinates and degrades women and incites sexual harassers, wife beaters, child molesters, rapists, and clients of prostitutes. Another feminist scholar believes that it is a violation of women's civil rights and that it links sex and violence by incorporating violent domination of women as a key element of sexual fantasy and incites men to sexual violence (Dworkin, 1991).

Not all women are anti-pornography, however, and there are different types of pornography. Screenseductress (2005) states that a great deal of pornography is fake and made for the male gaze, with the end result being the "money shot," the moment of male orgasm, often all over the woman's face and breasts while she gives a look of amazing ecstasy (Grindstaff, 2002). Of course, this is not real sex. It is scripted and many people, especially women, seem to dislike it. Cybersex puts sex back into the hands of real people who are able to make the pornography they enjoy. Some tape themselves having sex and upload it to the internet. Others have sex with another person online, tape it, and replay it over and over again. These people design the sexual script that they want, rather than watch traditional pornography that might not interest them. With the exception of those who are forced to perform for the camera, many people who participate in and make cyberpornography are open to what they want, say what they want, and typically receive what they want via their computer and their own hands. This is very different from traditional pornography.

While pornography remains a controversial issue that some say is bad for women and children and leads to all sorts of deviant behavior, it can also be used positively. Those who want to use it have easy access to it via the internet, which has websites to suit each and every sexual preference. It can cause face-to-face relationships to end, or it can enhance them. It all depends on how it is used.

References

Alcoholics Anonymous (2002a). *Alcoholics Anonymous: The Story of How Many Thousands of Men and Women Have Recovered from Alcoholism*, 4th edn. New York: AA World Services.

Alcoholics Anonymous (2002b). *Twelve Steps and Twelve Traditions*. New York: AA World Services.

Ben-Ze'ev, A. (2004). Flirting On and Offline. *Convergence*, 10(1), 24–42.

Berne, E. C. (2007). *Online Pornography*. New York: Greenhaven Press.

Bright, S. (1992). *Susie Bright's Sexual Reality: A Virtual Sex World Reader*. California: Cleis Press.

Dworkin, A. (1991). *Pornography: Men Possessing Women*. New York: Plume.

Elmer-Dewitt, P. (1995). On a Screen Near You: Cyberporn. *Time Magazine*, July 3, 38–43.

Grindstaff, L. (2002). *The Money Shot: Trash, Class, and the Making of TV Talk Shows*. Chicago, IL: University of Chicago Press.

Kitzinger, C. and Powell, D. (1995). Engendering Infidelity: Essentialist and Social Constructionist Readings of a Story Completion Task. *Feminism and Psychology*, 5(3), 345–372.

Levine, D. (1998). *The Joy of Cybersex*. New York: Ballantine.

McKinnon, C. (1996). *Only Words*. Cambridge, MA: Harvard University Press.

Michael, R., Gagnon, J. H., Lauman, E., and Kolota., G. (1994). *Sex in America: A Definitive Survey*. Boston, MA: Little, Brown and Company.

Morahan-Martin, J. (2005). Internet Abuse: Addiction? Disorder? Symptom? Alternative Explanations? *Social Science Computer Review*, 23(1), 39–48.

Ross, M. W., Rosser, B. R. S., and Stanton, J. (2004). Beliefs about Cybersex and Internet-Mediated Sex of Latino Men who Have Internet Sex with Men: Relationships with Sexual Practices in Cybersex and in Real Life. *AIDS Care*, 16(8), 1002–1011.

Schneider, J. and Weiss, R. (2001). *Cybersex Exposed: Simple Fantasy or Obsession?* Center City, MN: Hazelden.

Screenseductress (2005). *Virtual Slut: I Was a Cybersex Addict*. London: Creation Books.

Sexaholics Anonymous (2001). *The Problem*. New York: Sexaholics Anonymous.

Stephenson, S. (2003). History of Sex. Retrieved from: www.slais.ubc.ca/COURSES/libr500/03-04-wt1/assignments/www/G_Abaee/history.htm.

US Census Bureau (2007). Table 1: Reported Internet Usage for Households, by Selected Householder Characteristics: 2007. *Current Population Survey*. Retrieved from: www.census.gov/population/www/socdemo/computer/2007.html.

VHR (2009). *Sex Rehab with Dr. Drew*. Retrieved from: www.vh1.com/video/browse/index.jhtml?id=sex_rehab_with_dr_drew.

Whitty, M. T. (2003). Cyber-Flirting: Playing at Love on the Internet. *Theory Psychology*, 13(3), 339–357.

Whitty, M. T. (2005). The Realness of Cybercheating: Men's and Women's Representations of Unfaithful Internet Relationships. *Social Science Computer Review*, 23(1), 57–67.

Whitty, M. and Carr, A. (2006). *Cyberspace Romance: The Psychology of Online Relationships*. New York: Palgrave.

Wysocki, D. K. (1998). Let Your Fingers Do the Talking: Sex on an Adult Chat-Line. *Sexualities*, 1(4), 425–452.

Wysocki, D. K. and Childers, C. (Forthcoming). "Let My Fingers Do the Talking": Sexting and Infidelity in Cyberspace. *Sexuality and Culture*.

Wysocki, D. K. and Thalken, J. (2007). Whips and Chains? Fact or Fiction? Content Analysis of Sadomasochism in Internet Personal Advertisements. In M. T. Whitty, A. J. Baker, and J. A. Inman (eds.) *Online Matchmaking* (pp. 178–196). New York: Palgrave.

Young, K. S. (2004). Internet Addiction: A New Clinical Phenomenon and Its Consequences. *American Behavioral Scientist*, 48(4), 402–415.

Young, K. S. (2008). Internet Sex Addiction: Risk Factors, Stages of Development, and Treatment. *American Behavioral Scientist*, 52(1), 21–37.

Part VII

Self-destructive behavior as deviance

Overview

Much deviant behavior can be considered antisocial in that it victimizes others or harms society in general. Some forms of deviance, however, effectively victimize the perpetrator him- or herself. This part examines and analyzes several such modes of deviant behavior.

The chapters begin with explorations of alcohol abuse and alcoholism, and drug use, abuse, and addiction. Individuals may consume alcohol and drugs for a number of reasons, including psychological support, being constituent to some patterns of social recreation, and/or for personal pleasure. Alcohol and drugs are seldom viewed as self-destructive by the users, but because they are addictive, their use can become habitual and harmful. Their continued use can lead to loss of control, which may result in dangerous behavior and harm to self and others, as well as serious health problems and even death. Such use can also become a factor in the commission of other types of deviant behavior and crime.

The next chapter addresses eating disorders, which do not represent consumption but rather non-consumption behaviors. The resulting disorders, such as anorexia nervosa and bulimia nervosa, can cause serious physical and psychological problems, and in some instances such food and nutrient denial may lead to the death of the victim.

The next chapter explores cutting, piercing, and self-mutilation. Such behavior varies from culture to culture. Some such behavior may be viewed as a benign statement of social fashion, but more realistically it must be seen as dangerous and pathological as it is patently self-destructive and deviant.

The final chapter in this part discusses suicide as the ultimate mode of self-destructive behavior. It resolves personal problems with absolute finality. The cultures of almost all societies are life affirming and have norms that discourage, denigrate, and prohibit suicide. Committing suicide therefore becomes the consummate defiance of cultural norms and values, and, as such, is deviant behavior of heroic scale.

Alcoholism and alcohol abuse

The consumption of alcoholic beverages plays a significant role in the patterns of everyday life in many societies, and this has been the case throughout history. Alcohol fulfills a number of personal and social functions in social life and possesses numerous benefits. At the same time, its consumption can be quite dysfunctional at both the personal and the societal levels, and it creates numerous social problems, ranging from drunk driving, to domestic violence, to extensive health problems. At the personal level, alcohol use and its potential harm can sometimes be conceptualized as self-destructive behavior and deviance.

David Allen addresses heavy alcohol consumption as a self-destructive practice and points out that approximately 7 percent of the American population abuse alcohol; 85,000 people die each year as a result. Drinking in an abusive fashion costs the US taxpayer $185 billion each year.

The use of alcohol has historically been very controversial, and the practice of abusive drinking has had many social meanings. The National Institute on Alcohol Abuse and Alcoholism indicates that alcoholism (or alcohol dependence) has four symptoms: physical dependence, tolerance, craving, and an inability to stop once drinking has begun. The American Psychiatric Association, in its *Diagnostic and Statistical Manual of Mental Disorders* (*DSM*), conceptualizes alcohol problems as medical problems. The *DSM* makes a distinction between alcohol dependence and alcohol abuse. The former is demonstrated by loss of control and possibly physical dependence, and is a chronic condition. The latter is not chronic but is a "bad habit," medically speaking.

Allen reveals that in the colonial era, alcohol consumption per person was several times greater than it is today, and even drunkenness "was for the most part tolerated,." By the late 18th century, some physicians viewed alcoholism not as evil but as pathological. The drunk was deemed "incapable of control." Later, the Temperance Movement saw alcoholism as a disease, but contended that even moderate drinkers would fall into "its grip." Abstinence was the only way for "the inebriate to return to normal." By the late 19th century, the Temperance Movement had become quite militant and sought to solve drinking through coercion. After the First World War, the nation was pushed into national Prohibition. However, by the time of Franklin Roosevelt's inauguration in 1933, public sentiment had changed and Prohibition was soon repealed.

Alcoholics Anonymous was founded in 1935 and asserted that many people had a "defect" that made it impossible for them to drink moderately. According to AA, "the alcoholic must come to the realization that his/her life is unmanageable and turn it over to a higher power." It advanced the "Twelve-Step Program," a complex, long-term process of rehabilitation. Allen engages in an extensive examination of this process and the emergence of various other models to treat alcohol problems.

More recently, the disease concept of alcoholism gained new popularity, although the medicalization notion has met criticism from some scholars. Allen reports that after "the decoding of the human genome," there was a move toward genetic studies in regard to alcohol problems. He discusses new studies examining possible links between child abuse and neglect and alcohol problems, and the link between having an alcoholic parent and alcohol dependence. College binge drinking has also generated significant research interest recently. Allen concludes by reporting that there was a downward trend in alcohol dependence between 1992 and 2002, but an increase in alcohol abuse. He interprets this as an indication "that more heavy drinkers are encountering interpersonal conflicts or legal troubles."

Drug use, abuse, and addiction

Stephen Bahr, in his chapter, provides an overview of drug use and abuse in the United States. He reports that public concern about drugs dates back to the late 19th century, when various state and local ordinances were passed to limit commerce in opium, marijuana, and cocaine. He also points out that the Eighteenth Amendment of the United States Constitution prohibited the sale of alcohol from 1920 to 1933. Many laws were designed to limit and control the distribution and sale of drugs. Bahr suggests that perhaps the most significant single event in research on drug use and abuse was the creation of the US National Institute on Drug Abuse (NIDA) in 1973. Prior to the creation of the NIDA, drug prevention efforts had focused on reducing the supply of drugs. The NIDA sought to generate a knowledge base on the use and abuse of drugs that would contribute to reducing drug demand. This resulted in a large amount of research that addressed trends, epidemiology, addiction, and treatment of drug abuse.

This research included a number of national surveys and longitudinal studies on drug use and abuse. Bahr reviews various drug use and abuse rates and trends, and reports that in 2008, 8 percent of Americans aged twelve and over had used an illicit drug during the past month. He also indicates that although large numbers of adolescents and young adults still use drugs, this practice (particularly the use of cocaine) has declined in recent years. The US federal government spent a total of $14.8 billion on drug prevention, drug treatment, and law enforcement and intervention to control the supply of drugs in 2008. Drug use and abuse are quite prevalent among individuals who are involved in the criminal justice system, with 73 percent of US prison inmates admitting that they used drugs regularly prior to their incarceration.

Bahr defines drug addiction as a "compulsion to take a drug that results in a loss of control regarding the amount consumed." Some scholars use the phrase "substance dependence" rather than "addiction" and apply this diagnosis when there is a pattern of use that results in impairment or distress.

Bahr examines the motivation for drug use and suggests that there are six broad reasons for such behavior: because friends or acquaintances are using drugs; because it is enjoyable; to relieve stress or block physical or emotional pain; to improve performance; to make a statement, be different, or rebel; and curiosity. Although there are a number of explanations for why individuals use and abuse drugs, Bahr asserts that five theories are particularly useful in increasing understanding of drug use and abuse. These theories include: social learning theory, social control theory, strain theory, the social development model theory, and neuro-biological theory. He then defines and explains the dynamics of these theories in terms of their bearing on drug use and misuse.

Bahr concludes his chapter with a review and examination of prevention and treatment programs. He believes that three treatment programs are particularly effective in dealing with drug use and abuse: cognitive-behavioral, therapeutic community, and drug courts. He then goes on to describe the dynamics of these treatment programs and notes that "aftercare tends to increase program effectiveness."

Eating disorders as deviance

In their chapter, Diane Taub and Penelope McLorg note that the concept of deviance is related to an individual's attitude, behavior, and/or physicality, and eating disorders encompass all three. Eating disorders related to food consumption or non-consumption include anorexia nervosa (self-starvation) and bulimia nervosa (binge–purge syndrome). Both disorders derive from a fear of fatness and a distorted self-body image, or an exaggerated sense of being fat. Anorexics seek to reduce their weight by minimizing food intake, excessive exercising, self-induced vomiting, and misuse of laxatives, diuretics, or enemas. Bulimics engage in binge eating and self-induced purging, use of ipecac, and excessive use of laxatives and enemas. They tend to maintain near normal weight.

Taub and McLorg point out that eating disorders do not occur randomly in the population: some 90% of those with eating disorders are female, of whom most are young (in adolescence or young adulthood) and white. Larger bodies are more accepted among African Americans, whereas slim bodies are the cultural norm among white females, and are regarded as the most beautiful body type. Young white females internalize the thinness norm and seek to avoid fatness by dieting and exercise. The age periods of adolescence and young adulthood are very important "in the development of a female's identity and self-image." Taub and McLorg also suggest that these periods are "times in which peer-group influences are notable, with appearance norms keenly felt."

In contemporary society, the ideal of female slimness is pervasive and enforced by the mass media and advertising for all kinds of products that often feature young, slim females. Taub and McLorg also indicate that traditional female role models, such as television and movie stars, fashion models, and beauty contestants, are almost always thin. Losing weight is a major theme in books, periodical articles, television advertising, and gyms and spas. Anorexia and bulimia are simply deviant responses to the cultural norms that mandate dieting and achieving slimness.

Taub and McLorg report that specific social contexts may encourage eating disorders. As an example, they suggest that participation in certain organized sports, such as figure-skating, diving, cross-country running, swimming, and gymnastics, may heighten female vulnerability to anorexia and bulimia. This is the result of the belief that extra weight may slow movement and hinder performance in athletes. While most deviants are viewed as nonconformist, those who engage in disordered eating may be seen as social conformists because they participate in organized sports that are socially approved and valued.

Like some other forms of deviance, eating disorders have been highly medicalized. Anorexia and bulimia are viewed as illnesses or diseases that require intervention and control by qualified medical personnel. In many instances, the medicalized perspective has tended to ignore the cultural and societal causes and contexts of eating disorders.

The authors suggest that the prognosis of eating disorders lies in the cultural norms of female body shape and idealized standards of beauty, and the social pressures to achieve and maintain slimness. Initially, individuals with eating disorders may not consider themselves deviant, but once they have been labeled as "anorexic" or "bulimic" they may well internalize these labels and develop a deviant self-concept and identity. This new identity may then become a master status.

Taub and McLorg conclude their chapter with a detailed examination of the stigma of eating disorders and the management of this stigma. They end with the observation that "anorexia nervosa and bulimia nervosa are maintained by the visual objectification of females, the powerful medical complex, and the pervasive mass media that endorse a cult of thinness for females."

Cutting, piercing, and self-mutilation

In his chapter, Jimmy Taylor addresses the broad category of self-injury-related deviant behavior, explores its parameters, provides an overview of the separate bodies of research dedicated to the various modes of self-injury, and offers a variety of explanations in regard to motivations for self-injury. He asserts that the "social and private worlds of self-injurers" have remained "elusive and shrouded in mystery" as a research topic within the social sciences.

However, a plethora of recent research literature on the topic has solved much of the mystery by revealing a wide range of reasons for such behavior.

This research suggests that approximately 4 percent of adults and 23 percent of adolescents practice some form of self-injury. Such practices are most common among adolescent and early adult women, but in recent years there has been an increase in reported cases of self-injury among teenage boys and young adult males.

Taylor reveals that the majority of the self-injury literature derives from medical and psychiatric research. There was some debate among scholars regarding the most appropriate label for behavior of this type, but the name "self-injury" seemed to be the least judgmental. He points out that Emile Durkheim posited that marking the body is a means of expression and shared meaning. Accordingly, it plays an integrating role in the sense that distinctive body marking allowed members of a common culture to recognize each other as kindred. Contemporary scholars speak more of the body serving as an artistic canvas for sending messages. This process is facilitated by "the rapid interpretation and reinterpretation of the 'normal' body, based in part on constantly updated and highly circulated popular media images."

Taylor briefly discusses female genital mutilation as practiced in many societies in Africa and the Near East. This type of mutilation is culturally mandated and not volitional or self-inflicted, but it has been included because young girls willingly submit to it.

There is a much lengthier discussion of the practice of cutting. Taylor differentiates between cutters who are characterized as "individual deviants" and those who are characterized as "loner deviants." The former have personally acquired the skills for self-mutilation by themselves and for themselves. Such deviants may, however, have a support network, and may commit their acts of deviance in the presence of subcultural supporters. The latter dwell in isolation, without social networks. They commit their deviant mutilation without training, assistance, or support from others.

Some scholars have asserted that all cutters are essentially practicing for their own suicide, but others challenge this and view cutting as an act of renewal and restoration.

Taylor devotes the final part of his chapter to a discussion of body piercing. This practice is controversial and contentious, with some seeing it as deviant, "highly dangerous, and pathological," while others view it as a "seemingly harmless peer-group fashion statement."

Taylor urges scholars to de-stigmatize self-injury, which would make it easier for self-injurers to find help. He speaks of the need for more research and especially "nationally representative and international comparative, longitudinal studies, as well as critical ethnographies."

Suicide as deviant behavior

Suicide is the ultimate act of self-destruction, and in his chapter Steven Stack examines the parameters of suicidal behavior. He defines suicide "as the willful taking of one's own life," and reports that there were 877,000 cases of suicide worldwide in 2002. In 2005, in the US alone, 32,657 people committed suicide, making it the eleventh most common cause of death in the country. It is believed that there are 225 attempted suicides for every completed suicide.

In general, the public is more fearful of being killed by someone else than dying through suicide. This fear is misguided, as the annual suicide rate for the period 2003–2005 was 11 per 100,000 population, almost double the homicide rate of 6 per 100,000.

A number of demographic factors have a bearing on suicide rates. One of these is age. The elderly have the highest suicide rate of all age categories, although this has been declining in recent years. At the same time, the suicide rate for the "heart of the boomer cohort (ages 45–50) . . . has been increasing." Stack suggests that financial support (state assistance for medical bills, pensions, and so on) may decrease in the future and this may result in a significant increase in both the absolute number and the rate of elderly suicide, in the US and elsewhere. Another important demographic factor is gender. The suicide rate for men is approximately four times greater than that for women. Meanwhile, the official suicide rate for blacks is less than half of that for whites.

Many risk and protective factors also contribute to variable suicide rates. Stack discusses a number of psychiatric factors that may contribute to suicide, such as severe depression, anxiety disorders, panic disorders, recurrent hallucinations, schizophrenia, and substance abuse. He reports that there are also numerous sociological factors that have a bearing on suicide rates, such as marriage, which increases meaning in life, promotes integration, and helps protect against suicide (whereas divorce increases suicide risk). Cohabiting couples have a higher risk of suicide than married couples, but less suicide risk than individuals who live alone. Parenthood is another protective factor. Having children can increase one's sense of responsibility to others and provide a purpose in life. Accordingly, parenthood is a protective factor. Economic strain (low income) and unemployment both increase the risk of suicide. The unemployed have a suicide rate that is at least double that of the general population. The mass media, in some instances, may also increase the risk of suicide. Movies, news stories, and books about suicide may "suggest that suicide is a solution to various problems of living."

Stack concludes his chapter with a discussion of treatment and social policy. Various solutions to suicide have included "control of opportunity for suicide (gun control), prevention programs that feature education in schools and media campaigns, talk therapies . . . and pharmacological treatments, such as lithium and anti-depressants."

33

Alcoholism and alcohol abuse

David Allen

Alcoholism is a contributor to a wide range of illnesses, including cirrhosis of the liver, hepatitis, and several immune disorders. According to the National Institute on Alcohol Abuse and Alcoholism (NIAAA, 2000), approximately 7 percent of the American population drinks in an abusive or dependent manner, costing $185 billion and killing 85,000 people each year. While the number of alcoholics was estimated at 100,000 in 1940 and a million in 1946, in the 1980s the number quoted was 15 million, and it had reached 18.7 million by 2007 (Peele, 1989:238; Lemonick, 2007:44).

Definitions

In many countries, alcohol and its uses have a history of great controversy. Alcoholism and other terms denoting the socially undesirable or harmful use of alcohol have played a part in the unfolding of numerous political, moral, social, and intellectual issues. Understanding of these terms is very much tied to the interests, prejudices, and goals of those using them. As social processes, naming and identifying alcohol problems and those having alcohol problems have generated considerable interest. When the term "alcoholism" is used in conversation, it may convey a variety of meanings ranging from drunkenness to disability.

The NIAAA states that alcoholism (or alcohol dependence) consists of four symptoms: craving, inability to stop once drinking has begun, physical dependence (withdrawal symptoms), and tolerance. Other definitions are less specific and often do not include physical dependence.

The standard reference for objective characterization of alcohol dependence and alcohol abuse is contained in the *Diagnostic and Statistical Manual of Mental Disorders* (*DSM*) of the American Psychiatric Association (1994). The *DSM* has grown in size as the process of medicalization has continued. It has come to serve as the sole vehicle for making insurance claims and so has acquired considerable power. Because the *DSM* does not specify the causes of alcohol dependence, physicians and treatment personnel are free to supply their own. This is by design, as adherents to different frames of reference on these and other designated disorders are able to use the *DSM* as a tool. *DSM* designations are developed by committees with representatives of various constituencies. This process gives the American Psychiatric Association considerable control over the framing of the various conditions. It institutionalizes the position that alcohol problems are medical conditions.

Recent editions of the manual have done away with definitions in favor of listing a series of possible symptoms for psychiatric disorders and indicating *how many* of these symptoms must be manifested for a diagnosis to be made. A diagnosis of substance dependence specifies that the subject must display a "maladaptive pattern" of behavior over a period of twelve months and must manifest at least three of seven listed symptoms: tolerance; withdrawal; frequent inability to control the quantity consumed; a persistent desire or unsuccessful attempts to quit or moderate; spending inordinate amount of time acquiring, consuming, or recovering; giving up important activities; and continued use despite knowledge of harm being done. Thus, alcohol dependence may take a variety of forms and may or may not involve physical dependence, loss of job or family, and so on.

The current (fourth) edition of the *DSM* makes a distinction between dependence and abuse. The latter is "a maladaptive pattern of substance use" involving one or more of the following: failure to fulfill major obligations; recurrent use in dangerous situations; recurrent legal problems; and continuing use despite recurrent social or interpersonal problems. Moreover, the diagnosis of abuse indicates that the subject does not meet the criteria of substance dependence. While both dependence and abuse are medical conditions, and qualitatively different from heavy drinking, alcohol dependence is regarded as a chronic condition while alcohol abuse is not, at least beyond the term of twelve months. Abuse is a bad habit, while dependence is shown by the loss of control and, possibly, physical dependence.

The World Health Organization (1992) has developed a similar system of classification of drinking problems called *The ICD-10 Classification of Mental and Behavioural Disorders*. It uses the term "harmful use" instead of "abuse" and expressly acknowledges that uses that are sanctioned in some societies may not be considered harmful in others.

Historical considerations

The view of alcoholism as a progressive illness has quite a long history in the United States. In the colonial era, however, drunkenness—even habitual drunkenness—was for the most part tolerated. Alcohol consumption per capita was several times what it is today and increased well into the 19th century (Lender and Martin, 1982:205). Habitual drunkards were from time to time treated negatively and some received corporal punishment (Lender, 1973), but it was thought that they were addicted to drunkenness, not to liquor. Nor was the drunk viewed as drinking compulsively. To the extent that they were condemned, it was for their *love* of drink (Levine, 1978:147–151).

Late in the 18th century, physicians began to put forth the view that many behaviors were not evil but pathological. Habitual drunkenness, in this view, was beyond the control of the drunk. Rather than desiring to be drunk, the subject was incapable of control. To Dr. Benjamin Rush (1823 [1784]), the drinker of ardent spirits was at risk of losing control over drinking, resulting in misery, destructiveness, and poverty. This view of alcoholism was picked up by various religious groups, who took up the issue of drunkenness with considerable vigor and to significant effect. By 1830, the consumption of alcohol had dropped by at least half, and a significant movement was in the ascendancy.

For the Temperance Movement, the cause of inebriety was alcohol, especially in its distilled forms. Anyone who drank ran the risk of falling into its grip. Following Rush, this desire was often referred to as a disease. Avoiding it required abstinence, and abstinence was the only way for the inebriate to return to normal because moderate drinkers would eventually find themselves unable to resist. (Today they would be considered to be "in denial.") Strangely enough, moderate drinkers were often treated worse than drunks (Levine, 1978:159). Many temperance organizations took on a fraternal form, structured to help each other avoid drink and help drinkers reform.

In the late 19th century the Temperance Movement lost its benevolent and fraternal aspects as the Anti-Saloon League and the Prohibition Party attempted to solve the drinking problem by means of coercion (Gusfield, 1963). Prohibition was seen as a way to end many social ills, especially those associated with cities. This also resulted in the production of the drunk as skid row bum (Lender and Martin, 1982:103) and the movement lost most of its benevolent aspects. US entry into the First World War and the ensuing anti-German frenzy provided the final push for national Prohibition (Lender and Martin, 1982:129). During the 1920s, alcohol consumption declined, but smuggling and political corruption flourished. By 1930, however, enthusiasm for Prohibition had waned in the wake of some successful urban reform, the loss of insularity in the aftermath of First World War, and finally the beginning of the Great Depression (Lender and Martin, 1982:150). It was repealed shortly after Franklin Roosevelt's inauguration in 1933.

The Twelve-Step Program

It was not until 1935 and the founding of Alcoholics Anonymous that a new, more coherent view of alcoholism emerged (Levine, 1978:162). This organization holds the view that a minority of the population has a defect—the early movement referred to it as an allergy—that makes it impossible for them to drink moderately. It rejects the idea that alcoholism is caused by—or does itself constitute—mental illness. The alcoholic must come to the realization that his/her life is unmanageable and turn it over to a higher power. (AA rejects the notion that it is a religious organization, preferring the word "spiritual," but this claim is the subject of debate (Peele *et al.*, 2000).) This is the beginning of a long-term process of "working the steps," by attending meetings, praying, acquiring a "sponsor," and carrying AA's message to the outside world. The AA member must make an inventory of his/her faults, confess them, ask God to remove them, make amends to those who have been wronged, and continue this process of social and meditative modification of the self. The member thus submits to the will of a higher power as mediated by intense group interaction (O'Halloran, 2008).

AA has been, and still is, an inward-looking organization. In its own principles, it refuses affiliation with any other creed or religion. It does not specify the nature of the higher power and therefore isn't easily identified with Christianity. It does not actually define alcoholism, but uses statements that begin with something like "We have found . . ." or "We admitted . . ." It considers itself open and willing to help anyone who needs help. It has very little organizational structure or hierarchy. It does not own buildings, preferring to borrow space from community and religious organizations to hold its meetings. This means that it has avoided the dilemmas of stratification between layperson and professional and the necessity of raising large amounts of money faced by many successful movements and organizations. The local autonomy of AA meetings has allowed it to spread to different racial and ethnic groups and to many other countries, where its activities may be modified in order to suit the local culture (Makela *et al.*, 1996). AA does not have a strong public presence and cannot be considered an active player in the medicalization movement. Nevertheless, its humility, its resonance with the popular American theme of the repentant sinner, and its reputation for bringing about major changes in many people, coupled with the fact that it has never attempted to stop the rest of the population from drinking, have given it a favorable reputation. Its perceived heroism has formed the backdrop for a much more active and assertive alcoholism movement.

The post-Prohibition decades saw a considerable interest in science. The Yale Center for Alcohol Studies, set up in 1940, soon came under the leadership of E. M. Jellinek, whose work and summer seminars are probably responsible for the slogan "alcoholism is a disease" (Schneider, 1978:365). Jellinek's research gave scientific credibility to the disease view. In 1960 he published *The Disease Concept of Alcoholism*, in which he interviewed about a hundred members of AA and discovered that the disease progresses through a series of stages. The activities of the center gave rise to the National Council on Alcoholism (NCA; now the National Council on Alcoholism and Drug Dependence), founded by Marty Mann, a former member of AA who also funded the Jellinek survey. It saw its mission as supplanting the work of AA by educating the public about what it considered the nature of alcoholism. The inward message and meaning of AA was translated into an outward-facing propaganda campaign now phrased in terms the public could readily understand: alcoholics are sick people and worthy of being helped. The NCA and the Yale Center provided the impetus for the founding of the National Institute on Alcohol Abuse and Alcoholism. The endorsement by the American Medical Association in 1956 of the proposition that alcoholism is a disease, along with the growth of medical insurance in subsequent decades, provided the financial basis for a large for-profit treatment industry. Careers and financing by both public and private sources have thus come to give institutional status to the disease concept.

The work of Jellinek and the promise of applying science to the treatment of alcohol problems led to considerable popularity of this model. In the United States, residential treatment programs increased in number throughout the 1980s. The Minnesota Model, combining medical care with AA meetings, group therapy, and individual counseling, became the dominant treatment model. Many hospitals, having overbuilt, developed substance treatment facilities or leased space to treatment programs (Weisner and Room, 1984). Subsequent decades have seen a decrease in the use of residential treatment (Schmidt *et al.*, 1984) as well as a shortening of the typical stay in a residential facility. This has occurred for reasons of economy—insurance policies have become less generous—and as a consequence of findings that question the contention that residential programs are more effective than other modalities. The American system of treatment and trends in treatment strategies are very different from those in other countries, and treatment strategies vary considerably from one nation to the next (see Klingemann *et al.*, 1992).

This instilling of an alcoholic identity—albeit that of a *recovering* alcoholic—has been criticized on a number of fronts. Fingarette (1988) prefers the term "heavy drinking," which can take a number of forms, allows drinkers to seek help sooner, and does not impose a dogmatic program of recovery. Peele (1989) sees the alcoholic identity as a sort of self-fulfilling prophecy: when abstinent alcoholics are told that they can never drink again, they are more likely to see any relapse as a complete loss of control and are less able to maintain a sense of perspective once they do begin drinking. In a study of "naturally recovering" alcohol and drug addicts, Granfield and Cloud (2008) found that former addicts who quit without the assistance of formal treatment or participation in self-help groups hold a generally negative opinion of such groups (i.e. AA) and treatment programs. They tend to feel that their recovery has been due to their finding other meaningful activities and goals—work, family, and so on—and *marginalizing* their addicted selves. They feel that self-help groups retard the process of moving on in life by making alcoholism a salient component of the self.

Most sociological theories of deviance do not specifically make reference to addiction or distinguish between heavy use and harmful use. However, Peele (1985) develops what he calls a "life process" model of addiction. It contains components of strain, self-control, and social learning models. He advocates the idea that people become addicted to experiences rather than to drugs. Potential addicts receive messages and develop beliefs which facilitate the development of addiction. These include such early experiences as abuse and neglect (strain), which instill the message that life is unpleasant and uncomfortable; the "simplification of experience," or the message that one should not work hard to achieve pleasurable experiences (self-control theory, which would root this inability to defer gratification in faulty parenting rather than differential association); and the belief that drug or alcohol use is an effective and easy way to bring about desired feelings (social learning). This model situates addiction in the world of typical life experience and maintains that positive nondrug experiences and the acquisition of personal goals and a sense of self-efficacy both protect against and effect recovery from addiction.

Constructionist sociologists have been critical of the trend toward medicalization (Conrad, 1992, 2007). However, it has been pointed out (Appleton, 1995) that alcoholism—especially viewed from an AA perspective—is not medicalized in the sense of being under the control of physicians. Medical students seldom study alcoholism and most treatment modalities make little or no use of physicians. Rather, Appleton suggests, this view of alcoholism is holistic in nature; it is a disease of body, mind, and spirit and requires a treatment approach involving all three. Treatment based on the Twelve-Step Program has continued to be the dominant modality in America, even though more supportive and more scientific methods have been found to be as successful. The adoption of more thoroughly scientific modes of treatment has been inhibited by a persistence of moralistic discourse and entrenched biases in the training of treatment professionals (Quinn et al., 2004).

It must be noted, though, that the disease concept of alcoholism is no longer confined to AA and other Twelve-Step treatment programs. Research funding, the decoding of the human genome, brain imaging, and psychopharmacology have produced a more truly medicalized discourse which has, in many ways, bypassed the Twelve-Step movement. Genetic typing has brought about inconsistent results, but this has not led to a loss of faith on the part of either scientists or funding agencies. In fact, federal funding of research and support of access to databases have tilted away from social science and toward genetic studies (Duster, 2006). Addiction is seen as a *brain disease* (Leshner 1997), best treated by a combination of therapy (whatever works) and medication. While this viewpoint has not yet come to dominate the treatment field, we should, perhaps, think of two disease models—hard and soft.

Abuse and violence: recent research

Having alcoholic parents, as well as suffering abuse and neglect as a child, has often been found to correlate with alcohol dependence and abuse in adulthood. It has also been found that the experience of abuse "may delay or prevent normal maturation out of problematic alcohol use" (Widom et al., 2007:319). The relation between past abuse and problematic drinking extends into middle age among women.

Alcohol consumption has been found to be connected with practically every form of violence and is seen as a direct cause of violence, a component of unstructured and potentially violent social settings, and an excuse for violent conduct. It has also been found to be associated with violent conduct among gang members, both as a precursor to intra-gang confrontations and as an "enabling mechanism" in the minds of gang members (Hunt and Laidler, 2001).

Trends in prevalence

While there has been much recent concern over the phenomenon of binge drinking among the underage population, survey statistics fail to bear out the claim that this has increased in recent years. One survey (Monitoring the Future, 2009) shows a moderate decline since 2000 in annual prevalence of "being drunk" among twelfth-graders. College binge drinking has remained steady in spite of education and prevention efforts by colleges and universities (Johnston et al., 2007).

There have also been slight increases in both abstinence and "frequent" binge drinking (the latter increased from 20 percent to 22 percent between 1993 and 2001 (Wechsler *et al.*, 2002). Even colleges and universities that participated in a special program to decrease heavy drinking showed no evidence of a decline from 1993 to 2005. However, while efforts at diminishing bingeing have achieved little success (Nelson *et al.*, 2009), there is no evidence of an epidemic.

Downward trends have also been noted in heavy drinking and in the prevalence of consuming more than five drinks in the last month in the general population (Grant *et al.*, 2004:232). Interestingly, there was a downward trend in alcohol dependence between 1992 and 2002 but an increase in alcohol abuse (as defined by the *DSM*). The latter finding is particularly striking since it suggests that more heavy drinkers are encountering interpersonal conflicts or legal troubles.

References

American Psychiatric Association (1994) *Diagnostic and Statistical Manual of Mental Disorders*, 4th edn. Washington, DC: American Psychiatric Association.

Conrad, P. (1992) "Medicalization and social control." *Annual Review of Sociology* 18:209–232.

Appleton, L. (1995) "Rethinking medicalization: alcoholism and anomalies." In J. Best (ed.) *Images of Issues: Typifying Contemporary Social Problems*, 2nd edn (pp. 59–80). Piscataway, NJ: Aldine.

Conrad, P. (2007) *The Medicalization of Society: On the Transformation of Human Conditions into Treatable Disorders*. Baltimore, MD: Johns Hopkins University Press.

Denzin, N. (1993) *The Alcoholic Society: Addiction and Recovery of the Self*. New Brunswick, NJ: Transaction.

Duster, T. (2006) "Comparative perspectives and competing explanations: taking on the newly configured reductionist challenge to sociology." *American Sociological Review* 71:1–15.

Fingarette, H. (1988) *Heavy Drinking: The Myth of Alcoholism as a Disease*. Berkeley: University of California Press.

Granfield, R. and Cloud, W. (2008) "The elephant that no one sees: natural recovery among middle-class addicts." In J. Inciardi and K. MacElrath (eds.) *The American Drug Scene: An Anthology*, 5th edn (pp. 440–451). New York and Oxford: Oxford University Press.

Grant, B., Dawson, D., Stinson, F., Chou, S., Dufour, M., and Pickering, R. (2004) "The 12-month prevalence and trends in DSM-IV alcohol abuse and dependence: United States, 1991–1992 and 2001–2002." *Drug and Alcohol Dependence* 74:223–234.

Gusfield, J. (1963) *Symbolic Crusade: Status Politics and the American Temperance Movement*. Urbana: University of Illinois Press.

Hunt, G. and Laidler, K. (2001) "Alcohol and violence in the lives of gang members." *Alcohol Research and Health* 25(1):66–71.

Jellinek, E. (1960) *The Disease Concept of Alcoholism*. Highland Park, NJ: Hillhouse.

Johnston, L., O'Malley, P., Bachman, J., and Schulenberg, J. (2007) *Monitoring the Future: National Survey Results on Adolescent Drug Use: Overview of Key Findings*. Bethesda, MD: National Institute on Drug Abuse.

Klingemann, H., Takala, J., and Hunt, G. (eds.) (1992) *Cure, Care, or Control: Alcohol Treatment in Sixteen Countries*. Albany: State University of New York Press.

Lemonick, M. (2007) "The science of addiction." *Time*, July 18.

Lender, M. (1973) "Drunkenness as an offense in early New England: a study of Puritan attitudes." *Quarterly Journal of Studies on Alcohol* 34:353–366.

Lender, M. and Martin, J. (1982) *Drinking in America: A History*, rev. edn. New York: The Free Press.

Leshner, A. (1997) "Addiction is a brain disease—and it matters." *Science* 278(5335): 45–47.

Levine, G. (1978) "The discovery of addiction: changing conceptions of habitual drunkenness in America." *Journal of Studies on Alcohol* 39(1):493–506.

Makela, K., Arminen, I., Bloomfield, I., Eisenback-Stangl, K., Bergmark, N., Kurube, N., Mariolini, H., Olafsdottir, J., Peterson, M., Phillips, J., Rehm, R., Room, P., Rosenqvist, H., Rosovsky, K., Stenius, G., Swiatkiewicz, B., Woronowicz, P., and Zielinski, A. (1996) *Alcoholics Anonymous as a Mutual-Help Movement: A Study in Eight Societies*. Madison: University of Wisconsin Press.

Monitoring the Future (2009) Survey. Available at: www.monitoringthefuture.org/data/08data.html.

National Institute on Alcohol Abuse and Alcohol Dependence (2000) *Alcohol and Health: Tenth Special Report to the US Congress*. Rockville, MD. NIAAA.

Nelson, T., Ziming, X., Lee, H., Weitzman, E., and Wechsler, H. (2009) "Persistence of heavy drinking and ensuing consequences at heavy drinking colleges." *Journal of Studies of Alcohol and Drugs* 70:726–734.

O'Halloran, S. (2008) *Talking Oneself Sober: The Discourse of Alcoholics Anonymous*. Amherst, NY: Cambria Press.

Peele, S. (1985) *The Meaning of Addiction: Compulsive Experience and Its Interpretation*. Lexington, MA: Heath.

Peele, S. (1989) *The Diseasing of America: Addiction Treatment out of Control*. Lexington, MA: Lexington Books.

Peele, S., Bufe, C., Brodsky, A., Horvath, T. (2000) *Resisting 12-Step Coercion: How to Fight Forced participation in AA, NA, or 12-Step Treatment*. Tucson, AZ: See Sharp Press.

Quinn, J., Bodenhamer-David, E., and Koch, D. (2004) "Ideology and the stagnation of AODA treatment modalities in America." *Deviant Behavior* 25:109–131.

Rush, B. (1823 [1784]) *An Inquiry into the Effects of Ardent Spirits upon the Human Body and Mind, with an Account of the Means of Preventing and the Remedies for Curing Them*. Boston, MA: James Loring.

Schmidt, L., Weisner, C., and Wiley, J. (1984) "Substance abuse and the course of welfare dependency." *American Journal of Public Health* 88(11):1616–1622.

Schneider, J. (1978) "Deviant drinking as disease: alcoholism as a social accomplishment." *Social Problems* 25(4):361–372.

Valverde, M. (1998) *Diseases of the Will: Alcohol and the Dilemmas of Freedom*. Cambridge: Cambridge University Press.

Wechsler., H, Lee, J. E., Kuo, M., Seibring, M., Nelson, T. F., and Lee, H. (2002) "Trends in college binge drinking during a period of increased prevention efforts: findings from 4 Harvard School of Public Health college alcohol study surveys: 1993–2001." *Journal of American College Health* 50(5):203–217.

Weisner, C. and Room, R. (1984) "Financing and ideology in alcohol treatment." *Social Problems* 32(2):167–184.

Widom, C., White, H., Czaja, S., and Marmorstein, N. (2007) "Long-term effects of child abuse and neglect on alcohol use and excessive drinking in middle adulthood." *Journal of Studies on Alcohol and Drugs* 68(3):317–326.

World Health Organization (1992) *The ICD-10 Classification of Mental and Behavioural Disorders: Clinical Descriptions and Diagnostic Guidelines*, 10th edn. Geneva: World Health Organization.

34

Drug use, abuse, and addiction

Stephen J. Bahr

Introduction

The purpose of this chapter is to provide an overview of scholarly research on drug use, abuse, and addiction. I begin with a brief historical review of the field followed by a summary of rates and trends of drug use in the US. This is followed by a definition of addiction, a summary of why people take drugs, and a review of research on prevention and treatment.

For more than a century there has been concern about drug abuse in the United States. In the late 19th century state and local ordinances were passed to limit commerce in cocaine, marijuana, and opium (Gray 2001). From 1920 to 1933 the sale of alcohol was prohibited by the Eighteenth Amendment of the United States. Since the Second World War, numerous laws have been passed to control and limit the sale and distribution of drugs. The Controlled Substance Act of 1970 was designed to control and reduce the abuse and diversion of pre-scription and illicit drugs (Schnoll 2009).

A turning point in research on drug use came in 1973 with the creation in the United States of the National Institute on Drug Abuse (NIDA). Prior to that time drug prevention efforts in the US had focused primarily on reducing the supply of drugs. NIDA became the center of a new commitment to demand reduction and had a group of scholars who were committed to creating a knowledge base through scientific research (DuPont 2009). Research funding grew and the study of substance abuse became a legitimate academic field. Drug abuse research became institutionalized with qualitative and quantitative studies on trends, epidemiology, addiction, and treatment (McCoy 2009; Clayton *et al.* 2009; Carlson *et al.* 2009; Hubbard *et al.* 2009).

In order to estimate the incidence and prevalence of drug use, two ongoing US national surveys were instituted in the 1970s. First, to assess adolescent substance use, NIDA began funding Monitoring the Future (MTF) in 1975, an annual school survey of approximately 2,500 students in grades 8, 10, and 12. In addition, a sub-sample of the students was tracked longitudinally (Johnston *et al.* 2009). Respondents were re-interviewed every two years through age 30, after which they are surveyed every five years. Second, the National Household Survey of Drug Use and Health was an annual US survey of approximately 67,500 persons on the use of alcohol, tobacco, and illicit drugs (Substance Abuse and Mental Health Services Administration 2009).

Rates and trends in the US

In 2008, 8 percent of Americans aged 12 and over had used an illicit drug during the previous month. Among young adults aged 18–25 the figure was 20 percent, while it was 9 percent among those aged 12–17 (Substance Abuse and Mental Health Services Administration 2009). Among US high school seniors, 28 percent reported "getting drunk" during the past month, 19 percent had used marijuana, and 22 percent had used an illicit drug (Johnston *et al.* 2009). In 2008, 4 percent of the population aged 12 and over reported driving while under the influence of illicit drugs, and 12 percent drove while under the influence of alcohol (Substance Abuse and Mental Health Services Administration 2009).

Although large numbers of adolescents and adults use various drugs, the trends have been downward in recent years. There were decreases from 1980 to 1990, modest increases from 1990 to 2000, and modest decreases from 2000 to 2008 (Johnston *et al.* 2009). There were particularly sharp declines in the prevalence of cocaine use but also steady decreases in cigarette use and heavy drinking.

In 2009, the US federal government spent $1.4 billion on drug prevention and $3.4 billion on drug treatment. In addition, $9.6 billion were spent on law enforcement and interdiction to control the supply of drugs. The total federal expenditures on drug control and treatment were $14.8 billion in 2008 (White House 2009). This does not include costs by state governments or amounts spent by the criminal justice system on drug-related items.

Substance use is particularly common among individuals involved in the criminal justice system. Among prison inmates in the United States, 73 percent had used drugs regularly prior to their incarceration (Petersilia 2005). At the time inmates committed their latest offense, 50 percent were under the influence of alcohol or drugs (Karberg and James 2005). From 1975 to 2000, there was a 400 percent increase in the US incarceration rate, due primarily to a rapid growth in incarceration for drug offenses (Blumstein and Beck 2005).

Addiction

Drug addiction may be defined as a compulsion to take a drug that results in a loss of control regarding the amount consumed (Koob and Simon 2009). There is a tendency to increase the dosage to achieve the same effect. According to Koob and Simon (2009), addiction is a disorder with three recurring stages: preoccupation/anticipation, binge intoxication, and withdrawal/ negative affect.

Many professionals use the term "dependence" rather than "addiction." *The Diagnostic and Statistical Manual of Mental Disorders* (American Psychiatric Association 2000) defines substance dependence as a condition where a person exhibits at least three of nine possible symptoms and if some of the symptoms have persisted for at least one month or have occurred repeatedly over a longer period of time. To receive a diagnosis of substance abuse, one must have a pattern of use which results in impairment or distress, as indicated by one of the following: substance use which results in failure to meet obligations at home, school, or work; substances are used when it is physically hazardous; substance use continues despite having problems caused or exacerbated by use. In addition, usage has not met the criteria for dependence for a particular type of substance (American Psychiatric Association 2000).

Why people use drugs

The various reasons why people use drugs can be grouped into six broad categories. First, people take drugs because others around them are using the substance. In other words, they use them to gain acceptance from their peers. Drug use is a social activity and individuals rarely begin using on their own. Second, people use drugs because it is enjoyable—the drug makes them feel better or gives them a "high." Third, individuals often use drugs to relieve stress or block pain, be it physical or emotional. Fourth, some may use drugs to improve performance. Fifth, some use drugs to make a statement, be different, or rebel. Finally, some try drugs because they are curious.

Although there are many different explanations as to why individuals use drugs, five theories appear to be particularly useful in increasing understanding of drug use. First, much of the research on peers and drug use is based on social learning theory (Akers 1998). According to this perspective, an individual learns to use drugs in small, informal groups, such as peer groups and families (Akers and Sellers 2004; Petraitis et al. 1995). It is in these intimate settings that individuals are taught to hold certain attitudes regarding drugs and their use (Reed and Rountree 1997). The causal mechanisms are modeling, rewards, punishments, and direct teachings through networks of peers.

Second, social control theory is based on the premise that deviance is normal and conformity, rather than deviation, must be explained (Akers and Sellers 2004; Hirschi 1969). Given the pervasiveness of alcohol and drug use in American culture, most adolescents and adults are exposed to drugs and may be inclined to use them (Fisher et al. 2007). Individuals may act on those impulses if no social controls are provided through families, peers, and religious organizations (Hirschi 1969). Social control theory focuses on how bonds help constrain individuals from taking or abusing drugs.

Third, according to strain theory, drug use and abuse are responses to various types of stress. Agnew (2006) postulated that strains tend to result in negative emotional states, such as anger, frustration, jealously, depression, and fear. These emotions lead to pressure for corrective citation, reduce ability to cope in a legal manner, and reduce concern with the costs of crime. Furthermore, strains may reduce social control and foster the social learning of crime (Agnew 2006; Agnew et al. 2000). The key concept is how decisions to use or not use are influenced by strains.

Fourth, Hawkins and Weis (1985) have set forth the social development model (SDM), a general theory that integrates concepts from social control and social learning theories into a developmental framework. Catalano et al. (1996) identified pro-social and antisocial rein- forcements as key concepts which influence drug use. In addition, they hypothesized that strong attachments and commitments to pro-social others and institutions will serve as barriers to drug use by diminishing delinquent beliefs. On the other hand, attachments and commitments to antisocial others and institutions will encourage the learning of attitudes favorable toward drug use.

Fifth, according to the neurobiological perspective, drug addiction is a chronic brain disease and needs to be treated, in much the same way as other chronic diseases, such as hypertension and diabetes, are treated. Although the initial consumption of drugs may have been voluntary, once someone becomes addicted they no longer have control over their drug-taking behavior. The prolonged use of drugs will have produced changes in the structure and function of the brain (Leshner 1997; Powledge 1999). Researchers have studied the neurobiological mechanisms in the brain involved in the addiction cycle. This perspective leads to a multimodal approach which includes medication along with more traditional behavioral therapies (Leshner 1997; Poling et al. 2006). The focus is on how drug use and abuse change the structure and functioning of the brain and how this impacts behavior.

Although these five theories are all important and have received considerable empirical support, they do not exhaust the theoretical perspectives that have been employed to explain drug use. Theories of deterrence, self-esteem/self-derogation, rational choice, and various combinations of these perspectives have also been used to describe the etiology of drug use and abuse.

Prevention and treatment

One of the major shifts in the study of drug use and abuse is increased emphasis on prevention and treatment. A summary of prevention efforts during the past forty years has been provided by Sloboda *et al.* (2009). They suggest that national surveys, such as Monitoring the Future and the National Household Survey of Drug Use and Health, have provided information that could be used to target prevention efforts. Much of the work on prevention has focused on peers and has been guided by social learning theory. NIDA has supported the implementation and evaluation of drug prevention programs.

There have been a number of large evaluations of treatment programs (Adrian 2001; Fletcher *et al.* 1997; Galaif *et al.* 2001; Johnson and Gerstein 2000; Orwin *et al.* 2000). Key findings are that treatment effectiveness tends to be associated with length of stay in the program, treatment intensity, and amount of time spent in individual and group counseling. A historical overview of treatment research was provided by Hubbard *et al.* (2009).

In the past two decades there is evidence that three types of treatment program may be particularly effective: cognitive-behavioral; therapeutic community; and drug courts. I turn now to a brief summary of research on those three programs. Here I build on the work of Sherman *et al.* (2002) and use the Maryland Scale to evaluate the different studies. This scale required that studies had at least a quasi-experimental design in which a control group could be compared to a treatment group. I rate a treatment as effective if at least two quality studies showed it to be so.

Cognitive-behavioral

Cognitive-behavioral (CB) treatment programs focus on thoughts and attitudes as well as on building skills (Milkman and Wanberg 2007). The programs help patients recognize and react to cravings for drug use on the thought and behavioral levels. The research indicates that participants in CB programs tended to have lower rates of drug use than comparable groups that did not receive treatment (Dutra *et al.* 2008; Magill and Ray 2009). Cognitive-behavioral programs have been shown to be effective among juveniles, adults, and criminal offenders (Lipsey and Landenberger 2006; Pearson *et al.* 2002; Waldron and Kaminer 2004).

Therapeutic community

A therapeutic community is a highly structured residence program where the clients are organized into groups, and leaders are chosen from within the group. The purpose is to give governance and accountability to the clients themselves. Because of the responsibility of the clients for their group, peer pressure within the group helps constrain individuals and encourage compliance with rules. It is a structured environment where they are taught rules, given individual and group responsibility for following rules, and given positive reinforcement for complying with the rules. There is emphasis on respect and one's responsibility to the community. Those in the therapeutic community engage in a variety of activities, including therapy, work, education classes, and recreation. Individuals receive various types of treatment, including cognitive therapy, individual counseling, group counseling, and twelve-step programs.

The therapeutic community is a widely used treatment modality both within and outside correctional facilities. Researchers have reported that individuals who were involved in therapeutic communities in prison were more likely to remain drug free and arrest free than comparable individuals who were not treated in a therapeutic community, particularly when accompanied by after-care programs (De Leon and Wexler 2009; Inciardi *et al.* 2004; Knight *et al.* 2003; Wexler *et al.* 1990).

Drug court

A drug court is a specialized program that is designed to use the power of the court to encourage individuals to receive treatment. It is based on the belief that incarceration by itself will not help individuals overcome drug dependency. It is estimated that there are more than 1,200 drug courts in the United States.

Typically, individuals who participate in a drug court are required to plead guilty to their charges. If they choose to participate in a drug court, the charges to which they have pleaded guilty are held in abeyance as long as they comply with all requirements of the court. If they do not comply with these requirements, the judge may sentence them to prison since they previously pled guilty to the charges. If they do comply with the requirements and successfully graduate from the drug court, the charges are dropped and expunged from their record.

In addition to the judge, there is a case manager who oversees each individual case. Each drug court participant is given a drug assessment and then a specific, individualized treatment plan based on the nature of the drug dependency. This often requires participation in several different types of treatment, such as group therapy, individual therapy, and Twelve-Step Programs. It may include a short term in a residential facility and then out-patient treatment.

As the number of drug courts has grown, there have been numerous evaluations of their effectiveness. Although the research has not been entirely consistent, the evidence indicates that drug courts tend to be effective in reducing drug use and criminal recidivism (Banks and Gottfredson 2003, 2004; Goldkamp *et al.* 2001).

Summary and conclusions

Although national surveys indicate that the prevalence of drug use has decreased somewhat, large numbers of adolescents and adults still use various substances. Drug use and abuse are costly in terms of health, safety, and crime. Attempts to decrease drug use by law enforcement appear to have been ineffective. The "War on Drugs" and other policy decisions have resulted in the incarceration of large numbers of persons, particularly minorities. In an effort to reduce the level of drug use and the number of persons incarcerated, a major trend in drug research has been a focus on the treatment of offenders. The empirical evidence indicates that a variety of programs tend to reduce drug use and recidivism, particularly cognitive-behavioral programs, therapeutic communities, and drug courts. There is also evidence that aftercare tends to increase program effectiveness.

Another major trend in the study and treatment of drug use has been research on how drugs impact the brain—the neurobiology of addiction (Koob and Simon 2009). Viewing drug abuse as a brain disease has important implications for treatment. First, if individuals have a disease that they can no longer control, they need treatment, not criminal sanctions. Just as many people who wish to lose weight are unable to do so, many individuals wish to stop taking drugs but are unable to do so. It is not a matter of gaining more knowledge or of changing one's attitude. Because of changes in the brain caused by prolonged use of drugs, drug use may no longer be a matter of choice.

Second, the focus may need to shift from *curing* the disease to *managing* it. A chronic disease cannot be cured through treatment.

Third, treatments may need to include pharmacological as well as behavioral methods. If addiction is a disease which has altered brain functions, then treatments could include medications designed to alter brain functions. There is a growing body of research on the brain and addiction by neuroscientists which has produced pharmocotherapies—treatments that include the administration of drugs along with behavioral methods to help manage drug abuse (Balster *et al.* 2009).

Future research into and treatment of drug abuse needs to take a life course perspective. Research demonstrates that drug dependence is a chronic disorder that needs to be studied and treated throughout life (Hser *et al.* 2009). Therefore, research and treatment need to take a life course perspective where drug dependence is studied over an extended time period. This will require the coordination of different service agencies, particularly the criminal justice system and mental health agencies. Furthermore, there will need to be cooperation across disciplines so that neurobiology and behavioral research and treatment can be integrated.

References

Adrian, M. (2001) "Do treatments and other interventions work? Some critical issues." *Substance Use and Misuse*, 36: 1759–1780.

Agnew, R. (2006) *Pressured into Crime: An Overview of General Strain Theory*. Los Angeles, CA: Roxbury.

Agnew, R., Rebellon, C., and Thaxton, S. (2000) "A general strain theory approach to families and crime." In G. L. Fox and M. L. Benson (Eds.) *Families, Crime and Criminal Justice* (pp. 113–138). Amsterdam: JAI.

Akers, R. L. (1998) *Social Learning and Social Structure: A General Theory of Crime and Deviance*. Boston, MA: Northeastern University Press.

Akers, R. L. and Sellers, C. S. (2004) *Criminological Theories: Introduction, Evaluation, and Application*. Los Angeles, CA: Roxbury.

American Psychiatric Association (2000) *Diagnostic and Statistical Manual of Mental Disorders*, 4th rev. edn. Washington, DC: American Psychiatric Association.

Anglin, M. D., Brown, B. S., Dembo, R., and Leukefeld, C. (2009) "Criminality and addiction: Selected issues for future policies, practice, and research." *Journal of Drug Issues*, 39: 89–99.

Balster, R. L., Walsh, S. L., and Bigelow, G. E. (2009) "Reflections on the past 40 years of behavioral pharmacology research on problems of drug abuse." *Journal of Drug Issues*, 39: 133–152.

Banks, D. and Gottfredson, D. C. (2003) "The effects of drug treatment and supervision on time to rearrest among drug treatment court participants." *Journal of Drug Issues*, 33: 385–412.

Banks, D. and Gottfredson, D. C. (2004) "Participation in drug treatment court and time to rearrest." *Justice Quarterly*, 21: 637–658.

Blumstein, A. and Beck, A. J. (2005). "Reentry as a transient state between liberty and recommitment." In J. Travis and C. Visher (Eds.) *Prison Reentry and Crime in America* (pp. 50–79). New York: Cambridge University Press.

Carlson, R. G., Singer, M., Stephens, R. C., and Sterk, C. E. (2009) "Reflections on 40 years of ethnographic drug abuse research: Implications for the future." *Journal of Drug Issues*, 39: 57–70.

Catalano, R. F., Kosterman, R., Hawkins, J. D., Newcomb, M. D., and Abbott, R. D. (1996) "Modeling the etiology of adolescent substance use: A test of the social development model." *Journal of Drug Issues*, 26: 429–455.

Clayton, R. R., Sloboda, Z., and Page, B. (2009) "Reflections on 40 years of drug abuse research: Changes in the epidemiology of drug abuse." *Journal of Drug Issues*, 39: 41–55.

De Leon, G. and Wexler, H. (2009) "The therapeutic community for addictions: An evolving knowledge base." *Journal of Drug Issues*, 39: 167–178.

DuPont, R. L. (2009) "Reflections on the early history of National Institute on Drug Abuse (NIDA): Implications for today." *Journal of Drug Issues*, 39: 5–14.

Dutra, L., Stathopoulou, G., Basden, S. L., Leyro, T. M., Powers, M. B., and Otto, M. W. (2008) "A meta-analytic review of psychosocial interventions for substance use disorders." *American Journal of Psychiatry*, 165: 179–187.

Fisher, L. B., Miles, I. W., Austin, B., Camargo, C. A., and Colditz, G. A. (2007) "Predictors of initiation of alcohol use among US adolescents: Findings from a prospective cohort study." *Archives of Pediatrics and Adolescent Medicine*, 161: 959–966.

Fletcher, B. W., Tims, F. M., and Brown, B. S. (1997) "Drug abuse treatment outcome study (DATOS): Treatment evaluation research in the United States." *Psychology of Addictive Behaviors*, 11: 216–229.

Galaif, E. R., Hser, Y., Grella, C. E., and Joshi, V. (2001) "Prospective risk factors and treatment outcomes among adolescents in DATOS-A." *Journal of Adolescent Research*, 16: 661–678.

Goldkamp, J. S., White, M. D., and Robinson, J. B. (2001) "Do drug courts work? Getting inside the drug court black box." *Journal of Drug Issues*, 31: 27–72.

Gray, J. P. (2001) *Why Our Drug Laws Have Failed and What We Can Do about It*. Philadelphia, PA: Temple University Press.

Hawkins, J. D. and Weis, J. G. (1985) "The social development model: An integrated approach to delinquency prevention." *Journal of Primary Prevention*, 6: 73–97.

Hawkins, J. D., Catalano, R. F., and Miller, J. Y. (1992) "Risk and protective factors for alcohol and other drug problems in adolescence and early adulthood: Implications for substance abuse prevention." *Psychological Bulletin*, 112: 64–105.

Hirschi, R. (1969) *Causes of Delinquency*. Berkeley: University of California Press.

Hser, Y., Hamilton, A., and Niv, N. (2009) "Understanding drug use over the life course: Past, present, and future." *Journal of Drug Issues*, 39: 231–236.

Hubbard, R., Simpson, D. D., and Woody, G. (2009) "Treatment research: Accomplishments and challenges." *Journal of Drug Issues*, 39: 153–166.

Inciardi, J. A., Martin, S. S., and Butzin, C. A. (2004) "Five-year outcomes of therapeutic community treatment of drug-involved offenders after release from prison." *Crime and Delinquency*, 50: 88–107.

Johnson, R. A. and Gerstein, D. R. (2000) "Treatment populations, services, and outcomes for cocaine and crack-cocaine dependence." *Journal of Psychopathology and Behavioral Assessment*, 22: 339–351.

Johnston, L. D., O'Malley, P. M., Bachman, J. G., and Schulenberg, J. E. (2009) *Monitoring the Future National Results on Adolescent Drug Use: Overview of Key Findings, 2008*. Bethesda, MD: National Institute on Drug Abuse.

Karberg, J. C. and James, D. J. (2005) *Substance Dependence, Abuse, and Treatment of Jail Inmates, 2002*. Washington, DC: Bureau of Justice Statistics, Office of Justice Programs, US Department of Justice.

Knight, K., Simpson, D. D., and Hiller, M. L. (2003) *Outcome Assessment of Correctional Treatment*. Washington, DC: US Department of Justice.

Koob, G. F. and Simon, E. (2009) "The neurobiology of addiction: Where we have been and where we are going." *Journal of Drug Issues*, 39: 115–132.

Landenberger, N. A. and Lipsey, M. W. (2005) "The positive effects of cognitive-behavioral programs for offenders: A meta-analysis of factors associated with effective treatment." *Journal of Experimental Criminology*, 1: 451–476.

Leshner, A. I. (1997) "Addiction is a brain disease, and it matters." *Science*, 278: 45–47.

Lipsey, M. W. and Landenberger, N. A. (2006) "Cognitive-behavioral interventions." In B. C. Welsh and D. P. Farrington (Eds.) *Preventing Crime: What Works for Children, Offenders, Victims, and Places* (pp. 57–71). Dordrecht: Springer.

Magill, M. and Ray, L. S. (2009) "Cognitive-behavioral treatment with adult alcohol and illicit drug users: A meta-analysis of randomized controlled trials." *Journal of Studies on Alcohol and Drugs*, 70: 516–527.

McCoy, C. B. (2009) "Institutionalization of drug abuse research in academia: One professor's view." *Journal of Drug Issues*, 39: 15–20.

Milkman, H. and Wanberg, K. (2007) *Cognitive Behavioral Treatment: A Review and Discussion for Corrections Professionals*. Washington, DC: National Institute of Corrections, US Department of Justice.

Orwin, R. G., Ellis, B., Williams, V., and Maranda, M. (2000) "Relationship between treatment components, client-level factors, and positive treatment outcomes." *Journal of Psychopathology and Behavioral Assessment*, 22: 383–397.

Pearson, F. S., Lipton, D. S., Cleland, C. M., and Yee, D. S. (2002) "The effects of behavioral/cognitive-behavioral programs on recidivism." *Crime and Delinquency*, 48: 476–496.

Petersilia, J. (2005) " From cell to society: Who is returning home?" In J. Travis and C. Visher (Eds.) *Prison Reentry and Crime in America* (pp. 15–49). New York: Cambridge University Press.

Petraitis, J., Flay, B. R., and Miller, T. Q. (1995) "Reviewing theories of adolescent substance use: Organizing pieces in the puzzle." *Psychological Bulletin*, 117: 67–86.

Poling, J., Oliveto, A., Petry, N., Sofuoglu, M., Gonsai, K., Gonzalez, G., Martell, B., and Kosten, T. (2006) "Six-month trial of bupropion with contingency management for cocaine dependence in a methadone-maintained population." *Archives of General Psychiatry*, 63: 219–228.

Powledge, T. M. (1999) "Addiction and the brain." *Bioscience*, 49: 513–519.

Reed, M. D. and Rountree, P. W. (1997) "Peer pressure and adolescent substance use." *Journal of Quantitative Criminology*, 13: 143–180.

Schnoll, S. H. (2009) "Reflections of an academic clinical researcher on the past 40 years of addiction development." *Journal of Drug Issues*, 39: 21–28.

Sherman, L. W., Farrington, D. P., Welsh, B. C., and MacKenzie, D. L. (2002) *Evidence-based Crime Prevention*. London: Routledge.

Sloboda, Z., Cottlelr, L. B., Hawkins, J. D., and Pentz, M. A. (2009) "Reflections on 40 years of drug abuse prevention research." *Journal of Drug Issues*, 39: 179–195.

Substance Abuse and Mental Health Services Administration (2009) *Results from the 2008 National Survey on Drug Use and Health: National Findings*. Rockville, MD: Office of Applied Studies.

Waldron, H. B. and Kaminer, Y. (2004) "On the learning curve: The emerging evidence supporting cognitive-behavioral therapies for adolescent substance abuse." *Addiction*, 99: 93–105.

Wexler, H. K., Falkin, G. P., and Lipton, D. S. (1990) "Outcome evaluation of a prison therapeutic community for substance abuse treatment." *Criminal Justice and Behavior*, 17: 71–92.

Wexler, H. K., Melnick, G., and Cao, Y. (2004) "Rick and prison substance abuse treatment outcomes: A replication and challenge." *Prison Journal*, 84: 106–120.

White House (2009) *National Drug Control Strategy: FY 2010 Budget Summary*. Washington, DC: White House.

35

Eating disorders as deviance

Diane E. Taub and Penelope A. McLorg

The deviance of eating disorders

Within the field of the sociology of deviance, the term deviance connotes a variety of associations. For example, deviance can be described as being related to an individual's attitude, behavior, or physicality. Eating disorders comprise all three of these areas of deviance, with extreme internalization of the societal emphasis on thinness, aberrant behavior in response to the thinness norm, and altered appearance that embodies the thinness norm.

Eating disorders are related to food consumption or to non-consumption, and include anorexia nervosa (self-starvation) and bulimia nervosa (binge–purge syndrome). Both of these eating disorders involve a fear of fatness and a distorted body image, or exaggerated sense of being fat. Specifically, anorexia nervosa entails self-starvation alone or in combination with excessive exercising or occasional binge eating, self-induced vomiting, or misuse of laxatives, diuretics, or enemas. An individual with anorexia nervosa refuses to maintain minimum weight for age and height and is at least 15 percent below normal weight. Bulimia nervosa involves a recurrent activity of binge eating and self-induced purging. In this eating disorder, rapid consumption of a large number of calories (binge eating) is followed by actions to compensate for the binge (purging). An individual's purging may consist of self-induced vomiting, ipecac use, or excessive use of laxatives and enemas. An individual with bulimia nervosa is usually normal or close to normal in weight (Haller, 1992).

As types of deviance, eating disorders do not occur randomly in the population. Instead, like other deviance, eating disorders have higher prevalence among certain groups. Further, specific cultural contexts provide a setting in which disordered eating is more likely to occur.

Eating disorders and the demographic context of deviance

Eating disorders are most prevalent in females who are young and white. At least 90 percent of individuals with eating disorders are female (Haller, 1992). Adherence by females to the cultural norm of the female body is crucial to understanding the gender distribution of this deviance. Among females, the internalization to be slim is so ingrained that even when they are not overweight, females frequently perceive themselves as such (Wiseman *et al.*, 1998). Slim bodies are regarded as the most beautiful and worthy of admiration; fatness is viewed as not only unhealthy but offensive, objectionable, and deviant (Harrison and Cantor, 1997).

Internalization of the pervasive thinness norm for females and the corresponding desire to avoid fatness at all costs perpetuate continuing attempts by females to diet and lose weight. Eating disorders can be viewed as extreme or deviant responses to the thinness norm. For males, the ideal body is muscular, not skinny or weak. In contrast to females, males generally want to gain weight and size from muscle development (Harrison, 2000).

Regarding age distribution, anorexia nervosa and bulimia nervosa commonly have their onset and greatest prevalence during adolescence or young adulthood (Haller, 1992). Such age periods are especially significant for development of a female's identity and self-image. The teen and young adult years are times in which peer-group influences are notable, with appearance norms keenly felt. In terms of ethnicity, eating disorders are most prevalent among whites. Traditionally, larger bodies have been more accepted, and the slimness norm less salient, among certain ethnicities, such as African Americans, than among whites (Lovejoy, 2001).

The eating disorder deviance of anorexia nervosa and bulimia nervosa can be viewed as illustrating a rare type of deviance participation in its occurrence among white females. Stereotypically, deviance occurs more among non-whites than whites, and more among males than females.

Eating disorders and the cultural context of deviance

Along with the thinness norm, cultural factors that influence the prevalence of the deviance of eating disorders include role models of beauty, mass media messages perpetuating thinness, and the ubiquitous emphasis on dieting and weight-reducing behavior. These factors have been shown to affect the genesis and maintenance of eating disorders (Harrison, 2000). In addition, certain organized sport activities heighten the vulnerability of females to engage in disordered eating (Hausenblas and Carron, 2002).

Traditional female role models consistently support the thinness norm for females. Fashion models, beauty contestants, and television and movie stars are uniformly thin, with a pattern of these role models becoming increasingly thin over the past 30 years (Sypeck et al., 2004). Such bodily displays by these role models perpetuate disordered eating by promoting the acceptance of a certain ideal body type for women.

Mass media messages, including advertisements and articles, also encourage a uniform standard of thinness and beauty for females (Silverstein et al., 1986). Advertisers use slim female models to sell a variety of merchandise, including items that are not connected to beauty products. Further, diet and exercise ads have proliferated over the past 30 years. These ads promote a range of diet foods and diet aids, the safety of which is often questionable, and frequently showcase unproven exercise equipment and devices. Articles dealing with testimonies or struggles about losing weight, as well as with body shape or size, have similarly increased in number. Under the critical gaze of the public, female celebrities endorse particular weight-loss plans and reveal their perennial efforts to lose weight and maintain a lower weight. Books detailing diet plans and exercise programs are frequently at the top of bestseller lists. The topic of weight control is likely to be included in female-oriented magazines (Silverstein et al., 1986).

Beginning in childhood and continuing into later adulthood, concern about weight and weight-loss efforts is so common among females that such preoccupation is viewed as normative (Pliner et al., 1990). Along with the mass media encouragement of dieting, pervasive weight-reducing centers and spas promote women's self-consciousness about their weight and body shape. A history of repeated weight-loss efforts is quite common among anorexics and bulimics, and is considered a major risk factor for eating disorders (Wiseman et al., 1998). Anorexia nervosa and bulimia nervosa represent extreme or deviant responses to female socialization toward dieting and achieving slimness.

Specific social contexts encourage the deviance of anorexia nervosa and bulimia nervosa. In particular, participation in certain organized sports heightens female vulnerability to eating disorders (Hausenblas and Carron, 2002). Such physical activity involvement includes swimming, diving, figure-skating, cross-country running, dance, and gymnastics. Among athletes and coaches, extra weight is often thought to slow movement and hinder performance. The risk of eating disorders is increased when gender role expectations of thinness interact with an athletic environment that has an aesthetic focus or emphasizes body shape and control. Specifically, eating disorders are more common in sports that are individual rather than team in nature; include appearance as an element of the overall performance evaluation; involve airborne movements; and have a competitive uniform that illustrates body size and form. Further, rates of eating disorders increase as the level of the sport activity becomes more competitive (Hausenblas and Carron, 2002).

Again, due to their social status, participants in the deviance of anorexia nervosa and bulimia nervosa are atypical deviants. Individuals who are more likely to engage in disordered eating are often viewed as social conformists who participate in socially approved and valued activities (such as organized sports). Stereotypically, deviants are viewed as nonconformists who are not heavily involved in conventional activities.

The medicalization of eating disorders

Most literature on eating disorders focuses on the medical and psychiatric aspects. This emphasis facilitates the beliefs that eating disorders require medical intervention and control, and that anorexia nervosa and bulimia nervosa are illnesses or diseases that need to be treated by medical personnel. Such a portrayal of eating disorders supports the medicalization of these conditions (Conrad, 2007). Individuals who have eating disorders are considered patients, and the medical profession is considered expert in treating anorexia nervosa and bulimia nervosa. Under a medicalized orientation, the cultural and societal causes and contexts of eating disorders are less salient than medical testing and treatment. Anorexia nervosa and bulimia nervosa thus constitute a social problem and societal condition that the medical profession has coopted and claimed as its own. Similarly, problems associated with gambling, shoplifting, and number of sexual partners have recently been designated as medical concerns.

Notably, eating disorders are included in the *Diagnostic and Statistical Manual of Mental Disorders*, with specific diagnostic features and treatment regimens. Professional medical reference works, such as the *Merck Manual of Diagnosis and Therapy* and *Physicians' Desk Reference*, have entries discussing these disorders under medical and psychiatric domains. Emphases are placed on bodily and mental deviations and biochemical abnormalities. In the medicalization of eating disorders, attention is paid to the acute medical treatment of the problem and to medical and psychiatric etiology. The focus is on dealing with the medical symptoms and outcomes of the eating disorder and not on underlying individual and social causes. Many hospitals now have special floors or wings for patients with eating disorders and often isolate these patients from family and friends while they receive medical treatment and psychiatric counseling. Such treatment includes force-feeding, regimented diets, psychoactive drugs, and electrolyte correction. Once discharged and away from this institutional environment, patients often relapse and need to be re-hospitalized. Other inpatient and outpatient psychiatric treatments are drug therapies to deal with the diagnosis of depression that often accompanies eating disorders, as well as with the reported anxiety and obsessive aspects of these conditions (Haller, 1992).

Eating disorders and the progression of deviance

Individuals who become anorexic or bulimic begin their path toward developing eating disorders by internalizing the negative or deviant connotations of fatness, and the positive associations with slimness. Fatness is viewed in society as quite undesirable and as a personal failing; women who are fat are devalued and treated as deviant in social interactions because they are viewed as violating norms of body shape and self-control (Harrison and Cantor, 1997).

In contrast, a thin body symbolizes an idealized standard of beauty and personal achievement. Females are vulnerable to the ideal body norm as they are more likely than men to be judged by their appearance and physical aesthetics (Pliner et al., 1990). With gender socialization mandating visual attractiveness, women alter their bodies to conform to appearance expectations.

Females constantly strive to achieve thinness by dieting and losing weight. On any given day in the United States, for example, over half of all women may be on a diet (Haller, 1992). The reason for women's dieting is generally appearance, not health. In an environment of constant pressure to be thin, women engage in persistent weight-loss efforts. As many diets are not successful, females are on a constant mission to find another weight-loss program (Silverstein et al., 1986).

Those females who become anorexic or bulimic are at first conformist and try to abide by the thinness norm. The degree of contentment they feel about their bodies is influenced by the verbal and nonverbal reactions regarding their appearance they receive from others. Not feeling thin enough impels these females to undertake more extreme weight-loss measures, such as very restrictive food intake, excessive exercising, and purging after eating a normal meal. Eating disorders begin as extreme manifestations of dieting and the striving to avoid the negative label of being obese or fat (McLorg and Taub, 1987).

In his seminal work, Lemert (1951) outlines the progression to developing a deviant identity. With primary deviance, individuals engage in a transitory period of norm violations, which are generally not known to others. In this stage, individuals rationalize their deviant acts so that their self-concept and performance of social roles are not affected. Concerning anorexia nervosa, primary deviance entails episodic starvation for weight management, often for the express purpose of losing weight for a special event, such as wanting to wear a particular bathing suit during spring break or trying to fit into a certain dress for an upcoming school dance. For an individual initiating bulimic behavior, primary deviance comprises trial periods of maintaining or losing weight by purging after overeating or following a large meal. In the stage of primary deviance, individuals do not consider themselves deviant or as having an eating disorder (McLorg and Taub, 1987).

Other people's increased awareness of the starving and binging and purging behaviors leads to application of the "anorexic" and "bulimic" labels. For anorexics, other individuals become increasingly knowledgeable about their escalating weight loss and ritualistic eating and exercising patterns. For bulimics, others witness acts of purging or begin to question how weight can be maintained with such extreme intake of calories. Application of the deviant labels of anorexic and bulimic occurs prior to secondary deviance (McLorg and Taub, 1987).

According to Lemert (1951), in secondary deviance, individuals continue the norm violations, which are now responses to the deviant labels applied by others. The deviant acts, once occasional, are now continuous and prolonged. In the case of anorexia nervosa, an individual has a strict regimen of exercising and dieting behavior. The routine of a bulimic consists of frequent binge-eating and purging episodes. The deviant labels of anorexic or bulimic affect the performance of individuals' social roles, as others relate to them predominantly based on their eating disorder. Being anorexic or bulimic becomes the new master status, or the status most identified with the person. Such interactional responses to an individual with an eating disorder reinforce the anorexic and bulimic behaviors, and strengthen the individual's internalization of an anorexic or bulimic social identity (McLorg and Taub, 1987). Thus, during secondary deviance, the self-concept is transformed from a non-deviant to a deviant image.

Stigma and the management of eating disorders

Goffman (1963) suggests that individuals who have an attribute that is deeply discrediting possess a stigma. He differentiates three types of stigma: physical (i.e., abominations of the body), blemishes of individual character (e.g., former mental patient or prisoner), and tribal (i.e., race, religion, gender, and nation). Stigma develops from cultural standards and reflects the values and norms of individuals in the powerful group. The "spoiled" identity of the stigmatized person becomes known from the negative reactions of "normals" to the possessor of the discrediting quality. Individuals who are stigmatized need to create and defend a claim to a legitimate status.

One response of a person who is viewed as deviant, or as possessing a spoiled identity, is to engage in stigma management. Through various techniques, individuals attempt to control negative reactions or consequences from a discrediting attribute. The various methods used by stigmatized individuals depend on the degree to which their stigma is known or obvious to others. Goffman (1963) differentiates between stigmatized individuals with a visible or perceivable attribute (the discredited) and individuals whose stigmatized attributes are not easily identifiable (the discreditable). Individuals with a discredited stigma attempt to manage their stigma by controlling tension in social interactions, while people with a discreditable stigma strive to manage their stigma by controlling information that may expose their deviance.

Concerning eating disorders, individuals with anorexia nervosa often have to manage both discredited and discreditable stigmas due to their emaciated appearance and aberrant eating and exercising behaviors (McLorg and Taub, 1987). One stigma management technique used by anorexics is concealment—hiding or disguising their eating disorder. To control discredited stigma, anorexics wear big clothes to try to conceal their body size. To manage discreditable stigma, anorexics serve themselves food during meals with others to give the impression that they are normal eaters. However, rather than eating, they unobtrusively just play with the food on their plate. Individuals with anorexia nervosa also exercise secretly for hours by themselves.

Another stigma management technique used by individuals with anorexia nervosa is normalization—efforts to redefine the stigma and reeducate normals. In this strategy, anorexics confront the stigma of anorexia nervosa directly in the hope that the discrediting attribute may lose its stigmatizing quality. To manage discredited stigma, anorexics argue that their bodies are normal size, not so slim as to be defined as "too thin." To control information for a discreditable stigma, anorexics tell others that they are ultra-healthy because of their eating and exercising behaviors, and try to convince others that they are not deviant or extreme enough in their behaviors to be labeled sick (McLorg and Taub, 1987).

Further, attempts at redefinition by individuals with anorexia nervosa emphasize the positive attributes of the bodies of anorexics and of having total control over one's body. Various "pro-ana" websites reinforce this stigma management strategy, as these sites promote the uniqueness of anorexics' routines and the superior qualities of their bodies. Testimonies from anorexics appearing on these sites endorse anorexia nervosa as a lifestyle choice rather than an eating disorder. Reeducation as a stigma management strategy dictates that the condition of anorexia nervosa should not be an issue.

In contrast to anorexics, bulimics often do not have to manage discredited stigma because their weight remains normal or close to normal (McLorg and Taub, 1987). In addition, certain physical markers of bulimia nervosa, such as loss of tooth enamel or calluses on knuckles from self-induced vomiting, are not easily discernible by others. Thus, individuals in social encounters with someone with bulimia nervosa would not normally suspect that they are bulimic, and tension from a discredited stigma would not need to be controlled.

However, individuals who are bulimic do need to manage information associated with their discreditable stigma (McLorg and Taub, 1987). Like anorexics, bulimics use concealment as a stigma management strategy. Individuals with bulimia nervosa must attempt to hide their eating disorder by concealing their binge eating and purging. In public, or when eating with others, for example, bulimics attempt not to binge or eat too much or to be caught vomiting after eating. In addition, to reduce stigma and minimize disparaging responses, bulimics try to control information about their eating disorder by avoiding discussions of eating and weight-control issues.

Again in contrast to the stigma management techniques of anorexics, individuals who are bulimic do not normally engage in normalization, or attempts to redefine the stigma and reeducate normals. Bulimics tend to be more stigmatized than anorexics, as binging followed by purging to lose or maintain weight is viewed as more deviant than restricting food intake. Thus, bulimics are more likely than anorexics to internalize a deviant label from their binge-eating and purging behavior, and are not as likely as anorexics to argue that their weight-control behavior is normal or has desirable outcomes (McLorg and Taub, 1987).

Conclusion

The demographic distribution and cultural contexts of eating disorders demonstrate that a society acquires the deviance it perpetuates. Occurrences of anorexia nervosa and bulimia nervosa reflect the social conditions that promote the development of these eating disorders. Paralleling other types of deviance, anorexia nervosa and bulimia nervosa are more likely to be represented in certain demographic groups. However, eating disorders are most likely in the uncommonly deviant subgroup of white females. Further, participation in specific organized sports increases susceptibility of females to eating disorders. This dedicated involvement in conventional activities also distinguishes individuals with eating disorders from stereotypical deviants.

While dieting reflects normative acceptance of the ideal body shape for females, eating disorders represent deviant or extreme responses toward achieving slimness. Although having membership in the privileged group of white ethnicity, females with eating disorders are stigmatized and denied full societal acceptance. As labeled deviants, anorexics and bulimics must continually manage their stigma either by controlling tension in social interactions or by controlling information that may expose their eating disorder. With overzealous internalization of the thinness norm, consequent behavioral manifestations, and altered physicality, individuals with eating disorders engage in a deviance that mirrors societal norms. Anorexia nervosa and bulimia nervosa are maintained by the visual objectification of females, the powerful medical complex, and the pervasive mass media that endorse a cult of thinness for females.

References

Conrad, Peter. 2007. *The Medicalization of Society: On the Transformation of Human Conditions into Treatable Disorders*. Baltimore, MD: Johns Hopkins University Press.
Goffman, Erving. 1963. *Stigma: Notes on the Management of Spoiled Identity*. Englewood Cliffs, NJ: Prentice-Hall.
Haller, Ellen. 1992. "Eating Disorders: A Review and Update." *Western Journal of Medicine* 157:658–662.

Harrison, Kristen. 2000. "The Body Electric: Thin-Ideal Media and Eating Disorders in Adolescents." *Journal of Communication* 50:119-143.

Harrison, Kristen and Joanne Cantor. 1997. "The Relationship between Media Consumption and Eating Disorders." *Journal of Communication* 47:40–67.

Hausenblas, Heather A. and Albert V. Carron. 2002. "Assessing Eating Disorder Symptoms in Sport Groups: A Critique with Recommendations for Future Research." *International Sports Journal* 6:65–74.

Lemert, Edwin M. 1951. *Social Pathology*. New York: McGraw-Hill.

Lovejoy, Meg. 2001. "Disturbances in the Social Body: Differences in Body Image and Eating Problems among African American and White Women." *Gender & Society* 15:239–261.

McLorg, Penelope A. and Diane E. Taub. 1987. "Anorexia Nervosa and Bulimia: The Development of Deviant Identities." *Deviant Behavior* 8:177–189.

Pliner, Patricia, Shelly Chaiken, and Gordon L. Flett. 1990. "Gender Differences in Concern with Body Weight and Physical Appearance over the Life Span." *Personality and Social Psychology Bulletin* 16:263–273.

Silverstein, Brett, Lauren Perdue, Barbara Peterson, and Eileen Kelly. 1986. "The Role of the Mass Media in Promoting a Thin Standard of Bodily Attractiveness for Women." *Sex Roles* 14:519–532.

Sypeck, Mia Foley, James J. Gray, and Anthony H. Ahrens. 2004. "No Longer Just a Pretty Face: Fashion Magazines' Depictions of Ideal Female Beauty from 1959 to 1999." *International Journal of Eating Disorders* 36:342–347.

Wiseman, Claire V., Wendy A. Harris, and Katherine A. Halmi. 1998. "Eating Disorders." *Medical Clinics of North America* 82:145–159.

36

Cutting, piercing, and self-mutilation

Jimmy D. Taylor

Few topics within the social sciences have remained as elusive and shrouded in mystery as the social and private worlds of self-injurers. Rapid social and technological change, cultural diversity, and blurred categorical lines lie at the heart of this highly controversial and philosophically contested topic. The purpose of this exploration is to address some of the more frequently registered concerns, key issues, and innovations in research in the areas of "cutting," "piercing," and "self-mutilation." Although there is some considerable overlap in these areas, special attention will be paid to the separate bodies of research dedicated to each.

As with so many socially constructed forms of deviance, cultural relativity and the susceptibility to change serve to preclude fixed definitions of self-injury-related areas of deviant behavior. One aspect of self-injury that is widely agreed upon is that there are multiple reasons for these physical acts. Common reasons cited for engaging in related activities are as dissimilar as they are unifying, and include depression, past sexual abuse, fitting in, standing out, simultaneously fitting in while standing out, cathartic release, expressions of emotional turmoil, anger, grief and other forms of dissatisfaction to others, peer pressure, identity crises, narcissism, self-loathing, to feel euphoric, and to experience a form of self-nurturing as wounds literally heal. It has been estimated that as many as 4% of adults and 23% of adolescents practice some form of self-injury (Holmes 2000; Jacobson and Gould 2007). These practices are more frequent among adolescent to early adult women, although increased instances of self-injury by teenage boys and young adult males have been reported from the mid-1990s to present (Williams 2008).

The majority of published research involving self-injury has emerged from medical and psychiatric studies. Various studies (Adler and Adler 2005; Bates 2005; Guertin *et al.* 2001; Soloman and Farrand 1996) indicate that this has resulted from the refuted but once widely held notion that self-injury is a type of suicidal tendency that requires medical treatment or intervention. Although the "deliberate harming of skin tissue" of one's own body is often referred to as "body modification" (Featherstone 1999; Myers 1992; Pitts 2003), "self-mutilation" (Holmes 2000; Ross and Heath 2002; Williams 2008), "self-cutting" (Levenkron 1998; Bates 2005), "self-harm" (Cohn 2004; Gardner 2001; Schmidt and Davidson 2004), and "self-injury" (Adler and Adler 2005; Hodgson 2004; Walsh 2005), such prominent deviant behavior scholars as Adler and Adler (2005) and Thio (2009) have appealed to scholars researching related topics to adopt the term "self-injury." It is their contention that the other terms for these patterns of behavior are too judgmental, less applicable, and too closely tied to widely held notions of extreme violence or even evil. The term "self-injury" is also said to resonate more strongly with the actual practitioners of these activities (Adler and Adler 2005), such as intentional bone-breaking, branding, burning, cutting, pricking, scratching, hair pulling and skin picking, to name a few.

Durkheim and the sociological origins of self-injury

Emile Durkheim (1965 [1915]) helped to elevate the priority of analyzing the cultural significance of marking the human body as a means of expression and shared meaning. He noted that "the best way of proving to one's self and to others that one is a member of a certain group is to place a distinctive mark on the body" (p. 265). The body, not just written or spoken forms of communication or other cultural products, is used to convey meaning to the social world. This has been reiterated by Shilling (2005), who suggests that the literal, physical symbols left on the body as the result of such practices as cutting, scarification, tattooing, painting, and other means of "decoration" serve an integrating role by enabling members of a common, shared, but often obscured culture to recognize one another as kindred (p. 29).

It is important to make a distinction between the type of body markings and self-injury noted by Durkheim—which occur among highly homogeneous and cohesive (mechanical) cultures that emphasize the good of the collective—and those that occur within highly specialized (organic), more diverse cultures that espouse individuality and freedom of expression. Contemporary ethnographers such as Clifford (1988) and Mascia-Lees and Sharpe (1994) highlight the significance of the tentative symbolic value placed on different body alterations. The meanings assigned to some of the markings/alterations that are tied to deep cultural roots remain relatively intact over time, whereas more fleeting meanings were noted for alterations within modern societies.

Other scholars (e.g., Maguire 2002) have focused on how the practices of body modification are particularly well suited to modern, capitalist social systems, in that the body is adorned in response to market changes and demands. The body becomes something of an artistic canvas, or a billboard for sending out messages to a target audience. This process is said to be facilitated by the rapid interpretation and reinterpretation of the "normal" body, based, in part, on constantly updated and highly circulated popular media images (Shilling 2003). Other researchers (DeMello 2000; Kosut 2006; Pitts 1999, 2003) have chosen to focus on the influence of media outlets in casting certain forms of body modification in a deviant light.

A last key social force that has been found to have a profound influence on modes of self-injury is technology. Cerulo (1997), Foster (1997), and Adler and Adler (2008) have emphasized the significance of evolving technology and how this impacts forms and functions of deviant behaviors related to self-injury. They report that innovations in information technology (particularly personal digital assistants and other web-based technologies) are changing the way deviance is defined and performed by individual actors and their deviant communities. Now deviant actors can simultaneously find other deviant subculture participants with whom to interact and to foster group solidarity—instead of remaining in "loner" isolation as was more often the case with previous generations of deviants—while also being able to maintain strict anonymity whenever desired.

Female genital mutilation

Female genital cutting is a good illustration of body modification with deep cultural meaning, indicative of a more "mechanical" and collective-oriented interpretation of the body. Although the procedure is not self-inflicted, many girls do willingly submit to the ritual, in the belief that it makes them a "real woman" and "more desirable" (Thio 2009). The practice of female genital cutting involves alteration or removal of some of the female genitalia of girls aged between four and fourteen (Gruenbaum 2001; Hassanin *et al.* 2008). It is viewed within societies where it is frequently practiced as similar to other forms of common cosmetic surgery, such as breast augmentation, that are used to make women more appealing by Western standards (Hernlund and Shell-Duncan 2007; Thio 2009).

Genital cutting has been framed as deviant by Western media, even though practices involving extreme physical discomfort (Holmes 2000) and major cosmetic alterations (Parens 2006) are rampant within US subcultures. Negative attention is due to such problems as hemorrhaging, recurring infections, death (Cook *et al.* 2003), psychological side-effects (Behrendt and Moritz 2005) and decreased sexual pleasure (Lightfoot-Klein 1989; Catania *et al.* 2007).

Cutting

As indicated in the introductory remarks, cutters are by no means a unified group. The reasons frequently cited for engaging in self-injury practices by cutting are varied and highly complex. Although scientific studies pertaining to cutting practices are limited in terms of the number of studies published and their scope, existing literature suggests substantial variation among cutters in terms of function and form of cutting practices. It is also important, however, to consider the rapid change in public perception and awareness of cutting activities, and the social forces driving this dynamic form of deviance.

Inside the social structure and organization of cutting

Forms of deviant behavior are often identified and defined according to recognizable or predictable ways in which they are organized, maintained, transmitted and conducted. Seminal studies on cutting conducted by sociologists Patricia and Peter Adler (2005, 2008) have helped to illuminate the tentative nature of cutters and fragility of cutting categories. Adler and Adler (2005) analyzed cutting categories by adopting and applying Best and Luckenbill's (1982) theoretical typology of "individual" and "loner" deviance. According to this typology, "individual" deviants have gained all of the skills necessary to enable them to enact and participate in forms of deviance by themselves and for themselves. Some of the distinguishing characteristics of individual deviants center on the notion that although they (the cutters) are independent in the sense that they are free to engage in their chosen forms of deviance on their own, it is not necessary that they remain isolated from other like-minded deviants (Deshotels and Forsyth 2007). Individual deviants, such as skydivers (Anderson and Taylor 2010), military gun collectors (Taylor 2009) and the homeless (Snow and Anderson 1993), to name a few, may operate within support networks conducive to their deviant tastes and needs and even commit their independent acts of deviance in the presence of subcultural supporters. This would also include acts of deviance that are performed on the body of the individual deviant participant, such as the self-injury practice of cutting.

In contrast to "individual deviants," "loners" or "loner deviants" are individuals who dwell primarily in social isolation, without notable support networks to share in their deviant experiences or lifestyle choices. Consequently, they commit deviant acts on their own, without training, assistance or support from other deviants who perform similar or identical acts. Similar to other loner deviants, such as drug addicts who work in medical or related professions (Dabney and Hollinger 1999), people with eating disorders (O'Shaughnessy and Dallos 2009) and even child pornographers (Jenkins 2001), individuals who self-injure are unlikely to be associated (to their knowledge) with others who are engaged in the same or similar behavior. Therefore, loner deviants must typically seek out and develop the skills necessary to perform their acts of deviance on their own, in relative isolation.

Adler and Adler (2005, 2008) illuminate rapid change in the cutting world due to ways in which public awareness and technology—specifically, internet resources and chat-room-style support networks—have informed a broader population about the ways of cutting. They found that as cutting populations have begun to "find" one another, and talk more openly about their self-injury practices, a slow-moving de-stigmatization campaign has ensued. As the stigmatizing stronghold on cutting has started to weaken, it has fostered a new era of possibility for those who cut. Contributing to this new era is the burgeoning subcultural networking component ushered in by the internet. The cyber world has made it increasingly more practical for the practitioners of cutting—a group who were once primarily limited to pursuing their cutting practices in extreme isolation, amid the widespread (and persistent) belief that the practice is a shameful, dirty secret (Adler and Adler 2008; Holmes 2000; Klonsky 2009; Kibler 2009)—to feel more normal and find groups that help meet their individual needs (McKenna and Green 2002).

As a result of these changes, cutters are more difficult to situate in one specific category of deviance, including the "individual"/"loner" typology. Instead, cutters appear to be constantly negotiating the boundaries of their new options and possibilities. On the one hand, it is still a highly stigmatized form of deviance; however, the rapidly growing network systems and public information available to cutters make the transition from loner to individual deviant (and back) much more feasible. Additionally, the technologically evolved modern state of cutting sets the stage for a cutter simultaneously to hide their cutting life from the non-cutting world (and from the online community by remaining anonymous), while engaging the deviant social support network and information banks. A tech-savvy cutter can be simultaneously alone and interacting with countless others. Also, depending on the desire and needs of a cutter, internet and other deviant support networks may be used to self-educate for the purposes of disengaging from self-injury, or to seek support and self-educate for the purposes of continuing cutting as a type of life maintenance (Whitlock et al. 2006). The latter perspective assumes that cutting is a reasonable and legitimate, multi-purpose coping strategy (Adler and Adler 2008).

Cutting and suicide

The topic of suicide is prominent in most of the studies on cutting. This persistent focus is primarily due to a longstanding (and seemingly false) assumption that all cutters are simply practicing for their eventual suicide attempts (Soloman and Farrand 1996; Bates 2005). However, as more detailed data unfold, it has been suggested that many or most cutters do so more frequently as an extreme effort to self-heal, rather than destroy (Bates 2005; Guertin et al. 2001; Klonsky 2009; Whitlock et al. 2009). As the respondents of one study who had engaged in self-injury and then attempted suicide explained, they relied on cutting and other forms of self-mutilation to cope, or as a sort of patchwork self-treatment. They considered their suicide attempt to be exactly the opposite—cutting was set aside as an aspect of renewal and restoration, while the suicide attempt was compartmentalized as expressly for total self-destruction (Adler and Adler 2005).

As a logical outcropping of these and related findings, a move towards separate classifications of self-injury based on the presence of suicidal intent has been proposed and recently implemented (Muehlenkamp 2005; Richardson et al. 2007). Accordingly, Muehlenkamp (2005) has appealed to the field of psychiatry to list "non-suicidal self-injury" as a unique category of disorder in the next edition of the *Diagnostic and Statistical Manual of Mental Disorders*, due to the notable lack of suicidal intent among cutters and other self-injurers. Similarly, Richardson *et al.* (2007) suggest new official names for the proposed categorization scheme: non-suicidal self-injury (NSSI) and suicidal self-injury (SSI). It is important to note that this new form of categorization does *not* imply that no cutters are at risk of suicide. The focus is simply on intent. Even among cutters with no obvious, conscious suicidal intent there remains a concern over the persistent link between self-injurers who exhibit signs of depression and suicide (Adler and Adler 2005; Holmes 2000; Kibler 2009).

Body piercing

Although it has been noted in the discussion of other forms of self-injury up to this point that classification schemes and typologies pertaining to self-injury remain sources of contention and uncertainty, nowhere is this more evident than in research exploring the social world of body piercers. Although body piercing is often referred to as a form of self-injury or "self-mutilation" in popular media outlets (Mascia-Lees and Sharpe 1994; Pitts 2003), academic body piercing studies more typically rely on a body modification (BM) framework (Favazza 1996; Shilling 2003). Leading research on body piercing as BM reveals less about deviant behavior and more about the constant interpretation and re-interpretation of the meaning of the human body (Featherstone 1987) and attempts to communicate with the social world using the flesh as a working canvas (Shilling 2003). In this light, piercings are tantamount to a "body project," both responsive to and representative of the changing foci of social institutions—especially consumer media images (Pitts 2003; Shilling 2003).

Of all forms of BM, piercing and tattooing are the most common globally (Favazza 1996; Stirn 2003). BMs cover a wide variety of decorative body practices, ranging from the highly dangerous and pathological to seemingly harmless peer-group fashion statements (Stirn and Hinz 2008). However, media attention paid to body piercing and other BM practices remains overwhelmingly negative (DeMello 2000; Pitts 2003), and several studies have indicated high instances of negative traits among body piercers, such as an "anger trait" (Carroll and Anderson 2002), thrill seeking (Roberti *et al.* 2004), and risky adolescent sexual behavior (Roberts *et al.* 2004).

Concluding comments

As is evidenced by the literature explored in this chapter, self-injurers are far more dynamic and diversified in their activities and reasons for engaging in their chosen forms of deviance than is typically portrayed. While self-injury studies are still in their infancy, a growing body of research in this area continually highlights the difficulties of situating self-injurers within specific analytical frameworks. These difficulties hinge on the heightened influence of rapidly evolving and expanding technological resources, shifting public awareness and media-driven fluctuations in the perception of the body and identity (which help to shape these self-injury and body modification practices). All of these social forces serve to keep categorical lines blurred.

What remains unclear is the point at which BM or self-injury practices, such as cutting, piercing and tattooing, transition to legitimate harm from merely being forms of pseudo-artistic expression on a living canvas, attempts to signal individuality to the social world or efforts to fit in. Future research objectives are clear. We must be more proactive about countering media-driven misconceptions about self-injury in a collective effort to de-stigmatize these activities. This will benefit self-injurers by making it easier for those who need help to seek it out, while also fostering a better sense of trust and openness among the research community and self-injurers. Consequently, richer data will be accumulated. In order to facilitate future studies of self-injury and BM practices, there is a need for nationally representative and international comparative, longitudinal studies, as well as critical ethnographies in the spirit of the Adler and Adler (2005, 2008) research that continues to explore the new worlds that self-injurers are creating for themselves.

References

Adler, Patricia A. and Peter Adler. 2005. "Self-Injurers as Loners: The Social Organization of Solitary Deviance." *Deviant Behavior* 26(4):345–378.

Adler, Patricia A. and Peter Adler. 2008. "The Cyber Worlds of Self-Injurers: Deviant Communities, Relationships, and Selves." *Symbolic Interaction* 31(1):33–56.

Anderson, Leon and Jimmy D. Taylor. 2010. "Standing out While Fitting in: Serious Leisure Identities and Aligning Actions among Skydivers and Gun Collectors." *Journal of Contemporary Ethnography* 39:34–59.

Bates, Betsy. 2005. "Cutting May Be More Widespread Than Imagined." *Family Practice News* 35(6):50.

Behrendt, Alice and Steffen Moritz. 2005. "Posttraumatic Stress Disorder and Memory Problems after Female Genital Mutilation." *American Journal of Psychiatry* 162:1000–1002.

Best, Joel and David F. Luckenbill. 1982. *Organizing Deviance*. Englewood Cliffs, NJ: Prentice-Hall.

Carroll, L. and R. Anderson R. 2002. "Body Piercing, Tattooing, Self-Esteem, and Body Investment in Adolescent Girls." *Adolescence* 37(147):627–637.

Catania, Lucrezia, Omar Abdulcadir, Vincenzo Puppo, Jole Baldaro Verde, Jasmine Abdulcadir, and Dalmar Abdulcadir. 2007. "Pleasure and Orgasm in Women with Female Genital Mutilation/Cutting (FGM/C)." *Journal of Sexual Medicine* 4(6):1666–1678.

Cerulo, Karen A. 1997. "Reframing Sociological Concepts for a Brave New (Virtual?) World." *Sociological Inquiry* 67:48–58.

Clifford, James. 1988. *The Predicament of Culture: Twentieth-Century Ethnography, Literature and Art*. Cambridge, MA: Harvard University Press.

Cohn, Leigh. 2004. *Self Harm Behaviors and Eating Disorders*. London: Routledge.

Cook, Rebecca, Bernard Dickens, and Mahmoud Fathalla. 2003. *Reproductive Health and Human Rights*. Oxford: Oxford University Press.

Dabney, Dean A. and Richard C. Hollinger. 1999. "Illicit Prescription Drug Use among Pharmacists: Evidence of a Paradox of Familiarity." *Work and Occupations* 26:77–106.

Demello, Margo. 2000. *Bodies of Inscription: A Cultural History of the Modern Tattoo Community*. Durham, NC: Duke University Press.

Deshotels, Tina H. and Craig J. Forsyth. 2007. "Postmodern Masculinities and the Eunuch." *Deviant Behavior* 28:201–218.

Durkheim, Emile. 1965 [1915]. *The Elementary Forms of Religious Life*. New York: The Free Press.

Favazza, Armando. 1996. *Bodies under Siege: Self-Mutilation and Body Modification in Culture and Psychiatry*. Baltimore, MD: Johns Hopkins University Press.

Featherstone, Mike. 1987. "Lifestyle and Consumer Culture." *Theory, Culture, & Society* 4:55–70.

Featherstone, Mike. 1999. "Body Modification: An Introduction." *Body & Society* 5:1–13.

Foster, Derek. 1997. "Community and Identity in the Electronic Village." Pp. 23–27 in *Internet Culture*, edited by D. Porter. New York: Routledge.

Gardner, Fiona. 2001. *Self-Harm: A Psychotherapeutic Approach*. London: Routledge.

Gruenbaum, Ellen. 2001. *The Female Circumcision Controversy: An Anthropological Perspective*. Philadelphia: University of Pennsylvania Press.

Guertin, Tracey. 2001. "Self-Mutilative Behavior in Adolescents who Attempt Suicide by Overdose." *Journal of the American Academy of Child & Adolescent Psychiatry* 40(9):1062–1069.

Hassanin, Ibrahim M. A., R. Saleh, Ahmed A. Bedaiwy, Rachele S. Peterson, and Mohamed A. Bedaiwy. 2008. "Prevalence of Female Genital Cutting in Upper Egypt: 6 Years after Enforcement of Prohibition Law." *Reproductive BioMedicine Online* 16:27–31.

Hernlund, Ylva and Bettina Shell-Duncan. 2007. *Transcultural Bodies: Female Genital Cutting in Global Context*. Chapel Hill, NC: Rutgers University Press.

Hodgson, Sarah. 2004. "Cutting through the Silence: A Sociological Construction of Self-Injury." *Sociological Inquiry* 74(2):162–179.

Holmes, Ann. 2000. *Cutting the Pain away: Understanding Self-Mutilation*. Philadelphia, PA: Chelsea House.

Jacobson, Colleen and Madelyn Gould. 2007. "The Epidemiology and Phenomenology of Non-Suicidal Self-Injurious Behavior among Adolescents: A Critical Review of the Literature." *Archives of Suicide Research* 11(2): 129–147.

Jenkins, Philip. 2001. *Beyond Tolerance: Child Pornography on the Internet*. New York: New York University Press.

Kibler, Jackie. 2009. "Self-Injury in the Schools: An Exploratory Analysis of Midwest School Counselors' Knowledge and Experience." *North American Journal of Psychology* 11(2): 309–322.

Klonsky, David E. 2009. "Assessing the Functions of Non-Suicidal Self-Injury: Psychometric Properties of the Inventory of Statements about Self-injury (ISAS)." *Journal of Psychopathology and Behavioral Assessment* 31(3): 215–219.

Kosut, Mary. 2006. "An Ironic Fad: The Commodification and Consumption of Tattoos." *Journal of Popular Culture* 39:1035–1048.

Levenkron, Steven. 1998. *Cutting: Understanding and Overcoming Self-Mutilation*. New York: Norton.

Lightfoot-Klein, Hanny. 1989. "The Sexual Experience and Marital Adjustment of Genitally Circumcised and Infibulated Females in the Sudan." *Journal of Sex Research* 26(3):375.

Maguire, Jennifer. 2002. "Body Lessons: Fitness Publishing and the Cultural Production of the Fitness Consumer." *International Review for the Sociology of Sport* 37:449–464.

Mascia-Lees, Frances and Patricia Sharpe. 1994. "The Anthropological Unconscious." *American Anthropologist* 96(3):649–660.

McKenna, Katelyn Y. A. and Amie S. Green. 2002. "Virtual Group Dynamics." *Group Dynamics: Theory, Research and Practice* 6:116–127.

Muehlenkamp, J. J. 2005. "Self-Injurious Behavior as a Separate Clinical Syndrome." *American Journal of Orthopsychiatry* 75(2):324–333.

Myers, James. 1992. "Nonmainstream Body Modification: Genital Piercing, Branding, Burning and Cutting." *Journal of Contemporary Ethnography* 21:267–306.

O'Shaughnessy, Ruth and Rudi Dallos. 2009. "Attachment Research and Eating Disorders: A Review of the Literature." *Clinical Child Psychology and Psychiatry* 14(4):559–574.

Parens, Erik. 2006. *Surgically Shaping Children: Technology, Ethics and the Pursuit of Normality*. Baltimore, MD: Johns Hopkins University Press.

Pitts, Victoria. 1999. "Body Modification, Self-Mutilation and Agency in the Media Accounts of a Subculture." *Body & Society* 5:291–303.

Pitts, Victoria. 2003. *In the Flesh: The Cultural Politics of Body Modification*. New York: Palgrave Macmillan.

Richardson, E. E., N. Perrine, L. Dierker, and M. L. Kelley. 2007. "Characteristics and Functions of Non-Suicidal Self-Injury in a Community Sample of Adolescents." *Psychological Medicine* 37(9):1372.

Roberti, J. W., E. A. Storch, and E. A. Bravata. 2004. "Sensation Seeking, Exposure to Psychosocial Stressors, and Body Modifications in a College Population." *Personality and Individual Differences* 37:1167–1177.

Roberts, T. A., P. Auinger, and S. A. Ryan. 2004. "Body Piercing and High-Risk Behavior in Adolescents." *Journal of Adolescent Health* 34:224–229.

Ross, Shana and Nancy Heath. 2002. "A Study of the Frequency of Self-Mutilation in a Community Sample of Adolescents." *Journal of Youth & Adolescence* 31(1):67.

Schmidt, Ulrike and Kate Davidson. 2004. *Life after Self-Harm: A Guide to the Future*. New York: Routledge.

Shilling, Chris. 2003. *The Body and Social Theory*. London: Sage.

Shilling, Chris. 2005. *The Body in Culture, Technology and Society*. Los Angeles, CA: Sage.

Snow, David A. and Leon Anderson. 1993. *Down on Their Luck: A Study of Homeless Street People*. Berkeley: University of California Press.

Solomon, Yvette and Julie Farrand. 1996. "Why Don't You Do It Properly? Young Women Who Self-Injure." *Journal of Adolescence* 19(11):10–19.

Stirn, Aglaja. 2003. "Body Piercing: Medical Consequences and Psychological Motivations." *The Lancet* 361(9364):1205–1215.

Stirn, Aglaja and Andreas Hinz. 2008. "Tattoos, Body Piercings, and Self-Injury: Is There a Connection? Investigations on a Core Group of Participants Practicing Body Modification." *Psychotherapy Research* 18(3):326–333.

Taylor, Jimmy D. 2009. *American Gun Culture: Collectors, Shows and the Story of the Gun*. New York: LFB.

Thio, Alex. 2009. *Deviant Behavior*, 10th edn. New York: Pearson.

Walsh, Barnet. 2005. *Treating Self-Injury*. New York: Guilford.

Whitlock, J., Powers, J., and Eckenrode, J. 2006. "The Virtual Cutting Edge: The Internet and Adolescent Self-Injury." *Developmental Psychology* 42(1/2):407–417.

Whitlock, Janis, Greg Eells, Nina Cummings, and Amanda Purington. 2009. "Nonsuicidal Self-Injury in College Populations: Mental Health Provider Assessment of Prevalence and Need." *Journal of College Student Psychotherapy* 23(3):172–183.

Williams, Mary. 2008. *Self-Mutilation: Opposing Viewpoints*. Detroit, MI: Thomson Gale.

37

Suicide as deviant behavior

Steven Stack

Suicide is defined as the willful taking of one's own life. In 2002 an estimated 877,000 persons committed suicide throughout the world. In 2005, suicide was the eleventh most common cause of death in the United States, with 32,657 people taking their own life. This amounts to 89 people every day, or one suicide every 16 minutes. Further, it is estimated that there are approximately 25 suicide attempts for every completed suicide. In terms of people admitted to emergency rooms, 372,722 individuals were treated for suicide attempts in 2005—more than 11 times the number of completed suicides that year (Wasserman and Wasserman 2009).

While people often fear being killed by another, they are actually twice as likely to die by their own hand as to be killed. For the US between 2003 and 2005, the annualized rate of suicide was 11 per 100,000 population, nearly double the annualized rate for homicides (6 per 100,000 population) (Centers for Disease Control and Prevention 2008).

Table 37.1 provides basic demographic data on the numbers and rates of suicide per 100,000 persons in each demographic category. Over a relatively short time frame (1995–2005), suicide rates remained relatively stable. The rate for the general population declined somewhat from 11.9 to 11.0 per 100,000.

Age groups

Rates fell most notably for the elderly, with the rate for the young old (65–74) falling from 15.8 to 12.6, but the retired or elderly (especially males) still have the highest suicide rate of any age group. By contrast, rates rose for the cohorts of the large postwar "baby boom." For those in the heart of this group (ages 45–54), the suicide rate increased from 14.6 to 16.5. The large postwar baby boomer generation will begin to reach age 65 in 2011. In the decades thereafter, especially given the projected shortfalls in social security, Medicare, pensions, and related financial supports for the elderly, suicidologists predict a significant increase in the number and rates of elderly suicide in the US and abroad (Stack 2000a).

Gender

The suicide rate for males declined slightly, but it remains approximately four times greater than the rate for females (17.7 versus 4.5 in 2005). There are at least ten explanations in the

Table 37.1 Suicide rates per 100,000 in 1995–2005 by age group, and number of suicides in 2005

Age group	1995 Suicides per 100,000	2005 Suicides per 100,000	2005 Number of suicides in age group
5–14	0.9	0.7	272
15–24	13.3	10.0	4,212
25–34	15.4	12.4	4,990
35–44	15.2	14.9	6,550
45–54	14.6	16.5	6,991
55–64	13.3	13.9	4,210
65–74	15.8	12.6	2,344
75–84	20.7	16.9	2,200
85+	21.6	16.9	860
All ages, including missing data	11.9	11.0	32,637
Males	19.8	17.7	25,907
Females	4.4	4.5	6,730
White	12.9	12.3	29,527
Black	6.7	5.1	1,992
All non-white	6.9	5.5	3,110

Source: Centers for Disease Control and Prevention 2008

literature for the gap between male and female suicide rates. For example, the incidence of alcoholism, a risk factor for suicide, is five times higher among men than women. Further, women are significantly more integrated than men into organized religion, a social tie that protects against suicide. However, the relative merits of these explanations have not been rigorously evaluated (Lester 2000; Stack 2000a).

Race

The official rate for black people remains less than half of that for white people (12.3 versus 5.1 in 2005). Since black peoples' involvement in suicidogenic risk factors, including depression, economic strain, and marital disruption, is equal to or even exceeds that of white people, this social fact has been termed the "racial suicide paradox." Part of the racial divide in suicide is believed to be an artifact, since black deaths are considerably more likely than white deaths to be classified into causes of death apt to include disguised suicide (e.g., "violent death—specific cause undetermined," "unintentional drowning," and "unintentional poisoning"; Rockett *et al.* 2006). However, part of the race suicide paradox may be real. Societal discrimination against African Americans has contributed to a cultural response: the externalization of aggression. When confronted with stressful life events, black people are more likely to blame others than themselves. As a consequence, black homicide rates are five or more times those of white (Stack 2000a). Further, the tolerance of suicide—suicide acceptability—is considerably lower among black people than white people. Finally, religiosity levels are higher among black people than white people, and all religions tend to condemn suicide (Stack 2000a). No rigorous work clarifying these and related potential explanations has yet been completed.

Locating the problem: numbers versus rates

Rates of suicide, while important, may mask the locations of the sheer numbers of persons suiciding in social groups. Importantly, while those over 85 have a higher rate than the 45–54 age group, there are far more suicides among the latter: 6,991 compared to just 860. Hence, in terms of sheer numbers, people in mid-life account for the bulk of the suicide problem (Lester 2000; Stack 2000a). The average age of a suicide victim is 44.

Explanations of suicide have included many risk and protective factors at the individual and aggregate levels. For example, certain psychiatric disorders, themselves often studied as deviant behavior, contribute to suicide risk. Social relationships, including marital strain and social isolation, can increase the odds of suicide, too. Economic strain, including unemployment, underemployment, home foreclosure and eviction, also increase suicide risk. Highly publicized suicide stories often contribute to suicide through copycat effects, especially if the story involves a celebrity. Protective social factors include parenting, economic security, and a high level of religiosity and involvement in religious organizations.

This chapter will focus on four of the better-researched risk factors for suicide. These are organized according to a continuum starting with individual or trait explanations (psychiatric disorders), and continuing through more sociological conditions, including those in primary groups (marital strain) and then secondary groups (economic strain and mass media impacts).

Suicide and psychiatric risk factors

Over a century ago, Emile Durkheim (1966 [1897]) helped found the discipline of sociology with a work which stressed suicide as a result of factors external to the individual, principally inadequate ties to social groups. He argued that psychiatric morbidity was not a cause of suicide. Over the next 100 years, nevertheless, psychiatry has continued to dominate the study of suicide. To illustrate the point, of over 30,000 works on suicide published since 1980, only 400 have appeared in sociology journals. The large body of research on suicide has overwhelmingly stressed such individual traits as severe depression, high anxiety, and other psychiatric disorders. These conditions are often viewed as deviant behavior in themselves. Such conditions as lifelong depression, anxiety disorders, including panic disorders, and years of recurrent hallucinations suffered by schizophrenics can wear people out; then the terrors of death can either be welcomed or at least seem less daunting than continuing with the terrors of life.

The risk of suicide among persons with severe psychiatric disorders is often very high. The largest systematic review of the research analyzed a total of 249 studies (Clare and Barraclough 1997). Fully 36 of the 44 psychiatric disorders studied were marked by elevated risks of suicide. A summary of the average degree of suicide risk found in sets of these studies is provided in Table 37.2. Schizophrenia, a condition marked by perceptual distortions of reality, including auditory and visual delusions, generally begins to develop in early adulthood. It has biological and genetic roots. On average, across studies, schizophrenics are 8.5 times more likely than non-psychiatrically disturbed persons to die by their own hand. Persons suffering from major depression, a type of depression that lasts for at least two weeks at a time and during that period one cannot perform one's normal daily routines, were 20.4 times more likely than average to die through suicide. These elevated risks are much higher than those reported for social risk factors. For example, divorced persons are typically between two and four times more likely to suicide than married persons.

Thirty studies have followed samples of schizophrenics over time to track what percentage of them die through suicide. A review of this body of work determined that 37.7% of male

315

Table 37.2 Average risk ratio for selected psychiatric disorders

Psychiatric disorder	Number of research studies	Number of persons studied	Combined relative risk of suicide for persons with the disorder versus controls
Eating disorder	13	1,300	23
Alcohol dependence and abuse	32	45,000	6 (range 1–60×)
Opioid dependence and abuse	9	7,500	14 (range 3–36×)
Schizophrenia	38	30,000	8.5 (range 0.8–115×)
Major depression	23	8,000	20.4 (0–200×)
Bipolar disorder	14	3,700	15.1 (0–133×)
Dysthymia	9	50,000	12 (3–100×)
Mood disorders	12	10,000	16 (4–38×)
Epilepsy	12	6,500	4.88
Suicide attempts by self-poisoning	11	8,000	40 (20–120×)
Suicide attempts any method	9	2,700	38 (0–77×)

Source: Clare and Barraclough 1997

schizophrenics and 27.0% of female schizophrenics had suicided by follow-up. By contrast, only 1–1.5% of the general population die by suicide (Lester 2006).

Substance abuse is another well-researched deviant behavior. It is a powerful correlate of suicidality. Substance abusers have greater opportunity for suicide, given their access to drugs as a means for killing themselves. Further, drugs desensitize persons and promote impulsive acts, such as suicide. According to a review of 42 relevant investigations, alcohol use disorders increased risk for suicide by 9.7 times, opiate use disorders by 13.51 times, intravenous drug use by 13.73 times, mixed drug use by 16.85, and heavy drinking by 3.51 times, over that of the general population (Wilcox *et al.* 2004).

While the psychiatric perspective is useful in helping to explain why some individuals are at higher risk of suicide than others, it does not offer a full explanation of secondary variation in suicide risk. For example, it is not able to explain the large gap in suicide rates between men and women. It does not fully explain why suicide rises after publicized news stories about the suicide of a celebrity. It also cannot fully explain why suicide rates vary considerably among ecological areas such as cities, states, and nations. Work on other risk and protective factors therefore needs to be considered in order to improve our understanding of the causes of suicide. This chapter now turns to a review of three of the better-researched sociological explanations: marital strain, economic strain, and media coverage of suicide.

(The psychiatric risk factors and sociological risk factors are not meant to be mutually exclusive. Sociological risk factors, such as divorce and unemployment, can, for example, contribute to psychiatric morbidity, such as major depression. However, relatively little empirical work to date has tested the psychiatric and sociological perspectives simultaneously.)

Suicide and sociological risk factors

Marital integration/strain

Durkheim (1966 [1897]) contended that marriage was a key social source of integration. The institution of marriage provides and expects emotional support from a partner. Marital ties assist the individual in avoiding preoccupation with their own personal problems through helping another. By promoting integration and regulating sexual appetites, marriage increases meaning in life and should reduce deviant behavior, including suicide. In contrast, divorce would be expected to enhance suicide risk, to the extent that it breaks integrative bonds between the individual and their partner.

Divorce

The most widely researched sociological risk factor for suicide is divorce. Over 115 years, 132 studies appeared on the subject. These investigations contained 789 research findings. Fully 78% demonstrated a link between divorce and suicide risk. In Austria, for example, the suicide rate for divorced persons was 128.6 per 100,000, 4.22 times greater than their married counterparts' rate of 30.5 per 100,000. This ratio of 4.22 is termed a coefficient of aggravation (COA), the extent to which the status of divorce aggravates the problem of suicide. Generally speaking, the COA varies between 2 and 4 in most age groups and nations of the world. In the US, for example, for men it varies from 3.53 for those aged 60–64 to 4.58 for those aged 40–44. For women, it ranges from 2.10 for those aged 60–64 to 4.15 for those aged 25–29 (Stack 2000b).

Cohabitation

In recent decades ever more people have elected to live together without the legal bond of marriage. Therein, emotional support can be regularly provided to and received from a partner. The extent to which such cohabitation protects against suicide, relative to marriage, is unclear in the US, but European-based research has found that cohabitants have a significantly higher risk of suicide, yet are much less likely to suicide than members of the single population. For example, in Denmark, cohabitants have a risk of suicide that is 54% higher than married persons. However, single persons have a much more elevated risk: 3.17 times that of married persons (Qin *et al.* 2003).

Living alone

Many single persons have roommates or still live with their parents or other relatives. In such arrangements, emotional support can be provided. A substantial proportion of adults, however, live alone. This contributes to suicide through minimizing emotional support from intimate relationships. While not as well researched as divorce, findings have been fairly consistent on the impact of this factor on suicide potential. Living alone is, however, correlated with many other predictors of suicide potential, including marital status and depression. In the most rigorous analysis to date, such confounding factors were held constant. An analysis of the US National Center for Health Statistics' (2001) National Mortality Follow Back Survey (consisting of in-depth psychological autopsies of 9,869 adult deaths, including 948 suicides), controlling for 17 other risk factors, demonstrated that persons who lived alone were 1.58 times more likely to die through suicide than persons not living alone (Stack 2009).

Parenthood

One correlate of being married is having children. Ties to children can increase one's sense of responsibility to others and give a purpose to life. Parents may endure hardships and persevere for the sake of their children. Married persons with children tend to have a lower rate of suicide than married persons without children (Stack 2000b). For example, in Denmark, parents with a young child are 50% less likely to suicide than persons without a young child (Qin *et al.* 2003).

Economic strain

Suicide research has conceptualized economic strain principally in two ways: low income and unemployment. It is presumed that these groups would be among those experiencing financial stress, given their impoverishment and/or sudden loss of means of livelihood. Economic strain can also affect other suicidogenic conditions, including both sociological ones (e.g., marital strain) and psychiatric ones (e.g., substance abuse and depression).

Unemployment

Unemployment can erode not only the income but the self-esteem of the individual. Ties to co-workers are also typically lost or minimized. Research has typically found that the unemployed have a suicide rate at least double that of the general population. For example, in London, the difference was 73.4 per 100,000 versus 14.1 per 100,000 for the general population. In France in the 1990s the suicide rate among unemployed males was 74.9 per 100,000, more than double that of employed men (32.3 per 100,000). In Hong Kong, the ratio was nearly 3:1 (37.2 versus 13.2 per 100,000) (Stack 2000a). Unemployment is intermingled with other forms of deviant behavior, so there is a need to determine the independent influence of unemployment on suicide, preferably in long-term research where existing depression levels (i.e., depression before unemployment) can be measured.

To date, there have been 27 long-term investigations of unemployment and suicide. Surprisingly, however, only a few have measured depression. The best-designed investigation followed 189,000 persons from 1982 to 1997 in Denmark. After controlling out psychiatric disturbances and numerous socio-economic factors, persons who were unemployed during the last year of life were between 1.31 and 1.39 times more likely than employed persons to die of suicide (Agerbo 2005).

Low income

While Durkheim (1966 [1897]) contended that poverty was a school of "social restraint" and, as such, the poor should have a low suicide rate, the opposite has generally been found to be the case in modern empirical work (Stack 1982, 2000a).

For example, in the largest and best-designed investigation to date—a Danish study comprising 444,297 persons, including 21,169 suicides—found that persons in the lowest quartile in income were 5.52 times more likely to die of suicide than persons in the top quartile in income (Qin et al. 2003).

Mass media as a risk factor for suicide

Media effects

Durkheim (1966 [1897]) speculated that imitation had little or no real impact on suicide rates. However, starting in the late 1960s, evidence emerged that questioned Durkheim's assertion. Such media venues as books, movies, and news stories often suggest that suicide is a solution to various problems of living. It seems that, through social learning and other mechanisms, media stories on suicide can affect the social suicide rate.

For example, the book *Final Exit*—which rationalizes suicide and offers a guide on how to commit suicide with plastic bags—was associated with a substantial increase in suicide by that method in the year of its publication. Researchers found that suicide by plastic-bag asphyxiation increased by 313% in New York City. Further, 27.3% of these suicides were found with a copy of the book next to them (Stack 2005).

However, many studies report no copycat effect. This is associated with the notion that certain types of story are apparently more lethal than others. People identify with certain narratives of suicide more than other narrative types. The most extensive meta-analysis to date reviewed 419 findings contained in 105 studies of media effects on suicide. This analysis determined, for example, that investigations that explored the impact of the suicide of a well-known celebrity were 5.27 times more likely than other studies to report a copycat effect (Stack 2005). In contrast, stories about well-known criminals (such as mobsters or terrorists) had no discernible effect on the social suicide rate.

Treatment and social policy

A wide variety of solutions to suicide have been proposed. These include control of opportunities for suicide (gun control), prevention programs, including education in schools and media campaigns, talk therapies, including cognitive-behavioral treatments, and pharmacological treatments, such as lithium and anti-depressants. Most of these solutions have not been rigorously evaluated (Mann *et al.* 2005).

However, some pharmacological treatments for suicidal patients with affective disorders have shown promise. For example, a recent meta-analysis was done on 31 research studies which collectively covered 85,229 persons. The overall risk of suicide among those treated with lithium was 4.91 times lower than that for those not treated with lithium (Baldessarini *et al.* 2006). Another recent analysis used the rate of prescriptions for antidepressants to predict youth suicide rates in the US. Even after controlling for a host of socio-economic confounders, the higher the rate of antidepressant prescriptions, the lower the suicide rate (Gibbons *et al.* 2006).

References

Agerbo, E. (2005). Middle life suicide risk, partner's psychiatric illness, spouse and child bereavement by suicide or other means of death: a gender specific study. *Journal of Epidemiology & Community Health*, 59:407–412.

Baldessarini, R. J., Tondo, L., Davis, P., Pompili, M., Goodwin, F. K., and Hennen, J. (2006). Decreased risk of suicides and attempts during long term lithium treatment: a meta analytic review. *Bipolar Disorders*, 8:625–639.

Centers for Disease Control and Prevention (2008). *Deaths: final data for 2005*. National Vital Statistics Report Vol. 56, No. 10. Atlanta, GA: Centers for Disease Control and Prevention.

Clare, H. E. and Barraclough, B. (1997). Suicide as an outcome for mental disorders: a meta analysis. *British Journal of Psychiatry*, 170(3):205–228.

Durkheim, E . (1966 [1897]). *Suicide*. New York: The Free Press.

Gibbons, R. D., Hur, K., Bhaumik, D. K., and Mann, J. (2006). US youth suicide rates lower in counties with high SSRI use. *American Journal of Psychiatry*, 163:1898–1904.

Lester, D. (2000). *Why People Kill Themselves*. Springfield, IL: Charles Thomas.

Lester, D. (2006). Sex differences in completed suicide by schizophrenic persons: a meta analysis. *Suicide and Life Threatening Behavior*, 36(1):50–56.

Mann, J. J. , Apter, A., Bertolote, J., Beutrais, A., Currier, D., et al. (2005). Suicide prevention strategies: a systematic review. *Journal of the American Medical Association*, 294:2064–2074.

Qin, P., Agerbo, E., and Mortensen, P. B. (2003). Suicide risk in relation to socio-economic, demographic, psychiatric, and familial factors: a national register based study of all suicides in Denmark, 1981–1997. *American Journal of Psychiatry*, 160:765–772.

Rockett, R. H., Samora, J. B., and Coben, J. H. (2006). The black–white suicide paradox: possible effects of misclassification. *Social Science and Medicine*, 63:2165–2175.

Stack, S. (1982). Suicide: a decade review of the sociological literature. *Deviant Behavior*, 4:41–66.

Stack, S. (2000a). Suicide: a 15-year review of the sociological literature. Part I: Cultural and economic factors. *Suicide and Life Threatening Behavior*, 30:145–162.

Stack, S. (2000b). Suicide: a 15-year review of the sociological literature. Part II: Modernization and social integration perspectives. *Suicide and Life Threatening Behavior*, 30:163–176.

Stack, S. (2005). Suicide and the media: a quantitative review of studies based on nonfictional stories. *Suicide and Life Threatening Behavior*, 35:121–133.

Stack, S. (2009). The suicide of Ajax: a note on occupational strain as a neglected factor in suicidology. In S. Stack and D. Lester (eds.) *Suicide and the Creative Arts* (pp. 49–53). New York: Nova Science.

US National Center for Health Statistics (2001). *Mortality Follow Back Survey, 1993: Codebook*. Ann Arbor, MI.: Inter University Consortium for Political and Social Research.

Wasserman, D. and Wasserman, C. (2009). *Oxford Textbook of Suicidology and Suicide Prevention*. London: Oxford University Press.

Wilcox, H. C., Connor, K. R., and Caine, E. D. (2004). Association of alcohol and drug use disorders and completed suicide: an empirical review of cohort studies. *Drug and Alcohol Dependence*, 76S:S11–S19.

Part VIII

Deviance in social institutions

Overview

Deviant behavior does not take place in a social vacuum; rather, some configurations of deviance are linked to, and occur within, particular contexts. Much deviance takes place within the context of social institutions. Social scientists have traditionally articulated five basic or core social institutions: family, education, religion, the polity, and the economy and work. More recently, additional social institutions have been identified, including the military, medicine, and sports and recreation. Some scholars have asserted that certain forms of deviance are unique to particular social institutions. Some prime examples of this might be adultery as family deviance, and heresy as religious deviance. The nature of the normative system of each social institution and the opportunity structure attendant to particular social institutions would appear to engender unique configurations of deviance and crime. Chapters in this part will address deviance component to some social institutions, including family deviance, political deviance, organizational and occupational deviance, sport and leisure deviance, and medical deviance. These essays will examine both the normative system and the opportunity structures of each social institution.

Family deviance

Every social institution is a fertile context for deviant behavior and the family is no exception. The family harbors a variety of unique configurations of deviance. In their chapter, Angela Gover and Stacey Bosick explore some of these unique forms of deviance, and focus especially on family behaviors that are criminalized by public policy. The authors indicate that, historically, "problems within the family were typically viewed as 'private' and consequently outside the purview of public policy and criminal law." By the 1970s, however, the feminist movement had lobbied for a new perspective on the family that viewed physical and sexual victimization within the family as behavior that justified legal intervention.

The authors begin their survey of family deviance with an examination of family norms— legal and illegal, and "normal" and deviant. They point out that the US Census defines a family as "a set of two or more people living together, who are related by birth, marriage, or adoption," but this is a relatively narrow definition. Gover and Bosick elect to use a somewhat broader definition for their discussion. Only a relatively small percentage (12.1%) of families in the US conform to the idealized notion of the "nuclear family" (a married couple with children). Many marriages are not monogamous. Research has shown that 14.7% of males and 13.5% of females in self-identified relationships have been guilty of infidelity (sex with someone other than one's marital partner). One recent study estimated that there were more than three million same-sex cohabiting couples in the US. Today, more than 40% of children are born to unmarried parents, and there are 109 million single-parent American families. While infidelity is usually clandestine, sometimes it is open and consensual. "Swinging" couples consensually exchange spouses with other couples for the purpose of engaging in sex; however, it is believed that this practice is restricted to just 1–2% of married couples. All of these variations of family behavior are legal.

There are, though, illegal types of marriage arrangement, too. One example is bigamy, where an individual is married at the same time to two spouses, who typically are not aware of the other spouse. Polygamous marriages involve an individual having two (or more) spouses and usually living with both (or all) in a single home. Even though such marriages are consensual, they are illegal. This marital arrangement is relatively rare.

One of the more frequently encountered forms of family deviance is child abuse and neglect. An article titled "The Battered Child Syndrome," published in 1962, focused national attention on this problem. Four categories of child maltreatment have been identified: neglect; physical abuse; sexual abuse; and psychological abuse. Gover and Bosick indicate that 794,000 children were victimized by abuse or neglect in the US in 2007. Some 1,760 of them died as a result. Most perpetrators of abuse are male, while the majority of perpetrators of neglect are female.

A less frequently encountered form of family deviance is incest. This has been culturally, religiously, and legally sanctioned throughout history. The authors assert that the victims of incest frequently experience "devastating behavioral, psychological, and social consequences . . . ranging from self-esteem issues to personality disorders."

Domestic violence is a third form of family violence. Gover and Bosick indicate this type of violence "refers to the exertion of power and control by one intimate over another intimate partner." Other terms for domestic violence used by scholars include: spousal abuse, partner violence, battering, and wife abuse. Domestic violence occurs throughout the population in all income levels, social classes, ethnic groups, and religious groups. Partner violence results in approximately 2 million injuries per year, with some 500,000 of the victims requiring medical treatment annually. Domestic violence may take the form of physical violence, threats of physical violence, psychological/emotional abuse, or sexual violence. Victims of domestic violence may experience a variety of physical and psychological problems.

Yet another variety of deviance that occurs within the context of the family is alcohol and drug addiction. The authors report that "substance abuse is most prevalent among single, young adult males." Nevertheless, substance abuse does occur within families, and when this happens "the impact on family life is especially pronounced." Gover and Bosick suggest that when parental substance abuse occurs, it may contribute to a variety of negative outcomes for children, including behavioral problems, poor cognitive functioning, and low self-esteem. Parental substance abuse often leads to family conflict and stress, which may contribute to substance abuse by adolescent children. Drug and alcohol use in adolescence may encourage a "precocious" transition to adulthood, which may result in teenage parenthood. Substance-abusing children may well become substance-abusing parents. The authors conclude their chapter with the observation that the legalization of same-sex marriages (in some states) "illustrates that the concept of 'family deviance' has changed and continues to change over time."

Political deviance

In his chapter, Pat Lauderdale undertakes a theoretical analysis of political deviance and the power dynamics that result in the definition of deviance and the ability to label certain behavior as deviance. Lauderdale's exposition is basically an analysis of power. He begins with the cogent observation that "defining a particular action or behavioral pattern as deviance is inherently political since power is used to impose the definition or label."

He argues that political intent is socially negotiated. Further, he posits that some actions that are objectively harmful may, through political dynamics, come to be reclassified as socially acceptable. As illustrations, he offers Martin Luther King and Nelson Mandela, who at one time were considered to be dangerous deviants. Because of changing political circumstances, they are now known as famous leaders. Conversely, Henry Kissinger was originally thought to be a great statesman. More recently, he has been criticized, and even labeled by some as a war criminal, because of the policies he promoted during the Vietnam War.

Lauderdale asserts that the attribution of deviance has been a central ingredient in the construction of deviant definitions. He goes on to indicate that the attribution of consequences is also a significant variable in the construction of deviance, but adds that consequences are socially negotiated. He suggests that the present field of political deviance was derived from "a succession of relevant theories." Included here are social class theories, strain theory, and labeling theory, to mention some.

He suggests that the political deviance perspective focuses on how the definition of deviant behavior is creative, the actors intimately involved with the creation of the definition, how the definition is maintained over time, and the effects of that definition. He reports that prevailing research in political deviance focuses on conflicts between status groups, interest groups, economic groups, professions, and the state. Social movements, social organizations, media, and the state also play significant roles "in creating, maintaining, or transforming deviance and politics now concentrate on the media."

He suggests that an examination of court trials reveals that the law is very political, and trials based on society's system of law are "intrinsically political." To illustrate this, he offers as examples the trials of Nelson Mandela, Leonard Peltier, Socrates, Angela Davis, Jesus, and Alcibiades. He stresses the importance of reexamining trials using a political deviance framework.

Lauderdale concludes his chapter by raising questions that call for further research. These include: "Under what conditions is deviation seen as creative rather than destructive?" and "Under what circumstances are deviations viewed as leadership rather than stigmatized?" He also reports that one scholar has suggested that there are two possible perspectives of political deviance: "focusing on the nature of power relations in society and the ability of certain forces to label or categorize behavior as deviant" and "viewing deviance as a means of asserting power in resistance to such encompassing forces." Lauderdale finally reasserts that the political deviance approach requires the interaction of the study of power.

Organizational and occupational deviance

The social institution of economy, work, and the division of labor is also the context of a wide variety of deviant activities, some lawful and some illegal. In their chapter, John and Leonard Minkes survey and analyze these configurations of norm violations in the workplace.

They point out that the concept of deviance in the world of organizational work is difficult "without an understanding of the nature of organizations and the opportunities and constraints they offer to those who work in them." The authors indicate that the notion of organizational deviance refers to the proposition that an organization as an entity itself can commit deviant acts and be held responsible for them. Some scholars have argued that this is so because of three distinct characteristics of organizations that make them "more than just the sum of their parts": organizational structure; shared goals; and the fact that the individuals who work in them can be replaced without changing the nature of the organization. Thus, the organization can be held responsible for its deviance.

The authors indicate that organizational deviance may be unlawful or lawful. Furthermore, deviant acts may incur civil liability or criminal liability. Beyond this, there are both administrative and criminal penalties. In all cases, however, the prime beneficiary is the organization.

Some scholars prefer the phrase "organizational deviance" rather than "corporate crime," because the former covers unethical behavior as well as unlawful behavior. Research interest has extended beyond corporate deviance to deviant governmental agencies, such as police corruption. Yet another area of research interest is organizational "bullying," which is related to authority and power, and to competitive strategies in organizations. Sometimes it is used as a leadership style. The authors suggest that "bullying" may be used to coerce subordinates to engage in unethical or illegal behavior, such as "cooking the books." Even gender may contribute to organizational deviance. Minkes and Minkes point out that "corporate decision-making processes are dominated by stereotyped masculine behavior." They further suggest that inasmuch as "real men take risks," the organization may promote risk taking as a policy that may be defined as normality. This, in turn, may lead to decisions that prove to be dysfunctional and disastrous, which may lead to danger and harm to the employees and/or the wider public.

In regard to occupational deviance, the authors indicate that this label "refers to individual deviance within the work environment which, in contrast to organizational deviance, is intended to benefit the individual." This behavior may be unlawful or lawful. An example of unlawful deviance would be stealing money or property from an employer. An example of lawful deviance might be rule breaking or time wasting, such as viewing porn on an office computer. Scholars have identified three forms of individual deviance in the workplace: occupational crimes, such as financial offenses; occupational deviance, such as activities that are not criminal but deviate from professional or occupational-setting norm (e.g., professional misconduct by a physician or sexual harassment); and workplace crime—conventional crime (e.g., assaults or homicides) that occurs in the workplace but is not connected to the work itself.

Occupational crime dates back several thousand years, and is still relatively common today. Over the years, many occupations have been studied using ethnographic methods. More recently, occupational research has increasingly relied on quantitative methodology. The authors indicate that there are no authoritative statistics on occupational deviance because most employee theft goes undetected, and, if discovered, employers frequently deal informally with the offender. Estimates of annual losses from employee theft in the US range from $40 billion to $400 billion. Studies of blue-collar theft in the UK suggest that it represents 1.25% to 2% of gross national product.

Self-report studies have indicated that 75% to 92% of workers have admitted to stealing from employers. Some scholars have suggested that job design may facilitate or encourage theft. Even though employees admit to stealing on the job, they usually have "a common sense of how far to go." When caught, employees often rely on neutralizations and denials rather than admit to their criminal activities. Some employees try to justify their thefts by asserting that they receive low pay.

Minkes and Minkes conclude their chapter with a discussion of "whistleblowers," who may "decide that 'loyalty' to the organization is less important than moral action." They define whistleblowing as "the dynamic network between organizational and individual responsibility."

Sport and leisure deviance

In his chapter, Robert Stebbins examines two perspectives of the chapter topic: deviance as leisure and deviance in sports. In explaining sport, he observes that "an essential element in true sport is inter-human competition based on a recognized set of rules." Accordingly, his chapter omits any discussion of competition among birds and non-human animals.

In his exploration of the literature of deviance as leisure, he cites one early scholar who observed that "the pleasurable nature of certain forms of deviance has long been recognized." Another early scholar asserted that "adolescents do regard much of their deviance as fun." Some research has suggested that sex should be regarded as leisure, with sexual activities, such as group sex, prostitution, and mate-swapping, classified as deviant leisure. It has been asserted that leisure studies, in general, have tended to turn "a 'blind eye' to deviant leisure." The author suggests that studying deviant leisure will "contribute to a clearer understanding of how the rules which shape normal leisure practice operate."

In this regard, Stebbins posits two relevant perspectives for viewing deviant leisure. These are *tolerable deviance* and *serious and casual leisure.* In an earlier chapter in this volume, Stebbins discussed the notion of tolerable deviance, which refers to behavior that may violate a moral norm, but because it is only mildly threatening, it is tolerated and accorded some degree of legitimacy, albeit perhaps grudgingly. Although such behavior is tolerated, most others choose not to adopt or even accept it themselves. The author suggests that those who engage in tolerable deviance view it as something that is fun or interesting to do in their leisure time, and indicates that tolerable behavior is "justified" because it is leisure, and represents the "pursuit" of pleasure. Stebbins indicates that much deviant leisure fits in the category of casual leisure, which he defines as "immediately, intrinsically rewarding, relatively short-lived pleasurable activity requiring little or no special training to enjoy it." Deviant casual leisure is mostly "sensory stimulation."

Stebbins suggests that beyond tolerable and intolerable deviant casual leisure is the concept of deviant *serious leisure.* "Profound and involved" serious leisure might include such pursuits as "aberrant religion, politics, and science." Stebbins then discusses a variety of deviant leisure. Some examples of deviant sexual expression might be "group sex, homosexuality, pornography, and heterosexual transvestism." In a similar fashion, mind- and mood-altering drugs have become a "prominent means of enjoyment in the Western world." They are subject to some degree of control, but they can be categorized as tolerable deviance. Similarly, he suggests that excessive alcohol use and deviant (nonmedical) consumption of marijuana and prescription drugs, even if still socially stigmatized practices, could now be labeled as tolerable deviance. Gambling and nudism might be classified in the same way. Following this argument, Stebbins observes that "Western political, religious, and scientific institutions have inadvertently encouraged their own set of heretics." In this regard, he cites the Communist Party, the Unification Church, and a coven of witches. All of these have provided deviant serious leisure as a hobby. Even in science, "the occult has emerged as a renegade movement in response to the perceived inadequacies of science."

Stebbins devotes the remainder of his chapter to a discussion of deviance in sports. He points out that deviance does occur in sports, but generally tends to be tolerated. He articulates three ways that tolerable deviance demonstrates itself among athletes and fans: *deviance for sport; deviance for fun and need;* and *deviance with sport.* Regarding deviance for sport, he suggests that athletes deviate from the norms of their sport for two reasons: in the hope of gaining a particular advantage; and to express negative emotions, such as anger or hate. Athletes sometimes violate the norms of the sport by cheating. This might be intentional, to gain monetary advantages, or they might inadvertently be involved in some behavior that represents an illegal play. Another example of norm violation is the use of performance-enhancing drugs ("doping"). Elevated athletic output, strengthened muscles, and momentarily aiding endurance may well contribute to victory. Inasmuch as athlete drug use is seldom detected, Stebbins labels this behavior as noncriminal tolerable deviance.

He concludes by discussing some other forms of deviant leisure—violence, juvenile delinquency, recreational drug use, deviance out of need (hard drug use because of addiction), deviant gambling, and hooliganism—and observes that "tolerable deviant leisure and deviant sport require much more exploratory investigation before it may be said that they are truly understood."

Medical deviance

In his chapter, Paul Jesilow explores miscreance among physicians. He points out that "deviance in medicine has a long history" and that the Hippocratic Oath was an indication that some physicians were acting less selflessly than its author. This, presumably, was why Hippocrates felt the need to swear that he would "act only in the interest of his patients."

Jesilow informs us that "the practice of medicine is not an exact science and there are few iron-clad rules." Physicians can differ in their diagnosis of an ailment, and in the treatment of that condition. There is no black or white in the practice of medicine, only "gray areas." In the face of uncertainty, physicians have to make decisions. Of course, these should always be made in the best interest of the patient, but sometimes they are made in the self-interest of the physician. Such decisions may constitute deviance.

Jesilow reports that medical deviance is rife today and articulates various forms of such deviance: the violation of prescription laws; cooperating with corporate entities to steal billions of dollars from private insurance entities and public insurance entities (Medicare and Medicaid); sexually abusing patients; and so on. He discusses three types of medical deviance in greater depth.

The first of these is fee splitting, such as when a physician sends a patient to whichever surgeon will pay the largest referral fee, rather than to the most skilled surgeon. Other examples include "arrangements between physicians and hospitals," such as when a hospital gives a kickback to a community-based physician for referring a patient. Another variation is when hospital-based physicians, such as emergency room doctors, anesthesiologists, and radiologists, are "paid less by the hospital than the fair market value of the services they provide."

Jenilow's second type of medical deviance is unnecessary surgery. Research conducted in the 1970s suggested that at least 10% of the 20 million operations performed each year in the United States were unwarranted. More recent research has indicated that single opinions facilitate unnecessary surgery. Some unnecessary surgeries are criminal, inasmuch as they are performed only if an insurance company will pay for them. There have been cases of physicians frightening patients with bogus diagnoses of cancer so that they agree to operations that are billed to insurance companies and Medicare.

Jesilow argues that cesarean sections are unnecessary in many instances. Such surgery can, in some circumstances, be a "saving" operation, but it can also be dangerous to both mother and child. He reports that the rate of c-sections has been rising. The World Health Organization believes that c-sections should not exceed more than 15% of all births. In the US in 2006 they accounted for 31.1% of all births. Jesilow indicates that the prevalence of c-sections is the result of several factors. Some women request them for reasons of convenience or because they wish to avoid the anxiety and pain of vaginal childbirth. In terms of cost, c-sections are about twice as expensive as a vaginal birth, so are more profitable to the obstetrician. Perhaps one of the more significant reasons for their prevalence is that obstetricians are particularly vulnerable to malpractice lawsuits. Malpractice insurance fees are very high, and many believe that the high rate of c-sections is simply evidence of doctors practicing "defensive medicine." This is a controversial issue within the medical profession.

The third type of medical deviance discussed by Jesilow is fraud against third-party payment programs. Examples here include unnecessary surgery conducted only because insurance will pay for it. Other examples might be charging for a more expensive procedure than the one performed, ordering unnecessary visits, and unnecessarily extending treatment. One study showed that "about half of the physician-participants were willing to deceive third-party payers in this matter." Accordingly, some physicians rationalize such practices by saying that they are underpaid by Medicaid for their services, and insurance fraud is a means of compensating for this in order that they might provide services to the poor.

38

Family deviance

Angela R. Gover and Stacey J. Bosick

Introduction

General characterizations of deviance define the concept as behaviors differing from an accepted norm or standard of society. This chapter will more specifically operationalize family deviance as behaviors or forms of family that are criminalized by public policy. Although there are many competing concepts of deviant behaviors within every culture, we selected legal standards as a measure of family deviance due to the omnipotent presence such standards impose on every citizen.

When discussing what is considered to be criminally deviant in the family, it is relevant to consider the legal history of the criminal justice system's relationship with family. Problems within the family were typically viewed as "private" and consequently outside the purview of public policy and criminal law until around the 1970s, when the feminist movement established the necessity of legal intervention regarding physical and sexual victimization within the family (Schechter, 1982). Cultural norms previously had considered family violence as involving "mutually combative" couples whose violence did not affect public order, and therefore was irrelevant to the criminal justice system. Further, until recently, a dominant family court philosophy involved family systems theory, a perspective that viewed these issues as having roots in family interactions. In order to assist an abused partner or child, the state would treat the whole family through examination and therapy, rather than impose punitive measures on abusers (*Harvard Law Review*, 2003). Through activism by the feminist, child rights, and domestic violence movements, the public's increased awareness of family violence spurred the government to shift its perspective on families from "private" to necessitating intervention in the event of violence, neglect, and/or exploitation (Schechter, 1982).

This chapter will first cover general patterns of more normative, or legal, family behaviors. We will subsequently discuss family behaviors that are more transparently considered to be deviant due to criminalization of the behaviors. Through an examination of prior and current scholarship, we will provide a representation of legal and illegal family patterns from a research perspective.

Statistical patterns of legal family forms and behaviors

While the following forms of family may be legal, it is crucial to acknowledge that some of the following research may be hindered by participants' concerns over social desirability to researchers, or possible negative consequences for disclosing information, particularly with academia's problematic history of misrepresenting and categorizing lower-status citizens as disordered or "deviant." This section does not categorize the included families as culturally deviant, but rather as legally normative, and will cover research estimates of the varying legally normative family forms and behaviors. According to the US Census Bureau (2008), a family is a set of two or more people living together who are related by birth, marriage, or adoption. This definition is fairly narrow, and consequently, this section will consider family in a very broad sense, including family members not residing in the home, or even singles residing alone, comprising their own family.[1] Currently, there are 56 million married households in America, with 24 million of those married families including children under the age of 18 (US Census Bureau, 2008). New marriages have around a 51% divorce rate (National Vital Statistics Reports, 2008). Consequently, only about 21.1% of families adhere to the concept of the "nuclear family"—a married couple with children. There are 122.1 million singles in the US (50% of Americans over the age of 15), 10.9 million single-parent families (9.6% of households), and almost a million families with teenage parents (US Census Bureau, 2008). Nearly 40% of children are born to unmarried parents (Ventura, 2009), and over 1.7 million children in the United States have parents who are in jail or prison (Mauer et al., 2009). While estimates of gay and lesbian households vary widely, one study estimated that there were a little over 3 million same-sex cohabitating couples in America (Smith and Gates, 2001).

Most Americans practice monogamy, meaning that they form relationships with only one partner at a time (Treas and Giesen, 2000). It is important to note that infidelity is illegal in many, though not all, US states. Research on the success of adhering to a monogamous model finds mixed results. One recent study on infidelity (sex with someone other than one's partner), conducted with participants in self-identified monogamous relationships, found male infidelity rates to be 14.7% and female infidelity rates to be 13.5% (Gotta et al., 2009; see also Blumstein and Schwartz, 1983). Rates of infidelity have dramatically decreased since the 1970s, possibly due to increased openness and communication about sex among couples (Gotta et al., 2009). While infidelity is typically conducted under clandestine circumstances, sex or emotional intimacy can occur candidly, in open relationships. One such type of relationship, known as "swinging," occurs when couples consensually exchange partners for sexual purposes. Attention to swinging spread throughout the 1960s and research from that period indicated just 1–2% of married couples self-reported engaging in the practice, with a large proportion participating only once (Jenks, 1998). Another type of relationship, polyamory, involves forming romantic relationships with others besides one's partner. These relationships are also typically sexual. It is estimated that there are almost 500,000 openly polyamorous families in the United States (Bennett, 2009). Unlike infidelity, such relationships involve consent, open communication, and a lack of deception.

This section has offered an overview of general family patterns and behaviors. Departures from monogamous relationships hint at the diversity and complexity of American families. The following section will present family behaviors that are considered to be sufficiently dangerous or deviant to warrant their criminalization under American law.

Illegal forms of family deviance

Polygamy and bigamy

Monogamous marriages are the most dominant and culturally accepted form in the United States. By contrast, if a person is married to more than one spouse, he or she is in a plural or polygamous marriage, with bigamy specifically referring to a form of polygamy in which a person has two spouses. In the US polygamy is commonly associated with the Church of Jesus Christ of Latter-Day Saints, known colloquially as Mormonism. Polygamy violates the modern-day doctrine of that Church, however, and is practiced only by small, fundamentalist splinter groups. All forms of plural marriage are illegal in the United States, and such marriages are viewed fairly negatively (Hassouneh-Phillips, 2001).

Evidence is mixed regarding women's power and sense of control in polygamous relationships. Some research suggests conflict permeates polygamous marriages not only between husbands and wives but between co-wives who struggle to secure economic resources for themselves and their children (Ware, 1979). Women in polygamous marriages have been shown to have poorer mental and physical health outcomes, including a greater risk of contracting HIV (e.g. Hassouneh-Phillips, 2001). Children of polygamous marriages also show poorer health outcomes as well as lower academic achievement and increased behavioral problems (Eapen *et al.*, 2000). Additionally, one emerging problem in Utah and Arizona, titled the "Lost Boys," involves the Fundamental Church of Latter-Day Saints excommunicating large numbers of young males from their communities and families. Officials from the two states report that up to 1,000 boys have been abandoned outside their home towns, and indicate the problem is rooted in a need to maintain an asymmetrical gender balance to permit multiple wives per man, and to reduce young male competition for young wives (Borger, 2005). Church officials maintain the boys were excommunicated for behavioral problems.

Conversely, some research views opposition to polygamy as ethnocentric and patronizing, arguing that polygamy fulfills men's biological inclination for a greater number and variety of sexual partners, provides a legitimate sexual outlet for men during lengthy postpartum taboos, and maximizes opportunities for females to marry when men are in short supply (e.g., Arrington and Bitton, 1979).

Child abuse and neglect

Today, the abuse and neglect of children are considered to be serious social problems in the United States and worldwide. Child abuse and neglect can have short- and long-term physical, psychological, behavioral, and societal consequences. While the first organization focused on child maltreatment in the US was founded in 1874, the issue did not receive much attention until the 1960s. In 1962 the publication of physician Henry Kempe's landmark article "The Battered Child Syndrome" drew national and international attention to the issue of physical child abuse. By 1967, each state, the District of Columbia, and the US Territories passed legislation obliging certain professionals who interact with children in the course of their jobs (educational, legal, social service, and medical personnel) to report cases of suspected child abuse to their state's child protective services (CPS) agency.

While definitions of child abuse and neglect are determined by individual states, these generally include four types of maltreatment: neglect, physical abuse, sexual abuse, and psychological abuse. Neglect is considered to be a series of "inactions," such as failing to provide nourishment, clothing, shelter, healthcare, education, and supervision. Physical abuse refers to acts committed against a child that result in major or minor injuries, including death. Sexual abuse is considered to be any acts or situations involving children that are committed for sexual pleasure, or use sex as a tool of social dominance. Psychological abuse includes entrapment, verbal or emotional abuse, and other types of psychological cruelty and torture, such as withholding food, shelter, and bathroom access, or preventing sleep (Clark *et al.*, 2001).

National Child Abuse and Neglect Data System (NCANDS)[2] data for 2007 indicated that 794,000 children were victims of abuse or neglect, resulting in a victimization rate of 10.6 per 1,000 children in the population. The majority of victims experienced neglect, followed by physical abuse, sexual abuse, and psychological maltreatment. During 2007 an estimated 1,760 children died due to abuse or neglect, a rate of 2.35 deaths per 100,000 children in the general population. Girls experienced victimization at slightly higher rates than boys, with 52% of the victims being female. This was more pronounced for certain types of child abuse, such as sexual abuse. Victimization and age were inversely related, such that rates were highest for the youngest children. Approximately one-third (32%) of all victims of maltreatment were younger than four years old, 24% were between the ages of four and seven, and 19% were between the ages of eight and eleven (US Department of Health and Human Services, Administration on Children, Youth and Families, 2009). The majority of victims were white (46%), 22% were African American, and 21% were Latino. The NCANDS report indicated that most perpetrators of child abuse were parents (80%). Of perpetrators who acted alone, 38.7% were mothers and 17.9% were fathers. Children were abused by both parents 17% of the time. Regarding sexual abuse, the majority of perpetrators were male; with neglect, most perpetrators were female.

Incest

A second type of family violence, incest, is defined as sexual contact between related persons. Generally, sexual contact between related individuals has been considered a form of deviance that has resulted in negative cultural, religious, and legal sanctions throughout history. According to the empirical literature, incest is a particularly traumatic experience that has devastating behavioral, psychological, and social consequences for victims, ranging from self-esteem issues to personality disorders (Lev-Wiesel, 2006). Because children are physically and emotionally dependent on their families, incest replaces one's sense of security with fear and terror (Davis *et al.*, 2001).

Williams and Finkelhor (1990) suggest that common characteristics of incest offenders include passive, dependent personalities, child abuse and neglect histories, marital dissatisfaction, sexual dissatisfaction, and problems with empathy and bonding (see also Copps Hartley, 2001). Attempts to explain this type of deviant behavior have included biological, sociological, psychological, moral, legal, and economic approaches.

Fathers and stepfathers sexually assaulting daughters accounts for the largest proportion of sexual assaults within the family. The second most common form is father–son incest, followed by mother–son incest. Cases of mother–daughter incest are the least frequently documented. Although incest involving siblings is reported less often than cases involving a parent and child, some believe that it occurs much more frequently than is documented. The majority of sibling incest cases involve a male older child who forces the behavior on a younger sister, and the behavior may occur over a long period of time (Caffaro and Conn-Caffaro, 1998). Families that experience sibling incest have been characterized as having a lack of parental warmth, poor supervision, and misinterpretations about appropriate boundaries between individuals. Clinicians have documented sibling incest cases involving girls as perpetrators, although these cases are less likely to be reported than cases involving girls as victims.

Domestic violence

A third form of family violence, domestic violence, refers to the exertion of power and control by one intimate partner over another. Other terms used for domestic violence in the scholarly literature include intimate partner violence, spousal abuse, dating violence, family violence, battering, and wife abuse. Domestic violence occurs within the traditional family but also among married, cohabitating, same-sex and other types of couples. Although both men and women perpetrate domestic violence, women are overwhelmingly the victims and males the perpetrators.

One study estimates one out of every four women will be victimized by partner violence at some point in their life (Tjaden and Thoennes, 2000). The high incidence of partner violence is noted in medical data, with approximately 2 million injuries per year and 500,000 victims needing medical attention due to domestic violence (National Center for Injury Prevention and Control, 2003).

Domestic violence may occur in the form of physical violence, psychological/emotional abuse, threats of physical violence, or sexual abuse. Many domestic violence victims report that their initial experiences with psychological abuse escalated into physical or sexual violence. Domestic violence is not specific to certain cultures, ethnic groups, religions, or sexual orientation, nor is it related to one's socioeconomic status or level of education. According to empirical research, it can lead to physical and psychological consequences, including depression, anxiety, post-traumatic stress disorder, substance abuse, suicide attempts, and difficulties with general physical health (Bennice et al. 2003; Coker et al. 2000; Kernic et al., 2000; Downs and Rindels, 2004; Lang et al., 2004; Woods, 2005).

Domestic violence may consist of one violent incident or may be a pattern of systematic, coercive behavior. According to Walker (2000), it occurs in three stages: the tension building stage, the explosive stage, and the honeymoon stage. The three stages form a pattern of abuse that begins with the victim's fear increasing, moves to experiencing violence, and continues to a period of apologies and promises that the violence will stop. Individuals in relationships can become extremely emotionally and financially dependent on their partners, and those in abusive relationships are no exception. Of female victims who manage to leave their abusers and seek out a battered women's shelter, some reports estimate 60% return to their abusers within a two-month period (Brown, 1997).

Children additionally suffer from domestic violence. Approximately 10 million children observe parental violence in the US each year (Strauss, 1991). Children who have witnessed domestic violence display long-term adjustment problems, show higher rates of antisocial behavioral problems, experience depression and violence in dating relationships, and show greater amounts of post-traumatic symptoms than those who had not witnessed domestic violence during childhood (Maker et al., 2001).

Alcohol and drug addiction in the family

Substance use is most prevalent among single, young adult males. However, when parents drink and use illegal drugs, the impact on family life is especially pronounced. Addiction is widely held to undermine labor market and economic success, leaving families in severe cases without the resources necessary to meet basic needs (but see Schmidt et al., 2002). Parental substance abuse is also known to contribute to a host of negative outcomes for children, including low self-esteem, poor cognitive functioning, and behavioral problems. Evidence suggests that the impact of substance abuse on families generally operates indirectly through marital conflict and disruption, and it is commonly associated with spousal abuse (Kandel et al., 1994).

Family structure and conflict, in turn, contribute to substance use by adolescent children. Risk of adolescent drug use, for instance, is highest in father-custody families and lowest when both parents are in the home (Hoffmann and Johnson, 1998). Risk is also heightened in homes in which parents and close family members are substance abusers. Despite exposure to public service messages promoting parent–child communication about drug and alcohol use, substance-using parents are often unsure about the appropriate messages to communicate to their children. Interestingly, some evidence suggests that drug- and alcohol-related communication, even by non-substance-using parents, is typically unhelpful or even detrimental to adolescent outcomes (Ennett et al., 2001). More important are parental support and monitoring. Low parental control, high parent–child conflict, and a number of other family life events, including family violence, can influence youthful substance use. These family factors are largely mediated through adolescents' self-control and peer relationships (Thomas et al., 2003).

Among other consequences, drug and alcohol use in adolescence increases the risk of making "precocious" transitions to adulthood, including teenage parenthood. Early transitions, in turn, contribute to ongoing substance use in adulthood. In this way, substance-abusing children are disproportionately likely to become substance-abusing parents (Krohn et al., 1997).

Conclusion

While the family was historically considered to be a private entity, and therefore outside of the domain of the legal system, various social movements influenced the government to view the family as necessitating intervention to prevent violence and exploitation. The bulk of this review has centered on illegal forms of family deviance. It is important to acknowledge that we did not include all illegal forms of family (for example, most US states do not currently permit same-sex marriage). The fact that recent policy changes have legalized same-sex marriages in some states illustrates the important point that the concept of "family deviance" has changed and continues to change over time. Definitions of deviance are largely contingent upon social and political contexts.

Notes

1 However, all reported US Census data do conform to their conceptualization of family.
2 NCANDS data are collected and analyzed by the Children's Bureau in the Administration on Children, Youth, and Families, US Department of Health and Human Services.

References

Arrington, L., and Bitton, D. (1979). *The Mormon Experience: A History of the Latter-Day Saints*. New York: Alfred A. Knopf.

Bennett, J. (2009). Only you. And you. And you. Polyamory—relationships with multiple, mutually consenting partners—has a coming-out party. *Newsweek Web Exclusive*, July 29. Retrieved September 10, 2009, from: www.newsweek.com/id/209164/page/3.

Bennice, J. A., Resick, P. A., Mechanic, M. B., and Astin, M. (2003). The relative effects of intimate partner physical and sexual violence on PTSD symptomatology. *Violence & Victims*, 18(1), 87–94.

Blumstein, P., and Schwartz, P. (1983). *American Couples: Money, Work, Sex*. New York: William Morrow and Company.

Borger, J. (2005). The lost boys, thrown out of US sect so that older men can marry more wives. *Guardian*, June 14. Retrieved September 10, 2009, from: www.guardian.co.uk/world/2005/jun/14/usa.julianborger.

Brown, J. (1997). Working toward freedom from violence: The process of change in battered women. *Violence Against Women*, 3, 5–22.

Caffaro, J. V., and Conn-Caffaro, A. (1998). *Sibling Abuse and Trauma: Assessment and Intervention Strategies for Children, Families, and Adults*. New York: Haworth Maltreatment and Trauma Press.

Clark, R. E., Clark, J. F., and Adamec, C. A. (2001). *The Encyclopedia of Child Abuse*. New York: Facts on File.

Coker, A. L., Smith, P. H., Bethea, L., King, M. R., and McKeown, R. E. (2000). Physical health consequences of physical and psychological intimate partner violence. *Archives of Family Medicine*, 9, 451–457.

Copps Hartley, C. (2001). Incest offenders' perceptions of their motives to sexually offend within their past and current life context. *Journal of Interpersonal Violence*, 16, 459–475.

Davis, J. L., Petretic-Jackson, P. A., and Ting, L. (2001). Intimacy dysfunction and trauma symptomology: Long-term correlates of different types of child abuse. *Journal of Traumatic Stress*, 14, 68–80.

Downs, W. R., and Rindels, B. (2004). Adulthood depression, anxiety, and trauma symptoms: A comparison of women with nonabusive, abusive, and absent father figures in childhood. *Violence Victimology*, 19, 659–671.

Eapen, V., Bart, W., and Hektner, J. (2000). Mental health problems among schoolchildren in United Arab Emirates: Prevalence and risk factors. *Journal of the American Academy of Child and Adolescent Psychiatry*, 37(8), 880–886.

Ennett, S. T., Bauman, K. E., Foshee, V. A., Pemberton, M., and Hicks, K. A. (2001). Parent–child communication about adolescent tobacco and alcohol use: What do parents say and does it affect youth behavior? *Journal of Marriage and Family*, 63(1), 48–62.

Gotta, G., Rothblum, E. D., Balsam, K., Solomon, S., Schwartz, P., and Green, R. J. (2009). Monogamy in heterosexual and same-sex couples: Changes over 25 years. Poster session presented at the annual convention of the American Psychological Association, Toronto, August.

Harvard Law Review (2003). Developments: The Law of Marriage and Family. *Harvard Law Review*, 116, 1996–2122.

Hassouneh-Phillips, D. (2001). Polygamy and wife abuse: A qualitative study of Muslim women in America. *Health Care for Women International*, 22(8), 735–748.

Hoffmann, J. P., and Johnson, R. A. (1998). A national portrait of family structure and adolescent drug use. *Journal of Marriage and Family*, 60(3), 633–645.

Jenks, R. (1998). Swinging: A review of the literature. *Archives of Sexual Behavior*, 27(5), 507–521.

Kandel, D. B., Rosenbaum, E., and Chen, K. (1994). Impact of maternal drug use and life experiences on preadolescent children born to teenage mothers. *Journal of Marriage and Family*, 56(2), 325–340.

Kernic, M. A., Wolf, M. E., and Holt, V. L. (2000). Rates and relative risk of hospital admission among women in violent intimate partner relationships. *American Journal of Public Health*, 90, 1416–1420.

Krohn, M. D., Lizotte, A. J., and Perez, C. M. (1997). The interrelationship between substance use and precocious transitions to adult statuses. *Journal of Health and Social Behavior*, 38(1), 87–103.

Lang, A. I., Stein, M. B., Kennedy, C. M., and Foy, D. W. (2004). Adult psychopathology and intimate partner violence among survivors of childhood maltreatment. *Journal of Interpersonal Violence*, 19, 1102–1118.

Lev-Wiesel, R. (2006). Intergenerational transmission of sexual abuse? Motherhood in the shadow of incest. *Journal of Child Sexual Abuse*, 15, 75–101.

Maker, A. H., Kemmelmeier, M., and Peterson, C. (2001). Child sexual abuse, peer sexual abuse, and sexual assault in adulthood: A multirisk model of revictimization. *Journal of Traumatic Stress*, 14, 351–368.

Mauer, M., Nellis, A., and Schirmir, S. (2009). *Incarcerated Parents and Their Children: Trends 1991–2007*. Washington, DC: The Sentencing Project.

National Center for Injury Prevention and Control (2003). *Costs of Intimate Partner Violence against Women in the United States*. Atlanta, GA: Centers for Disease Control and Prevention.

National Vital Statistics Reports (2008). *Births, Marriages, Divorces, and Deaths: Provisional Data for 2008*. Washington, DC: US Government Printing Office. Retrieved September 25, 2009 from: www.cdc.gov/NCHS/data/nvsr/nvsr57/nvsr57_19.pdf.

Schechter, S. (1982). *Women and Male Victims: The Victims and Struggles of the Battered Women's Movement*. Boston, MA: South End Press.

Schmidt, L., Dohan, D., Wiley, J., and Zabkiewicz, D. (2002). Addiction and welfare dependency: Interpreting the connection. *Social Problems*, 49(2), 221–241.

Smith, D. M. and Gates, G. J. (2001). *Gay and Lesbian Families in the United States: Same-Sex Unmarried Partner Households*. Washington, DC: Urban Institute.

Strauss, M. (1991). Discipline and deviance: Physical punishment of children and violence and other crimes in adulthood. *Social Problems*, 38, 133–154.

Thomas Ashby, W., and Alison, M. Y. (2003). Family factors and adolescent substance use: Models and mechanisms. *Current Directions in Psychological Science*, 12(6), 222–226.

Tjaden, P. and Thoennes, N. (2000). *Extent, Nature and Consequences of Intimate Partner Violence: Findings from the National Violence against Women Survey*. Washington, DC: Office of Justice Programs, US Department of Justice.

Treas, J., and Giesen, D. (2000). Sexual infidelity among married and cohabiting Americans. *Journal of Marriage and Family*, 62(1), 48–60.

US Census Bureau (2008). *American Community Survey*. Washington, DC: US Government Printing Office. Retrieved September 21, 2009, from factfinder.census.gov/servlet/DatasetMainPageServlet?_program=ACS&_lang=en&_ts=100621288252.

US Department of Health and Human Services, Administration on Children, Youth and Families (2009). *Child Maltreatment 2007*. Washington, DC: US Government Printing Office. Retrieved September 21, 2009, from: www.acf.hhs.gov/programs/cb/pubs/cm07/index.htm.

Ventura, S. J. (2009). *Changing Patterns of Nonmarital Childbearing in the United States*. Washington, DC: US Government Printing Office. Retrieved September 21, 2009 from: www.cdc.gov/nchs/data/databriefs/db18.pdf.

Walker, L. (2000). *The Battered Woman Syndrome*. New York: Springer.

Ware, H. (1979). Polygyny: Women's views in a transitional society, Nigeria 1975. *Journal of Marriage and the Family*, 41, 185–195.

Williams, L. M., and Finkelhor, D. (1990). *The Characteristics of Incestuous Fathers*. New York: Plenum Press.

Woods, S. J. (2005). Intimate partner violence and post-traumatic stress disorder symptoms in women: What we know and need to know. *Journal of Interpersonal Violence*, 20, 394–402.

39

Political deviance

Pat Lauderdale

Introduction

Defining a particular action or behavioral pattern as deviant is inherently political since power is used to impose the definition or label (Ben-Yehuda 1985, Schur 1980, Lauderdale 1976). The study of political deviance is the study of differential power via departures from social norms or expectations that are believed, or are purported, to have positive intent and/or consequences for society. First, we need an understanding of the definitional processes involved in deviance designations because determining the intent of the actors and the consequences of their behavior is only part of a more complex picture. Intent and consequences are socially negotiated, which has become obvious in and out of courtrooms and throughout societies. The actions of relevant moral entrepreneurs, social movements and protests, public opinion, and the role of agents of social control, for example, are important in determining social perceptions of the deviants' actions and their consequences. To understand such struggles over social definitions, we can heuristically consider the tension between deviance, politics, and diversity.

Most individual diversity is categorized as normal variation, a small fraction as apolitical deviance, and an even smaller fraction as political deviance. The issue is how the boundaries of these categories are drawn and what determines the placement of specific actors and acts within any given category (Erikson 1966, 2004). Erikson focuses on a variety of central issues in politics, power, and who and what might account for the shift in the boundary between good and bad. He suggests the conditions under which the boundary might shift by focusing upon a realignment of power within the group, for example, or the appearance of new adversaries outside it (Erikson 1966: 68). The creation of categories and the placement of individuals within these categories are two basic processes of social definition that are outcomes of political variables (Becker 1963, Gusfield 1963). The social organization of the definition of deviance suggests the relevance of an examination of how political intent is socially negotiated and how objectively harmful social actions are often relabeled as socially acceptable (Lauderdale and Cruit 1993). These changing definitions become evident when we consider the varying reactions over time to the actions of such people as Martin Luther King, Nelson Mandela, and Henry Kissinger. King and Mandela went from being considered dangerous deviants to famous leaders. Kissinger initially was heralded as a great statesman but is now criticized and accused of war crimes for the policies he promoted during the Vietnam War and for his role in the establishment of dictatorial regimes in Latin America.

Other examples illustrating the question of political intent can be found throughout history. By offering millions of dollars of aid to the Contras in Nicaragua, was Ronald Reagan fighting for a people's right to live in a democratic society or acting to subvert a legitimate government to achieve the political and economic goals of his administration? Are the Zapatistas in Chiapas terrorists or patriots, defending themselves and the land they inhabited for thousands of years from further plunder and exploitation? When studying deviance, many researchers ignore the importance of political factors. Typically, when researchers do examine political factors, they focus upon individual actors. But what differentiates a "politically" deviant actor from an apolitical actor? Is a political deviant simply someone who disagrees with the existing political system? Perhaps the American society's political deviant of the last ten years is an animal rights activist, a conservationist, an opponent of the World Trade Organization, or a "new" war resister. Is the leader of loose-knit bands of hit-and-run killers of British soldiers a deviant or terrorist? This question raises the issue of the changing definitions attached to the actions of George Washington. And the political and historical factors behind related changes are significant. For example, in the 18th century, scholars such as Rousseau and Voltaire were defined not only as treasonous but as mentally disturbed (Oliverio 1998: 31).

The intent of a person has been a central ingredient in the construction of deviant definitions. An emphasis on the role of intent, however, has the unintended negative consequence of injecting into our analysis all the uncertainties associated with applying the *mens rea* criterion of crime in the law (Oliverio and Lauderdale 2005). Consider the insanity defense as only one example, the legal controversy surrounding one exemption from *mens rea*. The shooting and killing of a person may not be a crime if the shooter was incapable of telling right from wrong and/or was driven by an uncontrollable impulse. Uncontrolled impulses may be momentary, making it very difficult to distinguish between sane and temporarily insane actors. The result is that the insanity plea often turns into a bargaining device, with the status of sanity becoming something to be negotiated. Reliance on an individual's own interpretations places a heavy burden of proof upon observers to determine whether the person's justifications are legitimate or simply intended to mitigate the perceived severity of their actions. An attribution of intent is an important variable in the creation of deviance, but it is not sufficient in and of itself (Merton 1938, Goode and Ben-Yehuda 1994).

Another common conception of deviance views the actions of the deviants as intrinsically political or apolitical in terms of their consequences (Farrell and Case 1995). Some scholars have suggested that political deviance is the use of illegal and unethical means to gain, retain, or enlarge political power, as demonstrated in case after case of bribery, extortion, and kickbacks (Simon and Stanley Eitzen 1993). The Watergate Affair is a prime example of this approach, which examines the web of relationships between political and organized crime. This type of perspective also examines governments resorting to political imprisonment and state agencies engaging in official violence, such as police brutality. Internationally, political deviance is seen in the activities of the CIA, in "war crimes" such as the My Lai massacre and the "genocide" in Vietnam. While these are important examples of deviance, they seem to represent and fit into the significant literature on corruption or "high crimes." The perspective maintains that certain acts are inherently criminal or deviant depending on the magnitude of harm they create. The seriousness of "real crimes"—for example, sexism, racism, imperialism, ageism, consumer fraud, and economic exploitation—are defined by their harmful consequences (see Garland 2002, Cooney and Burt 2008). From this perspective, if the action (for example, a collective protest) has "positive" social consequences, then it is not deviant. Yet, while the attribution of consequences is an important variable in the creation of deviance, it is not sufficient in and of itself because consequences also are socially negotiated (Amster 2004). Ironically, the development of the sociological study of deviance traditionally has been psychologically trying to explain the ostensible problematic behavior of the isolated individual. Since the problem of deviance was essentially dictated by a research tradition that took individual personality as the unit of analysis, the role of power and social organizations in separating deviance from normality was not seen as an important issue (Liazos 1972). Each new set of researchers modified the psychological tradition in the study of deviance without considering how the behavior being studied first came to be defined as deviant via political processes (Inverarity et al. 1983).

Contemporary analyses of political deviance

Political processes are central to any analysis of deviance since all forms of deviance have a political dimension. Definitions of political deviance are created, maintained, and revised through processes of power in which the manipulations of political symbols are used for hegemonic control (Ben-Yehuda 2002, Oliverio and Lauderdale 2005). Accordingly, a political deviance perspective focuses upon how the definition of behavior as deviant is initially created, the actors intimately involved with the creation of the definition, how the definition is maintained or adjusted over time, and the effects of that definition. Moreover, the following factors are important: the status of the definer (e.g., is the actor doing the defining a well-respected opinion leader or a criminal?); the historical period during which the debate emerges (e.g., someone who is labeled as deviant during a period of social unrest may not be considered deviant during a period of strong social cohesion); and the ideological differences between the conflicting parties (e.g., is the content of the actors' behavior directly related to the power of the defining agent?). By exploring each of these areas, we can derive a perspective on how definitions are created and applied. These concerns highlight the primacy of precipitating factors of political power in the creation of deviance that can and should be distinguished from structural conditions of deviant behavior, raising important questions concerning the role of the state, hegemony, mass media, and information networks in constructing and perpetuating definitions of political deviance (Lauderdale 2011).

Prevailing research examines the overt political conflicts among economic groups, status groups, interest groups, professions, and the state (Lauderdale 2003, Henry 2009). A well-known argument contained within most of this research suggests that the study of political deviance should not concentrate on the deviations of lower-class individuals, but should rather include broader problems, such as economic advantages and disadvantages, civil rights and race, residential migration, and bias in gender and ethnicity (Kirk 2009). It should be noted that this position was first presented almost 70 years ago in a penetrating article by C. Wright Mills (1942). The more recent development (enactment and/or enforcement) of particular laws, and the criminalization of homelessness, for example, focus upon the recent spate of laws defining such conduct as sitting on sidewalks as criminal acts punishable by imprisonment in many cases (Amster 2004). The more subtle role of political power and its relationship to rule-making is presented by Henry (2009), who extends the seminal analyses of Garfinkel (1956) and Goffman (1963). The politically relevant dimension of deviance is most clearly demonstrated when new categories of deviance are being created or old categories are being transformed. Under the Fugitive Slave Laws of the 1850s, for example, aiding and abetting an escaped slave was an act of severe deviance; in fact, it was defined as a crime. Yet, with the passage of the Fourteenth Amendment less than a decade later, slavery itself was the crime. Similarly, in 1800 the organization of a labor union was a crime (conspiracy in restraint of trade). However, by 1940, not only were unions legal, but employers were required by law to engage in collective bargaining. Through political processes, then, an accepted and socialized form of activity can become delegitimized, or vice versa (Cohen 2004, Maratea 2008). The political deviance approach examines the processes that maintain, create, and change the definition of such important actions. One heuristic framework for this type of research focuses upon moral entrepreneurs, social movements, professional organizations, and the state (Lauderdale 2003).

Moral entrepreneurs usually initiate public discourses on specific issues, garner the resources to have their voice heard, and try to persuade the public and the state of their view of the truth (a Weberian view might examine these agents of charismatic law constructing the revolutionary elements that undermine the stability of tradition). The prior sociological literature on the changes in status of such moral entrepreneurs as Harry Anslinger and Eugene McCarthy is being extended to examine other entrepreneurs working on various crusades or programs. Such contemporary entrepreneurs include Al Gore, Pat Robertson, Ralph Nader, Oprah Winfrey, Caroline Myss, Louis Farrakhan, Russell Means, Michael Moore, Bobby Seal, the Dalai Lama, and Christiane Northrup.

Social movements include those movements protesting in numerous arenas, such as the diverse movements demanding an end to colonization, racism, and sexism, and those concerned with free access to water, air, and public space. Other movements campaign on more specific issues, such as the "Borgen Project," which attempts to put global poverty at the center of the US political agenda, supporters of the legalization of medical marijuana, Mothers Against Drunk Driving (MADD), and anti-abortion, pro-gun, anti-gun, and anti-pornography groups. The contemporary political deviance approach also explores the factors that lead to the trans-formation of social movements into social organizations, especially in light of the fact that most social movements do not become institutionalized (Gamson 1975, McAdam and Su 2002).

The research on the role of social organizations in creating, maintaining, or transforming deviance and politics now concentrates on the media. This thrust can be complemented by examining organizational forces influencing the media (Sacco 2003, Altheide 2006). Moreover, the historical overview of scholars such as Maria Mies (1986), including her research on witchcraft, suggests the importance of unraveling the deep connection between expanding organizations, the law, trials, and the state. Mies (1986: 83) notes in her discussion of the demonization of midwives as witches that the state

> was directly connected with the emergence of modern society: the professionalization of medicine, the rise of medicine as a natural science, the rise of science and of modern economy. The torture chambers of the witch-hunters were the laboratories where the texture, the anatomy, the resistance of the human body, mainly the female body, was studied. One may say that modern medicine and the male hegemony over this vital field were established on the base of millions of crushed, maimed, torn, disfigured and finally burnt, female bodies. There was a calculated division of labor between Church and State in organizing the massacres and the terror against the witches.

The role of the state is also evident in a political analysis of trials (Oliverio 1998). Here, political life is the principle of organization of all social fields and power relations. Deleuze and Guattari (1988) suggested long ago that politics is present everywhere, and before anything else in social life there is politics. Law, as an institution, has many political dimensions, and is a formal system defining what can be done, what cannot be done, and the sanctions for such actions. Law via the state determines some of the basic relations among people, arranging, for example, an authoritarian set in the courtroom, expressing the modern society, representing the state and its basic principles, reproducing state power, manifesting particular social norms, and being able to remove people from normal society, among many other powers. From this view, law as an agent of the state is deeply political, and trials based on this system are intrinsically political. The "criminal" trials of such people as Alcibiades, Socrates, and Jesus, or Angela Davis, Nelson Mandela, and Leonard Peltier, have been transformed over time into political, often famous, events. The political, legal, and economic reasons that lead to approximately 90% of felony charges ending in plea bargaining to current processes of jury selection suggest the relevance of the state's framework in all trials. The framework suggest the importance of reexamining trials in the study of political deviance. Recent analyses also include research on nuclear waste by Hanson (2009), relational processes and terror by Tilly (2005), and global change and state terrorism by Oliverio and Lauderdale (2005). This type of research is connected directly to the framework of political deviance and embraces a wider range of phenomena, including labor relations, ethnic cleavages, global resources, and the changing collective recognition of social harm.

Conclusion

A number of years ago, Colin Sumner (1994) wrote what he thought was the obituary on the sociology of deviance. He was particularly critical of the puritan nature of much of the writings. However, the field continues with much vibrancy. And in the expanding research on political deviance there is an expanding connection to the study of stratification and social mobility, and analyses of the shifts of moral boundaries resulting in the amplification or creation of deviance (see Gould 2002 on status hierarchies). Deviants often struggle to overcome their positions at the bottom of a status hierarchy, and/or others attempt to shift the balance of power (Lauderdale 2003). In his research on moral boundaries, Ben-Yehuda (1985) reveals some of the processes by which people attempt to legitimate their own views and actions of themselves or others while trying to neutralize negative ones. At least, we have to examine issues of intent and consequence in the larger context of shifting moral boundaries via differences in time and space, and factors such as moral entrepreneurs, social movements, organizations, the state, and globalization (Toggia et al. 2000, Kellner 2002, Nader 2002, Marshall et al. 2007).

The political deviance approach also leads to critical questions. Under what conditions is deviation seen as creative rather than destructive? Under what conditions are deviations defined as leadership rather than stigmatized? Pfohl (1994) suggests that defining particular acts as deviance can be one method of suppressing the resistance of those who threaten power arrangements. And Downes and Rock (2007) continue to raise at least two possible perspectives on political deviance: one a deep analytic view focusing on the nature of power relations in society and the ability of certain forces to label or categorize behavior as deviant; and the another viewing deviance as a means of asserting power in resistance to such encompassing forces. The political approach also calls for investigating the celebration of diversity within most universities, and examining the factors that often lead to a façade rather than a celebration. What, for example, determines whether someone or something is seen as diverse rather than deviant? Or, from a boarder historical perspective, under what conditions was an American Indian seen as good or bad? Vine Deloria, Jr. (1992: 25) emphasizes American Indians were stereotyped, that is, "They were either a villainous warlike group that lurked in the darkness thirsting for the blood of innocent settlers or the calm, dignified elder sitting on the mesa dispensing his wisdom in poetic aphorisms."

Finally, the integration of the study of power is essential to a political deviance approach. For example, where power is increasingly concentrated, the hegemonic forces that prescribe rules and laws, and proscribe certain conduct as deviant, play a concomitantly greater role in the promotion, revision, and maintenance of demonizing categories and labels. Where power is more diffuse, deviance may still persist but is more likely to be construed positively as political deviance, as with the work of certain geniuses, artists, musicians, scientists, or leaders. And where power approaches complete diffusion, political deviance might come to be seen as "diversity" and not as abnormal, immoral, or unlawful. Thus, the consolidation of power and the persistence of categories of deviance correspond in a manner that highlights the utility of an approach that incorporates analyses of both power and deviance. The political deviance perspective continues to examine how defining a particular action or behavioral pattern as deviant is inherently political since social power is used to impose the definition or label. And the political deviance approach continues the study of power by explicating departures from social norms or expectations that are believed, or are purported, to have positive intent and/or consequences for society.

References

Altheide, D. (2006). *Terrorism and the politics of fear*. Walnut Creek, CA: Alta Mira.

Amster, R. (2004). *Street people and the contested realms of public space*. New York: LFB Scholarly.

Becker, H. S. (1963). *Outsiders: Studies in the sociology of deviance*. New York: Free Press.

Ben-Yehuda, N. (1985). *Deviance and moral boundaries*. Chicago, IL: University of Chicago Press.

Ben-Yehuda, N. (2002). *Sacrificing truth: Archaeology and the myth of Masada*. New York: Humanity Books (Prometheus).

Cohen, C. J. (2004). Deviance as resistance: A new research agenda for the study of Black politics. *Du Bois Review* 1 (1), 27–45.

Cooney, M. and Burt, C. H. (2008). Less crime, more law. *American Journal of Sociology* 114, (2), 491–527.

Deleuze, G. and Guattari, F. 1988. *A thousand plateaus: Capitalism and schizophrenia*. London: Athlone.

Deloria, V., Jr. (1992). *God is red* (2nd edn). Golden, CO: North American Press.

Downes, D. and Rock, P. (2007). *Understanding deviance: A guide to the sociology of crime and rule-breaking* (5th edn). New York: Oxford University Press.

Durkheim, E. (1973 [1899]). Two laws of penal evolution (trans. T. A. Jones and A. Scull). *Economy and Society* 2, 285–308.

Erikson, K. T. (1966). *Wayward Puritans: A study in the sociology of deviance*. New York: John Wiley.

Erikson, K. T. (2004). *Wayward Puritans: A study in the sociology of deviance* (classic edn). New York: Allyn & Bacon.

Farrell, R. A. and Case, C. (1995). *The black book and the Mob: The untold story of the control of Nevada's casinos*. Madison: University of Wisconsin Press.

Gamson, W. A. (1975). *The strategy of social protest*. Homewood, IL: Dorsey Press.

Garfinkel, H. (1956). Conditions of successful degradation ceremonies. *American Journal of Sociology* 61, 420–424.

Garland, D. (2002). *The culture of control: Crime and social order in contemporary society*. Chicago, IL: University of Chicago Press.

Goffman, E. (1963). *Stigma*. Englewood Cliffs, NJ: Prentice-Hall.

Goode, E. and Ben-Yehuda, N. (1994). *Moral panics: The social construction of deviance*. Cambridge, MA: Blackwell.

Gould, R. V. (2002). The origins of status hierarchies: A formal theory and empirical test. *American Journal of Sociology* 107, 1143–1178.

Gusfield, J. R. (1963). *Symbolic crusade: Status politics and the American temperance movement*. Urbana: University of Illinois Press.

Hanson, R. (2009). *From bad to goods: Marketing nuclear wastes to American Indians*. Minneapolis: University of Minnesota Press

Henry, S. (2009). *Social deviance*. London: Polity Press.

Inverarity, J., Lauderdale, P., and Feld, B. (1983). *Law and society*. Boston, MA: Little, Brown and Company.

Kellner, D. (2002). Theorizing globalization. *Sociological Theory* 20, 285–305.

Kirk, D. S. (2009). A natural experiment on residential change and recidivism: Lessons from Hurricane Katrina. *American Sociological Review* 74 (3), 484–500.

Lauderdale, P. (1976). Deviance and moral boundaries. *American Sociological Review* 41, 660–676.

Lauderdale, P. (2003). *A political analysis of deviance* (new edn). Toronto: de Sitter.

Lauderdale, P. (2011). *A political analysis of deviance* (third edn). Ontario: de Sitter.

Lauderdale, P. and Amster, R. (2008). Power and deviance, Vol. 3: 1911–1923. In *Violence, Peace and Conflict* (2nd edn), edited by Lester Kurtz. New York: Academic Press.

Lauderdale, P. and Cruit, M. (1993). *The struggle for control: A study of law, disputes, and deviance*. Albany, NY: SUNY Press.

Liazos, A. (1972). The poverty of the sociology of deviance: Nuts, sluts, and perverts. *Social Problems* 20, 103–120

Maratea, R. (2008). The rise and fall of social problems: The blogosphere as a public arena. *Social Problems* 55, 139–160.

Marshall, H., Douglas, K., and McDonnell, D. (2007). *Deviance and social control: Who rules?* Oxford: Oxford University Press.

McAdam, D. and Su, Y. (2002). The political impact of the war at home: Antiwar protests and congressional voting, 1965–1973. *American Sociological Review* 67, 696–721.

Merton, R. K. (1938). Social structure and anomie. *American Sociological Review* 3, 672–682.

Mies, M. (1986). *Patriarchy and accumulation on a world scale*. London: Zed Books.

Mills, C. W. (1942). The professional ideology of social pathologists. *American Journal of Sociology* 49, 165–180.

Nader, L. (2002). *The life of the law*. Berkeley: University of California Press.

Oliverio, A. (1998). *The state of terror*. New York: SUNY Press.

Oliverio, A. and Lauderdale, P. (2005). *Terrorism: A new testament*. Whitby, ON: de Sitter.

Pfohl, S. J. (1994). *Images of deviance and social control: A sociological history*. New York: McGraw-Hill.

Sacco, V. F. (2003). Black Hand outrage: A constructionist analysis of an urban crime wave. *Deviant Behavior* 24, 53–77.

Schur, E. M. (1980). *The politics of deviance*. Englewood Cliffs, NJ: Prentice-Hall.

Simon, D. R. and Stanley Eitzen, D. (1993). *Elite deviance*. New York: Allyn & Bacon.

Sumner, C. (1994). *The sociology of deviance: An obituary*. Buckingham: Open University Press.

Tilly, C. (2005). Terror as strategy and relational process. *International Journal of Comparative Sociology* 46, 11–32.

Toggia, P., Lauderdale, P., and Zegeye, A. (2000). *Crisis and terror in the Horn of Africa: Autopsy of democracy, human rights, and freedom*. Aldershot: Ashgate.

40

Organizational and occupational deviance

John P. Minkes and Leonard Minkes

Definitional issues: whose deviance?

In this chapter, it would be simplest to define deviance as failure to conform to societal norms or organizational requirements. It is important to note, however, that defining deviance at work can be fraught with difficulties. As Friedrichs (2002: 249) puts it: 'any invocation of the term "deviance" in this context has to clarify whether deviance from formal or informal societal norms, from formal or informal organizational norms, from formal or informal professional peer association norms, or from informal norms of workgroup peers, is involved'. Or, to put it another way, dictionary definitions of deviance are of limited use without an understanding of the nature of organizations and the opportunities and constraints they offer to those who work in them. Furthermore, as is true of discussions of deviance generally, the question of power relations and who defines what is deviant cannot be ignored. In capitalist economies, commercial corporations exert considerable influence over norms of acceptable business behavior and the determination of the appropriate responses to misconduct. Sutherland (1949) made this point very clearly in his pioneering study, arguing that the essential difference between corporate offenders and conventional criminals is that the former have the power to avoid criminal prosecution. In addition, large organizations, commercial or otherwise, create internal rules and regulations for those who work in them and decide how to enforce those rules. Thus, these powerful entities will attempt to impose their own definitions of normal and deviant behavior on their own employees, but also on society as a whole.

This influence extends over the gathering of knowledge. Thus, while there is extensive literature written for management students and scholars on the business world (and how to succeed in it), funding for criminological research into organizational misconduct is very limited. Much of what is published relies on media reports and autobiographical accounts, rather than the in-depth studies of the offenders and their criminal careers characteristic of most criminological research. Furthermore, as will be noted later, research into occupational deviance has shifted from ethnographic studies of the meaning of such conduct to the actor to quantitative surveys and experiments in crime prevention. Disseminating research can also prove difficult. Mars (2001) reports that the *Harvard Business Review* once turned down an article which suggested tolerating occupational theft in order to preserve morale, and he himself was not allowed to give a series of lectures on occupational crime to managers attending a leading business school because 'managers would find them disturbing'.

Organizational deviance

Organizational deviance relates to the idea that an organization as an entity can commit and be held responsible for deviant acts. This involves recognizing the limitations of the methodological individualism which asserts that only individuals make decisions and not organizations as such. Harding (2007) usefully summarizes the three distinct characteristics which make them more than just the sum of their parts: organizational structure, shared goals, and the fact that the individuals who work in them can be replaced without changing the nature of the organization. The argument of this chapter is that it is legitimate to hold an organization responsible because of the inescapable influence of its cultures and power structures on the behavior of decision-makers. A good example of this is given by Geis (1967) in his account of price-fixing in the heavy electrical equipment industry: official company policy was that meetings with competitors were illegal and therefore forbidden but managers knew that the reality was different and that their careers depended on participating in the conspiracy.

Organizational deviance may be lawful or unlawful. It is clearly possible for behavior to be within the law but to be regarded as ethically deviant; there are also distinctions between criminal and civil liability, and between criminal and administrative penalties. But the essential point about organizational deviance is that although individuals are involved in the conduct, the prime beneficiary is the organization. In the case of the pharmaceutical industry (Braithwaite, 1984), a company's management may encourage over-prescription of their products or suppress negative drug test results in order to increase the company's sales and profits. Or, in the Guinness scandal (Kochan and Pym, 1987), senior executives conspired to boost the company's share price by creating a false market in order to increase the value of a takeover bid.

The term 'organizational deviance' is preferred by some to the widely used 'corporate crime', partly because it covers unethical as well as unlawful behavior, but also because it can include non-commercial bodies, such as government departments and other state agencies. Criminological interest in the activities of the state has grown considerably in recent years (see, e.g., Cohen, 2001). Another area which currently attracts considerable interest is police corruption (Punch, 2009); although the focus is often on individual wrongdoing, Punch argues that deviance is generated by the nature and structure of the organization and that attention should be directed not toward 'bad apples' but to the orchard. Similarly, the MacPherson Report (MacPherson, 1999) into the failed police investigation of the murder of Stephen Lawrence concluded that the root cause was 'institutional racism' in the Metropolitan Police.

As noted, not all deviance is unlawful. There is now a voluminous literature on bullying in the workplace and indeed as a strategy within organizations. Its inclusion in a study of deviance is interesting in itself but also provides another link between the individual and organizational categories. There is debate on definitions, but for the present purpose bullying is taken to refer to behavior unwanted by the victim, designed to attack or humiliate, using differential power, which in organizations may be a deliberate, competitive strategy to secure compliance. As with deviance in general, there may be difficulty in defining what is meant by 'norm'; in the case of workplace bullying, the answer must be related both to ethics and to undesired organizational losses, for example in productivity, absenteeism, or high turnover of employees.

As an instance of bullying in furthering unethical behavior, McCarthy et al. (2003: 15) refer to the Enron collapse: an 'Enron vice-president turned whistleblower' alleged at an American congressional inquiry 'that intimidation by an ex-chief executive and an ex-financial officer acted to perpetuate unethical accounting practices and duped the Enron board in respect of financial obligations generated in "off-the-books partnerships"'.

It is clear that bullying in the workplace is associated with authority and power and that there are gradations in the way these are exercised: it would be absurd to say that every authoritative instruction is an exercise in bullying. It is another matter, however, if power is used to enforce, as indicated above, unwanted behavior, or, as Salin (2003: 41) comments, 'sexual harassment can be used as a means for men to control women who try to challenge male authority and compete for "male jobs"'.

A number of writers have argued that there is a link between bullying and organizational politics and that it is used as a competitive strategy within organizations. It is also related to style of leadership, to reward systems, and to the culture of organizations in respect of supporting or accepting bullying behavior.

Gender considerations raise further complications in the consideration of organizational deviance. Maier (1997) argues persuasively that corporate decision-making processes are dominated by stereotypical masculine behavior. He shows how this was a major causal factor in the *Challenger* disaster as a 'real men take risks' (Maier, 1997: 959) attitude was normalized and thus concern for the safety of the mission was overruled during the fatal debate over the launching of the Shuttle. The same could be argued about the world of banking and the excessive risk-taking that caused the credit crunch in 2008. But this again raises questions about what is normality and what is deviant: in a male-dominated sector of a traditionally patriarchal society, can stereotypical masculine behavior be labeled deviant, even when it results in dysfunction and disaster?

A different lesson about deviance and *Challenger* is suggested by Vaughan (1996). She makes three critical propositions in her examination of deviations from the norm:

- In NASA, problems were the norm.
- The whole Shuttle system operated on the assumption that deviation could be controlled but not eliminated.
- Conflict between cost and safety is an endemic struggle.

Vaughan goes on to introduce the idea of the 'normalization' of deviance: at NASA, risk-taking became normal behavior. This can perform a useful function for an organization, for example by reducing uncertainty, and, indeed, 'deviation from specifications was common in an innovative design' (Vaughan 1996: 223). Moreover, she comments that the decision to accept risk and proceed with flight exemplifies what Simon (1957) referred to as a tendency for organizations to 'satisfice' rather than 'optimize' when making decisions – that is, to make an acceptable decision, based on the information they have, rather than to aim to make the 'perfect' decision.

This treatment of organizational deviance may be regarded as simply an expression of the problems encountered in situations of innovative design. In the context of this discussion, however, it is important to emphasize, as Vaughan does, that what may happen is the development of a work culture which leads to mistakes and even disasters. Furthermore, it may lead to the intrusion of non-technical issues into engineering considerations.

Many of these issues of organizational behavior are explicitly addressed by Ermann and Lundman (1978). They add to them by arguing that deviance by organizations is so labeled 'because it violates the normative expectations surrounding an organization' and 'the action is peer and elite supported, although it is inconsistent with stated goals of the organization' (Ermann and Lundman, 1978: 9). Among their examples, they include the scandal which surrounded the Nixon Reelection Committee and the chemical workers who die of work-related cancers, due, they state, to corporate homicide. They consider the reason for deviant acts is still an unanswerable question.

Occupational deviance

Occupational deviance refers to individual deviance within the work environment, which, in contrast to organizational deviance, is intended to benefit the individual. The person concerned may be working within an organization or as an individual producer or trader. Again, the behavior may be lawful or unlawful. Unlawful deviance would include stealing from the employer or customers or evading obligations to the state, such as the payment of taxes; lawful deviance might involve conduct which raises ethical issues or simply conflicts with an employer's interests, such as rule breaking, time wasting or transmission of information.

The boundary between individual and organizational responsibility can sometimes be blurred. In the well-known case of Barings Bank, the 'rogue trader' Nick Leeson acted on his own, but the failure of both his employers and the regulatory system to stop him has led such writers as Punch (2008) to attribute the collapse of the bank to systemic failure as well as individual fault.

Occupational deviance by individuals or groups of individuals in organizations is concerned with such matters as 'fiddling', 'casual' theft of materials, deliberate 'cooking' or withholding of information, and so on. In addition to matters which are unlawful or contrary to established rules of procedure in an organization, there are ethical considerations. Friedrichs (2002) notes that three forms of individual deviance in workplaces have been identified:

- occupational crime – financial offenses committed by individuals in the course of a legal occupation;
- occupational deviance – activities which are not necessarily criminal but deviate from the norms of a profession or occupational setting; and
- workplace crime – conventional crimes that occur at the workplace but are not connected with the work itself.

The first category includes stealing from the employer or from customers. The second concerns professional misconduct and sexual harassment or bullying where the perpetrator takes advantage of higher status. The third relates to common crimes, such as assault and homicide, committed in the workplace. Friedrichs argues persuasively that these should not be considered as occupational deviance.

There is evidence of occupational crime going back over 3,000 years. An Egyptian papyrus describes pilferage from a temple grain store by the temple officials (Peet, 1924), and two centuries ago Colquhoun (1806) wrote about the systematic theft of cargo by ships' crews and dock workers in London. More recent research has studied specific occupations, such as retail pharmacists (Quinney, 1963), dock workers (Mars, 1974), bread salesmen (Ditton, 1977), and fast-food restaurant workers (Hollinger et al., 1992). This diversity of occupations has led to controversy about the description of occupational 'fiddles' as 'white-collar crime', since many of those studied were in blue-collar jobs. The emphasis in much of this research was on ethnography: Mars (1974) observed dockers at work, Nicod (in Mars and Nicod, 1981) worked undercover in hotels, and Ditton (1977) worked as a bread salesman for a year. Their approach was sociological and anthropological and their aim was to understand the nature and meaning of the practices they encountered. The focus of research has now changed: more recent work seeks to quantify employee theft and recommend ways to prevent it (e.g., Oliphant and Oliphant, 2001; Bamfield, 2004).

There are no authoritative statistics on the costs of occupational deviance. Evidence of non-criminal forms of deviance is often anecdotal while crime statistics are not useful as most employee theft goes undetected and employers frequently deal informally with those they do catch; dismissing an employee is simpler than prosecution and avoids adverse publicity. Thus, Oliphant and Oliphant (2001), noting that definitions of employee theft can include misconduct, unethical behavior, and 'employee deviance' as well as stealing, cite estimates of annual losses in the USA which range from $40 billion to $400 billion. In the UK, Ditton (1977), referring only to blue-collar theft, cited a total figure equivalent of 1.25–2% of gross national product. From his own research, he estimated that the bakery salesmen he worked with added 10% to their salaries dishonestly. In terms of prevalence, self-report studies reviewed by Henry (1981) showed that 75–92% of workers admitted to pilfering or stealing from their employers. (Which again raises the question of what deviant behavior is. Can something so widespread be described as deviant?) More recently, Bamfield (2004) surveyed major retailers in Europe. Their responses showed that just 5.1% of those arrested for theft were employees. However, they stole seventeen times more than the average shoplifter, so staff theft accounted for 28.8% of shrinkage (compared to 41.4% through consumer theft and 18.3% through internal error). Thus, occupational deviance is clearly widespread but so much is undiscovered or unquantifiable that estimates are bound to vary widely.

Mars (2001) in his introduction to the anthology *Occupational Crime*, reviews the many different concepts and explanations given by the contributors to the anthology. In his own previous work (Mars, 1982), he emphasized the importance of job design in facilitating or encouraging theft. He also established that occupational crime has rules and limits: dock workers had institutionalized theft and cooperated to thwart management strategies to change work practices, but they had a common sense of how far to go; this extended to breaking into a workmate's car when he stole too much.

Ditton (1977) observed the conduct of his colleagues in the bread company. Most of the salesmen stole from the company or cheated customers, but they did not think of their behavior as criminal. If caught, they used neutralizations and denials rather than admitted to stealing. Some of them admitted to greed, but then justified their actions by reference to their low pay. Ditton (1977) thus referred to their illicit additional earnings as 'invisible wages' and, along with others, suggested that workers stole to inflate what they perceived as inadequate salaries.

Henry and Mars (1978) took an anthropological and sociological approach to illicit trading, arguing that pilfering was a way of personalizing trade, a more sociable and traditional way of doing business than modern trading. It was characterized by informality rather than a strictly business approach. As with dockers, there was an unwritten code about how far one should go. Within this, the common feature of all the fiddles is that 'they are acts of dishonesty which the people involved don't consider to be dishonest' (Mars and Nicod, 1981: 69). Again, this begs the question of whose perceptions of deviance hold sway. Ditton (1977) concluded that society is ambivalent because so much occupational theft is 'enterprise' – it epitomizes the capitalist spirit.

A different perspective was offered by Quinney (1963), who studied retail pharmacists and their propensity to carry out a particular type of fraud – prescription violation. He found that, like other professions, pharmacy has an in-built tension between the professional and the business aspects. Pharmacists with a professional outlook were less likely to commit prescription violations than those with a business orientation (with those who were indifferent or mixed coming somewhere between).

Finally, there is the issue of 'whistleblowers'. The relevance of this to the study of organizational and occupational deviance lies in the tension which it may reflect between individual and corporate responsibility, since whistleblowers may experience conflict between their own moral beliefs and organizational pressure to conform. A determined whistleblower, faced with deviant behavior, lawful or unlawful, may decide that 'loyalty' to the organization is less important than moral action. Alternatively, such an individual may not, and may perhaps be guilty of what has been termed the 'crime of obedience'. This is related, though not identical, to a situation discussed by Provis (2004), where a female employee asked a female superior for help over a problem of sexual harassment. The superior woman faced a dilemma because helping her junior colleague might damage her own prospects of advancement. This and the issue of whistleblowing may reflect the pressures of responsibility which is both individual and organizational in the context of the institutional settings within which employees live and work. The 'unbending whistleblower' asserts the significance of individual responsibility in response to what s/he regards as deviance and may pay a heavy price for resisting the institutional setting in which it has to be exercised (Glazer, 1983).

References

Bamfield, J. (2004) 'Shrinkage, shoplifting and the cost of retail crime in Europe: a cross-sectional analysis of major retailers in 16 European countries', *International Journal of Retail and Distribution Management*, 32 (5), 235–41.

Braithwaite, J. (1984) *Corporate Crime in the Pharmaceutical Industry*, London: Routledge & Kegan Paul.

Cohen, S. (2001) *States of Denial*, Cambridge: Polity.

Colquhoun, P. (1806) 'On river plunder', extract reprinted in G. Mars (ed.) (2001) *Occupational Crime*, Dartmouth: Ashgate.

Ditton, J. (1977) *Part-Time Crime: An Ethnography of Fiddling and Pilferage*, London: Macmillan.

Ermann, M.D. and Lundman, R.J. (1978) 'Overview', in M.D. Ermann and R.J. Lundman (eds.) *Corporate and Governmental Deviance: Problems of Organizational Behavior* (1st edn), New York: Oxford University Press.

Friedrichs, D. (2002) 'Occupational crime, occupational deviance, and workplace crime: sorting out the difference', *Criminal Justice*, 2 (3), 243–56.

Geis, G. (1967) 'White-collar crime: the heavy electrical equipment antitrust cases of 1961', in M.B. Clinard and R. Quinney (eds.) *Criminal Behavior Systems: A Typology*, New York: Holt, Rinehart & Winston.

Glazer, M.P. (1983) 'Ten whistleblowers: what they did and how they fared', reprinted in M.D. Ermann and R.J. Lundman (eds.) (1996) *Corporate and Governmental Deviance: Problems of Organizational Behaviour* (5th edn), New York: Oxford University Press.

Harding, C. (2007) *Criminal Enterprise: Individuals, Organisations and Criminal Responsibility*, Cullompton: Willan.

Henry, S. (1978) *The Hidden Economy: The Context and Control of Borderline Crime*, Oxford: Martin Robertson.

Henry, S. (1981) 'Introduction', in S. Henry (ed.) *Can I Have It in Cash?*, London: Astragal Books.

Henry, S. and Mars, G. (1978) 'Crime at work: the social construction of amateur property theft', *Sociology*, 12, 245–63.

Hollinger, R., Slora, K., and Terris, W. (1992) 'Deviance in the fast-food restaurant: correlates of employee theft, altruism and counterproductivity', *Deviant Behavior*, 13, 155–84.

Kochan, N. and Pym, H. (1987) *The Guinness Affair*, London: Christopher Helm.

MacPherson, Sir William (1999) *The Steven Lawrence Inquiry*, London: HMSO.

Maier, M. (1997) 'Gender equity, organizational transformation and *Challenger*', *Journal of Business Ethics*, 16, 943–62.

Mars, G. (1974) 'Dock pilferage', in P. Rock and M. McIntosh (eds.) *Deviance and Social Control*, London: Tavistock.

Mars, G. (1982) *Cheats at Work: An Anthology of Workplace Crime*, London: Allen & Unwin.

Mars, G. (2001) 'Introduction', in G. Mars (ed.) *Occupational Crime*, Aldershot: Ashgate.

Mars, G. and Nicod, M. (1981) 'Hidden rewards at work: the implications from a study of British hotels', in S. Henry (ed.) *Can I Have It in Cash?*, London: Astragal Books.

McCarthy, P., Sheehan, M., Barker, M., and Henderson, M. (2003) 'Ethical investment and workplace bullying: consonances and dissonances', *International Journal of Management and Decision Making*, 4 (1), 11–23.

Oliphant, B.J. and Oliphant, G.C. (2001) 'Using a behavior-based method to identify and reduce employee theft', *International Journal of Retail Distribution and Management*, 29 (10), 442–51.

Peet, T.E. (1924) 'A historical document of Ramesside Age', reprinted in G. Mars (ed.) (2001) *Occupational Crime*, Aldershot: Ashgate.

Provis, C. (2004) *Ethics and Organisational Politics*, Cheltenham: Edward Elgar.

Punch, M. (2008) 'The organization did it: individuals, corporations and crime', in J. Minkes and L. Minkes (eds.) *Corporate and White-Collar Crime*, London: Sage.

Punch, M. (2009) *Police Corruption*, Cullompton: Willan.

Quinney, R. (1963) 'Occupational structure and criminal behaviour: prescription violations by retail pharmacists', reprinted in G. Geis and R.F. Meier (eds.) (1977) *White-Collar Crime*, New York: Free Press.

Salin, D. (2003) 'Bullying and organisational politics in competitive and rapidly changing work environments', *International Journal of Management and Decision Making*, 4 (1), 35–46.

Simon, H.A. (1957) *Administrative Behavior* (2nd edn), New York/London: Free Press/Collier Macmillan.

Sutherland, E. (1949) *White-Collar Crime*, New York: Yale University Press.

Vaughan, D. (1996) *The Challenger Launch Decision: Risky Technology, Culture, and Deviance at NASA*, Chicago, IL: Chicago University Press.

41

Sport and leisure deviance

Robert A. Stebbins

This chapter looks at deviance in sport and leisure from two perspectives: deviance as leisure and deviance in sport. The distinction is easy to make, though only so long as the search for deviant sport is limited to the present. The gladiators of ancient Rome fought other gladiators (or sometimes wild animals) to the death, a practice regarded as criminal today. Gladiatorial activity was, most likely, work for participants, but it was clearly entertainment for the crowds watching from the stands. Likewise, boxing in Rome was little different in its intent to kill the opponent. Romans added iron or brass studs to each glove to create the cestus, which could be a deadly weapon. Then they went even further, developing a cruel, spur-like instrument of bronze called the myrmex ("limb piercer"). Boxing in the Roman Empire was not so much a sport as a bloody amusement for spectators, just like the gladiatorial contests, with slaves pitted against one another in fights to the death (www.hickoksports.com/history/boxing, retrieved December 3, 2008).

Although these sports were acceptable entertainment at the time, they would surely be criminalized in the modern Western world.

An essential element of true sport is inter-human competition based on a recognized set of rules (Coakley 2001: 20). Competition among birds and non-human animals is therefore omitted. Deviance as leisure is considered first. A discussion of deviance in sport follows.

Deviance as leisure

The field of deviance as leisure has led a schizophrenic existence in the two areas of research where, as argued here, it should play a far more central theoretic role: crime and deviance (hereafter referred to as deviance) and leisure studies. The pleasurable nature of certain forms of deviance has long been recognized. Becker (1953: 43), for instance, in writing about marijuana, noted that "the most frequent pattern of [its] use might be termed 'recreational.'" Cohen (1954: 26) asked of juvenile stealing: "Can this stealing be accounted for simply by describing it as another form of recreation, play, or sport? Surely it is that." Writing many years later, Jeffrey Riemer (1981) concluded that adolescents do regard much of their deviance as fun.

In leisure studies, Neulinger (1993) described sex, whether within or outside the family, as leisure, effectively classifying the latter as deviant when he exemplified it with mate-swapping, group sex, and prostitution (seen from the customer's perspective). Rojek (1997: 392–393) has

351

been virtually alone in his critique of leisure studies as having, in general, "turned a blind eye" to deviant leisure. Nevertheless, studying deviant leisure is extremely important for leisure research, for "students of leisure will not only throw light on a shadowy area of leisure activity; they will also contribute to a clearer understanding of how the rules which shape normal leisure practice operate." In the years since Rojek made that prediction, a modest literature on deviant leisure has begun to appear (e.g., special issue "Deviant Leisure" of *Leisure/Loisir*, 30 (1), 2006).

Until recently the fields of deviance and leisure studies lacked significant theoretical elaboration of the idea of deviant leisure. Now, however, the author, working in both fields, has developed two relevant perspectives: tolerable deviance (Stebbins 1996) and serious and casual leisure (Stebbins 2007). Both, incidentally, directly address themselves to Rojek's concern about how rules shape normal leisure practice.

The remainder of this section contains the main principles of these two perspectives as they relate to deviant leisure. Since much of deviant leisure can be classified as tolerable deviance, this concept is discussed next.

Tolerating deviant leisure

With tolerable deviance having been defined and described in Chapter 3 of this volume, it is now possible to apply it to leisure. Note first, however, that many who engage in tolerable deviance argue that their values and activities are merely different, and they readily offer views of and reasons for doing what the community regards as wayward behavior. Hence society should be tolerant, if not accepting, of their differentness. For deviance is their most effective means of expressing certain interests or fulfilling a particular part of human potential in post-industrial society, where these goals are met at least as much in leisure as in work.

These views and reasons constitute "justifications" for tolerable deviance: as leisure, work, or personal adjustment (Stebbins 1996: 7–15). Some forms of deviance are justified predominantly in just one of these ways; others require two or all three justifications. Moreover, these justifications are often used to challenge the label of deviance itself, at bottom a derisive community judgment. In general, the deviants hold that their behavior carries no real threat; it causes no significant harm to the community or themselves. Only the leisure justification is systematically considered in this chapter.

Many people who pursue tolerable deviance see it as something interesting or fun to do in their free time. It is leisure—defined here as uncoerced activity engaged in during free time—which people want to do and, in a satisfying or a fulfilling way (or both), use their abilities and resources to succeed at this (Stebbins 2007: 4). At times, certain forms of intolerable deviance are also sought as leisure: for instance, pre-addictive drug use, youthful rolling of drunks, or juvenile vandalism. But for most who practice intolerable deviance, it is likely to be explained either as full- or part-time work or as personal adjustment to an uncontrollable mental or physiological condition. Neither is leisure.

The idea that leisure can occasionally be deviant is old. Early in the 18th century, Isaac Watts wrote, "for Satan finds some mischief still for idle hands to do." By the mid-19th century in Europe and North America, leisure had, with the weakening of the Protestant ethic, nonetheless gained a degree of respectability. Gelber (1999: 1) says that, in those days, Americans saw hobbies as countering the threat posed by leisure and mischievous idle hands.

Most deviant leisure has the pursuit of pleasure as a main justification. In this regard, much of it fits well the definition of *casual leisure*: immediately, intrinsically rewarding, relatively short-lived pleasurable activity requiring little or no special training to enjoy it (Stebbins 2007: 5). More precisely, most deviant leisure is "sensory stimulation," one type of casual leisure.

Still, beyond the broad domains of tolerable and intolerable deviant casual leisure lies that of deviant *serious leisure*, composed primarily of aberrant religion, politics, and science. In contrast to casual leisure, serious leisure is profound and evolved. It is the systematic pursuit of an amateur, hobbyist, or volunteer core activity that participants find so substantial, interesting, and fulfilling that, in the typical case, they launch themselves on a leisure career centered on acquiring and expressing a combination of its special skills, knowledge, and experience (Stebbins 2007: 5).

Deviant leisure, whether casual or serious, is therefore never solely or principally motivated by pecuniary ends, as is much of criminal intolerable deviance. This is not to argue, however, that the latter might not sometimes be fun. The occupation of striptease—a form of tolerable deviance—well exemplifies those activities where monetary return is clearly more important to the participant than its sporadic pleasure (Ronai and Ellis 1989).

Varieties of deviant leisure

On the whole, sensually stimulating casual leisure is a main motive driving pursuit of most known forms of tolerable deviance in present-day industrial society. Thus, modern sexual expression is, according to some experts, used these days for fun at least as much as for procreation (e.g., Neulinger 1993). Today's aberrant, pleasurable solutions to the problem of sexual expression include group sex, homosexuality, pornography, and heterosexual transvestism.

The same holds for mind- and mood-altering drugs. Szasz (2003) points out that, whatever the society or its historical period, drug use tends to come under a measure of control. In the tolerable deviance framework this may be understood as an institutionalized solution to a major community problem. These drugs have recently become prominent means of enjoyment in the Western world. Here excessive alcohol use and deviant (nonmedical) consumption of marijuana and prescription drugs are stigmatized practices, now tolerable alternatives subject to control.

Gambling and nudism represent direct, deviant challenges to the institution of leisure. According to this institution, it is still morally improper to wager extensively for pleasure; to try to earn a living by gambling rather than by gainful employment; and to engage in various semi-public activities in the nude, especially in mixed company. In the latter case, there has been a recent shift in emphasis to relaxation and sociability from one of physical health. In North America before 1950 (and in contemporary Europe), nudism was justified as an alternative to mainstream health practices, with the curative rays of the sun and exercise in the buff being regarded as highly beneficial (Stebbins 1996: 211).

Lastly, Western political, religious, and scientific institutions have inadvertently encouraged their own sets of heretics. While important non-leisure reasons often encourage joining, say, the Communist Party, the Unification Church, or a coven of witches, their role in providing, in this case, deviant serious leisure as a hobby or volunteer work seems equally strong (for a discussion on volunteering as leisure, see Stebbins 2007). The growth of cults and sects is a sign of dissatisfaction with today's established faiths (Hiller 1978). The same is happening in science. The occult has emerged as a renegade movement in response to the perceived inadequacies of science (sometimes mixed with those of religion) (Truzzi 1972).

Deviance in sport

Sport is not generally the scene of serious player deviance, such as crime of the mugging, murder, and mayhem varieties. Yes, as in every other walk of life, deviance occurs in sport, but here it tends, with some notable exceptions, to be tolerated. Even bench-clearing brawls in baseball and man-to-man punch-ups in hockey fail, at bottom, to qualify as anything other than minor infractions of society's moral norms.

This section examines three different ways in which tolerable deviance is manifested among athletes and, more selectively, among fans. These are deviance for sport, deviance for fun and need, and deviance with sport (see Stebbins 2003 for more detail). Only deviance by athletes is considered in this chapter.

Deviance for sport

Athletes may deviate from the moral norms of their society or their sport for at least two reasons, both justified in the name of the sport they play. One, they may hope to gain a particular advantage while competing against other athletes, whether on their own team or a competing team. Two, athletes may deviate while expressing negative emotions, usually anger, and more rarely hate. Sometimes deviance for sport occurs as cheating, sometimes as use of performance-enhancing drugs. Violence and eating disorders have also been justified in the name of sport. With partial exception of the second, all seem best classified as either noncriminal or legitimate tolerable deviance. The first three are examined in this section.

Cheating

When athletes cheat, they intentionally violate one or more rules of the game, with the object being to gain momentary advantage in the ongoing contest. According to this definition, certain judgments by officials, however accurate, erroneously suggest cheating when the athletes implicated in them had no intention of breaking rules. For example, players explained in a study of amateur and professional football (Stebbins 1993) that "face-masking" calls by referees in football can be of this sort; they are not evidence of cheating, because a man's hand may accidentally slip around the mask of a player on the other team in the course of intense and rapidly moving action. Still, academic cheating by student athletes whose grades determine whether they play school-sponsored sport does, according to this definition, qualify as cheating.

Performance-enhancing drugs

To use performance-enhancing drugs, called "doping," is to take or have administered to humans (or animals) a substance designed to elevate athletic output. Some of these substances have been demonstrated to change the body more or less permanently, as do anabolic steroids, whose principal effect is to strengthen muscle. Others, notably amphetamines and, in large doses, caffeine, have been demonstrated to aid endurance momentarily and help overcome fatigue. Barbiturates and benzodiazepines work momentarily to control tremors.

These substances are legal, even if some are available only on prescription in some countries. But apart from caffeine, all are scorned by official sports organizations, which nowadays go to great lengths to ensure that only drug-free athletes compete at events within their jurisdiction. Hence, taking them is a special kind of cheating. The effectiveness of this control is unclear, however. On the one hand, very few contemporary athletes are apprehended for use of performance-enhancing drugs as a result of extensive random and announced testing. On the other hand, an unknown but probably large number of athletes, aided by some doctors and pharmacists, outsmart the tests. So the doping problem in modern sport remains clouded in ambiguity and inconclusiveness, nicely adding up to a textbook case of noncriminal tolerable deviance.

Violence

Smith (1983: 8–21) has identified four types of violence in sport: brutal body contact, borderline violence, quasi-criminal violence, and criminal violence. Presented here along a continuum of increasing seriousness and disapproval, the first two can be said to be tolerable and the second two intolerable. All can also be conceived of as varieties of cheating.

Smith observes that brutal body contact conforms to official rules and is more or less accepted by players. It includes such bone-jarring incidents as tackles, blocks, body checks, and collisions. Some of these, it turns out, can be delivered with such enthusiasm as to be considered excessively brutal—more force is used than is necessary to do the job. Thus body contact shades into borderline violence. The latter, though prohibited by official rules, is still more or less accepted by all concerned. The celebrated hockey fist-fight, the late hit in football, the high tackle in soccer, and the knock-down pitch in baseball exemplify this type.

Quasi-criminal violence, says Smith, violates official rules, player expectations (to a significant degree), and even criminal law. It is more or less unacceptable (i.e., intolerable) primarily because it is, in legal terms, a type of assault resulting in serious injury.

Criminal violence is so serious (often death results) that it falls squarely within the jurisdiction of the law. Most of the time, this type occurs just before or just after a contest.

Deviance for fun and need

When athletes engage in deviance outside sport they do so primarily for fun or to meet a need. Three deviant leisure activities are considered: juvenile delinquency, recreational drug use, and deviance out of need.

Juvenile delinquency

The commonsense idea that regular participation in organized sport insulates many adolescents against organizing their leisure lifestyles around delinquent activities, it turns out, lacks scientific support. Coalter's (2007) exhaustive review of research in the area reveals widespread ambiguous and inconclusive evidence stemming from conceptual and methodological weaknesses. Another part of the problem, he says, rests on lack of practical detail needed to generalize lessons learned from projects and programs.

Recreational drug use

Why do athletes use recreational drugs? One possible answer, according to Iso-Ahola and Crowley (1991) is boredom, though the causal relationship between these two variables still remains to be established. Surprisingly, the bored male adolescent drug abusers these authors examined turned out to be more active than the control group of non-abusers in such sports as football, baseball, gymnastics, skateboarding, and roller-skating. That the first were still bored even though they participated in active serious leisure lifestyles led the authors to suggest that therapists could possibly discourage further recreational drug use by providing the abusers "with copious opportunities to experience leisure activities that potentially meet the same needs that were formerly met through substance abuse" (Iso-Ahola and Crowley 1991: 269): that is, thrilling and adventurous pursuits rather than those considered repetitious and constant (e.g., football).

Because athletes are often in the public spotlight, there is a certain curiosity in the wider community about their use of alcohol and drugs. Press coverage tends to suggest that use of drugs and alcohol is rampant among athletes. But are the rates of use in sport different from those of comparable age and sex categories in the general population? Alas, research in this area is equivocal for both alcohol and marijuana use (for a review, see Stebbins, 2003: 82–83).

Deviance out of need

For want of a better word, "need" refers here to deviance enacted in response to some kind of inner force, as expressed in assault (anger), hard drug use (addiction), and drug trafficking (need for money). All qualify as intolerable deviance. The public is also highly curious about these forms of deviance among high-profile athletes. And here, too, sociologists have been trying to determine if rates of such criminality in sport differ from rates of comparable age and sex categories in the general population. Unfortunately, in this instance, systematic research is in extremely short supply, with nothing whatsoever available on drug trafficking among athletes.

Deviance with sport

This section examines two of the many ways people use sport to engage in their own peculiar forms of deviance: excessive gambling and hooliganism.

Deviant gambling

The deviant side of gambling, since it is examined elsewhere (Stebbins 1996: 9–10), will not be discussed here. Of interest in this chapter is gambling on the outcomes of games and competitions in a wide range of sports. Chief among these are football, hockey, soccer, and baseball as well as basketball, horse racing, and car racing. With off-track betting illegal in many parts of North America, gamblers there are limited to pari-mutuel systems, wherein they wager against each other rather than against a bookmaker. Horse racing is by far the most popular form of pari-mutuel gambling in North America (Stebbins 1996: 151). Also highly popular is illegally betting with bookies on horse races and team sports, primarily football, hockey, basketball, and baseball.

Sports events offer interesting and socially acceptable ways to enjoy free time by wagering, as long as the wagers are, according to local standards, moderate and infrequent. But people push the moral limit when they gamble regularly with large sums two to three times a week, thereby turning acceptable behavior into a form of tolerable deviance (Dickerson 1984: 38). The public attitude at this point is that the money lost could be better spent on family needs. The internet has greatly expanded opportunities for sport gambling.

Hooliganism

To the extent that hooliganism is about violence, it can be classified as intolerable, criminal activity. But it is not wholly that, even if inter-fan fighting, which is part of it, is seized on by the press and the general public. Rather, as Guilianotti (1999: 49) observes: "football hooliganism in its contemporary sense refers not to 'traditional' outbreaks of disorder, but instead to the social genesis of distinctive fan sub-cultures and their engagement in regular and collective violence, primarily with rival peers," who support the other team. Moreover, hooliganism is intolerably deviant leisure. Guilianotti (1999: 52–53) points out that participants get an "emotional buzz" when fighting with opponents. The hooligan's goal is to enter and leave the fray with body and mind intact, a sign of skill and competence in such circumstances that gains high respect from peers.

Conclusions

Employing the perspectives of tolerable deviance and casual and serious leisure helps explain the two main foci of this chapter—deviance as leisure and deviance in sport—their motivational bases, and their socio-cultural context. These perspectives also provide a broad and flexible framework of sensitizing concepts for future research in this area, where exploration is still, of necessity, the dominant approach to data collection. Nearly all the activities covered here as tolerably deviant leisure and deviant sport require much more exploratory investigation before it may be said that they are truly understood. Scientific interest in deviance in sport and leisure is, in general, in its infancy.

References

American Psychiatric Association. (2000) *Diagnostic and Statistical Manual of Mental Disorders*, 4th rev. edn, Washington, DC: American Psychiatric Association.

Becker, H. S. (1953) "Becoming a marijuana user," *American Journal of Sociology*, 59: 235–242.

Coakley, J. (2001). *Sport in Society: Issues and Controversies*, 7th edn, New York: McGraw-Hill.

Coalter, F. (2007) *A Wider Social Role for Sport: Who's Keeping the Score?*, London: Routledge.

Cohen, A. K. (1954) *Delinquent Boys*, Glencoe, IL: Free Press.

Dickerson, M. G. (1984) *Compulsive Gamblers*, London: Longman.

Gelber, S. M. (1999) *Hobbies: Leisure and the Culture of Work in America*, New York: Columbia University Press.

Guilianotti, R. (1999) *Football: A Sociology of the Global Game*, Cambridge: Polity Press.

Hiller, H. H. (1978) "Continentalism and the third force in religion," *Canadian Journal of Sociology*, 6: 189–202.

Iso-Ahola, S. E. and Crowley, E. D. (1991) "Adolescent substance abuse and leisure boredom," *Journal of Leisure Research*, 23: 260–271.

Neulinger, J. (1993) "Sex and leisure, or sex as leisure," *Leisure Information Quarterly*, 19 (1): 6–7.

Riemer, J. W. (1981) "Deviance as fun," *Adolescence*, 16: 39–43.

Rojek, C. (1997) "Leisure theory: retrospect and prospect," *Loisir et Société / Society and Leisure*, 20: 383–400.

Ronai, C. R. and Ellis, C. (1989) "Turn-ons for money: interactional strategies of the table dancer," *Journal of Contemporary Ethnography*, 18: 271–298.

Smith, M. D. (1983) *Violence and Sport*, Toronto: Butterworths.

Stebbins, R. A. (1993) *Canadian Football: The View from the Helmet*, Toronto: Canadian Scholars Press.

Stebbins, R. A. (1996) *Tolerable Differences: Living with Deviance*, 2nd edn, Toronto: McGraw-Hill Ryerson.

Stebbins, R. A. (2003) "Deviance and sport," in J. Crossman (ed.), *Canadian Sport Sociology*, Toronto: Nelson Canada.

Stebbins, R. A. (2007) *Serious Leisure: A Perspective for Our Time*, New Brunswick, NJ: Transaction.

Szasz, T. (2003) *Ceremonial Chemistry: The Ritual Persecution of Drugs, Addicts, and Pushers*, rev edn, Syracuse, NY: Syracuse University Press.

Truzzi, M. (1972) "The occult revival as popular culture," *Sociological Quarterly*, 13: 16–36.

42

Medical deviance

Paul Jesilow

Deviance in medicine has a long history. The ancient Hippocratic Oath reflects this fact. Stated about 2,500 years ago, the pre-eminent Greek physician of his day swore to act only in the interest of his patients "and never do harm to anyone." That other physicians were acting less selflessly can be deduced from the fact that Hippocrates saw it necessary to proclaim that "in every house where I come I will enter only for the good of my patients." Hippocrates' oath also reveals a basic underlying factor with respect to medical deviance: there is enduring controversy about what constitutes appropriate medical care. Among these matters in Hippocrates' statement are his prohibitions against euthanasia, abortion, and surgeries performed by non-specialists, issues that remain controversial. It is an overabundance of these gray areas in healthcare that continues to give rise to medical deviance.

The practice of medicine is not an exact science and there are few iron-clad rules. Physicians often have differences of opinion about the proper treatment for the same set of symptoms and there are considerable variations in medical practice (Wennberg, 2002). Doctors' decision-making when dealing with uncertainty may be influenced by a number of factors. Concern for their patients and society plays some role, but self-interest often seems to be a major factor, too. Physician choices on some occasions appear to be little more than rationalizations to excuse their misconduct. The lack of agreed rules in medicine allows physicians to excuse their self-interested behavior as the fault of others (Jesilow *et al.*, 1993). The result is often questionable behavior by doctors.

Today there are numerous acts of deviance in which some physicians engage: they sexually abuse patients (Jesilow, 2000); violate prescription laws (Storr *et al.*, 2000); cooperate with corporate entities to steal billions of dollars from private (e.g., Blue Cross/Blue Shield) and public (e.g., Medicare and Medicaid) insurance entities (Sparrow, 2000); and take part in other illegal activities (Liederbach, 2001). There is insufficient space to discuss them all here, so I focus on a few issues that illustrate how gray areas contribute to deviance by doctors.

Fee-splitting

Today, medical deviance falls within the rubric of white-collar crime, a term coined by Edwin H. Sutherland (1940) in his presidential address to the American Sociological Society in 1939. He defined his topic "approximately" as "crime committed by a person of respectability and high social status in the course of his occupation" (Sutherland, 1983: 7). Sutherland, at least in his writings, was not very concerned with illegalities by doctors. He mentions them as an example in his 1949 monograph on white-collar crime "because it is probably less criminal than other professions." He is, however, able to offer a litany of acts, including "illegal sales of alcohol and narcotics, abortion, illegal services to underworld criminals, fraudulent reports and testimony in accident cases, extreme instances of unnecessary treatment and surgical operations, fake specialists, restriction of competition, and fee-splitting" (Sutherland, 1983: 1). Only the last of these comes in for further explication. The fee-splitting physician, Sutherland explained sixty years ago, sends his patients to the surgeon who will pay the largest referral fee, rather than to the one who will do the best work; and, typically, the less skilled the surgeon, the higher the kickback he must give in order to generate business. Thus split-fee cases gravitate to the highest bidders, the most dangerous surgeons.

There is no doubt that old-style fee-splitting is still occurring between general practitioners and specialists who await referrals from them, but it is not the type of arrangement that dominates contemporary discussions on the matter. Rather, current concern focuses on arrangements involving physicians and hospitals. In one scheme, community-based physicians are overcompensated by hospitals as a means to entice the doctors to send patients their way (Vandenburgh, 2001). In another, hospital-based physicians—such as emergency room doctors, anesthesiologists, pathologists, and radiologists—are paid less by the hospitals than the fair market value of the services they provide or they are charged more than the going rate for services provided by the hospitals at which they work. These contractual relationships are of concern to the federal government because they often involve Medicare payments. The hospital obtains a portion of the physician-generated fees for overhead expenses. The government's position is that the hospitals have entered into these financial arrangements as a means to obtain illegal kickbacks from physicians in exchange for the physicians being able to provide (and be compensated for) services to government beneficiaries at the hospitals (Kusserow, n.d.).

Unnecessary surgery

Unnecessary surgery, also on Sutherland's 1949 list of physicians' offenses, illustrates the relationship between medical deviance and disagreement among practitioners regarding appropriate behavior. In the 1970s, researchers at Cornell University studied the impact of mandatory second opinions before an insurer paid for elective surgeries. The rate of surgeries declined because the second opinions did not always support the initial conclusions that surgery was needed. The researchers reasoned from the evidence that at least 10 percent of the 20 million operations then performed annually in the United States were unwarranted (McCarthy and Finkel, 1978; see Axon et al., 2008 for a review of ethical and legal considerations with respect to medical second opinions).

A recent case before the California Medical Board illustrates how single opinions facilitate unnecessary surgeries. A California doctor got into trouble for conducting cardiac surgeries based only on the recommendations of a second cardiologist; the physician had not confirmed for himself that the surgeries were necessary. The operations became suspect after the medical board pulled the license of the recommending cardiologist, whom they charged "with dozens of counts of gross negligence, incompetence, dishonesty and corruption, filing false or fraudulent claims, failure to maintain adequate records and repeated negligent acts" (Sabalow, 2008a: B1). An administrative law judge ruled that several of the operations he had recommended were unnecessary and that the performing surgeon had departed from accepted medical standards by relying solely on the recommendation of the now defrocked cardiologist. The judge further noted that the two doctors appeared to have used collusion to stop the patients from obtaining a second opinion that might have prevented the surgeries. The judge barred the operating surgeon from practicing medicine for 120 days and placed him on probation for eight years. No criminal charges were filed (Sabalow, 2008b).

A certain percentage of unnecessary surgeries are likely criminal—undertaken only because an insurance company will pay for them. These acts can be regarded as equivalent to assault— that is, as a crime that involves both theft of money and personal injury (Lanza-Kaduce, 1980). A Michigan dermatologist, for example, frightened his patients with diagnoses of cancers they did not have so that he could then bill Medicare and Blue Cross/Blue Shield for the unnecessary surgical procedures he performed (Shellenbarger, 2007).

We do not know the percentage of unnecessary surgeries that are criminal. Prosecutions are rare. The behavior is difficult to uncover and presents unusual problems for prosecutors who are more comfortable with cases that involve street criminals (Jesilow et al., 1993). Still, there are some prosecutions. One recent case illustrates just how egregious the practice of unnecessary surgery needs to be before it is handled criminally. More than 2,800 healthy, insured patients were paid between $300 and $1,000-plus to undergo unnecessary surgery for sweaty palms, hemorrhoids or cysts. Insurance companies were then billed more than $150 million for the procedures. One of the surgeons in the case received five years' imprisonment and another is serving a ten-year prison term for his actions. The latter's medical license was also revoked (Perkes, 2009). Such blatant frauds are likely rare, but when they do surface the extent of their costs and the evident disregard for patients make them efficient fodder for hungry news networks and undermine physicians' claims to be a selfless profession.

The largest percentage of questionable surgeries is the result of the normal practice of medicine and they differ from the acts that are tried in criminal courts. The rise in the use of cesarean sections in place of vaginal births may make this matter clear.

Cesarean section (c-section) can be a saving operation when certain problems arise either before or during birth. There are agreed-upon situations when it should be considered, but its actual use is a decision made by physicians and patients (Bailit et al., 2004; Currie and Macleod, 2008). Generally c-sections go well, but it is a major surgery that carries with it the same dangers that are associated with other operations, as well as a few more: for example, non-emergency c-sections are too often performed before the unborn babies' lungs are fully developed (Alan et al., 2009), and if a woman undergoes multiple c-sections there as an increased risk of the surgery causing problems (National Institutes of Health, 2006).

Concern has arisen because the rate of c-sections has been rising. The World Health Organization (1985) suggests that the cesarean section rate should not be higher than 15 percent, but achieving this rate in the near future seems unlikely. The US rate did decline from 22.6 per 100 births in 1991 to 20.7 in 1996 (Menacker and Curtin, 2001). But there has been a rapid increase in the use of c-sections ever since. The rate in the United States had climbed to 31.1 percent by 2006, an all-time high (Martin et al., 2009). And rates have risen in many other regions of the world, too (Armson, 2007; Pai, 2000). In Canada, the rate of cesarean births increased from 5.2% in 1969 to 25.6% in 2003 (Canadian Institute for Health Information, n.d.). In Iran, it is reported that 40 percent of children are delivered by c-section (Farmani, 2008).

Physicians offer a number of explanations for why c-sections are increasing. The most common stems from doctors' ideology about civil suits: they believe they are likely to be sued and they must take every precaution to avoid liability (Baker, 2005; Hyman, 2001–2). Concerns about malpractice are particularly acute for obstetricians and gynecologists who have a high rate of suits compared to other specialties (Studdert et al., 2006) and their malpractice insurance fees are, as a result, relatively expensive (MacLennan et al., 2005). The result of the concern about malpractice, according to the medical profession, is "defensive medicine": the ordering of additional diagnostic tests and performing tangential procedures; or refraining from performing procedures that they feel pose too much legal risk if a positive result is not obtained; or simply refusing to treat some patients or to practice in certain states for fear of litigation (General Accounting Office, 2003). Increased use of c-sections, many in the medical profession posit, is defensive medicine, the result of litigious patients and their greedy attorneys.

Obstetricians and gynecologists tell us they also conduct a sizable portion of c-sections because the expectant mothers request them, although the extent of this practice is unknown (National Institutes of Health, 2006; Norwitz, 2009). These elective cesarean deliveries occur without any medical indication that a vaginal birth would be unsafe. The women, the argument goes, are attempting to avoid the anxiety and pain of childbirth, while seeking the convenience of a scheduled delivery (Armson, 2007; Bewley and Cockburn, 2002). An editorial by the American College of Obstetricians and Gynecologists (ACOG) supported the practice in some situations, based on the belief that informed patients have a right to select among all their healthcare options (Hale and Harer, 2005). ACOG's (2008: 4) Committee on Ethics added:

> If the physician believes that cesarean delivery promotes the overall health and welfare of the woman and her fetus more than vaginal delivery, he or she is ethically justified in performing a cesarean delivery. Similarly, if the physician believes that performing a cesarean delivery would be detrimental to the overall health and welfare of the woman and her fetus, he or she is ethically obliged to refrain from performing the surgery.

The difficulty with such advice stems from the fact that there is not universal agreement on the advantages and disadvantages of c-sections. For example, obstetricians, in response to survey questions, indicated their belief "that women had the right to request a caesarean section without maternal/fetal indications" (Reime et al., 2004: 1388). Midwives and family practitioners were more likely to object to c-sections in such circumstances (Reime et al., 2004). Obstetricians were more likely than midwives and family practitioners to rely on technology and interventions and to believe that "increasing caesarean rates were a sign of improvement in obstetrics" (Reime et al., 2004: 1388)."[1] Lack of agreement on the correct course of action when expectant mothers request cesarean delivery is particularly evident among female obstetricians and gynecologists: "36% say they would not perform a cesarean at a woman's request if not medically necessary, 32% say they would, and 28% say it would depend upon the woman's circumstances" (ACOG, 2003).

Differences of opinion about c-sections allow some delivery physicians to view the surgeries as ethical behavior under circumstances that suggest otherwise. For example, research has indicated that higher fees for surgeries may influence physicians' decisions to operate; c-sections are paid about twice the fee for vaginal births (Currie and Macleod, 2008). Physician convenience may also play a role. Researchers compared deliveries at a group-model health maintenance organization (HMO) (Kaiser hospitals), where physicians are salaried employees who work a specific shift, to deliveries by fee-based physicians at other hospitals. The researchers (Spetz et al., 2001: 536) found:

> The probability of cesarean sections for patients insured by a group-model HMO is more stable during the course of a day than that for patients insured by all other insurance plans. Group-model HMO patients with previous cesarean sections are less likely to have cesarean sections in the evening hours and are less likely to be diagnosed with fetal distress or prolonged/dysfunctional labor.

The suggestion is that physicians who work a shift have no incentive to speed deliveries, while fee-based doctors may take action so that they can go home to bed.

Evidence that the increasing numbers of cesarean sections may in part be due to obstetricians' and gynecologists' attitudes that favor intervention and neutralize any feelings of wrongdoing undermine the perceived ethics of the profession. The argument that its members are acting to prevent civil suits likely has a similar impact. C-sections from this perspective are performed for the benefit of the delivering doctors and not because the medical conditions warrant them. It is likely that attitudes favoring intervention and blaming others for causing the use of questionable actions are common throughout the medical profession. These beliefs substantially contribute to the rate and cost of unnecessary surgeries and other procedures, while allowing physicians to see themselves as blameless.

Fraud against third-party payment programs

One final area of medical deviance to be discussed here is fraud by physicians against public and private insurance entities. Such acts have already been mentioned—unnecessary surgeries conducted only because a third party will pay for them being a prime example. But there are other areas of concern. Doctors have obtained additional income by charging for a more expensive procedure than the one performed, double-billing for services, ordering unnecessary visits, and unnecessarily extending treatment. These behaviors, although illegal, garner some support from other physicians, particularly with respect to Medicaid, the US government program to provide healthcare to the indigent. Medicaid pays physicians less than private insurance and this provides some doctors with an excuse to steal from the programs. They argue that the government payments barely cover the cost of treatment (Pittman, 2007) and that they must cheat Medicaid in order to continue to provide services to the poor (Jesilow et al., 1993). The excuse allows doctors to steal from the program while continuing to see themselves as selfless.

Self-serving explanations by physicians for criminal behavior are not limited to government programs. Physicians believe that there should be few restrictions on their practice of medicine. One outcome of this belief is that they may put false information in patients' medical records so that their treatments of those patients will be reimbursed, whereas otherwise they would not have been compensated (Bogardus et al., 2004). One survey found that about half of the physician-participants were willing to deceive third-party payers in this manner (Freeman et al,, 1999). The ideology allows physicians to collect payments for services that would not otherwise be covered by the insurance companies, while arguing that their actions are selfless and taken on behalf of patients.

Discussion

The delivery of healthcare services in the US has dramatically changed since Sutherland outlined his ideas on medical deviance. The sole practitioner no longer dominates healthcare and the medical profession has had its social privilege, economic power, and political influence eroded by HMOs; insurance companies, hospitals, and other healthcare facilities have merged into larger and more powerful corporate systems. As corporate forces continue to move into key management roles in medicine, doctors become employees, further eroding their once dominant position in healthcare.

Physicians' illegal, unethical, and questionable acts undermine the profession's claim of selfless behavior and further undermine the ability of its members to impact public policy. Physicians' attitudes were important considerations more than forty years ago, during initial legislative hearings on Medicare and Medicaid (Jesilow *et al.*, 1993). By 2009, that voice seemed much weaker as Congress debated national healthcare. We need the profession to take a strong stance in favor of the public good in order for it to regain our faith and confidence. Any indication that physicians may be acting in their own best interests will defeat their efforts and leave the debate over healthcare in the hands of corporations that may have little interest in helping anyone other than their stockholders.

Note

1   Although only about 9% of the obstetricians felt this way.

References

Alan T., Tita N., Landon, M., Spong, C., Yinglei, L., Leveno, K., Varner, M., Moawad, A., Caritis, S., Meis, P., Wapner, R., Sorokin, Y., Miodovnik, M., Carpenter, M., Peaceman, A., O'Sullivan, M., Sibai, B., Langer, O., Thorp, J., Ramin, D., and Mercer, B. (2009) "Timing of Elective Repeat Cesarean Delivery at Term and Neonatal Outcomes," *New England Journal of Medicine*, 360: 111–20.

American College of Obstetricians and Gynecologists (ACOG) (2003) "Gallup Survey Reveals Women Ob-Gyns Benefit from 'Insider Knowledge,'" 9 December. Online. Available: www.acog.org/from_home/publications/press_releases/nr12-09-03-2.cfm (accessed 31 July 2009).

—— (2008) "Surgery and Patient Choice" [ACOG Committee Opinion 395], *Obstetrics and Gynecology*, 111: 243–7. Online. Available: www.acog.org/from_home/publications/ethics/co395.pdf (accessed 1 August 2009).

Armson, B. (2007) "Is Planned Cesarean Childbirth a Safe Alternative?," *Canadian Medical Association Journal*, 176: 475–6.

Axon, A., Hassan, M., Niv, Y., Beglinger, C., and Rokkas, T. (2008) "Ethical and Legal Implications in Seeking and Providing a Second Medical Opinion," *Digestive Diseases*, 26: 11–17.

Bailit, J., Love, T., and Mercer, B. (2004) "Rising Cesarean Rates: Are Patients Sicker?," *American Journal of Obstetrics and Gynecology*, 191: 800–3.

Baker, T. (2005) *The Medical Malpractice Myth*, Chicago, IL: University of Chicago Press.

Bewley, S. and Cockburn, J. (2002) "Responding to Fear of Childbirth," *The Lancet*, 359: 2128–9.

Bogardus, S., Jr., Geist, D., and Bradley, E. (2004) "Physicians' Interactions with Third-Party Payers: Is Deception Necessary?," *Archives of Internal Medicine*, 164: 1841–4.

Canadian Institute for Health Information (n.d.) *CIHI Health Indicator Reports*. Online. Available: www.cihi.ca/hireports/search.jspa (accessed 11 January 2007).

Currie, J. and Macleod, W. B. (2008) "First Do No Harm? Tort Reform and Birth Outcomes," *Quarterly Journal of Economics*, 123: 795–830.

Farmani, H. (2008) "Too Posh to Push? Iran Seeks to Curb C-sections," *Anthropologist Community*. Online. Available: www.community.livejournal.com/anthropologist/1246675.html (accessed 26 July 2009).

Freeman, V., Rathore, S., Weinfurt, K., Schulman, K., and Sulmasy, D. (1999) "Lying for Patients: Physician Deception of Third-Party Payers," *Archives of Internal Medicine*, 159: 2263–70.

General Accounting Office (2003) *Medical Malpractice: Implications of Rising Premiums on Access to Health Care*. Online. Available: www.gao.gov/new.items/d03836.pdf (accessed 30 July 2009).

Hale, R. and Harer, W. (2005) "Elective Prophylactic Cesarean Delivery. Editorial," *ACOG Clinical Review*, 10: 1, 15.

Hyman, D. (2001–2) "Medical Malpractice and the Tort System: What Do We Know and What (if Anything) Should We Do about It?," *Texas Law Review*, 80: 1639–55.

Jesilow, P., Pontell, H., and Geis, G. (1993) *Prescription for Profit: How Doctors Defraud Medicaid*, Berkeley: University of California Press.

Jesilow. P. (2000) "Sexual Misconduct by Physicians," in C. D. Bryant (ed.) *Encyclopedia of Criminology and Deviant Behavior*, Philadelphia, PA: Taylor and Francis: 387–90.

Kusserow, R. (n.d.) "Financial Arrangements between Hospitals and Hospital-Based Physicians," Department of Health and Human Services, Office of Inspector General. Online. Available: www.oig.hhs.gov/oei/reports/oei-09-89-00330.pdf (accessed 1 August 2009).

Lanza-Kaduce, L. (1980) "Deviance among Professionals: The Case of Unnecessary Surgery," *Deviant Behavior*, 1: 333–59.

Liederbach, J. (2001) "Opportunity and Crime in the Medical Profession," in N. Shover and J. P. Wright (eds.) *Crimes of Privilege: Readings in White-Collar Crime*, Oxford, New York: Oxford University Press: 144–56.

MacLennan, A., Nelson, K., Hankins, G., and Speer, M. (2005) "Who Will Deliver Our Grandchildren?" *Journal of the American Medical Association*, 294: 1688–90.

Martin, J. A., Hamilton, B. E., Sutton, P. D. Ventura, S. J., Menacker, F., Kirmeyer, S., and Mathews, T. J. (2009) *Births: Final Data for 2006*, National Vital Statistics Reports, Vol. 57, No. 7, Hyattsville, MD: National Center for Health Statistics.

McCarthy, M. and Finkel, M. (1978) "Second Opinion Elective Surgery Programs: Outcome Status over Time," *Medical Care*, 16: 984–94.

Menacker, F. and Curtin, S. (2001) *Trends in Cesarean Birth and Vaginal Birth after Previous Cesarean, 1991–99*, National Vital Statistics Reports, Vol. 49, No. 13, Hyattsville, MD: National Center for Health Statistics.

National Institutes of Health (2006) "NIH State-of-the-Science Conference Statement on Cesarean Delivery on Maternal Request," *NIH Consensus and State-of-the-Science Statements*, 23: 1–29. Online. Available: www.consensus.nih.gov/2006/CesareanStatement_Final053106.pdf (accessed 1 August 2009).

Norwitz, E. (2009) "Cesarean Delivery on Maternal Request," *UpToDate*. Online. Available: www.uptodate.com/patients/content/topic.do?topicKey=~/hw1WZMCqim2ZX (accessed 1 August 2009).

Pai, M. (2000) "Unnecessary Medical Interventions: Caesarean Sections as a Case Study," *Economic and Political Weekly*, 35: 2755–61.

Perkes, C. (2009) "O.C. Doctor Loses License in Sweaty-Palm Surgery Case," *Orange County Register*, 21 April. Online. Available: www.ocregister.com/articles/hampton-insurance-surgeries-2370833-medical-surgery (accessed 28 July 2009).

Pittman, D. (2007) "Medicaid Holds up Doctors," *Amarillo Globe-News*, 22 December.

Reime, B., Klein, M., Kelly, A., Duxbury, N., Saxell, L., Liston, R., Prompers, J., Entjes, R., and Wong, V. (2004) "Do Maternity Care Provider Groups Have Different Attitudes towards Birth?," *BJOG: An International Journal of Obstetrics and Gynaecology*, 111: 1388–93.

Sabalow, R. (2008a) "RMC Surgery Case," *Redding Record Searchlight*, 19 March: B1.

—— (2008B) "Dr. Brusett's License Revoked," *Redding Record Searchlight*, 15 August: A1.

Shellenbarger, P. (2007) "Feds Want Stokes to Do Hard Time," *Grand Rapids Press*, 18 December: A1.

Spetz, J., Smith, M., and Ennis, S. (2001) "Physician Incentives and the Timing of Cesarean Sections: Evidence from California," *Medical Care*, 39: 536–50.

Sparrow, M. (2000) *License to Steal*, Boulder, CO: Westview Press.

Storr, C., Trinkoff, A., and Hughes, P. (2000) "Substance-Using Health Professionals: Similarities of Substance Use between Medical and Nursing Specialties," *Substance Use and Misuse*, 35: 1443–69.

Studdert, D., Mello, M., Gawande, A., Gandhi, T., Kachalia, A., Yoon, C., Puopolo, A., and Brennan, T. (2006) "Claims, Errors, and Compensation Payments in Medical Malpractice Litigation," *New England Journal of Medicine*, 354: 2024–33.

Sutherland, E. (1940) "White-Collar Criminality," *American Sociological Review*, 5: 1–12.

—— (1983) *White-Collar Crime*, New Haven, CT: Yale University Press.

Vandenburgh, H. (2001) "Physician Stipends as Organizational Deviance in For-Profit Psychiatric Hospitals," *Critical Sociology*, 27: 56–76.

Wennberg, J. (2002) "Unwarranted Variations in Healthcare Delivery: Implications for Academic Medical Centres," *British Medical Journal*, 325: 961–4.

World Health Organization (1985) "Appropriate Technology for Birth," *The Lancet*, 326 (8452): 436–7.

Part IX
Sexual deviance

Overview

No form of human behavior is more subject to social control than sexual behavior. This is because those behaviors attendant to sexual gratification are potentially disruptive to the social order. As Bryant (1982: 11) has observed:

> The sexual urge is a powerful component in physiological motivation and plays an equally intense role in the shaping of the social configurations, which accomplish to externalize carnal desire and provide for its satisfaction through institutionalized behavioral means. The carnal urge can also be, and often is, equally cohesive, in affecting social solidarity through bonding and concerted social efforts to facilitate and routinize opportunities for sexual gratification.

Throughout human history, one of the tasks of society has been to monitor, channel, and control sexual behavior. Sexual gratification may be physiologically simple, but the sociological behaviors that attend this goal are widely varied, complex, intricate, and often convoluted (Bryant 1982: 1).

The normative systems attempt to speak to the appropriate circumstances, conditions, and participants constituent to numerous varieties of sexual expression and carnal gratification (Bryant 1982: 11–12). The notion of sexual deviance is relative to time, place, and circumstances. Social sanctions for violations of sexual norms range from inconsequential admonition, or symbolic punishments, to death. Perceptions of, and attitudes toward, sexual deviance have differed over time, and that which was abhorrent two centuries ago may well be tolerated, if not accepted, today. The future may well see drastic changes in comparison to today in the way society views various kinds of sexual deviance. Some sociologists have speculated that there will likely be much more public toleration of even serious sexual crimes. Bryant (1982: 376), for example, has speculated that, "It may well be that, in time, the very concept of 'sex' crime itself will be eliminated from our legal perspective."

Female prostitution

Female prostitution is, arguably, one of the oldest forms of sexual deviance. Prostitution has assumed many configurations over the centuries. In the first chapter in this part, Mary Dodge examines contemporary prostitution and points out that prostitutes vary from street "hookers" (some of them may be narcotics addicts trying to earn money to pay for their habit) to expensive "call girls" who operate out of luxury hotels or are "referred" to well-to-do clients by telephone madams. Call girls often practice their trade under the guise of being an "escort" for an escort service. Such companies may even advertise in the Yellow Pages. Other guises might include posing as "artists' models," private "modeling" agencies, or masseuses in massage parlors. Some of the latter offer "full services," including intercourse, while others restrict the sexual services to masturbation by "hand whores," as they term themselves (see Bryant and Palmer 1973).

Prostitutes often specialize, with some accommodating bondage, discipline, dominance, and submission, inflicting pain and humiliation on their clients. Others service sadistic clients by letting them spank or whip them, or in some instances enduring severe physical beatings, known as "dumpings." Such prostitutes charge high fees and the cost of their medical or dental treatment. Dodge also informs us of the serious victimization problem of child prostitution, with some as young as eight years old.

Male prostitution

Over the years, most research on prostitution has tended to focus on female prostitutes. But Ronald Weitzer, in his chapter, points out that males and transgenders constitute a significant percentage of the prostitute population in many locations. Male prostitutes usually cater only to a male clientele, but some serve only female clients. A few cater to both markets.

These men are often selective in the services they offer. Some engage only in oral sex, others are willing to penetrate their clients, and yet others will engage in many kinds of sexual activity. Some male prostitutes provide their sexual services under the guise of working for an escort agency. Being an escort seems to help neutralize the stigma that attends being a prostitute. Some men seek male prostitutes in other countries.

Other than a few studies on women engaging in sex tourism and going to other countries for paid sex with male prostitutes, there has been little research on male prostitutes and female customers. Weitzer reports that the Caribbean is a favored location for many US female tourists looking for paid sex. The tourists meet men in clubs or bars, or on the beach. They become acquainted, date, and often develop affectionate relationships (or at least the women do), and have sex. The women usually pay for the meals and drinks, lodgings, incidentals, and frequently give gifts or money to their male escorts. Research has found that the women do not define themselves as "customers," but rather view their encounters with the men as "holiday romances" or even "love affairs." Similarly, the male escorts do not view themselves as prostitutes.

Sex tourism

Historically, many American men have believed that sex in foreign lands is more exotic, more pleasurable, and more satisfying than sex in the US. Such fantasies have been fueled by the sex stories that soldiers and sailors related after returning home from wars—especially the Second World War, Korea, and Vietnam. There were multitudes of cheap prostitutes, and the range of sexual services they offered was far more elaborate than that offered by their American equivalents. Non-prostitute women were also available for sex. It was during the Vietnam War that sex tourism truly began to blossom. US troops would periodically be given a week of "R & R," during which they were permitted to travel to other countries. Three very popular destinations were Taipei, Manila, and Bangkok.

In her chapter, Jody Miller examines the parameters of sex tourism today. She defines the phrase as tourists who travel for the purpose of participating in commercial sex. Sex tourism involves not only sex shows and prostitution, but specialized travel agencies, hotels, and other businesses. She asserts that "Sex tourism has developed to cater primarily to heterosexual Western and Japanese men who travel for business and leisure activities, though additional niche markets—serving gay men, heterosexual women, and pedophiles—have emerged as well."

The exact number of sex tourists visiting particular countries is not known but can be readily inferred. Miller reports that Thailand had two million international tourists in 1981. By 1996, this number had more than tripled to seven million. Of these, more than 70 percent were unaccompanied men, a significant proportion of whom were probably sex tourists. Miller points out that "an estimated 500,000 to 700,000 women work in commercial sex" in Thailand and claims that sex is part of the tourist experience for many travelers to the country.

The author stresses that one of the most abhorrent aspects of sex tourism is the involvement of children, who often play a substantial role. Some American pedophiles who have traveled abroad to have sex with children have been arrested and convicted upon their return to the US.

Pedophilia, child porn, and cyberpredators

In contemporary times, perhaps one of the most heinous sexual crimes is child molestation. Public concern about this phenomenon is connected to increasing awareness of technology-mediated offending. The computer and the internet have facilitated a wide array of criminal activity and/or deviant behavior. Among other deviant temptations afforded by the computer is the availability of a vast amount of pornography, including a copious supply of child pornography.

For decades, there has been an ongoing disputatious debate concerning the effect of pornography on society, with no definitive conclusion thus far. More recently, though, public concern about the impact of pornography on adults and their subsequent behavior has decreased and adult pornography has been more tolerated, if not accepted. On the other hand, public anxiety and concern about the danger of child pornography has increased. Ethel Quayle, in her chapter, asserts that many believe that there is a causal relationship between child pornography and sexual offenses, such as molestation, committed against children. Many also hold the view that those individuals who commit such offenses are inevitably pedophiles.

The Diagnostic and Statistical Manual of Mental Disorders (DSM) defines pedophilia as the erotic preference for prepubescent (aged thirteen or younger) children, but this would exclude offenders who are sexually attracted to slightly older children who are simply physically immature. The modal age for the victims of child sexual abuse in the US is fourteen.

Pedophiles may engage in a variety of erotic acts with children, ranging from undressing the child and viewing their nude body to oral sex and/or penetration. As there have been no reliable large-scale epidemiological studies of the general population, the prevalence of pedophilia is not known. Generally, though, it can be stated that pedophiles are more likely to be male than female.

Quayle indicates that child pornography dates back historically to the advent of photography. But as pornography can include drawings, paintings, block prints, and sculpture, the historical roots of child pornography go back much further in history. Child pornography is not a discrete type of image, but rather is represented in a wide array of images, ranging from clothed children, to naked children, to children in erotic poses, to children being sexually assaulted. It can be arranged in a continuum of "increased deliberate sexual victimization." Such a continuum is often a factor in determining the degree of guilt and the severity of punishment in criminal court trials.

The internet is often implicated in child pornography and other offenses against children. Child pornography can be produced, acquired, stored, retrieved, downloaded, and/or distributed via the internet. Because the computer is such a ubiquitous communication device in homes and places of business, the opportunity structure for child-related sexual offenses is vast and the number of internet sex offenders who are interested in children is substantial. Quayle reveals that there is "little information to indicate what risks are posed by internet offenders with no known history of sexual contacts with children."

In addition to providing a conduit for child pornography, the internet helps facilitate physical offenses against children, who can be encountered via chat-rooms or other internet locations, engaged in ongoing conversations of a sexual nature—"groomed" in a pseudo-intimate relationship—and then invited to a rendezvous for sexual purposes. Such internet users are known as "cyberpredators." It is generally believed that these online predators lure their victims to a meeting where the predator inflicts sexual violence on the unsuspecting victim. However, Quayle suggests that this scenario is "largely inaccurate." She reports that in the majority of cases the victim is fully aware that he or she is communicating with an adult. The victim tends to have normal interests in romance and sex and might well be willing to engage in sex with the cyberpredator, which "would suggest that these encounters often seem closer to models of statutory rape rather than a forced sexual assault or a pedophilic attack."

Erotic dancing

In their chapter, Carol Rambo and John Pruit suggest that "erotic dancing" includes "stripping, burlesque, belly dancing, table dancing, topless dancing, lap dancing, nude dancing [and] exotic dancing." Basically, it involves exhibiting one's body in some degree of nudity and in a sexually titillating fashion for financial reward. In some form or fashion, this practice dates back to ancient times.

Rambo and Pruit indicate that, over the centuries and in many cultures, erotic dancing has been admired as an art form or condemned as wickedness and depravity. It might be considered a "useful high-status occupation" or viewed through the "Victorian discourses of deviance and pathology," depending on the era and culture. As the authors explain, "It transforms a sexually idealized fantasy into reality, for a fee." Erotic dancing may take place in theaters, restaurants, "gentlemen's clubs," go-go bars, strip clubs, lingerie boutiques, wedding parties, or even a spa showroom, to mention but some venues.

The authors inform the reader that it first appeared in the US in burlesque theater in the late 19th century. This evolved into the more contemporary "review dancing," which involves groups of strippers or go-go girls, who dance both individually and collectively in choreographed routines.

Today, in addition to erotic stage dancing, many striptease and go-go establishments offer more individualized performances, such as tabletop dances, table dances, booth dances, and lap dances. Such individualized routines require a negotiated price and often also require the purchase of some expensive drinks, such as champagne.

Regardless of the venue or the variety of erotic dancing, and whether it is legal, such behavior is considered to be deviant. In spite of the traditional American values concerning the privateness and sacredness of the human body, nude or partially nude erotic dancers and striptease "artists" have evaded the norms of modesty and the community standards of anatomical propriety with their epidermal exposure and ecdysiast eroticism. As one researcher (Salutin 1971: 13) phrased it: "Strippers are viewed as 'bad' . . . because they strip away all social decorum with their clothes; they taunt the public with their own mores by teasing them and turning them on."

Erotic dancers, like strippers, are, in effect, exploiting their bodies and their sexuality and are accordingly prostitutes, of sorts. Many members of the public view erotic dancers simply as a depraved occupational group serving a depraved clientele.

Aberrant forms of sexual behavior

The sexual normative system of all societies specifies the parameters of "normal" sexual behavior, implicitly, if not explicitly. These prescriptions and proscriptions regarding sexual behavior are component to the cultures of those societies. Sexual norms are relative and vary from culture to culture. They also vary from time period to time period.

In his chapter, Thomas Weinberg notes that there is a section on paraphilias in the DSM. Here, there are discussions regarding a range of deviant sexual behaviors, including sexual sadism, sexual masochism, transvestic fetishism, voyeurism, frotteurism, exhibitionism, and pedophilia. In another section of the DSM, there are discussions of other paraphilias, such as necrophilia, zoophilia, and others.

Such sexual behaviors as the paraphilias list in the DSM can be better understood within a sociocultural context, rather than a clinical or psychoanalytic context. In fact, it could be said that all sexual behavior can be better understood within a sociocultural context, as this allows us to explore the social dimensions of its commission and context.

Weinberg examines a few of the sexual behaviors presently labeled "aberrant." He begins with sadomasochism, which is relatively widespread and has been extensively researched. Weinberg describes it as "the eroticization of dominance and submission, [which] has traditionally been viewed as an individual psychopathology." Recent research suggests that it is a complex social phenomenon, and psychoanalytical analysis does not appropriately or accurately describe it or explain it. Sadomasochism often occurs within a subcultural context.

Weinberg then addresses the topics of fetishism and partialism, two of the paraphilias listed in the DSM, and makes a distinction between the two. He indicates that partialism is sexual arousal by a body part—such as female breasts or thighs, or male biceps—while fetishism is the generation of sexual excitement by an inanimate object, such as a shoe or a pair of panties.

Frottage involves rubbing one's genitals against the body of another person, and deriving sexual gratification from this practice. For instance, a man may routinely ride crowded buses with many fellow passengers tightly bunched together and rub his genitals (within his trousers) against women in the crowd. Weinberg suggests that there is "the beginning of a subculture of frotteurs," with at least one website dedicated to the practice.

Weinberg concludes his chapter with a discussion of bestiality and zoophilia. These two paraphilias are the most pathological of all, and both are illegal in almost all of the states of the USA. Bestiality involves having sexual contact with an animal. Although empirical research on human–animal sexual contact has been limited, some such studies have found that a small

Clifton D. Bryant

percentage of both men and women have practiced it. Zoophilia relates to having a sexual preference for animals, and developing real love and affection for the animal sex partner. Weinberg reports that in a study of men who practiced zoophilia, the interviewees said that they sought sex with animals because of a desire for affection and pleasurable sex. These men felt that animals were more honest and unconditionally loving than humans.

References

Bryant, C. D. (1982) *Sexual Deviance and Social Proscription.* New York. Human Sciences Press.
Bryant, C. D. and C. Eddie Palmer (1973) "Massage parlors, sexual service, and 'hand whores': Some sociological observations," *Journal of Sex Research* 2 (3): 227–241.
Salutin, M. (1971) "Stripper morality," *Transaction: Social Science and Modern Society* 8 (8): 12–22.

43

Female prostitution

Mary Dodge

Prostitution evokes a wide spectrum of images and vernacular but can be defined in the most basic terms as the performance of sexual activities in exchange for money. Prostitutes are referred to by various labels, including whores, hookers, street walkers, working girls, escorts, call girls, and ladies of the evening. Prostitution on a service continuum may range from drug-addicted crack whores waiting for johns (customers) on the street to chic, expensive, call girls operating at luxury hotels. References to prostitution are common in popular culture, which often romanticizes or parodies sex work. In the movie *Pretty Woman*, Julia Roberts' character was rescued from a life of prostitution after being hired by a handsome, serious-minded, and rich corporate tycoon played by Richard Gere. As a fairy-tale ending would predict, they fall in love and live happily ever after. *The Best Little Whorehouse in Texas* musical and comedy starred Dolly Parton as a madam and Burt Reynolds as a sheriff in the roles of star-crossed lovers on opposite sides of the law. The daily realities of prostitution, however, are not those portrayed in the movies or media-driven incidents of high-class call girls with rich, famous customers.

Public scandals involving the so-called sordid behavior of high-profile prostitute–client relationships are fodder for the media. Transactions with escort services often include madams who offer "quality" women at exorbitant costs. Sydney Biddle Barrows, labeled the "Mayflower Madam" because she was a member of an upper-crust family, provided expensive services to wealthy and powerful men. Her Cachet escort service operated in the late 1970s and early 1980s. After her arrest, Barrows pled guilty to promoting prostitution and published an autobiography, aptly titled *Mayflower Madam*. Heidi Fleiss became well known in the 1990s after news leaked that the Hollywood madam provided prostitution services to wealthy men. Clients allegedly paid from $1,500 to $1 million for high-end services. Fleiss, who spent a short time in prison for tax evasion, is now residing in Nevada and is planning to open a brothel for female customers. In 2008, a federal wiretap provided information that New York Governor Eliot L. Spitzer, also known as Client-9, allegedly arranged to pay $4,300 to a prostitute for a rendezvous at the Mayflower Hotel in Washington, DC. Spitzer who had built his reputation prosecuting white-collar criminals and prostitution rings, resigned from office. Although elite escort services are available to those who can afford them, most prostitutes use the Yellow Pages, local newspapers, and the internet to advertise. High-end call girls charge clients $300 to $500 an hour for services; the average street worker receives $30 to $50 an hour.

Prostitution services

Prostitution services often hide under the guise of seemly legitimate businesses. Some massage parlors and private modeling agencies, for example, may offer hidden sex services. Bryant and Palmer (1974) identified four types of massage parlor. Genuine parlors found in health clubs, spas, and hotel resorts offer legitimate massage therapy. Rip-off parlors seduce customers with erotic promises, but merely provide inept massages and refuse to engage in physical sexual acts. Other massage parlors are actually brothels that offer a wide range of sexual services. And massage and masturbation parlors employ young women who describe themselves as "hand whores."

Prostitutes may specialize to accommodate customers who have a particular sexual penchant. Sadomasochistic clients, for example, take pleasure in inflicting or enduring pain or humiliation. Prostitutes may offer bondage, discipline, dominance, and submission. In clever marketing schemes, some have outfitted vehicles with restraints, cages, gags, chains, whips, and, of course, soundproofing. Prostitutes on wheels can quickly service specialized clients who, in some cases, require no actual intercourse. At the far end of the spectrum, some prostitutes will accommodate sadistic clients by enduring physical beatings for a substantial fee that also includes ensuing medical and dental treatment.

Prostitution is far more complex than a simple consensual economic exchange of goods and services for money. Deeply embedded controversies surrounding prostitution include moral, monetary, medical, and hegemonic issues related to basic sexual instincts. Sexual drives have created profitable illegal and legal markets in societies that hold diverse viewpoints on appropriate and inappropriate sexual behavior. Advocates, feminist theorists, law enforcement, and community members disagree on the form, function, and fit of prostitution in contemporary and sexually liberated cultures. The tenet that the subjugation and degradation of women sex workers undermine equality between the genders is a primary source of contention, though males, to a much lesser degree, also engage in prostitution. The somewhat sordid, yet intriguing, history of prostitution has resulted in a large body of research and perspectives that examine a wide variety of topics, including historical roots, myths and realities, violence, policing, and legislation.

The functions of prostitution

From a functionalist's perspective, prostitution may serve several purposes in society by providing an outlet for men who experience uncontrollable lust, thereby reducing rape and promoting healthy courtships and marriages. Meier and Geis (1997: 50) note that the absence of prostitution may result in sexually deprived men engaging in increased acts of "masturbation, more intense courtships or seduction patterns, sex by force, or behavior patterns that psychiatrists label as inhibitions and sublimations." A husband visiting a prostitute may alleviate the burden on a wife who is so overly taxed with home and childcare responsibilities that sex is a low priority for her. Sex for money may, in such a case, result in increased satisfaction levels for the husband and relief for the wife. Of course, such scenarios ignore the secretive nature and duplicity involved in sex-for-money transactions, especially considering the intricate nature of relationships between genders.

Men offer numerous reasons for engaging a prostitute. More often than not, they view such liaisons as mere business transactions. Puritanical notions of marriage and sexuality also influence encounters. In one case, a police officer asked an arrested, married john (slang for customer) why he had sought out a street walker's services. The man, who had paid for oral sex, responded,

"I kiss my wife." According to some research, men indicated that they seek out prostitutes so that they can be with a woman who "likes to get nasty" (Weitzer, 2000). Men also noted the excitement and thrill of approaching a prostitute, the need to experience a variety of sexual partners, and the desire to have a different kind of sex or change from their regular partners. Weitzer says fellatio is the most common activity requested from a prostitute. Prostitution also offers men the opportunity to engage in sex without emotional investment, and a sex worker can be found in each and every socioeconomic level.

Motivation for prostitution

Street-level prostitution often develops out of need and desperation as a means of survival for runaway teenagers and drug-addicted women. Street prostitutes may be pimp controlled or independent. In many cases, the women are addicted to crack or methamphetamine, and prostitution merely provides enough money to score another hit. In most major cities, prostitution areas are well known by johns and the police. Women will wait on the sidewalk or at truck stops for a customer to cruise by, known in England as kerb-crawling, and when approached will suggest that the transaction be conducted in the car or a nearby hotel room. Prostitutes on the streets are not "pretty women." Street-level prostitutes' lives are marked by violence, exploitation, and poverty which results in severe health issues that are often left untreated.

Prostitutes, according to many research findings, have frequently been subjected to sexual abuse at an early age. In most qualitative studies, a high percentage of juvenile and adult female prostitutes self-report unwanted sexual behavior before the age of sixteen (Earls and David, 1989). Additionally, studies report a strong correlation between prostitution and running away from home. Young women who lack legitimate opportunities may believe that prostitution represents the only way to obtain substantial incomes. Indeed, many prostitutes report that money is their primary motivation for sex work.

But financial concerns represent only one of the many motivations that contribute to decisions to perform sex work. Women may engage in prostitution because legitimate opportunities are limited or unattractive. Alternative jobs for prostitutes are likely to offer low wages, consist of dull, routine tasks, and demand long hours (Hoigard and Finstad, 1986). Other researchers have identified behavioral characteristics such as promiscuity, disassociation, and isolation as motivating factors. Some prostitutes also enjoy the independence and excitement of sex work (Weidner, 2001).

The proposition that prostitution is a victimless crime is easily countered by research findings that show drugs, violence, and sexual diseases commonly affect sellers, buyers, families, and law enforcement. Research concerning violence against prostitutes often focuses on street-level workers who are controlled by pimps. Violence and exploitation by pimps includes physical, emotional, and financial abuse. In interviews with former prostitutes, Williamson and Cluse-Tolar (2002) discovered a pattern of violence by pimps including savage beatings used to exert control and dominance over the women.

Prostitutes are also targeted by violent customers and sometimes corrupt police officers. Sadistic customers perpetrate physical and sexual assaults. However, the illegal nature of sex work prevents victims from reporting such crimes. In some cases, when prostitutes do report crimes by customers, their victimization is trivialized by law enforcement officials and prosecutors who see the violent consequences as an expected "part of the job."

Policing and programs

Generally, police focus on arresting individual women in stings using male undercover officers who pose as customers, though an increasing number of agencies are conducting reverse sting operations and cracking down on the customers in a bid to reduce demand. In the United States, however, only 10 percent of prostitution arrests are male customers (Weidner, 2001). In California, one prostitute appealed her conviction, claiming sexual discrimination by the police department. She noted that the more common use of male decoys compared with female decoys in police stings resulted in biased arrests. Court documents in this case revealed that 1,160 women were arrested for solicitation by male undercover officers in 1973 and 1974, compared to 57 men arrested in reverse sting operations (Kay, 1982). Supportive evidence was provided by Lefler (1999), who discovered that Boston courts arraigned 263 women in 1990 on charges of prostitution but no male customers. The California Superior Court denied the prostitute's appeal and outlined three reasons justifying the use of male officer decoys rather than female. First, a working prostitute will see several customers each night, hence committing several crimes, whereas a customer will typically hire only one prostitute for the evening and therefore commit only one crime. Second, arresting prostitutes is a stronger deterrent on other women in the business who communicate with each other as compared to male customers who are unknown to each other. Third, the use of female decoys is more expensive because of safety issues, equipment, and back-up teams that require the presence of male officers.

Creative policing and prevention programs have developed as law enforcement agencies struggle with improving practices and policies. Arrest patterns are troubling and police officers complain about repeat offenders who are granted bail and therefore return to the streets almost immediately. In San Francisco, police officers frustrated with the rapid release of a particular prostitute issued 54 citations over a three-month period for "obstructing the sidewalk," which eventually resulted in a 60-day jail sentence (Pearl, 1987). Some cities control street prostitution by implementing area restrictions that prevent a woman from being in a certain neighborhood. The likely result of such ordinances or statutes is merely the displacement of the activity. Other cities have established mandatory licensing for prostitutes which requires a background check and is renewable annually. Violations of licensing policies can result in one year in jail and a $1,000 fine. This approach is primarily a law enforcement tool to increase conviction options with low expectations that prostitutes and pimps will be lining up at the court house to purchase a license. Police argue that aggressively arresting johns and prostitutes will reduce drug crimes, sexual assault, robberies, and homicides.

Police agencies' focus on johns in the last ten years has increased the number of reverse sting operations and promoted innovative tactics to deter men from engaging in future transactions. Many major cities in the United States have programs designed to deter and humiliate customers, including driver's license revocation, john television, and vehicle seizure (Dodge et al., 2005). John TV features mug shots of convicted offenders on local television stations or the internet. In some cities, billboards and paid newspaper advertisements expose customers to public scrutiny. Efforts to shame and humiliate customers are believed to serve as general and specific deterrence, though the effectiveness of such methods remains unknown. "John schools" have become popular. Customers are ordered by a court to attend the classes, where they learn of illicit sex dangers through graphic representations of sexually transmitted diseases and narratives from former prostitutes. However, law enforcement efforts that focus on johns remain futile because of the low number of overall male arrests.

Social programs for prostitutes strive to divert women from the profession to a more stable lifestyle. In Washington, DC, the Bridges Program offers education and therapeutic groups that address addictions and early childhood trauma. Salt Lake City's Prostitution Diversion Project (PDP) has shown some level of success for women who have been arrested. It keeps the women out of jail and offers networking in the community by employing a collaborative approach that emphasizes harm reduction through treatment, therapy, and abstinence. As one of the few projects designed specifically for commercial sex workers, the PDP appears to provide useful recovery services across community agencies and saves the city money (Wahab, 2006). Resource referrals give women information on substance abuse, domestic violence, rape, self-defense, housing, and welfare.

Legalization

In the United States, brothels (also known as houses of ill repute, bordellos, and cat houses) are legal only in rural counties of Nevada. These brothels operate under strict regulatory law, including licensing fees (ranging from $200 to $100,000), minimum age requirements (ranging from 18 to 21 years old), weekly checks for certain sexually transmitted diseases (gonorrhea and chlamydia), and monthly examinations for HIV and syphilis. Condoms are mandatory for oral sex and sexual intercourse. Additionally, any brothel prostitute with HIV who knowingly engages in sex work is subject to felony charges and may face ten years in prison or a $10,000 fine.

Researchers have identified and studied three types of violence in legalized brothels in Nevada: interpersonal violence against prostitutes; violence against community order; and sexually transmitted diseases as violence against the backdrop of government regulation that allegedly provides a safe and hygienic outlet for prostitution (Brents and Hausbeck, 2005). Legalization, according to Brents and Hausbeck, increases public scrutiny and official regulation, thereby decreasing all three types of violence. This "challenges assumptions that prostitution and violence necessarily and inevitably coexist in predictable ways," though a lack of sophistication in analysis fails to address the inherently oppressive nature of the commercial sex trade (Brents and Hausbeck, 2005: 294).

In Rhode Island, transactions involving sex for money are not defined as illegal, although brothels, pimping, and street prostitution are statutorily defined and carry legal sanctions. The "loophole" in the state's law that allows acts of prostitution to take place in private is relatively unknown except among sex trade workers, and efforts are being made in the legislature to introduce changes to criminalize all acts of prostitution. Politicians, including Providence Mayor David N. Cicilline, argue that the proliferation of indoor prostitution "spas" has a negative impact on quality of life in high-traffic neighborhoods and damages the city's reputation (Cicilline, 2009).

In 1973, Margo St. James, a former prostitute, founded COYOTE (Call Off Your Old Tired Ethics) as an organization to help end the stigma of sex work, further public education, and offer support groups and referrals to service providers. St. James became well known for her quip that "a blow job is better than no job." As noted by scholar and author Valerie Jenness (1993) the group's potential lay in its ability to represent disreputable causes and gain legitimacy for disenfranchised deviants, such as prostitutes, strippers, pornography actresses, and phone-sex operators.

The controversy over the efficacy of legalized prostitution is far from resolved. The arguments for decriminalization focus primarily on the heavy-handed tactics that infringe on a woman's civil rights and cause further oppression. Current laws encourage corruption, unfairly penalize prostitutes by forcing them to work on the streets, reinforce negative labeling, and waste taxpayers' money on prosecutions and imprisonment (Meier and Geis, 1997). The voices of women prostitutes are silenced by fears borne of "intimidation, terror, dissociation, and shame"

(Farley, 2004: 117). Many commentators and scholars, however, argue against legalization or decriminalization. They contend that prostitution can be costly in terms of disease, drug addiction, and moral degradation, and assert that prostitution results in high rates of violence throughout the world, with between 60% and 94% of prostitutes reporting physical assault and rape, including in the Netherlands where prostitution is legal (Farley, 2004).

The division among feminist theorists also reflects a deep schism in the field. Jolin (1994) identified two primary approaches among feminist scholars that are inherently impossible to resolve. First, the sexual equality first (SEF) approach asserts that prostitution is dependent on the sexual subordination of women and, if allowed to continue, will prevent women from obtaining true equality. The SEF position is clearly articulated by the radical feminists Catherine MacKinnon and Andrea Dworkin, who suggest that all heterosexual sex demeans and subordinates women. The refusal by some feminists to accept prostitution as legitimate work marginalizes sex workers, though many adopt values aligned with the feminist movement, including "independence, financial autonomy, sexual self-determination, personal strength, and female bonding" (Kesler, 2002: 220). Second, the free choice first (FCF) approach gives women the freedom to choose with no restrictions or controls over decisions related to sexuality and reproductive rights. The catch-22, according to Jolin (1994: 77), is that "one can either believe that true equality for women will not exist so long as women sell their bodies to men or one can believe that true equality will not exist so long as women are prevented from exercising choice, including the choice to sell their bodies to men."

Future frontiers

In many ways, technology has transformed the business of prostitution and has resulted in women leaving the streets. Craigslist, for example, offers "erotic services" by city. In one Colorado case, an internet site offered potential customers full services from "nineteen-year-old Amanda." Monitoring by police employees of sites known to promote prostitution resulted in a sting and arrest after the girl was driven to a motel room by her pimp. In reality, Amanda was just fifteen years old. Nevertheless, she had already earned approximately $150,000 for her pimp, according to police reports. Meanwhile, Craigslist's erotic services came under fire after a masseuse was allegedly killed at the Marriott Hotel in Copley Square by a Boston University medical student, Phillip Markoff. Craigslist has promised to relabel its erotic services "adult services" and to prescreen the paid advertisements.

Child prostitution represents perhaps the most serious victimization problem. In America alone, according to the Department of Justice, an estimated 293,000 youth are at risk of being victimized by some form of commercial sexual exploitation. Juveniles who are recruited into sex work by force or pressure from parents are subjected to violence, drugs, and threats. Though little research is available, very young girls are involved in prostitution and pornography. Researcher and scholar James Inciardi (1990) interviewed nine girls between the ages of eight and twelve who were introduced into sex work by parents, siblings, or relatives. Known as "baby pros," these elementary school girls were living at home with parents or other relatives. They described performing masturbation and oral sex, and, in a few cases, engaging in sexual intercourse. Several of the girls worked in massage parlors as hand whores. Inciardi discovered that the girls participated because of fear of rejection by their parents or guardians and to gain attention from indifferent adults, in addition to covert coercion. However, they rightly and understandably expressed a deep disdain for the male clients.

References

Brents, B. G, and Hausbeck, K. (2005). Violence and legalized brothel prostitution in Nevada: Examining safety, risk, and prostitution policy. *Journal of Interpersonal Violence*, 20(3), 270–295.

Bryant, C. D., and Palmer, C. E. (1974). Massage parlors and "hand whores": Some sociological observations. *Journal of Sex Research*, 11(3), 227–241.

Cicilline, David N. (2009). Mayor Cicilline urges RI Senate to pass prostitution legislation. Press release, May 18. Available at: www.providenceri.com/press/article.php?id=515 (accessed June 1, 2009).

COYOTE (n.d.). Website. Available at: www.coyotela.org/what_is.html#who_gets (accessed June 1, 2009).

Dodge, M., Starr-Gimeno, D., and Williams, T. (2005). Puttin' on the sting: Women police officers' perspectives on reverse prostitution assignments. *International Journal of Police Science & Management*, 7(2), 71–85.

Earls, C. M., and David, H. (1989). Male and female prostitution: A review. *Sex Abuse*, 2, 5–28.

Farley, M. (2004). Bad for the body, bad for the heart: Prostitution harms women even if legalized or decriminalized. *Violence Against Women*, 10(10), 1087–1125.

Gusfield, J. (1994). Making it work: The prostitutes' rights movement in perspective (book review). *Contemporary Sociology*, 23(3), 379–380.

Hoigard, C., and Finstad, L. (1986). *Backstreets: Prostitution, money and love*. University Park: Pennsylvania State University.

Inciardi, J. A. (1990). Little girls and sex: A glimpse at the world of the "baby pro." In C. D. Bryant (Ed.), *Deviant behavior: Readings in the sociology of norm violations* (pp. 303–310). New York: Hemisphere.

Jenness, V. (1993). *Making it work: The prostitute's rights movement in perspective*. New York: Aldine de Gruyter.

Jolin, A. (1994). On the backs of working prostitutes: Feminist theory and prostitution policy. *Crime & Delinquency*, 40, 69–83.

Kay, H. H. (1982). *Sex-based discrimination: Test cases and materials* (2nd edn). St. Paul, MN: West.

Kesler, K. (2002). Is a feminist stance in support of prostitution possible? An exploration of current trends. *Sexualities*, 5(2), 219–235.

Lefler, J. (1999). Shining the spotlight on "johns": Moving toward equal treatment of male customers and female prostitutes. *Hastings Women's Law Journal*, 10, 11–35.

Meier, R.F., and Geis, G. (1997). *Victimless crime?* Los Angeles, CA: Roxbury.

Pearl, J. (1987). The highest paying customers: America's cities and the costs of prostitution control. *Hastings Law Journal*, 38, 769–800.

Wahab, S. (2006). Evaluating the usefulness of a prostitution diversion project. *Qualitative Social Work*, 5, 67–92.

Weidner, R. (2001). *"I won't do Manhattan": Causes and consequences of a decline in street prostitution*. New York: LFB Scholarly.

Weitzer, R. (2000). *Sex for sale: Prostitution, pornography, and the sex industry*. New York: Routledge.

Williamson, C., and Cluse-Tolar, T. (2002). Pimp-controlled prostitution: Still an integral part of street life. *Violence Against Women*, 8(9), 1074–1092.

44

Male prostitution

Ronald Weitzer

Traditionally, scholars have focused their attention on female prostitution and have ignored male and transgender prostitution, despite the fact that males and transgenders comprise a substantial percentage of the prostitutes in many cities (Weitzer 1999). In the past decade, however, a growing body of literature has examined male sex workers. Most male prostitutes sell sex to other men.

Male providers, male customers

There are some basic similarities as well as some important differences between male and female prostitution. For instance, there is a similar hierarchy in each—stratified by whether the worker sells sex on the street, in a bar or a brothel/club/massage parlor, through an escort agency, or as an independent call boy. Like female street workers, young men on the street often enter the trade as runaways or to support a drug habit, and they engage in "survival sex." Like upscale female workers, call boys and escorts possess social skills that allow them to relate to educated, upper-class customers, and they may develop emotional attachments to some of their regular clients (Smith *et al.* 2008; van der Poel 1992). And, like female workers in the mid- and upper-level tiers, similarly situated males are more likely than street workers to hold positive views of their work and themselves (Koken *et al.* 2010; West 1993). Interviews with 185 male prostitutes in three Australian cities found that two-thirds felt good about being a sex worker (Minichiello 2001). A study of male escorts reported that, as a result of being generously paid for sex, the escorts felt desired, attractive, empowered, and important; they also developed greater self-confidence and more positive body images over time (Uy *et al.* 2007). As a male brothel worker stated, it was "so wonderful to have love made to me by so many wealthy and socially elite men" (Pittman 1971: 23).

Economic motives are central for both male and female sex workers, but some males are also motivated by the potential for sexual adventure that prostitution may offer (van der Poel 1992). Differences in the ways male and female prostitutes experience their work are evident in the following areas. Males tend to be:

- involved in prostitution in a more sporadic or transitory way, drifting in and out of prostitution and leaving the trade earlier than women (Aggleton 1999; Weinberg *et al.* 1999);

- less likely to be coerced into prostitution, to have pimps, and to experience violence from customers (Aggleton 1999; Weinberg *et al.* 1999; West 1993);
- in greater control over their working conditions, because few have pimps (West 1993);
- more diverse as to their sexual orientation: some self-identify as gay; others as bisexual; and others insist that they are heterosexual despite engaging in homosexual conduct, an identity–behavior disparity typically not found among female prostitutes (Aggleton 1999);
- less stigmatized within the gay community (Aggleton 1999; Koken *et al.* 2010) but more stigmatized in the wider society because of the coupling of homosexuality and prostitution.

Like female sex workers, males draw boundaries around the services they are willing to perform. Some limit their activity to oral sex; some engage in penetrative but not receptive oral or anal sex; and others engage in all types. Some limit their encounters to sexual exchanges, while others are open to more comprehensive interactions, including cuddling, massage, and conversation. This has come to be known as the "boyfriend experience," a quasi-romantic, yet paid, encounter.

Although most research focuses on street prostitution, a thriving indoor market has been studied by some researchers. Male brothels are fairly rare, though a few have been studied (Pittman 1971). One hybrid brothel–escort agency, a business that provided services to about 200 clients per month, was studied by Smith, Grov, and Seal (2008). Most of the sexual encounters took place outside the agency, but some were "in-call," occurring in a designated room at the agency. Some of the workers even lived at the agency. When not working, some of the men engaged in social activities with other men at the agency, including the manager and friends of their fellow escorts. The manager served as a mentor to the escorts and was well liked by them. Like madams in female brothels, the manager screened clients and sought to ensure a safe and pleasant working environment for his employees. The benefits of working for this agency were that it provided a "sense of community" for the workers, "shielded escorts from potential stigma," and was "a source of positive support" for their work and lifestyle (Smith *et al.* 2008: 206, 208).

Most escort agencies do not double as brothels, resulting in much more social distance between the employees. Salamon's (1989) study of an escort agency in London that did not provide in-call services reported very little social interaction between the manager and the workers, and few workers knew any of the others.

Research on street prostitution offers a picture of a very different world—more risky for the workers but also potentially exciting. McNamara's (1994) ethnographic study of male street prostitutes in Times Square, New York, in the early 1990s found a community involved in selling sex on the street and at peep shows, gay bars, the bus terminal, and hotels. Most were Hispanic youths, and most of the clients were white men. The sex trade was remarkably well ordered: "very few problems occur either between the hustlers and the clients or among the boys themselves. In the vast majority of cases, the activities are completed without incident" (McNamara 1994: 62). The police generally left the prostitutes alone unless there was a disturbance.

Although most of the research on sex tourism centers on female prostitutes and foreign male clients, sometimes men travel abroad to meet and pay for sex with other men. Padilla's (2007) ethnographic study in the Dominican Republic provides a unique window into gay male sex tourism. Many of the workers do not self-identify as gay—in fact, many are married—and they service men simply because they comprise a much larger market than female sex tourists who are willing to pay for a sex encounter. Many sex tourists eroticize this, as it seems to accord with the fantasy of having gay sex with a heterosexual male. While some male prostitutes aim to avoid long-term or serial relationships with particular clients, due to the potential emotional risks involved, others cultivate long-term clients, develop affectionate feelings toward them, and await their next visit. The latter put a premium on meeting customers who will continue to send money or gifts after they return home. Padilla found a connection between the material and emotional aspects of these relationships: workers who received the most economic rewards were most likely to develop affectionate feelings toward a customer. Older clients were more likely to seek stable and more intimate relationships with a specific worker, while younger clients sought sex with multiple partners.

Male providers, female customers

Relatively little is known about male prostitutes who sell sex to women, and the few studies on this topic all center on tourist destinations. A handful of studies have examined contacts between affluent Western female tourists and young Caribbean men, who meet at clubs and on beaches (Phillips 1999; Sanchez Taylor 2001, 2006). There are some basic similarities between female sex tourism and male sex tourism (e.g., economic inequality between buyer and seller) as well as some differences (e.g., female sex tourists rarely act violently against male prostitutes). There is a profound economic inequality between the buyer and seller, and this gives the buyer a similar level of control over the worker, whether the latter is female or male. Like male sex tourists, female sex tourists use their economic power to buy intimate relations with local men, and during these encounters they assert control over the men. One study in the Caribbean concluded:

> The kind of control exercised in their relationships with local men is actually very similar to that exercised by male sex tourists in sexual economic relationships with local women . . . They are able to use their economic power to limit the risk of being challenged or subjugated.
>
> *(Sanchez Taylor 2006: 49–50)*

Female customers may become long-term companions or benefactors to the men, and in some cases this can lead to marriage.

Many of the female sex tourists do not define themselves as "customers" who buy sex from local men. Instead, they construct the encounters as "holiday romances" or "real love," and almost none describe their affairs as "purely physical" (Sanchez Taylor 2001: 755). The women do not see themselves as sex tourists and the men do not see themselves as prostitutes. However, the latter do receive material rewards for the time they spend with foreign women, including meals, lodgings, gifts, and money. According to Sanchez Taylor, these relationships therefore have all the hallmarks of sex tourism, irrespective of whether they are short or long term or whether money is exchanged, provided that the man receives at least some material benefits. Similarly, Phillips (1999: 191) argues that these transactions can be "easily fitted under the umbrella of prostitution," even though both the tourist and the provider do not perceive their liaison as such.

The "host club" in Japan is another example of male sex work involving female clients. Similar to the hostess clubs where women entertain male customers, host clubs are locations where women go to enjoy themselves in the company of attractive male hosts, which may include sexual encounters. Such bars have flourished in the past decade, with approximately 200 now operating in Tokyo alone. The hosts serve exorbitantly expensive alcoholic drinks to their clients and lavish praise, compliments, and advice upon the specific women to whom they attach themselves. The nature of this phenomenon is captured in the concept of "commodified romance" (Takeyama 2005), which involves nonsexual intimacy but may also include sexual services.

Why do women seek out these paid encounters? An ethnographic study of host clubs revealed that "customers claim that there are few other places in Japan's male-centered entertainment world where women can safely enjoy romantic excitement" (Takeyama 2005: 204). According to this study, the vast majority of hosts have had sex with at least some of their customers, although they prefer to avoid sexual intercourse in order to keep the woman coming back to the club and paying the high prices (the host gets a cut). Some hosts sleep with their customers without having sex with them.

Conclusion

Further research on male sex workers who service women will help address the question of whether the customer's gender influences the character and subjective meaning of the encounter. To what degree, if at all, is gender inequality or domination present in exchanges between female customers and male workers? Do female customers engage in less objectification of the workers, or is objectification evident irrespective of the customer's gender? Do female customers expect more emotional involvement from sex workers than is true for male customers? When the customer is a woman, is there less likelihood of violence from either party? These questions have yet to be investigated, but such research would be invaluable in answering the theoretical question of whether prostitution has certain "fundamental" or "essential" qualities, irrespective of the gender of the worker and the customer, or whether it varies significantly according to the actors involved. To answer these questions, we need systematic examinations of male prostitutes who service men in comparison with those who service women, and of male and female prostitutes working in the same tier, such as the comparative studies by Koken *et al.* (2010) and Weinberg *et al.* (1999).

References

Aggleton, P. (ed.) (1999) *Men Who Sell Sex*, Philadelphia, PA: Temple University Press.

Koken, J., Bimbi, D., and Parsons, J. (2010) "Male and female escorts: a comparative analysis," in R. Weitzer (ed.) *Sex for Sale: Prostitution, Pornography, and the Sex Industry*, 2n edn, New York: Routledge.

McNamara, R. (1994) *The Times Square Hustler: Male Prostitution in New York City*, Westport, CT: Praeger.

Minichiello, V. (2001) "Male sex workers in three Australian cities: socio-demographic and sex work characteristics," *Journal of Homosexuality*, 42: 29–51.

Padilla, M. (2007) "Western Union daddies and their quest for authenticity: an ethnographic study of the Dominican gay sex tourism industry," *Journal of Homosexuality*, 53: 241–275.

Phillips, J. (1999) "Tourist-oriented prostitution in Barbados: the case of the beach boy and the white female tourist," in K. Kempadoo (ed.) *Sun, Sex, and Gold: Tourism and Sex Work in the Caribbean*, Lanham, MD: Rowman & Littlefield.

Pittman, D. (1971) "The male house of prostitution," *Transaction*, 8: 21–27.

Salamon, E. (1989) "The homosexual escort agency: deviance disavowal," *British Journal of Sociology*, 40: 1–21.

Sanchez Taylor, J. (2001) "Dollars are a girl's best friend: female tourists' sexual behavior in the Caribbean," *Sociology*, 34: 749–764.

Sanchez Taylor, J. (2006) "Female sex tourism: a contradiction in terms?," *Feminist Review*, 83: 43–59.

Smith, M., Grov, C., and Seal, D. (2008) "Agency-based male sex work," *Journal of Men's Studies*, 16: 193–210.

Takeyama, A. (2005) "Commodified romance in a Tokyo host club," in M. McLelland and R. Dasgupta (eds.) *Genders, Transgenders, and Sexualities in Japan*, New York: Routledge.

Uy, J., Parsons, J., Bimbi, D., Koken, J., and Halkitis, P. (2007) "Gay and bisexual male escorts who advertise on the internet: understanding the reasons for and effects of involvement in commercial sex," *International Journal of Men's Health*, 3: 11–26.

van der Poel, S. (1992) "Professional male prostitution: a neglected phenomenon," *Crime, Law, and Social Change*, 18: 259–275.

Weinberg, M., Shaver, F., and Williams, C. (1999) "Gendered prostitution in the San Francisco Tenderloin," *Archives of Sexual Behavior*, 28: 503–521.

Weitzer, R. (1999) "New directions in research on prostitution," *Crime, Law, and Social Change*, 43: 211–235.

West, D. (1993) *Male Prostitution*, Binghamton, NY: Hayworth.

45

Sex tourism

Jody Miller

The term "sex tourism" refers to the development and expansion of industries that provide sexual services to tourists, and/or travel for the purpose of participating in commercial sex. Those who participate in or profit from sex tourism include not just establishments that provide sex shows and prostitution, but travel agencies, hotels, and other businesses, as well as workers in the informal economy. Sex tourism has developed to cater primarily to heterosexual Western and Japanese men who travel for business and leisure activities, though additional niche markets— serving gay men, heterosexual women, and pedophiles—have emerged as well (see Frohlick, 2008; O'Connell Davidson, 2005; Padilla, 2007; Pruitt and LaFont, 1995). Consider the growth of sex tourism in Thailand—a common destination for sex tourists. In the year 1981, Thailand received two million international tourists; by 1996, this number had more than tripled to seven million. Notably, the vast majority of these tourists—five million in 1996, or more than 70 percent—were unaccompanied men, "a significant portion [of whom] were sex tourists" (Bales, 1999: 75–76).

Understanding sex tourism requires consideration of several related issues: the embeddedness of the practice within broader patterns of tourism as a developmental strategy; its linkages to global patterns of economic, gender, and racial inequalities across nations; and, at the interactional level, the range of tourist–local relations that include sex as a component. As O'Connell Davidson (2005: 126) asks of the definition of "sex tourist":

> Does the term only refer to those who travel with the explicit and conscious intention of buying sex, or does it also include those who travel for "ordinary" reasons, but happen to buy sex one night because they are approached by a sex worker and think . . . "why not?" And what of those who enter into what they consider to be a holiday romance with a local, but also buy meals for or give gifts to their "boyfriend" or "girlfriend"?

O'Connell Davidson's questions suggest that sex tourism is a complex set of economic and social relations inextricably linked to the growth of tourism in general. It involves a range of sexual exchanges, from those formally purchased through legal, semi-legal, or illicit establishments, as well as more informal economic/sexual exchanges that occur within the borders of the formal tourist and sex tourist industries (Cohen, 1982; Dahles, 1998; Kempadoo, 2004; Padilla, 2007). In fact, sex is so common to the tourism experience that the latter is often said to comprise the four "S"s: sun, sea, sand, and sex (Waters, 2001: 179).

Sex tourism, tourism, and global inequalities

Experts link the growth of sex tourism to broader patterns of tourist growth. According to the United Nations World Tourism Organization, tourism is "one of the fastest growing economic sectors in the world" (UNWTO, 2011). Worldwide, tourism was a $3.5 trillion industry by the mid-1990s (Kattoulas, 1995). It has been promoted extensively as a developmental strategy for Third World countries, based on the imposition of Western developmental policies and global corporate influence (Enloe, 1989; Truong, 1990). As Crick (1994: 4) notes, tourism is "an industry which was from the onset encouraged by international agencies such as the United Nations and the International Monetary Fund and which is now dominated by multinational corporations."

Local governments have actively promoted tourism as well, and it is increasingly important in sustaining their economies. Consider the case of Sri Lanka. Though relatively late to develop international tourism (Crick, 1994), in recent decades tourism has become a key fixture of its economy. Suffering from both a civil war and an insurgency, by 1989 it faced an intense fiscal crisis. "A slump in traditional agricultural export markets coupled with spiraling foreign debt forced the Sri Lankan government to offer foreign investors a lucrative package of incentives to invest in . . . tourism" (Beddoe, 1998: 46). Part and parcel of this increased reliance on tourism was the evolution of a sex tourism industry along the island's southwestern coastal belt, primarily involving young men and adolescent boys (Beddoe, 1998).

Yet, despite the economic gains tourism brings to Third World countries, the vast majority of economic benefits are funneled to the West, and most economic gains within the host country disproportionately benefit the elite (Crick, 1994). This is also the case where sex tourism has flourished—whether in a formalized way, as in Thailand, or where it remains at the periphery of informal work in the tourist economy, as in Sri Lanka. Thus, as Crick (1994: 50) explains, "When a Third World country acquires a tourism industry, it does so as part of the overall international division of labour, where economic and political power are already very unequally distributed."

Sex tourism is well documented in a number of countries, including Thailand, the Philippines, China, Vietnam, Laos, Cambodia, Brazil, the Netherlands, and the Dominican Republic (Flowers, 1998). In Thailand, for example, an estimated 500,000–700,000 women work in commercial sex, with the vast majority in Bangkok. A third are believed to be minors (Lim, 1998). If these estimates are accurate, upwards of 10 percent of all young women in Thailand between the ages of 15 and 25 are involved in the sex industry (Scibelli, 1987).

As the Thai example illustrates, sex tourism has been especially pronounced in Asia, and its roots there are linked to the impact of the US military presence in the middle of the 20th century. Though prostitution has a long history in the region, sex tourism is a direct outgrowth of US military bases and "rest and recreation" centers established in Southeast Asia during the Vietnam War (Enloe, 1989; Phongpaichit, 1982). These centers were created to provide sexual services to American GIs serving in the region, and relied on the sexual labor of local women. This was nothing new. Prostitution regularly flourishes during wartime, with the tacit approval of military leaders and with little concern for harms caused to the women involved. It is often justified as a means of channeling men's presumed sexual "needs" (Enloe, 1989). In Southeast Asia, the early growth in international tourism—made possible by the expansion of commercial airlines and other leisure services—occurred around the time American troops were stationed in the region. The infrastructure put in place to serve American military personnel was well suited to the expansion of sex tourism after military withdrawal (Truong, 1990).

Gender inequality and sex tourism markets

As sex tourism markets have grown, the structure and operation of the industry continue to be shaped by Western imperialism, colonial legacies, and racialized notions of sexuality (Kempadoo and Doezema, 1998). Sex tourism is often promoted as beneficial to Third World economies and individual sex workers and their families, thus encouraging sex tourists to see their exploits as "beneficial" (Truong, 1990). Moreover, tourism promotions advertise the sexual availability of young women to tourists, highlighting the notion that Asian women are submissive, exotic and thus sexually desirable. In these ways, sex tourism is built on the idea of male entitlement to sex, casts men's involvement in a paternalistic framework, and hinges on stereotypical images of the femininity and sexual availability of young women in the Third World—images grounded in notions of racial hierarchy. Crick (1994: 4) explains, "image constructors make . . . Third World tourist destinations into veritable paradises where time-honoured themes in the depiction of the 'other'—primitivism, simplicity, sensuality, excess, harmony . . . are fervently recycled." As illustration, consider the following travel brochures (cited in Bales, 1999: 76–77):

> Slim, sunburnt, and sweet, they love the white man in an erotic and devoted way. They are masters of the art of making love by nature, an art that we Europeans do not know.
>
> *(Life Travel, Switzerland)*

> [M]any girls from the sex world come from the poor north-eastern region of the country and from the slums of Bangkok. It has become a custom that one of the nice looking daughters goes into the business in order to earn money for the poor family . . . you can get the feeling that taking a girl here is as easy as buying a package of cigarettes . . . little slaves who give real Thai warmth.
>
> *(Kanita Kamha Travel, the Netherlands)*

In addition to the prominent role of global inequalities, stable and changing features of local cultures help sustain the sex industry, including sex tourism. For instance, growing consumerism in the Third World is a factor: families in rural areas able to purchase consumer goods from the profits of their daughters' labor often achieve high status within their communities (Bales, 1999). Young women's sense of obligation to their families, and in some cases the economic benefits they receive, often result in acceptance of the circumstances of their work. Religion and the cultural devaluation of women also provide important justifications. For example, like most major religions, Thai Buddhism regards women as "distinctly inferior to men" and as "impure, carnal, and corrupting" (Bales, 1999: 39). Moreover, "Thai Buddhism also carries a central message of acceptance and resignation in the face of life's pain and suffering" (Bales, 1999: 39). The concept of karma, a key religious principle, teaches Buddhists that the pains they endure in this lifetime are the result of their actions in previous lives. Simply being born female is indicative of failures in past lives.

Who benefits from sex tourism?

Gender inequality and the cultural devaluation of women help explain why prostitution itself has proliferated, and why the brunt of the industry is borne by young women. However, global capitalism and its push for profits are equally at the root of why these young women have become "cheap and expendable commodities" (Bales, 1999: 234). As noted, the growth of sex tourism has strong roots in international policies and the practices of multinational corporations, with the majority of profits generated from tourism channeled to Western multinationals.

Nonetheless, tourism—including sex tourism—is recognized as a means of increasing foreign revenue in countries where it flourishes. For example, one study suggests that prostitution is Thailand's largest underground industry, generating between 10 and 14 percent of the country's gross national product (Lim, 1998). Bales (1999) examined the accounts of one brothel in Thailand and found a net monthly profit of $88,000. The result is tacit acceptance and encouragement of the industry by local officials, albeit amid the continued criminalization of the sex workers themselves (Truong, 1990).

Those who benefit from sex tourism are wide ranging. A study conducted by the International Labor Organization found that

> more than one third of the employees [in the sex industry] did not sell sex but gained their livelihood from the industry. Supporting employees include parking attendants, waiters, guards, drivers, cashiers, cleaners, cooks, barmen and laundry workers . . . [A] host of other people participate: investors in property, entertainment and tourism; business owners and entrepreneurs; lawyers; accountants; airlines, limousine and taxi services; telecommunications businesses.
>
> *(Agustín, 2007: 65–66)*

Internet services, newspapers and magazines that receive advertising revenue, money management businesses, and manufacturers could be included in the list, too. Wilson (2004: 79) reports that the sex trade in Patpong—a well-known red-light district in Bangkok—has stimulated the growth of many other local industries, including "pharmacies, medical clinics, a supermarket offering Western products, ATM machines, beauty salons, and a slew of Western restaurants: Brown Derby, McDonald's, Pizza Hut."

Consequently, while providers of sexual services are stigmatized and face law enforcement sanctions, the infrastructure of the sex industry itself—and those who profit from it—remains untouched. An additional benefit of this businesses model is that when young women become older, contract HIV or are otherwise too sick to work, they can be easily disposed of, because the police are often in collusion with the businesses that profit from prostitution. This is not just the case in Thailand: it is a global phenomenon (Kempadoo and Doezema, 1998). While those who profit from the sex industry are typically men, those at the bottom of the hierarchy—typically women and girls—suffer the negative consequences.

Thus, some commentators are critical of the disproportionate attention and stigma brought to bear on those who sell sex in tourist markets. Wilson (2004: 73) notes that the discussion of "the international sex trade is predicated on its sensational and spectacular qualities." Researchers' and policy-makers' overemphasis on sex tourism—divorced from the broader inequalities on which it is built—further marginalizes those involved. In addition, this focus obscures other forms of global labor exploitation that may be equally harmful but receive less attention because "sex sells"—not only in the sex industry itself, but in the global formation of moral panics (Altman, 2001).

Child sex tourism

Nowhere is this more apparent than in debates about child sex tourism—the sale or participation of children and adolescents in sex tourist markets—an issue that has dominated discussions of and interventions on sex tourism. The participation of children in sex tourism is undoubtedly a real problem, and it has received a great deal of international attention over the last few decades (see Anderson et al., 2000; Beddoe et al., 2001). Most available data focus on Asia, though child prostitution is a global problem. For example, according to an estimate by the United Nations International Labor Organization, upwards of a million children in Asia may be involved in the sex trade (Kaban, 1996), with Thailand, Sri Lanka, the Philippines, Cambodia, and India among the main centers of child sex tourism (Boyes, 1996). Other evidence suggests that many youths work in the sex tourist industry to support their families (Montgomery, 2001). Sex tourists from Western Europe, Australia, Japan, and the United States participate in the trade.

Experts suggest that child sex tourism has increased for several reasons. There is some evidence that Western tourists fearful of HIV and other sexually transmitted diseases now demand sex from younger individuals (Boyes, 1996). The internet has facilitated the growth of pedophile networks that provide information about traveling abroad to abuse children sexually (O'Connell Davidson, 2005). And, most importantly, developmental processes within the global economy have contributed to a rise in the earning activities of children in the Third World. Thus, many commentators argue that children's involvement in sex tourism must be addressed "in the context of the global exploitation of child labor" more generally (Kempadoo, 1998: 7; see also Montgomery, 2001).

However, these commentators lament that most interventions on child sexual abuse have focused too narrowly on child sex tourism and the prosecution of individual pedophiles. This narrow focus has been problematized in several ways. First, Anderson and her colleagues (2000: 480) point out that the "commercial sexual exploitation of children [is] just the tip of the iceberg . . . Far more child abuse takes place behind closed doors within the family, child care institutions, and other places which should be safe places for children." Thus the focus on children's involvement in sex tourism does little to reduce the widespread sexual abuse of children.

In addition, children in the sex trade often work in the same locations, under the same conditions, and serving the same clients as adults. Thus, "the same structural factors can underpin both adults' and children's entry into the sex trade and make them vulnerable within it" (O'Connell Davidson, 2005: 3). While it is doubtless true that niche markets have developed to serve the sexual needs of pedophiles, the near-exclusive focus on this phenomenon "is often emotive, salacious and panicky and the magnitude of the problem [is] grossly exaggerated" (O'Connell Davidson, 2005: 127). The result is a failure to examine the primary causes of children's participation in sex tourism.

As Montgomery (2008: 912) highlights, within sex tourist markets, "childishness, beauty and ethnicity have been intentionally collapsed into each other and ideas of innocence have been deliberately manipulated and commoditised." Thus, the qualities that sex tourists seek in adult sex workers are strikingly similar "to those that paedophiles find sexually attractive in children." As a consequence:

> Childlike and youthful sexuality commands a price in which age, except to a small group of preferential abusers, is not the main issue. Women who appear very young may well be as sought-after as those who really are young, but to a foreigner who is unable or does not want to guess ages, any distinction becomes meaningless.
>
> *(Montgomery, 2008: 913)*

Thus, the narrow focus on child sex tourism committed by pedophiles misses the basic inequalities on which the industry is built and fails to capture the experiences of most children involved in sex tourism.

Moreover, the focus on individual pedophiles places "prostitution firmly in the realms of morality," and ensures that "any discussion of economics, or structural inequalities, can be ignored" (Montgomery, 2001: 156). As O'Connell Davidson (2005: 138) explains:

> Because campaigns against "child sex tourism" focus attention on the minority of "deviant" tourists who travel in pursuit of sex with very young children, they actually ask very little of the tourism industry . . . Very few campaigners insist that the industry address questions about the derisory wages paid to hotel workers, or think about how this might contribute to their willingness to accept "bribes" and "tips" for turning a blind eye to the activities of tourists.

Such campaigns have lent

> legitimacy to violations of sex workers' rights (both adult and children) by police and other state actors, who have in many places responded to international pressure to end "child sex tourism" by simply clamping down on those working in informal sector prostitution . . . [T]he number of women and teenagers who have ended up deported, behind bars, or in "re-education," "rehabilitation" or whatever euphemism is preferred, as a result of international concern about "child sex tourism" far outstrips the number of Western paedophiles . . . who have been similarly treated.
>
> *(O'Connell Davidson, 2005: 139)*

Conclusion

Thus, as with sex tourism more generally, these commentators argue that child sex tourism must be defined broadly, explicitly to emphasize poverty and economic inequalities exacerbated by Western imperialism. Attempting to ameliorate children's and adults' participation in sex tourism without broadly addressing global exploitation and the gender and economic inequalities on which it is based remains a truncated approach with harmful effects for those involved. Instead, given the economic benefits derived from sex workers' exploitation within tourist markets and the gendered hierarchies upon which the industry is built, policies need to address these root causes by targeting those organizations and businesses that ultimately profit and providing real economic alternatives for those who currently support themselves through commercial sex.

References

Agustín, Laura María (2007) *Sex at the margins: Migration, labour markets, and the rescue industry.* London: Zed Books.

Altman, Dennis (2001) *Global sex.* Chicago, IL: University of Chicago Press.

Anderson, Sarah, Stan Meuwese, and Annemieke Wolthuis (2000) "Policies and developments relating to the sexual exploitation of children: The legacy of the Stockholm Conference." *European Journal on Criminal Policy and Research.* 8: 479–501.

Bales, Kevin (1999) *Disposable people: New slavery in the global economy.* Berkeley: University of California Press.

Beddoe, Christine (1998) "Beachboys and tourists: Links in the chain of child prostitution in Sri Lanka." Pp. 42–50 in *Sex tourism and prostitution: Aspects of leisure, recreation and work,* edited by Martin Oppermann. Elmsford, NY: Cognizant Communication Corp.

Beddoe, Christine, C. Michael Hall, and Chris Ryan (2001) *The incidence of sexual exploitation of children in sex tourism.* Madrid: World Tourism Organization.

Boyes, Robert (1996) "How the sex tourists evade justice." *The Times.* August 22.

Cohen, Erik (1982) "Thai girls and farang men: The edge of ambiguity." *Annals of Tourism Research.* 9: 403–428.

Crick, Malcolm (1994) *Resplendent sites, discordant voices: Sri Lankans and international tourism.* Chur: Harwood Academic.

Dahles, Heidi (1998) "Of birds and fish: Street guides, tourists, and sexual encounters in Yogyakarta, Indonesia." Pp. 30–41 in *Sex tourism and prostitution: Aspects of leisure, recreation and work*, edited by Martin Oppermann. Elmsford, NY: Cognizant Communication Corp.

Enloe, Cynthia (1989) *Bananas, beaches and bases: Making feminist sense of international politics*. Berkeley: University of California Press.

Flowers, R. Barri (1998) *The prostitution of women and girls*. Jefferson, NC: Macfarland and Company.

Frohlick, Susan (2008) "Negotiating the public secrecy of sex in a transnational tourist town in Caribbean Costa Rica." *Tourist Studies*. 8: 19–39.

Kaban, Elif (1996) "ILO says 250 million children are workers." *Reuters World Service*. November 12.

Kattoulas, Velisarios (1995) "World tourism industry dodges child sex-tour issue. *Reuters North American Wire*. November 30.

Kempadoo, Kamala (1998) "Introduction: Globalizing sex workers' rights." Pp. 1–28 in, *Global sex workers: Rights, resistance, and redefinition*, edited by Kamala Kempadoo and Jo Doezema. New York: Routledge.

Kempadoo, Kamala (2004) *Sexing the Caribbean: Gender, race, and sexual labor*. New York: Routledge.

Kempadoo, Kamala and Jo Doezema, editors (1998) *Global sex workers: Rights, resistance, and redefinition*. New York: Routledge.

Lim, Lin Lean, editor (1998) *The sex sector: The economic and social bases of prostitution in Southeast Asia*. Geneva: International Labor Organization.

Montgomery, Heather (2001) *Modern Babylon? Prostituting children in Thailand*. New York: Berghahn Books.

Montgomery, Heather (2008) "Buying innocence: Child sex tourists in Thailand." *Third World Quarterly*. 29: 903–917.

O'Connell Davidson, Julia (2005) *Children in the global sex trade*. Cambridge: Polity Press.

Padilla, Mark B. (2007) "'Western Union daddies' and their quest for authenticity: An ethnographic study of the Dominican gay sex tourism industry." *Journal of Homosexuality*. 53: 241–275.

Phongpaichit, Pasuk (1982) *From peasant girls to Bangkok masseuses*. Geneva: International Labour Office.

Pruitt, Deborah and Suzanne LaFont (1995) "For love and money: Romance tourism in Jamaica." *Annals of Tourism Research*. 22: 422–440.

Scibelli, Pasqua (1987) "Empowering prostitutes: A proposal for international legal reform." *Harvard Women's Law Journal*. 10: 117–157.

Truong, Thanh-Dam (1990) *Sex, money and morality: Prostitution and tourism in Southeast Asia*. London: Zed Books.

United Nations World Tourism Organization (UNWTO) (2011) "Why tourism?" Available at: unwto. org/en/about/tourism (accessed February 9, 2011).

Waters, Malcolm (2001) *Globalization*, 2nd edn. London: Routledge.

Wilson, Ara (2004) *The intimate economies of Bangkok: Tomboys, tycoons, and Avon ladies in the global city*. Berkeley: University of California Press.

46

Pedophilia, child porn, and cyberpredators

Ethel Quayle

Our understanding of pedophilia and its relationship with child pornography has become more critical with the advent of technology-mediated offending. The internet has led to an overall increase in the availability of all pornographic materials, and sexually related online activities have become routine for many adults and young people in the Western world (Döring 2009). This has also led to concerns, from professionals and public alike, about the effect of porno-graphic materials on society (Diamond 2009) and on young people in particular (Perrin *et al.* 2008). However, Cassell and Cramer (2008: 70) have argued that throughout history there has been a recurring moral panic about the potential danger of communication technologies (particularly for young women) but that when investigated it is less the technology that appears to be to blame, but rather the potential sexual agency of young women, parental loss of control, and the 'specter of women who manifest technological prowess'. Much of the debate has been about whether there is a causal relationship between viewing child pornography and the commission of a contact offense against a child (e.g. Endrass *et al.* 2009) and whether those who view images of children are inevitably pedophiles (Seto *et al.* 2006; Seto 2009).

Pedophilia

In the sex offender literature, internet offenders are often called pedophiles (Durkin 1997) however, *The Diagnostic and Statistical Manual of Mental Disorders* (*DSM*; APA 2000) criteria used to diagnose pedophilia have in more recent times been extensively criticized. Studer and Aylwin (2006) argued that the category adds little to our understanding of a person, beyond being a description of their behavior and that the pedophilia diagnosis actually subsumes a 'continuum' of sexual responses rather than dichotomous or exclusive groups. They concluded that the criteria are too broad to allow for any meaningful discrimination between child molesters and pedophiles, and too narrow where arousal by adult–child sex is ego-syntonic and not acted upon, a more relevant point with the huge increase in child pornography available on the internet (Quayle 2008).

The *DSM* (APA 2000) defines pedophilia as the erotic preference for prepubescent children. Blanchard *et al.* (2009) point out that if taken literally this would exclude from diagnosis a proportion of those men whose strongest sexual feelings are for physically immature persons. A review by these authors of the relevant evidence suggests that pubescent children are generally those aged between 11 and 15 years, and as the modal age for victims of child sexual abuse in the United States is 14 years, this would imply that the majority of offenders would not meet the criteria for pedophilia. One conclusion from this is that we should either expand the criteria for pedophilia to include children who are pubescent, or add a separate diagnosis of hebephilia, which would specify a preference for pubescent children.

Authors such as Hall and Hall (2007) have also pointed out that pedophiles may engage in a wide range of sexual acts with children, including exposing themselves to children (exhibitionism); undressing a child; looking at naked children (voyeurism); masturbating in the presence of children; rubbing their genitalia against a child (frotteurism); fondling a child; engaging in oral sex with a child; or penetrating the mouth, anus and/or vagina or a child. Seto (2009) has suggested that the prevalence of pedophilia in the general population is unknown as there have been no large-scale epidemiological studies, and we know very little of this population outside of clinical or correctional settings. However, a recent study by Goode (2010) draws on research with self-identified pedophiles living ordinary lives in the community who may or may not have been involved in criminal activity. The existence of such people is clearly evidenced in the number of internet communities who draw support from online fora (O'Halloran and Quayle 2010), which may lead us to conclude that the number of people with a sexual interest in children exceeds those within the criminal justice system. A related debate with regard to pedophilia is whether it should be classified as a mental disorder (e.g., Tromovitch 2009).

In general, most people who are classified as pedophilic are male, although more recently there has been growing literature about women who commit sexual offenses against children. Gannon and Rose (2008: 458), in their review of published literature, concluded that while female child sex offenders are a heterogeneous group, it appears that they

> are more likely to offend in the company of a male, are highly likely to have experienced both childhood and adulthood victimization at the hands of men, and are likely to display some profound disturbances in their ability to seek and maintain appropriate adult intimate relationships ... relationships, personality traits, and perceptions of men and boys are relatively immature, profoundly disturbed, and inextricably linked to their offending behavior.

To date, there have been very few reports of women whose offenses relate to child pornography, although in the UK the case of Vanessa George, a female nursery worker who admitted sexually assaulting very young children in her care and making and distributing indecent photographs of them through a social networking site, has been the cause of great concern (*Times Online* 2009).

Child pornography

Child pornography is not a new phenomenon, and there are historical accounts that would suggest that sexualized images of children became both available and collectable with the advent of photography (Taylor and Quayle 2003). While the term child pornography is used widely across most jurisdictions (Akdeniz 2008), more recently concerns have been expressed as to whether this reflects actual content or implies consent (Quayle 2009b). The term 'abusive images' is now widely used by those who advocate for children's rights in relation to sexual abuse through photography (Jones and Skögrand 2005) although it might be argued that such terms fail to capture the wide array of material depicting abusive and exploitative sexual practices towards children in the online environment (Quayle *et al.* 2008). The criminalization of such practices has led to an increase in the number of people within the criminal justice system who have been given the label of 'internet sex offender'. In the UK by 2005, internet-related sexual offenses accounted for one-third of all sexual convictions (Middleton *et al.* 2009).

Clearly not all sexualized images of children demonstrate the same degree of sexually abusive or exploitative practices, nor are all of these images illegal across many jurisdictions. If we look at the material found in the collections of offenders, the pictures range from images of clothed children, through nakedness and explicit erotic posing, to sexual assault. We can make some objective sense of this by thinking of the pictures in terms of a continuum of increased deliberate sexual victimization (Taylor *et al.* 2001). This continuum ranges from everyday and perhaps accidental pictures involving either no overt erotic content or minimal content (such as showing a child's underwear), at one extreme, to pictures showing rape and penetration of a child or other gross acts of obscenity, at the other. Taking this perspective focuses attention not just on illegality as a significant quality of pictures, but on the preferred type of pictures selected by the collector, and the value and meaning pictures have to collectors (Taylor and Quayle 2003).

In trying to understand the ways in which children are victimized within the images, Taylor *et al.* (2001) generated a typology based on an analysis of publicly available images obtained from newsgroups and websites (made possible under Irish law). This 'COPINE Scale' had ten levels, ranging from indicative images to those depicting sadism or bestiality. In 2002, in England and Wales, the Sentencing Advisory Panel (SAP) published its advice to the Court of Appeal on offenses involving child pornography. The SAP believed that the nature of the material should be the key factor in deciding the level of sentence, and adapted the COPINE Scale to five levels. It dropped Levels 1 to 3 completely, arguing that nakedness alone was not indicative of indecency. The proposed structure was therefore that COPINE Levels 5 to 6 constitute Sentencing Level 1, and COPINE Levels 7 upwards each constitutes an individual sentencing stage (Gillespie 2003). One consequence of using such a measure has been that it provides a means of communication about the images without, for most people, the images ever having been seen (Quayle 2009a).

Internet sex offenders

In relation to people convicted of internet sexual crimes against children, there are demographic consistencies between study samples, the most notable of which relate to gender and ethnicity. Wolak *et al.* (2005), in their study of internet crimes against minors, reported that 99 percent of their sample was male. This is similar to the findings of other studies (Sullivan 2007; Finkelhor and Ormrod 2004; Seto and Eke 2005; Webb *et al.* 2007; Bates and Metcalf 2007; Baartz 2008). The majority of offenders are not only male but white Caucasians (Sullivan 2007; O'Brien and Webster 2007; Wolak *et al.* 2005). Webb *et al.* (2007) indicated that their internet-related offenders were predominantly white, which appeared different from their child molester sample within the same study that came from a more mixed ethnic group. Within an Australian sample, the majority of internet sex offenders were identified as Caucasian (86 percent), with minimal representation in the Asian, Mediterranean and Aboriginal ethnic groups (Baartz 2008). Coward *et al.* (2009), in their analysis of an ongoing US research project, examined 405 cases made up of 277 convicted offenders with no known or reported internet sex offenses who had access to the internet and 128 with a charge or arrest for an internet sex offense. Ninety-two percent of the internet sex offenders were Caucasian males, compared to 73 per cent in the comparison group (which had a higher proportion of African Americans and Hispanics).

Given the volume of internet sex offenders, whose offenses largely relate to downloading, distribution and production of child pornography, it is unsurprising that there has been concern about the relationship between viewing abusive images, pedophilia and the commission of further offenses against children. Seto *et al.* (2006) studied a group of men whose offenses related to child pornography using a bio-signal measure of sexual arousal (penile plethysmography). Within their sample, 61 percent of child pornography offenders showed greater penile responses to stimuli depicting children compared to those depicting adults, and this was greater than those offenders who had committed contact offenses against children. Seto (2009: 396) has hypothesized that 'child pornography offenders with more child pornography images, a higher ratio of child to adult images, and images depicting younger children and both boys and girls are more likely to be pedophilic and thus more likely to seek sexual contacts with children'. However, there is still limited data to support this claim, and to date there are considerable differences across studies in the number of people convicted of child pornography-related offenses who have previous convictions for contact offenses against children (Hanson and Babchishin 2009).

Clearly, as yet, we have little information to indicate what risks are posed by internet offenders with no known history of sexual contacts with children, although a study by Seto and Eke (2005) indicated that child pornography offenders with any kind of prior criminal history were more likely to commit a contact offense, or an offense of any kind, during the study follow-up period of two and a half years.

Cyberpredators

Child pornography offenses are not the only internet sex offenses committed against children. Television programs such as *To Catch a Predator* have alerted us to the fact that some people (usually men) go online in order to engage with children and young people in a sexual way, and that a proportion of these people will have sexual contact with that young person in the offline world. Clearly such activity may target adults as well as children, and such terms as 'cyber-predators' have been used to describe this type of behaviour (Philips and Morrissey 2004). Kierkegaard (2008) makes reference to the 'grooming' of children in relation to this, and there have been changes in UK law to reflect growing concerns about such online activity, as well as an increase in proactive 'sting operations' by police to interrupt the process before a child can be sexually assaulted. Research by Davidson and Martellozzo (2008) with the UK Metropolitan Police would suggest that such offenders demonstrate a tendency to minimize their intention to abuse a child sexually. Several of the offenders in their study claimed that the online communication was about sharing fantasies with people whom they thought to be adults.

However, researchers from the University of New Hampshire alert us to what they believe are the myths and realities of online 'predators' (Wolak *et al.* 2008). Their studies of American youth suggest that the publicity about online 'predators' who engage with naive children through trickery and develop a relationship with them that culminates in violence is largely inaccurate. Their data suggest that these encounters are often closer to models of statutory rape, rather than forced sexual assaults or pedophilic attacks.

Much of this research has come from two studies (YISS-1 and YISS-2), which conducted telephone interviews with national samples of young internet users (aged 10 to 17 years) in 2000 and 2005 (Finkelhor *et al.* 2000; Wolak *et al.* 2006). This US research suggests that most internet-initiated sex crimes involve adult men who use the internet to meet and seduce underage adolescents into sexual encounters. 'The offenders use Internet communications such as instant messages, e-mail, and chatrooms to meet and develop intimate relationships with victims. In the majority of cases, victims are aware that they are conversing online with adults' (Wolack *et al.* 2008: 112). The implication of this research is that we should be paying particular attention to those youths who are most vulnerable. This would include those with histories of sexual abuse, those with concerns about their sexual orientation, and those who have patterns of risk taking across all domains. The research would also support the idea of developmentally appropriate prevention strategies that acknowledge normal adolescent interests in romance and sex.

The Internet Safety Technical Task Force (2008) argued that, although they are frequently reported in the media, US internet sex crimes against minors have not overtaken the number of unmediated sex crimes against minors, nor have they contributed to a rise in such crimes. The report states that the increased popularity of the internet in the United States has not been correlated with an overall increase in reported sexual offenses. Evidence is cited from the US that, overall, sexual offenses against children have declined in the last 18 years (National Center for Missing and Exploited Children 2006), with research indicating a dramatic reduction in reports of sexual offenses against children from 1992 to 2006 (Calpin 2006; Finkelhor and Jones 2008). What is still not known is whether we will continue to see a decrease in sexual offenses against children across other countries, and whether this will be paralleled by an eventual increase in technology-mediated sexual crimes.

References

Akdeniz, Y. (2008) *Internet Child Pornography and the Law: National and International Responses*, Aldershot: Ashgate.

American Psychiatric Association (APA) (2000) *The Diagnostic and Statistical Manual of Mental Disorders*, 4th rev. edn, Washington, DC: American Psychiatric Association.

Baartz, D. (2008) *Australians, the Internet and Technology-Enabled Child Sex Abuse: A Statistical Profile*, Canberra: Australian Federal Police.

Bates, A. and Metcalf, C. (2007) A psychometric comparison of internet and non-internet sex offenders from a community treatment sample, *Journal of Sexual Aggression*, 13, 1: 11–20.

Blanchard, R., Lykins, A.D., Wherrett, D., Kuban, M.E., Cantor, J., Blak, T., Dickey, R. and Klassen, P.E. (2009) Pedophilia, hebephilia, and the *DSM-V*, *Archives of Sexual Behaviour*, 38: 335–350.

Calpin, C.M. (2006) *Child Maltreatment*, US Department of Health and Human Services. Available: www.acf.hhs.gov/programs/cb/pubs/cm06/cm06.pdf (accessed 5 June 2007).

Cassell, J. and Cramer, M. (2008) High tech or high risk: moral panics about girls online, in T. McPherson (ed.), *Digital Youth, Innovation, and the Unexpected*, John D. and Catherine T. MacArthur Foundation Series on Digital Media and Learning, Cambridge, MA: MIT Press.

Coward, I.A., Gabriel, A.M., Schuler, A. and Prentky, R.A. (2009) Child internet victimization: project development and preliminary results, paper presented at the Annual Conference of the American Psychology-Law Society, San Antonio, March.

Davidson, J.C. and Martellozzo, E. (2008) Protecting vulnerable young people in cyberspace from sexual abuse: raising awareness and responding globally, *Police Practice and Research*, 9, 4: 277–289.

Diamond, M. (2009) Pornography, public acceptance and sex related crime: a review, *International Journal of Law and Psychiatry*, 32: 304–314.

Döring, .M. (2009) The internet's impact on sexuality: a critical review of 15 years of research, *Computers in Human Behavior*, 25: 1089–1101.

Durkin, K. (1997) Misuse of the internet by pedophiles: implications for law enforcement and probation practice, *Federal Probation*, 61, 2: 14–18.

Endrass, J., Urbaniok, F., Hammermeister, L.C., Benz, C., Elbert, T., Laubacher, A. and Rossegger, A. (2009) The consumption of internet child pornography and violent and sex offending, *BMC Psychiatry*, 9: 43–49.

Finkelhor, D. and Jones, L. (2008) *Updated Trends in Child Maltreatment, 2006*, Crimes Against Children Research Center. Available: www.unh.edu/ccrc/Trends/index.html (accessed 11 January 2009).

Finkelhor, D., Mitchell, K. and Wolak, J. (2000) *Online Victimization: A Report on the Nation's Youth*, Alexandria, VA: National Center for Missing and Exploited Children.

Finkelhor, D. and Ormrod, R. (2004) *Child Pornography: Patterns from the NIBRS*, Washington, DC: US Department of Justice Programs, Office of Juvenile Justice and Delinquency Prevention.

Gannon, T.A. and Rose, M.R. (2008) Female child sexual offenders: towards integrating theory and practice, *Aggression and Violent Behavior*, 13: 442–461.

Gillespie, A.A. (2003) Sentences for offences involving child pornography, *Criminal Law Review*, February: 80–92.

Goode, S.D. (2010) *Understanding and Addressing Adult Sexual Attraction to Children*, Abingdon: Routledge.

Hall, R.C.W. and Hall, R.C.W. (2007) A profile of pedophilia: definition, characteristics of offenders, recidivism, treatment outcomes, and forensic issues, *Mayo Clinic Proceedings*, 82, 4: 457–471.

Hanson, R.K. and Babchishin, K.M. (2009) How should we advance our knowledge of risk assessment for internet sexual offenders?, paper presented at the Global Symposium for Examining the Relationship between Online and Offline Offenses and Preventing the Sexual Exploitation of Children, Chapel Hill, NC, April.

Internet Safety Technical Task Force (2008) *Enhancing Child Safety and Online Technologies: Final Report of the Internet Safety Technical Task Force to the Multi-State Working Group on Social Networking of State Attorneys General of the United States*, Cambridge, MA: Berkman Center for Internet and Society, Harvard University.

Jones, V. and Skögrand, E. (2005) *Position Paper Regarding Online Images of Sexual Abuse and other Internet-Related Sexual Exploitation of Children*, Copenhagen: Save the Children Europe Group.

Kierkegaard, S. (2008) Cybering, online grooming and age play, *Computer Law and Security Report*, 24: 41–55.

Middleton, D., Mandeville-Norden, R. and Hayes, E. (2009) Does treatment work with internet sex offenders? Emerging findings from the internet Sex Offender Treatment Programme (i-SOTP), *Journal of Sexual Aggression*, 15, 1: 5–19.

National Center for Missing and Exploited Children (2006) *CyberTipline Annual Report Totals*. Available: www.cybertipline.com/en_US/documents/CyberTiplineReportTotals.pdf (accessed 4 June 2007).

O'Brien, M.D. and Webster, S.D. (2007) The construction and preliminary validation of the Internet Behaviours and Attitudes Questionnaire (IBAQ), *Sex Abuse*, 19: 237–256.

O'Halloran, E. and Quayle, E. (2010) A content analysis of a 'Boy Love' support forum: revisiting Durkin and Bryant, *Journal of Sexual Aggression*, 16, 1: 71–85.

Perrin, P.C., Madanat, H.N., Barnes, M.D., Corolan, A., Clark, R.B., Ivins, N. *et al.* (2008) Health education's role in framing pornography as a public health issue: implications, *Promotion and Education*, 15: 11–18.

Philips, P. and Morrissey, G. (2004) Internet cyberstalking and cyberpredators: a threat to safe sexuality on the internet, *Convergence: The International Journal of Research into New Technologies*, 10: 66–79.

Quayle, E. (2008) Internet offending, in D.R. Laws and W. O'Donohue (eds), *Sexual Deviance*, New York: Guilford Press.

Quayle, E. (2009a) Assessment of internet sexual abuse, in M.C. Calder (ed.), *Complete Guide to Sexual Abuse Assessments*, 2nd edn, Lyme Regis: Russell House.

Quayle, E. (2009b). Child pornography, in Y. Jewkes and M. Yar (eds), *The Handbook of Internet Crime*, Cullompton: Willan.

Quayle, E., Lööf, L. and Palmer, T. (2008) *Child Pornography and Sexual Exploitation of Children Online*, Bangkok: ECPAT International.

Seto, M. (2009) Pedophilia, *Annual Review of Clinical Psychology*, 5:391–4079.

Seto M.C., Cantor, J.M. and Blanchard, R. (2006) Child pornography offenses are a valid diagnostic indicator of pedophilia, *Journal of Abnormal Psychology*, 115: 610–615.

Seto, M.C. and Eke, A. (2005) The criminal histories and later offending of child pornography offenders, *Sexual Abuse: A Journal of Research and Treatment*, 17, 2: 201–210.

Studer, L.H. and Aylwin, A.S. (2006) Pedophilia: the problem with diagnosis and limitations of CBT in treatment, *Medical Hypotheses*, 67, 4: 774–781.

Sullivan, C. (2007) *Internet Traders of Child Pornography: Profiling Research*, New Zealand: Censorship Compliance Unit.

Taylor, M. and Quayle, E. (2003) *Child Pornography: An Internet Crime*, Brighton: Routledge.

Taylor, M., Holland, G. and Quayle, E. (2001) Typology of paedophile picture collections, *The Police Journal*, 74, 2: 97–107.

Times Online (2009) Child abuse: the camera doesn't lie, 25 October. Available: www.timesonline.co.uk/tol/news/uk/crime/article6886186.ece (accessed 26 October 2009).

Tromovitch, P. (2009) Manufacturing mental disorder by pathologizing erotic age orientation: a comment on Blanchard *et al.* [Letter to the editor], *Archives of Sexual Behavior*, 38, 3: 328.

Webb, L., Craissati, J. and Keen, S. (2007) Characteristics of internet child pornography offenders: a comparison with child molesters, *Sex Abuse*, 19: 449–465.

Wolak, J., Finkelhor, D. and Mitchell, K.J. (2005) *Child-Pornography Possessors Arrested in Internet-Related Crimes: Findings from the National Juvenile Online Victimization Study*, Alexandria, VA: National Center for Missing and Exploited Children.

Wolak, J., Mitchell, K. and Finkelhor, D. (2006) *Online Victimization: 5 Years Later*, Alexandria, VA: National Center for Missing and Exploited Children.

Wolak, J., Finkelhor, D., Mitchell, K.J. and Ybarra, M.L. (2008) Online 'predators' and their victims: myths, realities, and implications for prevention and treatment, *American Psychologist*, 63, 2: 111–128.

47

Erotic dancing

Carol Rambo and John Pruit

Stripping, burlesque dancing, belly dancing, table dancing, topless dancing, lap dancing, nude dancing, exotic dancing—all of these and more are labels for an activity that will be labeled here as erotic dancing. Erotic dancers use "the sensual exhibition of one's body for financial remuneration" (Boles and Garbin 1974a:114). Erotic dancing has a unique history, takes place in many settings, and encompasses a variety of interaction motifs. Throughout history, the definition of erotic dancing has been in flux. In some cultures it is accepted as a useful high-status occupation. At other times and places it has been framed through the Victorian discourses of deviance and pathology. Still others have politicized erotic dance, framing it through the discourses of domination, resistance, and liberation. Social science researchers have replicated these discourses across the pages of their publications (Rambo, Presley and Mynatt 2006). Now, more than ever, with the onset of the global financial crisis, people are turning to sex work, and in particular to erotic dancing, as their occupation of choice. For these reasons and more, erotic dancing as an occupation warrants social scientists' attention.

Erotic dancing, which titillates the sexual imagination without necessarily delivering whole-sale sexual services, has been in existence for hundreds of years. Whether at a wedding party, in a theater, a strip club, a go-go bar, a gentlemen's club, a restaurant, a lingerie boutique, or a spa showroom (Ronai and Trautner 2001), erotic dancers bring a fantasy to life, and transform sexuality into a commodity (Rambo, Presley and Mynatt 2006).

No discussion of erotic dancing would be complete without considering belly dancing, which originated in North Africa, Asia, and the Middle East. There are two forms of belly dancing set either in a cabaret or in formal celebrations, such as wedding ceremonies: *raqs sharqi* and *raqs baladi* (both Egyptian terms) (Lorius 1996a, 1996b). *Raqs sharqi*, meaning "Oriental dance," is a classical interpretation of traditional songs in which the hips, torso, and arms flow rhythmically to create a harmonious performance. In Cairo, this form is associated with the 1940s dancers who were classically trained by religious sheikhs. Modern *raqs sharqi* belly dancers base their performances on the same traditional forms.

Raqs baladi, meaning "of the country," uses the same movements as *raqs sharqi*, but emphasizes improvisation. Set to contemporary popular music, it may include rap, wit, and street humor (Lorius 1996b). Performers interact with guests, using phrases with double meanings and innuendo. This dance may be performed solo or in groups of two or more. When performed for wedding celebrations, as per ancient customs, the belly dancer performs separately for the groom's party and the bride's party. The dancer serves as a guide for the inexperienced newlyweds as they prepare for their journey into eroticism. For the men, it is similar to an American bachelor party, except that the dancer is considered a professional and given great respect. Strict norms govern interaction between the belly dancer, the groom, and his party. Inappropriate remarks, gestures or advances are absent from the interaction. The men, especially the groom, are expected to practice restraint, as disrespectful behavior toward the dancer is considered unmanly. If disrespectful behavior does occur, bouncers will deal with the offender. The only touching that occurs is to place a tip in the hand of the dancer.

In contrast to the men's, the women's party is lively, exuberant, and joyful. The belly dancer is an instructor of sorts, teaching the bride the sensual and seductive movements of the dance. As a way of paying homage to the bride, the members of her party will often join in the instruction. The intended result of both performances is that the couple will lose their childlike innocence and embrace their bourgeoning sexuality.

Eroticism infused working-class US culture in the late 19th century with the emergence of burlesque theater (Allen 1991). Actresses would appear on stage wearing flesh-colored, decorated body stockings. Their subversive sketch humor mocked contemporary morals, gender norms, and corrupt authority figures. Politicians, judges, and policemen were frequent targets of their cynical performances. At the height of their popularity, the shows attracted more upscale audiences. Once those who were being mocked attended the shows, they were frequently raided and shut down for public indecency. Ironically, the more the shows featured erotic dance, the less likely they were to be raided. In order to stay in business, burlesque theater evolved into the form with which we are familiar today: strippers who disrobe to music and stand up comedians who tell jokes and emcee the shows (Allen 1991).

Evolving from burlesque shows, contemporary "revue dancing" is a form of traveling striptease or go-go dancing which features performers that might be all male, all female, or mixed groups. Similar to the performers in burlesque shows, revue dancers often have a gimmick, such as acting out sexual mini-dramas, mud wrestling, or boxing. Dancers appear individually and as a group in choreographed routines. They are compensated with a flat rate for their stage performance. They may also leave the stage and dance table-to-table to encourage audience participation and solicit tips. Depending on local ordinances, dancers may receive tips in their g-strings, garters or hands.

Some erotic dancers, both male and female, contract to perform at private parties, typically bachelor or bachelorette parties (Ronai and Cross 1998). A twist on this is the traveling "strip-o-gram." Customers phone in and book an erotic dancer to surprise a recipient with a striptease. Often there will be a motif, perhaps a "policeman" arrives to tell birthday party attendees that they are too loud and need to quiet down. Later, the policeman turns on portable music and dances while removing his clothes for the guests. Other motifs include pizza-delivery person and repair person. At the end of the performance, the dancer will announce that the recipient has received a strip-o-gram and tell them from whom.

Within striptease and go-go establishments (businesses set up for the purpose of showcasing erotic dancers), both stage performances and more private dances are available. The latter include: tabletop dances, table dances, lap dances, and booth dances. Most go-go clubs are full liquor bars, while some serve only wine or beer. Dancers typically strip to a bra-like top and briefs or a thong. At the other end of the continuum, in fully nude establishments, no alcohol is allowed. In general, the more nudity there is, the less liquor and touching there will be.

During a tabletop dance, the dancer will dance on the table or countertop for a fee, which increases as nudity increases. Aside from the process of tipping, touching is usually not allowed. Some tabletop dances are accompanied by the purchase of alcohol, usually champagne, which is consumed by both the customer and the dancer. Later, the dancer typically receives half of the price of the alcohol, which might range from fifty to several hundred dollars a bottle.

There are several components to the performance in a strip club. The performer dances on stage, stripping away some or all of his or her clothing for tips and as a way to advertise for future interactions. After the performance the dancer exits the stage and walks around the room, available to share drinks and conversation with customers, as well as to dance privately. The process of negotiation between the dancer and customer is complex, as the dancer attempts to decode the intentions of the customer and balance them with his or her personal boundaries. The dancer negotiates with both the customer and his or her self, appearing open to the desires of the customer while attempting to remain true to the self (Boden 2002; Boles and Garbin 1974a, 1974b; Egan 2000; Enck and Preston 1988; Ronai and Ellis 1989; Thompson, Harred and Burks 2003; Wesely 2001, 2003).

Upon reaching an agreement for remuneration, the table dance takes place. The performance may occur on the floor or in a more private setting. The area designed for table dancing is divided from the general audience by a partition, walls, railing or partial curtains and is often elevated to give the customer a clear view of the stage. Table dances are usually sold by the song and can range from five dollars to over a hundred dollars, depending on the club, the degree of nudity, whether touching is permitted, and any other agreements made prior to the dance.

Local ordinances dictate the attire of the dancers, with men usually wearing a g-string or t-back and women a bra-like top and panties or a thong. Most local ordinances also dictate the proximity of the customer and dancer while the dancer is performing. Officially, this usually ranges from six to eighteen inches of separation, but this is often ignored unless law enforcement officers are suspected of being present. Higher-status clubs may have security measures to enforce both local ordinances and house rules.

While the private table dance takes place, the dancer stands between the open legs of the customer, bracing him or herself against the wall, on the arms of the chair, or on the customer's shoulders. Once both are in place and the song begins, the performer dances to the music. In some locations touching is not permitted by either the customer or the dancer, while in others the customer is permitted to touch the dancer's back, waist, hips and outside of the legs (Ronai and Ellis 1989). In clubs where touching is not allowed, the dancer may face away from the customer to be certain bouncers are not watching, and then turn around to allow the customer to touch him or her. This typically results in more tips. This type of touching is at the discretion of the dancer, and may have repercussions for each of them. If spotted by security, the customer may be escorted from the club and banned. The dancer might also be subject to discipline, ranging from pejorative labeling by other dancers, to fines or termination. When the dancer is fully nude, touching of any sort is prohibited, although some customers succeed anyway. With the exception of Nevada, where prostitution is legal, sexual activity during a table dance is always illegal. Rarely, intercourse, oral sex or masturbation occurs.

A more common occurrence during a table dance is the "rub off." The customer will slide to the edge of the seat, spread his or her legs and pull the dancer closer. A dancer is known to have "talented knees" (Ronai and Ellis 1989) when he/she can discreetly create body-to-genital friction. While breaking the law in this way will generate more money for the dancer, it may also result in stigmatization by other dancers as they feel the pressure to compete for tips by performing similar acts (Salutin 1977; Ronai and Cross 1998) and, of course, his or her arrest.

In some locations, lap dancing is illegal but may be tolerated by local law enforcement. During a lap dance, the dancer straddles the legs of the customer, swaying to the music. Facing toward or away from the customer, the dancer often makes contact with their lap, rubbing back and forth. Often the dancer deliberately stimulates the customer, being careful not to stimulate them to climax before maximizing the amount of money earned.

Couch dancing is a variation of lap dancing often practiced in "gentlemen's clubs." These establishments cater to business- and middle-class men, have designer furniture, and often demand membership or a higher admission price than strip clubs. Security is always present and local laws and house rules are enforced. All owners risk forfeiting investment capital and possibly the entire business if a liquor license is revoked due to a bust. Furthermore, if a gentlemen's club is to remain a high-status operation that attracts and retains the best dancers and clientele, it must maintain a reputation for being safe and clean.

As with the lap dance, the couch dancer will straddle the legs of her customer, resting her knees and shins on the sofa, and perform to the music. The dancer is allowed to touch the patron, but the gentleman is never allowed to touch or act inappropriately toward the dancer. The norms of the gentlemen's club stipulate that a client be just that—a gentleman who practices restraint and courtesy toward the dancer. Although body-to-penis friction might occur, it must do so discreetly, since the norms of a gentlemen's club and those of a strip club differ considerably.

Private booths are sometimes located in strip clubs, adult cinemas, adult entertainment retailers, and adult restaurants. Booth dancing takes place in a booth behind a Plexiglas partition with a slot for tips, with the customer seated in front of the partition. Customers enter the booth anticipating a more explicit performance than what might occur on the general stage. Although not necessarily the norm, some booth dancers admit to illegal activity, such as masturbation with or without objects and "showing the pink" (Ronai and Cross 1998; Ronai and Trautner 2001). As a security measure, there may be a camera present to prevent the customer from masturbating. On occasions when the customer does masturbate, there will then be evidence for the authorities that the customer, not the dancer, was in violation of the law.

Some restaurants feature erotic dancing to compete in the adult entertainment market. Although there is some evidence that these establishments are becoming more geographically mainstream (Hubbard, Matthews, Scoular, and Agustin 2008), they are usually located near interstate highways for the ease of the traveler who wishes to participate. These restaurants charge more for food and beverages than traditional restaurants. Lacking liquor, this setting features fully nude dancing on various stages throughout the restaurant. Table and booth dancing takes place in seclusion from the eating area.

For a fee, some lingerie boutiques offer the opportunity to see lingerie on "models." Some also offer private booths where the model dances for the seated customer. A limited number of lingerie boutiques are fronts for prostitution, but certainly not all. Similar to lingerie boutiques, some establishments advertise nude modeling for artists and photographers. The artist or photographer books the model for a set period of time at a set price. Once the session begins the customer may inquire about further services, or the model may offer additional services, such as table dances or sexual favors.

Some sales showrooms for spas offer special demonstrations by a model chosen by the customer. Once the door to the showroom closes the model may offer to dance around the spa for a fee. The fee increases if the customer desires the dancer to move closer or remove clothing. Knowledgeable customers desiring more advanced sexual favors know to remove all clothing, including shoes and watches, and place them on a loudspeaker. This is done to drown out any evidence that may be obtained by undercover police with hidden electronic equipment. These businesses are generally short lived, moving to a new area every three to six months.

A survey of the literature on erotic dancers reveals that the bodies and selves of the dancers are contested and claimed by researchers (Rambo, Presley and Mynatt 2006). This is carried out through the application of specialized technical discourses (Foucault 1977) in the framing of research projects and their descriptions of erotic dancers. Salutin (1977) notes that strippers are viewed as "bad" because they show no inhibitions or shyness about the body or sex. Through the Victorian discourses of deviance and pathology, dancers are frequently evaluated in terms of "What is wrong with them?"; "How can they be fixed?"; and "How can we prevent erotic dancing from occurring in society?" When sex is sold, it becomes simultaneously a commodity and an object of discourse, "invested with symbolic meanings and symbolic value—use-value, sign-value, exchange value, and sign-exchange value—through the functioning of a discursive and material order" (Waskul and Vannini 2006:10). These meanings, in turn, guide how we will approach the topic as researchers.

Other research discourses eschew deviance and pathology frames in favor of more politicized ways of viewing erotic dancers. In these dialogues, feminist researchers pose the question: "Are erotic dancers being exploited or liberated by their participation in the occupation?" In some radical feminist literatures, the dancers are positioned as passive sex objects who lack agency and unwittingly reinforce traditional patriarchal values. They are characterized as exploited and oppressed, perpetuating societal norms of "a culture in which sex is defined in terms of dominance and submission" (Kitinger 1994:209). Boden (2002) also draws on the exploitation discourse to frame his work on gay male dancers, observing that central to the virtual self is a constructed sexuality that is not reflective of the desires of the dancer; rather, it reflects the desires of the consumer.

Utilizing the alternative frame—liberation—pro-sex feminists and others claim women who dance for a living are exercising power and freedom when they work in the sex industry. For instance, Bruckert (2001) notes that erotic dancing affords women a level of autonomy, flexibility, and economic compensation rarely available to working-class women in the labor force. In another application of the liberation frame, Barton (2001) discusses how the sex industry can be viewed as a site which encourages women to expand their notions of their own sexuality and invites them to break taboos. Similar to burlesque dancing in the late 19th century, nude dancing is represented as a form of class opposition to dominant neo-puritan norms. In a twist on the exploitation and liberation discourse, some view it as a dualistic trap into which social science researchers fall. It is positioned as an artificially imposed construct that is potentially harmful. In everyday life, an erotic dancer may experience empowerment *and* oppression (Egan 2000; Barton 2001; Wesely 2001). Researchers in this camp seek to problematize the polarization of exploited victim and liberated woman as it is theorized in both radical and pro-sex feminist paradigms (Egan 2000). However, as these authors seek to challenge the exploitation and liberation frames, they inadvertently replicate the discursive order imposed by these assumptions inherent in the language of commodification of the body, thus further establishing and reinforcing existing power relations between erotic dancers and society (Rambo, Presley, and Mynatt 2006).

Though there is a healthy body of literature in existence on the occupation of erotic dancing, it is still a research site with the potential to offer up novel insights. Some of the research pathologizes and/or politicizes the bodies and selves of erotic dancers. We hope future projects investigate the case of the erotic dancer and sidestep these discourses altogether.

Back in 1986, Chaftez and Dworkin noted that gender bias was a general trend in deviance research. Similarly, Millman (1975:251) noted that "sociological stereotypes of deviance closely resemble those that appear in popular culture." Over three decades later, little has changed. More work has been done on female dancers than male dancers (Rambo, Presley, and Mynatt 2006). Furthermore, there is a dearth of research on customers who frequent erotic dance performances (Rambo, Presley, and Mynatt 2006). Both of these observations and more mirror the mainstream culture's attitudes toward exotic dancing: it is a curiosity for men and something deviant and problematic for women; it is normal for customers (mostly men) to participate in these settings, but problematic for the dancers themselves. These inequities and more exist in the literature, and future research would benefit from taking them into consideration.

References

Allen, Robert C. 1991. *Horrible Prettiness: Burlesque and American Culture*. Chapel Hill: University of North Carolina Press.

Barton, Bernadette. 2001. "Inside the Lives of Exotic Dancers." *Dissertation Abstracts International, A: The Humanities and Social Sciences* 61(9):3775–A.

Boden, David Michael. 2002. "A Wink and a Smile: Titillation and the Alienation of Sexuality within the Occupation of Male Erotic Dancing." *Dissertation Abstracts International, A: The Humanities and Social Sciences* 62(11):3951–A.

Boles, Jacqueline M. and Albeno P. Garbin. 1974a. "The Choice of Stripping for a Living: An Empirical and Theoretical Explanation." *Sociology of Work and Occupations* 1:110–123.

——. 1974b. "Stripping for a Living: An Occupational Study of the Night Club Stripper." Pp. 312–335 in *Deviant Behavior: Occupational and Organizational Bases*, edited by C. D. Bryant. Skokie, IL: Rand McNally.

Bruckert, Christine M. 2001. "Stigmatized Labour: An Ethnographic Study of Strip Clubs in the 1990s." *Dissertation Abstracts International, A: The Humanities and Social Sciences* 61(8):3378–A.

Chaftez, Janet S. and Anthony G. Dworkin. 1986. *Female Revolt: Women's Movements in World and Historical Perspective*. New York: Rowman & Allanheld.

Egan, R. Danielle. 2000. "The Phallus Palace: Stripping Spaces, Desiring Subjects and the Fantasy of Objects." *Dissertation Abstracts International, A: The Humanities and Social Sciences* 61:2066–A.

Enck, Graves E. and James D. Preston. 1988. "Counterfeit Intimacy: A Dramaturgical Analysis of an Erotic Performance." *Deviant Behavior* 9(4):369–381.

Foucault, Michel. 1977. *The History of Sexuality*, Vol. I: *An Introduction*. New York: Pantheon.

Hubbard, Phil, Roger Matthews, Jane Scoular, and Laura Agustin. 2008. "Away from Prying Eyes?' The Urban Geographies of 'Adult Entertainment.'" *Progress in Human Geography* 32(3):363–381.

Kitinger, Celia. 1994. "Problematizing Pleasure: Radical Feminist Deconstruction of Sexuality and Power." *Power and Gender* 9:104–209.

Lorius, Cassandra. 1996a. "Desire and the Gaze: Spectacular Bodies in Cairene Elite Weddings." *Women's Studies International Forum* 19(5):513–523.

——. 1996b. "'Oh Boy, You Salt of the Earth': Outwitting Patriarchy in Raqs Baladi." *Popular Music* 15(3):285–298.

Millman, Marcia. 1975. "She Did It All for Love: A Feminist View of the Sociology of Deviance." *Sociological Inquiry* 45(2–3):251–279.

Rambo, Carol, Sara Renee Presley, and Don Mynatt. 2006. "Claiming the Bodies of Exotic Dancers: The Problematic Discourse of Commodification." Pp. 213–228 in *Body/Embodiment: Symbolic Interaction and the Sociology of the Body*, edited by D. Waskul and P. Vannini. Burlington, VT: Ashgate.

Ronai, Carol Rambo and Rebecca Cross. 1998. "Dancing with Identity: Narrative Resistance Strategies of Male and Female Strippers." *Deviant Behavior: An Interdisciplinary Journal* 19:99–119.

Ronai, Carol Rambo and Carolyn Ellis. 1989. "Turn-ons for Money: Interactional Strategies of the Table Dancer." *Journal of Contemporary Ethnography* 16:271–298.

Ronai, Carol Rambo and Mary Nell Trautner. 2001. "Table and Lap Dancing." Pp. 402–405 in *The Encyclopedia of Criminology and Deviant Behavior*, Vol. III, edited by C. D. Bryant. Philadelphia, PA: Taylor & Francis.

Salutin, Marilyn. 1977. "Stripper Morality." Pp. 191–208 in *Deviant Life Styles*, edited by J. M. Henslin. New Brunswick, NJ: Transaction.

Thompson, William E., Jack L. Harred, and Barbara E. Burks. 2003. "Managing the Stigma of Topless Dancing: A Decade Later." *Deviant Behavior* 24(6):551–570.

Waskul, Dennis and Phillip Vannini. (2006). "The Body in Symbolic Interaction." Pp. 1–17 in *Body/Embodiment: Symbolic Interaction and the Sociology of the Body*, edited by D. Waskul and P. Vannini. Burlington, VT: Ashgate.

Wesely, Jennifer K. 2001. "Lived Experiences and Negotiated Gender: Female Exotic Dancing, Body Technologies and Violence." *Dissertation Abstracts International, A: The Humanities and Social Sciences* 62(2):782–A.

——. 2003. "Where Am I Going to Stop?: Exotic Dancing, Fluid Body Boundaries, and Effects on Identity." *Deviant Behavior* 24(5):483–503.

48

Aberrant forms of sexual behavior

Thomas S. Weinberg

From a symbolic interactionist perspective, the label "aberrant" is problematic, because such a label and its application are dependent upon some social audience with the power to make it stick. In turn, how these labelers see behavior is reliant upon the social context, which changes over time and from place to place. For example, the psychiatric profession is one of our society's most powerful labelers. The American Psychiatric Association's *Diagnostic and Statistical Manual of Mental Disorders* (*DSM*) defines many psychiatric behaviors. Yet, these definitions have changed over the years and through several editions of the *DSM*. At one time, for instance, homosexuality was defined as pathological. Later, at a meeting of the APA in 1974, it was decided to remove homosexuality from the *DSM*. Nymphomania, first defined as a form of mental illness in 1882 by the physician E. C. Abbey (Abbey 1882) and discussed in Richard von Krafft-Ebing's *Psychopathia Sexualis* four years later (Krafft-Ebing 1965 [1886]), is no longer in the *DSM*. Instead, there have been discussions about adding a category of sexual addiction or hypersexuality to the next edition.

There is a section on paraphilias in the fourth, revised edition of the *DSM*. Included in this section are exhibitionism, fetishism, frotteurism, pedophilia, sexual masochism, sexual sadism, transvestic fetishism, and voyeurism. There is also a category for "paraphilia not otherwise specified," which includes less common paraphilias, such as necrophilia, zoophilia, and others. These categories, closest to the label of aberrant sexuality, have been devastatingly critiqued by Moser and Kleinplatz (2005), who question the categorization of the paraphilias as mental disorders by the *DSM*. By so doing, they attack the underlying psychoanalytic assumptions of the paraphilia section.

In their analysis, Moser and Kleinplatz make a number of important points. They begin by using a social constructionist approach to point out that conceptions of mental disorders are made within a sociocultural context, thus making scientific definitions of healthy sexual behavior difficult to find. They deny that the paraphilias are mental disorders, noting that research has not provided data in support of this classification. In fact, they emphasize that non-clinical studies of individuals with unusual sexual interests do not distinguish them from those with conventional sexual interests. Additionally, Moser and Kleinplatz point out inconsistencies and contradictions within the *DSM* classification. They also provide specific instances in which statements appearing as fact in the section are not supported by research, including assertions about the sex ratio among masochists, the extent of injuries stemming from this behavior, and the prevalence of certain sexual practices. Claiming that the paraphilia section is not consistent with the current state of knowledge, they assert that criteria for such diagnoses rest on unproven and untested assumptions. Similarly, Reiersol and Skeid (2006) critique the usefulness of the classification of fetishism, fetishistic transvestism and sadomasochism in the *International Classification of Diseases* of the World Health Organization.

Traditionally, discussions of aberrant sexuality have taken a clinical approach, seeing these behaviors as individual psychopathology and utilizing case histories to validate their assertions (Caprio 1955; Chideckel 1963 [1935]; Krafft-Ebing 1965 [1886]; Stekel 1964 [1930]). However, many of these behaviors are also subcultural, which fundamentally alters how we view and understand their origins and practice. The advent of the internet, with its plethora of blogs, chat-rooms, web pages, and the like illustrates the subcultural nature of many of these forms of non-normative behavior.

Keeping these caveats in mind, this paper will discuss a few behaviors presently labeled as "aberrant."

Sadomasochism

Like many other forms of aberrant sexual behavior, sadomasochism, the eroticization of dominance and submission, has traditionally been viewed as an individual psychopathology (Freud 1938, 1953 [1905], 1959 [1924], 1961 [1920]; Krafft-Ebing 1965 [1886]; Ross 1997; Stekel 1965 [1929]). It was only four decades ago, beginning with the pioneering work of anthropologist Paul Gebhard (1969), that a more comprehensive view of this behavior as subcultural began to develop. Scores of articles on various social aspects of sadomasochism have been published since Gebhard's seminal paper, employing a variety of methodologies, including content analyses, survey research, in-depth interviews, and ethnography, and utilizing various theoretical perspectives, including symbolic interactionism, frame analysis, and postmodernism. Writers have noted that rather than being an isolated subculture, aspects of sadomasochism have found their way into popular culture and fashion (Falk and Weinberg 1983; Weinberg and Magill 1995). Social science research in sadomasochism over the past four decades indicates that this is a complex social phenomenon, not easily or accurately summed up by psycho-analytical perspectives. Contrary to the psychoanalytical view that SM is an individual psychopathology, sociological, social psychological, and anthropological studies see SM practitioners as emotionally and psychologically well balanced, generally comfortable with their sexual orientation, and socially well adjusted.

Characteristics of sadomasochism

Sociologists and social psychologists have identified a number of defining characteristics of sadomasochism. It is about the ritualization of dominance and submission and not necessarily about pain. SMers often consider their behavior to be a power exchange (Ernulf and Innala 1995; Hoople 1996; Moser 1988). SM is recreational or play-like behavior (Moser 1998), which is set aside from other aspects of life. Sadomasochistic behavior thus involves fantasy in varying degrees. Frequently, sadomasochistic scenarios are scripted; individuals play designated roles during their interaction. This serves to confine the behavior only to that episode, keeping it from spilling over to other aspects of life. Using fantasy, sadomasochistic scenes are framed by social definitions that give the behavior a specific contextual meaning (Weinberg 1978). It is this fantasy frame that allows participants to engage in behaviors or roles that are usually not permitted in everyday life, enabling them to enjoy themselves without feeling guilt (Weinberg 1978).

Sadomasochistic scenes are both consensual and collaboratively produced (Newmahr 2008; Weinberg 1978, 1987, 2006; Weinberg and Falk 1980). What may appear to the uninitiated observer to be spontaneous behavior is often carefully planned. Forced participation is not acceptable within the subculture; it is only the *illusion* that individuals are coerced that is approved by sadomasochists. Participants must agree on what will take place during the scene and carefully discuss limits to the interaction, as well as specific fantasies or scenarios (Moser 1998), insuring that both derive pleasure from their participation. Moser (1998) notes, however, that when SMers know each other well, this discussion may not always take place. Kamel (1980) points out that risk is reduced through agreement on norms and values within the subculture.

Sadomasochistic behavior is highly symbolic; a variety of devices, such as clothing (Brodsky 1993), the use of language, the utilization of restraints, and so forth, serve to indicate a participant's role, either dominant or submissive, in the interaction.

Sadomasochistic identity

Kamel (1980; see also Kamel and Weinberg 1983) demonstrated that for gay leathermen, becoming a sadomasochist was part of an interactive process or "career," during which the individual becomes aware of role expectations and is socialized into the community. The first sadomasochistic experience often, but not always, precedes "coming out," which refers to the process of coming to terms with a sadomasochist self-identity and entry into the subculture (Moser and Levitt 1987). There may be gender differences in this process, although the literature on coming out is unclear. Some people who have not previously recognized any SM interests become involved in sadomasochism through a variety of relationships. Breslow *et al.* (1985) found that another person had introduced over 60% of the women they studied to SM. While Breslow *et al.* found that men reported first developing an interest in SM on average six years earlier than females (14.99 years versus 21.58 years), Moser and Levitt (1987) found that women and men came out and participated in sadomasochistic behavior at about the same age. Coming out in the Moser and Levitt sample occurred at 22.9 years for males (Moser and Levitt 1987) and 22.7 years for females (Levitt *et al.* 1994). Bezreh (2009: 28) found that "13 of 20 respondents reported that they were aware of fantasies or feelings related to SM by age 15. Seven respondents reported that awareness by age ten."

Sadomasochistic subcultures

It is inaccurate to speak generically of the sadomasochistic subculture. There are many different sadomasochistic worlds organized around sexual orientation, gender, and preferred activities. For example, there are heterosexual, gay male "leathersex," and lesbian subcultures. There are more specialized subcultures devoted to bondage and discipline (B & D), which is used to describe the combination of restraint and control with punishment or humiliation, and body modifications like genital piercing, branding, burning, and cutting. Some SM practitioners make distinctions between sadomasochism, dominance and submission, and bondage and discipline. Often, however, there are blendings and overlaps among these subcultures, and a variety of practitioners may interact in parties or clubs (Moser 1998).

Sadomasochists enter their subcultures in a variety of ways. In addition to being introduced to these practices by another person, they meet others by placing and responding to advertisements in specialized publications, through chat-rooms on the internet, and by joining formally organized SM clubs, such as the Eulenspiegel Society and the Society of Janus. These societies function as support groups and agents of socialization into SM. They provide information about sadomasochistic practices and develop and maintain justifications, ideologies, and neutralizations, which allow members to engage in these activities while avoiding a deviant self-identity. There are also SM bars in which sadomasochists can find one another and engage in sadomasochistic scenes. Additionally, sadomasochists hold private parties, sometimes with more than 500 participants (Moser 1998).

Fetishism and partialism

Fetishism is sexual arousal by an inanimate object, while partialism refers to the generation of sexual excitement by a body part. Both of these behaviors have been traditionally dealt with as clinical aberrations. Caprio (1955: 265), for example, defines fetishism as "a form of sexual deviation in which the person's libido becomes fixated to something that constitutes a symbol of the love-object." Stekel (1964 [1930]: 3) notes that:

> The personal form of sexual attraction varies with different persons on the basis of a kind of fetishism, i.e., everyone prefers certain characteristics or attributes in his sexual objects ... We call them normal fetishes. They become pathological only when they have pushed the whole love object into the background and themselves appropriate the function of a love object.

Many of the erotic attractions of fetishists are learned within the larger culture and reflect knowledge of culturally learned symbols of sexuality. For instance, the fascination large female breasts hold for some men may have its roots in popular culture. The 1950s icon Dagmar, for example, was a celebrity so well known for her mammary endowment that car bumpers of the day were named after her. Women undergo breast enhancement partly because of the societal norm that larger breasts are more attractive. Some fetishes seem to be traceable to the era in which fetishists grew up. For example, preoccupation with separate garter belts and stockings in an earlier era appears to have been replaced with erotic attraction to pantyhose.

As with many other sexual variations, there are subcultures for fetishists and partialists. The advent of the internet not only facilitates communication among fetishists but provides materials for their satisfaction. Both pay and free internet sites enable fetishists to indulge their fantasies. There are, for example, sites for those interested in shoes, feet, smoking, face-sitting, pantyhose, cheerleaders, hairy women, female body builders, and so on.

Weinberg, Williams, and Calhan (1995) used mailed questionnaires to study a non-clinical sample of 262 gay and bisexual men who belonged to a mail organization catering to foot fetishists. They found that "it does not appear that our group of fetishists is much different in the extent of their psychological problems than wider populations ... fewer than one in four clearly fit the picture of the psychologically troubled fetishist found in the literature" (Weinberg, Williams, and Calhan 1995: 24).

Frottage

Frottage, also called frotteurism, the rubbing of one's genitals against another's body for sexual gratification, has barely been noted in the sociological literature. It may be either consensual or non-consensual. Consensual frottage was discussed by Paul Cressey (1968 [1932]) in his study of taxi-dance halls. Some of the female employees in these halls engaged in "sensual dancing," allowing their paying dance partners to rub their genitals against them. This was one of several techniques used to increase their customer base and, hence, their earnings. Generations of teenagers have practiced "dry humping" as a way of avoiding actual sexual intercourse. Sexual rubbing is also engaged in by gay men and women.

Non-consensual frottage is a form of sexual assault. It occurs in crowded public situations like bars, subway trains, and buses:

> I was seated in a crowded streetcar with standing room only during rush hour. An elderly man, probably in his mid-seventies, climbed aboard. Almost immediately, he found a spot behind a young woman, reaching over her to grasp the hanger. As the streetcar lurched forward, he pressed against her backside. I would not have paid much attention to this except that he maintained his position, even when additional space became available.
>
> After several blocks had passed, the young woman exited the streetcar. Quickly, the man found another young woman and positioned himself similarly behind her. After this woman left the car, he once again found a young woman and pressed against her. Finally, he left the streetcar.
>
> *(Author's field notes)*

This episode is instructive as an example of how one frotteur selected his victims and was able to carry out his private sexual aberrance within a very public setting. First, all of his victims were similar in appearance, although two were Caucasian and one was Asian. They were young, probably in their late teens or early twenties, petite, slim, and had long, straight hair. Second, the man used the ambiguity of the situation—a crowded vehicle that swayed back and forth, starting and stopping abruptly—to conceal his deviant motives. By selecting young women, he was probably assuming that they would be somewhat naive and less likely to confront him than an older, more experienced individual. He also used the possibility that the setting provided for multiple explanations of his behavior, which may have made the women reluctant to confront him and cause a public scene. He could, if challenged, use the ambiguity of the setting to proclaim his innocence.

While frottage is an individual behavior, there is some indication of the beginning of a formation of a subculture of frotteurs. For instance, there is an anonymous web group called "I Like Frottage" (www.experienceproject.com/groups/like-frottage/230720). However, it claims only three members and has no posts.

Bestiality and zoophilia

Sexual contact with animals (bestiality) and sexual preference for animals (zoophilia) are depicted in myth and legend (Cornog and Perper 1994; King 2002; Rathus, Nevid, and Fichner-Rathus 2008). They have also been the subject of films and plays (*Equus*, 1977; *Futz!*, 1969). Yet, sex researchers other than psychiatrists (Caprio 1955; Krafft-Ebing 1965 [1886]) have not paid much attention to these forms of sexuality, and as Williams and Weinberg (2003) point out, even sexuality texts devote little space to this behavior. There are exceptions to the general avoidance of this topic, however. In Alfred Kinsey's pioneering studies (Kinsey, Pomeroy, and Martin 1948; Kinsey, Pomeroy, Martin, and Gebhard 1953), he presented data indicating that a small percentage of both men and women engaged in sex with animals. Hunt (1974) also found a small proportion of men and women in his sample had had sexual contacts with animals. In August B. Hollingshead's classic study of *Elmtown's Youth* (1949: 416), he describes contact between young men and farm animals:

> During these early adolescent years a considerable proportion of these boys develop a behavior pattern which brings them into contact with farm animals on a scale that has only

recently been emphasized. Young farm boys have relations with animals more frequently than the town boys, but town boys often visit friends in the country and in the course of their play a visit to the barn is not unusual. Twenty-six boys admit that they have had intercourse with animals at one time or another—calves most frequently, but mares, sows, and ewes are included.

Sexual contact with animals is not confined to youths. In July 2009, a 50-year-old South Carolina man was arrested and charged with having sex with a horse. This was the second time he had been arrested for the same offense with the same animal. The horse's owner had installed a surveillance camera in the stable and caught him *in flagrante*. He had previously been ordered to undergo psychiatric treatment and had been given medication (Associated Press 2009).

Sex with animals remains controversial. Wisch (2008) notes that 30 states have passed legislation that prohibits sexual contact between humans and animals. Beirne (2001) makes a strong case that human–animal sex is wrong because it involves coercion, produces pain and suffering, and violates the rights of another being.

The definitive work on zoophilia to date has been done by Williams and Weinberg (2003). They studied a sample of 114 self-identified zoophile men, obtained through an internet website and snowball sampling. Additionally, they attended a gathering of some of these men and conducted face-to-face and telephone interviews. The men were well educated, most of them were single and had never married, and many were working in technical fields. Their median age was 27. The subjects made a distinction between bestiality and zoophilia, noting that the former simply indicated having sex with animals, while the later indicated real love and affection for them. The major reason for having sex with animals, according to these men, was the desire for affection and pleasurable sex. They saw animals as more honest and unconditionally loving than humans. Williams and Weinberg emphasize the importance of the internet in bringing zoophiles together as a subcultural community.

Conclusion

This brief survey of a few types of aberrant sexual expression indicates that these behaviors have to be explored sociologically as well as psychiatrically to be fully understood. They are not merely individual behaviors but socially reinforced and supported by subcultural groups, which provide their members with accounts, justifications, rationalizations, and neutralizations, enabling them to normalize their desires and behaviors and make them appear to be acceptable. The ubiquity and accessibility of the internet facilitates contact among like-minded individuals, thus promoting the formation of these subcultures.

References

Abbey, E. C. (1882) *The Sexual System and Its Derangement*, Buffalo, NY.

American Psychiatric Association (2000) *Diagnostic and Statistical Manual of Mental Disorders*, 4th rev. edn, Washington, DC: American Psychiatric Association.

Associated Press (2009) "Stable owner catches man having sex with horse," July 29. Online. Available at: www.chron.com/disp/story.mpl/bizarre/6553012.html (accessed September 29, 2009)

Beirne, P. (2001) "Peter Singer's 'heavy petting' and the politics of animal sexual assault," *Critical Criminology* 10:43–55.

Bezreh, T. (2009) "The dilemma of disclosure: developing resources for 'coming out' about sadomasochism," unpublished thesis, Emerson College.

Breslow, N., Evans, L., and Langley, J. (1985) "On the prevalence and roles of females in the sadomasochistic subculture: report on an empirical study," *Archives of Sexual Behavior* 14: 303–317.

Brodsky, J. I. (1993) "The mineshaft: a retrospective ethnography," *Journal of Homosexuality* 24(3/4): 233–251.

Caprio, F. S. (1955) *Variations in Sexual Behavior*, New York: Grove Press.

Chideckel, M. (1963 [1935]) *Female Sex Perversions: The Sexually Aberrated Woman as She Is*, New York: Brown Book Company.

Cornog, M. and Perper, T. (1994) "Bestiality," in V. L. Bullough and B. Bullough (eds) *Human Sexuality: An Encyclopedia* (pp. 60–63), New York: Garland.

Cressey, P. G. (1968 [1932]) *The Taxi-Dance Hall: A Sociological Study in Commercialized Recreation and City Life*, New York: Greenwood Press.

Ernulf, K. E. and Innala, S. M. (1995) "Sexual bondage: a review and unobtrusive investigation," *Archives of Sexual Behavior* 24: 631–654.

Falk, G. and Weinberg, T. S. (1983) "Sadomasochism and popular Western culture," in T. Weinberg and G. W. L. Kamel (eds) *S and M: Studies in Sadomasochism* (pp. 37–144), Buffalo, NY: Prometheus Books.

Freud, S. (1938) *The Basic Writings of Sigmund Freud*, trans. A. A. Brill, New York: Modern Library.

—— (1953 [1905]) "Three essays on sexuality," trans. J. Strachey, in J. Strachey (ed.) *The Standard Edition of the Complete Psychological Works of Sigmund Freud*, vol. VII (pp. 135–230), London: Hogarth Press.

—— (1959 [1924]) "The economic problem in masochism," trans. J. Riviere, in E. Jones and J. Riviere (eds) *Sigmund Freud, Collected Papers*, vol. II (pp. 255–276), New York: Basic Books.

—— (1961 [1920]) *Beyond the Pleasure Principle*, trans. J. Strachey, New York: Liveright.

Gebhard, P. (1969) "Fetishism and sadomasochism," in J. H. Masserman (ed.) *Dynamics of Deviant Sexuality* (pp. 71–80), New York: Grune & Stratton.

Hollingshead, A. B. (1949) *Elmtown's Youth: The Impact of Social Classes on Adolescents*, New York: John Wiley & Sons.

Hoople, T. (1996) "Conflicting visions: SM, feminism, and the law, a problem of representation," *Canadian Journal of Law and Society* 11(1): 177–220.

Hunt, M. (1974) *Sexual Behavior in the 1970s*, Chicago, IL: Playboy Press.

Kamel, G. W. L. (1980) "Leathersex: meaningful aspects of gay sadomasochism," *Deviant Behavior: An Interdisciplinary Journal* 1: 171–191.

Kamel, G. W. L. and Weinberg, T. S. (1983) "Diversity in sadomasochism: four S&M careers," in T. Weinberg and G.W. L. Kamel (eds.) *S and M: Studies in Sadomasochism* (pp. 113–128), Buffalo, NY: Prometheus Books.

King, B. M. (2002) *Human Sexuality Today*, 4th edn, Upper Saddle River, NJ: Prentice-Hall.

Kinsey, A. C., Pomeroy, W. B., and Martin, C. E. (1948) *Sexual Behavior in the Human Male*, Philadelphia, PA: W. B. Saunders.

Kinsey, A. C., Pomeroy, W. B., Martin, C. E., and Gebhard, P. H. (1953) *Sexual Behavior in the Human Female*, Philadelphia, PA: W. B. Saunders.

Krafft-Ebing, R. von (1965 [1886]) *Psychopathia Sexualis*, trans. F. S. Klaff, New York: Stein & Day.

Levitt, E. E., Moser, C., and Jamison, K. V. (1994) "The prevalence and some attributes of females in the sadomasochistic subculture: a second report," *Archives of Sexual Behavior* 23: 465–473.

Moser, C. (1988) "Sadomasochism," *Journal of Social Work and Human Sexuality* 7(1): 43–56.

—— (1998) "S/M (sadomasochistic) interactions in semi-public settings," *Journal of Homosexuality* 36: 19–29.

Moser, C. and Kleinplatz, P. J. (2005) "*DSM-IV-TR* and the paraphilias: an argument for removal," *Journal of Psychology & Human Sexuality* 17(3/4): 91–109.

Moser, C. and Levitt, E. E. (1987) "An exploratory-descriptive study of sadomasochistically oriented sample," *Journal of Sex Research* 23: 322–337.

Newmahr, S. (2008) "Becoming a sadomasochist, integrating self and other in ethnographic analysis," *Journal of Contemporary Ethnography* 37: 619–643.

Rathus, S. A., Nevid, J. S., and Fichner-Rathus, L. (2008) *Human Sexuality in a World of Diversity*, 7th edn, Boston, MA: Allyn & Bacon.

Reiersol, O. and Skeid, S. (2006) "The ICD diagnoses of fetishism and masochism," in P. J. Kleinplatz and C. Moser (eds) *Sadomasochism: Powerful Pleasures* (pp. 243–262), New York: Harrington Park Press.

Ross, J. M. (1997) *The Sadomasochism of Everyday Life*, New York: Simon & Schuster.

Stekel, W. (1964 [1930]) *Sexual Aberrations*, New York: Grove Press.

—— (1965 [1929]) *Sadism and Masochism: The Psychology of Hatred and Cruelty*, vol. II, New York: Grove Press.

Weinberg, M. S., Williams, C. J., and Calhan, C. (1995) "'If the shoe fits . . .' exploring male homosexual foot fetishism," *Journal of Sex Research* 32: 17–27.

Thomas S. Weinberg

Weinberg, T. S. (1978) "Sadism and masochism: sociological perspectives," *Bulletin of the American Academy of Psychiatry and the Law* 6: 284–295.

—— (1987) "Sadomasochism in the United States: a review of recent sociological literature," *Journal of Sex Research* 23: 50–69.

——(2006) "Sadomasochism and the social sciences: a review of the sociological and social psychological literature," in P. J. Kleinplatz and C. Moser (eds) *Sadomasochism: Powerful Pleasures* (pp. 17–40), New York: Harrington Park Press.

Weinberg, T. S. and Falk G. (1980) "The social organization of sadism and masochism," *Deviant Behavior: An Interdisciplinary Journal* 1: 379–393.

Weinberg, T. S. and Magill, M. S. (1995) "Sadomasochistic themes in mainstream culture," in T. Weinberg (ed.) *S & M: Studies in Dominance and Submission* (pp. 223–230), Amherst, NY: Prometheus Books.

Williams, C. J. and Weinberg, M. S. (2003) "Zoophilia in men: a study of sexual interest in animals," *Archives of Sexual Behavior* 32(6): 523–535.

Wisch, Rebecca F. (2008) "Overview of state bestiality laws," East Lansing, MI: Animal Legal & Historical Web Center. Online. Available at: www.animallaw.info/articles/art_details/print.htm (accessed October 19, 2009).

Part X
Crimes of the times

Overview

Some forms of crime date back to ancient times and are as durable as granite. Other configurations of crime are relatively new or newly emerging—crimes of the times, as it were. Many types of crime and deviance are linked to the development of new technology.

This part contains chapters that address some of these crimes of the times, beginning with an examination of "cyber crime." The computer has spawned a vast array of criminal opportunity structures and miscreants have not let these go by, but rather have seized and exploited most of them. The next chapter also deals with computers and examines identity theft. One's identity can be appropriated through a number of techniques, but computers will likely be involved at some stage in the process. Identity theft is reaching epidemic proportions and can have very serious implications for the victims.

Intellectual property misappropriation has been a crime since the inauguration of copyright laws, but the range of products now labeled as intellectual property has increased significantly. Beyond this, the techniques for reproducing books, pictures, recordings, movies, and so on have advanced to the point where intellectual property theft can be accomplished with the push of a button and on a massive scale.

In recent years, the workplace has become something of a "combat zone." Acts of physical violence and/or psychological abuse have occurred with some degree of frequency in today's workplaces. Employees may be victims of such harm committed by outsiders, customers or clients, someone with whom they may have a personal relationship, or even the organization itself. Workplace violence can have serious consequences for employees, employers, and the public.

The computer can be used as an instrument of harm. There are emerging patterns of harm perpetrated by some who wish to inflict verbal abuse on others. These patterns of harm include cyberbullying, cyberharassing, and cyberstalking. The perpetrators may view such activities as malicious fun, but the victims of such abuse may experience anxiety, fear, and other types of emotional distress, which, in some cases, have motivated them to commit suicide.

Recent years have seen the social and economic value and worth of natural resources and the environment in which they exist soar. Western society has become very protective of the environment and ecology, and degrading either is being redefined as a crime.

Terrorism on a massive scale has become almost commonplace. The new awareness of this global threat has brought about social challenges of a very profound nature. The enemies of the West seek its destruction, and terrorism has become a major tool in trying to accomplish this.

Cybercrime

In the initial chapter in this part, Stephen Rosoff and Henry Pontell explore the world of "cyber-crime." Perhaps no device in history has opened the door for, or facilitated, new configurations of crime more than the computer. It has offered vast vistas of criminal opportunities and these new vistas of crime will undoubtedly expand in the future.

Rosoff and Pontell provide several definitions of computer crime, including the all-encompassing and very generic definition of "computer crime as any intentional act associated with computers where a victim suffers a loss and a perpetrator makes a gain." Computer crime began with the "blue box," a device developed by young technological wizards who called themselves "phone phreaks," which made it possible to gain unauthorized access to the telephone network for the purpose of making long-distance calls without paying charges. Toll fraud losses today are now almost $4 billion annually.

The number of computers has increased exponentially in the last few decades, and they are now available to almost everyone in the Western world, including both amateur miscreants and career criminals. The authors assert that computer crime is "the fastest-growing category of crime in America." The same is true internationally.

Computers have been used to submit false income tax refund claims, to exchange child pornography, to "launder" drug money, to facilitate prostitution, and to maintain illegal gambling records, to mention but a few of their illicit uses. Hardware theft for illegal resale is a major criminal activity. Software is expensive and, accordingly, it is pirated (known as "soft-lifting") and counterfeited. It is estimated that in many European and Asian countries, between 75 and 90 percent of the total software in use is pirated US software. The computer has also been an enormous aid and facilitator of embezzlement and financial theft.

Hacking is perpetrated for both fun and profit. Hackers comprise a creative subculture and subscribe to their own peculiar code of ethics, known as the "cyberpunk imperatives." Malicious hacking has even posed a threat to national security.

Computers have also been used to perpetrate sophisticated identity theft scams. "Viruses" and "worms" are sometimes used to attack computer systems, doing very costly damage. "Phishing" is a technique used to obtain passwords and codes that are useful to hackers in illegally accessing computer systems and accounts for fraudulent or larcenous purposes.

Rosoff and Pontell point out that "the misuse of computers as tools for industrial, political, and international espionage is another cause for major concern." They also warn that even though computer security technology is improving all the time, miscreants have thus far tended to keep one step ahead of it.

Identity theft

In their chapter, Henry Pontell and Gregory C. Brown provide an overview of "the fastest-growing crime in America." Identity theft may involve the theft of driver's licenses, credit cards, social security numbers, or other identifying documents. It can also involve the creation of a fictitious identity to facilitate criminal acts. A state law in Arizona, passed in 1996, legally defined identity theft. A federal law, passed two years later, made it a matter of national concern.

Identity theft is linked to other new forms of crime, such as computer crime, and to new financial and organizational arrangements that involve large amounts of identity information being stored in massive databases. The chapter articulates three configurations of identity theft: financial identity theft, criminal identity theft, and identity cloning. Identity information can be obtained through theft of identity documents, hacking into databases, bribing employees of database organizations, sorting through trash ("dumpster diving"), or "phishing" (using e-mails to dupe someone into providing their personal information), among other ploys.

It is a major form of new crime. Between 2000 and 2005, there were 27 million victims of identity theft. Victims are harmed in two ways. They may suffer significant financial loss, but they may also spend considerable time and effort trying to reestablish their economic identity. Side-effects of this process may include physical and psychological problems, family dysfunction, damaged financial reputation, and anger and frustration that attend efforts to "coordinate legal responses and contact official agencies."

Pontell and Brown indicate that identity theft is increasingly taking on an international scale. Not only individuals but corporations and large government agencies are being victimized. Identity theft is generally not a white-collar crime, inasmuch as most "offenders possess no legitimate occupational status." Organized crime is involved, too.

Until recently, criminologists have had only modest interest in identity theft. One industry response has been the selling of identity theft insurance to the public. The authors conclude with the observation that "official responses that encourage citizens to guard their information more carefully are certainly important, but so, too, is the fact that their personal information is no longer entirely in their control."

Intellectual property offenses

In the United States, intellectual property includes the rights conferred by copyright, patent, and trademark law. The violation of these rights is a civil offense, but when the rights are violated in a willful fashion, and oriented toward financial gain, it is a criminal offense. The unauthorized duplication of computer software for commercial gain is a criminal offense.

David F. Luckenbill and Kirk Miller indicate that there are two principal intellectual property offenses—piracy and counterfeiting. An example of piracy would be copying a DVD. An example of counterfeiting would be making a cheap imitation of a consumer good, putting the trademark of a famous brand on it, and selling it as if it were genuine.

Intellectual property owners wish to maintain a monopoly over the use of their property in order to reap profits from its use. Consumer rights groups and scholars feel that people should be able to draw freely on intellectual objects in order to create new creative entities, and pursue personally and socially fulfilling ends. The conflict is complex.

Intellectual property offenses are almost endemic throughout the world, as a result of the availability and accessibility of inexpensive and effective copying devices, such as personal computers, optical scanners, paper duplication machines, and audio and visual recorders. In some countries, intellectual property piracy is big business.

While property owners have mobilized the legal system to strengthen their exclusive rights, consumers and consumer groups have been very vocal and vigorous in their opposition, insisting that "locking up virtually every use" of intellectual property impedes creativity and "makes for an intellectually weaker and less vibrant society."

Violence in the workplace

The workplace can be, and often is, hazardous and dangerous. The hazardous context may be a matter of unsafe working conditions, unsafe work processes, working with unsafe products or materials, and/or the possibility of accidents and even death. The workplace can also be dangerous because of the possibility of physical violence and/or psychological abuse while at work.

Spyridon Kodellas, Bonnie Fisher, and Martin Gill address the latter in their chapter. They indicate that workplace violence can have dire consequences for the "physical and psychological well-being of employees (and possibly their families) and can result in significant economic costs to the employers and social costs on the public." They suggest that such workplace violence has not been fully researched.

There are multiple definitions of workplace violence and little consensus on any. These definitions constitute a continuum ranging from serious harm, such as murder, to simple verbal abuse. The authors articulate four types of workplace violence: external or intrusive violence (committed by an outsider); consumer-related violence (customer becomes violent while being served); relationship violence (employee attacks a colleague, or violent acts committed by someone who has a personal relationship with an employee); and organizational violence (violent acts committed by the organization against staff or customer/clients).

Kodellas, Fisher, and Gill also bifurcate workplace violence into physical violence and psychological abuse and provide examples of each. They discuss a number of organizations and government agencies that collect data on workplace violence around the world.

Various risk factors are associated with workplace violence, and some occupations are more at risk than others. The authors list a number of risk factors and the most vulnerable occupations, as well as a variety of preventative measures.

Finally, they discuss the impact of workplace violence, and examine several negative consequences for organizations, employees, and their families. Costs to society include "healthcare (including mental health) and medical treatment costs, the loss of a productive workforce, and those associated with early retirement, long-term unemployment, and welfare dependency." Behavioral scientists have much more to learn about the etiology of workplace violence, and research opportunities in this sphere are quite broad.

Cyberbullying, cyberharassing, and cyberstalking

Recently, the media has reported on several adolescent victims of cyberbullying who consequently committed suicide. Cyberbullying is not an innocuous, humorous teasing activity among teenagers. Rather, it is a sinister and serious means of inflicting harm on others, and it may have fatal consequences.

In their chapter, Keith Durkin and Denay Patterson indicate that "cyberharassment" refers to a variety of behaviors that utilize the internet and other communication devices to menace someone. They advise that when cyberharassing involves young people, the label "cyberbullying" is more appropriate. This type of communication can range from insults or name-calling to death threats. Techniques used in cyberharassment might include attempts to ruin the reputation of, and stigmatize, the victim. This is known as "cybersmearing." The posting of sexually defamatory messages about, or pictures of, an individual on the internet is termed "cybersexual defamation." The aim of such efforts is to humiliate or embarrass the victim. Sometimes victims may be sent unsolicited, hostile text messages or e-mails. This is known as "cyberstalking." Victims of the various types of cyberbullying often experience anxiety, fear, and other types of emotional distress. Victimization may lead to poor academic performance and, in some instances, school dropout.

Relatively little empirical research has been conducted on cyberbullying, but one study indicated that 22.8% of women and 13.5% of men reported being a victim of it. Another revealed that 18% of boys and 16% of girls had been perpetrators at one time or another.

Cyberharassment and related behaviors seem to be linked to heavy internet usage and the nature of the internet, which offers anonymity and therefore has a "disinhibition effect." Perpetrators are "physically removed from their victims." Durkin and Patterson assert that, inasmuch as computer-mediated communication provides anonymity, it also tends to encourage anti-normative behavior.

Ecological crime

In his chapter, Rob White explores the parameters of the criminalization of ecological and environmental harm, or "green criminology," as he terms it. He points out that this is a relatively new area of research and scholarship, developed as a means to "stretch the boundaries of mainstream criminology to accommodate issues of global significance," such as the protection of the environment and the world's flora and fauna.

The development of green criminology was facilitated by the publication of a number of books that presented a new vocabulary of new terms and concepts, such as "ecological citizenship," "environmental justice," "crimes against nature," and "environmentalism," to mention but a few.

The concept of transnational environmental crime encompasses a multitude of deviant acts, ranging from the illegal transport and dumping of toxic waste, to the safe disposal of old ships and airplanes, to illegal trade in flora and fauna. The existence of such practices calls for new ways of conceptualizing matters relevant to environmental harm. One such matter has to do with the distinction between what is legal and what is illegal, inasmuch as many forms of environmental harm are currently still legal.

The concept of environmental crime has inevitably generated initiatives among groups on either side of the issue to protect their interests. For example, some campaigners have committed crimes themselves, such as tree spiking or damaging earthmoving equipment, in defense of the environment. The most serious of these acts—such as liberating animals from fur farms or laboratories and firebombing SUVs—are labeled "ecoterrorism." On the other side of the issue, large corporations have filed SLAPPs (Strategic Lawsuits Against Public Participation) to thwart public debate and involvement in regard to controversial developments that might be harmful to the environment. Another tactic is "greenwashing," propaganda that puts a corporate "spin" on environmental issues and problems.

White concludes his chapter with the assertion that "Eco-global criminology entails the exposure of [destructive or eco-harmful] practices as negative, degrading and hazardous by reconceptualising the nature of harm and putting the case for the banning and close control of such practices."

Terrorism and terrorists

In the final chapter of this part, Emilio Viano provides a very comprehensive and detailed socio-historical overview of terrorism and terrorists. He initially informs the reader that the definition of terrorism used by the United States government is "premeditated, politically motivated violence perpetrated against non-combatant targets by subnational groups or clandestine agents, usually intended to influence an audience." Thus, according to Viano, to be classed as terrorism, an act must be premeditated; have political motivation; attack people who cannot defend themselves or respond in kind; and be planned and carried out by a group. Viano emphasizes that "terrorism is . . . a method rather than a group of enemies or the objectives they want to realize."

He indicates that the word "terrorism" originated in the French Revolution and the "reign of terror" which followed it. The revolution provided inspiration for independence and nationalist movements, while the massive industrialization of Europe and the subsequent alienation and exploitation of workers created the conditions that nourished the creation and "growing of new 'universalist' ideologies like socialism and communism." By the late 19th century, the anarchist movement was seeking to bring about revolutionary change through the use of "tyrannicide and terrorism."

In time, "terrorism" came to refer to "the politics and practices of mass oppression and repression utilized by dictatorships against their own citizenry," such as the regimes of Hitler, Mussolini, and Stalin. In the decades after the Second World War, dictatorships emerged in South and Central America, Africa, Asia, the Middle East, and Europe. Soon, the indigenous populations of many African and Asian nations sought "liberation, decolonization and self-determination, and depended on uprisings and terrorism to achieve these goals." This was followed by "the growing menace of state-sponsored terrorism."

More recent times have seen the growth of criminally sponsored "narcoterrorism," while the dawn of the 21st century witnessed the emergence of another form of terrorism, sponsored by al-Qaeda, which seeks to destroy the West and all secular state systems. The world now lives in fear of terrorists obtaining weapons of mass destruction and mounting major cyberterrorist attacks that could result in "Cybergeddon."

49

Cybercrime

Stephen M. Rosoff and Henry N. Pontell

Cybercrime, or computer crime, has been defined broadly as "the destruction, theft, or unauthorized or illegal use, modification, or copying of information, programs, services, equipment, or communication networks" (Perry 1986). Donn B. Parker (1983), one of the United States' leading computer crime researchers, offers a less formal definition of it as any intentional act associated with computers where a victim suffers a loss and a perpetrator makes a gain. Under these definitional guidelines, the following offenses could all be classified as computer crimes:

- electronic embezzlement and financial theft;
- computer hacking;
- malicious sabotage, including the creation, installation, or dissemination of computer viruses;
- internet scams; and
- the utilization of computers and computer networks for purposes of personal, commercial or international espionage.

Before examining each of these offenses, however, we will consider the history of this problem and how fast it has grown.

For obvious reasons, computer crime has a relatively short history. Its most immediate precursor was the invention of the so-called "blue box" in the early 1960s. This was an illegal electronic device capable of duplicating the multifrequency dialing system developed by AT&T. The telephone company had described its new direct-dialing technology in its technical journals, apparently confident that no one in the general public would ever read (or at least understand) such esoteric information. "Ma Bell" became the first casualty of the first law of electronic crime: if it can be done, someone will do it. Motivated by a curious blend of mischievousness and greed, a cadre of young wizards tape-recorded piccolos and other high-pitched sounds to create the blue box, which gave them unauthorized access to the entire Bell network. They called themselves "phone phreaks." One ingenious phreak even discovered that a free whistle, given away in Cap'n Crunch cereal packets, produced a perfect 2,600-cycle tone that allowed him to place overseas telephone calls without paying charges.

A 1992 congressional committee estimated that toll fraud cost $2.3 billion annually (Quinn 1992; Taff 1992). The following year, the International Communications Association complained to the Federal Communications Commission (FCC) that 550 incidents of toll fraud had cost its members $73.5 million over a five-year period (Dodd 1993). Long-distance carriers are reluctant to reveal how much they lose each year to computer fraud, but in the mid-1990s one expert estimated that losses approached $4 billion. Of course, these costs were subsequently passed on to customers as a covert "fraud tax" (Titch 1994).

By the time the phone phreak subculture had established itself, the fledgling computer industry had graduated from the self-contained mainframe to interactive linkage and primitive networks. Once again, the first law of electronic crime was activated, as computer buffs could now use terminals to explore powerful mainframes that had previously been off-limits. A new term entered the public lexicon—"hacker." In the 1970s, the early hackers began using school computers for a variety of misdeeds—most notably the alteration of grades. However, since few schools even had computers then, hacking was a relatively minor nuisance.

Today, of course, that is no longer the case. Virtually all schools in the United States have computers—and hackers. By the end of the 1970s, modems and computerized bulletin board services (BBSs) had appeared; and by the early 1980s, the home PC had become increasingly common. This was the missing ingredient for the hackers—a high-tech skeleton key that could open myriad locked doors. For example, in 1985, twenty-three teenagers broke into a Chase Manhattan Bank computer by telephone, and proceeded to destroy accounting records and change passwords. No money was stolen, but customers were effectively denied access to their own files (Francis 1987).

Predictably, the first generation of hackers, for all their mischief, were only setting the stage for far more insidious types of computer crime. What may have begun as a questionable hobby shared by a network of adolescent misfits has been coopted by a much more malevolent class of white-collar criminal. Some individuals began employing the basic hacker methodology to break into systems, not as a prank, but to steal. "Computers have created opportunities for career criminals, an increasing number of whom are becoming computer literate" (Parker 1989: 15). An early (and ongoing) example involves the planting of an unauthorized program known as a Trojan horse. This program can transfer money automatically to an illegal account whenever a legal transaction is made (Perry 1986). To many skilled thieves and embezzlers, this was akin to striking the mother lode.

Computer crime was soon being labeled the fastest-growing category of crime in America (Meyer 1995). A 1993 survey reported that 70 percent of the 400-plus companies responding admitted to at least one security infringement in the previous twelve months; 24 percent put the loss per incident at more than $100,000 (*PC User* 1993).[1] Of the 150 large companies surveyed by Michigan State University in 1995, 148 said they had suffered from computer crime; 43 percent said they had been victimized 25 times or more (Anthes 1995).

By the early 1990s, computer crime was well established throughout the developed world, for instance in Canada (Wood 1988), Mexico (Sherizen 1992), the United Kingdom (Sykes 1992;[2] Hearnden 1986; Evans 1991), Sweden (Saari 1987), the Netherlands (Norman 1989), Germany (Hafner and Markoff 1991), Switzerland (Bird 1994) and Italy (Rockwell 1990). Viruses were being created everywhere from Bulgaria to South Africa (Sherizen 1992). Hackers were plying their trade in France and Israel (Major 1993), India and Singapore (Gold 1993), and Russia (where they are called "chackers") (Sherizen 1992; McHugh 2000). Likewise, computer security was a major concern in Japan (Sherizen 1992), Hong Kong (McGrath 1995) and Australia (Hooper 1987). More recently, India (Crime-research.org 2007), the Ukraine and Estonia (Moscaritolo 2009) have become centers of cybercrime.

It is almost impossible to make an accurate estimate of the annual losses due to computer crime, with estimates even in the early days ranging from $550 million (National Center for Computer Crime Data) to $15 billion (Inter-Pact, a computer security organization) (Major

1993). Such wide variance is due in part to disagreement over what actually qualifies as computer crime. Thieves might steal anything from entire systems (McLeod 1987), to individual laptops (Daly 1993), to integrated circuits, semiconductors, or memory chips (Bloombecker 1991), all of which can then be resold for their illicit "street value." But is straightforward theft of hardware truly computer crime? Tens of millions of federal tax returns are now filed electronically. In 1989, IRS agents arrested a Boston bookkeeper for electronically filing $325,000 worth of phony tax refund claims (Flanagan and McMenamin 1992). A 1993 report by the General Accounting Office warned the IRS of its potential vulnerability to a number of new electronic schemes (Quindlen 1993). But should this be classified as tax fraud or computer crime? The internet offers sociopathic young malcontents an opportunity to download "The School Stopper's Textbook," which instructs them how to blow up toilets and "break into your school at night and burn it down" (Diamond and Bates 1995). Is this criminal incitement or free speech? Dealers in child pornography utilize the internet and BBSs to advertise materials and exchange information (Torres 1993; Snider 1995). Pedophiles also use the internet to "troll" for potential adolescent victims (Wickham 1994; *Bay Area Advertiser* 1995; Villafranca 1995; Aol.com 1998; Rather 2001). This is obviously felonious conduct of the most offensive sort, but is it computer crime? Computer systems have assisted the daily operations of prostitution rings (McEwen 1991). Illegal gambling records are now routinely computerized (McEwen 1991). Organized crime uses computers in many of its operations, from bribery to hijacking, and drug cartels employ computers to keep track of clients and distribution networks (Chester 1986). The computer has also become an indispensable tool for "laundering" drug money (Moore 1994) and other organized crime revenues. Money laundering was a $100-billion-a-year industry in the United States by the early 1990s (Kerry 1991). Should all those billions of dollars be considered part of the cost of computer crime? There is little consensus in these matters. In fact, some experts have adopted an "agnostic" position and admitted that the true cost will never be known. To complicate estimation further, some have suggested that virtually *all* business crime must now involve at least some degree of computer crime (Major 1993).

Another gray area in estimating the losses from computer crime is software piracy. No one knows the full cost of such offenses, but a study conducted by the Software Publishers Association (SPA) back in 1993 claimed that $7.4 billion worth of business application software was counterfeited in that year—a figure nearly equal to the total *legitimate* revenues for the entire industry (*Houston Post* 1994). In addition to business applications, piracy entails the illegal copying of software for personal use, known as "softlifting" (Simpson, Banerjee, and Simpson 1994).

Foreign piracy of American software is an extremely costly problem. Some countries provide no copyright protection at all for software, and many that do have copyright laws find it almost impossible to enforce them (Taft 1994). Computer software is predominantly an American asset (American companies control about 80 percent of the world market), so other nations often do not focus on protecting it (Taft 1994).[3] In 1993, activities in just seven countries—South Korea, Spain, France, Germany, Taiwan, Thailand, and Poland—reportedly cost American software companies more than $2 billion. In each of these countries, pirated American software was said to account for between 75 and 90 percent of the total software in use (Taft 1994).

A newer form of piracy involves internet sites known as Warez. These are subterranean—though often "conspicuously subterranean"—websites which provide copyrighted programs for downloading. Most computer games, as well as popular movies, are available illegally on Warez sites before they have even been released (Rosoff and Pontell 2000).[4] People who create Warez sites are known as "crackers" because they "crack" copy protection codes. Most of them are teenage boys, who trade Warez like baseball cards. They use a program called a machine code monitor, which allows them to read protected disks one byte at a time—an operation known as "boot tracing." At critical points in the sequence they insert new instructions and "liberate" the disk.

The ultimate cost of computer crime is further clouded because there is a huge "dark figure" of unreported cases. Because of public humiliation, liability issues, and security inadequacies, many corporations do not report computer crime losses, especially large ones. Furthermore, when information is stolen, rather than money, the loss may be incalculable in terms of dollars. A survey of major corporations conducted by the Computer Security Institute and released in 1996 found that only 17 percent of those suffering electronic intrusions notified the authorities (Zuckerman 1996). Finally, the estimation of computer crime losses is perhaps most complicated by the clandestine nature of the crimes themselves. The most proficient electronic thieves are able to cover all traces that a crime has even been committed (Roufaiel 1994).

To understand the dimensions and the dangers of computer crime, we must examine the crimes themselves.

Embezzlement and financial theft

Without a doubt, the modern thief can steal more with a computer than with a gun.[5] According to Cressey (1971), embezzlers typically go through a three-stage process. In stage one, they are faced with what they perceive to be an unshareable financial problem: that is, a need for money which they cannot share with spouses, relatives, or friends. In stage two, they recognize an opportunity to solve that problem secretly. This opportunity rests in the positions of trust which they hold. Finally, in stage three, they manage to avoid internalizing a criminal identity by rationalizing their acts as borrowing rather than stealing.

Embezzlement is a traditional crime, but computers have done for it what the microwave did for popcorn. It is no coincidence that between 1983 and 1992—the years of the computer revolution—arrests for embezzlement rose 56 percent (Touby 1994).

As already noted, some embezzlers employ a Trojan horse—a "bad" program concealed inside a "good" program—as a means of diverting cash into fraudulent accounts. This is the most common method used in computer fraud (Hancock 1993). Dishonest programmers have also planted "trapdoors" or "sleepers" into the instructions which allow them to bypass security safeguards and siphon off cash using an imposter terminal (Prasad et al. 1991). A common variation on this method involves a practice known as "salami slicing." This type of fraud has been around for many years and was formerly known as "rounding down" (Francis 1987). Salami techniques divert (or, in keeping with the metaphor, "slice off") very small amounts of assets from very large numbers of private accounts. The stolen assets are so small, sometimes just a fraction of a cent per transaction, that they do not make a noticeable dent in any single account (Francis 1987).

When the computer fraud is committed by someone outside the victimized organization, embezzlement becomes theft. Here again, banks are frequent targets.

Hacking

In its original sense, the word "hacker," coined at MIT in the 1960s, simply connoted a computer virtuoso. "However, beginning in the 1970s, hackers also came to describe people who hungered to know off-limits details about big computer systems—and who were willing to use devious and even illegal means to satisfy this curiosity" (Roush 1995: 34). The pioneer hackers of the 1960s and 1970s probably exemplified sociologist Edwin Lemert's classic concept of primary deviance (Lemert 1967): that is, their conduct would have been described by observers as "norm violating." But computers were so new then that there may have been few clear norms to violate. If their intent was not to destroy private files, could they be considered vandals? If their intent was not to steal data, could they be considered thieves? Perhaps the least ambiguous way to characterize them was as trespassers.

On the other hand, there was likely little, if any, of Lemert's notion of secondary deviance (Lemert 1967): that is, no deviant self-identification on the parts of the hackers themselves. Indeed, their mastery of skills that may have seemed more magic than science to the general public endowed them with a sense of intellectual elitism. As one of these experts, commenting on the first generation of hackers, observed: "To be a computer hacker was to wear a badge of honor" (Hafner and Markoff 1991: 11). Most hackers display what Jay "Buck" Bloombecker, director of the National Center for Computer Crime Data, terms a "playpen mentality."[6] They see breaking into a system as a goal, not a means to some larcenous end.

At least two categories of "playpen" hackers have been identified: creative "showoffs" who break into databases for fun, rather than profit; and "cookbook hackers," the most common category, defined as computer buffs who coast along the global internet computer network without any specific target, twisting electronic door knobs to see which systems fly open (*Houston Post* 1995).

Hackers comprise a deviant subculture. They subscribe to norms that they apparently take very seriously, but which often conflict with the norms of the dominant society. Included in these are their own peculiar code of ethics, known as the "cyberpunk imperatives" (Stephens 1995). For instance, they believe computerized data are public property and that passwords and other security features are only hurdles to be jumped over in pursuit of these communal data (McEwen 1991).

Another way of looking at young hackers is from the perspective of Sykes and Matza's well-known "drift" theory of juvenile delinquency (Sykes and Matza 1957). Hackers might be viewed in this manner as fundamentally conforming youths who drift into occasionally deviant behavior through the use of such "neutralizations" as the claim that they are only trying to expose lax security systems (Kabay 1992)[7] or merely learn more about computers (Keefe 1992).

Beyond the "playpen mentality," however, there is a dark side to hacking, personified by a very different species of "stunt hacker" whose motivations are undeniably malicious. The infamous case of Kevin Mitnick is a vivid example of how a hacker can degenerate from prankster to public enemy. Computers have also become the principal tool in sophisticated identity theft scams. "Hackers are exploiting Internet auctions, non-regulated money transmittal systems, the ability to impersonate lottery and sweepstake contests, and other types of imaginative scams" (McCarthy 2007).

One of the most disturbing aspects of malicious hacking involves national security. A report from the American military's inspector-general found "serious deficiencies in the integrity and security" of a Pentagon computer used to make $67 billion a year in payments (Collins 1993: 5A). Cyberattacks on the government are an escalating problem. It is now believed that at least six or seven government computers are hacked successfully every day. Moreover, many government systems are invaded for months before the violation is even noticed (Goldman and McFarlane 2000).

An especially costly form of hacking is the "denial of service" attack, which involves the deliberate bombardment of a commercial website, causing it to crash. In late 2005, international crime rings utilized hacking in large-scale identity theft operations and extortion plots involving denial of service attacks (Theage.com.au 2006).

Viruses and worms

Computer viruses became an epidemic in the early 1990s (Powell 1992), and there is little sign of them being eradicated in the near future. A virus is an instructional code lodged in a computer's operating system that is designed to copy itself repeatedly. It may have four different phases: dormancy, when it does not destroy files, thus establishing a false sense of trust and complacency on the user's part; propagation, when it begins to replicate; triggering, when it is launched by an occurrence, such as a particular date; and damaging when it carries out the actual harm intended by its author (Greenberg 1989).

A computer can be infected with a virus for months or even years without the user's knowledge (Hancock 1993). When an infected computer comes into contact with an uninfected piece of software, the virus will be transmitted. Bulletin boards are major targets for infection. A worm is similar to a virus, although it is not contagious so infects only its host computer.

Viruses are sometimes placed in so-called "logic bombs." In other words, the virus program contains delayed instructions to trigger at a future date or when certain pre-set conditions are met, such as a specific number of program executions (Adams 1988). So-called "macro viruses" pose a significant threat to computers. These are actually worms, but they spread fast because they can be transmitted through e-mail and infect documents, rather than programs.

Internet scams

"The Internet has accelerated almost every aspect of modern life" (Npros.com 2002), including white-collar crime. For years, the FBI has been warning citizens that thousands of con artists, grifters, fraudsters, and other denizens of the dark are trolling for online victims. Cyberspace is full of millions of "exotic" offers, with everything from ostrich farming to Russian mail-order brides presented as a not-to-be-missed opportunity. The reported losses from internet fraud topped $239 million in 2007 (Claburn 2008). This was an all-time high, easily eclipsing the previous year's figure of $198.44 million (Vilches 2008).

Although Ponzi schemes, investment scams, and other con tricks seemingly have been around for ever, the Computer Age has added a new element: the internet's ability to spread these frauds at the speed of light. As a result, "fraud burns through the Internet in a matter of days" (Npros.com 2002). Mass e-mailings—"spam"—circulate word of new get-rich-quick schemes to millions of potential marks with a single click (Hiltzik and Piller 2002).

"Phishing" is a particularly prolific and costly type of internet fraud. The term was first coined in the 1990s by hackers who were stealing AOL accounts by scamming passwords from unsuspecting subscribers. By 1996, hacked accounts were called "phish" and were traded routinely by hackers as a form of electronic currency. Over the years, the definition of what constitutes a phishing attack has expanded. It now includes illegally accessing all personal and financial data (Ngssoftware.com 2005).

Phishing is a blend of technical deceit and what hackers call "social engineering" (manipulation and deception of designated victims). In the scam, the attacker sends an e-mail purporting to be from a valid financial or e-commerce provider—a technique known as "spoofing." The e-mail often uses fear tactics in an effort to prod the intended victim into visiting a fraudulent website: for example, "We've lost your password." Phishing e-mails normally utilize copied images and text styles that are used on the legitimate company website in order to give the impression that the e-mail is genuine. Many consumers are fooled into thinking the e-mail is authentic simply because it contains, for example, their bank's logo. However, to enhance authenticity, some phishing e-mails also include genuine links to the company's privacy policy and other pages on the legitimate website. Fraud sites supporting phishing e-mails are designed to mirror real sites in order to trick consumers into thinking they are at a trusted company's genuine website. Once there, they tend to be happy to disclose personal information. According to a study by Message Labs, a New York e-mail security firm, the number of phishing e-mails increased by 1,200 percent in 2004 alone (Gaudin 2004). In 2007, a survey by Gartner, one of the world's leading information technology research and advisory companies, reported that the cost of phishing attacks in the United States had soared to $3.2 billion, with 3.6 million citizens losing money through them (Gartner.com 2007). The security division of technology giant EMC reported that phishing scams rose another 66 percent in 2008, and that 68 percent of US bank brands were attacked (Siciliano 2009).

Much of the recent success of phishers lies in their use of "flax flux" attacks, a technique with which botnets hide phishing delivery sites behind an ever-changing network of compromised hosts ("zombie" computers) that act as proxies. The most serious consequence of phishing scams is identity theft. The pilfered personal information—including the victim's name, credit history, and billing address—can be used to apply for credit cards and other financial products and services.

Espionage

The misuse of computers as tools for industrial, political, and international espionage is another cause for major concern. Back in 1982, a major FBI sting operation targeted more than twenty employees of the Hitachi and Mitsubishi corporations of Japan, who were suspected of stealing data from IBM (Parker 1983). Thereafter, though, industrial espionage by means of computer exploded, increasing by a reported 260 percent between 1985 and 1993 (Lee 1993). Computers have also been used illegally to obtain confidential information for (or against) political candidates (Forscht and Pierson 1994).

Computer crime in the area of international espionage is more difficult to assess. The covert nature of spying makes it hard to determine the actual number of incidents (Lee 1993). Moreover, since this brand of white-collar crime often involves material classified as secret by a government, details of certain cases have probably been concealed from public scrutiny. Nevertheless, as equipment has become increasingly sophisticated, the threat of computer espionage has certainly grown more serious. Compression technology has already reached a level where vast amounts of data can be stored on a single memory stick.

Like viruses and worms, spyware has become another scourge of free enterprise. As a tool for corporate espionage, it represents a serious security threat to companies.

Anti-fraud systems, such as voice-recognition spectrographs, have long been on the market (Quinn 1992). Similarly, unauthorized computer access can be obstructed through biometric technology, including retina scanners, hand-print readers (Falconer 1995), and DNA identification devices (Stephens 1995), as well as by sophisticated "firewall" software that shields private information from hackers, thieves, and spies (Cheswick and Bellovin 1994). But computer criminals respond consistently to improved security technology with improved criminal technology,[8] and they will no doubt find a way to keep pace. This, in turn, will encourage still more advances in security and perpetuate a never-ending cycle of thrust and parry.

Notes

1 As testimony to how fast computer crime had grown, surveys conducted just five years earlier had reported the cost of most computer crime to be less than $10,000 (Gilbert 1989).

2 This article notes the exploits of England's "Mad Hacker."
3 Copyright protection is one of the most complicated areas of international law. Some nations take a very territorial approach, usually providing protection for works first published in that country (Forscht and Pierson 1994).
4 We can assume that the cracker subculture includes moles as game producers and within the technical side of the movie industry.
5 For a detailed consideration of electronic bank robbery, see Radigan 1993, 1995; Sherizen 1988, 1989, 1991; Sobol 1987.
6 Quoted in Beyers 1995.
7 The claim of helping to expose lax security is not limited to juvenile hackers. In the late 1990s, a 41-year-old man using a so-called "John the Ripper" internet password-cracking tool broke into computers at NASA's Sonny Carter Training Facility in Houston. His lawyer argued that he had performed a service for his country by calling attention to NASA's security deficiencies. The prosecutor scoffed at this claim: "Patriots don't use 'John the Ripper' to hack into government computers" (Brewer 1999).
8 For example, criminologist Gene Stephens (1995: 27) has warned that the development of virtual-reality technology will lead to fantastic new varieties of computer fraud: "In the future, a virtual-reality expert could create a hologram in the form of a respected stockbroker or real estate broker, then advise clients in cyberspace to buy certain stocks, bonds, or real estate. Unsuspecting victims acting on the advice might later find that they had enlarged the coffers of the virtual-reality expert, while buying worthless or nonexistent properties."

References

Adams, T. (1988) "Of viruses and logic bombs (part 1)," *Australian Accountant*, 58:83–85.

Anthes, G.H. (1995) "Security plans lag computer crime rate," *Computerworld*, 29:20.

Aol.com (1998) "Disgrace follows child porn bust," November 7.

Bay Area Advertiser (1995) "Cyberspace porn figures in assault cases of two teens," December 6:1–2.

Beyers, B. (1995) "Are you vulnerable to cybercrime: hackers tap in for fun, profit," *USA Today*, February 20:3B.

Bird, J. (1994) "Hunting down the hackers," *Management Today*, July: 64–66.

Bloombecker, J.J. (1991) "Computer ethics: an antidote to despair," *Mid-Atlantic Journal of Business*, 27:33–34.

Brewer, S. (1999) "Man pleads no contest to computer hacking," *Houston Chronicle*, October 9:36A.

Chester, J.A. (1986) "The mob breaks into the information age," *Infosystems*, 33:40–44.

Cheswick, W.R. and Bellovin, S.M. (1994) *Firewalls and Internet Security: Repelling the Wily Hacker*, Reading, MA: Addison-Wesley.

Claburn T. (2008) "Internet fraud loss for 2007 tops $239 million," InformationWeek.com, April 4.

Collins, C. (1993) "Hackers' paradise," *USA Today*, July 6:5A.

Credit Union Management (1989) "Operations: a viral epidemic," 12:28.

Cressey, D.R. (1971) *A Study in the Social Psychology of Embezzlement*, Belmont, CA: Wadsworth.

Crime-research.org (2007) "Top computer crime in 2007," May.

Daly, J. (1993) "Out to get you," *Computerworld*, 27:77–79.

Diamond, E. and Bates, S. (1995) "Law and order comes to cyberspace," *Technology Review*, 98:29.

Dodd, A. (1993) "When going the extra mile is not enough," *Network World*, 10:49–50.

Evans, P. (1991) "Computer fraud—the situation, detection, and training," *Computers & Security*, 10:325–327.

Falconer, T. (1995) "Cyber crooks," *CA Magazine* 128:12–17.

Flanagan, W.G. and McMenamin, B. (1992) "The playground bullies are learning how to type," *Forbes*, 150:184–189.

Forscht, K. and Pierson, J. (1994) "New technologies and future trends in computer security," *Industrial Management & Data Systems*, 94:30–36.

Francis, D.B. (1987) *Computer Crime*, New York: Dutton.

Garfinkel, S.I. (1989) "Lax security lets hackers attack," *Christian Science Monitor*, October 13:12–13.

Gartner.com (2007) "Gartner survey shows phishing attacks escalated in 2007," December 17.

Gaudin, S. (2004) "Phishing scams increase 1,200% in 6 months," Esecurityplanet.com, April 23.

Gilbert, J. (1989) "Computer crime: detection and prevention," *Property Management*, 54:64–66.

Gold, S. (1993) "Two hackers get six months jail in UK," *Newsbytes*, May 24:1–2.

Goldman, J.J. and McFarlane, U.L. (2000) "Man accused of hacking into NASA computers," *Los Angeles Times*, July 14:A15.

Greenberg, R.M. (1989) "Know thy viral enemy," *Byte*, June:175–180.

Hafner, K. and Markoff, J. (1991) *Cyberpunk*, New York: Touchstone.

Hancock, W. (1988) "Computer viruses," *American Agent & Broker*, 60:14–18.

Hancock, W. (1993) "Understanding computer viruses (part II)," *American Agent & Broker*, 65:61–63.

Hearnden, K. (1986) "Computer crime: multi-million pound problem?," *Long Range Planning*, 19:18–26.

Hiltzik, M. and Piller, C. (2002) "Internet snares scam victims," *Los Angeles Times* (online), November 10.

Hooper, N. (1987) "Tackling the techno-crimes," *Rydge's*, September:112–119.

Houston Post (1994) "Pirates cheat computer software industry out of billions by illegal copying, study says," July 5:C.

Houston Post (1995) "'Billy the Kid' hacker was not a threat to networks," February 17:15.

Kabay, M.E. (1992) "Hackers are no vigilantes," *Computing Canada*, 18:36.

Kabay, M.E. (2007) "Mail-order bride scams," Networkworld.com, September 11.

Keefe, P. (1992) "Portraits of hackers as young adventures not convincing," *Computerworld*, 26:33.

Kelly, K. (1993) "Cyberpunks, e-money, and the technologies of disconnection," *Whole Earth Review*, Summer:40–59.

Kerry, J. (1991) "Where is the s&l money?," *USA Today*, September:20–21.

Lee, M. (1993) "The rise of the company spy," *Christian Science Monitor*, January 12:7.

Lemert, E.M. (1967) *Human Deviance, Social Problems, and Social Control*, Englewood Cliffs, NJ: Prentice-Hall.

Major, M.J. (1993) "Taking the byte out of crime: computer crime statistics vary as much as the types of offenses committed," *Midrange Systems*, 6:25–28.

McCarthy, C. (2007) "Study: identify theft keeps climbing," Cnet.com, February 22.

McEwen, J.T. (1991) "Computer ethics," *National Institute of Justice Reports*, January/February:8–11.

McGrath, N. (1995) "A cleft in the armor," *Asian Business*, 13:26.

McHugh, D. (2000) "Hackers, pirates thrive in Russia's tech underworld," *USA Today*, June 1:17A.

McLeod, K. (1987) "Combatting computer crime," *Information Age*, 9:32–35.

Meyer, M. (1995) "Stop! Cyberthief!," *Newsweek*, February 6:36–38.

Moore, R.H., Jr. (1994) "Wiseguys: smarter criminals and smarter crime in the 21st century," *Futurist*, September/October:33–37.

Moscaritolo, A. (2009) "TJX hacker gets 30-year prison sentence," Scmagazineus.com, January 8.

Ngssoftware.com (2005) "The phishing guide," October 14.

Norman, A.R.D. (1989) *Computer Insecurity*, London: Chapman and Hall.

Npros.com (2002) "'Net fraud is tangled web for victims,' police," June 3.

Parker, D.B. (1983) *Fighting Computer Crime*, New York: Scribners.

Parker, D.B. (1989) "Computer crimes, viruses, and other criminoids," *Executive Speeches*, 3:15–19.

PC User. (1993) "Security Survey Reveals Huge Financial Losses," April 21:20.

Perry, R.L. (1986) *Computer Crime*, New York: Franklin Watts.

Powell, D. (1992) "Mopping up after Michelangelo," *Toronto Globe and Mail*, March 7:D8.

Prasad, Jyoti N., Kathawala, Yunus, Bocker, Hans J., and Sprague, David. (1991) "The global problem of computer crimes and the need for security," *Industrial Management*, 33:24–28.

Quindlen, T.H. (1993) "IRS computer systems are catching more fishy tax returns: GAO praises agency for reeling in electronic cheaters but urges tighter controls," *Government Computer News*, 12:67.

Quinn, B. (1992) "$2.3 billion: that's about how much toll fraud is costing us a year (maybe more)," *Teleconnect*, 10:47–49.

Radigan, J. (1993) "The growing problem of electronic theft," *United States Banker*, 103:37–38.

Radigan, J.(1995) "Info highway robbers try cracking the vault," *United States Banker*, 105:66–69.

Rather, D. (2001) "Cybercrime: oh what a wicked web we weave," *Houston Chronicle*, January 28:6C.

Rockwell, R. (1990) "The advent of computer related crimes," *Secured Lender*, 46:40, 42.

Rosoff, S.M and Pontell, H.N. (2000) "Who carez about Warez?," paper presented to the Western Society of Criminology, Hawaii, May.

Roufaiel, N.S. (1994) "White-collar computer crimes: a threat to auditors and organization," *Managerial Auditing*, 9:3–12.

Roush, W. (1995) "Hackers taking a byte out of computer crime," *Technology Review*, 98:34.

Saari, J. (1987) "Computer crime-numbers lie," *Computers & Security*, 6:111–117.

Sherizen, S. (1988) "Criminologist looks into mind of high-tech thief," *Bank Systems & Equipment*, 25:80–81.

Sherizen, S. (1989) "Future bank crimes," *Bank Systems & Technology*, 26:60, 62.

Sherizen, S. (1991) "Warning: computer crime is hazardous to corporate health," *Corporate Controller*, 4:21–24.

Sherizen, S. (1992) "The globalization of computer crime and information security," *Computer Security Journal*, 8:13–19.

Siciliano, R. (2009) "Phishing attacks rise dramatically in 2008," Finextra.com, February 20.

Simpson, P.M., Banerjee, D., and Simpson, C.L., Jr. (1994) "Shoplifting: a model of motivating factors," *Business Ethics*, 13:431–438.

Snider, M., (1995) "On-line users cheer arrests for child porn," *USA Today*, September 15:1D.

Sobol, M.I. (1987) "Computer crime trends: a brief guide for banks," *Bank Administration*, 63:52.

Stephens, G.M. (1995) "Crime in cyberspace," *Futurist*, 29:25–28.

Sykes, G.M. and Matza, D. (1957) "Techniques of neutralization: a theory of delinquency," *American Sociological Review*, 22:664–666.

Sykes, J. (1992) "Computer crime: a spanner in the works," *Management Accounting*, 70:55.

Taff, A. (1992) "Users call for toll fraud laws to distribute loss," *Network World*, 9:27–28.

Taft, D.K. (1994) "Software piracy rates tied to cultural factors," *Computer Reseller News*, 585:69, 72.

Theage.com.au (2006) "International crime rings, not hackers, true internet villains," August 6.

Titch, S. (1994) "Get real about fraud," *Telephony*, 227:5.

Torres, V. (1993) "New puzzle: high-tech pedophilia," *Los Angeles Times*, March 5:3.

Touby, L. (1994) "In the company of thieves," *Journal of Business Strategy*, 15:24–35.

Vilches, J. (2008) "US citizens lost $239 million from internet fraud in 2007," Techspot.com, April 8.

Villafranca, A. (1995) "Ex-guard jailed in computer porn case," *Houston Chronicle*, December 6:25A, 33A.

Wickham, S.K. (1994) "Crimes in cyberspace posing new challenges for law enforcement," *New Hampshire News*, March 6:1A.

Wood, C. (1988) "Crime in the computer age," *Maclean's*, 101:28–30.

Zukerman, M.J. (1996) "Businesses bypass law to fend off hackers," *USA Today*, June 6:3A.

50

Identity theft

Henry N. Pontell and Gregory C. Brown

Since the classic writings of Donald Cressey (1953) on embezzlement and Edwin Lemert (1958) on check forgers, new financial frauds have emerged as a costly problem throughout the world, including bank frauds, credit card frauds, and computer-assisted thefts. Such offenses are increasingly associated with the phenomenon of identity theft, which has been called "the fastest growing crime in America" (O'Brien 2004). Identity theft includes crimes in which a person's identifying material, such as a driver's license, credit card, or social security number, is stolen. It can also involve the creation of a fictitious identity in order to engage in criminal acts. Many different offenses have been carried out after the theft of someone else's identity. The most common is the purchase of goods by use of an illegally acquired credit card in the name of another person.

Identity theft was legally defined in the United States only in the mid-1990s. The Arizona legislature enacted a barebones statute in 1996 (Arizona 13-2008). This was followed by the federal Identity Theft and Assumption Deterrence Act of 1998 (18 USC §1028). The core outlaw behavior specified: "Knowingly transfers or uses, without lawful authority, a means of identification of another person with the intent to commit, or to aid or abet, any unlawful activity that constitutes a violation of Federal law, or that constitutes a felony under any applicable State or local law" (18 USC §1028(a) (7)). Later law specified that the possession of document-making equipment to produce false identifications was also forbidden (Pastrikos 2004; Towle 2004).

Identity theft as a crime category includes both old and new offenses. It facilitates and is related to new crimes, made possible by technological advances (most notably the networked computer) and new financial and organizational arrangements that include large amounts of identity information stored in numerous public and private databases (e.g., online banking, credit information, and e-business records). These new technologies and means to conduct financial transactions have unintentionally facilitated the theft of highly valued identities through such practices as hacking into large databases. The new economic order, much of which is based upon electronic transactions and similarly stored identity data, has produced a "crime facilitative environment" (Needleman and Needleman 1979) in which new forms of lawbreaking flourish.

Identity theft also characteristically involves older forms of crime. The term is used to denote a wide variety of offenses, such as checking frauds, financial crimes, counterfeiting, forgery, auto theft using false documentation, human trafficking, and terrorism, all of which existed as crime categories before the term "identity theft" was coined (Cole and Pontell 2006). Widespread publicity regarding the dire and dramatic impact on victims has been one of the major reasons for the creation of the new offense of identity theft (Newman and McNally 2005:12).

Some criminologists consider "identity theft" a less comprehensive term than "identity fraud," and see the former as a subcategory of the latter (Pontell 2003; Newman and McNally 2005). Alternatively, to the extent that many "thefts" of personal information are never turned into fraud, it may be argued that frauds are a sub-set of (virtual or real) thefts.

Caponetto (2004) notes three major categories of identity theft:

- *financial identity theft*, which entails the use of personal identifying information, primarily a social security number, to establish new credit lines in the name of the victim (such as telephone service, credit cards, or loans), buying merchandise, and leasing cars or apartments;
- *criminal identity theft*, which involves a criminal giving another person's identifying information to law enforcement in place of his or her own; and
- *identity cloning*, when imposters use victims' personal information to establish a new life. This may include financial and criminal identity theft as well. Persons who attempt this form of fraud are usually undocumented immigrants, wanted felons, individuals who are avoiding paying child support, those escaping from an abusive situation, and others who wish to leave behind a poor work, marital or financial situation. They might also file for bankruptcy after purchasing merchandise using another's personal information.

There are numerous means by which criminals can obtain personal information in order to commit identity offenses. Identity theft is a means to an end. It can begin through the commission of other crimes, such as stealing wallets and purses that hold identifying information, purloining mail that contains tax, banking, and credit card information, diverting mail to a new location by filing change of address forms at a post office, posing as a legitimate organization online (known as "phishing"), obtaining information from the workplace by bribing employees, stealing it themselves if they are an employee, fraudulently obtaining credit reports, and hacking into databases (known as "business record theft"). Identity information can also be obtained by rummaging through trash for personal information (known as "dumpster diving"), finding others' personal information in one's own home, using identity information shared on the internet, or obtaining such information from e-mails.

The growth of identity theft

To put the recent increase in identity theft in perspective, in 2005 the Federal Trade Commission (FTC) suggested that there had been over 27 million victims of the crime in the previous five years. An FTC survey polled 4,000 consumers and found that 507 had been victims of identity theft. This led to the estimate that about 4.25 percent of the US population had been victimized in this way. The survey found that Hispanics and African Americans were twice as likely as Asians or Whites to experience the most serious type of fraud, and that middle-aged people tended to lose the largest sums of money. During the twelve months covered by the survey, businesses and financial institutions suffered about $48 billion in losses because of identity theft, and victimized consumers paid out more than $5 billion to regain their financial identities (FTC 2005).

Family members targeting their own kin were reported as the most common perpetrators, and about half of the victims knew how their identities had been stolen. Children were often targeted, which is hardly surprising, as the crime is not usually uncovered until later in life when they attempt to establish credit. The survey suggested that victims play a major role in discovering that their identity has been stolen. More than half reported the theft after their purse or wallet had been stolen or after noticing aberrations on their paper or electronic financial account statements. Stolen information was typically used for about six months, although low-income and poorly educated individuals' information was in play for longer periods. After discovery, it usually took three months to restore the victim's financial status (FTC 2005).

Additional information is provided by the results of a major survey conducted by the Identity Theft Resource Center (ITRC), a large victim-assistance organization located in San Diego (Pontell, Brown, and Tosouni 2008). Two-thirds of those surveyed responded that they were victims of financial identity theft (as opposed to criminal ID theft, or cloning). The same number reported that their identity was used to open new credit accounts, and over a quarter were aware of charges to an existing credit card account. In addition to the significant amount of financial losses involved in these crimes, there was the personal trauma of victims who can spend months or even years trying to reestablish their economic identity. Victims reported considerable expenditure of both time and money to achieve this. They had to fend off creditors, coordinate legal responses, and contact official agencies. They also suffered health problems and accumulated medical expenses, experienced family dysfunction, and felt anger, powerlessness, and fear, among other emotional consequences (Pontell *et al.* 2008).

Identity theft has increasingly displayed an international component for US victims. The Federal Bureau of Investigation reports that many identity thefts and cybercrimes that occur in the United States originate in other countries, notably Russia, Romania, and West Africa. The Federal Deposit Insurance Corporation, a leading bank regulator, warned in June 2004 that increased corporate outsourcing of call-center tasks and other jobs to overseas sites had increased the risk of identity theft for Americans, whose personal and financial information was now being "outsourced" as well (O'Brien 2004).

In considering the cost of identity theft, it is undoubtedly the case that the total of crimes against persons is dwarfed by financial identity thefts that directly victimize large government assistance programs and, correspondingly, citizens and taxpayers at large. However, while reasonable information exists regarding financial identity frauds against consumers, there are no systematic data on such losses to government benefit programs. In the US, a number of scams against various government agencies have been uncovered which involve the use of social security numbers (*Government Computer News* 2000). In Australia, identity fraud has been found to account for substantial losses to the nation's tax system (Pontell 2003). The lack of data detailing government victimization creates a myopic view of what is already considered a mammoth social problem that has thus far been measured only by losses suffered by individuals, private organizations, and companies.

Despite its dramatic rise, identity theft is generally not the sort of offense that comes to mind when citizens discuss "the crime problem." It is non-violent, generally involves only modest sums of money for each individual crime, and in some cases results in no direct financial loss whatsoever for the victim. As such, it is sometimes viewed as lying on the border between crime and mere inconvenience; but in reality it is much more serious than that. As one commentator noted, "You have this seemingly low-level crime that cumulatively is a national crisis" (O'Harrow, Jr. 2003:1). A distinguishing attribute of identity theft is that financial displacement from victim to thief is usually the least destructive—and, in many cases, the least expensive— aspect of victimization. The more serious damage lies in the sense of personal violation, psychological trauma, possible medical care, family issues, and other ill effects, including the time and expense involved in trying to restore one's financial identity (Pontell *et al.* 2008). In this sense, identity theft is a second-order crime in that the value of the object stolen is generally far less than the value of goods whose security is endangered by the theft, such as bank accounts and credit ratings (Cole and Pontell 2006).

White-collar, common, or organized crime

Contrary to many media depictions and characterizations by law enforcement, identity fraud does not always constitute what most criminologists would class as white-collar crime. Many financial cases of identity fraud are the work of con artists and organized crime rings, where offenders possess no legitimate occupational status, generally a major prerequisite of inclusion in the ranks of white-collar criminals. With the exception of insider thefts committed by employees who use or sell personal data kept by their companies ("business record theft"), identity thefts can have little in common with white-collar crimes, other than that they can be financial in nature, remain hidden from victims for extended periods of time, and leave confusing paper and electronic trails for investigators. Identity frauds are economic crimes in that they involve monetary loss, but they are not likely to be carried out by relatively high-status offenders in legitimate occupational or organizational roles. Yet accounts of ID theft rings reveal the considerable degree of organization involved in criminal operations that affect large numbers of victims simultaneously.

Categorizing financial identity theft as organized, common, or white-collar crime is not merely a matter of semantics or academic interest, but has practical consequences in terms of enforcement and policy responses. Levi (2007) notes the importance that crime labels have on public attitudes and responses from the justice system. Treating financial identity theft as a form of organized crime rather than white-collar offending or an altogether "new" crime form allows criminal justice responses to target it more efficiently. This stands in sharp contrast to current legal and popular perception that sees identity theft as simply resulting from technological advances, individual carelessness with personal information, the growth of the internet, and legal and regulatory deficiencies. Organized crime exploits and may even help create systemic weaknesses and vulnerabilities. The rapid growth in financial identity theft is in no small measure a result of that exploitation.

Phishing e-mails are currently among the more widely used means to deceive large numbers of people into releasing their personal information to identity thieves. The biggest danger posed by this relatively new form of identity theft is that by stealing the identity of an organization a thief can obtain personal information on many individuals, which in turn can be used to commit a great number of financial crimes. Phishing has thus exponentially increased the ability of thieves to engage in identity theft. In 2005, about 30 percent of US phishing expeditions were limited to eBay and PayPal, and 60 percent to US Bank or Citibank (Lynch 2005). Phishing exemplifies what researchers have termed the first law of electronic crime: "if it can be done, someone will do it" (Rosoff et al. 2010:534). Banks are currently overwhelmed by customer service calls because of such thefts.

Responses

Mainstream criminology has, by and large, missed the major transformation in the nature of crime in the 21st century, or at least has been slow in taking up such issues as measured by work published in major journals or presented at professional meetings. Technology and information sharing, including the interconnectivity of large databases within and beyond national borders, combined with cultural and enforcement lags and inadequate policies, have created new criminogenic environments supportive of a variety of identity thefts related to financial frauds. The industry response to losses—to pay them and then push the resulting costs on to retailers and consumers—is no longer viable. For one, losses have mounted. For another, online banking systems present new risks and challenges to financial institutions that are responsible for protecting the electronic transfer of clients' funds from internal and external threats. In what appears to be a major "irony of control" (Marx 1981), criminals have usurped the identities of financial institutions themselves in an effort to gain online access to client information through phishing.

One current industry response to this situation in the US entails the selling of identity theft insurance to the public. This is not designed to stop the crimes (in fact, the very existence of the insurance indicates that the financial institutions are unable to do this), but rather allows companies to generate profits via unnecessary safeguards, inflated prices, and ineffective services. In other words, the insurers (usually banks or other financial institutions) have formulated a means to profit from the very problem they helped to create. In this sense, financial identity theft becomes another "externality" created in the pursuit of corporate profit in the new electronic frontier, a problem that is to be dealt with by "someone else."

Law enforcement officials report that smaller, individual cases are sometimes ignored or delayed until they can be bundled into high-profile, high-impact prosecutions (O'Brien 2004). The US emphasis on terrorism and security issues also leaves correspondingly fewer resources available for other criminal areas, including financial identity theft. Reports suggest that local law enforcement agencies are swamped with identity fraud cases, which in some jurisdictions account for a third or more of reported crimes. On average, the authorities manage to apprehend only 5 percent of the perpetrators (O'Brien 2004). For deterrence advocates, who see changes in statutory criminal laws and increased penalties as the only solution, it appears that the floodgates are open and the system's current capacity is strained far beyond any potential for the delivery of substantial sanctions.

Conclusion

The core issues associated with identity theft involve explicit standards of privacy and a level of protection of personal information that is commensurate with the increasing pervasiveness of electronic commerce. This includes an effective system of regulation for businesses and government agencies that store and use personal information. In addition, new technologies providing coordinated mechanisms for identity authentication need continual development in order to ensure consumer safety. The values of the free market, which encourage such financial transactions as buying on credit and electronic forms of banking, currently take precedence over, and are generally at odds with, mechanisms that would prevent many forms of financial identity theft. Official responses that encourage citizens to guard their information more carefully are certainly important, but so too is the fact that their personal information is no longer entirely in their control.

From a sociological perspective, financial identity theft provides a new window from which to view processes of deviance and social control. The most sophisticated analyses of privacy, surveillance, and control tend to focus on state intrusions into individual privacy. Gary Marx (2003:388), for example, notes:

> The study of privacy and secrecy overlaps the study of deviance and social control. In many settings privacy and surveillance are different sides of the same nickel. Privacy can serve as a nullification mechanism for the power offered by surveillance. Surveillance seeks to eliminate privacy in order to determine normative compliance or to influence the individual for its own ends, as with voyeurism.

Surveillance used by criminals in order to commit offenses through identity theft appears immune from traditional means of control and attempts to break through personal borders by

431

exploiting weaknesses in current systems of privacy control. Criminal surveillance by identity thieves thus represents another form of "casing the joint."

Systems currently designed to guarantee privacy and anonymity reveal yet another "irony of control" in regard to identity theft. In attempting to protect privacy from state surveillance we have created conditions through which others could violate that privacy. The delicate balance between privacy rights and state surveillance now has to be weighed against the costs incurred from a different threat to individuals: a criminal element intent on wreaking economic and personal havoc through financial identity theft. While state intrusion into privacy has become a major issue in post-911 America due to provisions contained in the Patriot Act, there is an equally serious threat of criminal invasion of privacy through identity theft. State and corporate actors, typically conceived in the security literature as wishing to extend their surveillance capabilities as far as possible, are strangely resistant to citizens' calls for greater regulation and control regarding identity theft. Instead, they have sought to portray the protection of individual identities as the sole responsibility of each individual (Marx 2006).

Identity theft is one of the most formidable innovations in the field of criminal enterprise. Its toll is tremendous and its relationship with vital democratic issues of privacy and freedom make it a compelling issue for scholarly research and public policy programs.

References

Caponetto, T.R. (2004). "Identity theft is a major problem in America," *KansasCity infoZine*. Available at: 69.61.32.91/news/stories/op/storiesView/sid/2215/ (accessed October 10, 2004).

Cole, S.A. and Pontell, H.N. (2006). "'Don't be low hanging fruit': identity theft as moral panic," in T. Monahan (ed.), *Surveillance and Security*, London: Routledge.

Cressey, D.R. (1953). *Other People's Money: A Study of the Social Psychology of Embezzlement*, Glencoe, IL: Free Press.

Federal Trade Commission (FTC) (2005). "Identity fraud survey," report presented at the Identity Theft Research Focus Group, National Institute of Justice, Washington, DC, January 27.

Government Computer News (2000). "Data from federal records used to commit identity theft," *Government Computer News*, 29:8.

Lemert, E.M. (1958). "The behavior of the systematic check forger," *Social Problems*, 6:141–149.

Levi, M. (2007). "Policing financial crimes," in H.N. Pontell and G. Geis (eds.), *International Handbook of White-Collar and Corporate Crime*, New York: Springer.

Lynch, J. (2005). "Identity theft in cyberspace: crime control methods and their effectiveness in combating phishing attacks," *Berkeley Technology Law Journal*, 20:259–300.

Marx, T. (1981). "Ironies of control: authorities as contributors to deviance through escalation, nonenforcement, and covert facilitation," *Social Problems*, 28:221–233.

Marx, G.T. (2003). "A tack in the shoe: neutralizing and resisting the new surveillance," *Journal of Social Issues*, 59:369–390.

Marx, G. (2006). "Soft surveillance: the growth of mandatory volunteerism in collecting personal information—'Hey buddy can you spare a DNA?,'" in T. Monahan (ed.), *Surveillance and Security*, London: Routledge.

Needleman, M. and Needleman, C. (1979). "Organizational crime: two models of criminogenesis," *Sociological Quarterly*, 20:517–539.

Newman, G.R. and McNally, M.M. (2005). "Identity theft literature review," Identity Theft Research Focus Group, National Institute of Justice, Office of Justice Programs, US Department of Justice.

O'Brien, T.L. (2004). "Identity theft is epidemic: can it be stopped?," NYTimes.com. Available at: www.nytimes.com/2004/10/24/business/yourmoney/24theft.html?pagewanted=all&position= (accessed October 28, 2004).

O'Harrow Jr., R. (2003). "Identity crisis," *Washington Post Magazine*, August 10:1.

Pastrikos, C. (2004). "Identity theft statutes: which will protect Americans the most?," *Albany Law Review*, 67:1137–1157.

Pontell, H.N. (2003). "'Pleased to meet you, won't you guess my name?' Identity fraud, cyber crime, and white-collar delinquency," *Adelaide Law Review*, 23:305–328.

Pontell, H.N., Brown, G.C. and Tosouni, A. (2008). "Stolen identities: a victim survey," *Crime Prevention Studies*, 23:57–85.

Rosoff, S.M., Pontell, H.N. and Tillman, R. (2010). *Profit without Honor: White-Collar Crime and the Looting of America* (5th edn), Upper Saddle River, NJ: Pearson/Prentice-Hall.

Towle, H.K. (2004). "Identity theft: myths, methods, and the new law," *Rutgers Computer and Technology Law Journal*, 30:237–325.

51

Intellectual property crime

David F. Luckenbill and Kirk Miller

An important form of property is intellectual property, but the term "intellectual property" is ambiguous. From a legalistic point of view, it refers to the exclusive rights to intellectual objects. In the United States, intellectual property includes the rights conferred by copyright, patent, and trademark laws. Copyright law grants an author the exclusive rights to reproduce, distribute, perform, and adapt a literary, musical, or artistic work; patent law gives an inventor the exclusive right to make, use, and sell an invention; and trademark law grants a business the exclusive right to use a word or symbol to identify and distinguish its products. More conventionally, "intellectual property" refers to the intellectual objects themselves—the original expressions of ideas fixed in tangible forms, such as books and records, and novel applications of ideas embodied in machines and technical processes.

In the United States, violation of the rights to intellectual objects is a civil offense. The offender is liable to civil prosecution and remedial sanctions, such as compensation of the victim. For example, a person who wrongfully copies a book's characters or labels a product with a mark resembling the one used by a company for its product is liable for civil action. Forms of copyright and trademark infringement that are willful and oriented toward financial gain are also criminal offenses; the offender is eligible for criminal prosecution and punitive sanctions. The unauthorized duplication of computer software for commercial gain is a criminal violation of copyright law; and the fraudulent labeling of apparel as genuine designer clothes for commercial gain is a criminal violation of trademark law.

The politics of piracy and counterfeiting

Two principal intellectual property offenses are piracy and counterfeiting. Piracy is a violation of copyright law. It involves the unauthorized reproduction, distribution, or performance of a creative work. Counterfeiting is a violation of trademark law. It involves the unauthorized reproduction of a genuine product's brand name and packaging. In practice, piracy and counterfeiting can occur together. For example, an individual who unlawfully reproduces computer software, packages the disk so that it appears to be the genuine product, and sells it online engages in both piracy and counterfeiting.

What constitutes piracy and counterfeiting has been a subject of debate. Some people, including many intellectual property owners, embrace a broad definition, treating virtually any unauthorized use of an intellectual object as a form of piracy or counterfeiting. The Motion Picture Association of America (2005a), for example, defines piracy simply as "the unauthorized taking, copying or use of copyrighted materials without permission." Other people, including consumer rights groups, adopt a narrower view. They limit piracy and counterfeiting to misuse that is deliberate and oriented toward financial gain—to purely criminal violations of law. The Electronic Frontier Foundation and the Digital Freedom Campaign maintain that people should be free to draw upon and use creative works in pursuing personally and socially fulfilling ends and that such pursuits should be treated as legitimate.

This conflict is complex. It is grounded in different interests. Property owners wish to maintain a monopoly over the use of their intellectual objects in order to reap profits from their production and distribution. Consumers, creators, citizens, and scholars all wish to enjoy the freedom to use intellectual objects in ways that extend beyond simple, passive consumption. They want the freedom to employ familiar literary characters in crafting new stories, exchange audio bites and video clips, mix samples of sound recordings in the creation of unique music, parody popular films and brand icons, and so on.

The conflict features the mobilization of rhetoric aimed at garnering public and political support and shaping the law in ways that serve their interests. Property owners have attacked unauthorized users, demonizing them as predators. The Motion Picture Association of America (2005a), for example, asserts that "piracy is theft, and pirates are thieves, plain and simple. Downloading a movie off the internet is the same as taking a DVD off a store shelf without paying for it." Offenders are frequently depicted in even more sinister ways. Some trade associations claim that commercial pirates and counterfeiters are linked to organized crime and funnel their earnings into terrorism and other dangerous enterprises. Owners also portray unauthorized use as detrimental to society. They contend that piracy and counterfeiting undermine vital industries, cause a loss of jobs, reduce tax revenues, and kill the incentive to innovate, making for an intellectually weaker society.

Meanwhile, consumer rights groups have challenged owners. While these groups agree that certain unauthorized practices, such as the willful reproduction of works for commercial gain, should be unlawful, they oppose the treatment of all unauthorized uses as wrongful. They maintain that the need to acquire owners' permission for virtually any use beyond passive consumption violates cherished rights and chills innovation, engendering fear that almost any use might elicit legal action and thus dissuade people from pursuing the creative enterprise. They contend that locking up virtually every use not only reduces the public domain but makes for an intellectually weaker and less vibrant society.

The outcome of this conflict is uncertain. Clearly, owners have managed to strengthen their exclusive rights. Copyright law, for example, has extended the length of ownership of creative works and reduced consumers' rights to use such works; and trademark law has expanded protection against practices that might dilute trademarks even if there is little likelihood of confusion. Nevertheless, owners' efforts to garner broad support and full legal protection have been less than completely successful. This may be due, in part, to the fact that many of the people who have been demonized as offenders are otherwise respectable, well educated, and middle class. Moreover, consumers have had a greater opportunity to contest owners' claims. Through blogs, internet forums, and the like, they have challenged owners' assertions, such as the substantial harm unauthorized use causes, and articulated the dangers of owners' efforts, such as reducing the amount of creative achievement made possible by a vigorous public commons. Moreover, through collective action, they have managed to mute some of the more onerous policy proposals.

The political struggles over intellectual property rights and what constitutes their violation will likely continue for some time. Both owners and users of intellectual property will continue to press their positions, claim the moral high ground in the conflict, and declare success in advancing their views. Which side will ultimately prevail is by no means clear.

The incidence of intellectual property offenses

It is difficult to determine the incidence of intellectual property offenses, for statistics on these offenses are meager. Nevertheless, we can marshal some statistics on their incidence in the United States. In 2008, a total of 3,346 civil cases of copyright infringement and 3,411 civil cases of trademark infringement entered the federal district courts. These numbers represent an increase of 64 percent over the number of copyright cases commenced in 1999 but a decrease of 5 percent over the number of trademark cases commenced in that year (Administrative Office of the United States Courts, 1999, 2008). In 2008, a total of 76 criminal cases of copyright infringement were filed in the district courts, an increase of 230 percent over the number filed in 1999, and 118 criminal cases of trademark counterfeiting were filed in the district courts, an increase of 42 percent over the number filed in 1999 (US Department of Justice, 1999, 2008). Turning to the seizure of goods attempting to enter the United States, federal officials made 14,992 seizures of goods violating copyright and trademark laws in 2007. This represents an increase of 131 percent over the number of seizures made in 2003 (US Customs and Border Protection, 2009).

Although these figures are considerably smaller than the numbers of conventional property crimes processed through the criminal justice system, they reflect only a fraction of all intellectual property offenses. The figures refer to cases handled by the federal legal system. However, some property owners employ state law to manage offenses. Recognizing that federal officials often are reluctant to take action, the film and recording industries mobilize local officials to prosecute pirates under applicable state laws. The manufacturers of luxury goods also frequently prosecute the producers and vendors of counterfeit goods in state courts.

In addition, the number of incidents that do not come to the attention of any official is substantial. Some owners do not take legal action against relatively minor forms of infringement, such as making copies of creative works for personal consumption and using brand icons in purely sociable activities. Most owners are also unaware of many offenses. The diffusion of intellectual objects, people's access to them, and the difficulty of monitoring use make it practically impossible for owners to know whether or how frequently their rights have been violated. But while the number of incidents that escape official attention is unknown, it is likely to be large. In a survey of adult internet users, the Pew Internet and American Life Project (2005) found that 27 percent of the respondents had downloaded music or video files and more than half of them had discovered ways to download outside of legitimate online services. Along the same line, Gallup Consulting (2007) found that 22 percent of a national sample of adults had purchased, copied, or downloaded products that they knew or suspected were illegitimate.

Although statistics on the incidence of intellectual property offenses are meager, figures bearing on the magnitude of these offenses frequently appear in popular accounts of piracy and counterfeiting. These figures generally relate to the economic losses from these offenses and derive from the property owners themselves. The Motion Picture Association of America (2005b), for example, claimed that US film studios lost $6.1 billion in 2005 to piracy: $1.3 billion resulted from piracy in the United States itself and $4.8 billion resulted from piracy in other nations. The Software and Information Industry Association (2009) stated that piracy cost the industry some $2 billion a year in North America and $11 to $12 billion a year worldwide. The National Association of Manufacturers (2008) maintained that counterfeit products account for 5 to 7 percent of world trade, which translates into approximately $500 billion annually. Along the same lines, the Global Intellectual Property Center (n.d.), an affiliate of the US Chamber of

Commerce, asserted that counterfeiting and piracy cost the United States between $200 billion and $250 billion a year in lost sales and that the effect of intellectual property offenses on the global economy amounted to $500 billion to $600 billion a year in lost sales.

Such figures are impressive, yet questionable. Property owners typically do not explain how loss figures are calculated or identify the source of the data used to compute them. Accordingly, the figures can be easily inflated. And it behooves owners to inflate them: the larger the numbers, the bigger the problem; the bigger the problem, the stronger the case owners can make for policies supporting their interests.

Explaining intellectual property offenses

Intellectual property owners commonly explain piracy and counterfeiting in terms of easy access to information technologies coupled with a weak system of legal control. This idea may well flow from the risk-management perspective that pervades the corporate world, a view that adopts a rational choice conception of behavior, and it frequently appears in the rhetoric of owners. In the 1980s, for example, the film and recording industries advanced this idea when lobbying Congress to increase the penalties for film and record piracy. They claimed that piracy had become epidemic and that this epidemic could be explained in terms of two conditions: the proliferation of video and audio recorders, highly accessible devices for producing and con-suming unauthorized recordings; and mild penalties for piracy that neither deterred the practice nor inspired officials to take it seriously. Piracy could be controlled, they insisted, by subjecting it to greater punishment. Brand-name owners have advanced a similar conception of counter-feiting and promoted similar corrective measures in legislative campaigns to protect their property. Although this line of argument has intuitive appeal, the idea that intellectual property offenses stem from easy access to information technologies and a weak system of legal control oversimplifies the complexities of the behavior.

Routine activities theory provides a more comprehensive explanation of intellectual property offenses. This theory proposes that the offenses flow from the convergence in time and space of three elements: motivated offenders, suitable targets, and an absence of capable guardians.

An intellectual property offense requires a motivated offender, a person who is both willing and able to violate the law. In the United States, the desire to misuse intellectual objects appears pervasive. This may stem partly from the ideology that informs intellectual property law. While law endorses the economic principle that creators have a right to remuneration for their labor, it also endorses the principle that people have the right to as much information as they deem necessary. The idea is that if people are to lead meaningful lives, they must be able to draw upon and use the works of others. This principle encourages people to regard intellectual objects as public goods and to use them in almost any way they see fit. The desire to misuse intellectual objects also may flow from such dominant values as materialism and consumerism paired with a limited concern for the means for pursuing wealth. It is not surprising that the counterfeit goods most often produced and distributed are luxury goods that demonstrate a consumer's social status. Moreover, the desire to misuse intellectual objects may stem from the belief that the behavior is harmless. Intellectual property offenses lack the clear, tangible loss associated with conventional property crimes, and this seems to make the behavior justifiable, even acceptable. A Harris Interactive poll (2004) found that a large majority of the American public views downloading music for personal use as an innocent act that should not be prohibited. This is consistent with an earlier Harris poll (2003) that found that about 75 percent of adolescent respondents believed that downloading music files without paying and letting other people download files from them should be legal.

A person who is willing to engage in an intellectual property offense must also be able to do so. The offense is facilitated, if not made possible, by exploitative information technologies—devices that enable people to use intellectual objects in ways that violate the rights of owners. Personal computers, optical scanners, and digital recorders exemplify these technologies. Recent years have witnessed the development and proliferation of a variety of affordable, easily manageable exploitative information technologies.

An intellectual property offense requires a suitable target, an object that is both appealing and vulnerable. In the United States, intellectual objects have considerable value; they are in great demand and are thus sources of enormous wealth. Consider the copyright industries, for example. One investigation showed that these industries comprise one of the fastest-growing segments of the US economy. From 2002 to 2005, they grew at an annual rate of 7.3 percent, while the remainder of the economy grew at a rate of 3.5 percent. In 2002, they contributed $669 billion to the economy and accounted for 6.4 percent of the gross domestic product; in 2005, they contributed $819 billion to the economy and accounted for 6.6 percent of the gross domestic product (Siwek, 2006).

Intellectual objects also are vulnerable to misuse. These objects have some of the qualities of public goods. They are both inexhaustible (use does not deplete them) and nonexclusive (they can be in numerous places simultaneously). These qualities make them difficult to protect. At the same time, property owners seek to make intellectual objects accessible to consumers. These objects can be regarded as "diffuse private property," for they are spread across the landscape. Diffusion is a function of owners' economic pursuits. Owners sell tangible items—books, disks, and the like—not the intellectual objects embodied in them. Law permits consumers to do almost anything they want with these items, but it forbids them from exploiting the intellectual objects within them, as owners maintain dominion over these objects. To make a profit, owners want to market the tangible items widely. Yet wide distribution of the items means making the objects embodied in them accessible to consumers, including potential offenders, and this increases the vulnerability of the objects to misuse.

Finally, an intellectual property offense requires an absence of capable guardians. In the realm of copyright and trademark, capable guardians have been relatively limited. On the one hand, government efforts to protect intellectual objects have been modest. Historically, the government has done little to control misuse. For the most part, agencies have registered intellectual objects and assigned exclusive rights to them; owners have been responsible for guarding their rights and enforcing them. On the other hand, owners' efforts to protect intellectual objects have been constrained. The diffusion of these objects, people's easy access to them and exploitative information technologies, and people's rights to use these objects in private have made it difficult for owners to monitor consumption and ensure that their rights are respected.

Controlling intellectual property offenses

Over the years, intellectual property owners have made various efforts to control misuse. Many of these efforts also flow from a risk-management perspective, and they are oriented toward the prevention of misuse.

Owners have mobilized the legal system to control intellectual property offenses. In the United States, they have urged law-makers to provide better protection for intellectual objects. The film and recording industries, for example, asked Congress to increase the penalties for piracy. On another front, owners have urged law-makers to regulate exploitative information technologies. The copyright industries sought to control piracy by getting Congress to prohibit the manufacture, distribution, and use of technologies that defeat anti-copying treatments. In addition, owners have pressed law enforcement officials to identify and prosecute offenders, and many have developed programs to assist in this enterprise. Although owners have long emphasized the legal process in protecting against misuse, they recognize that it offers limited security and should be supplemented with other modes of control.

Some owners have engaged in third-party policing. They have tried to compel innocent but well-situated third parties to control the unlawful conduct of individuals. The recording industry, for example, has urged internet service providers to police the unlawful sharing of sound recordings among their clients. Likewise, some trademark owners have employed municipal abatement laws to press landlords to evict tenants vending counterfeit goods.

Owners have used technology to control intellectual property offenses. Recognizing the difficulty of identifying and prosecuting offenders, they have tried to make it difficult for people to misuse their works by erecting technological barriers to misuse. To protect against unauthorized reproduction of their works, recording companies have added digital watermarks and inaudible copy protection ciphers to recordings, and computer software manufacturers have used copy-resistant disks and encryption processes. Trademark owners have employed complex designs and special packaging to make counterfeit products harder to pass off and easier to detect. Although technology has become an important means for controlling piracy and counterfeiting, owners acknowledge that such barriers are more likely to thwart the average user than the sophisticated user.

Owners have used education to control offenses. In the hope of getting people to honor their proprietary rights, they have endeavored to shape popular attitudes toward the use of intellectual objects. Through various media, they have expressed the obligations of consumers and drawn on conventional cultural frameworks in arguing against deviation from these obligations. Copyright owners, for instance, have argued that piracy is "theft," a breach of "mutual trust," and detrimental to the national good and to everyone who benefits from the creative enterprise. It should be noted that persuading people to honor the rights of owners is a formidable task, as many people do not regard intellectual objects as meriting the respect they accord conventional forms of property.

Perhaps recognizing the limitations of these forms of control, some owners have turned to marketing as a more effective means of control. Rather than wage war against pirates and counterfeiters, they have sought to compete with piracy and counterfeiting, trying to win over consumers. Computer software companies, for example, have tried to reduce the appeal of pirated copies by offering updates and other services to those who purchase legitimate copies. Film studios have attempted to reduce the appeal of unlawful copies of films available online by offering DVDs with various extras. Some video game companies have recognized that the simultaneous release of games in different territories will reduce the drive among gamers in foreign countries to buy pirated versions of new games.

For years, intellectual property offenses were modest, for many people were limited technologically in their capacity to misuse intellectual objects. But the tide has clearly turned. The development and proliferation of exploitative information technologies, coupled with the diffusion of intellectual products, the ease with which these objects can be obtained and manipulated, and the circulation of values and beliefs encouraging misuse, have facilitated intellectual property offenses and exacerbated the difficulty of managing them. Not surprisingly, the viability of intellectual property has consequently become a matter of serious concern.

References

Administrative Office of the United States Courts. 1999. *Federal Judicial Caseload Statistics*. Washington, DC: Administrative Office of the United States Courts.

——. 2008. *Federal Judicial Caseload Statistics*. Available at: www.uscourts.gov/caseload2008/tables/C02Mar08.pdf.

Gallup Consulting. 2007. *Counterfeiting in the United States*. Princeton, NJ: Gallup Organization.

Global Intellectual Property Center. n.d. "Facts about IP: Intellectual Property Drives Economic Growth." Available at: www.thetruecosts.org/index.php/component/content/article/46.

Harris Interactive. 2003. "Two Out of Three American Teens Oppose Fines for Music File Sharers, Says Harris Interactive Youth Survey." Available at: www.harrisinteractive.com/NEWS/allnewsbydate.asp?NewsID=683.

——. 2004. "Americans Think Downloading Music for Personal Use is an Innocent Act." Available at: www.harrisinteractive.com/harris_poll/index.asp?PID=434.

Motion Picture Association of America. 2005a. "Anti-piracy." Available at: www.mpaa.org/piracy.asp.

——. 2005b. "The Cost of Movie Piracy." Available at: www.mpaa.org/leksummaryMPA%20revised.pdf.

National Association of Manufacturers. 2008. "Product Counterfeiting: Grand Larceny on a Massive Scale." Available at: www.nam.org/PolicyIssueInformation/TaxTechnologyDomesticEconomicPolicy.

Pew Internet and American Life Project. 2005. "Music and Video Downloading Moves beyond P2P." Available at: www.pewinternet.org/~/media/Files/Reports/2005/PIP_Filesharing_March05.pdf.

Siwek, Stephen E. 2006. *Copyright Industries in the US Economy*. Available at: www.iipa.com.

Software and Information Industry Association. 2009. "The Dimensions of the Piracy Problem." Available at: www.siia.net/index.php?option=com_content&view=article&id=172:about-ap&catid=162:anti-piracy-articles&Itemid=130#dimensions.

US Customs and Border Protection. 2009. *Intellectual Property Rights Seizure Statistics*. Available at: www.cbp.gov/xp/cgov/trade/priority_trade/ipr/seizure/seizure_stats.xml.

US Department of Justice. 1999. *FY 1999 Annual Accountability Report*. Available at: www.usdoj.gov/criminal/cybercrime/ipstats.htm.

——. 2008. *FY 2008 Performance and Accountability Report*. Available at: www.usdoj.gov/ag/annualreports/pr2008/appd/p254-285.pdf.

52

Violence in the workplace

Spyridon Kodellas, Bonnie S. Fisher, and Martin Gill

No employee in any occupation is immune from the risk of physical violence or psychological abuse while at work or on duty. Governments, union officials, and employers throughout the world recognize workplace violence as an occupational hazard. However, collectively, their responses have been neither proactive nor consistent. Workplace violence can have dire consequences on the physical and psychological well-being of employees (and possibly their families, too) and can result in significant economic costs to employers and social costs on the public. Despite its apparent widespread negative toll, workplace violence has not been fully researched. This neglect is partially due to methodological issues, such as a lack of consensus about the definition of workplace violence, rather than a lack of interest among researchers. The paucity of research globally has led to an inadequate information base for developing evidence-informed responses to workplace violence.

This chapter will assess these and related issues by presenting definitions and typologies of workplace violence, describing various sources of workplace violence data, summarizing the risk factors, vulnerable occupations, and preventive measures, and briefly discussing the impact of workplace violence.

Defining workplace violence

A review of the current state of workplace research reveals that there are various accepted definitions of workplace violence. Definitions provided by government agencies from various countries indicate that the term is not only historically grounded but socially and culturally influenced. The European Commission defines workplace violence as involving "incidents where persons are abused, threatened or assaulted in circumstances related to their work, involving an explicit or implicit challenge to their safety, well-being or health" (Wynne *et al.*, 1997: 1). In the United States, the National Institute for Occupational Safety and Health defines workplace violence somewhat more narrowly as "violent acts, including physical assaults and threats of assault, directed toward persons at work or on duty" (NIOSH, 1996: 6). The Australian National Occupational Health and Safety Commission defines occupational violence as "the attempted or actual exercise by a person of any force so as to cause injury to a worker, including any threatening statement or behavior which gives a worker reasonable cause to believe he or she is at risk" (NOHSC, 1999: 4). In the same country, the Australian Capital Territory Occupational Health and Safety Unit defines occupational violence even more broadly by incorporating violence against property as well: "occupational violence is any incident in which employees are threatened or assaulted in circumstances arising out of their work. This may include personal intimidation in the form of threatening phone calls received at work or at home and vandalism to personal property" (ACT Occupational Health and Safety Unit, 1993: 2). The International Labor Organization defines workplace violence as "any action, incident or behavior that departs from reasonable conduct in which a person is assaulted, threatened, harmed, injured in the course of, or as a direct result of, his or her work" (ILO, 2003: 4).

It is evident from these examples that the existing definitions of workplace violence form a continuum that ranges from narrow definitions, which include only physical assaults and injuries, to broader ones that also include non-physical acts, such as threats and intimidation, verbal and psychological abuse. In some cases sexual and racial harassment are included, too. It is important when comparing studies, and when assessing policies, that account is taken of the types of workplace violence that are being considered.

Typology of workplace violence

There is no consensus among researchers and governmental officials as to how to categorize workplace violence. One categorization commonly used is based on four "types" that are defined by the victim–perpetrator relationship (see Bowie *et al.*, 2005a):

- Type I. *External or intrusive violence:* violent acts by offenders who have no legitimate relationship to the business or its employees and are usually committing a crime (e.g., robbery) from which violence derives.
- Type II. *Consumer-related violence:* violent acts by people who have a legitimate relationship with the business and become violent while being served (e.g., customers, clients, patients, students, inmates).
- Type III. *Relationship violence:* violent acts by an employee of the business who attacks or threatens another employee; or violent acts by someone who has a personal relationship with an employee (e.g., current or former spouse, boyfriend/girlfriend) and threatens or assaults the employee at the workplace.
- Type IV. *Organizational violence:* violent acts committed by the organization against staff or customers/clients.

As shown in Table 52.1, another categorization is based on the distinction between two types of victimization: physical violence and psychological abuse. Examples of behaviors that constitute each type are presented in this table.

Sources of workplace violence data

A number of organizations and governmental agencies globally collect data on the extent and nature of workplace violence. Table 52.2 summarizes and describes data sources for different types of workplace violence that are collected in the European Union (the first five sources), the United States (the next five), and elsewhere (the final three). The table is not intended to be comprehensive and it does not include all relevant surveys. Rather, the aim is to focus on some key studies to illustrate the scale of research and the variations that exist.

Even though the data from these sources are publicly available, identifying workplace violence trends is impeded by the different interpretations of workplace violence among those collecting the data. Most national surveys include only incidents of physical violence that result in a serious injury and omit incidents of non-physical violence. The British Crime Survey (BCS) measures

Table 52.1 Types of victimization and examples of behaviors

Type of victimization	Behavior
Physical violence	• Simple assault/attack • Vandalism (against employer or company property) • Aggravated assault • Robbery • Rape • Homicide
Psychological abuse	• Cessation of verbal communication • Ostracism • Generation and dissemination of gossip or false information • Discrimination • Offensive gesturing • Threats or intimidation • Bullying (repeated inappropriate behavior which could reasonably be regarded as undermining the individual's right to dignity at work) • Mobbing (repeated psychological harassment performed by a group of workers towards a target) • Stalking • Harassment (sexual, racial, or ethnic)

only external or intrusive violence in the workplace and excludes relationship violence (e.g., violence between colleagues or domestic violence at work). Yet, the European Working Conditions Survey (EWCS) considers not only physical violence from individuals within or outside the workplace but psychological violence, such as bullying and intimidation. The Survey of Workplace Violence Prevention, implemented by the US Bureau of Labor Statistics in 2005, includes all types of workplace violence except for those committed by an organization. Some forms of workplace violence, such as violence committed by the organization (or business) against its own staff or customers, are under-researched.

Reporting and recording practices also have an impact, in that they too complicate the process of assessing workplace violence trends. Researchers estimate that approximately only one in five incidents of non-fatal workplace violent acts are reported to law enforcement agencies (Mayhew and Chappell, 2001). Cumulative evidence has shown that organizational culture, job insecurity, embarrassment, and seriousness of the act all influence the victim's decision about whether to report what occurred (Duhart, 2001; Mayhew, 2000; NIOSH, 1996; Rugala and Isaacs, 2004). Typically, the less severe incidents are less likely to be reported, and insecure workers are generally less willing to report violent acts because of fear of losing their jobs.

Overall, valid and reliable measurement of the extent of all forms of workplace violence is unavailable. With the exception of fatal incidents, which represent a very small portion of all workplace violent incidents, all other types of violence at work remain under-reported and therefore underestimated.

Risk factors, vulnerable occupations, and preventive measures

It is possible to identify a range of risk factors that can be associated with workplace violence, as well as more at-risk occupations, especially for selected Western industrialized countries.

Table 52.3 summarizes different *risk factors* (see, e.g., Chappell and Di Martino, 2006; NIOSH, 1996; Perrone, 1999; Upson, 2004) and *most vulnerable occupations* (see e.g., Duhart, 2001;

Table S2.2 Sources of workplace violence data

Data source	Description	Sponsor/author	Type of workplace violence examined
European Working Conditions Survey (EWCS)	First conducted in 1990/91, the EWCS is conducted every five years in all EU member states	Eurofound: European Foundation for the Improvement of Living and Working Conditions	• Physical violence from people within or outside the workplace • Intimidation • Bullying and harassment • Sexual harassment • Discrimination
British Crime Survey (BCS)	First administered in 1982, the BCS is a nationally representative, household survey	Home Office, Research Development and Statistics Directorate (RDS)	• Assaults in the workplace • Threats in the workplace
Commercial Victimization Survey (CVS)	Examines crime against small and medium-sized retail and manufacturing premises in England and Wales	Research Development and Statistics Directorate (RDS)	• Violent crime • Burglary • Theft • Fraud • Bribery and corruption • Electronic crime • Stolen goods
European Crime and Safety Survey (EU ICS)	The EU ICS was first conducted in 2005 in 18 EU member countries	European consortium comprising Gallup Europe, UNICRI, Gallup Hungary, the Max Planck Institute, CEPS/INSTEAD and GeoX Ltd, co-funded by the European Commission, DG RTD	• Vehicle-related crimes • Theft and burglary • Robbery • Sexual offenses • Assaults and threats • Consumer fraud
Finnish Quality of Work Life Surveys	First conducted in 1977, the QWLS is a personal interview survey to monitor employees' working conditions and their changes	Statistics Finland	• Mental strain of work • Social relationships, conflicts in the workplace • Experience of illness and accident risks • Fears and uncertainties: lay-off, dismissal, threat of unemploymentand transfer to other tasks
Census of Fatal Occupational Injuries (CFOI)	Published annually; uses multiple sources to identify, verify, and profile fatal worker injuries	Bureau of Labor Statistics (BLS), US Department of Labor	• Fatal occupational injuries with detailed case characteristics and worker demographics

Survey	Description	Source	Topics
Survey of Occupational Injuries and Illnesses (SOII)	The sample is selected to represent all private industries in the states and territories; participation in the SOII may vary by year	BLS, US Department of Labor	• Number and frequency (incidence rates) of nonfatal workplace injuries and illnesses
Survey of Workplace Violence Prevention, 2005	Data are available for private industry, state government, and local government by industry and size of establishment	BLS for the National Institute for Occupational Safety and Health (NIOSH)	• Criminal violence • Customer-related violence • Co-worker violence • Domestic violence at work
National Crime Victimization Survey (NCVS)	Initiated in 1973, data are collected for personal and household victimization that happened while working or on duty; NCVS redesigned in 1992	Bureau of Justice Statistics (BJS), US Department of Justice	• Rape • Sexual assault • Robbery • Assault • Theft
Workplace Risk Supplement (WRS)	The WRS to the NCVS explores safety issues related to work environments and risk factors contributing to nonfatal violence in the workplace	BJS, US Department of Justice	• Rape • Sexual assault • Robbery • Assault
International Crime Victims Survey (ICVS)	Initiated in 1987, ICVS is a program of standardized sample surveys that looks at households' experience with crime in a large number of countries	Selected European criminologists with expertise in national crime surveys	• Vehicle-related crimes • Theft and burglary • Robbery • Sexual offenses • Assaults and threats • Consumer fraud
International Crime Business Survey (ICBS)	Conducted in nine Central and Eastern European capital cities in 2000, the ICBS succeeded the International Commercial Crime Survey (ICCS)	Fieldwork was executed by Gallup, with funding provided by the Ministries of Justice and Foreign Affairs of the Netherlands and the Ministry of Justice of Hungary	• Burglary • Theft (by employees and customers) • Vandalism • Assault • Robbery
Australian Work-Related Fatalities Studies	Information is obtained primarily from coronial records of traumatic fatality	National Occupational Health and Safety Commission (NOHSC)	• Fatal occupational injuries with detailed case characteristics and worker demographics

Table 52.3 Risk factors, vulnerable occupations, and preventive measures for each type of workplace violence

Type of workplace violence	Risk factors	Most vulnerable occupations	Preventive measures
Type I. External/intrusive violence: Violent acts by criminals who have no other connection with the workplace or the victim, but enter only to commit crime.	• Exchange of money or other valuable goods • Working alone or in small numbers • Working late at night or during early morning hours • Having face-to-face contact with the public • Guarding valuable property or possessions	• Taxi drivers and chauffeurs • Convenience store owners • Gas station attendants • Sales counter clerks • Bus drivers • Delivery workers • Cashiers (in banks, post offices, etc.) • Retail sales staff • Amusement and recreational workers	• Control or limit access to the facility • Physical barriers • Silent alarm systems • CCTV • Effective lighting • Reduce the amount of cash or valuables readily available • Security guards/Place managers
Type II. Consumer-related violence: Violence directed at employees by customers, clients, patients, students, inmates, or any others for whom an organization or a professional provides services.	• Working with unstable or volatile persons • Having a mobile workplace • Having face-to-face contact with the public • Working in high-crime areas • Working alone or in small numbers • Working in community-based settings • Having an easily accessible worksite	• Police officers • Security personnel • Nurses • Detectives • Prison guards • Mental health workers • Social workers • Emergency department workers • Community welfare workers • Firemen • Teachers • Prostitutes	• Employees never work alone • Reduce frustration and stress • Avoid disputes and emotional arousal • Post instructions • Employees carry pagers, cellular phones and hand-held alarms or noise devices • Protective screens for drivers and tellers • Train employees how to react in a violent situation • Security guards/Place managers

Type	Risk factors	Sector data	Prevention measures
Type III.a. Relationship violence—Staff on staff violence and bullying: Violence against co-workers, supervisors, or managers by present/ former employee(s).	• Organizational culture or management style conducive to injustice • Highly competitive business environments • Failure to maintain equitable workloads • Insecure jobs • Workers facing unemployment • Poor systems design or work station architecture • Poor communications • Poor working conditions	• Occupations in the goods-producing industries usually report a higher percentage of co-worker violence than occupations in the service sector	• Written policy explaining acceptable contact between co-workers • Control drug and alcohol use in the workplace • Improve communication between co-workers • Maintain equitable workloads • Improve working conditions
Type III.b. Relationship violence— Domestic violence and sexual harassment at work: Violence committed in the workplace by someone who does not work there, but has a personal relationship with an employee, such as an abusive spouse or domestic partner.	• Alcohol and drug abuse • Accessible worksite • Recent episodes of violent behavior outside the workplace • Employees with history of violence • Home finance/ money problems • Stressful events at home (accidents, illnesses, etc.)	• Occupations in the service sector report much higher percentages of domestic violence than occupations in the goods-producing sector	• Control or limit access to the facility • Physical barriers • Control drug and alcohol use in the workplace • Security guards/Place managers
Type IV. Organizational violence: Violence committed by the organization or business against staff or customers/clients.	• Precarious employment • Insecure jobs • Quasi-military hierarchical and rigid management styles • Highly competitive business environments • Severe economic downturns	• No data yet available	• Labor inspections by state and local regulatory organizations to ensure compliance with the labor laws • Formation of labor/trade unions

NIOSH, 2004; Toscano and Weber, 1995; Sygnatur and Toscano, 2000) for the four types of workplace violence. A list of practical *preventive measures* for addressing types of workplace violence is also included (see, e.g., Rugala and Isaacs, 2004; Gill *et al.*, 2002; ILO, 2003; NIOSH, 2006; Standing and Nicolini, 1997; Wassell, 2009; Wynne *et al.*, 1997). However, a word of caution is necessary here in that any measures used to tackle a specific type of workplace violence need to be matched to the context in which the problem occurs. The preventive measures are merely examples of what might be considered.

Impact of workplace violence

Workplace violence can have a range of negative consequences on the organization, its employees, and their families, including physical, psychological, and financial ones. The most advanced cost analyses consider both *tangible costs*, such as medical bills or loss of income, and *intangible* costs, such as fear and pain or a reduction in quality of life, at the individual, organizational, and societal levels. The costs of workplace violence to *employees* include loss of income due to absenteeism or poorer performance at work, and medical-related costs. The costs to *organizations* are related to increase in sickness absenteeism, higher turnover of staff, reduced productivity, increased insurance premiums as well as compensation costs. Societal costs are related to healthcare (including mental health) and medical treatment costs, the loss of a productive workforce, and those associated with early retirement, long-term unemployment, and welfare dependency.

Quantifying the costs associated with workplace violence is a daunting task, although it has been attempted. For example, the Health and Safety Executive (HSE) estimates that the costs to British *employers* of workplace accidents and work-related ill health in 2001–2 ranged from £3.9 billion to £7.8 billion, for *individuals* from £10.1 billion to £14.7 billion, and for British *society as a whole* from £20 billion to £31.8 billion (HSE, 2004). A more recent study estimated that the total cost to employers in Britain of workplace injuries and work-related ill health in 2005–6 ranged from £2.9 billion to £3.2 billion (Pathak, 2008). In 2006 in the United States, employers spent nearly $87.6 billion on workers' compensation (Sengupta *et al.*, 2008). For 1992 through 2001, the total cost of the 7,925 workplace homicides in the United States was estimated at nearly $6.5 billion (Hartley *et al.*, 2005).

Conclusion

In this short summary it has been possible to discuss only some of the contextual issues that inform our understanding of workplace violence. This type of deviance appears in many forms, and research work has operationalized different definitions. Moreover, most forms of workplace violence are under-reported and so there is a large "dark figure" which further complicates attempts to identify trends. Nevertheless, work that has been undertaken suggests that workplace violence is not uncommon, particularly for some types of work, albeit for a variety of reasons (Bowie *et al.*, 2005b). While there are many ways to respond to workplace violence, relatively little is known about the effectiveness of the various programs, reflecting the general lack of research on program effectiveness that characterizes modern criminology (see Licu and Fisher, 2006; Rogers and Chappell, 2003; and, for a more general discussion, Tilley, 2009).

References

ACT Occupational Health and Safety Unit (1993) *Reducing Occupational Violence*, Canberra: Chief Minister's Department.

Bowie, V., Fisher, B.S., and Cooper, L.C. (2005a) "Introduction: New Issues, Trends, and Strategies in Workplace Violence," in Bowie, V., Fisher, B.S., and Cooper, L.C. (eds) *Workplace Violence: Issues, Trends, Strategies*, Cullompton: Willan.
—— (eds) (2005b) *Workplace Violence: Issues, Trends, Strategies*, Cullompton: Willan.
Chappell, D. and Di Martino, V. (2006) *Violence at Work*, 3rd edn, Geneva: International Labor Organization.
Duhart, D.T. (2001) *National Crime Victimization Survey: Violence in the Workplace, 1993–99*, Washington, DC: Bureau of Justice Statistics, US Department of Justice.
Gill, M., Fisher, B.S., and Bowie, V. (2002) *Violence at Work: Causes, Patterns and Prevention*, Cullompton: Willan.
Hartley, D., Biddle, E.A., and Jenkins, E.L. (2005) "Societal Cost of Workplace Homicides in the United States, 1992–2001," *American Journal of Industrial Medicine*, 47: 518–527.
Health and Safety Executive (HSE) (2004) *HSE Updates Costs to Britain of Workplace Accidents and Work-Related Ill Health*. Available at: www.hse.gov.uk/press/2004/e04139.htm (accessed 29 March 2011).
International Labor Organization (ILO) (2003) *Code of Practice on Workplace Violence in Service Sectors and Measures to Combat this Phenomenon*, Geneva: International Labor Organization.
Licu, E. and Fisher, B. (2006) "The Extent, Nature and Response to Workplace Violence Globally: Issues and Findings," in Gill, M. (ed.) *The Handbook of Security*, London: Palgrave.
Mayhew, C. (2000) *Violence in the Workplace—Preventing Commercial Armed Robbery: A Practical Handbook*, Australian Institute of Criminology, Research and Public Policy Series No. 33, Canberra: AIC.
Mayhew, C. and Chappell, D. (2001) *Occupational Violence: Types, Reporting Patterns, and Variations between Health Sectors*, Working Paper Series No. 139, Discussion Paper No. 1, Taskforce on Prevention and Management of Violence in the Health Workplace, Centre for Mental Health, Sydney: NSW Department of Health.
National Institute for Occupational Safety and Health (NIOSH) (1996) *Violence in the Workplace: Risk Factors and Prevention Strategies*, Current Intelligence Bulletin No. 57. Available at: www.cdc.gov/niosh/violcont.html (accessed 29 March 2011).
—— (2004) *Worker Health Chartbook, 2004*. Available at: www.cdc.gov/niosh/docs/2004-146 (accessed 29 March 2011).
—— (2006) *Workplace Violence Prevention Strategies and Research Needs*. Available at: www.cdc.gov/niosh/docs/2006-144/pdfs/2006-144.pdf (accessed 29 March 2011).
National Occupational Health and Safety Commission (NOHSC) (1999) *Program One Report: Occupational Violence*, 51st Meeting of NOHSC, Hobart, 10 March.
Pathak, M. (2008) *The Costs to Employers in Britain of Workplace Injuries and Work-Related Ill Health in 2005/06*, Discussion Paper Series No. 2, Analytical Services Division, Health and Safety Executive. Available at: www.hse.gov.uk/economics/research/injuryill0506.pdf (accessed 29March 2011).
Perrone, S. (1999) *Violence in the Workplace*, Australian Institute of Criminology Research and Public Policy Series No. 22, Canberra: AIC.
Rogers, K. and Chappell, D. (2003) *Preventing and Responding to Violence at Work*, Geneva: International Labor Organization.
Rugala, E.R and Isaacs, A.R. (eds) (2004) *Workplace Violence, Issues in Response*, Washington, DC: US Department of Justice, Federal Bureau of Investigation.
Sengupta, I., Reno, V., and Burton, J.F., Jr. (2008) *Workers' Compensation: Benefits, Coverage, and Costs, 2006*, Washington, DC: National Academy of Social Insurance.
Standing, H. and Nicolini, D. (1997) *Review of Workplace-Related Violence*, Health and Safety Executive Report No. 143/1997, London: Tavistock Institute.
Sygnatur, E.F. and Toscano, G.A. (2000) "Work-Related Homicides: The Facts," *Compensation and Working Conditions*, 5(1): 3–8.
Tilley, N. (2009) *Crime Prevention*, Collumpton: Willan.
Toscano, G. and Weber, W. (1995) "Patterns of Fatal Workplace Assaults Differ from Those of Non-Fatal Ones," in US Department of Labor Statistics, *Fatal Workplace Injuries in 1993: A Collection of Data and Analysis*, Bureau of Labor Statistics Report No. 891, Washington, DC: US Department of Labor.
Upson, A. (2004) *Violence at Work: Findings from the 2002/2003 British Crime Survey*. Available at: www.homeoffice.gov.uk/rds/pdfs2/rdsolr0404.pdf (accessed 29 March 2011).
Wassell, J.T. (2009) "Workplace Violence Intervention Effectiveness: A Systematic Literature Review," *Safety Science*, 47: 1049–1055.
Wynne, R., Clarkin, N., Cox, T., and Griffiths, A. (1997) *Guidance on the Prevention of Violence at Work*, Luxembourg: European Commission, DG-V.

53

Cyberbullying, cyberharassing, and cyberstalking

Keith Durkin and Denay Patterson

Cyberharassment is a form of online deviance that has received a tremendous amount of attention from the media, law enforcement, mental health professionals, and academics in recent years. While there is no standard definition of cyberharassment (Wolak, Mitchell, and Finkelhor 2007), the term normally refers to a variety of behaviors that use the internet and other computer media communication devices to menace someone (Basu and Jones 2007). Cyberstalking is one example of this type of deviance. When the harassment involves young people, the term "cyberbullying" is used. This has been defined as "willful and repeated harm through the medium of electronic text" using the internet, phone, or other personal communication devices (Hinduja and Patchin 2008: 131). It occurs via e-mail, instant messaging, chat-rooms, web postings, and social networking sites, such as MySpace and Facebook. Such behavior is increasingly occurring via text messaging (Raskauskas and Stoltz 2007). This conduct can range from relatively minor incidents, such as name calling, to very serious behavior, such as death threats.

Such behavior has also been labeled "internet bullying," "electronic bullying," and "online bullying." However, the various terms used to describe cyberharassment are frequently ill-defined and sometimes used interchangeably (Beran and Li 2005). Cyberharassment offenders may encourage others to harass the victim on their behalf (Goodno 2007; Roberts 2008). For example, the offender can use trickery to make it appear the victim has started some type of conflict with a third party (Miller 2006). Furthermore, the harasser can attempt to ruin the reputation of, and stigmatize the identity of, their victim. The term "cybersmearing" has been used to describe various attempts to harm the reputation of another person online (Roberts 2008). Hadler and Jaishankar (2008: 53) use the term "cybersexual defamation" to describe the posting of sexually defamatory messages about, or pictures of, an individual on the internet. Disinformation posted online is particularly harmful, since it is easily accessible to a wide variety of people (Basu and Jones 2007). Among adolescents, this may involve the misuse of images of peers in an effort to humiliate or embarrass them (Raskauskas and Stoltz 2007).

The prevalence and severity of this type of deviance have been evidenced by its frequent appearance in the news media. Several high-profile cases have come to light in recent years. Perhaps the best-known is the story of Megan Meier, who committed suicide at the age of thirteen. The victim of cyberbullying by many of her peers, Meier hanged herself after being rejected by a boy who had previously shown interest in her on MySpace. After her death, it was discovered that the person behind this MySpace profile was not a sixteen-year-old boy but the mother of Meier's rival, who had created the fake account to harass Meier. Another recent case of cyberstalking that has been featured in the media concerned ESPN reporter Erin Andrews. An unauthorized video of Andrews was posted on various sites across the internet. The video shows a nude Andrews, who did not know she was being filmed, alone in her hotel room. This incident falls under Hadler and Jaishankar's definition of "cybersexual defamation."

Like many other forms of deviance in cyberspace, there has been relatively little empirical research on the topic of cyberbullying. In a study of 788 college students, Holt and Bossler (2009) found that 22.8% of the women and 13.5% of the men reported being the victim of online harassment in the previous year. In a study of approximately 1,400 children, Hinduja and Patchin (2008) found that about one-third of the respondents (regardless of gender) reported cyberbullying victimization. The results also indicated that 18% of boys and 16% of girls reported engaging in this behavior. In another study on this topic, girls and boys reported similar rates of participation in cyberbullying (Williams and Guerra 2007). A study of 3,700 middle school students found that one-third of the girls and 10% of the boys reported being victims of cyberbullying (Chu 2005). In the same study, 17% of girls admitted to bullying others online, compared to 10% of boys. Finally, in a national survey of youths ages ten to seventeen, 9% reported experiencing online harassment during the previous year, while a similar percentage reported engaging in the behavior (Mitchell, Wolak, and Finkelhor 2007). In terms of prevalence, cyberbullying is thought to peak in middle school (Williams and Guerra 2007).

One of the primary reasons for social concern about this behavior relates to its perceived consequences. Such victimization can be particularly problematic during adolescence, since it can disrupt social and emotional development (Raskauskas and Stoltz 2007). Victims of cyberharassment report negative affective states, such as fear, anxiety, and other types of emotional distress (Beran and Li 2005; Holt and Bossler 2009). Research has found a link between cyberbullying victimization and depressive symptoms in young people (Ybarra 2004). Anecdotal reports have linked victimization with poor academic performance and school dropout among young people (Raskauskas and Stoltz 2007).

Research has identified some factors associated with cyberharassment. Although not found in every study, some evidence suggests that cyberbullying victimization is more common among girls (Chu 2005; Mitchell, Wolak, and Finkelhor 2007). Cyberbullying victims report experiencing higher levels of face-to-face harassment than their peers (Beran and Li 2005; Hinduja and Patchin 2008; Ybarra and Mitchell 2004). Moreover, youths who bully in the traditional sense are more likely to be cyberbullies (Raskauskas and Stoltz 2007). Regular use of computer chat-rooms has been identified as a factor increasing victimization risk (Holt and Bossler 2009). Moreover, the amount of time spent online is positively associated with both cyberbullying offending and victimization (Hinduja and Patchin 2008; Marcum 2008). Lastly, college students who commit acts of computer deviance (e.g., hacking and viewing pornography) have higher levels of cyberharassment victimization (Holt and Bossler 2009).

Another form of online harassment is cyberstalking. Although this term is frequently used by professionals and academics, as well as members of the general public, there is no universally accepted definition of it (Goodno 2007). However, it is widely recognized as involving "a pattern of harassing or threatening behavior" (Alexy, Burgess, Baker, and Smoyak 2005: 279). The concept of cyberstalking covers a variety of behaviors, including gathering information on the victim, repeatedly sending unsolicited messages or e-mails, posting or sending hostile materials, and manipulating other internet users into threatening or harassing the victim (Spitzberg and

Hoobler 2002). It shares some common traits with cyberbullying, but the behavior normally involves adults rather than children and adolescents. Like proximal stalking, it involves repeated actions that transpire over time, as well as evidence of a perceived threat (Spitzberg and Hoobler 2002). However, there are some features of cyberstalking that distinguish it from traditional stalking. According to Goodno (2007), the cyberstalker can be geographically removed from the victim and can easily impersonate the victim, as well as encourage third-party harassment of the victim. Moreover, the cyberstalker can identify and target their victim exclusively online (Alexy, Burgess, Baker, and Smoyak 2005).

There has been surprisingly little empirical work on this topic (Sheridan and Grant 2007). It is impossible to estimate the prevalence of cyberstalking in the population, since no empirically sound, community-based survey exists on the topic (Roberts 2008). In a study of 750 college students, 3.7% reported being cyberstalked (Alexy *et al.* 2005). Most research suggests that, as with cases of proximal stalking, the offender tends to be a former intimate of the victim (Sheridan and Grant 2007). According to an examination of New York Police Department records, 80% of cyberstalking offenders are males.

Gendered aspects

Gender appears to be an especially important variable in cyberharassment in general, and cyberbullying in particular. Although the latter appears to be as prevalent among girls as boys, there also appears to be gendered patterns in this behavior. For instance, adolescent males are more likely to intimidate other males and threaten violence when bullying online (Hinduja and Patchin 2008; Keith and Martin 2005). Boys also show a pattern of accusing their victims of being homosexual (Hinduja and Patchin 2008). This can be distressing to adolescents in two ways: first, it aligns the victim with a devalued group in society, causing them to feel unwanted and inferior; second, it is generally done with the intent to demasculinize the victim. This can be especially hurtful at this time in boys' lives, when they are fighting to be seen as men by an adult society that still views them as boys.

Unlike traditional bullying that takes place in the schoolyard, cyberbullying typically focuses on psychological torment, rather than physical violence. This psychological bullying is commonly seen among girls. Calling names, saying hurtful things, and spreading rumors about others are all common bullying tactics for girls. According to Alane Fagin, executive director of Child Abuse Prevention Services, adolescent girls may even use relationships as weapons, creating and ending friendships for the purpose of hurting others (Keith and Martin 2005). This behavior can be seen in the phenomenon Miller (2006) calls "Mean Girls" bullying. Using this approach, a group of girls gather together to bully one victim. At first the victim believes she is chatting with only one girl. She may say things to this girl that she would not say if there were other girls present. Soon it is revealed that multiple girls are on the computer. Each of them joins the original girl in harassing and berating the victim. She may be attacked for the comments she made, which she thought were said in confidence (Miller 2006; Keith and Martin 2005).

Explanation

The internet plays an integral role in the daily routine of most Americans, including youth. In essence, it has become part of our lifestyle or routine activities. Just as the internet has opened up new opportunities for young people to learn, communicate, and recreate, it has created new opportunities for them to become victims.

Routine activities theory, introduced by Lawrence Cohen and Marcus Felson (1979), considers crime to be a function of everyday life. The concept of routine activities describes where people go to work and shop, as well as what they do for leisure and recreation (Robinson 2001). Cohen and Felson (1979) posited that crime is situational and occurs when three factors converge. The first factor is *motivated offenders*—individuals who are seeking a criminal opportunity. Victimization risks are considered a function of an individual's exposure to offenders (Mustaine and Tewksbury 2000). The second factor is *attractive targets*, be they vulnerable individuals or valuable commodities that are worth stealing. The final factor is a lack of *capable guardians*—individuals who, "if present, would discourage a crime from happening" (Felson 2001: 338).

When applied to cybercrime and deviance, routine activities theory posits that online lifestyle directly influences the risk of victimization (Choi 2008). The noticeably high rates of cyberharassment victimization among children, adolescents, and college students may be a function of their high level of internet exposure (Holt and Bossler 2009). As such, some people are exposed to motivated offenders because of their online lifestyle. For instance, users of internet chat-rooms and dating services have been linked to cyberharassment victimization. Also, people who engage in online deviance (e.g., hacking, illegal file sharing, and viewing pornography) report higher rates of cyberharassment victimization. Moreover, online harassment occurs in the absence of capable guardians (Marcum 2008). It would be very difficult, if not impossible, for authorities to prevent such behavior through policing the internet. Additionally, most victims of cyberharassment do not report their victimization to the authorities (Alexy, Burgess, Baker, and Smoyak 2005; Li 2006).

The nature of the internet and online interaction may be a driving force behind cyberharassment and related behaviors. The anonymity of computer-mediated communication can encourage anti-normative conduct (Durkin 2007). The offender may perceive there is less risk of arrest or retaliation for antisocial behavior that occurs online (Beran and Li 2005). This anonymity can cause a "disinhibition effect," which contributes to deviant activities (Basu and Jones 2007; Sheridan and Grant 2007). In the online environment, people are removed from the conventional restraints associated with face-to-face interaction and are free to behave in a malicious or aggressive manner (Hinduja and Patchin 2008). Consequently, it is relatively simple for a person to disassociate herself or himself from the implications of their online activities (Finch 2003). Since perpetrators are physically removed from their victims, there is a reduced likelihood they will feel guilty about their actions (Raskauskas and Stoltz 2007).

Conclusion

Computers and the internet have revolutionized social life, creating a new social landscape replete with novel patterns of behavior, association, interaction, and even identity (e.g., YouTube, Facebook, and MySpace). The use of computer-mediated communications has become part of the daily activities for the typical citizen, particularly among American youth. Technological innovations frequently create new possibilities for the pursuit of criminal and deviant behavior (Durkin, Forsyth, and Quinn 2006). Accordingly, there has been a vast array of deviant practices surrounding the technological innovation of the internet. Some examples are hacking, illegal gambling, sale of illegal drugs, sexual tourism, terrorist networking, and internet crimes against children.

While harassment via computer-mediated communications is clearly a problem, it is difficult, if not impossible, to estimate its prevalence based on existing data. This problem is exacerbated by the lack of standardized definitions of cyberharassment and related behaviors. The concept of "cyberbullying," as it is currently conceptualized, is especially problematic. Yet, it does appear that online harassment is more common among young people, and victimization is linked to lifestyle variables (e.g., the use of chat-rooms and computer dating services). Accordingly, routine activities theory appears to be a useful framework to examine such victimization. However, there remains a need for solid empirical research that utilizes a standard conceptualization of cyberharassment to advance our knowledge of this behavior.

References

Alexy, E.M., Burgess, A.W., Baker, T., and Smoyak, S.A. (2005) "Perceptions of cyberstalking among college students," *Brief Treatment and Crisis Intervention*, 5: 279–289.

Basu, S. and Jones, R. (2007) "Regulating cyberstalking," *Journal of Information, Law, and Technology*, 1: 1–30.

Beran, T. and Li, Q. (2005) "Cyber-harassment: A study of a new method for an old behavior," *Journal of Educational Computing Research*, 32: 265–277.

Choi, K. (2008) "Computer crime victimization and integrated theory: An empirical assessment," *International Journal of Cyber Criminology*, 2: 308–333.

Chu, J. (2005) "You wanna take this online?," *Time*, 166(6): 52–55.

Cohen, L.E. and Felson, M. (1979) "Social change and crime rate trends: A routine activity approach," *American Sociological Review*, 44: 588–608.

Durkin, K. (2007) "Show me the money: Cybershrews and online money masochists," *Deviant Behavior*, 28: 355–378.

Durkin, K.F., Forsyth, C.J., and Quinn, J.F. (2006) "Pathological internet communities: A new direction for sexual deviance research in the postmodern era," *Sociological Spectrum*, 26: 595–606.

Felson, M. (2001) "Routine activity theory: The theorist's perspective," in C.D. Bryant (ed.) *Encyclopedia of Criminology and Deviant Behavior*, Volume I: *Historical, Conceptual, and Theoretical Issues*. Philadelphia. PA: Brunner-Routledge.

Finch, E. (2003) "What a tangled web we weave: Identity theft and the internet," in Y. Jewkes (ed.) *Dot.cons: Crime, Deviance, and the Internet*. Cullompton: Willan.

Goodno, N.H. (2007) "Cyberstalking, a new crime: Evaluating the effectiveness of current state and federal laws," *Missouri Law Review*, 72. 66–159.

Hadler, D. and Jaishankar, K. (2008) "Cyber crimes against women in India: Problems, perspectives, and solutions," *TMC Academic Journal*, 3: 48–62.

Hinduja, S. and Patchin, J.W. (2008) "Cyberbullying: An exploratory analysis of factors related to offending and victimization," *Deviant Behavior*, 29: 129–156.

Holt, T.J. and Bossler, A.M. (2009) "Examining the applicability of lifestyle-routine activities theory for cybercrime victimization," *Deviant Behavior*, 30: 1–25.

Keith, S. and Martin, M.E. (2005) "Cyberbullying: Creating a culture of respect in a cyber world," *Reclaiming Children and Youth*, 13: 224–228.

Li, Q. (2006) "Cyberbullying in schools: A research of gender differences," *School Psychology International*, 27: 1–13.

Marcum, C.D. (2008) "Identifying potential factors of adolescent online victimization of high school seniors," *International Journal of Cyber Criminology*, 2: 346–357.

Miller, C. (2006) "Cyber harassment," *Law Enforcement Technology*, 33: 26–30.

Mitchell, K.J., Wolak, J., and Finkelhor, D. (2007) "Trends in youth reports of sexual solicitations, harassment, and unwanted exposure to pornography on the internet," *Journal of Adolescent Health*, 40: 116–126.

Mustaine, E.E. and Tewksbury, R. (2000) "Comparing the lifestyles of victims, offenders, and victim-offenders: A routine activity theory assessment of similarities and differences for criminal incident participants," *Sociological Focus*, 33: 339–362.

Raskauskas, J. and Stolz, A.D. (2007) "Involvement in traditional and electronic bullying among adolescents," *Developmental Psychology*, 43: 564–575.

Roberts, L. (2008) "Jurisdictional and definitional concerns with computer-mediated interpersonal crimes: An analysis on cyber stalking," *International Journal of Cyber Criminology*, 2: 271–285.

Robinson, D.M. (2001) "Routine activity theory: The commentator's perspective," in C.D. Bryant (ed.) *Encyclopedia of Criminology and Deviant Behavior*, Volume I: *Historical, Conceptual, and Theoretical Issues*. Philadelphia, PA: Brunner-Routledge.

Sheridan, L.P. and Grant, T. (2007) "Is cyberstalking different?," *Psychology, Crime and Law,* 13: 627–640.

Spitzberg, B.H. and Hoobler, G. (2002) "Cyberstalking and the technologies of interpersonal terrorism," *New Media and Society,* 4: 71–92.

Williams, K. and Guerra, N.G. (2007) "Prevalence and predictors of internet bullying," *Journal of Adolescent Health,* Supplement: S14–S21.

Wolak, J., Mitchell, K.J., and Finkelhor, D. (2007) "Does online harassment constitute bullying? An exploration of online harassment by known peers and online-only contacts," *Journal of Adolescent Health,* Supplement: S51–S58.

Ybarra, M.L. (2004) "Linkages between depressive symptomology and internet harassment among young regular internet users," *CyberPsychology and Behavior,* 7: 247–257.

Ybarra, M.L. and Mitchell, K.J. (2004) "Youth engaging in online harassment: Association with caregiver–child relationships, internet use, and personal characteristics," *Journal of Adolescence,* 27: 319–336.

54

Ecological crime

Rob White

Introduction

Matters of ecology and environmental harm have come to prominence in recent years due to a conjunction of social activism and greater public acknowledgement of profound changes happening worldwide linked to climate change. This has led to greater interest within the social sciences to questions of eco-crime and deviancy surrounding environmental issues generally.

Green criminology and eco-global criminology

The link between environmental issues and criminology finds its expression in environmental or green criminology, itself a development that has arisen from advances and concerns from outside the field. In this relatively new area of research and scholarship the concern is to stretch the boundaries of mainstream criminology to accommodate issues of global significance, while also utilising the insights of conventional criminology, to illuminate ways in which to understand and respond to environmental harm (White, 2008: 3; see also Beirne and South, 2007; South and Beirne, 2007) .

The expansion of scholarly interest and academic study within criminology on environmental matters is also associated with the development of new ways in which to articulate the issues. For example, recent books such as *Crimes against Nature* (White, 2008), *Global Harms* (Sollund, 2008), *Defining Environmental Justice* (Schlosberg, 2007), *Environmental Justice and Environmentalism* (Sandler and Pezzullo, 2007) and *Resisting Global Toxics* (Pellow, 2007) not only offer new insights into the nature of justice, crime and harm but find the voice to do so through their use of new terms and new concepts by which to describe the world around us. Terms such as 'environmental justice', 'speciesism' and 'ecological citizenship', for example, now feature regularly in such work. The language of green or environmental criminology is thus developing in the same moment as it approaches the study of harm in exciting, novel and critical ways.

Contemporary discussions of transnational environmental crime (e.g., White, 2008, 2009) are highlighting such issues as:

- Illegal transport and dumping of toxic waste.
- Transportation of hazardous materials such as ozone-depleting substances.

- The illegal traffic in real or purported radioactive or nuclear substances.
- Proliferation of 'e'-waste generated by the disposal of tens of thousands of computers and other electronic equipment.
- The safe disposal of old ships and airplanes.
- Local and transborder pollution that is either systematic (via location of factories) or related to accidents (e.g., chemical plant spills).
- Bio-piracy in which Western companies are usurping ownership and control over plants developed using 'traditional' methods and often involving indigenous people in the Third World.
- Illegal trade in flora and fauna.
- Illegal fishing and logging.

The transnational nature of much environmental harm – in terms of perpetrators (such as transnational corporations and organised criminal syndicates), in terms of transference (such as cross-national movement of polluted air and water), in terms of victimisation (such as universalising effects of climate change) and in terms of social conflict (such as increasing tensions and conflicts over goods, water and other resources) – demands new ways of analysing and responding to environmental issues. Eco-global criminology refers to a criminological approach that is informed by ecological considerations and by a critical analysis that is global in scale and perspective. Based upon eco-justice conceptions of harm, it considers transgressions against environments, non-human species and humans. One consequence of global trends, for example, is an expected upsurge in social conflict. These conflicts include those pertaining to diminished environmental resources, to the impacts of global warming, to differential access and use of nature, and to friction stemming from the cross-border transference of harm.

Environmental crime and ecological harm

To speak of 'environmental crime' or 'eco-crime' is to acknowledge some kind of specificity in the act or omission that makes it distinctly relevant to environmental considerations. Yet, as with crime generally, there is much dispute over what is defined as environmental harm, and in particular what ends up in the legal statutes as a 'crime' *per se*.

Issues of pollution and illegal disposal of toxic waste, among others, have generated various legal and law enforcement responses, including the development of environmental protection agencies. Local and national interest in environmental issues, including specific incidents and harms (e.g., Love Canal in the US) have further led researchers to undertake specifically criminological investigations of such harms (Situ and Emmons, 2000). The post-Second World War period has also seen major growth in the internationalisation of treaties, agreements, protocols and conventions in relation to environmental protection and with respect to the securing of environmental resources.

Conventional criminological conceptions of environmental harm tend to be based upon legal conceptions of harm as informed by laws, rules and international conventions. The key issue is one of legality, and the division of activities into legal and illegal categories. Typically, from this perspective, environmental crimes include such things as the illegal taking of flora and fauna (for example, related to fishing, logging and trade in wildlife), pollution offences (for example, illegal dumping through to air, water and land pollution associated with industry), and the transportation of banned substances (for example, illegal transfer of hazardous waste).

A basic premise of green or environmental criminology, however, is that we not only need to take these sorts of environmental harm seriously but we need conceptualisations of harm that go beyond conventional understandings of crime (Beirne and South, 2007). For instance, if ecological (and social and economic) welfare is to be maximised, we need to expand our notions of what actually constitutes environmental crime. Harm, as conceived by critical green criminologists, for example, demands more encompassing definitions than those offered by conventional law and mainstream criminology. This is because some of the most ecologically destructive activities, such as clearfelling of old-growth forests, is quite legal, while more benign practices, such as the growing of hemp (an extremely strong fibre), is criminalised.

Not surprisingly, environmental crime is defined variably by different authors, but in ways that include reference to transgressions against humans, transgressions against environments, and transgressions against non-human animals (see White, 2009). Specific instances of harm and criminal activity range from lobster and abalone poaching, through to pollution and the generation of toxic waste. Environmental harm frequently involves the simultaneous exploitation of particular biospheres, of particular plants and animals, and of the poorest, most vulnerable sections of the human community. Environmental crime and ecological injustice take place within certain historical and social contexts. One consequence of this is the phenomenon of differential victimisation, where different species, biospheres and human population groups are disproportionately subject to criminal and/or harmful activities.

Global warming, oil spills, widespread extinctions, reduction in biodiversity, toxic environments, the disappearance of the Arctic ice, poisonous water, unbreathable air, burning of garbage, clearfelling of forests, the list goes on as to how planetary well-being is being destroyed and diminished in many different ways. Broadly speaking, eco-crime is associated with harms against humans, against specific environments and against animals. Some of these harms are legal (such as the clearfelling of old-growth forests). However, to some degree, they are all now being identified as problematic due to the work of those activists and academics who are defining harm in more expansive ways.

Recent years, for example, have seen greater legislative and judicial attention being given to the rights of the environment *per se*, and to the rights of certain species of non-human animal to live free from human abuse, torture and degradation. This reflects both the efforts of eco-rights activists (e.g., conservationists) and animal rights activists (e.g., animal liberation movements) to change perceptions, and laws, in regard to the natural environment and non-human species. It also reflects the growing recognition that centuries of industrialisation and global exploitation of resources are (now rapidly) transforming the very basis of world ecology. Global warming threatens us all, regardless of where we live or our specific socio-economic situation.

Social constructions of environmental deviancy

A distinction can also be made between environmental crime and crimes associated with the environment. The latter includes what has been described as eco-terrorism or ecotage, acts that are sometimes committed by environmental activists involved in specific campaigns (e.g., tree spiking and damaging earthmoving equipment), and which are, in themselves, legally defined as criminal (Martin, 1990; Amster, 2006). These are crimes committed on behalf, or in defence, of the environment, rather than crimes against the environment. There is nevertheless an important connection between the two sorts of activity (damage to the environment and criminality related to protests over environmentally harmful activities). Moreover, each type of 'crime' calls forth major arguments over definition and what are deemed to be appropriate social responses. As will be seen, deviancy is not only in the eyes of the beholder, but is actively constructed through interaction with others.

SLAPPs

The term SLAPP refers to 'Strategic Lawsuits Against Public Participation'. Generally speaking, a SLAPP is a civil lawsuit filed against private individuals or organisations that have spoken out on issues of public interest or social significance (see Beder, 1997; Walters, 2003). SLAPPs are commonly filed by larger corporations to prevent the public from intervening in disputes and to protect themselves against any claims that could jeopardise their image or reputation. Typically, such suits are cloaked as claims for defamation, nuisance, invasion of privacy, and interference with contract.

Ogle (2007) emphasises the need to distinguish a SLAPP as an effect, rather than intent. He argues that Pring and Canan (1996), who first coined the term in the US, used it to refer to the effect of the suits. They acknowledged that legitimate litigation could be a SLAPP if it had the effect of 'chilling public debate'. As Ogle (2007) observes, the effect on public participation is the same regardless of the merit of the case or the intention of those suing. The real issue around SLAPPs is their impact not just on the defendants but on the broader community's right to public participation. SLAPPs can effectively intimidate people by literally scaring them into silence on issues of public concern. Second, if motive is hard to discern, then accusations of using legal action as a SLAPP can themselves lead to further lawsuits. In other words, calling a suit a SLAPP (when narrowly defined in terms of motive) can call forth a countersuit because it is defamatory (since the label, as narrowly defined, carries the imputation that the plaintiff is abusing the legal system).

SLAPPs have other attributes as well. As indicated, the point of SLAPPs is not to 'win', in the conventional legal sense, but to intimidate those who might be critical of existing or proposed developments. Beder (1997: 65) observes that 'the cost to a developer is part of the cost of doing business, but a court case could well bankrupt an individual or environmental group. In this way the legal system best serves those who have large financial resources at their disposal, particularly corporations.' Claims of defamation, and for damages to company reputation and potential profits, associated with campaigns against certain developments on environmental or social grounds have started to feature more prominently in the corporate arsenal. Public discussion and attempts to regulate corporate activity more strictly become even more difficult in such an intimidating atmosphere.

Greenwashing

In a manner analogous to the denial of human rights violations, environmental issues call forth a range of techniques of neutralisation on the part of nation-states and corporations which ultimately legitimate and justify certain types of environmentally unfriendly activity. For example, this takes the form of 'greenwashing' media campaigns which misconstrue the nature of collective corporate business in regards to the environment.

The phenomenon of greenwashing has been incorporated into many companies' operational practices in one way or another. It refers to putting a particular corporate 'spin' on environmental issues and problems. Much of it has to do with image-making, and hence it is heavily tied up with public relations and the manipulation of ideas through the mass media (see Athanasiou, 1996; Beder, 1997).

Techniques of greenwashing include publishing annual reports on recycled paper or only online; establishing and participating in business environment institutes and awards; and sponsoring World Environment Day. It can also involve manipulation of statistics:

> 3M claims in its promotional materials that 3P [Pollution Prevention Pays] prevented
> seventy-two million pounds of pollutants from being released every year between 1975 and

1989. It does not say that because of dramatic increases in production its total output of pollutants actually increased during that period.

(Athanasiou, 1996: 236)

What you see is not always what you get. This extends in other directions as well.

For instance, an insidious aspect of greenwashing is the creation and use of 'front organisations' (Athanasiou, 1996). Innocuous or misleading titles are intended to hide a multitude of industry interests and links (e.g., Global Climate Coalition, an industry group that is resistant to moves to restrict carbon emissions). Investigation of front groups often reveals direct funding by industry and strong personal ties between the 'community group' and the industry in question. Public relations firms have also been implicated in their establishment, as well as in creating situations which discredit 'real' community groups. Front groups are successful to the extent that they are not challenged and dismissed by journalists, government and the public; too often, the constructed veneer of such groups as community groups is taken at face value and they are given more credence than they deserve (Burton, 1997; see also Beder, 1997).

While greenwashing in its many and varied forms does exist, its success is less than definite. For example, ordinary people now have access to multiple sources of information. They are also frequently hit with the material realities of environmental degradation in their daily lives (such as toxic waste, oil spills and bad drinking water). There is thus a material basis for continuing concern, and protests, about environmental destruction, regardless of how powerful the corporate sector might appear to be.

Eco-terrorism

Another inhibiting factor when it comes to taking action over environmental issues relates to the alleged link between environmental activism and 'terrorism'. Consider, for example, the following list of direct actions taken by some individual environmental activists and activist groups (Brisman, 2008: 754):

> firebombing, defacing, or slashing the tires of SUVs; vandalizing business walls and windows with glass-etching cream and spray-paint; damaging construction equipment used for housing developments or mega-stores; burning buildings (such as laboratories, horse corrals, and unoccupied housing developments); tree-spiking (placing spikes in trees to fend off loggers' chainsaws); 'net-ripping' (which, similar to tree-spiking, involves dumping into the ocean tonnes of steel I-beams welded together to form large spikes that destroy bottom-trawling nets); blocking access to forest land that would otherwise be logged; disrupting hunts or otherwise preventing recreational hunters from hunting; sabotaging research or facilities using animal-testing techniques; and liberating or removing animals from fur farms or laboratories and industries that conduct animal-based research.

Many of these activities are harmful, dangerous and serious in their consequences. Many are also illegal or criminal. Yet all are defended on the basis of fighting for the general interest or some higher good.

This raises the issue of how far can or should one be allowed to go in order to defend environmental interests (as variously defined)? The rationale for such actions is generally along the lines of breaking the law for the sake of environmental/animal protection. Indeed, social change has long been based upon such principles, which argue that if existing laws and practices are unjust or unfair, then justice itself demands that they must be challenged. Such was the case with the suffragette movements of the late nineteenth and early twentieth centuries, the civil rights struggles of the 1960s and 1970s, and, today, the social movements that focus on environmental issues and animal rights.

Further ambiguity on these issues stems from two quarters. On the one hand, as scientific evidence firms up about certain harms (for example, global warming), public support is likely to grow in favour of actions that appear to address these issues (for example, attempts to stop the cutting down of old-growth forests). Political support from mainstream parties will also be reflected in such trends, and indeed a general greening of politics is now taking place worldwide. Thus, what was once seen as the preserve of extremists is presently being transformed into the concerns of the mainstream, albeit generally excluding more extreme forms of direct action.

On the other hand, different jurisdictions view and respond to acts of environmental 'resistance' in different ways. For example, in the US, the recent tendency has been to brand damage-causing acts of protest as ecotage or environmental terrorism, and to prosecute and sanction offenders heavily (Rovics, 2007; Brisman, 2008). By contrast, consider a recent court case in England that featured six Greenpeace activists (McCarthy, 2008). The six had been charged with criminal damage after scaling and defacing a chimney at Kingsnorth, a location earmarked for the development of a new generation of coal-fired power plants. At the conclusion of the eight-day trial, the jury decided that the activists had been justified in causing damage due to the larger threat of global warming. The jurors thus accepted the defence argument that the defendants had 'lawful excuse' (under the Criminal Damage Act of 1971) to damage the chimney in order to prevent even greater damage caused by climate change.

Mass public opinion, as affected by both sustained greenwashing campaigns and specific kinds of environmentalist attack, will influence legal decision-making and legislative change in this area. A polarisation of views can be one consequence of this. In the United States, for example, there are two opposing understandings of environmental activism as this pertains to civil disobedience and the employment of direct action tactics. These are encapsulated in the following phrases:

- *The Threat of Eco-terrorism* – which refers to extremism in the animal rights and environmental movements, and typically involves causing damage to the operations of companies or terrorising executives and employees of companies. A key emphasis is on the portrayal of environmental extremism as terrorist activity (ADL Law Enforcement Agency Resource Network, 2009).
- *The Green Scare* – which refers to a systematic movement, similar to the Red Scare of the 1950s, to discredit and penalise environmental and animal activists through application of new laws and punitive prosecutions in ways that involve heavy-handed government interventions and crackdowns, accompanied by sustained scaremongering fostered by corporate and media interests, around the theme of terrorism (Potter, 2008).

The social construction of environmental activism is a collective process involving many different players and interests. The justification for legal and illegal actions around environmental and animal issues relates to perceptions that many presently legal activities in fact constitute crimes against nature (whether this be a forest or in relation to animals). Conversely, some of the actions to protest against these alleged crimes are themselves subject to considerable criticism on the basis of their present illegality (and, indeed, the harm they inflict on others).

Whether construed as eco-terrorism or justified resistance, it is clear that the more extremist acts demand ethical parameters that can constrain both the acts themselves and the circumstances in which they may be undertaken (see Vanderheiden, 2005). This is a crucial point, for otherwise the potential to do good – on both sides – is undermined by ideological blindness, personal vindictiveness and wilful denial of consequence.

Conclusion

Many areas of harm to humans, environments and non-human animals are presently not criminalised. This includes such destructive, degrading and de-humanising practices as clearfelling of old-growth forests, reliance upon battery-hen egg and poultry production, and use of depleted uranium in weapons. Eco-global criminology entails the exposure of such practices as negative, degrading and hazardous by reconceptualising the nature of harm and putting the case for the banning and close control of such practices.

References

ADL Law Enforcement Agency Resource Network (2009) 'Ecoterrorism: Extremism in the Animal Rights and Environmentalist Movements', www.adl.org/learn/ext_us/Ecoterrorism_print.asp (accessed 6 April 2009).

Amster, R. (2006) 'Perspectives on Ecoterrorism: Catalysts, Conflations, and Casualties', *Contemporary Justice Review*, 9(3): 287–301.

Athanasiou, T. (1996) *Divided Planet: The Ecology of Rich and Poor*. Boston, MA: Little, Brown and Company.

Beder, S. (1997) *Global Spin: The Corporate Assault on Environmentalism*. Melbourne: Scribe.

Beirne, P. and South, N. (eds) (2007) *Issues in Green Criminology: Confronting Harms against Environments, Humanity and Other Animals*. Cullompton: Willan.

Brisman, A. (2008) 'Crime-Environment Relationships and Environmental Justice', *Seattle Journal for Social Justice*, 6(2): 727–817.

Burton, B. (1997) 'Invisible PR: Dirty Tricks for Media Consumption', *Australian Journalism Review*, 19(1): 133–143.

Martin, M. (1990) 'Ecosabotage and Civil Disobediance', *Environmental Ethics*, 12: 291–310.

McCarthy, M. (2008) 'Cleared: Jury Decides that Threat of Global Warming Justifies Breaking the Law', *Independent*, 11 September 2008, www.independent.co.uk/environment/climate-change/cleared-jury-decides-that . . . (accessed 10 October 2008).

Ogle, G. (2007) 'Beating a SLAPP Suit', *Alternative Law Journal*, 32(2): 71–74.

Pellow, D. (2007) *Resisting Global Toxics: Transnational Movements for Environmental Justice*. Cambridge, MA: MIT Press.

Potter, W. (2008) 'What is the "Green Scare"?', www.greenisthenewred.com/blog/green-scare/ (accessed 6 April 2009).

Pring, G. and Canan, P. (1996) *SLAPPs: Getting Sued for Speaking out*. Philadelphia, PA: Temple University Press.

Rovics, D. (2007) 'Pivotal Moment in the Green Scare', *Capitalism Nature Socialism*, 18(3): 8–16.

Sandler, R. and Pezzullo, P. (eds) (2007) *Environmental Justice and Environmentalism: The Social Justice Challenge to the Environmental Movement*. Cambridge, MA: MIT Press.

Schlosberg, D. (2007) *Defining Environmental Justice: Theories, Movements, and Nature*. Oxford: Oxford University Press.

Situ, Y. and Emmons, D. (2000) *Environmental Crime: The Criminal Justice System's Role in Protecting the Environment*. Thousand Oaks, CA: Sage.

Sollund, R. (ed.) (2008) *Global Harms: Ecological Crime and Speciesism*. New York: Nova Science.

South, N. and Beirne, N. (eds) (2007) *Green Criminology*. Aldershot: Ashgate.

Vanderheiden, S. (2005) 'Eco-Terrorism or Justified Resistance? Radical Environmentalism and the "War on Terror"', *Politics & Society*, 33(3): 425–447.

Walters, B. (2003) *Slapping on the Writs: Defamation, Developers and Community Activism*. Sydney: UNSW Press.

White, R. (2008). *Crimes against Nature: Environmental Criminology and Ecological Justice*. Cullompton: Willan.

White, R. (2009) *Environmental Crime: A Reader*. Cullompton: Willan.

55

Terrorism and terrorists

Emilio C. Viano

The definition of terrorism

The statutory definition of terrorism that the United States government uses is: "premeditated, politically motivated violence perpetrated against non-combatant targets by subnational groups or clandestine agents, usually intended to influence an audience" (22 USC 2656f (d)). Thus, terrorism has several elements:

- *Premeditation*—there must be an intent and a prior decision to commit an act that entails this type of violence.
- *Political motivation*, thus eliminating criminal violence for monetary gain or personal revenge.
- *Attacking people who cannot defend themselves or respond in kind.*
- *Planned and carried out by a group.* (Whether there can be a case of "individual" terrorism is debated. The place and the role of clandestine agents and subnational groups are delicate because many governments, including the United States, have utilized both.)

Some consider the threat of violence as terrorism as well.

It is essential to remember that terrorism is first and foremost a method rather than a group of enemies or the objectives they want to realize; and that it centers on what people do rather than who they are and what they are attempting to achieve.

The history of terrorism

Terrorism is basically and fundamentally political—very much about pursuing, acquiring, and using power to cause political change. Consequently, it is also violence or the threat of violence utilized and aimed in the pursuit of or in the service of a political objective.

The word "terrorism" initially became popular during the French Revolution, when it had a pro-governmental, "positive" connotation. The *"regime de la terreur"* of 1793–4, from which the English word originates, was established as a means to impose and consolidate power during the transient anarchical time of disorder and unrest that followed the revolution of 1789. Thus, far from being an anti-government operation, the *"regime de la terreur"* was actually a government tool. It was meant to consolidate and firm up the power of the new government by intimidating, terrifying, and eliminating counter-revolutionaries, political opponents, and any other dissidents labeled "enemies of the people." In other words, it was state-sponsored terror enforced through the liberal use of the guillotine. The word "terrorism" was popularized in English by Edmund Burke in his polemic tract against the French Revolution where he wrote about "thousands of those Hell hounds called Terrorists . . . let loose on the people" (Hoffman 1998: para. 14).

The French Revolution did inspire independence and nationalist movements that flourished and created modern nation states in Europe, such as Germany and Italy. Contemporaneously, dramatic socioeconomic changes were the consequence of massive industrialization, particularly in England and Germany. The alienation and exploitation of workers by 19th-century capitalism provided fertile ground for the sprouting and growing of new "universalist" ideologies like socialism and communism. During this period of intense change in Europe the concept of terrorism was developed and expanded. An Italian revolutionary, Carlo Pisacane, leading a rebellion against the Bourbon monarchy in southern Italy, developed the influential idea of "propaganda by deed." Pisacane wrote: "The propaganda of the idea is a chimera. Ideas result from deeds, not the latter from the former. The people will not be free when they are educated. They will be educated when they are free" (quoted in Ruby 2002). He argued that violence is needed not only to attract attention to the cause or to generate publicity but to inform, educate, and in the end get the masses behind the revolution. Pamphlets, wall posters or gatherings will never effectively substitute for the didactic value of violence.

One of the most notable groups to practice Pisacane's theory was Narodnaya Volya (People's Will or People's Freedom), a small group of Russian proponents of constitutional government founded in 1878 to limit the unconstrained power of the tsar. Because the Russian impoverished and illiterate masses were apathetic, fearful, and alienated, the group resorted to spectacular, violent acts to attract attention to its cause and to demonstrate that the tsarist government was not invulnerable or omnipotent. Narodnaya Volya refined the "propaganda by deed" approach by avoiding mass casualties and focusing instead on specific targets selected especially for their symbolic value, such as the tsar himself. Ironically, the success of the group in assassinating Tsar Alexander II on March 1, 1881 led to its complete suppression.

The message of Pisacane and Narodnaya Volya deeply impacted the growing anarchist movement. An anarchist conference in London in 1881 supported the idea of tyrannicide to achieve revolutionary change. At that conference, an "Anarchist International" (or "Black International") was established, spurring the growth of the mythology of a global revolution in the offing.

Following the assassination of President McKinley in 1901 by a young Hungarian refugee, the US Congress quickly approved legislation barring anyone who did not believe in or rejected organized government from entering the country. From 1887 until the end of the 1920s, anarchists succeeded in a series of political assassinations and several well-publicized bombings. However, these had little overall impact. The anarchists also produced widely available "how to" manuals for bomb-making and other violent acts.

During the last two decades of the 19th century, increasing unrest and liberation movements troubled the decaying Ottoman and Hapsburg empires. Notably, the Armenians undertook a strong campaign against the Ottoman Empire in eastern Turkey. Unfortunately, their quest for freedom and autonomy brought upon them the first holocaust of the 20th century. An estimated one million Armenians were slaughtered by Turkey. Some other revolutionary organizations in that region eventually degenerated into organized crime groups. A similar movement in Bosnia made up mostly of young Bosnian Serbs, Mlada Bosnia (Young Bosnia), approved of assassination to establish a Southern Slav political entity. This eventually led to the assassination of Archduke Franz Ferdinand on June 28, 1914 and subsequently to the outbreak of the First World War.

By the 1930s, "terrorism" meant mostly the politics and practices of mass oppression and repression utilized by dictatorships against their own citizenry, especially in Nazi Germany, Fascist Italy, and the Stalinist Soviet Union. Total compliance was guaranteed through various violent measures, including fear, coercion, political violence, street attacks, and the widespread persecution of Jews, Gypsies, homosexuals, religious figures, and others who protested. At the head of the Soviet Union, Stalin learned from Hitler how to transform a political party, in his case the Communist Party, into an instrument totally submitted to his will, and the state's law enforcement, military, and intelligence agencies into servile tools of repression, coercion, and oppression. Stalin's repressive purges, mass exiles, mass forced labor, mass transportation to Siberia, and gulags were planned and carried out as a progressive conspiracy to seize total power and completely silence any dissent through state terrorism.

Similar forms of state-planned violence have occurred in various parts of the world ever since, such as the right-wing military dictatorships in Chile, Argentina (Buchanan 1987; Cox 1983), and Brazil in South America; Greece, Spain, and Portugal in Europe; various African countries; and the Philippines, Indonesia, Myanmar, and Pakistan in Asia. It has even affected elected governments in the 1980s, for instance in El Salvador, Guatemala, Nicaragua, Colombia, and Peru, and today, for instance in Zimbabwe, Uzbekistan, Egypt, and other states of the Middle East. The Cultural Revolution in the People's Republic of China in the 1960s under Mao Zedong and in Cambodia in the late 1970s under the Khmer Rouge are examples of left-wing state terrorism.

The meaning of terrorism changed after the Second World War by reclaiming the revolutionary reputation with which it is associated today. At that time, in the late 1940s, 1950s, and even into the 1960s, it was associated with the uprisings by indigenous populations in Africa, Asia, and the Middle East to expel European colonial powers from their countries, especially through guerrilla warfare. Well-known examples are Algeria, Cyprus, Israel, Kenya, and Vietnam. The Cuban Revolution became a model for left-wing ideologues in their own struggles against capitalist powers. Because these movements were perceived internationally as a struggles for liberation, decolonization, and self-determination, thanks in part to adroit public relations campaigns by the insurgents and their supporters in the First World, their members were called "freedom fighters." This was also part of the Cold War's psychological and political warfare between the Soviet Union and its supporters, who praised the insurgents for their fights against capitalism, and the United States and Western Europe, who resisted them, for instance in the Philippines and Puerto Rico in the case of the United States. Thus, for example, the United States in the 1980s called the guerrillas in El Salvador, Guatemala, and Honduras "terrorists" because of their left-wing leanings and invested considerable military and counter-insurgency resources to defeat them. Meanwhile, it considered the mujahedin fighting the Soviet occupation of Afghanistan "freedom fighters" and gave them ample assistance, training, and arms, unaware that it was setting in motion the process leading to 9/11.

Several Third World and Communist Bloc countries described insurgency and rebellion in this way—not as terrorism but as fighting for freedom. For instance, this view was famously expounded by the chairman of the Palestine Liberation Organization (PLO), Yasser Arafat, when he appeared before the United Nations General Assembly in 1974: "For whoever stands by a just cause and fights for the freedom and liberation of his land from the invaders, the settlers, and the colonists, cannot possibly be called terrorist" (Arafat 1974: para. 48).

At the end of the 1960s and in the 1970s, terrorism was still viewed within a revolutionary framework. Ethnic minorities seeking independence or autonomy used terrorism not only to inflict casualties and serious damage on the dominant group but to attract international attention, sympathy, and aid. Among them were (and still are, in some cases) the PLO, Canada's separatist

Front de Libération du Québec, the Basque ETA (Euskadi ta Askatasuna or "Freedom for the Basque Homeland"), a South Moluccan group seeking independence from Indonesia and striking out in the Netherlands, the PKK (Kurdistan Workers' Party), the Irish Republican Army (IRA), which renounced armed struggle only in 2005, and others (Criss 1995; Bell 1996).

In the mid-1980s, a series of suicide bombings aimed mostly at American diplomatic and military targets in the Middle East abruptly called attention to the growing menace of state-sponsored terrorism. Several renegade foreign governments, such as Iran, Iraq, Libya, and Syria were suspected and indeed accused of being actively involved in sponsoring or commissioning such terrorist acts. Examples included the bombings of the Marines' barracks in Lebanon in 1983, attributed to Hizbollah ("The Party of God") but supported by Iran and Syria, and of Pan-American Flight 103 over Scotland by Libyan agents on December 21, 1988, killing 250 passengers and crew, mostly Americans.

In the early 1990s, two new expressions appeared: "narcoterrorism" and the "gray area phenomenon." The former is the alliance of completely criminal, violent, and economically driven organizations with terrorist and guerrilla entities using violence both for the advancement of their business activities and for political ends. The best-known example is the close alliance between Colombian cocaine cartels and left-wing terrorist groups like the FARC in Colombia and Sendero Luminoso in Peru. The CIA was also alleged to have engaged in drug trafficking, mostly directed at minority communities in Southern California, to finance arms deals for "freedom fighters" against the Sandinista regime in Nicaragua (Brown and Merrill 1995).

The "gray area phenomenon" refers to the difficulty of pinpointing precisely where and what terrorism is. This approach reflects the growing fluidity and chameleon-like changeability of subnational conflict in the post-Cold War era. Terrorism, in this sense, represents threats to the stability of nation-states by non-state actors and violence impacting large regions of the world, or major urban areas where the central government has lost its influence and control to new half-political, half-criminal groups. It also includes conflicts that do not fit well into traditionally recognized concepts of war as the fighting between clearly marked armed forces of two or more recognized countries. Instead, it involves irregular forces as one or more of the combatants. The shift here is clearly toward non-state conflict.

In a sense, terrorism is always changing and new. It must be kept in mind that terrorism has also existed and thrived in Europe and in North America. In the United States, the most notorious example is the 1995 Oklahoma City bombing, carried out by people with strong right-wing tendencies. Similarly, the front-lawn cross burnings and other menacing rituals of the Ku Klux Klan were designed to terrorize minorities demanding their rights and their white sympathizers (Baumel 1999; Smith 1994; Stern 1999; Walter 1995; Corcoran 1995; Coates 1987).

The new terrorism

The United States and the rest of the Western world were awakened to the existence of a new form of terrorism based in the Middle East by a series of events that culminated in the September 11, 2001 attacks in New York and Washington, DC. Since then, the names Osama Bin-Laden and al-Qaeda have become universally known and immediately connected with a violent struggle against the United States and Western interests more generally, based in the Middle East but with an international reach and a strong religious dimension (Stern 1999).

The danger of the new terrorism stems in particular from the fact that its activists form loosely linked cells that do not depend on a single leader or state sponsor. It is transnational, borderless, and carried out by non-state actors. There are several differences between the "new" and "old" forms of terrorism:

- The new terrorism is more violent. In the old model, terrorists mostly wanted to generate attention, not mass casualties. The new terrorists want both.
- The most dangerous terrorists today are transnational, non-state actors who want to inflict damage and even destroy the West and all secular state systems, including the current Islamic ones. Previous terrorists had mostly local agendas and aspirations.
- Today's terrorism is global in reach and has strategic objectives. Its activists are loyal to a cause, not to a particular state or political entity. This presents considerable challenges to governments that are accustomed to operating on a state-to-state level. A state wants to know who to threaten with force, with whom to negotiate, and who to sanction. The new terrorism makes this practically impossible.
- The new terrorists are much better financed than their predecessors, who depended mostly on state sponsors. They can access income generated from legal and illegal sources (e.g., drug trafficking, arms dealing, raw materials, precious stones, and people trafficking) and are not reliant on state sponsors. Al-Qaeda, for example, is a rich, multinational organization with many sources of income. This wealth can be used to buy entry and safe haven in certain countries; to subcontract certain missions to local organizations that know the terrain well; and to compensate the families of terrorists killed in action.
- Contemporary terrorists are much better trained in military, special operations, and intelligence functions. They are also less easy to infiltrate than earlier groups. The cellular structure of al-Qaeda and similar terrorist organizations is especially hard to penetrate, particularly for bureaucratic and hierarchical security organizations like those of the United States and other Western countries. The attempted terrorist attack on Northwest Flight 253 at Christmas 2009, the intelligence failures that made it possible, and the growing presence of al-Qaeda in Yemen and the Horn of Africa all point to this fact. It is extremely difficult to identify, locate, and infiltrate decentralized organizations whose members are unknown to one another, have never met in one place together, and utilize strict discipline during essential communication. Moreover, religious and highly motivated extremists are difficult to entrap using the traditional methods of money, entertainment, and sex. They cannot be easily bought, bribed, or blackmailed. As evidence of this, at the time of writing, the large rewards offered by the United States for the capture of Osama Bin-Laden and Mullah Omar remained uncollected.

Weapons of mass destruction

The reputed availability of weapons of mass destruction has raised the bar on the threat posed by today's terrorists and the potential damage that they might inflict. Up to now, terrorists have relied on small arms; explosives, particularly Semtex or plastique; rocket-propelled grenades; and, every once in a while, a shoulder-fired anti-aircraft missile. While these weapons continue to be used, more concern is now focusing on nuclear, radiological, chemical, and biological weapons, all potentially catastrophic weapons of mass destruction originating mostly in Russia and Eastern Europe, Pakistan, and North Korea (Gavel 2002).

New technologies

Information technologies, like the internet, cellular phones, instant messaging, and real-time photographic and filming capabilities, have facilitated and amplified the global reach of several terrorist organizations. There have already been sizeable cyberterrorist attacks. A new term, "Cybergeddon," relates to the potential loss of intellectual property, intelligence infrastructure, data exchange, or storage. Terrorists may be attempting to create a "virtual 9/11" by inflicting even more damage through a cyberattack but without commensurate levels of visible destruction. Russian hackers allegedly mounted this type of internet attack on networks in Estonia and Georgia in 2008. Cybersecurity is hampered because the threat is largely invisible, not taken seriously, or sometimes not even recognized while it is happening. Yet hacking has been widely utilized. Internet sites have come under attack; websites have been hijacked or defaced; there have been cases of denial of service, automated e-mail bombings, and web "sit-ins."

New technology has also been used by terrorists to increase their efficiency and reach. Management and administrative functions of terrorist organizations, coordinating operations, recruiting new members, improving communications between existing members, attracting people sympathetic to the cause, collecting, managing, and transferring funds, and spreading the group's message and philosophy have all been greatly facilitated by the impressive advances in information technology and communications.

Abolition of borders

Globalization and regional trading zones such as the European Union, Mercosur, NAFTA and others have made it easier for terrorists to expand their activities internationally. It is not only legitimate commerce and trade that gain from the abolition of border controls but organized criminals, drug traffickers, and terrorists. Their work is made easier and their movements are less easily detected. This has facilitated the territorial expansion of terrorist groups, the establishment of cells abroad, and the free movement across vast regions of the world in the planning and execution of terrorist activities. It is now much easier for terrorists to avoid detection and capture. And even if they are arrested, their prosecution is hampered because of the complexities of extradition treaties and procedures. Briefly, what is good for international commerce and communications is equally good for international terrorism (White 2002).

Terrorism, guerrillas, and crime

Terrorism is commonly confused with guerrilla activities. Guerrillas and terrorists frequently employ the same techniques—assassination, kidnapping, bombing of public places, hostage taking—to intimidate or coerce, thus impacting behavior through fear. Additionally, both are frequently undistinguishable from non-combatants. However, an important difference is that guerrilla generally refers to a numerically larger group of individuals who act as a military unit, attack military forces or the police, seize and hold territory (if only for a few hours), and control a defined geographical area and its population.

Terrorists are also frequently confused or equated with common violent criminals, who utilize similar violent acts to achieve specific goals (e.g., kidnapping, shooting, and arson). However, their motives are very different. The criminal is driven foremost by personal greed and the desire for personal gain and does not necessarily intend for his act to have long-lasting consequences, make a political statement, or impact public opinion (Turvey et al. 1999).

The terrorist is also different from the lone assassin, whose goal is often personal and egocentric. John Hinckley, who tried to kill President Ronald Reagan, was trying to impress the actress Jodie Foster. His was purely a personal quest.

References

Arafat, Y. (1974) "Speech by Yasser Arafat at the United Nations General Assembly, New York." Available at: www.mideastweb.org/arafat_at_un.htm (accessed July 5, 2009).

Baumel, J. T. (1999) Kahane in America: "An Exercise in Right Wing Urban Terror," *Studies in Conflict and Terrorism*, 22: 311–29.

Bell, J. B. (1996) "Ireland: The Long End Game," *Studies in Conflict and Terrorism*, 21: 5–28.

Brown, D. J. and Merill, R. (1995) *Violent Persuasions: The Politics and Imagery of Terrorism*, Seattle, WA: Bay Press.

Buchanan, P. C. (1987) "The Varied Faces of Domination, State Terror, Economic Policy and Social Response during the Argentinean 'Proceso,' 1976–1981," *American Journal of Political Science*, 31: 336–80.

Coates, J. (1987) *Armed and Dangerous: The Rise of the Survivalist Right*, New York: Hill & Wong.

Corcoran, J. (1995) *Bitter Harvest: The Birth of Paramilitary Terrorism in the Heartland*, New York: Penguin.

Cox, R. (1983) "Total Terrorism: Argentina, 1969–1979," in M. Crenshaw (ed.) *Terrorism, Legitimacy and Power*, Middletown, CT: Wesleyan University Press.

Criss, N.B. (1995) "The Nature of PKK Terrorism in Turkey," *Studies in Conflict and Terrorism*, 18: 17–38.

Gavel, D. (2002) "Can Nuclear Weapons Be Put beyond the Reach of Terrorists?," *Kennedy School of Government Bulletin*, Autumn.

Hoffman, B. (1998) *Inside Terrorism*, New York: Columbia University Press. Available at: www.nytimes.com/books/first/h/hoffman-terrorism.html (accessed July 5, 2009).

Ruby, F. (2002) "Anarcha-Feminism." Available at: www.anarcha.org/sallydarity/AnarchaFeminism byFlickRuby.htm (accessed March 2, 2011).

Smith, B. (1994) *Terrorism in America: Pipe Bombs and Pipe Dreams*, Albany: State University of New York Press.

Stern, J. (1999) *The Ultimate Terrorists*, Cambridge, MA: Harvard University Press.

Turvey, B. E., Diana T., and Jerry C. W. (eds.) (1999) *Criminal Profiling: An Introduction to Behavioral Evidence Analysis*, San Diego, CA: Academic Press.

Walter, J. (1995) *Every Knee Shall Bow: The Truth and Tragedy of Ruby Ridge and the Randy Weaver Family*, New York: HarperCollins.

White, J. R. (2002) *Terrorism*, Belmont, CA: Wadsworth Thomson.

Wilkinson, P. (1994) *Terrorism: British Perspective*, New York: Hall.

Zanni, M. (1999) "Middle Eastern terrorism and Netward," *Studies in Conflict and Terrorism*, 22: 247–56.

Part XI

Crime: traditional non-violent modes

Overview

One of the more common categories of criminal deviance is that of traditional non-violent crimes. Part XI includes four chapters that address particular forms of this category of deviance. The forms of deviance explored are fraud and embezzlement, burglary, motor vehicle theft, and arson. The combined cost to society of these four crimes is enormous, perhaps more than the cost of most other types of crime combined. The number of victims affected by such is equally enormous. With the exception of motor vehicle theft, which is little more than a century old, the other three have their roots in antiquity. Interestingly, although numerous counter-measures have been developed to prevent the occurrence of these offenses, or at least to minimize the frequency of their commission, none of these countermeasures has ever been successful. Examples here might be burglar alarms in homes, surveillance cameras in businesses, and electronic immobilizers on motor vehicles. The criminal mind is fertile, and no matter what the pace of development of "target hardening" strategies and devices, the offenders have always been able to defeat them.

Although classified as "non-violent" in this volume, these crimes sometimes do become violent. The burglar breaking into a home may be killed by the homeowner, or vice versa. "Carjacking" may result in the death of the driver or passenger. Arson, regardless of the original motivation of the offender, could result in death.

Traditional non-violent crimes are a constant threat to individuals and society itself, and they seem to be as durable as granite.

Fraud and embezzlement

In his chapter, Robert Morris provides an overview of the current state of research addressing fraud and embezzlement, focusing on the prevalence of certain types of fraud, the harms associated with fraud and embezzlement, the characteristics of offenders, and victimization statistics.

The US Department of Justice defines fraud as "when a person or business intentionally deceives another with promises of goods, services, or financial benefit that do not exist, were never intended to be provided, or were misrepresented." The label "fraud" refers to a very wide variety of violation of trust crimes, ranging from counterfeiting to telemarketing scams, and from tax evasion to Ponzi schemes. Morris articulates a number of such crimes and discusses some in detail. He also reveals the cost of such crimes: in 2004, they cost US employers more than $660 billion.

Morris's examination of specific forms of violation of trust crime begins with his discussion of embezzlement. He defines this crime as "the destruction or fraudulent appropriation of another's money or merchandise which has been entrusted to one's care." This differs from larceny in that the offender usually enjoys a fiduciary relationship with the victim. Morris reports that bank embezzlement is unique because of the characteristics of its offenders, who tend to be younger than those who commit other offenses. They are also much more likely to be female (45%), with many coming from "stable 'working' families." These female embezzlers tend to occupy clerical positions at banks, whereas male embezzlers tend to hold managerial positions.

One research study suggested that embezzlers could be classified on the basis of their motivation. Apparently, some embezzlers take a job with no initial intention to embezzle, while others seek jobs specifically for that purpose. Male embezzlers tend to rationalize their activities as mere "borrowing," while female embezzlers are more likely to view their actions as violations of trust. Men tended to embezzle to increase their social standing or to cover up errors. Female offenders did so for family welfare, to garner affection from their husbands, or through self-serving interest or greed.

Morris reports that credit card theft is an understudied crime, even though it has been a multi-billion-dollar problem since at least the mid-1990s. Offenders differ from other white-collar criminals in that they are less likely to be white or male, tend to be younger, and display lower levels of social stability. In other words, credit card offenders reflect the characteristics of many street-level offenders.

Morris differentiates between check fraud and check forgery. The former refers to offenders who write bad checks on their own accounts, or write checks for amounts that exceed their account balance. Check forgers manufacture counterfeit checks for fraudulent purposes. Research has shown that "naive check forgers tend to be male, white," "older than traditional criminals," "intellectually stronger," and possess "educational levels that were equal to or surpassed the general public of the time."

Fraudulent insurance claims have also been under-researched, according to Morris. This type of fraud is very expensive, costing the industry about $120 billion each year. Morris advises that "some 20 percent of all insurance claims submitted are fraudulent and fraudsters are rarely, if ever, arrested."

Currency counterfeiting has become much more widespread in contemporary times because of the amazing advances in printing technology. Morris indicates that approximately $300 million in counterfeit currency was seized in the US between 2003 and 2008, but even more fake US bills are in circulation in other countries.

Morris discusses tax evasion at length. Annual losses from tax evasion are approximately $300 billion annually in the US. About 25 percent of US taxpayers admit that they intentionally under-report their income level. Non-compliance offenders tend to be "male, younger, less educated, in low- or high- but not middle-income brackets." They usually live in areas with higher levels of minority residents and have friends who also evade paying tax.

Morris continues his chapter with an examination of identity theft and confidence games and concludes with a discussion of evidence from self-report research. He offers the observation that "our transition into the digital age will undoubtedly result in increased levels of fraud and new offenses that cannot yet be imagined."

Burglary

In his chapter, Jim Hawdon provides a concise yet detailed overview and analysis of the crime of burglary, defined by the FBI as "the unlawful entry of a structure to commit a felony or theft." "Structure" does not have to mean a house. It is used in a very generic fashion and could equally be a house trailer, houseboat, railroad car, store, sailing vessel, office, stable, apartment, or barn. Burglary also does not require the use of force to acquire entry.

It is the second most common type of crime in the US, with 2,179,140 burglaries recorded in 2007. Two-thirds of these burglaries were of residential households, most of which occurred during the day. Burglaries of offices and stores are most likely to occur at night.

Despite its continuing prevalence, rates of burglary have declined significantly in the United States in recent years. However, it remains costly, resulting in a $4 billion economic loss in 2007—approximately $2,000 per incident. In addition to the economic loss, victims often experience emotional distress and quality of life impacts.

Hawdon reports that studies of burglary can be divided into three broad categories: research on burglars, research on victims, and research on where burglaries occur. These three topics are interrelated. In regard to research on the burglars themselves, he indicates that 85% are male. They are also young, with approximately 60% of arrested burglars in the US under the age of 25, and 25% under the age of 18. Approximately 68% of them are black.

Effective burglars need technical and social skills to accomplish their criminal task. They often work in teams, and rely on networks of individuals, such as "tipsters," "fences," lawyers and bondsmen, and pawnshop owners, to mention but a few. Like many other career criminals, burglars often receive informal training. Research has shown that they are rational, employing and weighing a variety of environmental cues to select their targets. These include "gain cues" (perceptions of the quality and quantity of property to be burglarized) and "risk cues" (the likelihood that someone will detect the crime and apprehend the burglar).

As far as victims are concerned, African Americans are 1.5 times more likely to be burglarized than white households. Households with younger heads are more likely to be burglarized than those with older heads. And economically disadvantaged households are more likely to be burglarized than wealthy households. Leaving one's house unoccupied increases one's chance of being burglarized. Interestingly, being burglarized raises the chances of being burglarized again, often by the same perpetrators. People living alone—be they single, separated, or divorced—are approximately twice as likely to be reburglarized as a married household. There is even a correlation between the degree to which individuals worry about being burglarized and their likelihood of actually being burglarized.

In terms of environment, Hawdon indicates that burglaries are more likely to occur in urban areas, especially cities. Attractiveness, opportunity, and accessibility all tend to lure burglars to specific residential neighborhoods. They also target areas with which they are familiar, often because they are close to where they themselves live.

Hawdon concludes his chapter by discussing the theoretical integration of the research findings on burglars, victims, and the ecology of burglary using the routine activities perspective.

Motor vehicle theft

Heith Copes and Michael Cherbonneau, in their chapter on motor vehicle theft, point out that this crime is relatively under-researched. This is changing, however, and there has been increasing interest because of changes in motor vehicle theft rates and new laws to address the problem. Their chapter summarizes what is now a sizeable body of research literature, focusing on prevalence and trends, motivations, victimization patterns, and offender characteristics.

The authors define motor vehicle theft as "a form of larceny that involves the unlawful taking or attempted taking of a motor vehicle." In 2007 there were approximately 1.1 million stolen vehicles reported to the police in the US. This represents a property loss of $7.4 billion. The auto theft rate has fluctuated over the past 80 years, with Copes and Cherbonneau reporting that it rose gradually between 1933 and 1960, increased steadily over the next decade, underwent a series of precipitous declines and then annual stability from 1970 to 1983, and then rose dramatically up to 1991, when the theft rate hit an all-time high of 864 per 100,000 registered vehicles. Since then, the rate has fallen by more than 50%—in 2007, it stood at 431 thefts per 100,000 registered vehicles.

Considerable research has focused on auto theft motivation and several typologies have resulted from these studies. Perhaps the most durable of these typologies was one that articulated five distinct motivations for auto theft: "joyriding", short-term transportation, to keep the car for long-term personal use, for profit (through the sale of parts or the entire vehicle), and for use in another crime. Other typologies have essentially been variations of this one.

Copes and Cherbonneau report that auto theft victims are most likely to be young (20 to 34) and members of minority groups. Households with annual incomes between $15,000 and $35,000 are more likely to be victims than families with lower or higher incomes. Victimization likelihood is greatest for those in urban areas, especially renters who have lived less than one year in their current residence and inhabit a multi-unit dwelling with four or more occupants. The majority of auto thefts occur during the night or evening, and victimization is most prevalent in blocks that have bars and blocks that are adjacent to high schools.

In regard to offender characteristics, 38% were of those arrested for auto theft in the US in 2007 were non-white, 25% were under 18 (56% were under 25), and 82% were male. However, motor vehicle thefts have a very high reporting rate but a very low clearance rate (59% and 13%, respectively, in 2007). So the characteristics of offenders are difficult to determine with any certainty.

For young people, and especially deprived youth, motor vehicle theft provides "a degree of escape," excitement, status among peers, escape from boredom, and a sense of freedom. For novices, vehicle theft is usually a group activity, inasmuch as they need to acquire the skills necessary to steal a vehicle, and these are normally honed through an "apprenticeship."

Copes and Cherbonneau conclude their chapter with a detailed discussion of auto theft prevention and policy. They observe that "the opportunities structure for auto theft will undergo substantial change in the coming years," and future researchers will have "to think like auto thieves" in order to keep up.

Arson

Fires may occur for a number of reasons, such as accidents, lightning, fireplay, curiosity, and arson, among others. The FBI defines arson as "any willful or malicious burning or attempting to burn, with or without attempt to defraud, a dwelling house, public building, motor vehicle, or aircraft, personal property of another, etc."

In his chapter, Barry Goetz indicates that although arson rates have declined in recent years, it "remains a deathly and costly crime, the leading cause of structural fires in the United States and a significant number of costly wildland fires." He also points out that fire results in approximately 4,000 deaths each year in the US, with 28 percent of the civilian victims dying as a result of arson. In 2007, 64,332 arsons were recorded nationally.

In 1979, arson was redesignated as a Part I Crime by the FBI. It is the only index crime requiring proof (as opposed to being merely "reported") before it may be included in the FBI's *Uniform Crime Reports*. Although the casualty outcomes of fires in the US are about half what they were 35 or 40 years ago, the rate is still 2.5 times that of many countries of Europe.

Goetz suggests that arson may be viewed as "a means to an end, financial or otherwise, an act of mischief, or a source of fascination and personal satisfaction." The National Fire Protection Association reports that the most likely motives for committing arson fall into four primary categories: "fireplay" or "curiosity"; "motives of gain" (which can be subdivided into "indirect financial gain," "direct financial gain," and "gain may be or may not be financial"); "motives not including curiosity or gain" (including "personal motives," "excitement or attention," and "power over others"); and "unclassified suspected motives."

However, these motive categories do not reveal much information about the "behavioral dimensions of fire settings." Numerous researchers have offered a plethora of motives for arson, including psychological dysfunctions that are "manifest in criminality." For instance, one research study revealed a high degree of psychosis among arsonists. Others have linked sexual dysfunction, substance abuse, mental illness, homelessness, and being the victim of sexual abuse with arson. Spite–revenge is another commonly cited motive. This may originate in conflicts between rival gangs, employers and employees, intimate partners, or business associates. Some arson may represent political protest, sabotage, or attempts to intimidate employees at controversial workplaces, such as abortion clinics. Financially motivated cases of arson are relatively common, too, with a prime example being insurance fraud.

Goetz indicates that "the victims of fire are of an overwhelmingly low socio-economic status, and African Americans have among the highest death rates." He concludes his chapter with a detailed examination of enforcement agencies and their policies. He ends with the observation that "the incidence of arson will continue to vary, depending on social and economic conditions as well as the fiscal health and policy priorities of government."

56

Fraud and embezzlement

Robert Morris

The United States Department of Justice (n.d.) defines fraud as "when a person or business intentionally deceives another with promises of goods, services, or financial benefit that do not exist, were never intended to be provided, or were misrepresented." Many crimes fit under the general term "fraud," including credit card fraud, check fraud, forgery, embezzlement, tax evasion, currency counterfeiting, identity theft, insurance fraud, medical fraud, confidence games (cons), Ponzi schemes, online-auction scams, telemarketing scams, and others. Fraud is a complex phenomenon; however, it can be broadly conceptualized as intentional violations of trust between at least two parties (be they people or businesses) that result in financial harm (see Shapiro, 1990). Compared to index crimes, such as homicide, theft, and robbery, fraud and embezzlement have rarely been the focus of scholarly attention, in spite of several studies that suggest fraud (among other white-collar crimes) is a greater social harm (Glassner, 1999; Lynch and Michalowski, 2000; Shover and Hochstetler, 2006).

The goal of this chapter is to provide an overview of the current state of research surrounding fraud in general, with a particular emphasis on embezzlement. Here, information is provided on the prevalence of several types of fraud in the US in recent years (including specific definitions), the harms associated with fraud and embezzlement, offender and offense characteristics, and victimization statistics for several types of fraud, where such information is available.

In recent years, the estimated financial losses resulting from fraudulent crimes dwarf monetary losses associated with street crimes. As noted by Shover and Hochstetler (2006), the US General Accounting Office estimated losses to US employers resulting from fraud in excess of $660 billion in 2004 alone. Today, it is reasonable to assume that losses from fraud and embezzlement are even greater. Sadly, evidence that might help explain such losses are rare. Further, unlike street crime victims, a victim of fraud may be victimized for many years before they even realize that a crime is occurring, which makes estimation much more difficult, since the crimes often go unreported. Partly this is due to increased reliance on digital technology and digital record keeping, which has arguably increased opportunities for victimization via such crimes as identity theft and computer fraud.

Offense and offender characteristics of fraud

This section outlines several noteworthy types of fraud, their definitions, and the findings of relevant research.

Embezzlement

Embezzlement has been defined as "the destruction or fraudulent appropriation of another's money or merchandise which has been entrusted to one's care" (Altheide *et al.* 1978: 91). It differs from larceny in that the offender has been put in a position of financial trust prior to the criminal act and because "the thief usually holds a fiduciary relationship to the victim, such as trustee, guardian, agent, or employee" (Green, 1993: 96).

The Yale Studies on White-Collar Crime (see Wheeler *et al.*, 1982) focused on gathering court data specific to fraud and have resulted in numerous other studies. Embezzlement (in the form of bank embezzlement alone) is an offense that stands out compared to many related crimes. Researchers have found that, of the white-collar crimes explored, bank embezzlers tended to be younger and were much more likely to be female than for other offenses (45% of embezzlers were female). They also typically came from stable "working" families and did not have a high social status (Weisburd *et al.*, 1991: 59). The findings of Benson and Kerley (2000), which relied on similar data, suggest that most female embezzlers served in clerical roles at banks, while males more often served in managerial positions. The significance of educational attainment for bank embezzlers is more complicated. Embezzlers were found to score the highest (as a group) for graduating from high school, but the lowest for graduating from college. Regarding prior convictions, embezzlers scored very low, suggesting the need for more careful background checks for bank employees (Weisburd *et al.*, 1991: 60). Overall, Weisburd and his colleagues suggest the nature of jobs in the banking environment parallel increased opportunity to offend due to the heightened trust that is placed in employees.

Zietz (1981) interviewed a sample of convicted female embezzlers and identifies two distinct types. Some took up their positions with no intent to embezzle, while others purposefully sought out their employment position in order to embezzle. Zietz argues that male embezzlers rationalize their actions as mere "borrowing," whereas female embezzlers who had not sought their position specifically to embezzle viewed theirs as violations of trust. Further, the author suggests that men embezzle more for social uplift or to conceal errors, while women more often embezzle for family welfare. However, Daly (1989) found that both males and females embezzle for family welfare as well as for self-serving motives and greed. This latter finding is supported by the research of Weisburd and Waring (2001: 63). Zietz (1981) also notes that females may embezzle to increase the affection from their husbands.

Finally, Zietz (1981) found that women who took up positions of trust specifically in order to commit fraud tended to be vindictive, overly self-interested, and physically attractive. They also had higher than average IQs. These characteristics stood in contrast to those of the "honest" offenders (those who had not sought their employment specifically to embezzle).

Credit card fraud

Very little research exists regarding the social or behavioral characteristics of people who use credit cards fraudulently. This is most unfortunate, as credit card fraud resulted in losses of over $2 billion as early as 1994, according to Jackson (1994). Five years later, a report estimated that over 1,000 people are victimized by credit card fraud in the US every day (Lowry, 1999). Losses today are sure to be even more devastating because of the rise of identity theft and the expansion of the digital market place.

Weisburd *et al.* (1991) found that credit card fraudsters stood out in comparison with other white-collar offenders because they were less likely to be either white or male. They also tended to be younger and displayed lower levels of social stability (i.e., they were more likely to lack steady employment, have family troubles, and possess low net worth). In short, credit fraud offenders tended to reflect the characteristics of street-level offenders rather than other white-collar offenders. However, the vast majority of them still held respectable positions.

Ten years later, Weisburd and Waring (2001) found that most credit card fraud offenders were male and more were unemployed at the time of arrest when compared to higher-level white-collar offenses, such as antitrust violations and securities exchange crimes. However, nearly 90% of the credit card fraud offenders sentenced at the federal level held "white-collar" positions (e.g., manager, doctor, lawyer, or teacher).

Check fraud and forgery

Check fraud refers to using checks in a fraudulent manner and may involve someone writing bad checks using their own account or writing checks for an account that does not belong to them. Check forgery involves the manufacture of counterfeit checks for criminal purposes. For many years, there has been a paucity of research focusing on check fraud and forgery, as defined here. During the mid-twentieth century, however, criminologists did show some interest in explaining the nature of check fraud with regard to "check men." Lemert (1953) defines check forgery to include forgery, writing bad checks, creating counterfeit checks, and passing counterfeit checks. He was interested in explaining the behaviors of check forgers who were not likely to have a traditional criminal record and were unlikely to indulge in overt contact with traditional criminals. His data (Lemert, 1953, 1958) revealed that naive check forgers were typically male, white, of higher age than traditional criminals, intellectually stronger, and had educational levels that were equal to or surpassed the general public of the time.

Fraudulent insurance claims

It is surprising to note that little empirical research exists on the correlates of people who submit false insurance claims in the United States. Rather, the available research reflects corporate America's attempts to curtail the problem for the purpose of limiting losses (see Derrig, 2002). Friedrichs (2007) notes that insurance fraud costs Americans $120 billion each year (see Ericson and Doyle, 2004: 101). It has also been suggested that some 20 percent of all submitted insurance claims are fraudulent; and fraudsters are rarely, if ever, arrested (Friedrichs, 2007).

Currency counterfeiting

The advent of high-quality and affordable printing technology has resulted in large increases in the prevalence of counterfeit currency. The US Secret Service seized nearly $300 million in counterfeit bills from 2003 to 2008 in the US; however, most counterfeit US bills are circulated abroad (Morris *et al.*, 2009). Morris and colleagues provide the only systematic assessment to date of the correlates of currency counterfeiting and have done so relying on Secret Service case files. In all, they suggest that technological developments have "democratized" the crime, meaning that the characteristics vary by gender, race, age, criminal history, and so on.

Tax evasion

Tax evasion in the US constitutes a major source of revenue loss to the federal and state governments, with estimated annual losses at the federal level of about $300 billion (Friedrichs, 2007). Research suggests that tax non-compliance is common among taxpayers. In 1990, for example, about one-quarter of taxpayers intentionally under-reported their income level by $1,500 or more, probably knowing that the chance of their being audited by the IRS was extremely low (less than 1% according to Andreoni *et al.*, 1998). It has also been estimated that about 40% of US households under-report at least some of their annual income, which equates to about 16% of taxable dollars going unaccounted (Andreoni *et al.*, 1998; see also Internal Revenue Service, 2005). Much of this loss is surely due to more than mere accounting error.

The correlates of tax evasion have been the focus of many studies that have explored socio-demographics, economics, and behavioral characteristics of non-compliance. Some of these studies have utilized self-reports and randomized experimental trials, resulting in an extensive body of literature. However, most tax evasion research uses official sources of data from the Internal Revenue Service, and many social and behavioral components have remained unexplored.

Jackson and Milliron (1986) provide a comprehensive literature review on tax evasion and report a series of determinants of tax non-compliance. Their findings and those reported by Richardson (2006) suggest that being male, younger, less educated, in low- or high- but not middle-income brackets, residing in geographic areas with higher levels of minority residents, and having friends who themselves evade paying tax may each play a role in explaining tax evasion. Other research suggests that discontent with having to make extra payments for school loans, alimony, or child support may lead to an increased propensity to evade paying taxes as well (Ahmed and Braithwaite, 2004, 2005). The perception of unfairness has also been explored as a key predictor of tax evasion.

Unfortunately, much of the tax evasion literature can be considered dated, given the transition into the information age and increased social (and particularly gender) equality. The social ecology of American culture has shifted dramatically since the time when many of the above-mentioned studies were developed and published. Commerce has entered the digital age, as have paying taxes and submitting tax returns. Thus, findings based on more recent data would add to the knowledge base considerably. For example, findings on variation in non-compliance across gender have been inconsistent since the 1970s. Jackson and Milliron (1986) report that much earlier work found that men were more likely to be non-compliant in their tax returns, but changing roles for women may mean that the same is not true now.

Identity theft

Though no consensus exists with regard to defining identity theft, this crime generally refers to "the misuse of another individual's personal information to commit fraud" (President's Identity Theft Task Force, 2007: 2). As noted by Copes and Vieraitis (2009), the true extent of harm resulting from identity theft is difficult to ascertain. Reports have estimated losses between $3.2 billion (Bureau of Justice Statistics, 2006) and $15 billion (Synovate, 2007) in a single year. To date, only a few studies have presented findings specific to identity theft offender characteristics, none of which should be generalized to all offenders. Such studies have reported that identity theft offenders are rarely detected and therefore rarely brought to justice (see Allison *et al.*, 2005; Gayer, 2003; Owens, 2004). Relying on US Secret Service data, Gordon *et al.* (2007) found that offenders were typically between 25 and 34 years old. I explored identity theft incidents reported in American newspaper articles from 1995 through 2005 and extracted characteristics on 257 identity thieves from these articles (Morris, 2010). This analysis revealed that most identity theft offenders were male, typically under the age of 33, and commonly worked with an accomplice (42.5%).

Identity theft victimization is relatively common. This can be partially explained by the fact that an identity thief may target many victims. Findings from the National Crime Victimization Survey (NCVS) indicate that in 2004 over 6.4 million households included at least one member who had been a victim of identity theft in the six months prior to interview (Bureau of Justice Statistics, 2006). A similar study conducted by the Federal Trade Commission (Synovate, 2007) suggested that over 8 million people were identity theft victims in 2005.

Confidence games (conning)

Conning people is a commonly understood phenomenon dating back to ancient times. Numerous case studies focusing on various cons have been undertaken. Perhaps the best known is the Ponzi scheme, named after its inventor, Charles Ponzi. In this form of crime (and related cons, such as pyramid schemes) fraudsters rely on the greed and gullibility of potential "investors" to sell them worthless goods or shares. While many of these case studies constitute quality research, they do not usually involve an analysis of social and demographic correlates.

Today, internet cons and scams are running rampant and completely overwhelming law enforcement efforts (see Burns *et al.*, 2004). Trahan *et al.* (2005) have explored victims' motivations for participating in such schemes and found that these victims expressed strong desires to get rich quickly via the "American Dream."

Evidence from self-report research

Regarding the characteristics of fraudsters, several researchers have explored aggregate arrest data or court records at the federal level. More recently, however, Menard *et al.* (in press) have presented findings from a nationally representative longitudinal self-report survey that is specific to fraud-related crime (i.e., crimes of trust). Using data from the National Youth Survey Family Study (NYSFS), Menard *et al.* reported that, among over 1,600 respondents, 7.1% reported that they had embezzled money from their employers at least once between 1976 and 2003; 3.9% reported forgery; 9.1% reported check fraud; 3% reported credit card fraud; 2.3% reported insurance fraud; 10.3% reported "conning" someone; and 16.3% reported intentionally cheating on their income tax returns.

These findings are important in that they are not based on arrest statistics. The researchers reported positive correlations between participation in fraud and being male, white, having trouble with substance abuse, being divorced, and, to some extent, possessing above-average education. Their findings also suggest that the general prevalence rate of fraud during adulthood (i.e., the percentage of respondents reporting that they had committed some sort of criminal fraud) is comparable to peak delinquency rates during adolescence (reaching nearly 15% in the early thirties). This finding challenges the notion that crime is predominantly a phenomenon of youth.

Conclusion

Much remains to be understood about the etiology of fraud and related crimes, and how to prevent them from occurring. Our transition into the digital age will undoubtedly result in increased levels of fraud and new offenses that cannot yet be imagined. It will be difficult to keep up with the development of new types of fraud, but criminologists have a responsibility to start taking fraud-related crimes more seriously in their research, as these offenses are clearly distinct from traditional crimes and cause tremendous social harm.

References

Ahmed, E. and Braithwaite, V. (2004). When tax collectors become collectors for child support and student loans: Jeopardizing or protecting the revenue base? *Kyklos*, 3, 303–326.

Ahmed, E. and Braithwaite, V. (2005). Linking tax evasion with higher education funding. *Legal and Criminological Psychology*, 10, 291–308.

Allison, S., Schuck, A., and Lersch, K. M. (2005). Exploring the crime of identity theft: Prevalence, clearance rates, and victim/offender characteristics. *Journal of Criminal Justice*, 33, 19–29.

Altheide, D. L., Adler, P. A., Adler, P., and Altheide, D. A. (1978). The social meaning of employee theft. In J. Johnson and J. Douglas (Eds.), *Crime at the top: Deviance in business and the professions* (pp. 90–124). Philadelphia, PA: Lippincott.

Andreoni, J., Erard, B, and Feinstein, J. (1998). Tax compliance. *Journal of Economic Literature*, 36, 818–860.

Benson, M. L. and Kerley, K. R. (2000). Life course theory and white collar crime. In H. N. Pontell and D. Shichor (Eds.), *Contemporary issues in crime and criminal justice: Essays in honor of Gilbert Geis* (pp. 121–136). Upper Saddle River, NJ: Prentice-Hall.

Bureau of Justice Statistics. (2006). *Identity theft, 2004*. Washington, DC: Government Printing Office.

Burns, R. G., Whitworth, K. H., and Thompson, C. Y. (2004). Assessing law enforcement preparedness to address internet fraud. *Journal of Criminal Justice*, 32, 477–493.

Copes, H. and Vieraitis, L. (2009). Bounded rationality of identity thieves: Using research to inform policy. *Criminology and Public Policy*, 8, 237–262.

Daly, K. (1989). Gender and varieties of white-collar crime. *Criminology*, 27(4), 769–794.

Derrig, R. A. (2002). Insurance fraud. *Journal of Risk and Insurance*, 69, 271–287.

Edelhertz, H. (1970). *The nature, impact, and prosecution of white-collar crime*. Washington, DC: US Department of Justice, National Institute of Law Enforcement and Criminal Justice.

Ericson, R. V. and Doyle, A. (2004). Criminalization in private: The case of insurance fraud. In Law Commission of Canada, *What is a crime? Defining criminal conduct in contemporary society* (pp. 99–124). Vancouver: University of British Columbia Press.

Friedrichs, D. O. (2007). *Trusted criminals* (3rd edn). Belmont, CA: Thompson Wadsworth.

Gayer, J. (2003). *Policing privacy: Law enforcement's response to identity theft*. Los Angeles, CA: CALPIRG.

Glassner, B. 1999. *The culture of fear*. New York: Basic Books.

Gordon, G. R., Rebovich, D., Choo, K. S., and Gordon, J. B. (2007). *Identity fraud trends and patterns: Building a data-based foundation for proactive enforcement*. Utica, NY: Center for Identity Management and Information Protection.

Green, G. S. (1993). White-collar crime and the study of embezzlement. *Annals of the American Academy of Political and Social Science*, 525, 95–106.

Internal Revenue Service (2005). *Tax gap facts and figures*. Retrieved November 5, 2007, from www.irs.gov/pub/irs-utl/tax_gap_facts-figures.pdf.

Jackson, J. R. (1994). Fraud masters: Professional credit card offenders and crime. *Criminal Justice Review*, 19, 24–55.

Jackson, B. R. and Milliron, C. V. (1986). Tax compliance research: Findings, problems and prospects. *Journal of Accounting Literature*, 5, 125–165.

Lemert, E. M. (1953). An isolation and closure theory of naive check forgery. *Journal of Criminal Law, Criminology, and Police Sciences*, 44, 296–307.

Lemert, E. M. (1958). The behavior of the systematic check forger. *Social Problems*, 6, 141–149.

Lowry, T. (1999). Information brokers put on brakes, new limits to cut identity theft. *USA Today*, January 18, 3B.

Lynch, M. J. and Michalowski, R. (2000). *The new primer in radical criminology: Critical perspectives on crime, power, and identity* (3rd edn). Monsey, NY: Criminal Justice Press.

Mason, R. and Calvin, L. (1978). A study of admitted income tax evasion. *Law and Society Review*, 12, 73–89.

Mativat, F. and Tremblay, P. (1997). Counterfeiting credit cards. *British Journal of Criminology*, 37, 165–183.

Menard, S., Morris, R. G., and Gerber, J. (in press). Distribution and correlates of self reported crimes of trust. *Deviant Behavior*.

Morris, R. G. (2010). Identity thieves and levels of sophistication: Findings from a National Probability Sample of American Newspaper Articles. *Deviant Behavior*, 31(2), 184–207.

Morris, R. G., Copes, H., and Perry-Mullis, K. (2009). Correlates of currency counterfeiting. *Journal of Criminal Justice*, 37, 472–477.

Owens, M. (2004). *Policing privacy: Michigan law enforcement officers on the challenges of tracking identity theft*. Ann Arbor, MI: Public Interest Research Group in Michigan.

President's Identity Theft Task Force. (2007). *Combating identity theft: A strategic plan*. Retrieved February 18, 2011, from www.idtheft.gov/reports/StrategicPlan.pdf.

Richardson, G. (2006). Determinants of tax evasion: A cross-country investigation. *Journal of International Accounting, Auditing and Taxation*, 15, 150–169.

Shapiro, S. (1990). Collaring the crime, not the criminal: Reconsidering the concept of white-collar crime. *American Sociological Review*, 55, 346–365.

Shover, N. and Hochstetler, A. (2006). *Choosing white-collar crime*. Cambridge: Cambridge University Press.

Synovate. (2007). *Federal Trade Commission—2006 identity theft survey report*. Retrieved November 1, 2009, from www.ftc.gov/os/2007/11/SynovateFinalReportIDTheft2006.pdf.

Trahan, A., Marquart, J. W., and Mullings, J. (2005). Fraud and the American Dream: Toward an understanding of fraud victimization. *Deviant Behavior*, 26, 601–620.

Tremblay, P. (1986). Designing crime: The short life expectancy and the workings of a recent wave of credit card bank frauds. *British Journal of Criminology*, 26, 234–253.

US Department of Justice (n.d.). *Victims of fraud: Beyond financial loss*. Videotape. Washington, DC: Office for Victims of Crime.

Weisburd, D. and Waring, E. (2001). *White-collar crime and criminal careers*. Cambridge: Cambridge University Press.

Weisburd, D., Wheeler, S., Waring, E., and Bode, N. (1991). *Crimes of the middle classes: White-collar offenders in federal courts*. New Haven, CT: Yale University Press.

Wheeler, S., Weisburd, D., and Bode, N. (1982). Sentencing the white-collar offender: Rhetoric and reality. *American Sociological Review*, 47, 641–659.

Zietz, D. (1981). *Women who embezzle or defraud: A study of convicted felons*. New York: Praeger.

57

Burglary

Jim Hawdon

The Federal Bureau of Investigation defines burglary as the unlawful entry of a structure to commit a felony or theft (FBI 2007). A "structure" includes a house, apartment, barn, house trailer or houseboat, office, railroad car, stable, or sailing vessel. Burglary does not require the use of force to gain entry into the structure, and some states refer to burglary as "breaking and entering." A burglary conviction does not require theft: any unlawful entry into a building or other structure with the *intent* to commit a felony constitutes a burglary. The act of burglary is separate from any theft associated with the unlawful entry, and a person may be simultaneously charged with both burglary and larceny for the same criminal act.

Following larceny, burglary is the second most frequently committed index crime in the United States, and it accounts for over 20 percent of all property crimes committed each year. According to FBI data, 2,179,140 burglaries were committed in the US in 2007. Approximately two-thirds of burglaries are of residential households, and the majority of residential burglaries, occur during the day. Conversely, burglaries of non-residential structures, such as stores and offices, are more likely to occur at night. Nearly 60 percent of successful burglaries and 7 percent of unsuccessful burglaries involve forcible entry (FBI 2007).

As with other serious street crimes, burglary rates have decreased substantially since the mid-1980s, falling in almost every year between 1988 and 2007. The burglary rate in 1988 was 1,316 per 100,000 population; in 2007, it was 722 per 100,000 population. Between 1998 and 2008, the burglary rate decreased by 16.3 percent, although it has increased slightly since 2003 (FBI 2007).

While burglary rates have recently decreased in the United States, this trend has not occurred in other parts of the world. Now, compared to other countries, the United States has mid-level rates of burglary. For the period 1996–2005, households in urban Africa, Latin America, and Oceania are most at risk for burglary, while European, Asian, and North American households have burglary risks that are below the world average. Based on victimization surveys, the highest rates of burglary are in Cambodia, where they are over eight times higher than in the United States. Other nations with high burglary rates include Papua New Guinea, Mozambique, and Zambia. The lowest burglary rates are in Spain, Japan, Portugal, and Azerbaijan (Dijk 2008).

The costs of burglary

Over 90 percent of completed burglaries result in a loss of property. In the United States, burglary causes approximately $4 billion in economic loss each year. The average per-burglary dollar loss was $1,991 in 2007. Nearly 25 percent of completed household burglaries where the dollar value of the lost property is known result in losses of $1,000 or more (FBI 2007). While burglars in industrialized nations typically steal high-value objects, such as video equipment, jewelry, and computers, burglars in developing countries often steal food, household appliances, linen, or cutlery (Dijk 2008; Schneider 2005).

In addition to the economic costs of burglary, many victims report other losses, and approximately 20% of the total costs of burglary are intangible quality of life losses (Miller *et al.* 1996). These intangible losses include the victims suffering emotionally after their properties are burglarized. In a classic study, nearly half the victims reported feeling "annoyed" by the crime. Of more lasting effects, 41 percent of victims reported a sense of having their privacy and safety violated, and nearly 20 percent reported being emotionally upset because of the burglary. Women, people who express a sense of general insecurity in their lives, and people who attach greater importance to their private property are most likely to experience quality of life losses after a burglary (Maguire 1980).

However, despite the economic costs and emotional suffering associated with burglary, victims report only half of all burglaries to the police. Of those burglaries that are reported, approximately 12 percent are cleared by the police and result in an arrest (FBI 2007).

Research on burglary

Research on burglary can be divided into three general topics: research on burglars; research on burglary victims; and research on where burglaries occur. These topics are interrelated, and much of the most recent research on burglary deals with the intersection of burglar characteristics, the environment in which burglaries occur, and the characteristics and behaviors of victims.

Research on burglars

The most basic area of research on burglars concerns the demographic characteristics of such criminals. Based on US arrest data, approximately 85 percent of burglars are male. They are also disproportionately young, with nearly 60 percent of arrested burglars under the age of 25 and a quarter under the age of 18. Approximately 68 percent of those arrested for burglary are white, and roughly 30 percent are black. The latter figure is nearly 2.5 times the percentage of the general US population who are black. Therefore, blacks have disproportionately high arrest rates (FBI 2007).

One line of early research examined the skills burglars need to succeed. While some are crude thieves with few skills, good burglars possess a range of technical and social skills that allow them to succeed. A good burglar must know how to select lucrative targets that pose minimal risk of apprehension, spot valuable items that will be easy to sell, and use various tools to open safes, disable alarms, and gain easy entry to the targeted structure (Shover 1972). Good burglars also need networks of associates to succeed. Many work in teams, with one person serving as a lookout while the others enter the building to steal merchandise or cash. In addition, burglars use their networks as "tipsters" who provide information about potential targets in exchange for a portion of the profits. Burglars also use lawyers and bondsmen as "fixers" to try to avoid prosecution or reduce the consequences of prosecution (Shover 1972). Most importantly, they use their networks of friends, associates, and criminal receivers of stolen goods ("fences") to convert the stolen goods into money. In one study, over two-thirds of burglars used their network of friends and associates or residential fences to sell their stolen goods. The other means burglars used to dispose of stolen merchandise were to sell the goods to legitimate businesses, sell them at pawnshops, sell them on the street to strangers, trade them for drugs, or keep them for personal use (Schneider 2005).

In addition to the skills burglars need to succeed, there appears to be an informal training process that career burglars undertake. "Novice" burglars learn skills from more experienced burglars, and they may stay in training for long periods if they can continue to use their own networks of associates and fences to sell the stolen items. Once trained, novices become "journeymen" while they develop their reputations as experienced criminals. Finally, once their reputations are established and they have developed their skills and organizational abilities, burglars become "professionals." While a body of literature suggests many burglars follow this career path and specialize in burglary, recent research questions the extent to which they specialize and limit their criminal activities only to burglary. Many prolific, persistent burglars commit other economic crimes, such as larceny, and especially shoplifting (Schneider 2005).

Another line of research on the characteristics of burglars investigates whether burglars are rational. That is, do burglars weigh the potential risks and rewards of their criminal behavior prior to committing their crimes? This line of research has consistently revealed that burglars are indeed rational about their criminal activities. Skilled burglars use a variety of environmental cues to select a target. "Gain cues" refer to perceptions of the quality and quantity of property inside the household or business to be burglarized. "Risk cues" are perceptions of the likelihood that someone will detect the crime and apprehend the burglar (Cromwell *et al.* 1991). While the perception of both risks and rewards significantly influences a burglar's decision-making, the burglar's perceptions of potential rewards typically have the greater influence on their decision to engage in a residential burglary (Piquero and Rengert 1999). Still, in a longitudinal study of individuals, the possibility of punishment (a risk cue) significantly reduced the likelihood of committing a burglary even among the most criminally prone members of the study (Wright *et al.* 2004).

The body of research on how burglars assess gain cues is relatively limited. What research is available indicates that they target specific items, including electronic goods (televisions, stereos, computer equipment, etc.), power tools (drills, saws, etc.), gardening tools (lawnmowers, weed trimmers, etc.), jewelry and gold, cash, credit cards, cigarettes, and alcohol (Schneider 2005). In a recent study, some offenders selected higher-risk daylight burglaries because they offered higher rewards. The characteristics of the burglar seemed to determine their targeting strategies, including whether they committed the crime in the day or at night. The authors identified three distinct offender-type–burglary strategy combinations:

- older offender, low-risk, low-reward, nighttime burglaries;
- younger/mixed offender, high-risk, high-reward, daylight burglaries; and
- minority, oldest offender, low-risk, lowest-reward, daylight burglaries.

(Coupe and Blake 2006)

A larger body of research has investigated how burglars assess risk cues, including surveillability, occupancy, and accessibility (Cromwell *et al.* 1991). Surveillability cues refer to the extent to which a target is observable by neighbors or passers-by; occupancy cues are any indicators that someone is in the targeted site; and accessibility cues are indications of how easily the burglar can gain entry to residence. Important factors burglars consider when assessing the surveillability of a potential target include the type of street on which the targeted residence is located and the proximity of the residence to the street. Important accessibility cues that burglars consider include the location and types of doors and windows, if the residence is protected with locks or burglar alarms, and the number of escape routes from the site. In addition to the presence of someone being present in the targeted residence, other occupancy cues that burglars assess are the presence of guards, door attendants, and dogs.

Research consistently reveals the importance of these cues in shaping a burglar's selection of targets (e.g., Bernasco and Luykx 2002; Bernasco and Nieuwbeerta 2005; Cromwell *et al.* 1991; Coupe and Blake 2006; Wilcox *et al.* 2007). The more accessible a target is to potential offenders, and the less visible a target is to neighbors, the more vulnerable the target. Similarly, research consistently indicates that non-occupancy is associated with burglary. While burglars consider all three types of risk cue, occupancy cues may be the most important. In one classic study, 28 of the 30 burglars claimed they would never intentionally enter an occupied residence (Cromwell *et al.* 1991).

Although the research indicates burglars typically approach their crimes rationally, the extent to which they plan these crimes seems to have been exaggerated. While highly skilled burglars targeting potential residences that will be extremely lucrative typically plan their jobs, it appears that many burglaries are unplanned and opportunistic.

Research on the victims of burglary

The second broad area of research on burglary deals with the victims. The chances of being a victim of burglary are not equal for all subgroups of the population. Based on victimization data (US Department of Justice 2006), central city residents are more likely to experience a burglary than are suburbanites or those living in rural areas. Victimization is also related to race and ethnicity: households headed by persons of two or more races are approximately 1.8 times more likely to suffer a burglary than are households headed by white persons; and households headed by African Americans are approximately 1.5 times more likely to be burglarized than are white households. In addition, younger heads of households suffer higher burglary rates than older heads of households. Economically disadvantaged households are more likely than wealthy households to be burglarized: households with annual incomes of less than $7,500 have rates of burglary that are 2.5 times higher than those for households making over $75,000 per year. However, wealthy households have higher rates of victimization than middle-income households.

A consistent finding on burglary victimization deals with the danger associated with leaving one's home unoccupied (e.g., Cohen and Cantor 1981; Coupe and Blake 2006; Mawby 2001). Residential burglaries are more likely to occur during the day than during the night, with nearly 64 percent of offenses taking place in daylight hours (FBI 2007). Slightly more than 40 percent of all residential burglaries occur while people are at work or engaging in leisure activities away from home (US Department of Justice 2006). Thus, burglars often strike when one's home is unguarded.

Another consistent research finding is that past burglary victimization is one of the best predictors of future victimization (Sagovsky and Johnson 2007). Burglary victims have an elevated risk of repeat burglary that lasts for approximately six months after their first victimization, with the highest risk of re-victimization occurring between four and five months after the first burglary (Polvi *et al.* 1991). Research on re-victimization suggests that the same offenders commit both the initial and subsequent burglaries (Bernasco 2008). Re-victimization tends to occur at the same time of day as the first victimization. The probability of being victimized twice at the same time of day is highest for those re-victimizations that occur within seven days of the original burglary (Sagovsky and Johnson 2007). The victim's family structure and marital status also affect the probability of re-victimization. According to one study, those who live alone, regardless of whether they are single or separated/divorced, are approximately twice as likely to be re-victimized as those who are married. Moreover, poorer people are more likely to be re-victimized than wealthier people. Finally, repeat victims are more likely than first-time victims to leave their home unoccupied in the daytime for at least six hours (Mawby 2001).

Finally, a growing body of research indicates that people who are at high risk of burglary victimization are well aware of that risk. A study using the British Crime Survey to investigate if fear of burglary victimization matched the probability of being a burglary victim found a very strong relationship between how much respondents worried about burglary and their likelihood of victimization (Swaray 2007). These findings, and those from a handful of other studies, suggest that people's fears about burglary are not misplaced.

Research on the ecology of burglary

The third line of research on burglary concerns the areas in which burglaries are likely to occur. Like most street crimes, burglaries are more likely to occur in urban areas and are most common in cities with between 500,000 and a million residents, while rural areas have the lowest burglary rates (FBI 2007). With respect to non-residential burglaries, location of business determines the likelihood of burglary victimization. Businesses located within three blocks of heavily traveled areas are less vulnerable than those located in less traveled areas. In addition, the probability of burglary is inversely related to the length of time a business establishment has been in operation (Hakim and Shachmurove 1996).

An area's attractiveness, opportunity, and accessibility lure residential burglars to their target neighborhoods. Attractive areas—those that appear to offer valuable of goods to steal—have relatively high rates of burglary. Similarly, those areas where the likelihood of successfully completing the burglary is high (i.e., high opportunity) suffer more burglaries. Finally, accessibility is positively related to burglary rates. Thus, burglaries are most likely to occur in areas that are familiar to the burglar and relatively close to where the burglar lives (Bernasco and Luykx 2002). As with other street crimes, the likelihood of a burglar selecting a neighborhood increases with the area's ethnic heterogeneity and its percentage of single-family dwellings (Bernasco and Nieuwbeerta 2005). These areas with high levels of "social disorganization" typically lack social capital (as measured by levels of trust and civic engagement) and collective efficacy (as measured by trust and resident willingness to intervene on behalf of the neighborhood) (see Martin 2002; Wilcox et al. 2007).

Integrating the research on burglary

The insights from research on burglars, burglary victimization, and the ecology of burglary can be theoretically integrated using the routine activities perspective (Cohen and Felson 1979). This perspective considers crime as a function of the presence of motivated offenders and suitable targets, and the lack of capable guardians. The presence of motivated offenders is relatively consistent across areas, especially since burglars can travel to a location to commit their crimes. Thus, what determines the probability of being burglarized is the presence of suitable targets and the lack of capable guardians. Suitable targets are attractive in what they offer and are accessible to the burglar. They therefore have high gain cues and accessibility cues. Areas and households that are low in guardianship have low surveillability and occupancy cues. This perspective accounts for many of the facts about burglary victimization such as the highest rates of burglary being in both disorganized and affluent communities. While disorganized communities typically lack guardians, affluent areas are highly attractive and provide suitable targets. Similarly, this perspective can account for the high rates of victimization among the young, those who live alone, and those who are not home for long periods during the day. These individuals typically have daily routines that remove them from their households, thereby decreasing their guardianship.

The routine activities perspective and other research efforts offer suggestions for protecting oneself from burglaries. Varying one's routine by leaving and coming home at different times of the day and having a neighbor watch your household while you are away can decrease the likelihood of being victimized. These strategies increase guardianship and protect the household from intruders. In addition, "target-hardening" devices, such as locks, alarms, and dogs, may serve as deterrents for burglars by decreasing the target's accessibility and increasing the probability of a burglar selecting somewhere else. It should be noted, however, that some researchers have found that security devices do not deter burglars (Coupe and Blake 2006).

A multi-level approach promises to provide the best protection from burglary. And a neighborhood's level of collective efficacy enhances individual-level guardianship strategies: that is, individuals' efforts to protect themselves from burglary are most effective when they occur in neighborhoods where many people are making similar efforts (Wilcox *et al.* 2007).

References

Bernasco, W. (2008). "Them again?: same-offender involvement in repeat and near repeat burglaries," *European Journal of Criminology*, 5: 411–431.

Bernasco, W. and Luykx, F. (2002). "Effects of attractiveness, opportunity and accessibility to burglars on residential burglary rates of urban neighborhoods," *Criminology*, 41: 981–1002.

Bernasco, W. and Nieuwbeerta, P. (2005). "How do residential burglars select target areas?," *British Journal of Criminology*, 45: 296–315.

Cohen, L. and Cantor, D. (1981). "Residential burglary in the United States: life-style and demographic factors associated with the possibility of victimization," *Journal of Research in Crime and Delinquency*, 18: 113–127.

Cohen, L. and Felson, M. (1979). "Social change and crime rate trends: a routine activity approach," *American Sociological Review*, 44: 588–608.

Cromwell, P., Olson, J., and Avary, D. (1991). "How residential burglars choose targets: an ethnographic analysis," *Security Journal*, 2: 195–199.

Coupe, T. and Blake, L. (2006). "Daylight and darkness targeting strategies and the risks of being seen at residential burglaries," *Criminology*, 44: 431–464.

Dijk, J. V. (2008). *The world of crime: breaking the silence on problems of security, justice and development across the world*, Los Angeles, CA: Sage.

Federal Bureau of Investigation (FBI). (2007). *Crime in the United States, 2007*. Retrieved 4/23/2009 from www.fbi.gov/ucr/cius2007/index.html.

Hakim, S. and Shachmurove, Y. (1996). "Spatial and temporal patterns of commercial burglaries: the evidence examined," *American Journal of Economics and Sociology*, 55: 443–456.

Maguire, M. (1980). "The impact of burglary upon victims," *British Journal of Criminology*, 20: 261–275.

Martin, D. (2002). "Spatial patterns in residential burglary: assessing the effect of neighborhood social capital," *Journal of Contemporary Criminal Justice*, 18: 132–146.

Mawby, R. (2001). "The impact of repeat victimisation on burglary victims in East and West Europe," *Crime Prevention Studies*, 12: 69–82.

Miller, T., Cohen, M., and Wiersema, B. (1996). *Victim costs and consequences: a new look*, Washington, DC: National Institute of Justice.

Piquero, A. and Rengert, G. (1999). "Studying deterrence with active residential burglars," *Justice Quarterly*, 16: 451–471.

Polvi, N., Looman, T., Humphries, C., and Pease, K. (1991). "The time course of repeat burglary victimization," *British Journal of Criminology*, 31: 411–414.

Sagovsky, A. and Johnson, S. (2007). "When does repeat burglary victimisation occur?," *Australian and New Zealand Journal of Criminology*, 40: 1–26.

Schneider, J. (2005). "Stolen-goods markets: methods of disposal," *British Journal of Criminology*, 45: 129–140.

Shover, N. (1972). "Structures and careers in burglary," *Journal of Criminal Law, Criminology and Police Science*, 63: 540–549.

Swaray, R. (2007). "On the relationship between the public's worry about safety from burglary and probabilities of burglary: some evidence from simultaneous equation models," *Social Indicators Research*, 80: 361–378.

US Department of Justice. (2006). *Criminal victimization in the United States, 2006*. Retrieved 4/13/2009 from www.ojp.usdoj.gov/bjs/pub/pdf/cvus06.pdf.

Wilcox, P., Madensen, T., and Tullyer, M. S. (2007). "Guardianship in context: implications for burglary victimization risk and prevention," *Criminology*, 45: 771–802.

Wright, B., Caspi, A., Moffitt, T., and Paternoster, R. (2004). "Does the perceived risk of punishment deter criminally prone individuals? Rational choice, self-control, and crime," *Journal of Research in Crime and Delinquency*, 41: 180–213.

58

Motor vehicle theft

Heith Copes and Michael Cherbonneau

Compared to other Type I crimes (as defined by the Federal Bureau of Investigation), the theft of motor vehicles is relatively under-researched (Clarke and Harris, 1992). This pattern of neglect is beginning to change, however. In the past two decades, many studies of auto theft have been published that explore the offense in detail and at varying units of analysis. This growth in auto theft research is likely due to changes in motor vehicle theft rates and the passage of new laws to curtail the problem. In light of the recent developments in auto theft research, the goal of this chapter is to summarize the academic literature on this crime. We begin by discussing briefly the patterns about prevalence and trends, then discuss the motivations auto thieves offer for their crimes, victimization patterns, and offender characteristics. The chapter concludes with an overview of evaluations of various crime control strategies designed to curb auto theft.

Motor vehicle theft prevalence and trends

Motor vehicle theft is a form of larceny that involves the unlawful taking or attempted taking of a motor vehicle. Nearly 1.1 million stolen vehicles—one out of every 232 registered nationwide—were reported to US police in 2007, for an estimated total property loss of $7.4 billion, or an average loss per theft of $6,755 (FBI, 2008; FHA, 2008). Like other property crimes, motor vehicle theft rates have varied considerably over time. From 1933 through 1960 the rate of auto theft rose gradually. It is likely that this pattern simply reflected the threefold increase in motor vehicle ownership in the United States that occurred during this time. Supporting this claim is the fact that vehicle theft remained relatively stable throughout the Great Depression, when the demand for motor vehicles slowed. Greater increases in rates came after the Second World War, when the interstate highway system expanded and "urban sprawl" ushered in a renewed demand for motor vehicles among Americans. The rate of vehicle theft per 100,000 persons increased steadily between 1960 and 1970, but this was followed by a series of precipitous declines and annual stability until 1983, before a dramatic eight-year increase that peaked in 1991 at a rate of 864 motor vehicle thefts per 100,000 registered vehicles (FHA, 1997; FBI, 2008). Since reaching this high point, auto theft has dropped by 50%, standing at 431 thefts per 100,000 vehicles in 2007 (FHA, 2008; FBI, 2008).

Motivational typologies

Perhaps more than any other crime, auto theft is characterized by a wide variety of goals. Researchers have constructed auto theft typologies to reflect the varied nature of the offense, its offenders, and their motives, and to guide thinking about preventive measures with greater specificity (Challinger, 1987; Clarke and Harris, 1992; Copes, 2003; McCaghy et al., 1977). One of the most widely cited descriptions of auto thieves' motivations was developed by McCaghy et al. (1977), who identified five distinct motivations for the crime. The first and most common motivation is joyriding—the recreational, short-term use of a stolen car. Joyriding is thought to be motivated by a desire for excitement, to prove one's manhood, or to gain status among peers. In short, "the car is not stolen for what it does, but for what it means" (McCaghy et al., 1977, p. 378). The second motivational category is short-term transportation. This occurs when thieves steal the vehicle temporarily with the sole purpose of specific transportation and not for excitement. It is thought that the short-term car thief succumbs to situational pressures in which immediate transportation is seen as necessary (Copes, 2003). The third motivation for stealing a vehicle is to keep the car indefinitely: a thief steals the vehicle for their own long-term personal use. Profit is the fourth motivational category and includes those who steal vehicles to sell parts or the entire vehicle. The goal in this type of theft is purely economic. Theft of the vehicle is based on the automobile (or its parts) as a saleable commodity, not as a symbol or form of transportation. The final motivation involves stealing a vehicle for use in another crime. This is thought to be the rarest type of auto theft.

The McCaghy et al. typology is widely credited with identifying the common types of auto theft that exist in the United States and elsewhere (Challinger, 1987). Since publication of their typology, however, others have elaborated on it. Challinger (1987) reformulated the five-part McCaghy et al. typology into just three main motivational types—recreational, transport, and money-making—to allow for a more targeted approach to the prevention of various sorts of auto theft. In similar vein, Clarke and Harris (1992) proposed another three-part typology: theft for temporary use (namely, joyriding and short-term transportation); professional theft in which a thief intends to deprive the owner permanently of the vehicle for purposes of extended use, parts chopping, resale, or export; and thefts from vehicles of such items as car batteries, radios, and personal possessions.

Motivational typologies are common in auto theft research even though their theoretical value is suspect (Copes, 2003). They imply exclusivity and stability; and they assume that offenders in one group are qualitatively different from the others. However, this may not accurately represent auto thieves because it is common for such criminals to have multiple motivations over their careers and even for a single theft.

Victimization patterns

The National Crime Victimization Survey (NCVS, 2008) indicates that car owners most susceptible to auto theft are young (between the ages of 20 and 34) and members of minority groups. When considering risk based on household characteristics, households with incomes between $15,000 and $35,000 are more vulnerable than homes with higher or lower incomes. This is likely due to opportunity in terms of vehicle ownership and living in closer proximity to motivated offenders. Additional household characteristics associated with higher auto theft victimization risk include those in urban areas, renters rather than homeowners, household sizes of four or more people, occupants of multi-unit dwellings, and those who have lived less than one year in their current residence (Walsh and Taylor, 2007).

Some of the more robust auto theft patterns concern the time and place of occurrence. Beginning with theft location, victimization risks are highest in and around the immediate vicinity of the victim's household (Fleming *et al.*, 1994; Kinshott, 2001). Urban areas that have a large pool of potential offenders tend to have high rates of motor vehicle theft. City blocks with bars have nearly twice as many auto thefts as those without them (Roncek and Bell, 1981; Roncek and Maier, 1991). Further, blocks adjacent to high schools have higher levels of auto theft than those that are not (Roncek and Faggiani, 1985). Bars and schools are thought to attract those most likely to be motivated to commit a crime—namely, young males—thereby increasing the likelihood of crime.

The vast majority of auto thefts (70%) occur between 6:00 p.m. and 6:00 a.m., with a substantially greater number occurring in the latter half of this time period (NCVS, 2008). Of the 100 auto thieves interviewed by Light *et al.* (1993), a large proportion (40%) operated *only* after dark, while 52% claimed to steal at all times of the day. In addition, 80% of those who targeted vehicles outside homes did so only after dark, whereas 69% of those favoring car parks operated at any time of the day.

The intersection of time and place in auto theft can be tied to the routines of vehicle owners and motivated offenders as well as to target availability and levels of guardianship (Clarke and Mayhew, 1994; Hollinger and Dabney, 1999). In addition to the availability of automobiles and the size of the offender pool, there must be a sufficiently low level of capable guardianship for the offender to elude detection and arrest. Thus, parking lots with attendants have lower rates of auto theft than similar lots with no attendant on duty (Clarke and Mayhew, 1994). Some cars are chosen not because they can be stolen easily but because they can be concealed more effectively. Cars stolen for export to Mexico tend to be the same types of cars that are made and sold there (Field *et al.*, 1992). By choosing cars that are common in Mexico, thieves cut their chances of being easily recognized as such.

Note that guardianship refers not only to people protecting property but to "target-hardening" activities that make the vehicle more difficult to steal. In 1988, heavy trucks, buses, and motorcycles had significantly higher theft rates per 100,000 vehicles than did passenger cars. Harlow (1988) accounts for this by suggesting that trucks, buses, and motorcycles are simply easier to steal. This may be shown by the higher number of uncompleted thefts for cars than for trucks and motorcycles. Certain passenger cars are selected more often as targets because of their low level of security. For instance, the poor ignition locks of 1969–1974 Ford models has been suggested as a major cause of their disproportionately high rate of theft. Further evidence for this is the fact that theft rates for Fords fell by a quarter after their locks were upgraded in 1975 (Karmen, 1981). Similarly, the introduction of steering-column locks reduced car theft rates in the United States and the United Kingdom, but this had a comparatively longer-lasting impact on auto theft in West Germany, where they were made compulsory on the entire registered vehicle fleet (Webb, 1994).

Offender characteristics

The demographic profile of the typical thief is difficult to determine because the parameters of the total population of auto thieves are unknown. Official arrest records, however, can offer some guidance. Among persons arrested for auto theft in 2007, 82% were male, 25% were under the age of 18 (56% were under 25), and 38% were non-white (FBI, 2008). Of those serving a sentence for auto theft in adult state prisons in 2003, an estimated 95% were male and 60% were non-white (Harrison and Beck, 2006). However, we must be careful when generating offender profiles for auto thieves based on official records for two interrelated reasons. First, vehicle theft has an exceptionally high reporting rate—the police were notified of 89% of completed thefts in 2006 (NCVS, 2008). Second, it typically has one of the lowest clearance rates—only 13% of reported thefts were cleared by an arrest or exceptional means within the following year (FBI, 2008). Thus, the make-up of the total population of auto thieves cannot be determined with any precision because the vast majority of them go undetected each year.

For many marginalized youths, a stolen car can provide a degree of escape, if only temporarily, from their social and economic dislocation (Dawes, 2002). The pursuit of excitement, to alleviate boredom, and the influence of peers are the "main reasons" given by auto thieves for taking up the crime (Dawes, 2002; Light et al., 1993; Spencer, 1992). Indeed, the "excitement of theft and the status gained among peers must not be discounted as powerful sources of reinforcement of joyriding" (Clarke and Harris, 1992: 22). Few activities, legal or illegal, can trump the elation and sense of freedom derived from auto theft (Copes, 2003; Stephen and Squires, 2003). Beyond a search for excitement and to alleviate boredom, some car thieves wish to gain prestige and establish a reputation among their peers. Economic, family, and educational limitations can be assuaged by the status conferred through the social context of the peer group for their competence in car crime (Dawes, 2002).

For novices, car theft is almost invariably a group activity: very few offenders begin by stealing cars on their own (Light et al., 1993; Spencer, 1992). This is hardly surprising, given that entering cars and starting ignitions requires technical know-how and a degree of mechanical proficiency that transcend common sense. Auto theft involvement is facilitated through interaction with neighborhood peers, usually older and more experienced males (Spencer, 1992). Novices learn the skills needed to steal and drive cars from these "technical advisors" (Fleming et al., 1994) through a role best described as an "apprenticeship" (Light et al., 1993; Spencer, 1992). Status within the group is stratified by skill, whereby novices serve as lookouts and passengers before stealing themselves (Light et al., 1993).

Auto theft prevention and policy

Interviews with auto thieves show that they have a remarkable indifference to the risk of detection and arrest and to the legal ramifications even if they are apprehended. In general, they exhibit a carefree attitude when asked about the potential legal consequences of auto theft, which most calculate to be negligible. Few auto thieves think that continued offending will lead to their capture and most discount the potential for arrest by pushing such thoughts out of their minds. They typically display confidence in their skills for evasion and reducing risks, should they ever come under police scrutiny (Cherbonneau and Copes, 2006). Similarly, thieves in Fleming et al.'s (1994) sample were confident about their chances of avoiding punishment at every stage of the offense, including police pursuits and court proceedings following apprehension. Most interesting, however, was a view among younger thieves that their status as juveniles insulated them from the most serious repercussions.

Despite offenders' disregard of formal consequences for their actions, programs based on situational measures have been shown to produce meaningful reductions in auto theft, at least over the short term. The aim of such initiatives is to lessen criminal opportunities by increasing the perceived effort involved, enhancing the perceived risk of detection, or reducing the perceived rewards of the targeted crime. Opportunity-reducing techniques that serve to increase the perceived risks of auto theft include enhanced informal and formal surveillance. Examples of surveillance include security cameras placed in parking lots and active surveillance by employed security guards. Both of these measures have been shown to correspond with lower levels of theft in protected areas (Hollinger and Dabney, 1999; Webb et al., 1992). Similarly,

Lojack tracking devices have been shown to reduce auto thefts in the cities that implement the program (Ayres and Levitt, 1998).

The primary preventive approach to reducing the rewards of auto theft involves car part marking initiatives, the most common of which is the vehicle identification number (VIN). The Motor Vehicle Theft Law Enforcement Act of 1984 required manufacturers to stamp the VIN on fourteen different vehicle components. While parts marking serves many purposes, the primary preventive goal is to make it difficult to conceal the true identity of a vehicle and thereby reduce the number of vehicles stolen and dismantled in chop shops (Linden and Chaturvedi, 2005).

The most commonly used opportunity-reduction techniques to combat auto theft involve various forms of "target hardening." The goal of these strategies is to make it harder for would-be thieves to carry out the crime in question. West Germany made steering-column locks compulsory on all cars (and motorcycles) in 1961. The result was an immediate 20% reduction in motor vehicle thefts (Webb, 1994). A more recent target hardening development was the introduction of electronic immobilizers by automobile manufacturers. In 1995, the European Union mandated that all cars manufactured after October 1998 must be fitted with electronic immobilizers (Levesley et al., 2004). Police reports from Great Britain show that there was a decline in the rate of auto thefts for cars manufactured after 1998 (Levesley et al., 2004). Although such mandates are absent in the United States, immobilizers are becoming more commonplace on luxury and mid-range vehicles. Without a doubt, the introduction of compulsory immobilization reduced auto theft in Australia and the UK. However, the benefits of these programs must be tempered as partial displacement toward older, unprotected vehicles was evident in both countries (Brown and Thomas, 2003; Kriven and Ziersch, 2007). Additionally, some auto thieves have responded to increased vehicle ignition hardening by searching cars for hidden keys or even burglarizing dwellings to obtain keys (Copes and Cherbonneau, 2006; Donkin and Wellsmith, 2006). And some "professional thieves" apparently already know how to defeat immobilizers, as evidenced by the fact that an increasing number of vehicles fitted with such devices are being stolen and not recovered (Brown, 2004). To the extent that auto theft techniques are "cultural knowledge resources" (Stephen and Squires, 2003: 154) that are honed, updated over time, and passed on by the initiated to the uninitiated, history suggests that it is only a matter of time before such knowledge becomes diffused throughout the criminal subculture.

For all that has been learned about auto theft, a number of important questions about the offense remain. The one sure thing that can be concluded about the prevention of auto theft is that would-be thieves will likely adapt to any new target hardening initiative, so the best we can hope for is to stay one or two steps ahead of them. Like other thieves, those who steal vehicles are adaptable and willing to exploit emerging opportunities. For example, the increased use of electronic immobilizers has led to an increase in carjackings and key thefts. Additionally, the current economic downturn will likely increase the number of stolen cars sold on the underground market (e.g., chop shops) as more people will look to buy used parts instead of new vehicles. Certainly, the opportunity structure for auto theft will undergo substantial change in the coming years. Future researchers would be well advised to think like auto thieves in order to recognize and curtail emerging opportunities for auto theft.

References

Ayres, Ian and Steven Levitt. 1998. "Measuring Positive Externalities from Unobservable Victim Precaution: An Empirical Analysis of Lojack." *Quarterly Journal of Economics* 113:43–77.

Brown, Rick. 2004. "The Effectiveness of Electronic Immobilization: Changing Patterns of Temporary and Permanent Vehicle Theft." In *Understanding and Preventing Car Theft, Crime Prevention Studies*, Vol. 17 (pp. 101–119), edited by Michael G. Maxfield and Ronald V. Clarke. Monsey, NY: Criminal Justice Press.

Brown, Rick and Nerys Thomas. 2003. "Aging Vehicles: Evidence of the Effectiveness of New Car Security from the Home Office Car Theft Index." *Security Journal* 16: 45–53.

Challinger, Dennis. 1987. "Car Security Hardware: How Good Is It?" In *Car Theft: Putting on the Brakes, Proceedings of Seminar on Car Theft, May 21* (pp. 42–48). Sydney: National Roads and Motorists' Association and the Australian Institute of Criminology.

Cherbonneau, Michael and Heith Copes. 2006. "'Drive It Like You Stole It': Auto Theft and the Illusion of Normalcy." *British Journal of Criminology* 46:193–211.

Clarke, Ronald V. and Patricia M. Harris. 1992. "Auto Theft and Its Prevention." In *Crime and Justice: A Review of Research*, Vol. 16 (pp. 1–54), edited by Michael Tonry. Chicago, IL: University of Chicago Press.

Clarke, Ronald V. and Pat Mayhew. 1994. "Parking Patterns and Car Theft Risks: Policy Relevant Findings from the British Crime Survey." In *Crime Prevention Studies*, Vol. 3 (pp. 91–107), edited by Ronald V. Clarke. Monsey, NY: Criminal Justice Press.

Copes, Heith. 2003. "Streetlife and the Rewards of Auto Theft." *Deviant Behavior* 24:309–332.

Copes, Heith and Michael Cherbonneau. 2006. "The Key to Auto Theft: Emerging Methods of Auto Theft from the Offenders' Perspective." *British Journal of Criminology* 46:917–934.

Dawes, Glenn. 2002. "Figure Eights, Spin Outs and Power Slides: Aboriginal and Torres Strait Islander Youth and the Culture of Joyriding." *Journal of Youth Studies* 5:195–208.

Donkin, Susan and Melanie Wellsmith. 2006. "Cars Stolen in Burglaries: The Sandwell Experience." *Security Journal* 19: 22–32.

Federal Bureau of Investigation (FBI). 2008. *Uniform Crime Report: Crime in the United States, 2007.* Washington, DC: US Department of Justice.

Federal Highway Administration (FHA). 1997. *Highway Statistics, Summary to 1995.* Washington, DC: US Department of Transportation.

Federal Highway Administration (FHA). 2008. *Highway Statistics, 2007.* Washington, DC: US Department of Transportation.

Field, Simon., Ronald V. Clarke, and Patricia Harris. 1992. "The Mexican Vehicle Market and Auto Theft in Border Areas of the United States." *Security Journal* 2: 210–225.

Fleming, Zachary, Patricia Brantingham, and Paul Brantingham. 1994. "Exploring Auto Theft in British Columbia." In *Crime Prevention Studies*, Vol. 3 (pp. 47–90), edited by Ronald V. Clarke. Monsey, NY: Criminal Justice Press.

Harlow, Caroline. 1988. *Motor Vehicle Theft.* Washington, DC: US Department of Justice.

Harrison, Paige and Allen Beck. 2006. *Prisoners in 2005.* Washington, DC: US Department of Justice.

Hollinger, Richard and Dean Dabney. 1999. "Motor Vehicle Theft at the Shopping Centre: An Application of the Routine Activities Approach." *Security Journal* 12:63–78.

Karmen, Andrew. 1981. "Auto Theft and Corporate Irresponsibility." *Contemporary Crisis* 5: 63–81.

Kinshott, Graham. 2001. *Vehicle Related Thefts: Practice Messages from the British Crime Survey.* London: Home Office.

Kriven, Sophie and Emma Ziersch. 2007. "New Car Security and Shifting Vehicle Theft Patterns in Australia." *Security Journal* 20:111–122.

Levesley, Tom, Greg Braun, Michael Wilkinson, and Cymone Powell. 2004. *Emerging Methods of Car Theft: Theft of Keys.* Home Office Findings No. 239. London: Home Office.

Light, Roy, Claire Nee, and Helen Ingham. 1993. *Car Theft: The Offender's Perspective.* Home Office Research Study No. 130. London: Home Office.

Linden, Rick and Renuka Chaturvedi. 2005. "The Need for Comprehensive Crime Prevention Planning: The Case of Motor Vehicle Theft." *Canadian Journal of Criminology and Criminal Justice* 47:251–270.

McCaghy, Charles H., Peggy C. Giordano, and Trudy Knicely Henson. 1977. "Auto Theft: Offender and Offense Characteristics." *Criminology* 15:367–385.

National Crime Victimization Survey (NCVS). 2008. *Criminal Victimization in the United States, 2006 Statistical Tables.* Washington, DC: Bureau of Justice Statistics.

Roncek, Dennis and Richard Bell. 1981. "Bars, Blocks and Crime." *Journal of Environmental Systems* 11: 35–47.

Roncek, Dennis and Donald Faggiani. 1985. "High Schools and Crime." *Sociological Quarterly* 64: 491–505.

Roncek, Dennis and Pamela Maier. 1991. "Bars, Blocks, and Crime Revisited: Linking the Theory of Routine Activities to the Empiricism of Hot Spots." *Criminology* 29: 725–753.

Spencer, Eileen. 1992. *Car Crime and Young People on a Sunderland Housing Estate.* Crime Prevention Unit Series Paper No. 40. London: Home Office.

Stephen, Dawn and Peter Squires. 2003. "'Adults Don't Realize How Sheltered They Are.' A Contribution to the Debate on Youth Transitions from Some Voices on the Margins." *Journal of Youth Studies* 6:145–164.

Walsh, Jeffrey and Ralph Taylor. 2007. "Predicting Decade-Long Changes in Community Motor Vehicle Theft Rates." *Journal of Research in Crime and Delinquency* 44:64–90.

Webb, Barry. 1994. "Steering Column Locks and Motor Vehicle Theft: Evaluations from Three Countries." In *Crime Prevention Studies*, Vol. 2 (pp. 71–89), edited by Ronald V. Clarke. Monsey, NY: Criminal Justice Press.

Webb, Barry, Ben Brown, and Katherine Bennett. 1992. *Preventing Car Crime in Car Parks.* Crime Prevention Unit Series Paper No. 34. London: Home Office.

59

Arson

Barry Goetz

Arson in the United States

A little over 30 years ago, the federal government published a report entitled *Arson: America's Malignant Crime* (Suchy 1976). Rates of incendiary and suspicious fires (per 100,000) had increased by 234 percent between 1964 and 1974, compared to just 26 percent for accidental fires during the same period (Boudreau *et al.* 1977: 7). Arson rates have since declined. However, arson remains a deadly and costly crime, the leading cause of structural fires in the United States as well as a significant number of costly wildland fires (US Fire Administration 2004a; Prestemon and Butry 2005).

About 4,000 people die in fires every year in the United States, meaning our death rate is among the highest in the industrialized world (Hannon and Shai 2003). Arson is responsible for 28 percent of all civilian deaths caused by fire, more than any other single fire cause. Arsons are also responsible for about 9 percent of all firefighter deaths each year and the greatest dollar losses from fire (US Fire Administration 2004a)

Arson was redesignated a Part I crime by the FBI in 1979. This meant that its incidence and causes would be more carefully tracked and analyzed. Nevertheless, the data on arson remains problematic. The *Uniform Crime Reports* (UCR), published yearly by the Federal Bureau of Investigation, define arson as "any willful or malicious burning or attempting to burn, with or without attempt to defraud, a dwelling house, public building, motor vehicle or aircraft, personal property of another, etc." In 2007, the last full year for which data are available, the UCR reported that there were 64,332 arsons nationally, a 6.7 percent decline from 2006, consistent with a general decline in arson incidents since 1980 (Hall 2007). Only those fires that have been definitively determined to be arson are included in the FBI data (US Fire Administration 2004a). So incidents considered suspicious or where no case was opened are not reflected in FBI data. Moreover, arson is the only index crime where there has to be proof that it occurred (as opposed to "reported") to be included in the UCR. Arsons are also missed through the investigative process, misread as accidental or as causes unknown (Hall 2007; Jackson 1988). All of this leads to an undercount of the arson problem.

The FBI, the US Fire Administration (USFA), and the National Fire Protection Association (NFPA), a private non-profit organization, all collect and disseminate data on arson, leading to inevitable discrepancies over incidence rates (Jackson 1988). The USFA's National Fire Incident

Reporting System (NFIRS) is thought to provide the most accurate counts of the national fire problem. According to its 2006 figures, the latest year for which NFIRS data are available, there were 323,200 intentional fires nationally, about 87 percent of which occurred outside or in "other" circumstances (e.g., a dumpster). Structural fires represent 55,100 of these fires (17 percent) and vehicles represent 13 percent. There were 380 civilian and 10 firefighter deaths resulting from intentional fires, plus 1,200 civilian and a substantial 7,200 firefighter injuries (Flynn 2009). These casualty outcomes are almost half of what they were during the late 1970s and early 1980s, when arson was at its height, although the US fire casualty rates remain 2.5 times what they are in many European nations (US Fire Administration 2004a).

The term "intentional fire" was introduced by NFIRS in 1999. Before this, NFIRS used the designations "incendiary" plus "suspicious incidents," including some portion of undetermined cases, to assess the arson threat (Hall 2007). "Intentional fires" are defined as the "deliberate misuse of heat source or a fire of an incendiary nature" (Flynn 2009: 1). While many of these fires may be arson, Flynn (2009: 1) continues that "not all intentional fires are incendiary and intentional is not the same as arson." For example, fires set by the very young may be intentional but not malicious. There is some confusion over whether fires resulting from suspicious circumstances will be reflected in the intentional fires category (Hall 2007).

Structural fires represent 84 percent of the $1,184,000 in damage attributed to intentional fires in 2006. Of these, 54 percent occurred in residences, resulting in 85 percent of civilian deaths and 82 percent of civilian injuries attributed to intentional fires. Moreover, whether a property is occupied is predictive of intentional fires. Roughly 57 percent of all structural fires that involved vacant and unsecured buildings in the years 2003–2006 were intentional, compared to only 6 percent for occupied premises (Flynn 2009; Hall 2007).

Arsonists, motives, and victims

When the FBI first included arson in its list of index crimes, it was defined as a property crime. Now it is reported as a separate category because of the myriad motives and targets that it may involve. Arson may be viewed as a means to an end, financial or otherwise, an act of mischief, or a source of fascination and personal satisfaction (Prins 2001). Those arrested for arson are mostly male, young, and poorly educated (Sapp *et al.* 1994). Yet, arsonists may also be "white-collar" criminals or even firefighters (US Fire Administration 2003). The victims of fire are of an overwhelmingly low socio-economic status, and African Americans have among the highest death rates (Hannon and Shai 2003). One reason for this has to do with the high concentration of arson fires in low-income, urban communities (Munson and Oates 1983). Of special concern is the number of juveniles responsible for arsons. "Nearly half" of arrestees are under 18, and 59 percent are under 21 (Flynn 2009: 4). Still, investigators may fail to differentiate between arson and childhood fire setting. Approximately 12 percent of intentional fires are caused by children under the age of 12 (Flynn 2009: 55). Investigators may also fail to connect juveniles used as "torches" in arsons-for-profit to unscrupulous landlords (Sullivan 1991).

The NFPA has attempted to quantify the most likely motives behind arson using four primary categories (Flynn 2009: 22). The first is "fireplay" or "curiosity," estimated to be behind 23 percent of all intentional fires, although there is likely no true criminal motive. The second is "motives of gain," responsible for an estimated 21 percent. Motives of gain are further subdivided into "indirect financial gain," estimated at 11 percent (such as concealing an auto theft or burglary); "direct financial gain," accounting for 7 percent (with insurance fraud making up 5 percent); and "gain may be or may not be financial," accounting for 3 percent (including attempts to destroy evidence). The third primary category is "motives not involving curiosity or gain." These are divided into "personal" motives (17 percent), "excitement or attention" (15 percent), defined largely as "thrills," and "power over others" (12 percent), which includes acts of intimidation and domestic violence. Finally, the fourth primary category (11 percent) involves "unclassified suspected motives."

This categorization is useful in attempting to assess the degree of criminality associated with fire setting. Arson is a legal term and motive categories may yield little information about the behavioral dimensions of fire setting. Canter and Fritzon (1998) propose an "action system" model that considers the psychological and criminological motivations underlying arson and describe it as an expressive act (see also Kocsis 2004). "Personal" motives or "excitement and attention" can involve psychological dysfunctions that are manifest in criminality, but where experts may disagree over whether a criminal act was involved (Lowenstein 2001; Davis and Lauber 1999). Leong (1992) reports a high degree of psychosis among one cohort of individuals charged with arson, linking the crime to problems of homelessness and substance abuse. Prins (2001) links arson with sexual dysfunction. Lowenstein's (2001) review of recent major studies finds patterns of substance abuse, sexual abuse, and mental illness in the backgrounds of arsonists.

The report *Attacking the Violent Crime of Arson*, published by the US Fire Administration in 2004, presents less complex criminal justice-based motive categories. Here, spite–revenge is listed as the leading cause (33%), followed by vandalism (20%), fraud (16%), and crime concealment (9%). Rooted in NFIRS data, however, the proportion of unknown causes is high, caused in part by incomplete information provided from local officials (US Fire Administration 2004b).

The official clearance rate for arson is only 18 percent (Federal Bureau of Investigation 2007). This, coupled with the problems with NFIRS reporting, means that it is difficult to say with certainty which arson motives are predominant. Consistent with the US Fire Administration's (2004a) study, law enforcement officials argue that spite–revenge motives are the most common (Goetz 1997). This conclusion, however, has as much to say about solvability as it has to say about the universe of cases. Spite–revenge fires commonly involve conflicts between intimate partners, business associates, employers and employees, and rival gangs (National Gang Crime Research Center 2001; O'Connor *et al.* 1982). The anger associated with such disputes usually means that victims are able to identify their assailants, making clearances easier.

Some spite–revenge fires involve an amorphous assailant. Between 1995 and 1997, for example, hundreds of arsons occurred in churches throughout the South. Some argued that the fires were racially motivated because African-American congregations faced the highest risk of victimization (Soule and Van Dyke 1999). Nevertheless, arsons also occurred at white and racially mixed churches, leading some to speculate that the blazes were the result of simple vandalism and thrill seeking (Booth 1996). FBI data on arsons as hate crimes, however, suggest little association. In 2007, a scant 0.5 percent of hate crimes, just 40 out of 7,624, were linked to arson (Federal Bureau of Investigation 2007).

Arson, attempted arson, and bombs are also used for political protest and sabotage (Hinds-Aldrich 2007). Obvious examples include the Oklahoma City bombings, the World Trade Center attack of 1996, and the 9/11 attacks. Since 2000, there have also been at least fifteen cases of arson linked to intimidating workers at abortion clinics (National Abortion Federation 2009).

A British study on crime concealment and arson found that car thieves attempt to destroy evidence with fire, and that lawful owners also set fire to their abandoned cars in the hope that this will wipe out traceable registration information (Merrall and Chenary 2005).

Financially motivated arsons vary, and the organization of the crime can be complex. "Insurance fraud" is considered tantamount to these types of fires, but the broader term "arson-for-profit" better describes how various financial motivations are linked. Arson-for-profit is used as a form of speculation in lower-income neighborhoods, including clearing tenants from a building, clearing a structure from a parcel, or changing a building's or a parcel's occupancy or land use (US Senate 1978; Slade 1978; Lima 1977). Brady (1983: 1) has argued that arson-for-profit is linked to the "decisions undertaken by banking, real estate and insurance industries" that lead to neighborhood destabilization and "racketeering." This is exacerbated by banking and insurance disinvestment policies, or "redlining," and more recently by the sub-prime crisis (Birger 2008).

The use of high-risk insurance coverage for inner-city properties, such as Fair Access to Insurance Requirements (FAIR) plans and "surplus lines" lenders, have also been linked to arson because of lax underwriting (US General Accounting Office 1978). Arson-for-profit has also been linked to real estate upturns related to gentrification movements, so its prevalence may have more to do with economic shifts generally rather than specifically with downturns (Goetz 1997; Brady 1983). A recent upsurge of fires in the Greenpoint section of Brooklyn, for example, is associated with what some are calling an arson-for-profit ring linked to upscale residency conversions and construction (Jacobson 2006).

Several notable studies have attempted to link economic causes with increases in fire. Time series analyses done by Spillman and Zak (1979) show little evidence that arson and large-scale economic trends are correlated. Nevertheless, in more targeted analyses, arson rates have been found to be correlated with bankruptcies, falling house prices, insurance coverage amounts, and homeowner distress (Green and Seward 2004; Hershbarger and Miller 1978). Fire incidence and death rates generally are associated with the socio-economic status of individuals and spatial areas (Hannon and Shai 2003; Jennings 1999; Munson and Oates 1983), although there is disagreement over whether this is because of ecological factors (e.g., population density) or factors associated with social inequality, such as housing upkeep (Goetz 1997; Wallace 1978). Arsons are also positively correlated with the number of vacant structures (Flynn 2009; Hall 2007; Gunther 1981), suggesting a clear economic link to fire.

Enforcement

Arson is a difficult crime to discover. First, fires and firefighting destroy evidence. Second, overlapping agencies involved with investigating arson create potential inefficiencies (Jackson 1988). Typically, fire officials determine cause and the police are responsible for any criminal investigation, although sometimes these responsibilities will fall exclusively to one or other agency or a state-level fire marshal (Grimes 1977). Moreover, insurance officials may conduct their own independent inquiries. All of this makes for many different agencies vying for access to the same evidence and information. Third, there are questions of competence and expertise (US Fire Administration 2004a; Goetz 1997). Recently, Grann (2009) has reported how a shoddy arson prosecution may have led an innocent man to be executed in Texas.

These issues are even more pronounced where arson-for-profit is concerned. For example, a fire caused by leaving oil-based paints close to an open flame may be officially designated an accident but may also be viewed as highly suspicious by investigators. Fire and police investigators may also lack the specialized training needed to conduct a white-collar crime inquiry (Goetz 1997; US Senate 1978). Fire and police officials have also been associated with attempts to cover up arson-for-profit incidents (Slade 1978).

The focus on the national problem of arson during the 1970s and 1980s has led to the implementation of a number of important reforms. As has been said, arson is now designated a Part I crime by the FBI, meaning that local police departments are more attentive to clearance rates. The creation of the NFIRS in 1975 means that there is now a country-wide data-tracking source for fire officials using standardized motive categories. The US Fire Administration and the now-defunct Law Enforcement Assistance Administration have both funded arson task forces that have brought together specially assigned police, fire officials, and prosecutors in San Francisco, Seattle, Rochester, Chicago, New Haven, Phoenix, and other locations. These have been credited with professionalizing arson investigation methods (US Fire Administration 2004a; Longmire *et al.* 1983). Automated "arson information management systems" (AIMS) have helped track arson incidents and patterns related to location, victim, owner/lessee, and witnesses. The National Fire Academy, administered by the US Fire Administration, now provides federal support to local officials to improve their investigative skills. Fire and police officials now make more use of laboratory resources to test for flammable substances and other incendiary objects found at fire scenes. The FBI and US Department of Alcohol, Tobacco, and Firearms are now more commonly called in to assist local governments with complex arson cases (Goetz 1997).

Grassroots community movements have also helped deter arson through the use of "early warning systems" that rely on public records to help prevent arson-for-profit (US Senate 1978). The insurance industry has created its own fraud units and reformed the underwriting practices of high-risk FAIR plan programs to prevent inflated coverage (US General Accounting Office 1978).

Since the 1990s, however, ever more resources have been diverted from arson deterrence methods to help pay for America's "war on drugs" and, more recently, the "war on terrorism" (US Fire Administration 2004a). Clarke's (2000) research has also cast doubt on the effectiveness of multi-agency approaches to arson investigation, calling for jurisdictions to create distinct fire investigation agencies.

All of this suggests that the incidence of arson will continue to vary depending on socio-economic conditions as well as the fiscal health and policy priorities of the government.

References

Birger, J. (2008) "Will Foreclosures Spark an Arson Boom?," *Fortune Magazine*. Available at: money.cnn. com/2008/01/09/news/economy/birger_arson.fortune/ (accessed September 17, 2009).

Booth, W. (1996) "In Church Fires, a Pattern but No Conspiracy," *Washington Post*. Available at: www. washingtonpost.com (accessed August 20, 2009).

Boudreau, J., Q. Kwan, W. Faragher, and G. Denault (1977) *Arson and Arson Investigation: Survey and Assessment.* Washington, DC: US Department of Justice, Law Enforcement Assistance Administration, National Institute of Law Enforcement and Criminal Justice.

Brady, J. (1983) "Arson, Urban Economy, and Organized Crime: The Case of Boston," *Social Problems*, 33: 1–27.

Canter and Fritzon (1998), "Differentiating Arsonists: A Model of Firesetting Actions and Characteristics," *Legal and Criminological Psychology* 3: 73–96.

Clarke, M. (2000) "Arson: Whose Problem? A Question of Administrative Failure or of Professional Remit?," *Crime Prevention and Community Safety: An International Journal* 2: 19–32.

Davis, J. and K. M. Lauber (1999) "Criminal Behavioral Assessment of Arsonists, Pyromaniacs, and Multiple Firesetters," *Journal of Contemporary Criminal Justice* 15: 273–290.

Federal Bureau of Investigation (2007) *The Uniform Crime Reports 2007*, Washington, DC: US Department of Justice. Available at: www.fbi.gov/ucr/ (accessed September 13, 2009).

Flynn, J. (2009) *Intentional Fires*, Boston, MA: National Fire Protection Association.

Goetz, B. (1997) "Organization as Class: Bias in Local Law Enforcement: Arson-for-Profit as a Non-event," *Law and Society Review* 31: 557–588.

Grann, D. (2009) "Trial by Fire," *New Yorker* 85: 42–51.

Green, S. and J. A. Seward (2004) "The Economics of Residential Arson," unpublished manuscript, Hankamer School of Business, Baylor University, Waco, TX.

Grimes, M. (1977) "The National Problem of Arson," *Fire Journal* 71: 67–103.

Gunther, P. (1981) "Fire Cause Patterns for Different Socio-Economic Neighborhoods in Toledo, Ohio," *Fire Journal* 75: 52–53.

Hall, J. R., Jr. (2007) *Intentional Fires and Arson*, Boston, MA: National Fire Protection Association, 2007.

Hannon, L. and D. Shai (2003) "The Truly Disadvantaged and the Structural Covariates of Fire Death Rates," *Social Science Journal* 40: 129–136.

Hershbarger, R. A. and R. K. Miller (1978) "The Impact of Economic Conditions on the Incidence of Arson," *Journal of Risk and Insurance* 45: 275–290.

Hinds-Aldrich, M. (2007) "Visualizing Protest Arson: The Phenomenological Promise of Protest Photography," paper presented at the annual meeting of the American Society of Criminology, Atlanta, GA.

Jackson, P. (1988) "Assessing the Validity of Official Data on Arson," *Criminology* 26: 181–195.

Jacobsen, M. (2006) "Brooklyn is Burning," *New York* 39: 33–37.

Jennings, C. R. (1999) "Socio-Economic Characteristics and Their Relationship to Fire Incidence: A Review of the Literature," *Fire Technology* 35: 7–33.

Kocsis, R. N. (2004) "Psychological Profiling of Serial Arson Offenders: An Assessment of Skills and Accuracy," *Criminal Justice and Behavior* 31: 341–361.

Leong, G. P. (1992) "A Psychiatric Study of Persons Charged with Arson," *Journal of Forensic Science* 37: 1319–1326.

Lima, A. J. (1977) *Fires in Urban Residential Neighborhoods: A Survey of Causes and Local Efforts at Prevention*, Washington, DC: National Fire Prevention and Control Administration, US Department of Commerce.

Longmire, D., G. Vito, and J. Kenney (1983) "Combatting Arson: Detection, Arrest and Conviction," *Journal of Criminal Justice* 11: 359–368.

Lowenstein, L. F (2001) "Recent Research into Arson (1992–2000): Incidence, Causes and Associated Features, Predictions, Comparative Studies, and Prevention and Treatment," *Police Journal* 74: 108–119.

Merrall, S. and S. Chenery (2005) *Vehicle Fires: Explaining the Rise in Vehicle Arson*, London. Office of the Deputy Prime Minister.

Munson, M. J. and W. E. Oates (1983) "Community Characteristics and the Incidence of Fire: An Empirical Analysis," in C. Rapkin (ed.), The *Social and Economic Consequences of Residential* Fires, Lexington, MA: D. C. Heath & Co.

National Abortion Federation (2009) "History of Violence, Arson and Bombings." Available at: www. prochoice.org/about_abortion/violence/arsons.asp (accessed September 15, 2009).

National Gang Crime Research Center (2001) "Bomb and Arson Crimes among Gang Members: A Behavioral Science Profile," *Journal of Gang Research* 9: 1–38.

O'Connor, D.G., W. Parker, J. Phillips, J. Poulsen, D. Reichard, and L. Richardson (1982) "Identifying Revenge Fires," research paper, National Criminal Justice Reference Service.

Prestemon, J. P. and D. T. Butry (2005) "Time to Burn: Modeling Wildland Arson as an Autoregressive Crime Function," *American Journal of Agricultural Economics* 87: 756–770.

Prins, H. (2001) "Arson and Sexuality," in C. Bryant (ed.), *The Encyclopedia of Criminology and Deviant Behavior*, New York: Taylor and Francis.

Sapp, A. D., T. Huff, and G. Gordon (1994) *A Report of Essential Findings from a Study of Serial Arsonists*, Quantico, VA: National Center for the Analysis of Violent Crime, US FBI Academy.

Slade, S. (1978) "The Business of Arson," *The Nation*, March: 307–309.

Soule, S.A. and N. Van Dyke (1999) "Black Church Arson in the United States, 1989–1996," *Ethnic and Racial Studies* 22: 724–742.

Spillman, T. C. and T. A. Zak (1979) "Arson: An Economic Phenomenon?," *American Economist* 23: 37–43.

Suchy, J. (1976) *Arson: America's Malignant Crime*, Washington, DC: National Fire Prevention and Control Administration, National Academy for Fire Prevention and Control, US Department of Commerce.

Sullivan, M. (1991) "Crime and the Social Fabric," in J. Mollenkopf and M. Castells (eds.), *Dual City: Restructuring New York*, New York: Russell Sage.

US Fire Administration (2003) *Special Report: Firefighter Arson*, Washington, DC: Department of Homeland Security.

US Fire Administration (2004a) *Attacking the Violent Crime of Arson: A Report on America's Fire Investigation Units*, Washington, DC: Department of Homeland Security, 2004a.

US Fire Administration (2004b) *Fire in the United States*, 13th edn, Washington, DC: Federal Emergency Management Agency.

US Fire Administration/National Fire Data Center (2007) *Fire in the United States, 1995–2004*, 14th edn, Washington, DC: Federal Emergency Management Agency.

US General Accounting Office (1978) "Arson-for-Profit: More Could be Done to Reduce It," Document No. 79-664, Washington, DC: Office of the Comptroller General.

US Senate (1978) "Arson-for-Profit: Its Impact on States and Localities," hearings before the Subcommittee on Intergovernmental Relations of the Committee on Governmental Affairs, 95th Congress, First Session.

Wallace, R. (1978) "Contagion and Incubation in New York City Structural Fires 1964–1976," *Human Ecology* 6: 423–433.

Part XII
Crime: traditional violent modes

Overview

Sometimes deviance becomes very dark. Such is the case with violence. Violence runs the gamut from verbal abuse to mass murder. It is very disruptive and destructive of social order and the social fabric, and incurs the most severe sanctions. The victims of violence can experience an array of harm and suffering, such as fear, psychological distress, injuries, depression, physical disability, the possibility of suicide, and even death. Violence impacts on the victim's life and future. Not infrequently, there is collateral damage in the sense that spouse, children, and family may also experience harm and suffering. Violence also affects community and, indeed, society, inasmuch as the existence of violence diminishes the quality of life for all, and interferes with normal social life. This part examines a variety of configurations of violence, including spouse and intimate partner abuse, homicide, armed robbery, rape and sexual assault, and child abuse. The reader will be well acquainted with the nuances of these topics by these very comprehensive narratives.

Intimate partner violence

In her chapter, Donileen Loseke explores a range of violent behaviors between current and former spouses and dating partners. The violence "exists along a continuum from a single episode of violence to ongoing battering," and includes: "physical violence, sexual violence, threats of physical or sexual violence, and emotional abuse." Loseke points out that, in spite of the broad definition of intimate partner violence (IPV), the majority of attention is directed toward physical violence, rather than sexual or psychological abuse. Also, research on IPV has focused more on cross-sex rather than same-sex couples, with the majority of published articles on the subject examining violence where "men are the perpetrators and women are the victims."

Loseke reports that there are several methodological problems with the research in this area: too many different definitions; the sensitivity of the topic makes interviewing difficult; and most samples of victims and perpetrators are from social service programs and the findings are not easily generalized to non-clinical samples. These research problems have led to "often inconsistent and even contradictory findings."

Loseke focuses on four dimensions of IPV. The first of these relates to risk factors for perpetrators, such as alcohol consumption, individual psychopathology of the perpetrators, being uneducated, being a member of a minority group, being poor, marital dissatisfaction and discord, and growing up in a violent home.

The second dimension concerns contexts and meaning of violence. The evidence suggests that "women in cross-sex relationships use as much—or more—violence as men." There are gendered patterns of cross-sex perpetration and victimization. Loseke reports that there are four categories of IPV: "common couples violence," "intimate terrorism," "mutual violent control," and "violent resistance."

The third dimension relates to the consequences of IPV. Scholars agree that it has multiple negative consequences. It is recognized as a public health issue. Among the negative consequences of IPV are physical disability and psychological distress. Loseke reports that women are more likely to be physically harmed than men, and they take more time off work as a result of IPV. Although some research indicates that men are equally psychologically harmed by IPV, women tend to experience more depression, suicidal thoughts and attempts, and post-traumatic distress.

The final dimension Loseke addresses is social intervention. Some women victims seek informal help from family, friends, and neighbors, and look for formal help from police, medical personnel, or shelters. There has been considerable interest in IPV and criminal justice responses. There are no services to help men who are victims. Most intervention initiatives assist female victims and punish male perpetrators, but there is little evidence that existing intervention efforts are generally effective. Research on social intervention has been inadequate and insular. This, along with the problem of definitions, has hampered the accumulation of knowledge about IPV, and, as Loseke phrases it, "IPV research is not being informed by larger bodies of knowledge about violence."

Homicide, serial murder, and mass murder

In their chapter, Stephen Holmes and Ronald Holmes survey and analyze the crime of murder. Initially, they point out that this violent crime commands the attention of the public, and is a prominent theme in our mass media. Homicide is of special interest to academics in the fields of criminology and criminal justice because it is measured quite accurately, and it serves as a kind of "barometer of the true rate of violent crime in the United States and many developing countries." In the US, the homicide rate almost doubled between the mid-1960s and late 1970s, but it has declined since then and has been relatively stable since 2000. However, the annual number of homicides has increased over the years.

Homicide impacts on many people as well as the victims. Individuals who commit homicides tend to be young, between 18 and 24. Younger killers generally know their victims. After adulthood, the killers are about equally likely to know or be strangers to their victims. Most young homicides are gang-related, and members of the age group 18–34 commit the majority of felony-, sex-, drug-, and gang-related murders.

Holmes and Holmes assert that while homicide is interesting, serial and mass murders are even more interesting. They do not result from an argument, protection of turf, or a drug deal gone wrong. Rather, they occur because the offender enjoys killing or wishes to kill an entire class or group of people. There are significant differences between the two types of killers. Mass or "spree" murderers willingly kill multiple individuals in one place at one time. Serial murderers, on the other hand, kill "three or more people over a period of more than 30 days with a significant cooling off period between the killings."

Holmes and Holmes articulate a variety of types of both serial and mass killers. For instance, a serial killer may be a "visionary killer," a "mission killer," a "hedonistic killer," or a "power/control killer." He then distinguishes between three sub-varieties of hedonistic killer: the "lust killer," the "thrill killer," and the "comfort killer." Holmes identifies seven varieties of mass murderer: the "disciple," the "family annihilator," the "disgruntled employee," the "ideological mass killer," the "set and run killer," the "psychotic," and the "youthful school shooter."

They conclude with the observation that "it is not until we begin to understand the motivations, patterns, and anticipated gains of these offenders that we will truly begin to understand the reasons why they commit their murderous deeds and can start planning and implementing strategies to identify and treat them before they take the lives of the innocent."

Armed robbery and carjacking

In their chapter, Dee Wood Harper and Patrick Walsh address the topic of armed robbery, a crime that dates back to ancient times, and carjacking, a relatively recent variation of armed robbery. They point out that armed robbery and first-degree robbery occur on the streets/highways. Armed robbery involves "the taking or attempting to take anything of value from the care, custody, or control of a person or persons by force or threat of force or violence and/or putting the victim in fear." Carjacking combines armed robbery with auto theft and apparently came into existence when sophisticated theft-prevention equipment made it almost impossible to steal a car in the traditional manner. The highest rate of carjacking in the world is in South Africa, where the poverty, the culture of violence, lack of employment, and an ineffective criminal justice system create a context that encourages such armed robbery.

Street robbery is more frequent in large cities (those with populations above 250,000) than smaller communities (less than 10,000). Some 52.5% of street robberies occur in the large cities, while only 25.7% take place in small communities. In the US, the rate of reported robbery increased fourfold between 1960 and 1990. Harper and Walsh report that "Robbery is becoming a growing problem in Europe. For example, from 1997 to 2001, it increased in England and Wales by 92%, Austria 42%, France 75%, the Netherlands 48%, and Poland 72%."

They indicate that the highest victimization rate for robbery occurs among the poorest households. The perpetrator was a stranger in 74% of robbery incidents where the victim was male, but in only 48% where the victim was female. Victimization was highest for the 12–15-year-old age group in 2008. Of robbery offenders arrested in the US in 2008, 56.7% were black and 41.7% were white. The peak ages for robbery arrests are 17–19. In trying to understand the high incidence rates of robbery among young black males, some researchers have suggested that being "bad" is a socially desirable identity in the poor black urban community.

One criminologist classified robbers as "professionals," such as those who specialize in planned bank robberies, and "opportunists," who act randomly although take into account location, victim vulnerability, and the potential for getting money. He also spoke of the addict and alcoholic robbers who engage in robbery to support their habits. Robbery is predominantly a male crime (88.4%). As to motivation, "robbery is a quick way to secure money." It has also been suggested that "this violent crime is a means of [young, black males] expressing their masculinity."

The authors conclude by reporting that numerous counter-measures have been developed as a means of deterring robbery. These include environmental strategies such as alarm devices, bullet-resistant barriers, and closed-circuit television, and administrative strategies such as on-hand cash limits, multiple staffing, and robbery prevention training.

Rape and sexual assault

In her chapter, Lynn Pazzani explores facts, myths, stereotypes, and popular beliefs about rape and sexual assault. She points out that a popular stereotype of rape is that of a masked stranger armed with a weapon accosting a woman walking alone on a dark street and raping her. But only approximately 15% of sexual assaults are estimated to be committed by strangers. Pazzani indicates that a more common scenario is that of a woman being raped by a boyfriend or acquaintance.

She reviews legal definitions of rape, and reports that "the essential elements of a traditional rape were: force; absence of consent; and penile-vaginal penetration." Her own definition of rape is: "any sexual contact to the mouth, anus, or vagina committed by using a penis, finger or hand, or any foreign object, that occurs against an individual's will."

In her chapter, Pazzani focuses only on sexual assaults where a female is the victim and a male is the offender. Drawing on a widely circulated reference book on the subject, she reports that, in this source, rapists (stranger rapes) are divided into four categories: the *power reassurance rapist*, who "believes himself to be a loser and uses rape as a means of elevating his status"; the *anger retaliation rapist*, who "feels he has suffered great injustices at the hands of women in his life and commits rapes in order to hurt the victim and get back at all women"; the *power assertive rapist*, who "believes men are superior to women and that men are entitled to rape women as a matter of course"; and, finally, the *sadistic rapist*, who "uses rape as a means of expressing his aggressive sexual fantasies and will intend to inflict physical and psychological pain on his victim."

Pazzani chooses to divide rape and sexual assault into two broad categories, which she labels "real rape" and "non-deviant rape." The former refers to "actions involving strangers, violence, weapons, resistance, injury, and immediate notification of the police." The latter encompasses rape committed by persons known by the victim, such as family members, co-workers, friends, recent acquaintances, and boyfriends. Pazzani labels this "non-deviant rape" because it "more closely mirrors socially acceptable sexual behavior."

She then reviews a number of statistics regarding rape and explores the notion of "a rape culture" as well as a variety of rape myths, public perceptions, beliefs, and attitudes toward rape, and stereotypical justifications for rape. She concludes with the observation that rape has many negative outcomes for the victim, including mental and physical health problems, and opines that "changes to both the legal system and cultural views about rape are needed to improve the situation for victims and society in general."

Child abuse (sexual and physical)

In her chapter, Elizabeth Ehrhardt Mustaine examines in detail the societal problem of child abuse. She points out that, ideally, parenting should be "one of the most important, difficult, rewarding, and frustrating jobs a person will have in his or her lifetime." In spite of this social expectation, it is estimated that each day in the US (as of 2008) some 2,421 children are officially classified as having been abused or neglected.

There are both state and federal laws prohibiting child abuse. Statutes on child abuse include a wide variety of physical injuries, "ranging from minor bruises to severe fractures, to death." Sexual abuse includes such activities as indecent exposure, exploitation through prostitution or production of pornographic images, incest, rape, sodomy, or fondling a child's genitals, among others.

Mustaine indicates that there is a thin line between corporal punishment and physical abuse. The use of corporal punishment is discouraged. In regard to sexual abuse, she suggests that children are too young to understand sex; accordingly, they are unable to consent. She also reports that there are several antecedents to the sexual abuse of children. These include "a lack of internal inhibitors by the would-be offender" and "the overcoming of external inhibitors." A third antecedent is "the offender must overcome the child's resistance."

Mustaine also describes the six phases of the process of sexually abusing children: engagement; the pressured sex phase; the sexual interaction phase; the secrecy phase; disclosure; and, finally, the suppression phase. She then reports on patterns of child abuse.

There are various explanations of child abuse, and Mustaine analyzes several of them. One explanation centers on the pathology of an abusive parent or caretaker. Another explanation focuses on the interaction between the parent and the child. A third addresses what children learn when they witness or experience violence in the home. The fourth is the premise that common situational factors, such as family stress or social isolation, "influence families and parents and increase the risks for child abuse." Other theories that are used to explain child abuse include emotional congruence theory, sexual arousal theory, and blockage theory.

Mustaine concludes with some suggestions and strategies to help families and children experiencing abuse. She specifically urges that any suspected child abuse should be reported. There are a variety of agencies that aid families and children, and Mustaine calls for more inter-agency cooperation. She also stresses that there should be more educational efforts regarding punishment and discipline styles. Finally, she feels that we must alter cultural orientations about childbearing and child-rearing.

60

Intimate partner violence

Donileen R. Loseke

Intimate partner violence (IPV) is defined by the Centers for Disease Control (CDC, n.d.) as:

> violence that occurs between two people in a close relationship. The term "intimate partner"
> includes current and former spouses and dating partners. IPV exists along a continuum
> from a single episode of violence to ongoing battering. IPV includes: physical violence,
> sexual violence, threats of physical or sexual violence, and emotional abuse.

The label and this definition are very inclusive: IPV includes threatened and actual violence
that happens once or that is ongoing; it refers to violence among same-sex or cross-sex couples
in any type of current or former close relationship. Yet, in practice, this inclusive definition is
generally narrowed in three ways. First, the overwhelming majority of attention is directed to
physical abuse, with far less attention given to sexual abuse (see Black *et al.*, 2001) and psychological abuse (but see Schumacher *et al.*, 2001b). Second, research primarily concerns violence
in cross-sex, rather than same-sex, couples (see Renzetti, 1992, for the classic statement on lesbian
violence; see Stanley *et al.*, 2006, for a review of research on violence in gay relationships). Third,
regardless of the gender neutrality of the label, the majority of published articles with IPV in
their title or keyword are about violence in which men are the perpetrators and women are the
victims.

Characteristics of research on IPV

Research on IPV is characterized by severe methodological problems. Observers, for example,
complain that the results of studies often cannot be compared because IPV is defined and
measured in many different ways (Fincham, 2000). There also are problems in asking questions
about such a sensitive topic, in relying on retrospective reports, and with using a single informant
as the source of information about the characteristics of IPV in a couple (Ehrensaft *et al.*, 2003).
Moreover, IPV research often relies on clinical samples composed of victims and perpetrators
in social service programs and it is well known that findings from such samples cannot be
generalized to non-clinical populations (Ehrensaft *et al.*, 2003; Stith *et al.*, 2000). Finally, there
are questions about the "Conflict Tactics Scale" (CTS), which is commonly used to measure
IPV (see Straus *et al.*, 1996, for discussion of the scale and its psychometric properties). In brief,

the research literature is filled with complaints about the methodological problems of measuring IPV (see Hamby, 2005, for a review of these multiple problems).

These methodological problems underlying research on IPV lead to often inconsistent and even contradictory findings in studies examining four primary topics of interest: risk factors, contexts and meanings, consequences, and social interventions.

IPV risk factors

At first glance, research on IPV risk factors seems to confirm popular understandings: poor people, minorities, and uneducated people are more likely to be victims and perpetrators of IPV than are wealthy people, educated people, and Anglos (see Caetano *et al.*, 2008, for a review of these studies). In addition, alcohol consumption is associated with IPV perpetration and victimization (see Temple *et al.*, 2008), and there are relationships between IPV victimization and perpetration in adulthood and being an abused child or witnessing parental IPV as a child (see Ehrensaft *et al.*, 2003). Research also confirms common public beliefs that violence is a consequence of individual psychopathology: IPV perpetration is associated with particular constellations of psychological characteristics, such as impulsiveness, high levels of hostility, low levels of assertiveness, high need for control, and various types of personality disorder (see Dutton and Bodnarchuk, 2005, for a review). Not surprisingly, IPV is also associated with marital dissatisfaction and marital discord (Stith *et al.*, 2008); perpetration of physical violence is associated with attitudes condoning the use of violence (see Schumacher *et al.*, 2001a); and IPV in which men are the offenders and women the victims is associated with beliefs in traditional gender ideology promoting men's rights to control "their" women (see Stith *et al.*, 2004, for a review).

While seemingly confirming popular and commonsense notions of IPV risk factors, research actually is characterized by an extreme variability in its findings (Fincham, 2000). For example, while there are clear associations between *physical* violence and social class, no such relationship exists between *psychological* violence and social class (Schumacher *et al.*, 2001b). Factors associated with IPV perpetration are also not necessarily those associated with IPV victimization: one meta-analytic review, for example, found that a childhood history of "sexual victimization" was a risk factor for adult IPV *perpetration*, while a childhood history of "emotional/verbal victimization" was a risk factor for adult IPV *victimization* (Schumacher *et al.*, 2001a). Different studies also lead to different conclusions: some research shows that experiencing child abuse and/or growing up in a violent home is a "moderate to strong" risk factor for adult IPV perpetration (Schumacher *et al.*, 2001a), while other studies show such childhood experience is only a "weak to moderate" risk factor (Stith *et al.*, 2000). Furthermore, while some research finds little difference between risk factors for women and for men (Simmons *et al.*, 2008), other studies show a stronger relationship between growing up in a violent home and becoming an IPV *perpetrator* for men than for women and for becoming an IPV *victim* for women than for men (Stith *et al.*, 2000). In brief, and in sharp contrast to public images that IPV risk factors are simple, clear, and commonsensical, research on risk factors for IPV perpetration and victimization is characterized by complexity and inconsistent findings.

Further complexity in determining risk factors stems from the fact that the overwhelming majority of research on IPV is cross-sectional rather than longitudinal. Cross-sectional research, for example, can demonstrate the co-concurrence of parental IPV and child abuse but it cannot empirically demonstrate that parental IPV leads to child abuse, that child abuse leads to parental IPV, or that there tends to be a simple co-concurrence of IPV and child abuse (see McGuigan and Pratt, 2001). Similarly, although marital dissatisfaction and discord are often discussed as risk factors for IPV, cross-sectional research cannot rule out the possibility that IPV rather leads to a loss of marital satisfaction and an increase in marital discord (Stith *et al.*, 2008). Cross-sectional research cannot determine if alcohol use leads to IPV victimization or if victimization leads to alcohol use (Temple *et al.*, 2008).

Although research on IPV risk factors is important because effective prevention programs must be built upon adequate understandings of these factors (Ehrensaft *et al.*, 2003), research certainly has not yet established a firm knowledge base. On one point, however, there is general agreement: IPV cannot be understood to result from just one or a few risk factors (Stith *et al.*, 2004). What is needed are theories of risk that take account of individual characteristics as well as the immediate, social, and cultural contexts of violence (Fincham, 2000).

Contexts and meanings of violence

The common definition of IPV as violence that is unspecified in terms of its contexts and meanings leads to an assumption that all violence is equivalent. Yet this assumption has been questioned and lies at the core of the most long-lasting and frequent debates about IPV: there is considerable empirical data indicating that women in cross-sex relationships use as much— or more—violence as men (see Williams *et al.*, 2008, for a review of these studies). Does equivalence in the *use* of violence mean that women's violence toward men is the same as men's violence toward women? Traditionally, this question has been answered in two diametrically opposing ways. One answer dramatizes women as perpetrators of violence and argues that women's violence toward men is the same as men's violence toward women (see Carney *et al.*, 2007, for this argument). The other answer dramatizes women as victims of violence and argues that findings of equivalence in the use of violence obscure the fact that men's violence is done for the purpose of controlling women while women's violence is done in self-defense (see Temple *et al.*, 2005).

Rather than simply dramatizing women as either perpetrators or victims, it is far more productive to examine the *gendered* patterns of cross-sex IPV perpetration and victimization. For example, couples can be categorized as non-violent or violent. In turn, violence can be unidirectional (male or female as perpetrator) or symmetrical (both male and female are equally violent). Symmetrical violence can be further classified as having a primary perpetrator who is either male or female (Temple *et al.*, 2005). Gendered patterns can also be examined by focusing on the *context* of violence. In one model, for example, violence is categorized into four distinct types: "common couples violence," conceptualized as "minor" violence (e.g., slaps, pushes, shoves) done in the context of an argument; "intimate terrorism," which is more extreme violence done by one person who wishes to control the other; "mutual violent control," where both people use extreme violence to control one another; and "violent resistance," where the victim of intimate terrorism uses violence in self-defense (Johnson and Ferraro 2000; see also Leone *et al.*, 2007, for a review).

The debate about the meaning of men's and women's violence demonstrates a larger issue in theorizing about and doing empirical studies on IPV: the formal definition of IPV does not take into account the contexts or meanings of violence. Exploring the contexts and meanings of violence might lead to research that is not characterized by as many inconsistent and incongruent findings and it is also necessary because different contexts and different meanings lead to different consequences as well as to different kinds of help-seeking behavior (Leone *et al.*, 2007; Fincham 2000).

IPV consequences

There is universal agreement that IPV has multiple negative consequences. Widely recognized as a public health problem, IPV victimization of women *and* men leads to negative health outcomes, including increased risks of poor physical health, physical disability, and psychological distress (Office of Disease Prevention and Health Promotion, 2004). Yet, while both genders experience negative consequences, most research finds that women are far more likely than men to be physically harmed and to take more time off work because of injuries. The meanings of violence also tend to be different for women and for men: the former tend to experience more fear, depression, suicidal thoughts and attempts, and post-traumatic stress disorder than the latter (see Arias, 2000; Temple *et al.*, 2005; but see Carney *et al.*, 2007, and Hines *et al.*, 2007, for the counter-argument that men are equally psychologically harmed by IPV). Critically, particular kinds and extents of consequences cannot be assumed, because physical and psychological consequences depend upon the duration, extent, and context of violence (Leone *et al.*, 2007) as well as on the amount and quality of support available to victims (Roberts, 2006).

Considerable attention has also been paid to consequences for children who witness parental IPV. Research indicates that such children tend to display a range of behavioral and psychological problems, such as depression, anxiety, post-traumatic stress, aggression, hostility, social withdrawal, and low self-esteem (see Kaslow and Thompson, 2008). Consequences for children are such that there are calls to include "witnessing IPV" in the formal definition of child abuse (Norman, 2000).

In summary, while the consequences of IPV are highly variable, there is no debate: IPV is a public health problem because its results are manifold and negatively consequential. Clearly, then, IPV raises questions about how the public should intervene.

Social interventions

As far as social interventions are concerned, most attention has focused on services to assist women victims and to punish male perpetrators. One major line of research has been on addressing questions about victim help-seeking: when do women victims seek informal help from family, friends, or neighbors, and when do they seek formal help from medical personnel, police, or shelters? This research demonstrates that, contrary to public images of women victims as immobilized and unable to act on their own behalf, they actively seek both informal and formal help. The types and severity of violence women experience influence when they seek help and what type of help they seek (see Leone *et al.*, 2007, and Fugate *et al.*, 2005, for reviews of this literature).

Considerable attention has also been paid to examining criminal justice responses to IPV. Such research has explored the extent to which arresting perpetrators deters future violence, the effectiveness of prosecuting cases of IPV with or without the support of victims, and the effectiveness of using courts to mandate perpetrators into counseling (see Fleury, 2002, for a review).

Research focusing on services to assist women victims and to punish or rehabilitate male offenders reflects the characteristics of actual social interventions: most people assume women are victims and men are perpetrators of IPV. This has led to complaints that men are simply (and often wrongfully) assumed to be perpetrators (Carney *et al.*, 2007), and that there are no services for male victims (Hines *et al.*, 2007).

Characteristics of intervention programs reflect the multiple disagreements surrounding IPV. For example, how should "batterer intervention programs" be organized? Should they focus on punishment or rehabilitation? If the goal is rehabilitation, should this be achieved through therapy, education, or a combination of the two (Ehrensaft *et al.*, 2003)? Critically, regardless of which model these programs adopt, there is little empirical evidence that they succeed in reducing violence (Eckhardt *et al.*, 2006). This key problem is noted in the literature: while there have been innumerable interventions for IPV, there is little empirical evidence that *any* is generally effective. Medical providers, for example, have been encouraged—and sometimes even mandated—to screen their patients in order to identify abused women, but no research indicates that such screening results in any measurable good for these women (Wathen and MacMillan, 2003). Furthermore, research on criminal justice intervention shows that while prosecuting IPV perpetrators protects some women, it seemingly puts others into danger (Fleury, 2002).

The only summary that can be made about the current state of social interventions is that while there have been a great many of them, there remain disagreements about the form they should take as well as a lack of empirical support for their effectiveness. This should probably be expected: IPV encompasses many very different situations, so it follows that any particular social intervention will likely help some people, not help others, and perhaps even harm others.

Summary of knowledge about IPV

Although the literature on IPV is large and ever-growing, at least two problems prevent an accumulation of knowledge that would result in effective interventions to stop IPV from happening in the first place, to halt it once it starts, and to repair the effects of victimization. First, IPV research is increasingly insular (Hamby, 2005). Articles are found primarily in specialist journals dedicated to exploring issues relating to violence (e.g., *Violence and Victims*), violence in families (e.g., *Journal of Family Violence*), gender (e.g., *Violence Against Women*), and treatment (e.g., *Public Health Reports*). Furthermore, citations in these articles are overwhelmingly to other articles in the same journals. This means that IPV research is not being informed by larger bodies of knowledge about violence (Hamby, 2005). Second, the formal definition of IPV includes all violence, regardless of context, meanings, or consequences; it includes violence in present and past relationships in cross-sex and same-sex couples. So IPV encourages us to condemn *all* violence occurring among *all* adults who are other than strangers or mere acquaintances. Certainly, condemning all violence is a worthy political goal. Yet, simultaneously, the very inclusiveness of the label and definition of IPV leads to inadequacies in empirical research. Researchers tend to restrict their definitions of IPV (for example, by including only physical violence, only cross-sex couples, or only women as victims) yet continue to call the phenomenon they study "IPV." It is no wonder that the knowledge base for IPV is somewhat less than satisfactory.

References

Arias, I. 2000. Special series: Intimate partner violence introduction. *Behavior Therapy* 31:599–602.

Black, D. A., Heyman, R. E., and Slep, A. M. S. 2001. Risk factors for male-to-female partner sexual abuse. *Aggression and Violent Behavior* 6:269–280.

Caetano, R., Vaeth, P. A. C., and Ramisetty-Mikler, S. 2008. Intimate partner violence: Victim and perpetrator characteristics among couples in the United States. *Journal of Family Violence* 23:507–518.

Carney, M., Buttell, F., and Dutton, D. 2007. Women who perpetrate intimate partner violence: A review of the literature with recommendations for treatment. *Aggression and Violent Behavior* 12:108–115.

Centers for Disease Control. n.d. "Intimate Partner Violence." Available at: www.cdc.gov/Features/Intimate Partner Violence/ (accessed March 20, 2009).

Dutton, D. G. and Bodnarchuk, M. 2005. Through a psychological lens: Personality disorder and spouse assault. In D. R. Loseke, R. J. Gelles, and M. M. Cavanaugh (eds.) *Current controversies on family violence*, 2nd edn (pp. 5–18). Thousand Oaks, CA: Sage.

Eckhardt, C., Murphy, C., Back, D., and Suhr, L. 2006. Intervention programs for perpetrators of intimate partner violence: Conclusions from a clinical research perspective. *Public Health Reports* 121:369–381.

Ehrensaft, M. K., Cohen, P., Brown, J., Smailes, E., Chen, H., and Johnson, J. G. 2003. Intergenerational transmission of partner violence: A 20-year prospective study. *Journal of Consulting and Clinical Psychology* 71: 741–753.

Fincham, F. D. 2000. Family violence: A challenge for behavior therapists. *Behavior Therapy* 31:685–693.

Fleury, R. E. 2002. Missing voices: Patterns of battered women's satisfaction with the criminal legal system. *Violence Against Women* 8:181–205.

Frieze, I. H. 2005. Female violence against intimate partners: An introduction. *Psychology of Women Quarterly* 29:229–237.

Fugate, M., Landis, L., Riordan, K., Naureckas, S., and Engel, B. 2005. Barriers to domestic violence help seeking. *Violence Against Women* 11:290–310.

Hamby, S. L. 2005. Measuring gender differences in partner violence: Implications from research on other forms of violent and socially undesirable behavior. *Sex Roles* 52: 725–742.

Hines, D. A., Brown, J., and Dunning, E. 2007. Characteristics of callers to the domestic abuse hotline for men. *Journal of Family Violence* 22:63–72.

Johnson, M. P. and Ferraro, K. J. 2000. Research on domestic violence in the 1990s: Making distinctions. *Journal of Marriage and the Family* 62:948–963.

Kaslow, N. J. and Thompson, M. P. 2008. Association of child maltreatment and intimate partner violence with psychological adjustment among low SES, African American children. *Child Abuse and Neglect* 32:888–896.

Leone, J. M., Johnson, M. P., and Cohan, C. I. 2007. Victim help seeking: Differences between intimate terrorism and situational couple violence. *Family Relations* 56:427–439.

McGuigan, W. M. and Pratt, C. C. 2001. The predictive impact of domestic violence on three types of child maltreatment. *Child Abuse and Neglect* 25:869–883.

Norman, J. 2000. Should children's protective services intervene when children witness domestic violence? *Trauma, Violence and Abuse* 1:291–293.

Office of Disease Prevention and Health Promotion. 2004. *Intimate partner violence and healthy people 2010 fact sheet*. Washington, DC: Office of Disease Prevention and Health Promotion and US Department of Health and Human Services.

Renzetti, C. M. 1992. *Violent betrayal: Partner abuse in lesbian relationships*. Newbury Park, CA: Sage.

Roberts, A. R. 2006. Classification typology and assessment of five levels of woman battering. *Journal of Family Violence* 2:521–527.

Schumacher, J. A., Slep, A. M. S., and Heyman, R. E. 2001b. Risk factors for male-to-female partner psychological abuse. *Aggression and Violent Behavior* 6:255–268.

Schumacher, J. A., Feldbau-Kohn, S., Slep, A. M. S., and Heyman, R. E. 2001a. Risk factors for male–to–female partner physical abuse. *Aggression and Violent Behavior* 6:281–352

Simmons, C. A., Lehmann, P., and Cobb, N. 2008. A comparison of women versus men charged with intimate partner violence: General risk factors, attitudes regarding using violence, and readiness to change. *Violence and Victims* 23:571–585.

Stanley, J. L., Bartholomew, K., Taylor, T., Oram, D., and Landolt, M. 2006. Intimate violence in male same-sex relationships. *Journal of Family Violence* 21:31–41.

Stith, S. M., Green, N. M., Smith, D. B., and Ward, D. B. 2008. Marital satisfaction and marital discord as risk markers for intimate partner violence: A meta-analytic review. *Journal of Family Violence* 23:149–160.

Stith, S. M., Rosen, K. H., Middleton, K. A., Busch, A. L., Lundeberg, K., and Carlton, R. P. 2000. The intergenerational transmission of spouse abuse: A meta-analysis. *Journal of Marriage and the Family* 62:640–654.

Stith, S. M., Smith, D. B., Penn, C. E., Ward, D. B., and Tritt, D. 2004. Intimate partner physical abuse perpetration and victimization risk factors. *Aggression and Violent Behavior* 10:65–98.

Straus, M. A., Hamby, S. L., Boney-McCoy, S., and Sugarman, D. B. 1996. The revised conflict tactics scales (CTS2): Development and preliminary psychometric data. *Journal of Family Issues* 17:283–316.

Temple, J. R., Weston, R., and Marshall, L. L. 2005. Physical and mental health outcomes of women in nonviolent, unilaterally violent, and mutually violent relationships. *Violence and Victims* 20:335–358.

Temple, J. R., Weston, R., Stuart, G. L., and Marshall, L. L. 2008. The longitudinal association between alcohol use and intimate partner violence among ethnically diverse community women. *Addictive Behaviors* 33:1244–1248.

Wathen, C. N. and MacMillan, H. L. 2003. Interventions for violence against women: Scientific review. *Journal of the American Medical Association* 289:589–600.

Williams, J. R., Ghandour, R. M., and Kub, J. E. 2008. Female perpetration of violence in heterosexual intimate relationships: Adolescence through adulthood. *Trauma, Violence and Abuse* 9:227–249.

61

Homicide, serial murder, and mass murder

Stephen T. Holmes and Ronald M. Holmes

Introduction

The crime of homicide is a topic that has galvanized the attention of the American public and international audiences for the better part of the last 30 years. It is generally defined as the "killing of one human being by another." Homicide can occur as a result of a disagreement between two people, a lover's quarrel, or a crime gone wrong. It can also be a premeditated act, as in cases of serial or mass murder.

It is not necessary to look too far to see how it has influenced our society. If one looks at the bestseller lists, one is sure to find a book on a serial or mass killer. Further, when we scan our TV guides for shows to watch this week, inevitably some of the most popular and highly rated programs involve a police agency or profiler working to solve the heinous works of a homicide offender or serial killer. Further, some of the serial and mass murderers of years past are now household names. Any adult or college-aged student is likely to know more about Ted Bundy than about the current leaders of the US House and Senate.

Incidence and prevalence of homicide in the United States

To academics in the fields of criminology and criminal justice, the crime of homicide is especially important for two reasons. First, no other crime is measured as accurately as homicide because of the seriousness of the offense and the repercussions of the fatal event. Second, homicide is often viewed as a barometer of the true rate of violent crime in both the United States and many developing countries (Fox and Zawitz, 2007).

According to the Federal Bureau of Investigation's *Uniform Crime Reports* (FBI, 2007) the homicide victimization rate per 100,000 population almost doubled between the mid-1960s and the late 1970s. Thereafter, it declined, and it has remained relatively stable since 2000. This trend is illustrated in Figure 61.1.

Even though the homicide rate has stabilized in recent years, the number of homicides has increased dramatically over the years. In fact, if the trends illustrated in Figure 61.2 are reviewed, it is clear that, despite the recent decline, the trend line remains positive, pointing to an increasing number of homicide victims.

Perhaps these data are most telling of the problem. While victimization rates tell us the likelihood of falling victim to this heinous crime, the number of homicides is the prime indicator

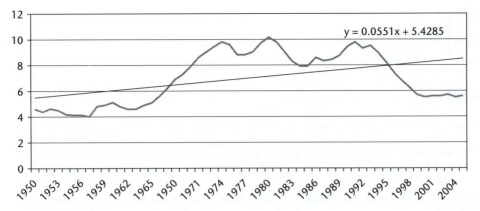

Figure 61.1 Homicide rate per 100,000 population, 1950–2004

Source: FBI, 2007

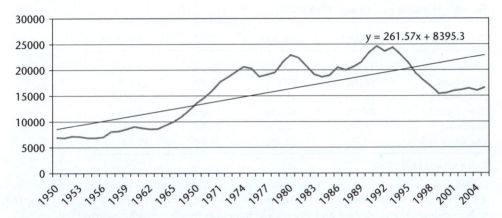

Figure 61.2 Estimated number of homicides, 1950–2004

Source: FBI, 2007

of the total number of people touched by the crime. Thus, while the victimization rate tells us we are now less likely to be a victim of this crime, the total number of homicides committed is generally thought to be a reflective indicator of the total human cost of homicide.

As far as the general characteristics of victims is concerned, most are older teens or young adults (18–34). Meanwhile, the modal age for perpetrators was between 18 and 24 (Fox and Zawitz, 2007). This is understandable because this is the age when youth are generally most involved in criminogenic activity.

Another commonly reported statistic on homicide is the relationship between the perpetrator and the victim. The data compiled by the FBI and the Bureau of Justice Statistics indicate that younger victims generally know their killers. However, adult victims are about equally likely to know or not know their killers. These data are presented in Figure 61.3.

As mentioned previously, there are a variety of reasons why people commit homicide. Official data collected by the Federal Bureau of Investigation in the Bureau of Justice Statistics' *Homicide Trends in the United States* report (Fox and Zawitz, 2007) shows that most youth homicides are gang-related. Further, those aged between 18 and 34 commit the majority of felony-,

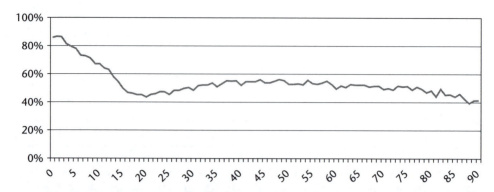

Figure 61.3 Percentage of homicides in which offender was known by victim, by victim age, 1976–2005

Sources: FBI, 2007; Fox and Zawitz, 2007

Table 61. Homicide type by age, 1976–2005

Circumstances	Under 18	18–34	35–49	50 and over
Felony murder	14.8%	72.9%	10.3%	2.0%
Sex related	10.7%	73.6%	13.7%	2.0%
Drug related	10.6%	76.9%	11.3%	1.2%
Gang related	28.9%	69.2%	1.6%	0.3%
Argument	6.9%	60.2%	23.1%	9.7%
Workplace violence	3.7%	53.1%	27.6%	15.5%

Source: Fox and Zawitz, 2007

sex-, drug-, and gang-related murders. Additionally, this age group is responsible for the majority of homicides in the workplace and when an argument between individuals turns fatal.

Serial and mass murderers

While the statistics and reasons why homicide is committed are interesting, there is a special class of homicide offender that in many aspects is more interesting than those that commit a single homicide. These offenders appear to be growing in frequency and notoriety (Holmes, Deburger, and Holmes, 1988). They generally do not kill because of an argument, a drug deal, or to protect their turf. Rather, they kill because they either enjoy the act or wish to wipe out an entire class or group of individuals. They are commonly referred to as serial or mass murderers.

In order to comprehend what a serial or mass killer is, it is best to start with some basic definitions. Holmes and Holmes (2009: 5–6) define serial murder as "the killing of three or more people over a period of more than 30 days, with a significant cooling off period between the killings." On the other hand, mass or spree killers are individuals who willfully kill a number of people at one time and in one place (Holmes and Holmes, 2001). Authors have different opinions about how many victims a person has to kill in order to be classified as either a serial or a mass murderer, but most agree on three as the baseline number (Hickey, 2006; Holmes and Holmes, 2009).

Differences between serial and mass murderers

There are fundamental differences between serial and mass murderers beyond mere definitional differences. These differences often hold the key to understanding the individuals who commit these crimes and hopefully catching them before they take another life.

Mass murderers generally take their own life either during their homicidal episode or shortly afterward. Should they not do so, they typically will place themselves in a position where the police or other authorities will take their life for them. For instance, James Huberty shot 40 people (killing 21) before a police sharpshooter fatally dispatched him. Only in rare cases will you find a mass murderer surrender to the police. Serial murderers, on the other hand, seek to avoid detection so that they may prey on more victims (Egger, 1998; Hickey, 2001; Holmes and Holmes, 2009). The one prominent exception to this rule was Edmund Kemper, who killed his mother and her best friend, realized that the killing must stop, and called the police to turn himself in.

Another difference between serial and mass murderers is that the latter generally see the killing of a group of people in a public place as their last act of defiance. They typically know that they will not live through to the end of the day. They understand the consequences of their actions and generally seek to punish their victims for the pain that they have caused them. There is also usually a connection between the place in which the homicidal event occurs and the perpetrator. With serial murder, the perpetrator typically seeks out a victim who matches their "ideal victim type." Thus, while the physical characteristics of the victim may be important (e.g., female, Caucasian, 18–25 years old), there is often no relationship between the perpetrator and victim or the place in which the incident occurs.

Another difference lies in how the community and indeed the nation respond to these incidents. In the case of mass murder, there is an immediate effect on the community and the nation as the incident is played out on local and national TV. If the mass murderer commits their crime on school grounds, a state of panic sets in as parents around the country check to make sure their children are safe. In the days and weeks following an attack, the community is mobilized and diligent concerning the security of their children and/or workplace. The police will be called whenever a suspicious person is seen on campus or even in the atriums of business offices across the country. Slowly, however, this effect dissipates and our communities return to normalcy.

In the case of a serial murderer, fear and panic often continue until the offender is either apprehended or killed. But it does not end there. Parents of the victims will often hold vigils for their children, and others will remind their children about the victims and warn them of the dangerous people who are out there. Thus the names of the killer and the victims become part of local legend and the community's folklore.

Another major difference between serial and mass killers is the behavior of the perpetrator before the homicidal episode begins. In general, the mass murderer will have experienced substantial discord in their personal or professional life. They may have lost their job, their marriage may have collapsed, and they may have been suffering from depression. The serial murderer, on the other hand, at least on the surface, is more in control of their attitude and demeanor. They often live a dual life (Carlisle, 1993). On the outside, they might be an outstanding or at least a respectable member of the community. For example, Ted Bundy was a law student and an assistant director of the Seattle Crime Commission (Michaud and Aynesworth, 1983). Other serial killers have held jobs as electricians (Jerry Brudos), engineers (Douglass Clark), and even social workers (Beoria Simmons) (Holmes and Holmes, 2001; Stack, 1983). However, deep inside their own mind, their personality is said to be in turmoil.

Types of serial killer

Just as there are important differences between mass and serial murderers, there are differences between the various types of killer within these two broad categories. Not all serial or mass murderers are alike or share the same motivations and anticipated gains. As far as serial killers are concerned, there are four primary types: visionary, mission, hedonistic, and power/control killers (Holmes and Deburger, 1985).

The visionary killer

The visionary serial killer often suffers a break with reality and commits heinous acts of violence. This type of killer cannot be called psychotic because, for the most part, they are in touch with reality, but they may at times suffer from psychotic episodes in which they hear voices or see visions that compel them to act. One of the most famous visionary serial killers was Joseph Kallinger ("The Shoemaker"). Kallinger claims to have seen a floating head (named Charlie) that followed him around, telling him to kill everyone in the world and then himself (Schrieber, 1983). In terms of the anticipated gain for this type of killer, it is intrinsic to the individual. The kill itself will often return the murderer to some form of psychological equilibrium by satisfying the craving of the entity with which they are communicating.

Unlike other types of serial killer, the visionary has no "ideal victim type," so they may choose male or female victims, depending on what the vision tells them to do. Sometimes, killer and victim may share nothing but the physical space in which the murder occurs (Holmes and Holmes, 2009).

The mission killer

The mission type of serial killer is different from the visionary in that they do not suffer from psychotic episodes. They do not hear voices or see visions; instead, in their own mind, they have decided the victim is an "undesirable person," often on account of their demographic or occupational status. In this killer's mind, such "undesirables" will have done something to hurt the perpetrator and thus must suffer the consequences.

Victims are therefore selected because they fit the killer's "ideal victim type." One of the most famous mission killers was David Berkowitz ("The Son of Sam"). Berkowitz claimed to have been commanded to kill by a black Labrador named Harvey that lived next door to him. However, he later retracted this statement and stated that he killed young women and their boyfriends because he was trying to stop the birth of illegitimate children. Berkowitz himself was illegitimate, and claimed that this had caused him great psychological distress.

Berkowitz and many other mission killers have stated that the kill itself provides them with a psychological reward. They often claim that they are providing a great service to society by eradicating a specific type of person or group.

The victims of the mission killer are usually strangers who conform to an "ideal victim type." The murderer will tend to choose a method that ensures a quick and certain demise of the victim. There is rarely a desire to prolong the act of killing itself.

The hedonistic killer

The type of serial killer that most often captivates the media is the hedonistic killer, of which there are three distinct types: the lust killer, the thrill killer, and the comfort killer. The first two of these have made a connection between personal and sexual gratification and fatal violence.

The third kills for financial reasons or some other type of personal gain. The methods used in the kill are often so bizarre that they are incomprehensible to the average person. Lust and thrill killers are often construed as sexual predators whose personal pleasure is dependent on the amount of violence and mayhem they are able to inflict on their victims. The more violent the act, the more rewarding it is to these killers.

The lust killer

Like the mission killer, the lust killer is very much in touch with reality. They kill primarily to fulfill a deviant sexual fantasy. Because fantasy and symbolism are highly involved in making the experience especially gratifying for the perpetrator, they follow a carefully prescribed ritual in the selection, abduction, and method of killing their victims.

Since sex is such a powerful motivating factor for this type of killer, they will typically select an "ideal victim type." During the kill itself, which usually occurs in a controlled environment, they are likely to torture and mutilate the victim both before and after death. Overkill—such as stabbing the victim dozens of times—may well occur, too. Strangulation is the most common method of murder employed by these killers, as it provides skin-to-skin contact with the dying victim.

The thrill killer

Like the lust killer, the thrill killer is hedonistic and motivated by sexual gratification. Usually a male, the thrill killer wants and needs to feel the excitement of the victim as they struggle to hold on to life. They typically choose female victims not only because they sexually excite them, but because they are more likely to scream, cry, and beg for their lives than men. While he shares many of the characteristics of the lust killer, the thrill killer usually loses interest in the body of the victim once they have died.

Like the lust killer, the thrill killer often demands complete domination and control over his victims. In the kill, he will often combine many aberrant sexual paraphilias and will take his time dispatching the victim in order to prolong his sexual pleasure. The longer pain and humiliation can be inflicted, the greater will be the sexual gratification. So victims will often be tortured before strangulation. However, they are unlikely to engage in either overkill or necrophilia, since their pleasure is dependent on a living, struggling, horrified victim.

The comfort killer

The comfort killer is very different from the other two types of hedonistic killer. These offenders are motivated not by sexual pleasure but by money, business gains, or other material rewards (Holmes and Holmes, 2009). They have made a rational choice to kill victims whom they believe are worth more to them dead than alive. Typically, then, the offenders know their victims, who may be family or friends. Alternatively, as in the case of Richard Kulinski, they murder people they have been paid to kill (Bruno, 1993).

The comfort killer will often plan their murders weeks or months in advance, and their methods vary: they may produce a slow death, as in the poisoning of a spouse, or be instantaneous, as in an assassination. Most comfort killers experience no real joy in the killing itself. Rather, it is simply viewed as a means to an end.

The power/control killer

Like lust and thrill killers, the power/control killer is compelled into action because of their fantasies and desires. However, their driving factor is not necessarily sexual. Sex may become part of this type of killer's ritual, but it is not at the heart of their motivation. Instead, they kill because of their thirst for absolute power and domination of their chosen victims.

The power/control killer will invariably have a deep and rich fantasy life. Many suffer from a "God complex" and gain satisfaction from deciding a victim's ultimate fate. For instance, Ted Bundy, a classic power/control killer, stated that his greatest satisfaction came from the life and death decisions he made for his victims (Holmes and Holmes, 2009).

Like other types of killer, the power/control murderer will carefully search for an "ideal victim type." This may be based on physical characteristics, but it is more often simply a particular type of person to whom the murderer has easy access. For instance, Douglas Clark preyed on prostitutes because they would willingly get into his car.

The power/control killer's personality is usually organized, and so is their crime scene. They typically lure the victim into a place of comfort (e.g., home or car), kill the victim, then humiliate the body for sexual gratification (for instance, indulging in piquerism and necrophilia) before dumping it. Some power/control killers continue to humiliate the body for several days before disposing of it.

Power/control killers consider themselves to be masters of their trade (Holmes and Holmes, 2009). They often practice until they are highly proficient at using restraints to control their victims. As they enjoy having the power of life and death in their own hands, they will often use strangulation as their preferred method of murder, so that they can feel the "life force" draining from their victims.

Types of mass killer

Mass killers typically share certain traits, including suffering episodes of depression, feeling hopeless, and believing that their victims are in some way directly or indirectly responsible for their suffering. However, they can be divided into seven different categories: the disciple, the family annihilator, the disgruntled employee, the ideological, the set and run, the psychotic, and the youthful school shooter.

The disciple

The disciple mass murderer kills not for their own pleasure or because they have been psycho-logically harmed by their victims, but because they have been directed to do so by a leader of a group to which they belong. Usually, this leader either directly instructs the killer to eliminate a group of individuals or suggests that it is "God's will" for this group to be eliminated. The Manson family were prime examples of this type of killer.

The family annihilator

The family annihilator fatally dispatches members of their own family. They do not hear voices or take instructions from others, but instead consciously decide to take the lives of those closest to them. Their motivations vary. Some feel the need to release family members from the shackles of the cruel world in which they live. Others target relatives because they feel they have brought shame on the family. Still others simply wish to start their lives over, free from the financial obligations of their family.

The disgruntled employee

The disgruntled employee kills individuals at their current or previous place of employment. Typically, they blame these people for all of their personal, psychological, or financial problems. The violence they enact usually takes one of two forms: they either prey on fellow employees or victimize customers. Many of these killers have claim to have been personally belittled by their co-workers and/or blame them for their inability to find suitable employment. In the mind of this type of killer, the reward is intrinsic to the individual: that is, the eradication of these "evil people" and the act itself will draw attention to the perceived atrocities that have been committed against them. Examples of this type of killer include Joseph Wesbecker and Frederick Davidson.

The ideological killer

Ideological mass killers often consider themselves soldiers in the fight against the repression of the people. Thus, the killer's belief system commands them into action to change the world by drawing attention to their cause. For these killers, there are no innocent victims. Instead, many of those who die at their hands are considered collateral damage.

The set and run killer

Set and run killers differ from most other types of mass murderer in that they do not tend to kill themselves at the crime scene or put themselves in a position where they are likely to be killed by the authorities. They may be motivated by ideology or simply by the desire to destroy the reputation of a company with which they have ideological or personal differences. Typically, they are not even present at the crime scene when their victims' lives are taken, as their weapons of choice are poison or bombs. While there are parallels between them and ideological killers, it is often best to conceptualize the set and run killer as a subtype of the ideological killer. A classic example in the United States is Timothy McVeigh, who blew up the Alfred P. Murrah Building in Oklahoma City.

The psychotic

This type of mass murderer typically has a severe psychotic condition during which they suffer a severe break with reality and common culture. They may hear voices or see visions, much like the visionary serial killer. Nettler (1982: 155) claims that the psychotic may have a distorted perception of reality, suffer serious mood swings, and have marked difficulties getting along with others.

A psychotic's victims are generally chosen randomly and have no prior relationship with the killer. Typically, they are simply at the wrong place at the wrong time. Examples of this type of killer include Priscilla Ford and William Cruse.

The youthful school shooter

Perhaps no other type of mass murderer captivates the attention of American society to the same extent as the school shooter. This individual is typically a young person, usually in middle or high school, who retaliates against those in their own social environment for the perceived ridicule that they have received. The school shooter is usually Caucasian, comes from a middle-class background, and interacts with other disenfranchised youth. Usually they have an interest in and experience with advanced weaponry. They will typically tell those closest to them what they plan to do. In some cases, they will even instruct others not to come to school on a specific day.

These killers and the heinous acts they commit are some of the most difficult to understand because the murderers have their whole lives in front of them. Examples include Michael Carneal, Kipland Kinkel, and, of course, Eric Harris and Dylan Klebold.

Conclusion

Serial or mass murder is a topic that has galvanized the attention of the public and media for many years. Those who engage in these offenses are viewed as the most evil, vile, and heinous criminals in our society. However, it is not until we begin to understand the motivations, patterns, and anticipated gains of these offenders that we will truly begin to understand the reasons why they commit their murderous deeds and can start planning and implementing strategies to identify and treat them before they take the lives of the innocent.

References

Bruno, A. (1993). *The Ice Man: The True Story of a Cold-Blooded Killer*. New York: Dell.
Carlisle, A. (1993). The Divided Self: Toward an Understanding of the Dark Side of the Serial Killer. *American Journal of Criminal Justice*, 17(2), 23–36.
Egger, S. (1998). *Serial Murder: An Elusive Phenomenon*. New York: Praeger.
Federal Bureau of Investigation (FBI) (2007). *Uniform Crime Reports, 1950–2005*. Washington, DC: US Department of Justice.
Fox, J. and Zawitz, M. (2007). *Homicide Trends in the United States*. Retrieved November 2009 from Bureau of Justice Statistics, US Department of Justice: www.ojp.gov/bjs/homicide/homtrnd.htm#contents
Hickey, E. (2001). *Serial Murderers and Their Victims*. Pacific Groove, CA: Brooks-Cole.
Hickey, E. W. (2006). *Serial Murderers and Their Victims* (4th edn). Belmont, CA: Thomson Higher Education.
Holmes, R. and Deburger, J. (1985). Profiles in Terror: The Serial Murderer. *Federal Probation*, 39, 29–34.
Holmes, R., Deburger, J., and Holmes, S. T. (1988). Inside the Mind of the Serial Murderer. *American Journal of Criminal Justice*, 13(1), 1–9.
Holmes, R. and Holmes, S. (2001). *Mass Murder in the United States*. Upper Saddle River, NJ.: Prentice-Hall.
Holmes, R. and Holmes, S. (2009). *Serial Murder* (3rd edn). Thousand Oaks, CA: Sage.
Michaud, S. and Aynesworth, H. (1983). *The Only Living Witness*. New York: Signet.
Mott, N. (1999). Serial Murder: Patterns in Unsolved Cases. *Homicide Studies*, 3, 241–255.
Nettler, G. (1982). *Explaining Murder*. Cincinnati, OH: Anderson.
Schrieber, F. (1983). *The Shoemaker*. New York: Signet.
Stack, A. (1983). *The Lust Killer*. New York: Signet.

62

Armed robbery and carjacking

Dee Wood Harper and Patrick Walsh

Introduction

The most common forms of armed robbery and first-degree robbery occur on streets and highways. In 2008, street/highway robberies in the United States accounted for 43.1 percent of the 441,855 robbery events known to the police (FBI 2009). This was an annual decrease of 0.7 percent, but the five-year trend (2004 data compared with 2008) showed an increase of 10.1 percent. These violent felony offenses involve the taking of anything of value from the person of another, or which is in the immediate control of another person, by use of force or intimidation while armed with a dangerous weapon, or when the offender leads the victim to believe he or she is armed with a dangerous weapon. The Federal Bureau of Investigation's annual *Uniform Crime Reports (UCR)* defines robbery as "the taking or attempting to take anything of value from the care, custody, or control of a person or persons by force or threat of force or violence and/or by putting the victim in fear" (FBI 2009).

In the United States the second most common form of robbery is residential, including home invasions, which accounts for 16.3 percent of all robberies, followed by businesses, at 13.8 percent. Gas station/convenience store robberies account for 8.1 percent. Bank robberies accounted for only 2 percent (7,278) of all robbery events, yet they yield the greatest average return of $4,854 (compared to the average robbery return of $1,315). Residential robbery was the only type of robbery that increased between 2007 and 2008 (by 2.5 percent) (FBI 2009).

Carjacking combines armed robbery with auto theft. The term came into common usage via the media during the 1980s. Some argue that carjacking came into existence because of the development of sophisticated theft-prevention equipment making it almost impossible to steal a car without the keys (Davis 2003). In the State of Louisiana Criminal Code, carjacking is treated as a type of armed robbery. The United States federal statute forbidding carjacking was enacted in 1992 and amended in 1994 (18 USC §2119). It reads as follows:

> Whoever, *with intent to cause death or serious bodily harm* takes a motor vehicle that has been transported, shipped, or received in interstate or foreign commerce from the person or presence of another by force and violence or by intimidation, or attempts to do so, shall (1) be fined under this title or imprisoned not more than 15 years or both, (2) if serious bodily injury results, be fined under this title or imprisoned not more than 25 years, or both, and

(3) if death results, be fined under this title or imprisoned for any number of years up to life, or both *or sentenced to death.*

(Italics added to indicate the 1994 changes to the statute)

In the United States, robbery rates were stable between 2000 and 2007, averaging 144 per 100,000 people. From 1988 to 1999, the average rate was 189 per 100,000 people, with the peak year, 1991, having a rate of 273. Carjacking between 1993 and 1997 averaged 21 per 100,000 people, but dropped to 13 per 100,000 people between 1998 and 2002 (Klaus 2004).

Carjacking, while receiving considerable media attention, has received little attention from criminologists. However, Bruce Jacobs, Volkan Topalli, and Richard Wright (2003) conducted an ethnographic study of twenty-eight active carjackers in St. Louis, Missouri, and found that their decision to commit carjacking was mediated and shaped by their participation in urban street culture.

Linda Davis (2003) reports that South Africa leads the world in its rate of carjacking: in 2000, it stood at 34.1 per 100,000 people. She contends that the country's history of apartheid and its associated culture of violence, rampant poverty and unemployment, and what appears to be an ineffective criminal justice system account for the high rate. Based on her interviews with twelve imprisoned carjackers, she discovered that carjacking is a large and rather lucrative business in South Africa. The cars are stolen to be sold in other African nations.

Because the victim's life is threatened, armed robbery is viewed as a serious crime warranting a severe penalty. As felony offenses, penalties for armed and first-degree robbery and carjacking range from three to ninety-nine years of hard labor without parole, probation, or suspension of sentence, and the death penalty under federal statute.

Patterns and trends

Robbery is not a recent creation of urban society. The New Testament records "a certain man . . . fell among thieves, which stripped him of his raiment, and wounded him, and departed, leaving him half dead" (Luke 10:30). This "certain man" was clearly the victim of a highway robbery. However, in contrast to the past, when robberies occurred in the hinterland, presently street robbery is a phenomenon of large cities, accounting for 52.5 percent of all robberies in cities with populations greater than 250,000, but just 25.7 percent of all robberies in cities of less than 10,000 (FBI 2009: Table 2).

The rate of reported robbery in the United States increased more than fourfold in the three decades from 1960 (60 per 100,000 people) to 1990 (257 per 100,000 people), before declining to slightly less than 186 per 100,000 by 1997. The overall rate stood at 154 per 100,000 people in 2008 (FBI 2009: Table 16).

International comparisons of robbery are difficult because no uniform standards for reporting or definitions for the crime currently exist. For example, a simple robbery in some countries may be categorized as a first-degree robbery or aggravated robbery in others. In some countries, burglary and robbery are lumped into one category. The Czech Republic, which has experienced a dramatic increase in robbery since the "Velvet Revolution" in 1989, treats robbery as a criminal offense against liberty, meaning it is viewed as an attack on both personal freedom and property (Rozum, Kotulan, and Tomasek 2006). Following the dismantling of apartheid in South Africa, the number of robberies increased dramatically, from 122,369 in 1997 to 208,932 in 2001, a 71 percent increase (Barclay and Tavares 2003). Thus, it can be concluded that rapid rates of social and economic change may exaggerate robbery rates.

Robbery is becoming a growing problem in Western Europe, too. For example, from 1997 to 2001, it increased in England and Wales by 92 percent, in Austria by 42 percent, in France by 75 percent, and in the Netherlands by 48 percent. While Spain showed only a 1 percent increase in this time-frame, it still had the highest rate for the continent (Barclay and Tavares 2003). In a Croatian study, robbery increased by 24 percent between 1997 and 2001, and it more than doubled between 1994 and 2003. Robbery in Croatia is also becoming more of an urban problem. In 1994, the Croatian capital and Zagreb County accounted for less than 50 percent of robberies in the country; in 2004, they accounted for 74 percent (Dujmovic and Miksaj-Todorovis 2004).

Victim characteristics

According to 2007's National Crime Victimization Survey (NCVS), in which the crime victimization experiences of people aged twelve and older in the United States are reported, 200 robberies were reported for every 100,000 persons. As we saw above, the following year, the *UCR* stated that 154 robberies were committed per 100,000 people. So, although the NCVS and *UCR* data sets are not exactly comparable, underreporting of robbery would appear to stand at roughly 25 percent. Data for 2005 indicates that the perpetrator was a stranger in 74 percent of robbery incidents where the victim was male, but only 48 percent were the victim was female. Both sources of data show fairly low and stable robbery rates for the period 2001 to 2008, and a steady decline over the last three decades. The rate of firearm crime victimization has declined from 59 per 100,000 (11 percent of all violent incidents) to 14 per 100,000 (7 percent of all violent incidents). In 2008, the victimization rate was highest among the 12–15-year-old age group (422 per 100,000). Victimization rates are also high for 16–19-year-olds (370) and 20–24-year-olds (378). The highest victimization rate (60 per 100,000) occurs among the poorest households (incomes of $7,500 or less), compared to just 10 per 100,000 in households with incomes of $75,000 or more (BJS 2010)

Offender characteristics

Arrest rates and offender characteristics have remained constant over recent years. Of those arrested in 2008, 41.7 percent were white and 56.7 percent were black (FBI 2009: Table 43). Robbery is an overwhelmingly male crime (88.4 percent) (FBI 2009: Table 42) and a crime of youth. The peak ages for robbery arrest in 2008 were 17 (8,904), 18 (9,464), and 19 (8,056) (FBI 2009: Table 38).

It is very difficult for social scientists to explain the high incidence of robbery among young black males. The correlation between robbery and race, according to LaFree (1995), is r = .98. However, LaFree (1995: 182) suggests that the theories advanced to explain black involvement in robbery are inadequate. The social disorganization perspective, for example, links black crime rates to high rates of female-headed households and low marriage rates. Comparative and historical research do not consistently support this view. For instance, some European countries have high levels of divorce and female-headed households and low crime rates. Some theorists argue that everyone is exposed to the goals of monetary success, but the means of achieving these goals through legitimate or conventional means are unequally structured. Given the relatively dire economic situation for many blacks, this argument seems relevant. However, when unemployment and income measures were examined, there was no significant effect on black crime rates (LaFree 1995: 182–186).

Katz (1988: 241) argues that the over-representation of blacks in the statistics for robbery is a result of being close to the seductions of stickup, and the social construction of the "hardman" as street robber. Moreover, at an emotional level, within the modern poor black urban community, being "bad" is often a collectively celebrated way of being that transcends good and evil.

Understanding robbery

No treatise on robbery is complete without a discussion of John Conklin's (1972) typology of the crime. Conklin classified robbers as professional, opportunists, addicts, and alcoholics. He concludes that the professionals—those who specialize in planned bank robberies, for example—are on the decline and that those who engage in these crimes currently do not differ significantly from the opportunistic robber. The opportunist acts randomly, although victim vulnerability, the potential for getting money, consideration of location, and escape are all taken into account before committing the act.

Often in street robbery, young males ranging in age from early teens to early twenties will operate as a team. Younger members of the team approach a potential victim to ask for directions, the time, a cigarette or spare change, a ploy designed to stop and "connect" with the target. An older member of the team will then approach from behind with a gun, announcing the stickup. The younger member of the team will then relieve the victim of money, jewelry, purse, or cameras (Harper 2005).

In some instances, victims unintentionally set themselves up for robbery. Single males drinking in bars might be approached by a friendly male or female who engages them in conversation. After a rapport is established, the conversation turns to whether the target would like sex or drugs. If the would-be victim answers "No," or "I don't have any money," the relationship will be terminated. But if the answer is "Yes," the robber will offer to accompany the victim to some unknown but not-too-distant location. The female robber usually has an accomplice who has left the bar and is waiting at a previously arranged location, where the robbery will take place. A male robber working alone will simply lead the victim to a nearby location and rob him (Harper 2005).

According to Conklin (1972), addicted and alcoholic robbers engage in robbery to support their habits. They have a low commitment to robbery as a favored type of crime, but they have a high commitment to theft in general. Physical force, rather than a weapon, is more often used to take money. In the last few years, one strategy employed in large urban areas by addicts, alcoholics, and so-called "gutter punks" is aggressive panhandling. In hotel districts, near convention center facilities, and near tourist attractions, aggressive panhandlers, acting individually or in groups, ambush pedestrians, pushing them, acting in a threatening manner, and demanding money. If the pedestrian is not forthcoming, she or he might be shoved, hit, or kicked (Harper 2005).

Why do people commit robbery? Aside from the simple answer that it is a quick way to secure money, there are a number of irrational elements to the crime. For example, the legal penalty does not depend on the amount taken, and the monetary return from a typical street robbery is rarely great. Even when tourists are targeted, the take will not often be more than $300 in cash (Harper 2005). So, given the risks and the low rate of return, why does the robber persist in this crime? Viewing the behavior from the perspective of the robber, Katz (1988: 167) distinguishes three phases in the robber's experience, which result in a customary style of attack and a particular understanding of self. The would-be robber must achieve a moral advantage over the target (gaining control of the situation), must commit to the act by declaring the crime (e.g., "Give it up!"), and must stick with the crime beyond reason (given the potential negative consequences). Spending money gained through robbery rapidly ("burning" money), the chaotic experience of the crime itself, and the experience of controlling it and the varieties of illicit action make up the life of the robber and account for his or her persistence in this crime.

As reported above, robbery is a predominantly male and black activity in the United States. Messerschmidt (1993) suggest that an "opposition masculinity" accounts for this disproportionate number of marginalized racial-minority boys being involved in robbery. He argues that this violent crime is a means of expressing their masculinity and it flows from their disconcerting school experiences and their life experiences with poverty, racism, negated futures, and lack of power. He argues that because of these conditions, young racial-minority boys are more likely to commit certain types of street crime and in the process construct a different type of masculinity outside of school. Robbery provides an ideal opportunity for them to act tough and male. According to Messerschmidt, for them, robbery becomes a rational practice of "doing gender."

Prevention and control of robbery

Due to the potential harm to victims as well as the potential fiscal losses associated with the crime of robbery, numerous countermeasures have been developed and implemented in an attempt to deter robberies, primarily in fixed-location businesses. Countermeasures are designed singularly or in combination to reduce the potential rewards of a robbery, increase the likelihood of failure of an attempted robbery, and/or increase the effort needed to achieve rewards.

There are two types of countermeasure, environmental and administrative. Environmental countermeasures increase the effort needed to complete the robbery and the likelihood of identification and apprehension. They include:

- Alarms: devices that either manually or automatically alert law enforcement to a robbery or robbery attempt being committed at a location (Ekblom 1987; Loomis et al. 2002).
- Bullet-resistant barriers (BRB): a physical barrier (pass-through window, pop-up screens, or an enclosed sales counter area) designed to separate employees from potential robbers (Kube 1988; Butterworth 1991; Grandjean 1990).
- Closed-circuit television (CCTV): increase an offender's likelihood of being identified and arrested (Crow and Bull 1975; Swanson 1986; Figlio and Armaud 1991).
- Door annunciators: an audible signal announces the entrance of someone (Swanson 1986; Jeffery et al. 1987).
- Height strips: color-coded markings on a door or in a doorway to assist victims in properly quantifying an offender's height (Hendricks et al. 1999; OSHA 1998).
- Lighting (quality and quantity): bright lighting provides for increased formal and informal surveillance (Butterworth 1991; Crow and Bull 1975; Erickson 1996; Farrington and Welsh 2002; Hunter 1988; Jeffery et al. 1987; Painter 1994).
- Time-accessed safes (often referred to as TACC—time-accessed cash-controller—safes): a time-delay feature which requires a robber to remain in a location for a period of time to gain access to cash in the safe (Dunckel 1988; OSHA 1998).
- Traffic flow devices: physical structures that impede an offender's ability to flee after the crime (Crow and Bull 1975; Erickson 1996; Hunter 1988, Swanson 1986; Jeffery et al. 1987).
- Visibility both into and out of a business is believed to reduce robbery (Bellamy 1996; Butterworth 1991; Crow and Bull 1975; Hendricks et al. 1997; Hunter 1988).

Administrative countermeasures are designed to increase the effort needed to complete the robbery, reduce rewards, and increase the likelihood of identification and apprehension. They include:

- On-hand cash limits (OSHA 1998; Hendricks *et al.* 1999).
- Hours of operation/hours of operation of BRB: ability either to close the establishment or utilize a BRB.
- Multiple staffing: the presence of two or more employees, often referred to as the "two-clerk" rule, is widely believed to deter robbery (Crow and Bull 1975; Jeffery *et al.* 1987; Vogel 1990; Figlio and Armaud 1991).
- Robbery prevention training (OSHA 1998).
- Signage: displayed information, often in English and Spanish, advising potential offenders of robbery countermeasures, such as "Cashier does not have access to safe" and "Store is under video and audio surveillance" (OSHA 1998).
- In addition to the above, there are industry-specific "denial of benefit" strategies, such as the use of exploding dye packs to deter bank robberies and acid packs to deter armored car robberies.

Slightly more than one in four of all robberies are cleared by arrest. However, the conviction rate for robbery is only about 66 percent of those arrested, with 90 percent of those convicted receiving jail sentences of less than ten years (Couture, Harrison, and Sabol 2007). The potential threat of severe sanction coupled with the judicial targeting of repeat offenders may have some, although as yet unknown, deterrent effect.

References

Barclay, G. and Tavares, C. (2003). *International Comparisons of Criminal Justice Statistics 2001*. London: Home Office. Retrieved 2/14/1011 from www.observatorioseguranca.org/pdf/01%20(23).pdf.

Bellamy, L. (1996). Situational Crime Prevention in Convenience Store Robberies. *Security Journal* 7 (1): 41–52.

Bureau of Justice Statistics, US Department of Justice (BJS) (1995). *Felony Sentences in State Courts, 1992*. Washington, DC: US Government Printing Office. Retrieved 10/20/2009 from www.ojp.usdoj.gov/bjs/abstract/felsent.htm.

Bureau of Justice Statistics, US Department of Justice (BJS) (2010). *National Crime Victimization Survey, 2008*. Washington, DC: US Government Printing Office. Retrieved 2/14/2011 from www.data.gov/raw/1526/.

Butterworth, R. (1991). *Study of Safety and Security Requirements for "At-Risk" Businesses*. Tallahassee, FL: Office of the Attorney General.

Conklin, J. E. (1972). *Robbery and the Criminal Justice System*. Philadelphia, PA: Lippincott.

Couture, H., Harrison, P. M., and Sabol, W. J. (2007) *Prisoners in 2006*. Bureau of Justice Statistics, US Department of Justice. Retrieved 2/14/2011 from bjs.ojp.usdoj.gov/index.cfm?ty=pbdetail&iid=908.

Crow, W. and Bull, J. (1975). *Robbery Deterrence: An Applied Behavioral Science Demonstration*. LaJolla, CA: Western Behavioral Science Institute.

Davis, L. (2003). Carjacking: Insights from South Africa to a New Crime Problem. *Australian and New Zealand Journal of Criminology* 26: 173–191.

Dujmovic, Z. and Miksaj-Todorovis, L. (2004). Basic Problems of Robbery Detection. In G. Mesko, M. Pagon, and B. Dobovsek (eds.) *Policing in Central and Eastern Europe*. Slovenia: University of Maribor. Retrieved 2/14/2011 from www.ncjrs.gov/pdffiles1/nij/Mesko/208002.pdf.

Dunckel, K. (1988). Holdup Delay Locks: Deterrent or Encouragement? *Security Management* 32 (1): 70–73.

Ekblom, P. (1987). *Preventing Robberies at Sub-Post Offices: An Evaluation of a Security Initiative*. Crime Prevention Unit Paper No. 9. London: Home Office.

Erickson, R. (1996). *Armed Robbers and Their Crimes*. Seattle, WA: Athena Research.

Farrington, D. and Welsh, B. (2002). *Effects of Improved Street Lighting on Crime: A Systematic Review.* Home Office Research Study No. 251. London: Home Office.

Federal Bureau of Investigation (FBI) (2009) *Crime in the United States, 2008: Uniform Crime Reports.* Washington, DC: US Government Printing Office. Retrieved 10/20/2009 from www.fbi.gov/ucr/cius2008/index.html.

Figlio, R. and Armaud, S. (1991). An Assessment of Robbery Deterrence Measures at Convenience Stores. In Association for Convenience & Petroleum Retailing (ed.) *Convenience Store Security: Report and Recommendations.* Alexandria, VA: NACS.

Grandjean, C. (1990). Bank Robberies and Physical Security in Switzerland: A Case Study of the Escalation and Displacement Phenomena. *Security Journal* 1 (3): 155–159.

Harper, D. Wood, Jr. (2005) The Tourist and His Criminal: Pattern in Street Robbery. In Y. Mansfield and A. Piazam (eds.) *Tourism, Security and Safety: A Case Approach.* Burlington, MA: Butterworth.

Hendricks, S., Amandus, H., and Zahm, D. (1997). Convenience Store Robberies in Selected Metropolitan Areas and Risk Factors for Employee Injury. *Journal of Occupational and Environmental Medicine* 39: 1233–1239.

Hendricks, S., Landsittel, D., Amandus, H., Malcan, J., and Bell, J. (1999). A Matched Case-Control Study of Convenience Store Robbery Risk Factors. *Journal of Occupational and Environmental Medicine* 41 (11): 995–1004.

Hunter, R. (1988). *The Effects of Environmental Factors upon Convenience Store Robbery in Florida.* Tallahassee: Florida Department of Legal Affairs.

Jacobs, B., Topalli, V., and Wright, R. (2003) Carjacking, Street Life and Offender Motivation. *British Journal of Criminology* 43: 673–688.

Jeffery, C., Hunter, R., and Griswold, J. (1987). Crime Prevention and Computer Analysis of Convenience Store Robberies in Tallahassee. *Florida Police Journal* 34: 65–69.

Katz, Jack (1988). *Seductions of Crime.* New York: Basic Books.

Klaus, P. (2004) *Carjacking, 1993–2002.* Crime Data Brief NCJ 205123. Washington, DC: Bureau of Justice Statistics, United States Department of Justice.

Kube, E. (1988). Preventing Bank Robbery: Lessons from Interviewing Robbers. *Journal of Security Administration* 11 (2): 78–83.

LaFree, G. (1995). Race and Crime Trends in the United States, 1946–1990. In D. F. Hawkins (ed.) *Ethnicity, Race and Crime.* Albany: State University of New York Press.

Loomis, D., Marshall, S., Wolf, S., Runyan, C., and Butts, J. (2002). Effectiveness of Safety Measures Recommended for Prevention of Workplace Homicide. *Journal of the American Medical Association* 287 (8): 1011–1017.

Messerschmidt, J. (1993). *Masculinities and Crime.* Lanham, MD: Rowman & Littlefield.

Occupational Safety and Health Administration (OSHA) (1998). *Recommendations for Workplace Violence Prevention Programs in Late-Night Retail Establishments.* Washington, DC: US Department of Labor.

Painter, K. (1994). The Impact of Street Lighting on Crime, Fear, and Pedestrian Street Use. *Security Journal* 5 (3): 116–124.

Rozum, J., Kotulan, P., and Tomasek, J. (2006). *Robbery Crime in Prague: Selected Results of Research Activities of ICSP in the Years 2004–2007.* Retrieved 2/14/2011 from www.ok.cz/iksp/docs/359.pdf.

Swanson, R. (1986). Convenience Store Robbery Analysis: A Research Study of Robbers, Victims, and Environment. Unpublished report for the Gainesville Police Department.

United States Department of Justice (1996). *Criminal Victimization in the United States, 1994.* Washington, DC: US Government Printing Office. Retrieved 10/20/2009 from www.ojp.gov/bjs/cvict.htm.

Vogel, R. (1990). *Convenience Store Robbery.* DeLand, FL: Volusia County Sheriff's Office.

63

Rape and sexual assault

Lynn Pazzani

When one thinks of a rape or sexual assault,[1] the image of a masked stranger with a weapon accosting a young woman walking alone in the dark tends to come to mind. Such scenarios are clearly deviant acts. They are frowned upon by society as a whole and are punished by our criminal justice system. But this clearly deviant act of rape is not, in actuality, the typical manner in which such assaults occur. A more common scenario is that of a boyfriend or acquaintance using pressure, threats, and/or intoxicants to coerce a woman or girl into engaging in sexual activity when she does not truly want to. These types of assaults, though extremely common, tend not to be viewed as deviant in our culture, and they are not punished by our criminal justice system to the same extent that deviant sexual assaults are.

This chapter will discuss both deviant rape and the more common forms of rape. For simplicity, it will focus on assaults where a female is the victim and a male is the offender. Of course, assaults with all possible combinations of victim and offender gender do occur, but such assaults are so different from male on female assault that it would be irresponsible to include them in this short entry as though they had the same causes and effects. Similarly, sexual assaults committed against young children will not be discussed because of their differences from sexual assaults involving adolescents and adults.

Rape defined

The definition of rape in colonial America was "carnal knowledge of a woman, not one's wife, by force and against her will," which only included penile-vaginal penetration. This excluded many other types of sexual assault, as well as rapes or sexual assaults committed by a spouse. The "essential elements of a traditional rape were (1) force, (2) absence of consent, and (3) vaginal penetration" (Spohn and Horney 1992: 22). In California, force is no longer required in a number of circumstances, including if the victim is in some way incapacitated from resisting or is not mentally capable of consenting. Absence of consent was originally demonstrated by the victim physically "resisting to the utmost," so if the woman did not fight for the entire duration of the attack it was assumed that she had consented (Samaha 2005). Absence of consent now can be indicated by verbal statements, or is not required if the victim is impaired or a minor. Moreover, rape and sexual assault now also include any type of sexual act, including oral copulation and penetration with a foreign object. Penetration can be extremely brief or incomplete, and there need not be thrusting after penetration for the act to be considered criminal.

Deviant rape

Holmes and Holmes (2002) summarize four types of rapists and the acts they commit, all of which fall outside of the norms of acceptable sexual behavior. For the most part, these rapists commit assaults that involve a stranger; they are not the sort of thing one could imagine occurring on a date or at a party. This typology was originally considered to cover all sexual assaults; however, in the second edition of their book, Holmes and Holmes (2002) caution that it should really only be applied to stranger rapes.

The power reassurance rapist

The power reassurance rapist, also known as the compensatory rapist, believes himself to be a loser and uses rape as a way to elevate his status. He is characterized as single, passive, having a low education level, and possibly coming from a home with a domineering or seductive mother. This type of rapist may engage in such behaviors as voyeurism or exhibitionism. Although it is generally believed that rape is not about sex, but rather an assault in which sex increases the impact, for the power reassurance rapist the assault *is* about sex. He is the least violent of the four types of rapist and uses only enough force to gain control over the victim. The sex makes him feel in control and important; something he does not feel during his daily life. He tends to believe that his victim enjoyed the rape, will often be concerned about her well-being, and will not harm her unnecessarily (Holmes and Holmes 2002).

The anger retaliation rapist

The anger retaliation rapist feels he has suffered great injustices at the hands of the women in his life and commits rape in order to hurt the victim and get back at all women. This type of rapist tends to have grown up in an unstable household, has hostile feelings about women in general, and perceives himself to be very masculine. He often has an action-based job and/or participates in contact sports. He is likely to be married and may have extra-marital sexual relationships with multiple partners as a means of supporting his highly masculine status.

He commits assaults in response to precipitating events involving a woman in his life. When he becomes angry, he may attack suddenly and with little planning. Such assaults are not specifically sexually motivated, but rather are aggressive acts that involve sex. This type of rapist intends to harm his victim and will use any weapons that are available, as well as directing profanity towards his victim. He associates sexual gratification with anger and rage, and will often force the victim to engage in particularly degrading acts (Holmes and Holmes 2002).

The power assertive rapist

The power assertive rapist has a strong belief in his own superiority simply because he is a man. He believes men are superior to women and that they are entitled to rape women as a matter of course. This type of rapist tends to have grown up in an unstable home and most will have suffered some form of physical abuse growing up. He will be concerned about his image, and his manner of dress and the vehicle he drives indicate his position in society and allow him to show off.

The power assertive rapist will often find his victims in bars. The rapes will involve verbal and physical assault and he will frequently commit multiple assaults against the victim during the attack. The rape is not specifically about sex; rather, it is an act of predation. His level of aggression may increase as he commits more assaults over time (Holmes and Holmes 2002).

The sadistic rapist

Like the power assertive rapist, the sadistic rapist tends to have grown up in an unstable or single-parent household. He also is likely to have suffered physical abuse. However, unlike the power assertive rapist, sadistic rapists often grow up in households where sexual deviance also occurs. The sadistic rapist will often be married, live in a middle-class neighborhood, have a high level of education and a white-collar job, and be viewed as a pillar of the community. He plans his assaults carefully and is skillful at evading detection by the police.

The sadistic rapist uses rape as a means of expressing his aggressive sexual fantasies and intends to inflict physical and psychological pain on his victims. This type of rapist often brings his victim to a secondary location which he controls and uses restraining items such as gags and handcuffs, not so much to control the victim as to increase her fear. He may also describe in detail to the victim what he intends to do to her to terrorize her before he commits the assault. This type of rapist is most likely to kill his victims (Holmes and Holmes 2002).

"Real rape"

Susan Estrich (1987) states that "real rape" is defined by actions involving strangers, violence, weapons, resistance, injury, and immediate notification of the police. She notes that women who are victims of a sexual assault that does not meet the "real rape" criteria often do not even identify the incident as a sexual assault themselves. Stories about rape that make the news tend to be in line with the "real rape" stereotype, and those that are not often include rape myths (Dowler 2006). When women are taught to protect themselves from rape, they learn about not going out alone at night, locking their doors, carrying pepper spray, and many other techniques designed to prevent someone from accosting them by surprise (Ullman 2007). These techniques are aimed at preventing the types of assault that would be committed by Holmes and Holmes' four types of rapist.

Unfortunately, this focus may be misplaced. Only approximately 15% of sexual assaults are estimated to be committed by strangers (Pazzani 2007). The rest are what Estrich (1987) says society considers "simple rape," although they are anything but simple when one examines all the factors associated with defining, identifying, and prosecuting these assaults.

Non-deviant rape

Much more common than the stereotypical "real rape" is a type of sexual assault that more closely mirrors socially acceptable sexual behavior. This is commonly referred to as "acquaintance rape," although it includes sexual assault committed by anyone known to the victim—family members, boyfriends, coworkers, friends, people the victim has just met, as well as acquaintances. Scholars have recently begun to differentiate between stranger and acquaintance rape (Pazzani 2007). However, there are significant differences in causes and effects within the acquaintance rape category depending on the relationship between the victim and the offender that have not yet been seriously studied.

In determining the nature and extent of sexual assault, victimization surveys tend to be preferred over police data because of the very low rate of reporting sexual assault to the authorities. In addition to an overall low rate of reporting, victims who do report their assault are more likely to have been assaulted by strangers, to have had a weapon used against them, and to need medical attention when compared to all rape victims identified in victimization surveys (Koss 1985).

Tjaden and Thoennes (2006) use the National Violence Against Women Survey to give us a picture of the types of sexual assault that are occurring and to whom. Of women over the age of 18, 14.8% report that they have been the victim of a completed sexual assault at some point in their lives. Rates are slightly higher for African American women and lower for Hispanic women. Victims tend to be young at the time of their first rape. Only 16.6% report that their first sexual assault occurred when they were 25 or older; 21.6% were under 12; 32.4% were between 12 and 17; and 29.4% were between 18 and 24. Results from this survey also indicate that, of women who identify themselves as rape victims, only 16.6% had ever been assaulted by a stranger. The rest had only been assaulted by people known to them: 20.2% were assaulted by a spouse or an ex-spouse; 4.3% by a cohabiting partner or ex-partner; 21.5% by a date or former date; 22.4% by a relative other than a spouse; and 27.3% by an acquaintance.[2] Most sexual assaults occur in a private setting (84.5%). Only 37.8% of assaults involved overt acts of physical violence, other than the sexual assault, and only 10.8% involved a weapon. Only 19.1% of these assaults were reported to the police[3] (Feild 1978; Gray 2006; Peterson and Muehlenhard 2004). This picture of sexual assault is significantly different from that suggested by the stereotypes relating to rape.

A rape culture

In a supposedly civilized society, why are so many women and girls being assaulted by people close to them? Many scholars theorize that we have a rape-supportive culture, making this type of behavior acceptable rather than deviant. We also live in a society where, although significant improvement has been made over the last 40 years, women are not entirely equal to men. According to feminist theory, patriarchy lies at the root of women's oppression (Donovan 1992). Rape is simply a way in which men oppress women by valuing their own right to sexual access above a woman's right to decide with whom she has sex.

Rape myths—false or stereotypical beliefs about rape and rape victims (Burt 1980)—play a large part in the rape culture. They indicate that women have multiple motivations for fabricating a charge of rape and that, should a rape occur, the woman likely did something to cause it. Assuming the charge is not made up, rape myths indicate that women want to engage in sexual activity even if it seems like they are resisting, and they serve to downplay or discard perceptions of harm to the victim of a sexual assault (Lonsway and Fitzgerald 1995). This impacts both potential perpetrators of sexual assault and those who respond to women claiming to have been victimized.

If women truly do want sex but are supposed to resist initially to seem like a "good woman," saying "no" would indeed sometimes means "yes." Saying "no" could easily be seen as the type of "token resistance" females are expected to give in order to preserve their reputation or "make it interesting," even when they really do want sex (Warshaw and Parrot 1991). If women truly do always want sex, using a bit of force may almost be considered doing the woman a favor. She is supposed to resist, but a heroic man overpowers her in order to give her pleasure. If women always want sex, then having sex with a woman who is intoxicated or even unconscious would not really be wrong because, if she could have consented, she would have. All of these acts are unmistakably criminal. However, in attitudinal surveys, people repeatedly give responses that are more consistent with rape myths than with the law (Feild 1978; Gray 2006; Peterson and Muehlenhard 2004). These perspectives can make potential perpetrators think that their actions are acceptable and make those responding to a claim of assault more judgmental and less sympathetic toward the victim.

The relationship between the victim and the offender is a major factor in determining whether the rape myth culture is relied upon in the response to a claim of rape. Women who are victims of a rape and sexual assault committed by a stranger tend to be believed and receive less blame about the assault than do women who were assaulted by someone they know, as numerous studies from different time periods have shown (Abrams *et al.* 2003; Bridges 1991; L'Armand and Pepitone 1982). Because acquaintance rape involves the behavior of the woman to a much greater degree than does stranger rape, it is easy for others to assume that the woman's behavior contributing to the rape is the same as the woman being to blame for it (Calhoun and Townsley 1991). Assaults committed by strangers are also considered to be more serious than assaults committed by acquaintances, probably because the assumed degree of harm to the female is reduced if there is a chance, or even an expectation, that she would consent to sex with her attacker (L'Armand and Pepitone 1982). Assaults committed by people close to the victim that do not include physical violence are generally not considered to be serious (Langhinrichsen-Rohling and Monson 1998).

Another factor in determining how a sexual encounter and a victim are perceived is the use of intoxicants. When a woman is impaired for any reason, including her voluntary use of drugs or alcohol, she is not able to give legal consent to engage in sexual activity. Although this person may not resist, or may even indicate that she wants to have sex, engaging in sexual activity with her is legally considered a rape/sexual assault. Yet research participants believe that if a woman is sexually assaulted, she is more likely to be responsible for the attack if she is intoxicated than if she is sober (Richardson and Campbell 1982). It is the woman's job to prevent sexual access (Warshaw and Parrot 1991) and she should have known better than to allow herself to become intoxicated and vulnerable to assault. Although a woman is considered more responsible when she is intoxicated, if a man is intoxicated, he is considered *less* responsible for committing an assault (Richardson and Campbell 1982). Men are supposed to be seeking sex constantly and they may become forceful when intoxicated, but they are not blamed for their actions because "it was the intoxicant that made them do it." The fact that the impact of intoxicant use on perceptions of responsibility is opposite for males and females is evidence of a culture that expects people to act within a narrow set of gender norms and becomes upset when those norms are broken.

Conclusion

Sexual assault is associated with a host of negative outcomes, including mental and physical health problems for the victim (Monroe *et al.* 2005) and significant others in the victim's life. With nearly one in six women reporting being victimized at some point in their lives, obviously a large number of people are affected. The focus on stranger rape and deviant sexual behavior may be misplaced, as these assaults are far less common than assaults that are culturally supported. In the United States, despite the legal sanctions against them, rapes and sexual assaults that include actions consistent with the social norms for sexual behavior are not as likely to be prosecuted (Bouffard 2000; Spohn *et al.* 2001). Changes to both the legal system and cultural views about rape are needed in order to improve the situation for victims and society in general.

Notes

1 The reader should note that, in this chapter, the terms "rape" and "sexual assault" will be used interchangeably. These terms are defined differently in legal systems throughout the United States, depending on the type of bodily contact, the relationship between victim and offender, age, and many other factors. The two terms refer here to any sexual contact to the mouth, anus or vagina, using a penis, finger or hand, or any foreign object, that occurs against an individual's will. This tends to encompass all the various legal statutes and definitions involving sexual contact, although they may have different legal terms associated with them, depending on the state in which they occur.
2 The percentages add up to more than 100 because some victims had been assaulted by more than one person, often from different relationship categories.
3 This could be an overestimation, given that those who did report could be more likely to disclose their assault to survey researchers than those who did not.

References

Abrams, D., Viki, T., Masser, B., and Bohner, G. 2003. Perceptions of stranger and acquaintance rape: The role of benevolent and hostile sexism in victim blame and rape proclivity. *Journal of Personality and Social Psychology*, 84(1), 111–125.

Bouffard, J. 2000. Predicting type of sexual assault case closure from victim, suspect, and case characteristics. *Journal of Criminal Justice*, 28, 527–542.

Bridges, J. 1991. Perceptions of date and stranger rape: A difference in sex-role expectations and rape-supportive beliefs. *Sex Roles*, 24(5–6), 291–307.

Burt, M. 1980. Cultural myths and supports for rape. *Journal of Personality and Social Psychology*, 38(2), 217–230.

Calhoun, K.S. and Townsley, R.M. 1991. Attributions of responsibility for acquaintance rape. In A. Parrot and L. Bechhofer (eds.) *Acquaintance Rape: The Hidden Crime*, New York: John Wiley & Sons, pp. 57–69.

Donovan, J. 1992. *Feminist Theory: The Intellectual Traditions of American Feminism*, New York: Continuum.

Dowler, K. 2006. Sex, lies, and videotape: The presentation of sex crime in local television news. *Journal of Criminal Justice*, 34(4), 383–392.

Estrich, S. 1987. *Real Rape: How the Legal System Victimizes Women Who Say No*, Cambridge, MA: Harvard University Press.

Feild, H. 1978. Attitudes toward rape: Comparative analysis of police, rapists, crisis counselors, and citizens. *Journal of Personality and Social Psychology*, 36(2), 156–179.

Gray, J.M. 2006. Rape myth beliefs and prejudiced instructions: Effects on decisions of guilt in a case of date rape. *Legal and Criminological Psychology*, 11, 75–80.

Holmes, R.M. and Holmes, S.T. 2002. *Sex Crimes: Patterns and Behavior*, 2nd edn, Thousand Oaks, CA: Sage.

Koss, M. 1985. The hidden rape victim: Personality, attitudinal, and situational characteristics. *Psychology of Women Quarterly*, 9(2), 193–212.

Langhinrichsen-Rohling, J. and Monson, C. 1998. Marital rape: Is the crime taken seriously without co-occurring physical abuse? *Journal of Family Violence*, 13(4), 433–443.

L'Armand, K. and Pepitone, A. 1982. Judgments of rape: A study of victim–rapist relationship and victim sexual history. *Personality and Social Psychology Bulletin*, 8, 134–139.

Lonsway, K. and Fitzgerald, L. 1995. Attitudinal antecedents of rape myth acceptance: A theoretical and empirical reexamination. *Journal of Personality and Social Psychology*, 68(4), 704–711.

Monroe, L., Kinney, L. M., Weist, M. D., Dafeamekpor, D .S., Dantzler, J., and Reynolds M. W. 2005. The experience of sexual assault: Findings from a statewide victim needs assessment. *Journal of Interpersonal Violence*, 20(7), 767–776.

Pazzani, L. 2007. The factors affecting sexual assaults committed by strangers and acquaintances. *Violence Against Women*, 13(7), 717–749.

Peterson, Z. and Muehlenhard, C. 2004. Was it rape? The function of women's rape myth acceptance and definitions of sex in labeling their own experiences. *Sex Roles*, 51(3–4), 129–144.

Richardson, D. and Campbell, J. 1982. Alcohol and rape: The effects of alcohol on attributions of blame for rape. *Personality and Social Psychology Bulletin*, 8(3), 468–476.

Samaha, J. 2005. *Criminal Law*, Belmont, CA: Thomson Wadsworth.

Spohn, C., Beichner, D., and Davis-Frenzel, E. 2001. Prosecutorial justifications for sexual assault case rejection: Guarding the "gateway to justice." *Social Problems*, 48(2), 206–235.

Spohn, C. and Horney, J. 1992. *Rape Law Reform: A Grassroots Revolution and Its Impact*, New York: Plenum Press.

Tjaden, P. and Thoennes, N. 2006. *Extent, Nature, and Consequences of Rape Victimization: Findings From the National Violence Against Women Survey*, Washington, DC: National Institute of Justice. Available at: www.ncjrs.gov/pdffiles1/nij/210346.pdf.

Ullman, S. 2007. A 10-year update of "Review and critique of empirical studies of rape avoidance." *Criminal Justice and Behavior*, 34(3), 411–429.

Warshaw, R. and Parrot, A. 1991. The contribution of sex-role socialization to acquaintance rape. In A. Parrot and L. Bechhofer (eds.) *Acquaintance Rape: The Hidden Crime*, New York: John Wiley & Sons, pp. 73–82.

64

Child abuse (sexual and physical)

Elizabeth Ehrhardt Mustaine

Overview

Parenting is perhaps one of the most important, difficult, rewarding, and frustrating jobs a person will have in his or her lifetime. Parents serve an essential role in the development of their children. They serve as the teachers and role models for the basis of the growth, development, and socialization of their children. Throughout adolescence, parents must teach their children how to become productive and positive functioning members of society. Ideally, parents provide security and stability for their children while teaching the lessons of life in a loving and enriching environment. Unfortunately, the messages conveyed to and actions against children by their families are not always the positive building blocks for which we would hope.

In 2008, the Children's Defense Fund reported that each day in America, 2,421 children are confirmed as abused or neglected, while 4 adolescents and 78 infants are killed by abuse or neglect. These daily estimates translate into shocking annual figures. Estimates further suggest that, of those children who were abused, 64 percent suffered neglect, 16 percent were physically abused, 9 percent were sexually abused, 7 percent were emotionally or psychologically maltreated, 2 percent were medically neglected, and 15 percent suffered "other" types of abuse (the percentages total more than 100 as some children are abused in multiple ways). Obviously, this problem is a substantial one (Finkelhor *et al.*, 2005).

Legalities

Most US laws about child abuse are enacted at state level and incorporate both civil and criminal statutes. Federal legislation provides a guide for states by identifying minimum sets of acts and behaviors that define child abuse and neglect. The Federal Child Abuse Prevention and Treatment Act (CAPTA), which stems from the Keeping Children and Families Safe Act of 2003, defines child abuse and neglect as, at minimum: "1) any recent act or failure to act on the part of a parent or caretaker which results in death, serious physical or emotional harm, sexual abuse, or exploitation; or 2) an act or failure to act which presents an imminent risk or serious harm" (42 USCA §5106g).

Statutes on physical abuse typically include elements of physical injury (ranging from minor bruises to severe fractures or death) as a result of punching, beating, kicking, biting, shaking, throwing, stabbing, chocking, hitting (with a hand, stick, strap, or other object), burning, or otherwise harming a child. Such injury is considered abuse regardless of the intention of the caretaker. Additionally, many state statutes include allowing or encouraging another person to harm a child physically (such as noted above) as another form of physical abuse in and of itself (Haley's Rights, 2009).

Sexual abuse usually includes activities by a parent or caretaker such as fondling a child's genitals, penetration, incest, rape, sodomy, indecent exposure, and exploitation through prostitution or the production of pornographic material (Haley's Rights, 2009).

Can children consent?

While there are some subcultures in society that argue that sex within the family is a safe and secure way for children to experiment and learn about sex, most views (including those represented in the law) are consistent with those of child advocates. These professionals and researchers suggest that society views appropriate sex as occurring between *consenting* persons. In order to consent, one must have knowledge and authority. Do children really understand sex well enough to make an informed decision? Can these children really say "no" to an adult wanting sex from them? Most experts believe that children are too young to understand sex or to turn down an offer from an adult effectively (Crosson-Tower, 2008).

Antecedents and progression of child sexual abuse

Most sexual offenders of children do not use physical force to gain access to their victims. But, as noted by experts, there are several preconditions necessary for child sexual abuse to occur. One such precondition is a lack of internal inhibitors by the would-be offender. These types of behaviors or conditions that overcome individual inhibition can be alcohol, psychosis, impulse disorder, senility, or more societal conditions, such as social tolerance for sexual interest in children, weak criminal sanctions, ideology of patriarchal prerogatives, and social tolerance for deviance committed while intoxicated (Herman, 2000).

A second precondition is the overcoming of external inhibitors. This can occur, for instance, when a mother is ill, absent, and/or not close to child, during social isolation of family, when there are opportunities to be alone with a child, and in unusual sleeping conditions. It might also be more structural, such as when there is a lack of social support for mothers, or when there are barriers to women's equality, erosion of social networks, and a decline in the ideology of family sanctity (Crosson-Tower, 2008; Herman, 2000).

Third, in order for child sexual abuse to occur, the offender must overcome the child's resistance. This can happen more readily with children who are emotionally insecure or deprived, with those who lack knowledge about sexual abuse, in situations of unusual trust between the child and the offender, or through coercion. Here, again, the problem might be more structural: for example, an absence of sex education for children and the social powerlessness of children in society (Crosson-Tower, 2008; Herman, 2000).

There are generally six separate phases in the sexual abuse of children. The first of these is engagement, when the perpetrator gains access to the child and indicates that this type of sexual behavior is appropriate, if not normal. In order to do this, the offender "grooms" the child by exploiting their need for affection, human contact, and adult approval, or by playing games and/or offering material rewards, in order to gain compliance (Crosson-Tower, 2008).

In the second phase, the pressured sex phase, the offender uses enticement to secure the child's cooperation. The strategy may be to make the child feel indebted or obligated in order to achieve their agreement. Here, though, the offender probably will not use physical force if the child refuses (Herman, 2000). This phase rarely involves forced sex, although the threat of harm or use of force may be used to complete the abuse. Or the offender might intimidate the child. In these rare cases, the child is seen as an object to be used for sexual gratification. A few offenders are sadistic.

The third phase is known as the sexual interaction phase. This is when actual sexual contact with the child occurs. Typically, the longer the abuse continues, the more complex and advanced the activity becomes (Herman, 2000).

Next, the offender typically uses threats or power to dominate, bribe, or emotionally blackmail to ensure the child does not report the abuse, which allows it to continue. This fourth phase is called the secrecy phase (Crosson-Tower, 2008).

After the secrecy phase, the child may disclose the abuse to a third party. This may occur during childhood or during adulthood. It also may occur purposely (the child tells) or accidentally (the third party finds out, for instance by noticing social or medical trauma) (Crosson-Tower, 2008; Herman, 2000).

Finally, the suppression phase may occur. In this phase, those close to the child, because of their own guilt, abhorrence of the activity, fear of scandal, stigma, or other feared consequences, force, compel, and/or encourage the child to recant or forget about the abuse. Many experts warn that the suppression phase can have the most serious consequences for a sexually abused child, suggesting that it can be even more damaging than the sexual abuse itself (Crosson-Tower, 2008; Herman, 2000).

Child abuse perpetrators

Research suggests that nearly 80 percent of child abuse perpetrators are parents of the victim. Other relatives account for nearly 7 percent, and unmarried partners of parents make up 4 percent. Of those perpetrators who are parents, 58 percent are women and 42 percent are men. Further, over 90 percent of parental abusers are biological parents, 4 percent are step-parents, and 0.7 percent are adoptive parents. Female perpetrators are typically younger: on average, they are 31 years old, while male perpetrators are 34 years old. Forty percent of women who abuse children are younger than 30 years of age, compared with 33 percent of male abusers. The racial distribution of perpetrators is: 54 percent white; 21 percent African American; and 20 percent Hispanic/Latino (National Child Abuse and Neglect Data System, 2006).

Explanations for child abuse

Many factors are associated with child abuse. Some of the more common/well-accepted explanations are individual pathology, parent–child interaction, past abuse in the family (or social learning), and situational factors. Each is summarized below.

The first explanation centers on the individual pathology of an abusive parent or caretaker. This theory focuses on the idea that people who abuse their children have something wrong with their individual personality or biological makeup. Such psychological pathologies may include:

- Anger-control problems.
- Depression.
- Having a low tolerance for frustration. Children can be extremely frustrating: they do not always listen, they constantly push the line regarding how far they can go, and once the line

has been established, they are constantly treading on it to make sure it has not moved. They are dependent and self-centered, so caretakers have very little privacy or time to themselves.

- Being rigid. This involves having no tolerance for difference: for example, if a son wanted to play with dolls, a rigid father might not let him, might ridicule him, or might punish him.
- Having empathy deficit. Parents who cannot put themselves into the shoes of their children cannot fully understand what their children need emotionally.
- Being disorganized, inefficient, or ineffectual. Parents who are unable to manage their own lives are unlikely to manage the lives of their children successfully. Many children want and need limits, but such parents are unable to set such limits and/or adhere to them (Iwaniec, 2006).

Biological pathologies that may increase the likelihood of child abuse include having substance abuse or dependence problems, or having persistent or recurring physical health problems. Such health problems can be extremely painful and can cause a person to become self-absorbed, two qualities that frequently give rise to a lack of patience, lower frustration tolerance, and increased stress.

The second explanation for child abuse centers on the interaction between the parent and the child. The theory is that certain types of parent are more likely to abuse, and certain types of child are more likely to be abused. So when these less skilled parents are coupled with these more difficult children, child abuse is likely to occur. Discussion then focuses on what makes a parent less skilled, and what makes a child more difficult? Unskilled parents tend to focus only on what their children do wrong, never giving any encouragement for good behavior and failing to be sensitive to the emotional needs of their children. They also have unrealistic expectations of their children. They may engage in role reversal—making the child take care of them, and believing that the child should assume responsibility for their happiness and well-being. Some parents view the parental role as extremely stressful and experience little enjoyment from it. Finally, less skilled parents tend to have unusually negative perceptions of their children. For example, they may criticize their physical appearance, accuse them of being manipulative (long before the child has this capability), or blame them for all of the family's problems. All parents with these characteristics are more likely to abuse their children. But that likelihood increases if they are coupled with a difficult child.

So what makes a child "difficult"? Through no fault of their own, some children certainly have characteristics that make childcare more demanding and difficult than in "normal" or "average" families. Such characteristics include physical illnesses and mental disabilities, such as autism, ADHD, hyperactivity, and recurring colic. Other children are simply more needy, or cry more often, than is considered "normal." Such children are more likely than placid children to be victims of abuse (Howe, 2005).

However, it is the interaction between "unskilled" parents and "difficult" children that is the key. Unskilled parents may produce children who are happy and not needy; consequently, they do not abuse because the child does not require them to be skilled. Meanwhile, "difficult" children with skilled parents who can manage the extra effort these children demand will probably not be abused either. Risks for child abuse only peak when unskilled parents must deal with difficult children (Howe, 2005).

Social learning or past abuse in the family is a third common explanation for child abuse. Here, the theory concentrates not only on what children learn when they see or experience violence in their homes, but on what they do not learn as a result of these experiences. Social learning theory in the context of family violence stresses that if children are abused or see abuse (toward siblings or a parent), those interactions and violent family members become role models for their future familial interactions. Children who witness or experience violence may learn that this is how parents deal with children, or may come to believe that violence is an acceptable method of child-rearing and discipline. When they themselves become parents, they may well declare, "I was hit when I was a child, and I turned out fine." They may learn unhealthy relationship interaction patterns by witnessing the negative interactions of parents, and they may adopt maladaptive or violent methods of expressing anger, reacting to stress, or coping with conflict (Crosson-Tower, 2008).

Equally important, though, is that they are unlikely to learn more acceptable and nonviolent ways of rearing children, interacting with family members, and resolving conflict. A parent who was abused as a child might well wish to be nonviolent toward his or her own child, but when the chips are down and the child is misbehaving, this parent will not have a repertoire of nonviolent strategies to employ. Consequently, they are likely to fall back on what they know— violence—to enforce discipline (Howe, 2005; Zielinski and Bradshaw, 2005).

It is important to note here that not all abused children grow up to become abusive adults. Those who break the cycle were often able to establish and maintain one healthy emotional relationship with someone during their childhood (or young adulthood). For instance, they may have received emotional support from a non-abusing parent; or they may have forged a positive relationship with another adult (e.g., teacher, coach, minister, or neighbor). People who were abused as children can also often break the cycle of violence through therapy. Even forming an emotionally supportive and satisfying relationship with a partner might be sufficient to allow an individual to make the transition to nonviolence.

Moving on to the fourth familiar explanation for child abuse, some common situational or environmental factors influence families and parents and increase the risks for child abuse. Typically, these factors increase family stress and/or social isolation. Specifically, they may relate to families that are receiving public assistance or have low socioeconomic status (a combination of low income and low education), and individuals who are experiencing unemployment, underemployment (working in a job that requires lower qualifications than an individual possesses), or part-time employment. Financial difficulties cause great stress for families in meeting the needs of their individual members. Single-parent households and larger families are also more likely to be stressed. Finally, social isolation can be devastating for families and their individual members. Having friends with whom we can talk, confide, and occasionally drop off the kids is tremendously important for our personal growth and satisfaction. Additionally, social isolation and stress can cause individuals lose their temper quickly, be less rational in their decision-making, and make mountains out of mole-hills. All of this can cause families to be at greater risk of child abuse (Reardon and Noblet, 2009).

While the above theories can aid our understanding of specific forms of child abuse as well as the occurrence of child abuse in general, some others specifically address child sexual abuse. One of the best known is Finkelhor's (1984) multifactor theory. This utilizes several different theories to explain the sexual abuse of children. First, emotional congruence theories suggest that the offender has always felt more comfortable with children. Consequently, they seek out children for many of their interactions in society: that is, for friendship as well as for sex. As a result, this individual often does not think that having sex with children is wrong. Second, sexual arousal theories focus on the idea that boys and girls often engage in sex play with their friends, cousins, siblings, and so on. Usually, in these circumstances, the sex play is quite innocent, safe, and mutually consensual. Crucially, though, this childhood sex play is the only time when sex is safe and enjoyable for some people. So, when they desire sex as adults, they remember this period in their life and consequently target children. Finally, blockage theories suggest that child sexual abuse results from the offender being unable to form a sexual relationship with another adult. This is most likely due to deficits within the offender: bad/hostile/negative personality, social isolation, antisocial behavior, an inability to engage others on an adult level, and so on. Thus, while the offender would like to have sex with adults, such opportunities are blocked to them. As a result, they turn to children to satisfy their sexual needs (Finkelhor, 1984).

How can society help abused children and abusive families?

Child advocates stress that we need to have greater interagency cooperation. This cooperation should be evident between battered women's shelters, child protection agencies, programs for at-risk children, medical agencies, and law enforcement officers. These agencies typically do not share information; if they did, more instances of child abuse would come to the attention of various authorities and could be investigated and managed. Along these lines, child protection agencies and programs should receive more funding. When budgets are cut, social services are often the first things to go or receive less financial support. Child advocates insist that, with more resources, child protection agencies could hire more workers, handle more cases, conduct more investigations, and follow up with more children and families (Guterman, 2001).

We must also institute more educational efforts on such issues as punishment and discipline styles and strategies, having greater respect for children, informing the community about what child abuse is and how to recognize it. Additionally, we must alter our cultural orientation about childbearing and -rearing. We must allow couples who wish to remain child free to do so without disdain. And we must acknowledge that raising children is very difficult, not always wonderful, and parents who seek help should be lauded rather than viewed with suspicion. With such efforts, more children will be raised in nonviolent, emotionally satisfying families, and will thus become better adults themselves.

References

Bancroft, L. and Silverman, J. 2002. *The Batterer as Parent*. Thousand Oaks, CA: Sage.
Children's Defense Fund. 2009. Accessed on 12/1/2009 at: www.childrensdefense.org/site/PageServer? pagename=research_national_data_each_day/.
Crosson-Tower, C. 2008. *Understanding Child Abuse and Neglect*, 7th edn. Boston, MA: Allyn and Bacon.
Finkelhor, D. 1984. *Child Sexual Abuse*. New York: Free Press.
Finkelhor, D., Ormrod, R., Turner, O., and Hamby, S. 2005. "The Victimization of Children and Youth: A Comprehensive, National Survey." *Child Maltreatment*, 10, 5–25.
Guterman, N. B. 2001. *Stopping Child Maltreatment Before It Starts: Emerging Horizons in Early Home Visitation Services*. Thousand Oaks, CA: Sage.
Haley's Rights. 2009. Accessed on 12/1/2009 at: www.haleysrights.org/.
Herman, J. 2000. *Father–Daughter Incest*. Cambridge, MA: Harvard University Press.
Howe, D. 2005. *Child Abuse and Neglect: Attachment, Development, and Interaction*. New York: Palgrave Macmillan.
Iwaniec, D. 2006. *The Emotionally Abused and Neglected Child*. West Sussex: John Wiley and Sons.
Myers, J. (ed.). 1994. *The Backlash: Child Protection under Fire*. Thousand Oaks, CA: Sage.
National Child Abuse and Neglect Data System. 2006. *Child Maltreatment 2006: Reports from the States to the National Child Abuse and Neglect Data Systems*. Washington, DC: Administration for Children and Families, US Department of Health and Human Services.
Reardon, K. K. and Noblet, C. T. 2009. *Childhood Denied: Ending the Nightmare of Child Abuse and Neglect*. Thousand Oaks, CA: Sage.
Thomas, P. M. 2003. "Protection, Dissociation, and Internal Roles: Modeling and Treating the Effects of Child Abuse." *Review of General Psychology*, 7(4), 364–380.
Zielinski, D. and Bradshaw C. 2005. "Ecological Influences on the Sequelae of Child Maltreatment." *Child Maltreatment*, 11(1), 49–62.

Additional online resources

- Administration for Children and Families, US Department of Health and Human Services: www.acf.hhs.gov/index.html
- Child Abuse Prevention Network: child-abuse.com/
- Childhelp: Prevention and Treatment of Child Abuse: www.childhelp.org/resources/learning-center/statistics
- Children's Bureau Express: cbexpress.acf.hhs.gov/
- Child Stats: www.childstats.gov/index.asp
- Child Welfare Information Gateway: www.childwelfare.gov
- Child Welfare League of America: www.cwla.org/
- Crimes Against Children Research Center: www.unh.edu/ccrc/
- Family Research Lab at the University of New Hampshire: www.unh.edu/frl/
- National Center for Missing and Exploited Children: missingkids.com/missingkids/servlet/PublicHomeServlet?LanguageCountry=en_US
- National Clearinghouse on Child Abuse and Neglect: www.happinessonline.org/LoveAndHelpChildren/p7.htm

Part XIII

Handicap, disability, and impairment as deviance

Overview

Some forms of deviance do not involve willful mischief or harm to self or others, but rather simply consist of deviation from cultural standards of physique and physiological normality, or cultural definitions of beauty or perfection, normal bodily functions, normal mental capability and acumen, or level of mental wellness and functioning.

Failing to possess or achieve such cultural standards and norms, by definition, constitutes deviance. Those who are "different" are socially discredited and stigmatized, and they and their physical or mental condition are labeled as deviant.

The chapters in this part address four such deviant conditions: deviant physical appearance, deviant physical function, mental retardation, and mental illness.

The stigma of deviant physical appearance

Druann Heckert, in her chapter, examines social constructions of the body. Similar to behavior, physical appearance is also subject to social evaluation and differential social reaction. There are expectations and norms regarding physical appearance. Those who do not resemble or conform to these norms, particularly in extreme ways, may be discredited and/or stigmatized. Some individuals with gross exceptions to the physical appearance norms may experience seriously degraded social reactions from others. Genetic variations of appearance, such as body or hair color, also impact the social response. Heckert offers examples of extreme appearance differences that are labeled by some scholars as "abominations" of the body, including those with physical deformities, such as conjoined twins.

Physical appearance norms are culturally constructed and include idealized models or portraits of the attractive and the unattractive. Heckert points out that "appearance norms are not benign; rather they are consequential." For the attractive, Heckert indicates that their appearance is a "facilitator for better life experiences" and elicits preferential treatment. In contrast, the unattractive may experience diminished life experiences and stigmatization. She also reports that appearance norms are both gendered and racial. Females have traditionally "been evaluated more harshly on the basis of appearance." Heckert asserts that Western cultural norms "have reified white beauty and marginalized other beauty."

Another source of inequality is age. In Western society, youth and youthful appearance have been idealized. Everyone seeks to remain youthful in appearance, and an astronomical amount of money is spent trying to achieve this.

In recent decades, people of size—overweight or obese—have been labeled as deviants. Heckert asserts that fat people are victims of discrimination, subject to harmful stereotyping, viewed as unattractive or undesirable, and even dehumanized in some instances. She reports that some women of size have experienced shame, reduced self-esteem, reduced human interaction, and a lack of fulfillment in their intimate relationships because of such stigmatization and stereotyping. Women with physical disabilities have reported similar experiences.

Appearance-challenged people have defensively relied on a very wide range of coping techniques, such as joining advocacy groups, becoming thick-skinned, walking away from negativity, focusing on personal gifts (such as intelligence), and salvaging their self-acceptance with a determination to enjoy life, among others.

Heckert concludes with the observation that "the stigma of physical appearance is an important issue that can impact the daily life of many people."

The stigma of deviant physical function

Individuals are stigmatized not only for not meeting societal norms regarding appearance, but for being unable to function in a normal fashion. Nancy Kutner, in her chapter, addresses social judgments regarding physical impairments that involve bodily functioning. Such conditions as blindness, deafness, paralysis, and epilepsy may elicit exclusionary social processes, including discrimination, greater social distance, and differential rejection.

Kutner reports that people with physical functioning disabilities are stigmatized and labeled as deviants. Stigma disrupts and strains social interaction with those considered normal. Kutner explains that those with physical functioning impairment, like those with deeply discrediting appearance, may resort to a "wide variety of concealing techniques in an effort to avoid the stigmatized label."

Individuals may have different levels of functioning, and this may result in differential disruptions to social interaction. Kutner notes that some of the negative social reaction may be the product of "existential" anxiety, in which the nondisabled people perceive in the disabled person the possibility of themselves having a functional impairment that would prevent a satisfactory life, or interfere with "important life activities."

Research has shown that physical disability may overwhelm all other identities and become a master-status that disrupts social interaction with others. Kutner suggests that contemporary healthcare campaigns may inadvertently exacerbate the plight of the disabled in that they may convey the message that "impairments are so undesirable that no one would want to accept living with such a condition."

She concludes with the observations that the US has an increasingly elderly population, and that the aging process, at some point, will involve impaired bodily functions. The increasing resource commitment to the physical functioning needs of the elderly may well moderate the stigmatization of the younger function-impaired population.

The stigma of mental retardation and intellectual disabilities

In the third chapter in this part, Steven Taylor informs the reader that in the late 19th and early 20th centuries many scholars accepted the notion that low intelligence was linked with various kinds of social pathology. A sociology textbook published in 1922 went so far as to suggest that the problem of "feeblemindedness" (mental retardation) was the result of "defective genes," and then called for such measures as involuntary sterilization, segregation, and even "compulsory elimination of the unfit." Morons were considered to be the "most dangerous of all" because many criminals, most prostitutes, and delinquent children in juvenile courts and reform schools could be so classified. As late as 1959, a leading criminology textbook called for the creation of special institutions for "defective delinquents."

Taylor points out that by the 1960s the harsh rhetoric of the past had moderated considerably, and mentally challenged individuals were now labeled as "mentally retarded." Some of the early sociological writings on stigma prompted a rethinking of the mentally retarded as more of a stigmatized identity than a social problem. The label of mental retardation was a deeply discrediting and stigmatizing attribute and some writers tried to sensitize professions "to the potentially harmful effects of diagnosing someone as mentally retarded."

Some research studies showed that a group of mildly mentally retarded, formerly institutionalized patients were aware of their stigmatized status and tended to deny it, hide their past institutionalization, and attempt to "pass" as normal individuals. They also had to rely on non-disabled "benefactors." A later follow-up study revealed that the former patients had become more independent and less concerned about passing, and that they relied less on "benefactors."

Taylor reports that, in time, a new concept in the field of deviance and stigma emerged: "normalization." This was defined as "making available to the mentally retarded patterns and conditions of everyday life which are as close as possible to the norms and patterns of mainstream society." This concept was to become a very powerful influence in the conceptualization, understanding, and management of mental retardation. Within the context of "normalization," the stigma of mental retardation is moderated, a more conventional life is possible, and the label "deviant behavior" is less appropriate and inevitable. Ultimately, advocacy groups and various scholars transformed the label "mental retardation" to "intellectual disability," which is less discrediting.

Taylor concludes with the observation that "the stigma of mental retardation and intellectual disability cannot be understood apart from the social institutions—professional diagnostic categories, school practices, human services arrangements—that created them."

The stigma of mental illness and psychiatric disorders

In the final chapter in this part, Jo Phelan and Bruce Link address mental illness as deviance through the social processes of labeling and stigmatization. They point out that society confers upon a limited group of professionals—including those involved in psychiatry and clinical psychology, clinical social workers, and psychiatric nurses—the license and mandate to define, diagnose, label, and treat mental illness. Phelan and Link's chapter focuses on the consequences of individuals being labeled in this way.

The authors examine the contentious debate among scholars of mental illness regarding the various dimensions of the conceptualization of labeling and their implications. They advance their own notion of modified labeling theory, developed as a synthesis of several other theories involving labeling, stigma, and mental illness. Modified labeling theory posits that labeling and stigma appear to degrade the life circumstances of individuals diagnosed as mentally ill, impacting their "employment chances, social networks and self-esteem." Because of this, mentally ill individuals are more likely to experience a "prolongation or recurrence of mental illness."

At this point, Phelan and Link dissect the process of conceptualizing stigma and offer arguments that support their perspective on stigma. They review trends in public attitudes relevant to stigma over time and suggest that "evidence challenges the idea that stigma will dissipate when the public adopts more medical views of mental illnesses."

They assert that being hospitalized for menial illness may result in the individual experiencing a variety of negative stigma outcomes, including status loss and discrimination. They then articulate and define in detail four configurations of discrimination: individual discrimination, discrimination operating through the stigmatized individual, interactional discrimination, and structural discrimination.

Phelan and Link conclude that "the public increasingly holds a medicalized view of mental illnesses"; nevertheless, "negative stereotypes and social distancing responses have changed little or become stronger."

65

The stigma of deviant physical appearance

Druann Maria Heckert

The body—socially constructed—is an important focus of sociology (Synnott 1993). An essential lens through which to examine the body is stigma. Erving Goffman (1963) famously wrote about stigma as a characteristic that is "deeply discrediting," since the attribute can be viewed by others as some sort of failing on the part of the bearer. Etymologically rooted in Greek, a stigma described a physical marking that carried disgrace; this is akin to stigmata, which were actual physical marks. Among the types of stigma that Goffman presented were "abominations" of the body, or physical deformities. Conjoined twins would fit his criterion here. Kitsuse (1980) expanded stigma to include "genetic stigmata," such as body or hair color. As an example, obese people are stigmatized.

Of further importance, Schur (1983) proposed the existence of "appearance norms" or culturally constructed norms depicting idealized portraits of favorable and unfavorable looks. As in the case of art, perhaps there is no simple answer to what is considered attractive, save for the meaning attached by a group (Gillespie and Perry 1973). Like other norms, variant images emerge across cultures, within cultures, and through time. Yet, within a specific context, culture powerfully creates reflections of the attractive and the unattractive. So widely shared are these norms that beauty is, in effect, not individually beheld but a cultural construct (Berscheid and Walster 1974; Hatfield and Sprecher 1986). For the attractive, the resulting positive consequences permeate life experience to such an extent that the phenomenon has been termed "what is beautiful is good" (Dion *et al.* 1972).

Appearance norms are thus not benign; rather, they are consequential. Those individuals deemed attractive within a cultural context find that their appearance is a facilitator for better life experiences because, overall, they are preferentially treated in various realms of life (Byrne 1971; Dion 1972; Landy and Sigall 1974). While there are a few disadvantages, such as slighting by the same sex, Krebs and Adinolfi (1975) maintain that the primary impact is positive. Reviewing multiple studies, Eagly *et al.* (1991) argue a more nuanced approach, concluding that physical attractiveness most impacts perceptions of social competence, but has less impact on potency, adjustment, and intellectual competence, and less again on integrity and concern for others. Still, positive outcomes ensue.

In stark contrast, those individuals deemed unattractive by culturally constructed appearance norms encounter diminished life experiences (Allon 1979; DeJong 1993). This stigmatization of the unattractive is indicative of the deviantization of physical attributes. Porter and Beuf (1991) state the case more boldly by designating vitiligo an "appearance impairment." Physical appearance is indeed a powerful variable.

Appearance molds negative experiences for those judged by societal appearance norms. Furthermore, the context of hegemonic appearance norms already creates inequalities. Both men and women are subject to appearance norms. In fact, in the case of redheads, men are more harshly judged than women (Heckert and Best 1997). Still, appearance norms are especially challenging for women in that they have traditionally been evaluated more harshly on the basis of appearance (Schur 1983; Mazur 1986). For example, Dellinger and Williams (1997) conclude that even though women are active agents in applying makeup to go to work, they do so in the context of the institutionalized dictates of appearance norms.

Further, appearance norms are not only gendered; they are raced (Robinson-Moore 2008; Gordon 2008). While appearance norms are culturally relative, in the United States, Eurocentric appearance norms have reified white beauty and marginalized other beauty (Patton 2006). Consequently, hair (texture and length) and skin color idealizations confront African American women as oppressive (Patton 2006). Additionally, Taub *et al.* (2003) note that appearance norms are centered on the able-bodied and exclude those with physical disabilities. Individuals with physical disabilities may also need to use a device such as a wheelchair, which further compromises appearance expectations. While Taub *et al.* found that women born with a physical disability were less likely to be impacted by the body image portion of appearance norms than those who acquired their disability at a later point in life, appearance norms still favor the able-bodied.

Another important source of inequality in appearance idealization is age. The preferred image of beauty is youth (Clarke *et al.* 2007). Consequently, the elderly are excluded. As an example, gray hair or decolorization has come to be symbolic of aging (Cooper 1971; Laz 1998) and can even hint at mortality (Synnott 1993). A content analysis of Grandparents' Day cards found that the typical representation of a grandparent included a youthful face but gray hair (Greene and Polivka 1985). Gray hair (Weitz 2001) and an aging appearance, once again, are especially problematic for women (Berkun 1985; Jedlicka 1978). Overall, appearance norms promote narrow—and even myopic—visions of beauty.

Stigma is clearly a central explanatory concept. Some appearance is stigmatized, and the sources of stigma in relation to appearance can be varied. Goffman (1963) argued that there are two types of stigmatized individual: the discredited and the discreditable. The discredited have stigmas that are apparent or visible on the surface. A short man—subject to more liabilities than a short woman—cannot hide his height (Jackson and Ervin 1992). Likewise, albinos (Wan 2003) or individuals with facial disfigurements cannot hide their attributes. Thus, the discredited person has to consider how to deal with the stigmatization of others. On the other hand, the discreditable have attributes that are not immediately visible on the surface. For example, a person with a strategically located disfigurement or scar, or a person with an offensive, yet concealed, tattoo (i.e., an achieved rather than an ascribed status), would be discreditable. The discreditable individual has to make decisions about whether to divulge information about their discreditable status. For example, they must choose which persons to share the information with or hide the secret from, and similarly decide upon the contexts (e.g., work) for providing it. Obviously, the discreditable person might experience the stress of worrying whether their "secret" will be revealed.

Labeling theory (Lemert 1972; Erikson 1964) is the theory that is perhaps most descriptive of how the stigma of physical appearance can impact individuals. It highlights three issues: the relativity of deviance, the societal reaction (e.g., stereotyping) to deviance, and the impact on the labeled. Clearly, there is cultural variation in which appearances are defined as deviant. For example, regarding the body, representations of the idealized have varied throughout history: for instance, thinness was popularized in the 1920s, only to be supplanted by curvaceous in the 1940s and 1950s, before thinness reemerged in the 1960s (Hurst 2000). Similarly, red hair has been adored in some cultures and reviled in others (Cooper 1971), and the path has been jagged. In some cases there may be less variability, as Wan (2003) notes that albinos have been stigmatized in many cultural contexts, including among the San Blas of Panama, in Zimbabwe, and in North America.

Labeling theory also includes analysis of the processes of the labeling, or the stereotyping (Schur 1971) that is involved. Stigmas are powerful because of this process of typification, which refers to the stereotypical terms under which culture has created a standardized and simplified category to describe all bearers of the deviance. Indeed, the stereotypes often extend beyond the attribute and constitute a master-status (Hughes 1945). As an example, redheads understand their societal typification and even participate in it, according to a study by Heckert and Best (1997). From the perspective of redheads, society stereotypes their rare hair color as indicating a fiery personality or a hot temper. They also consider that the stereotype of a redhead is that of a clown—often identified with a bold or unnatural shade of red—or caricature. Additionally, redheads feel that others view them as weird or goofy. Further, redheads think that other societal images include being Irish, sun challenged, and highly intelligent. Finally, they believe that redheaded women are viewed as wild or untamed, while redheaded men are believed to be wimpy or the sweet guy next door. Because this typification occurs at a societal level, it is undoubtedly powerful. Since these stereotypes go beyond the attribute of hair color, this hair color unmistakably constitutes a master-status.

Additionally, people of size are subjected to powerful stereotyping by society. In one study, female respondents felt that they were typified as having an unattractive or undesirable appearance (Sissem and Heckert 2003). They also thought that society viewed them as lazy or out of control, even if the stereotype is based on a fallacious assumption that weight is solely a consequence of individual behavior (Beller 1977). Third, the women believed that society construed them as incompetent, again reflecting the far reach of a master-status (Hughes 1945). Fourth, the respondents felt that society dehumanized people of size and created an image of a person less than fully human. Commonly, they reported that they had been subjected to appellations that served to remind them of their stigmatization.

Finally, labeling theory has examined the impact of labels. Because stigmas are powerful, they have great potential to mold the identity of individuals. Cooley (1902) created the notion of the looking-glass self; in the case of appearance, this is apt. In a sense, the deviant has a "spoiled identity" and this creates a social psychological problem. The identity of the stigmatized individual is threatened—at times severely—and thus they have to respond to that negative societal reaction. Regarding the labeling processes, Lemert (1972) described the transformation from primary to secondary deviance. As far as redheads are concerned, Heckert and Best (1997) found that they encountered negative peer treatment as children and adolescents, suffered lowered self-esteem, experienced feelings of differentness, and encountered incessant situations of being the center of attention.

As another example, Sissem and Heckert (2004) found that women of size were transformed in various ways. First, commonly, they felt shame. A few women externalized responsibility by blaming a prejudicial society. But most internalized the responsibility and experienced great shame and reduced self-esteem as a result. Many pointed to isolation or limiting human interaction so as to avoid painful, or potentially painful, situations. The respondents reported restriction in various life arenas, including full access to fair and non-discriminatory healthcare, clothing and fashion, physical activity, and self-development and awareness. Many thought the restrictions had begun early in life and felt that their marginalized status continued unabated throughout life. Finally, many reported being unfulfilled in various life arenas, including intimate relationships.

Additionally, Robinson-Moore (2008) concluded that racial appearance norms—rooted in skin color and texture of hair—impact socialization (alienation and academic achievement), higher rates of unemployment and greater rates of poverty, and marriage opportunities. Further, studying women with physical disabilities and how body image impacts their sense of self, Taub et al. (2003) reported that women accepted the dominant body image and reacted to this image emotionally, through anger and discontentment. They also utilized various forms of stigma management, such as concealment (e.g., clothing), deflection (e.g., emphasizing positive aspects of self through clothing), and normalization (e.g., educating the stigmatizers).

Individuals with the same stigma may respond differently, although all will be confronted with the same problem. For example, when studying albinos, Wan (2003) found that marginalization was experienced in many life experiences outside of the safety zone of home. However, individuals responded differently, allowing them to be categorized as one (or several) of the following: the defiant (responding to insults), the activist (educating the public), the serene (explaining the condition to people), the internalizer (directing their pain inward), the talker (venting about their problems with safe people), the hider (passing), the flamboyant (reveling in their uniqueness), or the positivist (incorporating their albinism into their identity).

Another example can be found in individuals who choose creative or alternative (self-defined by subject) hair (Heckert et al. 2005). The respondents in this study pointed to many negative cultural stereotypes of their hair, including being a subcultural follower, drug addict, criminal, or troublemaker, or being characterized by uncleanliness, rebelliousness, youthfulness/irresponsibility, or slow-wittedness/incompetence, or identifying with an issue of race, class, or sexuality. But they identified three potential impacts of the labeling on conceptualizations of self: a negative impact (the expected direction of labeling theory), no impact, and a positive impact. Regarding the last and least expected finding, the respondents felt that the creative hair enhanced their sense of self in that they saw themselves in the light of being unique, or bold, or some other desired characteristic. Stager et al. (1983) contend that in the case of a person rejecting the negative cultural construction and committing to the deviant identity, the labeling can improve a sense of self. An individual actively chooses alternative hair and purposefully refuses to comply with appearance norms. Thus, those who chose alternative hair might not see the societal label as related to their internalized self and they might not perceive that label negatively. Furthermore, Victor (2004) notes that emotional connections with other humans can diminish the impact of labels. So, those with creative hair are more responsive to their relationships with the members of their cliques than to the cultural constructions that they acknowledge exist. Furthermore, in the context of adult-onset vitiligo, those who already had high self-esteem dealt with it better than those who already had low self-esteem. Thus, the case of alternative hair is unique in that the person chooses the hair with an already formed self-esteem and has the power to change it at any particular moment.

Regarding human agency and societal stigmatization, Kitsuse (1980) refers to the deviant discarding the negative, embracing the marginalized identity, and creating a positive image of self. For example, redheads come to appreciate their uniqueness and the ways that red hair has singularly molded them by adulthood (Heckert and Best 1997). Further, Sissem and Heckert (2004) found that respondents in their study of women of size became tertiary deviants in the ways they chose to survive and thrive in life. A few joined advocacy groups, such as the National Association to Advance Fat Acceptance, which reject societal marginalization. Others emphasized their personal strength, salvaging their self-acceptance with a determination to enjoy life. They also utilized coping mechanisms, such as becoming thick-skinned, walking away from negativity, and focusing on personal gifts, such as intelligence.

Interestingly, as an achieved status, appearance norms can be flouted purposefully. Weitz (2001) contends that individuals can either oppose or give in to power relations embedded in social structure. Hippies and punks, for example, adorned their heads to mark themselves as members of a countercultural group. A popularized accoutrement of resistance, however, can become simply a fashion statement.

Deviance has always been complex and nuanced. Even in the context of idealized notions of beauty, stigma can surface. Blonde women present an interesting case in that they have benefited from social attributions of beauty. Nevertheless, simultaneously, stigma has been attached to their hair color in that their competence—indeed, their intelligence—has been subjected to incessant and unvarying critique (Kyle and Mahler 1996). So strong is this stigma that blonde women have to create coping mechanisms, such as ignoring or joking with the stigmatizer, fulfilling the prophecy, overcompensating (e.g., assuming the "ice princess" role or reducing emotional display), fighting back, and even passing (e.g., dying the hair black) (Heckert 2003).

As further example of nuance, the same physical appearance can be differentially judged. Irwin (2003) describes elite tattoo collectors as simultaneously positive and negative deviants, due to the highly divergent reactions that they generate—ranging from adulation to condemnation for refusing to participate in appearance norms mandating plain skin.

Overall, appearance is a potent shaper of how people define others and self. Clearly, the relationship between appearance and self is vital (Stone 1962). Mass media has heightened and continues to sustain attention on outward appearance. Anxiety about appearance persists; thus, the stigma of physical appearance is an important issue that can impact the daily life of many people. Although all humans know that they should judge a person by their character rather than their looks, the stigma of deviant appearance persists and is considerable. This area is ripe for further research and theorizing.

References

Allon, N. (1979) "Latent social services in group dieting," *Social Problems* 23:56–69.

Beller, A. (1977) *Fat and Thin: A Natural History of Obesity*, New York: McGraw-Hill.

Berkun, C. (1985) "Changing appearance for women in the middle years of life: trauma?," in E.W. Markson (ed.) *Older Women: Issues and Prospects*, Lexington, MA: Lexington Books.

Berscheid, E. and Walster, E. (1974) "Physical attractiveness," in L. Berkowitz (ed.) *Advances in Experimental Social Psychology VII*, New York: Academic Press.

Byrne, D. (1971) *The Attraction Paradigm*, New York: Academic Press.

Clarke, L., Repta, R. and Griffin, M. (2007) "Non-surgical cosmetic procedures: older women's perceptions and experiences," *Journal of Women and Aging* 19:69–87.

Cooley, C.H. (1902) *Human Nature and the Social Order*, New York: Charles Scribner's Sons.

Cooper, W. (1971) *Hair: Sex, Society, and Symbolism*, New York: Stein and Day.

DeJong, W. (1993) "Obesity as a characterological stigma: the issue of responsibility and judgments of task performance," *Psychological Reports* 73:963–970.

Dellinger, K. and Williams, C. (1997) "Makeup at work: negotiating appearance rules in the workplace," *Gender and Society* 11:151–177.

Dion, K. (1972) "Physical attractiveness and evaluations of children's transgressions," *Journal of Personality and Social Psychology* 24:297–313.

Dion, K., Berscheid, E., and Walster, E. (1972) "What is beautiful is good," *Journal of Personality and Social Psychology* 24:285–290.

Eagly, A., Ashmore, R., Makhijani, M., and Longo, L. (1991) "What is beautiful is good, but . . .: a meta-analytic review of research on the physical attractiveness stereotype," *Psychological Bulletin* 110:109–128.

Erikson, K.T. (1964) "Notes on the sociology of deviance," in H. Becker (ed.) *The Other Side*, New York: The Free Press.

Gillespie, D. and Perry, R. (1973) "Research strategies for studying the acceptance of artistic creativity," *Sociology and Social Research* 58:48–52.

Goffman, E. (1963) *Stigma: Notes on the Management of Spoiled Identity*, Englewood Cliffs, NJ: Prentice-Hall.

Gordon, M. (2008). "Media contributions to African American girls' focus on beauty and appearance: exploring the consequences of sexual objectification," *Psychology of Women Quarterly* 32:245–256.

Greene, R. and Polivka, J. (1985) "The meaning of grandparents' day cards: an analysis of the intergenerational network," *Family Relations* 34:221–225.

Hatfield, E. and Sprecher, S. (1986) *Mirror, Mirror . . . The Importance of Looks in Everyday Life*, Albany: State University of New York Press.

Heckert, D. (2003) "Mixed blessings: women and blonde hair," *Free Inquiry in Creative Sociology* 31:47–72.

Heckert, D. and Best, A. (1997) "Ugly duckling to swan: labeling theory and the stigmatization of red hair," *Symbolic Interaction* 20:365–384.

Heckert, D., Heckert, C., and Heckert, A. (2005) "Labeling theory and creative/alternative hair," *Sociological Imagination* 41:83–103.

Hughes, E. (1945) "Dilemmas and contradictions of status," *American Journal of Sociology* 50:353–359.

Hurst, C. (2000) *Living Theory*, Boston, MA: Allyn and Bacon.

Irwin, K. (2003) "Saints and sinners: elite tattoo collectors and tattooists as positive and negative deviants," *Sociological Spectrum* 23:27–57.

Jackson, L. and Ervin, K. (1992) "Height stereotypes of women and men: the liabilities of shortness for both sexes," *Journal of Social Psychology* 132:433–445.

Jedlicka, D. (1978) "Sex inequality, aging, and innovation in preferential mate selection," *Family Coordinator* 27:137–140.

Kilborne, B. (2002) *Disappearing Persons: Shame and Appearance*, Albany: State University of New York Press.

Kitsuse, J. (1980) "Coming out all over: deviants and the politics of social problems," *Social Problems* 28:1–13.

Krebs, D. and Adinolfi, A. (1975) "Physical attractiveness, social relations, and personality style," *Journal of Personality and Social Psychology* 31:245–253.

Kyle, D. and Mahler, H. (1996) "The effects of hair color and cosmetic use on perceptions of a female's ability," *Psychology of Women Quarterly* 20:447–455.

Landy, D. and Sigall, H. (1974) "Beauty as talent: task evaluation as a function of the performer's physical attractiveness," *Journal of Personality and Social Psychology* 31:245–253.

Laz, C. (1998) "Act your age," *Sociological Forum* 13:85–113.

Lemert, E.M. (1972) *Human Deviance, Social Problems, and Social Control*, Englewood Cliffs, NJ: Prentice-Hall.

Mazur, A. (1986) "US Trends in feminine beauty and overadaptation," *Journal of Sex Research* 22:281–303.

Patton, T. (2006) "Hey girl, am I more than my hair?: African American women and their struggles with beauty, body image, and hair," *NWSA Journal* 18:24–51.

Porter, J. and Beuf, A. (1991) "Racial variation in reaction to physical stigma: a study of degree of disturbance by vitiligo among black and white patients," *Journal of Health and Social Behavior* 32:192–204.

Robinson-Moore, C. (2008) "Beauty standards reflect Eurocentric paradigms—so what?," *Journal of Race and Policy* 4:66–85.

Schur, E. (1971) *Labeling Deviant Behavior*, New York: Harper and Row.

Schur, E. (1983) *Labeling Women Deviant*, Philadelphia, PA: Temple University Press.

Sissem, P. and Heckert, D. (2003) "The stigmatization of women of size," *Great Plains Sociologist* 15:52–69.

Sissem, P. and Heckert, D. (2004) "Acceptable the way that I am: labeling theory and women of size," *Humboldt Journal of Social Relations* 28:155–192.

Stager, S., Chassin, L., and Young, R. (1983) "Determinants of self-esteem among labeled adolescents," *Social Psychology Quarterly* 46:3–10.

Stone, G. (1962) "Appearance and the self," in A. Rose (ed.) *Human Behavior and Social Process*, Boston, MA: Houghton Mifflin.

Synnott, A. (1993) *The Body Social*, London: Routledge.

Taub, D., Fanflik, P., and McLorg, P. (2003) "Body image among women with physical disabilities: internalization of norms and reactions to nonconformity," *Sociological Focus* 36:159–176.

Victor, J. (2004) "Sluts and wiggers: a study of the effects of derogatory labeling," *Deviant Behavior* 25:67–85.

Wan, N. (2003) "Orange in a world of apples: the voices of albinism," *Disability and Society* 18:277–296.

Weitz, R. (2001) "Women and their hair: seeking power through resistance and accommodation," *Gender and Society* 15:667–586.

66

The stigma of deviant physical function

Nancy Kutner

Origin of the concept

Erving Goffman's work is the seminal social science contribution on the concept of stigma: "the situation of the individual who is disqualified from full social acceptance" (Goffman 1963:9). Goffman located stigma in social interaction processes, defining the framework of analysis as "the attitudes we normals have towards a person with stigma, and the actions we take in regard to him" (Goffman 1963:15). This chapter is concerned with social judgments associated with exclusionary social processes in response to physical impairments, which were categorized as "abominations of the body" in Goffman's taxonomy of stigmatizing conditions. Social judgments in response to deviant physical function may be enacted, perceived, or anticipated.

Evolution of scholarly interest in the topic

Safilios-Rothschild (1970) concluded that the position of disabled persons could be best analyzed using a general theory of deviance. Freidson (1965) and Scott (1965, 1969) also considered disability within a deviance or "societal reaction theory" framework (Gove 1976). The societal reaction theorist attaches little significance to primary deviance except insofar as others react to it. For example, according to Erikson (1964:11): "Deviance is not a property inherent in certain forms of behavior—it is the property conferred upon these forms by the audiences who directly or indirectly witness them. The critical variable is the social audience which eventually does the labeling."

Evolving literature on disability as deviance argued that, like other stigmatized groups, disabled persons tend to be evaluated as a category rather than as individuals. It was suggested that two predominantly negative stereotypes are likely to be applied: one stereotype of the particular impairment (blind, spastic, etc.) and one which is attached to the general label of "disabled" (Blaxter 1976). Freidson (1965) maintained that labeling, segregating, and feedback processes apply to the disabled as to other deviants; the disabled person is so defined because he deviates from what he himself or others consider normal and appropriate. Individuals may attempt a wide variety of concealing techniques in an effort to avoid the stigmatized label (Goffman 1963; Davis 1964; Hunt 1966), although opportunities for concealment may be limited in the case of many physical impairments.

Attribution of responsibility and disruption of social interaction have been proposed as potential explanations for social distance from individuals with various types of stigma. Using a modified Bogardus social distance scale, Albrecht *et al.* (1982) found in a study of professionals and managers holding key decision-making positions that respondents expressed greater social distance from such deviants as alcoholics and drug addicts than from disabled persons, such as paraplegics and the blind. The study found little support for the contention that attribution of responsibility determines variations in social distance across or within either stigma type. Rather, the data suggested that differential rejection stems from the disruption a stigma causes in social interaction.

West (1984) conducted in-depth interviews with 180 physically disabled, mentally retarded, and mentally ill persons from community and institutional residential settings to determine their perception of negative, stigmatizing attitudes toward the disabled, and the degree to which perceptions of community stigma restricted participation by the disabled in community recreation. This study found that many disabled people did perceive, and were affected by, stigma, and that those with highly visible impairments were most likely to have experienced negative community reactions.

In a series of experiments, Weiner *et al.* (1988) examined perceived controllability and stability of the causes of different stigmas. The investigators found that physically based stigmas were perceived as onset-uncontrollable and that they elicited pity, no anger and judgments to help. Mental-behavioral stigmas, however, were perceived as onset-controllable, eliciting anger rather than pity and judgments to help. In addition, physically based stigmas were perceived as stable, or irreversible, while mental-behavioral stigmas were generally considered unstable, or reversible.

Fine and Asch (1988) maintained that the experience of persons with disabling conditions varies in a number of ways that extend beyond the general rubric of stigma. Different physical impairments (e.g. deafness, paralysis, blindness, epilepsy) all pose problems of stigma, but persons with these impairments may be characterized by quite different levels of functioning. For example, although the need to manage stigma is important in the lives of persons living with epilepsy (Schneider and Conrad 1983), epilepsy may actually interfere minimally with individuals' daily functioning.

Gibbons (1986) claimed that "mildly stigmatized" persons, such as wheelchair users, seek out similarly disabled people with whom to compare themselves, avoiding interaction and comparisons with nondisabled people. Fine and Asch (1988) countered, however, that it should not necessarily be assumed that the "marked" person incorporates the mark as central to a self-definition. They suggested that perhaps disability is viewed as fearful, unacceptable, and different because the person with a disability is a reminder that it is impossible to control all life events. Attributing neediness and lack of control to people with disabilities may help those who are not disabled to attribute control and strength to themselves.

Perceiving a person with a disability as a suffering victim, a stimulus object, in need, or different and strange illustrates a view of the stigmatized person as "not quite human" (Goffman 1963:6). If a person is "not quite human," it is appropriate for that person to remain outside the community of those who "should" receive just distributions of societal rewards and resources (Deutsch 1985). At the same time, there is much historical and cultural variation in who becomes a stigmatized object (Ainlay *et al.* 1986). Impairment may be a ubiquitous "human constant," but response to it is not (Scheer and Groce 1988). Attending to all the aspects of life space that extend beyond the person with the impairment—that is, "beyond stigma"—should raise many new questions for social psychological research (Fine and Asch 1988).

Hahn (1988), expanding on issues noted by Fine and Asch (1988), maintained that the concept of "existential" anxiety summarizes the threat that nondisabled persons perceive in persons with disabilities. Existential anxiety refers to the threat of potential loss of functional capabilities thought necessary for a satisfactory life.

> Sometimes these concerns are evident in the silent thought that "There, but for the grace of God [or luck, or fate, or some other fundamental belief], go I." At other times, these worries may be verbalized in such statements as: "I would rather be dead than live as a paraplegic [or as blind, deaf, or immobilized]" . . . the social stigma of a disability fundamentally derives from the fact that the resulting functional impairments may interfere with important life activities.
>
> *(Hahn 1988:42–43)*

Hahn (1988) postulated that aesthetic anxiety, as well as existential anxiety, contributes to unfavorable perceptions of persons with disabilities. Thus, disabled individuals are devalued because they do not present conventional images of human physique or behavior. He suggested that aesthetic anxiety may actually be the stronger of the two influences in a society with a pervasive cultural emphasis on personal attractiveness. Consistent with this conclusion, research indicates that predominant attitudes toward persons with disabilities reflect aversion rather than more intense manifestations of anxiety.

Recent theory and research

The concept of stigma is an important research topic in social science and increasingly in public health as well, contributing to the burden of illness associated with many health conditions throughout the world.

Social psychology

Persons with physical disabilities may be perceived to be incompetent in areas that are actually unaffected by their specific disabilities. Houser (1997) proposed two hypotheses suggesting competing mechanisms for the impact of a physical disability on social interaction: the presence of a physical disability may overwhelm all other aspects of an individual's identity and in this way becomes the only cue used to characterize the individual's status in a group; physical disability may combine with other relevant cues to form a composite assessment of an individual's social standing. Houser experimentally manipulated the presence of a physical disability with other status cues to determine which interpretation best modeled the social effects of physical disability. A first experiment, in which presence/absence of a physical disability was the only salient status characteristic, showed that physical disability did affect social interaction in the experimental setting. Persons with physical disability were found to have less influence on group tasks, even if they were perceived as being more competent than nondisabled others. In a second experiment, in the presence of multiple status characteristics, the effect of a physical disability overwhelmed the other status cues. The findings of this study suggested that physical disability may operate as a master-status characteristic.

Based on fifteen years of research on the development of stereotyped responding toward physical differences among children as they mature, Harper (1999) noted that children tend to avoid peers whom they perceive as having difficulty completing the functional physical demands of a play situation, and that children who have had more personal contact with children with physical disabilities report more positive preferences and positive attributions toward those children. Thus, the more functionally limiting a particular disability, the more individuals with that disability are avoided by others, and the less desirable they are in children's expressed preferences. The less common (more rare) a particular disability, the more likely it is that this disability will violate expectations of the nondisabled observer. Harper suggested that this rarity may make such physical differences more salient. Unfavorable perceptions of disabled persons may indicate fear of associating or interacting with others who are considered alien or strange (Hahn 1988; Zola 1997). Dijker and Koomen (2006) proposed that it is likely that "universal psychological mechanisms" are causally involved in stigma responses.

Cross-cultural research

The relative degree of stigma attached to various disabilities has been found to be very similar among health practitioners in different countries. In all countries, people with arthritis seem to be among the most accepted, and people with cerebral palsy among the least accepted. These findings were remarkably stable in research conducted in the late twentieth century (Westbrook *et al.* 1993).

At the same time, developing countries tend to be more openly rejecting of disabling conditions than modern Western societies (Dijker and Koomen 2006). Weiss *et al.* (2006), commenting on Goffman's view of stigma, argued that a conceptual framework based on normalcy versus deviance cannot be applied in cross-cultural research. They argued that Goffman's reference to a dominant "normal" cannot accommodate recognition and appreciation of multiculturalism.

Health policy

Recent health policy studies have highlighted the potential production of stigma through health promotion campaigns. Paradoxically, health communication targeted to injury prevention with the implicit message "Don't let this happen to you" may portray people with disabilities in a stigmatizing way. Given the growing role of health communication in public health efforts, awareness of such unintended consequences is important (Wang 1992, 1998). Similarly, Hahn (1994) noted that efforts to prevent disability through genetic counseling convey a message that impairments are so undesirable that no one would want to accept living with such a condition. An ideology of "able-ism" has exclusionary social functions (Turner 2001), preserving and validating privileged designations of the body.

Sociological perspectives

Weiss *et al.* (2006) acknowledged that Goffman successfully shifted the conceptualization of stigma from a symbolic mark to social processes, but they also argued that his formulation stressed dyadic social interactions and gave little attention to social structural factors that influence social interactions. Scambler (2006) emphasized the causal importance of social structures for understanding stigma relations; the importance of understanding stigma relations in the context of wider societal change; and ways in which stigma relations interact with other relations, such as social class and power. According to Susman (1994:15), however, Goffman "does not view the link between stigma/deviance and disability as inexorable, nor does he claim that disabled people are inevitably passive and victimized. Rather, Goffman holds that the meaning of disability is a social, therefore changeable, construction."

Physical disability may frequently coexist with some type of psychiatric disability. Bahm and Forchuk (2009) found that people with a self-reported comorbid physical disability as well as a self-reported psychiatric disability perceived that they faced more overall discrimination/stigma than those with a psychiatric disability alone. Perceived discrimination/stigma was negatively correlated with self-reported general health, physical functioning, emotional well-being, and life satisfaction.

Stigma/deviance imputations may be challenged by physically disabled persons (Frank 1988; Susman 1994). In a sample of disabled activists, Hahn and Belt (2004) found that a personal affirmation of disability was a significant predictor of refusing medical treatment for disabling conditions. Age of onset of the individual's disability was also a predictor. Persons with an earlier age of disability onset were more likely to reject curative treatment. Hahn and Belt suggested two potential explanations for the latter finding. First, early disability onset is likely to lead to a stronger personal sense of disability identity. Second, early disability onset gives longer exposure to medical interventions that often prove disappointing because they do not provide a cure. In addition to affirmation of disability identity, communal attachments were strong values among the activists who were studied. Disability movements facilitated disabled persons' acceptance of self and a focus on positive identity.

A central feature of the disability "insider" experience may be a persistent and disquieting sense of mistaken identity, rather than "spoiled" identity (Goffman 1963). In one individual's words, "my disability is how people respond to my disability" (Craig Vick, cited by Gill 2001:352). Taub et al. (2004) explored disability status negotiation among female students with physical disabilities. Stigma management strategies included deflection, normalization, and disidentification. The women downplayed or claimed their disability status depending on whether the attached stigma was discredited or discreditable, whether the relevant relationship was formal or personal, and whether the other's reaction was perceived as accepting or questioning the legitimacy of the disability. Zola (1997) described an increase in his own comfort level regarding his physical disability when his young daughter conveyed to him her perception that he was comfortable with it. Cahill and Eggleston (1995) concluded that norms of public kindness, rather than stigma and deviance, are most salient for wheelchair users' functioning in public settings.

Because there are "seemingly infinite permutations of the experience of being physically different in a highly normalizing society" (Williams 2001:130), many scholars have advocated more analysis of variations in the ways in which different physical impairments translate into complex negotiated aspects of everyday life. Shuttleworth and Kasnitz (2004:147) asked, "Can use of the term stigma be applied equally as the negative response to divergent impairments?" It has been proposed that the more highly an attribute is valued, the more a person who lacks or is deficient in this attribute will experience a relative increase in degree of stigma and possible corresponding loss of self-esteem. More broadly, degree of stigma attached to particular impairments will vary depending on the different cultural values that are slighted. Other status characteristics (e.g., age category, race/ethnicity, economic level) that predominate among those who are perceived to carry a particular disabling condition also affect the stigma associated with that condition (Shuttleworth and Kasnitz 2004). The distinguishing features of stigma should be specified for particular groups of people in specific contexts.

Conclusion

Many important research questions regarding stigma of "deviant" physical function exist with respect to the individual and the larger society. How do individuals cope with ongoing stigmatization? What are the effects on their personal identity, social life, and economic opportunities? How do the medical establishment, media representations, and educational environments create and perpetuate the stigma of a particular condition? As Meyerson (1988) argued, if clinical psychologists and medical professionals focus attention on defects, deformities, and disease whose origin and treatment are viewed as "within the individual," the data that emerge are unlikely to support increased understanding of the disabled person within the larger environment. Wang (1992, 1998) has called attention to the role that public health messages in the media may play in societal acceptance of stigma. Variation across cultures in the definition, treatment, and experience of disability may illuminate processes by which a social barrier such as stigma arises.

Finally, the prevalence of persons living with physical impairments increases with population aging. Zola (1991) suggested that this phenomenon could create shared goals for the "able-bodied" and "the disabled," and Blaxter (1976) observed many years earlier that in the context of the aging process, disability and "normality" form a continuum. While valuation of youthful attributes is likely to remain strong in American society, growing resource commitment to physical functioning needs associated with the normality–disability aging continuum could have important implications for stigma associated with "deviant" physical function in American society.

References

Ainlay, S., Becker, G., and Coleman, L. (eds) (1986) *The Dilemma of Difference: A Multi-disciplinary View of Stigma*, New York: Plenum.

Albrecht, G.L., Walker, V.G., and Levy, J.A. (1982) "Social distance from the stigmatized: a test of two theories," *Social Science & Medicine* 16:1319–1327.

Bahm, A. and Forchuk, C. (2009) "Interlocking oppressions: the effect of a comorbid physical disability on perceived stigma and discrimination among mental health consumers in Canada," *Health & Social Care in the Community* 17:63–70.

Blaxter, M. (1976) *The Meaning of Disability: A Sociological Study of Impairment*, New York: Neale Watson Academic.

Cahill, S.E. and Eggleston, R. (1995) "Reconsidering the stigma of physical disability: wheelchair use and public kindness," *Sociological Quarterly*,36:681–698.

Davis, F. (1964) "Deviance disavowal: the management of strained identity by the visibly handicapped," in H.S. Becker (ed.) *The Other Side*, New York: Free Press.

Deutsch, M. (1985) *Distributive Justice*, New Haven, CT: Yale University Press.

Dijker, A.J.M. and Koomen, W. (2006) "A psychological model of social control and stigmatization: evolutionary background and practical implications," *Psychology, Health & Medicine* 11:296–306.

Erikson, K.T. (1964) "Notes on the sociology of deviance," in H.S. Becker (ed.) *The Other Side*, New York: Free Press.

Fine, M. and Asch, A. (1988) "Disability beyond stigma: social interaction, discrimination, and activism," *Journal of Social Issues* 44:3–21.

Frank, G. (1988) "Beyond stigma: visibility and self-empowerment of persons with congenital limb deficiencies," *Journal of Social Issues* 44:95–115.

Freidson, E. (1965) "Disability as social deviance," in M.B. Sussman (ed.) *Sociology and Rehabilitation*, Washington, DC: American Sociological Association.

Gibbons, F.X. (1986) "Stigma and interpersonal relations," in S. Ainlay, G. Becker, and L. Coleman (eds) *The Dilemma of Difference: A Multi-disciplinary View of Stigma*, New York: Plenum.

Gill, C. (2001) "Divided understandings: the social experience of disability," in G.L. Albrecht, K.D. Seelman, and M. Bury (eds) *The Handbook of Disability Studies*, Thousand Oaks, CA: Sage.

Goffman, E. (1963) *Stigma: Notes on the Management of Spoiled Identity*, Englewood Cliffs, NJ: Prentice-Hall.

Gove, W.R. (1976) "Societal reaction theory and disability," in G.L. Albrecht (ed.) *The Sociology of Physical Disability and Rehabilitation*, Pittsburgh, PA: University of Pittsburgh.

Hahn, H. (1988) "The politics of physical differences: disability and discrimination," *Journal of Social Issues* 44:39–47.

—— (1994) "The minority group model of disability: implications for medical sociology," in R. Weitz and J.J. Kronenfeld (eds) *Research in the Sociology of Health Care*, vol.11, Greenwich, CT: JAI Press.

Hahn, H. and Belt, T.L. (2004) "Disability identity and attitudes toward cure in a sample of disabled activists," *Journal of Health and Social Behavior* 45:453–464.

Harper, D.C. (1999) "Social psychology of difference: stigma, spread, and stereotypes in childhood," *Rehabilitation Psychology* 44:131–144.

Houser, J.A. (1997) "Stigma, spread and status: the impact of physical disability on social interaction," *Dissertation Abstracts International Section A: Humanities and Social Sciences* 58 (5-A).

Hunt, P. (ed.) (1966) *Stigma: The Experience of Disability*, London: Chapman.

Meyerson, L. (1988) "The social psychology of physical disability: 1948 and 1988," *Journal of Social Issues* 44:173–188.

Safilios-Rothschild, C. (1970) *The Sociology and Social Psychology of Disability and Rehabilitation*, New York: Random House.

Scambler, G. (2006) "Sociology, social structure and health-related stigma," *Psychology, Health & Medicine* 11:288–295.

Scheer, J. and Groce, N. (1988) "Impairment as a human constant: cross-cultural and historical perspectives on variation," *Journal of Social Issues* 44:23–37.

Schneider, J.W. and Conrad, P. (1983) *Having Epilepsy: The Experience and Control of Illness*, Philadelphia, PA: Temple University Press.

Scott, R.A. (1965) "Comments about interpersonal processes of rehabilitation," in M.B. Sussman (ed.) *Sociology and Rehabilitation*, Washington, DC: American Sociological Association.

—— (1969) *The Making of Blind Men*, New York: Russell Sage Foundation.

Shuttleworth, R.P. and Kasnitz, D. (2004) "Stigma, community, ethnography: Joan Ablon's contribution to the anthropology of impairment-disability," *Medical Anthropology Quarterly* 18:139–161.

Susman, J. (1994) "Disability, stigma and deviance," *Social Science & Medicine* 38:15–22.

Taub, D.E., McLorg, P.A., and Fanflik, P.L. (2004) "Stigma management strategies among women with physical disabilities: contrasting approaches of downplaying or claiming a disability status," *Deviant Behavior* 25:169–190.

Turner, B.S. (2001) "Disability and the sociology of the body," in G.L. Albrecht, K.D. Seelman, and M. Bury (eds) *The Handbook of Disability Studies*, Thousand Oaks, CA: Sage.

Wang, C. (1992) "Culture, meaning and disability: injury prevention campaigns and the production of stigma," *Social Science & Medicine* 35:1093–1102.

——(1998) "Portraying stigmatized conditions: disabling images in public health," *Journal of Health Communication* 3:149–159.

Weiner, B., Perry, R.P., and Magnusson, J. (1988) "An attributional analysis of reactions to stigmas," *Journal of Personality & Social Psychology* 55:738–748.

Weiss, M.G., Ramakrishna, J., and Somma, D. (2006) "Health-related stigma: rethinking concepts and interventions," *Psychology, Health & Medicine* 11:277–287.

West, P.C. (1984) "Social stigma and community recreation participation by the mentally and physically handicapped," *Therapeutic Recreation Journal* 18:40–49.

Westbrook, M.T., Legge, V., and Pennay, M. (1993) "Attitudes towards disabilities in a multicultural society," *Social Science & Medicine* 36:615–623.

Williams, G. (2001) "Theorizing disability," in G.L. Albrecht, K.D. Seelman, and M. Bury (eds) *The Handbook of Disability Studies*, Thousand Oaks, CA: Sage.

Zola, I.K. (1991) "Bringing our bodies and ourselves back in: reflections on a past, present, and future 'medical sociology,'" *Journal of Health and Social Behavior* 32:1–16.

—— (1997) *Meaningful Relationships/Moments in* Time, Boston, MA: Judy Norsigian.

67

The stigma of mental retardation and intellectual disabilities

Steven J. Taylor

Intellectual disability—or mental retardation, among other names—has long been considered a form of deviant behavior in sociology. Following the publication of hereditarian studies of feeblemindedness in the late nineteenth and early twentieth centuries (see, for example, Dugdale, 1877; Goddard, 1912), many sociologists accepted the presumed link between low intelligence and other kinds of social pathology. For example, a leading sociological text by Dow (1922), *Society and Its Problems: An Introduction to the Principles of Sociology*, characterized feeblemindedness as largely a problem of defective genes and endorsed such eugenics measures as segregation, involuntary sterilization, and even "compulsory elimination of the unfit" (p. 52). "Morons," the highest-functioning members of the feebleminded "class," were viewed as a special threat to society: "this class is the most dangerous of all, for it is the one which furnishes many of the criminals, a large percentage of our prostitutes, the delinquent children in our juvenile courts and reform schools, and the dull and backward children in our schools" (p. 539). As late as 1959, a criminology text by Barnes and Teeters endorsed the establishment of special institutions for "defective delinquents" (pp. 111–114), although it rejected the strident claims of earlier eugenicists.

Beginning in the late 1950s and 1960s, sociologists gradually shifted attention away from the presumed pathological nature of mental retardation to the processes through which people were labeled mentally retarded and the consequences of being so defined. In a series of articles published in the late 1950s and early 1960s, Lewis Dexter was one of the first sociologists to call for a rethinking of the "problem" of mental retardation. One of these articles (Dexter 1964) made an analogy between how mental retardation was viewed in Western societies and a mythical society in which the major targets of social discrimination were clumsy people, whom Dexter called the "gawkies." In the mythical society, people valued grace and style in movement, just as people in Western societies value intelligence. The system of writing and technology in this society would require grace for the performance of everyday tasks, not because gracefulness was necessary for the tasks at hand, but simply because things were designed this way. Dexter speculated on what would happen to clumsy people in the mythical society. Clumsy children would be social rejects, subject to pantomime jokes, and sent to custodial institutions. Academics and professionals would develop a grace quotient to rank all children in school. Scholars would present papers and have debates over the ability of clumsy people to function in society at the National Association on Clumsiness. Dexter used this analogy to call into question conventional thinking about mental retardation and to direct attention to how society contributed to making people disabled.

Erving Goffman's *Stigma* (1963) would eventually have a profound influence on thinking about various forms of disability, including psychiatric and intellectual disabilities. It had long been recognized that mental illness and mental retardation could be stigmatizing in society. In the late 1940s and early 1950s, for example, reformers waged campaigns to improve public understanding of these conditions and to reduce the stigma associated with them (Taylor 2009a: 331–332). Yet, stigma was only vaguely defined and associated with general public attitudes. Goffman directed attention to how people manage potentially discrediting characteristics in interactions with other people. For Goffman, a stigma was a discrediting attribute (physical disability, blemishes of individual characteristics, or racial, national, and religious background), but it was more than that, too. Stigma manifested itself in relationships between human beings:

> [S]tigma involves not so much a set of concrete individuals who can be separated into two piles, the stigmatized and the normal, as a pervasive two-role social process in which every individual participates in both roles, at least in some connections and in some phases of life. The normal and the stigmatized are not persons but rather perspectives. These are generated in social situations during mixed contacts by virtue of the unrealized norms that are likely to play upon the encounter.
>
> *(Goffman 1963: 137–138)*

Robert Edgerton elaborated on the application of Goffman's theory of stigma to people with intellectual disabilities in his 1967 book, *The Cloak of Competence* (Taylor, 2009b). Edgerton, an anthropologist, examined the experiences of 48 "mildly mentally retarded" former patients of the Pacific State Hospital in California. Having mental retardation, Edgerton concluded, was a deeply discrediting and stigmatizing attribute that could harm people's self-esteem. The former patients went to great lengths to deny their retardation, to hide their past institutionalization, and to "pass" as normal people. Edgerton also found that the former patients relied on nondisabled "benefactors" for assistance in managing daily problems and in denial and passing in the community.

Edgerton and his colleagues published follow-up studies of some of the former patients in the original study in 1976, 1984, and 1991. Of those who could be located, most were faring better in the community than Edgerton would have predicted in 1967. They had become more independent, less reliant on benefactors, and less consumed with denial and passing than when they had been studied initially.

The Cloak of Competence was widely read in the field on mental retardation in the late 1960s and 1970s. It helped to popularize sociological and anthropological methods and concepts in a field that had been dominated by medicine and psychology. Edgerton's work also sensitized professionals to the potentially harmful effects of diagnosing someone as mentally retarded. *The Cloak of Competence* would later be criticized by sociologists Robert Bogdan and Steven Taylor and historian David Gerber. In a 1982 book containing the life histories of people with mental retardation, Bogdan and Taylor argued that Edgerton did not question the concept of mental retardation itself and that mental retardation was a label imposed on people by others according to arbitrary standards. The title of Edgerton's book, claimed Bogdan and Taylor, suggested that people who were labeled mentally retarded tried to hide their incompetence. They maintained that people so labeled had a cloak of incompetence placed over them. Gerber (1990) questioned whether the former patients in Edgerton's study had an objective disability condition and suggested that social and economic factors had played a major role in their institutionalization.

In a revised and updated version of *The Cloak of Competence*, published in 1993, Edgerton defended his original study and expressed disagreement with what he referred to as the "extreme social constructionists' views" of mental retardation held by some of his critics.

In the late 1960s, a new concept informed by sociological theories on deviance and stigma emerged in the field of mental retardation. The concept was normalization (Taylor 2009a). It was developed in Scandinavia and incorporated into a 1959 Danish law governing services for people with mental retardation. However, the concept was not defined until the publication of an influential book in1969, *Changing Patterns in Residential Services for the Mentally Retarded*, edited by Kugel and Wolfensberger and published by the President's Committee on Mental Retardation. This book contained a chapter on "The Normalization Principle and Its Human Management Implications," written by Bengt Nirje, then executive director of the Swedish Association for Retarded Children. Nirje (1969: 181) provided the following definition of mental retardation: "The normalization principle means making available to the mentally retarded patterns and conditions of everyday life which are as close as possible to the norms and patterns of the mainstream society." He then gave eight implications of the principle of normalization (for example, normal rhythm of the day and normal routine of life).

In the introduction to *Changing Patterns*, Robert Kugel (1969: 10) wrote regarding the normalization principle:

> This construct has never been fully presented in the American mental retardation literature, but it is of such power and universality as to provide a potential basis for legal and service structures anywhere. Indeed, the editors of this book view the normalization principle as perhaps the single most important concept emerging in this compendium.

Gunnar Dybwad (1969: 385), past president of the National Association for Retarded Children, was more straightforward in the conclusion to the book: "Without a doubt, as far as the future of residential (as well as many other) services is concerned, the concept of normalization presented in Nirje's chapter has emerged as the most important one in this book."

Various contributors to *Changing Patterns* approached mental retardation from the perspective of the sociology of deviance. Dybwad described normalization as a sociological concept: "The normalization principle draws together a number of other lines of thought on social role, role perception, deviancy, and stigma that had their origin in sociology and social psychology" (p. 386). Wolf Wolfensberger's history of the origin and nature of institutions started with a review of the historical "role perceptions" of retarded persons (for example, as sick, as subhuman organisms, as a menace) and explained:

> Social scientists in the recent past have elaborated a concept of great importance to the understanding of the behavior and management of retarded persons. The concept is that of "deviance." A person can be defined as deviant if he is perceived as being significantly different from others in some overt aspect, and if this difference is negatively valued. An overt and negatively valued characteristic is called a stigma.
>
> *(Wolfensberger 1969: 65)*

Three years after *Changing Patterns*, Wolfensberger (1972) published another influential and widely read book, *The Principle of Normalization in Human Services*. In this book, Wolfensberger elaborated on the dimensions of normalization and offered a reformulated definition: "Utilization of means which are as culturally normative as possible, in order to establish and/or maintain personal behaviors and characteristics which are as culturally normative as possible" (p. 28).

Although mental retardation or intellectual disability is a stigmatizing attribute in society, it does not follow that people with intellectual disabilities will always be rejected or stigmatized by others or internalize cultural beliefs and the sentiments of others. Bogdan and Taylor (1989) studied the perspectives of nondisabled people who were involved in close relationships with people with severe intellectual disabilities. In contrast to theories of deviance and stigma, the nondisabled people in these relationships did not reject or stigmatize their severely disabled family members and friends. Bogdan and Taylor described four dimensions of the nondisabled people's perspectives that helped them maintain the humanness of severely disabled people in their minds: attributing thinking to the other; seeing individuality in the other; viewing the other as reciprocating; and defining social place for the other. In the conclusion of their article, they called for a less deterministic approach to the study of deviance and stigma.

Taylor (2000) described an extended family and social network of people who had been disproportionately defined as disabled or mentally retarded by public and private agencies, but who had constructed a life world in which disability was not stigmatizing or problematic to their identities. Members of the social network defined themselves and others in terms of their personal characteristics and social relationships, not disability labels. Taylor concluded that theories of deviance and stigma may be helpful in understanding casual encounters between people, the experiences of people enmeshed in human services agencies, and abstract cultural meanings, but do not necessarily account for the experiences of people embedded in different family worlds.

Groups of people with intellectual disabilities and their advocates have organized to fight the stigma associated with the label of mental retardation. The first "self-advocacy" groups for people with intellectual disabilities were organized in the 1970s. Many of these have taken the name "People First" to emphasize the humanity of their members and to downplay the significance of having been defined as mentally retarded (Shapiro 1993: 184–210).

Since the 1990s, the terminology "mental retardation" has been increasingly questioned. Some scholars have advocated abandoning it and using alternative language. Gelb (2002: 55) wrote:

> The reason that the name should be changed is that the term *mental retardation*, like its predecessors, long ago escaped from the clinical realm of classification into universal usage as a potent, utterly dismissive invective in the mouths of adults and school children. The injurious nominal form *retard* became a term of opprobrium alongside *moron*, *imbecile*, and *idiot*.

Others argue that as long as people with presumed low intelligence are viewed as inferior to others, changes in terminology will not make a significant difference. Thus, Danforth (2002: 54) has written: "The opportunity now is not to create new descriptions of diagnosed populations, for such descriptions have little chance of outrunning the pervasive ghost of cultural stigma." Mental retardation itself was viewed as being more positive and less stigmatizing than mental deficiency and other terminology (feeblemindedness, idiot, imbecile, moron) when it first became popular in the 1960s.

People First and other self-advocacy groups have strongly advocated abandonment of what they have called the "R word" (Carey 2009: 189–190). In response to these groups and concerns over the derogatory use of "mental retardation" in common language, the President's Committee on Mental Retardation was renamed the President's Committee for People with Intellectual Disabilities in 2003. The American Association on Mental Retardation, the oldest and largest professional organization in the field, changed its name to the American Association on Intellectual and Developmental Disabilities in 2007.

Mental retardation has long been a stigmatizing attribute in the United States and most, if not all, other Western countries. The stigma associated with mental retardation peaked in the early twentieth century, at the height of the eugenics movement, which linked feeblemindedness to social pathology and disorder. Although the hysteria surrounding the eugenics movement, with its claims that people with low intelligence were spreading their alleged defective genes throughout society, waned during the latter half of the twentieth century and the beginning of the current one, mental retardation remains a potentially discrediting characteristic in most situations. Yet, nondisabled people do not always reject and stigmatize those with presumed mental retardation, and those who have been defined as mentally retarded do not always internalize the stigma associated with that societal definition.

Changes in the terminology used to refer to any group of people may affect how they are viewed by others and how they view themselves, but more positive language cannot eliminate stigma in and of itself. New names can take on the same meanings associated with old ones.

Stigma is not inevitable for any group of people. Some extremely stigmatizing attributes in the past, such as being gay or lesbian, are no longer discrediting in many social circles. Other attributes and behaviors that were once relatively commonplace and tolerated, such as driving under the influence of alcohol, are becoming increasingly stigmatized In any society that places a high value on intelligence and literacy skills, people deemed lacking those attributes are likely to be devalued. Even so, it is always possible for any individual or group to be judged by others not on the basis of a single attribute, but on the full range of their personal characteristics. For instance, although athleticism is valued in many sectors of American society, many people lacking athletic ability are highly respected and have a high status in the United States.

Mental retardation—or intellectual disability, for that matter—is a social construction. Human beings vary according to reading, mathematical ability, reasoning, judgment, and other skills. The constructs of mental retardation and intellectual disability suggest that we can neatly distinguish between two categories of human being: the "normal" and the "other." Once this distinction is made, the "other" is likely to be associated with stereotypes and generalizations and subjected to a self-fulfilling prophecy in which a group of people is treated differently than others and behaves accordingly. The stigma of mental retardation and intellectual disability cannot be understood apart from the social institutions–professional diagnostic categories, schooling practices, human services arrangements—that created them.

References

Barnes, Harry Elmer, and Negley K. Teeters. 1959. *New Horizons in Criminology*. 3rd edn. Englewood Cliffs, NJ: Prentice-Hall.

Bogdan, Robert, and Steven J. Taylor. 1982. *Inside Out: The Social Meaning of Mental Retardation*. Toronto: University of Toronto Press.

Bogdan Robert, and Steven J. Taylor. 1989. "Relationships with Severely Disabled People: The Social Construction of Humanness." *Social Problems* 36, no. 2, 135–148.

Carey, Allison C. 2009. *On the Margins of Citizenship: Intellectual Disability and Civil Rights in Twentieth-Century America*. Philadelphia, PA: Temple University Press.

Danforth, Scot. 2002. "New Words for New Purposes: A Challenge for the AAMR." *Mental Retardation* 40, no. 1, 51–54.

Dexter, Lewis Anthony. 1964. "On the Politics and Sociology of Stupidity in Society." In *The Other Side: Perspectives on Deviance*, edited by Howard S. Becker, 37–50. New York: The Free Press.

Dow, Grove Samuel. 1922. *Society and Its Problems: An Introduction to the Principles of Sociology*. New York: Thomas Y. Crowell.

Dugdale, Richard L. 1877. *The Jukes: A Study in Crime, Pauperism, Disease, and Heredity*. New York: Putnam.

Dybwad, Gunnar. 1969. "Action Implications, USA Today." In *Changing Patterns in Residential Services for the Mentally Retarded*, edited by Robert Kugel and Wolf Wolfensberger, 383–428. Washington, DC: President's Committee on Mental Retardation.

Edgerton, Robert B. 1967. *The Cloak of Competence*. Berkeley and Los Angeles: University of California Press.

Edgerton, Robert B. 1993. *The Cloak of Competence: Revised and Updated*. Berkeley and Los Angeles: University of California Press.

Gelb, Steven A. 2002. "The Dignity of Humanity Is Not a Scientific Concept." *Mental Retardation* 40, no. 1, 55–56.

Gerber, David A. 1990. "Listening to Disabled People: The Problem of Voice and Authority in Robert B. Edgerton's *The Cloak of Competence.*" *Disability, Handicap & Society*, 5, 3–23.

Goddard, Henry. 1912. *The Kallikak Family: A Study in the Heredity of Feeblemindedness*. New York: Macmillan.

Goffman, Erving. 1963. *Stigma: Notes on the Management of Spoiled Identity*. Englewood Cliffs, NJ: Prentice-Hall.

Kugel, Robert B. 1969. "Why Innovative Action?" In *Changing Patterns in Residential Services for the Mentally Retarded*, edited by Robert B. Kugel and Wolf Wolfensberger, 1–14. Washington, DC: President's Committee on Mental Retardation.

Kugel, Robert B., and Wolf Wolfensberger (eds). 1969. *Changing Patterns in Residential Services for the Mentally Retarded*. Washington, DC: President's Committee on Mental Retardation.

Nirje, Bengt. 1969. "The Normalization Principle and Its Human Management Implications." In *Changing Patterns in Residential Services for the Mentally Retarded*, edited by Robert B. Kugel and Wolf Wolfensberger, 179–195. Washington, DC: President's Committee on Mental Retardation.

Shapiro, Joseph. 1993. *No Pity: People with Disabilities Forging a New Civil Rights Movement*. New York: Three Rivers Press.

Taylor, Steven J. 2000. "'You're Not a Retard, You're Just Wise': Disability, Social Identity, and Family Networks." *Journal of Contemporary Ethnography* 29, no. 1, 58–92.

Taylor, Steven J. 2009a. *Acts of Conscience: World War II, Mental Institutions, and Religious Objectors*. Syracuse, NY: Syracuse University Press.

Taylor, Steven J. 2009b. "The Cloak of Competence." In *Encyclopedia of American Disability History*, edited by Susan Burch, 188–189. New York: Facts on File.

Wolfensberger, Wolf. 1969. "The Origin and Nature of Our Institutional Models." In *Changing Patterns in Residential Services for the Mentally Retarded*, edited by Robert B. Kugel and Wolf Wolfensberger, 59–171. Washington, DC: President's Committee on Mental Retardation.

Wolfensberger, Wolf. 1972. *The Principle of Normalization in Human Services*. Toronto: National Institute on Mental Retardation.

68

The stigma of mental illness and psychiatric disorders

Jo C. Phelan and Bruce G. Link

Modern societies have created professions (including psychiatry, clinical psychology, psychiatric social work, and psychiatric nursing) upon whose members are conferred the authority to define, label, and treat mental illnesses. Social processes determine who encounters these professionals and many of the consequences that follow.

This chapter develops issues in mental-health sociology to provide a framework for examining current issues concerning labeling and stigma. It addresses the conceptualization of labeling and stigma, trends in public attitudes and beliefs, and how labeling and stigma affect individuals with mental illnesses.

The labeling debate

In Thomas Scheff's (1966) labeling theory of mental illness, labeling was driven as much by social characteristics of the labelers, the person being labeled, and the social situation in which their interactions occurred as it was by anything that might be called the symptoms of mental illness. Moreover, once a person is labeled, "persons around the deviant react to him uniformly in terms of the stereotypes of insanity, his amorphous and unstructured rule-breaking tends to crystallize in conformity to these expectations, thus becoming similar to behavior of other deviants classified as mentally ill and stable over time" (Scheff 1966: 82).

Critics of the theory, especially Walter Gove (1975), argued that labels are applied far less capriciously and with fewer pernicious consequences than labeling theory indicates. In Gove's view, if people with mental illnesses are rejected, it is because of responses to their symptomatic behavior rather than because of a label. Moreover, he argues, labeling is not an important cause of further deviant behavior.

Although some observers despaired at the protracted and seemingly irresolvable debate over labeling, the sharply opposed stances of Scheff and Gove clarified what was at issue and set the stage for subsequent theory and research.

Modified labeling theory

Link and colleagues developed a "modified" labeling theory that derived insights from Scheff's theory but stepped back from the claim that labeling is a direct cause of mental illness (Link

1982, 1987; Link *et al.* 1989). Instead, labeling and stigma were seen as jeopardizing the life circumstances of people with mental illnesses, harming their employment chances, social networks, and self-esteem. As a result of these disadvantages, people who have been labeled as mentally ill are put at greater risk of the prolongation or recurrence of mental illnesses.

Modified labeling theory also provided an explanation for how labeling and stigma might produce these effects: people develop conceptions of mental illness early in life as part of socialization (Angermeyer and Matschinger 1994; Scheff 1966). Once in place, people's conceptions become a lay theory about what it means to have a mental illness. Individuals form expectations as to whether most people will reject an individual with mental illness as a friend, employee, neighbor, or intimate partner, and whether most people will devalue a person with mental illness. If a person develops a serious mental illness, the possibility of devaluation and discrimination becomes personally relevant. If one believes that others will devalue and reject people with mental illnesses, one must now fear that this rejection applies personally. That perception can have negative consequences. Expecting rejection, people who have been hospitalized for mental illnesses may act less confidently and more defensively or avoid potentially threatening contacts altogether.

Evidence suggests that the processes described in modified labeling theory can result in strained interactions with potential stigmatizers (Farina *et al.* 1968), constricted social networks (Link *et al.* 1989; Perlick *et al.* 2001), a compromised quality of life (Rosenfield 1997), low self-esteem (Link *et al.* 2001, 2008; Wright *et al.* 2000), depressive symptoms (Link *et al.* 1997; Perlick *et al.* 2007), unemployment, income loss (Link 1982, 1987), and the discontinuation of treatment (Sirey *et al.* 2001).

Understanding the "package deal"

The evidence cited above indicates that labeling can have negative consequences. At the same time, a voluminous body of research indicates that many psychotherapies and drug therapies can be helpful in treating mental illnesses. Thus, the data do not justify a continued debate concerning whether the effects of labeling are positive or negative. Clearly they are both. Rosenfield (1997) demonstrated this in her examination of the effects of treatment services and stigma in the context of a model program for people with severe mental illnesses. Both the receipt of services and stigma (specifically, perceived devaluation and discrimination) were related—in opposite directions—to living arrangements, family relations, financial situation, safety and health. Similarly, in two longitudinal studies, Link *et al.* (1997, 2008) found evidence that symptoms improved with mental health treatment. However the effects of stigma and discrimination on depressive symptoms and self-esteem endured and were apparently unaffected by such benefits.

Thus, labeling effects are bundled in a "package deal." People seeking mental health treatment confront this deal in one way or another and face real choices and dilemmas as they navigate its parameters. If the balance of the package deal can be changed to one that delivers more benefit and less stigma, more people may choose treatment.

Conceptualizing stigma

The term "stigma" has been used to describe what seem to be quite different concepts, including the "mark" or "label" used as a social designation, the linking of the label to negative stereotypes, and the enactment of exclusion and discrimination. Even Goffman's (1963) famous book includes somewhat different definitions. Additionally, the concept has been criticized for at least two reasons. First, it identifies an "attribute" or "mark" as something residing in the person. The process of selecting and affixing labels has not been taken to be as problematic as it should be. Second, too much emphasis has been placed on cognitive processes of category formation and stereotyping and too little on discrimination and its influence on the distribution of life chances.

In light of this confusion and controversy, Link and Phelan (2001) proposed a conceptualization of stigma that recognized the overlap in meaning between such concepts as stigma, labeling, stereotyping, and discrimination. Their conceptualization defined stigma in the relationship *among* interrelated components. They also addressed criticisms of the concept by attending to the social selection of designations, by incorporating discrimination into the concept, and by focusing on the importance of social, economic, and political power in the production of stigma.

In Link and Phelan's (2001) conceptualization, stigma exists when the following interrelated components converge:

- People distinguish and label human differences. The vast majority of human differences—for example, toe length—are not considered to be socially relevant. However, some differences, such as skin color, are currently awarded a high degree of social salience. Both the selection of salient characteristics and the creation of labels for them are essential components of stigma.
- Dominant cultural beliefs link labeled persons to undesirable characteristics—to negative stereotypes, for example that a person with a mental illness represents a violence risk.
- Labeled persons are placed in distinct categories, accomplishing some degree of separation of "us" from "them." For example, certain ethnic or national groups or people with mental illness may be considered fundamentally different from "us."
- Emotional responses on the part of stigmatizers (anger, irritation, anxiety, pity, or fear) and stigmatized persons (embarrassment, shame, fear, alienation, or anger) are core parts of the stigma process (Link *et al.* 2004).
- When people are labeled, set apart, and linked to undesirable characteristics, a rationale is constructed for devaluing, rejecting, and excluding them. This occurs in several ways, described below.

A unique feature of Link and Phelan's (2001) conceptualization is that stigma is contingent on access to social, economic, and political power. Lower-power groups (psychiatric patients) may label, stereotype, and separate themselves from higher-power groups (psychiatrists). But in these cases, stigma, as Link and Phelan define it, does not exist, because the potentially stigmatizing groups do not have the social, cultural, economic, and political power to imbue their cognitions with serious discriminatory consequences.

Other conceptualizations of stigma are also useful. Jones *et al.* (1984) identify six dimensions of stigma, including concealability, course (how reversible the condition is), disruptiveness (the extent to which a designation leads to strained interactions), aesthetics, origin (how the condition came into being), and peril. Kurzban and Leary (2001) identify three potential evolutionary origins of stigma: the avoidance of poor social exchange partners (e.g., cheats); competition with out-groups; and avoidance of individuals likely to carry communicable pathogens. Phelan *et al.* (2008) identify three functions of stigmatization: exploitation and domination (keeping people down); norms enforcement (keeping people in); and disease avoidance (keeping people away). Readers interested in a mapping of concepts and theories relevant to stigma are referred to Phelan *et al.* (2008) and Pescosolido *et al.* (2008).

Trends in public attitudes relevant to stigma

Some argue that public attitudes and beliefs matter little and that acts of discrimination are much more important. But both modified labeling theory and Link and Phelan's conceptualization of stigma assign critical importance to the ambient attitudes, emotions, and beliefs of dominant groups in relations between a more powerful "us" and a less powerful "them."

The dangerousness stereotype from 1950 to 1996

In 1996, the MacArthur Mental Health Module of the General Social Survey (GSS) repeated a question originally asked of a similarly nationally representative sample in 1950: "When you hear someone say that a person is 'mentally-ill,' what does that mean to you?" Verbatim responses were reliably rated by trained coders with respect to whether the respondent's description referred to indicators of psychosis and whether it referred to violent behavior. The study thereby allowed a rare glimpse at trends in one key stereotype associated with mental illness. Remarkably, the analysis revealed that, despite massive efforts to educate the public about mental illness and enormous advances in treatment, respondents whose descriptions indicated a person with psychosis were more than twice as likely to mention violent behavior in 1996 (31.0%) as in 1950 (12.7%) (Phelan *et al.* 2000).

Trends in causal attributions, stereotypes, and social distancing responses, 1996–2006

In the interest of monitoring trends in public attitudes and beliefs, the 1996 GSS module was replicated in 2006, using identical vignettes describing individuals with major depression, schizophrenia, alcohol dependence, and a person with mild worries but no diagnosable disorder. Respondents were randomly assigned one of these vignettes and asked a variety of questions about the problem. In keeping with a strong push to educate the public that mental illnesses were just like other illnesses, the 2006 respondents were more likely to attribute the conditions to biological and genetic factors and to recommend medical and psychiatric treatment for the described cases. However, there was no evidence whatsoever that stereotypes of violence and incompetence, or willingness to interact with people with mental illnesses, had changed for the better over the ten-year period. This evidence challenges the idea that stigma will dissipate when the public adopts more medical views of mental illnesses (Pescosolido *et al.* 2008).

How labeling and stigma affect the lives of people with mental illnesses

People who have been hospitalized for mental illnesses fare worse on a wide variety of life chances, such as income, education, psychological well-being, housing status, medical treatment, and health (Druss *et al.* 2000; Link 1987). How does this happen? While part of the difference may be due to the directly debilitating consequences (given existing social circumstances) of the illness, stigma is involved in several ways.

Status loss

One consequence of negative labeling is a downward movement in status. One strand of sociological research on social hierarchies, the so-called expectation-states tradition, is particularly relevant to the study of stigma and status loss (Berger *et al.* 1977). This research shows that external statuses, like race and gender, shape status hierarchies within small groups of unacquainted persons even though the external status has no bearing on proficiency at a task the group is asked to perform. Men and whites are more likely than women and blacks to gain influence and attain positions of power and prestige. This research implies that status loss has immediate consequences for a person's power and influence, and thus their ability to achieve desired goals.

Discrimination

We conceptualize four mechanisms of discrimination as part of the stigma process: individual discrimination, discrimination operating through the stigmatized individual, interactional discrimination, and structural discrimination.

Individual discrimination

The term "discrimination" usually brings to mind the classic model in which Person A discriminates against Person B based on Person A's prejudicial attitudes connected to a label applied to Person B (Allport 1954). This is exemplified in Page's (1977) experimental study in which landlords who were informed that a potential tenant had a history of psychiatric hospitalization were much more likely to deny that an advertised apartment was available than when there was no mention of psychiatric hospitalization. This straightforward process doubtless occurs with considerable regularity, although it may often be hidden from the discriminated-against person; one rarely learns why one is turned down for a job, an apartment, or a date. Most discrimination, however, may be manifested subtly and occur without full awareness. For example, Druss *et al.* (2000) showed that people with schizophrenia were less likely to receive optimal treatment for heart disease even after controlling for the nature of the condition and availability of services. This is an instance of individual discrimination, as it results from the behavior of individual physicians making treatment decisions. Yet it is unlikely that the physicians are aware of their discriminatory behavior or the reasons for it.

Discrimination operating through the stigmatized individual

Another form of discrimination that is subtle in its manifestation and insidious in its consequences operates within stigmatized individuals themselves. As explicated above, modified labeling theory (Link *et al.* 1989, 1997; Link 1982, 1987) proposes that all people are exposed to common, ambient stereotypes about mental illness as part of socialization that become personally relevant if a person develops a mental illness. "Internalized stigma" consists of the devaluation, shame, secrecy, and withdrawal triggered by negative stereotypes one believes that others harbor (Corrigan 1998) and is central to understanding the psychological harm caused by stigma.

Interactional discrimination

A third type of discrimination emerges in social interaction. This form of discrimination is illustrated by an experimental study conducted by Sibicky and Dovidio (1986). Introductory psychology students were randomly assigned in mixed-sex pairs to one of two conditions. In one condition, a "perceiver" was told that a "target" (random assignment here as well) was recruited from the campus psychotherapy clinic. In the other condition, the perceiver was told that the target was recruited from a psychology class. In fact, the target was always recruited from the class. Both members of the pair completed a brief inventory of hobbies and activities. Then the experimenter exchanged the inventories and provided the perceiver with the labeling information (student or therapy client). Subsequently, the two engaged in a tape-recorded interaction that was later evaluated by raters blind to the experimental conditions. Even before meeting them, perceivers rated the therapy targets less favorably than the student targets. Moreover, the ratings of the blind judges revealed that, in interactions with therapy targets, perceivers were less open, secure, sensitive, and sincere. Finally, the results showed that the behavior of the therapy-label targets was adversely affected as well, even though they had no knowledge that they had been labeled. Thus, expectations associated with psychological therapy color subsequent interactions, actually calling out behaviors that confirm those expectations.

Structural discrimination

Structural discrimination occurs when laws or other institutional practices disadvantage stigmatized groups (Link and Phelan 2001). Examples are policies that provide less insurance coverage for psychiatric illnesses than for physical ones (Schulze and Angermeyer 2003) or laws restricting the civil rights, such as voting rights, of people with mental illnesses (Corrigan *et al.* 2004). Structural discrimination need not involve intentional discrimination by individuals in the immediate context (Corrigan *et al.* 2004); it can result from a practice or policy that is the residue of past intentional discrimination. For example, a history of not-in-my-backyard (NIMBY) reactions influences the location of board-and-care homes so that they are situated in areas high in crime, pollution, and infectious disease. This results in the exposure of people with serious mental illness to these noxious circumstances. Again, although the unequal outcomes resulting from structural discrimination may be readily apparent, the fact that these outcomes represent discrimination is obvious only upon reflection and analysis.

Summary

The strong positions taken in the labeling debate of the 1960s and 1970s brought into focus key issues that mental health sociologists have subsequently pursued. Growing evidence supporting modified labeling theory offered a potential resolution of the debate. Both positions were partially correct: labeling induced both positive and negative consequences in a "package deal." On average, treatments and services brought benefits, whereas stigma and the discrimination it entails produced harm. As evidence from modified labeling theory and other approaches within mental health sociology evolved, a parallel explosion of interest in stigma emerged in the social science literature more generally. With this growth came confusion about the stigma concept and questions about its utility. In response, Link and Phelan (2001) defined stigma as a phenomenon dependent on power that inheres in the confluence of labeling, stereotyping, setting apart, status loss, and discrimination.

Both modified labeling theory and Link and Phelan's conceptualization of stigma point to the importance of attitudes and beliefs, leading to questions about trends in such attitudes and beliefs over time. Here, research shows that the public increasingly holds a medicalized view of mental illnesses but that negative stereotypes and social distancing responses have changed little or have even strengthened over the years.

Finally, discrimination against people with mental illnesses occurs through multiple mechanisms, including direct person-to-person discrimination, discrimination operating through the stigmatized person, discrimination that emerges silently but perniciously through social interaction, and structural stigma.

References

Allport, G.W. (1954) *The Nature of Prejudice*, Garden City, NY: Doubleday.

Angermeyer, M.C. and Matschinger, H. (1994) Lay beliefs about schizophrenic disorder: The results of a population survey in Germany, *Acta Psychiatrica Scandinavica* 89: 39–45.

Berger, J., Fisek, M.H., Norman, R.Z. and Zelditch, M. Jr. (1977) *Status characteristics and social interaction*, New York: Elsevier.

Corrigan, P.W. (1998) The impact of stigma on severe mental illness, *Cognitive and Behavioral Practice* 5: 201–222.

Corrigan, P.W., Markowitz, F.E., and Watson, A.C. (2004) Structural levels of mental illness stigma and discrimination, *Schizophrenia Bulletin* 30: 481–491.

Druss, B.G., Marcus, S.C., Rosenheck, R.A., Olfson, M., Tanielian, T., and Pincus, H.A. (2000) Understanding disability in mental and general medical conditions, *American Journal of Psychiatry* 157: 485–491.

Farina A., Allen, J.G., and Saul, B. (1968) The role of the stigmatized in affecting social relationships, *Journal of Personality* 36: 169–182.

Goffman, E. (1963) *Stigma: Notes on the Management of Spoiled Identity*, New York: Simon & Schuster.

Gove, W.R. (1975) *The Labeling of Deviance: Evaluating a Perspective*, New York: Sage.

Jones, E., Farina, A., Hastorf, A., Markus, H., Miller, D.T., and Scott, R. (1984) *Social Stigma: The Psychology of Marked Relationships*, New York: Freeman.

Kurzban, R. and Leary, M.R. (2001) Evolutionary origins of stigmatization: The functions of social exclusion, *Psychological Bulletin* 127: 187–208.

Link, B.G. (1982) Mental patient status, work, and income: An examination of the effects of a psychiatric label, *American Sociological Review* 47: 202–215.

Link, B.G. (1987) Understanding labeling effects in the area of mental disorders: An assessment of the effects of expectations of rejection, *American Sociological Review* 52: 96–112.

Link, B.G., Castille, D., and Stuber, J. (2008) Stigma and coercion in the context of outpatient treatment for people with mental illnesses, *Social Science and Medicine* 67: 409–419.

Link, B.G., Cullen, F.T., Struening, E., Shrout, P., and Dohrenwend, B.P. (1989) A modified labeling theory approach in the area of the mental disorders: An empirical assessment, *American Sociological Review* 54: 400–423.

Link, B.G. and Phelan, J.C. (2001) Conceptualizing stigma, *Annual Review of Sociology* 27: 363–385.

Link, B.G., Struening, E.L., Neese-Todd, S., Asmussen, S., and Phelan, J.C. (2001) Stigma as a barrier to recovery: The consequences of stigma for the self-esteem of people with mental illnesses, *Psychiatric Services* 52: 1621–1626.

Link, B.G., Struening, E.L., Rahav, M., Phelan, J.C., and Nuttbrock, L. (1997) On stigma and its consequences: Evidence from a longitudinal study of men with dual diagnoses of mental illness and substance abuse, *Journal of Health & Social Behavior* 38: 177–190.

Link, B.G., Yang, L.H., Phelan, J.C., and Collins, P.Y. (2004) Measuring mental illness stigma, *Schizophrenia Bulletin* 30: 11–42.

Page, S. (1977) Effects of the mental illness label in attempts to obtain accommodation, *Canadian Journal of Behavioral Science* 9: 85–90.

Perlick, D.A, Miklowitz, D.J., Link, B.G., *et al.* (2007) Perceived stigma and depression among caregivers of patients with bipolar disorder, *British Journal of Psychiatry* 190: 535–536.

Perlick, D.A., Rosenheck, R.A., Clarkin, J.F., *et al.* (2001) Stigma as a barrier to recovery: Adverse effects of perceived stigma on social adaptation of persons diagnosed with bipolar affective disorder, *Psychiatric Services* 52: 1627–1632.

Pescosolido, B.A., Martin, J.K., Lang, A., and Olafsdottir, S. (2008) Rethinking theoretical approaches to stigma: A framework integrating normative influences on stigma, *Social Science & Medicine* 67: 431–440.

Phelan, J.C., Link, B.G., and Dovidio, J.F. (2008) Stigma and discrimination: One animal or two?, *Social Science and Medicine* 67: 358–367.

Phelan, J.C., Link, B.G., Stueve, A., and Pescosolido, B.A. (2000) Public conceptions of mental illness in 1950 and 1996: What is mental illness and is it to be feared?, *Journal of Health and Social Behavior* 41: 188–207.

Rosenfield, S. (1997) Labeling mental illness: The effects of received services and perceived stigma on life satisfaction, *American Sociological Review* 62: 660–672.

Scheff, T.J. (1966; reprinted 1984) *Being Mentally Ill: A Sociological Theory*, Chicago, IL: Aldine.

Schulze, B. and Angermeyer, M.C. (2003) Subjective experiences of stigma: A focus group study of schizophrenic patients, their relatives and mental health professionals, *Social Science & Medicine* 56: 299–312.

Sibicky, M. and Dovidio, J.F. (1986) Stigma of psychological therapy: Stereotypes, interpersonal reactions, and the self-fulfilling prophecy, *Journal of Consulting and Clinical Psychology* 33: 148–154.

Sirey, J., Bruce, M.L., Alexopoulos, G.S., *et al.* (2001) Perceived stigma as a predictor of treatment discontinuation in young and older outpatients with depression, *American Journal of Psychiatry* 158: 479–481.

Wright, E.R., Gonfrein, W.F.I., and Owens, T.J. (2000) Deinstitutionalization, social rejection, and the self-esteem of former mental patients, *Journal of Health and Social Behavior* 41: 68–90.

Part XIV
Exiting deviance

Overview

Some people become deviants, live their careers as deviants, and die as deviants. Most people who become deviant, at some point in their lives, however, escape or exit deviance. Individuals sometimes become "deviants" at very young ages. Children may engage in vandalism, such as throwing rocks at streetlights or at the windows of neighborhood homes. Other acts of deviance may be of more serious import, such as cruelty to animals or setting fires. Teenagers may sometimes become involved in "real" crime (economic or physical), such as shoplifting, burglary, serious vandalism, assaults, automobile theft, grand larceny, using narcotics, or even sexual escapades with underage females (thus, statutory rape). College students often get involved in deviant behavior. This is conceptualized simply as "college hijinks."

The perpetrators of such deviant acts almost always "outgrow" it, or "grow up," and turn to more conventional behavior as they pursue their occupational goals and careers, marry, and start a family. This type of behavior is seldom repeated later in life. "Maturing," "growing up," and "outgrowing" are major venues in exiting deviance.

A particular context may facilitate or precipitate deviant behavior. Soldiers sometimes commit unspeakable acts and engage in grand larceny on a grand scale in wartime but are not inclined to behave in the same way when they become postwar civilians. Individuals may give up or drift away from deviance because of boredom or lack of sufficient gratification, or because it is no longer "appropriate" behavior for a particular age and social status. Some narcotic addicts may elect to go into a rehabilitation program, or may simply go "cold turkey."

The process of exiting deviance can be bifurcated into two separate modes: *coerced and imposed* and *cessation and desistance*.

Coerced and imposed

If an individual commits a crime, he or she may be sentenced to jail or prison. Once incarcerated, the individual is no longer able to commit a crime or engage in deviant behavior (although, admittedly, narcotics may be smuggled into prisons to be used by inmates). Arguably, incarceration translates into incapacitation to engage in deviance. As James Quinn points out in his chapter, however, "Community-based corrections (i.e., probation and parole) are preferable to prisons and jails for most non-violent offenders. They are far cheaper than incarceration and reformative services are more available in the community than in penal institutions."

Recidivism rates after incarceration are quite high, strongly suggesting that it is ineffective at motivating change. Accordingly, community-based corrections have become the major venues for exiting deviance.

Quinn surveys and describes various modes of community control of deviants. Probation and parole are the most traditional mechanisms of community control and have proved to be relatively effective. ISP (intensive supervision probation/patrol) may be employed in the case of high-risk offenders. Quinn indicates that electronic monitoring of home confinement may be used in the cases of violent criminals, recidivist sex offenders, and high-flight-risk offenders. Other examples of community control mechanisms include: halfway houses and work release centers that "bridge the gap between institutional regimentation and normal life"; therapeutic communities or long-term residential facilities that employ a combination of self-help, counseling, and education in a structured setting with a supportive group of people with a common problem; boot camps; reporting centers; ignition interlock systems, which require passing a breath test before the car can be started; drug testing protocols; and drug and other specialized courts.

Quinn concludes that, "while incapacitation may contribute to public safety, it is unlikely to be successful in the long term unless combined with appropriate treatment."

Cessation and desistance

In many instances, individuals voluntarily leave a lifestyle of deviance for a variety of reasons and motivations. In his chapter, Stephen Farrall provides an overview of the transitions away from deviance on a volitional basis. He articulates a number of factors that impact the decision to desist. Among the external considerations for exiting deviance are marriage (or partnership), parenthood, engagement in the economy (employment or voluntary work), and moving away from where one grew up and therefore away from old (deviant) friends and acquaintances. After incarceration, some individuals may simply be "burnt out" and have no further interest in deviance.

Farrall also addresses some internal processes in the decision to abandon a sustained deviant career. These revolve around an "ongoing search for a meaningful identity on the part of individuals." In effect, some deviants seek to construct more positive images of self, more promising futures, and better lives. Farrall points out that these aspirations sometimes occur after an "epiphany—a moment or a point in time when clarity is observed for the first time or a sudden realization is made by an individual."

He also posits that deviants may seek a new sense of civic identity, active citizenship, and aspire to "make some important contributions to their communities." If deviants achieve some degree of upward mobility, they tend to assimilate the values of the stratum into which they move, providing motivation for exiting deviance. Finally, Farrall explores variations in exiting deviance by ethnicity.

69

Exiting deviance

Coerced and imposed

James Quinn

Society's ability to coerce an end to a deviant lifestyle is hotly debated. A shift to conventional behavior may result from many factors, some of which (e.g., brain maturity) are hard to measure. Deviance can legally be punished only where it overlaps with crime. The criminal justice system routinely uses incapacitation, deterrence, and treatment to force an end to criminality while striving to assure retribution to appease victims and the public. The type of offense, offender's background, and sentencing judge's beliefs determine how these goals translate into specific methods of inhibiting illicit behavior. Law presumes that incarceration is sufficient to motivate change, but recidivism statistics call this assumption into question. While some prisons and jails offer treatment programs, most efforts at reform are guided by probation and parole officers (PPOs).

Community control of offenders

Community corrections (i.e., probation and parole) are preferable to prisons and jails for most non-violent offenders. They are far cheaper than incarceration, and reformative services are more available in the community than in penal institutions. Probation/parole also allows offenders to pay fines and fees while avoiding the criminogenic influence of prison and supporting themselves (Clear 2008; Tonry and Petersilia 1999). Allowing non-dangerous offenders to avoid prison also assures institutional space for those who pose a clear threat to others (Gendreau *et al.* 2000).

Alternative sentences emerged in response to overcrowded prisons, loss of faith in treatment, and fear of crime. They are designed to cut costs and appeal to "get tough" sentiments by creating a graduated continuum of severity between traditional probation and prison (Merlo and Benekos 2000; Petersilia 1999). These sentences emphasize retribution, incapacitation, restitution, and deterrence as they strive to reform offenders and are more disliked than imprisonment by most offenders (Williams *et al.* 2008). These efforts to coerce an end of criminality may divert offenders from legal processing prior to trial, be part of a probated sentence, or an aspect of post-imprisonment parole supervision. In each case, the goal is to force compliance with the law and restrictions imposed by a judge or parole board.

When alternative sanctions are applied to offenders who would not otherwise be incarcerated, they merely inflate correctional costs and threaten civil rights. Use with low-risk offenders is nonetheless attractive to judges and agencies who fear the negative publicity of a single major crime by an offender under supervision. Despite public distrust, probation and parole are more likely to discourage long-term criminality than institutional confinement (Serin *et al.* 2009; Schlager and Robbins 2008).

Intensive supervision probation/parole

There is considerable variation in the degree to which offenders are supervised by PPOs. Intensive supervision probation/parole (ISP) doubles or quadruples the supervision received by regular clients. It is used with offenders felt to pose a high risk to the public and/or those at high risk of recidivism. ISP clients may sometimes transfer to normal supervision if they obey all laws and release conditions for a sufficient period of time. Unemployment and alcohol/drug abuse are the main predictors of recidivism among these clients. ISP may increase the rate of incarceration by facilitating the discovery of technical violations of release but may reduce long-term recidivism if designed to encourage intense involvement in a prosocial community and therapeutic activities (MacKenzie and Brame 2001).

Electronic monitoring of home confinement

Home confinement gained popularity in the US in the late 1980s, when monitoring devices and global positioning systems made it an enforceable extension of ISP. Typically, a transmitter is attached to the offender's ankle, and this relays information to a central office via the offender's phone. Hand-held ("drive-by") devices allow a PPO to determine if an offender is at home or work from up to a quarter-mile away using similar ankle bracelets. Although expensive, GPS monitors can track an offender's every move throughout the day. All activities outside the home must be scheduled and approved in advance. Offenders may leave home only to work, attend treatment sessions, and secure basic necessities.

Monitoring was designed for non-serious offenders who required more structure in their lives than afforded by traditional probation/parole, but it is most commonly used with violent criminals, recidivists, and sex offenders. PPOs trained in handling the monitoring equipment often lack training in dealing with such offenders, while PPOs trained to supervise these groups are often unfamiliar with the monitoring equipment (Demichele *et al.* 2008). There are "no replicated, well-designed studies showing that monitoring alone reduces recidivism after monitoring is terminated" (Burrell and Gable 2008: 101).

Halfway houses and work-release centers

Work-release centers are secure facilities associated with a jail or minimum security prison that confine offenders when they are not at their jobs in the community. Halfway houses are for people recently released from prison or other facilities and use rules rather than locks to control residents. Both bridge the gap between institutional regimentation and normal life. Halfway houses are crucial for prison releasees with no place to live while they search for jobs and housing, but few offer more than cursory supervision, shelter, a phone, and sometimes meals. They appear to reduce recidivism by about 6% in the first year after release but their long-term effects are unclear (Ohio Department of Rehabilitation and Correction 2003; Twill *et al.* 1998). Correctional authorities have very mixed opinions about these centers. Almost one in three agency directors feel the cost is not compensated by decreased recidivism. Prison administrators, however, support them because they reduce overcrowding, relieve tension, and keep inmates busy (National Institute of Justice 1995).

Therapeutic communities

Therapeutic communities (TCs) are long-term residential facilities for people with a common problem, such as substance abuse or mental illness. They assume that criminal behavior is socially learned and can be undone through similar processes. The specifics of treatment vary, but most use an intense mixture of counseling, self-help, and education in a supportive, structured setting that insulates clients from negative influences. Use of TCs in the community declined after 1985 but their use in prisons accelerated after 2000 because they are more effective than mere incarceration in reducing recidivism (Burdon et al. 2002). TCs are more expensive than other alternative sentences or imprisonment, and attempts to cut costs often threaten the value of treatment by reducing its length, quality, and intensity. The lack of aftercare services for TC graduates remains a serious problem, especially when the TC is located within a prison (Sullivan et al. 2007).

Split sentences

Split sentences consist of between two and twenty-five weeks of imprisonment followed by a much longer period of probationary supervision. Offenders must earn their way out of prison and then off ISP through continued good behavior. Community supervision may be handled by probation or parole authorities, depending on the state's procedural code. Early studies suggested that split sentences might reduce the reincarceration rate of probationers/parolees (Klein 1988), but more recent and comprehensive analyses have found that they serve no purpose, beyond retribution. Despite their costliness, they remain popular with some courts (Gottfredson 1999; MacKenzie and Brame 2001).

Boot camps

Correctional boot camps hold offenders for three to six months of rigorous discipline and labor. These residential facilities were designed to reduce prison costs and overcrowding by helping young, non-violent offenders with few prior arrests avoid prison and acquire self-discipline. The camps' tough, punitive image has great popular appeal, but their effects on recidivism differ little from imprisonment, despite their greater cost. Harsh drill instructors may even increase recidivism, but camps that emphasize treatment and aftercare, accept small numbers of inmates, and demand intensive interaction with staff members appear to be effective. The quality of treatment and staff is the most critical determinant of lowered recidivism (Parent 2003).

Day reporting centers

Day reporting centers (DRCs) hold unemployed offenders during weekday working hours. They discourage criminal contacts, prevent unemployed offenders from enjoying leisure, and can facilitate better use of community services. Attendance is closely monitored and absences are permitted only for job interviews and medical appointments. Economies of scale can be achieved by concentrating offenders in one location during business hours: PPOs can visit to conduct drug tests and gather information, and treatment providers can serve large numbers of offenders. DRC programs that focus on drug treatment, education, and employment encourage cessation of crime but most DRCs are merely incapacitative. Research shows that lengthy DRC participation can reduce recidivism if combined with intensive drug treatment, educational services, and strict weekend and evening surveillance (Craddock 2000; Kim *et al.* 2007).

Ignition interlock systems

An ignition interlock system is fitted to the starter mechanism of a drunken driver's car and requires a breath test prior to starting the vehicle. If alcohol is detected, the car will not start. Early versions of this technology were sometimes evaded with mechanical skills or simply by a sober person blowing into the device before switching places with the offender. Modern interlock systems prevent such evasions and force drivers to stop at random times to be retested. Offenders pay at least $750 for the unit's installation and about $100 a month thereafter. They also must visit service centers regularly to have the equipment checked. While effective in preventing offenders from driving while drunk, these units cannot detect drug use and they have no impact on recidivism once the device is removed. Victims' groups argue that the devices allow drunk drivers to evade punishment. Offenders see them as significant financial burdens (Robertson *et al.* 2001).

Drug testing

Drug testing, generally by urine analysis, is used by treatment facilities, correctional agencies, government agencies, and most large businesses. It is useful in identifying relapses that often lead to crime in persons under community supervision (Harrell and Kleiman 2002) and deters use among addicts in treatment (DeFulio *et al.* 2009). It also appears to reduce use among workers, although the strength of its workplace impact is arguable (Carpenter 2007). Workplace testing is more likely to identify marijuana use than use of other drugs and raises constitutional privacy issues (White 2003). More important, testing rarely checks for alcohol use, which is more closely related to workplace safety than is drug abuse. It also appears that both drug use and productivity are better predicted by the culture of the workplace than by drug testing (Bennett and Lehman 2003).

Drug and other specialized courts

Drug courts are the vanguard of an emerging array of specialized tribunals for offenders with specific problems that motivate their criminality, such as addiction or mental illness, as well as those charged with such crimes as DUI or domestic violence. Participants are required to appear for weekly or monthly case reviews in which the judge may threaten sanctions for continued deviance or reward compliance. Drug courts impose more varied sanctions for a wider range of behaviors than do traditional courts. More important, these sanctions are designed to complement the treatment needs of the individual rather than offer an equitable response to defendant behavior (Lindquist *et al.* 2006).

These courts have small caseloads, enabling the judge and staff to know each participant. Most have the power to impose jail terms to punish violations and all can terminate non-compliant participants, which usually leads to incarceration. Their primary focus, however, is to impose and monitor treatment along with vocational, educational, and other goals that will encourage a cessation of offending. The use of punishment does not appear to predict their success in reducing recidivism (Hepburn and Harvey 2007), but a high number of court appearances does predict longer treatment and a reduction in drug use and crime (Gottfredson *et al.* 2007).

Other types of specialized courts are newer and less well studied, but they appear to have similar effects on the defendants with whom they work.

Sex offenders

Control of sex offenders is a great challenge for modern corrections. Their recidivism rates vary across psychological categories that are difficult to correlate with legal charges. Contrary to popular belief, many sex offenders respond well to psychotherapy (Levenson *et al.* 2007). Convicted sex offenders must register with the state in which they live and these data are at least partially accessible to the public. Registered sex offenders (RSOs) are subject to residential restrictions and some jurisdictions notify residents when an RSO moves into the area. These restrictions are the product of "memorial laws" passed in response to infamous crimes. The statutes make no distinction between high- and low-risk offenders (Levenson 2008). Public registries and notification laws undermine RSOs' employment and family stability (Levenson and Tewksbury 2009), which retards reintegration efforts (Robbers 2009). Although RSO recidivism is not associated with residence (Meloy *et al.* 2008), residential restrictions are growing in number and severity. This creates clusters of RSO residences in disadvantaged areas, which may contribute to recidivism and decrease access to treatment services (Levenson 2008).

Castration of sex offenders deemed especially dangerous has also been used, largely on a supposedly voluntary basis to shorten confinement, especially indefinite civil commitment, which can be imposed by a court following a prison term. Drugs that temporarily reduce androgen levels theoretically render offenders impotent while reducing their aggressiveness and sex drive. Historical (Aucoin and Wassersug 2006) and clinical sources (Greenfield 2006) note that neither impotence nor diminished desire is assured with any form of castration. While many studies have found significantly lower recidivism among castrated RSOs (Kafka 2003), their methodological soundness is debated (Weinberger *et al.* 2005).

These laws have intuitive appeal, but disregard what is known about the antecedents of sexual offending and the process of successfully treating offenders (Berlin 2005). Neither residential restrictions nor castration assures an end to offending, and psychotherapy remains the paramount method of reducing sex offender recidivism (Greenfield 2006; Berlin 2005).

Conclusion: justice, public safety, and efficacy in altering offender behavior

The efficacy of efforts to force an exit from deviance varies across programs and people. The current data indicate that incapacitation may contribute to public safety, but it is unlikely to change behavior in the long term unless combined with appropriate treatment. This is especially true for alcohol and drug abusers who comprise a huge proportion of offenders. Less than a third of the prison inmates who need drug treatment actually receive it, and the type of treatment is determined mainly by administrative, rather than clinical, concerns (Office of National Drug Control Policy 2001). The punitive regimentation of the total institution reduces the efficacy of treatment and concentrates populations that live by norms of force and manipulation (De Leon and Wexler 2009; Tonry and Petersilia 1999). Thus, retributive incarceration serves society's desire for justice but reinforces offenders' estrangement from conventional norms. These goals must be balanced for each criminal case's disposition and policy must take into account the limits of coercion in shaping the behavior of deviants. Various means of coercing the cessation of deviance appear to provide only a hiatus in criminality in which treatment can be inserted to encourage the choice of more conforming behavioral choices. Coercion alone, however, seems incapable of assuring an end to offensive behavior in the community.

References

Aucoin, M. W. and Wassersug, R. J. (2006). "The sexuality and social performance of androgen-deprived (castrated) men throughout history," *Social Science & Medicine*, 63(12): 3162–3173.

Bennett, J. B. and Lehman, W. E. K. (2003). *Preventing Workplace Substance Abuse: Beyond Drug Testing to Wellness*, Washington, DC: American Psychological Association.

Berlin, F. S. (2005). "Commentary: The impact of surgical castration on sexual recidivism risk among civilly committed sexual offenders," *Journal of the American Academy of Psychiatry and the Law*, 33(1): 37–41.

Burdon, W., Farabee, D., Prendergast, M., Messina, N., and Cartier, J. (2002). *Prison-Based Therapeutic Community Substance Abuse Programs*, Rockville, MD: National Institute of Justice.

Burrell, W. D. and Gable, R. S. (2008). "From B. F. Skinner to Spiderman to Martha Stewart: The past, present and future of electronic monitoring of offenders," *Journal of Offender Rehabilitation*, 46(3–4): 101–118.

Carpenter C. S. (2007). "Workplace drug testing and worker drug use," *Health Services Research*, 42(2): 795–811.

Clear, T. R. (2008). "The effects of high imprisonment rates on communities," *Crime and Justice*, 37: 97–132.

Craddock, A. (2000). *Exploratory Analysis of Client Outcomes, Costs, and Benefits of Day Reporting Centers: Final Report*, Rockville, MD: National Institute of Justice.

DeFulio, A., Donlin, W. D., Wong, C. J., and Silverman, K. (2009). "Employment-based abstinence reinforcement as a maintenance intervention for the treatment of cocaine dependence," *Addiction*, 104(9): 1530.

De Leon, G. and Wexler, H. (2009). "The therapeutic community for addictions: An evolving knowledge base," *Journal of Drug Issues*, 39(1): 167–178.

Demichele, M., Payne, B. K., and Button, D. M. (2008). "Electronic monitoring of sex offenders: Identifying unanticipated consequences and implications," *Journal of Offender Rehabilitation*, 46(3–4): 119–135.

Gendreau, P., Goggin, C., Cullen, F., and Andrews, D. (2000). "Effects of community sanctions and incarceration on recidivism," *Forum on Corrections Research* 12(2): 10–13.

Glaz, L. and Bonczar, T. B. (2008). *Probation and Parole in the United States, 2007*, Washington, DC: Office of Justice Programs, US Department of Justice.

Gottfredson, D. C., Kearley, B. W., Najaka, S. S., and Rocha, C. M. (2007). "How drug treatment courts work: An analysis of mediators," *Journal of Research in Crime and Delinquency*, 44(1): 3–35.

Gottfredson, D. M. (1999). *Effects of Judges' Sentencing Decisions on Criminal Careers*, Rockville, MD: National Institute of Justice.

Greenfield, D. P. (2006). "Organic approaches to the treatment of paraphilics and sex offenders," *Journal of Psychiatry & Law*, 34(4): 437–454.

Harrell, A. and Kleiman, M. (2002). "Drug testing in criminal justice settings," in C. G. Leukefeld, F. Tims and D. Farabee (eds.) *Treatment of Drug Offenders*, pp. 149–171, New York: Springer.

Hepburn, J. R. and Harvey, A. N. (2007). "The effect of the threat of legal sanction on program retention and completion," *Crime & Delinquency*, 53(2): 255–280.

Hughes, L. A. and Kadleck, C. (2008). "Sex offender community notification and community stratification," *Justice Quarterly*, 25(3): 469–495.

Kafka, M. P. (2003). "Offending and sexual appetite," *International Journal of Offender Therapy and Comparative Criminology*, 47: 439–451.

Kim, D. Y., Spohn, C., and Foxall, M. (2007). "An evaluation of the DRC in the context of Douglas County, Nebraska," *Prison Journal*, 87(4): 434–456.

Klein A. R. (1988). *Alternative Sentencing: A Practitioners Guide*, Cincinnati: Anderson.

Levenson, J. S. (2008). "Collateral consequences of sex offender residence restrictions," *Criminal Justice Studies*, 21(2): 153–166.

Levenson, J. S., Brannon, Y. N., Fortney, T., and Baker, J. (2007). "Public perceptions about sex offenders and community protection policies," *Analyses of Social Issues and Public Policy*, 7(1): 137–161.

Levenson, J. and Tewksbury, R. (2009). "Collateral damage: Family members of registered sex offenders," *American Journal of Criminal Justice*, 34(1–2): 54–68.

Lindquist, C. H., Krebs, C. P., and Lattimore, P. K. (2006). "Sanctions and rewards in drug court programs," *Journal of Drug Issues*, 36(1): 119–146.

MacKenzie, D. L. and Brame, R. (1995). "Shock incarceration and positive adjustment during community supervision," *Journal of Quantitative Criminology*, 11(2): 111–142.

MacKenzie, D. L., and Brame, R. (2001). "Community supervision, prosocial activities and recidivism," *Justice Quarterly*, 18(2): 429–448.

Mauer, M. (2009). *The Changing Racial Dynamics of the War on Drugs*, Washington, DC: Sentencing Project.

Meloy, M. L., Miller, S. L., and Curtis, K. M. (2008). "Making sense out of nonsense: The deconstruction of state-level sex offender residence restrictions," *American Journal of Criminal Justice*, 33(2): 209–222.

Merlo, A. V. and Benekos, P. J. (2000). "Adapting conservative correctional policies to the economic realities of the 1990s," in B. W. Hancock and P. Sharp (eds.) *Public Policy, Crime, and Criminal Justice*, 2nd edn, Upper Saddle River, NJ: Prentice-Hall.

National Institute of Justice. (1995). *NIJ Survey of Probation and Parole Agency Directors*, Washington, DC: US Department of Justice.

Office of National Drug Control Policy. (2001). *Drug Treatment in the Criminal Justice System*, Rockville, MD: Drug Policy Information Clearinghouse.

Ohio Department of Rehabilitation and Correction. (2003). *Annual Report Fiscal Year 2003: Halfway Houses*, Columbus, OH: Ohio Department of Rehabilitation and Correction.

Parent, D. G. (2003). *Correctional Boot Camps: Lessons from a Decade of Research*, Rockville, MD: National Institute of Justice.

Petersilia, J. (1999). "Decade of intermediate sanctions: What have we learned?," *Justice Research and Policy*, 1(1): 9–23.

Robbers, M. L. P. (2009). "Lifers on the outside: Sex offenders and disintegrative shaming," *International Journal of Offender Therapy and Comparative Criminology*, 53(1): 5–28.

Robertson, R., Vanlaar, W., and Simpson, H. (2001). *Between the Lines: About Alcohol Ignition Interlocks*, Alexandria VA: National Traffic Law Center.

Schlager, M. D. and Robbins, K. (2008). "Does parole work? Revisited: Reframing the discussion of the impact of postprison supervision on offender outcome," *Prison Journal*, 88(2): 234–251.

Serin, R. C., Gobeil, R., and Preston, D. L. (2009). "Evaluation of the persistently violent offender treatment program," *International Journal of Offender Therapy and Comparative Criminology*, 53(1): 57–73.

Sullivan, C. J., McKendrick, K., Sacks, S., and Banks, S. (2007). "Modified therapeutic community treatment for offenders with MICA disorders," *American Journal of Drug and Alcohol Abuse*, 33(6): 823–832.

Tonry, M. and Petersilia, J. (1999). "Prisons research at the beginning of the 21st century," *Crime and Justice*, 26: 1–14.

Twill, S. E., Nackerud, L., Risler E. R., and Taylor, D. (1998). "Changes in measured loneliness, control and social support among parolees in a halfway house," *Journal of Offender Rehabilitation*, 27(3–4): 77–92.

Warner, T. D. and Kramer, J. H. (2009). "Closing the revolving door? Substance abuse treatment as an alternative to traditional sentencing for drug-dependent offenders," *Criminal Justice and Behavior*, 36(1): 89–109.

Weinberger, L. E., Sreenivasan, S., Garrick, T., and Osran, H.(2005). "The impact of surgical castration on sexual recidivism risk among sexually violent predatory offenders," *Journal of the American Academy of Psychiatry and the Law*, 33(1): 16–36.

White, T. (2003). "Drug testing at work: Issues and perspectives," *Substance Use & Misuse*, 38(11–13): 1891–1902.

Williams, A., May, D. C., and Wood, P. B. (2008). "The lesser of two evils? A qualitative study of offenders' preferences for prison compared to alternatives," *Journal of Offender Rehabilitation*, 46(3–4): 71–90.

70

Exiting deviance

Cessation and desistance

Stephen Farrall

This short essay will provide an overview of the main features of the literature surrounding the study of transitions away from deviancy. Although deviancy is taken to mean any form of non-standard behaviour, inevitably most of the material on exiting from deviant careers relates to the later stages of criminal careers. Although there is much literature on, for example, divorcees or retired people, since these are common features of human existence in most industrialised and post-industrialised societies, these do not fall within our definition of deviancy. This essay will provide an overview of the main processes associated with exiting from criminally deviant roles and behaviours, drawing on wider literature as it resonates with pertinent issues in these.

Interest in role exits and transformations of path trajectories has long been a feature of sociology. However, a number of key studies marked increases in interest in this aspect of social life. While Goffman's *Stigma* (1963) served as a useful overview of many aspects of deviant careers, there was little said directly about processes of exiting (most of the discussion being about the management of information, for example). Since then, however, academic criminology has grown, and alongside it there has been a growth of interest in explaining change over the life course (e.g. Ebaugh, 1984). This work has spawned a number of seminal studies (such as those by Meisenhelder, 1977; and Shover, 1983) that have contributed greatly to our understanding of exit processes among deviants and criminals.

The main factors associated with exit from a deviant career

In terms of criminal careers, a number of factors emerge as key associates or correlates of desistance. Such issues can – broadly speaking – be divided into two main forms: those which relate to processes outside of the individual; and those which relate to 'internal processes'. This divide is slightly artificial, since the social world impinges heavily on the 'inner' world, but it is nevertheless as good a starting point as any other. Some of the most consistent findings surrounding desistance revolve around marriage (or partnership) and parenthood, and engagement in the economy (employment or voluntary work). Such processes, however, often interact with age, as family and work responsibilities assume an increased salience for the individuals concerned after their mid-twenties (indeed, prior to this point, employment especially is associated with increased deviancy, via the consumption of alcohol and other proscribed substances). Leaving home, and/or moving away from where one grew up, and accordingly moving away from old (i.e. deviant) friends and acquaintances, has also been associated with leaving behind a period of involvement in crime. Similarly, the criminal justice system also appears to influence the nature and timing of exit from deviant careers. Some individuals, as we shall see, are 'burnt out' by the criminal justice system after a considerable period in prison or undergoing community supervision; whereas the same system's input seems to lengthen others' engagement in a deviant lifestyle. From the 1950s onwards, academics in the USA and Europe devoted much of their time to describing the above processes and their contours.

However, more recently, those interested in exit from deviant careers have started to focus on the 'internal' dynamics associated with change, especially when that change is associated with the abandonment of crime (e.g. Maruna, 2001; Giordano et al., 2002). Feeling shame or regret about past events, cognitive reorientations towards the behaviour in question, developing the motivation to stop previous behaviour, and having the resolve to make a decision to stop offending have all been identified as key internal processes associated with the abandonment of sustained deviant careers. Those more interested in what such feelings lead to have devoted their energies to studying and documenting the processes by which an individual identifies a 'blueprint' for a future self, and how they manage to 're-biographise' their past. Such studies have highlighted the importance of the role of hope in desistance, religious conversion and the adoption of citizenship values (or similar 'conventional' goals and values) in processes associated with exit from deviant behaviours, identities and pasts.

Giordano et al. (2002: 999–1002) outline a 'theory of cognitive transformation' to account for desistance from street crimes among female offenders. This process involves four stages. After a 'general cognitive openness to change', would-be desisters must be exposed to and react appropriately to opportunities for change for the exit process to be successful. Following this, the individual must start on the process of envisioning 'an appealing and conventional "replacement self"', which in turn leads to the fourth stage – a transformation in the way the individual views deviant behaviour. As noted by others (e.g. Cusson and Pinsonneault, 1986; Farrall and Bowling, 1999), a period of reflection and reassessment of what is important to the individual appears to be common among all successful exiters. Of course, this is insufficient in itself (Giordano et al., 2002: 1001; Farrall 2002: 225), as any would-be desister also needs to encounter opportunities to change their behaviour and/or way of being. Giordano et al. (2002: 1003), following work on the relationship between agency and structure (e.g. Farrall and Bowling, 1999), argue that 'the actor creatively and selectively draws upon elements of the environment in order to effect significant life changes'. In this way, they work towards a model of desistance that draws agency and structure together (see also Maruna and Farrall, 2004) via their notion of a 'blueprint' for a future self that resonates with Giddens' work on position practices (1984) and Sartre's notion of the being-for-itself (1958 [1943]).

Existential thinking has found a place in recent work undertaken by Farrall (2005, 2009) on the experiences of exiting from periods of excessive drug and alcohol use, and also of rebuilding lives shattered by wrongful arrest, conviction and imprisonment (see also Hunter, 2009, on the experiences of those leaving elite white-collar positions after allegations of financial wrongdoing). Key aspects of this approach include the emphasis that is placed on the ongoing search for a meaningful identity on the part of individuals, especially keenly felt during periods of dramatic change, slowly evolving a sense of one's inner self, beliefs about what is 'right' or 'wrong', problems of freedom and choice and, especially resonant for the wrongfully convicted, the loss of the assumptive world (see Kauffman, 2002, more generally).

Emotional trajectories

As an individual moves away from a deviant past, they inevitably encounter a series of sometimes powerful, sometimes mundane emotions. Some of these emotions may never previously have been encountered by the ex-deviant, or not encountered for many years. Ebaugh (1984: 164), for example, notes how her own emotional and sexual needs were awakened following her exit from life as a nun. Mundane experiences (such as eating chocolate (Ebaugh, 1984: 164) or being seen as an 'ordinary mum' (Clarke, cited in Farrall, 2009)) provide both a sense of satisfaction and a validation of one's status as 'normal'. Ambivalence about one's identity would also appear to be common among stigmatised individuals (Goffman, 1968: 130), and may be brought to the fore when those who have successfully exited from a deviant role (openly or via the successful 'covering up' of their past) are brought face-to-face with those who have not (Goffman, 1968: 132). Often, as beautifully charted by Maruna (2001), those leaving deviant careers want to 'give something back' to society or those people who now occupy the positions they once did. Farrall and Calverley (2006) charted the range of emotions encountered by those abandoning crime. Initially, respondents reported holding non-specific hopes and desires (for 'a better life') and reported few regrets about their past or feelings of guilt and shame, nor any sense of personal achievement. In subsequent phases, ex-offenders started to report fewer hopes for the future, but also started to report negative emotions about their past lives and behaviours. As they moved towards the status of 'non-offender', more of this group reported feelings of disgust and shame at their past lives while feelings of hope returned – but this time in more concrete forms (hopes for better homes, marriage, the chance to raise a family and so on). Feelings of pride in one's achievement (of having left behind a troubled period in one's life) and feelings of being trusted and 'belonging' also became more common over time. As such, there appears to be a trajectory of emotional experience which characterises the inner worlds of those exiting deviance. For some ex-deviants, there may be a period of 'phantom normalcy' (Goffman, 1968: 148), during which they move from 'deviant' to 'normal', and which is characterised by feeling as if one is learning or pretending to be normal in a socially acceptable manner.

The issue of epiphanies

In his studies of the processes of change among people recovering from alcoholism, Denzin (1987) introduces the concept of an epiphany – a moment or point in time when clarity is observed for the first time or a sudden realisation is made by an individual. Ebaugh (1984: 160) reports similar processes among nuns who decide to leave the convent. Can we assume that a similar process takes place in other exitings? The evidence from studies of the termination of criminal careers suggests that epiphanies are not common for this form of deviant cessation. As Bottoms et al. (2004: 383) write: 'Damascene conversions may happen for a few, but we suspect that, for many people, the progression is faltering, hesitant and oscillating.' Similarly, Farrall (2005) finds a number of 'staging posts', but no clear epiphany in his detailed examination of recovering from involvement in drugs, alcohol and crime.

Variations in places of 'exit'

Another growing area of interest is with *where* people who are exiting from a deviant lifestyle spend their time. Some have noted how important specific places are in the 'production' of criminal events, since the places where an individual lives out his or her life communicates some element of *who* they are and *what* they do (Meisenhelder, 1977; Goffman, 1963). But what of processes of exiting? Meisenhelder (1977) reminds us that not all 'places' (e.g. bars, snooker halls, railway stations, churches) are equal in terms of their ability either to facilitate or to confirm an 'ex-con's' status as an 'ex-offender'. For example, some places (bars, gambling halls, snooker halls, certain street corners) have a negative effect, suggesting that an individual has not abandoned their old ways and is still engaged in deviant activities. Other places suggest that an individual has made the break with crime; these include churches, reputable employers, domestic family homes and other 'conventional' civic associations. Still other places may convey neither positive nor negative messages (for example, a large out-of-town supermarket or a railway station). The list of places associated with signalling continuance/desistance from a deviant past or role will varying hugely depending on the role(s) the individual is leaving and the roles they are seeking to move towards. For example, attendance at AA groups or similar voluntary associations may convey the message that an alcoholic is either actively 'in recovery' or taking steps towards abstinence. Bars, liquor stores or other arenas which feature prominently in the 'nighttime economy' may convey the opposite.

This essay will now focus on two emerging issues from within the literature on processes of exiting from deviant careers. The first, the issue of exiting deviant roles/identities and adopting 'mainstream' values associated with citizenship, speaks to a wider set of debates around what society expects from its members. The second, the ways in which such processes unfold along ethnic lines, speaks to the structural and cultural variations associated with different ethnic groups in diverse societies.

Ex-deviants and citizenship

There have been relatively few explorations of deviant exits and the adoption of the behaviours and values associated with citizenship. Mercier and Alarie (2002: 234) reported that one ex-substance abuser related their reduction in drug usage to a new sense of civic identity:

> I am not a shame for society anymore. I am not living on society, giving back nothing. There was a time when my name did not appear on any computer, not even on social security databases, or electoral lists, or income taxes . . . Anonymous, completely anonymous . . . I did not want to be part of society, of the system . . . And now, my name is on many files, I even voted, I quitted anonymity . . . Now I have a bank book, my name is in the telephone book.

In many respects, this quote echoes observations from Maruna (2001: 12), who reminds us that 'desisting ex-offenders emphasise the desire to make some important contribution to their communities', suggesting that the process of desisting encompasses feelings which can be characterised as 'active citizenship'. Farrall and Calverley's (2006) examination of the citizenship values of fifty-one ex-probationers suggested that those who had stopped offending appeared to be more likely to support statements that emphasised liberal citizenship values (becoming involved in conventional political processes, tolerating differences, taking responsibility for oneself and being honest when dealing with state officials). Among those engaged in radical political groups, Sigel and Hoskins (1977: 266) note that those aged between twenty-five and thirty often experienced an increase in involvement in 'conventional' political groupings, a change that occurs in tandem with the assumption of family responsibilities. By this age, most men and women are married and have developed concerns over taxes, mortgage rates and schools. In a statement that echoes many of those from ex-offenders, the authors quote an ex-radical union president saying, 'It changes your outlook quite a bit when you have those mortgage payments, car payments and kids to feed.' In a similar vein, McEvoy and Shirlow (2009) reflect on the reintegration of former paramilitaries in Belfast following the Good Friday Agreement of 1998. They argue that, far from being passive recipients of reintegration, these former political prisoners have played key roles in the transformation of Belfast's political and crime landscape via their style of community leadership. They argue that the heavily politicised context of Northern Ireland illuminates central themes which are of direct relevance to both transitional and 'settled' societies concerning the reintegration of ex-prisoners and former combatants. Dowse and Hughes (1986: 204) report that the socially upwardly mobile take on the values of the stratum into which they move. Similarly, they find that migrants take on the values of the milieu into which they move (1986: 205). Glaser and Gilens (1997) provide evidence that migrants from the southern US states to the northern US states change their beliefs about different ethnic groups in line with the communities they join.

These studies highlight the role played by wider values and norms in processes of resettlement and exit. The ways in which ex-war criminals resume their lives after punishment is explored by Karstedt (2011), who, through an exploration of ex-Nazis, shows how their subsequent lives are shaped by wider normative expectations and the pressure towards change that German society in general, as well as families, friends and employers, expect from and exert on them. This, she argues, affects how such people perceive their moral and legal guilt, and whether they recognise any necessity to change their own values and beliefs.

Variations by ethnicity

As sociologists and criminologists have moved away from social class as a key explanatory variable, so they have highlighted ethnicity – alongside gender, age and sexual orientation – as a key explanatory variable in accounting for life opportunities and lifestyles that individuals pursue. Of course, this is not to suggest that ethnicity is paramount (after all, it is socially constructed, indexes other social processes and interacts with other variables), but simply to note that, along with a range of important socio-demographic variables, more attention has been paid to issues relating to ethnicity and race.

One of the oldest studies of this nature was undertaken by Finestone (1967), who studied the resettlement of Polish- and Italian-born ex-prisoners living in the US. Finestone found that, for the Italians, rehabilitation was a process in which both immediate and wider families played a key role. Release from prison saw a family gathering and the exchange of gifts among the family members. Little emphasis was placed upon the (im)moral aspects of deviancy and rehabilitation, and greater emphasis on 'growing up'. If asked, community workers would assist the family in helping with the ex-prisoner's rehabilitation.

In the Polish community, rehabilitation was experienced differently. Release from prison saw a re-establishment of social and emotional ties with only close family members (rather than the wider family). Polish family members tended, on the whole, to shun the released offender on moral grounds. In this respect, the ex-offender tended to become alienated, and more reported feelings of guilt about their past than did ex-prisoners from the Italian community.

In a more recent study, Reisig et al. (2007) studied prisoner release in Florida. They found that black males' reconvictions were highest in those counties with the greatest levels of economic inequality that disadvantaged black communities (i.e. where black communities were substantially poorer than non-black communities). They therefore concluded that black ex-prisoners return to communities that constrain (rather than support) their ability to desist.

Deane *et al.* (2007) explored desistance among North American Aborigines who were attempting to leave behind gang membership via a programme called Ogijiita Pimstiswin Kinamatwin. Interestingly, and unlike many such programmes, those enrolled could remain a gang member if they wished while they were in the process of exiting the lifestyle. This was allowed because such contacts were seen as being supportive during the transition from gang member to non-member. Key in facilitating their desistance was a recognition on the part of the (ex-)gang members that they were Aborigine (achieved via the (re)learning of traditional values and engagement in traditional ceremonies). The growing awareness of their ethnic heritage enabled the ex-gang members to realise that 'their' troubled pasts had been as much about wider anti-Aboriginal policies, practices and views as they were about their own behaviour.

Calverley (2009) studied three of the UK's most numerous ethnic minority groups (Indians, Bangladeshis and Afro-Caribbeans). Although many of his sample left behind lives of crime for reasons that one also finds in samples of indigenous white ex-deviants (marriage, family formation, employment and so on; see above), some intriguing patterns emerged when the life histories were analysed along ethnic lines. Indian families (who are very similar to the UK's white middle class in terms of economic position and aspirations) tended to rally around their sons, supporting both their deviant careers and their attempts to leave crime behind. For example, they would buy and even administer drugs for them. In order to maintain their status as 'respectable' in the local Indian community, Indian families frequently invented stories to account for their sons' imprisonment. On their release, they would often find them work in legitimate, family-run businesses.

On the whole, Bangladeshis in the UK are much poorer and have lower levels of educational attainment than Indians; they tend to live in poor housing with large families. Prison was important for the reform of this group, mainly as it reinitiated an interest in religion, which itself provided a 'script' for behaviour in the future that was incompatible with offending (see Giordano *et al.* 2008 on Christianity and desistance). Attendance at religious meetings additionally meant that Bangladeshi ex-offenders were seen by others at places of respectability (i.e. mosques), which acted as a form of re-labelling and allowed them to form new friendships. Bangladeshi ex-offenders slowly saw their families start to trust them again, a process that was often reinforced by the joint project of finding the desister a suitable marriage partner.

Black and dual-heritage ex-offenders were more likely to report feeling burnt out by prison. Religion was relatively unimportant in the accounts they gave, as were families (which were often fragmented and so of little practical use). Unlike either of the Asian groups, the black and dual-heritage ex-offenders spent a considerable amount of time in gyms as a way of avoiding old associates without 'dissing' them. As such, their route away from crime was much more individualistic.

Conclusion

Our understanding of why people leave behind deviant phases of their lives, and the processes involved in this transition, is now much more thorough than it was even ten years ago. During that time, we have witnessed a growth of interest in 'external' (i.e. social institutional) and 'internal' (i.e. emotional) processes and the ways these interact with one another. The importance of existential processes in 'rebuilding' one's sense of self and the ways in which this is shaped by wider social processes has come to the fore. Of late, greater attention has been paid to the roles played by gender and ethnicity in this, and the ways in which exit sites are spatially distributed. In this respect, the study of exits from deviancy looks likely to continue to be a central area of research.

References

Bottoms, A., Shapland, J., Costello, A., Holmes, D. and Muir, D. (2004) 'Towards Desistance', *Howard Journal of Criminal Justice* 43(4): 368–389.

Calverley, A. (2009) 'An Exploratory Investigation into the Processes of Desistance amongst Minority Ethnic Offenders', Ph.D. Thesis, Keele University.

Clark, S. (2003) 'Letter to Supporters', 11 April. Available at: www.sallyclark.org.uk/Sally0403.html.

Cusson, M. and Pinsonneault, P. (1986) 'The Decision to Give up Crime', in Cornish, D.B. and Clarke, R.V. (eds) *The Reasoning Criminal*, New York: Springer-Verlag.

Deane, L., Bracken, D. and Morrisette, L. (2007) 'Desistance within an Urban Aboriginal Gang', *Probation Journal* 54(2): 125–141.

Denzin, N. (1987) *The Recovering Alcoholic*, London: Sage.

Dowse, R.E. and Hughes, J.A. (1986) *Political Sociology*, London: Wiley.

Ebaugh, H. (1984) 'Leaving the Convent', in Kotarba, J. and Fontana, A. (eds) *The Existential Self in Society*, Chicago, IL: Chicago University Press.

Farrall, S. (2002) *Rethinking What Works with Offenders*, Cullompton: Willan.

Farrall, S. (2005) 'On the Existential Aspects of Desistance from Crime', *Symbolic Interaction* 28(3): 367–386.

Farrall, S. (2009) '"We Just Live Day-to-Day": A Case Study of Life after Release Following Wrongful Conviction', in Lippens, R. and Crewe, D. (eds) *Existentialist* Criminology, London: Routledge.

Farrall, S. and Bowling, B. (1999) 'Structuration, Human Development and Desistance from Crime', *British Journal of Criminology* 39(2): 252–267.

Farrall, S. and Calverley, A. (2006) *Understanding Desistance from Crime*, Crime and Justice Series, London: Open University Press,.

Finestone, H. (1967) 'Reform and Recidivism amongst Italian and Polish Criminal Offenders', *American Journal of Sociology* 72(6): 575–588.

Giddens, Anthony (1984) *The Constitution of Society*, London: Polity Press.

Giordano, P.C., Cernkovich, S.A. and Rudolph, J.L. (2002) 'Gender, Crime and Desistance: Toward a Theory of Cognitive Transformation', *American Journal of Sociology* 107: 990–1064.

Giordano, P.C., Longmore, M., Schroeder, R. and Seffrin, P. (2008) 'A Life Course Perspective on Spirituality and Desistance from Crime', *Criminology* 46(1): 99–132.

Glaser, J.M. and Gilens, M. (1997) 'Interregional Migration and Political Resocialization', *Public Opinion Quarterly* 61: 72–86.

Goffman, E. (1963) *Stigma*, Englewood Cliffs, NJ: Prentice-Hall.

Goffman, E. (1968) *Stigma*, paperback edn, Harmondsworth: Penguin.

Hunter, B. (2009) 'Desistance by White Collar Offenders', Ph.D. thesis, Keele University.

Karstedt, S. (2011) 'Life after Punishment for Nazi War Criminals', in Farrall, S., Sparks, R., Hough, M. and Maruna, S. (eds) *Escape Routes: Contemporary Perspectives on Life after Punishment*, London: Routledge.

Kauffman, J. (2002) 'Safety and the Assumptive World', in Kauffman, J. (ed.) *Loss of the Assumptive World: A Theory of Traumatic Loss*, New York: Brunner-Routledge.

Maruna, S. (2001) *Making Good: How Ex-Convicts Reform and Rebuild Their Lives*, Washington, DC: American Psychological Association.

Maruna, S. and Farrall, S. (2004) 'Desistance from Crime: A Theoretical Reformulation', *Kölner Zeitschrift für Soziologie und Sozialpsychologie* 43: 171–194.

McEvoy, K. and Shirlow, P. (2009) 'Re-imagining the DDR: Ex-combatants, Leadership and Moral Agency in Conflict Transformation', *Theoretical Criminology* 13(1): 31–59.

Meisenhelder, T. (1977) 'An Exploratory Study of Exiting from Criminal Careers', *Criminology* 15: 319–334.

Mercier, C. and Alarie, S. (2002) 'Pathways out of Deviance: Implications for Programme Evaluation', in Brochu, S., Da Agra, C. and Cousineau, M.-M. (eds) *Drugs and Crime Deviant Pathways*, Aldershot: Ashgate.

Reisig, M.D., Michael, D., Bales, W.D., Hay, C. and Wang, X. (2007) 'The Effect of Racial Inequality on Black Male Recidivism', *Justice Quarterly* 24(3): 408–434.

Sartre, J.-P. (1958 [1943]) *Being and Nothingness*, London: Routledge.

Shover, N. (1983) 'The Later Stages of Ordinary Property Offender Careers', *Social Problems* 31(2): 208–218.

Sigel, R.S. and Hoskins, M.B. (1977) 'Perspectives on Adult Political Socialization: Areas of Research', in Renshon, S.A. (ed.) *Handbook of Political Socialization*, New York: The Free Press.

Part XV
New horizons in deviance

Overview

Crime and deviance provide opportunities for the study of social constructionism, moral entrepreneurship, and the creation and management of numerous labels. The quantity, types, configurations, and recognition of forms of crime and deviance change with the march of time. This final section of the book offers the perspective that certain types of behavior may be essentially "neglected" and/or tolerated until "discovered" by those with enough social, political, or economic clout to bring a new conceptualization of such behavior to fruition.

Human beings may figure out new ways to act and new things to do as their changing social and cultural stages evolve. Also, signal events, dissemination of information about those events, and the willingness and ability of leaders to influence followers often prompt the creation and modification of rules and regulations surrounding new forms of deviance and crime. By identifying new contexts through which to view certain human actions, new formulations of crime and deviance are created.

Examples of these new formulations that are mentioned in Palmer and Bryant's final chapter are white-collar crime, zoological crime, briney crime, and khaki-collar crime, among others. The authors pay particular attention to zoological crime and offer a conceptual paradigm of how this type of crime may be viewed at individual, collective, and international levels.

The world in which we live is rapidly changing. Technological inventions and innovations are growing exponentially. Population growth continues. Stratification systems throughout the globe fluctuate, with gaps between the haves and have-nots apparent and divisive. So what does the future hold for the arenas of crime and deviance? The last chapter of this book calls attention to several new and/or expanding themes of crime and deviance, including terrorism, workplace violence, crimes related to health and medicine, computer-related crime, and new crimes brought about by technological advances, such as the internet.

Have scholars reached agreement about the cause and nature of crime and deviance? Will the future provide a consensus about how best to study these phenomena? Palmer and Bryant contend that these questions reveal the complexity of the issues. But while perspectives, approaches, methodologies, and theories will remain wide and discrepant, the authors submit that there is some agreement that crime and deviance are based on socially causative factors, that deviant behavior can be functional as well as dysfunctional, and that the processes involved in creating as well as managing (or attempting to manage) crime and deviance are of great social significance.

71

Neglected and new forms of deviance, and different conceptualizations of, and perspectives on, deviance

C. Eddie Palmer and Clifton D. Bryant

For a variety of reasons, some types of norm violation may go unnoticed or be ignored for long periods of time, even centuries. Business fraud has been the object of social proscription since the time of Hammurabi, but business crime, or crime in the office, was essentially overlooked or disregarded until 1939, when Edwin H. Sutherland "discovered" white-collar crime and informed the sociological community of its existence in his presidential address at the ASA Convention. Once alerted, sociologists and criminologists began to conduct research enthusiastically on this area of criminal activity.

Curiously, awareness of the existence of white-collar crime did not motivate behavioral scientists to examine the possibility of crime or deviance within the context of other types of work until several decades later. In time, behavioral scientists (and subsequently the public) were sufficiently sensitized to the notion of crime and deviance occurring within an occupational or organizational context that they began to turn their research attention to other occupational venues, where they "discovered" a variety of new forms of crime in relatively rapid succession. These new configurations included police or "blue-coat" crime (Stoddard 1968), "blue-collar" crime (Howning 1970), "political" crime (Boyd 1974), and military or "khaki-collar" crime (Bryant 1979). Some of these "discoveries" generated extensive interest among other scholars, while others did not, and have been neglected or ignored up to contemporary times. Similarly, "child battering" was essentially an unfamiliar, if not unknown, form of deviance until "discovered" in the early 1960s (see DeFrancis 1963).

Other "discovered" research venues that might have proved to be very promising but were essentially neglected or ignored were ocean-connected (or "briney") crime (Bryant and Shoemaker 1975), "rural" crime (Carter *et al.* 1982), and animal-related (or "zoological") crime (Bryant and Palmer 1976).

The deviance "discoveries" of the past few decades strongly suggest a probable direction of scholarly interest in the future. There will undoubtedly be similar new "discoveries" as students of deviance sift and examine the vagaries of deviant human social behavior and assemble their findings within new conceptual frameworks. With the development and perfection of these new conceptual configurations, all scientific disciplines are capable of new perceptual horizons.

A detailed account of one neglected form of crime and deviance may serve to illustrate the conceptual parameters of this type of crime and its research potential.

Zoological crime

Students of crime, deviance, and social control have paid little attention to zoological crime.[1] The label itself reflects that there is a complex framework of norms, laws, statutes, regulations, and sanctions that exist to regulate human animal-related behavior. This discussion includes a chart that depicts a conceptual paradigm of this configuration of crime and deviance. Hopefully, this will be instructive and provide an insight into nuances of zoological crime.

This conceptual paradigm posits three categories of the level of man/animal interaction: individual, collective, and international. It also differentiates broad categories or perspectives that permit viewing animals as property, food, participants in human social behavior, and sentient creatures. While the normative framework continues to grow in complexity as a result of social and global changes, this core typology provides a limited overview of this neglected form of crime and deviance, and within the cells of the matrix are examples of animal-related crime. Discussion of these various configurations of crime will provide further insight.

Table 71.1 Typological paradigm of "zoological crime"

	Instrumental perspectives		Affective perspectives	
Level of man/ animal interaction	Animals as property	Animals as food	Animals as participants in configurations of human social behavior	Animals as sentient creatures
Individual	Horse and cattle theft; "Dog-napping"; "Oyster-rustling"	Some species prohibited as food appropriate for human consumption	Violation of leash laws; Other laws governing ownership of pets; Anti-human–animal sex laws; Laws against serpent handling, etc.	Individual mistreatment of animals; Laws against "geek" acts
Collective	Violation of game laws; Wild game as "commonwealth" of people of state or nation	Violations of pure food laws, slaughterhouse regulations, sanitation laws, etc.	Laws against inappropriate use of animals in sports: e.g., cockfighting, dog fighting	Violations of humane slaughter laws; Laboratory laws, shipping regulations, etc.
International	Violation of endangered species laws; Wildlife as the "heritage" (property) of all people and generations	Violation of international efforts to regulate animals as food supply: e.g., international fishing treaties	Smuggling illegal animals; International efforts to stop hunting because it is "dehumanizing"	International efforts to stop "slaughter" of fur seals and inhumane practices involved

Animals as property: individual level

Some animals are considered to be private and personal ("chattels") and, accordingly, the theft of such an animal is larceny. As an example, cattle rustling, the scourge of the western frontier in the US in the 19th century, is still very prevalent today. To deal with this problem a 130-year-old trade organization known as the Texas and Southwestern Cattle Raisers Association employs 27 special rangers commissioned by the Texas Department of Public Safety or the Oklahoma State Bureau of Investigation. In a given year, these rangers might investigate more than 1,000 cases, primarily involving stray and stolen livestock, and recover or account for missing livestock with a value of approximately $5 million (Texas and Southwestern Cattle Raisers Association and *The Cattleman* n.d.)

Animals as property: collective level

Wildlife is considered to be public property in that it belongs to a political collectivity, such as a state or a nation—the "commonwealth," as it were. Wildlife is accordingly protected by laws that regulate hunting, fishing, trapping, and so on, with specialized law enforcement agencies charged with enforcing protective statutes.

Research (Palmer 1975b; Snizek *et al.* 1975) has shown that wildlife law enforcement officers routinely confront violators who consider wildlife to be the personal property of those skilled enough to take it from the wild. Resulting violations involve several basic forms of criminal activity, identified by Palmer (1975a: 3–5) as revolving around statutes governing time of harvest, method of catch, bag and creel limits, size and sex of game, species of animal, place of catch, and improper licensing.

Animals as property: international level

While state and federal regulatory guidelines attempt to control the illegal harvest of wild game within their territories, certain conditions arise that prompt international attention. Justification for this is based on the notion that some species of (usually exotic) fauna are conceptualized as being the "heritage" (property) of everyone in the world. Furthermore, such animals are believed to be the property of all future generations, and thus must be preserved for them. In effect, this generation must exercise the stewardship of these creatures to ensure that they can be protected and passed on to future generations.

Thus, one important dimension of zoological crime deals with violations of international sentiment concerning the conceptualization of the fauna of the world as being the universal property of the whole of mankind.

Animals as food: individual level

Individual violations of normative systems regulating the consumption of different types of animal flesh have been met with a variety of sanctions. Group avoidance of carnivorous activities is couched within a variety of cultural, religious, magical, totemistic, and hygienic belief systems of various groups or categories of people. Consequently, eating the meat of pigs, cattle, chickens and eggs, horses, camels, or dogs may be prohibited. While several of these proscriptions do not entail the attachment of the label of "criminal" for their violation, the assertion that one is zoologically deviant in one's selection of diet may well result in negativistic symbolic social sanctions.

Animals as food: collective level

There are public concerns at the societal level regarding the consumption of animals as food. Some of these concerns are based on cultural or religious ideologies, or collective sentiments. Others have to do with issues of health, safety, and the humane processing of animals into food. These concerns have resulted in the enactment of legal norms.

Complex sets of laws and regulations exist to prescribe and proscribe the conditions and circumstances by which animals are converted into food. These laws operate at a collective level in terms of acceptable species for food use, techniques of slaughter, conditions of processing and shipment, and packaging and sales.

Animals as food: international level

In US society, and many others, much food comes from other parts of the world, in both processed and unprocessed forms. There are numerous health and safety laws and regulations relating to foodstuffs, as well as international fishing and whaling treaties that regulate, limit, or prohibit the importing or exporting of certain animal products. For instance, whale meat cannot be imported into the United States, and horse meat cannot be exported. Violation of such laws may result in legal sanctions.

Animals as participants in configurations of human social behavior: individual level

Humans sometimes use animals to commit crimes. Poisonous snakes have been used to commit murder, a snapping turtle was once used as a weapon to rob a convenience store, and dogs have been kidnapped and ransomed.

Animals play seminal roles in many varieties of human social behavior, and laws and regulations governing such behavior are quite pervasive. In this regard, animals do have legal rights (Leavitt 1970). As an example of such regulations, many municipalities have "leash laws" that oblige the owner to have his or her dog on a leash and under control at all times. In some instances, there is also the legal requirement that dogs (particularly large dogs) wear a muzzle when not in a fenced area. Rabies shots for pets are legally required almost everywhere in the US, and the animals are required to wear a tag attesting to compliance. Many cities also have "dog poop" laws. When an owner is walking down the street with a dog on a leash, should the dog defecate on the sidewalk or street, he or she is legally obligated to scoop up the stool, place it in a bag, and take it home. In some localities, dog owners are also legally required to take out liability insurance for dogs that weigh over 30 pounds, as these are the ones most likely to bite. There are innumerable other laws involving humans and animals, such as those prohibiting bestiality.

Animals as participants in configurations of human social behavior: collective level

At the collective level, certain laws pertain to group activities involving animals. For instance, some southern US states have legal statutes that prohibit the handling of poisonous snakes during religious services. Similarly, there are laws in most states that criminalize cockfighting and dog fighting because they are violent, involve cruelty to animals, are centers of illegal gambling, and are believed to "brutalize" the human participants. In some states (and under federal law), cockfighting and dog fighting are felonies. Because of the possibility of harming others or creating a nuisance for others, owning a dangerous animal, such as a lion or a tiger, is either illegal or requires a special permit or license (which may specify certain conditions, such as very strong fencing or caging). Owning any animal that may annoy or offend neighbors because of its noise and/or smell may also constitute a crime.

Animals as participants in configurations of human social behavior: international level

Smuggling animals illegally across national borders is an extremely profitable criminal enterprise. Some endangered species of birds and animals fetch many thousands of dollars on the black market. The punishments may be severe, but the possibility of huge profits motivates many individuals to try, nevertheless. While smuggling such animals *into* a country such as the US is illegal, it is probably also illegal to smuggle them *out* of their country of origin.

Animals as sentient creatures: individual level

Animals have long been conceptualized by some people as sentient creatures. The law takes note of this, so cruelty to animals is illegal, with punishments sometimes severe. At the individual level, the owner of a dog, cat, or other animal who deliberately inflicted pain or other kinds of cruelty, such as starving, on their animal would be subject to arrest, prosecution, and a fine or even incarceration. The parameters and intensity of cruelty are subject to legal debate, however. Intentional neglect or failure to care for a pet or livestock properly is also subject to legal sanction.

Commercialized deliberate cruelty to a creature is considered to be especially reprehensible and depraved. For this reason, spectacles such as "geek" shows in carnivals are illegal in many areas. In such a show, a disheveled and "wild-looking" individual (often an alcoholic or a drug addict) might bite the head off a live chicken and drink its blood.

Animals as sentient creatures: collective level

At the collective level, numerous laws attempt to minimize the pain inflicted on animals that are used in legitimate commerce. Examples here include anti-cruelty laws governing the slaughtering of livestock. Other anti-cruelty laws regulate the use of animals in laboratory experiments. Using animals in movies is subject to legal regulation, as is exhibiting animals in zoos and circuses. Stingent governmental regulations relate to the humane shipping of animals. In addition, as was discussed earlier, cockfighting and dog fighting are illegal because they are perceived as cruel to the animals involved. All of these laws have serious legal consequences if violated.

Animals as sentient creatures: international level

Beyond the legal control of cruelty to animals, organized groups in the animal rights movement seek to extend the protection of animals, sometimes through vigilante initiatives. These groups believe in the concept of humane values that carry the weight of "natural laws," and they seek to enforce these. For instance, Greenpeace attempts to interfere with the activities of Japanese whalers, and activists attempt to stop the annual "slaughter" of fur-seal pups in the Canadian Arctic. Ironically, it is the members of these groups who are violating the law, because the actions of both the whalers and the seal hunters are technically legal under national legislation and/or international treaties. Of course, the animal rights organizations argue that they are operating under a "higher law."

The future

Terrorism

Several "themes" will likely dominate deviance in the immediate future. One of these is sure to be terrorism. Islamic terrorism, typified by suicide bombers and *jihad*, will almost certainly expand in scope and increase in frequency. Al-Qaeda appears to be growing in influence, and even American citizens of Middle Eastern extraction are succumbing to its doctrine, such as the Muslim army psychiatrist who committed mass murder at Fort Hood, Texas. The future will likely see many more such vengeful, militant Muslims turning to violence to vent their frustration, anger, and hostility toward the Western world, and especially the US. Some of their attacks will surely be massive in scope and terrifying in their number of victims.

Irrational violence

Growing numbers of people suffering from imagined victimization and other disgruntled individuals who feel hopelessness and disenfranchisement seem to be externalizing their anger and turning it into irrational violence. Examples include Eric Harris and Dylan Klebold, who committed the murders at Columbine High School; Timothy McVeigh, who bombed the Federal Building in Oklahoma City; and Cho Seung Hui, the student at Virginia Tech University who killed 32 fellow-students and faculty members before turning the gun on himself. There have been several more school shootings across the US since the Virginia Tech massacre.

Workplace violence

In today's society, much violence occurs in the workplace, ranging from altercations to mass murder. The workplace is often very stressful, and violence there may be a symptom of a larger societal malaise. In a seminal article entitled "Workplace as Combat Zone: Reconceptualizing Occupational and Organizational Violence," Knefel and Bryant (2004) examined this phenomenon and concluded that workplace violence is very widespread and will be better understood only if the context within which it occurs is taken into account.

Because a series of violent episodes took place in post offices, often involving postal employees killing fellow-workers, the process of losing control and committing multiple murders has become known in some quarters as "going postal."

Health- and medical-related crime and deviance

For much of America's history, one's health was simply taken for granted. Most people were generally healthy, albeit some had bearable chronic conditions, such as asthma. When an individual became ill, the ailment (often merely cold or flu) was usually treated with over-the-counter remedies. Those afflicted with more serious maladies might go to a physician (or have the physician visit them on a "house call") and consequently receive a prescription for more powerful drugs. Until the decade after the Second World War, however, very few prescription pharmaceuticals were actually available. When a patient had a serious condition, such as appendicitis, they were sent to the hospital for surgery. Recovery routinely took weeks. In the 1950s, physicians were finally able to prescribe sulfa drugs or penicillin, which were more effective than earlier remedies, albeit not always the "silver bullet." Over the next 50 years, however, science and technology (including medical technology) arguably advanced more than it had in the previous 500 years.

Now, the field of medicine is able to achieve seemingly miraculous results, through organ transplantation, reviving patients who have been "clinically" dead, and curing supposedly "incurable diseases." Medical miracles are not cheap, however, and the costs of medical care and drugs have risen (and continue to rise) at a near-astronomical rate. Consequently, neither private medical insurance plans nor Medicare will now cover certain procedures, treatments, and medicines. In the future, with continuing reform of the US healthcare system, even fewer procedures, treatments, and medications might will be covered. Certainly, some medical treatment will be "rationed," and particular categories of people (such as the elderly) may be systematically denied the coverage they need.

As a result of all this, medical- and health-related crime and deviance will inevitably rise. Medical insurance, Medicare, and Medicaid fraud, which is already prevalent today, will increase exponentially. Smugglers will "bootleg" ever more pharmaceuticals into the US, and a large, thriving, nationwide black market will develop for those who cannot afford to buy uncovered medications. More medicines and diagnostic equipment will be stolen, and back-street medical procedures using such stolen equipment may well be offered for cash with no questions asked. Armed robberies of valuable pharmaceuticals from drug stores and super-markets will increase, too. Bribery to obtain insurance-uncovered or rationed medical care (or, indeed, any kind of medical care where demand exceeds supply) will likely mushroom. This is already common in some countries around the world.

Counterfeiting expensive pharmaceuticals will be prevalent, and medical frauds of all kinds will be very widespread. Many of these frauds will be directed at the elderly population as it continues to increase in size. The elderly will be particularly vulnerable because they are most likely to be denied coverage for certain medical procedures or treatments. For instance, private health insurance and Medicare will both refuse to cover a woman in her mid-80s for potentially life-saving heart-bypass surgery. As a result, she will be a prime candidate for victimization by medical fraud that offers her affordable, but bogus, treatment.

There is already a thriving international black market in human organs (Schepter-Hughes 2009). Kidneys are obtained from poor individuals in impoverished countries for relatively modest sums of money. This cash allows the donors to purchase luxuries, such as a small automobile, educate their children, or simply sustain their families for a few months. The organs are sometimes transferred quickly to a hospital in the donor's own country for transplant surgery. But on other occasions they are transported to the US or another Western country. In the US, obtaining an organ for transplantation in this fashion is illegal. Nevertheless, the practice will undoubtedly increase greatly in the future.

Where medical care and medicines become exorbitantly expensive, cheaper ways to obtain them, even when these are illicit, will be sought. Where there are shortages of medical care or medicines, perhaps because of rationing, other means of obtaining them, even if deviant, will surely be employed. As the cost and the difficulty of obtaining medical care and medicines increase, the implications for increased crime and deviance become almost limitless.

Computer-related crime and deviance

Technological progress is a wondrous process, but its products, while often beneficial marvels, also have a downside. They are frequently dysfunctional as well as functional.

No other technological invention in history (aside, perhaps, from the printing press) has opened as many vistas of opportunity for crime and deviance as the computer. Why bother to rob a bank with a facemask and a gun? Those who have the appropriate computer skills can simply hack into a bank's system and transfer money to their own off-shore account.

The computer has revolutionized our society, with its utility ranging from household book-keeping to chain-store inventory control, and from fingerprint comparison to factory production close-tolerance machining. But it also has almost limitless potential for mischief. It has been used to find, create, store, and distribute pornography. Almost any telephone-related deviance can be duplicated on a computer. Each and every type of deviance, especially sexual deviance, has at least one website devoted to it, and these can be easily accessed by anyone who is interested. In effect, the computer now helps deviants connect with other deviants. It consolidates deviants.

Rosoff and Pontell (Chapter 49, this volume) indicate that computer crime can be classified into five distinctive modes:

- electronic embezzlement;
- hacking;
- malicious sabotage, including the creation, installation, or dissemination of computer viruses
- internet scams; and
- utilization of computers and computer networks for espionage.

They also mention software piracy as another form of computer crime.

However, computer crime is still in its infancy. The deviant mind is fertile and imaginative, and the possible deviant uses of a computer are almost infinite, so the opportunities for criminal activity using a computer are truly mindboggling. Every aspect of our lives and behavior that is touched by a computer may be the target of internet miscreants in the future. Computer crime already has an international flavor, as evidenced by the fact that con artists from all over the world routinely send scamming e-mail messages to unsuspecting victims in wealthier countries. Such messages typically advise the victim that they are the winner of an international sweepstake or competition, and that a check for a very large amount of money is ready to be sent. However, the victim must first send a modest amount of money to cover "administration costs."

The home computer is a fantastic device for committing all sorts of crimes, and its very low cost makes it available to almost anyone with a devious mind and a nefarious scheme.

Other directions

The future will see the development of new and very sophisticated technology to be used in the detection of crime and deviance. Preliminary work has already begun on a machine that will "read minds" by monitoring and analyzing subtle physiological variations in the body, and especially the brain. Although objections will certainly be raised against such intrusive technologies, the latter will prevail because they will be so effective.

The age-old search for the causation and cure of crime and deviance will continue. In the future, the search for biological and genetic factors will certainly persist and new findings will provide support for those of physiological conviction. Considerable attention is already being paid to possible biomedical factors in the causation of crime and deviance.

No clear and complete sociological consensus has emerged, but there is agreement that deviance is a function of definitional conception and, thus, is relative. There is further agreement that most deviant behavior is based directly or indirectly on socially causative factors, and can be functional as well as dysfunctional. Finally, there is accord that there is great social significance in the process that determines who, why, and under what circumstances individuals are labeled as deviants, and what is the outcome.

In the final analysis, the learned scholars of crime and deviance may have to recognize some wisdom in the explanation of the infamous bank robber Willie "The Actor" Sutton. When asked why he robbed banks, Mr. Sutton sagely explained, "Because that's where the money is."

Note

1   This section is a condensation of works produced by Bryant and Palmer (1976, 2005). Some material is taken verbatim from these works, some is paraphrased, and some is new.

References

Boyd, J. (1974) "The ritual of wiggle: From ruin to reelection," pp. 201–217 in C. D. Bryant (ed.) *Deviant Behavior: Occupational and Organizational Bases*. Chicago, IL: Rand McNally College.

Bryant, C.D. (1979) *Khaki-Collar Crime: Deviant Behavior in the Military Context*. New York: The Free Press.

Bryant, C.D. and C.E. Palmer (1976) "'Zoological crime': A typological overview of animal-related laws and deviant behavior." Paper presented at the annual meeting of the Southwestern Social Science Association, Dallas, TX, April.

Bryant, C.D. and C.E. Palmer (2005) "Zoological crime redux: The continued neglect of animal crime and deviance." Paper presented at the annual meeting of the Mid-South Sociological Association, Atlanta, GA, November.

Bryant, C.D. and D.J. Shoemaker (1975) "'Briney crime': An overview of marine and maritime law and deviancy." Paper presented at the annual meeting of the Southern Sociological Society, Washington, DC, April.

Carter, T. J., G. Howard Phillips, J. F. Donnermeyer, and T. N. Wurschmidt (eds.) (1982) *Rural Crime: Integrating Research and Prevention*. Totowa, NJ: Allanheld Osmun and Company.

DeFrancis, D. (1963) *Child Abuse: Preview of a Nationwide Survey*. Denver, CO: American Humane Association, Children's Division.

Howning, D. N. M. (1976) "Blue-collar theft: Conceptions of property, attitudes toward pilfering and work group norms in a modern industrial plant," pp. 46–64 in E. O. Smigel and H. L. Ross (eds.) *Crimes against Bureaucracy*. New York: Van Nostrand Reinhold.

Knefel, A. C. and C. D. Bryant (2004) "Workplace as combat zone: Reconceptualizing occupational and organizational violence." *Deviant Behavior* 25(6): 579–601.

Leavitt, E. S. (ed.) (1970) *Animals and Their Legal Rights*. Washington, DC: Animal Welfare Institute.

Palmer, C. E. (1975a) "Camouflage-collar crime and green-coat cops: A study of wildlife law enforcement." *Proceedings of the First Annual Meeting of the Mid-South Sociological Association*, November: 137–148.

Palmer, C. E. (1975b) "Wildlife law enforcement: A sociological exploration of the occupational roles of the Virginia game warden." Unpublished Ph.D. dissertation, Virginia Polytechnic Institute and State University, Blacksburg.

Schepter-Hughes, N. (2009) "The tyranny and the terror of the gift: Sacrificial violence and the gift of life." *Economic Sociology: The European Electronic Newsletter* 11(1): 8–16. Available at: econsoc.mpfg.de.

Snizek, W. E., Bryant, C. D., Blake, J. A., and Palmer, C. E. (1975) "Work roles and occupational ideologies of Virginia game wardens." Unpublished Hatch Project monograph, Virginia Polytechnic Institute and State University, Blacksburg.

Stoddard, E. R. (1968) "The informal 'code' of police deviance: A group approach to 'blue-coat' crime." *Journal of Criminal Law, Criminology and Police Science* 59(2): 201–213.

Texas and Southwestern Cattle Raisers Association and *The Cattleman* (n.d.). "A brief history of the cattle industry in Texas." Mimeograph.

Index

abortion 13–14, 22, 26, 41
acceptable deviance 4, 27–8, 29
"accounts", notion of 6, 36
action groups 51
addiction 286–7, 333
Adler, P. 193, 269, 270, 305, 306, 307, 308, 309, 310
Adler, P. A. 193, 269, 270, 305, 306, 307, 308, 309, 310
adolescence: cross-cultural lifetime deviance survey 83; cyberbullying in 450–1; parenting and self-control in 72, 180, 185–7; 'raging' hormones' of 159, 161; rates of self-injury in 305; risk factors for substance abuse in 334; teen pregnancy 261–2; *see also* premarital adolescent sexual activity; youth delinquency
age: and appearance norms 554; intersections in deviant behavior 8–9, 54–5, 57–8; intersections in labeling and social control 55–7; of onset of deviant behavior 184; and suicide rates 313
Agger, B. 35
Agnew, R. 55, 102–3, 114, 115, 116, 117, 118, 292
Akers, R. 12, 68, 70, 104, 106, 107, 108, 109, 110, 111, 112, 123, 185, 186, 292
al-qaeda 416, 466, 467, 604
albinos 554, 556
Alcoholics Anonymous (AA) 274, 285, 286, 287
alcoholism and alcohol abuse 277–8, 283–9; and alcoholic identity 286; binge drinking

287–8; control and urban immigrants 86; definitions of 283–4; historical attitudes to 284–5; impact on the family 333–4; neuroscience investigation of 162; Prohibition 18–19, 43–4, 285; a risk factor for suicide 314, 316; robbery to support 530; statistics 283; and Temperance Movement 18–19, 43–4, 284–5; treatment in prison for 587; trends in prevalence 287–8; Twelve-Step treatment programs 285–7; violence correlating with 287
alternative adaptation theory 161
The American Disease; The Origins of Narcotic Control 85
American Dream 99, 103, 104
American Psychiatric Association (APA) 22, 204, 225, 278, 283, 291, 403
analytic induction 67–8, 69
Anderson, E. 54, 55, 237, 261, 262
animal rights 13, 270, 458, 461, 603
animals: *see* zoological crime
anomie-strain theory 90, 99–105, 235, 292; general strain theory 55, 102–3; institutional anomie theory 103–4; recent developments 101–4; revisions of 100–1
anorexia nervosa 298, 301, 302
anthropology 84–5
antidepressants 49, 319
antiheros 29, 43

apparel (dress) behavior, deviant 210–11, 213–14
Arafat, Y. 465
armed robbery 507, 527–33; administrative countermeasures to 532; consensus of disapproval for 84; conviction rates 532; environmental countermeasures to 531–2; incidence of 527–8; offender characteristics 529–30; patterns and trends in 528–9; understanding 530–1; victim characteristics 529
arson 474–5, 498–504; characteristics of arsonists 499; correlations with economic causes 501; enforcement 501–2; incidence of 498–9; motives for 499–501; victims of 499
assisted suicide 22, 41
Athanasiou, T. 459, 460

Baldwin, J. D. 110
Baldwin, J. I. 110
Bandura, A. 108, 110
'The Battered Child Syndrome' 331
Beach, F. 85
Becker, H. S. 11, 12, 17, 25, 31, 33, 34, 122, 123, 138, 190, 191, 195, 197, 235, 254, 255, 337, 351
Becoming Deviant 185
Beemyn, B. G. 224
Being and Time 131
Bell, R. R. 40
Belt, T. L. 563
Ben-Yehuda, N. 43, 44n, 48, 51, 337, 338, 339, 341